COLONIALISM IN AFRICA
1870–1960

VOLUME 4
THE ECONOMICS OF
COLONIALISM

Edited by

PETER DUIGNAN *and* L. H. GANN

CAMBRIDGE UNIVERSITY PRESS

CAMBRIDGE

LONDON · NEW YORK · MELBOURNE

Published by the Syndics of the Cambridge University Press
The Pitt Building, Trumpington Street, Cambridge CB2 1RP
Bentley House, 200 Euston Road, London NW1 2DB
32 East 57 Street, New York, NY 10022, USA
296 Beaconsfield Parade, Middle Park, Melbourne 3206, Australia

Library of Congress Catalogue Card Number: 75-77289

ISBN: 0 521 08641 8

First published 1975

Printed in the United States of America
by Vail-Ballou Press, Inc., Binghamton
New York

Hoover Institution Publication 127

CONTENTS

v

CONTENTS

MAPS

TABLES

PREFACE

The first two volumes of *Colonialism in Africa* attempted to provide a survey of the history and politics of the imperial era. The third volume treated a variety of societal questions concerned with the impact of colonialism on African societies. The present volume is designed to furnish an analysis, as well as a convenient summary, of major economic trends and developments during the colonial period. As in previous volumes, we allowed our contributors a good deal of choice, and so gaps do remain.

Clearly, no work covering as enormous an area as the whole of sub-Saharan Africa can possibly be exhaustive. Had we tried to compile a comprehensive economic history, this volume would have turned into a series of its own. Our contributors deal with the major topics of economic development. Except for Kilby and the Dotsons, however, they do not provide case studies concerning the work of plantations, factories and mines; they do not supply detailed information concerning wages or productivity. We have not been able to go into technical questions concerned with subjects such as banking, currency or customs. We do not treat of institutional transfers—for example, with trade unions, private and public corporations, banks and so forth. Neither have we been able to say much about the services provided by co-operatives, insurance firms, shipping agents and stock-brokers in the economic development of the continent. We trust that the present volume will nevertheless prove of value by providing summaries of existing research, by furnishing new data and by stimulating debate concerning controversial issues.

We should like to express our thanks to our contributors and to the scholars who have helped us with advice. We are particularly indebted to Professors P. T. Bauer and Peter Kilby, who have perused most of this manuscript, and also to Professors Ralph A. Austen, Bruce F. Johnston, William O. Jones, Robert July and John Marcum, who have read individual chapters. We are grateful also to the copy editing done by Mrs Edna Halperin, to the typing, checking and other administrative chores performed by Miss Liselotte Hofmann and Mrs Bernadine Murray. Responsibility for documentation is the authors'.

We once more wish to express our appreciation of the support extended by Dr W. Glenn Campbell, Director of the Hoover Institution, Stanford University. Above all, we owe a debt to the Earhart Foundation of Ann Arbor, Michigan, whose financial generosity helped to make this project possible.

PETER DUIGNAN, LEWIS H. GANN
General Editors

June 1975

INTRODUCTION

In a country which has neither foreign commerce, nor any of the finer manufactures, a great proprietor, having nothing for which he can exchange the greater part of the produce of his lands which is over and above the maintenance of the cultivators, consumes the whole in rustic hospitality at home. If this surplus produce is sufficient to maintain a hundred or a thousand men, he can make use of it in no other way than by maintaining a hundred or a thousand men. He is at all times, therefore, surrounded with a multitude of retainers and dependants, who having no equivalent to give in return for their maintenance, but being fed entirely by his bounty, must obey him, for the same reason that soldiers must obey the prince who pays them.[1]

This form of clientage, argued Adam Smith, was a universal feature among all backward peoples, be they Scottish Highland clansmen, Arabian nomads or early Anglo-Saxon raiders. During the second part of the last century, Smith's analysis would also have had application to many parts of sub-Saharan Africa.

At the time when Rhodes and Leopold II, Chamberlain and Ferry and others like them were dreaming of great empires, the great majority of Africans subsisted in small village communities. Their technical knowledge and equipment were simple. Their main tools were the hoe, the digging stick and the axe. Manpower and technological equipment were in short supply. Only land was plentiful. In the more favoured parts, where the population was dense, where the land was exceptionally fertile or where soil might be claimed for incompatible purposes by competing claimants, some African communities developed long-term rights in cultivable acreages. But for most Africans, the very notion of permanently holding land for future use would have been quite unfamiliar.

Every recognized member of the community normally had the right to till a portion of the available soil. Except for a small minority, life for the average African centred on small villages or scattered hamlets. In the more backward parts of Africa, the greatest and wealthiest rulers could not accumulate large supplies of food, for they lacked secure storehouses, safe from the ravages of weevils, mice and rats. Even had they solved the problem of constructing and administering magazines, kings could not easily transport large quantities of maize or cassava from one part of their realm to another. Only merchandise of small bulk and high value could be traded long distances with reasonable ease. From ancient times Africans had exchanged commodities such as salt, iron, copper ingots, gold dust and kola-nuts. But cattle walking on their own feet comprised the only source of food that could easily be moved over long distances.

The majority of African societies therefore faced enormous difficulties in accumulating capital. The more developed urban cultures of the Western Sudan and of East Africa were familiar with complicated credit arrangements. The use of trade currencies such as cowrie shells and iron bars was widespread. Even so, the majority of African societies depended more on intricate networks of kinship support, of gift exchanges and of tributary relationships than on the ties of the market. Generally speaking, successful rulers had to be judicious distributors as well as warriors and judges. A Lozi or a Zulu monarch, like those

[1] Adam Smith, *An inquiry into the nature and causes of the wealth of nations,* Edwin Cannan, ed. (New York, 1937), p. 385.

I

Scottish Highland or Arabian chieftains described by Adam Smith, was expected to be a generous lord who made gifts to his followers and fed the hungry when the crops failed. In a society with few means of accumulating capital, generosity was indeed the best policy. The road to power commonly lay in a man's ability to secure by judicious presents and by personal protection both the loyalty of relatives and the allegiance of strangers.

Societies of this kind were beset by numerous technological weaknesses. For tasks as varied as bearing burdens, hurling missiles, paddling canoes or tilling the soil, Africans depended largely on the power of human muscle. Given the high cost of transport and the universal shortage of capital, traditional technology was by no means inefficient. But it was subject to numerous limitations. The indigenous people did not know how to harness the power of wind, water or steam. Fulani raiders or Sotho warriors might be expert horsemen, but no indigenous economy had developed the art of harnessing animals to the wagon or to the plough. For the average villager, a drought, an enemy assault or a great swarm of locusts was likely to cause disaster. Africans had few defences against human or animal diseases; they had only a rudimentary knowledge of metallurgy and no command over technical devices such as pumps and explosives required for deep-level mining. African farmers did not know how to breed improved strains of cattle or of plants; they lacked the very notion of scientific research.

Africans also had to contend with a wide variety of political difficulties. The forces of production might be shackled, for instance, by the absence of a widespread *pax*. Local wars, civil wars, slave raiding and various forms of servitude were endemic over wide areas before the imposition of European rule. Even in relatively developed regions like the Western Sudan, the absence of peace might stand in the way of economic progress. Bolanle Awe, a modern African historian, shows how many of the ingredients necessary for economic development were present in Yoruba country (Nigeria) during the nineteenth century. The Yoruba had plenty of land; labour was cheap; towns like Ibadan were well placed for trade and possessed a relatively developed material culture. Arts and handicrafts flourished; agriculture had made considerable advances. Yet, despite its military prowess, Ibadan could not impose peace in Yorubaland. On the contrary, during the course of a prolonged and bitter struggle for power, Ibadan took measures which jeopardized the chances of peaceful local economic development. Intermittent warfare and raiding interfered with trade and placed numerous constraints on economic growth. Militarism indeed seems to have dictated the pace of economic development, with far-reaching consequences for Yoruba prosperity.[2]

Economic development in pre-colonial Africa was, moreover, both promoted and restrained by the all-encompassing force of ethnicity. Rigid social stratification maintained by the coercive rule of one ethnic group over another was widespread in kingdoms as varied as those of the Ndebele, the Lozi, the Nupe, the Zande, the Ngoni and many others. In Rwanda, for instance, the dominant Tutsi reduced the Bantu-speaking Hutu to serfdom, virtually prevented intermarriage and organized the state in such a way as to reserve the great majority of positions of power and profit to the ruling group. Even advanced cities such

[2] Bolanle Awe, 'Militarism and economic development in nineteenth century Yoruba country: the Ibadan example', *Journal of African History*, 1973, **14**, no. 1, pp. 65–77.

as Timbuktu were divided into ethnic castes distinguished by language, status, occupation, kinship, local distribution, age organization, ritual practice and separate communities.[3]

Pre-colonial Africa, on the other hand, had shown a great capacity for adaptation, which had enabled Africans to colonize a continent, despite the vagaries of the climate and the difficulties posed by harsh environments. As Hogendorn, Newbury and Yudelman point out in this volume, African cultivators had adopted a great variety of new crops from afar, such as maize, cassava, sweet potatoes and yams. African agriculturists had elaborated a wide range of techniques for dealing with many different soils and climates. In a few favoured areas such as the Upper Zambezi, Africans had developed fairly intensive forms of farming. Trade was widespread; for some it included on a small scale various forms of international commerce in commodities like wild rubber, ivory, gold dust and palm-oil, as well as even more widely diffused local traffic in victuals, luxury goods and tools. Even a century ago rural people in many parts of the hinterland had already been drawn into the world economy. Boer trekkers, far from being self-sufficient, relied on travelling merchants for such merchandise as muskets and cloth. Duala chieftains on the coast of Cameroun knew all about the intricacies of the palm-oil trade. The fortunes of some Swahili-speaking hunter or a Nyamwezi transport-organizer might depend on price fluctuations of the ivory market in distant London or Bombay.[4]

In fertile regions, such as Yorubaland or the valley of the Luapula, there were populous agro-towns, substantial communities capable of sustaining large numbers of people, but dependent still on farming, some trade (including long-distance commerce) and tribute. The most advanced societies of sub-Saharan Africa included the maritime cities of the east coast, whose sailing ships carried on a far-flung trade with the other lands adjoining the Indian Ocean. In West Africa there were urban centres like Djenne, Timbuktu and Kano. Kano depended on crafts and commerce for its living. The Hausa exported artifacts and imported virtually all their food by water-carriage along the Niger. Sudanic artisans acquired a great reputation as leather-workers and smiths, as artists skilled in working gold and as potters. Their cities had a considerable amount of economic specialization; their way of life had something in common with that of urban centres in early mediaeval Europe.

Even the most highly developed African economies, however, were subject to serious limitations. The Sudanic industries, for example, were backward, not only by the standards of the steam-powered industries in eighteenth-century England, but also by those of, say, sixteenth-century England, where manufactures like fulling, dyeing, printing, sugar refining, soap boiling and shipbuilding had all, to some measure, begun to benefit from organization on a fairly large scale, from a relatively sophisticated technology and from a developing market economy. The economic gap between Africa and Europe kept increas-

---

[3] M. G. Smith, 'Pluralism in precolonial Africa', in *Pluralism in Africa,* Leo Kuper and M. G. Smith, eds. (Berkeley, University of California Press, 1969), pp. 91–151.

[4] Newbury, in his essay on modern labour problems, has ably criticized the concept of a dual economy. Proponents of the 'dual economy' school draw a sharp distinction between foreign economic enclaves and the rural hinterland, which supposedly depends on a subsistence economy. Newbury demonstrates that in modern Africa, rural markets are in fact interpenetrated by the import factor, and that these ties exert a far-reaching influence on the provision of manpower.

Table 1. *Trade of Africa in 1897*

	Imports £(000)	Exports £(000)		Imports £(000)	Exports £(000)
Southern Africa	23,915	20,467	Guinea	306	269
			Senegal	1,167	843
Lagos	771	811	Ivory Coast	188	189
Niger Protectorate	640	750	Dahomey	330	231
Gold Coast	911	858	French Congo	143	211
Sierra Leone	457	401			
Gambia	140	164	Total French	2,134	1,743
	2,919	2,984	German East Africa	479	262
			South West Africa	244	62
British Somaliland	348	350	Togoland	99	39
Egyptian Sudan	91	66	Kamerun	295	185
British East Africa	298	73			
Zanzibar and Pemba	144	81	Total German	1,117	548
British Central Africa	86	27			
			Congo Free State	950	537
	967	597			
			Grand Totals	37,391	28,347
Portuguese					
East Africa	4,350	273			
Angola	1,031	1,195			
Guinea	8	3			
Total Portuguese	5,389	1,471			

SOURCE: S. Herbert Frankel, *The tyranny of economic paternalism in Africa: a study of frontier mentality 1860–1960* (Johannesburg, 1960), p. 17.

ing, and within the framework of European commerce as a whole the trade of Africa was of but small importance. By 1897, for instance, only 4·3 per cent of British imports derived from Africa, and only 10·4 per cent of British exports went to Africa. As shown in Table 1, the most developed economies on the entire continent were to be found in the European settlement areas of southern Africa, which accounted for the bulk of Africa's foreign trade.

Yet, by the standards of Western Europe, South Africa remained a most backward country. Even after the economic revival experienced during the aftermath of the Boer War (1899–1902), the South African economy for long bore a typically 'colonial' character. Immigrants from Great Britain and, to a lesser extent, newcomers from the European continent provided the bulk of mine-owners, farming capitalists, professional men in industry and the more highly placed administrators, as well as the skilled white workers. The great majority of the white Afrikaners and the black Africans alike lived on the land; yet until the First World War the country was not even self-sufficient in food. As S. Herbert Frankel has demonstrated, the country depended heavily on foreign investment that largely centred on mining.

Backward though South Africa might appear at the turn of the century, it was an economic giant compared to the remainder of Africa. By the end of the last century, sugar was grown on plantations in Mauritius, cloves in Zanzibar and cocoa in the island of São Tomé. Peasant-grown ground-nuts and palm-oil were exported from West Africa. Cocoa was beginning to acquire some importance in the Gold Coast but had not yet become a major source of revenue. A large proportion of Africa's exports still derived from the collection of wild products or from hunting. Such merchandise comprised elephant tusks, ostrich plumes, gum, rubber, wax and other goods of the kind carried by camel caravans from the Western Sudan to the Mediterranean shore, or from the East African mainland to the littoral of the Indian Ocean. In addition, Africans sold rhino horns, gold dust, kola-nuts and palm products.

These commodities could all be furnished by traditional technologies, improved at times through the importation of foreign tools. The age-old art of hunting elephants or rhinoceroses required enormous skill and daring, though the hunter's chances greatly improved when he was enabled to purchase a Western-made rifle. But the export of ivory did not involve a basically new technology. The commerce in elephant tusks, moreover, easily turned into a kind of *Raubwirtschaft,* as elephants might be 'shot out' from entire regions. Alluvial gold deposits could easily be worked by traditional methods; rubber likewise formed a natural resource that could be worked by unskilled labour and required no more than tapping, a rudimentary form of processing and porterage.

Palm products were of special value to West Africa as Western markets expanded, and as industrialists found a growing range of new uses for palm-oil. The oil-palm was of particular importance to Nigeria, where rivers, creeks and lagoons provided a natural communications network long before railway tracks and motor roads had penetrated the interior. The Niger Delta, with its unique river system, its concentrated stands of oil-palms, and its trade-oriented political structure, dominated the palm-oil trade, though adjacent regions, such as the coastal areas of Cameroun, also played a part. In absolute terms, however, this traffic remained insignificant. In 1899, for instance, the value of Great Britain's imports from its four West African colonies amounted to no more than £2,021,250, less than 1 per cent of its total imports. Or, to put it another way, Great Britain in 1899 imported nearly six times as much from a small European state such as Denmark as from Nigeria, the Gold Coast, Sierra Leone and the Gambia combined.[5]

This traffic might not have mattered much to the British trade balance, but foreign commerce was of tremendous importance to the local African economies. The importation of liquor (gin and rum), muskets, beads and cloth altered local consumption patterns and profoundly affected the local balance of power, both between one community and another and within the various African poli-

---

[5] According to the *Statesman's yearbook* . . . (London, 1902), pp. 85, 195, 242–3, the value of British trade in 1899 (in pounds) was as follows:

British imports, total	485,035,583
Imports from the Cape	22,647,719
Imports from British West Africa	2,021,250
Imports from Denmark	12,432,977
British exports, total	264,492,211
Exports to the Cape	9,911,503
Exports to British West Africa	1,466,988
Exports to Denmark	3,961,807

ties. The business of slave-raiding had often enhanced the power of kings and warlords in command of powerful armies. The cultivation and sale of oil-palm products and ground-nuts, on the other hand, could be carried on equally well by smaller entrepreneurs. Hence new men arose capable of challenging existing political arrangements in West Africa. In its early stages, the traffic between Europeans and Africans involved a measure of rough equality. In the economic field, the whites perforce depended on indigenous methods of production. In the political sphere, they relied on the protection of African potentates. For example, German traders in Cameroun were confined to the hulks of superannuated ships anchored off shore, and had to utilize the services of Duala middlemen who jealously guarded their monopoly. In the same fashion, white pioneers who had made their way to the kingdom of the Lozi or of the Ndebele in south-central Africa looked to the favour of local monarchs for permission to shoot elephants or to sell guns and cotton cloth. Humanitarians might rail at 'low' white bush-traders who 'corrupted' blacks by selling them gin, or rendered them 'insolent' by providing them with fire-arms, but these strictures merely underlined the way in which the early white dealers had to operate within the framework of African political power.

Broadly speaking, the early West African entrepôt trade functioned only as long as whites were satisfied with the sporadic protection provided by consular courts and gun-boats dispatched by their home governments, and as long as the Europeans would content themselves with a relatively small range of goods derived above all from hunting, collecting and the most primitive forms of mining. The early entrepôt trade in commodities like palm-oil or ivory did not give rise to new methods of production. The forest states of West Africa might increase their production of palm products, but expanded output did not require new technological skills.

Many communities on the west coast did develop what might be called a proto-middle class. This group included chiefs with a stake in trade and farming, vendors and also African agents of European firms, some of them educated men who had acquired a form of standard English, French, Portuguese or an Africanized variety of these tongues as their native speech. But outside a few Atlantic ports, such as Freetown, Lagos or St Louis, there was no African bourgeoisie in the Western sense. Neither was there a manufacturing class. The artisans of Katsina, Kano or Zaria in Nigeria, for example, might be renowned for their skill in weaving, dyeing, leather-work and fashioning metals, but by the nineteenth century they could not easily outsell British iron goods made in Birmingham or textiles woven in Manchester. Surplus capital could not readily be invested. As a Nigerian put it with regard to Benin, a relatively advanced state: 'When anyone in Benin needs to borrow money it is customary to do so, not on [the security of] his goods but on his person, or that of his family. It is not usually done in lieu of payment of debt, or until that debt can be paid.' [6] In most parts of Africa, powerful men thus invested their surplus in men, in beasts or in prestige goods—in economic advantages derived from kinship, clientage and conspicuous consumption.

White entrepôt trade gave way to white conquest when the Europeans ceased to be satisfied with the existing economic relationships, and when they had

[6] Jacob U. Egharevka, *Benin law and custom,* 3rd ed. (Port Harcourt, 1949), p. 63.

acquired not only the military potential but also the medical knowledge and the transport facilities required to penetrate the interior. The precise economic motives for European territorial expansion varied greatly.[7] The Boer trekkers looked above all to new supplies of grazing land. In Kamerun, the Germans in the 1880s apparently became resolved to break the coastal trade monopoly of the Duala at a time when the world price of palm products slumped. From then onward, German rule inland seemed essential to protect German entrepreneurs anxious to cut out the Duala intermediaries, in order to deal directly with agricultural suppliers in the interior and to establish stores and plantations in the hinterland. In Matabeleland, to provide yet another example, white settlers in Mashonaland resolved to smash the Ndebele military monarchy when they became convinced, in 1893, that their own economy, based on simple forms of gold mining and cash farming, could not peacefully coexist with the raiding economy of an adjacent warrior state. Ndebele power, the whites argued, was incompatible with the physical security of European investment and the personal safety of black workmen in white employ. Moreover, the Ndebele state, in white eyes, was guilty of 'locking up' valuable labour, precious land and, possibly, great mineral wealth.

Colonial economic policies

As the Europeans gradually conquered Africa, they established new political systems, promulgated laws and set up administrative structures. Roughly speaking, the era of partition and occupation (from about 1885 to 1908) was commonly the period when white rule was at its harshest. African primary resistance to colonial governance was considerable. In many areas there were rebellions also against the new overlords, with their taxes, labour levies and personal abuses. European conquest of necessity involved the use of force; force in turn begat the most varied forms of economic coercion. The most straightforward form of exploitation involved the direct appropriation of movable wealth like cattle. This method was appropriate to older indigenous warrior economies such as those of the Ndebele, the Ngoni and the Masai. White pioneers likewise looted Ndebele cattle after they had overthrown Lobengula's kingdom in 1893. Direct appropriation of the frontier variety was, however, comparatively rare. In Africa the conquering Europeans found few currency hoards to loot and no industrial machinery to dismantle. The African precolonial economies rarely produced a surplus that would have made war a payable proposition from the white man's point of view.

Economic coercion was usually applied in different ways; the duration of its employment varied, though it was widespread throughout much of Africa until at least the 1920s. Pressure was applied against indigenous communities through the direct appropriation of land, the forcible or partly coercive recruitment of labour, the obligatory gathering or collection of crops, and taxes. In many colonies, the decade preceding the First World War and then the war itself and its aftermath formed an economic watershed; a philosophy of coercion gradually gave way to a new creed based on economic incentives. After the

---

[7] See L. H. Gann and Peter Duignan, 'Reflections on imperialism and the scramble for Africa', in *Colonialism in Africa 1870–1960*, vol. I: *The history and politics of colonialism 1870–1914*, L. H. Gann and Peter Duignan, eds. (Cambridge University Press, 1969), pp. 100–31.

war, the new approach to the colonial *mise en valeur* led to a greater concern for African well-being and to an increasing preoccupation with the economic importance of Africans both as producers and as customers.

Humanitarian and missionary attacks and parliamentary criticism at home, as well as the economic requirements of the more complex colonial economies, brought about a variety of administrative and other reforms. Especially the first decade of the present century saw numerous changes: for example, in Rhodesia after the rebellions of 1896–7, in the Congo Free State after 1908, in German Africa while Dernburg was in charge of colonial affairs from 1906 to 1910. Governments not only tightened up their control over European companies and officials, but also became more concerned with African interests and needs.

From the very beginning, colonial governments sought to make colonies pay. They encouraged investors, bankers, traders, plantation owners and business groups. Tax systems were drawn up to attract investment. Whereas the British expected each colony to pay its own way (with occasional help in the forms of loans and grants), the French and Germans put more money into their colonies from early on. The Belgians did likewise after Brussels had taken over from Leopold in 1908. To run the colonies, the new rulers levied import duties and imposed hut or head taxes. (Company taxes were paid in Europe and so were not always available to colonial administrations. Export duties, where levied, were used to funnel goods to the metropolitan markets, not to raise revenue.)

Political domination led to economic penetration. The policy of every colony was to attract and to serve European enterprises (settlers were not encouraged in West and Equatorial Africa, however) and, often, to stimulate African farming of export crops. The growth of the infrastructure of the colonies served these twin purposes. In West Africa essential services catered to the needs of African peasant-farmers and European commercial groups. In Southern Rhodesia, Kenya and the Belgian Congo, government was concerned, above all, with assisting white settlers or those engaged in mining, plantation or other commercial enterprises. In contrast, German Togo concentrated on economic development of African agriculture. In all cases, however, government services in Africa for a long time were funded directly by African tax revenue and forced labour and by subsidies provided by the metropole.

Economic penetration came not only through control of the import–export trade and of currency and banking, but also through control of the general relations of the colony to the metropole's economy. It was the colonial administration that determined laws on land and labour uses, on economic planning and control. Usually, the first sector of the economy to be regulated was commerce. European powers differed in their attitudes towards trade and the role of colonies in the metropolitan economies. Great Britain and Germany held largely to a policy of free trade in Africa and sought to persuade other powers to keep an open-door policy there. The Berlin Act of 1885 and the Brussels Agreement of 1890 guaranteed free commercial intercourse in the Congo Basin and in West, Central and East Africa.

British Africa was a free-trade area for most of the colonial period (except during wartime and after 1932, when the British imposed some restrictions and preferential duties). In general, the British did not control the colonial exchange economies for the exclusive benefit of the metropole; neither did they enforce a monopoly on the purchase of colonial products. British merchants and investors, moreover, played a substantial part in the economy of the former German colonies, which offered fairly favourable conditions to foreign enterprise.

France, on the other hand, was a protectionist country that tried to integrate its colonies into the metropolitan economy and to make the colonies serve the metropole. France followed an open-door policy only when obliged to do so by international treaties (as in the Congo Basin and in the League of Nations Mandates). Generally speaking, the Méline Tariff of 1892 brought French colonies under the control of metropolitan tariffs. There were some exceptions: colonial exports to France were admitted free or were given preferences, and French ships did not pay certain charges in colonial ports. These policies continued until 1928, when changes freed the colonies somewhat from the French tariff system. But all French colonies continued to be given a preference on goods shipped to France. French shippers enjoyed special privileges in the carrying trade to and from the colonies, and a quota system controlled the import–export trade. Except for Portugal, France dominated the export and import trade of its African colonies to a greater extent than did any other colonial power (see Table 2). Even after independence, France continued to sell the greatest percentage of goods imported into the former colonies and remained the most important purchaser of exports from the new states.

Despite the propagandistic claims made by many colonial statesmen, Europe's trade with the African colonies at first formed but a small percentage of total European trade. For Britain the African commerce was never very significant, especially if the British trade with South Africa is deducted from the total. Before 1914, British Africa received 5·26 per cent of Britain's total exports and accounted for an 8-per-cent share of imports to Britain. Africa became a somewhat more important market between the wars, but after 1955 the African share again declined to what it had been in 1914.

The French colonies took a relatively more prominent part in the French economy. By 1935, the French African colonies took 27 per cent of French exports and had 21 per cent of the French import market. And by 1949, France's

Table 2. *Relative importance of French African territories as proportion of total French overseas trade*

Percentage of total French exports		Percentage of total French imports	
1900	8·9	1900	5·0
1910	9·8	1910	9·1
1914	13·7	1914	7·5
1920	13·6	1920	5·0
(All French Africa)		(All French Africa)	
1926	12·2	1926	9·3
1928	14·5	1928	10·4
1935	26·9	1935	20·9
1938	22·5	1938	20·9
1951	29·6	1951	14·5
1954	29·0	1954	18·8
1959	28·2	1959	20·3

SOURCE: David K. Fieldhouse, 'The economic exploitation of Africa: some British and French comparisons', in *France and Britain in Africa: imperial rivalry and colonial rule,* Prosser Gifford and William Roger Louis, eds. (New Haven, Yale University Press, 1971), p. 642.

share of total exports from its African colonies was 80 per cent and French imports to its African territories represented 75 per cent of the total. Algeria was by far the greatest French colonial market—more important than all the other colonies combined. For example, in 1934 France's trade with all its colonies represented about 28 per cent of its total trade, of which Algeria had 14 per cent. Black Africa, therefore, usually did not have a large share of the total French commerce.

The Portuguese African colonies, on the other hand, were of considerable importance to the motherland, especially once large-scale development had begun to take place after the Second World War. By the early 1960s, about one-third of Angola's foreign trade was conducted with Portugal, which provided about half the territory's imports and bought one-fifth of its exports. Portugal also accounted for about 30 per cent of the imports to, and some 35 per cent of the exports from Moçambique.

Colonial control, however, did not imply a monopoly of colonial commerce. The French, Portuguese and Belgians sold more goods to, and bought more merchandise from their colonies than did their rivals. But even in these colonies, foreign merchants accounted for a considerable proportion of the trade. The British, German and Italian colonies, as Grover Clark shows in *The balance sheets of imperialism* (1936), did not play a major part in either the import or the export trade of their respective homelands. As regards Germany, the former colonies were negligible both as sources of supplies and as markets. Colonial imports were only 0·3 per cent and exports only 0·5 per cent of total German commerce between 1894 and 1913. For Italy it was only slightly higher—0·87 per cent between 1884 and 1932. The Germans had 3·5 per cent of the trade in its colonies from 1894 to 1903. This dropped to 2·8 per cent between 1903 and 1914.[8]

Up to about the 1930s, colonial governments normally believed that Africa should be developed by private enterprise. The government's task was to provide a basic infrastructure, to build roads, railways and harbours, and to protect persons and property, as well as to furnish a few essential technical services. (Only Rhodesia had an important privately owned railway system.) The basic services established by governments included some rudimentary educational and health facilities, city planning, the provision of water, electricity, sewerage and so forth. In addition, colonial research stations experimented with crops, and agricultural, forestry and veterinary officers provided some information with regard to technical problems. These services had to be paid for through local revenues, supplemented at times by metropolitan subsidies of a direct or an indirect kind. In addition, governments intervened in their constabulary capacity both for the purpose of protecting property and, initially in numerous cases, in order to exercise economic coercion.

Land

Throughout the colonial era, as before it, the overwhelming majority of Africans depended on the land for their livelihood. At the same time, indigenous

---

[8] Colonial powers often spent more in the colonies than they received as receipts. For example, between 1894 and 1913 Germany spent 1,002 million marks more than the local receipts of its colonies, and the total trade of Germany with all its colonies was only 972 million marks.

forms of land tenure continued to operate in one fashion or another. Traditional ways, far from being smashed by rapacious capitalists, were indeed widely sustained by colonial officials. Imperial paternalism often contributed to the survival of traditional systems into the post-colonial era and often impeded economic development by restricting African opportunities in trade and in land sales. On the other hand, colonial paternalism went counter to the requirements of settlers, planters and concessionaires, who competed with indigenous communities for land. White pressure on African acres was at its most severe in the temperate parts of the continent—in South Africa, in South-West Africa, in Algeria, in the highlands of Kenya, on the elevated plateau of Southern Rhodesia, in scattered parts of Tanganyika, Northern Rhodesia and Nyasaland. Company concessionaires acquired considerable acreage in the Belgian Congo, in parts of French Equatorial Africa, in the Cameroons and in other areas. Outside South Africa and South-West Africa, the European impact was most far-reaching in Southern Rhodesia, where by 1963 about 37 per cent of the land was allotted to the European areas and just under 46 per cent to African Trust Land and African Purchase areas.

Pressure on the land, moreover, varied enormously in relation to the total population at any given time and to the availability of water and of fertile soil. During the European conquest, land was a commodity in ample supply. Rhodesia at the turn of the century probably comprised fewer than one million Africans, who were distributed over an area three times the size of England. Population pressures were therefore at first localized. They became increasingly severe as Africans grew in numbers, as more immigrants made their way into regions of European settlement and as land came to be more intensively utilized. Land shortage then became itself a means of economic pressure.

The impact of white settlement was, however, always double-edged in its effects. In countries such as Kenya or Rhodesia, Africans lost the right to use a vast proportion of the available acreage, much of it in the proximity of the new railway lines. On the other hand, European settlement itself created new opportunities. The whites brought in new tools, new agricultural methods, new seeds, new crops, new species of trees, new breeds of animals and ways of breeding them and new veterinary devices. Within a few decades of the white occupation of Rhodesia, the number of acres under African cultivation had vastly increased. Cattle in African ownership, once the object of white cupidity, had multiplied. (The number of African-owned beasts in the country went up from 55,000 in 1902 to 377,000 in 1913; from 744,000 in 1920 to over 1,500,000 in 1930. The cultivated African acreage increased from 550,000 in 1902 to 730,000 in 1908; 1,224,000 in 1920, and 1,378,000 in 1930.[9]) For all the restrictions imposed by the conquerors on the indigenous people, African cash-farming was stimulated by white occupation.

Over most of the rest of Africa, land remained in Africa possession. The bulk of Africans under colonial rule, unlike Europe's white proletariat during the Industrial Revolution, retained a stake in their ancestral acres. In many regions, colonial policy itself deliberately prevented the alienation of African lands to foreign settlers or entrepreneurs. In the British West African colonies

[9] L. H. Gann, *A history of Southern Rhodesia: early days to 1934* (London, 1965), pp. 175 and 272. In Kenya, in the 1930s, Europeans had 16,700 square miles, Africans had 53,000 and the Crown held 99,000.

and in German Togo, white landownership was restricted in the real or supposed interests of Africans; the whites were confined to leasing land for mining and timber use. For instance, Pedler notes in his essay, the entrepreneur William Lever (later Lord Leverhulme) was refused permission to acquire land for oil-palm plantations under the Union Jack; instead, Lever's economic pioneering had to be done in the Congo (1902) under the Belgian flag.

In French West Africa (AOF), little land was alienated. A few land concessions were granted; for example, some 185,000 acres were alienated in the Ivory Coast. The French experience of the social evils of land alienation in Algeria and the failure of early French ventures in Senegal made the French unwilling to force Africans off their land in AOF. As a result, the economy in AOF was based on peasant farming, not on plantations or concessions. In French Equatorial Africa (AEF), a different policy was pursued in hopes of opening up the region. Large, thirty-year concessions were granted—forty companies received 70 per cent of the land of the Congo. Abuses of the African population led to reduction in the size and number of concessions in 1906 and 1930.[10] Even though Europeans ran the estates, development before 1945 was limited in AEF primarily because of transportation problems.

Extensive grants of land were made to concessionaires in the Congo Free State by Leopold II and after 1908 by the Belgian government. Railway companies received over 22·5 million acres. The concessions to mining companies in Katanga gave the companies administrative and commercial control over vast areas; 112·5 million acres were administered by a joint body, the Comité Spécial du Katanga. A third type of concession went to companies for marketing forest products—25·5 million acres. Various European enterprises and individuals also received blocks of land for commercial purposes; for example, Huileries du Congo Belge was granted land to promote palm-oil production. Not all this land was kept; all told, perhaps 51 million acres were alienated to Europeans by 1955 and Africans occupied about 120 million acres.

The Portuguese sought to attract settlers and concessionaires, by granting them land, in order to develop their African colonies. Vast estates were given to such groups as the Nyassa Company and the Moçambique Company late in the nineteenth century. These chartered companies ruled like governments; their charters were not revoked until 1929 and 1942 respectively. Mining, forestry and plantations received the largest units of land. Peasant farming schemes, which have mostly failed, received small pieces of land. Most Portuguese in the colonies have lived in cities and towns, but still large amounts of usable land have been alienated in Portuguese Africa. For example, in Angola, coffee plantations received 1,037,407 acres between 1950 and 1960; and mining companies were allotted a considerable area to work, for example, Diamang received 17,560 square miles and Lobito Mining Company 18,910 square miles. Still, there has been no shortage of land in Angola as only 1 to 3 per cent of the total land area of 481,351 square miles is cultivated.

Forced labour

When the Europeans tried to intensify the production of commodities such as wild rubber, they commonly faced a major labour problem. In most parts of

---

[10] See Catherine Coquery-Vidrovitch, 'French colonization in Africa to 1920: administration and economic development', in *Colonialism in Africa*, vol. I, pp. 165–98.

Africa, transport facilities were inadequate or nonexistent. Economic incentives were hard to supply as long as there was no network of trading stores where Africans might acquire new goods. Living conditions in pioneer mining areas in Northern Rhodesia or on railway construction jobs in the Cameroons were usually deplorable, not only for black workmen but also for white supervisors and foremen.

Europeans might talk about bringing the Industrial Revolution to Africa, but conditions in early colonial Africa were very different from those prevailing, say, in eighteenth-century England. The British Industrial Revolution had taken place in a country already supplied with an elaborate economic infrastructure and highly developed farming systems. Except for Irish immigrants, the majority of the early British labour migrants travelled only a short way to get to town. Africans, on the other hand, often had to undertake vast journeys. (By the 1880s, for example, there were some black mine-workers in Kimberley who had come down all the way from the Upper Zambezi in search of jobs and guns; theirs was an odyssey involving a trek over a thousand miles of inhospitable country.) And whereas most of the English countrymen who had lost their share in the village commons in eighteenth-century England had to make the best of life in the new towns, not so the Tswana, Lozi or Sotho workmen who had served their time in late nineteenth-century Johannesburg: the great majority of these labour migrants returned to their respective places of origin. The bulk of Africa's early black labour force remained seasonal in character. Indeed, in many parts of south-east Central Africa and East Africa, the first workmen solely dependent on cash wages were expatriates—say, mine supervisors from Wales, boiler-makers from Yorkshire, railway construction workers from Bombay.

Traditional land rights also impeded the influx into the countryside of urban capital (a form of investment which Adam Smith had considered to be an essential element in the economic development of England). The persistence of traditional land rights combined with official policies to retard or prevent the development of rural credit from land banks or village money-lenders. At the same time, the bulk of the African labour force retained an ambiguous character—part rural, part urban—and was thereby relatively inefficient and also hard to organize for industrial action. Migrant workmen preferred to go to the town, the farm or the mine without their wives. They were reluctant (or unable) to sell their land and settle permanently as wage labourers. Africans recognized the losses and gains involved, and chose to keep their traditional land and welfare rights in their villages and to work for cash to supplement their income. Because they were in town to make money, they lived cheaply, reluctant to pay much for food or housing.

According to some economists, the African migrant-labour system, with its seasonal supply of unskilled labour, was deliberately encouraged by white employers who looked on the African rural areas as a means of subsidizing cash wages and of providing old-age pensions and other welfare benefits at the expense of the indigenous economies. Early twentieth-century documents, such as Chamber of Mines minutes or company correspondence from early Rhodesia, tell a different story. Rhodesian employers, like their confreres in other parts of Africa, would have much preferred a 'non-spasmodic' labour supply of proletarians without a stake in tribal lands, men who were unlikely to desert, who depended entirely on their wage packet for their living and were hence willing to do more work and able to do it more efficiently than migrants. At the beginning of the present century, the white employers' demand for reliable, unskilled labour set off an intensive search for imported labour; but most of these foreign recruitment schemes came to nothing (Indians brought into East Africa were an exception). The colonial economies in the main had to depend on the unskilled labour of African countrymen. In its initial stages, the mobilization of labour often involved the use of compulsion.

For most people, the term 'exploitation' stands for a variety of abuses such as the payment of low wages (low in relation to profits, low in relation to wages in other countries or in other occupations) or the extortion of excess profits. Although the charge is rarely precise and sometimes contradictory, the supposed moral stigma seems inescapable. However, for serious analysis as opposed to political pamphleteering, this definition will not do. We offer David Landes's definition of exploitation linked to the exercise of political dominion: 'Imperialist exploitation consists in the employment of labor at wages lower than would obtain in a free bargaining situation; or in the appropriation of goods at prices lower than would obtain in a free market. Imperialist exploitation, in other words, implies nonmarket constraint.' [11]

During the colonial period there was forced labour and the appropriation of goods at lower than market prices. These policies varied in time and from colony to colony, but in many instances earlier forms of obligatory labour gave way to enforced cultivation of crops and the purchase of goods at lower than market prices.

The advocates of forced labour argued that Africa's main economic problem was a chronic manpower shortage. This notion went with demographic assumptions that Africa was gravely underpopulated and that, far from increasing, the population of certain areas might, in fact, be declining. Proponents of compulsion also believed, with good justification, that pre-colonial Africans had not been free economic agents, able to sell their labour and their crops to the highest bidder in a free marketplace. European conquest, said the advocates of empire, had moreover done away with pre-colonial forms of economic compulsion and indigenous forms of organized violence. Furthermore, Europeans generally believed that Africans were non-economic men, idlers who lived off the labour of their exploited wives. They argued that forced labour was a legitimate form of taxation—a facile assumption to make at a time when many African villages had not become fully enmeshed in a money economy, when peasants as yet had no money to pay their imposts in cash and when labour rather than land was the scarcest factor of production.

The term 'forced labour', of course, comprises within it an infinite number of gradations, not always considered by critics of the colonial system. In communities where tribal cohesion was strong, a recruiter in the early days could not make contracts with individuals without reference to the local political authority. If a pioneer missionary or merchant wanted men, he would have to approach a local dignitary who would supply workers in return for specified payments. This form of employment, though contrary to the notions of an individual wage economy, was miles away from cruder forms of coercion. But in many cases manpower was also recruited by the threat of brute force. The

[11] David S. Landes, 'Some thoughts on the nature of economic imperialism', *Journal of Economic History,* Dec. 1961, **21**, no. 4, p. 499.

employment of conscripted workmen commonly went with a primitive back-woods economy. Within the framework of undercapitalized pioneer enterprise, unskilled labour was apt to be at a premium; little machinery was employed; supervision was likely to be poor; labour yields were low; economic incentives could not easily be supplied in the absence of a developed trading network. Hence the demand for labour frequently exceeded the available supply, even though the best type of employer might be able to obtain all the workmen he needed. All too often, the colonists would not wait until African wants in-creased, and until Africans were motivated to go to work or to sell produce in order to buy imported goods. Mines, plantations and farms needed labour; gov-ernments wanted navvies for railway construction jobs and road-building; of-ficials and soldiers needed porters to carry supplies.

There were many different forms of obligatory labour. Government officials might resort to compulsion on their own; they might utilize African chiefs as labour recruiters; or they might apply indirect pressure through taxation and other fiscal devices. Forced labour for private employers was the first to be eliminated (by the 1920s it had been regulated, restricted and then abolished in most areas outside the Portuguese empire). Labour was conscripted for govern-ment projects for much longer periods. In the end, resort to compulsion came to be governed by international conventions and was restricted in the main to emergencies (such as floods or similar catastrophes), to certain communal un-dertakings or to wartime needs.

The coercion of labour was at its most brutal in the early days when whites attempted to intensify indigenous production derived from the collection of nat-ural products. The widespread atrocities committed in the Congo Free State and in AEF for the purpose of obtaining wild rubber are well known. But they are far from isolated. On a smaller scale, for instance, the Germans resorted to compulsion in Kamerun and elsewhere. Obligatory labour was also widely used in the construction of roads and railways, for porterage and for other govern-ment work.

Conscripts helped to build railways in the Congo, in the French colonies, in Nigeria and in British East Africa. Forced labour commonly suffered from a high rate of sickness and mortality; it also disrupted village life. Governments learned but slowly how to provide medical care for migrants; meanwhile, thousands died on mine, plantation and rail construction projects. Forced labour on public works diminished after 1919. Colonial governments attempted to limit the employment of draftees to the provision of essential government ser-vices. But porterage for officials was widely continued at least until the 1930s, when the increasing use of cars and trucks opened up even some of the more isolated areas.

Forced labour, however, ran counter to the views of 'scientific colonialism', which, at the beginning of this century, began to be propounded by men as diverse as Joseph Chamberlain and Bernhard Dernburg. Dernburg, head of German colonial affairs between 1906 and 1910, was perhaps one of the most gifted proponents of the new course. A banker, an efficiency expert skilled at restoring bankrupt firms to health, Dernburg believed that a proper combination of transport facilities, sound marketing methods, scientific research, technical training, scientific management and reliance on economic incentives would put the German colonies on their feet. He considered Africans to be valuable, not merely as wage labourers but also as customers of German-made goods. Far from being idlers, Dernburg argued, Africans were economic men: the 'Negro' was indeed peculiarly endowed with those virtues of thrift, foresight and hard work that some sociologists mistakenly attribute in a singular measure to Protestants. During the Dernburg period, therefore, the use of obligatory labour in the German colonies diminished.

There were reforms also in the Congo Free State (annexed to Belgium in 1908) and in Southern Rhodesia, where Sir William Milton (administrator from 1898 until 1914) introduced far-reaching improvements. Under the new dispensation, taxation was regularized and became a limited and predictable charge instead of an arbitrary and variable imposition. Working conditions improved in the mines; better food and medical attention resulted in a spectacular decline in the death rate of both white and black mine-workers. (In Southern Rhodesia, for instance, mortality among mine-workers dropped from 75·94 per thousand in 1906 to 21·68 in 1917 and 15·39 in 1925.) The use of economic incentives increased as bush-traders set up an increasing number of stores in the backveld.

The pace and scope of these reforms differed widely. By and large, the more developed regions like Southern Rhodesia changed first. The more backward territories, especially those under Portuguese rule, changed last. On balance, the British were more inclined to relinquish economic compulsion than were their continental rivals, though even in British territories there were considerable regional differences. In the Northern Territories of the Gold Coast, for example, the government continued to use official pressure to recruit workmen to the mines until after the First World War. Virtual compulsion did not cease until 1924, by which time the government had found that chiefs were apt to enlist the weakest and hence the least efficient members of the community for work in the mines.[12]

Compulsory labour was a ruinous burden on weak subsistence economies. This was true all the more when the whites demanded African services during the peak agricultural seasons. The brutality involved in direct coercion is widely documented. Its total impact remains much harder to assess. But clearly, direct compulsion was subject to numerous economic constraints. For instance, wild rubber could easily be tapped by unlettered villagers blackmailed to work in the bush, but the villagers' product was of poor quality and could not compete on the world market once plantations in South-East Asia began to produce a superior product with superior methods. The need for porterage might be widespread but porters found themselves without jobs, once bicycles and, later (in the 1920s and 1930s), cars and trucks made their appearance in the bush. Arbitrary impositions, such as the impressment of cultivators for labour or the requisitioning of food, might occasion both armed African resistance and bitter political polemics from metropolitan critics of the colonial government. Coercion was apt to produce inefficient and unwilling workmen; employers indeed were likely to complain that African chiefs would send only the local trouble-makers and ne'er-do-wells to work for the whites. Coercive methods tended to be unpopular among district officers charged with the unpleasant task of mobilizing labour. Moreover, they represented a concealed

[12] Roger G. Thomas, 'Forced labour in British West Africa: the case of the Northern Territories of the Gold Coast 1906–1927', *Journal of African History*, 1973, **14**, no. 1, pp. 78–103.

subsidy paid to the less efficient employers by the government at the expense of the more humane employers who could afford to attract labour by economic incentives.

The International Forced Labour Convention of 1930 was largely adopted by the British, French and Belgians but not by the Portuguese. The colonial rulers made some exceptions to the convention: compulsory military service, convict labour, civic obligation, emergency work and communal labour. The French kept forced labour for public works (*prestation*) until 1946. They also drafted soldiers, though labour on government projects could be substituted for military service (until 1950 such labour was used on public works). The Belgians and the British had done away with most forms of forced labour by the early 1930s. The Portuguese were the last colonial rulers to use forced labour. By 1960 they had apparently complied with many international regulations governing forced labour, but charges of official pressure to provide contract labour continued to be made during the 1960s.

Africans were also exploited by being compelled to cultivate marketable produce. Many were obliged to grow cash crops. The colonizers hoped thereby to develop their territories and to provide revenue for running the colonies. Africans received payment for their efforts, but, as Peemans shows in his essay, the remuneration fixed by the state was normally set at rates below those that cultivators might have received in the open market. The obligatory growing of specified crops, in other words, was a form of selective taxation directed against the villager, an impost from which African white-collar workers or artisans remained exempt. Though in this volume Peemans and Bauer each look at African history from very different standpoints, they concur on the deleterious effects of policies that withhold from the cultivator the full value of his crops in the assumed interest of the state. This particular form of government intervention diminished economic incentives for the cultivators; village traders were discouraged. Official planning, moreover, might involve mistaken choices. (In Northern Nigeria, for instance, indigenous cultivators disregarded official propaganda favouring the growing of cotton, and turned instead to ground-nut cultivation, a wise decision from the economic point of view.)

Economic development

For all the harshly coercive features of colonialism, European rule also represented an economically liberating element. The slave-trade was crushed. Domestic servitude in its various forms came to a gradual end. Because in most parts of Africa the whites acquired a monopoly of organized armed force, inter-tribal warfare became a thing of the past; so did the migrations of great armed hosts that had once shaken the weaker societies to their foundations. Freed from the menace of raiding bands, African farmers, herdsmen and traders could spread out farther afield. Fortified settlements, like the agro-towns of Kazembe's Lunda on the Luapula in Zambia, lost their military *raison d'être*. Over most of the continent agricultural production began to go up. Improved communications by road, railway and steamer permitted traders to distribute food over greater distances and in vastly greater quantities than had been possible in pre-colonial times. Merchants and migrants could now move over large areas with relatively few constraints. In the long run, government became more humane. Under the British rule in Northern Rhodesia, for example, barbarous punishments (such as condemning prisoners to be mutilated or to be eaten alive slowly by black ants or rapidly by crocodiles), once imposed by the ruling Lozi people, disappeared. A small minority of Africans began to acquire new skills; they found employment as drivers, telegraphists, printers, clerks, interpreters, mechanics—all new jobs that owed their existence to the European presence. Elementary health, agricultural and education services came into being, subsidized initially to a considerable extent by the private enterprise of metropolitan missionary societies. The colonizers created a host of new towns; they were Africa's city builders *par excellence*. The new settlements in turn began to be equipped in a more or less precarious fashion with electrical and water-purification plants, sewerage facilities and a host of other urban devices. These had been unknown in Europe at the time of the Industrial Revolution, but by the end of the nineteenth century their technology had been sufficiently developed to be applied in the tropical regions of the world. For all the misery suffered by the poor in new towns like Accra and Bulawayo, living conditions there probably never reached the depths of those experienced by the most poverty-stricken in the industrial cities of the early nineteenth century, when no European city had an adequate or a sanitary water supply, and when a modern urban technology and modern health services were unknown. The new towns also created demands for food and services that stimulated the rural economy.

Once the colonial administrations had emerged from the initial era of conquest, the conquerors began to set up regular bureaucracies, small in size, comparatively inexpensive to run, and motivated by psychic rewards in the share of honors, medals and a sense of mission more than by monetary incentives alone. Still, the colonial bureaucracy was the product of a money economy, and in turn worked for its extension. The bureaucracies, as Marx had pointed out earlier with regard to India, were agencies for the Westernization of indigenous society. They did away with traditional 'restraints on trade' occasioned by the tolls, tributes and other customary obligations once levied by African kings (although they imposed new ones in the form of licences for traders, enforced cultivation of crops, hut taxes, forced labour and so on). The bureaucracies shaped the colonies into administrative and political units of a new kind, units that survived their makers and later assumed the dignity of independent statehood. These new units of government were subject to rule from outside but were therefore exempt from the corruption, coups and counter-coups, the civil war and *caudillo* governance that beset, for instance, many Latin American countries during this period. In Western eyes, the colonial governments became credit-worthy and were able to raise money abroad for railways and other public works. Above all, the new bureaucracies functioned with astonishing economy of manpower. (In 1901, for example, the entire German administration of Kamerun comprised no more than seventy-seven whites, from the governor down to the gardeners in the botanical station in Victoria. Twenty-three Germans sufficed to run Togo.) The small numerical size of the administrative machine in turn imposed serious limitations both on the coercive power of the state and on its ability to shoulder more than a limited range of tasks.

In economic terms, Africa witnessed a remarkable degree of development before 1914. There was a staggering increase in exports, above all in West

Africa.[13] Given economic incentives and adequate communications, African cultivators made a striking response. In the Gold Coast, for instance, the Akwapim and Krobo acquired an enviable reputation as pioneers in the cocoa industry. Elsewhere, ground-nuts, cotton, coffee, maize, palm-oil and other crops became of major importance. This economic expansion was part of a wider movement that affected the entire tropical world. Sir W. Arthur Lewis demonstrates that during the period 1880–1913, tropical countries like the southern Gold Coast, Nigeria, Kenya and Uganda—that is to say, areas that had responded to the demand for export goods—did remarkably well. Their modern sectors grew as rapidly as the modern sectors of Western Europe.[14] For all its seamy side, the tale of empire in the pre-war period thus was in part an economic success story.

The economic impact of the First World War was double-edged. Africans conscripted as porters in colonial Africa or Africans sent to the Western front in the French army suffered terrible hardships. Africans were forced to grow crops for the metropole. Several small rebellions broke out in the French and Portuguese territories. There was a general rise in prices as the costs of imports went up. The hardships of war, however, were felt differently in various areas. In the north-eastern area of Northern Rhodesia the general rise in prices was not compensated for by increased opportunities for earning money as in the Gold Coast. On the contrary, the British impressed African carriers, and thereby artificially deflated wages for this particular form of labour. On the other hand, war benefited those producers able to take advantage of the rising prices of primary commodities. In all the more accessible parts of Africa, farmers got more for their crops. Mineral production went up in areas such as Katanga and Southern Rhodesia. In South Africa, moreover, entrepreneurs began to build more factories in order to replace products that could no longer be imported from Europe.

At the end of the war, there was a brief boom, followed by a lengthy period of depression and market instability, along with falling prices and reduced demand, especially for raw material. The countries of Africa were hit particularly hard because they were dependent on the sale of primary produce. Still, there was considerable development, though it was extremely uneven. Katanga and Northern Rhodesia experienced a far-reaching mining revolution; hence the value of their production increased at an immensely more rapid pace than, say, that of Tanganyika, which remained largely dependent on the export of a few agricultural products. Nevertheless, during the inter-war period a considerable portion of colonial Africa made substantial gains, and in the case of the mining and the cocoa-exporting areas, spectacular gains. Table 3, even though it does not allow for inflation, demonstrates that the inter-war period was not one of neglect and stagnation for tropical Africa as a whole.

Mining, along with agriculture, provided a major impetus for economic

[13] The index number of value of exports in 1913 (1883 = 100) was: West Africa, 584; Central Africa, 498; and East Africa, 372. By comparison, in Egypt it was 257, and in India, 235. W. Arthur Lewis, 'The export stimulus', in *Tropical development, 1880–1913*, W. Arthur Lewis, ed. (Evanston, Northwestern University Press, 1970), p. 15.

[14] Their overall growth rate *per capita* was lower—say, 1·0 to 1·5 instead of 1·5 to 2·0. But, Lewis argues, this difference was occasioned by the fact that in the tropical countries the traditional subsistence sectors were still large; they had started from a lower base of development. *Ibid.*, pp. 30–1.

Table 3. *Growing trade of French Africa and British Africa*

FRENCH AFRICA: value of exports (at current prices in million U.S. dollars)				
	1902	1913	1928	1938
French West Africa (incl. Togo)	13·1	29·2	88·0	40·5
French Equatorial Africa	1·6	—		
	(Congo)		} 20·0	7·5
Cameroons	—	—		7·2
Madagascar	1·8	9·4	—	23·5

BRITISH AFRICA: value of exports (in current prices, 1902–60, £000)				
	1902	1913	1921	1938
South Africa	1,548	66,659·5	62,381	28,074
Nyasaland	6	248	427	960
The Rhodesias	—	3,737	5,380	14,850
Zanzibar, Uganda, Kenya	20	2,116	5,022	8,473
Nigeria	1,337	7,352	9,690	9,286
Gold Coast	381	5,427	6,942	6,235
Sierra Leone	207	1,731	1,625	2,136
Gambia	228	867	793	256

SOURCE: David K. Fieldhouse, 'The economic exploitation of Africa: some British and French comparisons', in *France and Britain in Africa: imperial rivalry and colonial rule,* Prosser Gifford and William Roger Louis, eds. (New Haven, Yale University Press, 1971), pp. 659–60.

growth in Africa. Mining in its simple stage—that is, the extraction and export of untreated ore—did not contribute as much to economic development as did mining in its more sophisticated forms, supplemented by smelting and refining. But the large-scale working of copper, coal, gold and other minerals required a great variety of ancillary services. Telecommunication was needed, and railways, roads and harbours had to be built in order to export ores and to import mining equipment and stores. These facilities were almost always constructed with foreign capital. Later, domestic and foreign capital went into cement plants, electric plants, waterworks and workshops. Capital went also into mills, smelters and electrolysis plants to treat and process ores. Coal had to be provided for railways and power plants. Towns emerged to house the workers and technicians. There were new demands for building materials, fuels, food, clothing, and for health, training and other services. Mining townships required the skills of merchants, bankers and insurance agents. The growing compounds provided expanding markets for farmers and ranchers. This multiplier-accelerator process helped to push mineral-rich countries toward modernity.

Development, however, was extremely uneven, because the bulk of overseas capital had been invested in southern Africa, with the Belgian Congo coming second, British West Africa third, then French Africa and Portuguese Africa right at the bottom. The social ramifications and even the statistical amount of investment in Africa remain in dispute. But measured in terms of brick and mortar—roads, railways, ports, plants and cities—the period before 1939 was of great consequence. Before the outbreak of the Second World War, the colonizers provided the infrastructure for subsequent development. Between 1890 and 1939 more than 32,000 miles of railroad were built in black Africa. New cities like Ndola, Elisabethville and Dar es Salaam had sprung up. There were over 400,000 miles of roads. Plantations and light and service industries served mines, towns and farms. By the end of the 1920s the internal combustion engine had made its appearance in some of the backwoods as well as in the cities. Cars and trucks made the remoter regions more accessible to commerce. They reduced the isolation of distant villages, and at the same time they achieved what no missionary and no humanitarian had ever been able to accomplish: they put an end to the back-breaking labour of the porters in the bush.

The overall effects of foreign trade may be disputed, as Meier shows in his essay, but commercial statistics leave no doubt that there was a considerable influx of new commodities. People developed new skills and found greater opportunities. Some of the benefits of foreign trade trickled through even to the remoter villages in the shape of consumption goods (like coffee, tea, sugar, salt and matches), new means of transport such as bicycles and wagons, new forms of capital investment (such as ploughs, water pumps, sewing machines, cattle dips and fences)—investments that statisticians could not even attempt to measure and therefore go unrecorded as indicators of material well-being. In many parts of Africa, land had acquired commercial value. Village trade and international commerce increased alike. New crafts came into existence, such as those of the bicycle repairer, the motor mechanic, the truck driver, the photographer, the railway ganger, all occupations that had been unknown to pre-colonial Africa.

Mining and plantation work were done mostly by migrant workers. As long as many African workmen retained traditional rights in the land, they remained half peasant, half proletarian, with a stake both in the town and in the country. Critics of the system argued that the mines, plantations and cities thereby denuded the villages of their wealth and manpower, that African workmen could not become fully efficient, either as farmers or as industrial workers.

We have alluded to the employers' attitude in an earlier section. The impact of labour migration on the rural areas is much harder to assess. Much depended on local circumstances. For instance, among the Bemba of Northern Rhodesia, the departure of many able-bodied men from the villages probably had the most serious effects on a system of slash-and-burn agriculture requiring considerable physical strength. The Mambwe, on the other hand, developed new forms of cultivating fertile mounds, a type of agricultural work that could be done by women and older men as well as by youngsters. Hence labour migration for the Mambwe may have represented a more efficient way of mobilizing the available manpower resources. Labour migration did occasion a backwash of urban wealth and new goods and experiences into the countryside. According to a calculation made for Ghana in 1963, the urban-rural flow of wealth may have amounted to about 3 per cent of the national wealth, and a considerably larger fraction of the wealth comprised within the cash economy.[15]

[15] See, for instance, William Watson, *Tribal cohesion in a money economy: a study of the Mambwe people of Northern Rhodesia* (Manchester University Press, 1958), *passim;* and John C. Caldwell, *African rural-urban migration: the movement to Ghana's towns* (New York, Columbia University Press, 1969), p. 216.

Some of the new African entrepreneurs even received help from their former employers. There is, for instance, a Zambian economic success story concerning one Saulosi Dimba, an African economic pioneer from Mazabuka District, who used to work as a little boy on a European farm. After the First World War, Dimba became a waiter, but soon went back to farming, eventually rising from the lowly job of leading oxen to the more responsible task of driving a span. Having looked after his master's wagon for some time, Dimba wanted to become an employer. His white boss agreed to help him with farm implements to make a start. Dimba threw all his energy into his new enterprise, and having amassed some capital from the sale of maize, he decided to buy a wagon to trade in the Mazabuka area. He bought the old wagon of his accommodating former employer, which soon set him up on the road to a modest fortune. Africans and Europeans came along to have their wares carried, and—acting on his old employer's advice—Dimba got a hawker's licence. He then began to buy soft goods from the Mazabuka stores, loaded them onto his vehicle and took them to villagers farther afield, accepting in return for his merchandise not money but maize, which he sold at a profit along the line of rail. By 1937, Dimba felt that he had enough capital to put up a store of his own, and in time added a second and a third shop to his original enterprise.[16]

Men like Dimba, however, generally worked under severe disabilities. They commonly lacked capital, mercantile training and technical qualifications. Moreover, for reasons which are far from clear, some trading people who had done well in pre-colonial circumstances—people such as the Yao or the Bisa— often failed to make their mark under the colonial dispensation. In addition, the very nature of African land rights might militate against the provision of credit essential to a budding entrepreneur. Bankers or money-lenders could not give loans on the security of real estate as long as Africans did not own land in freehold tenure that they might freely mortgage. The structure of African land rights also helped to inhibit the growth of African capitalism in a more indirect fashion. Colonial governments, in protecting African land rights, often impeded or prevented the growth of capitalized agriculture under European leadership. As long as the majority of African workmen remained half peasant, half proletarian migrants with a stake in the land, employers looked upon their hands as though they were soldiers on a temporary engagement in an industrial army. Hired hands, especially the unskilled men, received only part of their wages in cash. A substantial portion of their remuneration was paid in lodgings and kind. Hence the problem of real wages hinged to a considerable extent on the question of improving the workman's food, his lodging and his medical care, as reflected in declining rates of disease and mortality.

The 'classical' period of colonialism had coincided, roughly speaking, with the age of pre-Keynesian economics. The government official was expected to be, above all, a specialist in law and order. He was expected to assist in the creation of an economic infrastructure, but he was not expected to transform the economy of traditional societies. The production of goods was to be left to individual entrepreneurs, many of them European, Indian, Lebanese (see the Dotsons' essay) or indigenous black people (such as the Yoruba élites described by Lloyd in his essay). The prevalent economic doctrines found expression in

---

[16] L. H. Gann, *A history of Northern Rhodesia: early days to 1953* (London, 1964), p. 288.

the ideal of financial self-sufficiency for each territory. With the exception of the Congo Free State, no colonial power ever transferred revenue raised by customs or taxation from an overseas dependency to the metropolis. On the other hand, before 1945 the metropolis did not feel required to play a major part in financing the development of the colonial areas, except in building roads, railways and ports, and in providing agricultural and technical services. Newly acquired territories obtained imperial subsidies; in addition, the imperial power guaranteed colonial loans. On the whole, however, the separate territories were expected to balance their own budgets. The richer colonies pushed ahead, while the poorer could hardly afford even the most essential services. The prevailing theory of government was based on the assumption of 'infinite time ahead', the belief that European governance in Africa would continue for many generations, if not for centuries to come, and that problems of administration must come first in the imperial order of priority. Government officials had neither the economic theory nor the economic tools to promote development; they saw themselves as guardians, not innovators, of economic growth.

From the end of the 1930s, the economic ethos of government gradually began to change. There was a rapid rise in world prices for primary products. The growing foreign demand for raw materials occasioned an increase in African exports (see Table 4). There was hardly an African colony whose trade did not increase.

Government officers at the same time began to tackle an ever-increasing number of economic tasks designed to stimulate and also to direct the growing economies. We have seen that the early colonizers had made extensive use of state power for mobilizing labour, for forcing Africans to grow specified crops, for compelling Africans to relinquish land and for other purposes. But, in addition, state power had begun to operate in a protective fashion, to assure industrial safety and minimum standards of food and accommodation in the mining areas, to protect migrant labour and to regulate traders. From the beginning the state also had to take a major share in investment. Frankel thus calculates that the majority of the listed capital invested in Africa between 1870 and 1936 derived from public sources.

In addition, the state took up many new functions. We have shown, in the introductory essay to the fifth volume of this series, how the imperialists had laid the foundations of an extensive network of research into all manner of subjects—from the sciences of medicine, veterinary science, plant biology, parasitology, geology and zoology to such non-utilitarian subjects as history and archaeology. All these studies owe their existence in Africa to the impact of empire. Their economic importance in the context of African development remains to be assessed.

World War II and its aftermath

During the Second World War and its aftermath the pace and scope of government intervention increased further. The British built up an elaborate network of marketing boards in West Africa and elsewhere. In Southern Rhodesia, Sir Godfrey Huggins, a prime minister of impeccable Tory antecedents, used the state power to organize an iron and steel industry. In 1947 the British Colonial Office started a heavily capitalized, publicly administered enterprise in Tangan-

Table 4. *Exports, by country, 1938–63*
(excludes gold imports)
(f.o.b. values in million U.S. dollars)

Country	1938	1946	1950	1960	1961	1962	1963
Total Africa	*862*	*1,512*	*3,222*	*5,930*	*6,076*	*6,459*	*7,031*
Total Africa south of the Sahara	*612*	*1,207*	*2,575*	*5,051*	*5,234*	*5,054*	*5,443*
Angola	15	39	75	124	135	148	164
Cameroun	7	n.a.	47	97	98	103	118
Congo (Leopoldville)	50	121	261	335	117	366	379
Central African Republic				14	14	15	22
Chad	7	n.a.	43	13	21	17	23
Congo (Brazzaville)				18	20	34	42
Gabon				47	56	59	72
Dahomey	3	2	13	18	14	11	13
Ivory Coast	11	15	79	151	191	193	230
Senegal	19	35	71	113	124	124	111
Niger	1	1	3	13	15	20	20
Ghana	52	57	192	294	292	290	273
Kenya	40	76	57	112	116	126	142
Uganda			81	120	116	115	153
Tanganyika	15	33	66	155	138	146	179
Liberia	2	12	28	83	62	68	81
Malagasy Republic	24	40	69	75	78	94	82
Mauritius	14	20	32	39	62	64	90
Moçambique	8	33	37	73	89	91	101
Nigeria	46	99	253	475	486	472	531
Réunion	6	19	19	36	37	33	38
Zambia	49	53	140				
Malawi	n.a.	n.a.	14	576	579	587	624
Rhodesia	24	68	117				
Sierra Leone	11	10	22	83	82	57	81
South Africa	157	394	626	1,238	1,329	1,336	1,387
Gambia	2	3	6	8	9	10	9
Zanzibar, Pemba	4	9	14	16	12	13	14
Togo	2	2	9	14	19	17	18
Guinea	3	5	11	52	61	45	55
Portuguese Guinea	1	n.a.	n.a.	4	7	7	8
Ethiopia	n.a.	20	27	73	76	80	90
Sudan	30	41	95	182	178	226	227
São Tomé and Príncipe	2	n.a.	n.a.	7	6	6	7
All other	2	n.a.	68	378	581	63	39

SOURCE: Adapted from Andrew M. Kamarck, *The economics of African development* (New York, 1967), pp. 254–6.

yika designed to grow ground-nuts by mechanized methods, which was an utter failure. Governments tackled an increasingly large number of tasks—supervisory, hortatory, educational, entrepreneurial—tasks that ranged from running radio stations to building roads and airports. A growing number of specialists invaded the field of government: anthropologists, agronomists, agricultural engineers, range experts and so forth. Hence the number of persons employed in the public sector increased sharply in the last years of colonial rule. (For instance, in the Gold Coast, the number of persons holding jobs in the public sector went up from 77,375 in 1950 to 189,990 in 1960.) For good and for ill, the power of the state vastly expanded, and with it the possibilities for political patronage and for gaining wealth by manipulating the state machinery.

At the same time, 'development' turned into a secular gospel, a creed that seemed to receive an added material impetus from a remarkable world-wide rise in prices for primary products. The coercion of labour was largely ended, even in its most indirect form, through the pressure of taxation. By the end of the Second World War, direct taxes on Africans had become but an insignificant proportion of the total revenue in the more advanced territories.[17]

Under the new dispensation, employers were no longer concerned with a shortage of unskilled manpower; only skilled men were at a premium. Moreover, attitudes towards labour began to change. As long as African miners and mill-hands had been short-term migrants, they were satisfied with what were, by African standards, acceptable dormitories owned by the employers and by the municipalities. But gradually, a portion of the African labour force became more stable. Urban incomes rose, and educational and medical facilities improved in comparison with those commonly available in the villages. Hence workmen began to bring their families to the city. (The Belgians led in the effort to stabilize labour and to provide family allowances and housing. The British and the French did less, and the Portuguese continued to rely on single migrant workmen.) The urban population steadily increased. African cities began to face the modern problems of unemployment, as many newcomers, and school-leavers without roots in the countryside, were unable to find suitable jobs. The importance of the urban markets also increased as African townsmen started to purchase a whole range of imported products: transistor radios, furniture and even new or second-hand motorcycles and cars.

[17] The percentage of total revenue from direct taxes on Africans for the years 1938 and 1951, in selected territories, was as follows:

	Percentage	
	1938	1951
Nigeria	14·2	1·4
Sierra Leone	9·9	3·0
Kenya	14·1	6·4
Uganda	30·9	3·6
Tanganyika	31·7	10·6
Northern Rhodesia	8·5	1·2
South Rhodesia	11·7	2·5
South Africa	1·1	0·6
Basutoland	44·1	23·6
Belgian Congo	24·4	3·4
Angola	21·9	10·6
Moçambique	?	15·2

Data from Lord Hailey, *An African survey: revised 1956* (London, Oxford University Press, 1957), pp. 682–4.

The speed of economic development differed immensely between the different parts of Africa, and even within the same territories. In spite of Leninist strictures that interpreted colonial expansion in terms of investment opportunities and superprofits, Africa as a whole did not prove particularly attractive to European investors. During the colonial period only 9·3 per cent of French overseas investment went to Africa, and only 21 per cent of British capital went there (South Africa got 15 per cent of the total funds invested in British Africa).

As shown in Table 5, government investment generally exceeded private investment in the African colonies except for the Belgian Congo. Fieldhouse estimated public investment at 47·7 per cent for British Africa and 61·2 per cent for French Africa. Before 1945, capital went where it could get the greatest return and could operate most easily. For some critics this meant that not enough capital was being invested to develop the colonies rapidly; after 1945, governments became more concerned to speed up development for the colonies.

Table 5. *Investment in Africa*
(in million U.S. dollars)

	Years	Public aid	Private investment
Great Britain	1956–63	2,867	2,791
France	1956–63	6,811	2,853
Belgium	1956–8	444	523

It is extremely doubtful, however, that capital was the major limiting factor in African development at any time. On the contrary, it seems more likely that much of the capital invested from abroad was wasted. Even in South Africa before 1910, there was excessive investment in railways from the Transvaal to the coast: five routes existed, any one of which could have carried all the traffic. Rhodes's Chartered Company never paid a dividend between 1890 and 1923. The railway inland from Luanda was unprofitable; the Benguela Railway did not pay a dividend for the first twenty years after its completion in 1929. What was lacking for African development was not capital but an efficient labour force capable of working in a modern economy. In any case, after 1945 governments became wedded to the idea of uneconomic, instead of economic, development. The results were to be very spotty.

There was a recrudescence of the belief, once held by the pioneers of empire, that Africa was a tropical treasure-house, capable of yielding enormous riches. According to many experts, the key to the coming miracle was to be found in an adequate supply of foreign capital (especially for the construction of huge projects like the Kariba Dam on the Zambezi), in central planning and in large-scale mechanization (of the kind unsuccessfully attempted by the British in the East African Ground-Nut Scheme, initiated after the Second World War). French and Belgian investments were especially large after 1945, although the British were the first (1929) to supply development funds through the Colonial Development and Welfare Acts. Belgian government and government-sponsored gross investments in the Congo amounted to 53,750 million francs between 1950 and 1958. In French Black Africa the Fonds d'Investissement pour le Développement Economique et Social des Territoires d'Outre-Mer (FIDES) did the planning for tropical Africa and provided the great bulk of funds estimated at $8,293 million between 1946 and 1964. This was a greater effort at development planning than any other colonial power put forth. Between 1946 and 1964 the British funnelled approximately $1,417 million into Black Africa.

Private investment in Africa remained relatively small, because earnings were low, the technical problems of operating in Africa were numerous, and there were greater advantages in putting money elsewhere. British private investment in Africa, for instance, was £693 million in 1962, or only 5·5 per cent of the total British overseas investment. Clearly, only a modicum of British investments went to Africa in the post-war period, for in 1936 the figure had been £413·3 million. A good deal of this money in turn was spent in Europe. For example, equipment had to be bought in Europe, salaries of European officials and technicians had to be paid, a large portion of the profits and of the salaries paid to company officials and company technicians working in Africa also returned to Europe. Nevertheless, in furnishing financial aid, the colonial powers did not so much look to immediate financial returns but to political advantages, to prestige and to the long-term development of markets capable of providing the metropolitan exporters with African outlets for more specialized products. Such manufactures included commodities like automobiles, trucks, typewriters, pharmaceutical goods and hydro-electric machinery, sophisticated merchandise that now began to supplement, and were later to displace, the simpler staple exports of old.

At the same time, the more advanced African countries made a start in manufacturing, beginning with the simpler kinds of goods. Industrialization in Africa had several sources. The introduction of steam-powered transport acted as a multiple-accelerator, for railways required repair shops, technical training facilities and a host of supporting services. Marx, writing of India in the 1850s, had already predicted that the British, in introducing the steam-engine to India, would of necessity lay the foundations of modern manufacturing enterprise: 'Modern industry, resulting from the railway system, will dissolve the hereditary divisions of labour, upon which rest the Indian castes, those decisive impediments to Indian progress.' [18] The creation of railways in Africa had similar effects. (During the Boer War of 1899–1902, for instance, when Southern Rhodesia had been settled by whites for little more than a decade, the Bulawayo railway workshops already made a small but welcome contribution to the Rhodesian war effort by fitting out several armoured trains and by manufacturing some matériel in a rudimentary fashion.)

As we have seen, the development of support industries for mineral production provided the major impetus to industrialization in Africa. Another industrial incentive derived from the needs for processing agricultural products like cotton, ground-nuts, cocoa, palm-oil, cheese, bacon and tobacco. Such industries included, for example, the cotton gins set up by Indians in Uganda. Among other early industries dependent on the rising demands for locally made consumption-goods were such light industrial products as furniture and building

---

[18] Karl Marx, 'The future results of British rule in India' [8 Aug. 1853], in *Karl Marx on colonialism and modernization* . . . Shlomo Avineri, ed. (New York, 1968), p. 129.

materials. Heavy industries tended to come last in chronological sequences. By the late 1940s, South Africa and Southern Rhodesia were the only African countries with established iron and steel industries of their own.

Speaking in a broad and general fashion, Africa's industrial revolution started in South Africa. Many critics of South African society had argued during the 1930s that the country was locked in a vicious circle of poverty from which it could not speedily emerge. But in fact South Africa enjoyed tremendous advantages. By earning large amounts of foreign exchange, thus providing government with extensive revenue and the country with substantial capital reserves, the gold-mining industry helped to accelerate development. South Africa had an elaborate system of harbours, roads and railways; industrialists were able to draw on ample supplies of coal and electricity. South Africa had a reasonably efficient system of technical education, of technical and scientific research. Successive governments had generally followed a fairly cautious financial policy, aimed at keeping the national debt to a moderate size in relation to the national income. South African politicians might condemn foreign capitalists in the harshest terms, but they took good care not to frighten away foreign investment by confiscating foreign property. South Africa possessed both a highly trained white managerial class and an extensive skilled labour force, which were largely, but by no means exclusively, of European origin. In addition, the country was able to draw on cheap, unskilled African labour, not merely from within its own borders but from as far afield as the Rhodesias, Nyasaland and Moçambique.

Industrialization got its true start during the First World War, and slowly accelerated during the 1920s, when the country embarked upon a protectionist policy under the premiership of General Hertzog. In 1934 the South African Iron and Steel Industrial Corporation (ISCOR), started six years earlier under government auspices, began the production of steel and thereby laid the foundations of a huge industrial complex. During the Second World War the country consolidated its industrial position; production increased at a phenomenal pace. In addition, manufactures became increasingly diversified and sophisticated. By the 1950s, South Africa was the first country in Africa to have attained industrial parity with the more developed nations of the world (see Table 6). An economically developed South Africa in turn became an exporter of capital, of specialized equipment such as mining machinery, and also of industrial, managerial and entrepreneurial skills, which in turn helped to change the economic fortunes of Southern Rhodesia, Moçambique and even Northern Rhodesia.

By this time, industrialization had also made considerable progress in Southern Rhodesia, and had begun to get under way in the mining territories of Northern Rhodesia and the Belgian Congo and in some of the more developed West African territories like Senegal and Nigeria. As Kilby points out in his essay in this volume, the main impetus came from European firms and, to a minor extent, from Lebanese and Indian entrepreneurs, who provided the managerial skill as well as the capital required to initiate manufactures of a more advanced variety. By the end of the colonial period, when even the remnants of empire had largely disappeared, South Africa was still the economic giant of Africa. But even beyond the Limpopo, many countries that for a generation or two had been dependent solely on the export of primary products had acquired

Table 6. *Growth of industries in South Africa, 1911–54*
(private, governmental, municipal, etc.)

	No. of employees (all races)	Fixed assets (in R million)	Gross value of output (in R million)
1911	65,916	—	34·4
1920	175,520	84·1	185·8
1930	218,298	133·0	223·5
1939	352,500	266·3	399·2
1945	488,661	340·2	750·6
1950	713,151	669·8	1,549·4
1954	855,295	1,208·9	2,459·5

SOURCE: *State of South Africa yearbook: economic, financial and statistical yearbook for the Republic of South Africa* (Johannesburg, 1963), p. 416.

secondary and, in some cases, even tertiary sectors of some importance. Africa was in the throes of an economic revolution, with incalculable consequences for the future.

In this introductory essay we have attempted to provide a partial outline for the economic history of the subcontinent during the colonial period. An over-view of the pre-colonial economies follows. Our contributors then discuss the economic mainsprings of imperialism, and offer interpretations concerning the different national styles of the European colonizers, British, French, Belgian, German and Portuguese. Next they provide data with regard to the main economic activities, including farming, mining and transport, trade and manufacturing. Subsequent essays cover some of the social implications of economic development, including labour questions, the evolution of new African élites, the role of immigrants from outside Africa and the increasing part played by the state in Africa.

BIBLIOGRAPHY

Awe, Bolanle. 'Militarism and economic development in nineteenth century Yoruba country: the Ibadan example', *Journal of African History*, 1973, **14**, no. 1.

Caldwell, John C. *African rural-urban migration: the movement to Ghana's towns*. New York, Columbia University Press, 1969.

Clark, Grover. *The balance sheets of imperialism: facts and figures on colonies*. New York, Columbia University Press, 1936.

Coquery-Vidrovitch, Catherine. 'French colonization in Africa to 1920: administration and economic development', in *Colonialism in Africa 1870–1914*, vol. I: *The history and politics of colonialism 1870–1914*, L. H. Gann and Peter Duignan, eds. (Cambridge University Press, 1969).

Egharevka, Jacob U. *Benin law and custom*. 3rd ed. Port Harcourt, 1949.

Fieldhouse, David K. 'The economic exploitation of Africa: some British and French comparisons', in *France and Britain in Africa: imperial rivalry and colonial rule*, Prosser Gifford and William Roger Louis, eds. New Haven, Yale University Press, 1971.

Frankel, S. Herbert. *The tyranny of economic paternalism in Africa: a study of frontier mentality 1860–1960*. Johannesburg, 1960.

Gann, L. H. *A history of Northern Rhodesia: early days to 1953*. London, 1964.
———. *A history of Southern Rhodesia: early days to 1934*. London, 1965.
Gann, L. H., and Peter Duignan. 'Reflections on imperialism and the scramble for Africa', in *Colonialism in Africa 1870–1960*, vol. I: *The history and politics of colonialism 1870–1914*, L. H. Gann and Peter Duignan, eds. Cambridge University Press, 1969.
Hailey, William Malcolm Hailey, 1st baron. *An African survey: revised 1956*. London, Oxford University Press, 1957.
Kamarck, Andrew M. *The economics of African development*. New York, 1967.
Landes, David S. 'Some thoughts on the nature of economic imperialism', *Journal of Economic History*, Dec. 1961, **21**, no. 4, pp. 496–512.
Lewis, W. Arthur. 'The export stimulus', in *Tropical development, 1880–1913*, W. Arthur Lewis, ed. Evanston, Northwestern University Press, 1970.
Marx, Karl. 'The future results of British rule in India' [8 Aug. 1853], in *Karl Marx on colonialism and modernization . . . ,* Shlomo Avineri, ed. New York, 1968.
Smith, Adam. *An inquiry into the nature and causes of the wealth of nations,* Edwin Cannan, ed. New York, 1937.
Smith, M. G. 'Pluralism in precolonial Africa', in *Pluralism in Africa,* Leo Kuper and M. G. Smith, eds. Berkeley, University of California Press, 1969.
Thomas, Roger G. 'Forced labour in British West Africa: the case of the Northern Territories of the Gold Coast 1906–1927', *Journal of African History*, 1973, **14,** no. 1.
Watson, William. *Tribal cohesion in a money economy: a study of the Mambwe people of Northern Rhodesia*. Manchester University Press, 1958.

PART ONE

EARLY PATTERNS

CHAPTER 1

THE PRE-COLONIAL ECONOMIES OF SUB-SAHARAN AFRICA

by

PETER DUIGNAN *and* L. H. GANN

My Illustrious Friend and Joy of My Liver! [wrote a Turkish governor in response to an Englishman's question] . . . The thing you ask of me is both difficult and useless. Although I have passed all my days in this place, I have neither counted the houses nor have I inquired into the number of the inhabitants; and as to what one person loads on his mules and the other stows away in the bottom of his ship, that is no business of mine. But, above all, as to the previous history of this city, God only knows the amount of dirt and confusion that the infidels may have eaten before the coming of the sword of Islam. It were unprofitable for us to inquire into it. O my soul! O my lamb! Seek not after the things which concern thee not. Thou camest unto us and we welcomed thee: go in peace.[1]

Many an administrator in modern Africa has been tempted to greet with similar impatience the well-meaning efforts of foreigners engaged in apparently useless research projects. Yet official obstruction and the ethnocentric bias of office-holders have been relatively minor problems facing investigators. Economic analyses or statistical data, for one thing, are often scarce, unreliable or totally unavailable for many periods of African history. Of course, the art of accurate counting is by no means a Western invention. Some pre-colonial monarchs, such as the kings of Ashanti (Asante) and Dahomey, managed to collect detailed figures concerning the agricultural production and the human and the livestock population within their dominions. Dahomean officials had long ago worked out an intricate system of accountancy based on the use of coloured pebbles. But the lords of Dahomey, like most pre-colonial princes, did not know how to read and write. Even literate potentates, such as the Muslim rulers of the Sudan, had great difficulties in keeping and preserving archives. Hence most of our knowledge concerning the economic life of pre-colonial Africa derives from European sources, many of them biased or inadequate. Historical generalizations concerning the growth of the population, the economic organization, the alleged increases or decreases in the gross national product, the flow of capital investment or the fluctuating volume of internal or external trade must therefore be treated with the greatest of caution.

The study of economic institutions in pre-colonial Africa involves other methodological difficulties. In the 1920s, an anthropological pioneer as distinguished as Malinowski assumed that such basic modern economic concepts as capital and entrepreneurship had no place in what he considered to be primitive economies. In the 1950s the 'substantivist' interpretation framed by the eco-

---

[1] Quoted from Sir Austen Henry Layard, *Discoveries in the ruins of Nineveh and Babylon . . .* (London, 1853), p. 663, in Jacques Barzun and Henry F. Graff, *The modern researcher* (New York, 1957), p. 3.

nomic historian Karl Polanyi likewise drew a sharp distinction between modern and 'archaic' economies. These issues have engendered a good deal of controversy. We ourselves are impressed by the variety of economic organizations found in pre-colonial Africa, though certain basic needs were common to all. Whether their medium of exchange consisted of bows and arrows, of herds or of crops or cloth or tools, the Pygmy hunters, the Zulu herdsmen and the Yoruba farmers employed some form of capital. All the peoples of Africa had to find ways of utilizing the available labour in order to put the available land to economic use. Most communities engaged in trade of some kind. Ancient Bushman paintings, for example, provide evidence concerning the exchange of goods between different bands in prehistoric times. And Africans, whatever their descent or their level of technical knowledge, had to adjust their way of life to the physical requirements of what often was a harsh land, with its climatic vicissitudes, its geographical obstacles, its Pandora's box of human and animal diseases and soil deficiencies. The African continent, which is three and a half times as large as the United States, embraces diverse geographic and climatic regions. Only 8 per cent of the total area is tropical rain-forest; over 60 per cent is arid wasteland. Poor soils and either a lack or an overabundance of rainfall have been the main physical obstacles to economic progress. To this day, these disadvantages impose serious limitations even on modern economies capable of damming great rivers, building large ports, fighting epidemics once held to be uncontrollable and performing similar prodigious feats. For technologically backward societies, these natural disabilities, which were of yet vastly greater moment, could hardly be surmounted.

The main types of pre-colonial economies

An historian making a survey of sub-Saharan Africa a hundred years ago would have found the greatest possible range of human conditions—from the age of the stone-tipped arrow to the era of iron-smelting and metal crafts. Daryll Forde, the British anthropologist, lists five main types of economies—collecting, hunting, fishing, cultivation and stock raising—though none of these is ever found to exist in a pure form. People lived rather by combining various types, herders by doing some cultivating, for instance, and farmers by keeping some cattle. We cite here a few examples of the wide range of economies present in pre-colonial Africa.[2]

The most ancient way of making a living was by hunting game and gathering food. Extensive areas of Africa were inhabited by small bands whose technology was still that of the later Stone Age. By the second half of the last century, these Stone Age peoples (Pygmies and Bushmen) had long since been pushed into the remoter and more arid regions of what is now South-West Africa, Botswana and Tanzania, or into forlorn stretches of the rain-forest in Zaire. Nevertheless, they still had at their disposal far more space than their descendants today. They subsisted in a state of ecological balance with their environment. As Livingstone wrote of the Bushmen in the Kalahari:

[2] For a detailed description of African political and social institutions around 1880, see Elizabeth Colson, 'African society at the time of the scramble', in *Colonialism in Africa 1870–1960*, vol. 1: *The history and politics of colonialism 1870–1914*, L. H. Gann and Peter Duignan, eds. (Cambridge University Press, 1969), pp. 27–65.

They are the only real nomades in the country; they never cultivate the soil nor rear any domestic animals, save wretched dogs. They are so intimately acquainted with the habits of the game, that they follow them in their migrations, and prey upon them from place to place, and thus prove as complete a check upon their inordinate increase as the other carnivora. The chief subsistence of the Bushmen is the flesh of game, but that is eked out by what the women collect of roots and beans, and fruits of the Desert.[3]

Africa also had communities of nomadic herdsmen such as the Somali, who had learned how to tame animals and whose economy revolved around the needs of their beasts and the vagaries of the climate. Donkeys were used as beasts of burden. Horses were sometimes ridden into battle, but more generally served as a means of rapid transport and a mark of social distinction. The Somali—like the Masai of Kenya—subsisted above all on milk, blood and meat. Life depended on the prosperity of the herds; and the well-being of the flocks depended in turn on the available supplies of water and good pastures. Of struggles over wells and grazing grounds there were many. Hence the Somali and people of their kind developed an extremely warlike way of life. They were also among the finest irregular cavalry in Africa, famed for their prowess and their pride. Warfare itself became a means of enriching the band, either through cattle-rustling or by the subjugation of men. Crafts such as leather- and metal-working were traditionally left to bondsmen, who were debarred from marrying into the ruling caste. The Masai, another nomadic, herding people, did some hunting and collecting to supplement their diet.

The great majority of Africans made their living primarily by tilling the land, and by hunting and fishing where possible. Some farmers in East-Central and southern Africa also kept cattle. An enormous variety of farming methods were employed. Nothing would be more misleading than to talk about 'traditional' ways of African agriculture, for these systems were themselves the product of centuries of experimentation and adaptation, involving the adoption of many new crops and the constant struggle to overcome the vagaries of different kinds of soil. Most soils of tropical Africa tend to be light, low in plant nutrients, and easily leached by heavy rains. High soil heat consumes organic material. African farmers learned to cope with these deficiencies by shifting cultivation, by resorting to slash-and-burn techniques and by planting varied crops to maintain green cover over the land to lessen the ravages of sun and rain. Though their method may appear rudimentary in Western eyes, it did protect the soil. Cleared patches returned to bush and forest, and fertility was thus renewed. Small fields received shade and protection from sun and erosion, and plant diseases could not easily spread from one small plot to another. Mixed fields guarded against total crop failure.

The majority of African farmers practised different forms of shifting cultivation that was dependent on careful soil selection and on the firing of forest and bush to enhance the fertility of cultivated gardens. This method produced low yields but required little labour. Fire, the most potent tool as yet invented by man, did most of the work. There was no need to remove tree stumps, clear out roots or manure the soil, for the ashes derived from controlled burning would enrich the earth. After being worked for a few years, the forest was allowed to lie fallow for lengthy periods; meanwhile the cultivators moved on to new land.

[3] David Livingstone, *Missionary travels and researches in South Africa* . . . (London, 1857), p. 49.

There was no need to construct elaborate buildings, irrigation facilities or indeed any other capital works that would have required a great deal of man-power. This system could not operate forever. Pressure of population growth on available land might increase, and the frequent use of land and shortening periods of fallow were apt to bring about changes in vegetation. Woodland might in time be replaced by bush, and bush in turn by grassland.[4]

The cultivation of bushland presented a variety of problems. Because of the many different kinds of bush, a great deal of expertise was required to make the best of its resources. By and large, however, slash-and-burn methods were apt to secure less ashes for fertilizing bushland than was available from the burning of forest. Hence farmers might have to improve the land by mixing burnt and unburnt leaves with the topsoil. This practice required a new tool, the hoe. Digging sticks, used by forest cultivators to scratch the ashes or to make holes for planting roots, no longer sufficed. In addition to hoeing, villagers had to weed the land and perform a variety of subsidiary jobs. Some writers have advanced the interesting hypothesis, therefore, that the more advanced forms of bush farming required more manpower than forest farming. Certainly the carrying capacity of the land under bush fallow varied considerably. For instance, the Bisa and Eastern Lala of what is now Zambia probably managed to feed only five people per square mile; the Western Lala supported perhaps seven persons per square mile; the Ngoni, Chewa and Nsenga perhaps maintained something like twenty-five per square mile.[5]

There were countless variations of these slash-and-burn systems that were commonly supplemented by hunting, fishing and sometimes by keeping small stock and cattle, if no tsetse-fly were present. Nevertheless there were also certain uniformities. In most parts of Africa bush and savannah land remained in almost limitless supply. There was no point in farming land intensively by placing cattle dung on the fields, by careful weeding, by rotating crops or by the use of similar methods, as long as capital and labour remained scanty, land remained plentiful and the fertility of the soil was preserved by lengthy fallow periods. Under such conditions there were no landless people; every recognized member of the community was entitled to stake out gardens for himself and his family. Strangers were usually welcomed, for they would provide manpower in time of peace and military assistance in time of war.

This condition, of course, was by no means universal. As the density of the population increased, some African communities were forced to work out more complex systems. The Lozi, dwelling in the fertile flood plain of the Upper Zambezi, evolved a peculiar form of riverine cultivation that appears to have sustained a relatively large number of people, and that even appears to have necessitated the importation of servile labour from outside. The Lozi system combined the use of cattle with the tillage of fertile mounds within the plain and of bush gardens on its margin. The Yoruba in what is now Nigeria managed to support even larger numbers of people. They grew a great variety of crops, such as maize, yams, ground-nuts, beans and cassava. They kept poul-

---

[4] Sir Dudley Stamp, a leading British expert, and other geographers cast doubt on the 'primeval' character of much of the savannah. A good deal of the tropical landscape is probably man-made. See Sir Laurence Dudley Stamp, *Africa: a study in tropical development,* 2nd ed. (New York, 1964), p. 108.

[5] William Allen, 'African land usage', *Rhodes-Livingstone Journal,* June 1945, pp. 13–14.

try, sheep and goats; and above all they had acquired a good knowledge of how to rotate crops.

By the end of the last century, the overwhelming majority of Africans lived in small hamlets or villages. In some of the more favoured areas, where the soil was fertile and the population had increased, travellers encountered much more substantial settlements, such as agricultural or trading towns. For instance, Kazembe, a Lunda chief in what is now north-eastern Zambia, controlled a stockaded town that gave him command over the Luapula valley, rich in fish and cassava. Kazembe's capital was a centre of worship, administration and commerce, depending on such tribute and trade goods as slaves and oxen, salt, ivory and malachite. Until the arrival of the British, Kazembe's town also provided physical security to its people. By the end of the nineteenth century, the total settlement, estimated at 1,000 yards in length and 200 yards in width, was surrounded by a great stockade that could not easily be levelled, except by European artillery. Essentially, however, the prosperity of Kazembe's town depended on the chief's political position rather than on its economic function. Once a British expedition armed with a machine-gun and light field-gun had chased Kazembe out of his stockade and had forced him to surrender, the settlement lost its governmental and military functions. Its *raison d'être* disappeared and its inhabitants found new homes for themselves on the Luapula river. This process of population dispersion was widely duplicated during the early colonial period as soon as peace obviated the need for stockaded settlements and at a time when land was generally still plentiful.

The *kibuga* (capital) of Buganda represented a more advanced level of urbanization. The *kibuga* formed the royal seat where the sacred fires and the sacred drums were kept, where matters of dispute were brought before a court of appeal and where major political decisions were made. The *kibuga* was an impressive agglomeration of buildings made of cane and rattan, divided by well-maintained streets and centring on the royal palace. At the height of its splendour, the capital may have maintained something like 40,000 people. The city dwellers still depended on agriculture. Retainers maintained gardens, but urban crops had to be supplemented by victuals brought in from country estates.

The Yoruba cities in Nigeria apparently began as fortified settlements put up by Yoruba settlers among more backward, and perhaps hostile, indigenous peoples. But their position did not depend solely on their function as centres of government. The Yoruba participated both in local and in long-distance trade, and their cities acted as market centres. There were craftsmen of many kinds— weavers and dyers, blacksmiths, carvers, leather-workers, makers of musical instruments, herbalists, carpenters, builders, salt manufacturers and numerous others. Some cities numbered as many as 40,000 inhabitants and required provisions from plantations run by slave labour to feed the population.

The Muslim cities of the Western Sudan stood for yet a higher degree of economic specialization. Timbuktu, in what is now Mali, depended above all on the entrepôt trade. By 1880, just before the era of colonial conquest, when Oskar Lenz, a German traveller, visited the settlement, he found that the city's prosperity was a thing of the past.[6] Gold from the south was in short supply

---

[6] See Oskar Lenz, *Timbuktu: Reise durch Marokko, die Sahara und den Sudan* . . . (Leipzig, 1884), esp. vol. II, pp. 141–69.

and its price had risen steeply. Worse still, the political decadence of Morocco, the constant struggles between Fulbe and Tuareg and the absence of a strong political authority to protect merchants rendered commerce unsafe. Nevertheless the city still contained something like 20,000 persons, most of them literate. There were no cultivated gardens, either within Timbuktu or in its vicinity. Provisions such as wheat, sorghum, vegetable butter, spices, fruit and fish had to be taken to the city from outside and were sold on the market. Timbuktu also conducted a long-distance trade to North Africa in commodities of small bulk and high value. These comprised slaves, as well as gold, salt, kola-nuts, ivory, indigo, gum and ostrich feathers. European imports included textiles, fire-arms, and the like, goods which indigenous artisans could not produce as cheaply, if at all.

Despite the enormous logistic difficulties in the way of the trans-Saharan trade, the volume of traffic was far from negligible. Modern research indicates that, so far from declining, the caravan traffic between North Africa and the Western Sudan actually increased before the period of colonial partition, reaching a peak about 1875, after which there was a slow decline. In addition to commercial centres like Timbuktu there were Sudanic communities whose livelihood depended largely on crafts. One of these was the settlement of Qualata (Walata) near Timbuktu, described by Lenz as 'a manufacturing centre of some importance'. Qualata artisans, like those of Hausaland, were famed for the excellence of their leather-work, which was sold far afield. Among other Sudanic manufactures were textiles, the preparation of hides and skins and iron goods.

Pre-colonial trading and exchange systems

Africans had traded commodities such as gold, iron, copper bars, malachite and ivory, and there was widespread traffic in food and other necessities. Salt was an ancient article of commerce over much of Africa. Where transport facilities were adequate, such as in the Niger Delta, canoes brought fish and salt from the coast to the hinterland in exchange for yams, plantains and livestock. Specialists also sold their wares along an east-west route, which carried dyewood, cloth, pots, canoes, bronze artifacts, and similar goods. The trade with Europeans, involving first gold and slaves, and later palm produce, was grafted on this pre-existing system of commerce. Pre-colonial commerce assumed many different forms. Richard Gray and David Birmingham in their excellent work on *Pre-colonial African trade* distinguish between subsistence-oriented and market-oriented trade. Subsistence-oriented trade revolved around agricultural products and depended on local kinship systems. Subsistence traffic in Africa had little impact on the basic economic and social systems, whereas market-oriented trade produced greater change and innovation.

Market-oriented exchange produced new forms of wealth, markets and the principles of supply and demand, production for the market, currency, economic specialization, the production of goods for exports and the development of professional merchants and long-distance traders. Most people of Africa continued to earn their livelihood by subsistence agriculture, but some groups and some localities were integrated into market-oriented trade governed in part by market principles and opportunities.

In West Africa the various geographic regions—desert, savannah, forest, river and coast—produced a wide range of food crops and other products that encouraged internal trade. The people of the rain-forest had yams, bananas, rice, okra, peas, gourds, pumpkins, beans, manioc, maize, ground-nuts and oil-palms. The savannah people specialized in cereals: pearl millet, sorghum and maize. They also grew tubers and other vegetables, cotton and indigo and collected from trees and bushes. Some groups raised cattle, sheep, goats, chickens and pigs. Africans living under different climatic and soil conditions would exchange goods with their neighbours. This exchange was, however, subject to many limitations. In most parts of the continent, commerce was conducted above all on the basis of kinship and tribal affiliation, more than on the principles of a market economy. Many villagers were, of course, familiar with market-places (that is to say, sites where sellers and buyers might meet). But few Africans traded according to the principles of a Western market economy (where the price of labour and of commodities is governed above all by the laws of supply and demand). Commodities might be subject to price fluctuations, but land and labour were seldom for sale according to market principles. And few Africans were dependent on the market-place for the basic necessities of life.

In the more developed parts of Africa, production had become more complex. In some West African states slaves and serfs were employed in the production of crops to feed royal courts and noble households. In addition, agricultural surpluses were sold in the market-place. Dahomey and Yoruba town slaves, for instance, worked on plantations to supply urban concentrations. In Djenne wealthy merchants had slaves who ran farms and provided food for Timbuktu. West Africa thus had at least three systems of food production: subsistence, cultivation for the nobility (a part of these crops was sold) and cultivation for the market.

Craftsmen labouring for local needs were common in West Africa. Large states like Ashanti, Dahomey, Benin and Nupe had specialist artisans and craft guilds to produce for the market. These craftsmen were jewellers, weavers, iron-workers, blacksmiths, carvers, leather-workers, glassmakers, potters, masons and carpenters. European visitors to the Sudanic cities (like Heinrich Barth in the 1850s) noted the presence of crafts and guilds housed in segregated parts of the city and producing a variety of goods. More than twenty kinds of cloth were made in Kano, for instance. But craftsmen in most of Africa were regarded as belonging to inferior castes.

Markets were to be found in almost all of West Africa except for parts of Liberia, the Ivory Coast and Nigeria. Local markets funnelled goods to more distant markets. Trade chiefs among the Yoruba, for example, organized exchange with Nupe, Hausaland and Dahomey. Markets were usually regulated as to time, prices and standards of workmanship. The Hausa markets were among the most important. Barth in 1851 estimated that £80,000 worth of bulk merchandise arrived in Kano each year. Coastal markets sent abroad gold and slaves, palm-oil and other goods in return for powder, iron goods, cloth, kerosene and knick-knacks. In the Sahara and the Western Sudan especially, dominant ethnic groups often managed to control particular routes, and commercial rivalry was apt therefore to engender or augment bitter struggles among neighbouring peoples.

In East Africa subsistence-oriented trade was dominant, but market-oriented trade developed (sometimes under the stimulus of Arab long-distance traders) among the Yao, Bisa, Kamba, Chokwe, Tonga and Nyamwezi who linked local markets to overseas trade.

An example of subsistence-oriented trade was that of the Tonga people of what is now Zambia. Their trade network exchanged approximately three hundred different goods with ten neighbours over distances up to 300 miles. The Tonga dealt in salt and other goods; they acted also as middlemen for local and overseas products. Trade, however, was seasonal; it did not produce specialist groups or an administrative class; nor did the Tonga have markets.

Market-oriented commerce especially had a widening effect on the lives and material well-being of the people; it promoted the circulation of new ideas, new techniques and new products. Technological advances and diffusion of new crops resulted from long-distance trading. Trade also created a new demand for imported objects (clothing, bracelets, beads, hatchets, guns, liquor). This rising consumer demand helped to transform subsistence economies. Centres of trade and industry sprang up throughout East and Central Africa, only to be smashed during the nineteenth century by the slave-trade and Ngoni invasions from the south. As Gray and Birmingham point out, most trade centres in this area were destroyed by the time that colonial rule was imposed.

In West Africa large kingdoms, such as Mali and Ashanti, were often associated with commerce by giving traders protection, supplying means of transport, maintaining roads and ferries, policing markets and settling disputes. In eastern Africa, on the other hand, the dealers themselves usually provided for their own protection and transport. Although the ancient empire of Monomotapa had once controlled trade over a great part of Rhodesia, many other trade networks developed without strong states or large political organizations. For instance, successful traffickers such as the Chokwe, Kamba, Bisa and Yao, lacked centralized kingdoms. Generally speaking, the trade in minerals and slaves appears to have fostered state-building. But the commerce in ivory does not seem to have done so.

East and Central Africa produced a number of trade-oriented empires such as the Lunda state in the Congo, as well as market-oriented traders such as the Kamba and the Yao. Yet their commerce failed to sustain economic growth in pre-colonial times because it depended too much on wasting assets—for example, ivory, rhino tusks, wild rubber, surface minerals and slaves. Transport difficulties and technological backwardness prevented the indigenous people from exploiting the agricultural and mineral wealth of the region. With the advance of the gunpowder and the slaving frontier in the nineteenth century and the spread of violence emanating from the Ngoni invasions, the commercial life of the area was disrupted. African traders and their trade routes declined. Colonialism brought peace and stability, but African traders could not stand before the onslaught of alien competition introduced by the new rulers.

Whatever its character, commerce normally involved the exchange of small lots of merchandise over relatively large areas. It thereby necessitated the employment of many middlemen, much patience and a great deal of time. This is how an early-nineteenth-century Portuguese explorer describes the trading methods of Africans in Kazembe's country:

The purchaser begins by putting on the ground a very small quantity of merchandise, to which he adds, as the vendor, examining it, lessens the price of the object; and as the price approaches the amount he wants, the purchaser keeps a little back to hand over at the conclusion of the deal. This kind of bargaining takes a lot of time, and much patience is required to bring it to a conclusion . . . And thus only natives are able to buy from natives because a European . . . only rarely has the patience needed to reap any advantage.[7]

Pre-colonial trade was necessarily limited in extent, as African commodity production was subject to inexorable limitations. Agricultural products could not easily be stored in great quantities and transport facilities remained inadequate. Hence over much of Africa the bulk of the existing agricultural production had to be consumed on the spot or traded nearby. Because generosity was usually the best policy, a substantial part of indigenous production was invested in feasts and ceremonies for lords, or in socially regulated gifts to kinsmen or followers who would be expected to reciprocate in times of need.

Societies of the kind which we have been describing could neither employ nor afford elaborate technologies. African miners, for instance, lacked pumps, explosives and a knowledge of engineering or of geology. Because they lacked the facilities for working metals at deep levels, they could barely scratch the surface of Africa's mineral wealth. Even had they been able to dig more ores, they could not have exported great quantities of copper or iron without wagons or steam-engines. African cultivators, who were dependent on digging sticks and hoes, faced similar obstacles. In a few favoured areas, such as Nigeria and Senegal, Africans did manage to produce palm-oil and ground-nuts and similar products for Western markets. Zanzibar became a major source for cloves. But indigenous planters and farmers usually lacked technical and scientific knowledge, and the total volume of Africa's trade remained small.[8]

There were exceptions. Dwellers in towns or entrepôts in touch with North Africa, or Africans in the vicinity of Arab or European forts along the coasts, gradually became involved in the market economy by selling either their crops or their labour. The price of goods such as ivory, used above all in the export trade, was clearly affected by the fluctuating demand in the overseas market. But throughout their history most Africans lived in communities where markets played but a peripheral role (that is to say, market-places might be available, but the allocation of land and labour was not determined by market principles).[9] African rulers commonly tried to increase their mercantile potential by extending their dominance over valuable trade routes. But local economies could not easily be integrated into wider systems. Loyalties were above all of an ethnic nature, though Islam was apt to create new ties based on a common literary culture that facilitated commerce. Even so, traffic was widely impeded

[7] A. C. P. Gamitto, *King Kazembe and the Marave, Cheva, Bisa, Bemba, Lunda, and other peoples of Southern Africa . . .* (Lisbon, 1960), vol. 1, p. 27.

[8] By 1880, for example, British trade with West Africa, commercially one of the most advanced parts of the subcontinent, amounted to no more than £8 million, barely more than 5 per cent of the value ascribed to Great Britain's principal exports during the year.

[9] Economists now model out household behaviour in subsistence economies so that each portion of working time at the margin in each line of activity, be it pot-making, collecting palm fruit or having sexual relations, gives exactly the same satisfaction. If taste change or outside opportunities change, there is going to be a reallocation of household labour time. Granted, market opportunities, even if very little used, do have considerable effect. But the more important point is that allocation was never static in traditional economies; it changed with technology, with external shifts and with changes in taste just as does any developed market economy. The views generally held concerning the allegedly static nature of subsistence economies reflect more than anything else an ignorance of their history.

by the absence of all-purpose money, by distance, by perils on the road and also by insufficient knowledge concerning market fluctuations in other regions.

Before the development of cash-crops such as cocoa, credit in the modern sense was unavailable. Of course, the lending of wealth was not unknown. Masai cattle-herders bought, sold and loaned stock. A powerful Ndebele chief might give horned beasts to a dependant to gain his good will. Cattle diplomacy would thus supplement military coercion as a means of cementing the state. In other parts of Africa—say, Nigeria—wealthy men might invest their surplus foods in slaves, who might serve as units of labour, as a form of stored wealth, as items of conspicuous display, as auxiliaries for defence or as human sacrifice. Ordinary farmers might lend grain or stock or cattle to a kinsman or neighbour. However, credit of the capitalist kind was confined mostly to areas where Africans were in touch with Arabs, Asians or Europeans. The Muslim peoples of the Sudan were familiar with credit in different forms. In Zanzibar, Indians furnished loans in slaves and ivory to Swahili-speaking dealers. On the west coast, European traders came to provide a wide variety of credit, consisting roughly of two categories. Importers might supply goods, with or without price fixing, to intermediate brokers who used this merchandise to purchase goods for export. In the Gambia, for example, traders were wont to obtain a supply of goods from European firms at Bathurst during November and December. Then the dealers would go up the river in search of customers, returning during June and July to make up their accounts. This system, which depended on a good deal of trust between supplier and middleman, had many forms. It prevailed in regions as far afield as the Niger Delta and the country adjoining the lower Senegal. On the other hand, there were some African merchant-importers, men like Richard Beale Blaize of Lagos, who dealt directly with firms in Great Britain, obtained credits from overseas houses and acted as both wholesaler and resaler.

The volume of these transactions, however, remained small. Banking institutions were confined to South Africa, where the Standard Bank opened its doors in 1862. Over most of the remainder of Africa, the shortage, or indeed the relative absence, of liquid capital prevented the development of rural credit. So did the nature of the indigenous social institutions in most parts of the subcontinent. Money-lenders could not have set themselves up in business under conditions where there was no freehold property, where there was no market in land, where no lender could recoup his losses by seizing the debtor's land and chattel and where the recipient of a loan would himself have had extensive obligations to a great circle of kinsmen. Even in a highly developed society such as that of Benin, with its great tradition of craftsmanship and trade, there was no credit system in the modern sense. A credit-seeker would borrow money, not on the security of his own land or goods but on the security of his own person or of his kinfolk. If the borrower defaulted on his obligations, the person in pawn would have to labour for the lender till the loan was paid. Credit, above all, was a matter of kinship.

Even communities with developed markets seldom depended on the market as the sole or even the dominant source of their livelihood. There were of course exceptions—the trading centres of the Sudan (Djenne, Gao, Timbuktu) and the cities of the Yoruba and Dahomeans, for instance. Supply and demand determined prices in the market, but unlike the situation in Western markets these prices had little effect on resource allocation and production. Goods changed hands in a variety of ways: by barter, gift exchanges, reciprocal exchanges or market-principle transactions. Money as such was usually absent (at least an all-purpose money) except in larger trading towns.

Small markets fed larger ones, and goods were slowly funnelled through the desert port cities or the factories and forts on the coast. Internal trade in foods and utensils was extensive. Professional dealers, often foreigners, controlled the external trade. Chiefs and kings commonly monopolized the commerce in luxury goods such as ivory and gold dust. They were entitled to a variety of tolls, dues and trade advantages, and in return were expected to give protection to merchants and presents to their own followers. In more complex systems there were interlocking currencies, such as iron bars, bales of cloth and cowrie shells, which themselves fluctuated in value. Cowrie shells, for example, had many of the characteristics associated with modern currencies. They were imported to West Africa from the Indian Ocean. Users could not arbitrarily expand their supply; shells could be transported like money, without much physical deterioration. Above all, cowries, like coins, served mainly for purposes of exchange; they could not be eaten or fed to cattle. Cowries were subject to inflation, like any other form of currency. Finally, Africans in some parts of the continent were getting used to coin. Maria Theresa dollars cast in silver and British guineas made of gold were more easily adjusted to large-scale trade with cowrie shells, which were fitted best for petty transactions.

The long-distance traffic involved the shipment of slaves and also of commodities such as salt, gold, ivory, palm-oil, palm-kernels, kola-nuts and metals. Sudanese merchants would import textiles, beads, perfumes, needles, swords and mirrors in exchange for other goods. Captives as well as gold dust and kola-nuts were imported from the south. Long-distance caravans likewise acted as moving retail markets, buying and selling along the road and breaking bulk as readily as urban pedlars. The long-distance trade was of considerable political importance, as it supplied kings and lords with ready sources of revenue. It accounted, however, for only a small proportion of the total trade. A relatively large amount of business was conducted at local markets, where sellers bought provisions—meat, fowls, guinea corn, sweet potatoes and so forth, as well as baskets, brooms, flints, knives and other articles of domestic use.[10]

The slave-trade

The commerce in human beings was Africa's earliest form of labour migration, plaguing the continent since ancient times. Slavery provided Africans with a scarce commodity, whose exploitation did not require much capital. The slave-trade meshed with existing forms of servitude, of which there were many kinds. Freemen might lose their liberty by being captured in war, by being convicted of crimes or by becoming the victims of political intrigues. There were even certain kinds of voluntary forms of slavery. The treatment of slaves varied widely. In some societies slaves might be regarded more or less as members of a family. Elsewhere their fate might be of the harshest, and captives might be

[10] Colin W. Newbury, 'Trade and authority in West Africa from 1850 to 1880', in *Colonialism in Africa*, vol. I, pp. 66–99 (see map facing p. 68 for cities and trade centres of the Sudan).

slain as a sacrifice to the gods—a common practice, for instance, in kingdoms like Dahomey or Benin.

In all probability the development of foreign trade and of mining caused existing forms of slavery to be put to new use. Slaves of both sexes were employed by the people of Monomotapa in mediaeval Rhodesia. This was true also of Ashanti, where slaves were apparently excluded from skilled crafts. (These crafts were endowed with religious significance and could be practised only by adherents of the national cult.) African slaves were employed on the land, for instance, by the Mandingo of Sierra Leone, in Dahomey and by the Yoruba of Nigeria. Pre-colonial Africa, however, never developed a large-scale plantation economy, although there was a variety of local markets for slaves, especially in the Islamic areas of Africa. The rich men of Bornu, in the Western Sudan, for instance, bought slaves as concubines, as eunuchs for their palaces, as domestic retainers, as wrestlers, as craftsmen and as field hands. From ancient times, moreover, African captives had been exported to the Near East and the Mediterranean basin in general.

The 'Christian' slave-trade, starting in the fifteenth century, at first followed a similar pattern. When the Portuguese set out on their career of conquest of Africa, they sought gold and spices rather than men. Unlike the Muslim countries adjoining the Mediterranean, Portugal had no large plantations with a vast demand for manpower. The early Portuguese slave-traffic, which was therefore of small proportions, served mainly to provide domestics and retainers for great households. The conquest of the New World, however, led to the creation of new plantation economies, dependent on the commercial cultivation of tropical crops. The plantations of the New World, and to a lesser extent those of small tropical islands like Réunion and São Tomé, created markets of monstrous proportions for African captives. African potentates supplied slaves in exchange for European manufactures. The slaves were then hauled across the Atlantic, where they produced sugar, tobacco, cotton, coffee and other commodities for sale.

The slave-trade was linked to the mercantilist system, and largely depended on powerful semi-official bodies such as the French West Indies Company (founded in 1664) and the Royal African Company (formed in 1672). These institutions received defined trading monopolies, in return for which they were expected to set up forts and 'factories' that would promote trade and defend their founders' interests against hostile interlopers, whether Swedes, Danes, Dutch, Brandenburgers or Courlanders, all of whom at one time or another tried their hand at the West African trade. European enterprise profoundly influenced the surrounding countryside. Foreign enclaves at the coast provided markets not only for slaves and gold but also for provisions. The commerce in captives, above all, resulted in one of the greatest enforced migrations of modern times. According to estimates recently made by Philip Curtin, an American scholar, up to nine million persons may have been shipped across the Atlantic in the course of four centuries. Of these, subtropical and tropical America, extending from the Caribbean to Brazil, probably absorbed about 90 per cent.

Historians continue to debate the effects of the slave-traffic on Africa. Some say that the abominable commerce led to economic decay as whole regions were depopulated and demoralized. Others point out that it was precisely the most advanced kingdoms of Black Africa, states like Benin and Dahomey, that were slave-traders. There is evidence, however, that Benin and Dahomey dealt in many different commodities in addition to captives and that the importance of the slave-trade to their economies has been much exaggerated. Moreover, Africa was shaped not merely by the 'Christian' slave-trade but also by the manner of its destruction. Abolition in the nineteenth century came essentially from without. The original traffic had rested on an Afro-European partnership in which white traders had to treat African potentates as their equals or even as their superiors. The destruction of the commerce during the nineteenth century owed little to the initiative of Africans. It came in response to Western pressures and linked Africa to the great revolution that destroyed serfdom in Europe, put an end to many hereditary caste distinctions, wiped out a host of established trading monopolies and created capitalist economies in which land and labour became freely saleable commodities. By the 1880s slavery had disappeared from Brazil and Cuba, the last American footholds of the institution, and slave-run plantations worked by African captives had become a matter of historical memory in the New World.

The abolition of the 'Christian' slave-trade by itself, however, entailed a measure of African subordination. British, American and French naval squadrons were employed to run down the slave-traders. European protectorates were set up along various parts of the West African coast to provide facilities for cruisers to protect traders and missionaries and to extend consular control. The abolitionist crusade, moreover, did not stop at ending the Christian trade. Abolitionists called for the abolition of slavery and the traffic in slaves in the Muslim parts of Africa, including the Western Sudan, and in East Africa. For a time slaves continued to be exported—for instance, from Zanzibar to the sugar plantations of Réunion and the great households of southern Arabia. Slave labour was also employed on Zanzibari estates that specialized in clove production for export. British pressure, backed by cruisers and gun-boats, gradually suppressed the maritime traffic, and in 1873 the Sultan of Zanzibar agreed to end the sea-borne slave-trade. Neither Royal Navy captains nor Her Majesty's consuls, however, could do much to stop the traffic inland, and the slave-trade away from the coast continued until Europeans established effective rule in the African interior.

The traffic in slaves had far-reaching consequences. Even if conventional exaggerations are discounted, the forcible appropriation of human muscle power was enormously wasteful of life and resources. As late as 1902, for example, slave-raiding armies in Northern Nigeria still devastated large stretches of land. The slave-raiders' record in other parts of Africa was no better, destroying alike life and wealth. Even where the ravages of the trade were held in check, the institution itself was one of many barriers in the way of economic change. Slave-owners generally felt little urge to apply new methods of production or to provide labour incentives. Indeed, the very notion of using manpower to its greatest economic advantage would probably have appeared strange to employers who, in many cases, treasured their slaves for purposes of prestige or conspicuous display or sensual indulgence rather than for the production of wealth. The slaves themselves had no reason to work hard or efficiently. From the European entrepreneur's standpoint, domestic slavery, however mild, was both an immoral and an uneconomic institution. As Lugard put it:

Slavery . . . is economically bad, for the freeman does more work than the slave, who, moreover, is indifferent to the productivity of the soil and careless of posterity. Barth noted . . . the more thorough agricultural methods of the independent tribes compared with the land under slave cultivation. Domestic slavery creates a demand for new slaves to replace losses, and hence encourages the slave-trade.[11]

The slave-trade in turn was incompatible with a system of free wage-labour that relied on monetary incentives instead of compulsion and provided workmen with a choice, however limited, of employers. Despite some rather romantic reconstructions of the patriarchical relations involved in domestic slavery, the slaves welcomed the abolition of their status by the colonizers. As experience in a country like Nigeria showed, 'those who have been brought into contact with the system of free labour learn to value freedom to earn wages, with which to buy what they like, for slavery and free labour cannot long exist side by side. If the slave asserts his freedom, it is generally in the form of an appeal for other employment.' [12] The abolition of slavery, effected under the colonizers' auspices, turned out therefore to be an indispensable step toward increasing both personal liberty and economic advancement.

African governmental systems and economic development

Nineteenth-century Africa supported an immense variety of political systems, ranging in size from small neighbourhood communities to great kingdoms.[13] Although generalizations with regard to their economic functions are therefore hard to make, they shared certain characteristics. Free trade in land was practically unknown. Gardens and estates were normally allocated according to political and social, rather than purely economic, criteria. Freemen rarely sold their labour for cash, except in European-settled areas such as the Cape, or in partly Westernized enclaves such as the coastal parts of Sierra Leone and the Gold Coast. Chiefs rarely relied on cash nexus. Normally they built up great followings by offering their subjects protection, favours and a host of religious, political or judicial services, by controlling fishing sites, by imposing labour services, by levying tolls and tribute and by monopolies in certain luxury goods like ivory or in imported muskets. Landowners in the modern sense were thus unknown, except among the Europeans of South Africa, the Swahili-speaking peoples of Zanzibar, Europeanized Africans in Sierra Leone or Senegal and a few other communities such as African *prazo* (estate) owners in Moçambique. Over the greater part of Africa, potentates or industrious farmers and herders could aggregate wealth in the form of wives, kinsmen, followers and slaves. Herds too could be multiplied. Prestige items like cloth or jewellery also set the wealthy apart. However, the most secure road to wealth and power lay not in making or selling goods but rather in working land and herds, in controlling men, in transmuting political or military power into tribute and that tribute in turn into conspicuous display.

Can such systems be regarded as feudal? Gallons of ink have been spilled over this question. Portuguese pioneers in the seventeenth century had no qualms about raising their African allies in the Congo to the dignity of dukes, counts and barons. British administrators in late-nineteenth-century Zambia were reminded of their own Houses of Parliament when they studied the workings of the Lozi national council. But appearances were deceptive. Feudalism in the European sense could operate only under conditions where the supply of

[11] Lord Lugard, *The dual mandate in British tropical Africa,* 5th ed. (London, 1965), pp. 364–5.
[12] *Ibid.,* p. 374.   [13] See Colson, 'African society', pp. 27–65.

land was limited and where, at least in theory, every piece of land was subject to a lord. Feudal lordship was a form of landed property that included social status together with public authority and, at any rate theoretically, a set of defined military obligations. In most parts of Africa, however, the limiting factor on production was not land but labour. African potentates controlled people rather than land. Public authority originally depended on kinship and ethnic affinity. In more warlike or in more highly developed societies these bonds were supplemented by patronage. Patronage implied a system whereby men offered themselves to a protector for whom they worked and for whom they fought, and who in turn bestowed gifts and favours. In many parts of the continent kings and minor chieftains alike came to rely increasingly on such fealties. Their existence of course was by no means tied to feudalism; they flourished in societies that had never known a feudal régime.

Trade was valued for political as much as for economic reasons. It is indeed tempting to argue that the more powerful states formed the political superstructure for societies distinguished by growing trade and more complex technology. Clearly, monarchs like Kazembe or the rulers of Benin derived both power and profit from their respective ability to control the long-distance exchange in commodities like slaves, guns and ivory. But no direct relationship exists between commerce and royal power. The kingdom of the Ndebele in nineteenth-century Rhodesia, for instance, was highly centralized, but the technology of the Ndebele was no more advanced than that of their neighbours. The Ndebele, moreover, conducted but little foreign traffic. They were raiders rather than traders. On the other hand, although communities elsewhere, such as the Kamba, the Yao, the Chokwe or the Nembe, carried on commerce on a comparatively large scale, they all lacked a strong state machinery. The so-called houses that made up many Niger Delta polities combined semi-capitalist modes of social organization with pre-capitalist institutions. Among the Nembe, for instance, a house formed a semi-autonomous community composed of a chief and his relatives, followers and slaves. The members of each house might reside in particular quarters of a city (petty chiefs might own smaller towns or a village), and its members might fish or farm. But above all the house acted as a trading corporation. At the same time it served as a military unit obliged to equip at least one war canoe for the navy of its respective city. The house was, besides, an association for the maintenance of law and order, a ritual body, a burial society and an organization for providing some sort of social security to its members.

Another interesting interpretation links the development of states to the means of destruction. Stone-tipped bows and arrows produced a democratic form of society because everybody could make these weapons. When iron was introduced, there was increased specialization, and rulers had to rely on blacksmiths. Where the employment of metal weapons could be combined with the use of horses and camels, warriors became capable of creating great empires depending on slave-raiding and servile labour. The Saharan and northern Sudanic city states were thus maintained by slave villages, dominated by armoured horsemen or camel-riders who could move rapidly across the savannah. Despotism, however, reached its apogee with the importation of European-made fire-arms, the manufacture of which was beyond the skills of local craftsmen. Access to guns could therefore be controlled by élites more compact than the ruling class of a cavalry state, where the breeding and purchase of animals and the production of trappings and armour could not be directly supervised by a royal court. In the forest belt, Sudanic cavalry was unable to operate because the horsemen were liable to be ambushed and their beasts to perish from disease. The footman with fire-arms prevailed on the battlefield and came to manage warlike dynasties in highly centralized kingdoms.[14]

This military-technological interpretation has many merits. The famed and resplendent kingdoms of the savannah clearly rested on ruthless exploitation of the villages. In seventeenth-century Songhai, the ruler's army, composed of cavalry and foot soldiers, had frequent skirmishes 'with those that refuse to pay tribute, and so many as they take, they sell unto the merchants of Timbukto'.[15] The importation of fire-arms likewise set up far-reaching disturbances, as the gunpowder frontiers steadily moved inland. By the end of the nineteenth century the Lovale of north-western Zambia, having access to Portuguese-imported weapons, were thus able to turn on the once-powerful Lunda, who then had to acquire muskets for self-protection. But again there is no necessary correlation between weapons and technology on the one hand and political centralization on the other. The simple Iron Age technology of Chaka's conquering Zulu was no different from that of their neighbours. The difference lay in the manner in which they trained their hosts and led them in battle. Guns were not necessarily decisive on their own. The military superiority of Dahomean armies rested not simply on the possession of muskets but on the splendid training that enabled Dahomean Amazons to load a Dane gun in thirty seconds—faster than a Prussian grenadier in the army of Frederick the Great.

The creation of African states was fraught with profound economic consequences, both positive and negative. Powerful monarchies facilitated the interchange of goods. Bantu rulers were 'distributor kings' who derived tribute, tolls, gifts and services from their followers; chiefs bestowed presents on their headmen, who in turn bestowed favours upon their followers. A monarchy such as that of the Lozi on the Upper Zambezi thus acted as the centre of a great network of provincial interchange, with a rudimentary degree of specialization of labour along ethnic lines. The Totela people, for example, supplied their lord with hoes, spears and axes; the Nkoya furnished canoes and nets; the Mbundu mats, baskets and wooden utensils; the Toka hides; and the Lunda tusks. Strong rulers protected traders and travellers. They safeguarded their subjects against foreign raiders and domestic evil-doers alike, thereby providing an essential economic service.

African state-building involved a substantial investment, and in some cases the social cost of this investment may have been high in relation to the services rendered. Long-distance trade certainly was facilitated by the existence of powerful monarchies. Commerce, however, as we have pointed out, could develop also among people without a strong political organization. In the eighteenth century, for example, the Bisa played an important role as middlemen in north-eastern Zambia and Moçambique; yet the Bisa managed to trade without bearing the cost of supporting a centralized state. The Nyamwezi of what is now

[14] Jack Goody, *Technology, tradition, and the state in Africa* (London, Oxford University Press, 1971), ch. 3.
[15] Leo Africanus, *History and description of Africa . . . done into English in the year 1600 by J. Pory . . .* (London, Hakluyt Society, 1896), p. 825.

Tanzania supplemented their income from agriculture by trade and by providing long-distance transport to other merchants. But again, Nyamwezi enterprise did not require investment in a costly state apparatus.

The precise relation between the social cost and returns derived from an 'investment' in state power remains hard to determine. But there is evidence that some African peoples may have bought the protection derived from a powerful state at too high a price, both in economic and in human terms. In Dahomey, for example, a great proportion of the population was employed as priests, diviners and novitiates. A vast material burden was thrown on the kinship groups who had to supply sacrifices, fees, gifts and so forth; hence 'the Dahomean sib compound was decapitalized by a permanent ecclesiastical draining'.[16] Worse still, the Dahomey, unlike say the Lozi monarchy, depended on an elaborate machinery of coercion, with great armies, a vast array of spies and human sacrifices. Prisoners were habitually massacred. Torture and killings on a massive scale were justified on the grounds of *raison d'état* combined with the rigidly observed precepts of ancestor worship. Needless to say, such killings entailed heavy social as well as economic costs.

Even when monarchs employed no terror, royal attempts at regulating the economy were apt to have unforeseen consequences. In Dahomey, public authorities set prices, fixed wages, controlled internal and external trade and adjusted agricultural production in accordance with real or assumed national needs. There were strict sumptuary laws that prevented commoners from living beyond their proper station in life. The cultivation of certain crops was restricted; some plants might be grown and distributed by royal officials only. Markets could not operate as price-setting mechanisms. Purchasers could not influence prices, and sellers had no incentive to improve their product or to lower their charges. Sir Richard Burton's observation of markets in late-nineteenth-century Dahomey would have struck a responsive chord in every British housewife during the Second World War, when a comprehensive rationing system prevailed. He was struck by 'a curious contrast, the placidity and impassiveness with which the seller, hardly taking the trouble to remove her pipe, drawls out the price of her two-cowrie lots, and the noisy excitement of the buyers, who know that they must purchase and pay the demand'. The monarchs of Dahomey were even sufficiently powerful to attempt long-term planning. According to Burton, King Gelele 'had resolved to grind the faces of his subjects for ten years, of which six are now elapsed. After that time they will be supplied to honest labour, and a man shall live on a cowrie a day, so cheap will provisions become.' But royal planning apparently did not do away with the shortages that beset Dahomey. If Burton is to be believed, Gelele's economic policy not only discouraged production in certain respects but also led to a sharp rise in prices.[17]

The Lozi monarchy was neither as centralized nor as bloodthirsty as the kingdom of Dahomey. Lozi kings, unlike their opposite numbers in Dahomey, were not much involved in the slave-trade, and Lozi priests did not practise human sacrifice. But in certain respects Lozi institutions may also have acted as

[16] Karl Polanyi, in collaboration with Abraham Rotstein, *Dahomey and the slave trade: an analysis of an archaic economy* (Seattle, University of Washington Press, 1960), pp. 78–80.
[17] Sir Richard Burton, *A mission to Gelele, king of Dahome* . . . memorial ed. (London, 1893), vol I, p. 49, and vol. II, p. 57 n. 1.

a brake upon the full development of the country's productive resources. The subject Subia, for instance, were not allowed to build in reed—apparently for reasons of prestige. Trade was subject to the most rigid restrictions. As François Coillard, a French missionary, put it:

> Not one man would dare to sell one of those bundles of rushes which he had cut, not one of those women, much as they long for white beads, would dare to do a day's work for me, without express permission from the king. We might starve to death at the gates of this large village without any one knowing it . . . no one would venture to visit us as long as His Majesty did not do so publicly. That is what prevented my vaccination from becoming popular, that is what stifles all innovation.[18]

African societies were commonly subject to rigid social differentiation. Stratification was as likely to occur in the economically backward as in the more advanced societies. For the Ndebele and kindred peoples warfare was an economic pursuit that enabled warriors to acquire women, cattle and grain, as well as serfs, who would supply both unskilled and skilled workmen—for instance, blacksmiths. Ethnic or supposedly ethnic divisions were quite rigid. The top layer among the Ndebele of Rhodesia consisted of the dominant group known as the Zansi, 'the people from upstream', followed by the Enhla, 'the people from downstream', who were mainly of Sotho descent. The lowest caste consisted of subject Shona-speakers, the Holi, who were virtually serfs and did the manual labour. Intermarriage between the three castes was forbidden, and most of the higher positions were reserved to the Zansi.

In Rwanda the conquering Tutsi, a pastoral warrior people, established a caste society in which the Bantu-speaking Hutu, reduced to serfdom, were denied the right to hold higher political office and were forbidden to intermarry with the ruling group. In nearby Burundi, the Tutsi further split into two endogamous castes, the lordly Tutsi-Banyaguru and the inferior Tutsi-Hima. In Rwanda and Burundi alike the king was regarded as a sacred personage. By these means the Tutsi conquerors sought to give divine sanction to their régime. The cavalry-dominated societies of the Western Sudan were no more egalitarian. Among the Mossi, for instance, commoners were not allowed to serve as horsemen lest they endanger the rulers' military monopoly. When Lenz visited the little town of Bassikunnu, he was struck by the way in which agriculture was confined to Muslim Negroes, who were relegated to a separate quarter. The Arabs, who were employed mainly in commerce, dwelt apart. In nineteenth-century Kano, for instance, the oldest and the most important quarter of the town was inhabited largely by Arab and Berber (principally Ghadasiye) merchants. There was also Agadesawa, a quarter largely occupied by people from Agades, as well as Yaawela and Marmara, which were largely for the Fulani. A similar system prevailed in the cities of the Yoruba, where the population was composed essentially of heterogeneous elements. Occupational differences provided a basis for social stratification—largely because of the way in which traditional skills were jealously guarded and handed down through specific lineages. Lineage membership thus helped to determine social status in the Yoruba towns.

---

[18] François Coillard, *On the threshold of Central Africa: a record of twenty years' pioneering among the Barotsi of the Upper Zambesi* (London, 1902), p. 487.

Pre-colonial societies: an assessment

The pre-colonial economies were extremely varied in their nature, in their ability to produce wealth and in their capacity for sustained growth or for maintaining different densities of population. Bushman hunters required an enormous amount of space to supply food for exiguous bands. Their 'capital', in the shape of bows and arrows and digging sticks, was almost negligible. Yoruba city dwellers, on the other hand, enjoyed an infinitely higher standard of living within the compass of walled towns that depended on the surrounding countryside for much of their provisions. Long before the Europeans set foot into the African interior, Africans had reached the Iron Age. They had perfected numerous crafts based on raw materials such as leather, wood and bone. Unlike the Maya and the Aztecs, Africans had become expert in the art of working copper and iron. Above all, African farmers had devised a great variety of techniques designed to cope with differing soils and harsh climatic conditions, which might vary all the way from desert to tropical rain-forest.

The obstacles facing the farmer were of many different kinds. A tropical climate does allow of long duration and of great intensity of sunlight throughout the year, thus providing energy for plant production. And the lack of frost and the minor seasonal variations offer an environment for continuous cropping. But high temperatures lead to high rates of evaporation and of plant transpiration, with a resulting loss of agricultural efficiency. Much of Africa suffers from these and other climatic handicaps: a great deal of the land is desert or savannah where rainfall is either scarce or briefly and perilously overabundant. This makes for a high rate of run-off and soil erosion as well as parched fields in the dry season. The combination of high temperature and high rainfall produces rapid loss of organic matter in tropical soils. This reduces the nutrient level of the soils as well as their ability to retain moisture. In addition, the tropical climate breeds enormous numbers and a great diversity of pests and parasites. There are considerably more natural enemies of man, plants and animals in the tropics than in temperate zones. Climate, diseases and pests combine to enervate man, and present numerous hazards to crop and animal production and storage. Eighty years of colonial agricultural research were unable to make up for all these disadvantages of tropical areas.

Over countless generations Africans had worked out flexible systems of food production to meet their peculiar conditions. Given their situation, in which labour and capital were usually in short supply and only land was plentiful, their systems were sound from both the ecological and the economic standpoint. African farmers had adapted a wide range of plants, such as cassava, maize and ground-nuts, to the African climate. During the nineteenth century the process continued. On the Gold Coast, by the late 1860s, for instance, British merchants were trying to promote the cultivation of cotton; German and Swiss missionaries of the Basel Mission Society had introduced coffee and Virginian and Kentucky tobacco. Nor were African peasants strangers to the work ethic. Villagers respected men who showed their prowess as hunters, who helped their neighbours and who laboured hard in the fields to support their dependants.

Traditional societies, however, had structural weaknesses that limited their productivity and impeded efforts at economic development. The traditional systems of agriculture depended on simple tools, appropriate to societies in which land was plentiful and capital scarce. Africans, for the most part, earned but slender rewards for the human labour involved. Agricultural output per head was generally low, for, in addition to the shortcomings occasioned by simple technologies and by unfavourable soil and climatic conditions, traditional agriculture had limited markets and little specialization. Except for export-crop production, the market demand for food crops was small even during the colonial period, because so few people lived away from the farm. The agricultural sector bought very little from other sectors of the economy. Farmers unable to buy what they needed for household and farm purposes had to make their own equipment. Hence they remained limited in their specialization and division of labour.

African social structures were organized to ensure against loss of income and to share the risks of food production. Seed varieties were chosen not for maximum average yields but to ensure minimum variation in yield. Although mixed and sequential planting in small plots required more labour, it reduced the chances of total crop loss. Large families were seen as an asset, for they provided not only a built-in labour force but also a guarantee that enough children would survive to care for the parents in their old age.

African kinship systems were, in an economic sense, a means of spreading costs. Kinship obligations required entire families, rather than one individual, to share burdens. A system of reciprocal rights and obligations sought to ensure security for all. Patience, endurance, honourable conduct and a high sense of family duty were the ideals of village and kinship communities. But the realities were often suspicion, envy, faction and fear. All too often village life aimed at economic levelling: no one should be so prosperous that he did not need to depend on others. The great majority of Africans thus lived in small-scale, non-monetized, subsistence societies, with simple technologies, limited division of labour and only a few specialized craftsmen.[19] Strong-minded men, such as the hero in Achebe's brilliant novel *Things fall apart,* might work like men possessed to harvest impressive crops and gain titles of honour; yet even for this hero the possibilities of economic innovation were strictly limited. In most parts of Africa there was no need for an entrepreneurial class, men who could mobilize capital, co-ordinate complex methods of production, and supply a wide market. Only rarely is division of labour for the production of a given commodity encountered among non-literate folk. The various pre-colonial African societies were by no means incapable of technological progress, as shown by advancement in the fields of farming and metallurgy. But innovation tended to be an extraordinarily slow process. Traditional societies could neither assimilate complex technologies in the technical sense nor make the required adjustments in the organizational field. By their very nature, societies of this kind were not organized in such a way that the production process could be divided among workers, supervisors and policy-makers. Status seldom came just from acquiring goods, although horses, cattle or wives in quantity were signs of wealth and prestige. Varying ideas of wealth also limited economic development. People usually did not try to maximize their profit or to work to get the best economic gains from land and labour.

[19] On weaknesses of African societies, see Peter Kilby, ed., *Entrepreneurship and economic development* (New York, 1971), *passim.*

Fear of foreign competition, mingled with religious or cultural prejudice, might also stand in the way of technological advancement. James Africanus Horton, a British army officer of African extraction, thus reported in the 1860s that the people living in the auriferous districts of the Gold Coast would not countenance competition from anglicized Africans using European methods of production. One Thomas Hughes, an educated black Gold Coaster, brought out expensive mining equipment to the gold-field of western Wassaw. But as soon as his workmen discovered a valuable vein, the locals smashed the machinery and expelled the miners in Hughes's employ, all under the guise of religion.[20]

Still other obstacles stood in the way of economic change. African farmers, as we have seen, seldom produced for the market. With land plentiful and labour scarce, there was no pressure for intensive land usage. Manure was rarely used; seeds were neither improved nor selected; planting was not done in a straight line; crop-rotation was rarely practised. The scientific breeding of animals was unknown, as were the principles of veterinary science, soil chemistry, parasitology and so forth.

Such division of labour as existed was generally based on sex and age. Men fought and hunted; men and boys tended cattle and did the heavy work of cutting bush and trees preliminary to planting and hut-building. Women prepared the food, did some gathering and water-portage, hoed, weeded, threshed and made beer. In tasks such as clearing fields or house-building, there was co-operative labour. Limited manpower and rudimentary tools restricted the amount of land that could be cultivated.

Economic development was subject also to serious technological restraints. The city folk of the Western Sudan used donkeys, mules, horses and camels for commerce and for war. In southern Africa a few communities such as the Sotho had learned the use of the pony from their European neighbours. But before the advent of Western veterinary science, no African, be he Boer trekker, Somali tribal chief or Ndebele cattle-keeper, knew how to cope with fly-borne diseases that struck down horses and cattle alike. And even people who had healthy cattle failed to use them as draught animals for ploughing or hauling.

Ploughs were unknown in most parts of sub-Saharan Africa; hence Africans could not farm heavy soil. Neither had they learned to harness oxen, water, wind or steam for the purpose of farming or industry. They depended largely or entirely on the strength of human muscles, whether for hoeing the fields, cutting down bushland, paddling canoes, carrying trade goods or hurling spears.

African husbandmen might attain some prosperity when times were good, but when drought or locusts hit the land, or when rinderpest decimated the herds, rural societies had few resources to tide the people over. Storage facilities for large quantities of food were nonexistent, and transportation was difficult. Despite these drawbacks, however, communities did try to cushion their members against acts of nature. In a year of good weather, as a safeguard against an occasional poor harvest, banana growers by Lake Victoria might cultivate an area much larger than the size necessary to feed their family. But if the crop was plentiful, the surplus would be left to rot in the fields for lack of a ready market. Add to these difficulties the ever-present threat of war. The destructive effects of internecine conflict or of slaving varied a great deal, of

[20] James Africanus Horton, *West African countries and peoples: 1868* (1868; reprint, Edinburgh University Press, 1968), pp. 238–9.

course. But when raiders burned a village, killed the men, took the women captive, looted the seed grain and made off with the cattle, recovery was difficult for people who had no means of readily replenishing their labour force or their food supplies.

Hence the population of the continent remained relatively small. In all probability manpower was also under-utilized. In the 1890s, for example, when cocoa came into wide use on the Gold Coast, indigenous farmers were suddenly able to produce this crop while continuing to grow their traditional foodcrops, even though the population had not as yet increased sizeably. Levels of production differed, but remained generally low. Seasonal hunger and disease were a common part of man's fate. In most areas of Africa, as we have seen before, the numerous geographical and technological obstacles left but few opportunities for economic choice either for producers or consumers. Regions such as the Niger Delta, where traders could transport goods for long distances by canoe, were exceptional.

Traditional societies could not easily innovate, primarily because of their levelling tendency and need to share in their social systems. There is little incentive to change if the innovator, the risk-taker, bears all the expenses and uncertainty and then must share what he produces. These societies had their own distinctive patterns of trust, but they all too often lacked the wider relationships—extending beyond those of a communal society—that would have created a favourable climate for innovation. Small-scale societies were severely limited also in their technical knowledge; they had few opportunities of acquiring expertise in this area, and little ability to evaluate possible uses of new technical knowledge. The division of labour remained circumscribed; there were few craft specialists. Moreover, life was generally precarious. People were far more exposed to the ravages occasioned by natural disasters than are the members of an industrial society.

Before the imposition of European governance, the majority of African societies had only limited opportunities for economic development. Living mostly in fairly isolated communities, African villagers were dependent to a large extent on self-generated change. They seldom had outside sources from which they might obtain capital equipment. They could not easily store their wealth. They could trade only on a small scale. Industrious and successful men might eat their crops, or give them away, or hold feasts or sometimes use them to acquire prestige items such as beads or cloth. But flocks and herds apart, they had no wealth that could be made to move or multiply.

As the peoples of sub-Saharan Africa came in contact with outsiders, they became increasingly dependent on imported commodities such as beads, knives, iron bars, textiles, axes, liquor and metal basins—goods that African artisans were often unable to turn out as cheaply or as efficiently as manufacturers in North Africa or Europe. In addition, there was a growing demand for such merchandise as muskets, rifles and mirrors, which Africans could not furnish at all with existing means of production. The economic history of nineteenth-century Africa hinges on the growing dependence of Africans on wider world market. In the 1870s, merchants in Timbuktu anxiously discussed news of the Franco-Prussian war. African cultivators in West Africa extensively cultivated ground-nuts, palm-oil and other produce for the world market. Elephant hunters in the bush of the Rhodesias had to reckon with price fluctuations brought about on the London ivory market by the Russo-Turkish conflict of 1877–8. Bemba warriors on the Zambezian veld learned the use of discarded British army muskets that had once done duty on the battlefield of Waterloo. And Gold Coast producers responded to rising world prices for monkey skins by catching more animals. Although Africans became increasingly avid for foreign-made goods, this merchandise had to be paid for by means of exports. Outside the more favoured parts of West Africa and Zanzibar, most indigenous Africans, however, had few commodities that could be produced at a small capital outlay and that were yet of sufficient value and small enough bulk to justify the cost of transportation to the coast. These commodities, as we have seen, included ivory, alluvial gold, rhino tusks and some wild crops such as bush-grown rubber and palm products. Much of this wealth, however, was irreplaceable. Once the elephants had been 'shot out' in a particular area, an African monarch faced serious economic trouble in finding an acceptable export substitute.

The only single commodity for which an ever-increasing market had been found for many centuries was human merchandise. The demand for foreign trade goods in Africa, combined with a ready market for servile labour in the Americas and the Muslim world, had resulted in the slave-trade. By the 1870s, however, the so-called Christian slave-trade had practically ceased. Slavery had disappeared from continental North America and, with the exception of Cuba, from the West Indies. Cuba as well as Brazil put an end to slavery in the 1880s. The Muslim traffic, however, continued in East Africa, in territories as far afield as the Sudan and Nyasaland. As the commerce in slaves, and in commodities such as elephant tusks, became more competitive, more and more African communities acquired fire-arms, with an accompanying increase in violence and destruction.

The long-term impact of the Muslim commerce is hard to evaluate. Muslim merchants imported a great many new products, such as food crops, textiles, guns and trinkets. Some Muslim chiefs, like Jumbe at Kota Kota in Nyasaland, became settlers in the true sense and improved indigenous agriculture by introducing rice cultivation to the country. There is also evidence of Muslim craftsmen who supplied the needs of inland communities. But man-catching or hunting economies could not provide the basis for lasting prosperity. Both depended on a wasting asset. The very existence of the slave-trade, moreover, militated against the introduction of new methods of production, the employment of labour-saving devices or incentives to improve output.

The same was true of ivory-hunters. Even entrepreneurs such as William Finaughty, an early pioneer in Rhodesia whose operations were run on the lines of a well-managed business, did not acquire great riches. The tall tales told by many European explorers concerning the assumed luxury and splendour enjoyed by Arab merchants on the east coast were heavily overdrawn. Gross profits of the ivory-trade must have been considerable, of course. But against these, entrepreneurs had to set the high cost of porterage, the substantial interest on borrowed capital, the sharp fluctuations of ivory prices on the world markets and the ever-present risk of total loss.

At the same time foreign trade created new political and social tensions in the societies of the interior. African rulers struggled hard to overcome these challenges. Some, like Lewanika, king of the Lozi, attempted to do away with the slave-trade altogether. But none commanded political or military power great enough to pacify large territories. None commanded technical resources sufficient to bring about basic changes in existing methods of production. For all the poets' praise of noble savages, for all the romantics' musings on traditional societies in a state of balanced social equilibrium, these cultures faced inner contradictions on an extraordinary scale. The polities of sub-Saharan Africa all succumbed to Western conquest. They collapsed not only because of the attackers' strength, but also because of the defenders' inherent weaknesses.

Europe in Africa before and during the 1880s

Before 1880 a mere handful of Europeans or Americans were apt to look upon Africa as anything other than a land of adventure, of heathendom and of horror. Still fewer regarded the continent as a field of economic opportunity. During the nineteenth century, Africa had attracted but a tiny proportion of the millions who had left Europe to seek new homes for themselves beyond the Atlantic. The bulk of South Africa's white population, by far the greatest concentration of whites in Africa, had been born on African soil and knew no other home. Potential European emigrants might consider North America, Australia, New Zealand or the Argentine, but rarely the Cape, Natal or the Boer republics beyond the Orange river. Outside South Africa, climate, disease and lack of economic opportunity had prevented the emergence of permanent white communities in all but a few trading posts. At the same time, Africa accounted for only a small proportion of the world's trade. By 1880, for instance, less than 5 per cent of British imports derived from the African continent.

Nevertheless African commerce was expanding at a considerable rate. The factories and workshops of Western Europe between them consumed a growing volume of tropical products. These included industrial raw materials, such as wool, cotton, palm-oil kernels and hard fibres; food crops such as cocoa and bananas; and raw materials for luxury industries, especially gems and ivory. At the same time, the application of steam-power to transportation would revolutionize the logistics of empire. Railways would provide not only a means of relieving sweating porters of their burdens, but would also vastly increase the volume of goods that could be carried overland. The Victorian era, above all, was the age of the steamship so eloquently praised in Kipling's poetry. For their motive power steam-powered vessels, unlike sailing ships, were independent of irregular winds. Because their size and carrying capacity greatly exceeded those of the old East Indiamen, freight charges dropped in spectacular fashion. For the first time in history, bulky merchandise could be moved over vast distances at moderate cash. Africa ceased to be dependent on the export of a few commodities of small weight and high value.

From the European merchant's standpoint, nothing mattered but the African periphery. During the early 1880s, the export trade conducted by the small islands of Mauritius and São Tomé, with their plantations producing respectively sugar and cocoa, was almost equal to that of Nigeria. Nigeria's commerce in turn amounted to more than four times that of the Gold Coast. The importance of West Africa itself was eclipsed by that of the South African colonies, where, from the seventeenth century, European immigrants had imported a new technology. Especially important was the commerce of the Cape. In 1880 the Cape Colony sold abroad goods worth £7,710,000, a paltry sum by the standards of contemporary British trade statistics, but still more than four times the value of the traffic between all British West African colonies and the United Kingdom.

The prosperity of the South African colonies, such as it was, depended on furnishing Europe with primary products. They comprised cane sugar, hides, skins, ostrich feathers, mohair and particularly merino wool. When the famous Kimberley 'Dry Diggings' were discovered in 1870, the South African back-woods economy, subjected as it had been to sharp price fluctuations, sudden gluts and extended periods of depression, underwent a far-reaching and dramatic change. By 1882 the Cape Colony had mined approximately £26 million worth of diamonds, an amount greater than its entire exports between 1826 and 1861. The value of the diamonds shipped abroad during the same year exceeded that of all merchandise sent overseas from the rest of the sub-Saharan subcontinent.[21] The extraction of gems provided new opportunities for skilled workers, professional men and entrepreneurs, many of them immigrants from Europe.

By the 1880s, only South Africa had the makings of a coal-mining industry. South Africans could obtain credit through a relatively intricate banking system, linked to the money markets of London. There were short stretches of railway, soon to be greatly enlarged; and there were fairly substantial port facilities, with the great Albert Docks operating at Cape Town. South Africa, especially the Cape, also pioneered in the provision of experimental farms and technical education on the soil of Africa. (In 1885, for instance, a viticultural station opened its doors at Groot Constantia, and four years later an agricultural school started at Stellenbosch.) The Cape Colony was thus the first territory in sub-Saharan Africa to acquire the rudiments of a modern economic infrastructure. The Cape Colony moreover was unique in possessing a diamond-mining industry capable of generating local capital on a substantial scale. These advantages, joined to the economic benefits derived from the presence of a relatively large white population with a substantial reservoir of skills, enabled the colony to play a primary role in the economic and political life of southern Africa.[22] The Cape developed an imperialist drive of its own, symbolized in the person of Cecil Rhodes, who was later to become both prime minister of the Cape and its major mining magnate. Cape predominance continued until a great gold industry was developed on the Witwatersrand in the Transvaal, where vast auriferous deposits were found in 1886. From then onward, the economic centre of South Africa gradually shifted into the interior beyond the Vaal river, hitherto one of the economically most backward parts of South Africa.

The Bantu-speaking peoples were no longer regarded by their white overlords as a major military threat, but merely as a 'security' problem. The ninth (and last) of the so-called Kaffir Wars ended in 1878. A year later the British routed the Zulu army at Ulundi, crushing the last independent military monarchy in South Africa. Conquest had far-reaching economic as well as political consequences. Tribal migrations became a thing of the past. Customary re-

[21] S. Herbert Frankel, *Capital investment in Africa: its course and effects* (London, Oxford University Press, 1938), p. 54.
[22] In 1876 the white population of the colonies within what is now the Republic of South Africa was estimated at 320,000, of whom 220,000 lived in the Cape Colony. Africans living within the borders of Natal, the Cape and the Boer republics of the Transvaal and the Orange Free State numbered approximately 1,200,000, and Africans outside these borders about 2 million.

straints on the mobility of labour disappeared, and so did the prestige associated with a way of life based on raiding and on the martial virtues. Successively more and more land passed into European ownership, and the acreage available for customary forms of slash-and-burn agriculture declined. At the same time as internecine warfare ended and food could more readily be distributed to relieve local shortages, the African population grew rapidly. New wants, new opportunities for spending money, the increasing pressure on African-occupied land and the need to find ready cash for the tax collector all combined to force Africans into earning money. Depending on local circumstances, they did so either by selling more grain and stock to traders or by earning wages in white employment as labour migrants. South Africa, in other words, was developing a substantial stratum of black labourers who were part tribesman, part proletarian, reliant both on traditional land rights and on wages. In addition, a new kind of African was making his appearance, a man who could no longer make his living as a cultivator but was fitted only for wage labour. People of this kind included some skilled workmen, painters, bricklayers and similar categories, as well as clerks, court interpreters, teachers and clergymen, trained in mission schools. In the second half of the century the number of African children receiving scholastic education of some kind increased roughly elevenfold, from 9,000 to 100,000, a development fraught with far-reaching economic and social consequences. Indirectly, the influence of the money economy extended far beyond the regions under direct European control. White traders travelled in ox-wagons to the distant Zambezi, and African labour migrants were coming to Kimberley from as far as Barotseland, nearly a thousand miles distant. Wage labour, migrant labour and cash cropping were to become the major forces of change throughout Africa during the colonial period.

Next to South Africa, the most important part of the continent from the economic historian's point of view was the west coast, especially the tropical forest belt.[23] The forest zone was rich in palm-oil, a valuable commodity with a variety of industrial and culinary uses. It could be produced by Africans using rudimentary methods, but was subject to sharp price fluctuations owing to competition from other products. The trade was rendered even more speculative by indigenous wars, which interfered with production, and by occasional deficien-

[23] According to Charles C. Stover, 'Tropical exports', in *Tropical development 1880–1913,* W. Arthur Lewis, ed. (Evanston, Northwestern University Press, 1970), pp. 46–7, in 1883 the probable value of exports in millions of U.S. dollars stood as follows:

Angola	2·0
Belgian Congo	2·2
French West Africa	4·0
Gambia	1·0
Gold Coast	1·8
Liberia	0·3
Mauritius	18·7
Moçambique	1·1
Nigeria	7·9
Réunion	4·5
São Tomé	3·0
Sierra Leone	2·2
Togo	0·1
Zanzibar	6·8

cies of rainfall, which rendered the fruit 'starved' and poor in oil. In the long run, moreover, African producers, used to the collection and preparation of the wild produce, could not compete against European entrepreneurs who turned out plantation-grown and factory-made palm-oil in Sumatra and other Eastern countries. The West African palm-oil industry, however, received a boost when industrial technologists discovered a use for palm-kernels, which had hitherto been regarded as useless. In the late 1860s, Hippolyte Mège-Mouriès, a French scientist, won a prize offered by Emperor Napoleon III by developing a butter substitute known as margarine. The manufacture of this new food created a vast new market for palm-kernels when industrialists found a means of using palm-kernel oil in its production, while the residue of the kernels was turned into oil cakes for stall-fed cattle. By the early 1880s, the West African oil trade was dominated by palm produce.

The expansion of trade was enormously aided by the arrival of the steamship. In the twenty years between 1864 and 1884 the tonnage of British ships visiting West Africa went up from 113,000 to 1,157,000 tons. Commerce between Western Europe and West Africa became more efficient and more regular. The arrival of the steamship also facilitated inland penetration. Nigeria, for instance, was fortunate in having a substantial network of rivers, creeks and lagoons that made transport by water simple and profitable. British shipbuilders learned how to construct shallow-draught, stern-wheel boats capable of going up the Niger river and other waterways. Moreover, sailors and merchants benefited from the prophylactic use of quinine, which safeguarded whites against malaria and its deadly concomitant, blackwater fever. The modern Niger trade was indeed the combined creation of the steamship and the cinchona bark.

The African palm-oil brokers in control of strategic river courses and creeks put up a determined resistance against white interlopers. British vessels steaming up-river encountered well-directed gunfire from fortified points along the bank. The merchants then called on their government for protection, and as long as vessels flying the White Ensign remained in the vicinity of the trading posts, merchants did good business. When the dry season set in and warships could no longer ascend the river, Africans resumed their attacks, with the result that barter and battle alternated with the regularity of the seasons. British traders could not be kept out, especially as their enterprise was strengthened by the creation of great shipping lines. They ceased to be merchants on their own account, but confined themselves to carrying other men's cargoes. For several decades, small entrepreneurs were able to avail themselves of these new logistic possibilities. European firms set themselves up in business along various parts of the coast and along the Oil rivers, where they made ample use of African, Eurafrican and somtimes Afro-Brazilian middlemen. Intense competition continued until prices fell. Finally, the West African trade, like the production of diamonds at Kimberley, entered an era of amalgamation. This first began in 1879, when Sir George Taubman Goldie succeeded in consolidating a number of rival firms into the United African Company.[24]

[24] The United African Company was formed by Sir George Goldie in 1879. Three years later it was reorganized and incorporated as the National African Company Ltd. In 1886 it was granted a Royal Charter and shortly afterwards changed its name to the Royal Niger Company. In 1922, the Royal Niger Company, the African Association, Miller Bros of Glasgow and a number of smaller firms were formed into the United Africa Company as a subsidiary of Lever interests.

Meanwhile, attempts were being made to adapt cocoa to West African conditions. From the late 1870s, for instance, a number of enterprising chiefs in Calabar tried to make money by investing in the new crop. Cocoa cultivators faced several obstacles, however. The trees bear fruit only after three or four years, and do not reach full maturity before about the eighth year, with maximum yield by the tenth to twelfth year. Cocoa cultivation thus entailed long-term planning and a lengthy waiting period before farmers could realize a return on their investment. Cocoa was also a purely commercial crop in that there was no internal demand for it anywhere in West Africa; growers depended for their livelihood solely on overseas buyers. Not until the 1890s, when black rural entrepreneurs, acting in concert with European traders and agricultural experts, brought about an economic revolution, did the cultivation of cocoa take hold in the Gold Coast.

In countries like Senegal and the Gambia, which lay outside the tropical forest zone, the place of palm-oil was taken by ground-nuts. This crop, which was introduced to Africa by the Portuguese and grown for African consumption, was used from the 1830s onward in the expanding French soap industry. African farmers successfully adjusted their production to the new demand, and exports from Senegal shot up from an estimated 1,000 kilos in 1841 to almost 5 million kilos in 1854. By that time the industry was firmly established. France dominated the ground-nut trade, which was extended inland by *métis* and French-speaking Africans whose desire for security and a settled administration contributed to a local variety of 'Senegalese imperialism'. French enterprise was strengthened when, in 1862, French engineers set to work at the port of Dakar. Four years later the Messageries Impériales opened a regular steamboat service, and Dakar ultimately developed into a great African metropolis.

South of Senegal, the British held a narrow strip of territory along the Gambia river. But Bathurst, the capital, stood right in the midst of mangrove-fringed marshes where disease ran rampant. The ground-nut trade remained so small that the British for a time even considered handing over their possession to the French in return for concessions elsewhere. The only other British outpost was Sierra Leone, with the splendid natural harbour of Freetown, where black colonists from the United States, freed slaves and missionaries had helped to create an English-speaking society. Sierra Leoneans benefited from missionary education and from the amenities offered by Fourah Bay (founded in 1827), the only institution of Western higher learning in West Africa at the time. Anglicized Africans helped to turn Freetown into an important centre, with shops, agencies and newspaper offices, and its own Afro-Victorian culture. Educated Sierra Leoneans played a part comparable to that of gallicized Senegalese pioneers; they pushed outward along the coast and inward into the hinterland as dealers, clerks, government officials and mission employees, carriers of European influence wherever they went. European-educated Africans, torn away from their traditional communities, were apt also to display a striking spirit of individualism and a greater willingness to accumulate capital than their neighbours. James Africanus Horton, a keen observer of West African society, thus noted how Sierra Leoneans resident in the Gambia were prone to get on in life—they had no voice in the local societies, but 'the spirit of parsimony exists among them, and they accumulate wealth, and are now building large and substantial houses . . . their children are sent to educational establishments in Sierra Leone and in England'.[25]

Before the mid-1880s, although Germany had no territorial colonies on African soil, its commercial stake and the extent of its informal influence were by no means negligible. Between 1879 and 1883 the value of Hamburg's trade with West Africa doubled. In 1883 the Germans imported from West Africa 9·2 million Reichsmarks' worth of goods, especially palm-oil, which was used as a machine lubricant and also for soap and candles. In exchange, the Germans exported liquor above all, and also salt, guns and gunpowder. Firms like Woermann or Jantzen & Thormählen controlled a network of trading posts in various parts of West Africa, and in 1882 Woermann started its own shipping service to West Africa. German influence was particularly notable in Kamerun, where the German merchants accounted for about half of the export trade, much of it consisting of spirits. British policy-makers and missionaries of all nationalities were fond of attacking these German liquor exports. However, the trade in liquor was profitable not only for merchants, but also supplied a valuable market for many German estate-owners, who did good business in distilling potatoes. Another centre of German trade was Zanzibar, where as early as 1859 the Hanseatic cities had managed to conclude a commercial treaty with the Sultan.

Portuguese power in Africa likewise depended more on indirect than on direct domination. The Portuguese possessions might loom large on a map, but by the late 1870s they in fact amounted to little more than a scattered network of ports and fortified posts surrounded by ill-defined zones of influence. Portugal lacked the resources and the will to develop its patrimony. The Portuguese colonies attracted few emigrants, as most would-be settlers from Portugal preferred to seek their fortunes in Brazil. Angola received an unduly high proportion of convicts or *degredados*. Slavery, though formally abolished in 1878, continued in disguised forms and probably restricted economic development. Moçambique especially was in a parlous state. Vast areas were controlled by the owners of *prazos,* half-Lusitanized magnates of mixed or sometimes even of purely African descent who governed their fiefs in a manner little different from that of African chiefs. Their power rested on the traffic in slaves and ivory and on private armies equipped with fire-arms. Until the 1880s the Portuguese did not even begin to assert their power effectively in the far interior, where expeditions could not be supplied and protected against a hostile climate. Portuguese influence inland, such as it was, depended on bush traders, ivory-hunters, and such *prazo* owners as chose to support their nominal sovereign. The internal slave-trade continued, and there was no plantation agriculture. By far the most important export was ivory for the markets of India. Moçambique seemed to be caught in a vicious circle of poverty and of maladministration or non-administration, from which most colonial theoreticians could see no possible avenue of escape.

Angola was somewhat more important to Portugal than was Moçambique. Luanda, its chief city, maintained close links with Brazil. The local settlers in Angola had adopted many facets of Brazilian civilization. Some even thought of joining Angola to the Brazilian empire. Though economically the country

---

[25] Horton, *West African countries,* p. 71.

was a backwater, there was nevertheless some growth. From the 1860s onward, steamers regularly plied from Luanda to the mouth of the Cuanza and thence up-river 100 miles to the market centre of Dondo. Between 1867 and 1873 the amount of produce brought to the coast increased sevenfold, especially in palm-oil, palm-kernels, coffee and ground-nuts. By the 1870s the total exports from Luanda, Benguela and Moçamedes were officially valued at about double the level of those of 1825, when they had consisted almost exclusively of slaves. Angola's total volume of trade, though small, exceeded that of the Gold Coast.

Control over the trade between the coast and the interior became a major issue from the mid-nineteenth century onward.[26] By the 1870s Europeans controlled small enclaves along the shores of the Atlantic and exercised some measure of consular supervision (see Map 1). But many merchants, whether Germans along the shore of Kamerun, Bordeaux businessmen with interests in Senegal, or British traders in Nigeria, were no longer satisfied with informal empire, with its dependence on consuls, gunboats and protected coastal enclaves. The need for greater physical security along a turbulent frontier and the commercial disruptions occasioned by internecine warfare seemed to dictate political intervention inland. Soldiers in search of glory and promotion were apt to agree readily with this position. So were officials, who assumed that trade would increase the revenue required to run the coastal enclaves. As Newbury concludes:

It followed that every coastal colony needed as large a hinterland as possible—at the expense of its neighbours. The political and international implications of this correlation of authority with trade occupied Africans and Europeans for the remainder of the century; and their decisions were to restructure the government and the economy of West Africa in the years to come.[27]

In the last quarter of the nineteenth century the west-coast merchants began to suffer from a serious trade depression that intensified competition between the various European groups on the one hand, and between Europeans and Africans on the other. White merchants became increasingly anxious to lower their costs by getting rid of tolls, customs and other restraints on trade in the interior, and by eliminating African middlemen. Africans, on the other hand, attempted to protect themselves against falling prices by deliberately obstructing supplies and by other devices. Hence many European merchants began to demand a more active policy in the interior. The need for commercial consolidation and desire for protection of inland trading posts and plantations against both white interlopers and black rivals led also to the creation of chartered companies that tried to combine commerce and government at no expense to the mother country. French competition along the Niger was a direct threat to the United African Company. In 1886, seven years after Sir George Goldie had brought the company into being, he received a charter from the British government that enabled his concern, now known as the Royal Niger Company, to administer the lands of the Niger. Goldie's company was only one of many that came into existence during this twilight era, when private capitalists were expected to create empires and colonialism had not yet become a nationalized enterprise. The formation of the Royal Niger Company was followed in 1888 by

[26] For trade in West Africa just before the partition, see Newbury, 'Trade and authority', pp. 66–99.　　　　[27] *Ibid.*, p. 94.

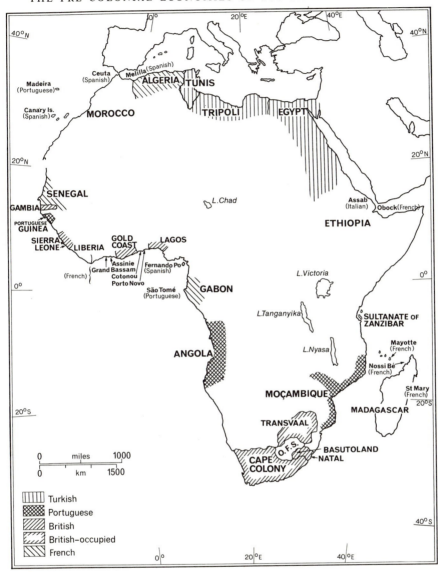

1. Africa in 1879

the creation of the Imperial British East Africa Company, and in 1889 by the emergence of the British South Africa Company. At the same time Germany attempted to carry out some of its early colonial expansion through chartered companies such as the Deutsch-Ostafrikanische Gesellschaft (1884) and the Deutsche Kolonialgesellschaft für Deutsch-Südwestafrika (1885).

On the face of it, chartered companies combined the advantages of *laissez-faire* capitalism with the merits of imperial conquest. They supplied—or pretended to supply—capital without making direct demands on the tax-payer at a

63

time when capital for colonial ventures was in desperately short supply, and when imperialism had not yet become a popular cause. Chartered companies could apparently take risks that governments were unwilling to shoulder. They seemed capable of building up pioneer administrations at a time when European governments as yet were often unwilling to take on more administrative responsibilities in the tropics. The sovereign powers of the new companies were limited and subject to control by the home governments, restraints which in fact proved difficult to exercise. Unlike the chartered companies of the sixteenth and seventeenth centuries, these companies did not normally receive officially recognized trade monopolies. Instead they were given specific administrative privileges. These might include rights in the disposal of land, the taxation of Africans, the exploitation of minerals and the power to assume control over territories not yet occupied by European powers.

The new companies were founded by strong-willed empire-builders like Sir George Goldie, Cecil John Rhodes and Sir William Mackinnon, whose motives seem to have been political as much as economic. Economically they did not succeed in their purpose. They were unable to raise sufficient capital for underdeveloped areas where opportunities for immediate profits were limited. The companies were formed at a period when the possibilities of quick gains from colonial territories were greatly overestimated, and when investors were often unaware of the need for elaborate administrative and economic infrastructures, in the absence of which investments would not pay dividends. Theoretically wedded to free trade, enterprises such as those run by Leopold II and Goldie could not function without establishing commercial monopolies of the most ruthless and exclusive kind. Rhodes's concern, although not interfering with private trade, could survive only by turning itself into a major investment trust, with stakes in mining, railway development and a host of other enterprises. In their pioneering stage the new companies might provide opportunities for a favoured few, directors and senior officials who held shares or directorships in well-placed concerns and who might thus profit from inside knowledge. Chartered companies also provided prestige and political power to their office-holders. They failed to give much satisfaction to the bulk of shareholders who, so to speak, acted as the 'forlorn hope' of colonial capitalism, before the imperial *mise en valeur* had got under way. The new companies did, however, succeed in their primary objective, which was to place vast areas of Africa under European rule. Hence the chartered companies bridged the gap between unofficial penetration and empire.

To sum up, by the beginning of the 1880s Africa had experienced a great variety of foreign contacts which had affected the indigenous societies in a number of ways. For countless centuries, Carthaginians, Romans, Byzantines and Arabs had traded with parts of Africa in order to acquire luxury goods such as gold, spices, hides, feathers, dyes and wild animals. In addition, Africa had been exploited by Muslims and Christians alike as the world's major source of slaves. Foreign traders, including Arabs and Europeans, had also brought new crops and new techniques to Africa. At first the impact was peripheral. Outside South Africa and a few enclaves like Senegal, whites had very little success in imposing their own forms of social and political organization on African societies.

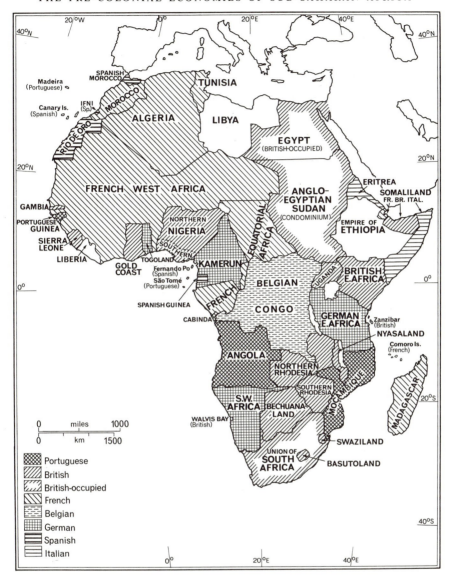

2. Africa in 1914

From the 1880s the Western economic impact quickened. Whether commerce preceded conquest or trade followed the flag, as European economic influence grew so did markets. All manner of new goods came into use—matches, knives, clothes, later on bicycles, ploughs and sewing machines. More Africans were induced or forced to sell their labour or their goods in the market; even land sometimes became subject to the market. As the market principle spread and as new technologies and new forms of social and economic or-

65

ganization were implanted on the soil of Africa, so did traditional institutions and ways of life, values and attitudes give way. Indeed, the thirty years between the scramble and the outbreak of the First World War (Map 2) saw extraordinary economic growth. Colonialism certainly was to have its grim and blood-stained side. The destructive impact of colonial violence in the initial phase of occupation, for instance, remains to be fully documented. But, as Marx had already pointed out in connection with India, Western colonization in the long run would serve a progressive function.[28] Westerners, unlike Arab or African conquerors before them, were victors of a different breed. The Europeans would bring to Africa a wholly new technology, new scientific concepts and new methods of education and of healing; they would make major contributions in education, in economic management and in political governance. The teacher and the technician, the merchant, the manager and the manufacturer were to follow in the soldier's footsteps. Between them, they would change the face of Africa and add immeasurably to the wealth of a continent.

BIBLIOGRAPHY

Africanus, Leo. *History and description of Africa . . . done into English in the year 1600 by J. Pory . . .* London, Hakluyt Society, 1896.

Alagoa, Ebiegberi Joe. 'Long distance trade and states in the Niger Delta', *Journal of African History,* 1970, **11,** no. 3.

The small brave city-state: a history of Nembe-Brass in the Niger Delta. Madison, University of Wisconsin Press, 1964.

Allen, William. 'African land usage', *Rhodes-Livingstone Journal*, June 1945.

Barzun, Jacques, and Henry F. Graff. *The modern researcher.* New York, 1957.

Bohannan, Paul, and Laura Bohannan. *Tiv economy.* Evanston, Northwestern University Press, 1968.

Bohannan, Paul, and George Dalton, eds. *Markets in Africa: eight subsistence economies in transition.* Garden City, N.Y., 1965.

Boserup, Ester. *The conditions of agricultural growth: the economics of agrarian change under population pressure.* Chicago, 1965.

Brewster, John M. 'Traditional social structures as barriers to change', in *Agricultural development and economic growth*, Herman M. Southworth and Bruce F. Johnston, eds. Ithaca, Cornell University Press, 1967.

Burton, Sir Richard. *A mission to Gelele, king of Dahome. . . .* Memorial ed. 2 vols. London, 1893.

Coillard, François. *On the threshold of Central Africa: a record of twenty years' pioneering among the Barotsi of the Upper Zambesi.* London, 1902.

Colson, Elizabeth. 'African society at the time of the scramble', in *Colonialism in Africa 1870–1960*, vol. I: *The history and politics of colonialism 1870–1914*, L. H. Gann and Peter Duignan, eds. Cambridge University Press, 1969.

Frankel, S. Herbert. *Capital investment in Africa: its course and effects.* London, Oxford University Press, 1938.

Gamitto, A. C. P. *King Kazembe and the Marave, Cheva, Bisa, Bemba, Lunda, and other peoples of Southern Africa. . . .* Lisbon, 1960.

Gluckman, Max. *Essays on Lozi land and royal property.* Rhodes-Livingstone Paper, no. 10. Livingstone, 1943.

[28] Karl Marx, 'The Government of India Bill' [1 July 1853], in *Karl Marx on colonialism and modernization . . .* , Shlomo Avineri, ed. (New York, 1968), p. 89.

Goody, Jack. *Technology, tradition, and the state in Africa.* London, Oxford University Press, 1971.

Gray, Richard, and David Birmingham, eds. *Pre-colonial African trade: essays on trade in Central and Eastern Africa before 1900.* London, Oxford University Press, 1970.

Hammond, Richard J. *Portugal and Africa, 1815–1910: a study in uneconomic imperialism.* Stanford University Press, 1966.

Herskovits, Melville. *Economic anthropology: a study in comparative economics.* 2nd ed., rev., enl., rewritten. New York, 1962.

Hopkins, A. G. 'Richard Beale Blaize: merchant prince of West Africa', *Tarikh,* 1966, **1,** no. 2.

Horton, James Africanus Beale. *West African countries and peoples: 1868.* Reprint of 1868 ed. Edinburgh University Press, 1968.

Hughes, A. B. J. *Kin, caste and nation among the Rhodesian Ndebele.* Rhodes-Livingstone Paper, no. 25. Manchester University Press, 1956.

Hunter, Guy. *Modernizing peasant societies.* New York, 1969.

Kilby, Peter, ed. *Entrepreneurship and economic development.* New York, 1971.

Latham, A. J. H. 'Currency, credit and capitalism on the Cross River in the pre-colonial era', *Journal of African History,* 1971, **12,** no. 4.

Layard, Sir Austen Henry. *Discoveries in the ruins of Nineveh and Babylon. . . .* London, 1853.

Lenz, Oskar. *Timbuktu: Reise durch Marokko, die Sahara und den Sudan. . . .* 2 vols. Leipzig, 1884.

Livingstone, David. *Missionary travels and researches in South Africa. . . .* London, 1857.

Lugard, Frederick John Dealtry Lugard, 1st baron. *The dual mandate in British tropical Africa.* 5th ed. London, 1965.

Mabogunje, Akin L. *Urbanization in Nigeria.* University of London Press, 1968.

McPhee, Allan. *The economic revolution in British West Africa.* 2nd ed. London, 1971.

Marx, Karl. 'The Government of India Bill' [1 July 1853], in *Karl Marx on colonialism and modernization . . . ,* Shlomo Avineri, ed. New York, 1968.

Meek, Charles Kingsley. *Land law and custom in the colonies.* 2nd ed. London, Oxford University Press, 1949.

Neumark, S. Daniel. *Foreign trade and economic development in Africa.* Stanford University, Food Research Institute, 1964.

Newbury, Colin W. 'North African and Western Sudan trade in the nineteenth century: a re-evaluation', *Journal of African History,* 1966, **7,** no. 2.

'Trade and authority in West Africa from 1850 to 1880', in *Colonialism in Africa 1870–1960,* vol. I: *The history and politics of colonialism 1870–1914,* L. H. Gann and Peter Duignan, eds. Cambridge University Press, 1969.

Polanyi, Karl, in collaboration with Abraham Rotstein. *Dahomey and the slave trade: an analysis of an archaic economy.* Seattle, University of Washington Press, 1960.

Stamp, Sir Laurence Dudley. *Africa: a study in tropical development.* 2nd ed. New York, 1964.

Stover, Charles C. 'Tropical exports', in *Tropical development 1880–1913,* W. Arthur Lewis, ed. Evanston, Northwestern University Press, 1970.

Wehler, Hans-Ulrich. *Bismarck und der Imperialismus.* Cologne, 1969.

White, C. M. N. *A preliminary survey of Luvale rural economy.* Rhodes-Livingstone paper, no. 29. Manchester University Press, 1959.

THE ECONOMIC ROLE AND MAINSPRINGS OF IMPERIALISM

by

CHARLES WILSON

The controversies that raged round the imperialism of the late Victorian Age were not in themselves novel. The debate had a long ancestry, dating back to the Spanish discovery and conquest of Central America. During that period, relations between metropolitan and colonial territories had immediately aroused bitter and recurrent quarrels, not only because they did not fit easily into the current framework of economic theory (such as it was), based largely on domestic experience, but also because they inevitably involved not merely economic judgements, but political, military, social and moral considerations, too. Spain had not long been in the Americas before a public debate was in progress between spokesmen of the special interests of the colonizers on the one hand and the humanitarian concerns of the missionaries on the other. From that debate emerged a ready-made body of law to justify the ideology of imperialism against all comers.[1]

Other empires—Portuguese, Dutch, British, French—beginning as trading, even piratical, ventures, developed vast commitments to defence, war and diplomacy on behalf of their overseas dependencies. In varying degrees, all were the objects of criticism. The economic problems created by expansion on an unprecedented scale and in strange and exotic lands were themselves puzzling to contemporaries. Trade to India and the East necessitated the export of large volumes of bullion and thereby contravened some of the most cherished convictions of the sixteenth and seventeenth centuries regarding the need to win and hold the largest stocks of precious metals. The monopolies created by governments for the great joint-stock companies trading to the tropics were likewise a permanent source of bitter controversy. The East India monopolies were under constant fire. Trade to Africa and the West Indies raised perpetual arguments about profitability. Who gained by it, planters or merchants? Where did the 'nation' come in, if at all? But worst of all, as Europe moved into the humanitarian age, these traders, depending as they did on the buying and selling of slaves, raised in most acute form grave moral issues, too.

I wish to record my gratitude to Dr. D. K. Fieldhouse of Nuffield College, Oxford, for allowing me to see and discuss with him the manuscript of his study of *Economics and empire 1830–1914* (to be published by Weidenfeld and Nicholson). My article reflects the influence of his arguments about the character of late Victorian imperialism in Africa. For the opinions expressed here, however, I take full responsibility.

[1] J. H. Parry, *The Spanish theory of empire in the sixteenth century* (Cambridge, 1940), ch. 1.

Metropolis versus empire: the long debate

When Adam Smith came to write the *Wealth of Nations,* it was the old colonial system that proved one of the most intractable lumps in his logic. The Navigation Laws, which constricted colonial trade and shipping into a compulsory nationalist mould, were economically indefensible; but what was indefensible economically became, on the political and strategic grounds of national defence, the best laws in the statute book. Smith was only, in fact, endorsing what an earlier exponent of mercantilist economics had said a century earlier: in the formulation of economic policy, Sir Joshua Child, the Grand Cham of the East India Company, had observed, 'Profit and Power must jointly be considered.' The dictum was especially true of colonial ventures. A century and a half later, Keynes, in destroying the historic bases of orthodox theory, found himself siding with practical statesmen who had never shared the presumptuous contempt of academics for the state of the balance of trade, a concept that had arisen not least from the practical conditions of trade with the colonial dependencies referred to above.[2]

Again, in describing some of the consequences of the vast disbursement of capital from Western Europe, and especially from Britain, which spread over the face of the whole world from 1815 to 1914, Herbert Feis has commented on the way in which the directions such capital took, and the uses to which it was put, were determined. Political circumstance rather than economic or financial calculation was often the criterion. The traditional theory of capital movements, where capital responds readily and flexibly to the beckonings of those who promise the highest return, is not adequate to explain its historical disposition in 'imperial' ventures as revealed by statistics. Considerations of national advantage, defence, extended dominion, favourable political sentiment towards allies, unfavourable towards enemies, all played their part in directing capital movements. Foreign capital was rarely, if ever, popular. Borrowers all looked forward to the day when debts could be redeemed. They did not have to await the prophetic revelations of Lenin to understand that borrowing had its disadvantages; they were only more conscious than he that it also brought rewards.

The consequences of international movements of capital and the influence of the capitalists who moved it were likewise controversial. For some—Hobson, Lenin, Kautsky, Hilferding and many others—they were a cause, if not the leading, even sole, cause of war. To others they created a community of interests which worked strongly for peace. In the judicious opinion of Herbert Feis, between 1870 and 1914 they worked in both directions, but seldom determined events in either.[3]

Yet even Feis was disposed to agree that capital movements were often the occasion of dispute, and that financial interests often hauled, or tried to haul, governments behind them in order to secure the optimum conditions for their operations.

Another analyst, S. H. Frankel, writing in the thirties, to whom African studies owe so much, also found himself compelled to modify some widely ac-

[2] John Maynard Keynes, *General theory of employment, interest and money* (London, 1936), p. 333.

[3] Herbert Feis, *Europe, the world's banker, 1870–1914* . . . (New Haven, Yale University Press, 1930), pp. 466–7.

cepted ideas about fundamental economic processes as a result of his African inquiries. The temptation to treat capital as money, or even as national equipment, had led to much error in policy and theory alike. Capital could not be created, nor future income realized, unless the organization of production was also changed. And in the case of primitive societies such as those of Africa, this meant contemplating changes in the whole organization of society and not merely in the economic apparatus in a narrow sense.[4] This combining of capital, technology and social organization seems a commonplace today. It is salutary to realize how novel it still was in the 1930s.

Thus it is evident that colonial trade and investment had always been problematical and controversial, never more so than during and after the sudden scramble for Africa during the last two decades of the nineteenth century. What was the *fons et origo* of the European drive into Africa that in a single generation turned Europe's 20-per-cent stake of 1878 into a grasp on the whole of Africa? For, by the 1930s, it could be said that only Liberia was still free of European control.[5]

Was the demonic force behind the expansion capitalist energy in general, for good or ill? Or did it represent, Hobson and Lenin argued, a highly specific stage of capitalist development that was reached precisely at the time of the 'new imperialism' (not before)—as Lenin put it: '*Imperialism, the highest form of capitalism*'? Or, to go to another extreme, had it no rational economic content or motivation whatever? Was it, as Joseph Schumpeter wrote in his *Imperialism and social classes*, 'object-less', a habit of mind deriving from the primitive, dynastic adventures associated with mediaeval princes or the absolute monarchies of the early modern period in Europe? Or was it expansion for the sake of expansion, or adventure, or fear or simply for the lack of anything else to do? William Lever, himself a pioneer of African development, expressed something of this merely functional (or functionless) view of imperialist activity when writing privately about his own enterprises in the Congo in 1913. 'One can go to the Congo and organize, organize, organize . . . But I don't work at business only for the sake of money . . . I work at business because business is life. It enables me to do things.' [6] This restless urge to activity for its own sake or as a source of satisfaction (satisfaction of urges good, bad and indifferent) undoubtedly entered into much 'imperialist' expansion, underlining the simple but often forgotten fact that systems of thought and government need to be operated by men, and that men's psychological needs and motives are strangely mixed.

As an explanation of the rapid annexation of vast areas of Africa, the Schumpeter theme may be compared with another recent interpretation, less theoretically positive but no less striking in its rejection of immediate economic benefit as the objective of the imperialists. This sees the annexation of Africa as incidental to other, more remote and even larger objectives, in particular to the British stake in India. Africa was annexed, in short, because it was on the way to India. The Dutch settlers in the Cape in the early seventeenth century had called their new home the 'Tavern of the Two Seas'. And so it was: the main victualling station of the Dutch East India Company for its ships voyaging be-

---

[4] S. Herbert Frankel, *Capital investment in Africa: its course and effects* (London, Oxford University Press, 1938), p. 6.

[5] *Ibid.*, p. 1.   [6] Charles Wilson, *History of Unilever* (London, 1954), vol. I, p. 187.

tween Amsterdam and Batavia. The opening of the Suez Canal had not altered the strategic and political importance of Africa as the hinge of the worlds, East and West. On the contrary, it meant that East, as well as West and South Africa were more than ever vital to Britain's Indian Empire and all it stood for east of Suez.[7]

Such theories certainly help to bridge the gap between the widespread distaste of most politicians, publicists and businessmen for any imperial involvements in Africa in the third quarter of the nineteenth century, and the revolution of the 1880s that swept nearly the whole of Africa into the net of European, and especially British, territorial control. Yet the statesmen themselves were no less puzzled by the nature of the drama in which they found themselves almost involuntary performers. 'I do not know exactly the cause of this sudden revolution', declared Lord Salisbury, addressing a Glasgow audience in May 1891, 'but', he ended, 'there it is.'

Probably few political contemporaries were much clearer than Lord Salisbury. However, economic interpretation was much in the air, economists omniscient as ever; and two economic interpretations stand out in the first fifteen years of debate in the twentieth century. Lenin's *Imperialism*, *pace* the editor of his *Works*,[8] is far from being 'his greatest contribution to the further development of the theories of Marxism'. It throws little light on 'imperialism' so far as it affects Africa (or other undeveloped continents), to which, indeed, it devotes scarcely any attention. It is primarily a violent denunciation of the monopolistic and corrupt condition of industrial capitalism in *Europe*.

Yet even Lenin's violence against capitalism has to yield repeatedly to his even more bitter violence against Kautsky and other enemies in the Second International, whose 'liberal reformist' tendencies were his true target. He confuses his accounts of capitalism in Britain, Germany and France; and, while quoting figures which show that rail-building, as might be expected, was proceeding more rapidly in the extra-European world than in Europe or in the United States, he accuses railway promoters of exaggerating the difference between developed and underdeveloped countries. No distinction, though it is crucial to his argument, is drawn, for example, between countries with which Britain *trades* and those in which it *invests*, nor between the countries of 'informal' and 'formal' empire. Yet for all its unsubstantiated assertions, its rhetorical spite, and the dissociation of its logic of convenience from known fact, Lenin's *Imperialism* must be taken seriously, for no other single work on the subject has acquired such a vast captive audience; and the assumptions of the work still help to determine acts and policies governing the lives and fortunes of millions. What are its main arguments?

Imperialism [wrote Lenin] is capitalism in that stage of development in which the domination of monopolies and finance capital has established itself; in which the export of

---

[7] For a fuller account of those arguments, see Ronald E. Robinson and John Gallagher, with Alice Denny, *Africa and the Victorians: the official mind of imperialism* (London and New York, 1965).

[8] V. I. Lenin, *Selected Works*, J. Fineberg, ed. (London, 1936), vol. v, p. xiv. For a critique of the theses of Lenin and Hobson, see L. H. Gann and Peter Duignan, 'Reflections on imperialism and the scramble for Africa', in *Colonialism in Africa 1870–1960*, vol. i: *The history and politics of colonialism 1870–1914*, L. H. Gann and Peter Duignan, eds. (Cambridge University Press, 1969), pp. 100–131; also, by the same authors, *Burden of empire* (New York, 1967), esp. pp. 55–72, 187–273.

capital has acquired pronounced importance, in which the division of the world among the international trusts has begun; in which the partition of all the territories of the globe among the great capitalist powers has been completed.

This sort of definition does not, of itself, get us very far. It does, however, establish certain basic assumptions beyond doubt if we wish to test the validity of the definition: capitalism *is* imperialism, capitalists *are* imperialists, capitalists collectively *are* government.

The relationship finance-capitalism-imperialism is developed as follows. As the accumulation of capital within Europe grew, the rate of profit declined. Surplus capital therefore sought bigger returns elsewhere, and where more profitably than in the underdeveloped areas of the world? Here raw materials were plentiful, labour cheap and—though this was purely hypothetical—yields on capital higher. Hence the renewed attractions, in the increasingly competitive conditions of Europe of the Great Depression (*c.* 1873–95), of extra-European investment and expansion. And because all the European powers were affected in some degree by the growth of monopolistic capitalism as well as by rising tariffs, sharper competition, falling profits and so on, one government after another was bullied, dragged, bribed or pushed into the new imperialism, especially into the scramble for Africa.

Before testing this theory against some basic historical facts, let us say a word about the provenance of Lenin's theory. First, since the onset of the depression in the 1870s, it had become increasingly fashionable to link together explanations of European economic troubles and of the swift spread of the new imperialism, especially in Africa. That is to say, long before Lenin's much more exigent theory of imperialism as a function of finance capital, theories of a 'commercial imperialism' were already popular. If the inventors of these theories were asked why territorial annexation became a feature of so many governments' policies round about 1880, they replied that the very intensity of competition for potential markets led the competitors to use all the weapons at their disposal to exclude all rivals from potential colonial markets. These included annexation, preferential tariffs, capital export and so on. And if the critics asked how this applied to the largest imperialism of all—the British—which was still free-trade, the answer came that Britain, faced by the exclusive practices of others, was forced back onto international agreements to secure its markets, and, if these were unobtainable or unsatisfactory, onto outright annexation.

Certainly there were plausible *a priori* grounds for such theories. Although European exporters suffered bad times in the last thirty years of the century, statesmen and businessmen alike were slow to adopt imperial annexation as a remedy for their economic troubles, and even tariffs were not really fierce until *after* the eighties. Yet by that time France was already launched into its expansion in Tunis, the Congo, Madagascar and West Africa. It was 1890 before Jules Ferry (already in retirement) provided a famous and eloquent exposition of the economic case for territorial colonial expansion. The theme of his argument was that colonial policy was 'the daughter of industrialization'. Industry needed colonial outlets if wages as well as profits, and indeed output itself, were not all to go into decline. Britain had already countered the threat to its colonial hegemony by laying siege to Africa at all points. Germany was meeting this initiative by its own rivalry. France must do the same. Colonization was 'an international expression of the external laws of competition'.[9] Yet no German—and Germany was far more highly industrialized than France—had seriously argued the economic case for imperialism before 1885. Bismarck shared the scepticism felt by most statesmen of the third quarter of the century over the utility of colonies. Germany did not get its Jules Ferry until Bernhard Dernburg emerged as secretary of state for colonies in 1906.

In Britain, the idea that overseas investment was a necessary stimulus to an over-capitalized and depressed home economy was much older. Long before Lenin, or Hobson or even Marx, the case had been argued by Edward Wakefield. Yet the 1830s had given little support to his theories, and the major movements of British capital to the United States had come in 1836 when the British economy itself was booming.[10] The whole subsequent history of white settlement had been economically disappointing. The general attitude of the mid-century thus became one of scepticism. Power might be used to protect and preserve existing interests. Gladstone and Morley maintained their reserve. Others, however, did begin to change their stance, but ostensibly for defensive reasons. In 1884, Salisbury told a Manchester audience that foreign encroachment might force Britain to annex territories to preserve its trading outlets. Four years later, Sir Harry Johnston, after discussing African policy with Salisbury, followed suit with a letter to *The Times* quoting Portugal and France as examples of the aggressive and exclusive policies to which Salisbury had referred. Thus, while Ferry attacked Britain, a growing group of public figures in Britain, who included Frederick Lugard, Sir Edward Grey, Salisbury and, above all, Joseph Chamberlain, were arguing that European rivals, especially France, were making it necessary for the British government not only to protect existing British commercial interests but also to prepare the way for further expansion—for example, by pre-emptive (if selective) annexations.

All this, however, fell a long way short of the actions and policies of which capitalist-imperialists were accused by their leading opponents. Of the non-Marxists, the most eloquent and persuasive was, without question, J. A. Hobson. Unlike Lenin, Hobson, in common with many other British liberals and socialists like H. N. Brailsford and Leonard Woolf, believed that the capitalist-imperialist error, which drew off vast quantities of capital badly needed to stimulate consumption and employment at home, into unprofitable imperial adventures, was remediable by government action. But, like Lenin, they believed also that the policies which they criticized were the result of a capitalist conspiracy by a knavish, malignant but infinitely elusive group of investors who bent governments, missionaries, engineers, administrators and others, all to their base end of maximizing their *rentier* incomes. Hobson's *Imperialism* was a classic of liberal-socialist thinking, eloquent and rhetorical but immensely dignified and persuasive. Its influence was great, not least on Lenin, who lifted much of its most telling argument for his own essay. The basic quantities were

---

[9] *Discours et opinions de Jules Ferry,* Paul Roubiquet, ed. 7 vols. (Paris, 1893–8), vol. v, pp. 194–6, quoted and translated by D. K. Fieldhouse. For general discussion, see especially Henri Brunschwig, *French colonialism 1871–1914* (London, 1964); M. E. Townsend, *Origins of modern German colonialism 1871–85* (New York, 1921); D. C. M. Platt, 'Economic factors in British policy during the new imperialism', *Past and Present,* 1968, no. 39; D. K. Fieldhouse, *The theory of capitalist imperialism* (London, 1967); and H. P. von Strandmann, 'Domestic origins of Germany's colonial expansion under Bismarck', *Past and Present,* 1969, no. 42.

[10] Leland Jenks, *The migration of British capital to 1875* (New York, 1927), p. 81.

that British capital investment between 1862 and 1893 had increased from £144 to £1,698 million. From 1884 to 1900 *rentier* income on overseas investments had risen from £33 to £60 million. Possessions during this period had grown by nearly 5 million square miles. All this seemed to confirm that capital export and the new imperialism marched together. Did they?

Testing the doctrines

By1914, Britain owned nearly £3,800 million of publicly issued capital overseas, of which about half was within the Empire. By comparison, French and German 'imperial' investments were small. France had only 9 per cent of its overseas total in its empire—and much of this was in the old colony of Algeria. German 'imperial' investment was negligible. Evidently the power of finance-capital, strongest in Germany, did not carry any concomitant imperial investment overtones. And of the British investment total, all but about £100 million was in the 'old' colonies. Canada accounted for £514 million, Australasia for £416 million, India for £378 million. The case for associating large capital exports with the imperialism of the post-1880s must rest on South Africa (which was only re-annexed *after* the Boer War) and, marginally, on West Africa.[11]

Such figures leave the Hobson-Lenin case badly weakened statistically. Does the argument that the 'new imperialism' nevertheless resulted from a corrupt conspiracy (or identification) between government and capitalism survive better? Were the governments of Britain, France, Belgium and Germany dragged into a scramble for Africa by finance capitalists representing vast monopolies of industry and banking who were anxious to refresh in the favourable virgin territories of Africa their depleted trade and falling profits from European enterprises now locked in suicidal competition?[12] A brief glance at the scramble for sub-Saharan Africa between 1880 and 1914 is necessary to answer these questions.

Of the Great Powers whose thrust was to change the face of Africa in the 1880s and after, France and Britain already had important African interests dating back, in the first case, effectively to the Napoleonic period, and in the second, to the seventeenth century. The French involvement in West and Central Africa cannot be understood without reference to French interests in the north and east. France's stake in Algeria went back to the 1830s, when the annexation of this area was deemed essential if the pirates who preyed on French Mediterranean shipping were to be stamped out. Morocco, an Islamic stronghold on Europe's doorstep, fell into the French sphere of influence as Algeria's neighbour, and Britain and Germany finally agreed to keep out of France's way. Yet in spite of important French financial interests in Morocco, Jules Ferry declined to take over Morocco in the 1880s, and only political disorders led to its oc-

---

[11] In 1914, British capital invested in South Africa was £370·2 million, or less than 10 per cent of the total; in West Africa, £37·3 million, or less than 1 per cent of the total. British investment in Latin America was nearly twice that in Africa; and China, Japan and Egypt all attracted larger British investment than any tropical African area. See Sir George Paish, 'Great Britain's capital investment in industrial, colonial and foreign countries', in *Journal of the Royal Statistical Society,* Jan. 1911, **74**, pt. 2, pp. 167–87; and Feis, *Europe, the world's banker,* p. 23.

[12] There was, of course, an awkward lesion in logic here. If capitalism in the West had arrived by its own expansive processes at a point of ultimate monopoly, it was not self-evident why it could not exploit its monopolistic situation to remedy its bankrupt condition without entering into another chapter of suicide in Africa.

cupation in 1911. Conversely, neither the pressure of British traders and ship-owners nor of German businessmen on their respective governments had any significant influence on events.

Similarly, the move into Tunis in 1881 came because the French business effort in Tunisia was slackening, while Italian enterprise was growing. Powerful sections of French opinion that were hostile to Tunisian involvement equally disliked the risks of Egyptian entanglement, and Britain had to take unilateral action to protect British interests threatened by the nationalist violence of 1881. So, while Britain became ever more embroiled in the problems of Egypt, the Sudan and indeed the whole of East Africa and the Upper Nile, France was given a free hand in North Africa, which Bismarck hoped might somewhat temper French bitterness over its defeat in Europe in 1871.

That business interests were concerned in some of these manœuverings is certain, and popular suspicions that some individuals were playing for high financial stakes are reflected in contemporary fiction (for example, in Maupassant's *Bel Ami*, written in 1885). But there is far more evidence that governments resisted such business pressures as did exist. The deciding influences were political and strategic, and they were linked physically with the European thrusts into sub-Saharan Africa.

The starting point was set before the economic crisis in Europe was really felt and certainly long before France had reached anything like Lenin's critical point in capitalist evolution. It consisted in the ambitious plans of the great French soldier and administrator Louis Faidherbe to rescue the Senegal from poverty by linking it with the Western Sudan, the Niger Basin and Algeria. When Louis Brière de l'Isle succeeded as governor of the Senegal in 1876, he revived this great project, whose life-blood was railways. This was characteristic of many of the great African projects of the day. Railways were to play the same role in Africa as in America, Germany and Russia. Yet, once again, the moving spirits were not 'capitalists' in any commonly accepted meaning of the word. They were soldiers, visionaries, explorers and fanatics, to whom railways were what spacecraft were to be to the space fanatics of the 1960s. In the event, much of the capital allotted to rail construction was used to conquer the Sudan, and a Sudanese army ranged through vast areas of the hinterland of the west coast. The capitalists proper, appalled at the prodigal waste of the Sudan enterprise, retreated.

British enterprise in the Niger Basin equally owed more to visionaries and soldiers than to merchants, who kept their ambitions to the coast. It was left again to a professional soldier, George Taubman Goldie, to forge the United African Company, the instrument of British penetration into the interior. This company concerned itself especially with the rivalry of French interests in the Niger (the Belgians were preoccupied with the Congo and Germany with the Cameroons). Yet again Jules Ferry (back in office in 1883) shied away from any plans for a French protectorate of the Niger. French strategy was only to secure access from the sea to the rivers. Goldie bought out the French tropical African companies, and a British protectorate was ultimately established from Lagos to Cameroun.

Yet all these British moves bespoke caution rather than aggression. At most, British statesmen like Salisbury and Rosebery were prepared to protect existing interests and to demand, diplomatically, fair parity for promising new enterprise. British merchants in Liverpool might complain bitterly that Britain was allowing French and German interests to predominate. Yet the other side of the coin was turned up by a Foreign Office spokesman with the remark: 'Not only do we not neglect Manchester interests, but we have to stir up Manchester to look after its own interests.' Government, in fact, did little more than reiterate its traditional concern for the security of profitable, legitimate British business operations. Power as yet hardly came into the picture, and did not until 1897–8, when Chamberlain introduced a new tone into the colonial debate. Railways, ports, technology were now to be the essential instruments of British expansion in West Africa. But was Chamberlain a tool of Goldie's company (now the Royal Niger Company)? Certainly he was a shareholder, but there the connexion ended. His objectives bore little resemblance to Goldie's. His imperial ambitions, right or wrong, entirely transcended any personal or immediate financial interest.

Like Salisbury, Bismarck, too, had to meet the demands of his trading community—Hamburg merchants, for example—for state assistance in their struggle to compete with British and French rivals. There is no evidence that 'capitalist-imperialist-finance interests' had the slightest influence on his annexation policy. The resort to action, in the mid-eighties, based on territorial rights, partition and annexation, came because all parties feared the loss of supplies and markets. But none of the merchant houses concerned was anywhere near the condition of high international finance-monopoly postulated by the cataclysmic school of anti-imperialists.

A similar situation applied in the case of the Congo Free State. For over a quarter of a century this was to remain, as it had begun, the personal creation of Leopold II, a masterful and princely entrepreneur allied with explorers and visionaries such as Stanley rather than with high finance. In its early days, Leopold's Congo enterprise was a purely commercial affair, entirely unconnected with the Belgian state. It grew as a territorial state only in response to the threat from the French protectorate on the north bank of the Congo and because here, as on the Niger, territorial rights seemed necessary to protect the vast outlay (much of it from Leopold's own pocket) on communications, transport and public services. As the demand for capital steadily outpaced his resources, he was compelled—like Britain and Germany—to call on favoured companies to provide capital. But the initiative came from Leopold, not from high finance.

It was the same in East Africa. Before 1884 there were old French and British interests, but no territorial annexation had been thought necessary to secure either economic or strategic concerns. Traditional British merchants here got on with their own business, asking only the traditional services of a government helping hand when needed. The 'new men' in East Africa, German and British—Carl Peters, Sir William Mackinnon, Thomas Buxton—were cast in the same mould as their contemporaries in West and South Africa. They were not, by training or nature, businessmen. They were patriots, idealists, often mistrusted and disliked by working merchants, bankers and government officials alike. The British East Africa Company of the eighties was even less a *bona fide* business company than Goldie's company, and its deserved epitaph at the end of a financially disastrous career was: 'an honest concern, not a money-making one.' The government's willingness to take it over, like its willingness in 1894 to declare a protectorate over Uganda and build a railway from Mombasa to Uganda, was rooted in fear for Britain's political and strategic position in the Indian Ocean, not in a concern for trade or private profit.

Crucial to the controversy is Cecil Rhodes and his British South Africa Company. Did it presage the sacrifice of British interests to capitalist profit? Was the later annexation of the Transvaal, in Harcourt's famous phrase, the manifestation of 'stock-jobbing imperialism'? The inference, against the background of Rhodes's entrepreneurial record, the connection with the Rand mines, the conflict of Boers and Uitlanders, seems plausible. Yet on closer inspection, difficulties begin to emerge. When the British South Africa Company received its charter to occupy the territories (later known as Northern and Southern Rhodesia), Rhodes was already the richest man in South Africa, having made vast fortunes successively out of diamonds, then gold.

The prospects for 'Rhodesia' were poor, the costs vast—so vast that professional financiers sheered off speedily from any connection with it. It survived only on the power of Rhodes's patriotic vision of a vast British imperial realm stretching from the Cape to Cairo, as well as on the British government's calculation that if successful it would counter the strategic and diplomatic threat from Germany and Portugal, saving the tax-payers their money and the government its unpopularity. But neither Westminster nor Whitehall liked or trusted Rhodes. Nor did the gold-mining companies. They much preferred to deal with the Transvaal, for all their grievances against it. The Boer War did not come because the Rand capitalists dragged the British government in to further their interests. It came rather because that government insisted on reforms (disliked by the Rand capitalists) that would have secured British *strategic* interests against Germany and to a lesser extent Portugal.

With the exception of Hobson, the other liberal, anti-imperialist voices that were raised during and after the Boer War—Hobhouse, Arnold White and C. F. G. Masterman, to mention only the most influential [13]—were more concerned with the political and social consequences of what they believed to be the domestically damaging, degrading and illogical aspects of imperial adventuring rather than with any precise or coherent theory of its economic motivation. They flung about the usual allegations of influence and corruption, but no more than was common form in any debate on government. Their chief concern was with the moral mess into which the nation had been led and with how to get out of it; and their arguments still have the authentic ring of deep convictions sincerely held, of moral shame and doubt, of high hopes shaken almost beyond repair. There is a bitterness here that goes far deeper than rejection of a politico-economic system.

The passions aroused by the war demand an analysis and an understanding of the African *débâcle* more profound than Lenin's simplistic explanation, his noisy rhetoric, his slap-dash statistics and his fundamental lack of concern with Africa itself. If the brief analysis of motive I have given is correct, there is little to be said for the Lenin theory. At hardly a single point is it possible to sub-

---

[13] L. T. Hobhouse, *Democracy and reaction* (London, 1904); Arnold White, *Efficiency and empire* (London, 1901); C. F. G. Masterman, *The heart of the empire* (London, 1901). See also Bernard Semmel, *Imperialism and social reform . . .* (London, 1960).

stantiate the allegation that governments were dragged into imperialism by rapacious monopoly-finance-capitalists. Can a more helpful interpretation be given?

The indirect explanation

One recent alternative has been expounded persuasively by Messrs Robinson and Gallagher.[14] They have emphasized the heavy involvement of Britain, during the half century before the scramble for Africa began, in a programme of economic expansion that accumulated vast investments overseas in Europe, in the Americas, in Australasia and in India. In that age of 'informal empire', power was not infrequently used to guard British trade, just as it was after 1880. The explanation of the revolution of the 1880s (so far as there can be any single coherent explanation) was that Africa was still as essential to Britain's eastern empire as it had been in the late eighteenth century, when Britain had annexed Cape Colony. Everywhere in Africa, Britain now took measures to protect the routes leading (by land and sea) to its Indian centre of military and economic power, where one-fifth of its overseas investments lay and to which one-fifth of its total exports was directed. At different times and in different places, France, Germany and Russia especially presented a potential or a real threat to Britain's eastern interests.

Such arguments have done much to clarify the confusion created by the rhetoric of the economic interpreters and the polemicists. They do not, of course, destroy the economic elements in the motivation of the 'new imperialism', nor do they remove imperialism into the category of 'objectless' activity. But Britain's African policy is transferred into a transitional position where its importance is related to a remoter but larger objective: India. Yet 'India' remains an *economic* objective, because its financial and commercial development meant that, along with other tropical areas of the British Empire, India discharged the unique function in the world network of trade and payments of helping, through its passive balance, to settle Britain's payment deficits with the rest of the world.[15]

Unquestionably, the role of Africa in the defence of Britain's eastern interests did much to break down the traditional reluctance of politicians and businessmen to become directly involved in territorial commitments in Africa. Yet the elevation of politics to a prime role and the relegation of economics to a 're-ferred' role may seem to obscure too much those aspects of African imperialism that were truly 'economic', though not in the sense in which either Hobson or Lenin or their followers used the term. Amongst modern scholars, both S. H. Frankel and D. K. Fieldhouse, each in his own way, have illuminated this natural economic drive.

Africa and the world economy

During the eighties, along with the political presence of the European powers that caused Britain's statesmen understandable anxiety, external pressures were

[14] Robinson and Gallagher, *Africa and the Victorians, passim.*

[15] Folke Hilgerdt, 'The case for multilateral trade', in American Economic Association, *Proceedings,* March 1943, **33**, no. 1, suppl. pt. 2; also S. B. Saul, 'Britain and world trade 1870–1914', *Economic History Review,* 1954, ser. 2, no. 6.

growing to bond Africa's economy into the world economy. A major problem common to all European societies was the accelerated growth of population, and the consequent demand for food and necessities that could be satisfied only by greater economic output. This in turn demanded and stimulated new and improved forms of transport. Unquestionably Africa was early seen as another source that could be tapped for such raw materials as palm products, ground-nuts and ground-nut oil, cocoa, wool, cotton and rubber. The diamond boom that had developed since the 1860s and had led in turn to the gold boom of the eighties raised prospectors' hopes of further mineral wealth.

Some of the new needs of Europe and America had a direct bearing on African resources. From the 1870s a new crop of industries grew up in Britain and Europe to serve the needs of the new urban masses. They manufactured soap and margarine, chocolate and cocoa, solid and (later) pneumatic tyres for bicycles and motor cars. Amongst the raw materials they began to search for to feed their rapidly expanding plant were some important products of Africa. Soap and margarine called for supplies of both animal and vegetable fats, but a chain of inventions made it possible steadily to enlarge the usefulness of African vegetable oils to both industries. Oil refining, hydrogenation (fat hardening) and refrigeration combined to make ground-nuts, palm-kernels, cotton seed and the oils and fats derived from them, increasingly useful to the soap and margarine manufacturers. The daily diet of Europeans, especially the millions of workers in the new industrial cities of Germany (and to a lesser extent of Britain, the Low Countries and Scandinavia) came to be linked with the fortunes of Africa, which by 1909 was supplying over 25 per cent of those world vegetable oils and fats that entered into export trade. (Half a century later, when total comparable supplies had increased between two and four times according to product, Africa's share had risen to nearly 30 per cent.) [16]

The nineties saw the rise of the chocolate and cocoa industry, whose products by 1900 were competing with tea and coffee as liquid beverages and with sugar confectionery in chocolate-bar form. The third group of industries that looked to Africa to meet its expanding needs was concerned with accessories for motor cars or cycles—belts, cushions and so on, but above all, tyres, solid and pneumatic. The world uses of diamonds and gold for technical as well as luxury purposes need here be mentioned only *en passant;* it is enough to remark that mining itself comprised a group of industries that more than any other, for good or ill, affected the economic destinies of the continent.

This is not the place for a detailed chronological survey of African economic development. But one point cannot be overstressed if the role of the pioneers who early glimpsed its vast possibilities and contrived its birth and development is to be understood. When the 'new imperialism' was launched, only a narrow band of territory, mainly along the northern coast and at the southern tip of the continent was at all developed. Here and there on the west and east coasts, there were points where sea traders picked up and exported supplies from the interior. But even here economic activity was spasmodic and fragmented. If the vision of an Africa yielding up its imagined mineral and natural

---

[16] K. E. Hunt, in *Margarine: an economic, social and scientific history, 1869–1969,* J. H. van Stuyvenberg, ed. (Liverpool, 1969), pp. 42, 78–9. For other trade and production statistics I am indebted to Mr P. A. Arden-Clarke of the United Africa Company, who kindly provided me with invaluable help.

wealth to the outside world and in return receiving a flow of manufactures was to materialize, the urgent need was to create a basic network—in current jargon an infrastructure—of harbours, railways, steamers, trucks, warehouses, machinery and telegraph and postal equipment, as well as the technology and skilled labour to operate it. The first prerequisite was exploration, surveys, maps. The second was capital in adequate supply. The third was an understanding of African society—not only as a source of labour and purchasing power, but as a living community with basic needs, most of them, even the most rudimentary ones, as yet unfulfilled, even unformulated.

In the early stages of development in Europe, similar problems had been encountered. They had evoked the response called by a later age 'mercantilist'—in reality the attempts, often on a grand scale, often unsuccessful, to provide just such another infrastructure of harbours, roads, merchant fleets, technology, and the rest. The architects in the early European saga were princes, statesmen or bureaucrats; rarely capitalists or tradesmen. The directing intelligence came from above—from Colbert in France, Peter the Great in Russia, Frederick the Great in Prussia, Prince Rupert or Sir George Downing in England. These were the Olympian contrivers of the *ancien régime* in its economic aspect, and they did not conceal the low esteem in which they held the mere capitalists who were their instruments, 'merchants' (as Colbert observed with some distaste) 'who only understand their own little commission and never the great forces which make commerce work'.

The pioneers

There was now something of the same attitude amongst the pioneers of Africa. The 'architects' here were not the old-fashioned capitalist African traders of Liverpool or Bristol, who were appalled by the immensity of the African task, the costs and risks it involved and the small and uncertain yield of profit it offered. It was a time for prophets and visionaries—of the stamp of the pioneers in Africa of the late nineteenth and early twentieth century—explorers like Stanley, missionaries like Livingstone, idealist administrators like Brière de l'Isle, Harry Johnston, or Buxton, entrepreneurs like Rhodes or Leopold II, politicians like Joseph Chamberlain, soldiers like Goldie or Lugard. The call of Africa was a call to a certain kind of imagination, to adventure and romance. Motives, as Frankel has said, were mixed; but on the whole they were in the first place political, patriotic or idealistic. Some of these men believed that a new Peru might be round the corner. Except in South Africa, they were to be sadly disappointed.

The essential and immediate fact was that this first phase of 'constructive imperialism', as Chamberlain labelled it, was too frightening and too costly to be financed by businessmen. Governments were still too hobbled by the cautious traditions of *laissez-faire* to take up a challenge so daunting. The job went, almost by default, to the chartered companies. Upon the Niger (later called the United Africa) Company, the East Africa Company and the British South Africa Company fell the duties of providing roads, rails, public services, even armies. This administrative and military 'investment' was essential if any economic development was to follow. Unlike the great trading companies of earlier times, which were in some sense their model, the new African companies received no officially sanctioned monopolies of trade. Only the Niger Company was to achieve a virtual, *de facto* monopoly through circumstances, not through law. The companies' privileges were to develop mineral resources, levy taxes and exercise a limited territorial sovereignty, always subject to the British government.[17] Their task was a vital, but essentially a transitory, one; and once it was completed the administrative company 'shell' fell away because it no longer served any purpose. By 1900 the charters of the East Africa and Niger companies were withdrawn. All had eventually to make way for the authority of a central government.

Though the chartered companies might pass away, the problems which they encountered were longer-lived: disease, poor water supplies, lack of navigable rivers, indeed lack of all forms of transport except the human pack-horse, labour shortage, depopulation in many areas, low and precarious labour productivity. Such were a few of the problems. But underlying the failure of the African economy to grow was the overall social stagnation. Long before the imperialists arrived, much of the accessible area of Africa had been exploited territory, where the rapacity of the slave-hunters was a curse added on to the plagues inflicted by nature. The belief of the pioneers that an injection of 'capital' was the cure-all slowly gave way to a realization that knowledge, social as well as technological, was equally necessary if the downward spiral of the African economy was ever to be halted and reversed. A reform and renewal of social institutions was essential, but its coming agonizingly slow. Except in South Africa and in parts of West Africa (Nigeria especially), economic development was very limited—some gold-mining south of the Zambezi, some experimenting with tobacco and other cash-crops in Rhodesia. The copper resources of the far north were known, but their exploitation was still in the future.

The second phase: development versus conservation

The business entrepreneur who followed in the wake of the pioneers faced, in some ways, even greater difficulties than his predecessors. They had commanded, at any rate, the support of officialdom. But when William Lever, a highly successful, forceful and imaginative British businessman attempted in the early years of the twentieth century to explore the 'inexhaustible supply of Palm Oil and Palm Kernels in the hinterland [of the west coast], only awaiting development and the opening up of markets', reported by his investigators, he was in for an unpleasant shock. For the Colonial Office was not only unenthusiastic; it refused point-blank to offer Lever any freehold whatever. A twenty-one-year lease was the farthest it would go; and to Lever, who contemplated heavy capital investment in scientific cultivation of the palm and mechanical milling of the fruit, this was totally inadequate. The gap between the entrepreneur's ideal of productive efficiency and (to his credit, let it be added) his concern for the welfare of the indigenous population, on the one hand, and the British government's concern to secure native rights over the ownership of land and its cultivation, on the other, was unbridgeable. Lever put the predicament vividly:

---

[17] The British South Africa Company was granted a monopoly of mining rights that enabled it to become a partner with, and to share the profits in, all mining companies operating within its sphere. The company developed into a financial trust as well, with major holdings in railways and other enterprises.

I sometimes wish [he wrote in 1905] that all native chiefs in . . . Africa . . . were made dukes. In my opinion we should then take the sensible view that this land was theirs for development and the advancement of civilisation, and just as we will not tolerate a duke keeping his land for his own pleasure or to lock it up, and have passed laws that make this impossible in the United Kingdom, so I can never understand why a black man should be allowed to assume a different attitude, and neither develop his own land nor allow other people to do so.[18]

But neither Lever's enterprise nor his chagrin impressed the Colonial Office, which, in this case as in numerous others, regarded it as a major part of its responsibilities to protect the inhabitants of British-occupied territories from the excessive economic zeal of British (and even more of non-British) business entrepreneurs. Lever's experience of British policy was not unique. Anton Jurgens, the leading figure in the Dutch margarine industry and a later partner of Lever, was similarly convinced that West Africa was ripe for intervention. In 1908 he contracted to buy 12,500 acres in the German Kamerun and even laid out much capital on preliminary development of a vast palm plantation. Alas! Two years later the German government followed the British example. The land was declared inalienable native property and the Jurgens enterprise collapsed with great financial loss.[19]

Much affronted by the Colonial Office's reception of his plans, Lever passed on to the Belgian Congo. Here the Belgian government was trying, with one hand, to redeem the reputation of the reformed Congo state, and with the other to attract capital to develop the Congo economy. At the same time, therefore, as it recognized the folly of the policies of forced labour that had led to despoliation and enslavement (especially under the old dispensation in the collection of wild rubber), it parted company with the policies of British and German West Africa by allowing industrial investors to buy land freehold for economic development. More than that, the Congo government made it clear that it was prepared to delegate powers to developers via a rights-cum-duties charter somewhat on the lines of the privileges granted to the Niger or East Africa companies. In 1911 Lever accordingly entered into a treaty with the Congo which brought into that state the Huileries du Congo Belge (HCB), in due course to develop into one of the largest private industrial concerns in Africa. With a concession of 750,000 hectares for plantations, the HCB was a powerful force, which by 1935 had lifted the Congo into third place as a world exporter of palm-oil.

This achievement came not without effort. In addition to the general problems already described—large areas of the HCB were still cannibal-inhabited jungle when Lever first visited them—the project soon came up against the productivity problem that underlay the whole stagnation of the African economy. 'The labour problem', Lever wrote in his diary in 1913, 'has grown into an ominous dark cloud.' The central difficulty was quickly discernible. He described it vividly:

The native has few wants, a little salt and a little cloth are his indispensables. After this, beads, brass rods and other luxuries. Chief Womba at Leverville can be taken as an example. Twelve months ago he and his people were poor and few in number and were keen to bring fruit. After twelve months or less of selling fruit he is rich and lazy, has

---

[18] Quoted in Wilson, *Unilever*, vol. I, pp. 166–7.   [19] *Ibid.*, vol. II, pp. 107–10.

ten wives and the village is almost four times the size it was, but he gathers little or no fruit . . . The Palm tree is in these parts the Banking account of the native and he no more thinks of going to the Bank for fruit [for money] when his wants and ambitions are supplied, than a civilised man would. His bank is always open when he wants to draw on it.[20]

Lever's predicament was the African predicament in miniature. Unconvinced by either Lenin or Hobson, his shareholders never ceased to criticize him for putting their money at risk anywhere overseas, let alone in Africa. Shrewder or more self-interested than the prophets, the shareholders sensed, even if they did not wholly understand, the colonial predicament. After all, it was not unique in history; many European economies, including seventeenth- and eighteenth-century Britain, had encountered this phenomenon in the early stages of development. While human expectations remained at such an abysmally low level, they were soon satisfied. The need to work thereupon fell away, the labour force disappeared and production along with it. Was not 'the creation of *wants*', Bishop Berkeley had asked in 1755, 'the likeliest way to produce industry in a people'? Perhaps, but it was to become plain also that the very concept of more 'wants' would have to be preceded by revolutionary changes in educational and social institutions, and these were an unconscionable time materializing.[21] So it was in Africa also. Capital investment alone could help only to solve the problems. And even this limited contribution meant not just capital in an abstract or monetary sense, but capital directed by individuals and groups with special knowledge of African conditions. What was needed, in short, was what a later age was to call a managerial class. But the emergence of this class was not helped by the fact that its objectives were frequently at variance with the principles and the convenience of the occupying powers and their dedicated servants. It is hardly surprising, therefore, that it was a long time before it appeared. (One or two areas of unusual advancement, mainly in South Africa, where mining investment grew at a spectacular pace, represent outstanding exceptions.) Nor is it surprising that during the process of gestation serious problems of *balance* emerged in the African economy that remained unsolved. If Africa was to develop, export markets were essential. Lacking exports, Africa could not afford the sophisticated technical equipment without which its economy would remain backward. But that the process of incorporation into the world economy raised grave problems and could carry grievous penalties was not long to be concealed.

Problems of balance

Every type of development in Africa raised its own crop of problems. In West Africa—the only area besides South Africa to get off to a relatively early start—reliance on the palm economy was dangerously wide. In 1920, for example, 63 per cent of Nigeria's exports by value were still palm products. And palm products were amongst the most notoriously unstable commodities on world markets so far as demand and price were concerned. Methods of collecting the wild fruit—there was little systematic cultivation—made heavy de-

[20] *Ibid.*, vol. I, p. 176.
[21] Charles Wilson, *England's apprenticeship, 1603–1763* (London, 1965), pp. 345–6. A combination of labour immigration and the bush-trader was ultimately to start an upward spiral of demand.

mands on labour. Preparation of fruit and kernels was largely a household industry carried on by women. Palm-oil was an important element in the local
diet, and perhaps half the total production went to domestic trade, the remainder to export. The next two decades, providentially, saw a fairly rapid
growth of ground-nut and cocoa production.[22] But the swift rise of competition
from the Netherlands Indies, Malaya and the Congo—all developing scientific
methods of palm cultivation superior to the natural growth of Nigeria—left the
export outlook far from bright. In East Africa, development was long held back
by the general absence of minerals and indigenous products, as well as by
disease, with the result that in Kenya, for example, three agricultural crops—
coffee, sisal and maize—provided more than half the exports. The Gold Coast
might diversify its industry—gold, manganese and diamonds were mined—but,
as elsewhere in Africa, natural-rubber output was hit by specialized production
in the east. Cocoa, therefore, emerged to account for a dangerously high proportion (82 per cent by 1920) of total Gold Coast exports by value. The Belgian
Congo, though badly placed for transporting to world markets, seems to have
diversified its production more successfully between 1900 and 1935. Rubber
output had declined to nothing, but palm products flourished. So did timber,
coffee, gold and copper. Yet the Congo economy pinpointed the major
weakness of the African position in world markets between 1930 and 1933.
During those critical years of depression, the value of the Congo's exports fell
by 50 per cent.

For Africa as a whole, diversification of exports had produced only limited
results. Gold remained far and away the most important single export, accounting for 46·7 per cent of total domestic exports by value in 1935—more than 5
per cent larger than its share in 1913.[23] (Historians of late mediaeval and early
modern Europe will be reminded of the functions of mining as a 'leading sector' in the economies of Bohemia and Hungary. There, gold, silver and lead

---

[22] The inter-war years were not, as is sometimes assumed, a period of economic stagnation. For
statistics on the growth of trade in these years, see L. H. Gann and Peter Duignan, 'Introduction', in *Colonialism in Africa 1870–1960*, vol. II: *The history and politics of colonialism
1914–1960*, L. H. Gann and Peter Duignan, eds. (Cambridge University Press, 1970), pp.
15–16. Exports from the Belgian Congo show the remarkable diversification of the inter-war
years:

	(In million francs)		
	1933	1937	1943
Palm-oil	70	183	452
Palm-kernels	64	144	—
Gold	180	378	627
Copper	102	828	1,041
Diamonds	58	143	186
Tin	18	235	516
Cotton	61	253	461
Coffee	37	68	224

(N.B. During this decade the value of the Belgian franc in terms of sterling fell by a half.)

[23] Frankel, *Capital investment in Africa*, p. 208.

became important items in the export trade. They were balanced by imports of textiles and manufactured goods from Britain, Holland and France. The export of precious metals certainly gave the exporting countries an important source of purchasing power. The mine-owners, governments and mine-workers all benefited in some measure. But did the flow of imports hinder the development of local manufactures? What was the balance of advantages? *Plus ça change . . .*) In Africa, wool, cotton, palm products, ground-nuts and cocoa all had a place averaging up to 4 or 5 per cent; but the proportionate share of rubber, diamonds and palm products had all declined relative to 1913. And the fall of diamond production (on an absolute as well as on a relative basis) reflected the peculiar problems of that industry, over which Rhodes had consolidated his grip by 1887. There had followed a steady policy of amalgamation between companies that created a highly centralized control of world diamond production and sale. Only thus was an industry that in its first half-century of life had produced over £300 million in precious stones enabled to save itself from threatened collapse through overproduction and wild fluctuations in price.

Such were some of the penalties of incorporation in the world market. Whether the industries were those producing agricultural crops through a multiplicity of peasant producers in the most primitive conditions, or highly capitalized and concentrated mining industries employing large aggregates of capital and a highly sophisticated technology, all faced one common problem: price fluctuations in world markets so large as to disrupt large areas of the African economy in bad times.

Africa's problem was made worse by the circumstances under which the original capital for the African infrastructure was raised and by the conditions imposed on the borrowings. Certainly a very large volume of capital was made available during and after the process of partition; and the flow of these funds was eased and accelerated by the British colonial stocks legislation. By 1900 this ensured that the issues of colonial authorities were, under certain safeguards,[24] accessible to trustee investors and thereby gave a considerable 'imperial preference in investment' (as it were) to colonial issues as compared with other, non-British securities. Thus the African states were able to borrow—at a price. Their basic needs were provided for largely by fixed-interest-bearing capital, obtained through either government or railway issues.

The age of partition itself was illuminated by a romantic glow that drew men and money into Africa. The African fever powerfully affected the popular imagination in all the great European states, but it was Britain that provided 80 per cent of the capital and secured the lion's share of political and economic control. The optimism that this engendered overrode or ignored such economic commonplaces as considerations of yield on capital. The magnetism of the name Rhodes enabled the British South Africa Company to continue to collect capital for thirty years without a dividend's ever being declared.[25] Investment in Africa offered different appeals to different investors: gilt-edged reliability to

---

[24] See Feis, *Europe, the world's banker*, pp. 92–5. See also *The British Empire: a report on its structure and problems by a study group of members of the Royal Institute of International Affairs* (London, 1937), pp. 290–1.

[25] The fortunes of the company improved after the British government relieved it of its administrative responsibilities in the Rhodesias, thus improving its liquid-cash position. See L. H. Gann, *A history of Southern Rhodesia: early days to 1934* (London, 1965), p. 248.

trustees and others concerned with a steady income, excitement to the speculator in mining shares, hopes of capital gain by appreciation of land values in areas of economic—especially of mining—expansion. All tastes and emotions were catered to, from patriotic idealism to uncomplicated greed.

Yet, *pace* the anti-imperialists, motive was of less importance than the nature of the investment. It was the allocation of the vast bulk of capital, not the rapacity of capitalists holding minority equities, that was to provide the greatest problems for Africa. In a situation in which, except for mining, genuine industrial or manufacturing investment represented a small proportion of the total, the scope for financing development through equity capital was small. Even the early euphoria for African industrial enterprises wore off as the real difficulties they faced were steadily and starkly revealed. The British South Africa Company was not the only one to feel the burden of its duties. Lever's Huileries du Congo Belge had accepted responsibility for providing, at its own expense, roads, canals, railways, telegraphs, telephones, schools, hospitals, medical staff, and so on. Lever had to guarantee agreed daily rates of pay to the workers, to encourage the circulation of money and in due time to provide guaranteed volumes of exports tied to the amount of land granted under his concession.[26] 'We have to take great risks, use an enormous amount of capital, and tax our energy and strength to get this business on a sound commercial footing,' said Lever in 1913. He had committed himself, in fact, to something not far short of an African welfare state in miniature. And it was fifteen years (1926) before the HCB paid a dividend.

Plainly, under African conditions, the scope for risk capital was severely limited. Even in South Africa, profits were to prove much lower than a hypnotized public had expected. Between 1887 and 1932 the annual average rate of return on the whole Witwatersrand mining industry was 4·1 per cent. Some mines naturally had much higher yields, but many were low; and everywhere the risks to capital were high and the period of exposure to risk and unprofitableness prolonged.[27] In Southern Rhodesia, £45 million invested by 1909 had yielded dividends of only £500,000. In industries not concerned with mining, the marginal efficiency of capital was exceedingly low.

Railways, which ate up a large proportion of capital invested in Africa, presented a specially intractable problem. In other continents railways were often built to serve growing urban or industrial areas or agricultural areas producing heavy crops. Elsewhere they were the instruments of general development, opening up new land and attracting immigrant settlers. This was rarely true in Africa. Except in southern Africa, sub-Saharan Africa for long counted its railway by hundreds of miles rather than by thousands.[28] Save in those areas where mineral traffic provided them with a captive market, railways were a losing investment. Indeed, their very purposes were more often strategic or political than economic. East Africa was especially dependent on government for railway capital. But it was only a degree worse off than many other areas. Most

---

[26] Wilson, *Unilever*, vol. I, pp. 167–87.   [27] Frankel, *Capital investment in Africa*, pp. 145–8.
[28] By 1900 there were 5,227 miles of railway in southern Africa, of which 490 miles lay in Portuguese East Africa and 586 miles in Bechuanaland (one of Rhodes's great projects). The longest lines elsewhere were in the Congo Free State (718 miles) and British East Africa (400 miles). These, added to the 246 miles in Senegal, 244 in Angola, 200 in the Gold Coast, 100 in Lagos, and 32 in Sierra Leone, totalled 1,940 miles. These figures may be compared with railway mileage in other developing areas at the same date: Australia had 13,000 miles, Canada over 17,500 and India about 4,000.

African railways were built by the state, or at any rate underwritten or sub-sidized by the state, which found it difficult to attract concessionaries to under-take construction simply because the traffic was not there and not likely to de-velop by any natural process of economic growth. Governments were not the only ones to be saddled with the financial burdens of railway economics. The British South Africa Company had to pay out millions of pounds as a result of guaranteeing the interest on railway debentures in the Rhodesias.[29]

Another heavy burden thus fell on Africa. Transport, like other services, had to be financed through guaranteed fixed-interest-bearing capital. Whether times were good or bad, prices high or low, the terms of trade favourable or other-wise, business brisk or stagnant, the interest on Africa's debts had to be paid.[30] In this respect, only South Africa and the Rhodesias possessed large sections of industry financed by equity capital that acted as an automatic cushion in bad times. By comparison with Malaya, for example, Africa's economic situation was rendered inflexible. Nor was there any obvious solution short of the cre-ation of interest-free capital funds from the developed world; and this—at any rate on any significant scale—was not yet practicable. (The British Colonial Development Fund's grants-in-aid before 1914 totalled only £30 million.[31]) Africa had to pay not for capitalist rapacity but for capitalist prudence.

The 'gearing' of its capital borrowings put Africa into the position of a com-pany whose equity was too small and whose preference–debenture ratio was too large; or (as a distinguished economist said of Southern Rhodesia) of a firm with heavy overhead expenses and an inadequate turnover.[32] Thus, once the first fine frenzy of pioneering was over, the pace of African development had slowed down until it seemed to be again little more than the pace of the ox. The creation of the original infrastructure had not been followed by the expected proliferation of secondary development; and although the entry into the stream of world trade had provided certain stimuli to the African economy, it had also created very serious problems. Much of the continent was more nakedly ex-posed to cyclical fluctuations by the weak and unbalanced character of its economy. In West Africa only limited progress had been made towards opening up the interior to commercial traffic or co-ordinating the regional economies. Only in South Africa and Southern Rhodesia was the motor lorry beginning to make its impact felt in the backveld by the 1930s. And the nature of the finance by which basic needs had been supplied bore heavily on an economy still largely agrarian and still dependent in many fundamental respects on the labour (and consumption) of a population living in accordance with ancient custom.

World War II and economic revival

The Second World War administered both a shock and a tonic to an economy still suffering from the depression of the early thirties. The years immediately preceding the war saw a distinct renewal of effort. West Africa, for example, at

---

[29] In fact, the British South Africa Company supplied the Rhodesias with their railways very cheaply. The cost per mile was less than half that for the Gold Coast construction, two-thirds that of South African and some three-fifths of Ugandan construction costs. See *Report by Brigadier-General F. D. Hammond, C.B.E., D.S.O., on the railway system of Southern Rhode-sia*, C.S.R. 2-1926 (Salisbury, 1925).

[30] The moratorium on the Southern Rhodesian railway companies' debts during the great slump was exceptional. [31] Frankel, *Capital investment in Africa*, p. 172.

[32] Henry Clay, *Report on industrial relations in Southern Rhodesia* (Salisbury, 1930).

last recognized the need to drop its former opposition to planned plantations if the competition of Sumatra and Malaya was to be countered. Machinery was developed for the crushing of oil-fruit, and milling and extraction was mechanized and improved. But in 1939, when the pace of growth was still slow, expert observers were pondering rather gloomily the dubious chances of obtaining the volume of capital necessary for African development and weighing these possibilities against the difficulties of planning how to guide and control the investment of such capital, given the not very rosy prospects of its becoming available.[33]

Then, for another ten years or more, and down to the coming of independence in most of North, West and East Africa, the old nagging problems seemed to be solved, or at any rate blanketed, by the war, which changed, for the time being, the nature of the world market and eased Africa's role in it. The comparative immunity of Africa (south of the Sahara, at least) from war damage stimulated the growth of industries that not only provided for Allied war needs but also were capable of conversion to peacetime production. The demand for iron, copper, manganese, platinum and so on, which seemed insatiable, was to continue. The routing of Allied shipping round the Cape likewise brought further activity. Africa was a little less restricted than formerly to the production of primary produce. Road construction, especially of the all-weather type, went on even in the depressed twenties and thirties, and increased both during and after the war. By 1966 Rhodesia, for example, had over 73,000 miles of roads, nearly 110,000 passenger vehicles and almost 33,000 commercial vehicles. Large stretches of the Congo were made navigable. In all, there were over 7,000 miles of navigable waterways within the Congo Basin by 1960.[34]

However, many of the old hindrances remained. Rivers were generally circuitous, and broken by falls and rapids that made it difficult to achieve continuous navigation without transhipment. The plateau that ended near the coast in much of Africa, as well as coastal swamps, prevented the use of the rivers for transport into the interior—hence the importance of railways and roads.[35] Yet railways were still inadequate and relatively unco-ordinated, the road system in many areas as yet skeletal. Because coal-mining was virtually restricted to South Africa and Southern Rhodesia, coal was scarce and costly.

So varied were the condition and the character of the congeries of states that composed Africa at the demise of imperialism, ranging as they did from prosperous industrial modernity to primitive agrarianism, that it is almost impossible to summarize the characteristics of their economic state. Yet, if we may assume that the first and second phases of economic change were represented by the construction of the original infrastructure and the transition to slow secondary development, the overall statistics of production and export suggest strongly that Africa entered its third phase before the final passing of imperial control. The new produce marketing boards began in Nigeria (with cocoa) in 1947. The idea behind this and later boards was that the farmer would be

[33] Frankel, *Capital investment in Africa,* pp. 421–9.
[34] See William A. Hance, *The geography of modern Africa* (New York, Columbia University Press, 1964), p. 310.
[35] See A. M. Kamarck, 'The development of the economic infrastructure', in *Economic transition in Africa,* Melville J. Herskovits and Mitchell Harwitz, eds. (London, 1964).

guaranteed a minimum price until a maximum price could be obtained in world markets.[36] The production of coffee, ground-nuts, palm-oil, cocoa and rice all reached record levels in 1959–60. Cultivated rubber production more than trebled between 1945 and 1960. Copper, diamond and gold output all forged rapidly ahead.[37] With production rising more steeply than export came a marked shift to policies of import substitution. A great foreign business organization such as the United Africa Company (linked since 1920 with Lever Brothers and later Unilever), deprived of its former business and revenue from primary produce dealing, redeployed its capital. The United Africa Company had long had close associations with European importers of consumer and capital goods. It now entered into partnership with its former import agents; that is, the company provided the capital and commercial expertise, the importers the necessary technology for local manufacture. The result was an impressive crop of industries throughout Nigeria, Ghana, French West Africa and East Africa, manufacturing machinery, motor bodies, electrical products, bicycles, cement, timber, beer, textiles and many other products.[38]

These new and welcome changes were not in themselves *simply* the product of political maturity—though growing political concern and new levels of training and education were admittedly indispensable to their progress—any more than the economic growth of the 1880–1914 period was *simply* the result of political imperialism. The early phases of change could not have happened without the technological revolution that made available railways, steamships, maps, telegraphs and so on. And the later developments were dependent on air transport, the motor truck, the bulldozer, aerial surveying, hydropower, new methods of oil exploration and drilling, road construction, radio-telephonic communication, pesticides, new tropical medicines and hundreds of other scientific or technological discoveries. Once more, it was not only the desire, or the urge or the will, but the scientific and technological skills and, above all, the ability to execute great programmes that were crucial.

Again, it was (and is) too soon to be over-sanguine. The post-war years, independence and post-independence were to be times of losses as well as of gains. World competition still faced an Africa modernized only in bits. Provision of capital was patchy. France was disposed to provide more capital for its colonies; Britain was unable to provide as much. After 1945, international aid

[36] For a critical view of these boards, see P. T. Bauer, *West African trade* . . . (Cambridge University Press, 1954).

[37] The rapid increase in African production is illustrated in the following figures:

	Coffee	Rubber	Cocoa	Rice	Gold	Diamonds
	Metric tons 000	Metric tons 000	Metric tons 000	Metric tons 000	Kg. 000	Carats 000
1929–30	52·7	—	352·7	—	—	—
1939–40	167·2	15·2	456·6	2,250	482·3	10,928
1949–50	234·5	45·7	486·1	3,200	419·8	13,831
1959–60	645·7	141·8	660·0	4,400	686·3	26,329

[38] See Wilson, *Unilever*, vol. II, chap. 8.

grew, especially from the United States. But suspicious voices from within Africa asked what strings were attached. Was this a form of neo-colonialism? Suspicious voices from without were, in turn, deeply mistrustful of the Left turn that seemed to align Africa too heedlessly towards Moscow. Above all, Africa pulsated with hidden resentments of territorial boundaries and political arrangements imposed by the imperialists. How much of the continent's slender resources were to be consumed by efforts to overthrow them? Many of the troubles of the future had been predicted in the 1940s and 1950s by those who knew Africa but were powerless to remedy the political and economic weaknesses from which it suffered.

Against increasing output had to be set the socio-political problems of achieving balance between agriculture and industry, between capital and consumer-goods production, between export advantage and the need for domestic development. Against the undoubted fact that a foreign investment that yields profits must increase the national income had to be set obstinate suspicions of neo-colonialism, the desire for greater economic independence and the willingness to assume burdensome régimes of austerity to wring savings even from the poor rather than accept 'imperialist' investment. The two most familiar elements in the African economy were the poor themselves and the traditions of state *dirigisme* that derived from imperialism itself. These two factors made a dangerous combination, and as Africa moved to independence, its chances of future economic progress hung in the balance. Africa remained poor; Africa remained basically agrarian; Africa remained economically unbalanced.[39] All are true. But the socio-economic evolution of a vast continent heavily burdened by man and nature cannot be easy, rapid or uninterrupted. In an age still suffering the disappointment of hopes repeatedly deferred, it is natural to lay much of the blame at the doorstep of the pioneers. In a better perspective, the achievements of these figures may come to seem greater, even their motives a little more creditable.

BIBLIOGRAPHY

Bauer, P. T. *West African trade: a study of competition, oligopoly and monopoly in a changing economy.* Cambridge University Press, 1954.
The British Empire: a report on its structure and problems by a study group of members of the Royal Institute of International Affairs. London, 1937.
Brunschwig, Henri. *French colonialism 1871–1914.* London, 1964.
Clay, Henry. *Report on industrial relations in Southern Rhodesia.* Salisbury, 1930.
Feis, Herbert. *Europe, the world's banker, 1870–1914: an account of European foreign investment and the connection of world finance with diplomacy before the war.* New Haven, Yale University Press, 1930.
Fieldhouse, D. K. *The theory of capitalist imperialism.* London, 1967.
Foster, Philip, ed. *Africa south of the Sahara 1971.* New York, 1971.
Frankel, S. Herbert. *Capital investment in Africa: its course and effects.* London, Oxford University Press, 1938.

[39] For a useful current survey, see Philip Foster, ed., *Africa south of the Sahara 1971,* (New York, 1971). The positive legacy of the colonial era to Africa today, however, seems to me to be often undervalued by some of the contributors.

Gann, L. H. *A history of Southern Rhodesia: early days to 1934*. London, 1965.

Gann, L. H., and Peter Duignan. *Burden of empire: an appraisal of Western colonialism in Africa south of the Sahara*. New York, 1967.

'Introduction', in *Colonialism in Africa 1870–1960*, vol. II: *The history and politics of colonialism 1914–1960*, L. H. Gann and Peter Duignan, eds. Cambridge University Press, 1970.

'Reflections on imperialism and the scramble for Africa', in *Colonialism in Africa 1870–1960*, vol. I: *The history and politics of colonialism 1870–1914*, L. H. Gann and Peter Duignan, eds. Cambridge University Press, 1969.

Hance, William A. *The geography of modern Africa*. New York, Columbia University Press, 1964.

Hilgerdt, Folke. 'The case for multilateral trade', in American Economic Association, *Proceedings*, March 1943, **33**, no. 1, suppl. pt. 2.

Hobhouse, L. T. *Democracy and reaction*. London, 1904.

Hunt, K. E. *Margarine: an economic, social and scientific history, 1869–1969*, J. H. van Stuyvenberg, ed. Liverpool, 1969.

Jenks, Leland. *The migration of British capital to 1875*. New York, 1927.

Kamarck, A. M. 'The development of the economic infrastructure', in *Economic transition in Africa*, Melville J. Herskovits and Mitchell Harwitz, eds. London, 1964.

Keynes, John Maynard. *General theory of employment, interest and money*. London, 1936.

Lenin, V. I. *Selected works*, J. Fineberg, ed. London, 1936.

Masterman, C. F. G. *The heart of the empire*. London, 1901.

Paish, Sir George. 'Great Britain's capital investment in industrial, colonial and foreign countries', *Journal of the Royal Statistical Society*, Jan. 1911, **74**, pt. 2.

Parry, J. H. *The Spanish theory of empire in the sixteenth century*. Cambridge University Press, 1940.

Platt, D. C. M. 'Economic factors in British policy during the new imperialism', *Past and Present*, 1968, no. 39.

Report by Brigadier-General F. D. Hammond, C.B.E., D.S.O. on the railway system of Southern Rhodesia. C.S.R. 2-1926. Salisbury, 1925.

Robinson, Ronald E., and John Gallagher, with Alice Denny. *Africa and the Victorians: the official mind of imperialism*. London and New York, 1965.

Roubiquet, Paul, ed. *Discours et opinions de Jules Ferry*. 7 vols. Paris, 1893–8.

Saul, S. B. 'Britain and world trade 1870–1914', *Economic History Review*, 1954, ser. 2, no. 6.

Semmel, Bernard. *Imperialism and social reform: English social-imperial thought, 1895–1914*. London, 1960.

Strandmann, H. P. von. 'Domestic origins of Germany's colonial expansion under Bismarck', *Past and Present*, 1969, no. 42.

Townsend, M. E. *Origins of modern German colonialism 1871–85*. New York, 1921.

White, Arnold. *Efficiency and empire*. London, 1901.

Wilson, Charles. *England's apprenticeship, 1603–1763*. London, 1965.

History of Unilever. 2 vols. London, 1954.

PART TWO

NATIONAL STYLES

CHAPTER 3

BRITISH PLANNING AND PRIVATE ENTERPRISE IN COLONIAL AFRICA

by

SIR FREDERICK PEDLER

From the standpoint of a Victorian businessman, Africa, for all its reputed romance, was but a continent of outposts. In 1880, when the 'New Imperialism' was just beginning to get under way, the British imported more goods from the few scattered white colonies in Australia than they did from the entire African continent. For the next thirty years or so, as shown in the Table 7, the importance of the African trade in relation to Great Britain's total commerce changed but little.

Table 7. *United Kingdom imports by continents, 1880 and 1910*
(in percentages)

Year	Europe	Africa	Asia	North America	South America	Australia
1880	39·1	4·9	14·1	29·5	6·1	6·3
1910	40·6	6·4	12·1	21·5	10·6	8·8

SOURCE: Werner Schlote, *British overseas trade from 1700 to the 1930's* (Oxford, 1952), pp. 156–7. See also Colin W. Newbury, 'Trade and authority in West Africa from 1850 to 1880', *Colonialism in Africa, 1870–1960*, vol. I: *The history and politics of colonialism 1870–1914*, L. H. Gann and Peter Duignan, eds. (Cambridge University Press, 1969), p. 91.

In East Africa, the bulk of the long-distance trade in the interior was controlled by Swahili-speaking merchants, sometimes financed by Indian capital. Porters bearing loads on their heads walked hundreds of miles into the interior to deal in slaves, ivory and other commodities. British pressure was beginning to reduce the importance of the slave-trade, and in 1873 the Sultan of Zanzibar signed a treaty whereby he agreed to abolish the export of human merchandise from his dominions. The traffic in 'black ivory' continued, of course, for many years. Nevertheless east-coast traders built up a variety of other exports, including wild rubber, gum-copal, sesame and cereals, as well as ivory and cloves.

In West Africa the slave-trade at long last was ceasing to be of significance. The Royal Navy effectively policed the Atlantic. Cuba and Brazil, the last two strongholds of the transatlantic plantation economy built upon servile labour, abolished slavery in 1886 and 1888 respectively. In West Africa the traffic in human beings gradually disappeared. Commerce founded upon the gathering of wild produce and on hunting gradually diminished in relative importance as against the export of such tropical crops as ground-nuts from the Gambia and Senegal and palm-oil from countries farther south. In exchange, Africans imported such luxuries as strong liquor, bangles, beads and cotton cloth, and

95

simple forms of capital goods such as hatchets, knives, guns and other implements useful in hunting or agriculture.

In 1870 this traffic was still so small that it afforded employment to no more than two dozen merchant houses and a steamship company. As a proportion of Britain's overseas trade as a whole, it represented less than 1 per cent. Nevertheless, in terms of local African interests, the British did exert considerable impact. Bathurst in the Gambia had developed into a commercial centre where several French firms had established themselves to ship ground-nuts to France, the main overseas market for this particular commodity. French and British traders had established posts all along the Gambia river. The British were established also in Freetown and Sherbro, in what is now called Sierra Leone, as well as on the Gold Coast, where in 1872 they acquired the remaining Dutch possessions in that part of Africa. English merchants did not hesitate to supply weapons of war to indigenous monarchs. A. and F. Swanzy, the leading commercial house in the area, shipped arms to the king of Ashanti. Hence, when war broke out between Britain and Ashanti, the London *Pall Mall Gazette* attacked Swanzy for supplying munitions of war to the enemy. Similarly, Thomas Chadwick of the firm of G. B. Ollivant in Sierra Leone furnished gunpowder to Bai Bureh, an indigenous chief who went to war against the British in 1895. Some British merchants, in other words, had a recognized stake in the existence of African kingdoms, and in turn enjoyed the favours of indigenous potentates.

In the Gold Coast, British power was likewise in the ascendant. In 1873 the Ashanti advanced across the river Prah, invading the Fanti country. When the Fanti looked for British protection, the British government decided to send an expedition inland. The British gained an overwhelming success, and in 1874 they administratively separated their possessions on the Gold Coast and Lagos from those farther west in Sierra Leone, creating a new dependency formally known as the Gold Coast Colony. Along the bights of Benin and Biafra, British merchants were obliged to deal with a congeries of city states, some of them kingdoms, others trading republics. For centuries the foreign trade of these communities had depended largely on the export of slaves.

The British policy of suppressing this commerce had far-reaching consequences for the economic structure of these states. Lagos, for example, had been occupied by the British as part of the struggle to suppress the traffic. By about 1870 the conversion from slave-trading to palm-oil trading had been largely completed. Not unnaturally this had caused some towns to decline in importance and others to increase. In 1869, for instance, a subject of King Pepple of Bonny named Ja-Ja left that town with a group of followers and set up an independent kingdom at Opobo. The British trading houses made arrangements with one or another of these African states, and the rivalries among them frequently extended to armed hostility. On one point, however, the African trading states were all agreed: they preserved for themselves the 'middleman trade' with the interior, and did everything possible to prevent European ships from sailing upstream. By the 1870s, however, steam-power and quinine between them were helping to change the balance of power inland. The British felt strong enough to send steamships up the fever-infested Niger even though they had to resort to the use of arms.

According to a widespread myth, accepted equally by missionary and Marxist propagandists, ignorant African chiefs were wont to barter away valuable concessions for a string of beads or a keg of gin. This belief, based on paternalist stereotypes of the mid-Victorian era, has little basis in fact, and takes no account of the Africans' sense of economic rationality. In the lands that fringed the bights, foreign traders were subjected to an elaborate system of dues known as 'comey'. In the rivers of Benin and Brass, comey was computed at a certain value of goods for each mast a vessel carried, and that value was the goods required for the purchase of two puncheons of palm-oil. Bonny and New Calabar took into account the registered tonnage of the ship, levying a comey of five iron bars for every registered ton. In Cameroun it was at the rate of ten 'crews' for every 100 tons of the ship's register, eight crews being worth one pound sterling.[1]

The captains of trading ships had been accustomed to depend on chiefs to help them in conducting trade, for the chiefs, wishing to attract Europeans to their ports, took care that their subjects settled their debts with traders who had paid dues correctly. By 1870, however, captains who anchored off the Gold Coast could no longer depend on chiefs to look after their credit risks. The authority of chiefs had been superseded by colonial law courts; but because the courts seemed to favour the debtors, the Bristol firms stopped trading in British colonies and confined their activities to places where they could deal with independent African authorities. 'The merchants had prospered most where the authority of the Colonial Office did not run, and they did not want colonial rule which would have to be paid for out of their profits.'[2]

The chartered companies

In the Niger Delta the Foreign Office was determined that trade should be open to all and should not be restricted by the old-established palm-oil merchants. Traders were encouraged to send ships up the Niger. The consul was happy that four firms had responded (1878), but in Downing Street the mood was one of anxiety lest it might not be possible to provide protection for this trade. At the conference of Berlin, the Foreign Office secured recognition of the lower Niger as a British sphere, but was not prepared to bear the cost of administration. A solution to this difficulty was found in 1886 by the grant of a charter to a company that then became known as the Royal Niger Company, under which 'the company was empowered to administer justice, to enforce treaty rights, to collect customs duties, and to spend the receipts solely on the expense of rule'.[3] Whereas the chartered companies of earlier eras had involved officially recognized trade monopolies, charters such as that conferred on the Royal Niger Company did not provide for commercial privileges. Under the terms of its charter, other traders, British or foreign, might have access to the area. On certain occasions French and German expeditions asserted their rights; but in general the Royal Niger Company made it very difficult for competitors to enter its territory, requiring them to report at certain points for customs examination.

On the east coast of Africa there was no British private enterprise in 1870. However, William Mackinnon, founder of the British and Indian Steam Navi-

---

[1] Thomas J. Hutchinson, *Journal of the Society of Arts*, 6 March 1874, **22**, no. 1111.
[2] Ronald Robinson and John Gallagher, *Africa and the Victorians: the official mind of imperialism* (London, 1965), p. 51. [3] *Ibid.*, p. 181.

gation Company, did contemplate an investment until he was warned by the Foreign Office (1877) that there would be no protection against foreign powers. After the scramble for Africa, the Foreign Office changed its policy; it hoped that inland territory—Uganda, for instance—might be effectively occupied by a commercial organization with a royal charter. The Imperial British East Africa Company, organized by Mackinnon, was chartered in 1888. This company went bankrupt in 1892, however, and the government set up its own administration.

In 1889 the British South Africa Company received a charter empowering it to negotiate with African chiefs, as well as to acquire rights from them, in the Rhodesias. The impresario of the BSA Company was Cecil Rhodes. The circumstances surrounding the formation of this firm would involve a far too detailed account of South African conflicts, international politics, financial combinations and philanthropic movements to fall within the limits of the present essay. For more than thirty years the BSA Company maintained in the Rhodesias its dual function of administrator and commercial entrepreneur. It incurred huge administrative charges that the British government was unwilling to bear and built railways in the expectation of recovering all this expenditure out of commercial profits; but it never paid a dividend until after it had given up its governmental functions.[4]

The charters produced as a side effect in West Africa a major concentration of British commerce that had an important influence on the attitude of colonial governments to private enterprise. Nine firms joined together in the African Association for the purpose of applying for a charter for the Niger Delta region. They hoped to secure in this region powers similar to those that the Royal Niger Company had gained in the more northerly part of the country. Their application for a charter, however, met with no success. Instead, the British government proclaimed a protectorate over the area and set up a colonial form of administration. But on the commercial side there was now one business combining the nine firms. By further amalgamations this combination became in 1919 the African and Eastern Trade Corporation and in 1929 the United Africa Company. The size and power of this concentration tended to upset the colonial governments and led to strained relations for many years in West Africa. On the eastern side, where no such concentration existed, the attitude of the governments to commercial enterprise was more friendly.

Wholesale and retail distribution

In tropical Africa the most important share of the retail trade, which is conducted in traditional markets, has always been entirely in the hands of Africans—before, during and since colonial times. Many market traders, women as well as men, have made a lot of money. An important effect of colonial policy on this kind of African private enterprise was that traders, encouraged by peaceful conditions and freedom of movement, commonly went far away from home. Among notable large-scale movements were those of the Ibo traders to Northern Nigeria, and Hausa butchers from the north plied their trade in mar-

[4] Peter Slinn, 'The role of the British South Africa Company in Northern Rhodesia 1890–1964', *African Affairs*, 1971, **70**, no. 281, 365–84.

kets throughout the south. 'Lagosians' in large numbers had stalls in the markets of Ashanti, and the Kwahus from the high land near Nkawkaw were well represented in the Accra markets. In East Africa there was less of this kind of movement, but there was some. Trading in Mombasa, for example, was conducted largely by Luo whose homes were hundreds of miles away. Somali traders, too, were much given to travelling about the countryside far from home.

The retail-market traders bought their supplies of imported goods from importers, who in 1870 were sometimes European firms established in Africa and sometimes African merchants who dealt with export houses in Liverpool and London. In the three decades 1870 to 1900, the number of European houses established in Africa increased, whereas the importance of Africans in the import trade diminished. It is thought that the principal cause of this change was the establishment of regular rapid steamship routes. These improved communications conferred important advantages on firms that enjoyed facilities at both ends, Africa and Europe. Several of the new European firms established themselves in Africa by taking over an African's business.

In the nineties the trading companies, because they were reluctant to leave their water-borne communications, remained on the coast or on the rivers. The African Association decided in 1893 against inland penetration, withdrew to the coast and compelled the only dissident, George Miller of Miller Brothers, to comply under threat of boycott by African traders. The Africans, wishing to preserve the inland trade for themselves, co-operated willingly with the African Association. Miller appealed to the colonial government that had recently been established, but was told that if the coercion with which he was threatened was a simple refusal on the part of the Africans to trade, no official action was possible. Also in the 1890s, the government of the Gold Coast urged expatriate firms to open posts in the interior. For a decade the firms held back, preferring to limit their activities to wholesale trading in the ports and relying on Africans for inland distribution. The government, dissatisfied with the facilities that resulted from these arrangements, set up trading stores itself to make good the deficiency in distribution. Not until 1905 did firms begin to open businesses inland.[5]

Europeans trading in West Africa must have felt that they had chosen a very hard way to earn a living. Health conditions were very bad. In 1894, for instance, more than half the white people in the Gold Coast died; and at Bonny nine men out of eleven perished of yellow fever.[6]

In 1900, after the Niger Company lost its charter, Sir Frederick Lugard was placed in charge of the government of Northern Nigeria. He undertook a series of military expeditions that brought the African states of the savannah under control. Lugard's hope that trade would follow the flag was doomed to disappointment. The Niger Company showed no inclination to move away from the rivers. It continued to trade for barter, whereas Lugard wanted produce to be bought for cash in order 'to promote the circulation of the coinage'. Under pressure the company agreed to this in 1904. Government officers differed in

[5] Robert Szereszewski, *Structural changes in the economy of Ghana, 1891–1911* (London, 1965), *passim*.
[6] Mary Henrietta Kingsley, *Travels in West Africa: Congo français, Corisco and Cameroons* (London, 1897), p. 32.

their attitude to private enterprise, for whereas Lugard would have liked trading companies to be more active, Charles Temple, an administrator and later lieutenant-governor, saw his duty 'in protecting the virtues of northern aristocratic life and its communal economy from the "barbarising" effects of European capitalism, democracy and individualism'. He was not exceptional. 'The kind of missionary spirit which bred the good district officer was often associated with a romantic revolt against industrial society.' [7]

Throughout this period trade tended to follow not the flag but the railway. In Kano, for instance, when the line was opened in 1911, eighteen firms came to buy ground-nuts. The farmers responded enthusiastically, and the quantities offered for sale were beyond all expectations. In 1913 the government laid out trading sites and auctioned them. Because the law restricted non-indigenous traders to certain sites, it effectively determined the places at which ground-nuts, cotton, hides and other products might be bought for export.

About this time—that is to say, in 1912–14—people in West Africa noticed the trading activity of immigrants from the Arab countries of the Middle East. At that time these countries were under the sway of the Turkish Empire. The Arab traders, who were very poor, became known collectively as 'Syrians', though many of them were Lebanese and some were Druses. They earned their living by trade, buying and selling. Many of them prospered and invited relations to come and join them. In less than twenty years they became a well-established community, supplying a significant volume of wholesale and retail distribution services. The Indian trading community in East Africa, beginning in much the same way and a little earlier in the century, achieved a similar position. These communities, which were founded entirely on private enterprise, owed nothing to any encouragement from the governments.

Economic and supportive infrastructure

The year 1895 witnessed a change at the Colonial Office when Joseph Chamberlain became the Secretary of State. He believed that the government should develop the Empire. He said that he regarded the colonies as 'undeveloped estates': 'If the people of this country are not willing to invest some of their superfluous wealth in the development of their great estate, then I see no future for these countries.' Here is an interesting use of the word 'undeveloped', with the germ of the idea of aid (superfluous wealth) and a hint of the capital-input theory of development. In Chamberlain's view, the colonizers should act as 'trustees for civilization for the commerce of the world'. Colonial raw materials and foodstuffs should be developed alike in the interests of the Africans and of the world at large. Chamberlain's version of the 'Dual Mandate' involved departmental planning. Chamberlain, a strong chief surreptitiously referred to by even the most highly placed civil servants as 'Our Master', instituted a number of reforms at the Colonial Office. In the various colonial territories, 'each administration was to be equipped with a strong agricultural department which would persuade the African Chiefs to grow cotton, kola nuts, fibres, cocoa and rubber'. Colonial governments were compelled to obtain their

---

[7] John Michael Lee, *Colonial development and good government: a study of the ideas expressed by the British official classes in planning decolonization 1939–1964* (Oxford, Clarendon Press, 1967), p. 73.

requirements, whether port or railway equipment worth millions or small articles worth only a few pounds, through the Crown Agents. This arrangement had the advantage of placing into competent and experienced hands the greater part of capital expenditure of colonial revenues. But it also assured an indirect preference for the home market and involved a limited form of public enterprise in economic management.

Chamberlain, a convinced advocate of 'scientific colonization', also took a major part in promoting research. By the time he took office as colonial secretary in 1895, the British had made considerable strides. Following on Queen Victoria's Golden Jubilee in 1887, the Imperial Institute had come into existence for the purpose of disseminating information and promoting scientific investigations concerning the Empire. This endeavour, much of which centred on problems of tropical medicine and agriculture, was supported by the Royal Botanical Gardens at Kew and the natural history section of the British Museum. Chamberlain played a particularly significant part in medical progress. To a considerable extent, the creation of an adequate medical service for the colonies was occasioned by Chamberlain's foresight. Government money helped to set up the Liverpool School of Tropical Medicine (1898) and the London School of Tropical Medicine (1889). These bodies played a major part in a medical revolution that had far-reaching effects both on the Africans' demographic structure and on the ability of Europeans to live and work permanently in regions that used to be known as the 'white man's grave'. In the early nineteenth century, for instance, the annual mortality rate of white soldiers in West Africa had amounted to 150 per thousand. By 1917, the rate had fallen to 9.87 per thousand for the Gold Coast, once one of the worst fever spots on the Gulf of Guinea.

Such a development could not have been achieved without money. Additional revenue was raised from European firms, and in some places taxes were imposed on Africans. The cost of several ports and railways was met by grants or by loans guaranteed by the British government.

The Kenya–Uganda Railway, commenced in 1896, reached Lake Victoria in 1902. Its cost, which exceeded £5½ million, was supplied in the form of a grant bearing no interest. The investment was eventually written off. The Nigerian line from Lagos to Kano was completed in 1911. The engagements of governments in railways led them, when motor transport began to compete, to restrain it by leaving gaps in the main roads. However, although the governments provided much of the infrastructure, especially railways and ports, there was no doctrinaire insistence that private enterprise must be excluded from this sphere of investment. As noted above, the Rhodesian railway was built by the BSA Company. The Niger Company created harbour facilities at Burutu, for many years the third port of Nigeria. In the thirties, when the Sierra Leone Development Company came forward with the novel idea that it might be profitable to ship iron ore intercontinentally, that company built a railway and constructed a port.

River transport was left to private enterprise on the Gambia and the Volta, the Niger and the Benue rivers. On these last two, the great rivers of Nigeria, there were privately owned fleets that came into strenuous competition with the government's railway. Swanzy had run ships on the Volta since 1891; and the manager of that enterprise, an African named Cato, took his car across the

Volta in 1917 on a raft of canoes, thus inaugurating the era of vehicular ferries which became a feature of road travel in Africa. At the invitation of the Gold Coast government, Swanzy set up an organization that maintained many ferries until after independence. In Sierra Leone the government, dissatisfied with the operation of ferries by its public-works department, invited the United Africa Company to take them over in 1931. This company made the ferries efficient, thus forcing the railway to take road competition seriously. A single 'zone rate', which made long road hauls uncompetitive, was therefore introduced, and on certain roads the conveyance of goods was prohibited. The company, which had supposed that it was performing a public service, was dismayed to find itself at the centre of these controversial measures and insisted on handing the ferries back to the public-works department.

Chamberlain's policy on colonial responsibilities changed the attitude to chartered companies. In Nigeria, when it became known that the charter would be revoked, a pool was formed in order to avoid ruinous competition. The arrangement was made in 1899 between the Royal Niger Company, the African Association, Miller and a lesser company. A committee called, perhaps unwisely, the Committee of Control was set up. All this the high commissioner of the Niger Coast Protectorate reported to Chamberlain, who invited the committee to meet him. Accordingly they went to Downing Street, where he asked them to explain the purposes of their association. After discussion he expressed himself as perfectly reassured. Through the next four decades, when pools were regarded by most commercial men as the normal way of trade in West Africa, the governments never liked them, regarding them as a means of rigging prices. It was mainly to satisfy the objections of the governments and of African opinion that the practice of trading in pools ceased in the 1940s.

In Nigeria the charter ended with the nineteenth century. In compensation the company received a cash payment. In addition the government undertook to impose royalties on any minerals that might be taken from certain lands and to pay half of such royalties to the company for ninety-nine years. These royalties, passing to the United Africa Company as successor of the Niger Company, exacerbated relations between that company and the government of Nigeria. The right to the half-share was sold to the government by the company in 1949 for £1 million which turned out to be three years' purchase.

In southern Africa in 1900 the British government, in the throes of the Boer War, was in no position to take over the Rhodesias from the chartered company. The British South Africa Company did not give up its administrative responsibility for Northern Rhoesia until 1924, but when it did so it retained the ownership of the minerals. During the 1920s geologists made new mineral discoveries. Metallurgists found ways of profitably working the low-grade ores of the Northern Rhodesian Copper Belt. Northern Rhodesia then built up a vast copper industry, the second largest in the world, yielding precedence only to that of the United States. The BSA Company's right to collect royalties was much criticized and the legal basis of its title was disputed. In 1950 the company agreed that 20 per cent of the royalties might go to the government until 1986, when it would surrender its right. However, the arrangement did not last so long, for in 1964, just before Northern Rhodesia became independent under the name Zambia, the BSA Company relinquished its rights in return for a payment of £4 million.

Private enterprise in mining

The BSA Company deserves credit for a wise selection of the companies to which it granted mining leases in Northern Rhodesia. These firms proved to be good operators in every sense of the word. The mines created markets for all kinds of products. The growing urban populations had to be fed. Money went into such enterprises as workshops, repair outfits, electric-power plants, cement factories and waterworks. The Northern Rhodesian mining companies had to build and manage their own townships. They also created medical facilities. Development in turn attracted a multitude of people anxious to supply the growing demand for building materials, fuel, clothing and all manner of personal services. No other colony had a mining industry as prosperous as that of Northern Rhodesia, but there were mines also in Sierra Leone, the Gold Coast, Nigeria, Kenya, Uganda and Tanganyika.

The attitude of the governments towards the mining companies appears to have been cordial. However, the company mining diamonds in the Gold Coast and Sierra Leone encountered difficulties. In Sierra Leone in the fifties illicit diamond-digging became common, inflicting loss on the company and depriving the government of important revenues. The company complained that the government was failing in its duty to suppress illicit digging and smuggling. In the course of the dispute, the whole basis of the company's concession was brought into discussion. The company agreed to increase its payments to the government to 60 per cent of its profits on condition that the government would take steps to suppress illegal mining. The government was unsuccessful, however, and the following year the company's concession was greatly reduced in area and the government compensated the company with cash. The government was now in a position to sell licences to African diggers and thus to bring them within the law. In general, therefore, colonial governments relied on private enterprise for the development of mineral resources, the only major exception being the coal mine that was an enterprise of the Nigerian railway. In the last phase of colonial rule, however, the Colonial Development Corporation, a United Kingdom government agency, supplied finance and management for the development of certain new mines.

Crops for export: market regulations

The half-century or so that elapsed between the onset of the New Imperialism and the outbreak of the Second World War saw a commercial revolution in Africa. Between 1886–8 and 1936–8 the trade of British West Africa alone, as shown in Table 8, had increased more than twelvefold, during a period when many theoreticians worked out elaborate analyses to account for the supposed stagnation of Britain's West African empire. The expansion of trade was far reaching in effect, introducing a vast array of imported wares to African villagers, ranging from all manner of consumption goods to new tools such as ploughs, sewing machines, bicycles and pumps. All these provided simple but effective forms of capital investment, though not easily measurable by statisticians. African farmers paid for this merchandise by vastly increasing their cash-crops. The planners had assumed originally that the principal export crop of Northern Nigeria would be cotton, but in fact the most profitable commerce

Table 8. *Trade of British West Africa*
(annual average)

Imports in £1,000		Exports in £1,000	
1886–8	1,179	1886–8	1,328
1911–13	13,074	1911–13	13,072
1936–8	22,803	1936–8	26,160

was established in ground-nuts. Because of a combination of circumstances, the growth of the ground-nut industry increased at a phenomenal rate. This resulted from the extension of government agricultural services and research, the development of the railway just at the time when Europe's need for ground-nuts was increasing, the conversion of that need into effective demand by the trading firms and the quick-witted, diligent response of the peasant farmers.

The cultivation of cotton owed a major debt to planning done by the British Cotton Growing Association. This association, formed in 1902 by private enterprise as a non-profit corporation, provided facilities in several colonies to promote the cultivation of cotton. For instance, the association issued high-quality seeds, offered copious advice on cultivation, installed central ginning facilities and performed a major service by raising cotton yields, both through experimentation and by assisting producers. Its collaboration with governments was so close that many believed it to be an official organization. In Nigeria and Uganda it helped to prescribe the type of seed that might be planted in order to maintain a standard high quality. Marketing was confined to a prescribed season, and in some dependencies buying had to be done within specified zones in order to avoid mixing varieties. The operation of gins was subject to licence.

The old trades, palm-oil in the Delta and ground-nuts in Gambia had been notorious for 'abuses'; but the firms grew tired of the trickery, an in 1929 they took steps to establish better standards of trading. As new trades opened, the established firms were not unwilling that marketing should be subject to rules—for instance, that purchases should be made only on weigh-scales located in certain places where their accuracy could be checked by inspectors. In many cases regulations required prices to be posted. Thus the government played an active role, in which the basic idea was not *laissez-faire* but fair play. The market rules, however, imposed some degree of restraint upon the entry of new participants in the trade, and had the effect of limiting the expansion of the activities of Asian traders, Indians in East Africa and Syrians in the west. Before markets were subjected to rules, there were many African produce-traders; but the rules bore heavily upon them, too. If they wished to buy in the gazetted markets, they had to pay for licences, to own scales and to fill in forms and pay the posted prices. The governments took credit for eliminating middlemen's profits, but middlemen's profits were livelihood and inducement for African entrepreneurs. If middlemen made money, it was because someone set value on their services. A farmer lacking means or inclination to take produce to the gazetted market might then employ a middleman; but market rules tended to peg him at the lowest level of the trade or even to push him into the penumbra of the law's shadow.

European settlers and plantation agriculture

Another form of private enterprise was the farms established by communities of European settlers in Kenya, in Northern Rhodesia, in Nyasaland and in Tanganyika, but nowhere in West Africa. It would not be possible in this brief essay to deal with the problems of the settler communities, but it is appropriate to note that wherever these settlements existed they were among the most vocal critics of the large trading and mining companies. Especially in Northern Rhodesia, the representatives of the settlers in the Legislative Council led the attack on the British South Africa Company's mining revenues.

In the legislative councils of the colonies, members of the commercial community were nominated by the governor to sit alongside the most senior government officers and representatives of other interests. Where mines were important, a leading member of the mining community would also be nominated as a member. Normally the nominated representatives of commerce and mines abstained by convention from voting on any politically controversial issue. Over a long period, their relations with African members of the legislative councils were for the most part cordial.

Policy on plantations falls within the main current of relations between governments and private enterprise, both expatriate and indigenous. In 1900 George Miller approached Sir Ralph Moor, high commissioner for Southern Nigeria, on the subject of rubber. He asked if land could be made available for plantations to be established by his company and by Africans, and offered to distribute plants to the Africans without payment; but his proposal was rejected because the government wished to preserve the communal ownership of the land. However, Moor was succeeded as high commissioner by Walter (later Sir Walter) Egerton, who had seen rubber in Malaya. Egerton chided Alexander Cowan, a director of the Miller company, that private enterprise in Nigeria had not had the initiative to start a rubber industry. Cowan told Egerton of Miller's experience with Moor, whereat Egerton arranged for the leasing of land to Miller. Miller's Nigerian rubber estates proved a success in every way. Farmers took up the industry as he had foretold, and by 1954 the area of smallholdings planted with rubber in Nigeria exceeded 100,000 acres.

William Lever (raised to the peerage as Viscount Leverhulme), who created an international soap business, was keen to promote the production of raw materials. He would have liked a partner relationship with African communities. He wanted to set up a mill, to which they would bring the fruit from wild farms in the forest, for processing into palm-oil and palm-kernel oil. At the same place he would develop a plantation of oil-palms, which would both augment supplies to the mill and show the local people how to cultivate improved strains of palms. Seedlings of such strains would be made available. Lever sent an agent to Africa in 1903 to seek concessions, but with no success. The governments saw danger in any alienation of land.

In 1923 a famous confrontation took place between Viscount Leverhulme and Sir Hugh Clifford, governor of Nigeria. Leverhulme expressed the view that 'the colonial system of administration was founded on the recognition of the principles that the encouragement of trade and commerce and the development of the colonies were of first consideration'. Clifford, in the Legislative Council in Lagos, described this as 'monstrous and mischievous heresy'. He added that these so-called principles died finally and forever when Warren Hastings was impeached, and he declared his adherence to the paramountcy of African interests. He then expressed a very interesting idea, the hope that the people of Nigeria would 'retain their independence' and would 'not fall into the temptation of producing any crop which is valueless to them unless they can dispose of it for export'. The public slanging match continued for another year, when, in 1925, Leverhulme anchored his yacht at Lagos. Clifford had him to dinner but refused to accept a return invitation to dine on the yacht.

Economically, the case for plantations rested upon the need to secure capital and management for the introduction of modern technology. Without advanced methods Africa could not compete with Malaya and Indonesia in the palm-oil and rubber industries. R. K. Udo, an African writer, holds that restrictions on the extension of plantations retarded the development of Nigeria. On the other hand, it was argued that when prices were low, peasants would carry on in cases where plantations could not. In Uganda, for instance, the agreements of 1900 and 1901 secured African interests in land while making it possible to grant areas for plantations. Thus 225 estates came into existence, growing sugar, sisal, rubber, coffee and tea. In the economic blizzard of the twenties, however, the number declined; and after that, peasant production increased in importance.

In most areas peasant and plantation forms of agriculture were regarded as distinct; but in the Anglo-Egyptian Sudan, expatriate capital and management had found a way of combining with peasants. In 1903 an American entrepreneur with the help of a London bank formed the Sudan Plantations Syndicate. This company evolved a method of operation in which capital and management played their parts while granting tenancies to local cultivators. The government had a large irrigation scheme on the Nile that the syndicate managed. The tenant provided seed, implements, animals and labour. He grew food on part of his plot. His title was subject to good performance in cultivation and he received 40 per cent of the profit. The government received 35 per cent, with the remaining 25 per cent going to the syndicate. This ratio was changed on renewal to 40:40:20. The shareholders had to wait ten years before they received their first dividend, after which they had good years and bad. In these circumstances, it was an appropriate investment for risk-bearing capital.

Government officers worried whether the scheme was being conducted with too much regard for private profit and too little for social welfare. The historian of the Gezira scheme, Arthur Gaitskell, commented that 'The emphasis on government control in many emergent territories was less an ideology than a legacy of paternalism based on the same outlook.' [8] It was agreed that village communities should be developed and that the civic and agricultural control of the farmers should be entrusted to them. In 1944 the government, influenced by its study of the Tennessee Valley Authority, decided that the syndicate would not be required after 1950, and in that year a government board took over the syndicate's functions. A numerous and prosperous community of peasants had been created, in which thousands of individuals had a personal interest in the continuing prosperity of the undertaking. Interesting features of the set-up were

[8] See Arthur Gaitskell, *Gezira: a story of development in the Sudan* (London, 1959).

the triple partnership (private enterprise, government, peasant) and the time-limit on foreign participation.

Between 1938 and 1960 many schemes for the settlement of peasants were undertaken in British tropical Africa. But there is no record here of any attempt to follow the Gezira model closely. There appear to have been two places where private enterprise was invited to help, both in 1950, at Bunyoro (Uganda) and at Shendam (Nigeria). The first petered out, but the second brought into existence a new agricultural community. At Damongo (Gold Coast) and Mokwa (Nigeria), the Colonial Development Corporation was invited to provide capital and management. The developer was to have two-thirds of the crop and the tenant the remaining third. The scheme did not succeed in either case; the peasants could do better on their own. One-third of the crop was evidently too small an incentive, but whether two-fifths (as in Gezira) would have provided the marginal unit of inducement will never be known.

Trade in local foodstuffs

In 1930 the United Africa Company started trading in locally produced African provisions. The memorandum presenting the proposals referred to 'the shortage of native foodstuffs which is bound to arise as more and more people are induced to give up work on farms'. [9] As matters developed, this was a very accurate forecast, for massive imports of food developed over the next thirty years. Sir Robert Waley Cohen, first chairman of the United Africa Company, discussed the proposals during a tour of West Africa. He received a letter of encouragement from the governor of Nigeria. He agreed with the governor of Sierra Leone to trade in rice and to provide a rice mill. However, African traders were furious because the company was offering food for sale at prices which affected their margins. The Nigerian government, fearing a riot, asked the company to stop. Meanwhile there had been a board-room revolution in London, and the new managing directors, convinced that African competitors would render trade in provisions unprofitable for the company, had no wish to engage in such activity. Accordingly, they dropped the whole idea. It was ironical that during the Second World War the Sierra Leone government asked the company to trade in local rice; and the Nigerian government, with a view to counteracting the rise of prices in the markets, asked the United Africa Company to buy local foodstuffs for resale in the markets under official control.

The cocoa hold-up and the marketing boards

From the last decade of the nineteenth century, indigenous cultivators began to realize the commercial possibilities of cocoa. With absolutely no European capital, African farmers near the coast, and later those in the interior, went ahead with the planting of trees. Output increased at a truly phenomenal rate, as shown in Table 9. This astonishing progress rested on an often unacknowledged partnership among African producers, local middlemen and the large

[9] T. M. (later Sir Malcolm) Knox, 'Report to the board on visit to W. A.', May 24, 1929, p. 18 (copy in U.A.C. archives).

Table 9. *Growth in cocoa production, 1891–1930*

Years	Five-year average by tons
1891–5	5
1906–10	14,784
1926–30	218,895

SOURCE: F. M. Bourret, *The Gold Coast: a survey of the Gold Coast and British Togoland, 1919–1946* (Stanford University Press, 1949), p. 26.

exporting firms that marketed the crop overseas. This partnership was an uneasy one, as the price of the crop tended to fluctuate sharply. By 1937 the export of cocoa thus amounted to some 236,000 tons, valued at nearly £10 million. Economists calculated that the output over the following year would at least be 10 per cent greater. The value, on the other hand, went down to £4.5 million, a drop of over 50 per cent. The firms were prepared for this decline, and proposed to keep the local price of cocoa from rising above the world market price. In 1937 sixteen companies (British, German, French and Swiss), all exporters of cocoa from the Gold Coast and Nigeria, entered into an agreement for 'eliminating harmful competition'.[10] Representatives of the group called at the Colonial Office to explain the situation. They suggested that the governments should name an observer to sit on the committee in London that would fix the prices to be paid for cocoa in Africa. Although this invitation was not accepted, the Secretary of State informed the governors that in his view the agreement was justifiable. At this moment, disastrously, the price of cocoa fell from £40 to £27. Africans blamed the drop on the agreed firms. In the Gold Coast, farmers refused to sell, and chiefs identified themselves with the boycott movement. Fetish oaths were sworn to enforce the boycott, and trucks attempting to carry cocoa on the roads were stopped by pickets. The Gold Coast government did not share the favourable opinion of the agreement that had been expressed by the Secretary of State, saw political danger in appearing to side with the agreed firms and gave no protection to trucks transporting cocoa. The Secretary of State thereupon sent a second message, advising the orderly sale of the crop. The governor, however, declined to communicate this message to the public. The firms therefore distributed copies of it, but it was not well received. A commission of inquiry was appointed. The firms abandoned the agreement and suffered a humiliating defeat. Their profits were very adversely affected.

Next their representative placed before the commission proposals for establishing an organization to be called Cocoa Union. This was to consist of the five largest firms, to be endowed with a statutory monopoly and to submit to various measures of control. The plan called for marketing all the cocoa through a monopoly established by law. It is highly significant that the proposal was brought forward by the companies. It implied an admission that competitive private enterprise at that time was not eager to undertake the job. The commission considered that the proposal would not be acceptable to African opin-

[10] Great Britain, *Parliamentary papers,* vol. IX, Cmd 5845, *Report of the Commission on the Marketing of West African cocoa* (London, 1938), appendix.

ion, but recommended instead that a statutory association of farmers should market the crop.

At this point the Second World War broke out. By way of intensifying their military effort, the British resorted to more and more economic planning. Domestic economic planning naturally spilled over into the colonies. One measure of wartime control adopted by the Colonial Office was to set up the West African Produce Control Board, which bought and sold cocoa and oil seeds. The details of the controversies that arose over the Association of West African Merchants (AWAM) do not fall within the purpose of this essay; but through this organization the business houses provided all sorts of services to the governments during the war, such as control of imports and exports and allocation of scarce supplies. In the Gold Coast the AWAM became very unpopular towards the end of the war; but the issue was not one in which government and private enterprise were ranged against each other. The AWAM, in spite of its name, had been acting on behalf of the governments.

After the war it was the simplest thing to hand over the trading in cocoa and oil seeds, together with the large balances that these functions had accumulated, to boards in the colonies. The companies that had been dealers in produce did not raise their voices against state monopolies. They were glad that they did not have to carry the market risk nor bear the blame when prices fell. They co-operated as buying agents for the boards. In East Africa, also, boards were set up to buy the crops. A Royal Commission expressed regret that this measure had destroyed the pricing function of the free-marketing system, because under that system the allocation of resources would have been more satisfactory.

Those who planned the marketing boards intended that surpluses earned in good years should be used to support the price in bad years; but the practice of the boards turned out to be very different, for surpluses were transferred to governments in large sums. More than any other single factor, the sense of power created by this windfall, and the impression that such funds could be easily accumulated, led colonial governments to the practice of forced saving for financing their plans. By 1951 it was 'frequently suggested that this constitutes the main justification for the accumulation of large reserves'.[11] Forced saving transfers resources from private individuals to public authorities. The progress of African private enterprise was generally held to be disappointing; but if forced saving siphons off the funds with which entrepreneurs might start, it is hardly surprising that small businesses are fewer than a healthy economy should generate. This state of affairs made it necessary to provide institutions for assisting small businesses. A member of the Colonial Office spoke of 'the proliferation of new development and financial institutions designed to deal with problems rather special to Africa, arising from the relative lack of an indigenous entrepreneurial class';[12] he went on to refer to loan boards. In one colony eleven agencies conducted small loan programmes for the benefit of Africans who wished to start small businesses.

[11] Great Britain, *Parliamentary papers*, vol. XIII, Cmd 9475, *Report of the East African Royal Commission, 1953–55*, (London, 1955), p. 80.
[12] A. Emanuel, 'The financing of the economic development of Africa', in *International days for African studies* (Ghent, International Fair 1956), p. 92.

Colonial Office confrontation with the United Africa Company

The largest of the sixteen firms in the cocoa agreement was the United Africa Company (UAC). No account of the attitude of governments to private enterprise would be complete without a reference to communications that passed between that company and the governments during this period. The UAC had been formed in 1929 when the African and Eastern Trade Corporation, which was having financial difficulty, amalgamated with the Niger group (companies owned by Lever Brothers). During the ensuing year, Lever Brothers amalgamated with the Margarine Union to form Unilever. The UAC suffered large losses in 1930; and because the African and Eastern Trade Corporation was too weak financially to bear its half-share of those losses, Unilever came to the rescue with millions of pounds, in return for which they took control. The UAC held a large share of the import and export trades, *grosso modo* 50 per cent in the Gold Coast and Nigeria and 35 per cent in the Gambia, though in Sierra Leone the UAC was not the largest company and in East Africa its share attracted no special notice.

In 1938, attacks were made on the UAC from several quarters. The Gold Coast government complained that the company's prices were too high. The Nigerian government reported that the company had been selling stockfish at low prices in order to embarrass an African importer. Several British export firms complained that the UAC was driving them out of business.[13] Because the company's vigorous defence of its actions did not please the Colonial Office, a long list of charges against the company was produced. Viscount Trenchard, chairman of the UAC, replied to the Secretary of State in seventeen foolscap pages, concluding by expressing 'the company's deep sense of the Government's prejudice against it', by declaring that the company's prosperity was linked with that of the African inhabitants, and by appealing for 'cordial co-operation of the colonial administration and business interests'. After discussion, the Secretary of State caused a letter to be sent to governors that concluded, 'The Secretary of State is aware of the danger of the government seeming to come in on the side of the company, but is anxious for co-operation where possible and for a just examination of the complaints against the company.'

The outbreak of war in 1939 inaugurated a period of close co-operation between the colonial authorities and the established firms. Though the wartime arrangements were discontinued when peace was concluded, they left behind personal relationships that promoted a better understanding between government and commerce. There were no doubt other reasons for this, besides the friendly co-operation in wartime. Because the large commercial companies were by now recruiting educated young men for service on 'career terms', the staffs of government and commerce were very much alike. The companies had given up 'pools' and could no longer be held responsible for the prices of crops. Furthermore, in tropical Africa the decade following the war turned out to be particularly prosperous, and it is always easier for private enterprise to enjoy cordial relations with other sections of the community when trade is good.

[13] Great Britain, Public Record Office, London, CO 15221/74/38, CO 33650/38, CO 33650/39; and Unilever, 'Managing directors committee minutes', 4 Aug. 1938 and 11 Aug. 1938.

The concern of colonial governments with welfare

The development of agriculture had many dimensions. Colonial governments not only encouraged export crops but also paid attention to the production of food. After the First World War, the British became increasingly conscious of the need to expand the scientific services. In order to meet this need Lord Milner, then Secretary of State for the Colonies, set up authoritative committees in 1919 to examine each of the three technical services in the colonies: the Colonial Veterinary Service, the Colonial Forestry Service and the Colonial Agricultural Service. Of the three, the most important was the Agricultural Service, which by 1938 numbered more than three hundred officers.

Progress was made both in the metropole and in the colonies. In Great Britain the authorities set up new bodies such as the Commonwealth Forestry Institute, established at Oxford in 1924, and also various Imperial Agricultural Bureaux. These applied themselves to a wide range of problems concerned with entomology, animal breeding, mycology, veterinary science, the study of soils and so forth. The British initiated a variety of geological, ecological and related surveys, some of which still rank as classics in their respective fields. Local agricultural departments began to play an important part in spreading more knowledge concerning crops, in teaching African farmers how to cope with soil erosion, in constructing cattle dips and in coping with animal diseases. In arid inland villages, cassava was introduced as a reserve against famine. The sweet potato, maturing quickly after rain, was established in areas where 'end-of-season hunger' was an annual affliction. Many other examples could be cited, but these suffice to indicate the concern of colonial governments with the nutrition of the people.

The 'development philosophy' had to contend with a conflicting philosophy, namely, that African tribal society should be protected against change.[14] This attitude sometimes accompanied a desire to protect Europeans against competition from Africans in the production of cash-crops. In Kenya, for instance, there were restrictions on the cultivation of coffee by black farmers. Such measures were defended on the grounds that black growers would not be able to cope adequately with diseases of the coffee plant. These restrictions continued in Kenya until the early 1950s, when the British began to encourage the cultivation of African coffee. African coffee-planting thus increased from about 4,000 to 26,000 acres between 1954 and 1959.

Development owed a good deal also to general administrators, no matter whether they worked in some remote out-station or in a gubernatorial office. Perhaps one of the most outstanding of these colonial 'developers' was Sir Gordon Guggisberg, who was appointed governor of the Gold Coast in 1919. Guggisberg, a former director of public works in the Gold Coast who had risen to the rank of brigadier general in the Royal Engineers during the First World War, was a man of administrative ability and managerial skill. On taking office, he outlined a 'Ten-Year Development Plan' that he hoped to put into effect during the 1919–29 decade. His main object was to raise the people of the Gold Coast towards what he regarded as 'a higher state of civilization'. Education was to be the main instrument of improvement, but schools and other

[14] See, for example, Great Britain, *Parliamentary papers,* vol. x, Cmd 4556, *Report of the Kenya Land Commission* (London, 1934).

social services required money. Hence the revenue of the dependency would have to be increased. This should be accomplished by extending the communication system, thereby opening new areas to the world market as well as reducing freight rates on imported and exported goods. The railway system was accordingly expanded and more roads were built. Motor trucks became an increasingly important means of transporting men and merchandise. Because the Gold Coast lacked a good natural harbour, Guggisberg made good this deficiency by constructing the port of Takoradi, which was opened for commerce in 1928. This port has proved invaluable in the country's development. Another lasting memorial of Guggisberg's stewardship was the school of Achimota. His work has received generous acknowledgement from the people of Ghana since independence.

The 'development philosophy' that inspired men like Guggisberg sprang from different sources. Chamberlain had spoken of the building up of the 'undeveloped estates' of empire. But historians can also trace a continuous evolution of this philosophy from the writings of Jesse Jones and the report of the Phelps-Stokes committee (1922–5), which indicate the early impact of American thought.[15] Following Jones's recommendations and with the aid of the Carnegie Corporation, Jeanes schools (named for Anna T. Jeanes, an American benefactress) came into existence in Kenya, Northern Rhodesia and Nyasaland. The aim of the training was to improve community life. Teaching maternity and child-welfare work to the students' wives was no less important than the village hygiene and practical agriculture that formed the curriculum for the husbands.

By 1930 this type of action was widespread in African colonies. Money was advanced to stock-owners in Tanganyika in 1930 to enable them to start co-operative dairies for making ghee. And in 1934 the same government, having proposals for stock-routes and cattle-markets, anticipated later planners in naming a target: to increase the number of cattle coming to market from 154,000 a year to a million. G. F. M. Swynnerton, of the Tsetse Research Department, propounded strategy for dealing with tsetse (1937), identifying areas that, though unpopulated at that time, were 'suitable for cheap attack'. Sierra Leone framed an agricultural policy in 1934, in which the first object was 'the improvement of swamp rice cultivation'.[16] In 1939 that government, reviewing the progress of the plan, stated that 'the agricultural development of the various types of country can be, has been, and will continue to be, pursued logically and expanded steadily'.

In 1938 Northern Rhodesia set up the National Development Board, placing at the board's disposal a fund to 'be used only for development'. The board encouraged government departments and Native Authorities to submit schemes that would achieve results within three years. Statements of policy were published for health, agriculture, education, forestry and veterinary services, with the help of a general ecological report and of a review of human nutrition.[17] That same year Northern Rhodesia adopted a five-year plan for the roads that was carried through. In 1939 Uganda had a seven-year programme for roads,

[15] Thomas Jesse Jones, *Education in East Africa* . . . (New York, Phelps-Stokes Fund, 1925).
[16] Sierra Leone, *Annual report of the Department of Agriculture, 1938* (Freetown, 1939).
[17] Northern Rhodesia, National Development Board, 'Minutes of proceedings at 1st and 2nd meetings' (Lusaka, 1938).

several of which were intended to encourage tourist traffic; and in 1940 the roads of East Africa formed the subject of a ten-year plan. On the suggestion of the advisory council set up under the Colonial Development Act of 1929, Nyasaland made a four-year development plan.

While the word 'plan' was being used in so many colonies in the thirties, academic circles and official classes in London were beginning to entertain the idea of planning material progress. Earlier talk of 'colonial development', such as Amery's contributions in the twenties and McLean's 'imperial development plan' of 1925, was inspired by thoughts of markets for exports and was in any case largely concerned with 'the Dominions'. Lord Hailey has been widely regarded as the main propagator of the 'new philosophy' that economic development must precede the grant of independence. His first contribution to the subject, however, was not made until 1938, and the *Report on nutrition in the colonial empire*, which has been described as epoch-making in converting opinion to the development idea, did not appear until 1939. By that year the governments were deeply involved in economic development. If one main cause for this involvement is sought, it may be found in the success of the government's peace-keeping and life-preserving activities. The situation was exemplified by Sir Philip Mitchell:

If natural causes had been allowed to have their way, the acute shortages of food which have resulted from the failure of the rains . . . would have caused the death by starvation of possibly sixty per cent of the population of the districts, and the problem would have been solved by Nature in her own brutal way. We have intervened to prevent Nature having her way, and there has been no abnormal mortality. But we delude ourselves if we suppose that we can leave the matter at that. We have also to interfere, as effectively as we do to prevent death from famine or epidemic, with the economic and social organisation of the people.[18]

The idea that the *increase* of population presented a problem was strange and new. As recently as 1925 Swynnerton, the tsetse-fly expert to whom reference has been made, had written, 'Increase of population must be fostered by every available means.' Thus in twenty years a demographic revolution had taken place. Colonial governments had 'upset the human ecological balance' [19] and the consequences had to be faced.

The Colonial Development Acts

The Colonial Office had its first experience in administering aid when the Colonial Development Act of 1929 made available £1 million a year. The sponsors of the Act hoped that it would serve two purposes, to help the colonies and at the same time to provide employment in Britain. Some schemes very conveniently served both these aims. The charge that employment in Britain was all that counted is unwarranted. For instance, money was provided to build aerodromes in several colonies. The shortcomings of the Act were attributable to other circumstances. The use of the money was braked by rules that were inspired by the thought that the metropolitan country must not be lured into any

---

[18] Sir Philip Mitchell, 'General aspects of the agrarian situation in Kenya', Dispatch no. 46 of 1946 (Kenya Archives).
[19] Lauchlin Currie, 'Planning and the free enterprise system in the developing world', in *Governmental planning and political economy* (Berkeley, University of California, 1967).

permanent commitments. For loans under the Act, the beneficiary government was required to accept responsibility for servicing or repaying the loan after ten years. When grants were made, the colonial government was usually required to bear part of the expenditure, but in every case to express ability to meet the annual charges resulting from the capital investment. These conditions inhibited poor colonies from submitting schemes. Sir Bernard Bourdillon uttered a *cri de cœur* from Nigeria: 'The doctrine of self-sufficiency has never been abandoned.'[20]

In spite of the rules, however, £8,800,000 was committed in eleven years. Among the schemes were two short-term loans to help mining companies over their construction period, when for some years they would commit their capital without receiving income. One was for iron in Sierra Leone, the other for copper in Northern Rhodesia. These were examples of the use of aid to prime the private enterprise pump.

In 1939 Sir Bernard Bourdillon asked the Secretary of State for a new deal. He wrote that his subject was the economic development of the African colonies and that he raised it with less diffidence than he would have done a year earlier, because he noted evidence that the British public was awakening from its complacency. Sir Bernard went on to explain why Nigeria had received in ten years only £250,000 from the colonial development fund, and had asked for little more: he blamed the restrictive rules. He quoted Lord Hailey and W. M. Macmillan. He made a plea for 'soft' loans. Then came his main proposal, that the British government 'should accept responsibility for financing the operations of the agricultural, forestry, geological survey, veterinary and co-operative departments' and that the work of those departments 'should form the subject of a ten-year programme'.[21]

About this time a Royal Commission reported on the West Indies and made recommendations about aid. The Colonial Development and Welfare Act of 1940 has sometimes been attributed to the influence of this commission. Sir Alan Pim's report on Northern Rhodesia, coming about the same time, also exerted considerable influence. The act made £5,500,000 available annually, of which £500,000 was earmarked for research. The government acknowledged that this arrangement had been made in response to Lord Hailey's suggestion. The Fabian Colonial Bureau raised its voice in favour of planning 'in a new economic direction',[22] but, in wartime, human and physical resources were lacking. When the end of the war seemed to be approaching, the Colonial Office published in 1944 *The planning of social and economic development in the colonial empire*. This report said that the objective should be to make people healthier, wealthier and wiser, and that the nearest approach to a single criterion was 'average income per head'. This is very like the goal set in the 1958 United Nations *Manual on economic development projects* fourteen years later: 'accelerating the rate of increase of *per caput* income'. The paper of 1944 foresaw that there would be 'steady growth in the planning activities of the state'. It urged that those activities should aim 'at the stimulation rather than the restriction of private enterprise'; but while stimulating private enterprise, governments must 'ensure that the benefit of economic development accrues to the people'. Forecasts, it said, were essential.

[20] Sir Bernard Bourdillon, confidential dispatch of 5 April 1939.
[21] *Ibid.*   [22] Rita Hinden, *Plan for Africa* (London, 1941).

The first ten-year plans

In order to lend strength to a request to Parliament for much larger sums than had been comtemplated in the 1940 Act, Secretary of State Oliver Stanley wished to secure some quantification of the effective demand. This was the occasion in 1944 for asking colonial governments to submit ten-year development plans. Since plans and programmes had been matters of frequent discussion in African capitals in the thirties, this request caused no surprise. Gambia had in fact already submitted a ten-year plan in 1943,[23] a plan that was a prototype of the first African wartime colonial plans in that it proposed the co-ordinated expansion of the government departments. Nigeria was quick to follow up with its ten-year plan. There was an impression that there might be an element of 'first-come-first-served' in the allocation of the money under the act-to-be, and few officers in the colonies had any idea how much Parliament was going to make available. The Act of 1945 increased the sums for development and welfare to £120 million for the ten years 1946–56, and for research to £1 million in any financial year.

The Nigerian plan claimed that it was 'drafted on the lines of a military plan of campaign covering intended policy, but which is nevertheless sufficiently flexible to meet changing conditions'. The proposed sources of funds were as follows:

From the Colonial Development and Welfare vote		£23,000,000
To be raised by loan, partly internal		8,000,000
From Nigerian revenues		22,000,000
	Total	£53,000,000

The plan consisted 'largely of extensions to existing departmental activities', but priority was given to supplying water, adequate and pure. The most important provision of the plan was said to be development services leading to economic betterment. A board was set up to determine priorities and to allocate resources.[24]

In Tanganyika's plan for 1947–56, the aim was to improve the lot of the African farmers, with emphasis on utilization and preservation of land. Swynnerton's anti-tsetse strategy was implemented, the most spectacular result being the move of 30,000 people from the overcrowded areas of Sukumaland into the unoccupied territory of Geita. The Uganda plan included the Owen Falls Dam on the Nile. Completed in 1954, the dam provided an important source of hydro-electric power. The Uganda Plan was favourable towards African private enterprise and took the initiative in helping African entrepreneurs 'united, where possible, in African co-operative organisations'.

For general objectives, the plans accepted the statement of 1944, but Northern Rhodesia set out three specific goals: firstly, to supply the bare essentials of social and economic services that all sections of the community require; secondly, to encourage development of national assets without permitting 'exploi-

[23] Sir Hilary Blood, Dispatch no. 48, 24 June 1943 (London, Foreign and Commonwealth Office, Library).

[24] Nigeria, *A ten-year plan of development and welfare for Nigeria, 1946* (Sessional paper of 24 Dec. 1945), Lagos, 1946.

tation' of these assets; and thirdly, to assist the African population to develop under its Native Authorities with all possible speed.[25]

The words 'under its Native Authorities' in the Northern Rhodesian plan are significant. At that time colonial governments, with the exception of Kenya, were committed to the policy of using Native Authorities as the main instruments of political and social progress. It is true that doubts had arisen about this policy and that Lord Hailey had discussed it in terms that lacked enthusiasm; but the policy was still there and it implied certain social objectives in upholding tribal structures and discipline. At that time any definition of social objectives inconsistent with such a policy would have stirred up a hornet's nest. In a sense, it was just too early. Before long, however, the Native Authority policy had withered away and new political objectives in tne form of parliamentary democracy were adopted.

The specific goals set forth in the plan did not define the function of private enterprise, though the reference to exploitation presumably meant that the colonial government would take a substantial proportion of profits in taxation. Speaking in the final year of the ten, however, the head of the development department in the Colonial Office said:

Most economic development is indeed outside the government sphere. Government can help to create favourable conditions by providing basic services and ensuring a healthy state of the economy as a whole. It is the productive work of the individual which constitutes the true development.[26]

By the time the Nigerian plan was published, a Labour government had come into power in London. Naturally they looked upon planning as an instrument of socialist policy. This had not been true of the Conservative Oliver Stanley, who had originally asked the colonial governments to produce the ten-year plans. Guidance was offered the governments on how to make the plans. A white paper was published with the title *Colonial mining policy*, in which state ownership of all mineral resources was recommended. The Fabian Colonial Bureau[27] held the view that local populations should be brought into consultation, and in some colonies at this stage various committees were consulted about the plan or about parts of the plan. The Colonial Office was given an opportunity of consulting distinguished people about the plans in 1946 when the Colonial Economic Development Council was set up; but this did not prove to be an effective body and its life was short. It was suggested that there was too much welfare and not enough economic development, and the British government caused adjustments to be made with a view to spending less on welfare services and more on economic services. In 1949 the Secretary of State told Parliament that of all new moneys being put into colonial development and welfare, at least half was going into productive economic activities and less than a sixth into social services.

Total expenditure contemplated in the original ten-year plans was £178 million, of which £56 million was to come from the Colonial Development and Welfare vote, £51 million from loans and £71 million from colonial revenues.

[25] Robert E. Baldwin, *Economic development and export growth: a study of Northern Rhodesia* (Berkeley, University of California Press, 1966), p. 193.
[26] Emanuel, 'Financing of the economic development of Africa', p. 90.
[27] See Rita Hinden, *Common sense and colonial development* (London, 1949), pp. 40–3.

During the period in which they were in effect, the plans were expanded; and in some cases the enlarged version was described as a new plan. By 1953 the projected expenditure (over the ten years) had increased to £282 million. Some increase would have been necessary in any case to keep pace with inflation of costs, but a large 'real' increase resulted from the fact that financial resources of colonial governments were greater than had been expected. This was attributable partly to policies of forced saving, as noted elsewhere, and partly to genuine growth. The British government increased the aid budget by the Acts of 1950 and 1955.

The Overseas Food and the Colonial Development corporations

The striving for development was not all comprehended within the scope of the ten-year plans. The war had left ideas such as the notion that human will-power with the resources of modern technology could do things hitherto deemed impossible. This was the basic idea behind the ground-nut scheme in Tanganyika, hailed by the author of *Africa emergent* as 'the most imaginative piece of constructive work'. It was the brain-child of Frank Samuel, managing director of the United Africa Company. Samuel was influenced by the writings of Lord Boyd-Orr, who had foretold a world shortage of food, especially of edible fats. It seems odd to look back at it, considering how hard it was to sell butter and margarine during the next thirty years. However, Samuel felt that he had a mission to relieve human suffering by growing ground-nuts—following the same capital-input theory of development that had been used in creating the Mulberry Harbour for the invasion of Normandy. In order to get this enterprise started, the United Africa Company was asked to manage it for the first year, after which the Overseas Food Corporation set up by the British government took over the management. The enterprise was a disastrous failure that carried several object-lessions for developers. It was the extreme example of the capital-input theory, but it showed that other considerations are important, too. It was inherent in the scheme that great economy could be achieved in agriculture by engaging in it on a vast scale; but, although different forms of agriculture may have optimum units of varying size, it is fallacious to suppose that biggest must be best. As for the spirit of Mulberry, men and women created Mulberry without counting the cost. They sacrificed themselves in a way that could not be expected in peacetime.

Parallel with the Overseas Food Corporation, which had been set up by the Ministry of Food, the Colonial Office created the Colonial Development Corporation. The CDC launched out on a number of enterprises that were inspired by the belief that given plenty of capital and determination, the time-consuming preliminaries such as research, testing and pilot projects could be dispensed with. Also implicit in the programme was the curious idea that 'colonial conditions were hardly suitable for discussions of marginal utility',[28] whatever that may mean. (A 1950 United Nations commission of experts was also troubled by 'the inadequacy of the marginal principle'.) The early experiences of the corporation resulted in a number of failures. It became painfully clear that

---

[28] Lee, *Colonial development and good government*, p. 116.

marginal utility was not irrelevant after all. The CDC, with a new chief (Lord Reith) and new money, adopted a new policy that paid heed to the rigorous disciplines under which business enterprises have to work. In any case, the prospect of having businesses owned and managed by a British government agency, even if it was not intending to make profits, did not in all cases commend itself to African colonies. They set up corporations of their own.

Development of manufacturing

During the war, when Lord Hailey was asked to preside over a committee on post-war planning in the colonies, one of the subjects that engaged his attention was manufacturing. Before the war there had not been many factories in British colonial Africa, though Lagos had a soap-works, beer was brewed in Kenya and the Gold Coast, cigarettes were made in several places and singlets were fabricated in Nigeria and the Gold Coast—all, of course, by private enterprise. The post-war planning committee inquired of the United Africa Company what its attitude would be towards manufacturing. In response the company resolved that it would expand its manufacturing activities,[29] that it could envisage African participation and that prospects would improve if the colonies would form a customs union. When the company informed the governor of Nigeria that it had five factories in view, the governor replied that they could count on his support.

As soon as peace came, the company went ahead in Nigeria with its plans for manufacturing plywood, beer and cotton prints. Technical partners of international repute joined the beer and cotton enterprises. For the brewery, a financial formula was adopted that was to become common in Africa for import-substitution industries; that is to say, the principal importers of beer were invited to subscribe to the equity. Arrangements were made also for African beer-sellers to acquire shares. The cotton-printing project was abandoned because of a quarrel with the government of Nigeria over the possibility that excise duty might be imposed. Nevertheless, the brewery, paying excise of course, went ahead, as did the plywood mill.

During the colonial period the United Africa Company was concerned in the operation of twenty-three factories, and many industrial enterprises were started by other companies as well. A number of these undertakings brought expatriate investors into partnership with governments. The cement factory at Enugu was the first private enterprise in Nigeria to invite the public to subscribe for equity shares and to secure a quotation on the Lagos stock exchange.

For the sake of encouraging industry in East Africa, an industrial council was set up that offered monopoly rights to private entrepreneurs for the whole region. This seems to have been a misjudgement of what investors wanted, for the response to this form of inducement was disappointing. The Uganda government put 'capital into a number of diverse industrial projects'; but a Royal Commission, expressing the view that better uses might have been found for this capital, discouraged the idea that the colonial governments should engage in industrial production.

[29] United Africa Company, Board Minutes of Sept. 1941 and Sept. 1943.

Government–private-enterprise relations in the fifties

It will have become apparent that the attitude of colonial governments towards expatriate private enterprise was more favourable in the fifties than it had been in the thirties. The merchant houses, which no longer had anything to do with fixing the prices of produce, had abandoned the practice of trying to influence the prices of imported goods by agreements. The leading companies had introduced pension schemes for their employees and had done a great deal for education, especially in the technical sphere. They were redeploying their activities into manufacturing, which was popular. Nevertheless, there had been some critical moments. The left wing of the Labour Party would have liked to nationalize the large companies working in the colonies; but the Labour Secretary of State, Arthur Creech-Jones, who did not hold those views, resisted the pressure. However, shortly after the riots of 1948, the government of the Gold Coast suggested to the UAC that the activities of the company in the Gold Coast should be entrusted to a new company having Africans on its board and offering opportunities to African investors.[30] In the course of years both those steps were taken by the company, but in 1948 the UAC board took the position that neither step would be appropriate. The issue to be faced at that time was not who should control the company, but who should control the government. That same year the House of Commons Select Committee on Estimates paid a visit to West Africa and displayed particular interest in the activities of private enterprise. There was a demand in political circles for an inquiry into 'monopolies' in the colonies. The upshot was that in 1949 the Colonial Economic Research Committee requested an economist, P. T. Bauer, to study the organization of trade in Nigeria and Gold Coast. Bauer's findings, which were published in 1954, provided a penetrating study of the oligopsonistic and oligopolistic tendencies in the private sector.[31] (Oligopsony denotes a market condition where there are few buyers; oligopoly, where there are few sellers.) The only monopolies that were discovered, however, were those established by the governments for handling the crops.

Second-generation plans

The decade of the plans slipped by and it was time to prepare some more. The second-generation plans were drawn up to cover five years.[32] Planners now had assistance from the International Bank for Reconstruction and Development, which sent missions to Africa. The United Nations had entered the planning business with its commission of experts in 1950, and the Food and Agriculture Organization helped the Tanganyika government in 1955. Not only advice but also money was now available internationally, and notably from the United States.

The federal government of Nigeria adopted an economic programme for 1955–60, the cost of which was to be £91 million. The regional governments in

[30] *Ibid.*, 3 March 1948.
[31] P. T. Bauer, *West African trade: a study of competition, oligopoly and monopoly in a changing society* (London, 1954).
[32] Great Britain, *Economic development in the United Kingdom dependencies* (London, 1957).

Nigeria also drew up plans, and together they proposed to spend more money than the federal government. The content of the regional plans reflected the powers that had been conferred on the regions by the constitution recently adopted. Whereas the federal government dealt with communications and power, the regions were concerned with education, health and agriculture. In Tanganyika the second plan (1957) consisted of schemes formulated on the initiative of African members of the Legislative Council.

By this time two major projects were engaging attention, the Kariba Dam on the Zambezi and the Akasombo Dam on the Volta. The decision to proceed with the Kariba Dam was taken in 1955. Towards the estimated cost of £114 million, contributions were made by the International Bank, the Colonial Development Corporation, the Commonwealth Finance Corporation, the companies mining copper in Northern Rhodesia, other private enterprise firms and the federal government of Rhodesia and Nyasaland. The Volta river project had begun as private enterprise. In the thirties a successful businessman named Duncan Rose decided that his next venture should take the form of developing a major source of electric power for converting bauxite into alumina. After seeking in several continents for a place where bauxite could be mined near a river capable of generating power, he chose the Gold Coast. He spent ten years in scientific exploration and in negotiating with chiefs and government to secure facilities. In 1949, when he was anxious to start, the government would not grant the final assent. After long delay, it said that the project could not go forward as private enterprise. By this time it was expected that the Gold Coast would shortly be independent, and it was felt wise to defer the scheme for consideration by the independent government.

Summing up

My original intention was to use the term 'laissez-faire' in the title of this essay. But unfortunately the phrase carries a variety of connotations. To some people it might mean letting private entrepreneurs do what they liked; to others it would reflect the attitude of the British government in leaving colonial governments to do the best they could with their own resources. Chamberlain's infrastructure policy signified a break from both those attitudes. The construction of ports and railways by governments took place long before any substantial section of opinion in Britain had embraced the view that public ownership of important services was theoretically desirable. The starting-point in Africa was different. Governments built railways and ports because they held out no hope of commercial returns on private capital. Hence activity of governments in this field was not a take-over from private enterprise. The intention was to help private enterprise by providing infrastructure. The 'mixed economy' that resulted has persisted in Africa and is a feature of recent statements of the philosophy of African socialism.

The infrastructure policy stimulated development, and crops increased. The governments stepped in to regulate the activities of private enterprise in purchasing and processing the yield. The regulation of marketing was sometimes welcomed by established firms. Although such regulation was motivated partly by the urge to protect supposedly unsophisticated Africans from private entrepreneurs, it also acted as a restraint on competition between private entrepre-

neurs. Africans who wanted to make money by trading in produce were sometimes placed at a disadvantage.

However, this was incidental, and it was certainly no part of the policy of
colonial governments to discourage African traders. If the import and export
trades were mostly in foreign hands, it was because such activity required much
capital and involved large risks that could be considered only by international
companies. During the Second World War, some colonial governments reserved quotas in these trades for Africans. Inland distribution, up to the end of
the colonial period, came progressively into the hands of Asian traders; and
since the opportunities they seized were open equally to others, their success
must be attributed at least to some degree to their propensity for hard work, as
well as to a willingness to operate with high risks and low profit margins. In
plantation agriculture the colonial governments placed severe restraints on international companies and reserved most of the major export crops for the indigenous cultivators. In trade, because foreign firms, especially French, held
large shares, British firms enjoyed no exclusive advantages.

In any case, the trading companies did not have a narrow, nationalistic attitude. Thus, it might happen that a French trading company represented an important British manufacturer, while the principal British trading house sold the
products of that manufacturer's American competitor. The imperial preference
system, under which imports from the British Empire were taxed at lower rates
than foreign goods, was adopted in Sierra Leone and the Gambia only, for in
Nigeria and the Gold Coast and in East Africa the British government was committed by international treaties to an open-door trade policy. In mining, the
British government was concerned to keep major resources under British control, though this policy did not entirely exclude foreign investors from mining.
In Northern Rhodesia, for instance, there was an important American stake in
copper.

With the advent of the era of planning, the function of increasing 'production' was left to private enterprise, both local and expatriate. For expatriate
capital, production could only mean manufacturing, because restraints on the
acquisition of land denied agriculture to foreign investors as a growth sector;
and in the tradition of the infrastructure policy, governments kept their hands
on the production of electricity, which included hydro-electric dams. Before the
end of the colonial period there was considerable investment in manufacturing
by expatriate private enterprise. When a report to the 84th Congress of the
United States indicated that the expatriate companies in Africa had 'no iden-
tifiable place in official development plans', colonial governments might have
replied that by omitting manufacturing industry from the plans they had identified that field as the area of growth for the companies.

What judgment may be passed on the ten-year plans? The plans were carried
through, for the most part, and in fact the only failure that attracted attention
was the rural portion of the Northern Rhodesian plan. The resources allocated
to this aspect of the plan proved inadequate, and the methods employed were
too paternalistic in that they ignored the fact that 'the African farmer is profit-
oriented'.[33] In general, the decade 1946–55 was prosperous. Revenue at least
trebled in most colonies. In Nigeria and Uganda it increased more than four-
fold, in the Gold Coast more than eightfold, as shown in Table 10.

[33] Baldwin, *Economic development and export growth*, p. 203.

Table 10. *Territorial revenue, selected countries*
(in £1,000)

Country	1946	1954–5
Gold Coast	9,328	77,100
Kenya	9,057	29,675 (1955–6)
Nigeria	13,200 (1945–6)	62,698
Northern Rhodesia	3,362	13,847
Nyasaland	1,287	4,303
Tanganyika	4,500 (1945)	15,042
Uganda	3,891	19,476

Between the late 1930s and the mid-1950s, as Table 11 demonstrates, imports and exports alike increased phenomenally. These indices of prosperity far exceed anything that occurred in later years when plans became more comprehensive. Yet in a later generation of planners there has been a tendency to decry the plans of the colonial era.[34] However, an authority on planning who in early years was very critical of the colonial plans, but who came to think better of them after twenty years, said:

The rate of economic growth depends not so much on government expenditure as it does on whether farmers plant more, the business men build more factories, and the mines increase their investment. If conditions are favourable to the expansion of such activities, the economy will grow rapidly whether there is a development plan or not. From this one may deduce the legitimate role of a development plan, which is to help create conditions favourable for growth . . . The earliest development plans did not pretend to be able to predict or control the rate of economic growth. They confined themselves to bringing order and co-ordination into the planning of government expenditures. This was a valuable and much-needed service.[35]

Table 11. *Imports and exports, selected countries*
(in £1,000)

Country	1938		1953	
	Imports	Exports	Imports	Exports
Gambia	277	289	2,219	2,860
Gold Coast	10,380	15,425	73,803	89,943
Kenya, Tanganyika and Uganda	13,116	2,555	105,834	87,445
Nigeria	11,567	14,391	108,291	121,988
Northern Rhodesia	5,234	10,135	51,833	93,742
Nyasaland	832	975	7,580	7,118
Somaliland	728	208	2,086 (1952–3)	1,030 (1952–3)
Zanzibar	994	845	5,940	7,967

SOURCE: *Whitaker's Almanack* and *Statesman's Yearbook.*

[34] Federation of Nigeria, *National development plan 1962–68* (Lagos, 1969), p. 6.
[35] W. A. (Sir Arthur) Lewis, *Aggrey-Fraser-Guggisberg memorial lectures summary* (Accra, 1968, third lecture).

If economic activity is to flourish, it is more important that governments should govern than that they should plan, and in the decade of the first plans the governments provided stability and confidence.

Colonial governments in 1945 possessed neither the powers to restrict the free choice of individual consumers and producers in the manner that is postulated by plans to direct the whole economy, nor the statistical basis for such planning. The earliest studies of national income in tropical Africa became available only in 1948.[36] Furthermore, no conscious direction of the monetary system was possible inasmuch as colonial governments had neither central banks nor national currencies.

Should social objectives have been defined more precisely? Colonial governments were committed, at the time of the inception of the plans, to two policies of great social significance: one, that the Native Authorities should constitute the social framework; and the other, that farmers should receive the full value of their crops. However, both these policies, as we have explained, were abandoned while the plans were being carried out. The social consequences of using the crop-marketing system to impose forced saving on the rural community, and of employing resources thus diverted to subsidize the urban community, were not foreseen. The Native Authority policy was abandoned because it became politically impossible to maintain any system that was not consistent with the most rapid movement towards independence on a basis of parliamentary democracy. Clearly, therefore, the ten-year plans were not related to consistently pursued social objectives; they nevertheless did provide a framework of action for making colonial governments more effective.

Private enterprise continued to be the mainspring of economic activity, though now excluded from the export trade in the main crops. In the era with which this book is concerned, private enterprise had played its part in rapid economic growth. The evidence for that has been given in the figures quoted and there is no need to repeat them. The most spectacular developments had been in the cultivation of cocoa and of ground-nuts for export; both were produced by the enterprise of African farmers and marketed by the enterprise of European merchants. The growth of these trades is, in itself, sufficient evidence that the merchant companies provided buying services that stimulated an enthusiastic response from farmers. The prices paid, clearly, were attractive. There was active competition between merchants at all times except during the brief episode of the cocoa pool, and this enabled the farmers to secure prices closely related to international market levels. The provision of credit in the form of advances during the growing season was a service on which the agricultural community set great value.

However, competitive private enterprise had produced a structure of trade that could hardly have been expected to win the approval of African nationalists as the continent moved into the era of independence. At the end of the colonial era, though the large operations of exporting had recently been taken over by government corporations, the large operations of importing were controlled by European companies. The vast retailing activities in the markets and villages were mainly in the hands of Africans, most of whom traded on credit supplied

[36] Phyllis Deane, *The measurement of colonial national incomes: an experiment* (Cambridge University Press, 1948).

by the European companies. The situation was complicated by the presence of Asian trading communities, Indians in the east and mainly Lebanese in the west. They competed with the Europeans as importers and also with the Africans as retailers, but sometimes they provided a service complementary to both importing and retailing by acting as large wholesalers. Occasionally an African, a man or woman with an aptitude for commerce, would establish a prosperous business that was able to import merchandise direct from other continents; but such persons were not numerous.

The division of functions in the distributive trades between Europeans, Asians and Africans was not supported by laws or rules, but it was reinforced by communal attitudes and aptitudes. Certain efforts of colonial governments to help African merchants to engage in the larger operations of commerce had met with little success. In this matter, as in others, the private-enterprise system carried on under its own momentum, without needing or wishing to depend on the favours of governments. This was perhaps best illustrated by the international composition of the trading community, where important elements from France, the United States, Switzerland, India, the Lebanon and other countries engaged in business no less successfully than the British.

BIBLIOGRAPHY

Baldwin, Robert E. *Economic development and export growth: a study of Northern Rhodesia, 1920–1960.* Berkeley, University of California Press, 1966.

Bauer, P. T. *Dissent on development: studies and debates in development economics.* Cambridge, Mass., Harvard University Press, 1972.

Economic analysis and policy in underdeveloped countries. Durham, N.C., Duke University Press, 1957.

West African trade: a study of competition, oligopoly and monopoly in a changing economy. London, 1954.

Bourret, F. M. *The Gold Coast: a survey of the Gold Coast and British Togoland 1919–1946.* Stanford University Press, 1949.

Burns, Sir Alan C. *History of Nigeria.* 7th ed. London, 1969.

Cairncross, Sir Alexander K. *Home and foreign investment, 1870–1913: studies in capital accumulation.* Cambridge University Press, 1953.

Cohen, Sir Andrew. *British policy in changing Africa.* London, 1959.

Deane, Phyllis. *Colonial social accounting.* Cambridge University Press, 1953.

The measurement of colonial national incomes, an experiment. Cambridge University Press, 1948.

Dike, Kenneth O. *Trade and politics in the Niger Delta, 1830–1885: an introduction to the economic and political history of Nigeria.* Oxford, Clarendon Press, 1956.

Emanuel, A. 'The financing of the economic development of Africa', in *International days for African studies.* Ghent, International Fair, 1956.

Frankel, S. Herbert. *Capital development in Africa: its course and effects.* London, Oxford University Press, 1938.

The economic impact on underdeveloped societies: essays on international development and social change. Oxford, 1953.

Gaitskell, Arthur. *Gezira: a story of development in the Sudan.* London, 1959.

Geiger, Theodore, and Winifred Armstrong. *The development of African private enterprise.* Washington, D.C., National Planning Association [1964].

Great Britain. *Parliamentary papers*. Vol. x, Cmd 4556. *Report of the Kenya Land Commission*. London, 1934.

Vol. ix, Cmd 5845. *Report of the Commission on the Marketing of West African Cocoa*. London, 1938.

Cmd 6950. *Statement of the future of marketing of West African cocoa*. London, 1946.

Vol. xiii, Cmd 9475. *Report of the East Africa Royal Commission*. London, 1955.

Hancock, Sir William K. *Survey of British Commonwealth affairs*. 2 vols. London, Oxford University Press, 1937–42.

Hailey, William Malcolm Hailey, 1st baron. *An African survey: a study of problems arising in Africa south of the Sahara*. London, Oxford University Press, 1938.

An African survey: revised 1956. London, Oxford University Press, 1957.

Hill, Polly. *The migrant cocoa farmers of southern Ghana: a study in rural capitalism*. Cambridge University Press, 1963.

Studies in rural capitalism in West Africa. Cambridge University Press, 1970.

Hinden, Rita. *Common sense and colonial development: report to the Fabian Colonial Bureau*. London, 1949.

Plan for Africa. London, 1941.

Hunter, Guy. *The best of both worlds? A challenge on development policies in Africa*. London, 1967.

Jones, Thomas Jesse. *Education in East Africa: a study of East, Central and South Africa by the Second African Education Commission*. New York, Phelps-Stokes Fund, 1925.

Kamarck, Andrew M. *The economics of African development*. New York, 1967.

Kingsley, Mary Henrietta. *Travels in West Africa: Congo français, Corisco and Cameroons*. London, 1897.

Knowles, Lilliam C. A. *The economic development of the British overseas empire*. London, 1924.

Lee, John Michael. *Colonial development and good government: a study of the ideas expressed by the British official classes in planning decolonization, 1939–1964*. Oxford, Clarendon Press, 1967.

Leubuscher, Charlotte. *Bulk buying from the colonies: a study of the bulk purchase of colonial commodities by the United Kingdom government*. London, Oxford University Press, 1956.

Tanganyika territory: a study of economic policy under mandate. London, 1944.

The West African shipping trade, 1909–1959. Leyden, 1963.

Lewis, Sir Arthur, ed. *Tropical development 1880–1913*. Evanston, Northwestern University Press, 1970.

Lugard, Frederick John Dealtry Lugard, 1st baron. *The dual mandate in British tropical Africa*. Edinburgh. 1922.

McPhee, Allan. *The economic revolution in British West Africa*. 2nd ed. London, 1971.

Masefield, Geoffrey Bussell. *Agricultural change in Uganda, 1945–1960*. Stanford University, Food Research Institute, 1962.

A short history of agriculture in the British colonies. Oxford, 1950.

Neumark, S. Daniel. *Foreign trade and the economic development of Africa: a historical perspective*. Stanford University, Food Research Institute, 1963.

Newbury, Colin W. 'Trade and authority in West Africa from 1850 to 1880', in *Colonialism in Africa 1870–1960, Vol. 1: The history and politics of colonialism 1870–1914*, L. H. Gann and Peter Duignan, eds. Cambridge University Press, 1969.

Nkrumah, Kwame. *Africa must unite*. London, 1963.

Pedler, Sir Frederick J. *Economic geography of West Africa*. London, 1955.

West Africa. London, 1959.

Robinson, Ronald, and John Gallagher, with Alice Denny. *Africa and the Victorians: the official mind of imperialism*. London, 1963.

Schlote, Werner. *British overseas trade from 1700 to the 1930's*. Oxford, 1952.

Segal, Harvey H., and Mathew Simon. 'British foreign capital investment, 1856–1894', *Journal of Economic History*, 1961, **22**, no. 4.

Shonfield, Andrew. *British economic policy since the war*. Harmondsworth, Middlesex, 1958.

Slinn, Peter. 'Commercial concessions and politics during the colonial period', *African Affairs*, Oct. 1971, **70**, no. 281.

Szereszewski, Robert. *Structural changes in the economy of Ghana, 1891–1911*. London, 1965.

Ward, W. E. F. *A history of Ghana*. London, 1963.

CHAPTER 4

FRENCH ECONOMIC POLICY
IN TROPICAL AFRICA

by

VIRGINIA THOMPSON *and* RICHARD ADLOFF

The colonial policy of France, like that of other Western imperial powers, was inspired to varying degrees by the profit motive, by the spirit of adventure and conquest and, above all, by nationalism.[1] The last-mentioned element was accentuated by the conviction felt by many Frenchmen that their institutions and their civilization were superior and universally valid and, specifically, that implanting them in their colonies would benefit the native populations. *'Mission civilisatrice'* was the euphemistic term devised to gloss over the incompatibility between their materialistic and their humanitarian objectives, as well as the contradictions inherent in France's own legacy of authoritarianism and liberalism.

One or the other of these conflicting tendencies dominated French colonial policy throughout the country's history, and none of the compromises by which successive French governments tried to reconcile them met with whole-hearted popular support. France's early overseas ventures caused such great financial and territorial losses to the state as to convince public opinion that colonies were an economic liability and not an asset. Eventually the French people were persuaded to accept the empire presented to them by enterprising individuals, but only when and in so far as this gratified their national pride. That feeling developed first around the concept of the colonies as satellites contributing to the metropole, then as an integral part of the republic and finally as members of a partnership in which the colonial peoples were bound to France by ties of culture and self-interest.

For nearly three hundred years trading monopolies, based on seventeenth-century mercantilism, characterized French economic operations in the colonies. They epitomized the view, widespread in France, that by virtue of conquest or by treaty the colonies were French property and, as such, existed to enhance the metropole's power and influence. To some extent, revolutionary changes in France itself and in the world led to liberalization of this mercantilist heritage with the passage of time. This was true more in the political and social domains, however, than in the economic sphere. Practical obstacles, imposed by diverse natural and cultural conditions, also breached the uniform administrative structure that France tried to create in all its colonies; but they did not alter its fundamental principles. These were the centralization of authority in Paris, the primacy of metropolitan over colonial interests and the unity of France and its overseas dependencies. However, the successive names by

[1] See Henri Brunschwig, *Mythes et réalités de l'impérialisme colonial français, 1871–1914* (Paris, 1960).

which France and its distant possessions were known—the Empire, the French Union and the Franco-African Community—as well as the term 'Overseas France', reflected changes in the temper of the times and greater flexibility in application rather than in basic tenets.

The revolutionary spirit of 1789 introduced the element of liberal egalitarianism into French colonial policy, and united those who opposed imperialistic expansion on financial or humanitarian grounds. After the Napoleonic wars, France was left with only remnants of the far-flung empire it had held a hundred years before. Later in the nineteenth century, however, France acquired a second group of colonies, mainly in the Far East and Africa, even larger and more dispersed than the first group. Its tropical African possessions, until then restricted to scattered coastal trading posts, comprised most of West and part of Equatorial Africa, the small enclave of Somaliland on the Red Sea and the great island of Madagascar off the continent's south-eastern coast. After the First World War, the major areas of German Togoland and Kamerun became French-administered mandates under the League of Nations and, after the Second World War, trust territories of the United Nations.

Because of adverse climatic conditions, soil deficiencies and the shortage of labour, none of France's new sub-Saharan African acquisitions was suited to European colonization or to plantation agriculture. Haphazard exploration and conquest, as well as international treaties, created artificial frontiers in West Africa both between the French dependencies themselves and between them and Liberia, the Spanish Sahara and the generally richer and more populous British colonies. In eastern Africa, French Somaliland and Madagascar were isolated from the bulk of France's colonial empire. Early in the twentieth century, France grouped its contiguous sub-Saharan colonies into two similarly structured federations, and with minor variations applied to them the same administrative and economic policies. The evolution of French Equatorial Africa (AEF), because of its greater distance from France, even smaller natural and manpower resources and international treaties that gave birth to the Belgian and French Congos, differed somewhat from that of French West Africa (AOF).

During the lull of nearly a half-century between its two empires, there occurred a temporary revision of France's colonial policy, in which religious considerations took priority over military and economic ones. The material support hesitantly given to persecuted Catholic missionaries led to territorial acquisitions in the Pacific and the Far East, but France stopped short of confrontations that would have involved it in hostilities with Great Britain. Indeed, an Anglo-French agreement in 1860, relaxed the trading restrictions theretofore imposed by France on its colonies—a policy known initially as the Colonial Pact and later as the *économie de traite*. Under either name, it required the French colonies to export their raw materials to France and to import French merchandise, in a closed economic circuit designed to exclude foreign traders and shipping. During the periods when the policy was enforced, a few trading companies profited by their monopolies, but the financial burden it placed on the state's revenues confirmed the anti-colonialism of those who opposed imperialism on moral or economic principles. In any case, throughout most of the nineteenth century, the French were generally indifferent to events outside France and felt no need of colonies as an outlet for their foreign trade or their surplus population.

The defeat of France by Prussia in 1870 and the development of French industry gave new impetus to empire-building. This was true especially among the military and with politicians, as well as among a few businessmen, journalists and explorers. In general, however, French capitalists preferred to invest in countries other than their colonies, and French traders and industrialists supported colonial expansion only on condition that their former monopolies be restored. Army officers, backed by small but dynamic groups, such as the Colonial Party in the Parliament and the Comité de l'Afrique Française, effectively propagated the view that France needed an empire to revive its military glory and to prevent Britain from dominating the world. Their activities were supported by the Union Coloniale, a congeries of industrialists, merchants and bankers actually or potentially interested in France's colonies. None of these colonial propagandists could have believed that imperialism would be financially profitable to France, but they argued cogently that it was indispensable for national prestige. As a sop to those Frenchmen who still actively opposed overseas conquest and colonial administration as more costly than rewarding, a law was passed at the turn of the century that required the newly acquired African colonies to become self-supporting except for military defence and such public works as were of 'imperial' interest.

In terms of economic development, the price that the French colonies paid for such a policy was high. Public investments, which were small, took the form of loans repayable with interest from the federations' revenues. French private capital invested in the colonies was even more meagre and was concentrated in trading enterprises, whose monopolies the state was expected to enforce. Such changes as occurred in this mercantilist tradition were not in its principles but in the methods employed and in the nature of Franco-African trade. Tariff barriers, not armadas, were the means now used to exclude foreign competition, and colonial exports no longer comprised bullion, slaves and wild produce but, increasingly, lumber and cultivated produce needed by France's expanding industries. Exports of French manufactured goods to the colonies were relatively insignificant, for the Africans had not yet acquired either the desire or the purchasing power for such merchandise.

The wars of 1870, 1914 and 1939, and the economic depressions of the inter-war years, were the catalysts that changed France's attitude toward its subject peoples, but they brought no loosening of French economic controls over the colonies. Because these events enhanced the colonies' value as sources of manpower and materials for France, a greater effort was made to increase their productivity and the well-being of their inhabitants. The goal of France's successive public-works programme for its dependencies, and of the imperial conference of 1935, was not to make the colonies self-sufficient but to integrate them more closely with the French economy. To this objective must be added, in all fairness, the French people's concern to express their gratitude for the heavy contributions made by the colonial peoples to the defence of France during the two world wars, when they suffered great losses and severe hardships. Consequently both liberals and businessmen gave their support to the policy known as 'assimilation', which assumed that the colonial peoples could have no higher ambition or good fortune than to be united with France and to achieve equal status with metropolitan Frenchmen. This belief was also widely shared by the Francophone African élite, until time proved it to be unrealistic and the rise of African nationalism made it appear to them less desirable.

Unfortunately for the effectiveness of France's three overseas development plans, their conception coincided with periods of severe financial stringency and they were carried out only in part and sometimes wastefully. Yet by the early 1950s massive injections of French public funds had given the two federations a modern infrastructure and had also helped to increase the volume, the value and the variety of African production and foreign trade. Furthermore, they were accompanied by political reforms that gave popularly elected Africans greater control over their budgets and development plans, as well as French citizenship and voting power in the French Parliament (1946). This was followed by the adoption of an enlightened overseas labour code (1952), the institution of elected municipal governments (1955), a larger measure of territorial autonomy (1956) and, finally, the grant of independence (1960). Economic emancipation, however, did not keep pace with political progress, and, despite their admission to the European Economic Community (1957), the newly sovereign African states continued to depend largely on French aid.

The elimination of federal subsidies and services in the course of Francophone Africa's rapid political evolution placed such a financial burden on the new national entities' meagre revenues as to make them economically unviable without large-scale foreign capital and technology. France assured both through bilateral treaties, negotiated with all the territories but Guinea on the eve of their independence, in return for their pledge to remain in the franc zone and to maintain French trading privileges. France's share of this *quid pro quo* included its continuing to pay the salaries of its technicians and teachers serving in Francophone Africa, as well as for the major educational development projects. Pre-independence status was also perpetuated for African civil servants, wage earners and export-crop farmers, and to a lesser degree for the immigrant Levantine merchants. In brief, thanks to France's sizeable subsidies, the nascent African bourgeoisie would share with transient foreigners the protection, the privileges and the monopolies that had characterized the economy of French Black Africa under the colonial régime.

Why French taxpayers should have been willing to support such a costly policy, after their former African dependencies had become associate members of the European Common Market and politically independent, can be explained only by a marked change in France's concept of national grandeur. To be sure, the French had never expected their colonies to be—nor had they ever been—a source of profit except to a few companies, businessmen and banks. Apparently, however, the burden imposed by the government's overseas policy, both militarily and financially, had been rising since the Second World War in reverse proportion to the satisfaction of national pride. In the mid-1950s, the revolt in Algeria and the loss of Indochina, Tunisia and Morocco caused a resurgence of anti-colonialism in France, notably among the conservatives, who urged that the public funds being allotted to Africa would be better spent in modernizing the French economy. They might well have carried the day had it not been for concurrent events in France and Africa, which more than any other factors accounted for Francophone Black Africa's swift and bloodless political emancipation and, to some extent, for its continued economic dependence. The two events chiefly responsible for this evolution were the granting of independence to Ghana in 1957 and General de Gaulle's return to power in France in 1958.

In conformity with his policy of reinforcing France's position as a great power, De Gaulle used French public funds, as had his predecessors, to perpetuate French influence and to promote French business interests in tropical Africa. Successively, however, he introduced changes to meet the Africans' rising demands for independence and economic development. First, in a referendum, he offered Africans a choice between immediate, total independence, on the one hand, and, on the other, autonomy with continuing French aid, in a Franco-African Community. Although all the sub-Saharan territories except Guinea opted for the second choice, by late 1950 they were asking for both independence and aid as their price for maintaining close relations with France. Faced now with a virtual ultimatum himself, De Gaulle decided to sacrifice France's political sovereignty in Africa so as to salvage its cultural and economic interests there. In this he succeeded brilliantly. He not only exercised throughout his lifetime an unrivalled personal influence over the leaders of Francophone Africa, but also made his African policy an integral part of the Gaullist heritage for his successor.

Planning

Until the post-World War I economic depression, French trading companies almost completely dominated the African colonies' economy. The government's role was confined to enforcing their monopolies against foreign intervention and to financing the construction of a few public works and military installations. In 1921, Albert Sarraut, then colonial minister, introduced the concept of state planning for the empire, with a view to making France and its colonies as self-sufficient economically as possible. Admittedly, this would further subordinate the colonies' economy to that of France; but for the first time the empire would be developed as an interrelated unit and French public funds would be used to promote the colonies' productivity. By 1922, however, France's empty treasury and the nonpayment of the expected German reparations caused the Sarraut plan to be abandoned after negligible accomplishments. The only major public works undertaken in the 1920s were improvements in the port of Dakar and the launching of a large-scale irrigation project in the central delta of the Niger river.

In 1931 the still-born Sarraut plan was revived and given new impetus by the world depression. Two laws passed that year initiated a program of public works for each colony and authorized the state to underwrite loans for their execution. This policy hastened the colonies' economic recovery, which began in 1934 and continued until it was interrupted by the Second World War. During the war, the economy of AOF retrogressed, but that of AEF and Cameroun forged ahead because of their political affiliations, respectively, with the Vichy régime and with the Free French. Even before the war ended, the Gaullist authorities drafted a new plan for the modernization and equipment of all the colonies.

The overseas plan of 1946 represented no departure from the principles laid down by Sarraut in 1921 or from the policy of state financial aid and the protectionist legislation of the 1930s. It was innovative, however, in vastly expanding the scope of its action, particularly in the social domain, and, above all, in providing the means for its implementation. It set up a Fonds d'Investissements pour le Développement Economique et Social (FIDES), which supplied annual subsidies from the metropolitan budget, supplemented by far smaller contributions from African territorial revenues, for the construction and upkeep, respectively, of the plan projects. Another novel institution was the Caisse Centrale de l'Outre-Mer (CCOM), created to handle the FIDES accounts and also to grant long-term, low-interest loans from other public funds to private firms and African public bodies whose operations would promote the overall objectives of the plan.

During the first decade of its execution, the plan's orientation, funding and management underwent significant changes. This metamorphosis resulted from the lessons of experience, from France's depleted financial resources and its conservative governments and from stronger African demands for more control over the plan projects. The credits initially allotted to the FIDES for the African territories were cut by 15 per cent, the original ten-year plan was replaced in 1949 by a series of four-year plans that were frequently revised and the Paris directorate of the FIDES was increasingly criticized for its cumbersome procedures and wasteful expenditures.

About two-thirds of the funds available to the African dependencies from 1948 to 1952 were allotted to the means of communication, less than one-fifth to the increasing of production, and the balance to social development. Moreover, as shown in Table 12, the fund's geographical distribution generally favoured the more developed coastal territories at the expense of the poorer and more populous hinterland, whose production stagnated and whose youthful inhabitants gravitated in growing numbers to the overcrowded towns. Territorial revenues were being rapidly depleted to pay for the maintenance of the plan projects, and French public funds were perforce financing an ever-larger proportion of the African development programmes.

By 1952, both French and Africans agreed that the plan must be revised so as to increase production for African consumers, to concentrate on projects that promised rapid financial returns, to make the management of the FIDES more efficient and to encourage the investment of more private capital to offset the shrinkage in public-funds allocations. Subsequently, price-support funds were created for certain African exports, FIDES grants were made for a longer period, the cost of some essential consumer-goods imports in Africa was re-

Table 12. *Distribution of FIDES funds, 1948–52*

Mauritania	$15,100,000
Senegal	140,500,000
Guinea	78,700,000
Ivory Coast	109,000,000
Soudan (Mali)	79,400,000
Upper Volta	44,700,000
Dahomey	49,000,000
Niger	25,200,000
Chad	55,800,000
Oubangui-Chari	50,400,000
Middle Congo	91,000,000
Gabon	49,600,000

SOURCE: France, Ambassade, Service de Presse et d'Information, *French Africa: a decade of progress, 1948–1958; achievements of FIDES* . . . (New York, Nov. 1958).

duced by subsidies and the transfer of French capital from Indochina was encouraged by fiscal concessions. As to the selection of projects to be undertaken in future plans, opinion was divided among both French experts and African politicians. Some advocated promoting large-scale mining and electric-power enterprises, whereas others preferred a modernization of the traditional African economy through scientific agricultural research and a programme of modest rural public works. A compromise between the two views was reached eventually, but it was weighted on the side of maximum industrialization.

Undeniably the plan's greatest material achievement was in transport and urbanization. Its outstanding failure was its inability to promote productivity sufficiently to keep pace with the growth in the African infrastructure and population. Before 1960, the plan's agricultural goals had been reached only for timber and certain export crops; the processing industries and mining had just begun to expand. Neither France's financial commitments to its erstwhile colonies nor the colonies' economic dependence on French aid had been appreciably reduced by their membership in the European Common Market. Yet, after the African territories became independent, considerations that were largely political induced France to maintain its financial contributions to the new African states, and, mainly for psychological reasons, the zeal of the new governments for planning continued unabated. The mere drafting of a plan has seemingly convinced the African leaders that they can control their economic future, even though none of the plans has ever been fully implemented or carried out without major foreign aid.

Finances

The financial history of the French Black African colonies falls roughly into four periods: from 1900 to 1931, from 1932 to the Second World War, through the first post-war decade, and from the *Loi-Cadre* of 1956 to independence in 1960. In each of these periods, official French policy was the decisive factor in the determination of private as well as public investments, in revaluation of the currency, and in African budgetary revenues and expenditures. The government's financial policy, in turn, was influenced by political and psychological considerations, as well as by international economic conditions and by the world wars and their aftermath. Nevertheless, certain constant elements characterized this whole evolution. These were the almost exclusively French origin of all the colonial investments; the predominance of French public over private capital, with the concentration of the public funds in the colonial infrastructure and of the private in commercial and allied enterprises; currency instability in the tightly structured franc zone; and the sparsity of African revenues.

The principle of colonial financial autonomy and self-sufficiency, laid down in the law of 13 April 1900, was generally adhered to until the world depression of the early 1930s. Throughout that period, French public expenditures in Africa were directly invested only in military and port installations and in the Office du Niger irrigation project. Indirectly they took the form of loans to finance other public works, notably railroad construction, repayable from federal revenues at interest rates ranging from 3·5 to 6·5 per cent. From the formation of the federations until the outbreak of the Second World War, France guaranteed six loans to West Africa and three to Equatorial Africa. Because accurate statistics are lacking and because the franc was twice devalued in the inter-war years, the worth of these loans in terms of contemporary currencies is hard to determine. Furthermore, the loans did not include the special budgets and the subsidies, both financed from French public funds, for projects such as the Office du Niger, radio stations, mobile health units and the like, or for meeting colonial budgetary deficits.

The most authoritative estimates of French investments in Black Africa, as shown in Tables 13 and 14, were those made by S. H. Frankel in 1936 and by

Table 13. *Capital investment in French Black Africa, 1870–1936*
(estimates in thousands of pounds sterling)

| Area | Investments | | Non-registered capital | General total |
	Public	Private		
AEF	15,248	5,000	1,012	21,260
AOF	16,477	12,500	1,449	30,426
Cameroun ⎫ Togo ⎭	11,306	6,431	887	18,624
Total	43,031	23,931	3,348	70,310

SOURCE: S. Herbert Frankel, *Capital investment in Africa* (London, Oxford University Press, 1938), Tables 28, 29, 48, as condensed by Jean Suret-Canale, *Afrique noire occidentale et centrale*, vol. II, *L'ère coloniale (1900–1945)* (Paris, 1964), p. 206.

Table 14. *Volume of French investments in AOF, AEF, Cameroun and Togo, 1900–40*
(in thousands of 1940 francs)

| Branch of activity | Investments of | | Total investments | Per cent by branch (or group of branches) of investments |
	Companies	Private individuals *		
Business	8,761,962	1,752,392	10,514,354	39 ⎫
Construction	814,953	81,495	896,448	3·5 ⎬ 48·5
Banking	1,556,732	—	1,556,732	6 ⎭
Industries	2,176,801	435,460	2,612,161	9·6 ⎫
Mines	1,860,304	186,030	2,046,334	7·5 ⎬ 17·1
Transportation	879,150	87,915	967,065	3·6 3·6
Plantations	2,451,848	2,451,848	4,903,696	18 ⎫
Livestock-breeding	71,450	14,290	85,740	0·3 ⎬ 30·8
Forestry	1,933,236	1,449,927	3,383,163	12·5 ⎭
Private investments, total	20,506,436	6,459,357	26,965,693	
Public investments (loans)	7,033,014	—	7,033,014	
Global total	27,539,450	6,459,357	33,998,707	

* Amounts given are estimates.

SOURCE: Jean Suret-Canale, *Afrique noire occidentale et centrale*, vol. II, *L'ère coloniale (1900–1945)* (Paris, 1964).

the Ministry of Colonies in 1943. The estimates diverged somewhat, partly because they did not cover precisely the same time span and partly because the Frankel estimate was calculated in sterling and the ministry figures were in francs. Nevertheless, both sets of figures show that the investments of French public funds were smaller than those made by any other European colonial power in Africa, although they were nearly double the total of private capital. French public investment was larger in West than in Equatorial Africa, and in both federations it was concentrated in public works. The Cameroun and Togo mandates borrowed less, not only because they were smaller in area and population than the federations, but also because they were able to finance their own development programme, as well as to meet their operating expenses from surplus revenues. Although the mandates received less income from customs duties and the head-tax than did the federal budgets, the mandates were not burdened with analogous expenditures for military operations, excessive European official personnel and interest on the public debt, which absorbed from one-third to one-sixth of the federations' revenues.

The tempo and total of France's financial contributions to its African colonies increased after the First World War, and especially during the depression of 1930–1. To offset the sharp decline in African export-crop production, a big colonial loans programme was voted by the French Parliament in 1931 to bolster the federal revenues. Both AOF and AEF had been financially structured so that the expenditures of their governments-general and of the services common to their respective colonies should be paid from federal revenues, which derived from indirect taxation, principally customs duties. The individual colonies, for their part, depended on direct taxes to pay for their own administrative expenditures. Of these, the essential was provided by the head tax, which was levied on all Africans from the age of fourteen (AOF) or eighteen (AEF), except in the mandates, where women and adolescent boys were exempted by international agreements. The rate of the head tax varied, not only from year to year but also between the colonies and between different categories of the population. On the whole, the head tax yielded far smaller revenues for the territorial budgets than did the indirect taxes for the federal budgets. Moreover, with the overall growth in Black Africa's foreign trade, the taxes for federal budgets were increasing.

To make this fiscal structure more flexible, the governments-general annually apportioned the surplus federal revenues to the colonial budgets that were in deficit. This practice, euphemistically termed 'federal solidarity', not only aggravated the colonies' subordination to the federal government, but caused resentment among the coastal peoples, whose export earnings were used not to develop their own economies but to subsidize the poorer hinterland territories. Aside from the moot question of its equity, this system created so great a financial interdependence that the spectacular decline in African exports in 1930 adversely affected the living standards of all Francophone Black Africans. It was to reactivate African export production that the French government launched the colonial loans programme of 1931. This move served not only to stimulate private investments in tropical Africa but, more important, introduced a new principle into French colonial policy. This was direct state intervention and financial aid for colonial development, which was to become the dominant principle of France's economic overseas policy in the ensuing years.

Until the First World War, only about one-fourth of the French private capital invested abroad had gone to France's colonies. During the 1920s, private investments in the French empire began to increase; but it was not until the pre-World War II decade that the proportion of foreign to colonial private investments was completely reversed. This geographical reorientation, however, was not accompanied by any change in the concentration of French private capital in Black African commercial enterprises, nor by any vast increase in its total amount. In the Equatorial federation, even after the disappearance of the last big concessionary companies financed by French, Belgian, Dutch and British capital, French private investors made no attempt to develop the rural economy. They simply moved in to replace other European merchants in so far as possible.

By the end of the inter-war period, French private capital invested in tropical Africa, as shown in Table 14, aggregated less than 35 billion francs. Of this total, about 30 per cent was invested directly in trading firms, and another 9·5 per cent in banking and real-estate companies, notably the Banque de l'Afrique Occidentale and Crédit Foncier de l'Ouest Africain, whose activities and some of whose directors were shared with those of the commercial companies. Of the 30·8 per cent invested in the rural sector, 12·5 per cent went to forest enterprises, 18 per cent to plantations, and less than 1 per cent to animal husbandry. The comparatively small allotment to industry (17·1 per cent) and to transport (3·6 per cent) reflected both the French capitalists' perennial preference for investments that would bring in quicker returns and involve minimal risks, and the limitations of the African markets. Despite frequent bankruptcies, especially of small businesses, the French firms generally prospered (see Table 15), notably those heavily capitalized and long established in Senegal, the Ivory Coast and Gabon. They preferred repatriating their profits, freely convertible inside the franc zone, to reinvesting them locally.

Even after the Second World War, when the French treasury assumed the burden of improving the infrastructure and undertaking geological prospecting

Table 15. *Volume of business of European enterprises in French Black Africa,*
1956
(in millions of CFA francs)

Territory	Agriculture and forests	Building and public works	Mines and industries	Total	Average per African inhabitant (in CFA francs)
Senegal	—	6,800	27,690	34,490	15,800
Ivory Coast	4,010	6,200	5,400	15,610	6,300
Guinea	1,010	3,100	4,200	8,310	3,300
Dahomey	—	1,700	870	2,570	1,600
Soudan (Mali)	—	3,500	3,510	7,010	1,900
Niger	—	1,600	420	2,020	900
Upper Volta	—	1,800	1,280	3,080	900
Middle Congo	1,340	1,770	3,960	7,070	9,000
Gabon	3,010			6,380	15,300
Oubangui-Chari	—	3,370			
Chad	—	1,760	5,900	7,660	2,900
Togo	—	420	320	740	700

SOURCE: Raymond Barbé, *Les classes sociales en Afrique noire* (Paris, 1964), p. 56.

in Africa, French capitalists were still disinclined to invest heavily there in any long-term industry except mining. The most common explanation of this reluctance was their fears of political instability and, even more, of another currency devaluation, for they had everything to gain from maintaining the *status quo*.

France created the CFA (Colonies Françaises d'Afrique) franc in 1945 and devalued it twice in 1948 and again in 1958. Except in Djibouti, which was given its own currency in 1949, the CFA franc remained pegged to the metropolitan franc, and at its third devaluation became worth two French centimes. The depreciation of the franc in terms of dollars and sterling caused prices to rise in France, which traded extensively with those blocs. This had repercussions in French Black Africa, largely because its foreign commerce depended on France. Francophone Africa's economy was more directly affected by the high value given to the CFA franc in relation to that of the metropole, for this created an inequitable disparity between the purchasing power of those residents in Africa who were paid in CFA or in metropolitan francs. The rising cost of French imports caused the already high cost of living in Africa to soar, particularly for officials whose salaries were paid in metropolitan francs. As to African exports, which were sold for the most part in the French market for metropolitan francs, their sales price remained low until price-support funds for certain crops were instituted. This was done at the expense of the French taxpayer and consumer, and to the benefit of the trading firms, whose profits were made in CFA francs, advantageously converted into metropolitan francs and repatriated for eventual spending in France.

It was allegedly as a result of the political pressure exerted by such powerful beneficiaries that the government refused to give the CFA franc a more realistic value.[2] This did not concern the majority of Africans, who lived by subsistence agriculture, but was essentially a controversy between different categories of Frenchmen. The overvaluation of the CFA franc affected only the African minority who participated in the money economy as export-crop farmers, wage earners, traders, or government employees. Following a widespread decline in African living standards during and immediately after the Second World War, the real incomes of French West African export-crop farmers and labourers increased with the overall rise in the prices paid for that federation's three main exports—ground-nuts, coffee and cocoa—between 1950 and 1960 (see Table 16). Concurrently, the purchasing power of African members of the administrative cadre increased after the passage of the Lamine Gueye law of 1950, which gave them parity with French officials in the same professional category. Small as was the total cash revenue of this moneyed élite compared with the earnings of French functionaries and businessmen (see Table 17), it was far higher than that of the African peasantry.

A main cause of Francophone Black Africa's inability to contribute more to its own economic development was the plan's failure to bring about an overall improvement in the living standards of farmers, herders and fishermen. Had a greater effort been made to increase rural production beyond the subsistence level rather than directly and indirectly to promote the modern trading sector, the benefits resulting from the expansion of French Black Africa's economy after the Second World War would have been more widely shared. Such a development would have made possible a basic reform of the budgetary structure,

[2] Teresa Hayter, *French aid* (London, Overseas Development Institute, 1965), pp. 70–1.

Table 16. *Indicators of changes in real incomes, French West Africa, 1946–60*
(1949 = 100)

	Terms of trade of farmers (net barter)			Wage-earners (unskilled)			Relative returns of export crops: wage earning (unskilled labour rate)	
Year	Ground-nuts (Senegal)	Cocoa (Ivory Coast)	Coffee (Ivory Coast)	Real wage (Dakar)	Import purchasing power of wages — Dakar	Abidjan	Coffee price (Abidjan)	Ground-nut price (Dakar)
1946	132	—	—	92	106	119	—	124
1947	123	—	—	87	105	131	—	117
1948	128	—	62	99	86	79	77	149
1949	100	100	100	100	100	100	100	100
1950	163	103	205	103	108	115	179	151
1951	115	149	280	111	112	120	234	103
1952	105	136	253	106	113	135	188	93
1953	130	334	437	112	142	183	239	91
1954	153	238	327	126	173	213	142	88
1955	144	153	303	127	175	243	125	82
1956	—	—	—	140	—	—	120	79
1957	—	—	—	130	—	—	129	77
1958	—	—	—	135	—	—	98	70
1959	—	—	—	148	—	—	76	63
1960	—	—	—	—	—	—	69	63

SOURCE: Elliot J. Berg, 'Real income trends in West Africa 1939–1960', in *Economic transition in Africa,* Melville J. Herskovits and Mitchell Harwitz, eds. (London, 1964), p. 224.

Table 17. *Volume of wages and salaries, French Black Africa except Oubangui-Chari*
(in millions of CFA francs)

Territory [a]	Europeans	Africans	Total
Senegal	5,300	11,100	16,400
Ivory Coast	2,000	4,600	6,600
Guinea	900	3,600	4,500
Dahomey	—	3,200	3,200
Soudan (Mali)	1,300	3,300	4,600
Niger	100	2,500	2,600
Upper Volta	1,900	1,100	3,000
Middle Congo	3,310	2,460	5,770
Gabon	520	600	1,120
Chad	2,140	1,520	3,660

[a] Data for AOF territories derived from *Comptes économiques de l'A.O.F., 1956,* vol. III; for AEF territories, from *Comptes économiques du Gabon, 1956, Comptes économiques du Congo, 1958* and *Comptes économiques du Tchad, 1958.*

SOURCE: Raymond Barbé, *Les classes sociales en Afrique noire* (Paris, 1964), p. 87.

which remained much the same as in colonial days. Even with the rapid growth in volume of the overseas budgets, and after the Africans acquired greater control over them in 1956, there was little change in the source of their revenues or in the orientation of their expenditures. Revenues continued to depend overwhelmingly on the fluctuating fortunes of foreign trade; and about half of all expenditures was accounted for by the salaries of a growing bureaucracy. This segment was progressively Africanized but comprised no more than 1 per cent of the total population. Moreover, because this minuscule, new-born African bourgeoisie used its surplus funds for usury or for land purchases, the financing of productive development projects continued to depend almost wholly on foreign capital.

By 1960 only a small proportion of the approximately $460 million allotted to the French Black African countries by the European Common Market development fund had actually been distributed. Hence, until independence enabled them to diversify their sources of foreign aid, they still depended financially almost wholly on France.

Land tenure and agricultural production

Traditionally, in Africa, all land was owned in some communal form and was periodically redistributed among kinship groups by their chiefs. The African farmer was granted usufructuary rights to the land that he cultivated, but the time-limit imposed eliminated any incentive to improve the soil or to produce crops beyond the satisfaction of his immediate needs. There was no association of animal husbandry with farming in the form of either traction or soil fertilization; the use of manure was rare. There was no limit to the area that could be left fallow or that could become eroded under the customary slash-and-burn method of cultivation. Such a system was incompatible with the production of export crops and with the growth of population—between 1 and 2 per cent a year—that occurred under the colonial administration. Both these phenomena called for intensive rather than extensive farming techniques, and the development of modern towns gave urban property a monetary value. Consequently the Africans were pressured into increasing their crop output (but for export more than for food) and into asserting individual ownership rights over their land.

The first treaties which France made with African chiefs guaranteed their traditional land rights, but these were soon disregarded. Under French law there was no provision for the collective ownership of real property. Besides, to all appearances, vast uninhabited areas in the two federations were ownerless. In AEF in 1899 and in AOF in 1904, therefore, France proclaimed the state's right to 'vacant and ownerless land'. The government also drew a legal distinction between the public and the private domains, and in the latter encouraged the registration of individual ownership titles. It was not until 1955 that traditional African land rights received stronger legal protection and those of the state were curtailed. By that time, however, economic forces were already promoting private land ownership and agricultural production.

Throughout French Black Africa, European colonization was soon discouraged by the poverty of the soil, irregular climatic conditions, the scarcity of labour and the large amounts of capital required to develop big plantations. In Senegal, the failure of plantation agriculture early in the nineteenth century caused France to encourage farming by Africans throughout AOF and in the mandates. In AEF, however, huge areas were ceded during the 1880s to a few European companies, which were granted a monopoly of their production and control over their inhabitants on condition that they respect African customary rights and undertake works of public utility. This experiment soon proved disastrous in both economic and human terms, but it was not until 1929 that the last concessionary company disappeared.

These failures did not wholly discourage the granting of land to Europeans and Africans; but the area so conceded was far smaller, land grants no longer included administrative rights and the state began to enforce fulfilment of the specific developmental terms on which it authorized leases or granted freehold titles to real property. By the eve of the Second World War, European properties in AOF covered only some 75,000 hectares, mainly in the Ivory Coast and Guinea; and in AEF the only surviving company with large landholdings was the Compagnie Française du Haut et du Bas Congo, whose original concession of 75,000 sq km had been reduced by half. Because the area formerly owned by the concessionary companies in AEF had gradually reverted to the state, there was an appreciable enlargement of the public domain. Moreover, this coincided with a steady decline in African landownership rights, despite the establishment of 'native reserves' in the areas formerly conceded.

The French laws passed in 1925 and 1935, although confirming the state's rights to 'vacant' lands, introduced the Torrens system of land registration. Although this system aimed at simplifying the procedures and reducing the expenses for Africans seeking ownership titles, it led to no marked increase in the registration of African land rights except in the towns. During the inter-war period, the only Africans who acquired extensive tracts of rural land were the 5,000 or so colonists who farmed the central delta of the Niger river in Soudan, under the auspices of the Office du Niger. The initial objective of this project—the growing of cotton for French textile manufacturers—conformed to the established policy of the colonial administration, but the operations of the Office du Niger included major innovations (and, later, greater stress on rice production). These were the unprecedented scope and funding of the whole scheme, the damming of the Niger river to provide irrigation, scientific experimentation to determine plant selection and cultivation methods, the importation of agricultural colonist-labourers and the ultimate grant to them of titles to the land they farmed. Little progress was made elsewhere in persuading the Africans to register land transfers. Not only did the Torrens system run counter to African traditions, but it had the further disadvantage in African eyes of placing their property under French civil law. By the end of the Second World War, in all AOF only some 29,000 hectares had been so registered by 1,742 African landowners.

Another paternalistic law, designed by the colonial administration to protect registered African urban land titles, also miscarried. To check the encroachments of Levantine and European speculators, who were buying up large plots in the coastal towns during the depression years, Africans were forbidden to alienate or mortgage their property to foreigners. Not only did this law prevent African landowners from raising needed capital, but it failed to protect them wholly from abuse. With similar motives and much the same results, the French authorities doubled the area classified as forest reserves so as to preserve African timber resources and prevent soil erosion. But the law was not always enforced against covetous foreigners, and it had the further disadvantage of impinging on customary African rights to clear the land for cultivation and even to gather firewood. In 1945, forest concessions to European companies covered about one-fourth of the wooded areas in the Ivory Coast and some one-sixth of those in Cameroun.

After the Second World War, when popularly elected Africans acquired more control over land, European concessions were no longer a burning issue. Subsequently, the only large land grants made to foreigners were those to French farmer-colonists in the Niari valley of Middle Congo. It was therefore to reducing the French state's existing land rights and to increasing those of Africans, collectively and individually, that the African leaders directed their efforts. As a result of these efforts, the French Parliament on 13 May 1955 passed a law restricting the state's right to own or expropriate land unless its 'vacancy' or indispensability for public utility could be effectively proved. By giving African landowners greater security, this law encouraged them to undertake long-term improvements on their property, but it also had unforeseen and unfortunate results. In the first place, the cession of tribal lands by chiefs in the coastal areas resulted in the creation of African plantations worked not by their owners but by unstable and poorly paid migrant labour. Secondly, freehold titles allowed Africans to farm their land without any of the restraints theretofore imposed either by custom or by French law.

As the French Black African territories moved towards autonomy, some but not all of the organizations created by the colonial administration in the rural areas disappeared. The outstanding institution eliminated was the Sociétés de Prévoyance (SIP), which had been progressively established throughout the two federations before the Second World War. Initially set up as a para-administrative body to constitute food granaries and to promote ground-nut production, the SIP gradually added new functions. In some areas they granted loans from funds borrowed from the administration, undertook small agricultural works, and transported, processed and sold their members' crop output. Aside from their effectiveness, which varied from region to region, it was the compulsory nature of membership in them and, even more, their subordination to the local French administrator that aroused widespread African resentment. From 1949 on, the SIP were progressively liquidated and some of their functions taken over by new federal services, agricultural credit banks and co-operative societies. But because of lack of funds, inexperience or incompetent or dishonest management, none of the co-operative societies became markedly successful.

Among the existing organizations taken over or expanded by the newly autonomous African territories were the scientific research and experimental stations created after the Second World War. These concentrated at first on export crops, but gradually they enlarged their activities to include African food crops and the training of farmers in modern agricultural techniques. Nationalist African leaders encouraged these operations as a means of increasing agricultural output, curtailing the urban influx and reorienting the African élite away from bureaucratic employment and toward economic productivity. By the end of the colonial period, progress was evident in crop yields and diversification, but little headway had been made against the educated Africans' distaste for manual work. Agriculture remained the occupation of some 85 per cent of the African population; but it was still unrelated to animal husbandry, techniques were archaic and farmers' cash earnings were discouragingly small. Subsistence agriculture in the hinterland areas continued to coexist with the more remunerative and technically advanced plantation farming in the coastal regions. There, on one-twentieth of AOF's total area, from 80 to 90 per cent of French Black Africa's export crops were produced.

Beginning early in the twentieth century, the export of wild-grown produce such as gums, wax and natural rubber declined steadily, until this activity was briefly revived to meet the Allies' demand for raw materials during the Second World War. Both before and after the war, it was the French trading companies, backed by the administration, that encouraged the production and export of cultivated produce but not of African food crops. Although handicapped by the shortage of labour, the coastal colonies were destined by their favourable climatic and soil conditions and geographical accessibility virtually to monopolize export-crop production, and in so doing they attracted seasonal workers from the more populous hinterland. This process began in Senegal with the introduction there of ground-nuts, the cultivation of which expanded rapidly eastward to the detriment of African food production. Senegal therefore became dependent on Soudan to meet its needs for millet and for migrant labour. The same development was repeated in other coastal colonies, mainly in AOF and to a lesser degree in the mandates and in AEF. Export-crop monoculture increasingly dominated the economy of specific coastal areas, either spontaneously or through pressure from the administration. Natural conditions, the attractions of a cash income and the needs of the French market combined to make cotton the chief export of Chad, Oubangui-Chari and northern Cameroun; bananas that of Guinea; oil-palm products of Dahomey; cocoa, coffee and lumber of the Ivory Coast; and okoumé wood of Gabon.

Africans were by far the largest producers of export produce, except for lumber and bananas; but the prices that they received for their output were determined by the French export firms in the light of the world market, with the aim of earning maximum profits (see Table 18). The big trading companies ignored African food crops, made little effort to improve the quality of export crops and took no steps to remedy the soil exhaustion and erosion that ensued from their promotion of exportable agricultural output. Not until after the Second World War, when it assumed a more active role in improving, increasing, diversifying and standardizing the agricultural output of the Black African dependencies, did the colonial administration move to mitigate the unfortunate consequences of this mercantilist policy.

Trade

Traditional African trade, based on the exchange of a few surplus commodities produced by a subsistence economy, survived its coexistence with the *économie de traite,* but underwent extensive modifications. With the importation of European merchandise and the availability of new shipping routes, African demand for such indigenous items as desert salt and iron objects was eliminated or reduced; but trading in other local products, such as colas, dried fish and livestock, increased. Under the colonial administration, inter-African as well as foreign commerce expanded as a result of greater security, improved means of communication and trading in new exports and imports. It was further facilitated by a common currency and by the lack of customs barriers between

Table 18. *Principal export crops of French Black Africa, 1956–9*
(random years)

Country	Principal crops	Overall value to producer (millions of CFA francs)		Average value per African farmer (CFA francs)
		European planters	African producers	
Senegal	Ground-nuts	—	10,000	5,830
Ivory Coast	Coffee, cocoa, palm-kernels, bananas	1,060	13,330	6,110
Guinea	Bananas, coffee, palm-kernels, pineapples	880	1,870	830
Dahomey	Palm-kernels, ground-nuts, coffee	20	1,940	1,330
Soudan (Mali)	Ground-nuts, cotton	—	1,700	490
Niger	Ground-nuts	—	1,750	770
Upper Volta	Ground-nuts, cotton, yams, karité	—	240	80
Middle Congo	Ground-nuts, palm-kernels, coffee, cocoa-beans, tobacco, sugar	380	250	410
Gabon	Coffee, cocoa-beans	—	240	640
Oubangui-Chari	Cotton, coffee	360	990	930
Chad	Cotton	—	1,640	670
Cameroun	Cocoa-beans, coffee, palm-kernels, bananas, cotton	1,500	6,350	2,230
Togo	Coffee, cocoa-beans, cotton, ground-nuts, palm-kernels	20	2,340	1,960

SOURCE: Raymond Barbé, *Les classes sociales en Afrique noire* (Paris, 1964), p. 26.

France's Black African colonies. Itinerant Diula and Hausa merchants enlarged the area of their operations and shared with immigrant Levantines the role of agents for European import and export companies.

In the nineteenth century, family-owned firms with headquarters in Bordeaux or Marseille established themselves in the French colonies, where they traded in a wide range of merchandise. Of the forty or so import–export companies operating in French West Africa during the colonial period, three limited-liability companies known as the Grands Comptoirs came to dominate trade and, to some extent, the related banking and transport businesses. Thanks to tariff protection and to their extensive network of branches throughout West Africa, the Big Three were able to set the prices for most African exports and for some imports. They purchased only such African crops as were abundant, cheap and readily saleable in France, and they repatriated their profits. Because of their ties with metropolitan buyers and provisioners, they long opposed the establishment in Africa of industries that would compete with those of France. Yet by bringing the French colonies into the modern economic circuit and by organizing their trade, the import–export companies performed useful services to African producers and consumers by bringing in new goods in wide variety, ranging from matches to bicycles and sewing machines.

With the promotion of new export crops by the European trading firms, a money economy was introduced into the coastal regions. This development, however, barely touched the hinterland, which long continued to grow only indigenous food crops. Although ground-nuts and cotton eventually became export crops for the landlocked colonies, these areas continued to grow enough millet, rice and manioc to help meet the growing deficiencies in foodstuffs of the coastal peoples. The sale of agricultural produce, either abroad or in neighbouring colonies, determined the purchasing power of the growers, who formed the great mass of the population and therefore largely accounted for the volume of imports. Because food crops for African consumers earned less than did export crops, and because heavy transport charges added to the already high price of French imported goods, the hinterland inhabitants were doubly disfavoured. Nevertheless, with the overall expansion of trade during the colonial period, imports grew in volume and variety to include luxury as well as essential consumer goods. This growth in their prosperity, however, made the African territories increasingly vulnerable to world market conditions beyond their control, and also made them more dependent on France.

Through a proliferating network of controls, France channelled the trade with its African dependencies. First tariff barriers, then imperial preference and finally currency restrictions ensured that specific African exports would be sold only to France and that French manufactured goods would be pre-eminent in the African market. Under the basic tariff régime established in 1892, French exports entered the colonies duty-free—though subject to fiscal charges in some cases—but only certain African exports received reciprocal treatment in France. Successive modifications of this régime did not alter its protectionist bias, for they were made mainly to meet France's subsequent treaty commitments in the Congo basin area and in the mandates. It was not until African cash-crop production fell sharply during the world depression in 1930 that France accorded certain African exports a quota and higher-than-world prices in the French market. Because this automatically increased France's share in the trade of its colonies, the granting of preferential treatment to African exports of oleaginous products, cotton and bananas became a permanent feature of French policy. No such favoured treatment was accorded, however, to African lumber, coffee and cocoa, the production of which became too large for French consumers to absorb. Hence most such exports were sold in non-franc markets.

During the Second World War, the French African colonies were perforce provisioned from Anglo-American sources, but this drastic reorientation of their trade was of brief duration. To restore France's previous domination of the African market and to ease its own shortage of dollars and sterling, the Paris authorities imposed a system of import licences and currency controls that, in effect, required the Africans to sell certain exports exclusively to France and to buy French commodities. Because France sold many of its imports from Africa abroad at prices higher than it paid to the producers, and then allotted to the African territories only from 10 to 25 per cent of the hard currency received for them, African leaders protested strongly and effectively. By 1949 most of the above-mentioned restrictions had been eased, French industry had recovered sufficiently to supply the African market in essentials and the pre-war trading pattern had been virtually restored.

Tables 19 and 20 show that Franco-African trade grew appreciably, if irregularly, from before the Second World War to 1955. By that time France was taking some 65 per cent of French Black Africa's exports and supplying about the same proportion of its imports, though there were variations between the two federations, the trust territories and the free-trade zone of Djibouti.[3] As regards African exports, the percentages were much the same as in the pre-war decade, but there was a marked increase in the volume of African imports from France, especially equipment goods. This rise in imports enlarged both the territories' revenues from customs duties and the unfavourable balance of trade, which had begun in the 1930s as a result of French protectionist measures (see Table 21).

To enhance the Africans' purchasing power and to offset the rising volume and cost of French imports in the 1950s, France instituted price-support funds for African growers of cotton, cocoa and coffee. Also, for African exports of ground-nuts, sugar, vegetable oils and bananas, the metropole paid prices higher than those prevailing in world markets by, respectively, 15 to 20 per cent, 100 per cent, 20 to 30 per cent, and 15 to 20 per cent. At the same time, Africans were buying such French consumer goods as cotton textiles and food-stuffs at prices that ranged from 23 to 105 per cent above world prices for analogous products.

So complex and unstable did this web of *surprix* on exports and imports become that its net impact on the economies of France and Africa can only be surmised. An estimate in 1964 by a neutral student of this trade indicated that it cost the African territories greater monetary losses than it did France.[4] But this calculation did not take into account the multiple loans, subsidies and other contributions made by France to its dependencies, which gave the dependencies a favourable balance of payments. In any case, by 1956 the growing burden on the French tax-payers that resulted from the government's African policy caused an upsurge of anti-colonialism in France. This was related also to France's insistence the following year that its overseas dependencies become associate members of the European Economic Community (EEC) established by the Treaty of Rome.

France's demand was reluctantly accepted both by its five partners, who could foresee no material benefits and only expenditures from this association, and by the Africans themselves, who feared it as a revival of the Colonial Pact on a European scale. To allay African misgivings, France pledged that there would be no appreciable diminution in its aid. France's partners, moreover, agreed to provide African exports not only with a protected market but also with funds for diversifying their economies, for developing local industries and for helping to reduce production costs to meet world competition.

Theoretically, the membership of the Francophone Africans in the EEC should have gratified their aspiration for larger development funds and for a more widespread and advantageous market in which to buy and sell. It should at the same time have lessened France's financial contributions to African development. Actually, however, satisfaction was limited on both counts. France gradually spread its aid throughout the Third World, but allotted nearly the same proportion of national revenues (approximately 1 per cent) to its former dependencies in return for maintaining its privileged position in their markets.

[3] Huguette Durant, *Essai sur la conjoncture de l'Afrique noire* (Paris, 1957), p. 85.
[4] Hayter, *French aid*, p. 73.

Table 19. *Volume (tonnage) of principal French Black African agricultural exports, 1925–55*

Year	Ground-nuts	Palm-oil and kernels	Wood	Cocoa	Bananas	Coffee (green)	Cotton
1913	242,000	54,700	193,400	150	30	10	300
1925	453,854	153,252	332,334	15,973	—	—	5,728
1926	494,861	161,163	388,196	17,470	—	—	6,849
1927	421,326	159,110	489,812	23,915	—	—	7,475
1928	429,934	131,780	519,097	28,365	—	—	7,347
1929	418,700	144,300	453,300	32,300	6,100	470	7,400
1930	521,320	170,400	636,000	39,500	8,100	460	7,600
1931	459,100	141,000	326,200	38,700	11,700	790	5,400
1932	203,900	153,800	320,600	45,900	16,800	1,550	4,300
1933	405,240	130,500	377,600	55,500	22,600	2,500	5,000
1934	548,513	161,000	447,900	67,400	29,600	4,200	8,600
1935	419,640	183,300	430,500	78,600	42,900	7,600	10,600
1936	550,450	234,000	388,900	84,600	68,600	10,000	11,700
1937	722,600	185,000	578,400	83,800	79,500	14,600	14,000
1938	585,100	157,600	382,400	92,300	91,200	21,000	16,500
1939	572,690	127,583	241,449	93,533	84,175	27,054	13,814
1940	375,178	103,689	102,971	75,972	46,405	23,700	9,180
1941	377,869	116,996	36,627	66,311	11,869	31,152	23,843
1942	95,271	104,031	50,716	47,240	762	29,226	28,231
1943	34,676	115,482	56,148	35,543	236	38,101	14,544
1944	148,486	122,982	94,879	51,761	2,648	32,713	28,032
1945	132,350	107,884	81,104	69,981	270	52,187	32,754
1946	201,832	76,016	195,268	67,101	12,787	45,610	27,804
1947	232,312	85,077	229,019	66,050	50,049	57,991	23,925
1948	297,094	125,500	354,139	93,232	82,358	67,595	35,196
1949	271,207	156,353	382,487	108,059	94,672	76,654	27,377
1950	280,250	154,467	445,392	112,191	116,540	71,248	25,674
1951	253,729	138,471	478,764	111,748	124,918	79,288	30,682
1952	273,943	112,610	388,800	108,500	131,257	88,112	33,891
1953	332,491	150,072	609,500	143,600	165,200	71,500	28,900
1954	382,889	135,163	606,770	117,174	177,704	115,076	37,185
1955	268,583	140,772	939,962	146,412	201,163	116,036	43,267

NOTE: Certain figures are only approximate, because of the transformation of products in the course of years. This is especially true of oleaginous products: ground-nuts and palm-kernels are increasingly processed into oil, which results in a decline in global tonnage but a rise in export value.

SOURCE: Huguette Durant, *Essai sur la conjoncture de l'Afrique noire* (Paris, 1957), p. 38.

As to the EEC, after independence all the states except Guinea twice renewed their associate membership voluntarily, if unenthusiastically. Yet they continued to complain that the tariff preference to which their exports were entitled in the EEC markets had been largely nullified by internal sales taxes, and that they had not been given enough help or time to make their economies viable.

In so far as France had developed the African economies to meet its own needs and as an integrated whole, and had also accustomed the Africans to protection and freedom from competition, their current plight might be largely at-

Table 20. *Volume of French Black African imports from France and other countries, 1938–55*
(in thousands of tons)

Year	AOF Total	AOF France	Togo Total	Togo France	Cameroun Total	Cameroun France	AEF Total	AEF France
1938	558	227	21	5	59	16	76	25
1939	636	314	23	—	60	16	70	—
1940	327	147	12	—	31	7	56	17
1941	225	128	6	—	36	—	74	1
1942	240	181	6	—	27	—	97	1
1943	202	25	9	—	40	—	93	—
1944	275	—	15	—	38	—	73	—
1945	345	18	10	1	36	1	86	1
1946	396	83	19	2	55	4	78	5
1947	595	152	23	5	77	22	125	39
1948	676	217	25	7	152	65	197	63
1949	919	426	38	22	212	85	309	144
1950	1,071	568	45	25	227	134	306	188
1951	1,471	777	57	22	337	197	363	197
1952	1,328	686	48	19	404	214	356	171
1953	1,257	653	51,7	23,7	288	134	293	131
1954	1,416	714	64	27	317	141	300	118
1955	1,489	675	66	26	339	176	311	132

SOURCE: Huguette Durant, *Essai sur la conjoncture de l'Afrique noire* (Paris, 1957), p. 148.

Table 21. *Trade balance of French Black Africa with various currency zones, 1938 and 1945–55*
(in millions of metropolitan francs)

Year	Franc	Sterling	U.S. dollar	Other currencies	Total
1938	+ 246	− 146	− 119	− 194	− 213
1945	+ 1,965	−1,242	− 1,364	− 206	− 867
1946	+ 5,308	−2,541	− 3,676	−1,054	− 1,959
1947	+ 559	−1,392	− 7,198	−1,046	− 9,073
1948	+ 8,172	−1,564	− 6,673	−2,746	− 2,927
1949	−14,212	− 668	−11,276	−2,903	−29,066
1950	−27,914	−1,896	−13,093	+4,623	−38,280
1951	−53,334	−2,285	−11,058	−1,790	−68,467
1952	−52,361	−8,011	−11,725	−5,357	−77,454
1953	−19,804	−4,556	− 4,559	+2,574	−27,176
1954	−19,931	−4,408	+ 3,898	−2,622	−23,065
1955	−40,381	−5,620	+ 2,398	+2,966	−40,637

SOURCE: Huguette Durant, *Essai sur la conjoncture de l'Afrique noire* (Paris, 1957), p. 92.

tributed to French commercial policy. But African grievances transcended those that were legitimately held against France or even the EEC, for they concerned the terms of world trade. Because prices for tropical produce were generally declining while those for manufactured goods were rising, the Africans had little financial incentive to increase their output or to improve its quality. Political independence has served to sharpen African insistence on stable, remunerative prices for their exports, on cheaper manufactured imports and on more aid in developing industries, without which they believe that they cannot raise the living standards of their populations.

Transportation

Because of the vast land area involved, the sparseness and dispersion of population and the scarcity of natural harbours and of permanently navigable waterways, Francophone Black Africa's transportation problem has always been critical. Military strategy and French commercial policy dictated the linking of the more populous hinterland to the exporting coastal regions. To facilitate the movement of troops and goods, the colonial administration early prepared an overall plan to build railroads between the ocean ports and the navigable stretches of the Senegal, the Niger and the Congo rivers. To finance construction, the two federations then borrowed funds from the French treasury.

According to calculations made by Frankel in the mid-1930s,[5] the railroad loans between 1887 and 1934 totalled roughly £32 million for building 2,888 miles of track in tropical Africa (see Map 3). Because of long delays imposed by difficulties with labour and with contractors and by the rugged terrain, the cost of construction far exceeded original estimates. Furthermore, the railroads, particularly those built for military rather than for economic objectives, were operated at a heavy loss to the state, which administered the whole system. After construction was interrupted by the First World War, the French government, disillusioned and short of funds, abandoned the original rail plan and turned to road-building. Subsequently, the only important additions it made to the rail network were the Congo-Ocean line, completed in 1934, and an extension of the Abidjan-Niger railroad to Ouagadougou in 1956, both undertaken for primarily political reasons. In strictly financial terms, the railroads were a failure, but they served two useful purposes: they carried bulk produce between the ports and some towns on the inland rivers, and they reduced human porterage.

Although truck transport became increasingly competitive with the railroads, road construction, because it was cheaper and served a wider area, proved a better investment for the state and more useful to the population. Roads could be built and maintained by forced labour, and more readily in the 'savannah corridor', where the soil was lateritic and less densely forested and the climate drier than in the coastal region. By 1940, most of the 105,200-km road network of AOF and Cameroun, and virtually all of the 15,800 km in AEF, were to be found in the interior colonies. To be sure, only the main towns had paved streets, and the vast majority of French Black Africa's so-called roads were no

[5] S. Herbert Frankel, *Capital investment in Africa* (London, 1938), p. 414.

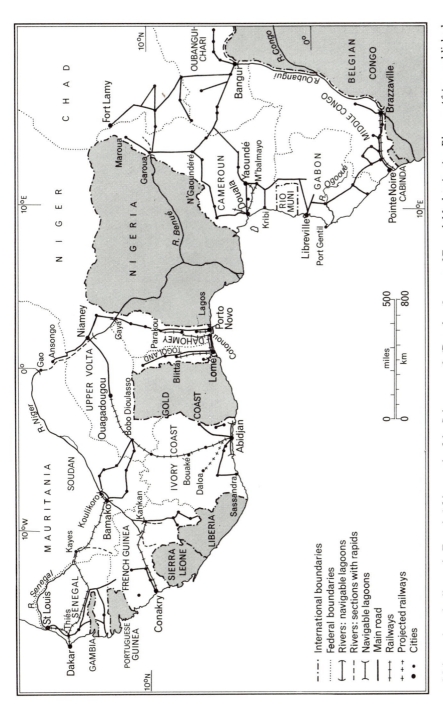

3. Main roads and railways in French Africa south of the Sahara, 1956. (Based on *Impact of French Modernization Plan on Africa*, published by Service de Presse et d'Information, Ambassade de France, New York, October 1956)

149

more than dry-season tracks; but they did facilitate the movements of men and merchandise between previously isolated regions.

Under the overseas plan, the improvement and extension of the road network and even more of the ports of Dakar, Abidjan, Pointe Noire and Douala, reinforced the orientation of the whole transport system to the western and southern coasts. In AOF, in 1956, five ports handled 95 per cent of the federation's passenger and freight traffic, and its four railroads carried 75 per cent of the tonnage passing through those ports.[6] In AEF, a similar role was played by Pointe Noire and Port Gentil on the Atlantic coast, but in that federation a larger share of the traffic was taken by the river ports of Brazzaville and Bangui. In both federations, however, air transport was still in its infancy. Their road and rail facilities together were unable to cope with the post-war growth in foreign and inter-African trade, and exorbitant transport charges added considerably to the cost of their imports and exports.

Industry

The slow development of industries in French Black Africa resulted from both internal and external factors. The most serious impediments were lack of capital, of a remunerative local market, of African skilled labour and of precise knowledge of the colonies' resources, as well as opposition from metropolitan manufacturers. It was not until the Second World War created shortages of essential imports in the African colonies and, above all, until French colonial policy changed course in 1946, that Francophone Black Africa was launched on the path to industrialization.

Until 1940, only 17.1 per cent of all French private capital investments in Black Africa went into industry and mining.[7] More than a third of the funds invested in industry were allotted to enterprises related to port and railroad construction and upkeep and to the generation (and distribution) of electric power from small thermal plants fuelled by imported oil. That an even smaller percentage was invested in mining (7.5 per cent) could be attributed to the lack of geological surveys, to the speculative nature of such ventures and to French laws that separated land rights from those for prospecting and extracting minerals. Consequently, such mining as was done before the Second World War remained largely in the hands of the thousands of Africans who had, since pre-colonial days, been panning gold in Guinea, in Soudan and throughout AEF. Only a few European companies, using archaic methods, extracted negligible amounts of gold, titanium, copper, lead, zinc and diamonds.

The only other existing industries were those processing local agricultural produce, notably vegetable oils, cotton and wood; and many of these owed their birth to the scarcity of shipping and, consequently, of French imports during the First World War. By the early 1920s, however, French manufactured goods once more flooded the African market, and the wartime industries either disappeared or curtailed their output. The only important West African enterprises that survived that period were the oil mills of Senegal and a textile factory in the Ivory Coast, both of which used local raw materials to produce

[6] B. E. Thomas, 'Railways and ports in French West Africa', *Economic Geography*, Jan. 1957.
[7] Jean Suret-Canale, *Afrique noire occidentale et centrale*, vol. II: *L'ère coloniale (1900–1945)* (Paris, 1964), p. 269.

for the internal market. A somewhat similar development occurred in AEF on a smaller scale. There the sole survivors were a few tanneries and soap factories. The industries of Cameroun and AEF, because these areas had a better network of internal communications, were less centralized than those of AOF. None of them, however, produced enough to meet more than a fraction of the local demand, or used processes that could be described as meeting more than a rudimentary mechanical standard.

The isolation of France from its colonies during the Second World War created far more serious shortages of essential goods than had been the case in 1914–18—a condition that stimulated African industrialization on an unprecedented scale. Throughout the federations there sprang up factories producing textiles, tinned foodstuffs, chemical products and edible and fuel oils, as well as quarries and mechanized workshops. By the end of the war, most of the area's new industries were rooted firmly enough to withstand the opposition of competitive French manufacturers, especially the Bordeaux and Marseille oil-millers and soap-makers. Moreover, official French policy, as reflected in the overseas development plan of 1946, currently accorded a high priority to African industrialization, especially mining, with the dual objective of promoting not only exports but the welfare of the Africans as well. At the same time, the potential market for local industrial products was growing because of the rapid increase of the population, as was also the demand for African minerals in world markets.

Beginning in 1947, the state undertook the first systematic survey of sub-Saharan hydro-electric and mineral resources, and also construction of the means of communication that would make the development of these facilities feasible and profitable for French entrepreneurs. Spared such expense, French capitalists did indeed invest heavily for the first time in mining enterprises, but only in the most accessible deposits. As time went on, the state geologists discovered huge deposits of more valuable ores in remote regions, but to mine and process these would require enormous investments. Access roads and railroads, and in some cases hydro-electric plants, had to be built, and housing had to be supplied for staff and labourers. Internationally financed companies were therefore formed to exploit the iron and copper of Mauritania; the manganese, petroleum and iron of Gabon; the diamonds of Oubangui-Chari; and the bauxite of Guinea (see Map 4).

It might be argued that this rapid development of mining by foreign companies was detrimental to the French Black Africans' future welfare in that it depleted their natural resources without ensuring commensurate benefits. Only to the extent that the new enterprises gave employment to a few thousand unskilled labourers, promoted a few auxiliary industries, developed some markets and contributed royalties to the territorial budgets did the Africans profit from them, for they had neither the capital nor the skills to participate in them directly. Yet most of the French territories were so poor and undeveloped that their leaders hailed with enthusiasm even a modest mineral find. In their eyes, industrialization was the *sine qua non* for raising mass living standards, and it had the additional attraction of making the Africans less dependent on French capital and trade.

The role of the French import–export firms also was being undermined by a concurrent proliferation, both in number and variety, of local consumer-goods

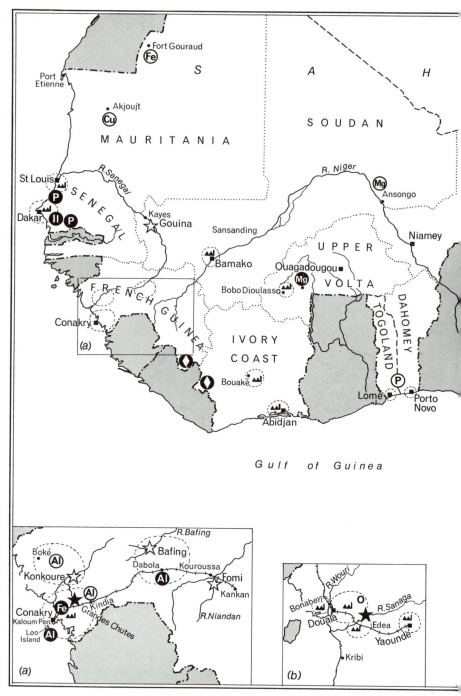

4. Main areas of hydro-electric, mining and industrial development in French Africa south
by Service de Presse et d'Information, Ambassade de France, New York, October 1956)

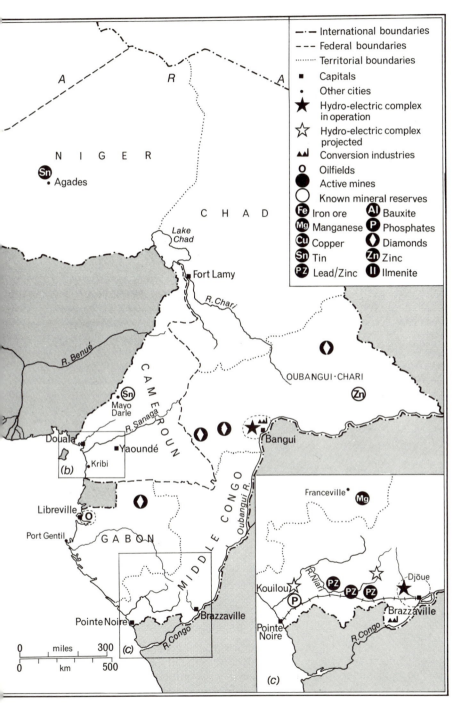

of the Sahara, 1956. (Based on *Impact of French Modernization Plan of Africa*, published

industries. To those already established in the two federations were added factories for making cement, plastics, plywood, pharmaceuticals, shoes, beer, cigarettes and so on. Because of the growth of foreign trade and the increase in the urban population, as well as the distribution of more electric power at cheaper rates, the coastal cities inevitably became the main industrial centres. Although detailed statistics are not available for all the newly developed industries, it appeared that between 1947 and 1957, AOF's industrial output tripled and was growing at an annual rate of 12 per cent.[8] The rate varied, however, from territory to territory and from one industry to another. As shown in Tables 22 and 23, growth was slowest in the hinterland agricultural processing industries, and most rapid in mining and electric power; but everywhere it was unmistakable.

Table 22. *Mineral production in AOF and AEF, 1939, 1949, 1955*

			AOF		
Year	Gold (kg)	Diamonds (carats)	Phosphates (tons)	Bauxite (tons)	Iron (tons)
1939	5,455·5	56,316	—	—	—
1949	90·1	94,996	5,675	10	—
1955	6·9	313,400	142,600	479,219	657,234

			AEF	
Year	Gold (kg)	Diamonds (carats)	Lead (tons)	Zinc (tons)
1939	1,793	17,491	6,907	3,314
1949	1,781	122,928	1,405	111
1955	1,448	136,900	6,407	—

SOURCE: Huguette Durant, *Essai sur la conjoncture de l'Afrique noire* (Paris, 1957), p. 143.

Table 23. *Electric-power production in French Black Africa, 1949 and 1954* (1,000 kwh)

Area	1949	1954
French West Africa	31,612	80,762
French Equatorial Africa	7,683	21,551
Cameroun	2,685	21,600

SOURCE: Huguette Durant, *Essai sur la conjoncture de l'Afrique noire* (Paris, 1957), p. 146.

Labour

As a reservoir of manpower for recruits needed by the French army and for a local labour force, Black Africa proved disappointing to the colonial authorities. Its inhabitants totalled only some thirty millions, and many young men were disease-ridden, unskilled and disinclined to labour either for the government or for European employers. In its effort to overcome the difficulties posed

[8] Marcel Capet, *Traité d'économie tropical: les économies d'A.O.F.* (Paris, 1958), p. 280.

by the Africans' physical and psychological handicaps, the administration experimented unsuccessfully with indentured Oriental and Mexican workers. Finally it had recourse to forced African labour.

The legal abolition of slavery in 1901, followed by the instituting of forced labour for public works and for the private sector, disrupted the traditional socioeconomic system. In time, a small but growing percentage of the active native population became government employees, wage-earners, planters and merchants, thus revolutionizing the communally oriented African society. The opportunities provided by the French for gainful employment, limited as they were for Africans, developed their individualism and their awareness of the outside world. For the first time Africans had the opportunity and the desire to earn money and to aspire to some degree of authority and security outside the tribal context, as well as to learn a new set of values related to regular working hours, efficiency and expertise.

Forced labour

Before the Second World War, virtually all able-bodied Africans, whether they were civilians, prisoners or military recruits, were liable for labour on public works. Unofficially the administration also requisitioned labourers for certain private enterprises exporting lumber and agricultural produce. Such measures were 'justified' on the grounds of overall benefits to the economy, of instilling in the Africans disciplined work habits and providing a modicum of training and of enabling them to pay the head tax.

During the inter-war period, the administration came to realize that the system lent itself to gross abuse and was moreover inefficient. Gradually the use of forced labour, as to numbers, duration and place, was restricted by laws, which also required that requisitioned workers be given some medical care, housing, food and clothing, as well as be paid standard wages promptly and in cash. Such protective regulations, however, were incomplete and ineffectively enforced. On 11 April 1946 the Parliament unanimously abolished forced labour throughout French Black Africa. The next year penal labour was placed on the same legal basis as free labour, and in 1950 the use of military conscripts on public-works projects was banned. Thenceforth, the only surviving form of forced labour was the domestic serfdom sanctioned by African custom.

Migrants

Spontaneous large-scale population displacements, which antedated the French occupation, increased greatly as a result of railroad construction and of the development of export crops and lumber camps in the coastal region. Migrants were attracted to the coast by their desire to escape the constraints and boredom of rural tribal life and to earn money to pay the bride-price, as well as to acquire social prestige. During each dry season in the hinterland, thousands of youths went to work in the underpopulated French and British coastal colonies, from which they sent money home to their families. Some, of course, never returned.

For many years, coastal employers welcomed the immigrants, despite their lack of skills and stability, because they worked for low wages and were unorganized. The hinterland economies benefited by the remittances of the migrants, and the coastal Africans accepted them as long as they remained temporary, rural labourers. In time, however, the disadvantages of such labour became more apparent, especially when the migrants became permanent urban residents and occupied white-collar jobs. The indigenous coastal peoples blamed the newcomers for the unemployment and for the social problems that were increasingly plaguing the fast-growing towns (see Table 24); and riots directed against Dahomean and Togolese civil servants and clerks erupted in Gabon (1953) and in the Ivory Coast (1958). With the growth of territorial nationalism after 1956, this hostility was extended to include hinterland migrant workers, whose presence was held responsible by local labour leaders for impeding wage increases and unionization. After independence it was obviously only a question of time before the movements of migrant workers would be curtailed by the African governments.

Table 24. *Population of French Black Africa, 1955–6*

Territory	Total (thousands)	Urban population (of towns with more than 7,000 inhabitants)	
		Total [a] (thousands)	Per cent of territorial population
Senegal	2,180	443	20·3
Ivory Coast	2,470	277	11·2
Guinea	2,497	187	7·5
Dahomey	1,612	143	8·9
Soudan (Mali)	3,637	137	3·8
Niger	2,333	51	2·2
Upper Volta	3,322	88	2·6
Middle Congo	749	137	18·3
Gabon	416	33	7·9
Oubangui-Chari	1,121	136	12·1
Chad	2,600	95	3·6
Cameroun [b]	3,183	318	10·0
Togo	1,093	135	12·3

[a] Based on *Outre-Mer—1958* (except Cameroun).
[b] Data derived from Yves Nicol, 'Cameroun—1959', *Marchés Tropicaux*, 21 Nov. 1959, pp. 2564–5.

SOURCE: Raymond Barbé, *Les classes sociales en Afrique noire* (Paris, 1964), p. 64.

Wage-earners and civil servants

As soon as forced labour was abolished, Africans abandoned their employers in droves. Within a few years, however, the number of African wage-earners had risen above the pre-war level. With the execution of the overseas-plan projects during the first post-war decade, the total of African wage-earners, excluding civil and domestic servants, grew everywhere except in Oubangui-Chari. But even then they represented only a fraction of the federations' active population. The proportion of unskilled to skilled workers, as shown in Tables 25, 26 and 27, was strikingly large. At the end of 1948, unskilled workers in AOF accounted for nine-tenths of the wage-earners in agriculture and about half of

Table 25. *Wage-earners in French Black Africa*
(except civil servants and domestic workers), 1947 and 1957

Territory	1947	1957
Senegal	80,864	83,160
Ivory Coast and Upper Volta	77,798	175,210
Guinea	35,965	84,900
Dahomey	12,467	16,910
Soudan (Mali)	29,647	33,910
Niger	5,003	10,460
Middle Congo	48,603	54,980
Gabon	24,593	36,800
Oubangui-Chari	51,094	41,400
Chad	a	26,220
Cameroun	109,000 [b]	124,200
Togo	3,794	8,260

[a] Data unavailable.   [b] Figure for 1948.

SOURCE: Raymond Barbé, *Classes sociales en Afrique noire* (Paris, 1964), p. 68.

Table 26. *Skilled and unskilled workers in certain sectors,*
French Black Africa, 1957

Territory	Total	Agriculture and forestry (number)	Non-agricultural sectors	
			Number	Per cent of active male population
Senegal	66,600	4,600	62,000	7·9
Ivory Coast	146,600	90,000	46,600	6·7
Guinea	75,900	32,000	43,900	6·1
Soudan (Mali)	27,200	7,300	19,900	1·5
Dahomey	12,800	1,700	11,100	2·1
Niger	9,700	200	9,500	1·3
Upper Volta	16,900	1,100	15,800	1·4
Middle Congo	41,800	12,000	29,800	13·8
Gabon	32,000	12,900	19,100	14·4
Oubangui-Chari	38,700	15,500	23,200	6·9
Chad	21,700	100	21,600	3·2
Cameroun	103,000	45,000	58,000	5·9
Togo	4,300	500	3,800	1·2

SOURCE: Raymond Barbé, *Les classes sociales en Afrique noire* (Paris, 1964), p. 72.

those in non-agricultural enterprises, whereas Africans holding skilled or managerial jobs averaged approximately 1 per cent of the total in all sectors of the economy. Almost a decade later this situation remained virtually unchanged, with even a slight decline registered in the number of Africans in top-echelon posts. Between 1948 and 1957, it was in the non-agricultural sector, and particularly in government service, that the greatest numerical gains were made by Africans, as well as by Europeans.[9] The proportion of gainfully employed Eu-

[9] Raymond Barbé, *Les Classes sociales en Afrique noire* (Paris, 1964), p. 73.

Table 27. *Total skilled and unskilled labour in the public and private sectors, French Black Africa, 1956*

Territory	Unskilled labour		Skilled labour		Total skilled and unskilled labour	
	Number	Per cent of total African wage-earners	Number	Per cent of total African wage-earners	Number	Per cent of total African wage-earners
Senegal	36,300	40·5	30,300	33·8	66,600	74·3
Ivory Coast	115,000	70·1	31,600	19·3	146,600	89·4
Guinea	50,600	47·5	25,300	23·8	75,900	71·3
Soudan (Mali)	18,600	47·0	8,600	21·7	27,200	68·7
Dahomey	8,400	39·6	4,400	20·8	12,800	60·4
Niger	5,600	45·5	4,100	33·6	9,700	79·1
Upper Volta	12,600	54·0	4,300	18·5	16,900	72·5
Middle Congo	30,500	50·1	11,300	18·6	41,800	69·7
Gabon	24,600	62·4	7,400	18·8	32,000	81·2
Oubangui-Chari	30,700	64·0	8,000	16·7	38,700	80·7
Chad	15,000	45·3	6,700	20·2	21,700	65·5
Cameroun	72,200	57·6	30,800	24·6	103,000	82·2
Togo	1,700	14·6	2,600	22·4	4,300	37·0

SOURCE: Raymond Barbé, *Les classes sociales en Afrique noire* (Paris, 1964), p. 71.

ropeans to Africans was very small. Table 28 indicates roughly the number of African wage-earners in the various sectors (except in that of civil servants, where Europeans were proportionately more numerous). Moreover, the geographical distribution of wage-earners clearly reflected the far greater economic development of the coastal territories in both federations, although the imbalance was less striking in AEF than in AOF.

In all categories of employment, Africans far outnumbered Europeans, but the Europeans held the top posts and many in the middle echelons and earned a much larger percentage of the revenues. New government posts created by the FIDES, beginning in 1947, brought to Africa some 66,000 new French immigrants attracted by salaries higher than those paid for equivalent services in France. In 1956 their number was further swelled by the transfer to the African territories of French officials and technicians evacuated from Indo-China, Tunisia and Morocco. The new arrivals monopolized many posts; they thereby restricted the opportunities available to educated Africans for upward mobility, for there was no adequate training of Africans for such employment, with the result that only a handful of trained and experienced African civil servants and technicians were available to hold responsible jobs after independence.

At the lower end of the economic spectrum, the tapering off of the FIDES-financed public-works programme in the late 1950s resulted in unemployment in the unskilled category of African wage-earners. This became acute in Dakar, in Abidjan and in Brazzaville, whose populations had more than doubled since the Second World War and continued to increase despite the shrinkage in job opportunities. Not only did the persistent rural exodus reduce agricultural production in the hinterland, but also the growing number of idle youths in the

Table 28. *African wage-earners in various sectors, French Black Africa, 1958*

Territory	Public sector		Private sector						
	Civil servants	Other government employees	Agriculture, fishing, forestry	Mines and quarries	Processing industries	Building and public works	Trade, banking, liberal professions	Transport and maintenance	Domestic servants
Senegal	5,550	15,200	4,650	1,000	12,550	11,600	20,750	17,500	11,500
Ivory Coast	6,000	22,000	90,000	2,000	8,000	11,000	12,000	10,000	10,000
Guinea	5,500	10,100	32,200	2,700	3,900	15,500	11,000	9,500	19,000
Soudan (Mali)	5,700	9,850	7,380	3,840		5,470	3,940	3,420	2,200
Dahomey	3,300	4,800	1,700	110	840	2,320	4,330	2,800	1,800
Niger	2,200	4,200	190	120	500	3,860	1,180	410	940
Upper Volta	2,650	9,050	1,120	320	1,560	5,100	2,230	690	1,780
Middle Congo	3,000	14,200	12,030	1,360	6,340	4,960	9,550	6,540	5,420
Gabon	2,000	6,500	12,940	6,230	2,400	3,840	3,220	1,670	2,800
Oubangui-Chari	2,200	3,200	15,520	5,750	7,220	4,200	3,800	1,700	5,000
Chad	3,250	8,000	140	330	4,770	5,760	5,350	1,870	5,330
Cameroun	8,000	17,900	45,150	2,500	12,300	12,950	25,400	8,000	7,500
Togo	2,040	3,420	470	260	300	620	1,410	1,780	1,650

SOURCE: Raymond Barbé, *Les classes sociales en Afrique noire* (Paris, 1964), p. 70.

towns aggravated urban social problems and jeopardized political stability as well as the investment of private capital.

Belatedly and ineffectually, the French administration urged unemployed youths to return to the land. They also instituted some rapid vocational-training courses in the towns. This, however, improved the situation only slightly, for the French school system in Africa was geared to training a limited number of Africans for clerical posts and even fewer in manual skills. In the private sector, educated African personnel had little prospect of advancement to managerial positions, nor did private employers make living and working conditions attractive enough to overcome the Africans' aversion to regular and monotonous work. Inasmuch as little was done to revitalize village life, young farmers naturally gravitated to the towns, where they could find shelter, diversion and an occasional job.

African traditions of hospitality required the urban wage-earner to support his less fortunate kinsmen, and the larger his salary the greater the number of drones he had to lodge and feed. This obligation, combined with rapidly rising prices, encouraged corruption, particularly among the civil servants, who were the best paid of all African wage-earners. Furthermore, they aspired to maintain the same ostentatious life-style as that set by expatriate officials. The grant of greater autonomy to the African territories in 1956 led to a rapid Africanization of the administration, by means of which political leaders sought to enlarge their following. Personal loyalty rather than professional competence became the yardstick for appointment to the bureaucracy. The numerical increase of this class was not matched by a corresponding growth in its efficiency and honesty, and both the territorial administrations and their revenues suffered accordingly.

Legislation

In the glow of post-World War II liberalism, the French Parliament moved to satisfy partially the Africans' aspiration for equality with Frenchmen in the economic as well as the political domain. This necessitated revising and supplementing the piecemeal labour legislation of the inter-war period, in the interests first of African civil servants and then of wage-earners. The Lamine Gueye law of 30 June 1950 guaranteed legal parity between African and metropolitan bureaucrats possessing the same professional qualifications, except for the latter's expatriate allowances. Educational facilities for Africans were still so limited, however, that few Africans could compete with metropolitan candidates for admission to the higher echelons of the administrative corps.

The *Loi-Cadre* of 23 June 1956, by dividing the overseas bureaucracy into state and territorial services, marked another step toward Africanizing the official cadres. France retained the right to appoint and pay the salaries of officials staffing the services of defence, finance, judiciary and transportation, the territorial governments' control being limited to functionaries of the local administration. Although the African ministers were thus enabled to Africanize the minor posts, this provision had the disadvantage of increasing the privileged status of the few African bureaucrats, thus widening the gap between them and the peasantry and also arousing the wage-earners' jealousy.

The Overseas Labour Code, finally promulgated in 1952, though it created a theoretical equality between African and French workers, required time and pressure from the African parliamentarians and unions to make this a practical reality. Eventually, the Code's provisions for a minimum wage, a forty-hour week, an eight-hour working day, pensions, paid leave, family allowances and safeguards for women and child labourers were enforced. Subsequent decrees closed the loopholes in regard to work accidents and occupational diseases, established labour exchanges and created the machinery for settling disputes between employers and employees. Concurrently, African wage-earners were encouraged to form unions, and the literacy qualifications initially required for election to union offices were eliminated.

Labour organizations

The first French Black African unions in AOF were organized in 1937 by France's socialist government, but in AEF the unions were not authorized until 1944. In neither federation, however, did they take firm root until they were promoted by the Overseas Labour Code, whose application required that African wage-earners be represented by elected spokesmen. Although the first significant labour strike in Francophone Africa was carried out in 1947 by the autonomous union of workers on the Dakar-Bamako railroad, it was the three main metropolitan labour federations that promoted unionization by forming branches throughout French Black Africa.

The Force Ouvrière (socialist), which was the first in the field, attracted both French and African civil servants. The strength of its branches ebbed, however, with the declining power of the socialist party in France soon after the Second

World War, while the Christian unions forged ahead, especially in the coastal territories where Catholic missions were entrenched. The most rapid progress of all, particularly among workers in the private sector, was registered by the Confédération Générale du Travail (CGT) unions, which during the early post-war years were effectively backed by the French Communist Party and by the strongest interterritorial African political movement, the Rassemblement Démocratique African.

The *Loi-Cadre* of 1956 encouraged an autonomous trend among the African trade unions, whose sponsorship by the metropolitan labour federations now seemed to their leaders to be a liability rather than an asset. To be sure, French labour officials had given a structure to their African branches and had supported their demands in the Parliament, besides giving their leaders training abroad. But by the mid-1950s the African unions' subordination to their French mentors, and their own division into organizations based on Western ideological divergencies, seemed artificial, and even harmful to effective bargaining with the colonial administration and private employers.

The Christian unions, which were the first to organize on a Pan-African basis, were soon overtaken by the Union Générale des Travailleurs de l'Afrique Noire (UGTAN), formed in the Francophone territories by the Guinean labour and political leader Sékou Touré. With its anti-colonial programme of African unity and independence of foreign labour movements, the UGTAN captured the membership of the CGT and of most of the autonomous unions in AOF and Cameroun. Although weak in AEF, the UGTAN for several years was the strongest organization of Francophone African wage-earners, until it was progressively undermined by regional, tribal, personal and ideological divisions. Fearing the UGTAN's radical orientation and its domination by Sékou Touré, the politically moderate African governments asserted greater control over their territorial labour unions.

From the outset, the effectiveness of French Black Africa's unions was hampered by their organizational and financial weaknesses. The vast majority of African workers, who were self-employed farmers or seasonal workers on isolated plantations, forest camps or mines, were not union members. Only those wage-earners who were comparatively stabilized, either geographically or by occupation, belonged to any labour organization, and even these paid their dues irregularly if at all. Unions therefore became dependent on outside financial sources, notably on a political party in Africa or in France, or on the international labour organization with which they were affiliated. This lack of independent funds, combined with the growth of the unemployed active population, prevented the unions from conducting prolonged strikes, particularly against the administration, which was everywhere the largest single employer of labour. Only when the unions made common cause with the urban proletariat, as they did in Dahomey in the 1950s, could they bring effective pressure to bear on the government and on private employers.

Until the French Black African territories became independent in 1960, the improvements made in the status of their wage-earners were due less to local union action than to legislation passed by the French Parliament on the initiative of liberal French politicians and African deputies. Without political pressure, African labour had little bargaining power of its own vis-à-vis the colonial administration and foreign employers. Its initial assets—low wages and the scarcity of labour in relation to the demand—dwindled steadily after 1946, while its perennial drawbacks of instability, preference for clerical employment and lack of skills remained almost unchanged. After the abolition of forced labour, the enforcement of the Overseas Labour Code and the official encouragement of unionization, employers in French Black Africa tried various expedients to reduce their dependence on unskilled African labour. Rapid vocational-training courses were instituted by chambers of commerce, forest and mining enterprises were increasingly mechanized and Italian labourers were imported to build the Edéa (Cameroun) hydro-electric dam. None of these measures, however, proved wholly satisfactory, because they were inadequate, were too costly or were strongly opposed by the African unions. To break this impasse and to give themselves and the unions more leverage, the African nationalist leaders politicized the labour movement. They succeeded in enlisting the unions' support for independence, but only at the cost of subordinating the professional interests of African wage-earners to the attainment of political objectives.

The granting of independence to the French Black African territories in 1960, a result in part of the combined efforts of African political and labour leaders, removed the cement that had held them together; and increasingly their interests diverged. Wage-earners of all categories tried to perpetuate and even to improve the privileged status they had acquired under the French administration. No longer would they accept the politicians' tutelage; and the contention that labour must adjust its demands to the new states' financial resources in the interest of the entire population fell on deaf ears.

BIBLIOGRAPHY

Barbé, Raymond. *Les classes sociales en Afrique noire*. Paris, 1964.

Berg, Elliot J. 'The character and prospects of African economics', in *The United States and Africa,* Walter Goldschmidt, ed. New York, 1963.

'The economic basis of political choice in French West Africa', *American Political Science Review,* June 1960, **54,** no. 2.

'Real income trends in West Africa 1939–1960', in *Economic transition in Africa,* Melville J. Herskovits and Mitchell Harwitz, eds. London, 1964.

Blanc, Paul. 'A propos des migrations dans l'ancienne "Afrique Française" ', *L'Afrique et l'Asie,* 1961, no. 54.

Brunschwig, Henri. *Mythes et réalités de l'impérialisme colonial français, 1871–1914.* Paris, 1960.

Buell, R. L. *The native problem in Africa.* 2 vols. New York, 1928.

Capet, Marcel. *Traité d'économie tropicale: les économies d'A.O.F.* Paris, 1958.

Charbonneau, Jean and René. *Marchés et marchands d'Afrique noire.* Paris, 1961.

Chauleur, Pierre. 'Les plans de modernisation de l'Afrique noire et de Madagascar', *Revue Juridique et Politique,* Jan.–March 1964.

Dia, Mamadou. *Réflexions sur l'économie de l'Afrique noire.* Paris, 1952.

Dresch, Jean. 'Les trusts en Afrique noire', *Servir la France,* April 1946.

Dulphy, G. 'La promotion des masses rurales africaines', *Marchés Tropicaux,* 15 Nov. 1958.

Dumont, René. *L'Afrique noire est mal partie.* Paris, 1962.

Durant, Huguette. *Essai sur la conjoncture de l'Afrique noire.* Paris, 1957.

'Enquête sur les banques et sociétés en Afrique noire', *Afrique Nouvelle,* 18 Sept. 1956.

Erhard, Jean. *Le destin du colonialisme.* Paris, 1957.

Esperet, Gérard. 'Syndicalisme croyant en Afrique française', *Le Mois en Afrique,* May 1967, no. 17.

'L'évolution des régimes douaniers des états de l'Afrique et de la république de Madagascar', *Marchés Tropicaux,* 15 July 1961.

France. Ambassade. Service de Presse et d'Information. *French Africa: a decade of progress, 1948–1958; achievements of FIDES . . .* New York, Nov. 1958.

Impact of French modernization plan on Africa. New York, Oct. 1956.

Frankel, S. Herbert. *Capital investment in Africa: its course and effects.* London, Oxford University Press, 1938.

Gandolfi, Alain. 'Réflexions sur l'impôt de capitation en Afrique noire', *Revue Juridique et Politique d'Outre-Mer,* April–June 1962.

Gerig, E. *The open door and the mandates system,* London, 1930.

Haight, F. A. *A history of French commercial policies.* New York, 1941.

Hailey, William Malcolm Hailey, 1st baron. *An African survey: revised 1956.* London, Oxford University Press, 1957.

Hance, William A. *Population, migration and urbanization in Africa.* New York, Columbia University Press, 1958.

Harmand, Jules. *Domination et colonisation.* Paris, 1910.

Hayter, Teresa. *French aid.* London, Overseas Development Institute, 1965.

Henry, Paul. 'The European heritage: approaches to African development', in *Africa Today,* C. Grove Haines, ed. Baltimore, Johns Hopkins Press, 1955.

Hoffherr, René. *Coopération économique franco-africaine.* Paris, 1958.

'Les investissements des sociétés dans les états de l'Afrique de l'ouest', *Marchés Tropicaux,* 8 July 1961.

Karp, Mark. 'The legacy of French economic policy in Africa', in *French-Speaking Africa,* W. H. Lewis, ed. New York, 1965.

Lokke, C. L. *France and the colonial question.* New York, Columbia University Press, 1932.

Mathieu, Gilbert. 'L'ensemble économique franco-africaine ne peut demeurer dans le status quo', *Le Monde,* 24–26 Sept. 1958.

Meynaud, Jean, and Anisse Salah-Bey. *Le syndicalisme africain.* Paris, 1963.

Moussa, Pierre. *Les chances économiques de la communauté franco-africaine.* Paris, 1957.

Pim, Sir Alan. *The financial-economic history of the African tropical territories.* London, Oxford University Press, 1940.

Plessz, N. G. *Problems and prospects of economic integration in West Africa.* Montreal, McGill University Press, 1968.

Priestley, H. I. *France overseas.* New York, 1938.

Richard-Molard, Jacques. *Afrique occidentale française.* Paris, 1952.

Roberts, S. H. *History of French colonial policy 1870–1925.* 2 vols. London, 1929.

Sarraut, Albert. *La mise en valeur des colonies françaises.* Paris, 1923.

Saxe, Jo. 'The changing economic structure of French West Africa', *Annals of the American Academy of Political and Social Science,* March 1955.

Schachter, Ruth. 'Trade unions seek autonomy', *West Africa,* 26 Jan. 1957.

'Social security in Africa south of the Sahara', *International Labour Review,* Sept. 1961.

Suret-Canale, Jean. *Afrique noire occidentale et centrale,* vol. II: *L'ère coloniale (1900–1945).* Paris, 1964.

Thomas, B. E. 'Railways and ports in French West Africa', *Economic Geography,* Jan. 1957.

Le travail en Afrique noire. Paris, 1952.

Wade, Abdoulaye. *Economie de l'ouest-africain.* Paris, 1964.

Zartman, I. W. *The politics of trade negotiations between Africa and the European Economic Community.* Princeton University Press, 1971.

CHAPTER 5

CAPITAL ACCUMULATION IN THE CONGO UNDER COLONIALISM: THE ROLE OF THE STATE

by

JEAN-PHILIPPE PEEMANS

The most elaborate and the most 'realistic' models of current development theory invoke the concepts of dualism and economic surplus. The purpose of this is to demonstrate the conditions under which the modernization of traditional society would be possible.[1] The realistic appearance of these models stems from their portrayal of modernization as an accumulation process rooted in the agricultural surplus built up by peasant labour.

On the one hand, these models, for instance, do not provide for an analysis of the relations between the social classes and of income distribution in pre-capitalist societies. In order to find a point of equilibrium based on their hypothesis of a constant wage, they have to fall back on the zero marginal productivity myth. In so doing, they reduce to a common denominator structures as different as colonial Jamaica, Meiji Japan and independent India. As a factor in the genesis and utilization of the economic surplus in pre-capitalist societies, the role of the state and of political power as a specific expression of class structure is completely neglected.[2]

On the other hand, these models are 'autocentric'. They analyse only the relations between agriculture and industry, with the agricultural surplus contributing effectively to the development of the industrial sector. But what happens when production for export is the predominant activity? Or when the agricultural surplus is absorbed by an industrial sector located abroad and does not contribute to the growth of a national industry? Or if there is a concurrent growth of agricultural and mining products for export? This is precisely what came about in African countries and in the Congo during the colonial period.

From the Leopoldian system to the Belgian colonial system

The striking image of a centre and a periphery seems to fit particularly the relations between industrial metropolises and their colonies exporting raw materials. In this case, in order to explain the extent to which the accumulation

---

[1] In particular, Sir Arthur Lewis, *Economic development with unlimited supplies of labour* (Manchester, 1954); and John C. H. Fei and Gustav Ranis, *Development of the labor surplus economy: theory and policy* (Homewood, Ill., 1964), p. 324.

[2] As an example of the opposite theory, which takes this role into consideration, we may cite Irfan Habib, 'Potentialities of capitalistic development in the economy of Mughal India', *Journal of Economic History,* March 1969, **29**; E. Herbert Norman, *Japan's emergence as a modern state: political and economic problems of the Meiji period* (New York, 1940); and Catherine Coquery-Vidrovitch, 'Recherches sur un mode de production africain', *La Pensée,* 1969, no. 144.

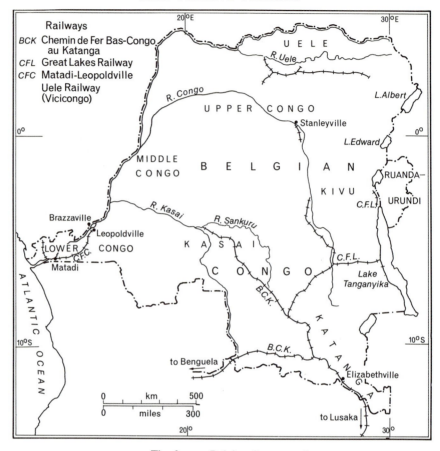

Railways
BCK Chemin de Fer Bas-Congo au Katanga
CFL Great Lakes Railway
CFC Matadi-Leopoldville
Uele Railway (Vicicongo)

5. The former Belgian Congo, 1960

progress in the periphery is slow and dependent, we must take into consideration the transfer of surplus to the metropolis, whether indirectly through unequal exchange [3] or directly through the repatriation of a large share of the profits earned locally.

However, the analysis of the centre-periphery relationship must not neglect the role of the state. Otherwise there is danger of giving an oversimplified explanation in terms of a dominant versus a dominated country. The other pitfall is to place undue emphasis on the economic aspects of the overseas expansion of the central economies and of their relations with the countries of the periphery. Here the state may play a dual role: first, in the expansion of the metropolitan economies; and second, in the peripheral economies.

In discussing the first, one must avoid the temptation of strict historical determinism to explain by so-called economic laws alone the overseas expansion

---

[3] Arghiri Emmanuel, *L'Echange inégal: essai sur les antagonismes dans les rapports économiques internationaux* (Paris, 1969), pp. 23–54, 86–188, 254–72; and Christian Palloix, *Problèmes de la croissance en économie ouverte* (Paris, 1969).

of mature capitalist economies looking for low-cost raw materials or markets for manufactured goods. This drive is, of course, one of the possible ways in which entrepreneurs try to overcome the tendency in mature capitalist economies for profit rates to decline.[4] But this policy, in order to become effective, does require state intervention. Hence we need an analysis of the social nature of state power [5] to explain why some mature capitalist economies have opted for colonial expansion, while others, faced with the same contradictions, have not.

In order to understand the differences in strategy between various social structures that have attained a given level of economic development, it is important to know the nature, the goals and the ideologies of the groups wielding state power. This applies to the mercantilist phase of capitalist development in the seventeenth and eighteenth centuries as well as to the 1880–1914 phase of maturity, during which imperialist expansion was renewed. But again we must avoid a mechanistic approach. What we are actually dealing with is the problem of competition between states that are political rivals, assuming specific interests of competing capitalist systems within a world-wide capitalist network organized solely on an economic basis. Nor is the state merely a simple instrument of the interests of finance capital. But, conversely, the importance of the role of the state does not allow us to make the analysis solely at the political level and in terms of political rivalries alone. The problem is to understand the interactions between the economic structure and the class structure, and the relative autonomy of political decisions of the state power that work inside these structures themselves.

The role of the state in the peripheral economies is important on a number of counts. First of all, it is the military force of the centre states that imposes on the peripheral countries a certain degree of subordination (as in the case of China after the unequal treaties of 1842),[6] or even complete subordination (as in the case of the colonies properly defined). The conquering state power can destroy the pre-existing state, or make it subservient to its own goals. For instance, it can use political power to promote new forms of production geared toward export. The state can also impose on the subject country a certain position in the international division of labour. Furthermore, it can establish through the use of political power a division of labour between the conquering minority and the conquered people inside the colony itself. For instance, state power may be used to concentrate the ownership of the means of production in the hands of the conquering minority. Through this means, the minority may become transformed into a bourgeoisie controlling the accumulation of capital. At the same time, state power becomes an efficient tool for depriving the labour force of its land, thus proletarianizing the cultivators. The control of state power by the foreign minority may thus play an important role in integrating the labour force into the world market at a lower income level than would be

---

[4] See, on this question, Christian Palloix, *L'Economie mondiale capitaliste* (Paris, 1971), vol. I, pp. 81–95.
[5] See, for example, the analysis proposed by Nicos Poulantzas in *Pouvoir politique et classes sociales de l'état capitaliste* (Paris, 1968), p. 398; and in his 'Le concept de classes sociales', *L'Homme et la Société*, 1972, no. 24–25, pp. 23–26.
[6] Jean Chesneaux, ed., *Histoire de la Chine*, vol. I: *1840–1885* (Paris, 1969), pp. 5–50.

obtained for the development of independent peasant production.[7] It is difficult, here, not to lose sight of the origins of a so-called dualism in traditional society itself: that is, the scarcity of land and the growth of population. What does exist is a new set of social relations having their origin in the use of political violence as an instrumentality of the state. The state, for instance, can create a scarcity of land if it uses its sovereignty to expropriate large tracts of land and cede them to a foreign minority.[8] In this way the state can check the development of autonomous forms of capitalism in the periphery country; and by breaking down the pre-capitalist society, it can halt the growth of an indigenous class structure. Such a policy leads instead to a polarization between the foreign bourgeoisie on one hand and a more or less uniform indigenous mass on the other.

In this respect the role of the state has been crucial in the Congo since the beginning of the Leopoldian conquest. Here, in fact, between 1885 and 1908, the state exercised active leadership in all fields of the colonization process. Nor can this activity be explained solely as a manifestation of King Leopold's exceptional personality. State power had an economic and social rationality that must be analysed in terms of the interplay between state power and foreign capital.

On the one hand, the state laid the foundations of the relations between foreign capital and the African labour force on a global scale. On the other hand, it arbitrated between the various foreign lobbies whose interests sometimes conflicted. After 1908, despite an apparent loss of power and autonomy, the colonial state continued to perform its previous role. It maintained close ties with foreign capital. It continued to utilize an elaborate set of constraints for the purpose of putting pressure on the labour force, thereby fostering the accumulation of capital. The state served as arbitrator between different groups of foreign capitalists competing for available labour supplies. The state also arbitrated between the short-term and the long-term interests of the colonial system in order to avoid the contradictions that posed a threat to the very existence of the system. Even though the role and the autonomy of the state may be objective facts, the importance of the state should not be overrated. The colonial state is a periphery state. It wields enormous power over the colonized society, yet it has no means of influencing the external conditions of the dependent development that it has helped to promote. The world market and the metropolis economy remain outside its range.

Moreover, although the close relations between the colonial state and finance capital made possible many compromises, this co-operation could not resolve the growing contradictions within the system after the Second World War. These contradictions led to the disintegration of rural society, to proletarianization without an adequate growth in employment opportunities, and to a heavy dependence on external debt to finance development projects. The partnership between the state and foreign capital failed to promote the development of an indigenous capitalism that might have stabilized the colonial society.

---

[7] See, on this question, C. Bundy, 'The emergence and decline of a South African peasantry', *African Affairs,* Oct. 1972, pp. 372–88.

[8] This has been vigorously demonstrated by Giovanni Arrighi, 'Labour supplies in historical perspective: a study of the proletarianization of the African peasantry in Rhodesia', *Journal of Development Studies,* April 1970, no. 3, pp. 197–234.

After the war, however, there was a real change in economic and social policy in this direction.

The present study analyses the decisive role played by the colonial state in establishing a certain mode of relations between foreign capital and indigenous labour in the Congo. We point out first of all the exceptional features of the Leopoldian régime in this respect, and show the continuity between the policy of the Congo Free State and that of the colonial régime after 1908. We then examine the interdependence between the colonial state and foreign capital. In this general framework, we emphasize the role of the state in building a transportation network. This development was a precondition for the integration of the African labour force into the world market and for the take-off of the accumulation process.

State constraint in the economic and social spheres

Between 1885 and 1908, the Leopoldian system took two fundamental steps in the Congo to assure control over the means of production. First was the appropriation of land by the state; and second, the enactment of a set of laws providing for mobilizing the labour force. The two measures tended to complement and to reinforce each other.

By a decree of 1 July 1885, the General Administration of the Congo Free State established the right of the state to dispose of all lands that were not effectively occupied by African tribes. The administration thus gained the right to exploit directly or to grant rights of exploitation over all uncultivated lands. In this way the state acquired an enormous capability for exerting pressure on the colonized society and for paralysing almost all the society's economic initiatives. In lineage-type societies the acreage required to maintain an economic equilibrium exceeds many times the acreage under cultivation. A great deal of land is needed both for shifting cultivation and for hunting. Indigenous land systems therefore cannot do without vast areas that are not actually occupied. Before colonization, all the Congolese territory was thus shared *de facto* between various communities that recognized common rights of occupation and circulation in empty areas. The rights of land use devoted to the members of each community were regulated by the elders by virtue of custom. But these notables could never cede the indivisible collective ownership to foreign people.

By its 1885 decree, the state gave the foreign colonists a legal device to take over all these lands. By a broad interpretation of the decree, as was the practice between 1891 and 1908, Africans could be forbidden to undertake any activity outside production for subsistence. They could be obliged to labour on the land belonging to the state or on the land granted to private companies, or to work as wage-earners for the same companies.

Under the Leopoldian régime, this decree was interpreted in various ways. After a period of very strict application (1891–1906), there was a certain softening of the system. The decree of 3 June 1906 allowed to the governor the right to leave to the African communities three times as much land as that effectively occupied. The decree of 1885 was not abolished after 1908. It was applied more or less extensively, but remained a pillar of the colonial system and rested on the grant of vast tracts of land to semi-public organizations or private companies. Its usefulness was indeed clearly understood by the Belgian colonial administration after 1908. For instance, the *Annual report on the colony* dated 1918 declared, 'In the interest of the Africans themselves, it is necessary to avoid making impossible or difficult the grant of land to Europeans by setting up over-sized native reserves. This would moreover keep the native away from industrial employment.' [9] The decree concerning vacant land had thus the same consequences as the reserve policy devised by the British in other territories. In both cases, during the first stage of occupation state power helped to take over control of the natural resources and to give to the colonizers a tool to reduce the colonized society to the role of a simple labour reservoir. In this manner the colonial society was forced to encompass in one leap all the stages that had created a proletariat in Europe over centuries of gradual economic and social transformation, especially through 'enclosures' and similar devices.

This acceleration of the process, however, required other complementary measures. One of the most important was the creation of a legal framework that allowed the state to mobilize the potential labour force by authoritarian means.

As early as 1892, the administration of the Congo Free State required the indigenous male adult population to collect marketable products and to deliver them to state agents. This measure complemented the establishment of a state monopoly on the products available on the 'vacant lands', most of which were from that time classified as 'state domain'. These decisions were a loose application of the principles of the 1885 decree on the vacant lands.

From 1885 to 1891 state ownership remained formal in nature. Foreign trade expanded and traders bought merchandise from Africans for export. Beginning in 1891, a change took place. The state did not formally outlaw this commerce, but it reserved to itself a virtual monopoly on purchasing marketable products from the so-called domain lands. This system prevailed in the newly occupied areas, beyond Leopoldville, towards the Kasai and the Upper Congo. In these areas were located the three most valuable products—rubber, copal and ivory—over which the state assumed control. In the Lower Congo, where trading activities were firmly established and centred on palm products, foreign commercial capital was able to continue its business; it contributed to state income through the classical method of export duties.

This policy enabled the state to increase its share of production. Between 1895 and 1906, state income rose from 30 to 49 per cent of export earnings. By 1906, 41 per cent of state revenue derived from direct taxes paid by the African population, 35 per cent from direct profits of the state monopolies and other economic activities, and 20 per cent from customs duties. These duties were a charge supported mainly by the African population: duties on exports were subtracted from the prices paid to producers, and duties on imported consumer goods were supported by mass consumption. Capital goods were not subject to taxation, and taxes on foreign enterprises represented only 2 per cent of state receipts.

Later the state substituted administrative constraints for commerce. The administration established a system of taxes in kind, according to which every adult was obliged to provide each month a certain volume of exportable products. The volume could vary from region to region and was imposed on every community. The intensity of the pressure on the population therefore depended

---

[9] Belgian Congo, *Rapport annuel sur la Colonie, 1918* (Brussels, 1919), p. 107.

on the local representatives of the state. But two elements joined to push this pressure to the limit. On the one hand, the central authority ordered its agents to increase state incomes by all available means. On the other hand, the agents themselves were directly interested in getting a high return on taxes through a system of bounties. Moreover, they knew that their performance in this area determined to a large extent their eligibility for promotion. The result was an expansion in production for export dependent on the use of force and even of terror. Since many reliable descriptions of this system have appeared, there is no need to provide details here.

From 1892 to 1903 the system had highly arbitrary features, as it was based only on a very general and vague decree of the secretary of state providing for all measures necessary to promote the development of the state private domain. During this period violence reached its height. After 1903, two elements combined to produce some restraints. The first was a press campaign organized both in England and in Belgium against the Leopoldian régime that led to political pressure on the king. Secondly, the reign of force had enabled the state to reach a level of production that could not be surpassed, given the physical limits of an economy based on gathering. This situation may be illustrated by the evolution of exports of gathered products between 1887 and 1913 (see Table 29). Following the administrative pressure and the occupation of the territory, by 1895–1900 production had reached a peak that was not exceeded before the First World War. Assuming that a system of gathering forest products could not be improved by technical means, output could be enlarged only by expanding the producing areas. But that would have required an important reinforcement of the military occupation—that is, increasing costs in order to reach marginal areas. Therefore the best policy was to concentrate the efforts

Table 29. *Exports of gathered products, Lower and Upper Congo,*
1887–1913
(in 1,000 tons)

| | Origin by regions | | | | |
| | Lower Congo | | Upper Congo | | |
	Palm-oil	Palm-kernels	Rubber	Ivory	Copal
1887	1·0	2·9	—	—	—
1890	2·3	6·5	0·1	0·2	—
1892	0·9	3·0	0·1	0·2	—
1895	1·8	4·9	0·6	0·3	—
1898	1·4	4·7	2·1	0·2	—
1900	1·6	4·8	5·3	0·2	—
1902	1·7	5·2	5·3	0·2	0·3
1904	1·7	4·5	4·8	0·1	0·9
1906	1·9	4·9	4·8	0·1	0·8
1908	2·1	5·2	4·5	0·2	1·6
1910	2·1	6·1	3·4	0·2	0·9
1911	2·2	6·7	3·4	0·2	2·1
1912	2·0	5·8	3·5	0·2	3·7
1913	1·8	6·6	3·5	0·2	4·1

SOURCE: Alexandre Delcommune, *L'avenir du Congo belge menacé*, 2nd ed. (Brussels, 1921), pp. 282–3.

on the regions already occupied, with easy access, controlled by a relatively small but highly mobile military force (the *promenades militaires* system). By this means, existing levels of production might be maintained, provided that the negative effects of excessive pressures could be avoided.

The decree of 18 November 1903 was thus a step in the direction of stricter control. It enabled the district commissioners to determine each year the importance of the *prestations* required from the populations under their jurisdiction. According to the local applications at that time every Congolese adult was obliged to perform forty hours of work each month to meet state requirements.[10]

A new decree issued in 1906 completed and defined more precisely the regulations of 1903. Its main feature was to determine the value of the products delivered, to pay taxes and to classify the African tax-payers according to this value. The real goal of this tax system was to extract from the African labour force a surplus for export at a price level below normal. The fiscal system was an institutional way to determine the level of the terms of trade and to establish a system of unequal exchange.

Clearly, the peculiar tribute system that existed between 1891 and 1908 played a major role in creating the economic and social structures of the colonized society. Administrative constraint was used to incorporate the African population into the world market at an arbitrary level of remuneration. By the same token, the use of political violence and institutional pressures to increase production eliminated the material basis of economic development within the normal framework of capitalism. It suppressed the profit motive in the development of production. The growth of an autonomous capitalist structure was hampered not only by political pressure, but also by the extreme variations in world prices of raw materials that occurred between 1910 and 1935. It is hard to discover a rationale for an economic system in which the same product, requiring the same amount of labour, could fluctuate in value by as much as 500 per cent from year to year.

During the colonial period, both economic and political elements militated against the development of an active capitalist market. One example, relating to the period 1919–20, may illustrate this situation. In 1919, the high prices paid for export crops stimulated the peasants to grow specialized crops and to buy their food on the market. The governor-general then issued a circular obliging the peasants to return to the cultivation of subsistence crops.[11]

This continuous interplay of political and economic elements interfered with the process of an autonomous capitalist development that in other circumstances might gradually have come about. The explanations for the delay are to be found in the very nature of a lineage society. One of the most important was

[10] Decree of November 18, 1903, *Bulletin Officiel de l'Etat Indépendant,* 1903, pp. 292–309, which specified: 'Chaque année, les commissaires de district dresseront les rôles des prestations à fournir en espèce et en durée de travail pour l'année suivante par chacun des indigènes résidant dans les territoires de leur district respectif.'

[11] Governor-General Eugène Henry, in his circular of 5 April 1920, on the problem of native subsistence crops: 'In certain areas, the natives, attracted by high prices, devote all their activity to export products, and neglect more and more their subsistence crops. They are buying food products, of which a part is even imported from Europe, because they have sufficient incomes . . . I strongly urge the territorial authorities to take all necessary measures; the decree of 20 February 1917 gives them the power to act if persuasion fails.'

the role of the traditional authorities. For instance, in the case of the French Congo, Pierre Philippe Rey has shown how trade failed to establish contacts between foreign traders and African peasants. The chiefs, because they controlled the work force of the youngest adults and could appropriate collectively the greatest share of the gains realized through the barter system, intervened between the two.[12] This explains why a large share of imported goods consisted of prestige items circulating among the chiefs, rather than consumer goods for mass markets that might have stimulated the growth of exports. In its initial stage this growth could thus be very slow because of its dependence upon the lineage structure. But at the same time, as this structure was geographically very fragmented, the required number of intermediaries between the producers in the interior and the trade centres on the coast was greatly increased, thus heightening the differentiation between the various lineages. Those located near the coast controlled the trade chains and obtained the greatest gains. At the same time, the chiefs needed middlemen who specialized in trade contacts with foreigners, such as the *'linguisters'* in the Lower Congo. These middlemen were in a peculiarly favourable position. Not only were they agents of the chiefs but they actually enjoyed great autonomy and were able to build up private businesses. In time they might have become a sort of comprador bourgeoisie. Under the Leopoldian régime, the state monopoly established after 1891 eliminated the foreign traders and their local African agents, at least beyond Leopoldville. However, the state agents were not put directly in contact with the African peasants. The tribute, which replaced trade, was levied through the traditional chiefs.[13]

Thus under the state monopoly régime, the traditional hierarchy was utilized to foster production; but at the same time, it was tied in with the system by being given a share in the production extracted by the system. This share was a sort of remuneration that had been allocated to the chiefs since before 1900. At that time, the régime instituted a system of compulsory cultivation, in order to promote coffee and cocoa crops for export for the state's benefit. For each tree planted, the chief received 0·10 francs. When he had delivered the crop, he was paid in addition 50 per cent of the purchase price paid by the state. The decree of 3 June 1906 on the native chiefdoms recognized very clearly this role of the chiefs as paid auxiliaries of the administration.

A marked continuity of policy may be observed here between the colonial régime and the Leopoldian. Controversies over direct or indirect administration focused on the level of autonomy left to the traditional hierarchy in its relation with the colonial administration. But no one questioned either the role of the headmen in their control over the population and the labour force or the remuneration they received for this service.

The decree of 2 May 1910 reinforced the tutelage of the administration over the traditional hierarchy; this became the lower grade of the executive and was used to collect taxes and to ensure compulsory works and the recruitment of workers and soldiers. There was a tendency to appoint puppet chiefs, who were

---

[12] Pierre Philippe Rey, *Colonialisme, néo-colonialisme et transition au capitalisme: exemple de la 'Comilog' au Congo-Brazzaville* (Paris, 1971), pp. 224–44.

[13] On this subject, the report of the governor-general for 1904 says: 'The facts show that the natives accept the new order of things much more readily when it is presented by their traditional chiefs' (*Bulletin Officiel de l'Etat Indépendant*, 1906, p. 199).

often rejected by the population and whose efficiency in obtaining the required *prestations* was very low.

After 1918, the Minister of Colonies, Louis Franck, gave a larger measure of autonomy to the chiefs. This did not diminish their economic role. Their economic stake even increased, for the decree of 31 August 1919 fixed the remuneration of chiefs at a level proportional to the number of adult males suited to manual labour and to the amount of taxes paid.

The years 1920–30 witnessed heavy pressures on the potential labour surplus because of the rapid pace of accumulation. During this period, traditional power was actively associated with the pressures exerted primarily by the state and by foreign capital. A recent article by Jan Vansina is very illuminating in this respect.[14] The author shows that in the Kuba kingdom, the district administration was looked upon as the new suzerain of the Kuba king, but that, at the same time, the administration helped the king to reinforce his political power. Their collaboration was particularly active in the economic field. The king provided workers for the construction of the Chemin de Fer du Bas-Congo au Katanga (the BCK railway), and for the various recruiters; he collected taxes required by the colonial administration and took for himself tribute that was as important as the tax burden. For his services he received from the administration a salary of 60,000 francs a year, this at a time when the ordinary worker was paid a daily wage of one franc. He received in addition numerous bounties from the companies for which he had recruited manpower.

The decree of 1933 on the *circonscriptions indigènes* (native districts) was still more precise in its definition of the role played by traditional chiefs in the mobilization of labour. The new regulations, however, were increasingly applied in a spirit of direct administration. The administration itself took over more and more the direct control of compulsory work and tax collection. At that time, the process of subordination of the customary power was almost completed.

The colonial state, which continued the work undertaken by the Leopoldian régime, fostered a process of simultaneous conservation and dissolution of the traditional structures. There was conservation because the social relations and the ideology of the lineage society were apparently kept alive. There was dissolution because, at the same time, traditional society was being progressively eroded without any possibility of finding a new and dynamic coherence within the new system. Political constraint rejected the colonized society on the periphery of capitalism, reducing it to the sole role of a labour force lacking any material stimulus to production. The resistance or the apathy provoked by this absence was interpreted by the colonial power as a feature of an irrational behaviour that had to be cured by reinforcement of the political constraint, with an educative emphasis. Thus the use of political violence for economic goals, as long as there were no normal economic incentives (higher incomes) or constraints (a high degree of complete proletarianization) to promote production, was the cause of its own perpetuation. Continuity in the utilization of political tools to determine certain types of economic and social structures manifested itself in other ways, too, mainly through the tax system and through compulsory work.

[14] Jan Vansina, 'Les Kuba et l'administration territoriale de 1919 à 1960', *Cultures et Développement*, 1972, **4**, no. 2, pp. 275–98.

The utilization of state power to shape a particular type of economic and social structure continued after 1908. The most drastic features softened, but the logic of the system survived. The main characteristic of the régime was the utilization of the tax system for economic purposes. After 1910, taxes in kind were replaced by money taxes, but, despite this change, the goal of the tax system did not become purely fiscal. It remained an instrument of pressure on the African labour supply. This goal was clearly defined in a letter written by two managers of one of the most important commercial companies operating in the Congo between 1910 and 1914. 'The goal of the tax system', they argued,

is not only to reimburse the government in some measure for the cost of occupying all the territories, and of providing protection for the native population. Taxes also have a higher purpose, which is to accustom the Negroes to work . . . The native from the Upper Congo region has not as yet reached that stage of evolution where he would increase his comfort by trade and work, and for this reason the tax system will continue to provide for a long time the main incentive to work. The trader can of course steer the native in the right direction, but in the long run he had to be helped by the state. A tax system judiciously and regularly applied is the only efficient tool that can do the job.[15]

An interesting sidelight to this letter is the fact that its authors were also ardent backers of a restriction of commercial freedom imposed between 1910 and 1914. According to them, commercial freedom tended to stimulate competition among traders and to increase the purchase prices paid to African producers.

Taxes thus exerted pressure on the supply of products or labour until the end of the Second World War. As late as 1954 a specialist in colonial studies could write:

The experience of colonization in the Belgian Congo and elsewhere shows that taxes are a powerful incentive to the natives to work, and contribute in this way to their social progress. A tax should therefore not be so low that it becomes ineffectual as a stimulus. Nor should it be so high as to discourage work.[16]

Table 30 shows how poll taxes levied on the incomes generated in the compulsory crops system contributed to extracting a surplus from peasant labour. The figures in this table show that around 1920 the direct taxes on African incomes provided an important part of state receipts. In time, this share declined as foreign companies expanded and paid an increasing share of public revenue in the form of taxes. However, the larger revenue represented only a light burden on the foreign companies and individuals, while the declining share of the poll taxes on African incomes represented a heavy burden. Before 1940, yearly poll taxes absorbed 20–60 per cent of the African's annual cash incomes. The only exception was in the Lower Congo region, where market production had been developed much earlier and where the tax burden was relatively lighter. Given the high share of taxes in the peasants' annual incomes, many young men were forced to seek wage employment. These migrants had to work for three to six months in order to earn enough to pay taxes and to buy a few necessities. In many regions the monthly wage was indeed lower than the tax.

[15] Letter of Albert Thys and A. Camille Delcommune to the government, cited by Alexandre Delcommune, *L'avenir du Congo belge menacé: bilan des dix premières années (1909–1918) d'administration coloniale gouvernementale; le mal—le remède*, 2nd ed. (Brussels, 1921).

[16] Georges Hostelet, *L'œuvre civilisatrice de la Belgique au Congo de 1885 à 1945*, vol. 1: *L'œuvre économique et sociale* (Brussels, Institut Royal Colonial Belge, 1954), pp. 184–5.

Table 30. *Comparison of tax burden on foreign bourgeoisie and on African population, Belgian Congo, 1920–40*
(in per cent)

	1920	1922–4	1930	1933	1937	1940
Taxes on foreign bourgeoisie						
1. Rate of tax on:						
personal incomes	0–4				0–9	
profits of joint-stock						
companies	0				0	
dividends	6				12	
2. Share of taxes listed in						
(1) in state receipts	6		22			15
Taxes on African population						
1. Share of poll taxes in						
state receipts	21		16			13
2. Burden of annual poll						
taxes on:						
annual income of						
peasants		25–65	20	60		
average wage in						
rural areas for: 1 mo.		75–95	110	150		
2 mos.		25–30	35	48		
1 yr.		5–8	9	12		

SOURCE: Jean-Philippe Peemans, *Progrès économique et convergence des prix: le cas Congo-Belgique 1900–1960* . . . (Louvain, 1968), pp. 326–30; and Hugues Leclercq, 'Un mode de mobilisation des ressources: le système fiscal; le cas du Congo pendant la période coloniale', Université Lovanium, Institut de Recherches Economiques et Sociales, *Cahiers Economiques et Sociaux*, 1965, **3**, no. 2, 116, 118, 131.

The tax system thus played a decisive role in creating a labour market characterized by migrant labour and a high turn-over.

In addition to the tax system, other means of constraint were utilized after 1908, notably labour recruitment for economic purposes, and compulsory cultivation. The recruitment for so-called public-works projects was undertaken by authoritarian means. According to the decree of 22 March 1910, the customary chief of each African community was responsible for supplying a specified number of men for the construction of roads, railways or public buildings. In addition, the administration put pressure on the chiefs to provide foreign entrepreneurs with an adequate labour supply. This pressure was so severe between 1920 and 1930 and between 1935 and 1945 that it sometimes occasioned sharp debate in the metropolitan consultative colonial institutions.

The compulsory system of cultivation was re-established by an ordinance promulgated on 20 February 1917, according to the policy proposed by the Direction de l'Agriculture of the Ministry of Colonies. The chief proponent of this system, Edmond Leplae, attributed to it the subsequent growth of Congolese agriculture. He wrote in 1933: 'Whatever growth has taken place in the agriculture of ten million Africans in the Belgian Congo has been made possible only by the regulation introduced in February 1917. This ordinance enables us to compel the natives to plant certain subsistence or industrial crops.' [17] This

[17] Edmond Leplae, 'Histoire et développement des cultures obligatoires de coton et de riz au Congo belge de 1917 à 1933', reprint from *Congo*, May 1933, **1**, no. 5, p. 2.

régime forced the various African communities to cultivate each year some specified crop on a specified acreage, as determined by the agricultural service. The district administration helped to enforce these regulations. Failure to meet quotas was penalized. Between 1920 and 1930 this system was progressively regulated and extended. The decree of 5 December 1933 laid down new rules, which ceased to be the chief instrument for increasing production after the Second World War; but the decree of 10 May 1957 still permitted that it be applied. During the years 1920–45, this system was a powerful means of expanding production while keeping prices and peasant incomes low.

After 1908, indeed, the state no longer used direct constraint for the benefit of its own enterprises. But state power continued to serve, in a direct or indirect manner, the needs of private foreign enterprise. In the eyes of the overwhelming majority of observers at the time, this change was radical as compared with the previous situation. The advocates of private foreign interests had very often viewed the policy of the state as being opposed to the aims of foreign capital.

For instance, Félicien Cattier wrote in 1906:

The state must renounced all trade activity, limit itself to colonization and leave to the traders the natural resources of the colony. It must eliminate taxes in kind, which weaken the colony and diminish its greatest asset: manpower. What is important is to replace taxes in kind by taxes in money in order to force the native to contribute to public expenses and to oblige him to supply a certain amount of labour.[18]

During the Leopoldian régime and even after, Leopold's policy was often interpreted as being in conflict with private interests. But this contradiction was only apparent. In fact, there was continuity, as we have already seen, in the use of constraint by the state, before 1908 and after. The use of constraint by the state for its own enterprises in a first phase, and for the sake of private interests in a second phase, actually represented two complementary aspects of the same process. The link between the two may be found in the privileged relations maintained by the state with certain sectors of foreign capital. The colonial power, before and after 1908, worked in close co-operation with foreign industrial and finance capital evincing strongly monopolistic leanings. This co-operation often clashed with the interests of other sectors of foreign capital, because economic policy was geared to the creation of optimal conditions for the development of this monopoly capital. In certain cases, the state even utilized political devices to hamper the development of other kinds of capitalist ventures, foreign or indigenous, in trade or in agriculture.

Relations between the state and foreign capital

The state monopoly set up by Leopold II from 1891–2 on was considered by his contemporaries as extravagant and dangerous. Many of the king's officials were opposed to it and left his service. Sharp criticisms were made in the Belgian newspapers and in Belgian political circles. Opponents viewed the new policy as an unjustified blow to the principles of economic liberalism. Later on there was a tendency to look at the policy in terms of Leopold's personality or as stemming from the constraints bearing upon his colonial enterprise. Whichever was the case, it was assumed that either Leopold's policy was shaped by mercantilism, an outdated colonial doctrine, or it derived from a difficult situation that called for undesirable countermeasures.

[18] Félicien Cattier, *Etude sur la situation de l'Etat Indépendant du Congo* (Brussels, 1906), p. 204.

But there is still another possible interpretation. State monopoly may be regarded as a tool for exerting rigorous control over the limited economic surplus that existed in the first phase of colonial occupation. This policy had a long-range goal—to create an infrastructure that would attract foreign finance and industrial capital to the Congo. But it was necessary at the same time that foreign commercial capital be prevented from mobilizing the potential economic surplus to its own advantage. By concentrating on this surplus, the state could finance the cost of a rapid occupation of the territory and ensure its active participation in the capital formation of certain important enterprises.

Yet even though state monopoly was used as an effective instrument to guarantee the supremacy of finance and industrial capital, it cannot be regarded simply as an archaic and irrational form of economic organization. On the contrary, this policy was well suited to the stage of capitalism prevailing in Europe at the time the colonization of the Congo was undertaken, and also to the peculiar problems encountered in this vast region of Africa.

These fundamental aspects, however, have often been concealed by facts that, though they may have been dramatic, were perhaps not particularly pertinent. One example is the net transfer of 20 million francs by the Congo Free State to Belgium to finance urban prestige projects favoured by the king. That has been viewed as a typical element of an archaic form of colonial exploitation. Granted, it was indeed a very rare case of net transfer of surplus from the colony to the metropolis during the first phase of colonization. But can we regard this transaction as the most significant element of state economic policy when we know that the total of the agricultural exports alone had amounted to more than 450 million francs between 1890 and 1908?

Of much greater importance seems to be the economic policy adopted in the Congo itself during this period. This policy hampered the development of petty trade and commercial capitalism; it favoured instead large, long-range capitalist undertakings.

A most interesting case in this respect is that of the Compagnie Congolaise pour le Commerce et l'Industrie (CCCI), founded in 1887 by a confidant of Leopold II to pursue various commercial, agricultural and industrial activities in the colony. The decrees of 1891-2, which put a stop to the commercial activity, caused strained relations between the company's directors and the king. But the king forced the CCCI to make major commitments in the transport sector of the economy. The company became active in the construction of the Matadi-Leopoldville railway (CFML, also known as CFC) and in mining explorations in the Katanga (by the joint foundation of the Compagnie du Katanga).

Other facts, moreover, clearly illustrate the real purpose of the state-monopoly policy. At the height of this system, between 1897 and 1905, the state signed agreements with the Empain group for the construction of the Great Lakes railway (CFL) in the eastern part of the Congo. Most important of all, the state established close links with the Société Générale de Belgique, the principal Belgian concern at the time. This association resulted in the foundation of the two leading mining enterprises (Union Minière and Forminière) and of various railway companies that had to build the network required for the export of minerals. These agreements necessitated close co-operation between the state and foreign finance capital. Leopold II's Free State succeeded in creating a favourable climate for foreign capital, and co-operated closely with investors to promote the development of transport and mining. The state provided guaranteed rates of interest and vast land concessions; and it set up privileged companies known as *compagnies à charte*. It bestowed other economic favours, too. For instance, when the railway company CFL was founded in 1902, the state guaranteed the Empain group the amortization of its loan and also a minimum rate of 4 per cent annual interest. In addition, Empain received a concession of 4 million hectares of land, including rights over the subsoil, and the right of eminent domain—that is, the power to grant exploitation rights on the land. For each new investment of 25 million francs, the company would receive a new concession of 4 million hectares. In exchange, the state received 47 per cent of the profits and 25 per cent of the votes. It has been estimated that the Leopoldian state conceded to foreign companies a total of some 27 million hectares of land.

The outstanding result of the close co-operation between the state and finance capital was probably the Comité Spécial du Katanga (CSK), a development company founded in 1900. This privileged company reorganized the Compagnie du Katanga, established by the CCCI and the Free State in 1891, in order to explore the Katanga for the state. By the 1900 agreements, the state received two-thirds of the capital and income of the CSK, and the Compagnie du Katanga one-third. The CSK at the same time was granted extensive powers of administration and management and a concession over 45 million hectares of its domain. In addition, the CSK was assigned sovereign powers, including the right to establish a police force. These rights were exercised until 1908. The CSK took the initiative in creating the Union Minière du Haut-Katanga (UMHK) and until 1960 remained its most important shareholder.

The state might thereby have exerted a dominant influence on the management of the largest producer operating in the Congo of the time. But management was in fact left to the most important Belgian financial group, the Société Générale, despite the fact that the Société controlled only one-sixth of the CSK stock. The same principle was applied to the management of the diamond mines (Forminière).

This policy of non-intervention in direct management was typical of the period following the Leopoldian régime. After 1910 the state no longer exercised direct control over the economic surplus, but it still provided active assistance to foreign capital, even though this help depended on more indirect means.

Co-operation between the state and foreign capital assumed new forms under the colonial régime. After 1910 the state continued to provide guarantees for railway construction. This policy was extended during the period 1920–35. Secondly, the state continued the concessionary policy initiated under the Leopoldian régime. The only difference was that the state put pressure on the earlier concessionaires when they failed to carry out the terms of their respective grants. This enabled the state to re-allocate land to new settlers. But as Table 31 shows, land concessions made to settlers were relatively unimportant until the end of the Second World War.

After 1945, state policy became more favourable to the settlers: the areas under their control increased to 0·6 million hectares. At the same time, the areas controlled by the big companies were reduced to 2·5 million. This did not imply a reduction of their economic power, however, but merely the con-

Table 31. *Areas of land legally alienated, Congo, 1885–1944*
(hectares in millions)

	Private companies	Missions	Settlers
1885–1919	7·1	0·01	0·01
1920–44	4·6	0·10	0·21
Total	11·7	0·11	0·22

centration of their efforts on more manageable concessions. Moreover, the reduction of the areas was compensated for by the grant of monopoly rights of purchase of agricultural products in these restricted zones. One of the most typical cases of this evolution was Lever Brothers, whose concession was granted in 1911, after the Leopoldian régime. The company nevertheless maintained many monopolistic rights. Initially, it was permitted to select 0·75 million hectares from land scattered in five areas comprising 5·60 million hectares. The initial grant was progressively reduced: to 0·35 million hectares in 1930, by which time the company had developed only 0·03 million hectares. But at the same time, monopoly rights for purchase of palm products were reinforced and remained in effect until 1958.

The creation of the Comité National du Kivu (CNKi) in 1928 affords another example of the continuity of the monopolistic policy. This was indeed an institution very similar to the privileged companies created by Leopold II, such as the CSK. The CNKi was developed on the basis of the concessions granted to the CFL in 1902. It extended the co-operation between the state and the Empain group by combining under its control the state domain and the 12 million hectares granted to the CFL. At the same time, other financial groups were associated with the new institution, which received a state guarantee for its new investments and the right to grant land to individual settlers. The CNKi was assigned broad powers to develop the infrastructure in the Kivu. But because of the crisis of 1930–4, it relinquished this right, and until 1960 contented itself with the role of ground-nut collector.

In the preceding analysis I have tried to establish the links of continuity between the Congo Free State and the colonial state in the field of economic and social policy. The Leopoldian state, far from being an irrational set of institutions rooted in archaic principles, played a decisive role in shaping the relations between foreign capital and indigenous labour in the colony. As I see it, the state in that period may be regarded as a typical case of state-monopoly capitalism in the periphery. There was, moreover, no real break between the Leopoldian state and the Belgian colonial régime. The colonial régime merely continued to use the tools of constraint left by its predecessor. Of course it softened the harsher features, but at least until 1945 it used the existing economic constraints to create a labour market and to facilitate the accumulation of capital.

Colonial state policy in the accumulation of capital, 1910–60

During the colonial period, the foreign minority exercised major control over the means of production. Two factors contributed strongly to this situation: the economic initiative itself was concentrated in the hands of that minority; and various measures were taken, at least until 1945, to hamper indigenous economic initiative.

Ownership of means of production and structure of capital accumulation

As shown in Table 32, the foreign minority in 1958, though it represented only 1 per cent of the population, controlled 95 per cent of the assets, 88 per cent of private savings and 82 per cent of all the firms. But within the foreign minority itself a great discrepancy existed between a restricted number of powerful groups and a much larger number of small owners and employees. These powerful groups provided the economic basis of what may be called the foreign bourgeoisie: mainly the high- and middle-level cadres of the great foreign companies, and also the more important traders, independent industrialists and settlers. In a purely legal sense, the cadres did not own the means of production. Nevertheless they did constitute a genuine colonial bourgeoisie because they enjoyed a considerable measure of autonomy in decision-making and in the organization and control of production in the colony.

The bourgeoisie of cadres and managers was close to the top of the hierarchy. The middle-ranking officials of the colonial administration constituted the other branch of the colonial bourgeoisie. The ties between the two were not only social—both enjoyed a similar level of personal incomes and a privileged way of life with many opportunities for social intercourse—but they had also an economic basis. Because of the economic role of the colonial state, the high- and middle-level officials were often involved in economic questions of common interest.

Throughout the colonial period, indeed, an overwhelming proportion of the capital invested in the Congo was controlled by four financial groups closely

Table 32. *Comparison of economic condition of foreign minority and African population, Belgian Congo, 1958*

	Foreign minority (per cent)	African population (per cent)
1. Total population	1	99
2. Total assets	95	5
3. Largest units of production	82	18
4. Cultivated land	15	85
Cattle	47	53
5. Value of agricultural output:		
Total	35	65
Marketed	58	42
6. National income (including		
subsistence crops)	42	58
Private consumption	31	69
Private savings	88	12
7. Private sector wage-earners	2	98
Wage incomes	45	55

SOURCE: *Bulletin de la Banque Centrale du Congo et du Ruanda-Urundi*, Nov. 1959, pp. 411–34; and Peemans, *Diffusion du progrès économique*, pp. 12 and 385–6.

associated with the colonial state. At the end of the Leopoldian régime, transportation and mines—two sectors in which the capital invested represented two-thirds of all the capital stock—were controlled jointly by the state and three of these four financial groups (see Table 33).

Table 33. *Valuation of firms operating in the Congo, 1908–12*
(in francs)

	1908	1912
Transportation	62,500,000	200,500,000
Plantations	8,700,000	40,100,000
Mines	38,000,000	37,840,000
Trade	46,362,000	65,360,000
Cattle breeding	1,200,000	2,200,000
Total	156,762,000	346,000,000

SOURCE: Delcommune, *L'avenir du Congo belge menacé*, p. 299.

Between the First World War and the slump of 1929–34, capital accumulation in the Congo proceeded at an accelerated pace. In 1932, however, mines and transport still represented 70 per cent of all the capital stock. The investment in agriculture was only 18 per cent and in the industrial sector 13 per cent.

A somewhat exceptional document provides valuable data for the study of the structure of the ownership of assets at that time. This is a report of the Commission for Colonial Affairs of the Belgian Senate on the 1934 budget.[19] According to this document, the four above-mentioned Belgian financial groups controlled 75 per cent of the capital invested in the Congo, with the largest group controlling 60 per cent alone. These four groups held sway over 72 out of a total of 200 joint-stock companies in the country; of these, 41 were under the control of a few large concerns. The main financial groups also had almost complete charge over the banking system, transportation and mining, and over about 45 per cent of the manufacturing enterprises (see Table 34).

According to the Belgian Senate's Commission des Colonies, the industrial enterprises were the most prosperous, because the state, the mining companies and the transport companies provided a market.

By 1950, the structure of capital ownership does not appear to have changed much, compared with the situation in 1930. A proper evaluation is not easy, however, because different sources of information often use different systems of calculation. According to independent sources,[20] the total capital invested in the Congo in 1950 by foreign companies was between 34 and 38 milliard

[19] Belgium, Sénat, Commission des Colonies, *Discussion du budget pour l'exercice 1934*, Sénat, 1933–4 Sess., Documents parlementaires, no. 85 (Brussels, 1934).

[20] See Jean Gonda, 'Les holdings belges et le financement de l'industrialisation au Congo belge', *Revue des Sciences Economiques* (Liège), 1956, no. 105, pp. 38–40; G. Verriest, 'Résultats des sociétés coloniales ayant leur siège administratif en Belgique, suivant la statistique de l'impôt complémentaire sur les revenus', *Bulletin de la Banque Centrale du Congo Belge et du Ruanda-Urundi* (hereafter cited as *Bulletin BCCBRU*), March 1954; and Yvan Delhaye, 'Les résultats fiscaux des sociétés coloniales soumises à la loi du 21.6.1927', *Bulletin BCCBRU*, Sept. 1955.

Table 34. *Distribution of capital assets between sectors and financial groups: cumulative assets, Belgian Congo, 1920–32*
(current francs in milliards)

	Société Générale	Empain group	Cominière group	Brufina group	Total 4 groups	Total Congo
Transport	2·8	0·40	0·21	—	3·41	3·9
Mines	1·6	1·10	—	—	1·70	2·0
Industry	0·5	—	0·03	0·05	0·62	1·2
Agriculture	0·1	1·04	—	0·02	0·16	0·5
Trade	0·2	—	0·03	—	0·29	0·3
Real estate	—	—	—	—	—	0·1 *
Banks	0·05	0·04	—	0·10	0·20	0·3
Total	5·35	0·58	0·27	0·17	6·38	8·3

* Subscribed capital.

SOURCE: Belgium, Sénat, Commission des Colonies, *Discussion du budget pour l'exercice 1934*, Sénat, 1933–4 Sess., Documents parlementaires, no. 85 (Brussels, 1934).

francs, of which 25 milliard was controlled by the four financial groups associated with the state.

Thus, according to these figures, in 1950 the four groups controlled almost 70 per cent of the capital stock. The most important of them still had an absolute preponderance because it represented around 17·5 milliard in assets—that is, 70 per cent of the total assets controlled by the four, and 45 per cent of all the colony's assets (see Table 35).

In short, the state was associated with the four financial groups with subsidiaries representing around 16 milliard of their assets worth 25 milliard francs.

Table 35. *Distribution of capital assets among the four financial groups, Belgian Congo, 1950*
(1950 francs in milliards)

	Holdings	Assets of holdings
Société Générale	CCCI, Compagnie du Katanga, Simkat, Compagnie du Kasai, Interfina, Petrocongo	3·5
	UMHK, Forminière, Géomines	9·8
	Cotonco	1·1
	CSK	3·6
Empain group	Auxilacs (CFL, MGL), CIM, CNKi	2·5
Cominière group	Vicicongo, Cotonco	1·3
Brufina group		0·9
Colonial state	Otraco, Mines Kilo-Moto	1·3
Total		24·0

SOURCE: J. Gonda, 'Les holdings belges et le financement de l'industrialisation au Congo belge', *Revue des Sciences Economiques* (Liège), 1956, no. 105, pp. 38–40.

Table 36. *Capital assets by sectors, Belgian Congo, 1951–8*
(francs in milliards)

Sector	Gross fixed assets *		New investments	
	1951	1955	1955–8	1958
Mines	13·72	22·44	10·70	33·14
Transport	5·47	6·36	3·60	9·96
Industry	4·91	8·82	4·00	12·82
Agriculture	3·37	4·17	3·00	7·17
Trade	0·34	1·76	1·50	3·26
Real estate	0·83	1·55	0·66	2·21
Other	0·66	0·91	0·70	1·61
Total	29·30	46·01	24·16	70·17
Mines and transport (per cent)	65	63		61

* The figures given here cannot be strictly compared with the figures given previously. They represent only gross fixed assets, with no coefficient taking account of the money depreciation.

SOURCE: *Bulletin BCCBRU*, Nov. 1953, pp. 384–5; Nov. 1956, pp. 419–30.

As shown in Table 36, the situation does not seem to have changed very much between 1950 and 1960. The transport and mining sectors remained in first place. The progress of the industrial and agricultural sectors, where the middle foreign bourgeoisie could develop some initiative, did not fundamentally change the existing structure.

Although the major share of capital was invested in the transport and mining sectors, this does not imply that these two areas contributed in the same proportion to production and employment. These are sectors with a high capital intensity and a high capital–output ratio, both of which have a tendency to increase with time. Those who control the two sectors do not directly control the bulk of production and employment; nevertheless, they exert a strategic influence over economic development because they control the sectors where accumulation is concentrated. What is important, indeed, is the utilization of a growing economic surplus generated in sectors with a low capital–output ratio and a low capital intensity. In a model such as that used by Fei and Ranis, for instance, the transfer of surplus from the pre-capitalist sector does play a decisive role in financing accumulation in the capitalist sector. Thus, if ownership of the means of production is highly concentrated in the capitalist sector, control over the utilization of the surplus originated in the pre-capitalist sector will also be highly concentrated.

What, then, is the nature of that surplus? Fundamentally, it is a labour surplus above the normal level of activity in the pre-capitalist sector. It can take two forms: either a direct migration of labour to the capitalist sector or production of an agricultural surplus that will be transferred to the capitalist sector. This agricultural surplus itself will be transferred in the form of products (cash-crops) or savings (difference between subsistence wages and sales receipts, which is the gross profit of the owners of the agricultural surplus). According to the Fei-Ranis model, the zero marginal productivity of labour in the pre-capitalist sector explains 'naturally' the subsistence level of wages, and therefore creates the conditions for growth of an economic surplus that will contribute to financing the accumulation of capital. At the same time, the working of the model is based on a simplified hypothesis: in order to develop, modern industry, where capital has to be accumulated, is located in the rural areas themselves, thereby reducing to a minimum the costs of transfer and migration of labour.

In the Congolese case, the low wage level was also an important element in promoting the growth of the economic surplus. But as we have seen, the conditions favouring that growth did not derive from the pre-capitalist society but were the result of a systematic use of political constraint for mobilizing the potential economic surplus.

Moreover, in the Congo, contrary to the oversimplified hypothesis of the Fei-Ranis model, the potential costs of transfer and migration were substantial. They were occasioned by the complete geographic separation between the densely populated areas and the mining regions, which in the first phase of development required a tremendous labour force. Thus the state had to intervene in order to minimize transfer costs and to stimulate migration flows at wages close to the subsistence level.

Still another problem analysed by the Fei-Ranis model is the conflict that can arise between the two types of labour surplus mobilization. The migration of surplus labour to the industrial sector may entail a drop in the available agricultural surplus at a time when labour in that sector is beginning to show a positive marginal productivity because of the continuous outflow of redundant labour. This situation may bring about a worsening of the terms of trade for the industrial sector that threatens the accumulation process. According to their model, this problem can be solved by the introduction of technical progress into the agricultural sector.

However, in a periphery country such as the Congo, the problem is more complicated. The agricultural surplus itself may take two competing forms: a surplus of export crops and a food surplus to be consumed by the mine-workers. These contradictions become even more marked when the mining sector, in its early phase of development, requires a great deal of labour, when the available supply of manpower is limited and when technical progress in the agricultural sector remains restricted. Moreover, these contradictions are exacerbated when competing groups of foreign capital attempt to accumulate different forms of surplus. Then the state must intervene in order to arbitrate between contradictory claims, to establish priorities and to decide which form of surplus accumulation and which sector of foreign capital should be favoured. This is what happened in the Congo. Between 1920 and 1950, agricultural production assumed considerable importance, coming second after mineral exports. It was only after 1950 that an industrial sector working for an internal market became a factor of some significance.

The figures in Table 37 indicate that as early as 1920 mineral exports represented the greatest share of total exports, and this relative importance further increased between 1920 and 1930. Whereas agricultural exports increased two and a half times, mineral exports rose sixfold. During the same period the value of mineral exports was three times higher than that of agricultural exports, whereas industrial output amounted to no more than 4 per cent of the production of all three sectors combined.

Table 37. *Agricultural and mineral exports and industrial output,
Belgian Congo, 1920–58*
(for 1920–39, in milliard 1948–50 francs; for 1950–8,
in milliard current francs)

	Agricultural exports	Mineral exports	Industrial output	Total
1920	0·5	0·6	0·05	1·1
1925	0·9	2·2	0·10	3·2
1930	1·3	3·6	0·18	5·0
1935	2·1	4·0	0·12	6·2
1939	3·0	4·8	0·22	8·0
1950	6·5	6·6	1·8	14·9
1955	8·1	14·8	4·5	27·4
1958	8·9	11·2	4·8	24·9

SOURCES: Gaston Vandewalle, *De conjoncturele evolutie in Kongo en Ruanda-Urundi* . . .
(Antwerp, 1966), p. 9; and *Bulletin BCCBRU,* Nov. 1959, pp. 412 and 453.

During the world slump, on the other hand, agricultural exports increased
much more (by over 60 per cent between 1930 and 1935), whereas the value of
mineral exports remained practically stagnant. This result is all the more striking because constant 1948–50 prices are used for valuation, although agricultural prices had fallen more than mineral products prices during the crisis.

Foreign capital controlling the mineral output was able to defend itself by
monopolistic practices and by limiting supply. The small and middle-sized agricultural sector, on the other hand, doubled its export volume.[21] This development, as we shall find, was linked with overt pressures exerted by the colonial
administration upon the African peasantry. Between 1935 and 1939 the value
of agricultural exports continued its relative progress; and by 1939 the ratio of
mineral exports to agricultural exports had been reduced to 1·6. At that time,
because of the absence of an internal market, industrial production held an even
weaker position than in 1930.

After the Second World War, agricultural exports continued to increase, and
by 1950 they had reached the same level as mineral exports. Between 1950 and

[21] The accompanying tabulation shows the evolution of the volumes and prices of mineral and agricultural exports during the great crisis. The data are from Marcel Van de Putte, *Le Congo belge
et la politique de conjoncture* (Brussels, Institut Royal Colonial Belge, 1946), p. 39.

	Price (1927–9 = 100)		Volume (1,000 tons)	
	Mineral products	Agricultural products	Mineral products	Agricultural products
1929	101	97	51	24
1930	83	72	60	24
1931	51	50	50	23
1932	42	39	29	26
1933	42	34	42	32
1934	38	30	45	38
1935	49	40	52	45

1955, mineral exports took the lead once more, but after 1955 began to drop back. In 1958 their share was down to the 1950 level—that is, 44 per cent of the total of the three categories. However, the most notable fact was the growth in industrial production, which shot up from 2 per cent of the total in 1939 to 20 per cent in 1958.

Until 1945, production was dominated by the growth in export of primary products. But this expansion created many tensions. The mobilization of labour posed many problems, such as the construction of a transport network in the absence of mechanization, and the production of a food surplus in order to supply the migrant labourers in the mines and urban centres. Normally, the competitive demands of the mining enterprises, the plantations, the export and local traders and the colonial administration itself would have considerably increased the wages and incomes of all the workers. On the contrary, as shown in Table 38, we can see that between 1912 and 1945 real wages deteriorated sharply.

Table 38. *Real wages for unskilled workers, Belgian Congo, 1910–50* (1958 = 100)

Relation between wages and textile prices in rural areas (Kwango, Equateur, Ubangui, Kasai, Sankuru, Uele, Ituri, Kivu, Maniema)							
	1911–13	1920	1924	1928	1933	1938	1944	1950
A. Nominal wages	2	3	6	12	9	11	34	53
B. Textile prices	5	19	28	47	24	29	74	103
C. Real wages A/B	48	16	22	26	44	40	45	55
The same relation including urban centres								
Real wages	56	22	23	29	44	44	44	50

SOURCE: Peemans, *Diffusion du progrès économique*, pp. 268 and 325. Wages include remuneration in cash and in kind.

How were all the demands satisfied while at the same time the average wage remained at a very low level and even declined in purchasing power? This paradoxical situation can be explained only in terms of the continuous intervention of the colonial state in order to shape the structure of labour and production that is, in order to realize an appropriate equilibrium between the various forms of surplus mobilization. As a means of reaching this goal, the state simultaneously arbitrated in favour of certain segments of foreign capital and exerted heavy pressure on African society. These two processes were interconnected: the pressure on African society was linked with the type of arbitrage ensured between the various segments of foreign capital.

In examining this situation and the fundamental problem it presents, we can distinguish three periods: 1910–15, 1915–45 and 1945–60. The first period, though short, was important. It was indeed the only period during which freedom of trade was fairly effective, because the 1910 decrees had suppressed the state monopoly. The Belgians reopened to trade activities the areas previously forbidden and replaced taxes in kind by taxes in money. At the same time, labour recruitment was made free, a situation that was very suitable for development of the mines in Katanga, which had just begun production. The grow-

187

ing freedom of trade quickly led to a huge increase in the number of foreign petty traders, most of them of Mediterranean origin and without much capital. Simultaneously, Congolese petty traders and middlemen came back in great numbers. The result was a rapid increase in prices paid to peasants and in wages, to a level that was not reached again before 1950. This state of affairs was sharply criticized by the representatives of the foreign import-export companies managed by Belgians. These companies demanded from the Ministry of Colonies that the activities of Congolese and foreign petty traders be restricted because the high prices paid to the peasants threatened the profits of enterprises making heavy investments. Alexandre Delcommune, in his famous book *L'avenir du Congo belge menacé,* put forward an alternative strategy of development. He argued that the big Belgian trade companies should be protected from the 'dishonest' competition of the petty traders. The cultivators would then be forced to market a certain volume of agricultural surplus as a result of the pressure of taxation, but they would retain enough material incentives for increasing output.

The administration, however, did not intervene against the petty traders. The situation was indeed favourable for tax purposes. The poll-tax rates were linked with the growth of incomes. The increases in purchase prices thus enlarged the fiscal base during a period of increasing expenditures, when the colony was obliged to rely entirely on its own budgetary resources, especially taxes on Africans.

During the same period, there was an attempt by Belgian settlers to develop food production in the Katanga to supply the mining and urban areas. Thus, during this short period conditions were favourable for a surge in the capitalist growth process, sparked by small and medium-size enterprises, both foreign and indigenous. This process could probably have led in the long run to the birth of a petty African bourgeoisie, in the towns as well as in the countryside.

In the beginning of the period 1915–45, the administration embarked on a policy of new economic constraints. These resulted in an authoritarian system of mobilization of the agricultural surplus, at a price level that could not stimulate a normal supply. The first measure arose from the needs occasioned by the First World War. The administration introduced compulsory rice cultivation in areas near the scene of military engagement in order to supply food for the troops. After the war, the system was kept alive to provide food for the miners. In this manner, the government fostered the growth of a marketable food surplus at low peasant wages. In 1917, the system was extended to the cultivation of cotton. This resulted in greatly expanding the yield. To some extent this system was justified on allegedly pedagogic grounds. As Edmond Leplae, a dedicated propagandist for the system, put it:

To oblige the native to know and to develop one or another crop for export is the only way to improve the material situation of the entire population in a relatively short period. . . But that method of compulsion is of course followed for educational purposes. It does not aim to keep the population under a régime of constraint indefinitely.[22]

But the plants built by the state for the treatment of cotton were rapidly handed over to Cotonco, a private company that was closely linked to financial

[22] Edmond Leplae, 'Cultures obligatoires: leurs résultats au Congo belge et dans d'autres pays tropicaux', *Revue des Questions Scientifiques,* March 1934, pp. 256–7.

groups and that was granted exclusive purchase rights in major areas. The same method was applied progressively to the areas granted to the Lever group in order to promote the production of palm-oil and palm-kernels. Between 1920 and 1930, more than a million African peasants were subjected to an authoritarian levy on the agricultural surplus. In 1933 there were 1 million women and 0·9 million men. In these areas, petty traders as well as big ones were eliminated for the benefit of monopolistic companies. As the level of peasant incomes remained low, it was easier to recruit young unmarried men for work in the mines at low wages. This situation is illustrated in Table 39. In 1924, in the cotton areas (Sankuru, Uele) it took three months' wages to buy a piece of cloth. In fact, the price exceeded the average annual income of the cotton grower (Uele).

Table 39. *Relation between peasant income, rural wages and price of ordinary textiles, Belgian Congo, 1924*
(monthly rural wage = 100)

	Annual money income per peasant	Price of an ordinary piece of cloth
Lower and Middle Congo	477	75
Sankuru	414	321
Uele	230	357

In the other areas, the level of prices and wages was higher, the Lower and Middle Congo being the most favoured areas. But here the administration had to arbitrate between various interest groups competing for the potential labour surplus. An economic boom of sorts occurred between 1924 and 1929. The state had undertaken many large public works using a good deal of manpower. Private construction—as yet unaided by mechanization—was being carried on in the urban areas. The mines required a large labour force, while traders and settlers were trying to get marketable products and cheap labour. Thus demand was active on all fronts, but each sector of foreign capital was trying to get agricultural products at the lowest price and manpower at the lowest wage. At the same time, each segment was vying for state aid in order to eliminate other competing interests and to increase the pressure on the African labour force. In an attempt to resolve matters, the administration took various measures, such as restricting the activities of petty traders and settlers and legislating minimum and maximum prices. It backed the development of the so-called labour auctions in order to stimulate agreements between employers for wage control and increased pressure to step up recruitment. Nevertheless, economic expansion was so rapid that the administration could not prevent a general increase in wages and prices. In the cities, however, the rise in food prices made the nominal wage increase almost meaningless.

At the same time, the agrarian social structure was subjected to a severe shock. Forced proletarianization and large-scale emigration of young adult men resulted in a demographic imbalance: the new cities were overwhelmingly populated by young unmarried men, while the rural areas were left with a majority of women. The high labour turn-over corrected this situation to a degree, but had little influence on long-range migration, with men staying away for years. Hence some missionaries and civil servants, backed by certain members of the metropolitan consultative councils, voiced strong protests against an imminent major social crisis. They called for restrictions on proletarianization and on the migration of labour. These critics were supported by settler spokesmen and by representatives of commercial capital who shared the views of Delcommune. They succeeded in appointing a commission to study manpower problems. The commission's report supported their claims and asked for limits on recruitment.[23] As economic expansion continued, these recommendations failed to be applied. From 1927 onward, however, the largest foreign company, the Union Minière, itself took the initiative in developing a labour-saving technology. It did so because of the increasing risks and costs of a recruitment policy entailing a high turn-over and high mortality and morbidity rates. Progress was rapid, as indicated by the evolution of the capital intensity index (1950 = 100): from 20 in 1920 and 21 in 1925, it climbed to 47 in 1930 and to 60 in 1940. This new departure entailed a policy of labour stabilization, combined with a search for improved productivity and a strongly paternalistic and authoritarian welfare policy.[24] It resulted also in a growing disparity of working and technical conditions between large enterprises linked with finance capital on the one hand and small and medium-sized enterprises on the other.

It was the world-wide depression of 1929–34, however, that contributed most to ease the tension. The colony was hard hit by the drop in the price of raw materials, even though the decline in agricultural export prices was compensated by a sharp increase in the volume of exports. This result was obtained only by the reinforcing of economic constraints. A new policy enforced a strict division of labour between African producers and foreign capital. African producers were restricted to the production of agricultural products (maize, rice, cotton, coffee) at prices fixed by the administration, whereas foreign interests obtained an effective monopoly over the industrial processing of these products, and thus were enabled to profit from the added value. Compulsory cultivation of crops at controlled prices in turn influenced wages in two ways. It prevented both the rise of urban living costs and an increase in wage levels that might have resulted from a sustained rise in peasant incomes.

This policy had a number of important consequences. In the first place, it entailed stagnation at the outset, and afterward, even a deterioration in the position of African agriculture relative to that of foreign settlers. The administration was unable to reverse this trend even after 1950, when it offered more favourable conditions for the development of African agriculture (see Table 40).

[23] Belgium, Commission pour l'Etude du Problème de la Main-d'Œuvre au Congo Belge (1924–5) and Comité Consultatif de la Main-d'Œuvre (1928), *Le problème de la main-d'œuvre au Congo belge* Rapports (Brussels, 1928); and Belgium, Commission de la Main-d'Œuvre Indigène (1930–1), *Le problème de la main-d'œuvre au Congo belge,* Rapport général (Brussels, 1931).

[24] EDITORS' NOTE: The companies thus began to improve health and labour conditions on the mines, with the result that the African death-rate on the Union Minière mines dropped from 10·6 per cent per annum in 1917 to 1·6 per cent per annum in 1930. According to an unpublished Ph.D. thesis on the history of Elisabethville by Dr Bruce Fetter at the University of Wisconsin, cash wages accounted for less than one-fifth of the labour costs incurred by the Union Minière. The rest was spent on food, lodgings, medical care, recruiting, etc. The Union Minière's total cost per worker per day rose as follows (in current francs): 2·16 in 1916; 5·17 in 1920; 8·80 in 1925; 28·00 in 1930; and 9·76 in 1935.

Table 40. *Relative position of marketed African production and European production, Belgian Congo, 1933–58*

	1933	1939	1950	1958
Marketed African production	100	100	100	100
European production	64	67	64	78
Value added by European section for treatment of African products			57	57

SOURCE: Vandewalle, *De conjoncturele evolutie*, pp. 9 and 31–2.

In the second place, administration policy delayed the development of an African rural capitalism. It also extended the process of proletarianization in the rural areas, as shown in Table 41.

Table 41. *African proletarianization in rural areas, Belgian Congo, 1936–58*

	Adult male population in rural areas (in millions)	Rural workers (in millions)	Rural manpower as percentage of adult rural population	Rural manpower as percentage of total manpower
1936	2·6	0·13	5·2	37·9
1939	2·5	0·15	6·0	36·4
1944	2·4	0·20	8·4	33·5
1950	2·3	0·24	10·0	30·8
1952	2·4	0·25	10·3	32·0
1954	2·4	0·27	10·8	23·1
1956	2·5	0·30	12·5	36·0
1958	2·6	0·31	12·0	42·2

SOURCE: Peemans, *Diffusion du progrès économique*, p. 304.

In the third place, official policy slowed down wage increases. The situation in 1933 and 1939, as shown in Table 42, indicates the relation existing between peasant income and rural wage levels. There is, of course, no strict interrelation

Table 42. *Relation between peasant income, wages and labour productivity, Belgian Congo, 1933 and 1939*
(in 1950–3 francs)

	1933	1939
Annual peasant income (average)	450	700
Rural wage for 3 months	450	450
6 months	900	900
1 year	1,800	1,800
Annual wage in mines or industry	3,900	3,900
Annual output per worker in foreign agriculture	5,750	8,100
in mines and industry	20,600	21,800

SOURCES: Vandewalle, *De conjoncturele evolutie*, pp. 31–2 and 47–8; and Jean Louis Lacroix, *Industrialisation au Congo* (Paris, 1966), p. 65.

between the two. The average annual peasant income equalled from three to six months' rural wages—that is, the normal labour-supply period for labourers who did not emigrate from rural areas. This level allowed foreign settlers to re-alize a sizeable surplus, even though their enterprises had a lower productivity than mines or industry. These companies had a higher surplus per worker, despite the fact that they had to pay a nominal wage twice as high as the annual income in rural areas, which had to cover all food and housing expenses plus a premium for emigration.

This atmosphere of constraint was still prevalent during the Second World War under the policy of 'the war effort'. By 1938 the manpower volume had again reached the 1929—that is, 480,000 workers; by 1945 there were 800,000 salaried workers. At the same time, compulsory cultivation was greatly ex-panded. The cotton areas increased from 70,000 hectares in 1933 to 375,000 in 1944. Between 1939 and 1943, the compulsory cultivation areas of palm trees, rice and manioc grew, respectively, from 18,000 hectares to 35,000, from 50,000 to 132,000 and from 157,000 to 340,000.

After 1945, economic expansion oriented towards export continued, but under different conditions. The pressures exerted during the war could not be maintained without risk of a social crisis much more serious than that of 1925. From about 1945 onward there was evidence of growing discontent among the African masses, even though it was as yet spontaneous and unorganized, that took the form of revolts, riots, strikes and mutinies, such as those in 1944 and 1945. In addition, civil servants were coming under the influence of a new ideological trend—the result of a new policy designed to stabilize the colonial system. Officials now favoured an improved standard of living for the African proletariat and the development of a small peasantry attached to its land and in-terested in more efficient methods of cultivation. From the standpoint of the ad-ministration, the best guarantee of survival for the colonial régime was the promotion of an African petty bourgeoisie composed of small traders, crafts-men and various kinds of clerks.[25]

The new course required increasing state expenditures in the field of educa-tion, social services and rural development. Thus the budgetary provision for social services and education increased from 18 per cent to 30 per cent of the normal allocation—from 0·7 to 4·3 milliard francs.

The explanation for this major shift in policy probably lies in the new stage of capital accumulation that had been reached and in the fresh ideas thus generated. Or at least these ideas were probably consonant with the predomi-nant interests in the short run and assisted the colonizers' long-run goals. The important sectors of the economy controlled by finance capital had reached a stage where net investment relied mainly on internal net profits; labour cost represented only a small fraction of total cost of production, given a relatively

[25] These ideas are developed in Belgium, Congrès Colonial National, 6th Sess. (Sénat de Belgique, 4–5 Oct. 1947), *Comptes rendus des séances et rapports préparatoires* (Brussels, 1948), pp. 123–31, 149–62, 303–9, 323–72; Belgium, Congrès Colonial National, 13th Sess., 1958, *La promotion des milieux ruraux au Congo belge et au Ruanda-Urundi,* Rapports, Assemblées Générales des 7 et 8 novembre 1958 (Brussels, 1958), pp. 111–320; Institut de Sociologie Sol-vay, *Vers la promotion de l'économie indigène* (Brussels, 1956); Guy Malengreau, *Vers un paysannat indigène: les lotissements agricoles au Congo belge* (Brussels, Institut Royal Colonial Belge, 1949); and Belgium, Congrès *Colonial National, Le problème de la main-d'œuvre,* Rap-ports, Assemblée Générale du 6.6.1952 (Brussels, 1952), pp. 69–97 and 145–81.

high capital intensity. The financial groups had thus no reason to resist a policy fostering a greater social stability, a condition which they now favoured. The new course, on the other hand, met strong resistance from those petty and middle foreign interests that had invested in the agricultural sector, where cost of labour represented the main production cost.

The strong demand for raw materials by the United States and Europe up to 1954 was still another element that favoured the new policy. The resulting economic expansion brought a general increase in wages and in peasant incomes. The administration no longer opposed this trend, and even began to ratify by decrees the increases brought on by normal market action. The general rise in incomes enlarged the internal market and tended to encourage import substitution of items for mass consumption (see Table 43).

Table 43. *Expansion of consumer-goods industries, Belgian Congo, 1950–8*
(in milliard francs)

	1950	1952	1954	1956	1958
Local industry	1·5	2·6	3·5	3·9	4·4
Imports	3·6	6·2	5·8	6·3	5·5
Total	5·1	8·8	9·3	10·2	9·9
Local industry as per cent of total	30%	29%	38%	39%	44%

SOURCE: Fernand Bézy, *Problèmes structurels de l'économie congolaise* (Louvain, Institut de Recherches Economiques et Sociales, 1957), p. 170.

The growth of industry itself contributed to an increased demand for labour. Because the accelerated pace of growth accentuated the disparities between towns and countryside, this demand could be met without too much difficulty. Thus we find a huge migration of young adults towards the cities. But as expansion continued in all sectors of the economy, competition among employers grew, and rising wages attracted more rural migrants. This situation characterized the period 1953–8. Industrial enterprises, controlled mainly by small and middle foreign capital, now reacted in a manner similar to that of the big mining companies between 1927 and 1930. They made a major effort towards mechanization and improved management, which resulted in a marked spurt in productivity, as shown in Table 44.

The increase in productivity was so marked in the mines and in manufacturing that these two sectors registered an absolute decline in employment. In this way the agricultural sector controlled by small foreign capital became the main source of employment, increasing its share in the total from 30 per cent in 1950 to 42 per cent in 1958. However, as indicated in Table 41, this sector absorbed only 12 per cent of the total number of men available in the rural areas. The wages of this new rural proletariat decreased in relation to the urban workers' wages, whereas the income of independent peasants deteriorated relative to rural wages and to the income of workers employed in foreign agriculture (see Table 45).

All the age categories therefore improved in purchasing power, but the relative deterioration of rural incomes revealed the absence of a real structural

Table 44. *Various productivity indicators, Belgian Congo, 1954 and 1958*
(1950 = 100 [at constant price])

	Foreign agriculture		Mines		Industry		Transport	
	1954	1958	1954	1958	1954	1958	1954	1958
Capital stock	145	215	153	180	190	214	110	113
Output	148	200	153	129	166	220	165	194
Labour	111	130	87	76	124	80	122	124
Output/Labour	136	155	176	170	134	275	127	156
Capital/Labour	130	165	176	236	153	267	90	92
Capital/Output	95	108	100	139	114	97	66	58

SOURCES: *Bulletin BCCBRU*, Nov. 1953, pp. 384–5; Oct. 1955, p. 410; Nov. 1955, pp. 443–55; Nov. 1959, pp. 424–5 and 438; Dec. 1958, pp. 412–13; and BCCBRU, *Rapport, 1959* (Brussels, 1960), pp. 71, 74, 79.

Table 45. *Peasant income, rural wages and urban wages:*
average, Belgian Congo, 1950 and 1958

	1950	1958
Average peasant income	100	100
Average rural wage	63	86
Production by worker in foreign agriculture	270	352
Price of piece of cloth as percentage of monthly wage		
rural areas	61	41
Leopoldville	26	13
Elisabethville	40	15

change. Between 1950 and 1960, the increased productivity in the mines and in industry widened the gap between these sectors and agriculture, both foreign and indigenous. By 1958 the mines, employing only 15 per cent of the total manpower, were producing 39 per cent of the total output controlled by foreign capital, whereas foreign agriculture, utilizing 55 per cent of the total manpower, was producing only 15 per cent of that output. Evidently, great disparities existed in the process of capital accumulation among the various sectors controlled by foreign capital. The imbalance in the African sector was particularly marked. This shows clearly the uneven structure of accumulation that prevails in a periphery economy. In 1958, as shown in Table 46, the African sector contributed only 11 per cent to the total market output, which involved 89 per cent of the active population.

Not surprisingly, the outflow of rural migrants to the cities continued unabated. Labour migration received an additional stimulus from the deterioration of the traditional social structure in the countryside, a process that in turn created new psychological pressures. The wage increase that took place between 1948 and 1955 therefore rested on weak economic foundations. After 1956 it was only state intervention that prevented a decline in wages occasioned by the falling demand for labour. After the state passed through a severe crisis in 1960, no braking power remained to check the rapid fall in urban wages.

Table 46. *Relative situation of foreign and African sectors, Belgian Congo,*
1950 and 1958
(in per cent)

	Value of output		Fixed assets		Active population and manpower	
	1950	1958	1950	1958	1950	1958
Total of African and European sectors	100	100	100	100	100	100
Total African output	35	30	—	4	89	89 [a]
Marketed African output only	12	11	—	—	89	89 [a]
European agricultural output, including processing of African products	15	15	13	15	4	5 [a]
Mines, industry, and transport	50	55	87	81	7	6 [a]
European sector only	100	100	100	100	100	100 [b]
Agriculture and processing of agricultural products	28	25	13	15	43	55
Industry	12	17	17	22	24	18
Mines	44	39	39	40	21	15
Transport	16	20	31	22	12	14

N O T E: The total active female population is included in the total because of the division of labour between men and women within African agriculture. Moreover, some women already worked for wages, even though they represented only a small proportion of the labour force. As regards fixed assets, official statistics are not very trustworthy, since they do not indicate any capital invested in African agriculture. Nevertheless, even if these figures were included, it seems clear that such investments were almost negligible.

[a] Male and female active population.   [b] Wage manpower only.

S O U R C E: Peemans, *Diffusion du progrès économique*, p. 304.

The fragile nature of urban wage increases explains the continuing disparity in income between foreign workers and Africans. As shown in Table 47, the ratio remained almost unchanged between 1925 and 1960.

Moreover, as has already been pointed out, every wage increase entailed the employment of new technologies, resulting in increased capital intensity, thus

Table 47. *Ratio of African to European wages in transport sector,*
Belgian Congo, 1927–58
(annual wage in 1,000 1959 francs)

	1927	1930	1935	1940	1945	1950	1955	1958
European salary	220	220	330	220	260	275	320	450
African wage	6	6	6	5	5	5	10	18
as percentage of European salary	3	3	2	3	2	2	3	4

S O U R C E: André Huybrechts, *Transports et structures de développement au Congo* . . . (Paris, 1970), p. 182.

siphoning off manpower from the capitalist sector. Because increased capital intensity was effected through the import of capital goods, labour displaced from the consumer-goods sector could not be utilized by a national sector for developing the means of production. This state of affairs was largely responsible for limiting internal consumer demand, because labour-saving techniques limited the level of employment. Thus, despite its apparently rapid growth between 1950 and 1960, the Congolese economy presented the typical structure of a periphery country. On the one hand, complete technological dependence on industrialized countries and on the profit system hindered the expansion of employment in the modern sectors with high productivity and under foreign control. On the other hand, the increasing agricultural surplus favoured only to a minor extent the growth of peasant incomes, because a large part of the surplus was taken by the foreign sector, which controlled the channels of added value formation. In addition, African producers suffered through the deterioration in terms of trade that favoured the industrial countries. Thus, the African peasants were left with only a small part of the yields of the growing agricultural surplus—yields that had the potential to expand their consumption as well as their savings.

It might well be asked, of course, whether this very unequal distribution was not itself favourable to the acceleration of an accumulation process. Many have argued that a distribution pattern favourable to the upper-income strata, given their high propensity to save, is consonant with a rapid growth pace. But this position lacks merit if there is no link between savings and investment. Such was the case in the Congo, as in other periphery countries. Moreover, the consumption of luxury goods absorbed an important share of those high incomes. In addition, much private saving was transferred to Europe. Even more disturbing was the extent of profits transferred to Europe by private enterprises of all sizes. Though these companies were able to finance their net investments internally, given the high rate of profit, the share of their surplus reinvested in the Congo was only a fraction of the total. The fundamental cause of this situation may probably be found in the uneven rate of profit realized by investors. The exceptional rate of profit in certain sectors could not be reproduced in others because of the limited size of the internal market and the unequal distribution of income. Thus profits flowed out of the country. Political considerations prompted by the general crisis of confidence in the colonial system from 1957 onward accelerated this movement. From that time, amortization compared to net investment increased sharply. Table 48 illustrates the change in levels of income for both Africans and foreigners between 1950 and 1958.

Once more, the state had to intervene actively in an attempt to solve the contradictions of colonial capitalism. But henceforth its role was materially altered. No longer did the state direct the mobilization of a labour surplus in order to foster the accumulation of an economic surplus. Now it was oriented instead towards solving the problem of utilizing the economic surplus. We have seen that after the Second World War the state favoured the broadening of the market for mass consumption, which created good opportunities for private investment. But we have seen, too, that this process was limited. Because outlets for profitable private investment were restricted, the state permitted the foreign bourgeoisie to utilize its economic surplus freely, even for transfers. It did not oblige capital investors to reinvest in the colony at a lower rate of profit, to aid,

Table 48. *Structure of income distribution and utilization, Belgian Congo,*
1950 and 1958
(in milliard francs)

	1950	1958
African incomes		
For wage-earners	5·1	14·1
For peasants, craftsmen and traders	3·6	6·8
Foreigners' incomes		
Salaries	5·6	12·9
Income from property and business enterprises	4·2	7·0
Amortization	1·8	5·9
Corporate savings	6·0	1·3
African consumption	7·6	19·0
Foreigners' consumption	6·4	12·1
Gross corporate investments	5·2	7·3

SOURCE: BCCBRU, *Rapport, 1959*, pp. 140–1 and 144–5.

say, the financing of the ambitious development programme proposed by the
Ten-Year Plan 1950–60. Although the huge public works programme in fact
needed a great amount of capital at a low interest rate, the state had to act to finance projects insufficiently attractive for private investors, and to compensate
for potential consequences of capital outflow. Between 1950 and 1960, therefore, the expenditure of the colonial state increased sharply. State investments
between 1950 and 1958 amounted to 51·5 milliard francs, whereas the capital
accumulated by colonial enterprises through their own profits stood at only
38·9 billion. The result, as shown in Table 49, was an enormous increase in
the public debt. The table shows how the tax burden imposed on foreign en-

Table 49. *Finance structure and utilization of surplus,*
Belgian Congo, 1950–8
(in milliard francs)

	Private enterprises				The state	
	Dividends	Amorti-zations	Reserves	Taxes	State savings	Cumulative public debt
1950	3·2	1·8	4·7	1·2	1·6	8·7
1951	3·6	2·2	6·7	1·3	3·1	10·5
1952	3·7	2·9	7·1	1·4	2·7	15·3
1953	4·0	3·8	4·8	2·0	3·2	15·4
1954	5·0	4·4	4·2	2·1	3·3	21·3
1955	6·2	4·9	3·7	2·2	2·9	26·4
1956	6·3	5·3	4·4	2·2	2·4	32·7
1957	4·8	5·5	1·7	3·3	3·1	31·4
1958	5·0	5·9	1·2	2·0	0·7	42·5

SOURCE: BCCBRU, *Rapport, 1959*, pp. 134, 153, 159.

terprises remained at a low level despite the increasing needs of the state budget—a situation quite typical of a periphery country.

In spite of the expanding direct economic role of the state in regulating the process of accumulation, public investments were not financed by fiscal mobilization of the surplus accumulated by foreign firms. On the contrary, the foreign bourgeoisie, as shown in Table 50, increasingly transferred its profits and savings to the metropolis. The financing of public investments by external sources through a growing public debt thus served a double function. It allowed the outflow of the economic surplus, but at the same time ensured investment for large public works and social welfare projects that were unattractive for private capital. The same policy helped also to solve balance-of-payments problems by massive public loans, particularly in Belgium. The price of this policy was, of course, a growing foreign debt.

Table 50. *Capital transfers by foreign bourgeoisie and external borrowing of the state, Belgian Congo, 1950–9*
(in milliard francs)

| | (1) | (2) Outside transfers | | | | (3) Foreign debt | |
| | | | | | | Long-term capital | |
	Trade balance	Transfer of profits	Private transfer	Outside private expenditure	Transport and insurance	Private	Public
1950	+ 6·9	−1·2	−0·9	—	−1·1	+0·3	+2·5
1951	+ 6·1	−1·3	−0·5	—	−2·5	+0·9	+0·1
1952	+44·0	−1·7	−0·4	—	−2·8	+0·7	+2·4
1953	+ 5·1	−2·2	−0·5	−0·6	−3·5	+0·1	+2·6
1954	+ 6·9	−2·4	−0·6	−0·8	−4·5	−0·3	+2·5
1955	+ 9·6	−3·2	−0·7	−1·0	−5·3	+1·3	+2·8
1956	+11·3	−4·4	−1·0	−1·3	−6·4	−0·6	+4·3
1957	+ 7·7	−3·5	−1·3	−1·5	−6·8	+0·3	+0·1
1958	+ 8·3	−3·4	−1·4	−1·7	−5·4	−0·1	+5·4
1959	+13·4	−4·0	−3·5	−1·7	−5·9	−4·4	+2·1

NOTE: Column (1) indicates the role played by the positive trade balance for financing transfers towards the metropolis. But that positive balance was itself the result of the unequal income distribution. Because of the low level of the African incomes, African consumption was oriented towards mass consumer-goods produced inside the colony. The Africans tended to import very little. By contrast, the tendency of the foreigners to import was very high but stable. Since the import substitution industries were for the most part established before 1952, the market expansion in the years following could be satisfied through an increasing utilization of output capacity. There was therefore a diminished import of capital goods (8·9 milliard francs in 1952, 6·6 milliard in 1955, 6·4 milliard in 1958). Thus the savings of the foreign bourgeoisie were only partly invested and could be sent abroad. But from 1953 on, the positive balance of trade was not big enough to finance all kinds of transfers, and the state had to borrow to make up the balance of payments.

SOURCE: Figures compiled from BCCBRU, *Rapport, 1959*, p. 103.

Thus the state played a crucial role during the 1950s in maintaining some kind of equilibrium in the accumulation structure, despite huge transfers of surplus made by private capital. The state took an important part, too, in solving an acute employment problem by itself becoming a big employer. Between 1950 and 1958, the salaries paid by the state jumped from 10 per cent to 25 per cent of the total wage bill. This became the economic basis of the development of a Congolese petty bourgeoisie composed of lower-ranking civil servants, whose claims played a major role in the political crisis leading to independence. However, despite growing intervention, the state could not prevent the development of the economic contradictions inherent in a dependent society of this nature. From 1957 onward, when an economic recession occurred that was linked to the international economic situation, these contradictions were exacerbated. They gave rise to a social, ideological and political crisis that shook the fragile equilibrium of the colonial system. When the crisis became general, the state appeared politically unable to cope with it. The programme of economic growth launched since 1950, with its long-range goal of social stabilization, had developed new economic problems and had set in motion social forces that the state could no longer control. These led in turn to the chaotic decolonization of the years 1959 and 1960.

The transportation network as a tool of colonial economy policy

State intervention played a decisive part in the construction of a transport network. As we have already shown, until the end of the colonial period the capital committed to mines and transport represented the major portion of the total funds invested in the Congo. Moreover, we have thrown some light on the close ties linking the state and large financial groups. However, the Congolese transport network was established to allow the development not only of the mining sector. In a country as large as the Congo, where human and material resources were so dispersed, the creation of a transport network was a precondition for the process of accumulation itself. In this process the colonial state played a decisive role. By studying the action of the state in this regard, we may come to understand its co-operation with the dominant sectors of foreign capital, and also to grasp the relative autonomy of state decisions and development strategy.

When all private and public investments are taken into account, the share of total capital invested in the transport system and in transport equipment appears even larger than the figures in Table 36 would indicate. Public investment financed also the road-building for the equipment of Otraco, the semi-public transport corporation. By the end of the colonial period, as shown in Table 51, transport still represented almost 30 per cent of the total assets of the colony.

Table 51. *Total transport assets, Belgian Congo, 1928–53*
(in milliard 1953 francs)

	1928	1938	1948	1953
Total fixed assets (private, semi-public, and public sectors)	21	33	48	93
Total fixed assets in transport sector	7	11	17	27
Roads	3	6	10	12
Trucks, rolling-stock and river boats	3	4	5	12
Other	1	1	2	3
Transport as percentage of total	30	30	29	29

SOURCE: Peemans, *Diffusion du progrès économique*, p. 43.

The state throughout played a major role in the capital formation of this sector. According to André Huybrechts, the state financed directly or indirectly 30 per cent of the total transport investment during the colonial period.[26] If we take the figures of cumulative gross investment during this period and reevaluate it in 1959 francs, the state spent 38 milliard through the extraordinary budget and 22 milliard in the form of subsidies to or shares in the transport corporations—that is, 60 milliard out of a total of 75 milliard. Thus the greatest part (two-thirds) of public expenditure was financed through the extraordinary budget, of which more than 35 per cent was always devoted to transport, as shown in Table 52.

Table 52. *Cumulative extraordinary outlays of the state,*
Belgian Congo, 1909–59
(in milliard 1959 francs)

From 1909 to	Total extraordinary outlay (A)	Extraordinary outlay devoted to transport (B)	Percentage $\dfrac{(B)}{(A)}$
1914	6·6	3·4	52·6
1920	9·5	4·9	52·1
1925	12·4	6·5	52·1
1930	23·7	11·0	46·4
1935	30·6	12·7	41·6
1940	37·1	16·5	44·5
1945	42·5	16·8	39·6
1950	50·2	19·0	37·8
1955	80·5	31·5	39·0
1959	106·3	38·1	35·8

SOURCE: Huybrechts, *Transports et structures de développement*, pp. 134–5.

There were two major spending periods, 1920 to 1930 and 1950 to 1960. The first was occasioned by the great public-works programme framed by Louis Franck in his capacity as colonial minister. Of the total spent, 75 per cent went to railway and river transport. The First Ten-Year Plan (1950 to 1960) again involved large-scale expenditure. A total of 50 milliard francs was disbursed, of which 21 milliard was devoted to transport, 50 per cent going to railways and river transport and 40 per cent to roads and airports. One-third of the total state expenditure went into subsidies, guarantees or the purchase of shares in the various transport enterprises in which the state was linked to major financial groups (see Table 53).

The state thus contributed almost 50 per cent of the capital of the transport corporations established together with various financial groups: the Société Générale (Unatra, CFML and BCK), the Empain group (CFL), and the Comcinière group (Vicicongo). Moreover, it gave 6 milliard 1959 francs in the forms of subsidies and loans. Subtracting from that total the 3.1 milliard income from its capital shares leaves a deficit of 2.9 milliard. The subsidies were paid

[26] André Huybrechts, *Transports et structures de développement au Congo: étude du progrès économique de 1900 à 1970* (Paris, 1970), p. 162.

Table 53. *Share of public funds in capital formation of transport enterprises, Congo, 1889–1958*
(in milliard 1959 francs)

Corporation	Total assets	State share	Per cent of state share
CFML (Matadi-Leopoldville railway)	11·5	6·2	54
CFL (Great Lakes railway)	5·2	0·2	5
BCK (Katanga railway)	15·9	9·4	58
Vicicongo (Uele railway)	2·3	0·4	19
Unatra	0·8	0·3	40
Total	35·7	16·5	47

SOURCE: Huybrechts, *Transports et structures de développement*, p. 109.

mainly to the CFL Company (2.2 milliard), to whose capital the state had contributed little, and from which it received only a small income (0·2 milliard). In this case, as in the case of the Vicicongo, as early as 1930–40 official voices had condemned the collusion existing between the state and the financial groups. In 1933–4, for instance, the Senate Commission on the Colonial Budget censured the state for paying guaranteed dividends and interest to the CFL and Vicicongo companies. The Vicicongo had an apparent deficit, which supposedly justified the grant of subsidies; but this deficit had arisen because the company had carried out all its profitable activities through subsidiary companies, which legally, however, were completely independent of the parent company.

Abuses of this kind, however, inherent in a system based on profit-seeking and characterized by a close interdependence between political and economic powers, should not be confused with the deeper logic of the system itself. It would be easy, of course, to show that many political figures and high civil servants concerned with colonial problems closed their careers in the service of one or another of the financial groups controlling the Congolese economy. Many instances could be cited also of the influence exerted by such officials to steer policy decisions in a direction favourable to monopoly interests. Yet, can we conclude therefore that there was a complete and one-sided dependence of the entire state superstructure on the financial groups? The state is never a pure reflex nor a simple, docile tool. One cannot deny to the state *a priori* a certain degree of autonomy within a system whose global coherence must be assured by the state. It therefore seems more appropriate to speak of interdependence between the state and the financial groups rather than of dependence of the state. Through its relative autonomy, the state has to arbitrate between conflicting interests, between various sectors of capital, between short-term and long-range interests of the system. Above all, the state has the responsibility to ensure the expansion, the stability and the continuity of the predominating economic and social patterns.

The economic policy of the colonial state in the field of transport seems to illustrate the double aspect of interdependence and relative autonomy. In this sense the situation bore a strong resemblance to that linking the state with financial groups in nineteenth-century Europe during the construction of a railway network. The Congolese case was by no means unique. But here the essential purpose of the co-operation between the state and private finance was completely different. In Europe, the transport policy aimed at developing internal markets by encouraging the growth of the self-centred aspects of national capitalism. In the Congo, official policy sought to develop the primary exports and fostered an extroverted and dependent structure of production. It was the transport policy that gave the Congo the status of a periphery country. The railway network built after 1895 and the improvement in the river system aimed at linking the enormous hinterland of the colony to Matadi, the only ocean outlet controlled by Belgium. The co-operation between the state and foreign capital must be regarded in this context. In promoting and financing the transportation network, the state created the conditions for profitable exports from the mines controlled by the financial groups. But this does not mean that the transportation policy was oriented entirely in favour of the mines. Historically the policy was inaugurated with the building of the Matadi-Leopoldville railway in order to export animal and vegetable products from the Upper Congo. From this period onward a certain ambiguity is apparent in the relations between the state and the transport companies. The state made a heavy contribution to the capital of the CFML; the company itself enjoyed a *de jure* and a *de facto* monopoly that it tried to utilize for fixing tariffs at a level almost as high as the portage tariffs. The managers of the company were certainly interested in reaping exceptional profits. The state, on the other hand, wished to develop exports to the maximum, and thus to reduce the tariff. Vice Governor-General Moulaert thus clashed with private river-transport companies, which desired a cartel aiming at tariff increases.[27] Through sustained pressure, the state finally succeeded in getting a progressive decrease in tariffs.

After the First World War, two networks (BCK and CFL) were developed in order to serve the mines. The state once again faced a conflict between monopolistic transport companies and various other firms. The transport companies set charges that discriminated in favour of firms belonging to the same financial groups as the transport companies, to the detriment of outsiders. The state tried to prevent economic discrimination of this kind. It attempted also to impose two major goals on the monopolies: first, to develop the export capacity of all sectors, including low-value products; and second, to promote a preference for using the Congolese network—namely, the 'national way' policy. The state never opposed the controlling interests of finance capital but did attempt to arrive at compromises with these interests in order to secure long-term objectives.

Before 1920, co-operation between the colony and the monopolies had been effected through bilateral discussions. After 1920, policy was guided by a new institution set up as a general co-ordination device, the Comité Permanent de Coordination des Transports au Congo, established in 1926. After the Second World War, however, the state encountered more and more difficulty in imposing its goals within this committee because the private companies had almost transformed it into a professional board. Under the pressure of an increasingly centralized colonial administration, the Belgian Minister of the Colonies tried to reassert the state authority. In 1954, he dissolved the Comité Permanent and

---

[27] Georges Moulaert, *Problèmes coloniaux d'hier et d'aujourd'hui* (Brussels, 1939); and André Lederer, *Histoire de la navigation au Congo* (Tervuren, Musée Royal de l'Afrique Centrale, 1965), pp. 162–7.

replaced it with the Conseil Supérieur des Transports, which exerted a more active form of supervision.

The two goals of the state were realized in two ways: by the promotion of technical progress in order to reduce costs and by the selective use of that cost reduction to foster low-value exports produced in remote areas.

Between 1900 and 1960, technical progress was important in all sections of the transport network. Table 54 shows that the quantitative growth was accompanied by a real improvement in quality. Transport costs, as shown in Table 55, thus decreased sharply compared both with the costs of traditional portage and with the transport costs in Belgium.

Table 54. *Expansion and improvement of transport network,
Belgian Congo, 1911–59*

	1911–13	1938–9	1958–9
Expansion			
Length of network (*in 1,000 km*)			
Navigable river network	7·7	11·6	14·5
Railway network	1·1	4·6	5·0
Total road network	6·0	68·1	140·0
Total river engine-power (*1,000 hp*)	4·5	15·9	71·9
Locomotives (*units*)	129	304	458
Goods-vans (*units*)	1,045	4,370	9,130
Improvement			
River facilities (Otraco)			
Average tonnage pulled by a			
tugboat (*in 1,000 t*)	0·2	1·8	2·1
Average capacity pulled by a			
power unit (*t/hp*)	1·9	6·6	6·2
Rolling-stock			
Tons/kilometres per locomotive			
(*in million t/km*)	0·4	2·0	4·1

SOURCE: Peemans, *Diffusion du progrès économique*, pp. 46–57.

The requirements of technical progress shaped the tariff policy adopted by the administration. The government tried to make available to all exporters the benefits derived from lowered costs, and the promotion of exports remained a high-priority target throughout the period 1910–60. The state and the transport companies thus experienced no difficulty in arriving at agreements favouring exports and the import of capital goods. Imported merchandise for mass consumption, on the other hand, as shown in Table 56, received relatively unfavourable treatment. The state thus made a macroeconomic choice that favoured profits and investments, as against wages and consumption. Such an implicit choice seems a more satisfactory explanation than the official one that justified discrepancies in the tariff structures by regional differences in transport costs. The higher transport charges on the upper rivers were said to have been responsible for higher tariffs on imported goods. Yet imported capital goods received favourable treatment as compared to imported textiles for African consumers.

Table 55. *Decrease in transport costs in the Congo, 1914–58* *

	1914	1936–8	1956–8
Congo			
Import price	100	750	2,800
River transport cost	100	122	527
Railway transport cost			
CFML	100	127	157
BCK	100	482	600
CFL	100	206	386
Road transport cost			
per truck	100	685	592
per porter	100	428	3,571
Belgium			
Wholesale price	100	650	2,795
River transport cost	100	503	1,750
Railway transport cost	100	972	2,722

* Comparison between wholesale price index and transport costs in the Congo and in Belgium. All tariff classes average.

SOURCE: Peemans, *Diffusion du progrès économique*, pp. 60 and 93.

Table 56. *Tariff differences by product classes, Belgian Congo, 1912–58*
(Belgian tariffs = 100)

	1912–13	1936–8	1956–8
River tariffs			
Agricultural exports (average)	138	18	52
Cement	421	50	48
Industrial material	421	50	139
Cotton textiles for Africans	593	259	151
Railway tariffs			
CFML:			
Agricultural exports (average)	121	69	67
Food products (average)	1,000	31	52
Cement	1,500	151	62
Machines and machine parts	500	94	122
Cotton textiles for Africans	3,950	414	204
CFL:			
Agricultural exports (average)	270	102	95
Food products (average)	500	87	75
Cement	6,500	469	225
Machines and machine parts	2,160	292	256
Cotton textiles for Africans	2,160	506	303
BCK:			
Agricultural exports (average)	305	92	80
Food products (average)	500	106	62
Cement	750	315	126
Machines and machine parts	250	196	180
Cotton textiles for Africans	833	480	253

SOURCE: Peemans, *Diffusion du progrès économique*, pp. 94–5 and 99. The comparison between Congolese and Belgian tariffs is made for products of the same category, e.g., manioc and rice with wheat, etc.

Those discrepancies, however, were corrected in three ways. In the first place, the discriminatory tariff policy was applied in a general context of downward tariffs. Secondly, after the Second World War, the more favourable policy towards mass consumption entailed a reduction in the tariff gaps. Thirdly, the primary subsistence goods benefited early from low tariffs in order to lower the urban wages.

In addition, transport enterprises themselves initiated a tariff cut to reduce the labour cost for other urban enterprises dependent on the same financial group. For instance, as early as 1928, the BCK, under pressure from the administration, established favourable tariffs in order to supply the workers' camps of the Union Minière du Haut-Katanga with maize cultivated by Kasai peasants located alongside the railway line.

State intervention was particularly active in providing favourable tariffs for agricultural exports. In this sphere, agreement of the transport enterprises could of course be easily obtained, provided that the favoured product derived from allied enterprises. In this case, the low profitability of transport enterprises concealed in fact a transfer of productivity, through lower prices, to allied enterprises, which thereby improved their rate of return and their capacity for expansion. The evolution of the profit rate of the transport enterprises relative to other sectors, as shown in Table 57, illustrates the strategy followed between 1920 and 1950. The state favoured this strategy, which provided the financial groups a better rate of return on their agricultural subsidiaries rather than profits on their associated transport enterprises. After 1930, the state applied the same

Table 57. *Rate of return of transport sector relative to other sectors, Belgian Congo, 1910–59*
(in per cent)

	Transport	All sectors except transport	Mines	Industry	Agriculture
1910	8·9	−0·5	−5·1	—	—
1915	0·4	−0·5	—	—	−3·1
1920	−3·2	6·7	—	—	−8·3
1925	0·9	15·3	41·0	0·5	11·3
1930	3·9	10·3	28·5	14·1	1·0
1935	5·5	9·0	25·7	4·2	5·4
1940	1·0	14·9	39·4	14·7	5·3
1945	3·9	14·9	26·1	19·4	8·5
1950	7·9	23·5	40·0	22·1	23·4
1955	10·5	19·4	40·5	17·9	15·8
1959	8·4	12·2	28·2	13·1	7·8

NOTE: The figures cited are calculated according to the formula $r = P/K$, where r is the sectoral rate of return, P the total sectoral balance of the profit and loss accounts, and K the total sectoral assets. The figures for transport are based on the data of eleven enterprises; for the mines of three; for industry of nine; and for agriculture of three. The largest enterprises are included: Union Minière, Géomines, Unilever, Cotongo, Utexleo, Tabacongo, Chanic, Afridex, Brasseries de Léopoldville et du Katanga.

SOURCE: Huybrechts, *Transports et structures de développement*, pp. 322–3.

policy in favour of the small capital of foreign settlers not directly dependent on the financial groups. In both cases, the goal was to use more African labour in production through incentives to the various segments of foreign capital able to mobilize the labour surplus. Low transport tariffs for exports were a complementary device added to fixed low purchase prices to peasants and to administrative constraint exerted upon the peasants. After 1950, however, the policy of low tariffs for agricultural products was designed also to give incentives directly to the peasants. The margin allocated as the purchase price to the peasants was increased. But the positive effect of this measure over effective price increases was lessened because, at the same time, transport prices were affected by fluctuations on the international market. The colonial state agreed to compensate firms for possible losses that might be incurred when earnings fell below a fixed rate. State intervention was especially strong during the Great Depression, when the state directly subsidized those tariff reductions that had been agreed upon with the transport enterprises. Between 1928 and 1934, the amount of capital guaranteed by the state rose from 711 million francs to 2,646 million, of which 2,366 million represented the capital of transport enterprises. In 1934 the subsidies granted to the transport companies by the state stood at 104 million francs—that is, one-third of the total public debt. From 1928 to 1934 the change in this figure increased from one-fourth the total of other administrative expenses to three-fourths.

State intervention favoured the financial groups in two ways. First, it allowed them to limit the losses sustained by their mining and agricultural subsidiaries through a lowering of transport costs. In addition, it helped the transport enterprises to achieve a more or less normal rate of profit, thanks to the subsidies. During the crisis the rate of profit realized by transport was even higher than in other sectors: 5·3, 3·5, 3·7 and 4·6 per cent, respectively, for 1931, 1932, 1933 and 1934, against 3·1, 0·6, 1·2 and 1·7 per cent.

During the same period, and according to the same logic, the state regrouped in a single public corporation (Otraco, created by royal decrees of 1935 and 1936) the river network and the CFML, which previously had been managed by a subsidiary of the Société Générale. The lake, railway and road networks of the Kivu region were joined to it. With the creation of Otraco, the state assumed the burden entailed in eventually granting lower tariffs to the purely agricultural areas where the greater part of the African labour force working for export was located. In a period of recession, however, the exploitation of these regions required low transport costs and low purchase prices. This policy benefited various foreign interests: individual settlers in Kivu and Equateur provinces; and large monopoly groups interested in the purchase of compulsory cultivated products, such as cotton in Uele and Kasai, palm products in Kwango and Upper Congo. The creation of Otraco also effectively increased African agricultural production, despite the drop in agricultural prices. Moreover, Otraco provided the state with a new tool for promoting the national-way policy. This policy aimed at the complete integration of all the eastern regions of the Congo with the Matadi hinterland despite the fact that they belonged normally to the Indian Ocean hinterland. The realization of these goals required two complementary measures: first, the construction of a network completely oriented towards Matadi; and second, a tariff policy that equalized the tariffs between

Matadi and the eastern regions and those of foreign routes, despite the greater distances involved.[28]

From 1930 on, this policy was followed through the new long-distance tariffs. The low tariffs were financed by a discriminatory geographical distribution of the gains realized through lowered cost. They were imposed mainly for the benefit of the eastern regions and the exports originating from those areas. This system gave rise to sharp controversies, but it was finally supported because of the general downward trend in transport costs.

How shall we explain the systematic and recurrent devices resorted to in favour of this national way? The national way represented a choice reflecting fundamentally the role of the state in a world capitalist system where national capitalism had competing or antagonistic interests. Under Leopold II, the problem was to attach Katanga firmly to the rest of the colony and to protect it from British expansion. After the First World War, when the issue of nationalism was even more highly charged, the colonial policy-makers were resolved to provide for the Congo a complete, independent transport network even though this represented a costly solution. The lower transport costs of other colonial networks were looked upon as a danger to the Congo.[29]

Moreover, mastery over a vast economic area integrated through an autonomous transport network facilitated control of the growing economic surplus extracted from the Congolese labour force. It permitted policy-makers to shape the form of that growth by a selective distribution of the results of technical progress, and of the lowered costs, between foreign capital, the state and African peasants, according to the priorities established by the state.

Between 1933 and 1945 these lowered transport costs resulted in the allocation of a growing share of the surplus to foreign capital, whereas prices paid to African peasants did not increase. After 1950, greater importance was attached to the development of a mass-consumption market. The peasants benefited through minimum prices paid for their crops even when commodity prices fell

[28] Distances between Kivu, Katanga and the Atlantic and Indian oceans:

	Total length in km	Number of transfer points	First year of service
Kivu and Nord Katanga			
Via Matadi national way I	3,615	5	1915
Via Matadi national way II	3,520	5	1928
Via Dar es Salaam	1,610	1	1914
Sud Katanga			
Via Matadi national way I	3,920	6	1911
Via Matadi national way II	2,788	2	1928
Via Beira	2,608	0	1910
Via Lobito	2,070	0	1931

[29] See Pierre Fontainas, 'Rapport sur la politique des transports', in Belgium, Congrès Colonial National 1920, Compte rendu des séances (Brussels, 1921), pp. 153–214; P. Fontainas, 'La politique des transports au Congo belge', Bulletin de la Société Belge des Ingénieurs et des Industriels, 1921, 2, 163–220; and Ronald de Briey, ed., Notes sur la question des transports en Afrique, précédées d'un rapport au Roi (Paris, 1918).

Table 58. *World cotton price, Uele-Antwerp transport cost and price paid to peasants, Belgian Congo, 1923–58*
(in current francs and in per cent per ton)

	1923		1929		1933		1952		1958	
	Francs	Per cent	Francs	Per cent	Francs	Per cent	Francs	Per cent	Francs	Per cent
World price	5,000	100	16,000	100	5,000	100	40,000	100	36,000	100
Uele-Antwerp transport cost	1,000	20	3,000	18	1,000	20	2,400	6	2,200	6
Purchase price to peasants	350	7	1,100	7	600	12	8,000	20	5,500	15
Import price (1959 = 100)	14		27		22		94		114	

SOURCES: Edmond Leplae, 'La question agricole', in Belgium, Congrès Colonial National, Comité Permanent, *La politique économique au Congo belge*, Rapport au Comité Permanent du Congrès Colonial (Brussels, 1924), pp. 145–51; Edmond Leplae, 'Histoire et développement des cultures obligatoires de coton et de riz au Congo belge de 1917 à 1933', reprint from *Congo*, May 1933, I, no. 5, p. 43; and Edmond Leplae, 'Cultures obligatoires: leurs résultats au Congo belge et dans d'autres pays tropicaux', reprint from *Revue des Questions Scientifiques*, March 1934, p. 58.

on the world market. In addition, they obtained more for their produce when international commodity prices rose (see Table 58).

More often still, the state itself compensated for the lower share of transport cost in the world price by increasing export duties in the same proportion.[30]

The decrease in the share of transport cost in the world price was a significant feature of the colonial period in that it contributed to the integration of the entire Congolese territory in the world market as a producer of raw materials. Moreover, the national way was an efficient device for shaping a unified Congolese economic policy for imported and local manufactured goods. This is borne out by the impressive reduction in inter-regional price disparities between 1910 and 1960, as shown in Table 59.

As far as imported goods were concerned, this decrease strengthened the integration of the colony as a periphery country, importing manufactured goods and exporting raw materials. After 1950, when the import substitution process

[30] Huybrechts, *Transports et structures*, p. 230, gives the following percentage of land transport costs (1), of sea transport costs (2), and of taxes and duties (3) in total transfer costs (1928–55):

	1928	1934	1949	1955
Cacao (1)	34	26	19	13
(2)	48	72	25	18
(3)	18	2	56	69
Palm-oil (1)	48	14	20	30
(2)	46	86	25	39
(3)	6	0	55	31
Tin (1)	58	53	21	28
(2)	20	14	9	12
(3)	22	33	70	60

Table 59. *Price disparities among various regions, Belgian Congo, 1910–58*

	Goods consumed by foreign bourgeoisie (Belgian prices = 100)					
	Matadi and Leopoldville			Elisabethville		
	1910–14	1936–8	1956–8	1910–14	1936–8	1956–8
Food products	227	175	131	548	239	150
Household articles	229	155	132	396	167	146

	Goods consumed by African population (Boma and Matadi prices = 100)				
	Coquilhatville	Luluaburg	Stanleyville	Kindu-Bukavu	Elisabethville
Food products (1912)	155	225	265	203	227
(1937)	72		112	87	196
(1957)	88	90	90	85	96
Household articles and clothing (1912)	181	97	237	200	135
(1937)	103		125	111	142
(1957)	102	96	100	105	114

SOURCE: Peemans, *Diffusion du progrès économique,* pp. 414–18 and 428–30.

was limited, it eased the concentration of industrial activity in the two growth centres, at Leopoldville and Elisabethville, because these areas could extend their outlets to the entire country.

Let us note finally that though the national-way policy was clearly a state goal, it was never put into effect independently or against the interests of the financial groups with which the state was associated. For instance, in favouring the promotion of imports from Matadi to the eastern regions, it contributed to balancing the traffic networks of those regions (CFL and BCK), which were managed by the financial groups. But it never required these groups to export only in accordance with the national way.

To sum up briefly the results of the transport policy, we may say first of all that the development of the transport network occupied an important place in the first phase of capital accumulation in the Congo. Its orientation reflected the role assigned to the country by the colonial policy within the international division of labour. In this respect, the state played a decisive role. It associated itself closely with the ruling segment of foreign capital, to which it granted privileges, advantages and subsidies of all kinds. Its strategic goal was to integrate into the world market the largest possible volume of the available labour force, and to do away with all obstacles to profitable investments by various foreign-capital interests. The realization of that goal did not occasion any problems when it coincided with the immediate interests of the financial groups. The state was particularly active where the long-range interests of foreign capital as a whole outran the short-term interests of the dominant group. The colonial power never opposed the fundamental interests of the financial groups, but it did negotiate with them in order to secure its own general goal. Where necessary, the state also utilized public funds in order to reach its goal. By pursuing this policy, the state was able to integrate the entire Congo and its labour force into the world market. This achievement stands out as a striking instance of state-monopoly capitalism on the periphery.

BIBLIOGRAPHY

Anstey, Roger. *King Leopold's legacy: the Congo under Belgian rule 1908–1960*. London, Oxford University Press, 1966.

Arrighi, Giovanni. 'Labour supplies in historical perspective: a study of the proletarianization of the African peasantry in Rhodesia', *Journal of Development Studies*, April 1970, no. 3.

Banque Centrale du Congo et du Ruanda-Urundi. *Bulletin*, Nov. 1953, Nov. 1956, Nov. 1959.

Rapport, 1959. Brussels, 1960.

Belgium. Commission de la Main-d'Œuvre Indigène (1930–1). *Le problème de la main-d'œuvre au Congo belge*. Rapport général. Brussels, 1931.

Belgium. Commission pour l'Etude du Problème de la Main-d'Œuvre au Congo Belge (1924–5) et Comité Consultatif de la Main-d'Œuvre (1928). *Le problème de la main-d'œuvre au Congo belge*. Rapports. Brussels, 1928.

Belgium. Congrès Colonial National. *Le problème de la main-d'œuvre*. Rapports, Assemblée Générale du 6.6.1952. Brussels, 1952.

Belgium. Congrès Colonial National, 6th Sess. (Sénat de Belgique, 4–5 Oct. 1947). *Comptes rendus des séances et rapports préparatoires*. Brussels, 1948.

Belgium. Congrès Colonial National, 13th Sess., 1958. *La promotion des milieux ruraux au Congo belge et au Ruanda-Urundi*. Rapports, Assemblées Générales des 7 et 8 novembre 1958. Brussels, 1958.

Belgium. Congrès Colonial National. Comité Permanent. *La question sociale au Congo*. Rapport au Comité Permanent du Congrès Colonial. Brussels, 1924.

Belgium. Sénat. Commission des Colonies. *Discussion du budget pour l'exercice 1934*. Sénat, 1933–4 Sess. Documents parlementaires, no. 85. Brussels, 1934.

Bézy, Fernand. *Problèmes structurels de l'économie congolaise*. Louvain, Institut de Recherches Economiques et Sociales, 1957.

Briey, Renaud, comte de, ed. *Notes sur la question des transports en Afrique, précedées d'un rapport au Roi*. Nancy, 1918.

Bulletin Officiel de l'Etat Indépendant. Brussels, 1903.

Bundy, Colin. 'The emergence and decline of a South African peasantry', *African Affairs*, Oct. 1972.

Cattier, Félicien. *Etude sur la situation de l'Etat Indépendant du Congo*. Brussels, 1906.

Chesneaux, Jean, ed. *Histoire de la Chine*, vol. 1: *1840–1885*. Paris, 1969.

Congo, Belgian. *Rapport annuel sur la Colonie, 1918*. Brussels, 1919.

Coquery-Vidrovitch, Catherine. 'Recherches sur un mode de production africain', *La Pensée*, 1969. no. 144.

Cornet, René Jules. *La bataille du rail: la construction du chemin de fer de Matadi au Stanley Pool*. Brussels, 1947.

Delcommune, Alexandre. *L'avenir du Congo belge menacé: bilan des dix premières années (1909–1918) d'administration coloniale gouvernementale; le mal—le remède*. 2nd ed. Brussels, 1921.

Delhaye, Yvan. 'Les résultats fiscaux des sociétés coloniales soumises à la loi du

21.6.1927, *Bulletin de la Banque Centrale du Congo et du Ruanda-Urundi*, Sept. 1955.

Dupré, Gérard. 'Le commerce entre sociétés lignagères: les Nzabi dans la traite à la fin du XIXe siècle (Gabon-Congo', *Cahiers d'Etudes Africaines*, 1972, no. 48.

Emmanuel, Arghiri. *L'échange inégal: essai sur les antagonismes dans les rapports économiques internationaux*. Paris, 1969.

Fei, John C. H., and Gustav Ranis. *Development of the labor surplus economy: theory and policy*. Homewood, Ill., 1964.

Fontainas, Pierre P. 'La politique des transports au Congo belge', *Bulletin de la Société Belge des Ingénieurs et des Industriels*, 1921, **2**.

'Rapport sur la politique des transports', in Belgium, Congrès Colonial National 1920, *Compte rendu des séances*. Brussels, 1921.

Gonda, Jean. 'Les holdings belges et le financement de l'industrialisation au Congo belge', *Revue des Sciences Economiques* (Liège), 1956, no. 105.

Gouverneur, Jacques. *Productivity and factor proportions in less developed countries: the case of industrial firms in the Congo*. Oxford, Clarendon Press, 1971.

Habib, Irfan. 'Potentialities of capitalistic development in the economy of Mughal India', *Journal of Economic History*, March 1969, **29**.

Hostelet, Georges. *L'œuvre civilisatrice de la Belgique au Congo de 1885 à 1945*, vol. I: *L'œuvre économique et sociale*. Brussels, Institut Royal Colonial Belge, 1954.

Huybrechts, André. *Transports et structures de développement au Congo: étude du progrès économique de 1900 à 1970*. Paris, 1970.

Institut de Sociologie Solvay. *Vers la promotion de l'économie indigène*. Brussels, 1956.

Joye, Pierre, and Rosine Lewin. *Les trusts du Congo*. Brussels, 1961.

Lacroix, Jean Louis. *Industrialisation au Congo: la transformation des structures économiques*. Paris, 1966.

Leclercq, Hugues. 'Un mode de mobilisation des ressources: le système fiscal; le cas du Congo pendant la période coloniale', Université Lovanium, Institut de Recherches Economiques et Sociaux, *Cahiers Economiques et Sociaux*, June 1965, **3**, no. 2.

Lederer, André. *Histoire de la navigation au Congo*. Tervuren, Musée Royal de l'Afrique Centrale, 1965.

Leplae, Edmond. 'Cultures obligatoires: leurs résultats au Congo belge et dans d'autres pays tropicaux', *Revue des Questions Scientifiques*, March 1934.

'Histoire et développement des cultures obligatoires de coton et de riz au Congo belge de 1917 à 1933', *Congo*, May 1933, **1**, no. 5.

'La question agricole: possibilités et méthodes de développement de l'agriculture au Congo belge', in Belgium, Congrès Colonial National, Comité Permanent, *La politique économique au Congo belge*. Rapport au Comité Permanent du Congrès Colonial. Brussels, 1924.

Lewis, Sir Arthur. *Economic development with unlimited supplies of labour*. Manchester, 1954.

Lux, André. *Le marché du travail en Afrique noire*. Louvain, Institut de Recherches Economiques, Sociales et Politiques, 1962.

Malengreau, Guy. *Les droits fonciers coutumiers chez les indigènes du Congo belge: essai d'interprétation juridique*. Brussels, Institut Royal Colonial Belge, 1947.

Vers un paysannat indigène: les lotissements agricoles au Congo belge. Brussels, Institut Royal Colonial Belge, 1949.

Mendiaux, Edouard. 'Le Comité National du Kivu', *Zaïre*, Oct. 1956, **10**, no. 8.

Merlier, Michel. *Le Congo de la colonisation belge à l'indépendance*. Paris, 1962.

Moulaert, Georges. *Problèmes coloniaux d'hier et d'aujourd'hui*. Brussels, 1939.

Mouttoule, Léopold. *Politique sociale de l'Union Minière du Haut-Katanga pour la main-d'œuvre indigène, et ses résultats au cours de vingt années d'application*. Brussels, Institut Royal Colonial Belge, 1946.

Norman, E. Herbert. *Japan's emergence as a modern state: political and economic problems of the Meiji period*. New York, 1940.

Palloix, Christian. *L'économie mondiale capitaliste*. 2 vols. Paris, 1971.

Problèmes de la croissance en économie ouverte. Paris, 1969.

Peemans, Jean-Philippe. *Diffusion du progrès économique et convergence des prix: le cas Congo-Belgique 1900–1960; la formation du système des prix et salaires dans une économie dualiste*. Louvain, 1968.

Poulantzas, Nicos. 'Le concept de classes sociales', *L'Homme et la Société*, 1972, no. 24–25.

Pouvoir politique et classes sociales de l'état capitaliste. Paris, 1968.

Rey, Pierre Philippe. *Colonialisme, néo-colonialisme et transition au capitalisme: exemple de la 'Comilog' au Congo-Brazzaville*. Paris, 1971.

Roeykens, Auguste. *Le baron Léon de Béthune au service de Léopold II: conflit de l'Etat du Congo avec certaines compagnies commerciales belges (juillet-octobre 1892)*. Brussels, Académie Royale des Sciences d'Outre-Mer, 1964.

Stengers, Jean. *Combien le Congo a-t-il coûté à la Belgique?* Brussels, Académie Royale des Sciences Coloniales, 1957.

'The Congo Free State and the Belgian Congo before 1914', in *Colonialism in Africa 1870–1960*, vol. I: *The history and politics of colonialism 1870–1914*, L. H. Gann and Peter Duignan, eds. Cambridge University Press, 1969.

Tibbaut, E. 'L'action agricole et sociale de Lord Leverhulme au Congo', *Revue Economique Internationale* (Brussels), Jan. 1926.

Van de Putte, Marcel. *Le Congo belge et la politique de conjoncture*. Brussels, Institut Royal Colonial Belge, 1946.

Van der Kerken, Georges. *Les sociétés bantoues du Congo belge et les problèmes de la politique indigène*. Brussels, 1920.

Vandewalle, Gaston. *De conjoncturele evolutie in Kongo en Ruanda-Urundi van 1920 tot 1939 en van 1949 tot 1958*. Antwerp, 1966.

Vansina, Jan. 'Les Kuba et l'administration territoriale de 1919 à 1960', *Cultures et Développement*, 1972, **4**, no. 2.

Verriest, G. 'Résultats de sociétés coloniales ayant leur siège administratif en Belgique, suivant la statistique de l'impôt complémentaire sur les revenus', *Bulletin de la Banque Centrale du Congo et du Ruanda-Urundi*, March 1954.

CHAPTER 6

ECONOMIC DEVELOPMENT IN GERMANY'S AFRICAN EMPIRE, 1884–1914

by

L. H. GANN

The Kaiser's Kolonialreich was the most short-lived of the colonial empires in sub-Saharan Africa. German rule lasted for little more than three decades. Yet, considering the brief duration of German domination, probably more ink has been spilt per square mile of colonial territory under German sway than over any other part of colonial Africa. The Wilhelmian period produced an extensive number of official reports and statistical and technical publications, some of them so thorough that the reader is enabled to trace the precise value of all the horns, hoofs and antlers sent year by year from each colony to the Fatherland.[1] There are reminiscences, polemical discussions and down-to-earth treatises with blunt titles such as 'How do we make our colonies pay?'[2]

This self-assured approach gave way to polemics after the Versailles settlement. According to the victors, Teutons were unfit to rule backward races. To substantiate this argument the British, for instance, compiled detailed reports on the way the Germans had robbed their subjects and stolen their land. The Germans in turn attacked what they called the *Kolonialschuldlüge* (imputation of Colonial culpability), and replied in kind with accusations against Germany's former enemies. German nationalists thereby made a formidable, though unintended, contribution to the critique of Western imperialism in general. German post-war publicity not only pushed the notion that Germany's role in the colonies had been beneficial, but also heightened the guilt feelings of many liberal-minded Englishmen who, after the First World War, began to worry about 'the clever men who forced upon Germany the Treaty of Versailles, and thereby sacrificed the moral gains of the war'.[3] Later on, Nazi propaganda contributed further to early imperial notions of the Carl Peters and Cecil Rhodes variety to the effect that colonization in Africa was or could be turned into an immensely profitable undertaking. This concept was familiar also to Marxist-Leninists, who drew totally different conclusions from similar premises.

After the Second World War, German writing on the colonies entered a new era when the colonial archives became available to historians and economists. Scholars in both Germanys now began to re-evaluate the German past in Africa. East Germany, calling itself the first Workers' and Peasants' State, became the first legatee of a former colonial power whose official policy obliged contemporary historians to condemn the records of all preceding gov-

---

[1] See the detailed tables for German imports and exports to the colonies appended in Otto Mayer, *Die Entwicklung der Handelsbeziehungen Deutschlands zu seinen Kolonien* (Munich, 1913).

[2] Paul Rohrbach, *Wie machen wir unsere Kolonien rentabel? . . .* (Halle, 1907).

[3] William Harbutt Dawson, 'Introduction' to Heinrich Schnee, *German colonization past and future: the truth about the German colonies* (London, 1926), p. 39.

6. German Africa before 1914

ernments. Marx, during the nineteenth century, had still assigned a historically progressive function to British colonialism in India. Engels had welcomed the French conquest of Algeria as the victory of civilization over barbarism. Lenin's subsequent approach, however, stripped colonialism of all progressive function, and Lenin's heirs in the German Democratic Republic could not help but follow suit. They paid special attention to the numerous abuses inflicted by colonial rulers on their subjects. Hence their writing sometimes bore an odd resemblance to the revelations regarding the evils of Portuguese or Belgian colonialism published during the first part of the twentieth century by bourgeois reformers such as E. D. Morel and Sir Roger Casement. At the same time, East German writers tended to play down the more positive aspects of German economic development. Nor did they use the argument, implicitly accepted by Wilhelmian imperialists as well as by Marx himself, that force was the midwife of history and an engine of progress.

The Federal German Republic, unlike its eastern neighbour, lacked an officially sanctioned party line. Some writers continued to defend the German past, including Germany's colonial record. But there was a widespread ideological preference in favour of re-evaluating Germany's historical legacy. What were the origins of totalitarian terror? How far could the roots of Nazism be traced to earlier epochs?[4] The West German state, moreover, was created and maintained above all by the heirs of the old Centre Party and the Social Democratic Party, by the very groups who had most bitterly condemned Germany's colonial record in the Wilhelmian Reichstag. Their adherents were the men whom militant nationalists had been wont to denounce as *vaterlandslose Gesellen* (men without a country), and who were naturally apt to stress the element of discontinuity in German history. All traditional German institutions began to draw fire, including the defunct colonial establishment.

The attempts of German scholars to come to terms with their own past have thus produced new schools of colonial historiography. There are now valuable monographs on specialized topics, including studies of particular territories, based on newly available archival sources. These include works such as Detlef Bald's book on German East Africa, which, though harshly critical of Germany's colonial record, also goes into what the author regards as positive aspects of German colonization.[5] But apart from propaganda works of World War I vintage, there is as yet no overall assessment in English of the German

---

[4] Helmut Bley, *Kolonialherrschaft und Sozialstruktur in Deutsch-Südwestafrika 1894–1914* (Hamburg, 1968), translated into English as *South-West Africa under German rule 1894–1914* (Evanston, Northwestern University Press, 1971), is in some ways perhaps even more harshly critical of Germany's economic and social record than the East German study by Horst Drechsler, *Südwestafrika unter deutscher Kolonialherrschaft: der Kampf der Herero und Nama gegen den deutschen Imperialismus (1884–1915)* (Berlin, 1966). Bley, like Hannah Arendt, sees colonialism abroad as a source of fascism at home. In a comparable vein, Hans-Ulrich Wehler, in a brilliant re-evaluation, *Bismarck und der Imperialismus* (Cologne, 1969), interprets Bismarckian colonialism, among other things, as a means of trade promotion, and also as a defensive mechanism against democratic tendencies arrayed against Bismarck's 'Bonapartist dictatorship'. The last of the gubernatorial reminiscences was Oskar Hintrager, *Südwestafrika in der deutschen Zeit* (Munich, 1955), written by a one-time deputy-governor of South-West Africa.

[5] Detlef Bald, *Deutsch-Ostafrika 1900–1914: eine Studie über die Verwaltung, Interessengruppen und wirtschaftliche Erschliessung* (Munich, 1970); see also Rainer Tetzlaff, *Koloniale Entwicklung und Ausbeutung: Wirtschafts- und Sozialgeschichte Deutsch-Ostafrikas 1885–1914* (Berlin, 1970), written from a sociological viewpoint.

colonial impact on Africa. There is not even a straightforward economic history of German colonial enterprise. The present essay cannot hope to fill the gap, but aims to serve merely as a preliminary review.

An overview

During the thirty years that elapsed between Bismarck's colonial initiative and the outbreak of the First World War, the Germans acquired numerous overseas dependencies, which were centrally administered from Berlin. In effect, however, there was not one German colonial empire but many. The Kaiser's colonial dependants, who between them made up something like one-fifth of his subjects, differed enormously from one another. Fula and Bushmen, Ewe and Nyamwezi, Herero and Nama were indeed far more unlike one another than Germany's minority citizens in the metropole, be they Poles, Danes, Jews or Franco-Alsatians. The German colonial empire contained a tremendous diversity of socio-economic systems. There were, for instance, Stone Age people such as the Bushmen of the Kalahari, who made their living by gathering food and hunting game with bow and arrow; there were Iron Age cattle-keepers such as the Herero; and there were sophisticated merchants such as the Swahili-speaking traders of Dar es Salaam. Similarly, geographers could find almost every possible climate and topography, from the snows of Mount Kilimanjaro to the tropical rain-forest of southern Kamerun. There were even enormous differences to be found within the boundaries of the same colony; for instance, there was not one but several German East Africas, with widely varying conditions of climate and vegetation.

During the mid-1880s Germany established a far-flung network of colonial claims, and German cartographers proceeded to paint large patches of Africa in Prussian blue. In the end, the German colonial empire was much larger than the Reich itself [6] and required a considerable time to conquer. Even after twenty years of formal occupation and after lengthy campaigns in different parts of the empire, there remained large areas where German authority was represented not by a regular civilian administration but merely by soldiers. In the remoter parts of Kamerun and in parts of East Africa, German authority remained even more tenuous. Here German colonial administrators were apt to look with favour on 'aristocratic' races like the Tutsi or the Fulani. Germans in charge of remoter *Residenturen* worked out their own form of 'indirect rule', which differed sharply from the direct administration characteristic of regions under immediate German sway, and which implied a minimum of governance in the accepted sense.

The development of the empire was a vast undertaking, requiring much expertise and huge outlays of cash. Yet during the first two decades of German colonization, the Germans had little capital to spare for colonial ventures. The explanation for Germany's failure to invest large sums in its overseas possessions must be sought largely in domestic terms. The three decades that elapsed between the foundation of the Kolonialreich and its dissolution represented a period of tremendous economic growth within the metropolis. Between 1880

[6] The total area of East Africa was 384,000 square miles, of South-West Africa 322,000, of Kamerun 305,000 and of Togo 34,000, whereas that of the Wilhelmian Reich was 209,000 square miles.

and 1914 the population of the Wilhelmian Reich rose from 45 million to nearly 68 million. Germany developed immense industries, great cities and a vast mercantile marine.

The pace of foreign and colonial lending picked up after the turn of the century; but even so, only about one-tenth of current savings between 1900 and 1914 went abroad. Of this, the bulk was placed in Europe (the Austro-Hungarian Empire alone absorbed as much capital as the entire African and Asian continents). In Africa, the capital invested outside the German colonies, especially in South Africa and Egypt, exceeded the sums placed within the German possessions.[7] German investors remained chary of putting their savings into the colonies, despite the exertions of the government and despite the tremendously powerful position held on the German money market by a few great banks. These banks, especially the 'four D's,—the Deutsche Bank, the Disconto-Gesellschaft, the Dresdner Bank and the Darmstädter Bank—would respond to official suggestions for colonial lending not merely to make money but also as a matter of prestige and patriotic duty.[8] Nevertheless, within the total context of German capital investment, the colonies played but a negligible part. By 1907, German private investors, planters, mine-owners, merchants, railway builders and so forth had placed some 229 million marks into the overseas possessions of the Reich. This sum amounted to no more than the combined share capital and reserves of just *one* major metropolitan enterprise, such as the Dresdner Bank (231 million marks) or the Disconto-Gesellschaft (227 million marks). Some of these colonial enterprises (such as the Deutsche Kolonialgesellschaft für Südwest Afrika) did exceedingly well. But the great majority of colonial firms had to struggle hard. Their annual dividends (meticulously listed in publications like *Von der Heydt's Kolonialhandbuch: Jahrbuch der deutschen Kolonial and Überseeunternehmungen* [Berlin]) were mostly modest and often non-existent. The stock promoter's expectation of golden super-profits usually turned out to be no more than an insubstantial dream.

The colonial empire likewise accounted for only a small fraction of Germany's overseas trade. (Between 1891 and 1910 the colonial share of Ger-

---

[7] By 1914 something like 23·5 milliard marks had been invested abroad; of this, 12·5 milliard went to Europe, 2 milliard to Africa, and 1 milliard to Asia. See Herbert Feis, *Europe, the world's banker* . . . (New Haven, Yale University Press, 1930), pp. 60–78.

[8] According to a talk given by Secretary of State Bernhard Dernburg in the Frankfurt Chamber of Commerce, German capital in the colonies amounted to over 300 million marks, and in 1907 was distributed as follows:

	Private capital (in marks)	Capital invested by the Reich, including loans to Togo and Kamerun (in marks)
East Africa	92,687,231	15,730,026
South-West Africa	45,848,021	37,877,028
Kamerun	42,661,858	5,489,910
Togo	12,914,000	9,759,723
Pacific colonies	35,020,448	11,114,743
Total	229,131,558	79,971,430

Data are from Bernhard Dernburg, *Koloniale Finanzprobleme* . . . (Berlin, 1907).

many's exports rose only from 0·17 per cent to 0·73 per cent of the total.) Social Democratic critics of imperial colonization never tired of pointing out that Germany's traffic with a small country like Norway was worth far more than Germany's commerce with all its overseas dependencies. As late as 1912 Germany exported more than five times as much to Belgium as to all its colonial dependencies, and eighteen times as much as to South-West Africa, a territory for which so much blood and treasure had been spilt. (The respective figures were 493,300,000 marks for Belgium, 91,323,000 marks for the African colonies and 26,442,000 marks for South-West Africa.)

The financial means available for colonial purposes were likewise exiguous. By 1913, just before the colonial empire was lost, Germany spent ten times as much on its postal administration as on all the colonies; and the budget of Berlin University for that year was substantially greater than that of the 'model colony' of Togo.[9]

During the pioneering years, Germany, like its competitors, had to contend with lack of experience and, in many cases, with lack of colonial realism. German diplomats, for instance, spent much time to secure access to the Zambezi river for their South-West African colony. The occupation of this connecting link, popularly known as the *Caprivi Zipfel,* made sense to Europeans, who thought in terms of using a great navigable waterway such as the Rhine, where tug-steamers pulled barges up-stream and down-stream. In the African context, however, the very idea of securing a great stretch of veld, some seven hundred miles away from the nearest port, to promote steam transport along a river broken by some of the world's greatest and most spectacular waterfalls, had a surrealist touch.

At the outset, of course, there was a very general lack of expertise. As late as 1913, J. K. Vietor, a Bremen merchant with extensive interests in Togo, still argued that except in the case of large-scale mining the real problem in the colonies was not so much lack of money as lack of good men. Too many colonial ventures, including both plantations and diamond mines, had been ruined by incompetent or dishonest management. Hence large and small investors alike had become suspicious of colonial enterprise.[10]

German colonization had other weaknesses. For all the Germans' deserved reputation for scientific thoroughness, scholarly exploration was at first sketchy. This was particularly serious in countries like South-West Africa, where the Germans aimed at establishing a white farming colony. Yet as late as 1907 Paul Rohrbach, a staunch advocate of colonialism, could still criticize harshly the German failure to make any scientific preparations for agricultural settlement in South-West Africa.

[9] In 1913, Germany disbursed 675,861,000 marks on posts and telegraphs, and 92,030,000 marks on the colonies, of which 51,900,000 was raised within the dependencies. Berlin University in 1913 spent 4,927,000 marks, while Togo's expenditure was 4,060,000 marks. Data from *The New International Yearbook . . .* (New York, 1916); *Minerva: Jahrbuch der gelehrten Welt . . .* (Strassburg, 1914); and Alfred Zimmermann, *Geschichte der deutschen Kolonialpolitik* (Berlin, 1914).

[10] J. K. Vietor, *Geschichtliche und kulturelle Entwicklung unserer Schutzgebiete* (Berlin, 1913), pp. 192–31. Vietor had acquired practical experience as a planter as well as a trader. He was a member of the progressively minded faction within the *Kolonialrat* (an imperial advisory body), a supporter of the missions and an opponent of large-scale concessions.

It was a fundamental mistake . . . that from the very beginning nothing serious was done to promote scientific research through public funds . . . Nothing has been achieved for zoological research since the studies of Andersson half a century ago; nothing has been accomplished in botanical studies since the work of Schinz twenty years earlier, and both were private individuals depending on private means. Despite the presence of ore bodies and a small amount of surface mining, geological exploration remains in its earliest beginnings . . . The meteorological service is somewhat better, but nevertheless is by no means adequately organized.[11]

The Germans were slow to create a modern transport system. When Dernburg took over colonial affairs in 1906, the German railway system in the colonies was negligible in every territory except South-West Africa. In the absence of steam-engines and trucks, the Germans had to rely on porters, usually impressed by force. In South-West Africa the pioneers had to rely on donkeys and ox-wagons. The lack of harbours created another logistic bottleneck. In 1904, for instance, military operations in South-West Africa might have come to a standstill but for the ingenuity of a private concern, the Woermann shipping line, in utilizing and improving the truly miserable facilities available at Swakopmund and Lüderitz. The German run-of-the-mill administrators, even at their best, were for the most part ill-trained to cope with issues concerning economic development, a weakness not cured by the specialized legal training received by the higher class of German civil servants.

Yet, when all is said and done, the thirty years of German rule in Africa, especially the last decade, saw progress on an impressive, and indeed on an accelerating, scale. None can tell how the German colonies might have fared had some other occupying power been in charge. But certainly the Germans achieved a great deal. Trade figures, of course, are not the only indicator of economic development. But they do at least provide some relevant data. Following a period of relative stagnation in the 1880s and 1890s, colonial export figures showed a sharp increase after the turn of the century. (Within the space of only five years—from 1907, when the effective conquest of the empire had been largely completed, to 1911—the commerce of the colonies doubled from 217,885,000 to 433,440,000 marks.) The colonial economies were beginning to change in character. A small new stratum of Africans had come into existence, educated at mission and at government schools, capable of reading not only the Lutheran Shorter Catechism, but also, in some cases, the *Vorwärts,* the leading Social Democratic paper. The overall impact of the imperial economy was exceedingly uneven. Conditions varied widely. German West Africa was looked upon as a tropical region, totally distinct from South-West Africa, which the Germans meant to turn into a white man's country. Within each colony the rate of development would differ in startling fashion from region to region.

Broadly speaking, development was marked by certain distinct stages. During the early years of German colonialism, Afro-German contacts were largely limited to coastal entrepôt trade. Subsequent German conquests might or might not be followed by a period of *Raubwirtschaft* dependent on direct coercion and

---

[11] Paul Rohrbach, *Deutsche Kolonialwirtschaft,* vol. I: *Südwest-Afrika* (Berlin, 1907), p. 509. These weaknesses had begun to be remedied just before the First World War.

entailing the use of forced labour, the displacement of Africans from their land or even the appropriation of African cattle. Such a system of exploitation in German (as well as non-German) colonies was often linked to concessionary régimes, whereby overprivileged and undercapitalized concerns were entrusted with areas equal in size to European principalities. In economic terms, the colonies remained largely underdeveloped estates, acquired for speculative purposes, famed more for their scandals than for their productivity.

During the first decade of the present century, major changes began to get under way. Abuses within the empire were coming under closer scrutiny from the Reichstag, which jealously defended its political and fiscal prerogatives in the colonies. Private bodies such as the Basel Mission Society pleaded for a more humanitarian policy with regard to Africans. Opposition parties, especially the Social Democratic Party and the Centre, attacked corrupt practices both for the sake of the Africans and as a means of belabouring the government. There were official inquiries into cruelties that were publicly documented. The new departure was described as the era of 'economic reform', entailing limited and piecemeal improvements applied in varying and uneven fashion in different parts of the empire.

'Economic reform' implied the end of *Raubwirtschaft* and concessionary monopolies, in favour of a more rational and intensive form of colonial development. In the political field, the system was represented by Bernhard Dernburg, previously a director of the Darmstädter Bank, an advocate of 'American' methods of business efficiency, who had charge of colonial affairs between 1906 and 1910. Under the new régime, which is discussed in greater detail below, the use of terroristic or arbitrary measures of government diminished, or was ended altogether. More capital flowed into the colonies. Between 1904 and 1913 the investments made by German companies in the colonies rose from 185 million marks to 506 million. There were solid advances in medicine, in scientific research, in transport, as well as in other areas. The Germans developed more specialized forms of plantation agriculture. In the tropical possessions they made attempts to encourage African crop production, with reliance on market incentives gradually replacing simple coercion. Finally, there were the first feeble beginnings of secondary industries. At the outbreak of the First World War, when the Germans were about to lose their empire, Wilhelmian colonialism had assumed a more or less modern form.

Coastal transit trade

Mein Feld ist die Welt (the world is my field) was the motto chosen by the Hamburg-America Line when it began operations in 1847. These words, for all their Disraelian ring, were aptly chosen. Not only did they symbolize the spirit of one particular firm and its founder, Albert Ballin, but they also gave evidence of Hamburg's special position within Germany, a country which at the time still depended mainly on agriculture for its living. Hamburg, like its Hanseatic sister cities of Lübeck and Bremen, was a Free City within the German Confederation, largely dependent on commerce, shipping, insurance and similar services. Hamburg was anglophile in sentiment, cosmopolitan by inclination and wedded to free trade by self-interest.

During the second half of the nineteenth century, railway and canal traffic vastly increased the trade of Hamburg's hinterland. Germany became increasingly industrialized. The economy of the North American continent grew rapidly, and Hamburg's commerce with the New World greatly expanded. Hamburg enjoyed a special position in Germany's overseas traffic. Even when the city joined the newly united Reich in 1871, Hamburg for a time managed to enjoy a peculiar status. Still, Hamburg merchants could not prevent Germany's drift to protection in 1879, and they had but a limited stake in the new tariff partnership between the great Prussian landowners and heavy industry, which, from 1879 onward, helped to cast Wilhelmian Germany into a new protectionist mould. But Hamburg did not fully join the German customs union until 1888, when the last of its port privileges disappeared and the so-called free zone within the Hamburg port became an historical memory.

One of Hamburg's many overseas markets was found in West Africa. There the Germans enjoyed a good reputation among abolitionists, for they had never taken an appreciable share in the slave-trade and there was no pro-slavery lobby in any German states.[12] From the commercial standpoint, the original centre of Hamburg activities in West Africa was Lagos, where Hamburg merchants had begun to operate from 1848. For instance, the firm of A. Woermann and of Jantzen & Thormählen then set up chains of 'factories' in many parts of the coast, all the way from Liberia to Gabon. German commerce had assumed such great importance in Kamerun that in 1882 Woermann instituted a regular shipping line to West Africa. Woermann's ventures signalled a major departure in the history of German maritime enterprise. Woermann, among others, realized that the future lay with the steamship, not with the sailing vessel. He understood also that shipping could no longer form an appendage to mercantile enterprise. Steamships were expensive investments, and the days were numbered when every big export firm in Hamburg would try to have at least one boat of its own to serve as a prestige symbol as well as a means of transport. The Germans in West Africa purchased all manner of tropical goods, especially palm-oil, which they used as a lubricant for engines and also for the manufacture of soap and candles. In South-West Africa, missionaries of the Rhenish (or Barmen) Missionary Society supported an associated concern that carried out legitimate trade in cattle purchased from the pastoral Herero and sold in South Africa.

Hanseatic traders also facilitated exchange between the west coast and the Indian Ocean. Especially during the earlier part of the nineteenth century, Ger-

---

[12] Germans were active not only as merchants but also as preachers. The pioneer Protestant mission on the Gold Coast was the Basel Mission Society, most of whose clergymen came from Germany. Basel set up schools, translated the Bible into indigenous languages, fought disease and helped to introduce such crops as coffee, cocoa and Virginia and Kentucky tobacco. Educated Africans such as James Africanus Horton, an Afro-British medical man, thought highly of the Baselers, who were indeed proud to call themselves Germano-Africans. See James Africanus Horton, *West African countries and peoples, 1868* (reprint, Edinburgh University Press, 1969), pp. 132–4. Another area of mission work was Togo, where the North German Missionary Society had begun to work among the Ewe with the encouragement of British Methodists.

Anglo-German missionary co-operation was equally marked in South Africa, where the Rhenish Missionary Society had sent out its first contingent in 1829 at the instigation of the London Missionary Society. In 1842, the Rhenish Society extended its operations into what is now South-West Africa. Dr Friedrich Fabri, the director of the missionary society, famous as a theoretician of early German colonialism, stood for missionary enterprise of the anglophile kind, which stressed the benefits of trade and the real and assumed benefits of European trusteeship.

mans shipped cowrie shells from the Indian Ocean to the countries along the Gulf of Guinea. From the coast, cowries passed into the interior, to places like Bornu and Timbuktu. The Germans thus performed a valuable function in supplying a currency useful especially in small transactions where dealers required 'coins' of minute denomination. Initially, the traffic in cowries was a most profitable undertaking. The firm of A. J. Hertz, for instance, at one time managed to clear $18 per hundred pounds of Maldive cowries. But the trade grew to such proportions that the shell currency became subject to inflation, and in 1859 Hertz was forced to close its supply depot in Zanzibar. The Germans sold other merchandise, too, such as salt, cloth and fire-arms. Dealers from Hamburg and Bremen, like their European competitors, had not the slightest compunction about selling guns to Africans, even the most modern breech-loaders. Indeed, without foreign rifles, nations such as the Herero and the Nama of South-West Africa could not subsequently have resisted the Kaiser's forces with such tenacity.

Gin was a mainstay of the west-coast trade. Tastes varied among the various African customers—the people of the Gold Coast liked rum, but elsewhere *Branntwein* came to dominate the trade in spirits. The traffic in cheap liquor, much of it manufactured from potatoes in distilleries on great estates in East Germany, set up a tacit partnership between Hanseatic merchants and Prussian noblemen that played a major part in shaping the traffic on the African coast. By the 1880s, much to the displeasure of missionaries, schnapps amounted to between 30 and 60 per cent of the Hanseatic trade in the area. As Woermann stated in a Reichstag speech: 'It is the traffic in spirits which is viewed with the greatest jealousy by nations, indeed by most other nations. It was the means whereby the Germans were able in the first place to worm their way into the commerce of West Africa.' [13]

Compared with Germany's West African trade, its East African commerce amounted to little. (Between 1881 and 1885 the average value of Hamburg's exports to East Africa stood at 1·5 million marks, as compared to 10·1 million marks to West Africa.) Because orthodox Muslims had no use for schnapps, the Germans sold mainly textiles, guns, beads and other manufactures in return for such items as ivory, gum, spices, hides and coconuts. But though the volume of German traffic might be small, the Hamburgers managed their affairs to such good effect that they were among the foremost trading partners of Zanzibar, more important even than their Indian, Arab, British and French competitors.

In a general way, this German pioneering trade with Africa had certain distinctive characteristics. It centred mainly on West Africa, where between 1871 and 1883 Hamburg's exports rose by 560 per cent.[14] But in terms of Germany's total traffic, colonial business transactions were insignificant. (In 1891, for example, Germany's total exports to all its colonies amounted to 6 million marks out of a total of 3,504 million marks.) Germany's commerce to colonial Africa was relatively small, even by comparison with German traffic to South Africa, where German mine-owners, wine growers, merino sheep-breeders and businessmen had acquired substantial fortunes under the protection of the Union Jack or the Transvaaler *Vierkleur*.

---

[13] Quoted by Helmut Washausen, *Hamburg und die Kolonialpolitik des deutschen Reiches 1880 bis 1890* (Hamburg, 1968), p. 184, fn. 18.

[14] Mayer, *Die Entwicklung der Handelsbeziehungen Deutschlands*, p. 33.

German colonial trade was channelled through a few cities. Bremen merchants, such as A. Lüderitz, had staked out a claim in South-West Africa. The bulk of Germany's African trade passed through Hamburg. Even Hamburg's African commerce, however, was of small proportions. A good deal of money was made by transhipping British-made goods. The dependence on the British connexion lessened only during the latter part of the nineteenth century, when German factories began to compete in an increasingly successful manner against British rivals, and the inscription 'made in Germany' became a badge of honour rather than a mark of inferior craftsmanship. The Hamburgers were reluctant to tie up large sums in African ventures over long periods. They had accordingly little interest in permanent colonization as against informal influence. In some areas, as on the coast of Kamerun, German merchants did not even have permanent stations on land. They preferred to settle down in the hulks of superannuated sailing ships anchored off-shore, where they were secure from African interference. From these floating depots, the Germans supplied credit to African agents who returned with palm-oil and palm-kernels.

German exports, such as guns and liquor, were intensely unpopular with imperialists of a later vintage, who thought that liquor made Africans lewd and lazy, while fire-arms turned them insolent. The Hamburg pioneers thought otherwise, and, not surprisingly, at first had little desire for official supervision that might interfere with the traffic in rifles and schnapps. Hamburgers felt quite capable, moreover, of maintaining good relations with African rulers without relying on the help of German civil servants. Originally, Afro-German relations were of a strictly egalitarian kind. If anything, the advantage lay with African chiefs, whom the Hamburgers learned to humour. The Hamburgers in turn were apt to resent official interference. For instance, they defended the sovereignty of the Zanzibari Sultanate, which looked with favour on German traders. A majority of the Hamburg Senate thus opposed annexation right up to 1890, several years after formal German empire in Africa had become an accomplished fact. In West Africa, the old order ended when falling prices for African-grown products impelled German businessmen to push inland so as to reduce costs by circumventing local African monopolies. Once firms such as Woermann or Jantzen & Thormählen had begun to set up plantations and stores on the mainland, they required direct German protection, and therefore came to favour territorial expansion.

The economics of coercion

The pastoral frontier

South-West Africa is a harsh land. Though it covers an area more than six times the size of England, its population remains small. Except in the extreme north, the coastal lands are the most forbidding of all.

The aspect of Angra Pequena is as dreary and melancholy as it is possible to conceive . . . scarcely a vestige of vegetation is to be found within some miles of the place; dry sand and rocks, time-worn and buffeted by centuries of bad weather, constitute the whole landscape. Moreover, there is no fresh water to be had here.[15]

[15] Charles John Andersson, *The Okavango river: a narrative of travel, exploration and adventure* (London, 1861), p. 287.

Where rainfall is adequate, the natural conditions are not a great deal more attractive. Rainfall is not only low, but also irregular (with an average of 300 to 400 mm in the central Windhoek area, and 50 to 100 mm in the southern Keetmanshoop zone). In something like 70 per cent of the territory, even dry-land cropping is out of the question. Grazing is the only possible form of agricultural enterprise. Even so, the pastures have a low carrying capacity. In some areas underground water comes to the surface in the form of springs, but for the most part, it cannot be tapped except by sinking bore-holes. Over recent years modern technology has vastly added to the country's wealth. The construction of dams, fences, cattle-dips and bore-holes and up-to-date methods of stock-breeding, pasture management and disease control have helped to make farming an infinitely more profitable and a less hazardous occupation than in the past. In addition, the introduction of new breeds of animals, new varieties of trees and new forms of forage have helped to change the character of the economy. The creation of port facilities and rail and road services had revolutionized the economy of a country where nature has failed to provide navigable waterways. Modern fishing vessels now exploit the country's fishing grounds.

These improvements, however, have all required a great deal of time, as well as capital and technical know-how of a kind unavailable to the pastoral peoples who inhabited the greater part of the country at the time of the German occupation. The pre-colonial communities were scanty in number.[16] They had no defence against the ravages of locusts, rinderpest or other cattle diseases. Much depended on the possession of adequate springs, and bitter feuds were fought over cattle and the control of water-holes. In all probability, the introduction of fire-arms through white traders rendered warfare more destructive than in the olden days, when warriors had depended on bow, spear and knobkerry. Some communities, such as the Hottentots originating in the Cape Colony, had acquired increased mobility through the importation of horses from the south, and thereby added materially to the range of their military operations.

When the Germans first hoisted the Imperial Eagle on the South-West African coast, they came to a strife-torn country. The Nama had waged long and bitter wars against the Herero, in which the Rhenish Mission Society had sided with the Herero. More backward communities had been reduced to a state of virtual serfdom by their stronger neighbours. The Germans had no ready-made base, because the British had by 1878 annexed Walvis Bay, the country's main port. There were no natural lines of communication. To reach the interior, the newcomers had to cross an inhospitable desert. The Germans had little or no knowledge of the country's natural conditions. They had to contend with brave and often well-armed warrior communities. They lacked the experience of veldcraft, acquired both by the indigenous people and by immigrant trekboers from the south. The Germans' only existing economic stake was a petty traffic in dried beef, hides, ostrich feathers, rifles, schnapps and trinkets. Even this did not amount to much, for the main market for cattle was to be found in South Africa, whence itinerant traders came to buy beasts for the markets of Kimberley and other centres. Such was the land which German policy-makers

---

[16] In 1966 the territory's estimated population was 601,000. At the beginning of the German era, it was probably less than one-fourth that number. The most numerous group was the Ovambo in the relatively well-watered north, who were little touched by German rule. The largest groups who clashed with the Germans were the Herero, about 80,000 people, and the Nama, about 20,000.

meant to turn into a settlement colony capable of competing on the world markets with pastoral countries such as Australia and the Argentine; this was to be a new German Fatherland in the Antipodes.

According to the Bismarckian concept, the colonizing task was to be done by private companies, which would supply the capital, run the risks and administer the country. The intended instrument was the Deutsche Kolonialgesellschaft für Deutsch-Südwestafrika, founded in 1885 with a capital of 500,000 marks (soon increased to 1 million marks), a petty sum in terms of big business in the Wilhelmian era (the kind of money that would make a suitable dowry for the daughters of a provincial banker). From the start, the Kolonialgesellschaft lacked the cash needed to govern, and in 1885 the German government had to appoint an imperial commissioner. In the economic sphere, however, the concessionary régime continued. The Kolonialgesellschaft, as well as other concerns, including the South-West Africa Company, a British enterprise linked to Cecil Rhodes's group, acquired gigantic areas. By 1903 the six major concessionary companies in the country laid claim to 29,500,000 hectares, more than one-third of the entire territory.

The companies did little or nothing to develop these enormous holdings. Initially, they looked to future profits from mining gold and copper. In 1890, however, German troops penetrated into the interior and occupied the area round the present Windhoek, then part of the unoccupied no-man's-land between the warring Herero and Nama communities. Because the region seemed suitable for white settlement, the German authorities in 1891 provided a small subsidy to encourage sheep-farming. The concessionary companies, being too undercapitalized to carry out much development of their own, began to look to future profits accruing from the influx of white colonists that would cause land values to rise.

Concessionary capitalism derives from several different sources. The bulk of the German bourgeoisie was unwilling to risk its savings in the colonies, where conditions were little known and profits seemed uncertain. The Reichs-Schatz-amt (the imperial treasury) was wedded to a doctrine of economy as rigid as the financial creed of the British Treasury. The Reichstag, by the turn of the century, had become disillusioned with the colonies, where a great deal of money had been lost in risky or dishonest ventures and where many scandals had taken place. So low stood the reputation of the colonies, in fact, that even senior officials were apt to regard volunteers for the colonial service as prodigal sons, who had probably chosen a career overseas to escape their debts or to lead a life of idleness and profligacy. But capital was sorely needed, and according to men like Gerhard von Buchka, head of the Kolonial-Abteilung (1898–1900) cash could be attracted only by the grant of large-scale monopolies. But concessionary monopolies were apt to engender the most brutal forms of exploitation. In Germany even *Raubwirtschaft* had its theoreticians. The most extreme advocate of direct exploitation, for instance, was one Julius Scharlach, a Hamburg lawyer, a speculator in South-West African and Kamerunian concessions, an influential member of the Kolonialrat (an imperial advisory body) and a friend of Buchka. According to Scharlach, the government neither could nor should initiate any form of economic enterprise in the colonies. Investors would have to be tempted into investing money in the dependencies by grants of monopolies and large estates. Companies should raise capital by issuing stock in small denominations. In this fashion, small men could also profit from colonial ventures, and thereby strengthen the colonial lobby. Concessionary enterprise, moreover, was not concerned with national boundaries. Thus Scharlach was anxious to co-operate with foreign interests, both British and Belgian, which played a considerable part in financing concessionary ventures in South-West Africa and Kamerun, respectively. The African population, according to Scharlach, had no economic value. Colonization was a matter not of civilizing savages, but of pushing them to the wall and ultimately destroying them. Countries unwilling to act upon these principles should not acquire colonies in the first place.[17]

Moral considerations apart, however, concessionary capitalism was not economically viable in the long run. The concessionaires did little real development work of their own. They failed to mobilize capital in large quantities. They were ill-fitted for economic innovation. In South-West Africa the real pioneering was done for the most part by small men, by trekboers and by more substantial settlers from South Africa, by ambitious German farmers willing to take risks and also by a host of amateurs, ex-officers, technicians, demobilized German soldiers or German navvies and artisans brought to the country to build the railway. These would-be farmers usually had little capital. Opportunities for obtaining agricultural credit were scanty. (The Landwirtschaftsbank, the first major body providing loans to farmers, began to operate only in 1913.) Markets were at first scarce. Communications were inadequate, and haulage contracting was an important subsidiary industry. A pioneering existence was harsh, entailing great risks and limited profits. Concessionary lands thus tended to be out of the reach of these frontiersmen, who soon began to call for the appropriation of African pastures.

Although they contended with Africans for grazing grounds, the frontiersmen depended also on their African neighbours. The most important part of a farmer's capital was his cattle, especially his breeding stock, which no intelligent pioneer would have thought of selling. But this was always in short supply, especially because the German authorities at first had neither the means nor the inclination to import beasts from abroad. German colonists therefore had to purchase animals from Africans, who in turn put a high value on *their* quality breeding cows. The average German pioneer often began his career as a bush-trader—a hard and risky occupation, yet one that gradually grew more profitable as Herero in the vicinity of white settlements became more used to imported products such as clothes, coffee, sugar and tobacco.

The turning-point came with the outbreak of the great rinderpest epidemic of 1896–7 that swept through the whole of southern Africa. The Germans were able to save a substantial portion of their herds by inoculating their beasts, but the Herero herds were decimated. For the first time the settlers were enabled to

---

[17] Julius Scharlach, 'Kolonien und die Presse', cited by Vietor, *Geschichtliche und kulturelle Entwicklung*, p. 62. Scharlach's ideas were developed in *Koloniale und politische Aufsätze und Reden* (Berlin, 1903). For details concerning Scharlach's financial interests, his stake in German banks, plantations and railway enterprises, his links with foreign, especially British, capitalists, and his official appointments, see Jolanda Ballhaus, 'Die Landeskonzessionsgesellschaften', in *Kamerun unter deutscher Kolonialherrschaft*, Helmuth Stoecker, ed. (Berlin, 1968), vol. II, pp. 107–8, an excellent essay.

compete successfully with the Herero in selling cattle. At the same time, European labour costs fell as impoverished Herero were forced to hire themselves out as workmen. The epidemic also occasioned widespread destruction of draught animals. The Germans therefore decided to build a railway inland from Swakopmund. Railway construction increased the size of the internal market, and indirectly increased the demand for cheap land and the appropriation of African grazing grounds. The German authorities preferred to incur the hostility of African tribesmen (whose fighting skills were greatly underestimated) rather than meddle with powerful concession companies with the right connections in Berlin. The result was disaster. The ravages of the rinderpest, brutalities inflicted on Africans by individual Germans, a pervasive sense of insecurity, the forfeiture of land and the fear of future deprivations all combined to produce an explosion.[18] In 1904 the Herero rose, and were soon joined by their erstwhile enemies, the Nama. The Bergdamara, on the other hand, refused to join the insurrection, whereas the so-called Basters, a people of mixed Euro-African origin, fought on the side of the Germans.

According to the official German war history, Germany's opponents were equal in skill and marksmanship to the Boers, and surpassed them in military efficiency and resolute action.[19] Lothar von Trotha, commander of the German troops during 1904–5 and a protégé of the famed Count von Schlieffen, carried out a *Vernichtungsstrategie,* designed to annihilate the Herero in a classic battle of encirclement of the kind taught in German staff colleges. Trotha's methods were abhorrent to the civilian authorities in South-West Africa, including Governor Theodor Leutwein, and also to the settlers, who feared for the country's economic future and for their labour supply. But Trotha, like his mentors, was the prototype of a pure technician, concerned only with destruction and not with the political or economic consequences of his strategy. As a result of the Trotha method of waging war, a large portion of the Herero nation perished miserably in the desert. Trotha and his kind, moreover, failed to understand that seizure of the enemy's cattle should have been the key both to victory and to the conclusion of a profitable peace, an axiom known to every frontier fighter in southern Africa. Nothing was done to save the Herero cattle. The Germans did not even bother to loot the enemy's beasts, but left them to die.

The war against the Nama, who put their trust in guerrilla struggle of the mounted kind, was also fought with great bitterness. Scattered partisan operations continued in the southern part of the country as late as 1909. In the end the Germans won, but their colony was left impoverished. After protracted fighting, in which more than 17,000 white troops were engaged, the majority of German settlers were poor, bankrupt or dead. The Herero nation had been decimated. Outside Ovamboland, which had remained untouched by the conflict, most Africans were in a deplorable condition. War had smashed their social institutions, destroyed their property and spread epidemics and sickness.

---

[18] According to Oelhafen, at the beginning of the rising, out of 83,500,000 hectares in the colony, the Africans owned 31,400,000, the companies 29,175,000, the government 19,250,000, and the settlers 3,684,500 (Hans von Schöllenbach Oelhafen, *Die Besiedlung Deutsch-Südwestafrikas bis zum Weltkrieg,* Berlin, 1913, p. 76).

[19] Germany, Grosser Generalstab, Kriegsgeschichtliche Abteilung, *Die Kämpfe der deutschen Truppen in Südwestafrika* (Berlin, 1906–7), vol. I, p. 19.

The tropical frontier

Kamerun differs from South-West Africa as day from night. Beyond the coastal swamps and plains the land rises to a densely wooded plateau covered with different varieties of rain-forests. This characterizes most of southern Kamerun. In the interior, where the elevation is even higher, forests give place to savannah, where cattle flourish and where in days gone by Islamic horsemen were able to operate with ease. The ethnographic map of Kamerun is as varied as the physiographic map. Before the arrival of the Germans, the north had been invaded at one time or another by Fulani, Hausa and other Islamic peoples. The invaders in each case had forced the pagan tribes into submission. The Fulani established large states, of which Adamawa was the most important. These monarchies were built on slavery, trade, pastoral farming and craft industries. Muslim cavalry, however, could not penetrate into the forest regions, where the indigenous races lived in smaller communities.

The peoples dwelling in the forests and along the Atlantic littoral had acquired tenuous links with the Western world through the slave-trade with the New World. During the nineteenth century, Western merchants gradually switched to 'legitimate trade'; palm-oil became an important export product, and the Duala people along the coast acquired a dominant position in the local traffic. German influence was at first confined to the shores and creeks along the Gulf of Guinea, and the Europeans remained dependent on the goodwill of the Duala. The expansion of the African palm-oil trade, however, contributed to a drop in world prices, which itself formed part of a much wider recession. White merchants had hitherto been content with local German protection exercised through consular courts and warships. But now German traders called for inland expansion, so as to break the Duala mercantile monopoly and deal directly with the producers of the interior. Between 1884 and 1895 the Germans established their rule over the coastal regions. Later on, German traders, backed by German *Schutztruppen* commandos, pushed inland where they dealt in palm products, in ivory and above all in wild rubber.

From the economic standpoint, the Kamerun share in the German trade balance was infinitesimal. By 1898 the colony's exports were worth little more than 4,500,000 million marks, considerably less than one-thousandth of the total value of the merchandise imported by Germany at the time (nearly 6 milliard marks). But opportunities offered by the development of the automobile and electrical industries, and the profits made in the Congo Free State by the exploitation of rubber, persuaded German speculators that Kamerun could be squeezed in a similar fashion. In 1898 Scharlach and other investors, backed by German banks as well as by Belgian Congo concerns, created the Gesellschaft für Südkamerun (GKS). The new concern received an enormous concession comprising some 5 million hectares. Another major concessionaire was the Gesellschaft für Nordwest-Kamerun, which likewise obtained a princely stake in the country.

Concessionary capitalism was strongly supported by Jesco von Puttkamer, Governor of Kamerun between 1895 and 1907 and the son of an ultra-conservative cabinet minister who had been responsible for purging the Prussian civil service of its more liberal members. According to Puttkamer, Africans were naturally idle, and African forest-farming was incompatible with economic progress, merely tending to devastate the land. Therefore, if the country were not to continue to vegetate in a state of 'un-culture', capitalists would have to be encouraged to invest their money in plantations.[20] Puttkamer was profoundly impressed by the cocoa and coffee plantations which he had seen on the Portuguese island of São Tomé. He therefore resolved to introduce agricultural enterprise of a similar kind in Kamerun, and made the required land grants to German pioneers. Puttkamer was equally optimistic with regard to rubber. But his views were based on a lack of understanding not merely of indigenous methods of African farming, but also of the difficulties faced by plantation companies in many other countries, such as Sumatra, where Bremen entrepreneurs had lost a great deal of money.

Despite Puttkamer's endeavours, the Germans were unable to transform Kamerun into a plantation economy. The bulk of Kamerun's exports continued to derive from trade. Indeed, the plantation companies themselves engaged in commerce as well as in agriculture. The impact of this new rubber economy was fraught with disastrous consequences for many African communities. The indigenous subsistence economies became subject to heavy strain. The Germans needed an ever-increasing number of labourers to work on plantations, tap wild rubber, carry loads, construct railways and perform a host of allied tasks. Work on the plantations was at first bitterly unpopular. Among Africans the mortality of the hired hands was high, their pay was poor and their treatment bad, though some companies, such as the Westafrikanische Pflanzungsgesellschaft Viktoria, made serious attempts to improve conditions. Because plantations were unable to secure sufficient voluntary workers, the government began to recruit labour by force. German exactions—sometimes accompanied by vicious cruelty—led to widespread resistance; between 1904 and 1907, for instance, there was fighting in many parts of southern Kamerun; armed repression produced loss of life in battle, and even more so, through disease and famine.

The growth of the money economy was, however, double-edged in its effects. Some enterprising coastmen joined trading caravans into the interior where literate Africans, often immigrants from Gabon or the Gold Coast, set up branch factories to collect rubber in exchange for merchandise. Hausa merchants benefited from the German *pax* by extending their operations from the north to the forest region and the coast. Here the northerners exchanged meat for rubber, which they then sold to the Germans. German plantations also began to grow new experimental crops such as cocoa. In time Africans also discovered the value of this, and developed cocoa on their own initiative as a peasant cash-crop.

The Germans, for their part, discovered that coercion entailed severe economic costs. Moreover, the Germans' ability to govern by naked force alone was strictly limited. By the turn of the century, there were only forty permanent civil servants (*etatsmässige Beamten*) in the whole of Kamerun, including the governor, three district commissioners (*Bezirksamtmänner*) and their respective staffs. The white establishment as a whole, including gardeners, technicians and supervisors, comprised only seventy-seven persons. German military strength at the end of the Puttkamer régime was little more impressive. The

[20] Jesco von Puttkamer, *Gouverneursjahre in Kamerun* (Berlin, 1912), pp. 103–4.

armed forces comprised but nine companies of askaris, commanded by a handful of German commissioned and non-commissioned officers. This force was expected to control a territory six times the size of England with totally inadequate communications, a country where the invaders encountered the most extraordinary climatic, topographical and medical difficulties.

German abuses in Kamerun never approached those committed in the Congo Free State. The German concessionaires, unlike those in the Congo, had no recognized sovereign powers. Throughout its history, Kamerun incurred heavy annual budget deficits, a condition that gave the Reichstag whatever excuse it may have needed to intervene in the affairs of the colony. The 'Scharlach System' therefore met with a wide range of opposition. Critics included the Basel Mission Society, which condemned the concessions, whereas the Catholic Pallotine Mission tended to defend Puttkamer. German merchants bitterly censured concessionary monopolies. So did British traders like John Holt, whom the German authorities did not wish to alienate lest the British should interfere with German commerce in British possessions. Parliamentary opposition came from many sources—from the Social Democrats and the Centre, as well as from various conservatives, including the Pan-Germans, who objected to the stake held by foreign capitalists in German concessionary companies.[21]

In the long run, moreover, *Raubwirtschaft* was not necessarily profitable. Many companies suffered serious losses. Forced labour, moreover, was inefficient. Thus Puttkamer remarked that chiefs were reluctant to send their best men to work in European employment, and often dispatched the weakest they could find. When the Gesellschaft für Südkamerun between the years 1899 and 1908, paid almost no dividends, the size of its concession was substantially reduced. *Raubwirtschaft,* dependent on the tapping of wild trees, led to widespread destruction. In time, wild-grown produce from Kamerun had to compete with superior rubber obtained from well-run plantations in South-East Asia. The company was therefore forced gradually to introduce a more efficient kind of cultivation. The Gesellschaft für Nordwest-Kamerun, on the other hand, failed to adjust its methods, incurred heavy losses and finally lost its territorial stake in the colony.[22] An economy of coercion, moreover, produced widespread inter-white dissensions. Plantation managers, merchants and officials competed for the available supplies of manpower, and sometimes censured one another in unmeasured terms. At the same time, the widespread African unrest, the scandals and abuses associated with the Puttkamer régime combined with metropolitan criticism to produce demands for a more rational form of colonization. Governmental exactions, though still onerous, ceased to be arbitrary

[21] For a detailed account, see Ballhaus, 'Die Landeskonzessionsgesellschaften', pp. 99–257.

[22] Nevertheless, rubber remained the colony's most important product. The value of rubber exports in 1910 amounted to 11,071,000 marks out a total of 19,924,000 marks. This was the year when plantation-grown rubber first reached the world market in substantial quantities. The world output of plantation-grown rubber increased from 11,000 tons in 1910 to 567,000 tons in 1927, by which time wild rubber accounted for only 6 per cent of world production. The most important recent studies on Kamerun include Helmuth Stoecker, ed., *Kamerun unter deutscher Kolonialherrschaft,* 2 vols. (Berlin, 1960–8), written from the Marxist-Leninist standpoint; Karin Hausen, *Deutsche Kolonialherrschaft in Afrika: Wirtschafts- und Kolonialverwaltung in Kamerun vor 1914* (Zurich, 1970); and above all, Albert Wirtz, *Vom Sklavenhandel zum kolonialen Handel. Wirtschaftsräume und Wirtschaftsformen in Kamerun vor 1914* (Zurich, 1972), an important work which successfully combines authropology with economic history.

and were strictly regulated, and Africans at last came gradually to be looked upon no longer as savages, but as economic men.

Kamerun, in the German colonial hierarchy, was a backwater. German East Africa, on the other hand, was regarded as a prize possession; and German officials considered the governorship of East Africa as the most prestigious appointment in the empire. German East Africa, with its ancient links to the Orient and India, had an air of romance that no other colony could rival, and for long the image of German East Africa dominated popular imagination concerning the colonies. German scientists and scholars devoted more attention to East Africa than to any other colonies. Up to 1904, when South-West Africa started to move into first place, German East Africa's annual trade was normally larger than that of any other German-dominated territory. No wonder that German colonial enthusiasts were wont to refer to the country as the German India.

The economic realities of German East Africa, however, were far different. The colony was a meeting-ground of many different cultures, a land where indigenous people like the Chagga had developed flourishing agricultural systems and where communities like the Nyamwezi had come to play an important part as porters and traders. But East Africa was also a region riddled by internecine strife. Rwanda and Burundi in the far interior were warlike kingdoms dominated by the Tutsi pastoral conquerors. In addition, German East Africa formed the extreme northern frontier of Ngoni expansion. During the nineteenth century, raiding states, which in their constitution and raiding habits resembled those of the Ndebele and Zulu, were set up in parts of what are now southern and western Tanzania. The coastal regions and part of the hinterland were dominated by Swahili-speaking merchants of Muslim faith, often backed by Arab and Indian financiers and indigenous African allies. The pre-colonial export trade hinged on ivory and slaves, as well as on some tropical products such as spices, sesame and palm-oil.

During the 1880s and 1890s the Germans, British and Belgians between them crushed the Muslim slave-trade. The widespread destruction of elephant herds largely eliminated the traffic in ivory. The Muslims ceased to be a ruling class, though they continued to play an important part through such minor positions of authority as guides, foremen, leaders of caravans and also as subordinate officials within the German colonial hierarchy. German conquest in fact had the unintended effect of further spreading the use of Swahili into the interior. But in the commercial field, Arabs could not easily compete with Indians, who came to play an important part in the country's economic life as traders, money-lenders and clerks. By 1909 the Indian community in the country numbered no more than 4,300 persons. Yet Indians came to play an indispensable part as middlemen in the African trade, and German opinion was itself divided with regard to their value. Most administrators (and many colonial theoreticians such as Hans Meyer and Kurt Hassert) branded them exploiters and usurers, the 'Jews of Africa', whose activities helped to guide a considerable part of the colony's export trade to India and Great Britain. On the other hand, many German entrepreneurs in Zanzibar and other coastal cities who dealt with Indian merchants felt convinced that the country could not prosper without the aid of Asian middlemen.

In addition to Indian immigrants, a few thousand Europeans entered the country. Initially the Germans thought in terms of placing white peasants on the land. But colonists recruited from among German settlers in Russia and Palestine failed to make good in Tanganyika, where conditions were totally dissimilar to those in their home countries, where sickness was rife, and where the newcomers lacked markets for their produce. Governor Count von Götzen (1901–6) took a more cautious attitude towards white settlement than had his predecessor, Eduard von Liebert (1896–1901). Only a few thousand whites entered the country during the German period, and these newcomers did not quite attain an importance comparable to that of the Europeans in Kenya. The area of European settlement was relatively dispersed. There were no gigantic land alienations on the South-West African or Kamerunian scale. The European immigrants, moreover, included a substantial number of foreigners (especially Greeks and Afrikaners) who lacked political influence in the metropole.[23] The Germans gradually became convinced that only well-capitalized plantations, producing specialized crops such as sisal, would succeed financially, and that African cash farmers would have to play a major part in the economic development of the colony.

The Germans encouraged the production of African food-crops such as ground-nuts, especially as German sisal planters and other employers had a vested interest in obtaining cheap food for their workmen. The Germans spread the commercial cultivation of cotton, too. In 1900 the Kolonial-Wirtschaftliche Komitee (a semi-official corporation set up in 1896 under the chairmanship of Karl Supf, a manufacturer) engaged a number of black Americans to pioneer the cultivation of cotton in Togo. Beginning in 1902 the Komitee went about cultivating cotton in East Africa. They set up an experimental station as well as a cotton inspectorate designed to improve the quality of the crop.[24] But again, the Germans proceeded on the assumption that Africans were insensitive to economic considerations, that they were congenital idlers who would not work except under the threat of compulsion. Africans were forced to grow crops. They were expected to devote a month a year to the cultivation of cotton. Of the total proceeds of their labour, one-third went into the treasury of the local government, one-third was paid to Swahili foremen and one-third went to the producers. The Germans made themselves hated in other ways also, by levying heavy taxes, by impressing labour for the use of private employers, by interfering with elephant hunting and by similar repressive measures.

German policy therefore created widespread discontent. Revolutionary activity centred not on the areas of white settlement but on the southern parts of the colony, geographically the most remote and economically among the more backward portions of German East Africa. The rebels united in a supratribal coalition. They determined to wipe out not only the whites, but also the Europeans' real or assumed henchmen, the Muslim officials in German employ, the Indian traders and the Westernized Africans. The Maji-Maji fighters put their

[23] In 1905, there were 1,873 Europeans in the country, of whom 180 were planters, farm managers and truck farmers. By 1913, the total number of Europeans had risen to 5,336; of these, 882 were employed in agriculture. By 1912 a total of 313,161 hectares of Crown Land had been sold. Of the white population 29 per cent were non-Germans.

[24] Vietor, *Geschichtliche und kulturelle Entwicklung*, p. 84; Germany, Reichskolonialamt, *Die Baumwollfrage* . . . Veröffentlichung no. 1 (Jena, 1914), pp. 115–16.

trust in magic, which would make them invulnerable to German bullets, and looked forward to the restoration of a supposedly happier past, when men dwelt in peace and freedom. But the Germans struck back hard. They defeated the insurgents in battle and they systematically destroyed the economic foundations of resistance. Between 1905 and 1907 something like 75,000 Africans were said to have lost their lives in battle, through epidemics or from famine. When the war was over, the southern parts of German East Africa had suffered a catastrophe comparable in extent to the earlier one in South-West Africa.

To sum up, the faults of German administration were not to be sought simply in atrocities committed by individuals, or in brutalities engendered by large-scale campaigns. Reform required a thorough-going change in the entire power structure, a shift to economic incentives from economic coercion. Reform called for a logistic system based on steam-power rather than on carriers; a military supply system dependent on central stores rather than on *ad hoc* requisitions; a form of labour management founded on skilled and willing volunteers rather than on unwilling draftees capable of performing only the most menial tasks. Reform required reliance on African entrepreneurial ability in farming and commerce. Reform, however, was hard to carry out before the Germans had acquired an effective monopoly of armed power and had completed the conquest of their colonies.

The 'new course'

In Germany the colonial risings, especially the South-West African disaster, occasioned bitter opposition to the colonial authorities and to the government. The Social Democrats, the Centre Party and the Progressives were up in arms, and in 1906 Reich Chancellor Prince von Bülow then decided to take what his contemporaries regarded as a remarkable step. Prince von Hohenlohe-Langenburg, a well-connected but ineffective aristocrat, was replaced as head of the Kolonial-Abteilung by Bernhard Dernburg, son of a Jewish National Liberal politician and writer. A year later the colonial section within the German Foreign Office became a separate ministry, with Dernburg as its first secretary of state. Dernburg, a banker known for his ability to restore the financial stability of tottering companies, was determined to run the empire in businesslike fashion. He travelled widely through the colonies, and for his companion and adviser selected Walther Rathenau. Rathenau possessed an unusual combination of talents. Not only was he a highly literate though confused intellectual, but he was also a successful organizer, a prominent industrialist and director of the Allgemeine Elektrizitätsgesellschaft.[25] Dernburg was influenced in addition by Governor Albrecht von Rechenberg, a Catholic, an aristocrat, a Swahili scholar and an outspoken reformer. Rechenberg felt convinced that the bloody East African rising had been provoked by his predecessor's policy with regard to forced labour and the compulsory cultivation of crops, rather than by the Africans' supposed barbaric state.

[25] Walther Rathenau (who later quarrelled with Dernburg) subsequently took a major part in running the German war economy during the First World War, became foreign minister under the Weimar Republic and was assassinated in 1922. His 'Erwägungen über die Erschliessung des Deutsch-Ostafrikanischen Schutzgebietes', published in *Reflexionen* (Leipzig, 1908), pp. 143–97, made a major contribution to the shaping of German colonial policy.

Dernburg, though often attacked for his 'negrophilist' views, was in no sense anti-European. Like the missionary imperialists such as David Livingstone and John Mackenzie, he was convinced that Europeans had an essential part to play in Africa. (South-West Africa, Dernburg believed, could accommodate 100,000 Europeans.) Europeans should come to the colonies as capitalists, as entrepreneurs, as managers, as specialists and as technicians. There were opportunities also for planters and farmers possessed of sufficient capital and specialized agronomic skills to start new agricultural industries. Indians had a valuable part to play in East Africa as merchants. But, according to Dernburg, there was no room for unskilled white workmen or peasant farmers. He resisted also the claims for internal self-government put forward by the settlers in South-West Africa. In this respect, his views were shaped, not merely by his belief in imperial trusteeship for Africans, but also by a profound conviction that the colonists were too few in number, in experience and financial resources to run the colony. When diamonds were found in South-West Africa in 1908, and when settler interests clashed with those of metropolitan investors, Dernburg opposed the settlers, who, for their part, believed that the overseas capitalists were over-favoured and inadequately taxed.

Dernburg's main interest, however, centred on the Africans. In his view, the main economic asset of the colonies lay in their people. His views were shaped to some extent by the demographic predilections of the time. In his day colonial theoreticians concerned themselves less with African unemployment than with the supposed inadequacy of industrial manpower. The possibility of a future population explosion did not trouble them, for they believed that Africa lacked a sufficient number of people, or that the population might remain stationary or that it might even be declining. Depending on their own preconceptions, they would attribute the supposed deficiencies either to the evils of colonial capitalism or to the Africans' presumed idleness and immorality. Since no 'reliable' demographic data are available for the pre-war period, most figures depend on guess-work. It seems probable, however, that at least in some areas observers confused the dispersion of the African population with depopulation. The pacification of the colonies, for all its violence, did away with the slave-trade and internecine African wars. Moreover, the effect of rinderpest or the spread of the tsetse-fly was apt to cause demographic shifts that were not necessarily connected with German employment, but with the inadequacy of contemporary medical services.

Dernburg was determined to pursue a policy that would be *negererhaltend* (designed to safeguard Africans). Black people, Dernburg said, were not lazy savages, but economic men.

Speculations concerning the Negro's invincible idleness should be consigned to the realm of fables. Given wages commensurate with the value of his labour, the Negro will work as hard as a European. Indeed, of all the Negro's instincts, his impulse for acquiring wealth and holding property is perhaps the strongest.[26]

Africans should therefore be encouraged to enter the market economy as workmen, and above all as producers of cash-crops. Government should stimulate peasant farming by creating a more adequate system of transport, by promoting education and research, by improving the administration and by protecting the

[26] Bernhard Dernburg, *Südwestafrikanische Eindrücke* . . . (Berlin, 1909), p. 85.

rights of African employees. Coercion, whether direct or indirect, must give way to economic incentives. Only the government, not the settlers, could be expected to promote black advancement.

A rational native policy, Dernburg believed, would combine philanthropy with profits. Once African producers became more prosperous, he argued, they would produce more goods for the world market and would buy more German merchandise. Instead of having to fight costly and unpopular campaigns against African rebels, the Reich would be able to count on the loyalty of contented African subjects. Well-to-do peasant farmers would also be in a position to pay higher imposts into local exchequers. The colonies would thus become financially self-sufficient, and a weight would be taken off the German tax-payers' shoulders. Economic advance would lead to cultural progress. German rule could therefore be morally justified in terms of reciprocal benefits, as expressed in the Latin tag *do ut des* (I give in order that thou mayest give).

Dernburg's policies were in no sense original. They owed a great deal to work of existing bodies, such as the Kolonialwirtschaftliche Komitee, and to senior German officials like Adolf Count von Götzen and Albrecht Freiherr von Rechenberg. But Dernburg's views were a far cry from those of Scharlach or of Gerhard von Buchka, head of the Kolonial-Abteilung between 1898 and 1900 and an admirer of Scharlach. They were formulated at a time when the effective conquest of the colonies had been largely completed and the era of open violence was coming to an end. German ability to employ naked force was, moreover, limited. In South-West Africa a total of over 17,000 men, most of them volunteers from the metropole, had to be mobilized to put down the Herero and Nama risings. But the South-West African campaign (Germany's colonial equivalent of the Boer War) was expensive in men, money and political commitment. The Reichstag was always reluctant to vote money for colonial armaments. In South-West Africa the very townsmen in Windhoek who loudly called for a tough policy regarding the Africans in South-West Africa, were most unwilling to pay for an adequate police force. By and large, the Germans had to make do with small forces. Despite wartime Allied charges to the contrary, they never tried to militarize their empire. By the outbreak of the First World War, the entire military establishment in Germany's African colonies amounted to less than 8,000 men, most of them askaris, commanded by German officers and sergeants.[27] These troops were expected to hold down an African population numbering altogether at least 12 million, and in addition they had to defend a vast empire against greatly superior Allied forces.

The impact of German violence, or indeed of colonial violence in general, has as yet never been properly assessed in economic terms. Armed repression could be devastating in its consequences. 'My heart bled', wrote Hans Dominik, a German soldier,

when I traversed the Jaunde [Yaoundé] country [which had just been subjugated by a punitive expedition of the *Schutztruppen* in Kamerun]. Instead of the rich villages and flourishing fields which I had visited three months ago, and where prosperous people had greeted me everywhere, everything was devastated and abandoned. Only black,

[27] These were distributed as follows: German East Africa: 14 companies, 2,732 men; German South-West Africa: 9 companies, 3 batteries, 2,556 men; Kamerun: 12 companies, 1 artillery detachment, 1,855 men; Togo: some 800 armed police.

burnt logs, broken pots and ravaged plantations reminded the beholder of former home-steads. Up to the Njong river I saw no people whatever. Only beyond the river, where I knew every chief in person, the people had more confidence.[28]

Colonial violence, though extremely uneven in its impact, could be most destructive on a local scale. A 'pacification' expedition might resort to acts of brutal indiscipline or to bloody reprisals. But even where the soldiers acted under restraint, the conscription of carriers or the requisitioning of food might disorganize a local economy and provoke the very unrest that the employment of the military was designed to repress in the first place. According to Vietor, Togo's relatively peaceful development as a 'model colony', in contrast, say, to Kamerun's, was occasioned at least in part by the requirements of fiscal economy. There was little money available to undertake military ventures. Only a small force could be kept under arms. Thus the Africans had to be treated with caution, and the colonial authorities had to rely more on negotiations than on armed might. But the employment of violence also had positive features from the economic standpoint. The Germans, like all other colonizers, created for themselves a monopoly in the use of military force. Once German rule was established, internecine wars, armed feuds and slave raiding ended. Ideas, men and merchandise could circulate more easily than before, with profound consequences for the economic development of the colonies.

By the time that Dernburg assumed office, the era of conquest had been largely completed. 'Economic reform', moreover, was now assured of a considerable measure of support within the ranks of the German colonial establishment. Colonial scandals were aired in the Reichstag and the press. The worst culprits, men like Waldemar Horn, Governor of Togo from 1902 to 1905, and Jesco von Puttkamer, were driven from office. Administrators such as Rechenberg in East Africa, Theodor Seitz, Governor of Kamerun from 1907 to 1910, and of South-West Africa from 1910 to 1915; and Count Julius von Zech, Governor of Togo from 1905 to 1910, displayed a more enlightened outlook. For all their various disagreements regarding colonial matters, they were in accord that Africans must play a more active part in the economic development of their respective countries. Germany could not afford to rule through coercion alone. (Seitz, to give just one example, felt convinced that Africans should take a limited part in the local self-government of Kamerun. Education, he argued, should not be designed merely to turn blacks into 'tools' of the white man. The future of Kamerun's economy would rest on the cultivation of indigenous food crops, rather than on the production of rubber for an unstable world market.[29]

Dernburg's logistic programme emphasized the construction of railways and port facilities. Such projects not only appealed to soldiers and administrators, but also served the interests of heavy industry. More capital flowed into the colonies, where the big banks began to set up a network of branches. 'Economic reform' met the wishes of merchants like Vietor, who considered Africans not merely as producers, but also as actual or potential customers. In Dernburg's day, and indeed long afterwards, many missionaries, administrators and settlers

[28] Cited by Puttkamer, *Gouverneursjahre in Kamerun*, p. 68. Puttkamer himself saw nothing wrong with these proceedings, as he was convinced that 'before the Negroes become reliable subjects, they first have to be taught a bloody lesson' (p. 65).

[29] Theodor Seitz, *Vom Aufstieg und Niederbruch deutscher Kolonialmacht*, 3 vols. (Karlsruhe, 1927–29), vol. II, pp. 36–8.

were still in the habit of denouncing, in a highly moralistic fashion, the increasing popularity of 'luxuries' among Africans, who supposedly spent their hard-earned cash on 'useless' merchandise. But Dernburg and his kind realized that the increasing sale of clothes, tools, utensils and consumption goods such as tea, matches or salt, in fact implied a rise in the customers' living standards and a rational economic choice.

The very settler communities who accused Dernburg of 'negrophilism' were in fact riddled by economic contradictions. There was, for instance, competition for African labour. As an East African labour commissioner argued, 'The planters were heaping up trouble on their own heads by outbidding one another with regard to wages and work quotas.' [30] Whether they realized it or not, 'economic reform' in practice corresponded to the interests of the more efficient employers who could attract workmen by providing better conditions, and who saw no reason why the government should subsidize their competitors by supplying them with forced labour below market cost. Again, the value of conscripts diminished when German plantation companies began to use steam-ploughs, expensive and complex machinery that could not be entrusted to unwilling and unskilled draftees. Moreover, the very planters who denounced African villagers for their assumed laziness were happy enough to buy African-grown provisions to feed their workmen. And farmers who censured missionaries for educating blacks beyond their proper station in life, themselves did not scruple to employ mission-trained artisans to construct a barn, or to hire a literate African to run a farm store.

Dernburg's 'new course' had other apparent merits. It did not imply a totally new departure. Togo, where access to navigable waterways had favoured commerce in tropical crops, owed its prosperity to African farmers who sold palm-oil, palm-kernels and similar products. Taxation remained relatively low. (In the southern districts, Africans were expected to work for twelve days a year on public works, but could obtain exemption from these dues in return for a small payment). In Kamerun, as well as in Togo and East Africa, the Germans had already initiated a programme of agricultural instruction in the cultivation of cotton. They had set up experimental stations, one at Nuatjä in Togo, for instance, and an even more prominent research institute at Amani in East Africa (founded in 1902). Dernburg and his associates were able, therefore, to build on existing foundations; and the new economic policy, despite its many limitations, exerted considerable impact on the empire.

Progress, of course, was intermittent and limited to enclaves. Dernburg was subject to severe pressure during his tenure. His policies conflicted with those of right-wingers within the ruling coalition of Conservatives, National Liberals and Progressives, who denounced him for being a pro-British liberal and negrophile Jew. On the other hand, his views were supported by the very Centre Party which he had previously denounced. After a few years, the Bülow coalition collapsed, and in 1910 Dernburg resigned from office. Friedrich von Lindequist, a man sympathetic to settler interests, continued as secretary of state. In South-West Africa the Germans intensified control over African workers by a comprehensive system of pass laws and contracts. Obligatory paid labour continued in various forms; and though measures began to be taken to

---

[30] Cited by Tetzlaff, *Koloniale Entwicklung und Ausbeutung*, p. 250.

protect workmen against the grosser forms of abuse, corporal punishment was still administered. Legally, workmen had few rights, and were permitted to break their contracts only if exposed to severe physical ill-treatment.[31]

Nevertheless, a shift in German policy did occur. During Dernburg's tenure of office, a crucial period in the economic history of the African colonies, trade increased in dramatic fashion. The Germans improved their agricultural, medical and educational services. In West Africa, German employers, including both government offices and mercantile houses, employed an increasing number of educated Africans in order to keep down administrative costs. African agricultural production increased in various parts of the empire. Even in East Africa, where settler influence was considerable, the European planters were never sufficiently influential to eliminate competition from African producers of coffee, cotton and rubber. Economic rivalry between black and white not only benefited the metropolitan consumer, but also helped to promote the growing of specialized crops like arabica (high-grade) coffee and sisal that could best be produced on plantations. In South-West Africa the clash of colour continued; yet the European economic lobbies diverged in their interests. German workmen, for instance, looked to the creation of a legalized colour bar. But lacking both trade unions of their own and representation in the Landrat, they had as yet no means of creating a comprehensive system of white labour monopolies, which would have injured the interests of farmers, railway companies and mine-owners alike.

Above all, the metropolitan climate of opinion was beginning to change, a fact noted with some bitterness by German hard liners. By the beginning of 1914, the powerful Budget Commission of the Reichstag had passed a major resolution, which was accepted by the legislature.[32] By the terms of this instrument, the Germans officially committed themselves to a form of colonial paternalism more comprehensive than any other existing in Africa at the time. Practice, of course, differed sharply from theory. Forced labour and other abuses continued in many parts of the German empire. By the time that German dominion collapsed in Africa, Dernburg's ideal of creating a free labour market, dependent on economic incentives rather than on coercion, was far

---

[31] For the legal position as it existed about the end of the Dernburg era, see Paul Class, *Die Rechtsverhältnisse der freien farbigen Arbeiter in den deutschen Schutzgebieten Afrikas und der Südess* (Ulm, 1913).

[32] Germany, Reichstag, *Verhandlungen*, XIII Legislaturperiode, 1 Session, *Anlagen zu den stenographischen Berichten*, vol. 304, no. 1421, pp. 2918–19. The chancellor was requested to 'safeguard life, liberty and property of the natives in the colonies'. Forced labour was to be eliminated in every form. African workmen were not to be separated from their wives. African workers on European plantations were to be entitled to work and own their plots, to receive an adequate amount of land for the purpose and to live in villages of their own. Steps were to be taken to reduce African mortality by improving medical services and by prohibiting recruitment in areas where climatic conditions were greatly different from those prevalent in the workmen's new place of work. The government was to promote the settlement of workers' families at or near the breadwinner's place of work. African labourers were not to be recruited in such numbers as to lead to the destruction of indigenous economies and family life. More legislation was to be enacted to improve the conditions of both white and black workers in industry and farming. The government was to regulate working hours and to impose minimum wages. The number and size of plantations were to 'correspond correctly to the existing number of the African population'. This resolution was accepted by the Reichstag on 10 March 1914. The accompanying debate (*Verhandlungen*, XIII Legislaturperiode, 1 Session, vol. 294) gives further insight into the state of parliamentary opinion just before the outbreak of World War I.

from achievement. But the new creed of *Fürsorge* (public welfare) nevertheless was a major step forward. German legislators now insisted on the preservation of the African family structure, on the stabilization of labour and on the fixing of minimum wages and working hours. Just before the collapse of their empire, the Germans had elaborated, at least in theory, a creed of African welfare which, in its implications, went a good deal beyond the much better-known British doctrine of native trusteeship. Social paternalism, originally developed in Germany to cope with the rising working class of the metropole, began to be adapted to colonial use.

The creation of an infrastructure

Transport and communications

The greatest achievement of the 'new era' was the completion of a fairly extensive transport system. The Germans set up telegraph lines and connected their colonies to a world-wide system of cable communications. They improved shipping services. In addition, just before the outbreak of the First World War, they installed a great wireless station at Kamina in Togo. The largest in Africa, it was intended to be the chief receiving and distributing center for all other stations in the German colonies. (Ironically enough, the announcement concerning the declaration of war was probably the last important message the German operators received from Berlin before the station was overrun by Allied troops.) Above all, the Germans began to build railways at a furious pace. Dernburg, largely because of his business background and his connections in high places, managed to circumvent the reluctance of the Reichs-Schatzamt regarding loans for railway development. He succeeded in mobilizing the required capital, which came mainly from the leading banks and other large enterprises. During his administration the Reichstag voted a total of 265 million marks for building railways or for guaranteeing private loans. Eight years after Dernburg came to office, the German colonial empire could boast an operating railway system with something like 4,500 km of track, a noteworthy achievement. The German accomplishment far exceeded the colonizers' record in French West Africa, for instance, where just over 2,000 km had been built; in the Belgian Congo, where just over 1,200 km were in operation by 1912; and even in the Rhodesias, where about 3,200 km were in working order. The construction of the rail network, often under the most difficult climatic and topographic conditions, brought profound changes at every level. Railway transportation, which was infinitely cheaper than porterage, was indispensable as a means of agricultural development. (Kurt Hassert, an economic geographer, calculated that a single railway carriage could carry as much as ten ox-wagons or three hundred carriers.) Railway transport, moreover, greatly speeded up traffic. A caravan, for instance, would formerly have spent about two months on the road from the Indian Ocean to Lake Victoria. The Uganda Railway was able to traverse the same distance in two days. In all essentials, the existing railway systems of the African countries once under the Kaiser's sway were built during the Wilhelmian period.

The railway network was supplemented by feeder roads. The road-building programme was especially successful in Togo, which was provided with a network of routes and rest-houses covering the entire country. Some roads were built with an eye to future motor transport. But the most useful vehicle of all was the bicycle, which, in Togo at any rate, was already being widely used by Africans during the first decade of the present century. The Germans also created telegraph lines and port facilities in various parts of their empire. Among them, these innovations changed the logistics of Germany's dependencies beyond recognition.

In building this new infrastructure, the Germans relied overwhelmingly on public initiative. Nearly all colonial railways were publicly owned. One of the few exceptions to state capitalism was found in Kamerun, where the so-called Nordbahn went inland from the port of Bonaberi to a distance of about 160 km. The railway was owned by the Kamerun Eisenbahn und Betriebsgesellschaft, founded in 1905 with a capital of 17 million marks. This company, which received an imperial guarantee of 3 per-cent interest on a maximum of 110 million marks, was so successful that dividends could be paid one year after the line had begun to operate in 1911. The construction of the railway provided transportation right through the difficult forest zone, and enabled the Germans to reach the savannah belt. In 1908 the Reichstag voted funds to guarantee a loan to the value of some 40 million marks for a state-owned line, the so-called Mittellandbahn. The railroad was to proceed from the port of Duala to the Njong riger, whence transportation would be continued by water. Further extensions were planned but not completed. In addition, the Germans created new port facilities, especially at Duala, where a dry dock was opened in 1905. In Togo, the transport system hinged on Lomé. The Germans built three different railway lines, which were designed to promote trade, to unify the country from a logistic standpoint and to reduce the country's further dependence on outlets in British territory.

The East African interior at first depended to a considerable extent on the British Uganda Railway. The existence of transport facilities stimulated African cash-crop cultivation in the Lake Victoria region, with the result that the German colony became the foremost producer of ground-nuts in East Africa. Such planners as Rathenau were profoundly impressed by what they considered the bold conception of the British, who, at great initial expense and risk, built the Uganda line in advance of economic development. Despite considerable opposition, Dernburg and Rechenberg decided, therefore, that the existing short line from Dar es Salaam to Morogoro was useless unless extended right to the Great Lakes. This central line would later become, in effect, the spinal column of a more extensive system opening up the entire territory. In addition to promoting economic development, especially African farming, the project would be helpful to the army. Strategic considerations were always present in the minds of staff officers, who, during the Maji-Maji rising, had relied on the goodwill of their British neighbours to rush a detachment to Lake Victoria by means of the Uganda Railway in order to abort a threatened revolt among the Sukuma and the Nyamwezi. By 1912, when the line had been completed to Tabora, plans were approved for its extension to Lake Tanganyika. The Germans also began the construction of the so-called Nordbahn, which went from Tanga inland and was designed especially to facilitate European settlement and to compete with the Uganda Railway. In their turn the railways were the making of the ports of Tanga and Dar es Salaam, though the Germans never had an opportunity of fully utilizing the economic potential of their new railways. In order to open up the south of their colony, the Germans finally considered running a track from Kilwa to Lake Nyasa; but again they lacked the time to bring the project to fruition.

Of the railway systems in all the German colonies, the most extensive was that of South-West Africa. By 1912, when the main port had been completed, the territory was covered by some 2,100 miles of track. The oldest line, which opened in 1902 and ran from Swakopmund to Windhoek, had been put in by the German military and played an essential part in the conquest of the country. In building the line, the Germans had pursued a labour policy exceptional in southern Africa: they had imported white workmen in some numbers to do rough navvying as well as skilled and supervisory work. (By 1902, 370 whites were employed as workmen.) In addition, Swakopmund, despite its many deficiencies as a port, served as the outlet for a line running northward to Tsumeb. The northern railway served primarily the needs of the mining industry. The track was laid by the private enterprise of the Otavi Minen und Eisenbahngesellschaft, which was formed to exploit the copper deposits in the northern part of the colony. In addition to using African prisoners of war, the Germans hired a number of Italian labourers. But not only were these immigrants apt to strike, they were also sufficiently sophisticated to sue their employer in local courts over the terms of their engagement. The Germans therefore came to rely mainly on Africans both to build and to run the line, a policy that necessitated the creation of a special training school for African personnel.

The so-called Südbahn linked Lüderitz (formerly Angra Pequena), the colony's only reasonably good port, with Keetmanshoop, the main communications centre in the south. Keetmanshoop in turn was connected to Windhoek, and, by means of a southerly extension, to Warmbad. The railway system as a whole played an indispensable part in facilitating European land settlement, in the exploitation of the country's mineral resources and in the transportation of those African workmen without whose labour the colony could not have functioned.

Technical services

During the last decade of German colonization in Africa, the Germans began to take enormous pride in their success as 'scientific colonizers'. Though it may be difficult to make generalizations for such a far-flung empire, the extent and scope of German experiment and research provided a high degree of justification for their claim. The transfer of agricultural skill was effected both by private and by public enterprise. In South-West Africa, for example, German farmers improved the indigenous Damara breed by crossing beasts with Simmental, Pinzgau and Shorthorn bulls. They introduced a variety of new crops. They built cattle-dips and dams, fenced pasture land and sunk bore-holes, as well as making many other improvements. In East Africa, German settlers, after a great deal of experimentation, brought in the sisal plant from Florida and built up a new industry. Although German experiments with coffee were less successful, Africans, working with lower overhead costs than planters, took up the cultivation of this crop and developed it into a valuable export commodity.

Officially sponsored research had its origin with the Kolonial-Wirtschaftliche Komitee, a quasi-official body originally founded in 1896. The Komitee aimed at combining scientific research with practical experimental work and colonial propaganda. It issued technical publications such as *Der Tropenflanzer* (an agricultural journal), as well as specialized monographs. The work of the committee received support from the Botanische Zentralstelle in Berlin, an organization that functioned above all as a clearing-house for botanical and related studies and received information from various institutions set up in the colonies.

These new bodies included the Biologisch-Landwirtschaftliche Institut, in Amani, East Africa, created in 1902. The institute was designed to study the flora and fauna of the territory, to carry out agricultural experiments, to investigate and improve existing agricultural practices and to disseminate information by means of publications and a programme of instruction. Research on a large scale was carried out also at the botanical gardens at Victoria in Kamerun (which later developed into a full-fledged research station). The institute contained botanical and chemical laboratories. It carried out work in the raising of tropical plants, manuring and other agricultural problems. In addition, experimental gardens were set up in the more important administrative stations, which furnished additional data.

Above all, the Germans paid special attention to the cultivation of cotton, as experts feared that the textile industries of the Reich might have to face severe price fluctuations, or even a world-wide scarcity of this vital raw material. As previously mentioned, from 1900 the Kolonial-Wirtschaftliche Komitee began to promote cotton farming as far afield as Togo, Kamerun and East Africa. This work was soon intensified. In fact, between 1910 and 1914 alone, the Germans set up six additional cotton-research stations and three general experimental stations. Coercion of the kind used before the Maji-Maji rebellion disappeared. Instead, the Germans began to rely more on economic incentives and on persuasion. African agricultural demonstrators, for instance, provided expert advice; and the government furnished seed free of charge, with the result that cotton became an important cash-crop. At the same time, the Germans realized that both for technical reasons and in order to increase general productivity, the cultivation of cotton would have to be integrated with other agricultural activities. Thus the experimental stations devoted to cotton were designed also to help other forms of farming.[33]

By 1910, development had progressed to such an extent that an administrative division of labour had become indispensable. The Kolonial-Wirtschaftliche Komitee was charged with the technical aspects of cotton cultivation, the construction of ginning stations, the purchase of cotton at guaranteed prices, the distribution of prizes, the provision of loans, the control and inspection of cotton qualities and similar functions. The German colonial administration took on the responsibility for setting up experimental stations, for conducting campaigns against plant diseases and for the organization of meteorological and related services. Separate agricultural departments were set up in each of the colonies. By 1914 the agricultural staff of Togo, for example, consisted of fifteen officers of various grades, five assistant agriculturalists and a number of subordinate instructors.

By way of broadening the base of the agricultural programme, the Germans

[33] Germany, Reichskolonialamt, *Der Baumwollbau in den deutschen Schutzgebieten: seine Entwicklung seit dem Jahre 1910* (Jena, 1914), pp. 292–3.

provided instruction at a number of technical institutions. In Togo, for instance, they created an agricultural school at Nuatjä where students were given a three-year course in arable farming, cattle raising, the art of ploughing and similar agricultural techniques. Their training completed, the alumni were furnished agricultural equipment and set off to farm on their own. In addition, experiments were conducted with many varieties of cotton, as well as with maize, beans, ground-nuts, and other food crops. Pastoral farming and planning techniques were studied, too. In Kamerun Africans were trained as plantation managers at an agricultural school attached to the institute at Victoria. In addition the Germans created cattle-breeding stations, a network of experimental gardens at the main administrative centres, a forestry department, and a rubber inspectorate with its own stations.[34]

In South-West Africa the government joined private enterprise in building bore-holes and dams. A Water Department came into being, with two geologists providing technical advice. The Germans thereby extended considerably the area suitable for settlement. In addition, they carried out research on a solid scale. By 1914 the government was operating an experimental station for arable farming, a tobacco station, an experimental horse ranch, a sheep ranch and an ostrich farm, as well as five experimental stations for truck farming. Between them, scientifically trained agriculturists and ordinary farmers adapted a large variety of fruit, including grapes and dates, as well as grain and vegetables. Besides all these advances, they introduced many new strains of animals to the country. One of the most successful of these ventures was the importation of the karakul sheep from Bokhara and southern Russia. The karakul herds flourished under South-West African conditions, and karakul breeding developed into a valuable industry. The government also planted many varieties of new trees, including the eucalyptus, whose presence in the country helped to change both the appearance of the countryside and its ecological features.

Technical education likewise played a prominent part in Germany's colonial calculations. The Germans were among the first, for instance, to give practical training to some of their emigrants to Africa. Students received instruction in agricultural and related subjects at the Deutsche Kolonialschule at Witzenhausen, founded in 1899, and at the Kolonialakademie at Halle, where there was also an institute for natural science. The prestigious Kolonialinstitut at Hamburg, created in 1908, was a product of the Dernburg era. In addition, linguistic and ethnographic instruction was provided at the Seminar für Orientalische Sprachen at the University of Berlin. A medical man anxious to serve in the colonies would find facilities available for specialized study at institutes in Berlin, Hamburg and Tübingen.[35] The very existence of such facilities provided a reservoir of skills that played a valuable part in the *mise en valeur* of Germany's African dependencies.

[34] For a general account of these activities, see Albert C. Calvert, *The German African empire* (London, 1916), pp. 132–8, 230–4, 312–16. This is particularly interesting inasmuch as the author is generally hostile to the Germans. For the work in East Africa, see especially Bald, *Deutsch-Ostafrika,* pp. 161–78.

[35] For a detailed study of German administrative methods and educational institutions available for the purpose, see Jake Spidle, 'The German colonial civil service: organization, selection and training' (Ph.D. dissertation, Stanford University, 1972); and Ralph A. Austen, *Northwest Tanzania under German and British rule . . .* (New Haven, Yale University Press, 1968).

In the field of African education, the Germans, like their neighbours, relied mainly on the private enterprise of missionaries, subsidized to a limited degree by public funds. The extent of missionary penetration remains hard to assess, because statistics vary in their accuracy. Certainly, by 1913 there were something like 150,000 baptized Africans in the various German colonies, men and women who were in some measure affected by Westernization.[36] Nearly 120,000 students were attending school, most at the elementary level.[37]

Missionary enterprise exerted a far-reaching impact on the economy as well as on religion and education. Missionaries created a host of new wants. And they spread a wide range of new skills, marketable only in a Western economy, with the result that the great majority of missionary alumni became wage or sal-

[36] Anton Mayer, ed., *Das Buch der deutschen Kolonien* (Potsdam, 1933), pp. 297–301, gives the following figures on German missionary penetration, 1912–3:

	European clergymen, layworkers, sisters	Baptized Africans
Togo		
Catholics	80	14,657
Protestants	12	7,780
	92	22,437
Kamerun		
Catholics	103	21,272
Protestants	41	15,255
	144	36,527
German East Africa		
Catholics	696	61,135
Protestants	98	10,605
	794	71,740
German South-West Africa		
Catholics	90	2,600
Protestants	68	26,499
	158	29,099
Total	1,188	159,803

[37] For a detailed breakdown, compiled on the basis of extensive questionnaires, see Martin Schlunk, *Die Schulen für Eingeborene in den deutschen Schutzgebieten . . .* (Hamburg, 1914), *passim*. The following summary of German schools in 1911 is based on Schlunk's work:

Togo
Primary schools *   315
Post-primary schools **   5
Trade schools ***   4
Total number of students   13,746
Post-primary and technical students   395
      *including 2 government schools
      **including 1 government school
      ***including 2 government schools

(Continued on p. 245)

ary earners. By 1911 graduates of mission schools in Togo were being employed as interpreters, clerks and supervisors in government service, as telegraphists and assistants in the post office, as engine drivers, conductors and station masters on the railway, as salesmen, buyers and cashiers with commercial firms, and as teachers and evangelists in missionary employ. In East Africa, mission-trained Africans found employment also as supervisors on plantations. Some of these became successful cotton farmers, while others joined the police or even the military signalling units of the *Schutztruppen*. In addition, the missions trained printers, painters, builders, shoemakers and other artisans. Even in South-West Africa, where Africans had to meet competition from Europeans, there was a demand for German-speaking Africans. Suitably trained candidates were able to obtain positions in the service of the government, the police, the post office or commercial firms.

The missionary impact was uneven, and it is not easy to assess its effects. In comparative terms, the Germans clearly did well. German East Africa, which absorbed more European workers than all the other colonies between them, was the main frontier of Germany's missionary effort. By 1921, British reports stated that literacy was widespread.

It must be admitted that the degree of usefulness to the administration of the natives of the Tanganyika territory is in advance of that which one has been accustomed to associate with the British African Protectorates. Whereas the British official may often have had to risk the mutilation of his instructions to a chief by having to send them verbally, the late German system has made it possible to communicate in writing with every Akida and village headman, and in turn to receive from him reports written in Swahili.[38]

(footnote 37 continued)

Kamerun

Primary schools *	499
Post-primary schools **	21
Trade schools ***	11
Total number of students	34,117
Post-primary students	2,061
*including 4 government schools	
***including 2 government schools	

South-West Africa

Primary schools	48
Post-primary schools	1
Trade schools	5
Total number of students	3,698

German East Africa

Elementary schools *	955
Higher-level schools **	48
Trade schools ***	17
Total number of students	66,647
Post-primary and technical students	2,163
*including 78 government schools	
**including 2 government schools	
***including 3 government schools	

Total number of students: 118,288
Total number of post-primary and technical students: 4,583

[38] Cited in Raymond Leslie Buell, *The native problem in Africa* (London, 1965 ed.), vol. 1, p. 478.

Over the territory as a whole, school attendance figures were not greatly inferior to those of the neighbouring Gold Coast, probably more populous than Togo, and educationally one of the most developed parts of the British African empire. In 1913, for instance, almost 18,000 Africans went to school in the Gold Coast, as compared to some 14,000 in Togo by 1911. Just before the outbreak of the First World War, Vietor, the merchant, reported that on a tour of the country he had been able to invite some fifty educated Africans, all of whom had been trained to occupy positions of greater or lesser responsibility, working for his firm. The remote north, on the other hand, was little affected. The same was true in Kamerun, where the Islamic regions remained almost untouched by missionary enterprise.

Missionary linguistic policies varied just as greatly as did the educational practices. Missionaries were responsible for reducing a considerable number of African languages to writing and for spreading their use as a language of scholastic instruction. In Kamerun, for example, the Basel Mission Society would have liked to use Duala as a lingua franca in all its schools, a policy rejected by Governor Seitz, who in 1910 enforced a comprehensive system of regulating schools, providing government subsidies to approved institutions, and insisted that German must be taught wherever schools placed a second language on the syllabus.

In addition to subsidizing missions, the colonial governments established *Regierungsschulen* of their own, designed to supply the growing demand for junior officials. The schools were located in such a way as to supplement missionary enterprise. In Kamerun, for example, the Germans deliberately put a *Regierungsschule* at Garua to provide instruction to the Muslim population, thus preventing an undue preponderance of coastal people in government service. By 1911, the students in government schools numbered 4,312 in East Africa, 833 in Kamerun and 449 in Togo.

The transfer of medical skills likewise involved far-reaching economic adjustments. Permanent European settlement, administration and long-term economic development were unthinkable as long as the German empire-builders were susceptible to the ravages of malaria, gin, opium and blackwater fever. In the early days, the Germans, like all the colonial invaders, suffered from a high death-rate in the tropics. From the beginning of the present century, they managed to control some of the more important insect-borne diseases, especially malaria. Sewerage services were set up in the fledgling towns, and arrangements were made for proper water supply. By the end of their period of colonization, the Germans had gone a long way towards enabling whites to live under reasonably healthy conditions.

The impact of German conquest on the medical conditions of the Africans was double-edged in character. Warfare and conquest brought in their train not only hunger and sickness, but above all venereal disease. Labour migration entailed innumerable abuses. Particularly in the early days, Africans succumbed to all manner of afflictions, especially disorders of the lungs and nutritional deficiencies. In Kamerun, for example, the death-rate of plantation labourers during 1905–6 has been estimated at 10 per cent per annum, a rate comparable to that of an army in action. But there were improvements. The Germans began to take measures to better the lot of labour migrants by providing rest-houses on the road to work, by insisting on better food and better accommodation and sanitary facilities. Because of extraordinary variations in the conditions prevalent in a single colony, the total effect of these measures remains hard to assess. The 1912 official report for East Africa, for instance, still complained that the planters in the Morogoro district continued to resist health measures that had long been accepted by employers in the north of the colony. Water supplies, sanitation facilities and medical treatment for workers remained inadequate. This state of affairs, said the report, was occasioned by the fact that the Morogoro plantations were still being developed and had as yet failed to yield profits. Conditions in the older-established plantations in the Arusha district, on the other hand, were far superior, largely because the employers were able to hire local rather than migrant workers.[39]

The Germans made further efforts to ameliorate health conditions by inoculating Africans against smallpox, by isolating lepers in special villages, by attempting to treat sleeping-sickness and by setting up hospitals. By 1913, German doctors at work in the colonies numbered 120; and the number of Africans treated in government institutions had increased from 4,516 in 1904 to 100,348.[40] The first beneficiaries of the new medical services were probably the members of the African élite, soldiers and junior civil servants, whereas Africans in remoter areas remained little affected. It seems likely nevertheless that the demographic expansion which has characterized the former German territories over the past half-century or so had its beginning during the German era.

German colonialism: material achievements and demise

In 1879 Friedrich Fabri, a former mission inspector, wrote what has since become a famous book in German colonial historiography, entitled *Does Germany need colonies?* Fabri's work argued that the Reich needed colonies as a market for its exports, as a source of raw materials and as a place where German emigrants might find new homes under German rule, thereby saving the Fatherland from the menace of overpopulation. Fabri believed also that colonization would provide a social safety-valve and would impede the revolutionary aspirations of the Social Democrats. In the colonies, the Germans would help to civilize and Christianize the indigenous peoples. Fabri's study was therefore an essay both in political advocacy and in futurology. But none of his predictions came true. German colonization helped to spread the Gospel in Africa, but the Germans did not 'civilize' their dependencies in the sense understood by Fabri. German enterprise in turn played a part in creating a new African élite, a thin stratum of literate craftsmen, junior civil servants, teachers and cash farmers. But these men were never regarded as part of German society overseas, and few Germans bothered to accord to Africans even the polite address of *Sie* as distinct from the familiar *Du*. As for trade and investment, the importance of the colonies for the German metropolitan economy remained negligible. The structure of exports altered, as consumption goods like gin and

---

[39] Reichskolonialamt, *Medizinalbericht über die deutschen Schutzgebiete 1911–12* (Berlin, 1915), p. 163.
[40] Mary Evelyn Townsend, *The rise and fall of Germany's colonial empire, 1884–1916* (New York, 1930), p. 298.

beads increasingly gave way to sophisticated merchandise such as mining equipment and rolling-stock. This change reflected the wider transformation of the German economy. German businessmen, however, had only a marginal interest in the colonies. British trade remained important throughout the German colonial empire. German businessmen failed to create a colonial economy for themselves, although the volume and the proportionate share of the Reich in colonial commerce increased during the Dernburg era.[41]

Some colonial propagandists, such as Gustav Schmoller, the social historian, had assumed that Germany's external empire would help to solve Germany's internal problems. The colonies, for example, might ease academic unemployment by supplying jobs for surplus university graduates. In practice, however, the colonies were too insignificant to function as a social safety-valve. The colonies continued to be ruled and policed by a tiny élite whose numbers were too small to affect the employment situation at home. The colonies, moreover, were far from the El Dorados pictured by chauvinist propaganda and the more dishonest kind of stock-exchange prospectuses. The dependencies failed to yield substantial public revenues and had to be subsidized by the German taxpayers.[42] Although some colonial entrepreneurs did make a great deal of money, the majority of these enterprises failed to meet their founders' expecta-

[41] The trade of the German colonies in 1910 is shown in the following tabulation:

	Imports (in 1000 marks)		Exports (in 1000 marks)	
	Total	From Germany	Total	To Germany
German East Africa				
1903	11,118	2,969	7,054	2,674
1910	38,659	19,677	20,805	12,585
Kamerun				
1903	9,426	6,782	7,139	4,490
1910	25,480	19,991	19,924	17,248
Togo				
1903	6,105	3,509	3,616	1,668
1910	11,466	6,298	7,222	4,526
South-West Africa				
1903	7,931	6,712	3,443	380
1910	44,344	34,455	34,691	28,674

SOURCE: Otto Mayer, *Die Entwicklung der Handelsbeziehungen,* appended table [13].

The German mark, like the U.S. dollar and the British pound sterling, were based on the gold standard. By 1914 their comparative value was as follows:
1 mark = $2.386
£1.0.0 = $4.86,65

[42] The colonies raised their own revenue through taxation, customs and other imposts. The Reich covered deficits through a variety of subventions. After 1908, a number of major items concerning colonial expenditure were derived from loans guaranteed by the Reich. Togo, German East Africa and Kamerun raised loans of their own. Exceptional expenditures in South-West Africa—e.g., railways and major public-works projects—were financed directly through Reich loans.

The following tabulation, from Zimmerman, *Geschichte der deutschen Kolonialpolitik,* pp. 307–8, shows the expenditure for all colonies since the creation of the Reichskolonialamt:

tions.[43] The colonial reality in fact turned out to be far different from the dream world of superprofits depicted by stock-exchange prospectuses, as well as by some subsequent socialist polemics. The colonies did not succeed in resolving the real or supposed contradictions of German capitalism. Neither did they have any impact on Germany's anticipated population problem. By the 1890s the great stream of German emigration had largely dried up. Even South-West Africa, the great projected settlement colony, had only 14,830 whites by 1914,

(footnote 42 continued)

	Total expenditure (in 1000 marks)	Revenue raised within the colonies (in 1000 marks)
1907	73,130	23,580
1908	155,530	24,110
1909	68,200	42,630
1910	82,430	48,720
1911 (projected)	97,130	47,990
1912 (projected)	90,100	49,900
1913 (projected)	92,030	51,900

[43] Some major colonial enterprises by 1914:

Type of activity	Number of firms in business	Number of firms having paid dividends	Highest rate paid in any one year (in per cent)
Diamond mining	48	3	55
Rubber plantations and trade	58	8	15
Cocoa plantations and trade	22	4	10
Sisal plantations	19	8	20

Data from Zimmermann, *Geschichte der deutschen Kolonialpolitik*, pp. 310–11.

By 1913, the total number of firms working in all German colonies (including the South Seas) was 399. Their capital amounted to 506·08 million marks. According to *Grosser Brockhaus* (Leipzig, 1931), vol. x, p. 328, they were distributed as follows:

Type of company	Amount of capital (in million marks)	Number of firms
Mining, including diamond mining with 29·99	141·90	217
Mixed enterprises—trade, industry, etc.	133·48	109
Plantations and pastoral farming	117·72	138
Transport (shipping 41·8; railways, telegraphs, etc., 60·04	101·84	16
Banking	11·14	10

less than half the number of German-speaking people in the Union of South Africa. German social democracy, which Fabri and others had feared so greatly, never developed into a revolutionary force. The German workers, on the other hand, failed to acquire much interest in the colonial empire, which remained mainly a middle-class achievement.

In African terms, however, a major change occurred. The Germans laid the foundations of the infrastructure for Kamerun, Togo, Tanganyika and South-West Africa. They pioneered modern health, educational and agricultural services, albeit on a small scale. During the last decade of German rule, each of the German colonies achieved a miniature *Wirtschaftswunder* (economic miracle). The export of tropical crops expanded considerably.[44] In South-West

[44] Exports for key commodities increased as follows (in tons):

	German East Africa	Kamerun	Togo	Total
Palm-kernels				
1905	—	9,518	3,200	12,718
1913	—	15,999 (1912)	7,140	23,139
Palm-oil				
1905	—	2,606	425	3,031
1913	—	3,595 (1912)	1,174	4,769
Copra				
1905	3,729	—	14	3,743
1913	5,477	—	163	5,640
Ground-nuts				
1905	1,422	—	49	1,471
1913	8,960	—	80	9,040
Sesame				
1905	1,111	—	—	1,111
1913	1,476	—	—	1,476
Rubber				
1905	326	1,034	115	1,475
1913	1,367	2,926	91	4,384
Cocoa				
1905	0·2	1,414	13	1,427
1913	12 (1912)	5,157	335	5,504
Coffee				
1905	641	—	—	641
1913	1,059	—	—	1,059
Sisal				
1905	1,140	—	—	1,140
1913	20,835	—	18 (1912)	20,853
Cotton				
1905	189	—	134	323
1913	2,192	—	503	2,695

SOURCE: Figures for German East Africa, Kamerun and Togo are from Heinrich Schnee, ed. *Das Buch der deutschen Kolonien* (Leipzig, 1937), pp. 426–8.

Africa the Germans re-created a pastoral economy that was a great deal more productive than the one destroyed by German conquest.[45]

The Germans also introduced modern mining methods to South-West Africa. The industry was left to private enterprise, for administrators like Seitz soon convinced themselves that mining was too complex and too risky to be run by the state. The discovery of diamonds in 1908, as well as the successful exploitation of copper, rapidly changed the economic configuration of South-West Africa and turned the country from an agricultural state into a producer of minerals.[46] At the same time, the character of German exports to the colonies altered greatly: instead of guns, gin and beads, the Germans sold an ever-increasing variety of textiles, machinery, vehicles and other more complex kinds of merchandise. By 1910, German West Africa was importing commodities to the value of 14,275,000 marks, as against 2,653,000 marks twenty-five years earlier. The bulk of the imports, including textiles, provisions and other commodities, were destined for the African trade. The rise in imports therefore reflected a rise in African consumption, and thereby, to some extent, a rise in African living standards.

The German era finally saw the first feeble beginnings of a secondary industry in the colonies. Manufacturing hinged largely on South-West Africa, where skilled white labour was available. The initial ventures were concerned mainly with the processing of agricultural products and with the supply of building materials, electric power, and repair facilities for mines and railways.[47] The First World War impelled the Germans to set up in East Africa

---

[45] Between 1907, at the end of the rising, and 1913, the number of beasts in the country supposedly rose as follows, according to Hintrager, *Südwestafrika*, p. 175:

	1907	1913
Cattle	52,531	205,643
Horses	3,119	15,916
Sheep bread for meat, and goats	204,954	957,986
Sheep bred for wool	3,526	53,691
Angora goats	3,696	31,400
Pigs	1,202	7,772
Ostriches	0	1,507

[46] Between 1908 and 1913 the value of the main exports rose as follows: (in 1,000 marks)

	1908	1913
Diamonds	51	58,910
Copper	6,296	7,929
All products	7,795	70,303

Data from *ibid.*, pp. 177 and 178.

[47] In 1914, South-West Africa had four machine works, two railway depots, a wagon-building shop, two electricity works, three quarries, a cannery, two breweries, two distilleries, two tanning works and an ice-making factory. In addition, there were numerous small workshops belonging to individual artisans. *Ibid.*, p. 178.

some short-lived ersatz industries. On a very small scale, the Germans manufactured textiles, pharmaceutical supplies and a substitute for petrol made from
copra, as well as rubber products, medicaments and footwear.

The wider social impact of German colonization was extremely uneven. Outside South-West Africa, the German invaders had occupied only a small proportion of the available acreage. The mass of the Kaiser's African subjects kept
their links with the land. The Germans, like their colonial contemporaries,
helped to create a small semi-proletariat—half wage-labourers, half subsistence
farmers—who remained tied to their ancestral villages. But even in South-West
Africa the economy was beginning to absorb a small group of self-employed
Africans—transport drivers, cattle-breeders and a handful of artisans.[48] Though
precise statistics concerning the extent of African entrepreneurship are now
hard to obtain, African cultivators were making a substantial contribution to the
export economy in the German tropical colonies. The Germans finally developed a small group of African functionaries, clerks, interpreters, telegraphists,
police sergeants, agricultural demonstrators and teachers, who formed the non-
commissioned officers of empire, and who, between them, must have numbered at least several thousand.

The German colonial empire failed to survive the First World War. The
Allies conquered Germany's overseas dependencies, and thereby helped to
prevent the emergence of a Germanophone Africa, tied by language, commerce
and administrative tradition to Central Europe. Under the terms of the peace
treaty, moreover, the Germans lost a substantial number of their colonial assets
under the guise of reparations. The colonial powers themselves thereby set a
precedent for the expropriation of private property on political grounds, and
indeed pursued a policy more rigorous in this regard than that followed by
many African successor governments toward their former rulers. In Africa, the
sudden change of colonial régimes led to some temporary disorganization. For
instance, a good deal of the agricultural research done by the Germans was suddenly discontinued, and its findings were lost. But the infrastructure created by
the Germans remained intact, as did a host of other German-initiated enterprises. Perhaps the most important legacy unwittingly bequeathed by the

[48] In 1912 the black South-West African labour force consisted of the following:

Total number of indigenous Africans	78,810
Self-employed workers	
Transport drivers and cattle farmers	1,230
Arable farmers	154
Artisans	34
Total	1,418
Wage workers in white employment	
Domestic servants and farm workers	12,091
Employees of large enterprises	7,571
Workmen and artisans employed by the administration, military and police	2,482
Non-indigenous Africans	4,173
Total	26,317

Data from Oelhafen, *Die Besiedlung Deutsch-Südwestafrikas, passim.*

Germans to modern Africa lies in the field of state-building. The three independent republics of Tanzania, Togo and Cameroun owe their geographical configuration essentially to Germany's colonial effort. The same holds true for South-West Africa (Namibia), which first became a united territory under German rule. Ironically enough, these three former states continue to exist as political entities, with their own economic framework, long after the German Reich, their one-time colonial sovereign, has passed into historical oblivion.

BIBLIOGRAPHY

Ar.Jersson, Charles John. *The Okavango river: a narrative of travel, exploration and adventure.* London, 1861.

Austen, Ralph A. *Northwest Tanzania under German and British rule: colonial policy and tribal politics, 1889–1939.* New Haven, Yale University Press, 1968.

Bald, Detlef. *Deutsch-Ostafrika 1900–1914: eine Studie über die Verwaltung, Interessengruppen und wirtschaftliche Erschliessung.* Munich, 1970.

Bley, Helmut. *Kolonialherrschaft und Sozialstruktur in Deutsch-Südwestafrika 1894–1914.* Hamburg, 1968.

Buell, Raymond Leslie. *The native problem in Africa.* 2 vols. 2nd reprint. London, 1965.

Büttner, Kurt. *Die Anfänge der deutschen Kolonialpolitik in Ostafrika: eine kritische Untersuchung an Hand unveröffentlicher Quellen.* Berlin, 1959.

Calvert, Albert C. *The German African empire.* London, 1916.

Class, Paul. *Die Rechtsverhältnisse der freien farbigen Arbeiter in den deutschen Schutzgebieten Afrikas und der Südsee.* Ulm, 1913.

Cornevin, Robert. *Histoire de la colonisation allemande.* Paris, 1969.

Dawson, William Harbutt. 'Introduction' to Heinrich Schnee, *German colonization past and future: the truth about the German colonies.* London, 1926.

Dernburg, Bernhard. *Koloniale Finanzprobleme: Vortrag gehalten auf Veranlassung der Handelskammer in Frankfurt.* Berlin, 1907.

Südwestafrikanische Eindrücke: industrielle Fortschritte in den Kolonien; zwei Vorträge. Berlin, 1909.

Zielpunkte des deutschen Kolonialwesens; zwei Vorträge. Berlin, 1907.

Drechsler, Horst. *Südwestafrika unter deutscher Kolonialherrschaft: der Kampf der Herero und Nama gegen den deutschen Imperialismus (1884–1915).* Berlin, 1966.

Feis, Herbert. *Europe, the world's banker, 1870–1914: an account of European foreign investment and the connection of world finance with diplomacy before the war.* New Haven, Yale University Press, 1930.

Full, August. *Fünfzig Jahre Togo.* Berlin, 1934.

Gärtner, Karl. *'Togo': finanztechnische Studie über die Entwicklung des Schutzgebietes unter deutscher Verwaltung.* Darmstadt, 1924.

Germany. Grosser Generalstab. Kriegsgeschichtliche Abteilung. *Die Kämpfe der deutschen Truppen in Südwestafrika.* Berlin, 1906–7.

Germany. Reichstag. *Verhandlungen.* XIII Legislaturperiode. 1 Session. *Anlagen zu den stenographischen Berichten,* vols. 294 and 304.

Germany. Reichskolonialamt. *Der Baumwollbau in den deutschen Schutzgebieten: seine Entwicklung seit dem Jahre 1910.* Jena, 1914.

Medizinalbericht über die deutschen Schutzgebiete, 1911–12. Berlin, 1915.

Gifford, Prosser, and Wm. Roger Louis, eds., with the assistance of Alison Smith. *Britain and Germany in Africa: imperial rivalry and colonial rule.* New Haven, Yale University Press, 1967.

Grosser Brockhaus (Leipzig, 1931).

Hallgarten, Georg Wolfgang Felix. *Imperialismus vor 1914: die soziologischen Grundlagen der Aussenpolitik europäischer Grossmächte vor dem ersten Weltkrieg.* Rev. and extended ed. 2 vols. Munich, 1963.

Hausen, Karin. *Deutsche Kolonialherrschaft in Afrika: Wirtschaftsinteressen und Kolonialverwaltung in Kamerun vor 1914.* Zurich, 1970.

Hintrager, Oskar. *Südwestafrika in der deutschen Zeit.* Munich, 1955.

Horton, James Africanus. *West African countries and peoples, 1868.* Reprint. Edinburgh University Press, 1969.

Ibbeken, Rudolf. *Das aussenpolitische Problem Staat und Wirtschaft in der deutschen Reichspolitik, 1880–1914: Untersuchungen über Kolonialpolitik, internationale Finanzpolitik, Handelsverträge und die Bagdadbahn.* Schleswig, 1928.

Iliffe, John. *Tanganyika under German rule, 1905–1912.* Cambridge University Press, 1969.

Kaiserlich-Biologisch-Landwirtschaftliches Institut Amani. *Jahresberichte. . . . 1903–4.*

Kurtze, Bruno. *Die Deutsch-Ostafrikanische Gesellschaft: ein Beitrag zum Problem der Schutzbriefgesellschaften und zur Geschichte Deutsch-Ostafrikas.* Jena. 1913.

Leutwein, Theodor. *Elf Jahre Gouverneur in Deutsch-Südwestafrika.* Berlin, 1908.

Loth, Heinrich. *Die christliche Mission in Südwestafrika: zur destruktiven Rolle der Rheinischen Missionsgesellschaft beim Prozess der Staatsbildung in Südwestafrika, 1842–1893.* Berlin, 1963.

Mayer, Anton, ed. *Das Buch der deutschen Kolonien.* Potsdam, 1933.

Mayer, Otto. *Die Entwicklung der Handelsbeziehungen Deutschlands zu seinen Kolonien.* Munich, 1913.

Meyer, Hans Heinrich Joseph, ed. *Das deutsche Kolonialreich: eine Länderkunde der deutschen Schutzgebiete.* 2 vols. Leipzig, Bibliographisches Institut, 1909–10.

Minerva: Jahrbuch der gelehrten Welt . . . Strassburg, 1914.

Müller, Fritz Ferdinand. *Deutschland-Zanzibar-Ostafrika; Geschichte einer deutschen Kolonialeroberung 1884–1890.* Berlin, 1959.

—— ed. *Kolonien unter der Peitsche: eine Dokumentation.* Berlin, 1962.

The New International Yearbook. . . . New York, 1916.

Oelhafen, Hans von Schöllenbach. *Die Besiedlung Deutsch-Südwestafrikas bis zum Weltkrieg.* Berlin, 1913.

Puttkamer, Jesco von. *Gouverneursjahre in Kamerun.* Berlin, 1912.

Rathenau, Walther. 'Erwägungen über die Erschliessung des Deutsch-Ostafrikanischen Schutzgebietes', *Reflexionen.* Leipzig, 1908.

Rohrbach, Paul. *Deutsche Kolonialwirtschaft,* vol. I: *Südwest-Afrika.* Berlin, 1907.

—— *Wie machen wir unsere Kolonien rentabel? Grundzüge eines Wirtschaftsprogramms für Deutschlands afrikanischen Kolonialbesitz.* Halle, 1907.

Rudin, Harry Rudolph. *Germans in the Cameroons, 1884–1914: a case study in German imperialism.* London, 1938.

Sander, Ludwig. *Geschichte der Deutschen Kolonialgesellschaft für Südwest-Afrika, von ihrer Gründung bis zum Jahre 1910.* Berlin, 1912.

Scharlach, Julius. *Koloniale und politische Aufsätze und Reden.* Berlin, 1903.

Schlunk, Martin. *Die Schulen für Eingeborene in den deutschen Schutzgebieten am 1. Juli 1911: auf Grund einer statistischen Erhebung der Zentralstelle des Hamburgischen Kolonialinstituts dargestellt.* Hamburg, 1914.

Schnee, Heinrich, ed. *Das Buch der deutschen Kolonien.* Leipzig [1937].

—— *Deutsches Kolonial-Lexikon.* 3 vols. Leipzig, 1920.

Schwabe, Kurd. *Im deutschen Diamantenland: Deutsch-Südwestafrika von der Errichtung der deutschen Herrschaft bis zur Gegenwart 1884–1910.* Berlin, 1910.

Seitz, Theodor. *Vom Aufstieg und Niederbruch deutscher Kolonialmacht.* 3 vols. Karlsruhe, 1927–9.

Spidle, Jake. 'The German colonial civil service: organization, the question of selection and training' Ph.D. dissertation, Stanford University, 1972.

Stoecker, Helmuth, ed. *Kamerun unter deutscher Kolonialherrschaft.* 2 vols. Berlin, 1960–8.

Tetzlaff, Rainer. *Koloniale Entwicklung und Ausbeutung: Wirtschafts- und Sozialgeschichte Deutsch-Ostafrikas 1885–1914.* Berlin, 1970.

Townsend, Mary Evelyn. *The rise and fall of Germany's colonial empire, 1884–1916.* New York, 1930.

Trierenberg, Georg. *Togo: die Aufrichtung der deutschen Schutzherrschaft und die Erschliessung des Landes.* Berlin, 1914.

Vietor, J. K. *Geschichtliche und kulturelle Entwicklung unserer Schutzgebiete.* Berlin, 1913.

Walter, Heinrich. *Die Farmwirtschaft in Deutsch-Südwestafrika: ihre biologischen Grundlagen.* Berlin, 1940.

Washausen, Helmut. *Hamburg und die Kolonialpolitik des deutschen Reiches 1880 bis 1890.* Hamburg, 1968.

Wehler, Hans-Ulrich. *Bismarck und der Imperialismus.* Cologne, 1969.

Wirtz, Albert. *Vom Sklavenhandel zum kolonialen Handel: Wirtschaftsräume und Wirtschaftsformen in Kamerun vor 1914.* Zürich, 1972.

Zache, Hans, ed. *Das deutsche Kolonialbuch.* Berlin [1926].

Zimmermann, Alfred. *Geschichte der deutschen Kolonialpolitik.* Berlin, 1914.

CHAPTER 7

SOME ECONOMIC ASPECTS OF PORTUGUESE AFRICA IN THE NINETEENTH AND TWENTIETH CENTURIES

by

RICHARD J. HAMMOND

Close on half a century ago, in 1924, Vicente Ferreira, who was one of the most experienced and influential of Portuguese colonial administrators, wrote that an economist might consider the whole colonial enterprise of Portugal absurd, but that a mystic or a simpleton might describe it as a miracle. A generation later, the Brazilian sociologist Gilberto Freyre was to attribute the miracle to a unique Portuguese ability to create a *luso-tropical* civilization, largely through miscegenation. This explanation would not have satisfied Ferreira, for whom miscegenation was at best a 'necessary mistake' to be avoided in the future; it was apparently at his instance that the white settlers in the government's new agricultural colony at Cela in Angola, started in 1952, were forbidden to employ African labour. The critical period, between 1885 and 1910, in establishing Portugal's African empire within its present boundaries was one in which miscegenation was in some degree officially frowned on; and though current Portuguese governmental thinking—in contrast to the views of Ferreira and the nineteenth-century proconsul António Enes (Ennes)—emphasizes the multi-racial character of the overseas territories, current settler practice tends in the opposite direction. White women are no longer rarities in Luanda, the capital of Angola, as they were as recently as the beginning of the present century.

It is not necessary to invoke miraculous explanations of the continued Portuguese presence in Africa, even though that presence breaks the rules that historians of modern imperialism have come to think of as normal. Portugal, at the time of the nineteenth-century scramble for Africa, held title to a few bits of African seaboard and little besides: no industries seeking overseas markets, no middle class seeking overseas fortunes, no capitalists seeking overseas investments, no large military forces seeking overseas employment. Portugal was a net importer of capital. As late as 1900, 78 per cent of Portuguese adults were reckoned as unable to read; fifty years later the figure was still 40 per cent. There was indeed continual emigration, mainly from the north of Portugal and of poor, illiterate peasants; not, however, save in a trickle, to Africa, but to Brazil. Such as went to Africa, wrote António Enes in 1893, were 'useless people without a trade, led astray by the belief that in Africa one digs gold with one's fingernails'. It was the remittances of emigrants to Brazil that until 1890, when an economic crisis in Latin America reduced them to vanishing point, kept the Portuguese balance of payments in equilibrium. The failure of remittances helped to drive Portugal off the gold standard and to compel an arbitrary reduction in interest on its foreign debt (June 1892). The decisive years when it established itself in Moçambique were years when the kingdom was an un-

7. Portuguese Africa, 1960

discharged bankrupt; not until 1902 was an agreed settlement reached with the foreign creditors, who were chiefly French and German.

The fact that the foreign-debt negotiations were allowed to linger over ten years suggests that the governments in question were anxious to do nothing that would threaten the existence of monarchy in Portugal (and consequently in the Iberian peninsula); an abortive Republican revolution did break out in Oporto

257

on 31 January 1891. For more than a year, during the protracted negotiations between Portugal and Great Britain that followed the British 'ultimatum' of January 1890, counsels of moderation had been urged on the British government by the crowned heads of Europe.[1] The territorial settlement that ensued in 1891 fell far short of the expectations of opponents of Portugal in Africa like Cecil Rhodes, just as the territory included in Angola after the Berlin West African Conference of 1884–5 had been huge compared with that over which the Portuguese could claim effective authority. In each instance the moderation displayed by governments that could readily, had they wished, have put Portugal out of business as an imperial power rested largely on the belief that there was no need to hasten the inevitable. It was the impatience of one government, that of post-Bismarck Imperial Germany, with the slow process of inevitability that led to the notorious secret Anglo-German treaties of 1898, providing for a contingent partition of the Portuguese colonies. These treaties, however, constituted an aberration from the generally indulgent attitude of the powers towards Portugal.

What might have been expected to end Portuguese dominion overseas before long was the sheer expense and difficulty of the tasks—establishing boundaries, ensuring settlement and promoting economic development—that were implicit in the new rule on 'effective occupation' laid down at the Berlin West African Conference.[2] Until then, the Portuguese empire had consisted mainly of a series of isolated coast communities, dating back for many centuries, and inhabited (apart from a handful of officials) by Africans, persons of mixed Portuguese and African blood, and criminals exiled from continental Portugal. The primary purpose of these posts, centuries earlier, had been to serve as stages on the sea route to the Indies; they had been chosen for their merits as harbours and for their ease of defence against local tribesmen, rather than for trading with the interior. Several of them—Bolama in Portuguese Guinea (Guiné), Ibo, and Moçambique in Moçambique—were on offshore islands. As early as the sixteenth century also, the Portuguese had established settlements well up the Zambezi, at Sena and Tete; in the seventeenth century, they had added a number in the Cuanza river basin behind Luanda, and in the hinterland of Benguela.

These settlements have persisted to the present day. It is evident that continuity, particularly in those up-country, was often tenuous and even broken for years at a time. It is evident also that even at the height of Portuguese influence, the number of white men in Africa cannot have been more than a very few thousand. When historians speak of the Angolan wars of the seventeenth century they mean not wars between European and African but wars between African and African in which Europeans joined: sometimes, as with the Portuguese and the Dutch there, on opposite sides. The Portuguese settlements in Africa rested at bottom on a *modus vivendi* with the surrounding African tribes. In Moçambique there was a further element: Indians from Goa, who were more adaptable to the East African climate than Europeans, and who came to dominate the great estates (*prazos*) of Zambézia as early as the seventeenth century. The basis of this *modus vivendi* was, of course, the slave-trade, for which

---

[1] For a detailed account of the Anglo-Portuguese negotiations, see Eric Axelson, *Portugal and the scramble for Africa* (Johannesburg University Press, 1967), pp. 232 ff.

[2] Sybil E. Crowe, *The Berlin West African Conference, 1884–1885* (London, 1942).

Brazil provided a principal market and the Arab countries a secondary one. Nothing useful can be said about the slave-trade from the economic point of view by people who forget that it, as a member of the British Foreign Office wrote in 1888, was 'a state of things founded on religion, custom, profit, and taste, and handed down from time immemorial'.[3] Slaves appear to have been the only African export that had, for hundreds of years, a consistent large-scale market; they were hence the only means by which Africans could obtain imports they desired or needed; their capture required little capital investment; and they were not only self-transporting to seaboard, but might serve as porters for another valuable export—ivory. To say, as has been said, that the development of Portuguese Africa over centuries of slave-trading was hindered by the existence of the trade seems perverse; it implies that there was some unrealized alternative export that would have provoked greater development. Yet, quite apart from the environmental obstacles in Africa itself—climate, disease, absence of skilled labour, want of transport—there was no sizeable market abroad for anything new that might be produced there, except the precious metals. Again and again this point has been ignored by promoters of development schemes. It is inconceivable, for instance, that the Zambézia *prazos* could at any time before the present century have found an export market for substantial quantities of cultivated crops. Yet the mistaken belief that their original purpose had been agricultural underlay the ineffective *prazo* legislation of Lisbon from the mid-eighteenth century onwards.

It would be truer to say, therefore, that the economic development that occurred in Portuguese Africa before the nineteenth century and that is reflected in the buildings that survive in some of the coast towns, came either from the slave-trade or from without—from the silver and gold of Brazil, which from about 1700 onwards replaced the Indies as a source of treasure for the Portuguese kingdom. These buildings bear witness to another long-standing trait of Portuguese settlement: the export to Africa of numbers of craftsmen and artisans, trained to build in the European style. The un-African appearance of towns like Luanda, Moçambique and Bolama was remarked upon by nineteenth-century travellers, who frequently went on to note, however, that the buildings were in decay.

The process of economic decline appears to have begun, at any rate in Zambézia, a century at least before the abolition of the slave-trade, which was itself a relatively unprofitable substitute for the acquisition of the precious metals that had originally been hoped for. On the west coast, there had never been any substantial alternative to the slave-trade, and the economic history of Angola and Portuguese Guinea in the second half of the nineteenth century can be read in terms of an effort to find one. Only painfully and gradually did it come to be recognized that economic development in Portuguese Africa, as elsewhere in the 'underdeveloped' world, called in the early stages for capital investment disproportionate to the immediate financial reward that might be expected from it.

The settlement of Portuguese families in the African provinces to engage in farming had been a recurrent will-o'-the-wisp for centuries. It had been pre-

---

[3] Villiers Lister; quoted in Richard J. Hammond, *Portugal and Africa, 1815–1910: a study in uneconomic imperialism* (Stanford University Press, 1966), p. 61.

scribed in such early *donatárias* as that to Paulo Dias de Novaes (Luanda, 1575) and was implicit in the decree of 1760 that sought (vainly) to limit the size of the Zambézia *prazos*. In the second quarter of the nineteenth century a renewed attempt was made. In 1840 the *presídio* of Moçâmedes was established on the arid southerly coast of Angola; in 1845 that of Huíla, inland on the healthy southern plateau; and in 1854 that of Porto Alexandre, south of Moçâmedes. Both Moçâmedes and Porto Alexandre succeeded in becoming permanent, though small, civilian settlements whose economies were based, not on agriculture, but on the rich fisheries off the coast. The fishing industry was analogous to peasant proprietorship in that its labour, as well as its meagre capital, was exclusively white. About the same time, the ports of Angola became bases for whaling, carried on mainly by Americans. The settlement at Huíla, however, was abortive; not until the 1880s did white men (mainly at first Boers) establish themselves as farmers there. In 1857 an unsuccessful effort had been made to plant a farm settlement at Pemba Bay in northern Moçambique. Contemporaries put down these failures to poor, 'utopian' planning; but it is questionable whether the conditions for success were ever present. (It is perhaps worth mentioning that native African opposition was not held responsible for any of these failures.)

How insignificant, economically, the possessions in Angola and Moçambique were a century ago can be judged from the colonial budgets of the 1860s: the revenue and expenditure figures for the tiny enclave of Portuguese India considerably exceeded those of Angola, which in turn were nearly twice those of Moçambique. Some progress was registered in Angola in the 1870s. Between 1865 and 1875, for instance, the Banco Nacional Ultramarino (founded 1864), whose Luanda branch was managed by a British citizen, multiplied its cash turnover there ten times. A line of river steamers under Anglo-American management began operations between Luanda and Dondo, two hundred miles up the Cuanza river, in 1867, but its traffic amounted to only a few thousand tons a year. Even so, exports from Angolan ports in the early 1870s were valued at twice what they had been half a century earlier when, of course, they consisted almost exclusively of slaves.

In 1886, work began on a railway inland from Luanda the title of which, Grand Trans-African Railway, reflected a current Portuguese preoccupation: that with establishing a belt of territory across Africa from Angola to Moçambique in accordance with the claims on the 'rose-coloured' map, published that same year. There were hopes that the new line would encourage large increases in plantation agriculture. It received a heavy government subsidy that guaranteed its *gross* revenues per kilometre, so that it was encouraged to be roundabout (when it came to be rebuilt in the 1920s it was shortened by 100 km, or one-fifth) and to keep its traffics, and hence its expenses, as low as it dared. Twenty years later, the quantity of products reaching Luanda annually by rail was no more than had been carried by the Cuanza steam-boats the railway had superseded: less than ten thousand tons. The subsidy, as a governor-general of the time wrote, was being used for 'putting a muleteer's load on wheels . . . the less traffic the more profits'. By that time the railway had reached Ambaca, about two hundred miles inland. It was subsequently extended to Malange, a further hundred miles or so, and has not been extended since, though there are plans to do so.

Contemporary critics pointed to the Ambaca railway guarantee as a typical example of the restrictive practices that, they implied, were strangling the growth of Angola. On every side, indeed, such practices were evident: the national shipping line, enabled by flag discrimination to keep its rates high; the Banco Nacional Ultramarino, likewise a monopoly that could get on quite well without actively promoting trade and agriculture; the Moçâmedes Company (formed in 1894 under mainly French auspices to develop the extreme south of Angola), which sixteen years later was reported to be completely inactive. The question is whether these attitudes were not a reflection as much as a cause of Angolan economic stagnation. Time and time again there had been hopes of some commodity development that would replace the slave-trade and make the colony's fortune. At the time of the American Civil War, there had been cotton; in the eighties and early nineties, coffee and wild rubber successively formed the principal exports; but the tonnages were all but insignificant even at their peak. The rubber boom in the late nineties was held responsible for generating another mushroom industry: the production of sugar for making into rum, the favourite barter object of the African gathering rubber or beeswax for export. The rum industry had been made profitable by a series of increases in import duties on spirits, introduced partly as a result of the Brussels Convention (1890) aimed at discouraging their use by black Africans, but not matched, as they logically should have been, by rises in excise duties. By 1899, imports of gin into Angola had been all but wiped out, but production there of *aguardente* had risen to 15 million litres a year. At this point an additional excise tax was imposed on the industry, the proceeds of which were eventually used to extend the Ambaca railway to Malange. The pressure of world humanitarian opinion, however, made it impossible for the Portuguese to allow the industry to continue; and after some years of fruitless tinkering the decision was taken to prohibit distilling outright. There was left an industry producing raw cane sugar for export, which competed for the small protected metropolitan market with the older-established industry in Moçambique. The colonial sugar surplus that resulted began to disappear only in the 1950s, when rising consumption in Portugal itself at length caught up with supplies.

The predominance of spirituous drinks in the economy of early twentieth-century Angola could be matched in Moçambique. 'The measure of the state of trade [of Lourenço Marques]', wrote António Enes in his *Relatório* of 1893, 'is the importation of intoxicants'; the favourite occupation of immigrants from Portugal was that of innkeeper. Alcoholic drinks were the only commodity for which the natives' demand was unlimited; they would distil or ferment them themselves if they could not get them otherwise. In the coastal areas near Quelimane and Moçambique town, where the cashew tree grows wild, there had long been annual saturnalia on liquor made from the fruit, which was sold to the natives in 'small drinking houses usually kept by [Portuguese] convicts'. Moçambique south of the latitude 22°S (roughly, south of the Save river) was, moreover, outside the application of the anti-alcoholic rules prescribed by the Brussels Convention. A law was actually enacted for Moçambique in 1902, in the supposed interest of wine-growers in continental Portugal, prohibiting distilling and the brewing of 'fermented Kaffir drinks' such as *sopé* and *sura*. But the imported substitute, fortified grape wine, proved unacceptable; Africans declined to work for white men who could not supply them with their customary drinks; and in the end the law had to be abandoned. As late as 1919 it was asserted that the majority of white farmers in Southern Moçambique lived by growing sugar-cane, the juice of which they fermented and sold to the blacks. The sale of liquor was said to be virtually the only commercial activity engaged in by Portuguese, petty trade in other things being, as it had been for centuries, in the hands of Indians.

This situation was irksome to believers in colonial development. The economic state of Angola, wrote Governor-General Paiva Couceiro of the period 1907–9, was the same as if the first stone monument (*padrão*) set up by Diogo Cão in 1482–3 had been established yesterday. Other colonial writers pointed out that the very existence of a colonial budget surplus was evidence that much-needed development had not been undertaken. Colonial budget surpluses, except in Moçambique and the tiny 'cocoa province' of São Tomé, were not indeed the rule in the last years of the monarchy; but the greater part of the deficits, mostly in Angola, were accounted for not by development but by military expenditures. (The chief exception was the subsidy to the Trans-African railway.) Even these were below the optimum for swift and effective pacification of the remote interior; it was not the strength of African opposition so much as the want of Portuguese financial and military resources that delayed the complete conquest of southern Angola, northern Moçambique and Portuguese Guinea until the second decade of the twentieth century. But until complete conquest was attained, the funds available from a bankrupt central government for development had to be few. What is doubtful is whether, had funds been more plentiful, the rate of development would have been substantially quicker.

The only territories in Portuguese Africa, except for the extreme south of Moçambique, that showed any substantial signs of economic development under the monarchy were the tiny volcanic islands of São Tomé and Príncipe in the Gulf of Guinea. These were uninhabited when the Portuguese occupied them, about 1485, and by the late nineteenth century had acquired a small but heterogeneous population: owners, some white and some *mestiço,* of large estates; a substantial number of tenant farmers and peasant proprietors; a number of *Angolares,* descended from the survivors of a slave-ship wrecked centuries before, who lived in a village of their own apart from the remainder of the population; and a large contingent of former slaves, emancipated in 1876. None of these people was willing to work regularly on plantations for wages, and such was the natural fertility of the islands that men could live without doing more than an occasional job of work.

The ending of slavery and of the slave-trade had destroyed the economic base on which the little province, as a statutory port of call *en route* for Brazil, had lived for centuries. Labour on the islands for the new crops of coffee and cacao became unavailable overnight; and it was in these circumstances that the shipment of contract labourers (*serviçaes*) from the Angolan mainland was started, in 1877. For a generation these shipments continued, and after 1890 their numbers sharply increased, thanks to the growing demand for São Tomé cocoa; moreover, no *serviçal* who went from Angola to the islands was ever known to return. Anxiety was already being shown in Angola about the traffic, which was causing a shortage of plantation labour there, and measures were being taken at least on paper to deal with it before Henry Nevinson, by his articles in *Harper's Magazine,* let loose the humanitarians of the world on the

Portuguese government.[4] From the subsequent boycott of São Tomé cocoa the industry never completely recovered; though cocoa still constitutes some three-quarters of exports by value, it accounts for only 1 per cent of world production. Only a quarter of the crop is absorbed by Portugal.

The triangular enclave of Portuguese Guinea was saved from a French take-over in the mid-nineteenth century largely by the efforts of its famous (and only) black governor, Honório Pereira Barreto.[5] Shortly afterwards, the then capital of the territory, Bolama, which lies on an offshore island, was threatened with conquest by the British, who had vague claims to the island dating back to 1792. They were eventually persuaded to submit these claims to arbitration by United States President Grant, who in 1870 awarded the disputed territory to Portugal, an award that earned him a statue that still stands in Bolama. In 1879, Portuguese Guinea was made into a separate province from the Cape Verde Islands. A substitute for slaves as exports was found in ground-nuts, which were being exported from Bissau (now the capital) as early as 1846. But the interior remained unsubdued until the second decade of the twentieth century; climate and tropical disease made European settlement impracticable, and plantation agriculture was not even attempted. Until after the First World War, such wholesale trade as existed was in the hands of French and German commercial houses; European residents numbered fewer than a thousand. Portuguese Guinea, like São Tomé before foreign humanitarians discovered it, was until recently a province without a history.

Much the same can be said of the Cape Verde Islands (Cabo Verde), a semi-arid, mainly mountainous group some 300 miles west of Dakar in Senegal, which were uninhabited when the Portuguese discovered them in 1457, and have long been predominantly *mestiço* in population. The spoken language is a creole dialect of Portuguese; some customs of apparent African origin have survived, but no racial feeling along with them. Since the invention of the steamship and the submarine telegraph, the principal importance of Cabo Verde (or rather of one of the islands, São Vicente) to the outside world has been as a cable station and a refuelling station: fuel oil, like coal before it, is at once the principal export and the principal import. There is a trickle of agricultural exports, such as arabica coffee and bananas, but the majority of the population (some 225,000) is engaged in subsistence agriculture, a pursuit unrewarding in view of the heat and frequent drought. Density of population is high, nearly 150 per square mile, and many are driven to emigrate, some to Portuguese Guinea and latterly to São Tomé and Angola. The absence of serious political problems for the Portuguese rulers during the centuries is perhaps an index of economic stagnation, due to the unfavourable natural conditions, rather than of positive content of the islanders with their lot.

In Moçambique, the problem of development was long by-passed, and still is to some extent, by the geographical circumstance that Lourenço Marques and Beira happen to be the most convenient ocean ports for neighboring land-locked temperate territories, the Transvaal and Rhodesia, and that these territories are both short of black labour. One might say, indeed, that the export of

---

[4] See my earlier essay in vol. 1 of this series, pp. 373–5. A fuller discussion appears in Hammond, *Portugal and Africa*, pp. 313–25.
[5] There is an excellent biography by Jaime Walter, *Honório Pereira Barreto* (Bissau, 1947). See also Hammond, *Portugal and Africa*, pp. 46–50.

workers from Moçambique to the Rand gold-fields, for which the export trade through Lourenço Marques is a *quid pro quo,* was functionally a substitute for the slave-trade; though it would be wrong to infer, as some Portuguese critics did, that it hindered development within Moçambique. It was of course true that, as late as the outbreak of the First World War, investment there, both Portuguese and foreign, had been concentrated in the port and railway of Lourenço Marques, which, as Governor-General Freire de Andrade indignantly wrote, were 'tied to the destinies of the Transvaal'.[6] But everything, not least the surplus that the province contributed to the total colonial budget during the last decade of the monarchy, points to an economic justification for this policy. By contrast, the chartered companies that had come into existence in Moçambique in the 1890s were a disappointment to their shareholders no less than to the Portuguese government that had counted on them to promote land settlement. Neither the Moçambique nor the Nyassa Company fulfilled the intent of its charter that, in phraseology redolent of the *donatária* given to the founder of Luanda in 1575, provided that it should establish one thousand Portuguese families within its territory within five years. The Nyassa Company never built a mile of the railway, some 400 miles long, it was charged with building from Porto Amelia to Lake Nyasa. The failure of these companies to come up to expectations was only partly, if at all, due to bad management; it was due, rather, to over-sanguine expectations that, for instance, precious metals might be found, or to overconfidence in the ability of ports and railways to generate development by themselves. One cannot say too often that the provision of economic infrastructure in any country is a necessary, but not a sufficient, condition of economic development.

Such provision had not, indeed, gone very far in either Moçambique or Angola by the time the monarchy was overthrown in 1910. By far the most important developments were the port and railway of Lourenço Marques, which continued to be the preferred route for Transvaal transit trade in spite of British efforts to divert it to less convenient ports under their political control. The Portuguese were able to exploit the need of the Transvaal gold-mines for Moçambique labour so as to secure a guarantee of a minimum proportion of rail traffic for the Lourenço Marques route; and the 1909 treaty with the Transvaal to this effect was specifically incorporated in the British Act of Parliament establishing the Union of South Africa, passed later the same year. It is of some technical interest that the agreement was formally unconstitutional in monarchical Portugal, though as events turned out this proved to be of no importance.[7]

Other colonial railroads were comparatively insignificant. That from Umtali (Rhodesia) to Beira had been completed, though initially only in narrow (two-foot) gauge, at the turn of the century; but the development of Rhodesia, and hence the transit traffic, disappointed expectations when the massive gold finds forecast by Rhodes failed to materialize, and that of the Moçambique Company's territory was no less disappointing. The management of this territory was almost exclusively in the hands of the British: 'saints' days and Portuguese festal days are not observed in Beira', wrote an indignant Portuguese observer in 1896. It was, indeed, only the Anglo-German secret treaties of 1898 (which

[6] Afredo Freire de Andrade, *Relatórios de Moçambique* (Lourenço Marques, 1909), 1,103; translation in Hammond, *Portugal and Africa,* pp. 294–5.
[7] The Act is 9 Edw. 7, c.9. See Hammond, *Portugal and Africa,* pp. 326–32.

would have called for an equivalent concession to Germany) that prevented moves towards acquisition of the Moçambique Company by close allies of the 'Chartered', the British South Africa Company of Cecil Rhodes. The Benguela Railway in Angola, started in 1904, proved so difficult and expensive to build that its promoters, also former associates of Rhodes, ran out of capital at the end of 1908 and construction was halted for a time. By 1911, however, it had reached Huambo (later Nova Lisboa) on the central plateau.

The first years of the republic were marked by little economic progress in either Angola or Moçambique. The level of colonial administrative competence was lowered by the exile or retirement from public life of a number of leading royalist figures, such as Aires de Ornelas; Freire de Andrade was almost alone in continuing to serve under the republic. The principal preoccupation of the governor-general of Angola in these years, Norton de Matos, was with the growing boldness and insolence of German designs on the territory, designs encouraged by the complaisance of the British Foreign and Colonial secretaries, Sir Edward Grey and 'Lulu' Harcourt. Actions like the German demand for low transit duties on goods passing through Angolan ports *en route* for South-West Africa, and the foundation in that colony of the *Angola Bund,* with the proclaimed purpose of creating in Angola an indispensable complement to German South-West Africa, naturally alarmed the Portuguese. The governor-general was convinced that these and other activities were preliminaries to a military invasion: a view that was borne out, after the First World War had started, by the discovery in September 1914 of a series of clandestine depots in Angola, containing food for men and horses, along the routes which an invader would take from the southern frontier to the Benguela Railway.

A German invasion of Angola, however, would have been practicable only with the acquiescence of the British. Once general war had broken out, the German African colonies were isolated from Germany: first by British naval supremacy in the South Atlantic and Indian oceans, secondly by British control of the submarine cable-telegraph systems at a time when radio-communications were in their infancy. South-West Africa's only hope of survival after 1914 lay in the possible neutrality of the Union of South Africa, and this was in the end denied it. So too in East Africa the outbreak of the First World War alone prevented the Niassa Company from coming under German control; but there was no possibility of a permanent conquest of Moçambique by German forces. The fantastic exploits of von Lettow-Vorbeck, who responded to defeat in German East Africa by invading Moçambique with his askaris in November 1917, penetrated as far south as Quelimane, and was still undefeated, on Northern Rhodesian soil, when the Armistice was signed in Europe a year later, were a military irrelevance that was made partly possible by incompetence on the part of the Portuguese defenders of the province.

Military glory so persistently eluded the Portuguese forces, whether in southern Angola, northern Moçambique or on the Western Front in Europe, as to make highly questionable the arguments of those Portuguese who had urged that the government declare war on Germany. In the end, it is true, it was the Germans who declared war on Portugal, in February 1916; but even so, the dispatch of troops to the Western Front, where they constituted no more than an embarrassment to their allies, might well have been avoided. The Portuguese delegation to the Peace Conference of 1919 was, partly if not wholly in consequence of the poor military performance of its troops, subjected to a series of slights; the only reward for belligerency was the tiny Kionga triangle in northern Moçambique, which had been taken from the Portuguese by the Germans in 1894. A Portuguese request for a colonial mandate, prompted by the award to Belgium of Ruanda-Urundi, was not taken seriously by the remaining Allies.[8]

The Peace Conference in fact provided an opportunity for the other Allies to lecture the Portuguese on their failure to develop Angola and Moçambique, and to suggest that their continued possession of the territories might turn on their ability to develop them. Such assertions were, of course, in line with the spirit of the times, as expressed in the establishment of League of Nations mandates for the conquered German territories: a system that some would have liked to extend to those of Portugal. They were not accompanied by any serious analysis of the problems that Portuguese colonial development presented, or by any acceptable proposals that would help Portugal to deal with them.

It is indeed difficult to believe that the other powers, and particularly the 'ancient ally', Great Britain, had any real interest in developing the Portuguese colonies. For it must have been clear to anyone giving thought to the question that Portugal lacked the resources to develop them itself and would have to rely on foreign help; that it would leave them undeveloped rather than allow foreign developers and foreign capital to act as Trojan horses for a foreign conquest; and that a guarantee of continued possession, rather than vague threats of dispossession, was therefore essential if foreign capital were to be let into Moçambique and Angola. It does not, of course, follow that if more capital investment had been permitted and forthcoming it would have been fruitful. One can argue that too much, not too little, capital had been put into African infrastructure around the turn of the century—witness the five separate railways from the Transvaal to the coast, any one of which could have carried all the traffic, and those to Luanda and Beira, which were likewise under-employed.

In any event, the disorganized political and financial condition of Portugal in the decade between the Armistice and the appointment of Dr Oliveira Salazar as Minister of Finance in 1928 was such as to discourage any foreign investment in its overseas territories. That this condition did not result from anything except bad administration is demonstrated by the ease, technically speaking, with which Salazar was able to deal with a situation that his predecessors had thought insoluble without a League of Nations loan. His financial miracle was produced, not by brilliance as an economist, but by single-minded determination backed by military force. In the long run it has undoubtedly assisted Portugal to secure a modicum of foreign investment, both at home and in the overseas territories. But in the short run it produced painful results, particularly in Angola.

Angola rather than Moçambique tended to receive the greater solicitude from Portuguese governments under the republic, for a number of reasons: its greater need for economic help, in the absence of a large source of invisible exports comparable to the ports and railroads of Lourenço Marques and Beira; its more exclusively Portuguese character, in the absence of the sizeable influence of Great Britain and the Union of South Africa on Moçambique; and the greater suitability of its central and southern plateaux, compared with any part of

[8] William Roger Louis, *Ruanda-Urundi, 1881–1919* (Oxford, Clarendon Press, 1963), pp. 233–55.

Moçambique, for settlement by Portuguese peasants. There were sometimes complaints of discrimination in favour of Angola, notably by the (partly British-owned) cane-sugar industry of Moçambique, which by itself was capable of supplying metropolitan Portugal's requirements and found its output artificially restricted to make room for sugar produced by the former rum industry of Angola.[9] The long-standing custom of relieving Angola's budget deficits from the surpluses in the budgets of São Tomé and Moçambique had been an earlier source of criticism.

The period when attention was most sharply focused on Angolan economic problems was the 1920s. The decade had begun auspiciously: the diamond field in the district of Lunda, discovered just before the First World War, had proved sufficiently important to justify the grant of a mining monopoly to an *ad hoc* associate of the De Beers organization in South Africa, the Companhia de Diamantes de Angola (Diamang). For the next two decades, diamonds were to be Angola's leading export and a substantial contributor to provincial revenues; they are still important fifty years later. Diamang is reputed to be a model employer, and its provision for education and health among its African employees is said to be noteworthy. But its operations are confined to one remote inland corner of the province that, if the boundaries of 1885 had been settled on ethnic grounds, might well have been included in the Congo Free State. Its influence on the mass of the Angolan population is negligible.

In 1922 a British writer published a book—*Angola, a coming colony*—that radiated optimism about the province's future.[10] In 1923 the Moçâmedes Railway reached Sá da Bandeira, on the plateau. Thereafter, however, everything began to go wrong. Norton de Matos, who had been governor-general in the immediate pre-war years and afterwards the principal instigator of Portugal's ill-starred military activity on the Western Front in Europe, was sent back to Angola for a second term, this time as high commissioner, with his mind full of devices for economic and social development. In principle some of these made sense. But in Portugal in the mid-twenties there was neither the money to finance them nor the trained men to carry them out; the want of qualification of Norton de Matos' recruits for Angola became a national laughing-stock. Severe parliamentary criticism, led by the formidable Cunha Leal, followed; and in June 1924 the high commissioner resigned, leaving a legacy of unfinished projects, financial confusion and commercial depression.

It was in this situation that one Alves Reis conceived a scheme for bringing prosperity to Angola and fortune to himself by founding a new bank—the Angola e Metropole—that would break the banking monopoly of the Banco Nacional Ultramarino in Angola and remedy the shortage of capital there. The new bank's initial capital was obtained in a unique way: a forged letter from the Bank of Portugal to its bank-note printers, the highly reputable British firm of Waterlow and Sons. On the strength of this, Alves Reis and his fellow-conspirators obtained the printing and personal delivery of $5 million worth of 500-escudo notes that, being printed from the same plates, were indistinguishable, except for a secret printer's mark, from the genuine article. It had been represented to Waterlow's that the notes would be overprinted 'Angola'

[9] Sena Sugar Estates, Ltd., *Moçambique e o problema açucareiro* (Lisbon, 1945).
[10] J. C. B. Statham, *Angola: a coming colony* (Edinburgh, 1922).

before issue—a point that should have aroused suspicion, inasmuch as the sole bank of note issue for the Portuguese colonies was not the Bank of Portugal but the Banco Nacional Ultramarino.

In June 1925 the new bank received its official charter and began to open offices in Angola and to lend money. The false notes—not, of course, overprinted—began to be circulated in Portugal itself, where alone they could escape detection. The bank's activities began to arouse gossip and hostile criticism in at least one influential Lisbon newspaper; but the bubble was burst in December through the individual activity of a single, completely obscure citizen of Oporto, who read the newspaper articles and jumped to the conclusion that the new bank's notes were forged. His views reached the Bank of Portugal's Oporto office, which examined the 500-escudo notes in its possession and found that they were all apparently genuine, but that some had duplicate numbers. There was nothing for it but to call the whole issue in, replacing it all by genuine notes of other kinds. The Bank of Portugal eventually sued Waterlow for damages in the British courts and won, though not without going as far as the House of Lords, and then only by a vote of three law lords to two: the minority held that, because the notes had no gold backing, the Bank of Portugal had failed to prove loss beyond its printing bill. Allowing for the assets of the defunct Banco Angola e Metropole and the part of the false note issue that had not found its way into circulation, the total damages were rather more than $2 million. Efforts have since been made, though without any attempt at proof, to represent Alves Reis (who was given a long prison sentence by the Portuguese courts) as a Keynesian before his time.[11]

It is not clear how far this bizarre episode, reflecting on the methods of British business rather than those of Portuguese government, was responsible for the next move, in 1926: the transfer of the rights of note issue and commercial banking in Angola away from the privately owned Banco Nacional Ultramarino to a newly created semi-public body, the Banco de Angola, and the replacement of the heavily discounted Angolan escudo by a new currency unit, the angolar, of a nominal par value with the metropolitan escudo but, like its predecessor, not freely exchangeable against it or directly into foreign currency. It is not easy to see why this measure was expected to help with the chronic problem of Angolan currency between the two world wars—shortage of metropolitan and foreign exchange—because this was inherent in the province's trade situation, and not to be remedied by any administrative device. Unless an undeveloped country has some extremely valuable export in quantity, such as gold or diamonds in South Africa at the end of the nineteenth century, it will seldom if ever be able to pay out of export earnings for the imports it needs for development. In Angola's case, even with the earnings of Diamang, there was often difficulty in converting into escudos current demands in angolares, such as those represented by funds belonging to persons returning to Portugal from spells of duty. It was rare for such people to settle permanently in Angola, or to wish to keep their surplus funds there. Currency transfer continued to be a cause of complaint, along with the banking monopoly of the Bank of Angola to

---

[11] A contemporary account of the case is in Sir Cecil H. Kisch, *The Portuguese bank-note case* (London, 1932). A more recent full account, journalistic in manner and title but based on much research and marred chiefly only by superficiality and error about Portuguese affairs in general, is by Murray Teigh Bloom, *The man who stole Portugal* (New York, 1966).

which it was linked, throughout the inter-war period. Indeed, as late as 1960 an informed critic wrote that the main result of exchange control in Angola had been to promote illegal exchange transactions, speculation and flights of capital.[12] These problems were less consistently troublesome, perhaps, in Moçambique, but they have persisted there also.

Complaints from the overseas territories became more vociferous when, after 1928, the extravagances of the Norton de Matos era were suddenly replaced by the budget austerities of Salazar, the like of which had never been experienced in Portugal. The Salazar remedy for financial extravagance—an insistence that the annual budget for each province, at least in appearance, be in balance or surplus, an insistence that was, moreover, written into the new 'corporative' constitution—did nothing in the short run for colonial economic development. Nor was the austerity made easier to accept in the overseas territories by the fact that at no time in his forty years of virtually unchallenged power did Salazar visit a single one of them. It is easy to understand why the series of budget surpluses overseas immediately before the outbreak of the Second World War should have been pointed to with pride. On a longer view, however, the critics who referred to these 'housekeeper's balances' as 'merely the privilege of theorists in the study, adherents of a narrow-minded fiscal policy' and called for a positive policy of help for Angola, were surely in the right.[13]

Nevertheless, without the administrative discipline that the budgetary reforms embodied, it might have been hard for Portugal to retain Angola and Moçambique at all, particularly after 1933 when the Germans were clamouring for colonial territories. The dilemma remained inescapable right up to the Second World War: either keep control in the hands of Portugal, which though now financially solvent had insufficient resources in capital and skilled labour to develop even its metropolitan territory; or let control slip into the hands of foreign-controlled and foreign-financed companies and thence, at least indirectly, into those of foreign governments. It is, let it be repeated, by no means certain that economic development would have been more extensive or more rapid under different political control. As in many other economically backward regions, such as southern Italy and much of Latin America, the return on investment was inadequate, the skilled and literate manpower required for industrialization absent, and the market for increased agricultural and other production remote, inaccessible or non-existent. In any case, the ban on foreign investment in Portuguese Africa was not absolute, nor would that investment have been substantial in the economic climate of 1929–39.

One large enterprise was completed in Angola during this period: the building of the Benguela Railway, which reached the border of the Belgian Congo in 1928 and the Katanga copper mines, the prime object for which it was built, in 1931. Its completion coincided with the worst of the world slump and a fall in the price of copper to $25 a ton. The Benguela Railway was yet another example of unprofitable, because premature, colonial railway investment. Grossly underestimated in cost; forced, for the first and most difficult phase of its construction, to import East Indian coolie labour from Natal in default of local

---

[12] Roberto S. de Medeiros Fernandes, 'Portugal and its overseas territories: economic structure and policies, 1950–1957', Ph.D. dissertation (Harvard University, 1960).

[13] Manuel Domingos da Cruz, *A Crise de Angola* (Lisbon, 1928), p. 60; Francisco Pinto da Cunha Leal, *Subsídios para o estudo do problema do crédito em Angola* (Lisbon, 1930).

labour; compelled to resort to the costly rack-rail system (since replaced by the normal adhesion system) for the steepest part of its climb to the plateau; unable to raise extra capital in Great Britain before 1914 by reason of the Anglo-German secret agreements of 1898, and halted completely in building during the First World War, the line did not pay a dividend until 1948, more than forty-five years after the grant of its ninety-nine-year concession.

Between the world wars, the economy of Moçambique continued to be dominated by the transit trade with the Union of South Africa and Southern Rhodesia. The agreement tying a minimum quota of trade through Lourenço Marques to a regulated supply of labour for the Rand mines was renewed with minor modifications in 1928. In 1935 a two-mile-long railway bridge over the Zambezi at Sena was completed, the principal engineering work on the mainly British-owned Trans-Zambézia Railway, linking the Beira-Umtali line at Dondo with Nyasaland (now Malawi). In 1938 a Cotton Export Board (Junta de Exportação de Algodão) was set up to promote cotton-growing by Africans, mainly in the northern part of the province, for export to Portugal. There appears to be no doubt that the introduction of an unaccustomed cash-crop, together with an organized system of road transport to bring it to market, brought about a 'general economic awakening' of northern Moçambique.[14] But the compulsion on Africans to grow cotton, coupled with the fixing of a buying price well below the world price, was to arouse much foreign criticism in the 1950s. These arrangements could not have been brought into full being but for the disappearance, with the expiry of its concession in 1929, of the Nyassa Company, which had inconspicuously failed to develop the northernmost part of the province over a forty-year period. It was to be followed into obscurity twelve years later, in 1941, by the somewhat more successful Moçambique Company based in Beira, once thought of as the vehicle by which disciples of Cecil Rhodes might attain British control over the whole of Moçambique.

Portuguese neutrality in the Second World War, made possible by the disappearance in 1919 of the German African colonies, ensured that Angola and Moçambique did not once again become the scene of military operations. Moreover, in the later years of the war, exports of tropical products from the Portuguese territories were not subjected to the bulk-purchasing operations of the Allied Combined Food Board, but left as an uncontrolled source of supply for neutral countries. The provinces appear to have prospered during the war years, and they shared in the post-war economic boom. Financial revenues were sufficient, and tax revenues buoyant enough, to justify the authorities in launching a series of development schemes.

The scale on which these schemes were launched and the confidence with which the government embarked on them were something new in Portuguese history. The confidence can be explained partly by twenty years of political and financial stability, partly by awareness that the outcome of the Second World War had removed, at long last, any European threat to the Portuguese African dominions. The character of the schemes, however, was not new: it combined the long-standing—and very necessary—attention to economic infrastructure with an even longer-standing aim that elsewhere in tropical Africa had never

[14] The phrase quoted is Irene S. van Dongen's; in David M. Abshire and Michael A. Samuels, eds., *Portuguese Africa: a handbook* (London and New York, 1969), p. 270.

been attempted—namely, the settlement of European peasant farmers on the land. By this means the Portuguese intend to permeate Angola and Moçambique with their particular form of European culture; the peasant settler is to be the leaven that leaveneth the whole African lump. To quote from the preamble to the second overseas development plan, published in 1958:

The state of peace in the Portuguese territories . . . is in itself an important contribution towards the solidity of the defence of the values we have sustained for centuries . . . our indestructible belief in the equality of the human species and . . . a conception of human democracy wholly alien to the idea of conflict, to the feeling of racial superiority or inferiority.

The Portuguese settler is carrying out a national mission that transcends the national self-interest, and this historic mission must be justified; the development plan for Angola in particular must be judged exclusively by its effects on white settlement.

This criterion [the preamble goes on] will not be understood by one who seeks to transform the African native into an abstract type of civilized man . . . For us . . . Africa is also our motherland and we wish to make the natives into Portuguese and not simply *civilizados*. We must therefore people Africa with Europeans who can assure the stability of our sovereignty and promote the 'portuguesation' of the native population.[15]

These views are seriously meant, for all that they represent only an uncontradicted minority (though perhaps a majority among the politically conscious) in Portugal itself; the African majority in the overseas territories is naturally not consulted. Leaving aside the possibility that Africans might not co-operate in being made into Portuguese, the question arises whether enough Portuguese settlers can ever be found to do the job. It is not enough to point to the vertiginous increase in the European population of Angola, which quadrupled between 1940 and 1960 and may now (1972) be more than a quarter of a million, compared with perhaps five million Africans. The European population of Moçambique likewise quadrupled between 1940 and 1960, but was still under 100,000 at the latter date, compared with an African population of nearly six and a half million. However, the Europeans in both provinces are predominantly town-dwellers, remote from the rural African: more than one-third of the European population of each province lives in the respective capitals, Luanda and Lourenço Marques, and some towns, such as Sá da Bandeira and Moçâmedes in Angola, have more white and *mestiço* inhabitants than Africans.

There are, it is true, a handful of rural settlements for whites, most of them heavily financed by government, that are pointed to with pride as offering opportunities for the settlers and Africans to work side by side. However, the best known of these, Cela in Angola, was designed to be entirely white, settlers being forbidden to employ African labour. This decision is traceable, as was noted earlier, to the influence of Vicente Ferreira, who shared his great predecessors' views on the undesirability of miscegenation—views nowadays so out of fashion that attempts are made to deny that they were ever held. Later settlements both in Angola and Moçambique have specifically provided for both immigrant Portuguese and Africans to serve as part-time labour on European

[15] Translation from: Portugal, Presidéncia do Conselho, *Relatório final preparatório do II plano do fomento (IX) Ultramar* (Lisbon, 1958), p. 12.

lands. The Cela project, moreover, now admits *mestiços;* and the original plan of 1952 for as many as two thousand subsistence (50-acre) holdings has been modified to allow for some holdings as big as 250 acres, employing hired labour recruited in Portugal.[16]

It is too early to say whether these schemes will turn out to be permanent successes, although they embody a determination and a care in planning that were conspicuously absent from earlier proposals of the kind. In any case, their extent has been too limited to have serious impact on the problem that the government sees itself facing in Africa, and the prospect of enlarging their scale significantly appears to be dim. Already there have been complaints of bad choice of colonists for the schemes, including some who cannot read and write; the colonizing power, it is pointed out, loses face when the black man has to write the white man's letters for him.[17] Insistence on farming as a principal employment for settlers from Portugal goes strongly against the grain for the majority of those wishing to emigrate, who, on reaching Brazil and Africa alike have traditionally chosen to work otherwise than on the land. Nearly a century ago a district governor of Moçâmedes scornfully noted the propensity for petty trade: 'Trading is here a vice; the aim of the majority is to fill up time without working, neglecting the advantages offered by tillage.' A modern official echoes him: 'The prime objective of every *civilizado* [in the district of Huíla] is to obtain a nest-egg and a connection, so as to devote himself to storekeeping, either as an employee or on his own account. Not because this business always brings evident profits, but because sometimes it is highly lucrative, and principally because it allows a life without physical effort.' The principal commodity sold to the African is said to be wine, which is in accordance with long-standing tradition.[18]

It seems out of the question that peasant agricultural settlement in Angola, let alone in Moçambique where climatic conditions are less favourable to white men, could ever be on a scale that would do much more than demonstrate its feasibility. It is true that emigrants are available in Portugal; as many as 100,000 have been leaving each year for the last decade (1961–70), nearly half of them for France. But the proportion going to the overseas provinces has been diminishing, even though Brazil has, temporarily at any rate, ceased to be a major recipient of Portuguese immigrants; and of the 12,000 or so who have been going to Angola and Moçambique annually, the majority stay in the towns. In many areas of the interior, 'the only props of the colonizing power's culture and civilization are the district officer and the missionary'.[19] It is hard to see how this situation can alter in the foreseeable future.

This does not mean that very considerable economic development has not taken place in both Angola and Moçambique since the Second World War. It does mean that a great number of Africans remain peripheral to the modern money economy, something that can be said, for that matter, of a substantial number of country people in Portugal itself. In neither instance is self-suf-

[16] Irene S. van Dongen in Abshire and Samuels, eds., *Portuguese Africa,* pp. 280–4.

[17] José Maria Gaspar, 'A colonização branca em Angola e Moçambique', in Junta das Investigações do Ultramar, *Colóquios de política ultramarina internacionalmente relevante* (Lisbon, 1958), pp. 42–53.

[18] Afonso Mendes, *A Huíla e Moçâmedes: considerações sobre o trabalho indigena* (Lisbon, 1958), pp. 34–35. [19] Gaspar, 'A colonização branca', pp. 42–53.

ficiency absolute: there is always something that has to be obtained from outside the local community and some surplus commodity, or service, to be exchanged for it. The subsistence economy differs in degree, not in kind, from the exchange economy. But in extent of dependence on the exchange economy, the peasant in Portugal and the tribesman in Portuguese Africa are comparable, each being far removed from the Portuguese governing class.

Portuguese critics have sometimes remarked of the official Overseas Development Plans, of which the first covered the years 1953–8 and the second the years 1959–64, that they overemphasized additions to economic infrastructure and did not invest enough in social development or in improvements to the native economy. It is hard to say how much there is in these criticisms. The plans did not cover the total of public expenditures, and in many instances they set maxima for expenditure that proved impossible of fulfilment. The first plan, for instance, allocated 235 million escudos for the extension of the northern Moçambique railroad towards Lake Nyasa; but by September 1957 nothing had been spent. By the same date, only one-eighth out of a 1-million-escudo allocation for land drainage and reclamation in Sâo Tomé–Príncipe had been spent. There has, in fact, been a chronic tendency—as so often in Portugal itself— for colonial public-works projects to fall behind schedule. In a way, this offers an insurance against over-sanguine budgeting, or against the tendency—which Portuguese critics have also pointed out—to ignore the possibility that changes in economic circumstances (for example, in the terms of trade) might prevent development plans from being accomplished. In fact, however, it seems that though budgeted improvements in infrastructure have not always been carried out on time, they have been carried out eventually. The northern railroad from Nacala, for instance, has now (1972) reached the border of Malawi, so providing that country with an alternative outport to Beira, which has frequently been congested in recent years. The resulting transit traffic may make the line profitable for the first time.

Another important rail link, completed in 1955, is the Limpopo branch of the Lourenço Marques system, which joins the Rhodesian railways at Malvernia, so providing another alternative to the Beira railway, particularly for Zambian copper. The Beira railway was itself bought from its British owners by the Portuguese government in 1949; in 1951 a convention between Great Britain and Portugal guaranteed the line's transit traffic in return for a Portuguese undertaking to make improvements in the port of Beira. In Angola the most significant railway development in recent years has been the extension of the Moçâmedes railway to Serpa Pinto, nearly 500 miles inland, and the construction of a branch line from it to serve the newly exploited haematite iron-ore workings at Cassinga, 400 miles from Moçâmedes. Yearly shipments of iron ore through that port, which was very substantially improved in the 1950s, are expected to reach more than 5 million tons; as late as 1966 the line carried less than 300,000 tons. Another huge iron-ore deposit is about to be exploited near Nacala, in northern Moçambique, by building a special railway line and export quay.

Apart from improvements in ports and railways, the most striking developments of infrastructure have been in hydro-electric power. Five hydro-electric plants have been completed in Angola since the Second World War; the largest of them is at Cambambe, on the Cuanza river at the head of navigation, near the market town of Dondo. It supplies electricity to the city of Luanda. A much larger scheme is planned to grow out of the existing Matala project on the middle Cunene, near the border with South-West Africa; this plant will ultimately have a capacity of 300,000 kilowatts, and the dams will irrigate over a million acres. These plans are being concerted with those of the government of South-West Africa. Similar international co-operation lies behind the huge Cabora Bassa scheme on the Zambezi in Moçambique, situated, incidentally, in an area handed over to Portugal by the British in 1891 to compensate Portugal for the seizure of the (supposedly gold-rich) plateau of Manica by agents of Cecil Rhodes's Chartered Company. Proponents look forward to the ultimate generation of 50,000 million kilowatt-hours a year, to the irrigation of over 3·5 million acres, and to making the Zambezi navigable all the year round from Tete to the Indian Ocean, about 400 miles. These prospects have been made possible because the Republic of South Africa will be the principal buyer of Cabora Bassa power. Hydro-electric and irrigation projects have already been built on the Revué and Limpopo rivers in Moçambique; the Limpopo Dam serves also as a bridge for the new rail link to Rhodesia, and irrigates the lands of the Limpopo agricultural settlement scheme.[20]

The most important new industrial developments to occur so far in Angola are the iron-ore mines of Cassinga and the discovery of petroleum, both on-shore and off-shore. On-shore, substantial oil reserves have been found near Luanda, and a refinery with a capacity of 1 million tons a year has been built. Even more important is the off-shore field of the tiny enclave of Cabinda, which by itself will produce twice Portugal's current oil needs. Oil and iron ore already rival coffee and diamonds as sources of export income, which now appears to be large enough to contribute substantially towards a favourable balance of payments—an achievement that has eluded Angola through most of its existence—and to relieve the dependence on coffee exports that has characterized the economy of the province since the Second World War. The chief agent, indeed, in the post-war economic transformation, and a wholly fortuitous one so far as Angola was concerned, was the development of the 'instant coffee' industry in the United States, which provided a huge new market for the hitherto cheap and despised *robusta* coffee in which the province specializes. By the 1960s, coffee had far outstripped diamonds as the most valuable single export, accounting for close to half the total. For the first time in its history, Angola appeared to have found a means of paying for the imported capital goods it needed for development; in only four of the fifteen years 1952–66 did the official accounts not show a favourable balance of external trade. The balance-of-payments situation is somewhat less favourable when 'invisibles' are taken into account, which explains why the Angolan escudo—formerly called the angolar—still stands at a varying but substantial discount from the metropolitan escudo on the free currency market.[21]

The currency situation in Moçambique remains similar—if anything rather worse—inasmuch as no money-making physical export comparable with coffee

---

[20] For a map of the Cabora Bassa plan and a full discussion of all these hydro-electric schemes, see David M. Abshire in Abshire and Samuels, eds., *Portuguese Africa*, pp. 301–3 and 311–13.

[21] There is a huge literature on the currency question. The most useful discussions in English are in the unpublished dissertation of de Medeiros Fernandes, already cited, and by Frank Brandenburg in Abshire and Samuels, eds., *Portuguese Africa*, pp. 238–52.

or iron ore has so far been found, and 'invisibles', mainly transit trade, earnings of migrant labour and tourist expenditures, continue to bulk large on the credit side of the provincial balance of payments. The Moçambique escudo likewise stands at a considerable discount from the metropolitan escudo on the free market, and various administrative devices have not, apparently, been able to solve the problem of currency transfer to continental Portugal. The declared ideal of a common currency for the whole 'escudo area' appears to be as far from effective realization as ever; it is maintained in principle only by rationing the supplies of metropolitan currency available to the provinces, and by imposing many months' delay on the settlement of their accounts.

These changes have had widely differing effects for the economies of Angola and Moçambique, viewed as wholes. The development of Angolan exports of coffee, about one-third of which is grown by Africans, and of cotton exports from Moçambique, virtually all of which are grown by Africans, has brought substantial numbers of country people into the exchange economy. The same is true of the export from Moçambique of cashew nuts, which are mostly gathered by Africans from trees growing wild, but are now being grown on European-owned plantations. The oil and iron-ore enterprises, on the other hand, are essentially European enclaves employing little African labour. It seems likely that the variety of comparatively minor industrial enterprises that has grown up, more particularly around Luanda, and the growth of 'service' industries that has gone along with it, have had more direct effect on the African population. Half a million people, or one-tenth of the total population of Angola, are now said to live in Luanda and its environs; Europeans account for rather less than one-third of these. Such an increase in urban living, much of it in hastily erected slums, is, of course, common to many African cities in the last quarter of a century. It means that Luanda is outdistancing Oporto as the second city of Greater Portugal. It means also that the capital city, not the peasant settlement, is likely to be the chief agent of Portuguesation among Africans. Lourenço Marques, by reason of its eccentric situation on the extreme southern border of Moçambique, is less well placed to perform this task, and it is anyhow growing far less fast than Luanda.

The influx of Africans into Luanda and other cities may suggest that traditional tribal links in Angola are beginning to break down. They have, of course, never existed in the Cape Verde Islands or in São Tomé–Príncipe. It seems possible also that within the past twenty years or so the exchange economy has at long last been able to recruit enough African labour more or less freely, so that the long-standing device of a compulsory labour contract for male Africans, reinforced by a hut tax, can be dispensed with. Compulsory labour has, of course, long been a target for missionary and other critics of Portuguese colonial administration. Criticism has tended to be levelled not so much at compulsion for public purposes (such as road-making) but at that for the benefit of planters and other private employers. This used to be common (and not only in Portuguese territories), but it was explicitly forbidden in the new Native Labour Code that was introduced in 1928; what many critics have doubted is whether the new Code was strictly, or at all, enforced. Obviously it is never easy for an unlettered African to insist on his rights against a European administrator, or for sympathizers to get a hearing for complaints against the administration under a dictatorship that censors the press. Even before Salazar, moreover, it was common ground among foreign critics that the letter of the law and its enforcement were two different things.

In 1960 the Portuguese government ratified the 1957 ILO Convention for the Abolition of Forced Labour, an act that was immediately followed by a complaint by Ghana, supported by the United Arab Republic, that Portugal continued to rely on forced labour as the pivot of its native policy, and that the ratification was only a subterfuge. The visiting commission, comprising experts from Switzerland, Uruguay and Senegal, that was appointed by the ILO to investigate the complaint, unanimously rejected the charge of bad faith; the changes in policy were, it declared, real. The commission made one comment, however, that points up, more clearly than most of the writing on the subject, the difficulty about establishing firm conclusions about the quality of administration in a primitive country: that in some cases, notably that of the Cassequel sugar plantations near Lobito, 'the bulk of the working force is at so backward a stage of development that the question whether the labour exacted from them is forced labour becomes virtually meaningless'. The lives of such people (the commission went on) 'are a series of conditioned reflexes which are less than human . . . An order is an order; a suggestion is indistinguishable from an order; and the inertia of ages maintains a social pattern in which people do what they are told to do because they have always done so.' [22]

Much the same, however, might be said of the masses in Portugal itself; they have always been separated from the government and the ruling class by a gulf of poverty and illiteracy. This was just as true under the liberal monarchy and the democratic republic as it was under Salazar; in 1915, for instance, the number of persons who might legally vote was less than half a million, one-tenth of the population. The earlier régimes allowed more freedom than did that of Salazar to the minority interested in politics; but the vast majority of the nation has always been completely outside political activity. Moreover, the absence until recently of industrial development in Portugal would have prevented the rise of strong trade unions, even had not the unions been deprived of political significance under the Salazar régime. [23]

The close analogies between the social structures of continental Portugal and Portuguese Africa seem to have escaped most foreign critics. In neither has there ever existed any force capable of defending the rights of the majority of poor citizens, white or black, against abuse or neglect by government. In these circumstances the effectiveness of laws, however wise and good they may appear to be in principle, cannot but be decidedly limited. This, presumably, is what the ILO commission meant to imply by its comment on the Cassequel sugar workers. There is no lack of enlightenment on paper, any more than there was in earlier colonial labour legislation that equally came under foreign criticism for insincerity. There is no necessary lack of good intentions on the part of government. But there is no external check on the conduct of bureaucrats in the field, no freely elected legislature that can question their behaviour, no independent judiciary, no uncensored press that can expose scandals and no inter-

---

[22] International Labour Office, *Report of the Commission appointed . . . to examine the complaint filed by the Government of Ghana concerning the observance by the Government of Portugal of the Abolition of Forced Labour Convention, 1957 (no. 105)*, March 1962, p. 378.

[23] One of the few foreign writers who have fully noted the class-bound character of Portuguese society is Frank E. Huggett, in *South of Lisbon* (London, 1960).

ested and sizeable public opinion to which appeal can be made. There is not even, for what it might be worth, a single political party with a mass following, as there was in fascist Italy and Nazi Germany, and as there is in the Soviet Union. Of course, this situation is the normal one of mankind through the ages; the Portuguese government and bureaucracy, regarded historically, are not exceptionally inhumane or irresponsive. Rather do they represent a survival that to many outside the Portuguese dominions appears an intolerable anachronism. Mutual want of sympathy is so great as to make mutual understanding out of the question; the Portuguese government and its critics are not talking the same language.

It is against this background that one has to consider what at first sight might appear to be a revolutionary economic and social change: the abolition, in September 1961, of the special status of non-assimilated Africans in the territories, the *indigenato*. This removed at a stroke the legal obligation to be contracted for labour service, formerly imposed on non-assimilated male Africans who could not show themselves to be already at work either on their own or another's account. (It has never been clear how, in the absence of an independent appeal tribunal, this demonstration could be made good.) What was not removed was the chief sanction behind the legal obligation—namely, the head tax on African males, which in February 1962 was extended to all male inhabitants between eighteen and sixty, along with females employed by the government. Moreover, the contract labour system was continued on a voluntary basis, in accordance with a new and (on paper) enlightened rural labour code. What is difficult, as the ILO inquiry of 1962 found, is to discover how much practical difference these legal changes have made.

It is likewise difficult to know what the real effect of the Angolan 'revolt' of 1961 and the corresponding movements in Moçambique and Portuguese Guinea, has been. Those events postdate the period of history with which this volume is concerned, and the time has not yet come when a full account of them can be written. Nevertheless, some comment on them by way of conclusion is possible.

The movements were made feasible by the fact that the frontiers between all three Portuguese territories and their neighbours did not correspond to ethnic boundaries between African tribes and were not physically closed. It was therefore possible for dissidents, unobserved by Portuguese authorities, to use neighbouring states as their bases of operations. The government in Luanda, for instance, was taken completely by surprise by the events of early 1961; the Salazar secret police (PIDE) had recently, for the first time, established an office there, but this had been done to watch for individual opponents of the régime, European, *mestiço* or African, not to forestall an organized African movement directed from without.

None of the various opposition groups has ever commanded a mass intertribal following. The Portuguese have, as they have for centuries, been able to recruit Africans to fight alongside the European garrisons. The failure of the majority of African tribes in the territories to make common cause with such insurgent tribes as the Bakongo in Angola or the Makonde and Nyanja in Moçambique has been patent. Even in Portuguese Guinea, the largest single tribe, the Fula, has sided with the administration. Hence the claim of opposition leaders like Holden Roberto, the late Amilcar Cabral and the late Eduardo

Mondlane to represent the Angolan, Guinean or Moçambiquan peoples is without foundation—indeed without meaning, because now none of these peoples can be said to exist as political entities.

With a possible exception for Portuguese Guinea, it may be said now that the opposition groups have nuisance value but no more. So long as the Portuguese remain resolved to hold on in Africa, they will be able to do so, short of intervention by a major power from outside. The cost will be heavy, but not prohibitive.[24]

The striking economic expansion that has occurred, particularly in Angola since 1961, is a measure of the insignificant direct effect of the African disturbances. Except in Guinea, it must be repeated, the areas affected by guerrilla activity have affected but a small proportion of Portuguese Africa. In fact, the guerrilla campaigns may even have provided a stimulus to Portuguese activity. Certainly cities, Luanda in particular, have grown enormously. Military needs in some areas have necessitated the construction of airfields, all-weather roads, repair shops and other facilities that are useful for civilian purposes. Angola, for instance, now also has one of the most extensive civil air networks in Africa. The rate of school building has been stepped up and the beginnings of a university system created in both Angola and Moçambique.

In regions subject to partisan attacks, the army has set up a series of fortified settlements known as *aldeamentos*. The Portuguese have tried to collect the dispersed rural populations into these centres and to provide them with schools, dispensaries and other facilities. The Portuguese have claimed that these settlements, particularly in northern Moçambique and the Bakongo districts of Angola, have been successful in reconciling the people to Portuguese rule and freeing them from terrorist pressure. The *aldeamentos* are, of course, run almost entirely by Africans, just as the army is predominantly African.

Talk about 'self-determination'—handing over Angola and Moçambique to African rulers—in the near future is tantamount to suggesting that the territories be economically and politically disintegrated. There are simply not enough educated, Portuguese-speaking Africans yet to run an Angolan or Moçambiquan state, or its exchange economy. There is no alternative to Portuguese as a lingua franca for government and business; indeed, no alternative written language at all.

One does not have to endorse Portuguese claims for their system of government, or swallow the *luso-tropical* theories of Gilberto Freyre, to acknowledge that in present circumstances—say, for the rest of the twentieth century—there is no both practicable and desirable alternative to Portuguese rule in Angola, Moçambique or the South Atlantic islands. This is partly the result of Portuguese backwardness, until very recently, in developing the territories economically, socially and perhaps above all educationally. Such a judgement says nothing, of course, about the form that future Portuguese rule—particularly the form of association between the metropolitan country and the overseas territories—should take. It does say that the anti-Portuguese resolutions passed in the United Nations Assembly in the past few years have been totally irresponsible, offering as they do no solution to the problem, if problem there be. The

---

[24] The recent discussion by Andrew Wilson Green in Abshire and Samuels, eds., *Portuguese Africa*, pp. 345–63, seems pretty near the mark.

Portuguese would claim that the problem has been largely cooked up for them by foreign influences, and there is more in this claim than most non-Portuguese who have looked at the question will admit. Objection to 'colonialism' *per se* has led a number of American writers in particular to take the claims of self-appointed insurgent leaders at face value and to suppose that Portuguese obstinacy alone deprives the African peoples of freedom and self-determination. The fact of Portuguese obstinacy is undoubted; but for it, the Portuguese dominion would have crumbled long ago. Its immediate disappearance, nevertheless, would result in political and economic chaos, out of which political and economic freedom would be very unlikely to emerge.

Postscript (February 1975)

This chapter was completed long before the Portuguese revolution of April 1974, when the Estado Novo of the late Dr Salazar, which had never enjoyed any substantial popular support, collapsed at a touch. It was followed by a precipitate and irresponsible abandonment of colonial rule everywhere, amid general applause abroad. The problems indicated in the last two paragraphs of the chapter remain unsolved. Angola and Moçambique may be able to do without rule from Lisbon, and even to set up governments dominated by the handfuls of Portuguese-speaking Africans. But they will not be able to sustain their present level of economic development unless they make it worth while for the white settlers and administrators to remain. The absence of strong race feeling in Portuguese Africa makes this at least a possibility; but one can only wait and see.

BIBLIOGRAPHY

Abshire, David M., and Michael A. Samuels, eds. *Portuguese Africa: a handbook*. London and New York, 1969.

Anstey, Roger. *Britain and the Congo in the nineteenth century*. Oxford, Clarendon Press, 1962.

Axelson, Eric. *Portugal and the scramble for Africa*. Johannesburg University Press, 1967.

Bloom, Murray Teigh. *The man who stole Portugal*. New York, 1966.

Corvo, João de Andrade. *Estudos sobre as províncias ultramarinas*. 4 vols. Lisbon, 1883–7.

Couceiro, Henrique de Paiva. *Angola: dois anos de govêrno, junho 1907–junho 1909*. 2nd ed. Lisbon, 1948.

Crowe, Sybil E. *The Berlin West African Conference, 1884–1885*. London, 1942.

Domingos da Cruz, Manuel. *A crise de Angola*. Lisbon, 1928.

Ennes, António. *Moçambique: relatório apresentado ao govêrno*. 3rd ed. Lisbon, 1946.

Fernandes, Roberto S. de Medeiros. 'Portugal and its overseas territories: economic structure and policies, 1950–1957'. Ph.D. dissertation, Harvard University, 1960.

Ferreira, Vicente. *Estudos ultramarinos*. 4 vols. Lisbon, 1953–5.

Freire de Andrade, Alfredo. *Relatórios de Moçambique*. 6 vols. Lourenço Marques, 1906–10.

Gaspar, José Maria. 'A colonização branca em Angola e Moçambique', in Junta das Investigações do Ultramar, *Colóquios de política ultramarina internacionalmente relevante*. Lisbon, 1958.

Hammond, Richard J. *Portugal and Africa, 1815–1910: a study in uneconomic imperialism*. Stanford University Press, 1966.

Huggett, Frank E. *South of Lisbon*. London, 1960.

International Labour Office. *Report of the Commission appointed . . . to examine the complaint filed by the Government of Ghana concerning the observance by the Government of Portugal of the Abolition of Forced Labour Convention, 1957 (no. 105)*, Geneva, March 1962.

Kisch, Sir Cecil H. *The Portuguese bank-note case*. London, 1932.

Leal, Francisco Pinto da Cunha. *Caligula em Angola*. Lisbon, 1924.

Subsídios para o estudo do problema do crédito em Angola. Lisbon, 1930.

Lobato, Alexandre. *Colonização senhorial da Zambézia e outros estudos*. Lisbon, 1962.

Louis, William Roger. *Ruanda-Urundi, 1881–1919*. Oxford, Clarendon Press, 1963.

Lyne, Robert Nunez. *Mozambique: its agricultural development*. London, 1913.

Mendes, Afonso. *A Huíla e Moçámedes: considerações sobre o trabalho indigena*. Lisbon, 1958.

Moniz, Egas. *Um ano de política*. Lisbon, 1919.

Neumark, S. Daniel. *Foreign trade and economic development in Africa*. Food Research Institute, Stanford University, 1964.

Norton de Matos, José Mendes Ribeiro. *Memórias e trabalhos da minha vida*. Lisbon, 1944.

Pinheiro Chagas, Manuel. *As colónias Portuguesas no seculo XIX*. Lisbon, 1890.

Portugal. Presidencia do Conselho. *Relatório final preparatório do II plano do formento (IX) Ultramar*. Lisbon, 1958.

Sá da Bandeira, Bernardo de Sá Nogueira de Figueiredo, Marquez de. *O trabalho rural africano e a administração colonial*. Lisbon, 1873.

Saldanha, Eduardo d'Almeida. *O Sul de Save*. Lisbon, 1928.

Sena Sugar Estates, Ltd. *Moçambique e o problema açucareiro*. Lisbon, 1945.

Statham, J. C. B. *Angola: a coming colony*. Edinburgh, 1922.

U.S. Department of the Army. *Area handbook for Angola,* prepared by Alison Butler Herrick and others. Pamphlet no. 550-59. Washington, 1967.

Area handbook for Mozambique, prepared by Alison Butler Herrick and others. Pamphlet no. 550-64. Washington, 1969.

Vilhena, Ernesto de. *Questões coloniaes: discursos e artigos*. 2 vols. Lisbon, 1910.

Walter, Jaime. *Honório Pereira Barreto*. Bissau, 1947.

PART THREE

ECONOMIC MAINSTAYS

ECONOMIC INITIATIVE AND AFRICAN CASH FARMING: PRE-COLONIAL ORIGINS AND EARLY COLONIAL DEVELOPMENTS

by •

JAN S. HOGENDORN

The economic and social antecedents to the emergence of African cash farming have received much notice in recent literature. Attention has been focused also on the development during the early colonial era of new cash-crops by African farmers. The present essay utilizes these two areas of discussion to survey the link between pre-colonial African agriculture and its great growth, unexpectedly sudden to many contemporary observers, during the early years of European colonization.

Full realization that such a link existed was long delayed. Many observers used to argue that Africans were indifferent to material progress, lazy, shiftless and inefficient, with a very much higher preference for leisure than for consumer goods. In the related area of African reactions to changing market prices, many writers have taken the position that Africans respond unpredictably to price changes. Sometimes it is said that there is no response at all. At other times the argument is made that when prices rise, production falls, just as higher wages lead in perverse fashion to fewer hours worked. These speculations have reached the realm of economic theory in the writings of economists who postulate a backward-bending supply curve for labour as typical of the African environment.

By way of contrast, this essay takes the opposing view: that the pre-colonial period furnishes much evidence of economic behaviour by African farmers similar to their behaviour after colonization gave ready access to world markets; and further, that in this process rational economic response to the market incentives of supply and demand can be seen to operate. Because this line of reasoning can be abused, however, a disclaimer is in order. We do not mean to imply that such rationality was complete nor that it was the sole determining factor. Paralleling a recent study of the backward-bending supply curve, the argument is merely that African economic behavior may well have changed much less over time than has often been thought. We say nothing about all Africans being entirely rational either before colonial rule or now, any more than all Africans or all Europeans are entirely motivated by economic rationality.[1]

The essay is subject to four limitations. First, it is concerned solely with the output and trade of agricultural commodities—defined broadly, however, to include arboriculture, and thus including the oil-palm, kola, cocoa and so on. Second, it will not consider the institution of plantation agriculture. Third,

[1] Marvin P. Miracle and Bruce Fetter, 'Two causal models of African economic conduct: a reply', *Economic Development and Cultural Change*, Oct. 1972, **21**, no. 1, p. 171.

there is a limited geographical frame of reference, with attention directed primarily to sub-Saharan Africa exclusive of areas where extensive white settlement was present. Finally, there is a temporal limitation. In order to focus the discussion on the *transition* between the pre-colonial and the early colonial periods, the evidence presented will in the main refer to what Polly Hill has called the 'pre-lorry age', with the approximate terminal date being the outbreak of the First World War in 1914.

Economic initiative in the pre-colonial period: evidence from agriculture

Evidence of a desire for economic improvement among African cultivators in the pre-colonial era is constantly accumulating as area and crop studies proliferate. The case that African farmers have for many centuries and in many geographical locations been alert to improve their welfare is now very strong.

The first indications of such initiative in agriculture owe their existence to the botanical sciences. The highly developed, often controversial literature that discusses the geographical origins of plants makes it clear that the majority of food- and cash-crops grown today in Africa were introduced from abroad and had spread widely before the onset of colonial rule. This phenomenon, primarily non-market in nature, has received much notice among anthropologists and historians as well as botanists. However, it is of equal significance for the welfare economist because it demonstrates a willingness among both farmers and consumers to alter traditional patterns of behaviour when changes are manifestly advantageous. Given the tenacity with which consumers everywhere cling to their traditional foodstuffs, this process by itself is compelling evidence of pre-colonial initiative in agriculture.

All too little is known about the conditions under which new crops were introduced, and when and where they spread. Enough is known, however, to suggest some economic causes and effects of their adoption. Several crops appear to have had an African origin or to have been introduced long before the birth of Christ (sorghum, pearl millet, kola, the oil-palm). The source of other plants was apparently Asia, with arrival in Africa before the thirteenth or fourteenth century (yam, coco-yam, banana). Neither group will be discussed here.

After 1492, other plants—manioc, the sweet potato, maize and ground-nuts, among others—were introduced from the Americas, and these require closer attention. Although the question is debatable, it appears that Portuguese traders searching for more convenient foods to feed slaves awaiting shipment were responsible for the initial introduction. By the seventeenth century, shipment of these crops from Brazil to Africa was commonplace. Any excess supplies could be traded to Africans, and to save on transport costs the new foods could be planted in coastal areas. No doubt, as Pierre de Schlippe notes, the first varieties penetrating into the interior were degenerate. For this reason, the introduction of suitable strains was more significant than the first appearance of a plant.

Consider the rapidity with which the spread occurred. Manioc was introduced successfully around the mouth of the Congo river soon after the first contacts with the Portuguese, and several tribes in the region have traditions that it was grown in the 1600s. It was well established along the Guinea coast and in the Gambia area by the end of the eighteenth century. By that time it had also begun to penetrate East Africa, and by the 1850s occupied most of its present range. Ground-nuts, too, were commonly encountered through much of the continent within about two centuries of their introduction. Maize, the most widely distributed food plant in Africa today, was carried to both the east and the west coasts during the early days of the slave-trade. It had been seen 200 miles up the Niger in 1535, in the Congo in 1548 and in East Africa by 1597. Sweet potatoes also had crossed the Atlantic and were well established in the Congo and East Africa, particularly in Uganda, by the time the Europeans arrived.

Many different agents played their part in spreading the American plants. These included long-distance traders dealing in goods of relatively small bulk and high value, warriors and raiders on the march, slave-traders leading their victims to the sea and also humble villagers in contact with neighbouring communities. Migrant peoples were apt to take their plants with them when they moved. Stronger groups may have imposed new crops by coercion on their neighbours, though coercion probably played a less important part in the spread of American varieties than of earlier plants. Even more important in the diffusion of imported plants was the web of long-distance trade routes for ivory and slaves. Jan Vansina has shown that tribes in Central Africa not located near these routes were late in adopting the new crops, and Marvin Miracle has called attention to the role of Arab traders in their diffusion.

For our purposes, however, the most interesting question is why the new plants were accepted so widely. Most of the evidence points to normal economic calculations of benefit exceeding cost, with African farmers taking the initiative to change cropping patterns because their economic welfare would be improved thereby. Among the advantages offered were the addition of variety to the diet, a reduction in the cost of cultivation and a reduced dependence on any single crop, which lessened the risk of crop failure and gave greater protection against famine. Sometimes a new plant possessed particularly favourable attributes. Maize, for example, often gives far more calories per acre than other cereal crops. Manioc can be harvested throughout the year with little variation in output and is resistant to drought and locusts. It can also be cultivated more easily under conditions of deforestation than its competitor, millet, and yields are often higher than for other starchy staples.

The migratory process was made easier because the climate of much of tropical Africa is similar to that of Brazil, the native haunt of most of the American plants. Further, both maize and manioc are sufficiently similar in cultivation to the traditional yam. Therefore difficult problems of agricultural technique did not tend to arise. But these considerations do not alter the conclusion that the economic initiative shown by African peasant producers in the colonial period had widespread pre-colonial antecedents in the adoption of new crops from outside the continent.

The development of pre-colonial African agriculture also offers evidence of initiative and a desire for improved welfare in other ways. For instance, there was trade in agricultural commodities. Over the years, many authorities have written as if there were very little of such trade; historians have emphasized instead the traffic in slaves, gold and other metals, ivory, cowries, salt and the like. This traffic did indeed overshadow the contemporary commerce in agricultural products, probably in terms of volume as well as value. However, the rapidly expanding literature on early African economies makes clear the wide extent of trade in agricultural commodities in the pre-colonial period. In an essay of this scope, it is possible to indicate only something of the scale of the relatively sophisticated international and inter-regional exchange as well as the purely local commerce in these goods.

In general, *local* trade in foodstuffs seems to have been the most common form of exchange in Africa, although the area of supply for any particular market was usually limited to the distance a producer was willing to walk. Many farm commodities were traded in highly segmented markets that met periodically, with little interconnection and with participation restricted to local farmers and consumers.

The evidence for pre-colonial local trade in agricultural commodities is much the most impressive and comprehensive for West Africa. It is difficult to identify any West African peoples who in the mid-nineteenth century were so wedded to subsistence that they did not engage in local marketing. Local trade was carried on even where markets, properly speaking, were rare or absent, as in parts of the Nigerian plateau, in some areas of Liberia and in the south-western Ivory Coast.

Of Central and East Africa it is commonly said by contrast that local trade in agricultural commodities, as well as other economic activity, was at a far lower level than in West Africa. As William Barber puts it for the Rhodesias, in terms applicable to much of the east coast as well:

Broadly speaking, the indigenous economic structure . . . was much less differentiated than the one that had developed in parts of West Africa in pre-colonial days. Few of the tribal peoples . . . had participated in substantial exchange activity.[2]

The question why the East and Central African economic structure should have been more closed, more self-contained and more centred on the family group as the basic producing unit than that of West Africa remains highly debatable. The suggested causes include geographical, ecological, cultural, demographic and ethnic differences, as well as the greater political diversity that prevailed in that part of the continent and made household sufficiency desirable. Settled agriculture appears to have had a longer history of continuity in West Africa. The commercial contacts between West Africa and the Mediterranean area were more substantial and less intermittent than those of East and Central Africa. Some authors have called attention also to the cultural emphasis on cattle-owning among a good number of East and Central African tribes (for example, the Masai, the Nandi, the Turkana of Kenya and the Hima aristocracies of Uganda), an emphasis that relegated commercial agriculture to a minor role. Even among the Ganda of Lake Victoria, in many ways an innovating group, a cattle-cum-slave ethos had serious detrimental effects on trade.

Some tribes, such as the Kikuyu, do not fit this pattern, and the number of exceptions is steadily increasing as research progresses on the economic patterns prevailing in East and Central Africa. Even so, when later in this essay we come to concentrate on the economic initiative of African farmers in the

---

[2] William J. Barber, 'The movement into the world economy', in *Economic transition in Africa*, Melville J. Herskovits and Mitchell Harwitz, eds. (Evanston, Northwestern University Press, 1964), pp. 309–10.

early colonial period, we shall find that large-scale entrepreneurial response was clearly more pronounced in West Africa.

As distinct from local trade, pre-colonial inter-regional and international trade was subject to serious cost constraints. The theorems of location economics ensure that before the arrival of wheeled transport, only non-food items of high value in relation to their weight would be likely to stand the cost of transport by primitive methods—by canoe or on the heads of porters. (Even when slave-labour provided the transport services, such labour would have positive opportunity costs, because of the possibility of overseas sale.)

This was not always the case, however. When famine raised food prices to a sufficiently high threshold, bulky foodstuffs could stand the cost of long-distance transport. Luxuries or specialities, such as edible palm-oil in the Sudan zone, might also command a price high enough to overcome the barrier. Some areas of specialized production imported large quantities of foodstuffs (the Niger Delta, Timbuktu, Djenne) because of geographical factors; other areas exported surplus staples as standard practice when market prices were sufficiently attractive (the trade of Mali, capital of the Mali empire, with Djenne and Timbuktu; exports of yams from the Nigerian rivers to feed the human cargo of the slave-ships; the thriving traffic in millet, rice, manioc, groundnuts, shea butter and assorted vegetables to intra-Saharan oases and tribes along the major trade routes). Finally, foodstuffs also entered long-distance trade by means of local sale to members of caravans carrying slaves, ivory, kola and so on.

More typically, only a few specialized commodities (kola, cotton products, tobacco and coffee beans) had the requisite high value/weight ratio that enabled them to overcome the barrier of high inter-regional transport costs. By the eighteenth century, the kola-nut trade from Ashanti and the hinterlands of the Ivory Coast and Liberia was a large, highly developed commercial system involving thousands of merchants using caravans, credit and subsidiary dealers. This commerce from Ashanti is discussed in detail later in the essay. Trade in cotton textiles was pervasive also, with centres of cotton-growing and cloth production in the area of Kano and in Southern Nigeria. On the eve of colonial rule, Kano cottons were said to clothe two-thirds of the population in the Western Sudan. There were West African centres of inter-regional trade in tobacco (Katsina, Timbuktu and elsewhere), while in East Africa both Ukutu and Ankole tobacco was traded at long distance. Coffee beans produced in Bunyoro, Bukoba and Buganda also entered long-distance trade, as did cottons from near Lake Rukwa.

International trade in agricultural commodities, defined here as either intercontinental or trans-Saharan commerce, began at a very early date. The first such contacts probably involved incense exports from Somaliland (Punt) to Egypt about 3000 B.C. One source dating from classical antiquity, the *Periplus of the Erythraean Sea* (A.D. 60) notes exports of spice and frankincense from Somaliland, and coconut oil from Azania (the ancient name for the coastline further south). When the Portuguese arrived on the east coast, they found some trade in agricultural goods still continuing. Gums and palm products continued to be the chief east-coast agricultural exports well into the nineteenth century. The dry highlands were the world's most important source of gum copal, used as a base in varnish and lacquer preparation. But operations were on a small scale and no match either for the slave- and ivory-trade or for the economic activity in West Africa.

Doubtless far greater in amount was the commerce that flourished on the west coast from the fifteenth century. In return for goods such as woollen cloth, iron pots, weapons and jewellery, sent south by the Europeans in the first hundred years of trading contact are found various peppers, dyewoods, palm-oil, gums and cotton among the items exported in exchange by African traders. From the southern coast of West Africa, malaguetta and Benin peppers were exported from the first, and were the earliest staple commodities of overseas commerce. The 'Grain Coast' is said to have received its name from the granular nature of the spices involved. The original Portuguese monopoly on the coastal pepper trade was very short-lived—West African peppercorns were being shipped to England in English ships as early as 1553, with the French active in the trade even earlier. Even though it was soon surpassed by the traffic in slaves and ivory, pepper was originally the most prominent item exported from Benin. However, this promising start was cut short by the competition of pepper shipped from the Far East. There was also a less important trade in dyewoods, the extracted dyes of which were used in the textile industry, and in gums, which were utilized in printing and finishing textiles. Much of the world gum supply was obtained from the Mauritanian forests north of the Senegal until demand fell off in the nineteenth century. An embryo cotton trade also sprang up at an early date, with the first consignment of West African cotton cloth taken from Benin to England in 1558.

With the demand for raw materials growing in Europe, new forms of pre-colonial trade in agricultural commodities emerged. By the mid-nineteenth century, much of the west coast, especially the Oil Rivers area in what is now Nigeria, was already exporting large quantities of cotton for overseas export, while ground-nuts were being produced by peasants in uncolonized territory and then shipped from the European stations in both Senegal and the Gambia. These products are considered more fully later in this essay.

All the while the flourishing trans-Saharan trade was bringing high-value, low-bulk products by caravan from Europe to the great markets of the Sudan zone along three main routes, with gums, kola-nuts, cotton cloth, millet and shea butter representing agriculture among the many exports that went north towards the Barbary states as the *quid pro quo*.

As the colonial era approached, therefore, sub-Saharan Africa had already evidenced a substantial degree of economic initiative in peasant production. These pre-colonial origins make it far more clear why an 'economic revolution' in smallholder agriculture could take place when colonial Africa found itself fully exposed to the markets of the world. These origins also explain why Colin Newbury has suggested that the 'revolution' had already occurred in West Africa as long ago as the period 1820–50, when commodity exports had risen six times or more.

A model of the expanded production of cash-crops in the early colonial period

A familiar economic model, the 'vent for surplus', is useful in analysing the re-action of African farmers to the expanded opportunities for international trade under the colonial régimes. An early version of this model was mentioned by Adam Smith in his *Wealth of nations* of 1776. It has lately received wide attention in the works of Professor Hla Myint of the London School of Economics and a growing number of other scholars.[3] In Myint's view many traditional societies before the opening of trade had substantial underemployment of both land and labour. The introduction of new transportation facilities and trade goods provided both the means and the incentive to bring the under-utilized land and labour into the production of agricultural export goods. Yet at the same time there was little if any diminution of the production of subsistence foodstuffs. The export production and the trade goods were a net increment to production and consumption (exchanged, in essence, for leisure), with the world market providing, in the phrase coined by John Start Mill, a 'vent for surplus'. The model as it applies in African agriculture includes these elements:

(A) An area isolated from international markets by high transport costs, both internal and external, has a potential surplus capacity for production owing to the existence of underemployed factors of production.

(B) The major determinant of the capacity of the area for export is its population density. With land relatively more abundant than labour, it is the supply of labour that becomes the major constraining factor on potential exports when trade opens. Furthermore, an expansion of exports can occur without the necessity for reducing domestic food production. An economy that grows by shifting resources from subsistence food production to some other product clearly faces problems of reallocation. But the Myint version of the vent-for-surplus model presupposes that local food output can stay at former levels because the new exports are the result of the *surplus* of land and labour. The entry into international trade will entail far less risk where an area continues to be self-sufficient in food output.

(C) An essential function of international trade is to provide the effective demand for exports, and this demand is the catalyst that allows the surplus resources to be utilized. As an adjunct to the critical provision of effective demand from abroad, various internal changes, such as improved transport and communications, may be spurred by the onset of trade, thus tending to accelerate the process. As demand grows, there is a stimulus for improved transport facilities, not only internally within an area but in the handling of cargoes at the ports and in the quantity and quality of ocean freight as well. The profit expected from faster commercial decisions gives an impetus for improved communications. These combine with demand increases to promote the development of trade.

(D) Production for export that is carried on by the indigenous population of the newly opened area will be very much stimulated (and perhaps will not take place otherwise) by the availability of manufactured trade goods from abroad. The proceeds of an export trade will be of use to a near-subsistence economy only if there is the opportunity to acquire products hitherto scarce or unobtainable. This desire for imported goods will combine with the new demand for exports of primary products to increase the level of trade.

(E) Myint makes the point that indigenous capital formation, at a low level initially, will not alter to any great degree as trade develops. Here the original

---

[3] Hla Myint, *Economic theory and the underdeveloped countries* (London, 1971). See in particular ch. 5, a reprint of Myint's well-known *Economic Journal* article of 1958.

model is modified by the argument that capital formation, when defined to include direct investment in agriculture and working capital, did play a distinct role in the early colonial expansion of African agricultural exports.

(F) Also not emphasized by Myint was the role of colonial governments in stimulating trade. Money taxes, propaganda, compulsion, agricultural research and extension services were all utilized with varying effect.

(G) Finally, not predicted by Myint but central in the context of this essay, is the emergence of indigenous entrepreneurial ability in a wide variety of circumstances. These include entrepreneurship in trade, where domestic trading networks were redirected to conform with overseas trade, and in production, where new combinations of land and labour were undertaken and new production decisions made. The skills of farmers and traders in the period before 1914, in combination with the other elements of the model, were an essential factor in delimiting the path of African agricultural development.

Throughout the remainder of my discussion, this modified Myint vent-for-surplus model is the vehicle used to illustrate the experience of peasant production of goods with an overseas demand during the early years of the colonial period.

Items (A) and (B) of the model refer to surplus capacity at the beginning of the colonial period, with labour the major constraining factor on the potential for export. This state of affairs seems hardly to be doubted for most of the period of time and geographical area covered. Evidence of a land surplus can be deduced from a number of agricultural practices reported by observers. Shifting cultivation with 'bush fallowing', very widespread in Africa, is one such example. William Allan and Ester Boserup have pointed out the direct relation between low population density and the use of extensive methods of cultivation. Another indication of a surplus can be found in the communal land-tenure systems of Africa, with the relative rarity of individual land ownership associated by some authors with the abundance of land in relation to labour. Surplus labour must have been generated by the decline of warfare after the colonial pacification, which released manpower on a large scale from the need to serve in military levies—whether the large seasonal armies of strong central governments or the *ad hoc* bands raised for village defence. This view is reinforced by the prevalence of women as cultivators of food in the traditional economy. As women could often produce enough food crops for family needs, men were freed for a wide variety of non-economic activity (administration of justice, religious pursuits, tribal governance and so on). There was little to be gained from employing men in large-scale food cultivation. The surplus so obtained could not be sold as long as market size was limited by transport costs, and storage was equally difficult and high in cost.

Further evidence on the question of a surplus of land and labour is found in the field of subsistence output. Where labour is abundant relative to land, the average landholding may be so small as to allow little production over the margin essential for subsistence. But, quite the reverse, in sub-Saharan Africa a remarkable expansion in the output of cash-crops for export took place early in the colonial period *without* a large-scale reduction in the output of subsistence crops. There is a high risk of crop failure in much of Africa, combined with poor transport facilities. Even today, over most of sub-Saharan Africa, farmers try to grow their own basic food supply. This was even more true in the early colonial period, where great increases in exports of cotton, cocoa, ground-nuts, palm products and so on, were generated without causing a 'food deficit', so-called by Andrew Kamarck.

Finally, a surplus of land and labour with labour the major constraining factor is suggested by the very low population densities occurring through most of tropical Africa at the present time (following a half-century or more of population growth in most areas). With a few exceptions, such as Nigeria, Ghana, Rwanda, Burundi and elsewhere around the East African lakes, densities do not approach those found in the Far East. Some authorities suggest that a portion of these surpluses remains to be utilized in production, as when they report a continuing high elasticity of supply for foodstuffs.

Item (C) of the model postulates a new demand from the outside world impinging on the indigenous economy. For tropical Africa the century preceding the First World War was the period during which new effective demand became apparent. The four most important commodities involved were palm-oil, cotton, ground-nuts and cocoa, all of which are considered below.

The first manifestations appeared early in the nineteenth century, with initial impact on palm-oil production.

With the increasing population at the time of the industrial revolution in Britain came changes in social customs and industrial requirements. As British people began to take washing seriously, the demand for soap rose considerably, and palm oil was the chief constituent in its manufacture. The substitution of metal for wooden machinery and the development of railways caused a steep rise in the use of oil as a lubricant. The existing sources of animal fats were not only inadequate, but sometimes unsuitable. West African palm oil was found to satisfy these needs.[4]

In the 1830s, candles came to be made of palm-oil and its use for edible purposes in the kitchen expanded rapidly. Before the growth of the petroleum industry, thousands of tons of palm-oil were used to lubricate the wheels of railway carriages. (In the United Kingdom alone, more than 13,000 tons were used for this purpose in 1865.) British demand grew slowly at first, with imports rising above 1,000 tons by 1810. With the aid of a substantial duty reduction in 1817, they passed 5,000 tons in 1821, reached the 10,000 mark in 1830, 20,000 in 1842, 30,000 in 1851 and 40,000 by 1855. Elsewhere in Europe, large increases of population concurrent with and following the industrialization process added to the growing demand for oils. From the 1850s on, however, the discovery of large petroleum deposits in America, the establishment of the oil-seed industry in India and elsewhere in Asia, the development of the tallow trade in Australia and Europe, all served to cause a long-term fall in prices from an average of £43·6 per ton in 1856–60 to £20·4 in 1886–90. But this was somewhat offset by the long-term decline in ocean freight and by the discovery of palm-kernel oil, obtained through crushing the kernels of the oil-palm. Unlike the palm-oil itself, palm-kernel oil took far longer to spoil, and thus became a useful substitute for animal oleo in the manufacture of margarine. Even palm-oil underwent a resurgence of demand when the tin-plate and canning industries arose toward the end of the century, because it was the best agent at the time for fusing tin and other metals.

[4] K. Onwuka Dike, *Trade and politics in the Niger Delta, 1830–1885* (Oxford, Clarendon Press, 1956), pp. 49–50. Soap in particular was needed because of the dirty conditions in industry.

Ground-nuts, too, shared in the new demand for oils and fats. The original demand arose in France, where in the 1830s the nuts were being crushed commercially for their oil. This was preferred to palm-oil as a base in soap-making and was used for table or cooking purposes as a substitute for higher-priced olive oil. The Gambia began exporting nuts commercially in 1834, with exports reaching 671 tons in 1837. In the 1840s, Gambian exports were in the thousands of tons, reaching 12,000 tons by 1851. For a time, 1836–40, a large share of Gambian output was shipped to the United States for human consumption (about three-quarters by value in 1838 and 1839); but this commerce was much reduced by the U.S. Tariff Act of 1842, which curtailed imports of foreign nuts. Shipments from Senegal were initiated in 1840, with French tariff policy playing a part in the increased demand. Influential olive-oil producers had long benefited from duties on substitute fats and oils, which duties were substantially reduced in 1840. Continuing high demand in France led to exports from Senegal of 65,000 tons by 1894, in comparison with 3,000 tons in 1853, less than 9,000 tons in 1870, 34,000 in 1881 and 45,000 in 1885. Gambian exports, also largely to France, were in the vicinity of 15,000 or 20,000 tons during the last quarter of the century.

The discovery of margarine gave a sudden boost to ground-nut demand. By 1900, two Dutch companies, Anton Jurgens and Van den Bergh (today merged in the Unilever combine), had captured most of the margarine market in Germany, the Low Countries and Britain. The trade had been dependent for a long while on oleo, an extract of animal fat. As a result of higher personal incomes and increasing public acceptance, consumption of margarine more than doubled in Britain from 1906 to 1913, and was up by 250 per cent in Germany from 1906 to 1914. An effect of this was that oleo prices rose dramatically (£18 per ton at Rotterdam in 1906, £62 in 1912). The prices of several other fats and oils rose comparably during the period, focusing attention on the ground-nut. At £11 per ton c.i.f. in 1906 and still at only about £13 in 1912, the nuts were strongly competitive. The fact that ground-nut oil is a liquid at room temperature (the solidifying process called hydrogenation was not perfected until the mid-1920s), kept demand limited. Even so, margarine could include up to 20 or 30 per cent ground-nut oil, which resulted in a boom for this article. Most of the new demand came initially from Germany, where crushing plants in the Hamburg-Bremen area supplied margarine factories in that country, the Netherlands and Britain. These events, which are discussed below, were primarily responsible for bringing Northern Nigeria into ground-nut production.

The new demand for African cotton, unlike that for oil, arose because of difficulties with the traditional sources of supply. Britain's largest manufacturing enterprise in the nineteenth century was textiles, and the looms of Lancashire depended for the most part on New World supplies. But the cotton belt of the United States had failed to supply sufficient quantities of fibre on two occasions: first, during the American Civil War of 1861–5, and second, during the 1890s, when the boll-weevil plague infested the American crop. The stimulus of high prices led to plans for growing cotton in West Africa, and by 1868–70 an annual average of over 1 million pounds was being imported to England, mainly from Lagos. Although this first spurt receded when American production recovered, the boll-weevil epidemic brought renewed study of African production possibilities. The influential British Cotton Growing Association

(BCGA), founded in Manchester in 1902, lobbied industriously to encourage cotton production in Africa, particularly in Northern Nigeria and Uganda. The new demand generated a rapid increase in output in both areas, particularly in Uganda, where, just after the end of the First World War, output of ginned cotton had reached almost 20,000 tons—a much higher level than anywhere else in Africa.

The new demand for cocoa was more prosaic in origin and slow in development. Growing personal incomes in Europe, the Victorian breakfast, the 'sweet tooth' and improved processing techniques were all involved. Mechanical presses for processing the raw material were not patented until 1828. High import duties kept demand low in Britain until they were reduced in 1853. The highly popular milk chocolate was not introduced until 1876 (in Switzerland). But in the two decades before 1914, production swelled in response to demand, the main impact being in the Gold Coast (output over 50,000 tons in 1913) and in Western Nigeria (about 5,000 tons in 1914). By comparison, pre-war output in the rest of Africa was small.

These were the most evident examples of the new demand. Other commodities were involved as well, such as rubber, tobacco, coffee, timber, tea, rice, shea butter, benniseed, sisal, cloves and so on; but among African-produced export crops in the period of time considered, the four discussed above were pre-eminent.

The Myint model predicts that various internal changes will occur as a result of the new demand from abroad. In Africa, no such change was more important than the construction of railways and the improvement of ports early in the colonial period. Before the era of the railway, easy transport in sub-Saharan Africa was very much the corollary of navigable waterways. Inland areas without this access were often entirely without roads suitable for wheeled vehicles. In 1907, for example, in all of the Gold Coast only 32 miles were deemed 'motorable', and only 54 miles were thought so in Southern Nigeria. There were indeed passable roads in much of the Sudan zone north of the forest belt and in some parts of East Africa; but the tsetse-fly strictly curtailed the use of draught animals in many coastal regions, and the rainy season would bring impassable stretches and unfordable streams.

A number of waterways were open to cargo-carrying canoes, obviating the difficulties noted above. Especially on the west coast the Oil Rivers and the associated lagoons, the Niger and Benue, the Senegal and the Gambia, had been used for centuries as arteries of commerce. On the other hand, the usefulness of the Congo river and its great tributaries was much diminished by the extensive rapids and falls along its course. Furthermore, some coastal and inland water routes passable in the eighteenth and early nineteenth centuries had become unusable by the colonial period because of silt or other causes.

Away from the canoe traffic, costs of transport were far too high to make the export of most products economic. In dense forest where the pack-donkey could not survive because of tsetse-borne trypanosomiasis and other animal diseases, head-loading was required, with consequent ballooning of costs. A familiar estimate is that porterage of cargo equivalent to that which could be carried by one railway train would have taken more than twenty times as long as the train, would have involved 15,000 to 20,000 porters and would have cost an additional five to ten times as much. Head-loading inland from Mombasa to the Uganda region incurred costs between £100 and £300 per ton. The problem of cost must have been considerably exacerbated whenever the colonial authorities suppressed slavery, because in earlier times a large proportion of the porters in both East and West Africa were slaves. (S. D. Neumark argues that only after the abolition of slavery was the high cost of porterage revealed. However, the possibility of selling slaves to the trans-Atlantic traders must have meant that the cost of keeping them as porters was appreciated.)

The result was that bulky items could not be shipped profitably any great distance, thus precluding the development of agricultural exports over great stretches of the continent. This in turn led to concentration on those commodities that could stand the transport costs, primarily what Gray and Birmingham have called 'wasting assets': items such as ivory, slaves and, especially, valuable minerals. When the new demand for oils, cotton, cocoa and more minor crops began to make itself felt in the nineteenth century, it became clear that railways were a necessity for commercial expansion.

Originally it was thought that the lure of profit would lead to extensive private railway building, as was happening in Britain, Canada, the United States and other more developed areas. The chartered British companies, the French land concessionary companies and private firms were expected to finance and build lines on their own initiative. However,

well before 1914 the consequences were economically disappointing and morally disturbing. No new Rand was discovered, investors showed marked reluctance to risk their capital, and colonial governments were too poor and inexperienced to undertake essential public works. Clearly Africa was no treasure trove offering easy fortunes . . . The outcome was a serious reappraisal of African policies on both sides of the Channel which began about 1900 and continued to 1914 and beyond . . . During this second phase, neither France nor Britain discarded belief in the economic potential of Africa. The new factor was recognized that the state must play a more positive role . . . Colonial governments must become the agents of development by developing communications, stimulating all forms of economic activity, and planning for the future . . . So much was common ground between Britain and France.[5]

Private enterprise did finance the construction of some lines, perhaps the most successful being the Rhodesian system, which paid shareholders just over 3 per cent per annum over the first forty years of its existence. Two private railways were built in French West Africa (later purchased by the government amid revelations of their shoddy construction), and a number in German territories, but none in British West Africa. The famous Uganda Railway started as a venture of the East Africa Company, but until government funds became available it was a 'sorry fiasco' and was eventually completed under the supervision of a Foreign Office Committee. The reason for the widespread failure of private enterprise seems clear enough. Railway construction in Africa was very expensive, railways being an outstanding example of capital-intensive construction. Thus, attention devolved upon the metropolitan governments for the wherewithal to build the lines.

Once it was taken for granted that government assistance was necessary for railway construction, economic profitability became only one among several

---

[5] David K. Fieldhouse: 'The economic exploitation of Africa: some British and French comparisons', in *France and Britain in Africa: imperial rivalry and colonial rule,* Prosser Gifford and William Roger Louis, eds. (New Haven, Yale University Press, 1971), pp. 595–6.

motivating factors that propelled railway appropriation bills through the legisla-
tures of the colonial powers. The military strategy of imperial politics was one
very important consideration in the location of the lines, many of which were
built long before the regions they served had developed sufficient traffic to
make them pay. Another common denominator of railway construction was the
desire to extend and consolidate effective political control inland from the
coast.

Although agricultural produce became by far the most important cargo for
export on most African lines, a fair number were not constructed with this purpose uppermost. For example, the Gold Coast Railway, commenced in 1898,
was built primarily to exploit the gold-mines at Tarkwa and Obuasi. The first
suggestions for the Lagos Railway, eventually begun in 1896, were put forward
'as much from humanitarian as from mercantile motives',[6] and in Northern
Nigeria the Bauchi light railway was the outcome of tin discoveries on the Jos
plateau. The Eastern line in Nigeria, running north from Port Harcourt, would
probably not have been built but for the coal of the Udi coal-fields, whereas
across the continent the Uganda Railway was started at Mombasa in 1895 following an agreement at the Brussels Conference of 1890 for suppressing the
slave-trade by opening up the interior. Political, strategic and economic considerations also lay behind the construction of the Uganda Railway, but apparently
the cotton which was to make this line famous soon after its completion in 1902
did not. The potential for losses on what was thought to be an uneconomic line
was the factor largely responsible for the policy of settling emigrants from Britain along its route in the highlands of Kenya. Similarly, the railways built by
the Germans in East Africa were laid largely for political purposes and incurred
losses for many years.

The French, during their period of railway construction, concentrated on
West Africa to the exclusion of French Equatorial Africa. Even as late as 1924,
except for a tiny line built to evacuate copper from Mindouli, there was not a
kilometre of rails in French Equatorial Africa. But in the vast, underpopulated
west, construction had begun early. A connection between the old port of
Senegal, St Louis, and the city selected to succeed it, Dakar, was begun in
1882 and completed in 1885. Though intended to provide better port facilities
for traffic to and from the far interior, the line had the effect, as is pointed out
below, of transforming the nearby Cayor Plain into a major source of ground-
nuts for export. A Senegal-Niger connecting link was commenced in 1881 to
supplement the navigable stretches of those two rivers, but because of political
struggles at home, the Niger was not actually reached until 1904.

Under the auspices of Governor-General Ernest-Nestor Roume, railway construction became the central focus of economic policy between the turn of the
century and 1910. The Guinea railway was begun in 1900, the Dahomey line in
the same year and the Ivory Coast railway in 1903.

The Belgians, too, were active in railway-building from an early date, with
the Matadi-Leopoldville by-pass opened in 1898 to avoid the rapids and falls of
the lower Congo. For many years exports from the interior of French Equatorial
Africa were routed along the Congo, and thus were obliged to use this Belgian
line. However, such exports were small in any case, being exceeded over seven

[6] Allan McPhee, *The economic revolution in British West Africa* (London, 1926), p. 108.

times by the exports of French West Africa on the eve of the First World War.

Some railway building in Africa, unlike that described above, was undertaken with a specific agricultural export or combination of exports in mind. The German colonial administration in Togo went so far as to name the various short lines constructed in that colony after the products expected to make up the most important cargo: hence the coconut line, cocoa line, cotton line and palm-oil line (Ol-bahn). The main line of the Sierra Leone Government Railway was built primarily to tap the oil-palm areas. The second railway built in the Gold Coast, begun in 1909 and running from Accra north-east to Kumasi, was explicitly the result of a cocoa boom in the area. The extension of the Lagos Railway through Northern Nigeria to Kano, open for traffic in 1912, although built partly to ensure collection of customs duties heretofore accruing to Southern Nigeria, was very largely a result of the promotional efforts of the British Cotton Growing Association. Cotton was also a most important motivating factor behind the Busoga Railway in Uganda. (The Accra-Kumasi line, the Lagos extension and the Busoga Railway are discussed below.)

These railways, and other less significant lines not discussed here, were the most important form of capital supplied by the colonial powers, and were the vent through which much of the surplus capacity for agricultural production in Africa could be utilized. Although the development of road systems after the First World War had an undoubted effect in lowering the cost of moving goods, it is hard to over-emphasize the impact of trains. Transport costs per ton/mile by human porterage were three to as much as thirty times greater. Even where there were no feeder roads, production of bulky commodities could now be profitable as far as 30 to 40 miles from a railhead. These developments were fundamental for the growth of smallholder agricultural exports.

Where the colonial railways reached the sea, however, the vent for surplus was often unduly constricted by the very limited number of good natural harbours along both coasts of Africa. In Senegal, Dakar was a fine port, although St Louis was silting up with a sand spit and off-shore bar. Bathurst and Freetown were excellent, but both had a limited hinterland—Bathurst had no railway and Freetown only a small one. Conakry was shallow and exposed to northerly winds. Along the Gulf of Guinea in the year 1900, sand bars and unprotected stretches necessitated shipping cargo in surf boats or branch steamers before loading into ocean-going steamers anchored off-shore (control of the necessary lighterage and loading facilities helped to protect the shipping cartel in this area). Abidjan lay behind a great bar, and attempts to pierce it with a canal in 1904–7 failed. Neither Accra nor Sekondi nor Lomé nor Cotonou was a harbour; Porto Novo and Lagos lay on lagoons with restricted passage for deep-draught ships, while Port Harcourt was not yet to be discovered for a dozen years. Ships had to anchor 25 miles away from Duala. Libreville was a good port without a railway. Matadi had a railway (since 1898), but it was miles from the sea up the Congo, a stretch of river with sharp bends, strong currents and sand-banks. Farther south there were only a few primitive jetties in stagnant Angola. On the east coast, north of Moçambique and its fine harbour of Lourenço Marques, Dar es Salaam was a lighterage port and only Mombasa was adequate.

Chronic overcrowding of docking facilities, schemes for dredging, channel relocation, sea walls, causeways and the like were thus a continuing part of economic life in most places where the railways generated a substantial amount of traffic. All in all, the lack of good ports played an important part in the seemingly haphazard location of railways, and was an inhibiting factor in the development of cash-cropping for export in the early colonial period (and remains so today). But the port improvement plans of the colonial governments ensured that a potentially serious bottleneck was never so tight as to constrict the vent for surplus in any acute manner.

The Myint model suggests further that *external* developments in transport and communication will help to enlarge the vent for surplus. This was certainly true in the case of Africa during the latter half of the nineteenth century. Regular steamship service to West Africa began in 1852, the African Steamship Company running vessels between Liverpool and the coast, while the opening of the Suez Canal in 1869 speeded passage to East Africa. Coal-conserving compound-expansion steam-engines after 1854, then triple expansion in the 1870s, surface condensers for economizing on boiler water and steel construction that significantly increased cargo capacity—all had a favourable effect on transport costs. Thus ships of 1900 could carry three to four times more cargo per ton of displacement than could wooden sailing vessels. The under-sea cable and the telegraph on land permitted more efficient use of ships, trains and storage facilities. As early as 1886, Accra had a working cable to Liverpool, and most of the West African coastal cities were connected by 1894. Major East African ports soon had their own under-sea link as well.

The next section of the Myint model, item (D) in our version of it, emphasizes the role of imported trade goods. Such goods serve as an incentive for increased output of exportable commodities, and without them it is difficult to see why additional effort would have been forthcoming from African farmers in the absence of compulsion. Though data are meagre, it appears certain that everywhere that cash incomes were earned in tropical Africa, a varying but always large proportion of that income was spent for imported consumer goods.

There is a considerable body of economic theory that attempts to explain how and why such a reaction will occur. (The excellent short survey in P. T. Bauer and B. S. Yamey, *Economics of underdeveloped countries,* is a fine example.) This accretion of theory tends to support the view that in a wide variety of cases, after a period of exposure to imported goods, African farmers chose without compulsion to participate in large-scale production of cash-crops. Evidence of this change in taste, which long antedates the colonial period, appears to be a fairly consistent factor in African economic history. From the earliest contact between Africans and European traders, there was significant demand for trade goods. In West Africa, tastes ran initially to the more colourful items: beads, glass, brass pans, cheap ornaments and the like. However, it was not long before the composition of the imported items altered to a mix of rum (later gin), tobacco, muskets, powder and ball and, most noteworthy, cotton textiles.

In many areas both along the coast and at inland trading centres, a demand pattern for imports was established long before cash-crops for export became the chief means of payment. In one representative year, 1787, of total commodity imports into West Africa valued at substantially more than half a million pounds sterling, about 70 per cent by value were cotton textiles, 17 per cent metal and metal-wares, 7 per cent various liquors, and 7 per cent arms and ammunition. The percentages altered from year to year as tastes changed, but cotton cloth always ranked very high. In the 1830s, with the slave-trade moribund, cotton goods made up about a third of British exports to West Africa, and in the 1840s the figure had risen to over 50 per cent. Added impetus for obtaining such goods came from the general decline in f.o.b. prices caused by the economies of the Industrial Revolution in Europe. The impression that imports, sometimes speciality products not yet mentioned, had an important effect on local preferences is confirmed from studies of many geographical areas. For the Oil Rivers, G. I. Jones reports that during the nineteenth century Manchester cottons captured the cloth market and imported Cheshire salt virtually ended local production. Even the main product of the Niger Delta, dried fish, had stiff competition from imports by the end of the century, in particular from the Norwegian dried cod known in Nigeria as stockfish.

Farther west at Lagos, in 1886 out of a total import bill of £357,831, about 38 per cent was made up of cotton goods, 20 per cent wines and spirits, 8 per cent tobacco, and 34 per cent salt, hardware, haberdashery and building materials. All along this coast and farther west as well, imported tobacco was so much in demand that Mary Kingsley said it approached being a necessity. In the Popo towns of what is now Dahomey, the most desired goods were the same as along the coast to east and west—silks, Manchester cottons, guns and ammunition. Cottons made up over one-third of Guinea's imports just before 1900. Before the Wolof of the Gambia came under the British protectorate, their economy had already been altered radically by imports that created a new set of wants so strong that some goods, especially textiles, became established as necessities.

In the Western Sudan, imported trade goods brought in caravan across the Sahara were commonly found in large markets at least as early as the sixteenth century, when Leo Africanus was in the area. European cloth was especially in demand. Timbuktu, Djenne, Gao and other centres imported overland several varieties as well as the cooking-ware, weapons and so on that had become the standard imports along the coast. The selection of overseas merchandise had widened by the time of the nineteenth-century expeditions to the Sudan. Perhaps most familiar is Dr Barth's account of the Kano market in 1851, with its surprisingly wide and appealing range of consumer goods from Europe. In short, the desire for imported goods was seemingly as strong in the interior as on the coast, modified only by the virtual nonexistence of the trade in spirits because of the Muslim strictures against alcohol. In lieu of spirits, however, there was the very strong demand for kola-nuts, from the southern forests, which also served as 'incentive goods'.

The generally poor quality of the merchandise was a noteworthy aspect of the import trade. In particular, moralists lamented the obsolete and worn-out fire-arms that were passed off as serviceable weapons. Muskets with enlarged fire-holes or weakened, even ruptured, barrels would have taken their toll among users. When the Egba boycotted the Lagos palm-oil market for five months in 1855, this was one of their main points of protest, as well as the poor quality of the spirits and cotton goods. The rum most commonly traded in the eighteenth century, and the trade gin which superseded it in popularity in the nineteenth, gained a notorious reputation for low quality.

It must not be concluded from this that all of pre-colonial West Africa was carrying on a thriving commerce in European imports. With per capita incomes low, and transport slow and expensive, inland regions would not share in the trade to the extent that the coast did. Neither would luxuries become essentials with the ease with which this occurred near the sea. The salient feature in our context remains the same, however: familiarity with imported goods was already widespread before colonial rule. In many different geographical areas, often irrespective of tribal and religious differences, Africans had shown themselves willing to exert additional effort to acquire imported goods, which in turn were the incentive for the vent for surplus. The evidence suggests that in almost every case where agricultural produce was exported for cash, the importation of 'incentive goods' kept pace.

There appears to have been considerably less of a pre-colonial import trade in most of East and Central Africa, though the difference is one of magnitude only. In coastal areas an import trade had existed since classical times. The *Periplus* lists shipments from the Mediterranean of textiles, metals, glass artifacts, tools and weapons (some made especially for the African trade), as well as various luxuries. Before the end of the fifteenth century, coastal regions were receiving beads, porcelain and other ceramic ware, and a very few other luxury goods from Indian Ocean ports to the north and west. In the sixteenth century, as the Portuguese presence grew stronger, imports of luxuries became more common. Even far inland, the Central African empire of Monomotapa became familiar with shipments of cloth and beads from trading centres, especially Sofala, during the period of Portuguese maritime supremacy.

By the early nineteenth century, there was a steady flow of imports to Zanzibar and the coast, with American shippers dominating this commerce right up to the American Civil War. Coarse cotton cloth (called 'merikani') and arms and ammunition were the staples of the trade, along with the heavy, durable hatchets of New England manufacture. For the remainder of the century, cloth and guns were the most important means by which Zanzibari merchants paid for the slaves and ivory purchased inland.

For geographical, political and other reasons, however, trade goods from overseas penetrated the interior in much smaller quantity, and much later, than had been the case in West Africa. The state of Buganda provides an excellent illustration. Strong, cohesive and wealthy for its area, Buganda was largely unfamiliar with imports before the second half of the eighteenth century, and even these were only cups and plates brought in by Arab traders. Imported cotton goods, which were known by the early 1800s, soon became the standard dress of the Buganda ruling classes, while fire-arms came later in the century. Commoners were generally able to afford only some brass and copper ornaments. Elsewhere in the interior, imports were not widely available until about thirty years before the colonial period. Where they are mentioned in the literature, they are generally the staples of the western trade: cloth, powder and ball, beads, alcoholic drinks, hoes, knives and the like. However, even though the import trade was undoubtedly much smaller in pre-colonial East Africa than in West Africa, its role of incentive in the vent for surplus was still effective to a degree. Among the Buganda chiefs and farmers, for example, the developing taste for imported luxury goods helped to stimulate the growth of the Uganda cotton industry, which is discussed below.

The preceding pages have emphasized a new effective demand for export commodities coupled with an incentive for imported goods. Here the connecting link between the two, very often provided by European export–import firms, may be emphasized. These firms stood ready to collect produce and process it and to manage the transport to foreign markets. These same merchants offered the inducement for output increases by selling farmers imported goods. Expatriate firms and traders had moved ashore from ships or anchored hulks in some areas long before colonial rule, but there was usually a considerable influx of companies whenever European authority was established. It is certainly possible to overemphasize the effect of this inland spread of the European firms. To some extent it did not represent new economic services but instead the displacement of African traders and middlemen who had been in the field on their own account, as agents for the European firms or as the clients of African merchants. As the instrument for combining commodity exports with consumer imports, however, the expatriate firms greatly facilitated overseas commerce.

The model that has been illustrated thus far is the standard one as depicted by Myint. At this point several modifications that increase its descriptive accuracy are added. The first of these refers to the provision of indigenous capital formation in African cash-agriculture (item (E) above). Creation of capital occurred in ways and in amounts that have not always been appreciated, probably because of the tendency for observers to equate investment with new plant and equipment, as is so often the case in developed countries. In the African context, both domestic real and money capital had to be created if production and trade were to expand appreciably.

Among the items of real capital were tools, storage and transport facilities, the establishment of cleared land and tree crops and the withholding of seed for future increases of output. All of these were present within the vent-for-surplus framework, in different proportions for the various commodities considered. As already noted, the latter part of this essay considers kola, palm products, cotton, ground-nuts and cocoa in some detail. Among these products, domestically produced tools were utilized in all cases. The primary ones were clearing and cutting instruments (axes, machetes, knives) for kola, cocoa and palm-fruit; hoes for cotton and ground-nuts; and processing materials (pressing instruments, mats, containers, hand tools for decorticating and the like) for all the products. Indigenous storage and transport facilities (structures, containers, slaves and animals as beasts of burden) were present in quantity. Direct investment in agriculture by Africans by means of the clearing of land and the planting of tree-crops almost always occurred with cocoa, as it sometimes did with kola and palm products when these were deliberately planted in prepared groves. Finally, seed retention to increase the size of the ensuing crop is a form of capital formation that was especially important in the ground-nut trade.

Growth in financial capital was necessary also, and monetary expansion, as well as the development of credit facilities over wide geographical areas, was in large part the result, but also in part the cause, of growing agricultural output during the early years of the colonial period. Both West and East Africa had used 'native monies' for a very long time, at any rate before extensive contact with Europeans had occurred. Cowries apparently were introduced into the interior of West Africa during the Middle Ages, and by the seventeenth century they were reaching the coast in great quantity. Cowries were supplemented during the slave-trade by such currencies as manillas, brass and iron rods, trade gin and various European and American coins. In East Africa, experience with money was apparently neither so extensive nor so early, but nonetheless by the eighteenth century currencies including cowries, beads and metal ingots and bars were in fairly wide use.

The most significant aspect in terms of our model was not the mere existence of these indigenous currencies, but the experience with a money supply that they gave. When the colonial powers assumed authority, they invariably introduced a metallic currency, followed later (during and after the First World War for the most part) by paper notes. The metallic coinage was highly portable, recognizable, difficult to counterfeit and had high value in relation to weight. Given these advantages, together with the extended earlier experience with monies of various kinds, it tended to be adopted much more rapidly than had often been expected by contemporary observers. By the second half of the nineteenth century, colonial coinage was superseding local monies in the Senegambia, while specie imports rose considerably in the British and French territories to the east. (Some six and a half million pounds was shipped by the British mint to West Africa in the twenty years 1891 to 1910.) Banks charged with currency issue, such as the Banque de l'Afrique Occidentale and the Bank of West Africa, were in operation in most colonial territories by 1914. With cowries and other local monies demonetized by governmental order during this period, there was thus a widespread need to acquire the new European means of exchange. Monetary theory is explicit with regard to the adoption of a new currency. Holdings for the purposes of transactions must be accumulated by temporarily raising the level of economic effort until the desired amount of cash balances is achieved. As colonial coinage replaced other forms of money, then, the effect was to stimulate production over and above what would have been the case had transactions balances already been adequate.

At a time when transactions balances were being built towards desired levels, and with a formal banking system just coming into being and in any case not disposed to lend to African traders, indigenous credit institutions for supplying working capital were essential. Here, too, sub-Saharan Africa had long experience with credit. During the slave-trade, credit to Africans had been provided by Europeans on a large scale, as well as by Africans to fellow Africans. During the nineteenth century, the system was utilized for agricultural exports, and was available for expansion when trading opportunities presented themselves. Evidence of pre-colonial credit facilities is very widespread geographically, with 'trust' on the West African coast the most familiar. Middlemen were provided with goods on account by some patron, European or African, which the middlemen in turn would sell in exchange for produce to be delivered to the lender at some future time. Most often the price of goods distributed in trust would be marked up substantially because of risk and to secure an interest rate on the loan of working capital. Where European firms were concerned, goods worth thousands of pounds sterling might be entrusted to agents at any one time. In the Gold Coast, in Sierra Leone and at Lagos, credit evolved further, with emergent local groups of African and European importers able to secure credit direct from European exporters.

The patron–client relationship appears to have been a familiar credit mechanism almost everywhere, even though it did not approach in scale the trust system of the west coast. Under various linguistic guises, such as bara, mai gida, diatigi, jula-ba, jula-den and many others, working capital was made available to agents in quantity, and lack of it was not the constraining factor it might well have been. Several examples of this credit mechanism in operation are discussed later in this essay.

The next step of the model—item (*F*) above—states that the colonial governments commonly utilized two policies that tended to encourage the operation of the vent for surplus. The first was the imposition of direct taxation, payable in legal tender, which necessitated the earning of a cash income and helped to focus African attention on cash-cropping. The second was government encouragement of and support for cash agriculture by several different means: the propaganda of local officials, subsidization of seed supplies and transport costs, provision of processing facilities and sometimes coercion.

These two policies were motivated simultaneously by the desire to supply raw materials to European industry, to generate revenue sufficient to make colonial ventures self-supporting financially and to perform a 'civilizing mission' in Africa. Official involvement in cash agriculture for export would obviously meet the first test. As for revenue, the growth of income would make tax collection more lucrative and simpler to the extent that exports and the imports purchased with the new cash income could be taxed directly. In addition, other attractive possibilities might follow the stimulation of cash-crop exports. According to William Barber, colonial governments believed that Africans

could only be advanced from their rude state by educating them to new standards of taste and to higher levels of productive performance. Moreover, it was thought that in some areas the final suppression of the slave trade would not be complete unless an alternative 'legitimate' trade could be created. Where the traffic had flourished earlier, commercial channels—both within Africa and overseas—were too well established to remain idle. If they could not be diverted to other transactions, clandestine slaving might well recur. Mixed with these factors was a consideration of prudence. The *pax* in Africa, it was widely believed, depended on the provision of opportunities for Africans to earn money incomes. Otherwise, idleness among African men might well breed mischief and thereby expensive threats to the new order.[7]

Two of the responses to this situation, direct taxation in cash and government encouragement of agriculture, are examined below.

The economic philosophy behind a system of direct cash taxation in the African colonial context is simple enough. It was the most effective tool through which subsistence farmers could be drawn into the money economy; it could not be avoided even by those who did not want to buy imported goods or preferred leisure to work. Every tax-payer had either to work for wages or to sell some product for which there was a market.

The method used was ordinarily a flat-rate levy not based on ability to pay (which would partly have thwarted the work-incentive feature and was in any case an administrative impossibility), in its various guises called a head tax, a poll tax, a hut tax and so on. In general, direct taxes were established some time after a territory had been pacified and European law and order established, and about the same time that railway construction was undertaken. In many cases the imposition of such devices was made easier because pre-colonial régimes had employed them. This was especially true of Muslim states with their Koranic tax obligations.

[7] Barber, 'Movement into the world economy', pp. 300–301.

Early attempts to impose direct money taxes, as in the Gold Coast and Sierra Leone in the 1850s, were unsuccessful and were withdrawn after occasioning some violence; but during the 1890s such attempts were made again. Their effectiveness in forcing Africans into the cash economy was shown in the Cape Province of South Africa after the Glen Grey Act of 1894, and soon they were adopted by most colonial administrations. The aim of the tax differed depending on whether or not the colony concerned was opened to white settlement and/or European plantations. Where this was so, the tax was mainly intended to provide a black labour-force that could be employed for wages in the European sector of the economy. Elsewhere, the tax was expected to encourage the development of cash-cropping for export. Many colonies in the last-mentioned category established direct taxation within fifteen years after 1894. Among them were the Gambia, with a hut tax in 1896, Tanganyika with an 1897 house and hut tax, French Guinea with a poll tax in the same year, Sierra Leone with a hut tax in 1898, Dahomey with a head tax in 1899, Uganda with a hut tax in 1900, the Northern Nigerian taxes embodied in the proclamations of 1904 and 1906 and the Togo tax of 1907.

In combination with the other elements of the vent-for-surplus model, direct taxation may be considered something of a last step, taken on the eve of or just after a revolution in transport. Notwithstanding whether such taxes were morally defensible, they did help to shift the pattern of economic activity towards cash-cropping for export, reinforcing incentives that in many cases were already there. But it is interesting to note that direct taxes were not a factor in two major areas of pre-1914 smallholder initiative: the Gold Coast and Southern Nigeria. Neither area was so taxed in the period discussed above, and neither was to be until long after the First World War. The reason in both cases was that an export trade in palm-oil from Southern Nigeria and in rubber, later superseded by cocoa, from the Gold Coast was already well established. Furthermore, in the case of the Gold Coast there were memories of the Christianborg rebellion of 1854, a result of the early attempt at a poll tax mentioned above.

The second policy followed generally was government (and missionary) encouragement of and support for cash agriculture. In its broadest meaning this would include many factors such as pacification and the establishment of law and order, the first collection of economic statistics necessary for policy decisions, initial accumulation of data on climate, soils and crops, the first rudimentary efforts in education and public health, the beginnings of cadastral surveys and land-tenure investigations, as well as improved transport and communications. Only the last of these has been treated in the present study. As for the remainder, suffice it to say (as does Kamarck) that 'in almost every case they did make *some* contribution—small or large'.[8]

Attention will be directed here to the specific encouragement of cash-crops, either as a whole or of particular varieties. From a very early date, colonial authorities undertook to foster cash agriculture, although the large-scale development projects did not come until years after the period considered here. (The major dams of the Gezira Scheme were built in the 1920s, the Office du Niger was started in 1932 and the Volta River Project was first aired in 1938.) Even

[8] Andrew M. Kamarck, *The economics of African development* (New York, 1967), p. 12.

so, cash-crop promotion was far from rare in the early years of the colonial period.

Nowhere was research more extensive than in German territory. Before 1914, agricultural stations and special government institutes for crop development had been established in both Kamerun and German East Africa, where the research centre at Amani was well known. But these were basically for the benefit of settler plantations, though African farmers profited from them also. More interest attaches to the programme in Togo, where, as early as 1892, German authorities introduced almost 90,000 coffee bushes and 21,000 rubber trees. In the decade after 1900, Togo received an experimental station and an agricultural training school for Africans at Nuatja, which by 1911 had ninety-nine students and was conducting research on many crops. The government even invited six Negro agricultural students from Tuskegee Institute to demonstrate improved American methods of cotton cultivation. These efforts were parallelled by the work of the Kolonial-Wirtschaftliches Komitee (KWK), a semi-official body founded in 1896. The KWK sponsored numerous agricultural activities in Africa: scientific expeditions, the establishment of nurseries, seed research, crop evaluation, a cotton board and a rubber board. It was a German East Africa Company botanist who introduced the highly successful sisal from Florida. (For details of German activities, especially in pioneering cotton production, see Yudelman's essay in this volume, especially pp. 342–3 below.)

The intensive early research of the German territories was not in general matched by the other colonial powers. There had been some early efforts: demonstration farms on the Gold Coast early in the eighteenth century, a botanical garden in Sierra Leone in 1808 and another in Lagos in 1887. Between 1887 and 1900, seven agricultural stations were established elsewhere in Southern Nigeria. In the Gold Coast, following the foundation of the Aburi Agricultural Station in 1890, seven more stations were operating by 1910. By 1914, every British colony in Africa had a botanical garden undertaking plant research, with the sole exception of the Gambia. In French West Africa, a central station for research was established at Hann in 1903, whereas at specialized stations (Koulikoro, Banfofo, M'Bambey) the emphasis was on cotton and corn, rubber and ground-nuts respectively. Four other experimental gardens in Senegal and Guinea concentrated on cotton and rubber among other products. Across the continent in British East Africa, the first agricultural experiments were undertaken in 1896, and an experimental farm was founded at Nairobi in 1903. Elsewhere, small departments of agriculture, individuals serving as agricultural officers and local officials who promoted cash agriculture as one of their regular duties were at work in almost every colony in the decade before 1914.

However, expenditure for these purposes was low almost everywhere in the French and British territories, and even the establishment of an agricultural department was long delayed in some areas. As late as 1911, the important Gold Coast agricultural service, which aided in the remarkable expansion of the cocoa industry by distributing cocoa seedlings, had only twenty-seven staff members. Three years later, its budget still did not exceed a penurious £17,000. The small Uganda Agricultural Department, under pressure from the British Treasury to make the colony self-supporting, had already undertaken studies of a remarkable array of potential cash-crops by 1914. But in that year it consisted only of a director, two specialists, six agricultural officers, one ploughing instructor and a veterinary staff. Southern Nigeria did not have an agricultural department until 1910, and Northern Nigeria had none until 1912.

In spite of these limitations, good work was done in classifying plants and in identifying and coping with a number of plant diseases and pests. Helpful experiments improved the cultivation and preparation of cocoa and rubber, in particular. Ground-nuts, kola and palm products, on the other hand, were relatively neglected.

The picture drawn above is one of good intentions severely constrained by budgetary limitations. But in the case of one specific crop, cotton, the effort made to stimulate production was much more intensive. In Uganda, in Northern Nigeria, in French West Africa and on a smaller scale in other territories, colonial governments employed policies that differed in detail but not in the expected result. Specific official actions are considered here, whereas cotton as an example of smallholder initiative will be returned to below.

In Uganda, the encouragement of cotton cultivation took the form of the distributing of free seed in 1904, together with a small extension service and the provision of hand-gins, either free or at a low price. Strong pro-cotton persuasion was brought to bear on the chiefs of the protectorate by the colonial authorities. After the marketing difficulties encountered in 1907, caused by mixing different varieties in the same bale and by poor storage, which resulted in staining, stringent regulation of the crop was adopted. Government seed farms were established to ensure a standardized seed supply, and by 1908 instructions had been issued on approved planting and cultivating techniques. An experimental station for cotton was established in 1911, and research expanded greatly thereafter.

The pattern was similar in Northern Nigeria. Free seed, made available by the BCGA, was distributed to farmers by district officers on tour. Special low rates were charged by the railway for shipments of ginned cotton. The governor of the protectorate encouraged his officials to urge the cultivation of cotton and, meanwhile, several ginneries were constructed by the BCGA with the help of imperial financial grants.

In French West Africa after 1903, cotton received far more attention from the government than any other crop. However, because of budgetary constraints the major method of encouragement was compulsion. As in Northern Nigeria and Uganda, district officers would preach the advantages of cotton to the chiefs with accompanying seed distribution; but as distinct from these two areas, military personnel in French territory were assigned to bring conformity with the official instructions. But the long distances involved, the expense of irrigation facilities and the low fixed price paid by the Association Cotonnière Coloniale, all meant that even by the early 1920s cotton production was not a success in French West Africa. Compulsion in favour of cotton was emphasized among farmers in the plantation economies also, particularly in French Equatorial Africa and in the Congo. In most cases, however, this did not occur until during or after the First World War.

All too often, government promotion of cash-crops appears to have been thoroughly disappointing. Because the government had acted on inadequate information, the particular crop encouraged was found, after some time had passed, not to possess a comparative advantage in production. Nowhere was this more apparent than in the promotion of cotton growing. Government pressure for self-sufficiency in subsistence foodstuffs, a policy followed during this period in a number of colonies, was another form of neglect for economic rationality. Nevertheless, most authorities would probably agree that when economic incentives and the dispensing of information, rather than compulsion, were emphasized, government encouragement of cash-crops had a positive effect in helping to stimulate latent economic initiative.

The final element in the model—item (G) above—the role of indigenous entrepreneurial ability in the operation of the vent for surplus, needs little additional comment here. Its widespread pre-colonial existence in African agriculture has already been treated in this study, and it is discussed again in connection with specific products. Where these products were concerned, no new infusion of a Western business ethic was needed to marshal African entrepreneurial skills as the colonial period began.

Entrepreneurship is defined in its Schumpeterian terms as economic initiative, organization and risk-taking. These have all been seen in the pre-colonial adoption of new food-crops, and in the establishment of long-distance trade, often involving credit. The existence of brokerage arrangements, including supplier monopolies such as the Ashanti or Dahomey royal houses, the Ivory Coast Jack Jacks, the Niger Brassmen, the Delta Houses and the 'trading diasporas' of mainly Muslim co-religionists, all involve a relatively sophisticated form of entrepreneurship. In the remainder of the essay, the skills of initiation, organization and risk-taking are seen to be important in every case considered.

Five studies of initiative in African cash agriculture

A fairly large number of case studies have been made on the subject of growth in African cash agriculture. From these, five different products in a variety of geographical and pre-1914 temporal settings have been selected for inclusion here.

The first, kola from Ashanti, was grown and traded internally in Africa centuries before the colonial era. Its high value/weight ratio made it one of the very few products in which an extensive commerce could develop before the stimulus of the vent for surplus was felt. Apart from the introduction of new forms of transport, this situation altered little after the European occupation. A second product, the fruit of the oil-palm grown along the southern coast of West Africa, was used for culinary purposes long before the coming of the white man. It became the first great agricultural export to Europe in the century preceding the colonial period, and remained important thereafter. Here, many elements of the vent for surplus were operating before the colonial occupation. Cotton, the third product studied, had also been raised for centuries; but its large-scale entry into overseas trade came after colonization. In one instance, the encouragement of this crop by colonial authorities showed rapid success (Uganda), but in others progress was very slow, primarily because of insufficient economic incentives (Nigeria, French West Africa). Ground-nuts, the fourth product chosen, are considered in two regions: Senegal-Gambia, where most output came originally from areas not under colonial control; and Northern Nigeria, where the colonial conquest antedated production for export by nearly a decade. Finally, we shall survey the rise of the cocoa industry, the most capitalistic of the group, which occurred first in the Gold Coast and shortly thereafter in Southern Nigeria.

The view that emerges from these studies is the wide diversity of ethnological and geographical situations in which African economic initiative in agriculture made itself apparent.

Kola in Ashanti

Source material is scanty for kola production and trade, though scholars have recently begun to devote more attention to this subject. Kola-nuts, because they are one of the few stimulants in which Muslims are permitted to indulge, were and are exceedingly popular in West Africa. The variety *nitida* is highest in caffeine content and is thus usually the more valued. Consumption is in fact much lower in the producing areas than it is in the Sudan zone where Islam predominates. Kola was proffered to guests and to thirsty travellers as a sign of hospitality. It was used for both presents and alms. In all cases, it conferred status on the giver. As a luxury item, kola could stand the high cost of transport in the interior.

The nuts were grown in the humid forests of the Guinea coast, often in areas where cocoa later became established, but also farther north where marked leaf-fall occurs in the dry season. Production for trade took place only in certain districts between the Volta river and what is now Sierra Leone. The industry's growth was slow, no doubt correlated with the spread of Islam, but a strong impetus was received following the successful jihad in 1804 of the Islamic reform movement in Hausaland. As late as 1700 in Ashanti, the best-known source of pre-colonial output, the trade in gold is reported to have been more important than that in kola, although the situation was clearly reversed by the second half of the nineteenth century.

Kola trees begin to bear fruit after about seven years of growth, but output is commercially inconsequential until the twelfth to fifteenth year. Full production, which is attained after twenty years, continues for decades, often up to seventy or a hundred years. In Ashanti, trees were apparently not planted but allowed to propagate naturally. (In some other parts of West Africa, folk wisdom holds it unlucky for farmers to plant kola.) In the nineteenth century, Ashanti state traders were active in kola buying, as were private middlemen, but collection and processing were basically a family activity, with slaves and pawns often used to augment the supply of labour. Slaves represented a capital outlay sometimes financed by an indigenous co-operative credit mechanism (*abusa*) involving the pooling of funds. Producers often transported their own processed kola to the main export market at Salaga, which was also visited by professional large-scale traders, who bought at the farm and sold at Salaga.

The long-distance trade in kola-nuts is an instructive example in economic initiative. Professional dealers existed not only on the supply side as just noted, but also in the areas of greatest demand, particularly in Hausaland. Dr Barth and later writers justifiably emphasized the role of the Hausa trader, although the traffic with Ashanti had not actually begun on any scale until the early eighteenth century.

For several hundred years, long before the Hausa trade developed, Mande dealers had pioneered the commerce in kola through their wide-ranging commercial network, trading north to the great markets of the Western Sudan. But by the nineteenth century, three professional Hausa trading groups had arisen to dominate the trade: the Agalawa, the Tokarawa and the Kambarin Beriberi. These accumulated capital, acquired specialized knowledge of the kola areas, developed social relations attuned to the furthering of long-distance trade and benefited from the very favourable conditions granted to Muslims by the Ashanti government. The Hausa traders frequently bought their nuts direct from the farmer, but from the 1830s the Kumasi government put restrictions on how far south they could go.

Eyewitness accounts of the nineteenth-century kola caravans furnish impressive evidence of contemporary entrepreneurial ability. Commander Clapperton of the Royal Navy was one of the first to travel with Hausa kola *fatake* (long-distance traders) on his second expedition of 1826. In Borgu he fell in with a

Houssa goffle, or caravan, which is on its way from Gonja and Ashantee: they consist of upwards of 1000 men and women and as many beasts of burthen . . . The principal, part of the cargo of these Houssa merchants consists in gora or kolla nuts, which they receive in exchange for natron, red glass beads, and a few slaves . . . They carry their goods on bullocks, mules, asses, and a number of female slaves are loaded; even some women hire themselves to carry loads to and from Nyffe [Nupe]. Some of the merchants have no more property than they can carry on their own heads.[9]

A quarter-century later, Dr Barth noted the interdependency that this flourishing trade promoted:

Three points are considered essential to the business of the kóla trade; first, that the people of Mósi bring their asses; secondly, that the . . . natives of Asanti bring the nut in sufficient quantities; and thirdly, that the state of the road is such as not to prevent the Háusa people from arriving. If one of these conditions is wanting, the trade is not flourishing.[10]

The kola caravans were ordinarily routed via the Sokoto Caliphate through Borgu, Dagomba and Gonja to Salaga, sometimes continuing along the great Kumasi north-eastern road to the markets of Ashanti. They exchanged cloth, leather products, potash, dried onion leaves (*gabu*), and other commodities for kola-nuts. The journey was laborious and time-consuming, taking six months to a year for a round trip from Kano to Ashanti. Clapperton commented on the run-down condition of both the animals and the people in the group with which he travelled. In size, the caravans at their largest could be double the thousand that Clapperton saw, with an equal number of pack-animals. Some kola was sold on the return journey, but most was brought to Hausaland for sale from the traders' own compounds or in the market-place. Often the nuts were held in storage in anticipation of a price rise during the wet season, when caravan traffic was interrupted by impassable roads and rivers. The nuts would then be parcelled out in small lots to town and village kola retailers.

In the period just before the First World War, with the colonial powers now *in situ*, there was rapid change in the make-up of this trade. In 1896, on the eve of the British conquest of Northern Nigeria, C. H. Robinson had met a 1,000-man kola caravan almost identical to the ones described above. Almost fifteen

[9] Hugh Clapperton, *Journal of a second expedition into the interior of Africa from the Bight of Benin to Soccatoo* (London, 1829), p. 68.
[10] Henry Barth, *Travels and discoveries in North and Central Africa* (London, 1859), vol. III, p. 364.

years later, in December 1910, E. D. Morel described what could have been the same sight—a caravan on the move to kola country. But as soon as the Lagos-Kano railway was opened for traffic in 1912, African merchants began to substitute rail and water transport for the overland traffic. In 1913, over 1,000 tons of Ashanti and Sierra Leonean kola arrived at Kano by train, and the Ashanti caravan trade went into a rapid decline. In south-western Nigeria, perspicacious farmers began to plant trees in order to share in the new direction of the commerce, although these trees did not bear fruit on any scale until after the First World War. Thus, without European commercial participation, without any infusion of European capital except in transport, even without much awareness by Europeans of this trade, which is seldom given attention in the official sources, the kola traffic demonstrated a relatively high degree of mercantile awareness and organizational ability.

Kola production has further ramifications for African cash agriculture, in that it contributed significantly to the later development of cocoa production in Ashanti and to ground-nut output in Northern Nigeria. For Ashanti, farmers harvesting kola found that their equipment and tools (capital) could easily be shifted into cocoa output. The inspection mats for kola were used to dry cocoa. The large carrying-baskets were equally useful for either crop. The fermentation baskets used for removal of the kola-skin were used similarly for cocoa. The hooked plucking-pole could be used interchangeably, and the specialized knives and cutlasses used for kola cleaning and brush clearing were as essential in cocoa production. Ashanti kola buyers who bought from the farmers and transported the nuts to regional centers for resale to long-distance traders found their experience and capital accumulation very useful in the cocoa trade also. The employment of hired labour was familiar in kola purchasing and distribution. Loans to agents for kola-buying expeditions gave experience in the provision of credit, and village self-help groups active in kola harvesting found a second incarnation in the preparation of cocoa. Thus Kwame Arhin posits that nineteenth-century Ashanti

was used to types of capitalistic modes of organization, some sections of the people possessing resources that can be described as capitalistic accumulation in a form determined by Ashanti's cultural level; that those modes of capitalistic organization and resources were switched over to cocoa production; and that together with the equipment and tools brought over from kola to cocoa production, they account for the rapid development of the latter industry in Ashanti.[11]

In Northern Nigeria, experience in kola buying also had its further ramifications. We have already seen that Hausa trading groups had developed commercial forms of clientage involving credit long before the colonial hegemony. Merchants with financial capital had established clientage relationships with agents, who, entrusted with goods provided interest-free by the patron, engaged in long-distance trade for the patron's account.

When ground-nut production emerged unexpectedly in Northern Nigeria in the year 1912, it was the Hausa kola traders with their network of interlocking credit relationships who were primarily responsible. The four Hausas most important in spreading the ground-nut trade were originally participants in the

[11] Kwame Arhin, 'Aspects of the Ashanti northern trade in the nineteenth century', *Africa,* Oct. 1970, **40**, 372.

kola traffic. This 'business school' meant that the various clientage networks, tested for decades in pre-colonial economic experience, were thus available for immediate use in the new industry.

Palm products in West Africa

The production for the market of palm-oil, like that of kola, was well established before the colonial period, usually by a half-century or more. And as was the case with kola, in this period the collection of palm produce and its handling by middlemen were in African hands virtually without exception. Unlike kola, however, palm-oil was the first large-scale *overseas* export of agricultural produce; and from African middleman to final market the trade was conducted mostly by Europeans. When the commerce in palm-oil began, it came from areas without colonial officials, without consulates, forts or naval bases, and with white settlement limited to a few impermanent commercial agents located ashore or in hulks tied up in the coastal creeks. Finally—again, as was the case with kola—the colonial rule brought remarkably little change in the trade up to and even after the First World War, with the exception that the control of the large African middlemen was broken.

The oil-palm is native to West Africa, and for centuries its edible oil had been consumed in cooking and used for fuel, light and medicine, and its sap drunk as palm-wine. (Even today, about the same quantity is used domestically as is exported.) Palm-oil was first mentioned as an export in 1588–90, but the trade died out almost completely and was not rekindled until 1772. Regular shipments to Liverpool continued thereafter and, had reached 1,000 tons by 1810. During this period, exports to France grew rapidly also, but were not more than about 5 per cent of the British figure.

For the time and place, palm-oil had two paramount advantages. First, production was centred in the forest belt along the coast, often within a day's journey of the navigable coastal creeks and lagoons. Cost of transport was thus relatively low, an essential consideration in the era before the railways. Second, the intricate structure of middlemen, advances of credit and commercial knowledge built up in more than a hundred years of slave-trading by coastal Africans could be applied to the marketing of palm-oil.

In the nineteenth century, palm-oil was being shipped from most sections of the West African coast, including Sierra Leone, Ivory Coast, Dahomey and Western Nigeria. However, as is pointed out below, the famous Oil Rivers of the Niger Delta formed by far the largest centre of production, accounting consistently for more than half of West Africa's palm exports in the nineteenth century.

The fruit of the oil-palm, when ripe, was collected by local farmers and brought home for treatment. The oil was extracted by a crude process of boiling the husks and removing the oil as it rose to the surface. Females were especially active in preparing and transporting the oil to local markets, where African traders from coastal towns purchased it. The trees themselves, after taking about fifteen years to rise above the surrounding vegetation, have a life of up to a hundred years and propagate freely in the coastal forests. Much collection of palm-fruit thus fits the stereotype of produce growing wild and waiting only for the gathering. But, missed by Allan McPhee, who remarked that the industry was 'merely a collecting and preparing of sylvan produce',[12] the oil-palm was often established and maintained by African economic initiative. Farmers frequently planted the trees on land cleared for growing food. From the end of the eighteenth century, Ibo-speaking peoples

cut down the forests, replacing them by villages and hamlets surrounded by oil palm groves, farmlands, and forest remnants. The oil palm forest of south-eastern Nigeria is the product of this Ibo invasion and settlement. It provides a distinctive humanized landscape related to trading contact with Europe.[13]

In the Niger Delta, enterprising house companies (which owed most of their prosperity to their transport services and not to production) cleared land and planted palms, thus adding to the quantity of oil entering the trade. Organized planting and maintainance were also found elsewhere—sometimes under the direction of local merchants, as at Whydah, sometimes under royal auspices, as in the case of King Gezo's Dahomean palm-groves. Here Dahomean military aristocrats with the royal prerogative for oil production, using slaves as their labour force, ran what verged on a plantation economy. Unfortunately, lack of data makes it impossible to suggest an estimate of the proportion of palm-oil derived from trees occurring wild or from trees planted by man.

There was a well-developed mechanism for the collection of palm-oil that involved the use of money, middlemen and credit. This structure, as already mentioned, was a carry-over from the slave-trade. The currencies used, which varied from place to place, included manillas, brass rods, iron bars, and the puncheon and crewe of oil as well as the familiar cowrie. But the major form of exchange was oil for imported trade goods brought to local markets by African middlemen, who in turn had obtained the goods from European traders on the coast. The middleman did not ordinarily purchase the imports, however. He obtained them on credit, a system known in the Oil Rivers as 'trust', advanced either by another African middleman in the trading network or direct from the European. Along the Niger Delta, the most common period for trusting goods was from six months to a year, although more rarely pay-back was in two years. Africans receiving these advances were required to trade them for the palm-oil of the coastal districts and interior; the oil was then used to repay their European creditors. The system was an old one that had seen wide use during the heyday of the slave-trade, when similar advances had been made by Europeans to Africans in order to assure a steady supply of slaves. One effect of trust was to impose high capital requirements on firms exporting palm-oil to Europe. Whether firms were European or owned by Africans (there were many such, including those of the Yoruba and the Sierra Leoneans), the cost of trust helped to ensure a high rate of bankruptcy.

The African middlemen deserve closer examination. They were usually native to the coastal regions where they traded, although freed slaves from Sierra Leone and the Americas were important middlemen at Lagos and Badagry. They laboured assiduously to keep Europeans from direct contact with pro-

[12] McPhee, *Economic revolution,* p. 35.
[13] W. B. Morgan, 'The influence of European contacts on the landscape of Southern Nigeria', in *People and land in Africa south of the Sahara,* R. Mansell Prothero, ed. (London, 1972), p. 198.

ducers. Even as late as the 1880s the white traders in general were content to rely on the traditional commercial framework, confining their efforts to the coast. Why? Because the scope of the middlemen's enterprise was so large as virtually to preclude contemporary imitation. The two largest among the middlemen, Ja Ja of Opoba and Nana of Warri, covered hundreds of square miles in their respective trading domains and employed thousands of canoemen, labourers, warriors, traders and local buying agents. The middlemen were not loath to use military force to restrain competition, as in the Oil Rivers and in Western Nigeria, and were strong enough to impose various taxes and duties (comey, dash, canoe-house impost, work and customs bar and so on) that helped finance their activities. Such systems operated elsewhere on a smaller scale, as along the Ivory Coast.

All this was not to last indefinitely. European palm-oil merchants arrived at Lagos in 1852 on the heels of the establishment of consular authority. The opening of the Niger river for steam navigation, and the up-river activities of the National African (later Royal Niger) Company began the long process of by-passing the middlemen, which, however, was not in full swing until the last two decades of the century. The process was encouraged by the use of European arms: there were what might be called 'palm-oil bombardments' of Porto Novo in 1861, the Brass towns in 1877 and Onitsha in 1879, among others.

In the end, the largest of the African middlemen were deposed: Ja Ja in 1887 after he undertook to start his own export–import trade, Nana in 1894 and others of their ilk in the same period. But in large measure the African middleman was never truly by-passed. Neither the European traders nor the colonial officials of the Oil Rivers Protectorate and succeeding administrations were to comprehend the extent of the middleman's service. His local knowledge could not be matched by the expatriate firms. He could use this knowledge to advance goods or money to the producer where an outsider could not assess the risk. Above all, he was able to deal in very small amounts of both palm-oil and imported merchandise. The result was that, although the expatriate firms quickly became established inland, they continued to deal with middlemen who were as ubiquitous as ever; but these middlemen never again operated with the panache of Ja Ja and Nana.

Thus the trade in palm products, which exhibited a high degree of African organizational skill and economic initiative in the nineteenth century, continued to do so thereafter though in somewhat muted form.

Cotton in Uganda and Nigeria

Among the five products discussed in this section, cotton received by far the most support from colonial authorities. The outstanding success of this crop during the period before 1914 was gained in Uganda. Over most of that country physical conditions for the cultivation of cotton, including rainfall, temperature and soil, are hospitable. In the south-east, the area first tapped by the Uganda Railway, cotton and a food-crop could be grown on the same plot in the same year, so obviating the problem of subsistence. In any case, much unutilized land was available; and male labour was in surplus, too, because the establishment of colonial rule had brought an end to the large army of Buganda. Several varieties of cotton, as reported by Speke and Grant in 1862 and by Lugard in

1891–2, were already growing wild before the colonial period. The opening of the Uganda Railway to Kisumu in December 1901 had lowered freight rates by 48 shillings per ton, as compared to the £100 to £300 per ton in the days of head-loading. Cotton did not at first receive a great deal of attention and, in 1902–4, ivory still predominated among exports. To generate further traffic for the railway the government was investigating coffee, rubber, chillies, wheat, simsim, ground-nuts, sugar, sansevieria and ramie.

With the hut tax of 1900 and the foundation of the British Cotton Growing Association in 1902 and of the Uganda Company, Limited in 1903 came the strongest impetus for developing cotton cultivation in Uganda. During 1903, when there was a minor rush to import varieties suitable for use in the textile industry, the government brought in a ton and a half of Egyptian cotton-seed and the Uganda Company, two and a half tons of Egyptian and American strains. (G. B. Masefield claims that the 1903 date given by almost all sources is wrong by a year, because Uganda Company records state that the introduction took place in 1904.) Both government and company distributed the seed free of charge for trial, the Uganda Company utilizing twenty-seven tribal chiefs in eight districts of Buganda for eventual apportionment of the seed among farmers.

Considerable enthusiasm was aroused, especially among the chiefs in Buganda, and during the next year almost five hundred farmers applied for seed. The government had doubled its initial order even before the results of the first planting were apparent, and three tons were distributed, mainly in Buganda, Bunyoro and Busoga, during September 1904. The first results showed the American seed far superior to the Egyptian strains. The government therefore obtained one more ton of American seed through the BCGA, distributing it in Ankole, Buganda, Bunyoro and Busoga during April 1905.

The role of the chiefs in the spread of cotton cultivation is emphasized by most sources. By 1905, many were stockholders in the Uganda Company, which reported that they were fostering cotton cultivation enthusiastically. At first, cotton was established by what Cyril Ehrlich has called essentially collective means, in roadside fields under the watchful supervision of the chief. The chiefs themselves had only recently been granted freehold tenure over large areas by British administrative decision, and in these early stages their entrepreneurial initiative was noteworthy. As peasants began to appreciate the potential profits in cotton cultivation, a growing number began to produce the crop for themselves as well as for their chief. This development took place more quickly in Buganda than elsewhere, although even there it was a slow process. Although some Ganda leaders were particularly enterprising and commercial-minded, this was not true of all, as seen in the references to unenthusiastic chiefs who had to be encouraged by the Protectorate government. One letter to the District Commissioner at Masaka reads:

I regret to hear that the chiefs in your district show want of interest in this most important industry. There is no excuse whatever for Mugema, who as Saza chief must be made to understand that he is responsible to us for the progress of his country. If he had set an example as he should have done, instead of showing reprehensible lack of interest, his people would most certainly have exerted themselves more as they have done in other sazas. Please make the sub-chiefs responsible clearly understand that they will forfeit their positions unless they show more attention to their duties and send Mugema to me on my return to Kampala.[14]

More than a hundred hand-gins were either sold below cost or given away by the government; and when these were seen to be unsuitable, the government bought them back from their owners at their original price. After the hand-gin failure, the crop had to be sent to Kisumu in Kenya for processing until a power-gin was set up at Kampala by the Uganda Company with the help of the BCGA. Three gins followed in 1908, with twenty in all by 1913–14. The Uganda Company was the only buyer until 1907; but with the entry of private traders as buyers, marketing controls were imposed. This furnishes an example of that curious prejudice against middlemen that is characteristic of much of Uganda's later economic history, both before and after independence.

The efforts of the government, the Uganda Company, the BCGA, the chiefs and Uganda's farmers led to a spectacular rise in cotton exports. In 1904–5, the equivalent of 54 bales worth £236 was shipped (0.39 per cent of all exports). In 1907–8 the figures were 3,973 bales, £51,800, and 35 per cent, respectively. By 1910–11 they had risen to 13,378 bales worth £168,000 (55 per cent), reaching 32,535 bales valued at £369,300, or 71 per cent of all exports, in 1914–15. Most of the cotton was shipped to Liverpool. (After 1918, India and Japan became the main customers.)

Among the several factors helping to spur this growth, one was the desire for imported consumer goods. This is clearly reflected in the trade returns, which show £115,000 worth of all goods imported in 1904, as compared to £940,000 in 1914. Noteworthy among the goods listed are textiles: imports of superior cottons, woollens and silks rose by value in that period from £24,000 to £185,000, as compared to the slower rise for inferior unbleached calico from £21,000 to £108,000. Bicycles and accessories rose from nil to £27,000 during the same decade. The distribution of these imported goods was mainly in the hands of itinerant Indian traders and shopkeepers, who served as middlemen in the buying of cotton also.

The 1,900 Indians in Uganda at the census of 1911 were economically important far beyond their numbers. Living primitively, they penetrated far into the Uganda hinterlands, introducing the imported trade goods that provided the incentive for local production of cash-crops. Even the cotton ginneries soon came to be owned mostly by Indians.

There were also some African middlemen, mainly Ganda, active in the cotton trade. Most received advances from Indian and European ginners and traders at the start of each buying season, and some began to accumulate a stock of capital. The reason for their disappearance is controversial, involving both the fierce competition of the Indian traders and the discouragement they suffered at the hands of the colonial authorities.

Further stimulus to cotton-growing was received from railway extension, with the Busoga extension being opened in 1912. This allowed cultivation to expand far beyond the borders of Buganda, where between 1910 and 1915 the estimated area under cotton remained stationary at about 20,000 acres. In the same period, however, acreage estimates for Busoga rose from 8,000 to

---

[14] Quoted in Cyril Ehrlich, 'Cotton and the Uganda economy, 1903–1909', *Uganda Journal,* Sept. 1957, **21**, no. 2, p. 172.

15,000, for Bukedi from 6,000 to 13,000 and for Teso from 5,000 to 30,000. In the Teso area, the introduction of ox-drawn ploughs was important, while in some cases migration occurred from highlands to plains as farmers sought land suited for cotton. (Large-scale migration of labour from Rwanda did not begin until after the war.) A programme of road-building was helpful in extending acreage, as was the provision of ginning facilities in the production areas. Teso was served also by the new Lake Kyoga steamers.

A final element in the early growth of production, already noted on p. 305, involved government regulation of marketing following the difficulties encountered in 1907, controls over seed supply, the establishment of an experimental station in 1911 and continuing research thereafter.

Over the years since the First World War, cotton has slowly been overtaken in Uganda by other more profitable crops, especially coffee. The early growth of the cotton industry depended heavily on the influence of the colonial authorities over the chiefs and the influence of the chiefs on their subjects. The completion of the railway, the need to make it pay and the search for new sources of cotton for the looms of the English Midlands were the coincident factors that greatly altered the Uganda economy after 1903. In spite of all this, however, cotton would not have come to prominence without a strong desire for cash on the part of Uganda's peasants, first to pay taxes, and second in much larger measure to import the consumer goods made newly available by the railway and by expatriate traders.

All this is by way of contrast with the very poor results before 1914 of campaigns in Nigeria and French West Africa to promote the production of cotton for export. Both areas, as already noted, had a long tradition of cotton cultivation, textile manufacturing and trade, dating back at least four centuries. Why did they not follow the lead of Uganda? The main explanation lies in the lack of sufficient financial incentives that might have attracted farmers into production.

Southern Nigeria is an apt example of the central role of economic incentives in cotton output. Initial attempts instigated by the Church Missionary Society to export the crop from Yorubaland (chiefly the Abeokuta region) in the 1850s had little success, although by 1859 more than two hundred gins were operating and a fair number of energetic Sierra Leonean middlemen had been attracted to the trade. The cotton famine caused by the American Civil War brought a real impetus to the trade by raising buying prices so much that more than 2,500 bales (400-lb lint equivalent) worth £60,000 were being shipped annually on average in 1868–70. But then, after 1870, U.S. supplies recovered and prices fell, leading to the virtual cessation of exports.

The BCGA attempted to resurrect cotton exporting in Southern Nigeria after 1902. The transport situation was now improved, as the new Nigerian Railway had reached Ibadan in 1901. Cotton could now be evacuated by rail instead of along the old Ogun river canoe route. Once again, however, the problem of incentives put a brake on progress. The BCGA established a fixed buying price of approximately 1d per pound at its stations; but in the face of competition from substitute crops such as cocoa and palm-oil, and from local buyers purchasing cotton for the indigenous textile industry, exports performed far less well than they had in Uganda. Exports sputtered erratically upward, averaging 8,700 bales annually between 1906 and 1913 and reaching a pre-war maximum of

14,200 bales in 1913. In the decade after 1913, the annual average dropped back to 9,895 bales. Cotton's competitive disadvantage was made greater by the need to grow lower-yield local varieties, as American strains proved susceptible to various diseases and pests, and by the growth of the cocoa industry.

In Northern Nigeria, the reaction of farmers to the BCGA's low fixed price was even more pronounced. The association had very high hopes for the cotton-growing area around Kano, with Winston Churchill, its chief parliamentary spokesman in the Commons, arguing that Northern Nigeria was 'the best cotton-growing region . . . discovered in the wide reconnaissances of the B.C.G.A.' [15] But the free seed, the pro-cotton administrative pressure brought to bear on local authorities and the new railway to Kano opened on 1 April 1912 were to have unexpected results. Quite unforeseen by almost all observers, the money return for ground-nuts turned out to exceed that for cotton. Farmers and traders joined in a ground-nut boom (discussed in the following section), which soon pushed cotton off the light, sandy soils suitable for the ground-nut in the Kano area, a retreat that ended at the heavier soils of Zaria and Katsina. But this was not the only blow. The sudden influx of new income from ground-nut sales, which also stimulated demand for local textiles, led Hausa merchants to offer higher prices for Northern cotton than did the BCGA. The buying stations of the BCGA were thus able to purchase only enough to export about 2,600 bales in 1912 and about 1,600 bales in 1913. Of this, fewer than 100 bales came from Kano in either year. Following the war, cotton exports from the heavy-soil regions near the railway did increase substantially, but only after the problem of insufficient incentive to producers had been overcome. For the pre-war period, however, the experience with cotton in Northern Nigeria provides an excellent example of fruitless planning and policy, of a programme undermined by the Hausa farmer's economic acumen.

The general picture was much the same for French West Africa. The Association Cotonnière Coloniale, founded in 1903, embarked on a programme of encouraging cotton exports with government support. But here, too, the low producer-price failed to generate significant response among farmers. Results were even less encouraging than in Nigeria, with output averaging only 570 tons per year for the whole of that vast colony as late as 1918–22, even after the stimulus given by the war. For the most part, the natives 'stood aloof, because ground-nuts and cocoa paid far better than cotton, and what were the dictates of national policy to them? . . . Lacking incentives, they stood still.' [16]

(For an account of German efforts to grow cotton in Togo, see Yudelman's essay in this volume, pp. 342–3.)

Ground-nuts in Senegambia and Northern Nigeria

Ground-nuts, of American origin, were probably introduced into West Africa by the Portuguese early in the slave-trade. Because they could be interplanted with food-crops and involved no new technology, increased output was relatively easy to obtain in the presence of sufficient producer incentives and low-cost transport. In Senegal and the Gambia, the rapid growth of ground-nut cul-

---

[15] See J. S. Hogendorn, 'The origins of the groundnut trade in Northern Nigeria', in *Growth and development of the Nigerian economy,* Carl K. Eicher and Carl Liedholm, eds. (East Lansing, Michigan State University Press, 1970), p. 32.

[16] Stephen H. Roberts, *A history of French colonial policy 1870–1925* (London, 1929), p. 324.

tivation and exportation was the most significant economic event of the nineteenth century, as it was to be later in Northern Nigeria. These areas together became the world's largest commercial suppliers of the nuts, producing about two-thirds of world output.

In Senegambia, following the suppression of the slave-trade in the early nineteenth century, the only important export was gum, a trade that was not particularly lucrative. French schemes to establish production of cotton and indigo in the 1820s netted poor results. Nonetheless, French colonial authorities were intent on a policy of *mise en valeur:* making the most of the unutilized agricultural and mineral resources in territory under their control.

Ground-nuts attracted minimal interest in the early days of Senegambian colonization. Observers reported they were little used for food, grown mainly as insurance against a millet failure. As late as 1824, a European visitor noticed them in the Gambia only because horses were fed with the green parts of the plant.

The first commercial shipment, from the Gambia in 1834, followed investigation of potential uses for the nuts by the British firm of Forster and Smith. French demand brought about the major growth in exports. However, little was achieved until French oil-seed duties were substantially reduced in 1840; but after that date—as French housewives found ground-nut oil less expensive than olive oil, and as the French preference for blue marble soap with a ground-nut–olive-oil base vis-à-vis yellow soap made from palm-oil became established—development was swift. Bordeaux merchants, among them Hilaire Maurel, Hubert Prom and Charles Peyrissac, persuaded local chiefs that farmers under their rule should grow ground-nuts. They argued that the sale of this crop could replace the revenue lost from the suppression of the slave-trade—revenue that could be spent in imported goods made available by these same merchants. Some Senegalese rulers, such as Lat-Dior, *damel* of Cayor, also encouraged production. By about 1850, French companies dominated the trade in both Senegal and the Gambia, with most nuts shipped to France. French commercial dominance in the Gambia led to the acceptance of the five-franc piece as legal tender in 1843 (the use of francs remained legal until 1922), and official recognition of the French *bourdeau* (eight bushels) in 1848. Ocean shipping to France was monopolized by the French because of heavy tariffs on colonial products imported in foreign vessels. These tariffs were not removed until 1866.

A most interesting facet of the ground-nut trade during this early period, and one resembling the trade in palm-oil, was the large proportion of the ground-nut crop grown outside the area under colonial control. This was almost entirely true of Gambian exports. Wolof farmers, using their earnings for the purchase of powder, muskets, kola and, especially, textiles later in the century, selling to and buying from Wolof middlemen, were most conspicuous in this development.

Even with the French as ultimate buyer of most Senegambian nuts, however, exports from Senegal remained limited because of poor transport. The main production area was originally in the north-east, near St Louis, but output of 3,000 tons in 1853 and 8,700 tons in 1870 compared poorly with progress in the Gambia. After thirty years of trade, exports were still no more than 15,000 tons in 1872, gum remaining more valuable in the accounts of the colony. Two subsequent events contributed to a major expansion in ground-nut production. First, peace was restored for the time being to the Cayor region lying between Dakar and St Louis. Cayor, one of the few good ground-nut areas in Africa near the coast, was instrumental in raising exports from the 1872 figure of 15,000 tons to 40,000 tons by 1885. It was in 1885 that the 174-mile Dakar–St Louis Railway was completed, spurring another large increase in output from the fertile Cayor Plain. Exports climbed to 65,000 tons in 1894 and to over 140,000 tons by 1900. With the railway's completion, Dakar now became the outlet for the Cayor crop. Farther south, Rufisque, too, developed in the 1880s as a ground-nut port.

Further railway-building brought additional ground-nut cultivation along the path of the line, with the completion of the Thies–Diourbel section of the Dakar–Niger line in 1908 allowing farmers in the provinces of Baol and Sine-Saloum to enter the export economy. Shipments reached 240,000 metric tons in 1913. The steady growth in Senegambian ground-nut production in the seventy years before the First World War was carried forward with only slight direct encouragement from colonial authorities, although seed distribution by the Gambian government was undertaken in 1896 and then again in 1909 and subsequent years with the aim of improving quality. As in the palm-oil trade, extensive use was made of credit, with imported goods advanced to indigenous middlemen, who in turn used the goods to purchase nuts for export. At least as early as 1896, the practice of cash advances by middlemen to farmers before harvest had been noticed. Soon thereafter, about 1900, Lebanese merchants began to arrive, and almost at once they were involved in ground-nut buying and the sale of imports.

Evidence indicative of peasant initiative as early as 1848 is provided also by the large-scale seasonal migration of labour to ground-nut areas. Migrant ground-nut farmers known as *navétanes* (a word derived from the Wolof for rainy season) in Senegal and as 'strange farmers' in the Gambia, travelling 500 or 600 miles, cultivated and sold their own nuts after payment of a fee to the local chief. The 1848 Gambia *Colonial report* states that the majority of nuts exported were grown by these migrant farmers. According to Neumark, these wet-season migrations to Senegambia are among the oldest in Africa.

It is extraordinary that many years later, in 1912, when the railway from Lagos reached Kano in Northern Nigeria, ground-nuts were *not* expected to be a major export from that vast territory. The area around Kano, with its light, sandy soil and adequate rainfall, was suited for ground-nut production on an enormous scale. But conditions were suitable for cotton also, and as previously noted, the BCGA and the colonial government expected the new railway to result in a cotton boom. There were always a few sceptics, in particular E. D. Morel, editor of the *African Mail*. But in spite of the Senegambian example, no one anticipated the great scale of ground-nut exports that was to jam the railway with traffic within the year.

The reasons for the neglect of ground-nuts by European observers were five-fold. Firstly, the propaganda for cotton by the BCGA and the government distracted official attention from other crops. Secondly, the Niger Company, the largest trading firm in the north, had its own pet project, shea-nuts, which, according to its officials, was the oil-seed of the future in that area. Thirdly, there was no ground-nut crushing in Britain; and as the West African Shipping Ring forced almost all cargoes to be carried to Liverpool or Hamburg, Germany would stand to be the chief beneficiary of a ground-nut boom. (There was no sympathy for this idea.) Fourthly, because of an overstatement of yield per acre of perhaps 20–25 per cent, gross return per acre for cotton cultivation was overestimated by the authorities. At the same time, the European buying price of ground-nuts was advancing steadily in 1912–13, from about £13 per ton in 1912 to as high as £17–18 in 1913, because of the growth of the margarine industry. The authorities predicted a comparative advantage for cotton that, in the event, was reversed. Lastly, there was insufficient appreciation of the lower labour requirements and lower risk for ground-nuts as opposed to cotton. Ground-nuts are less susceptible to drought and can be consumed instead of being exported should other crops fail.

The population in the vicinity of Kano, which was relatively large for the day (one and a half to two million), pursued an agricultural and marketing system that utilized permanent cropping with manure. Farm tools were fabricated in quantity by Kano ironsmiths. Indigenous farmers were sufficiently skilful that should potential sources of new income offer themselves, a reservoir of agricultural experience lay ready to be tapped. Finally, the Hausa traders of Kano had long before developed an extensive system of clientage, with less well-to-do traders, who had been provided with merchandise or cash by the head of the clientage network, acting as buyers or sellers on account for rich merchants. This system tended to overcome the problems of the very long distances over which Hausa trade was conducted and the low level of working capital available to most individuals.

The initial decision of the European firms to buy ground-nuts is remembered by participants as prosaic. A price was established and the news was made public in the city market by interpreters. Though details are fragmentary, it appears that a number of successful Hausa merchants, already heads of their own clientage organizations, were sought out, particularly by the Niger Company. In turn, three or four of these merchants employed agents who carried pro-ground-nut propaganda to farmers, recruited the services of village heads with money gifts and advanced imported salt and cloth to farmers on the understanding that the farmers would repay the advance with ground-nuts during the coming season. Because this occurred concurrently with rising prices for nuts in Europe, farmers rapidly began to part with nuts formerly eaten for food. Stocks mounted swiftly in Kano, at 100 tons per day and more, and the railway found itself unable to handle shipments. There was no way to store them adequately. Referred to as an embarrassment, they had to be stacked in the streets. Finally, in February or March 1913, the railway could no longer guarantee evacuation, with the result that the companies discontinued buying entirely. About 6,000 tons had been purchased, with the new cash income being used largely to pay taxes and purchase imported and local cloth, salt and kola.

When stocks had been cleared about the end of April 1913, more than 4,000 additional tons were purchased. Now a new planting season was approaching. European prices were even higher, competition among expatriate firms more intense and the efforts of Hausa middlemen reached more farmers. When the first rains fell in May, it became clear almost immediately that the Hausa of Kano had taken to the ground-nut far more than in the previous year. The senior government official at Kano telegraphed: 'AN ENORMOUS INCREASE IN CULTIVA-

TION OF GROUNDNUTS IS APPARENT AND EVERY POSSIBLE PRODUCER . . . IS STRAINING EVERY EFFORT TO HAVE A SHARE IN THE BIG PROFITS ANTICIPATED . . .' while the BCGA noted apprehensively that 'the natives have . . . taken up the cultivation of groundnuts on a large scale, and there is some danger of this competing with cotton.' [17]

Exports would have increased by a large amount, probably to about the 40,000-ton figure that was the Kano area's average in the decade after 1913. However, the growing season of 1913–14 saw the worst failure of the rains in the twentieth century in Northern Nigeria, with an unprecedented famine and deaths estimated at 30,000 for Kano Province as a whole. Output was cut and many nuts were eaten, including some already shipped south to the ports, stopped *en route* and sent back by rail. The figure for exports in this second season of the trade, about 12,000 tons, is actually strong evidence for the contention that a widespread shift to ground-nuts took place during the planting of 1913.

The really large tonnages to which we are accustomed today date from the period of railway extension in 1929–30 and the extensive use of motor lorries after 1928. But exactly the same economic incentives operating at Kano in 1912–13 appear to have applied in the newly opened areas, and indicate that Kano's experience was widely recognized, appreciated and copied.

On reflection, this discussion shows that the Senegambian and Northern Nigerian cases have two major points in common. The first is that labour was a constraining factor on output once transport and incentives were provided, and that surplus labour was utilized in both areas. In the Senegambia, the surplus was largely in the form of incoming migrants from areas not yet open to trade. In Northern Nigeria, the surplus developed as cotton output collapsed and as farmers ceased paying local taxes in millet and guinea corn. Second, large increases in output were achieved by capital accumulation in the form of seed retention by farmers. About 6 or 7 per cent of the preceding crop must be retained to sustain current output. Large increases in acreage thus always necessitate prior seed retention and restriction of current income. For Hausaland, Polly Hill has suggested that retention and storage are usually undertaken by richer farmers, who then lend seed to their poorer neighbours. In short, the groundnut trade, both in Senegambia and Northern Nigeria, is an excellent example of pre-1914 African economic initiative.

Cocoa in the Gold Coast and Western Nigeria

The concluding case is that of the most capitalistic crop among those studied: cocoa in the Gold Coast and Western Nigeria. Originating in Central or South America, the crop was spread widely by the Spanish and Portuguese, and had reached São Tomé and Fernando Po by the early years of the nineteenth century. There is some controversy as to how the plant was introduced to the Gold Coast—the Basel Mission Society, Governor Sir William Brandford Griffith and a Ga blacksmith named Tetten Quashie all being claimants. Quashie's cocoa nursery in Mampong (Akwapim) appears to have been the initial source whence pods or seedlings were distributed to local farmers, in itself an important example of indigenous entrepreneurship. Governor Griffith's new botanical

---

[17] Quoted in Hogendorn, 'Origins of the groundnut trade', p. 39.

garden at Aburi was selling cocoa seeds and seedlings to farmers by 1892 or 1893, which sales had grown by 1899 to over 400,000 annually. However, as 750 to 1,000 seedlings are needed per acre, and as over 200,000 acres had been planted by 1903, government efforts could not have been nearly so important as the farmers' own efforts.

Cocoa seedlings were thus becoming available at a time when the industrious farmers on and near the Akwapim Ridge north of Accra were searching for new cash-crops. The search was engendered by the considerable decline in palm-oil prices after 1885, at a time when the chief cash-crop of Akwapim was the oil-palm. It was the era of the Gold Coast rubber boom. Little rubber was grown in Akwapim country, however, although some profit was gleaned from trade in that commodity.[18] Cocoa seedlings were consequently obtained for planting, and coffee as well, though the resulting coffee trees died or were rooted up in 1897 and after because of the inroads of boring insects. European merchants were willing to buy cocoa; but as their operations were confined to the ports, they had less to do with the growth of the trade than was the case with groundnuts.

However, the farmers of the Akwapim Ridge did not have sufficient land to cultivate cocoa on a large scale. Thus, as early as 1892 began the great migration of cocoa farmers first revealed to economic historians by Polly Hill. At first, pioneer Akwapim farmers moved north and west of their ridge, until in 1896 or 1897 they crossed the Densu river, moving west. Shai, Krobo, Ga and other farmers from the Accra plains soon joined the migration to areas where cocoa would grow. The forested lands to which they moved were almost uninhabited except by hunters, and belonged to a small group of Akim towns located to the north and west. The Akim chiefs and people were not (until later) cocoa farmers, and even if they had been, their lands would have been far too abundant to cultivate by themselves. Hence the Akim chiefs quickly sold large forest holdings to the entrepreneurial-minded Akwapim.

The migrants had at least enough cash for down pa
purchase price, small sums such as £5 having been earned by individuals from their participation in palm-oil production or the rubber trade. Slowly exports began to mount, from a mere 80 pounds in 1891 to 13 tons (worth £500) in 1895, and 530 tons (£27,000) in 1900. Much output in the 1890s, however,

---

[18] Aside from its truncated progress, West African smallholder production of rubber is another good example of pre-1914 African initiative and innovation. Rising demand, first recognized in the Gold Coast by a number of African merchants at Cape Coast, led to the dispatch of agents into the interior forests. The spread of tapping techniques, the development of special tools, the sale of imported merchandise on credit and the use of advances to farmers—all appeared independently in the rubber trade. Prices approximately doubled between 1886 and 1899, leading to a rise in Gold Coast rubber exports from a high of 1.5 million pounds in the 1880s to a peak of 5.99 million pounds in 1898. But these developments did not survive slaughter tapping, the competitive demand for labour from the new cocoa industry and the rise of the Malayan rubber industry. Thus Gold Coast exports declined rapidly after 1910.

In Lagos Colony, rubber production peaked earlier, in 1896 (6.5 million pounds), owing to slaughter tapping that ruined output. Farther east, in the Southern Nigerian Protectorate, a high of 2.4 million pounds was achieved in 1904, but the widespread destruction of the wild rubber trees led to a collapse of the industry after 1905. In French West Africa, the principal producer was Guinea, source of 42 per cent of French West Africa's maximum figure of 4,300 tons in 1909. In that year Senegal/Sudan and Ivory Coast, each with 29 per cent of output, were not far behind Guinea. As in the British territories, the industry went into precipitous decline after 1910.

had been devoted to establishing new acreage, as shown by exports of 5,100 tons (£187,000) in 1905, 22,600 tons (£867,000) in 1910; and 50,600 tons (£2,489,000) by 1913. By this last year, sufficient new trees were already established to provide a further export expansion of more than threefold by 1919. No group in Africa before 1914 was brought into the money economy at a more rapid rate and with such large sums available for spending. Farmers used their new earnings for the consumption goods discussed earlier for palm products, cotton and ground-nuts. But there was unprecedented economic activity of other sorts as well. In the cocoa zone, education of children was financed and house building proliferated. Even local public works were undertaken, the projects including a few roads and foot-bridges. Finally, large-scale purchase of new land was made possible because of the profits from cocoa. Land-purchase arrangements were altered over time as the migrant farmers evolved organizations for collective buying. Family syndicates bought land west of the Akwapim hills and then subdivided their new holdings into strips the width of which varied according to the syndicate members' cash contribution. Each participant farmed his own strip, using his own or hired labour.

In the years before the First World War, tens of millions of trees were planted annually on the new lands, and herein appears the capitalistic nature of the cocoa industry. The establishment of a cocoa farm is incontestably an act of capital investment. Investment is ordinarily defined as economic activity that does not raise present consumption but does raise future output. Amelonado cocoa trees fit this definition fully. They were usually planted in forest areas where new land had to be laboriously cleared. The trees take about seven or eight years to mature, during which time they must be cared for by the farmer. For two or three years, the interplanting of food-crops among the young cocoa trees will yield some income, but after that time the farm becomes too shady for food-crops. Thereafter, the farmer needs a stock of working capital from some source in order to tide him over the remaining non-productive years before the trees bear for the first time. Full bearing of the tree takes much longer, fifteen years or more, meaning that cocoa farmers had to have a more extended time horizon than is needed for many investment projects in the Western world. It is worth noting how seldom direct investment in agriculture, in the form of established tree-crops, is recognized in modern statistics of capital formation.

Migrants without the money to buy their own land for planting cocoa could become tenant-farmers in one or two different structural arrangements that flowered as the industry grew: *abusa,* where the tenant received one-third of the cocoa picked for his landlord; or *nkotokuano,* with a fixed payment for each load collected. By 1910, says Polly Hill, there may have been as many of these labourers as farmers. In his detailed study, Robert Szereszewski has depicted the extraordinary labour-using character of the cocoa industry, with labour input rising from 100,000 man-days in 1891 to 37 million in 1911. Materially aiding in the mobilization of this surplus labour, which Szereszewski argues was primarily sacrificed leisure, was the fact that the cocoa harvest occurs at a slack period in food farming.

Further demand for hired labour, most often migrant in nature, emanated from the necessary task of transporting the cocoa to the coast. For, unlike the Nigerian ground-nut industry, the first twenty years' growth in the cocoa industry was accomplished without easy access to a railway. Only in 1910 and

1911, with the opening of the first stations on the new Accra–Kumasi line, was a start made in replacing man as a beast of burden. Road-building programmes by then were causing cask-rolling to replace porterage in the area. Within a short period, Accra became the port most utilized for cocoa export.

The character of the industry was thus established in the two decades before 1914. With the help of seed sales by Akwapim farmers, cocoa spread into Ashanti in 1898–1900. Production expanded faster there than elsewhere with the help of migrant labour from the Northern Territories, and by 1911 the Gold Coast was the world's largest producer. From the beginning, Gold Coast cocoa farmers had shown a high degree of entrepreneurial ability, exceptional response to economic incentives and remarkable dedication to economic betterment. This judgement, confirmed by later events such as the great cocoa strike of 1937–8 in response to an expatriate buyer's combine, has now held true for over three-quarters of a century.

In many respects the Nigerian cocoa industry developed in a like manner to that of the Gold Coast, and the introduction of the plant was approximately contemporaneous. The seed is said to have been brought first to Bonny in 1874 from Fernando Po by a local chief named Squiss Ibaningo (Bamego, Banego), who had worked as a labourer on the island; and at about the same time it was introduced into Calabar by an African named David Henshaw. Soon after these abortive beginnings it made a separate début in Egbaland, Ondo and Ilesha districts, and the Ibadan area, probably spreading from a cocoa farm planted by J. P. L. Davies, an African, at Ijan near Agege. Beginning in 1893, the government botanical station at Lagos (Ebute Metta) distributed some cocoa seeds. Near Ibadan, some farms had already been planted with cocoa soon after 1892. However, several negative factors kept growth less dramatic than in the Gold Coast. The reaction of farmers was somewhat slower than it had been among the Akwapim, who had had more extensive experience with trade. Of greater importance, competing economic alternatives—palm-oil, cotton and rubber—were available in the area. Thus cocoa exports were no more than 202 tons in 1900, 470 tons in 1905 and 2,932 tons in 1910, worth in that year about £101,000 (12 per cent of that year's Gold Coast crop). Only 4,939 tons (£172,000) were exported in 1914, although by that year the trees had already been planted that would produce exports of over 17,000 tons worth £1,238,000 in 1920.

Except for the fact that the Nigerian industry developed more slowly, there remain many strong similarities with that of the Gold Coast. The spread of cocoa cultivation in Western Nigeria involved bringing into use much previously idle land. From the first, migrants from towns in the forest belt established the cocoa farms, although migration was primarily a post-war phenomenon. Around 1900, the practice of hiring migrant labour appeared also, as it had in the Gold Coast. Unfortunately, it is not possible to measure the extent to which this labour had been previously idle, sacrificing leisure to raise cocoa, or alternatively, what other forms of economic activity were reduced for the purpose. The decline of palm-oil and cotton production in Western Nigeria points to the second explanation, however.

Other similarities with the Gold Coast industry include the spread of cocoa in areas adjacent to the railway, which had reached as far north as Oshogbo by 1907, the development of methods for obtaining credit, the rise of a market for land usufruct rights and the especial use of cash proceeds to finance construction activity, particularly new houses. Nigerian cocoa farmers actively promoted public investment in new transport, while farmers in both Ibadan and Ondo organized agricultural societies to disseminate information on new crops and techniques in their areas. The society at Ibadan even established an experimental farm in 1903, with some financial support from the colonial administration at first that was later withdrawn for budgetary reasons. Perhaps most noteworthy, however, is that many farmers in Western Nigeria were willing on their own initiative to take the long view, engaging in capital formation with no chance of significant return for six or seven years, just as had been the case 400 miles to the west in the Akim forests.

Conclusion

Over the years since about 1950, economic evidence bearing on African pre-colonial and colonial experience has accumulated rapidly. Economists have come to see that this experience has been diverse, and often more sophisticated than expected earlier. As a result, they have become wary of generalities in their descriptions and analysis. Yet one thread may be seen to run through the period covered in this essay—namely, that the quest for higher real incomes by African farmers and traders of agricultural commodities has led directly to indigenous economic initiative in a wide variety of institutional, geographic and temporal settings. This initiative has not been confined to any particular period. Many of the cases surveyed here have evidenced a link between pre-colonial cash farming and its subsequent development in the colonial period. The spread of new crops throughout Africa and the existence of fairly extensive local, regional and overseas trade in agricultural produce have been used here to exemplify economic initiative in the pre-colonial era.

The *process* through which this initiative was mobilized, leading to very large increases in output and exports of cash-crops in the early colonial period, has been described with the use of a modified Myint vent-for-surplus model. Surpluses of land and labour, with labour the more important constraining factor, new effective demand generated abroad, improved transport facilities and the inducement to production of 'incentive' goods are the elements most emphasized in the original model. Attention has been directed further to several other components needed to give the model descriptive accuracy. Included are indigenous capital formation comprising both real and working capital, efforts by colonial government to stimulate production (by means of taxes, propaganda, compulsion and agricultural research), and lastly, the central topic of this essay, the development and redirection of African entrepreneurial ability.

The elements discussed have usually been operative at the same time, but as I have shown, their importance in any particular case varies considerably. Whatever the variation, the discovery and expression of African economic initiative serve as a unifying factor for all the products surveyed. That initiative, already evident in pre-colonial economic activity, led by way of the vent for surplus to a very large expansion in colonial output. Any stereotype or theory not taking this into account fails to grasp one of the central features of African economic experience.

BIBLIOGRAPHY

Ajayi, J. F. A., and Michael Crowder, eds. *History of West Africa, vol. I.* New York, Columbia University Press, 1972.

Alagoa, Ebiegberi Joe. 'Long distance trade and states in the Niger Delta', *Journal of African History,* 1970, **11,** no. 3.

Allan, William. *The African husbandman.* New York, 1965.

Arhin, Kwame. 'Aspects of the Ashanti northern trade in the nineteenth century', *Africa,* Oct. 1970, **40.**

Ayorinde, Chief J. A. 'Historical notes on the introduction of the cocoa industry in Nigeria', *Nigerian Agricultural Journal,* 1966, **3,** no. 1.

Barber, William J. *The economy of British Central Africa.* Stanford University Press, 1961.

Barth, Henry. *Travels and discoveries in North and Central Afria,* vol. III. London, 1859.

Bauer, P. T., and B. S. Yamey. *The economics of under-developed countries.* Cambridge University Press, 1957.

Berry, Sara S. 'The concept of innovation and the history of cocoa farming in Western Nigeria'. African Studies Association paper, Nov. 1972.

Bohannan, Paul, and George Dalton, eds. *Markets in Africa.* Evanston, Northwestern University Press, 1962.

Boserup, Ester. *The conditions of agricultural growth.* London, 1965.

Bovill, Edward W. *The golden trade of the Moors.* London, Oxford University Press, 1968.

Brand, Richard R. 'The role of cocoa in the growth and spatial organization of Accra (Ghana) prior to 1921', *African Studies Review,* 1972, **15,** no. 2.

Brooks, George E., Jr. *Yankee traders, old coasters, and African middlemen.* Boston University Press, 1970.

Chevalier, A., and E. Perrot. *Les végétaux utiles de l'Afrique tropicale française,* fasc. VI: *Les kolatiers et les noix de kola.* Paris, 1911.

Clapperton, Hugh. *Journal of a second expedition into the interior of Africa from the Bight of Benin to Soccatoo.* London, 1829.

Clark, J. Desmond. 'The spread of food production in sub-Saharan Africa', *Journal of African History,* 1962, **3,** no. 2.

Clendenen, Clarence C., and Peter Duignan. *Americans in black Africa up to 1865.* Stanford, Hoover Institution, 1964.

Crowder, Michael. *West Africa under colonial rule.* London, 1968.

Curtin, Philip D. *Trade and market mechanisms in the Senegambia.* Discussion Paper series EH 71–3. Madison, University of Wisconsin, 1971.

Daaku, Kwame Yeboa. *Trade and politics on the Gold Coast 1600–1720.*

De Gregori, Thomas R. *Technology and the economic development of the tropical African frontier.* Cleveland, Press of Case Western Reserve University, 1969.

Dike, K. Onwuka. *Trade and politics in the Niger Delta 1830–1885.* Oxford, Clarendon Press, 1956.

Dumett, Raymond. 'The rubber trade of the Gold Coast and Asante in the nineteenth century: African innovation and market responsiveness', *Journal of African History,* 1971, **12,** no. 1.

Ehrlich, Cyril. 'Cotton and the Uganda economy, 1903–1909', *Uganda Journal,* Sept. 1957, **21,** no. 2.

Eicher, Carl K., and Carl Liedholm, eds. *Growth and development of the Nigerian economy.* East Lansing, Michigan State University Press, 1970.

Elkan, Walter. 'A half-century of cotton marketing in Uganda', *Indian Journal of Economics,* April 1958.

Fynn, J. K. *Asante and its neighbours*. Evanston, Northwestern University Press, 1971.

Gabel, Creighton, and Norman R. Bennett, eds. *Reconstructing African culture history*. Boston University Press, 1967.

Gann, Lewis H. *A history of Northern Rhodesia: early days to 1953*. London, 1964.

A history of Southern Rhodesia: early days to 1934. London, 1965.

Gann, Lewis H., and Peter Duignan. *Africa and the world*. San Francisco, 1972.

eds. *Colonialism in Africa 1870–1960*, vol. I: *The history and politics of colonialism 1870–1914*. Cambridge University Press, 1969.

Gellar, Sheldon. 'The politics of development in Senegal'. Ph.D. thesis, Columbia University, 1967.

Gertzel, Cherry. 'Relations between African and European traders in the Niger Delta 1880–1896', *Journal of African History*, 1962 **3**, no. 2.

Gifford, Prosser, and William Roger Louis, eds. *France and Britain in Africa: imperial rivalry and colonial rule*. New Haven, Yale University Press, 1971.

Gray, Richard, and David Birmingham, eds. *Pre-colonial African trade*. London, Oxford University Press, 1970.

Green, R. H., and S. H. Hymer. 'Cocoa in the Gold Coast: a study in the relations between African farmers and agricultural exports', *Journal of Economic History*, 1966, **26**, no. 3.

Hance, William A. *African economic development*. New York, 1967.

Hargreaves, John D. *West Africa: the former French states*. Englewood Cliffs, N.J., 1967.

Harlow, Vincent, and E. M., Chilver, eds., assisted by Alison Smith. *History of East Africa*, vol. II. Oxford, Clarendon Press, 1965.

Herskovits, Melville J., and Mitchell Harwitz, eds. *Economic transition in Africa*. Evanston, Northwestern University Press, 1964.

Hill, Polly. *The migrant cocoa-farmers of southern Ghana: a study in rural capitalism*. Cambridge University Press, 1963.

Rural Hausa: a village and a setting. Cambridge University Press, 1972.

Studies in rural capitalism in West Africa. Cambridge University Press, 1970.

Hodder, B. W., and D. R. Harris. *Africa in transition*. London, 1967.

Hogendorn, J. S. 'The origins of the groundnut trade in Northern Nigeria'. Ph.D. thesis, University of London, 1966.

Hoyle, B. S., and D. Hilling, eds. *Seaports and development in tropical Africa*. London, 1970.

Ingham, Kenneth. *A history of East Africa*. London, 1965.

Johnson, Marion. 'The cowrie currencies of West Africa, parts I and II', *Journal of African History*, 1970, **11**, no. 1; and 1970, **11**, no. 3.

Johnston, Bruce F. *The staple food economies of western tropical Africa*. Stanford University Press, 1958.

Jones, G. I. *Trading states of the Oil Rivers*. London, Oxford University Press, 1963.

Jones, William O. 'Economic man in Africa', *Food Research Institute Studies*, 1960, **1**, no. 2.

'The food and agricultural economies of tropical Africa: a summary view', *Food Research Institute Studies*, 1961, **2**, no. 1.

Manioc in Africa. Stanford University Press, 1959.

Kamarck, Andrew M. *The economics of African development*. New York, 1967.

Kingsley, Mary. *West African studies*. London, 1901.

Kopytoff, Jean Herskovits. *A preface to modern Nigeria*. Madison, University of Wisconsin Press, 1965.

Lewis, W. Arthur, ed. *Tropical Development 1880–1913*. Evanston, Northwestern University Press, 1970.

Lovejoy, Paul E. 'The Hausa kola trade 1700–1900: a commercial system in the continental exchange of West Africa'. Ph.D. thesis, University of Wisconsin, 1973.

'Long-distance trade and Islam: the case of the nineteenth century Hausa kola trade', *Journal of the Historical Society of Nigeria*, 1971, **4.**

McPhee, Allan. *The economic revolution in British West Africa*. London, 1926.

Manning, Patrick. 'Slaves, palm oil, and political power on the West African coast', *African Historical Studies*, 1969, **2,** no. 2.

Masefield, G. B. *A history of the colonial agricultural service*. Oxford, Clarendon Press, 1972.

A short history of agriculture in the British colonies. Oxford, Clarendon Press, 1950.

Meillassoux, Claude, ed. *The development of indigenous trade and markets in West Africa*. London, Oxford University Press, 1971.

Miracle, Marvin P. *Agriculture in the Congo basin: tradition and change in African rural economies*. Madison, University of Wisconsin Press, 1967.

Maize in tropical Africa. Madison, University of Wisconsin Press, 1966.

Miracle, Marvin P., and Bruce Fetter. 'Backward-sloping labor-supply functions and African economic behavior', *Economic Development and Cultural Change*, 1970, **18,** no. 2.

'Two causal models of African economic conduct: a reply', *Economic Development and Cultural Change*, 1972, **21,** no. 1.

Morel, E. D. *Nigeria: its peoples and its problems*. London, 1911.

Murdock, George Peter. *Africa: its peoples and their culture history*. New York, 1959.

Myint, Hla. *Economic theory and the underdeveloped countries*. London, 1971.

Neumark, S. Daniel. *Foreign trade and economic development in Africa: a historical perspective*. Stanford, Food Research Institute, 1964.

Newbury, Colin W. 'Credit in early nineteenth century West African trade', *Journal of African History*, 1972, **13,** no. 1.

The western Slave Coast and its rulers. Oxford, Clarendon Press, 1961.

Northrup, David. 'The growth of trade among the Igbo before 1800', *Journal of African History*, 1972, **13,** no. 2.

Nye, G. W. 'Short account of the history and development of cotton in Uganda', *Empire Cotton Growing Review*, 1931, **8,** no. 4.

O'Connor, A. M. *Railways and development in Uganda*. Nairobi, Oxford University Press, 1965.

Oliver, Roland, and Gervase Mathew, eds. *History of East Africa*, vol. 1. Oxford, Clarendon Press, 1963.

Pim, Sir Alan. *Colonial agricultural production*. London, Oxford University Press, 1946.

Prothero, R. Mansell, ed. *People and land in Africa south of the Sahara*. New York, Oxford University Press, 1972.

Roberts, Stephen H. *A history of French colonial policy 1870–1925*. 2 vols. London, 1929.

Rodney, Walter. *A history of the Upper Guinea Coast 1545–1800*. Oxford, Clarendon Press, 1970.

Rodrigues, José Honório. 'The influence of Africa on Brazil and of Brazil on Africa,' *Journal of African History*, 1962, **3,** no. 1.

Schlippe, Pierre de. *Shifting cultivation in Africa: the Zande system of agriculture*. London, 1956.

Suret-Canale, Jean. *French colonialism in tropical Africa, 1900–1945*. New York, 1971.

Szereszewski, Robert. *Structural changes in the economy of Ghana, 1891–1911*. London, 1965.

Thomas, Harold B., and Robert Scott. *Uganda*. London, Oxford University Press, 1935.

Turner, Victor, ed. *Colonialism in Africa 1870–1960*, vol. III: *Profiles of change: African society and colonial rule*. Cambridge University Press, 1971.

Vansina, J. 'Long-distance trade-routes in Central Africa', *Journal of African History,* 1962, **3,** no. 3.

Vansina, J., R. Mauny, and L. V. Thomas, eds. *The historian in tropical Africa*. London, Oxford University Press, 1964.

Wrigley, C. C. *Crops and wealth in Uganda*. Kampala, 1959.

Yudelman, Montague. *Africans on the land*. Cambridge, Mass., Harvard University Press, 1964.

CHAPTER 9

IMPERIALISM AND THE TRANSFER OF AGRICULTURAL TECHNIQUES

by

MONTAGUE YUDELMAN

At the beginning of the period covered by this essay (1850–1960), most of the inhabitants of sub-Saharan Africa were living outside the money economy. Apart from the cities of the savannah belt in the Western Sudan, the towns of the West African forest zone, and the maritime entrepôts along the east coast and some comparable settlements, Africans largely depended on agricultural economies of the household type. There was little specialization of production. Producers relied, above all, on a plentiful supply of land to provide for their subsistence. Methods of production varied in accordance with the dictates of nature. Over the centuries, moreover, African farmers had managed to adapt a considerable number of foreign crops, such as maize, to local conditions. Nevertheless, methods of production generally remained rudimentary. There was rarely any population pressure to force an intensification of land use. The volume of trade was so limited that it was usually insufficient to induce tillers to increase their output beyond the immediate needs of the tribe or family.

By the end of the colonial era, however, the colonial impact had created conditions that had a substantial bearing on raising agricultural output and trade. The establishment of 'law and order' and the advent of the administrator, teacher, missionary, tax collector and trader all contributed to the need to produce a surplus to meet money obligations. The development of transport systems, especially railroads and low-cost shipping, facilitated such a rapid expansion of external trade that during the period under review a marketable surplus was produced above and beyond subsistence. The surplus was large enough to meet the demands of the expanding urban centres in Africa, as well as to provide the major exports to earn foreign exchange with which to finance imports needed to foster economic development.

Sub-Saharan Africa is still the least-developed region in the world in terms of the proportion of total resources used to maintain the population; for instance, agricultural productivity is still extremely low by international standards. Nonetheless, there has been a considerable increase in agricultural output since the middle of the nineteenth century, and most notably since the first decade of the twentieth century. Part of this increase has come from extending age-old methods of cultivation to new lands, and part from exploiting natural resources, such as wild rubber or oil-palms, when a market has opened for these products. The introduction of new, higher-value crops has undoubtedly contributed most to the expansion of output, but there have also been increases in productivity that have come from technological changes in the agricultural sector.

Technological changes in agriculture, which may be defined as the introduction of new or improved inputs in the production process, are changes that take place at the farm level. These new or improved factors of production can be developed within a given region or country, or they can be brought in from elsewhere. A new or improved item, such as a better farm implement, may be developed by a farmer or a group of farmers; but those that are derived from scientific research—and which are the basis of most technological changes in modern agriculture—are seldom invented, discovered or originated by farmers themselves. The discovery and development of 'high technology' factors of production, such as new or improved varieties of seeds, improved breeds of livestock, chemical fertilizers, new farm machinery and new drugs for animal disease control or new pesticides for crop protection, are the outcome of the efforts of scientists, technicians, engineers and other skilled persons. The adoption and spread of these inputs depend, in good measure, upon whether farmers find it profitable to use them, and profitability, in turn, will depend upon market conditions and prospects for trade. A minimum requirement for the development of a high-technology agriculture is that there be a cadre of scientists and technicians to work on problems of the agricultural sector. Because this minimum requirement was not fulfilled in sub-Saharan Africa in the mid-nineteenth century, the science-based technology had to be brought in. During the period under review, most of the scientists and technicians were expatriates; and though there was some progress in the development of indigenous institutions, much of the available technology was imported and nearly all the skilled persons developing new technologies in Africa were expatriates.

New technology and new factors of production can be introduced from abroad 'spontaneously', or they can be introduced by governments systematically as part of a deliberate policy. The first new inputs brought into Africa were new crops, which were introduced by travellers and traders coming from other regions of the world, notably the tropics of the New World. With the expansion of colonial hegemony, the policies followed by colonial administrations assumed increasing importance in determining the pattern of agricultural development in the region. The initial emphasis was on the expansion of exports that were already being produced. During this period, whatever innovations came about were largely the work of missionaries, private individuals and non-public entities such as chartered companies and business groups. In tropical Africa there was relatively little in the way of systematic government-sponsored research or training of scientists to undertake research. After the turn of the century, however, colonial policies began to place increasing emphasis on the 'application of science to agriculture'. There was a determined effort to learn more about African agriculture and to create institutions to promote agricultural development in tropical Africa. By the middle of the twentieth century, all colonial governments were increasingly involved in raising agricultural productivity with a view to enhancing the welfare of most of the population of sub-Saharan Africa.

The sections that follow examine selected facets of the problem of technological change and the international transfer of technology as part of the process of African agricultural development during this period. The first part elaborates on the meaning of technological change and the international transfer of technology and points out how the transfer of agricultural technology differs from the transfer of other technologies. The second part considers the first spontaneous technological changes arising from the introduction of new crops; thereafter, it considers the efforts made under colonial administrations to promote agricultural development and technological change, especially by promoting research. The conclusion gives a brief review of the scientific and technological legacy related to agriculture left by the colonial powers on the eve of independence in Africa.

Technological change and the transfer of technology in agriculture

In theory, technological change in agriculture is the same as that in any other sector of an economy: it involves the introduction of a new or improved input in the production process.[1] Emphasis is laid on this approach because technological change extends beyond the concept of more skilful management or better organization of existing resources—namely, there is a shift in the production function rather than a more efficient use of existing inputs. Examples in agriculture in contemporary Africa can illustrate this difference: farmers in many countries are advised to change from broadcasting seed to planting in straight rows so as to increase yields per acre. Where no new factors of production are used, then, this will represent a change in technique whereby the farmer expects yields to rise because of the benefits from improved spacing of his plants. However, if, as is the more usual case—as with cotton in Uganda—farmers introduce row planters or new seeds and chemical fertilizers at the same time as they shift to planting in straight rows, this represents a technological change. Technological changes involve the introduction of some form of additional capital in the production process. This, in turn, usually requires some change in the management and techniques of production if the capital is to be combined efficiently with other factors of production. The international transfer of technology involves the transfer of a new input developed and used in one country to another. If this item is to be used efficiently, the transfer usually requires a transfer of techniques as well.

Although the principles of technological change and the international transfer of technology tend to be applicable to all sectors of an economy, several aspects of this process are peculiar to agriculture, especially as they relate to transfers from Europe to Africa. The distinctive aspect of agricultural technology, for instance, is that it deals with inputs and end-products that have a life-cycle of their own. For analytical convenience, inputs used to produce agricultural products may be described as reproducible and non-reproducible. The reproducible, such as seed and animal breeding-stock, are those that have inherent qualities of their own, that are influenced by the physical environment and that reproduce themselves. These qualities can be modified by breeding programmes that change the genetic base of a specific plant or animal. Thus it is possible for plants or animals to evolve through a process of natural selection or to be bred in such a way as to flourish within a given physical environment. However, since all reproducible inputs are sensitive to their environment, a plant or animal that flourishes in one physical environment will not necessarily flourish in another. A reproducible input suited for conditions in temperate

[1] See Montague Yudelman, Gavan Butler and Ranadev Banerji, *Technological change in agriculture and employment in developing countries* (Paris, Organization for Economic Co-operation and Development, 1971), *passim*.

Europe may not be productive when used in tropical Africa; thus there may be a constraint on the ready transferability between different environments. In some instances the constraint can be removed by the process of adapting the seed or livestock, through a breeding programme, for use in the importing country.

In agriculture, then, there are physical or environmental obstacles to the transplantation of commodities from one environment to another. Indeed, the differences in the physical conditions necessary for production of, say, cacao and apples provide part of the basis for a given country's enjoying a comparative advantage in producing a particular commodity. Differences in physical environment also frequently necessitate differences in techniques of production and management of resources.[2] For example, the water régime in temperate Europe differs considerably from that in tropical Africa. In Europe, the pattern of rainfall and the relationship between precipitation and rates of evaporation combine to make droughts or floods a rarity, whereas in Africa production is frequently sandwiched between droughts and floods. Consequently, soil and water management and the timing of farm operations are much more important in Africa than in Europe. In addition, the differences in water régimes account for varying requirements in such procedures as the application of fertilizers and in techniques of plant protection. In temperate zones, living weeds can be controlled by deep ploughing at the beginning of a crop season; in the tropics, where weeds may be killed by drought before the crop season, shallow, primary cultivation may be adequate. Indeed, experiments have indicated that when techniques of 'clean weeding' after the European fashion, recommended to increase yields in Europe, are transferred to Africa, they actually reduce yields and are detrimental to the soil under tropical conditions.[3]

The importance of the environment and the evolution of techniques of plant and animal breeding have resulted in a pattern of the transfer of agricultural technology to sub-Saharan Africa that is not much dissimilar to the pattern of transfers to other parts of the tropics. With the introduction of new plants brought by travellers coming from areas with a similar physical environment, the initial transfers tend to be unsystematic. The second stage involves the deliberate selection and multiplication of varieties that are introduced because they have general qualities that are economically desirable. The third stage involves the development of a prototype of the input that has desirable physical and economic characteristics in the light of local requirements. In Africa, these three stages were represented first by the introduction of new crops by Portuguese sailors and travellers coming from the tropics of the Indies and the New World. The second stage followed on the establishment of colonial hegemony and the desire to develop export markets, and included the deliberate importation of sisal from Florida, long-staple cotton from the United States, high sucrose-content sugar from Java, high-yielding tea from Ceylon and so forth. The final stage involved the creation of adequate research facilities within Africa to develop local varieties, a stage that was well under way in South

[2] A. H. Bunting, *Effects of environmental differences on the transfer of agricultural technology between temperate and tropical regions* (Reading, Eng., 1972).

[3] G. B. Masefield, *A short history of agriculture in the British colonies* (Oxford, Clarendon Press, 1950), p. 88.

Africa and for most export crops by the 1940s, but that for most food crops was only getting under way in tropical Africa by the 1960s.

An important aspect of the final stages of the international transfer of technology is that research must be applied *in situ* within the host country. Basic research in plant classification, genetics, biology and physiology may be universal in character and may be undertaken in any location, provided that there are suitable facilities to simulate different physical conditions. In addition, the initial import of new inputs may be undertaken without localized research. Many tropical products, for example, have been transferred from Latin America to Africa or the Far East by way of the Herbarium at Kew Gardens. Transfers such as the importation of rubber seeds from Brazil (*Hevea brasiliensis*) into Ceylon and Singapore were facilitated by the classification and multiplication of seed in Kew Gardens and by the subsequent transfer of this seed to botanical gardens in the Far East, where there was further multiplication. However, once the stage is reached when it is necessary to adapt both inputs and techniques of production to local circumstances, this can be done only within the area where the commodities are to be produced. It is only there that it is possible to test, systematically, how an input or a package of inputs will perform in circumstances under which they may be used for production. Thus, in the final analysis, the creation of facilities for research, together with the creation of a capacity to undertake research—including the human capacity—is necessary if any region wishes to adapt imported technologies to a given physical environment. Research of this kind, intended to benefit producers in subtropical Africa, cannot be undertaken in Europe, for, unlike research related to other sectors of the economy, agricultural research and product development tend to be both product specific and location specific.

Thus far, my discussion has concerned itself with the problem of transferring biological inputs, but in agricultural production farmers the world over use a wide variety of manufactured goods. The non-reproducible goods that are used are associated with the level of development of the agricultural economy. In isolated, underdeveloped and primitive economies, these items are usually made within the family household, and might include tools such as digging sticks, simple hoes and sleds for transport. With the growth of trade there will be increased specialization of production and division of labour. An increasing proportion of the inputs purchased by farmers will be manufactured off the farm. These might be developed and produced by local artisans and small workshops or they might be imported. An increase in trade between the agricultural and non-agricultural sectors will give rise to a larger-scale, domestic manufacture of these goods. Alternatively, they will continue to be imported. These articles may well be manufactured by extremely large-scale, capital-intensive, high technology industries, such as the chemical fertilizer and pesticide industry or the tractor-manufacturing industry.

Unlike reproducible inputs, there are no physical constraints on the transfer throughout the world of such capital inputs as machines. Certain economic considerations do have a bearing on the appropriateness of the manufactured inputs that are transferred among nations. Because the largest markets for capital goods used in agriculture (such as tractors and heavy implements) are to be found in the high-income countries, these goods are largely designed for the conditions existing in these markets. Such conditions usually include a relative scarcity of labour and an abundance of capital. In the low-income countries, by contrast, there is a relative abundance of labour and a scarcity of capital. Thus the transfer of technology that is capital-absorbing and labour-displacing may be undesirable from the point of view of increasing returns to society. Such a transfer might be encouraged by economic policies in the importing countries that undervalue capital and foreign exchange while overvaluing the price of labour. In addition, some importing countries may be forced to fall back on capital-intensive technologies because no alternative intermediate system is available to them. The manufacturers of these capital-intensive technologies, for their part, may have very little interest in developing less sophisticated systems because of the low rate of return.

The availability of complementary skills is a necessary condition for the successful introduction of new technology. The more complex the technological change, the greater the skill component in effecting the change. The most successful technological changes in agriculture in colonial Africa tended to be those that were the least demanding in terms of additional skills. The successful introduction of new crops such as maize was due partly to the ease with which these crops were cultivated and harvested. Similarly, the ease of cultivation is largely responsible for the spread of some tree-crops such as cocoa.

The least successful attempts to foster technological change in colonial Africa were made in the post-World War II years when there were several schemes to encourage the use of machine technology, such as tractors. The costs of operation and maintenance of these machines tended to make the schemes impracticable. Part of the reason for these high costs was a shortage of trained and skilled personnel. This did not apply in areas such as those parts of southern and Central Africa settled by Europeans. Here the settlers brought with them skills acquired by education and experience that were transferred when they migrated. The pattern was similar to that in North America and Australasia; but, of course, the number of European migrants to Africa were a minute fraction of those who went to the temperate zone regions of North America and Australasia.

A further aspect of the transfer of technology relates to the diffusion of new inputs among farmers. In this regard it is axiomatic that producers must have appropriate incentives if there is to be widespread technological change. Because the number of individual decision-makers in agriculture is substantial, any widespread technological change must appeal to a large number of producers. In some instances changes might be enforced, as in the early 1900s when compulsion was used to force producers in Uganda or the Congo to grow cotton or food-crops. In the main, though, producers will adopt changes only when they consider it to be to their advantage.

During the colonial era it was not always appreciated that all indigenous producers might not see the desirability of change in the same light. Nor did policy-makers appreciate that there might be differences in outlook within the same societies and between societies. In some societies, for example, innovators might be highly motivated to increase output, even though the adoption of a technological change might require added inputs of labour. Others, who did not adopt the change, might have preferred added leisure to added output, especially if there was little opportunity to trade the increased output. In some societies—especially in poor subsistence economies—producers might not be interested in change because they might consider the inherent risks too great. Subsistence producers might have evolved methods of production by trial and error to maximize risk aversion, as the risk of crop failure might mean hunger and starvation. In the eyes of such a group the potential benefits from change might not be equal to the premium they placed on risk aversion. In other instances, the value that the local populace attached to a commodity—such as cattle in parts of South and East Africa—might far exceed the apparent market value because of the special role that cattle play in these societies. In very broad terms, though, as a society becomes monetized, so producers tend to adopt those changes that will add to their real incomes and so costs and prices per unit of output tend to become important determinants of the direction of technological change.

Once it is recognized that costs and prices influence the direction of technological change, then it may be seen that technological change in agriculture is not a phenomenon that is isolated from events outside the agricultural sector. The interdependence of agriculture and the other sectors of the economy and the subsequent inter-sectoral linkages influence both costs and prices in agriculture, and so the adoption of new inputs. The opening of railways, which were so important in African development, for example, may be a prime factor in encouraging technological change. Costs of transporting bulky crops may be sharply reduced, thus making it profitable for farmers to introduce new export crops into an area where formerly the marketing costs had been too high. The development of the mining industry, as happened in South Africa, can encourage technological change in agriculture; an expansion of a labour-intensive mining industry might result in a rising cost of labour, thus encouraging farmers to substitute animal or machine-drawn equipment for labour at the farm level. The development of a new low-cost method of producing chemical fertilizer, as occurred in the 1920s in Europe, may shift the cost–price ratio between chemical fertilizer and the price of a product to favour the use of fertilizer. Indeed, because agricultural progress in tropical Africa was closely linked to the development of world markets, the major impulses for introducing technological changes in African agriculture came in response to development outside Africa.

The transfer of technology and the spread of technological change in agriculture depend on a host of factors, cultural, social, economic and physical. Whatever the origins of a new input in a specific area, this input usually requires some adaptation in a given environment. This means there has to be localized research, which must frequently be financed out of public revenues. The allocation of public expenditures thus becomes an important factor influencing the transfer of technology and techniques of production. The diffusion of the new technology requires the spread of knowledge that makes it readily accessible to farmers. In the final analysis, though, the rate of adoption of the new input will depend on the extent to which farmers believe their best interests can be served. In the early pre-colonial period in Africa, the absence of an internal market of appreciable size limited the demand for agricultural output. It was the opening of the export markets that provided the major stimulus for both technological change and agricultural development.

The early colonial period

Africa is a vast continent that covers a multiplicity of climatically diverse regions, many of them isolated from one another by deserts, mountains or forests. Some nine-tenths of sub-Saharan Africa is situated within the tropics, with the temperate zones being primarily in the Republic of South Africa. The interior of tropical Africa remained for the most part isolated from the world, partly because of the effects of the tropical environment on Europeans and partly because of the inaccessibility of the African hinterland. With the exception of the salubrious areas, such as those in the Republic of South Africa and, to a much lesser extent, in Rhodesia and Kenya, there was very little permanent immigration from outside Africa. Thus the problems attendant on encouraging technological change in agriculture in Africa, unlike those in North America and Australasia, were related to encouraging change among an unlettered and unschooled indigenous population inhabiting an area about which very little was known even as late as the mid-nineteenth century.

Early African agriculture was based on a system of shifting cultivation that was rational from a technical and economic point of view in the circumstances that prevailed. Technically, it was a concession to the nature of the soil and the climate, especially the erratic rainfall. The soil is poor in many parts of tropical Africa, particularly in the semi-arid regions of Central and East Africa; and shifting cultivation has in the past prevented depletion of the soil in the absence of an appropriate technology to meet the requirements of sedentary cultivation. A relatively sparse population using primitive techniques of production was in ecological balance with its environment. Economically, within the limit of his horizons, the African producer was rational in his production methods. Land was plentiful, labour was relatively scarce and capital almost nonexistent. The plentiful and free land supply was substituted for any intensive labour effort that might have required extra energy-inputs (which undoubtedly had a cost). Thus land was used extensively to produce a limited output; output per acre and per man must have been low. Some of the larger centres, cities like Timbuktu, Kano and Ibadan, drew for their provisions on imports from the countryside. But in most parts of the subcontinent, the bulk of the crops was produced for consumption within the span of the season before the new harvest was brought in. There was little diversion of effort for 'round-about' production. Irrigation works, such as those built by the ancients in parts of East Africa, were few and far between. Capital formation consisted mainly of land clearance, the building of simple storage facilities and the production of uncomplicated tools. Economically, these were backward societies. The range of choice, both for producers and for consumers, was limited. Surpluses were limited; and even though there was usually some form of trade in salt, iron and other valuable commodities, producers had to live mainly on what they grew themselves or on what they could take away from others by force.

The first changes in African agriculture that followed on the expansion of European interest in the region were not so much changes in techniques of production as in the introduction of new crops. Before the advent of the Europeans the more important indigenous food-crops included sorghums, millets, yams, native rice, teff and certain wheats. A few crops, such as teff, had, and still have, a limited geographical range, whereas others, such as sorghum and

336

millet, provide the staple diet throughout the semi-arid areas of the continent—namely, from Senegal to the Sudan and southern Africa. As well as the indigenous crops came others, primarily by means of Arab traders from the East, and they included cloves and spices. Later, the Portuguese brought into the region major crops from the New World, such as cassava, sweet potatoes, ground-nuts and tobacco.

Perhaps one of the more important food-crops introduced into Africa in the sixteenth century was maize, which is now a staple food throughout much of the continent south of the Sahara. The introduction and the spread of this crop were not systematic, but seem rather to have taken place because the qualities of maize made it culturally and economically acceptable.[4] It was introduced at first on the east and west coasts in order to supply a suitable foodstuff for ships' crews. Later, the demand increased because maize seemed suitable for feeding to slaves on the long voyages to the New World. Thereafter, it penetrated the hinterland very rapidly. In Uganda, for instance, maize growing spread through much of the territory between 1840 and 1900. Here again, though the reasons are subject to speculation, the physical attributes of the crop seem to have encouraged its acceptance and diffusion. It is easy to plant and to harvest, and it can be stored and transported and converted into edible food without too much difficulty. Thus it was an ideal commodity for provisioning travellers, for trading and for use by marauding parties.

In contrast to maize, other commodities, such as Asiatic rice and cassava, spread much more slowly through the regions in which they could be cultivated. Asiatic rice is labour-intensive, and labour was scarce in Africa; and because the rice grew in the areas infested by tsetse-fly, it was not possible to substitute animal labour for human labour. Consequently, producers tended to prefer to grow the less labour-intensive crops that were less demanding. Cassava, for example, grows very readily in tropical Africa, but technology for converting it into an edible food-crop requires the removal of the prussic acid in this root crop. The difficulty in adopting this technology slowed down the spread of this crop. It was only when former slaves from Brazil returned to West Africa that a suitable technology for the preparation of manioc meal was diffused. Thereafter its production increased very rapidly.[5]

There were attempts before 1880 also to introduce new commodities and inputs into regions suited for European settlement. The major efforts in this direction were made in South Africa, where the earliest settlers grew maize and wheat. In addition, though, new crops introduced into South Africa included grapes brought into the Cape by the Huguenots, sugar cane introduced into Natal and merino sheep imported into the Cape. The settlers introduced horses as well, which provided mobility for the Voortrekkers.

During the period 1880–1950, the colonial powers gradually assumed increasing responsibility for the development of agriculture in sub-Saharan Africa. Before the Berlin Act and the subsequent scramble for Africa, they tended to follow a policy favouring the expansion of markets rather than developing new regions through government intervention. A variety of pressures—

[4] See Marvin P. Miracle, *Maize in tropical Africa* (Madison, University of Wisconsin Press, 1966), *passim*.
[5] Thomas R. De Gregori, *Technology and the economic development of the tropical African frontier* (Cleveland, Press of Case Western Reserve University, 1969), *passim*.

humanitarian, economic, financial, commercial and political—led the colonial powers to intervene in the economic development of these territories. Initially, though, in the absence of direct government intervention in agriculture, it was the private corporations or individuals, missionaries and traders who assumed important roles in developing agriculture.[6]

The humanitarian impulse of the missionaries was directed largely at the abolition of the slave-trade. However, slave porterage was essential for the ivory and rubber trades, so that if the slave-trade was to be ended, it was necessary to develop alternative exports and a supporting transport system. Traditional commercial activity fitted comfortably into this general scheme of expanding trade, so that mission societies soon became involved in promoting trade as well as agricultural development.[7]

Successful evangelization often began with the establishment of a plantation, or else economic necessity required that the mission station develop a plantation. Consequently, some missionaries imperceptibly became settlers (though early attempts to found self-supporting Methodist missions failed). The dual in-

[6] EDITORS' NOTE: The notion of planned economic development was becoming widely current by the beginning of the twentieth century. In Germany, Bernhard Dernburg (in charge of colonial affairs 1906–10) had very clear ideas on how to develop the colonies through the creation of a logistic infrastructure and of specialist services. The Germans founded African agricultural schools, such as Nuatja in Togo, and research centres, such as Amani in East Africa. The Kolonial-Wirtschaftliches Komitee promoted the cultivation of cotton. The British under Joseph Chamberlain, colonial secretary 1895–1903, had both planners and a plan. Pressure from shipping and merchant interests, cotton manufacturers and others pushed government into providing some infrastructure to develop West Africa. Railways and roads and ports were built. Humanitarian interests dictated health measures. The official plans called for the development of trade, and governors were appointed who had qualifications in port and railway construction and public health. For example, in South Nigeria, Governor William MacGregor and Sir Ralph Moor stressed agricultural development by experimentation, testing of plants for their economic value and supplying farmers with seed, seedlings and saplings from the government botanical gardens. The seedlings for coffee, kola, cocoa, maize, oil-palm and citrus and other fruits produced at the Royal Botanical Gardens at Kew helped to improve the people's diet and led to the development of economic crops. Farmers were given instruction in cultivation, and gardeners and demonstrators were provided. The new steel matchetes made it easier to clear the bush, and new crops were planted for food and export. Economic plants were brought from the West Indies, and American experts in cotton-growing and stock-raising came to Lagos. These people not only tried to develop new export crops, but planted new trees to conserve and develop forest resources as well. The Southern Protectorate of Nigeria also encouraged agriculture and market gardening. It introduced new crops and experimented in agriculture. It had botanical gardens and an experimental cotton plantation, and brought in cattle from Barbados. Although many ideas failed, some succeeded, notably those involving mangoes, tobacco, firewood plantations, cocoa, kapok, cinnamon, raffia and kola. The protectorate experimented also with jute, castor oil, bananas, maize, and ground-nuts. (See I. F. Nicolson, *The administration of Nigeria, 1900–1961* [Oxford, Clarendon Press, 1969], for details.) Similar work was done in Kenya, Uganda and Southern Rhodesia.

[7] For a fuller discussion, see Roland Oliver, *The missionary factor in East Africa* (London, 1972), pp. 172–8 and 213–15; M. F. Hill, *Planters' progress: the story of coffee in Kenya* (Nairobi, 1956), p. 47; J. D. Tothill, ed., *Agriculture in Uganda* (London, Oxford University Press, 1940), pp. 314–15; Seth La Anyane, *Ghana agriculture: its economic development from early times to the middle of the twentieth century* (London, Oxford University Press, 1963), p. 37; J. F. A. Ajayi, *Christian missions in Nigeria, 1841–1891: the making of a new élite* (London, 1965), pp. 114–16 and 141–2; C. G. Baëta, 'Introductory review: facts and problems', in *Christianity in tropical Africa: studies presented and discussed at the Seventh International African Seminar, University of Ghana, April 1965*, C. G. Baëta, ed. (London, Oxford University Press, 1968), pp. 13–17.

terest in evangelization and agriculture also inspired some crop experimentation and agricultural education. Missionaries were responsible for the introduction and dissemination of many important export crops in Africa.

Missionaries helped to lay the foundations of the cotton industry in Uganda. In 1903, the industrial mission of the Church Mission Society imported from the United States sixty-two bags of cotton-seed of five varieties. This seed, along with some imported from Egypt by the government, was distributed among the chiefs. It soon became apparent that the long-staple, American upland variety flourished in the environment of Uganda. From this seed, which in 1904 was given to about thirty growers of the Ugandan Trading Company, established by the mission, some forty-five tons were harvested. The crop was so successful, in fact, that whereas in 1904 there were 500 applicants for seed and more than 240 bales of cotton were exported, by 1914 some 27,000 bales were exported. Missionaries also introduced coffee into East Africa. The White Fathers' mission in Kenya brought arabica coffee to that country where, after many technical difficulties were resolved by the agricultural department, it became an important export crop. Missionaries introduced other minor crops, too, varying from cinnamon and ginger to potatoes and onions. They also helped with the dissemination of improved seed, playing an important part in fostering the rapid growth of the cocoa industry in the Gold Coast, tea and coffee in Malawi, and fruit and vegetables in Zambia.

In addition to these contributions, the missionaries helped to spread improved techniques of production. The Jesuits and Seventh-Day Adventists helped to introduce the ox-drawn plough to the Tonga of Northern Rhodesia. The London Missionary Society in north-eastern Zambia introduced the use of manure and the practice of laying out gardens in beds. In Malawi, missionaries and missionary workers played an important role in the introduction of cotton culture and dairy farming. Individual missionaries made lasting contributions to agricultural development. Among the most successful of the missionary teachers were two American agriculturists, George Arthur Roberts and Emory Alvord, both of whom worked in Southern Rhodesia. Roberts taught agriculture to Africans from 1908 to the 1960s. He introduced the plough and taught Africans to train and to use their cattle as draught animals to till soil that had previously been left idle. In 1914 he added dairy cows to his training programme, and soon after, the proper care and feeding of poultry. His innovations were numerous. He practised the first contour-ploughing to stop the erosion that accompanied tropical rains; he organized agricultural shows to stimulate improved farming and animal husbandry; he taught Africans to irrigate; and he tried new crops, vegetables, trees, pest controls and improved stock-breeding, ditching and draining. Significant as Roberts's contributions were, his influence was largely confined to the vicinity of his mission, whereas Alvord, in his efforts to improve African agriculture, covered the entire colony of Southern Rhodesia.

Alvord, who had a master of science degree in agriculture, came to Southern Rhodesia in 1919 to work with the Congregational Church Mission. For seven years he ran an agricultural course in the mission school and worked out a comprehensive scheme for demonstration and extensive work. In 1920, when he had been in Southern Rhodesia only a year, he was asked to assist in drawing up plans for a new government agricultural school at Domboshawa that had been authorized recently. He spent some time at Domboshawa instructing the staff and the African students in subjects such as crop rotation, proper ploughing, manuring, the use of legumes and row planting. Alvord was appointed agriculturist for the instruction of Africans in 1925, and spent the next thirty years training Africans in his demonstration techniques. Successful demonstrations of improved farming and animal-husbandry techniques required that Alvord-trained Africans live in the villages and actually plant and raise cattle. They were equipped with new knowledge, seeds, fertilizers and tools. Alvord also taught the use of the plough and introduced manuring, new crops and so forth. He taught Africans how to conserve and maintain their soil, how to plant and tend their crops, to care properly for their cattle and to maintain proper pasturage and to increase the amount of arable land; in addition, he introduced irrigation. He taught Africans to live in planned and well-constructed villages, rather than to scatter at will, planting their crops haphazardly wherever there seemed to be space. In this way it was possible to improve their water supplies, to achieve better sanitary conditions and to keep pastures and cultivated fields separate.[8]

In general, missions performed a valuable task in helping to create some of the conditions necessary for technological change in agriculture. They introduced new inputs such as the plough and seed and encouraged their diffusion; and they taught some of the complementary skills needed to utilize the new inputs. Through the spread of literacy, they paved the way to a better understanding of the scientific basis for agricultural production. Nonetheless, despite these efforts most missionaries were after all not agricultural scientists; their primary interests lay in other directions. Their main contribution to agricultural development and technological change in agriculture lay in their educational programmes and the spread of literacy. These programmes provided the first cadres of Africans who were to exert an influence on the development of their own educational systems, including those related to agriculture.

In the metropolitan powers there were commercial interests eager to exploit the resources of the colonies. Among the more successful of these was the British Cotton Growing Association (BCGA), financed largely by the cotton manufacturers of Liverpool, formed in 1902 to encourage cotton production in the hope of finding an alternative source of supply to the southern states of the United States.[9] The association itself financed research trials, distributed seed, guaranteed the price of cotton, assisted in arranging transport for cotton and established ginneries in parts of Africa. In co-operation with the missionaries and with some local governments, the association undoubtedly played an important part in creating the cotton-growing industry in sub-Saharan Africa—an industry

---

[8] EDITORS' NOTE: Another example of a missionary who revolutionized African agriculture was Sam Coles, an Alabama Negro who went to Angola in 1923 as an agricultural missionary and served for thirty years in southern Angola among the Ovimbundu. Coles had been trained in agriculture and industrial arts at Talladega College. He introduced the plough, taught Africans to train their cattle to pull the ploughs, to carry water, to stump trees and to transport logs and crops. He introduced new crops such as wheat and fruit and showed people in a 300-mile area around his mission station how to improve their crops and to farm previously unused land. See Samuel B. Coles, *Preacher with a plow* (Boston, 1957).

[9] Great Britain, *Parliamentary papers*, vol. LXVI, Cd 5215, *Memorandum on government action in encouragement of cotton growing in Crown Colonies* (London, 1910); and vol. XVI, Cmd 523, *Report on Empire Cotton Growing Association* (London, 1920).

dominated by small-scale African producers. In 1921 the association was super-seded by the Empire Cotton Growing Corporation, which was supported by the British government. The corporation focused its research on improving the genetic quality of cotton plants and worked closely with the Shirley Institute in England to enhance the ginning characteristics of African cotton. It operated a series of research stations in sub-Saharan Africa, including stations in South Africa, Sudan and Uganda. As the number of cotton growers expanded, the corporation's work shifted more towards resolving practical problems of cotton production, such as improving practices and techniques of production and pro-tecting crops. There is no doubt that between 1902 and 1920 the BCGA as-sisted substantially in the founding of the cotton industry in Africa; nor can there be any question that the corporation made a major contribution towards the expansion of that industry over the years 1920–60. The dramatic impact of its contribution may be gauged from the record of one country. Uganda, which in 1904 exported no cotton, exported 1.5 million 100-pound bales of cotton in 1959.

Other commercial interests that fostered technological change in African ag-riculture included processors of raw material, such as the manufacturers of tobacco. Tobacco companies, such as the Nigerian Tobacco Company and the East African Tobacco Company, assisted African producers to provide the raw material needed for their cigarette and tobacco factories.[10] To this end, the companies sponsored research and production of seedlings and of high-quality tobacco. The seedlings were then distributed to farmers who were given tech-nical advice, credit and supplies, including help in building small curing barns. The companies purchased this tobacco at a guaranteed price. In Nigeria, where the programme started in 1934, 400,000 pounds of tobacco was sold by the farmers by 1938.[11] In East Africa, the tobacco companies started somewhat later; but by 1960 both Nigeria and the three countries of East Africa—Uganda, Kenya and Tanzania, formerly known as Tanganyika—had a self-sufficient tobacco industry. In additon, large numbers of hitherto subsistence producers, such as those in the West Nile region of Uganda, were able to enter the money economy and to enjoy a much higher level of living than hitherto.

The trading companies were still another element in the private sector that contributed towards agricultural development and technological change in sub-Saharan Africa. These companies appeared to provide a means of resolving the dilemma of expanding colonial hegemony while limiting government enterprise and extending government administrative expenses. The chartered company became an important vehicle for this purpose and was used in the British, Ger-man and Portuguese colonies.

The three British chartered companies—the Royal Niger Company, the Im-perial British East Africa Company and the British South Africa Company—were founded in 1886, 1888 and 1889, respectively. Of the three, only one was a financial success, the Royal Niger Company, operating in the Niger basin. This may be partly explained by a sequence of technological changes outside

---

[10] Peter Kilby, *Industrialization in an open economy: Nigeria, 1900–1960* (Cambridge University Press, 1969), *passim*.

[11] EDITORS' NOTE: Over the succeeding years the Nigerian Tobacco Company encouraged and taught Africans to grow and to cure better varieties of tobacco and to form co-operatives and producer groups. They also gave technical advice and lent Africans money.

Africa that provided the stimulus for an expansion of trade in palm-oil products. The first of these changes was the invention and the increased use of the steamship, which reduced substantially the costs of ocean transport. This lowered the price of palm-oil and thereby increased demand until the expansion of this trade was limited by the substitution of petroleum for palm-oil. The decline in value of palm-oil exports, however, was offset by a further technological innovation that increased the use of palm-kernels. This innovation, called the Loder process, led to the manufacture of margarine and permitted palm-kernels to be used as a low-cost substitute for animal oleo. It was not long before palm-kernels, previously unused, surpassed palm-oil as an export.

The company's main interests were in trading in products already produced in the region rather than in developing new products or new techniques of production. Nonetheless, the company did undertake some experimental work in agriculture through the establishment of botanical stations manned by officers trained at Kew in London. At Abutshi, attempts were made to cultivate cocoa, coffee, fruit trees, cotton and indigo; and there was a small experimental rubber plantation at Koonini as well as an experimental garden at Asaba. Except for the Asaba garden, which was totally unfit for cultivation because of its unfortunate location on the sand-banks of the Niger river, little is known about the operation of these stations.[12]

The Imperial British East Africa Company, whose contribution to agricultural development was limited, was short-lived. The company established its own plantations for the production of coffee, undertook surveys and explored the possibilities of improving transport to the interior. The British South Africa Company looked to the exploitation of minerals in Central Africa for its main source of revenue. When its expectations were not realized, the company decided to capitalize on its very large concessions of land. Land was sold to companies, syndicates and individuals. In addition, the company hoped to attract European settlers and to exploit its own holdings for productive purposes. Although programmes for recruiting settlers never succeeded, the company made a major contribution to the development of the region by using its lands for investigating every branch of agriculture that might have held promise, especially the production and processing of tobacco, the growing of citrus under irrigation and the improvement of beef and dairy herds. However, these advances were confined to the European sector of the agricultural community, which in 1920 numbered some 20,000, compared with the 900,000 or so Africans who depended on the land for their livelihood. The research work initiated by the company laid the basis for one of the most successful programmes of research undertaken in Africa, which followed when Rhodesia became a self-governing colony in 1923.

Perhaps the most determined efforts were those of certain German Kolonialgesellschaften, which undertook the major task of agricultural development of the German territories in Africa between 1870 and 1915. These companies, backed by the German government, approached the development of agriculture in their colonies with a thoroughness that befitted the European country with the most advanced system for developing technological change in Europe. The Kolonial-Wirtschaftliches Komitee (KWK), founded in 1896, came to play an

[12] Major MacDonald, *Report on the administration of the Niger Territories 1890*, F.O. 84/2109 (London, British Public Record Office).

important role in promoting technological change in the German territories.[13] It concentrated on introducing rational methods of production in the German colonies: Kamerun, German East Africa, Togo and German South-West Africa. It mounted scientific expeditions to various tropical regions, established nursery gardens in the colonies and undertook the chemical testing of tropical agricultural products and seeds. The chartered companies and plantation interests established a private colonial training school in 1898 to train European staff. Pressure from German industries led to the creation of special institutions to undertake research into seed production and the production of implements for colonial use, and to the establishment of a cotton board and a rubber board.

The chartered companies and the KWK assisted in introducing new inputs into their colonies. In 1893, a botanist working for the German East Africa Company introduced sisal agave from Florida into East Africa. Ten years later, East Africa exported 422,000 kg of sisal. The companies also introduced coffee, cotton and potatoes into German East Africa. The KWK was instrumental in promoting cotton production in the German territories. Cotton plantations, on which the first steam ploughing-engines and fertilizers were used on irrigated lands, were established in East Africa. In Togo, the KWK attempted to encourage the Africans to grow cotton; and, as part of this effort to transfer technology and techniques of production, six Negro farmers were brought over from the Tuskegee Institute in North America to introduce the crops to the Africans.[14]

In other parts of Africa, notably in the French and Belgian territories, the private sector's contribution to agriculture was through the concessionaire system, which was also part of the effort to reduce administrative expenses. Large-scale concessions granted to European enterprises enabled them to exploit the natural resources through the establishment of plantations. The exploitation frequently consisted of using forced labour to harvest the products already growing in a region rather than the promotion of a new product or the introduction of new techniques of management. The extent of exploitation of the local

---

[13] See Karin Hausen, *Deutsche Kolonialherrschaft in Afrika* . . . (Berlin, 1970), pp. 36 ff; H. H. J. Meyer, ed., *Das deutsche Kolonialreich: eine Länderkunde der deutschen Schutzgebiete,* 2 vols. (Leipzig, 1909–10); and A. Schmidt, *Das KWK: ein Rückblick auf seine Entstehung und seine Arbeiten aus Anlass des Gedenkjahres 50 jähriger deutscher Kolonialarbeit* (Berlin, 1934).

[14] EDITORS' NOTE: The party of six Tuskegeeans arrived in Togo in 1901 and established an experimental farm. Among other things, they planted cotton, maize and ground-nuts. They had to overcome locusts, ants and chiggers, African indifference to cash-cropping, and seed failures. A hybrid was finally developed, and an agricultural school for over 200 students was in operation by 1907. Cotton production went from almost zero to 530,763 kilograms in 1911. Before 1914, Tuskegee also sent instructors to teach agricultural and industrial skills to Africans in the Sudan, Nigeria and the Belgian Congo.

The Tuskegee approach, as formulated by Booker T. Washington, emphasized practical education in agricultural and industrial skills (carpentry, blacksmithing, etc.). From 1900 on, hundreds of missionaries and colonial officials came to visit Tuskegee and Hampton institutes to learn how to offer practical education to Africans. The example and the lessons of Tuskegee were followed closely by many schools established in Africa. Included among these were the Zulu Christian Industrial School of Natal, the South African Native College, Fort Hare, the Lumbwa Industrial Mission of Kenya, the Mittel und Gehilfen Schule of German East Africa and Achimota College in the Gold Coast. After the First World War the Phelps-Stokes Fund carried forward the idea of practical agricultural education for Negroes in Africa and the United States. By supporting investigating teams and visits from Africa by missionaries and colonial officials, the Hampton-Tuskegee techniques of agricultural training were introduced into African schools.

populations led to a public outcry against the system, which, together with the lack of profitability of many concessions, resulted in the system's being abandoned or considerably modified.

By the turn of the century it was becoming increasingly accepted that the administration of the colonies was a public responsibility—a responsibility that the colonial powers gradually assumed along with the task of helping to develop the resources of the colonies. In this connection there was much disagreement as to how great a role private interests could play in agricutural development, especially as to whether large-scale European plantations were preferable to African smallholdings. In West Africa, climatic conditions more or less determined that development would rest in native hands and secured it there. European plantations were not allowed. In 1907 Lever Brothers failed to win plantation rights in Nigeria, and shortly thereafter, when a world shortage of vegetable oil and oil-seed increased the pressure for more efficient exploitation, the government promised its support for ground-nut cultivation. The government accepted responsibility for improving techniques of production. To this end, research was initiated into the improvement of the processing of oil so as to reduce the high wastage under peasant systems. In contrast to Nigeria, the Belgian authorities permitted Lever Brothers to have large-scale concessions in the Congo. These were administered so effectively by the local operatives that exports of oil-palm products from the Congo rose very rapidly. However, for many years there was no research into improving the technology of production, and the plantations were enclaves of development that had a minimal spread-effect regarding technological change among peasant producers of African oil-palm. It was only in 1936 that research was initiated into commodity problems and problems of establishing productive African farming systems.

In other regions, where the climate was more salubrious, governments encouraged policies of European settlement. The European settlers in South Africa, Southern Rhodesia and Kenya were pioneers and innovators. In areas such as South Africa, the immigrants brought European techniques with them to the Cape and Natal. In Southern Rhodesia they developed the tobacco industry, the main source of that country's agricultural income; and in Kenya, the coffee and dairy industries. In each instance, the largest proportion of the resources to develop new inputs and new techniques of agricultural production was allocated to the European settlers.[15] Nonetheless, there was considerable progress among African producers in these regions, as evidenced by the acceptance of new means of production, such as ploughs, wagons, the use of farm manure and the growing of cash-crops.[16,17]

As the notion of imperial responsibility developed, the public sector of the various governments assumed an increasing role in encouraging agricultural development and technological change in agriculture. Perhaps the most concerted effort was Germany's 'scientific colonialism'. Apart from the major efforts by

[15] Montague Yudelman, *Africans on the land . . .* (Cambridge, Mass., Harvard University Press, 1964), *passim*.

[16] See L. H. Gann, *A history of Southern Rhodesia: early days to 1934* (London, 1965); and Bryan Devereux Hickman, 'Kenya and Uganda', in *Tropical development 1880–1913*, W. Arthur Lewis, ed. (Evanston, Northwestern University Press, 1970), pp. 178–97.

[17] EDITORS' NOTE: The Southern Rhodesian government also sought to improve the African reserves. They built bore-holes, wells and cattle-dips, and they introduced ploughs, seed and new

the private sector, the government established what was probably the most advanced research station in Africa at Amani in East Africa. The government also introduced cocoa, rubber and coffee, promoted the cultivation of cotton, expanded palm-oil and coconut production, undertook reafforestation and planted sisal. This programme yielded dramatic results in the increase in exports. A special feature of German development was the attention given to subsistence agriculture, with agricultural advisers being sent to each district to give instruction on a local level.[18]

French and British efforts at research differed from German mainly in that they were less concerted. The French followed a policy of specialized monoculture rather than attempting to diversify, taking the path of least resistance indicated by the resources of their colonies. Rubber seemed a promising prospect for a long while until, with the exhaustion of forests and the rise of eastern competition, the industry declined rapidly. Efforts to retrieve it by fostering plantation cultivation and by reafforestation were ineffectual. Palm-oil products then became the mainstay of the economies of Dahomey and timber of the Ivory Coast. The ground-nut was always the staple in Senegal, its production booming with the construction of railways into the interior and bringing in its wake a serious problem of soil depletion.

As in other areas, cotton cultivation was encouraged for a while, especially breeds of cattle. From the early 1900s onward, there was, in fact, an astounding increase in African production of maize, beef, ground-nuts, etc.

	1904	1914
Area cultivated by Africans (in acres)	159,000	936,173
	1902	1913
African-owned cattle	55,155	377,000
	1902	1913
African-owned sheep and goats	257,000	893,000

Data are from Gann, *History of Southern Rhodesia,* pp. 185, 323.

The Southern Rhodesian government began to give more active support to African agriculture soon after responsible government was achieved. In 1924, government industrial and agricultural schools were set up at Domboshowa and Tjolotjo, where farming instructors were trained. In 1929, Alvord came under the newly organized Department of Native Education; and from the late 1920s, agricultural demonstrators began to work in the reserves. Southern Rhodesia was actually ahead in the provision of agricultural services for Africans in comparison with Colonial Office-administered territories like Northern Rhodesia and Nyasaland.

In Kenya, white farming did not prevent the emergence of African production for the market. Hickman notes: 'The year 1913 was prosperous for Africans as well as for the whites. The opportunity to export was beginning to make itself felt, and the shortage of land in the reserves would not reveal itself until after the war. Grain and pulses, mostly maize, simsim, beans and peas, headed the list of exports for the year ending March 31, 1913, with a value of £131,258, more than four times the amount exported just three years before.' ('Kenya and Uganda', p. 187.) In German East Africa, the development of German plantations producing commodities such as sisal did not prevent the rapid expansion of such African-grown crops as coffee and cotton.

[18] Kenneth Ingham, 'Deutsch-Ostafrika: ein wirtschaftliches Experiment in Afrika', *Afrika-Verein,* 1961, **3,** no. 1.

after palm production in Malaya began to undermine the profitability of African palm production, but with little success. As the vicissitudes of monoculture trade became apparent, attempts were increasingly made to vary production, again with little success. The full extent of these efforts may be appreciated from an examination of the Inspector of Agriculture's report, with its flower-bed by flower-bed account of the various plants grown in government research stations.[19] Under the control of the Fédération d'Afrique Occidentale Française was a Station Centrale Agronomique at Hann (founded 1903), which had a small laboratory and experimented with all types of soils and plants. Smaller, more specialized, stations existed at Koulikoro (1902) and at Banfofo (1904), the former experimenting with cotton and ostrich farming, among other things, and the latter dedicated largely to rubber-tree cultivation. By 1907, four other experimental gardens, specializing in cotton, rubber, fruits and sheep rearing, were established in Senegal and Guinea. A ground-nut research station at M'Bambey, founded in 1913, set the model for later specialized research stations. The work of such stations was often hampered by inadequate staffing and by a lack of knowledge about tropical conditions, knowledge that had to be acquired by trial and error.

Yves Henry, in his 1906 report on agriculture in French West Africa, emphasizes the limited role of these stations, announcing important departures in French agricultural policy.[20] His criticisms are similar to those found in many recent reports on agricultural development throughout the tropical world. He took issue with the old policy that gave every experimental garden the research capacity for independent existence—a garden, a collection of plant specimens, a laboratory and an experimental farm—assuring it independence and continuity in information services. Not only was this system expensive, but it was suitable only for areas of monoculture because individual research stations could not diversify their experiments widely.

Further flaws in the old system were a fondness for showy foreign plants and sensational novelties, experimented with on a small scale and not yielding anything but speculative results—itself a symptom of a narrowness of interest on the part of the directors 'qui s'hypnotisaient sur leurs carrés de cultures et, le plus souvent, ignoraient presque tout de la région dans laquelle ils se trouvaient placés'. This was accompanied by a tendency to implant European methods of cultivation in regions that were not ready for them, a tendency which forced the early closure of two stations which had over-ambitious plans involving full-scale European-style farms to teach Africans sophisticated agricultural techniques. In Senegal, large numbers of agricultural tools were given to stations for distribution to the Africans, but remained unused because it was not realized that success depended not simply on offering better tools, but on significant cultural changes to inculcate the concepts of individual property and industrialized production. Experimental gardens, which were of limited usefulness to African agriculturalists, were likely to fail when created with insufficient resources. They were dependent on a higher administrative bureau for their direction, and thus abrupt budget cuts and policy changes were often handed down.

---

[19] *Annuaire du Gouvernement Général de l'A.O.F., 1913–1914* (Paris, 1914), pp. 181–244, 295, 333, 354, 403.
[20] Yves Henry, *Afrique occidentale française: rapport agricole pour l'année 1906* (Paris, 1907), pt. 1.

Modest sums for crop experimentation were likely to be withheld in favour of grants for *culture maraîchère* for the direct support of the towns in which administration was centered. Henry embodied his administrative recommendations in a decree making agricultural services an independent branch of the federal administration.

The principle that each British colony should have a department of agriculture managing botanical gardens was endorsed by many governors before it was translated into action. Although government resources were scarce, the colonial governments did expand research efforts. This pattern of expansion may be illustrated by the experience of British West Africa.[21] In the Gold Coast the first research station, the Aburi Agricultural Station, was established in 1890. Thereafter, the following stations were established: the Christianborg Coconut Plantation, 1901; the Aburi Rubber and Kola Plantation, 1902; the Tarkwa Agricultural Station, 1903; the Lalolubo Cotton Farm, 1904; the Kumasi Agricultural Station, 1906; the Assuantes Agricultural Station, 1907; and the Tamali Agricultural Station, 1909. Although the results of the early work of these stations is difficult to assess, experience was gained in developing plant types, and knowledge was gained about pests and plant diseases. The experience proved valuable in subsequent breeding of improved plant types grown for distribution and in evolving methods of plant and disease control. In addition, the researchers discovered improved methods of rubber tapping, so making the rubber tree more productive as well as discovering methods of improving cocoa fermentation.

In Nigeria, developments were somewhat slower.[22] Despite sporadic attempts to establish botanical gardens, little was done until the agricultural department was founded in 1910. Before that time, there was a forestry department, of which agriculture had been a part during the first decade of the twentieth century. Northern Nigeria had no agricultural department until 1912 and no veterinary services until 1914. Thus, because of the slow start in establishing work in agricultural crops, the most interesting and useful experimental results pertained to tree-crops, especially rubber. Little, though, was done until 1907 on oil-palm trees and on diseases affecting them. This, together with the exclusion of plantations, was one of the factors that led to the decline of the Nigerian domination of the world market for palm-oil.[23] After a late start, there was some work on cotton and, after years of research, the Department of Agriculture was able to introduce the exotic American Allen type of cotton that gave higher yields so that cotton became an attractive crop for farmers. These higher yields and the opening of the railway to the coast soon resulted in a substantial upsurge of cotton production in Northern Nigeria. In addition, there was some research work on ground-nuts through the very rapid expansion of ground-nut production; and exports of this crop are attributable, in large measure, to the opening of the railway that provided access to world markets.[24]

In the British colonies, agricultural development always had a grass-roots

[21] A. Baron Holmes, 'The Gold Coast and Nigeria', in *Tropical Development*, pp. 147–77.

[22] *Ibid.*, p. 170.

[23] EDITORS' NOTE: See Pedler's essay in this volume, pp. 95–126, for the reasoning behind the rejection of plantations. The British excluded plantations in order to protect African land rights.

[24] EDITORS' NOTE: For a different view, see note 6.

orientation because responsibilities in this department, particularly in the initial stages of colonization, usually devolved on the individual district officer. Lord Lugard's directives to his district officers underlined their duty to encourage native farmers to grow export crops and to collect information as to the necessary conditions for production, including transport requirements. Although the principle of economic self-determination was inconsistent with applying pressures to produce any particular crops, officers were to make polite suggestions and to forward samples of promising crops to the Imperial Institute (created to assist in the marketing of tropical products). As enforcers of anti-adulteration and forest-preservation laws, they were generally to try to maintain high levels of produce by patient explanation that inferior produce fetched lower prices. It was considered desirable also for the heads of provinces and, if possible, for local officers to maintain gardens at their stations (for which purpose they could use prison labour if available), where vegetables, seedling trees of economic value and fruit should be planted as well as samples of improved crops.[25]

A personal account of the practical problems of administration in newly opened tropical territories written in 1914 reiterates the fact that the development of a district is very much a matter of how committed the individual officer is to his 'civilizing mission'. After considering the various advantages and disadvantages of native cultivation as the basis for agricultural development, the account offers two rules of thumb as guide lines in such matters: 'Encourage development of the slow but sure type,' not becoming discouraged by a failure to achieve quick results, and 'trust the bulk of the adminstration to the European', giving the African little say in policy matters. It considers a certain amount of coercion useful in the introduction of new methods to native farmers, proposing that the pressures of taxation be supplemented by compulsory (paid) labour on government plantations established solely for training purposes. After an initial period, this system could be altered; for example, the plantations could be run on a smaller scale as youth training colleges and for the growth of local seed supplies. This system would release agricultural superintendents for advice-giving tours of the region. More and better practical education is seen as the main hope for development. Examining attempts to develop various crops for export and local use, it is stressed that it is worse than useless to introduce new crops or improvements in techniques of cultivation that have not been thoroughly tested because governments thereby can easily destroy the whole credibility of their policy.[26]

Although closer co-operation between government agencies, private enterprise and missions was developing, African initiatives were seldom encouraged.[27] Some Gold Coast cocoa plantations were managed by Africans

[25] Lord Lugard, *Political memoranda: revision of instructions to political officers on subjects chiefly political and administrative, 1913–1918,* 3rd ed. (London, 1970), p. 30.

[26] C. H. Stigand, *Administration in tropical Africa* (London, 1914), pp. 6–8, 98–9, 102–15.

[27] EDITORS' NOTE: Holmes, 'The Gold Coast and Nigeria' (p. 151), gives a different interpretation: 'The Department of Agriculture [in the Gold Coast] played an absolutely vital role in distributing cocoa seeds and plants, and in demonstrating basic techniques to the Akwapim and Krobo peoples, but did not have sufficient resources (men or money) to introduce precise, exacting or complicated techniques to large numbers of people. It had to rely on the "grapevine" of information passed from one farmer to another. The basic techniques of cocoa-growing were fortunately simple enough for this method of transmission; therefore the efforts of a few persons proved to have a high multiplier effect in terms of information communicated.' Between 1900

with full government support, and the services of trained native agriculturists were used by the Fédération d'Afrique Occidentale Française in its 'cadre local d'agents indigènes du Service de l'Agriculture' (created in 1913); but there was no systematic organization of the indigenous cultivator into co-operatives. The French launched the first experiment in native co-operatives with the creation in 1910 of the Sociétés Indigènes de Prévoyance. These were semi-official agencies, in which membership was later made compulsory. Dues were collected and were meant to provide the basis for insurance, marketing and loan schemes, as well as finance for members of the co-operative farms. These ambitious schemes certainly did not begin to realize themselves in the early years of the Société's existence, when co-operative activities were limited to seed lending and tool sharing.

By 1914, tropical agriculture was being developed along several fronts. Every British colony except the Gambia had a botanical garden for localized research. Research and information services on all levels were beginning to be integrated with native welfare programmes, both medical (to alleviate chronic labour shortages) and educational public-works projects and commercial development plans. A few important successes in crop introduction—cotton in Uganda, coffee in Kenya, cocoa in the Gold Coast, ginger in Sierra Leone, cloves in Zanzibar—had been achieved along with the distilled experience of many failures.[28] The introduction of certain fruits and food-crops helped raise national productivity; there was a start on conservation and on experimentation with minor crops such as mangoes, raffia, and kapok in Nigeria. Cattle were imported from Barbados and work was initiated in combating sleeping-sickness. Simple ploughs, steel machetes and oil-expressing devices were being used to advantage, although, on the whole, new methods of production were much more difficult to introduce than new crops. The basis was established, though, for the expansion of exports, which was to be so important for the development of the region as a whole. If the agents of colonial policy in the years before the First World War did not have dramatic success in developing African agriculture, it is hardly surprising.[29] The lack of funds available for development made it difficult enough, but added to this was the tremendous lack of knowledge about the physical, social and economic conditions that prevailed in Africa.

Research and development after World War I

The years after World War I up to the beginning of the 1960s were years during which there was a determined effort to learn more about African agriculture. It was a period in which it was recognized that a greatly expanded research effort in the region was a necessary prerequisite for introducing technological changes

and 1913 the export of cocoa went up from 536 tons valued at £27,300 to 50,600 tons valued at £2,489,000. 'The Gold Coast', says Holmes, 'had become the world's foremost cocoa producer.'

[28] EDITORS' NOTE: To the list of successes, add cotton in Togo and in German East Africa, ground-nuts in Senegal.

[29] EDITORS' NOTE: The needs of the industrialized West stimulated tropical exports of cocoa, coffee, tobacco, palm-oil, palm-kernels and oil, ground-nuts, cotton, sisal and rubber. Charles C. Stover, 'Tropical exports', in *Tropical development* (p. 53), estimates that the period from 1880 to 1913 was one of spectacular growth in export crops.

into tropical Africa and that new approaches would be needed to organize, execute and finance such an effort. In this period, though, there occurred a time of great financial stringency—during the depression of the 1930s—and many of the programmes and projects for expanding research and inquiry in the colonies were curtailed. By the late 1940s and early 1950s, however, the financial situation had changed. The colonies themselves had surplus funds arising from the expansion of exports during the post-war boom, and the colonial powers made substantial allocations for agricultural development in the colonies. The last years of the colonial era culminated with a substantial effort to promote agricultural research and development in Africa along with the adjustment of many of the institutions in keeping with the change from colonial to independent status.

The nature and pace of change that did occur may be illustrated by the British experience with promotion of colonial research during this period.[30] The British war-time experience with government-supported research on developing substitutes for scarce raw materials led to the firm establishment of the principle that the government should accept responsibility for research. This principle, which was extended to the Colonial Office, resulted in the creation of the Colonial Research Committee. This committee, which remained in operation until 1933, disbursed a very modest amount during its existence. In 1925, the separation of the Colonial Office from the Dominions provided an opportunity for reorganizing certain aspects of direction of colonial agriculture. A series of advisory committees was established and an agricultural adviser for the colonies was appointed in 1929. The Empire Marketing Board, which was created in 1926 and was in operation until 1933, was set up to give preference to colonial food products. Because this policy could not be implemented without contradicting Britain's 'cheap food policy', it was decided to allocate £1 million a year for promoting schemes to encourage the sale of Empire produce in the United Kingdom. These schemes included research on projects of direct benefit to the colonies, such as assisting the Imperial College of Tropical Agriculture in Trinidad, which was to become a centre for training of colonial officers interested in tropical agriculture. In 1929, with the onslaught of the industrial recession, the government of the day introduced the Colonial Development Act, which established the principle of unilateral aid to colonial territories for development purposes. The Act, though, was acceptable only because it was seen as a means of reducing unemployment in Great Britain by promoting commerce and industry between the United Kingdom and the colonies.

By the late 1930s there was an increase in the interest in agricultural development in the colonies. However, there was still no overall policy—nor much in the way of financial resources—for agricultural research and agricultural development.

Nevertheless, some significant progress was made in the British territories during the inter-war years. Some of the work in cotton has already been mentioned. Additional progress was made at the Gezira Research Station in the Sudan, which was subsequently to become the Agricultural Research Institute. In Nigeria, the Northern Region Experiment Station was established at Samaru

[30] See Sir Charles Jeffries, ed., *A review of colonial research, 1940–1960* (London, HMSO, 1964), pp. 12–58.

in 1922 to work on cotton and ground-nuts. A breeding station for wheat was opened in 1930 in Njoro in Kenya. Some forty minor stations were developed to conduct research in the Rhodesias and Nyasaland. Four main research stations were developed in Tanganyika; two government-sponsored research stations were formed in Uganda and nine in Kenya.

The work that was undertaken covered a wide range. In broad terms, however, the research effort became more diverse, for as old problems were resolved new ones emerged. One of the principles of agricultural development is that each success generates a new set of problems, thus making it essential that there be a sustained research effort to maintain whatever gains are made. This may be well illustrated in the case of the Agricultural Research Institute in the Sudan, which made an important contribution to the success of the Gezira Scheme. The initial research at the institute made possible the control of two important diseases of cotton: blackworm and leaf curl. Strains were developed that were resistant to these diseases, thus enabling producers to get higher yields. Thereafter, the researchers turned their attention to developing varieties of higher ginning quality.

In the late 1930s, following excellent crops of high-quality cotton, a new pest, 'leaf-sucking' jassid insects, invaded the cotton fields. Experimental work resulted in the discovery of an appropriate application of insecticide that controlled the jassids and so saved the crop. Thereafter, with these diseases and pests under control, the research workers turned to examine a phenomenon that influenced the size of the harvest. This was a consideration of why yields fluctuated from season to season and from area to area. Careful research indicated that heavy rains increased yields but resulted in a high growth of weeds after harvest, and this depressed subsequent yields of cotton. The weeds, it was found, removed both moisture and nutrients from the soil. As a result of further experimentation, irrigation of fallow and the use of nitrogenous fertilizers were introduced to offset this effect and to give farmers sustained high yields. Irrigation out of season, however, encouraged the growth of unwanted seed grass. On the other hand, removal of this grass and weeds would deprive the farmers of Gezira of their main source of animal fodder and so cut down their production of high-protein meat and milk so necessary for good nutrition. The nutritional problem could be overcome by mechanization and fodder conservation, but its resolution was still perplexing the scientists at Gezira in the late 1950s and early 1960s.

Other research in the inter-war years included a sophisticated programme of corn-breeding in Southern Rhodesia. This programme began in Salisbury in 1932. Seventeen years later, Southern Rhodesia released its first hybrid maize, thus becoming the first country outside the United States to produce hybrid corn commercially. By the early 1960s most of the European-grown corn in the Rhodesias consisted of hybrids, which gave much higher yields than did the traditional varieties. In 1930, research was started on improving wheat at the wheat-breeding station at Njoro in Kenya. The scientists at this station developed a range of varieties of wheat. Their research in this direction saved the Kenya wheat crop in the post-war years when an outbreak of plant disease caused a breakdown of resistance of one of the most dependable high-altitude varieties of wheat. Fortunately, as a result of earlier research efforts, alternative disease-resistant varieties were made available for distribution to farmers, so cornering the wheat crop of Kenya.[31]

The tempo of research and promotion of agricultural development was stimulated in the years following the Second World War. General Smuts pointed out in his Rhodes Memorial Lecture delivered at Oxford in 1929 that there was need for a comprehensive survey of what was taking place in Africa so that a research programme could be formulated. In response to this suggestion, the Royal Institute of International Affairs sponsored such a survey under the direction of Lord Hailey. The major recommendation of the Hailey Report, which was accepted by the British government, was that the British government should provide substantial funds for research into African problems and that the funds should be administered by a central managing body that included representatives from scientific and academic institutions involved in the problems. Despite the outbreak of the Second World War, the British government created a new Colonial Development and Welfare Fund and a Colonial Research Fund—the latter being directly linked to the Hailey proposals. A Colonial Research Committee was appointed to administer the fund; and the committee recommended, *inter alia,* that centres of research and development should be established to help with the research programmes.

For the first time, substantial funds were available for research and development on problems of special interest in the colonies. In addition, there was a network of advisory boards covering most of the relevant areas of research. Regional research institutes were established in East and West Africa. In 1959, the Colonial Research Council was dissolved and its functions were transferred to a new Overseas Research Council. With the increasing independence of the colonies, a new Department of Technical Co-operation was established, which assumed some of the functions formerly carried out by the Colonial Office. Among its functions was the financing of research.

Between 1940 and 1960, through the Colonial Development and Welfare Acts, some £24 million was made available by Parliament for 'colonial research'.[32] About 6.5 per cent was earmarked for research into agriculture and related activities, with most of the funds being allocated for expenditure in East and West Africa. At the same time, the governments of countries such as the

---

[31] EDITORS' NOTE: Italy and Portugal, too, sponsored agricultural research for their colonies. The Italians founded the Istituto Agricolo Coloniale Italiano in Florence in 1903. The institute published an important journal, *L'Agricoltura Coloniale*. In the colonies themselves the Italians built a number of research centres. There were veterinary institutions at Asmara, Mercera and Addis Ababa. In the 1930s the Italians created also a network of agricultural offices and experimental farms. Agricultural experts provided advice both to Italian settlers and to indigenous farmers. Specialized commissions from Italy also investigated particular products, such as wool, oil seeds, bananas, etc.

In 1906 the Portuguese opened the Jardim e Museu Agricola do Ultramar, which made important contributions to the study of colonial plants and agricultural products. Then in 1930 the Portuguese reorganized their system of colonial studies into a central body, the Junta das Missões Geográficas e de Investigação do Ultramar. Special institutes dealt with plant and animal diseases. Also in the 1930s the Portuguese maintained a central laboratory for veterinary pathology as well as experimental farms in Angola and Moçambique. Their work on the breeding of cattle and sheep for export was of practical value for Angola. After the Second World War the Portuguese founded such groups as the Centro do Investigação Científica Algodeira (for cotton) and the Instituto de Investigação Agronómica de Angola. Similar bodies were opened in Moçambique as well. [32] Jeffries, *Review of colonial research,* pp. 12–58.

Gold Coast, Nigeria and Uganda had accumulated substantial reserves through state trading in export crops by statutory marketing boards. These boards were able to finance commodity research such as that undertaken on cocoa, coffee and cotton. The policy for the grants from the Colonial Development and Welfare Fund was to encourage regional research efforts so as to avoid duplication and to encourage regional and national institutions to become self-supporting. This was to be done by providing a part of the total resources needed, while the governments were to assume an increasing share of total costs. The research funds provided by the British government helped to finance a number of existing and new regional research stations: the West Africa Cacao Research Institute, the West African Oil Palm Research Institute, the West African Institute for Trypanosomiasis Research, the East African Veterinary Research Organization. Unfortunately, though, even in 1960, the strains of nationalism were already making it apparent that the idea of a regional approach was premature.

In the post-war years, substantial progress was made also in the French and Belgian territories. The French system was reorganized in 1943, when the central direction of research in the French colonies became the responsibility of the Office de la Recherche Scientifique et Technique Outre-Mer (ORSTOM), which is attached to the Ministry for Overseas France. The role of ORSTOM was to organize fundamental research or to provide 'orientated basic research', whereas a series of eight specialized institutions was to undertake applied research. These eight institutions included a group of development agencies, such as the Bureau pour le Développement de la Production, that helped in the execution of development projects. The French system had its headquarters in France and was supported by a central scientific service based near Paris. By 1960 ORSTOM had thirty research centres of a permanent nature distributed throughout the different ecological zones. ORSTOM's budget was directly paid for by French tax-payers, and the organization deployed a permanent staff far larger than that in most research organizations—more than five hundred research scientists complemented by nearly two thousand assistants and technicians.[33]

The eight specialized institutions differed slightly according to the circumstances of their establishment. Some were government-controlled companies, some non-profit-making private associations. But each had a central headquarters and laboratories in France to provide logistical and technical information and support for the stations abroad. In most cases, however, they were national stations managed by the institute on behalf of the host state. In 1960 there were seventy such stations. The French research programme has been notably successful in gathering basic information, in improving varieties and production of ground-nuts and cocoa, in developing new farming methods and in promoting agricultural development in general.

The French system differed from the British approach in that it was a tightly controlled system operated by French expatriates and financed largely by French tax-payers. It was assumed that the concentration of effort along functional lines made sense in a situation where many of the countries concerned

---

[33] G. Camus, 'L'Office de la Recherche Scientifique et Technique Outre-Mer: recherche et développement', *Le Progrès Scientifique*, July 1967, no. 110, 2–23; and M. Pagot, 'Les organismes français de recherches agricoles spécialisées outre-mer', *Le Progrès Scientifique*, Nov. 1968, no. 124.

were too small to afford their own research efforts. In addition, the shortage of indigenous skills and finance made it appear highly advantageous for the former colonies to participate in this programme. Unlike the British approach, it was accepted in the French plan that there would be a continuing commitment. No special provision or consideration was given to creating an independent research capacity in each of the colonies or in the colonies when grouped on a regional basis.

The Belgian system was somewhat similar to that of the French, with the central organization for agricultural research in the Belgian Congo being the Institut National pour l'Etude Agronomique du Congo Belge (INEAC). This institute was financed primarily from Belgian sources and was administered by a committee representing the Ministry of the Colonies and the Belgian universities. INEAC became 'one of the finest tropical research centers in the world.'[34] The station was notably successful in breeding oil-palms, which increased yields considerably.[35] INEAC contributed also to one of the few successful technical and social programmes to establish sedentary 'agriculture': the Paysannats settlement schemes. These schemes moulded the system of shifting cultivation into the pattern whereby the benefits could be maximized and the harmful effects minimized. Before the independence of the Congo, INEAC employed approximately 450 Belgian scientists and technicians. Following independence, as the administrative system collapsed, there was nearly complete disintegration of INEAC, and much of the best and most painstaking research on tropical agriculture was lost.

In the early post-war years, despite the increase in research, there was still an assumption that it was possible to transfer new technology into the region without constant investigation and sustained research in the field. The consequences of this assumption were highlighted by the failure of two important projects of agricultural development, both of which ignored this principle. The first scheme was the Ground-nut Scheme undertaken in Tanganyika in 1946. Some 20,000 acres were to be planted to ground-nuts so as to provide vegetable oils for the housewives of Britain. The operation was to constitute the largest single mechanized-farming operation in the world. The capital, management and expertise were to be provided from Britain. The scheme was a complete and costly failure. Undoubtedly the wash-out would have been mitigated had there been some experimentation that showed the true nature of the physical environment—the lack of rainfall, the difficult properties of the soil and the high cost of mechanized bush clearance.[36] The second scheme, though it too involved mechanization, was to encourage settlement in unoccupied but fertile land in Northern Nigeria and to lead to a substantial increase in the production

[34] John J. McKelvey, Jr., 'Agricultural research', in *The African world: a survey of social research,* Robert A. Lystad, ed. (New York, 1965), p. 345.

[35] EDITORS' NOTE: The Ecole de Médecine Vétérinaire de l'Etat was also important for veterinary research in the Belgian Congo. Agricultural problems were investigated at the State Botanical Gardens, at the Botanical Department of the Musée du Congo Belge at Tervuren, and at the University of Louvain. In 1931, Louvain initiated its own research centres in the Congo for the purpose of improving African agriculture. The new organization became known as CADULAC (Centres Agronomiques de l'Université de Louvain au Congo). INEAC also played a role in improving the cultivation of rubber and indigenous foods crops and worked on veterinary problems and the upgrading of African-bred cattle.

[36] McKelvey, 'Agricultural research', p. 333.

of ground-nuts and sorghums. The scheme was initiated in 1954. Many African peasants refused to be drawn into it, and it was effectively terminated in 1959. The scheme itself was uneconomic partly because there had been no research on the technical aspects of the programme; nor had there been any research on the economics of increased production.[37]

The lesson of these colonial failures, in so far as they relied on large-scale capital imports, appears to have been well learned. Most of the schemes initiated towards the end of the colonial era (and in the subsequent period of independence)—such as the Swynnerton Plan in Kenya—were based on technological changes that had been proved successful in the area in which they were to be adopted. This could be done only when there was investigation and research within the region in question and an appreciation of the social and economic factors involved. By 1960, the accumulated experience of the colonial era indicated that there were no short cuts in agricultural development and that there could be no wholesale transfer of technology from Europe to Africa. The lessons learned were that African agriculture would have to develop along its own lines and that a sound economic and technical base for development could emanate only from research and investigation in the tropical regions of Africa.

Conclusion

Technological change in agriculture is part of the dynamics of agricultural development; change takes place at the farm level when farmers use new inputs in the production process. If there is no indigenous capacity to produce those inputs, then they have to be imported. There are, however, physical constraints on the successful transfer of seeds and breeding-stock and techniques of production from one ecological zone to another. Historically, the first imports of new agricultural inputs are usually from countries with similar physical environments, and, over time, the importing country develops its own capacity to generate its own inputs—inputs adapted for use in local social, economic and physical circumstances.

At the outset of the period 1850–1960, the new inputs were introduced into tropical Africa by the private sector—missionaries, traders and private research groups. There was little desire for public involvement in the development of the colonies, much less any desire to allocate public resources for the development of a technology exclusively for the use of peoples living in tropical Africa. By the 1880s, though, there was a shift of attitudes. Over the next seventy years there was an increasing involvement of both the metropolitan powers and the administrations in tropical Africa in developing suitable inputs and technologies for localized use.

Nonetheless, it was only in the late 1940s that substantial public resources were made available for research and agricultural development. These resources included the first substantial grants made by the colonial powers for this purpose, and were in many respects the forerunner of the subsequent programmes of external aid for development of less-developed countries. By the 1960s there was publicly financed research in all the colonies or former colonies in tropical Africa. The pattern of research in Francophone Africa differed

[37] *Ibid.*, p. 334.

355

from that in Anglophone Africa in that research in the Francophone region was tightly controlled from France, whereas the emphasis in Anglophone Africa was to devolve responsibility onto local administrations.

During this period there were successes and failures in the spread of new inputs and the introduction of new technologies. The greatest success in agriculture in the colonial era was undoubtedly the rapid expansion of production for export. Part of this may be attributed to improved transport crops, but some credit should be given to the introduction and adaptation of new crops during the colonial era. In addition, the sustained increase in exports was made possible also by research and development on methods of disease and pest control and by research on the most suitable techniques of production. The failures, on the other hand, generally involved attempts to introduce advanced techniques of production, such as mechanization, imported from the colonial powers. One reason for the failures was the lack of adequate research and investigation into the social, economic and physical conditions in the areas in which the machine technology was to be used. Another explanation, especially outside of areas of European settlement, lay in the shortage of complementary skills.

Whatever the successes—and they were considerable—there was at least one great weakness in the colonial approach. This was the failure to develop institutions that could produce the skilled, indigenous manpower to undertake research and to participate in the management and direction of agricultural growth. At various times during the colonial era attempts were made to establish vocational and agricultural schools or to introduce agricultural training, but there was no sustained effort to provide the skilled élite of agriculture. By the time of independence there was only one agricultural faculty in sub-Saharan Francophone Africa; it was founded in the mid-1950s in the Belgian Congo. There were five institutions of higher learning in the British territories established in the early 1950s that provided an advanced degree in agriculture. Between 1952 and 1963 only four university graduates were trained in Francophone Africa and around 150 in Anglophone Africa.[38]

In 1960, in terms of overall economic development, the former colonial areas of tropical Africa included some of the least productive and most technologically backward economies in the world. By international standards, then, the colonial experience in economic and agricultural development might appear to have provided a limited base for future development. However, the real achievements during the period under consideration have to be seen in a perspective that incorporates some notion of the backwardness of the region as little as fifty to sixty years before 1960. This backwardness is well illustrated by Sir Philip Mitchell, a former governor of Kenya. He described the indigenous population at the turn of the century as follows:

Inland of the narrow coastal strip they had no units of government of any size or stability; indeed, with a few exceptions such as Buganda, nothing beyond local chiefs or patriarchs. They had no wheeled transport and, apart from the camels and donkeys of the pastoral nomads, no animal transport either; they had no roads nor towns; no tools except small hand hoes, axes, wooden digging sticks, and the like; no manufactures and no commerce as we understand it, and no currency, although in some places barter of produce was facilitated by the use of small shells; they had never heard of working for wages. They went stark naked or clad in the bark of trees or the skins of animals, and

[38] *Ibid.*, pp. 348–9.

they had no means of writing, even by hieroglyphics, notches on a stock or knots in a piece of grass or fibre; they had no weights and measures of general use.[39]

The transformation of the agricultural economy of the region between 1880 and 1960, when considered against the above background and with full account taken of the shortage of trained agricultural élites, has been remarkable indeed. By the end of the colonial era the agricultural economy was 'monetized', a transport system facilitated the movement of crops, and an expanding education system and expanding medical services were paid for out of an agricultural surplus. The indigenous producers of the region were using new inputs, including new seeds developed within the region as well as new implements and a few machine-powered inputs. The region had become an important exporter of agricultural surpluses, with the indigenous producers exporting a wide range of crops that were competitive in world markets. This could not have been accomplished without the importation of technology and a recognition of the importance of adapting this technology to local needs.[40]

BIBLIOGRAPHY

Allan, William. 'Studies in African land usage in Northern Rhodesia', *Rhodes-Livingstone papers,* no. 15. Livingstone, Oxford University Press, 1949.

Ajayi, J. F. A. *Christian missions in Nigeria, 1841–1891: the making of a new élite.* London, 1965.

Anyane, Seth La. *Ghana agriculture: its economic development from early times to the middle of the twentieth century.* London, Oxford University Press, 1963.

Baldwin, K. D. S. *The Niger agricultural project . . .* Oxford, 1957.

Boserup, Ester. *The conditions of agricultural growth . . .* London, 1965.

Brown, L. H. 'Agricultural change in Kenya: 1945–1960', *Food Research Institute Studies,* 1968, **8,** no. 5.

Brunschwig, Henri. *Mythes et réalités de l'impérialisme colonial français, 1871–1914.* Paris, 1960.

Camus, G. 'L'Office de la Recherche Scientifique et Technique Outre-Mer: recherche et développement', *Le Progrès Scientifique,* July 1967, no. 110.

Church, R. J. H. *West Africa: a study of the environment and of man's use of it.* London, 1957.

Cook, Arthur N. *British enterprise in Nigeria.* London, 1964.

Cooper, St G. C. *Agricultural research in tropical Africa.* Nairobi, 1970.

Cornevin, Robert. *Histoire du Togo.* Paris, 1962.

Crowder, Michael. *West Africa under colonial rule.* London, 1968.

De Coene, R. 'Agricultural settlement schemes in the Belgian Congo', *Tropical Agriculture,* 1956, **33,** no. 1.

De Gregori, Thomas R. *Technology and the economic development of the tropical African frontier.* Cleveland, Press of Case Western Reserve University, 1969.

Deherme, Georges. *L'Afrique occidentale française: action politique, action économique, action sociale.* Paris, 1908.

Doggett, H. 'Sorghum breeding for resistance', in *CCTA/FAO Symposium on Savannah Zone Cereals,* Agenda item III (b) (1); Dakar 1962, Aug. 29–Sept. 4.

[39] As quoted in Yudelman, *Africans on the land.*

[40] EDITORS' NOTE: See also, in this volume, both Hogendorn's essay and the relevant section in the Introduction, which gives a somewhat different interpretation.

Drachoussoff, V. 'Agricultural change in the Belgian Congo, 1945–1960', *Food Research Institute Studies,* 1965, **5,** no. 2.

Flint, John E. *Sir George Goldie and the making of Nigeria.* London, Oxford University Press, 1960.

François, Georges. *A.F.O. Le budget local des colonies.* Paris, 1908.

Gaitskell, Arthur. *Gezira: a story of development in the Sudan.* London, 1959.

Gourou, Pierre. *Les pays tropicaux . . .* Paris, 1948.

Great Britain. *Parliamentary papers.* Vol. LXVI, Cmd 5215. *Memorandum on government action in encouragement of cotton growing in Crown Colonies.* London, 1910.

Vol. XVI, Cmd 523. *Report on Empire Cotton Growing Association.* London, 1920.

Grigg, David. *The harsh lands: a study in agricultural development.* London, 1970.

Hadlow, Leonard. *Climate, vegetation and man.* New York, 1953.

Hance, William A. *The geography of modern Africa.* New York, Columbia University Press, 1964.

Harmand, Jules. *Domination et colonisation.* Paris, 1910.

Henry, Yves. *Afrique occidentale française: rapport agricole pour l'année 1906.* Paris, 1907.

Herskovits, Melville J., and Mitchell Harwitz, eds. *Economic transition in Africa.* Evanston, Northwestern University Press, 1964.

Hill, M. F. *Planters' progress: the story of coffee in Kenya.* Nairobi, 1956.

Horsfall, James G., *et al.* 'Tropical soils and climates', chap. 8 in *The World Food Problem: A report of the President's Science Advisory Committee.* 3 vols. Washington, D.C., U.S.G.P.O., 1967.

Hostelet, Georges. *L'oeuvre civilisatrice de la Belgique au Congo de 1885 à 1953.* Brussels, Institut Royal Colonial Belge, 1954.

Hunter, Guy. *Modernizing peasant societies . . .* London, Oxford University Press, 1969.

Hurwitz, Nathaniel. *Agriculture in Natal, 1860–1950.* Vol. XII of *Natal Regional Survey.* Cape Town, Oxford University Press, 1957.

Huxley, Elspeth. *White man's country: Lord Delamere and the making of Kenya.* 2 vols. London, 1935.

International Bank for Reconstruction and Development. *The economic development of Kenya.* Baltimore, Johns Hopkins University Press, 1962.

The economic development of Nigeria. Baltimore, Johns Hopkins University Press, 1955.

The economic development of Tanganyika. Baltimore, Johns Hopkins University Press, 1962.

The economic development of Uganda. Baltimore, Johns Hopkins University Press, 1960.

Irvine, F. R. *West African agriculture.* 3rd ed. London, Oxford University Press, 1970.

Jeffries, Sir Charles, ed. *A review of colonial research, 1940–1960.* London, HMSO, 1964.

Johnson, R. W. M. 'African agricultural development in Southern Rhodesia, 1945–1960', *Food Research Institute Studies,* 1964, **4,** no. 2.

Johnston, Bruce F. *The staple food economies of western tropical Africa.* Stanford University Press, 1958.

Jones, William O. 'Environment, technical knowledge, and economic development in tropical Africa', *Food Research Institute Studies,* 1965, **5,** no. 2.

Kamarck, Andrew M. *The economics of African development.* New York, 1967.

Kettlewell, R. W. 'Agricultural change in Nyasaland, 1945–1960', *Food Research Institute Studies,* 1965, **5,** no. 3.

Kilby, Peter. *Industrialization in an open economy: Nigeria, 1900–1960.* Cambridge University Press, 1969.

Kimble, George H. T. *Tropical Africa*. 2 vols. New York, 1960.

Laressan, Jean-Louis. *Les principes de colonisation*. Paris, 1897.

Leurquin, Philippe. 'Agricultural change in Rwanda-Urundi, 1945–60', *Food Research Institute Studies*, 1963, **4**, no. 1.

Lewis, W. Arthur, ed. *Tropical development 1880–1913*. Evanston, Northwestern University Press, 1970.

Lugard, Frederick John Dealtry Lugard, 1st baron. *The dual mandate in British tropical Africa*. London, 1922.

Political memoranda: revision of instructions to political officers on subjects chiefly political and administrative, 1913–1918. 3rd ed. London, 1970.

McDermott, P. L., comp. *British East Africa, or I.B.E.A.: a history of the Imperial British East Africa Company*. London, 1893.

MacDonald, Major. *Report on the administration of the Niger Territories 1890*. F.O. 84/2109. London, British Public Record Office.

McKelvey, John J., Jr., 'Agricultural research', in *The African world: a survey of social research,* Robert A. Lystad, ed. New York, 1965.

McPhee, Allan. *The economic revolution in British West Africa*. London, 1926.

Makings, S. M. 'Agricultural change in Northern Rhodesia/Zambia 1945–1960', *Food Research Institute Studies*, 1966, **6**, no. 2.

Masefield, G. B. 'Agricultural change in Uganda, 1945–1960', *Food Research Institute Studies*, 1962, **3**, no. 2.

A short history of agriculture in the British colonies. Oxford, Clarendon press, 1950.

Miracle, Marvin P. *Maize in tropical Africa*. Madison, University of Wisconsin Press, 1966.

Nicolson, I. F. *The administration of Nigeria, 1900–1961*. Oxford, Clarendon Press, 1969.

Phillips, John F. V. *Agriculture and ecology in Africa* . . . London, 1959.

Pim, Sir Alan. *The financial and economic history of the African tropical territories*. Oxford, Clarendon Press, 1940.

Robinson, E. A. G., ed. *Economic development for Africa south of the Sahara: proceedings of a conference held by the International Economic Association*. London, 1964.

Rudin, Harry R. *Germans in the Cameroons, 1884–1914.* . . . London, 1938.

Shaw, D. J., ed. *Agricultural development in the Sudan*. 2 vols. Khartoum, 1966.

Stigand, C. H. *Administration in tropical Africa*. London, 1914.

Taylor, A. R. 'The development of scientific societies in Rhodesia and Nyasaland', in *Proceedings of the First Federal Science Congress, Salisbury, May 18–22*. Salisbury, 1962.

Tothill, J. D., ed. *Agriculture in Uganda*. London, Oxford University Press, 1940.

Wood, Alan. *The groundnut affair*. London, 1950.

Worthington, E. B. *Science in the development of Africa: a review of the contribution of physical and biological knowledge south of the Sahara*. London, 1958.

Wrigley, Gordon. *Tropical agriculture: the development of production*. New York, 1969.

Yudelman, Montague. *Africans on the land: economic problems of African agricultural development in Southern, Central and East Africa, with special reference to Southern Rhodesia*. Cambridge, Mass., Harvard University Press, 1964.

Yudelman, Montague, G. Butler, and R. Banerji, *Technological change in agriculture and employment in developing countries*. Paris, Organization for Economic Co-operation and Development, Development Centre, 1971.

CHAPTER 10

THE MINER'S FRONTIER, TRANSPORT AND GENERAL ECONOMIC DEVELOPMENT

by

SIMON E. KATZENELLENBOGEN

Mining and metal-working have been part of Africa's economy and culture for centuries. At least as far back as the tenth century, gold was exchanged across the Sahara for salt, and was later traded with the Portuguese, British, Dutch and Danes. Iron and copper were also important, both having been smelted in Southern Rhodesia in A.D. 530 ($\pm$ 120). Unlike most of Europe, pre-colonial Africa would appear to have progressed directly from the Stone Age to the Iron Age without passing through the intermediate bronze period. One African observer, writing just over a hundred years ago, described the smelting techniques used, techniques that had changed very little through the generations:

In the interior of Gabon iron is found in considerable quantity, cropping out on the surface. To obtain the iron, they [the Fan people] build a huge pile of wood, heap on this a considerable quantity of the ore broken up, then come with more wood, and apply fire to the whole; wood is continually being thrown into it until the ore becomes fluid, when it is allowed to cool down, and cast iron is obtained. To temper it and make it malleable, they put it through a most tedious series of heating and hammering till at last they turn out a very superior article of iron and steel, which is much better than the trade quality brought out from Europe. Of this they make their knives, arrowheads and swords.[1]

Copper, the ancient symbol for which—$\female$—was derived from the metal mirror said to have been carried by Venus, is also found in many parts of the continent and was a major item of trade in Central Africa long before Europeans penetrated the area. The famous 'Katanga crosses' were spread far afield. Dutch traders on the west coast were buying copper from the Katanga region in the sixteenth century. Arabs from the East began acquiring it along with gold, ivory and slaves even earlier, sending some of it to India and China.

The extent to which the pre-colonial mining industry could develop was severely limited by the very narrow range of technical skills and capital resources available. In the absence of pumps, explosives and similar devices, only those deposits found on or near the surface—a minute proportion of the available ores—could be worked. Ore bodies covered by a mantle of sand or rock could not be located, and deep-level mining was impossible. Gold, iron and copper could be treated easily by relatively crude methods, but many of Africa's minerals, such as zinc, cobalt, aluminium and uranium, could be exploited only with the use of a complex technology originating in the West.

By introducing modern mining methods, Europeans began an economic revolution in Africa. A vast array of technical skills was transferred from the in-

---

[1] James Africanus Horton, *West African countries and peoples: 1868,* reprint of 1868 ed. (Edinburgh University Press, 1968), p. 7.

dustrialized societies, as an army of prospectors, geologists, chemists, surveyors, laboratory technicians and managerial staff was deployed. When aerial photography became increasingly important in prospecting work, even pilots and ground crews became part of the mining companies' personnel. In order to attract to Africa the skilled men required—and in the late nineteenth and early twentieth centuries Africa was quite justifiably regarded as a dangerous place in which to work—the mining companies not only had to provide sufficiently high salaries and fringe benefits; they also had to mobilize and train thousands of unskilled and semi-skilled workers. It was soon realized that in order to maintain an efficient labour force, it was necessary to create permanent townships, complete with housing, health services, water supplies, sanitation, training and recreational facilities and so on. Mining also required a host of ancillary enterprises—repair shops, smelting plant and facilities for the manufacture of iron and steel, cement and many other products—as well as service industries such as electricity-generating. The towns that grew up around the mines created a demand for food, clothing, fuel, housing and other supplies and services that entrepreneurs were eager to meet. Trading stores and banks opened their doors, while many craftsmen, such as bicycle repairers, motor mechanics and photographers, found employment. Mines also supplied substantial public revenues through taxation, licence fees, and, in some cases, the colonial government's shareholding in an enterprise, thereby helping to finance various state services or to subsidize other sectors of the economy. In general terms, mining was one of the fundamental multiplier-accelerators of economic growth.

A major aspect of this growth was finance. It was mining that initiated the great flow of money from Europe, primarily Britain, that was essential for economic development. It was one thing for a prospector or a geologist to locate a mineral deposit but quite another matter to convince investors—individuals, corporations or governments—to take the very high risks of supporting its exploitation. Technical obstacles had to be overcome, sometimes requiring the development of new mining methods or metallurgical processes either of a general nature or to cope with specific local conditions. When these basic problems had been solved, others remained. Mine-workers, sometimes numbering tens of thousands, had to be fed. Provisions had to be either brought from great distances or produced locally. The mines therefore gave an important stimulus to local agriculture. Farming expanded as the mining areas provided centralized domestic markets, while the extension of railway lines enabled cultivators to raise crops for export. As a major employer of Africans, the mining industry was also at the centre of far-reaching changes in traditional African society, crossing ethnic and political boundaries and gradually providing an increasing number of social and medical services as the work force tended to become stabilized and as the mortality of black and white miners alike declined with dramatic speed.

The relationship between the mines and the railways was particularly important. Most of the mines were a long way from the ocean or from navigable waterways. Supplies and equipment had to be shipped in over thousands of miles, and ores and metals transported back over the same route, initially entailing tremendous freight charges. Mining companies came to rely on railways for the dependable, cheap means of transportation that was essential for their success. Railways, on the other hand, relied on mineral traffic for the bulk of their revenues and profit, and could therefore charge lower rates for agricultural products than would otherwise have been possible. Without these lower rates, export agriculture could not have grown to its present proportions. So important indeed was the transport factor in the development of the mining industry, and of the economy in general, that special attention is devoted in this essay to the creation of the railway system.

Development of the mining industry

The first European mining frontier in Africa was on the banks of the Vaal river, to which hundreds of men flocked in the 1870s to stake claims to the large alluvial diamond deposits that had been discovered there in 1867. The early diggers, many of them farmers searching for diamonds in their spare time, had and required little in the way of capital. As diggings went deeper, however, money was needed for equipment to pump water out of pits and to clear fallen reef, or to sink shafts to begin underground operations. Restrictions on the number of claims which an individual could hold were gradually lifted, clearing the way for the formation of joint stock companies to take over mines and to begin the process of consolidation. By the beginning of 1880, twelve companies with a total share capital of £2·5 million had been formed. Eighteen months later, at the height of the diamond boom, the number of companies had risen to seventy-one, with a combined authorized capital of more than £8 million. The depression that inevitably followed brought the number of companies down to forty-two in 1885, by which time only fifty-nine private holdings had survived. The major problem then facing the industry was the wildly fluctuating diamond output that made it impossible to secure a consistently high price on world markets. In order to control supplies to meet the fairly inelastic demand and at the same time to enable the industry to expand, concentration of financial and operational control was essential.

Amalgamation plans were drawn up by a number of people, but it was Cecil Rhodes who took the lead. He gained control of the De Beers mine in 1887, and the following year took over the Kimberley Central Diamond Mining Company. The market value of the two companies concerned, which owned the richest mines in the area, has been estimated at nearly £18 million. The Dutoitspan and Bultfontein mines were also acquired by the new company that Rhodes and his associates formed, De Beers Consolidated Mines, as were others subsequently opened. Some smaller mines were brought under De Beers control by leasing arrangements. With the Anglo American Corporation (see below p. 363), De Beers came to control the production and distribution of diamonds throughout Africa, Europe and the Americas. As well as making trading agreements with producers, the two groups bought large shareholdings in companies operating or holding mining rights in Angola, the Congo, Sierra Leone, British Guiana and elsewhere.

One of the unique features of the South African diamond industry was that until the period of amalgamation, only a negligible amount of capital came from outside the country. Finance for expansion and development was provided by the industry's own profits; and, particularly during the 1881 boom, Cape banks prepared to advance considerable sums against the prospectors' and vendors' scrip, in which form most of the mining companies' share capital was held. Amalgamation required outside help, much of which came from the London Rothschilds, some from Paris and Hamburg. When the amalgamation had been completed, the industry's own profits were once again sufficient to provide most of the finance needed. Professor Frankel has estimated that by 1936 foreign investment in South African diamonds totalled only about £20 million, although some £340 million worth of diamonds had been produced and the companies concerned had declared dividends of more than £80 million. (See Tables 60 and 61 for capital issued and dividends declared after 1910.) In extending its control outside South Africa, Anglo-American did rely heavily on British, American and French capital, most notably from the house of Morgan and the Rothschilds.

Diamonds also provided much of the initial capital used in opening up the gold-fields of the Transvaal. People who had been bought out in the course of amalgamation, international firms that had profited from diamond dealing, and those who still retained an interest in the industry sought opportunities on the Witwatersrand to make or to increase their fortunes. As with diamonds, individual prospectors worked alluvial deposits and outcroppings, but it soon became obvious that considerably more funds than were available in South Africa itself would be needed to finance underground mining. Rhodes formed Gold Fields of South Africa in 1887, placing £100,000 of the company's first £125,000 share issue on the London market; the rest was sold in South Africa. (With the help of De Beers the company was reorganized in 1892 as Consolidated Gold Fields.) Investment in gold-mining has been compared to betting on horses: the risks of loss are enormous, and backing a favourite is not always successful. There is also a delay of five to seven years between opening a mine and bringing it in production. In South Africa, many problems arise from the fact that the gold-fields contain ores of low grade in narrow, fractured seams. Therefore capital, technical expertise and equipment beyond the resources of companies floated to work individual mines became necessary. The further need to spread the financial risk and to secure economies of scale led to the growth of the group system on which the finance and operation of the gold-mining industry has continued to be based.

Under this system one of the Rand's mining finance houses contracts with a mining company to provide the finance and the technical, managerial and administrative services essential for opening the mine, bringing it to production and subsequently operating it. The control of these large finance-houses over the separate companies is theoretically based on the contract rather than on major shareholdings. In practice, this is a distinction without a difference; none of the companies is in a position to go against the wishes of the group that finances and services it. Tables 62 and 63 show the relative importance of the different finance houses now existing, but indicate only part of the reason why the Anglo American Corporation of South Africa dominates the country's gold-mining industry. Anglo American was formed in 1917 by Ernest (later Sir Ernest) Oppenheimer, who first went to Africa in 1901 as the representative of a London diamond merchant and became very successful on his own account. He became mayor of Kimberley, but, because of anti-German feeling during the First World War, moved to Johannesburg and became interested in gold-mining. He formed the company with the support of an American mining engineer, W. L. Honnold, who was able to provide access to substantial American

Table 60. *Capital issued by South African mining companies, 1911–61*
(£000 for 1911–58; R000 for 1959–61)

| Year | Total | Type of mine | | | | Outside Union | In Union | Percentage in Union |
		Gold	Diamonds	Coal	Other			
1911 (£000)	93,196	73,855	8,619	7,734	2,988	—	—	—
1912	90,834	71,048	9,032	7,732	3,022	—	—	—
1913	87,319	68,205	8,503	7,716	2,895	—	—	—
1914	85,543	66,233	8,235	8,144	2,931	—	—	—
1915	82,702	64,565	7,603	7,507	3,027	—	—	—
1916	82,334	64,209	7,655	7,390	3,080	—	—	—
1917	82,059	64,371	7,675	6,798	3,215	—	—	—
1918	81,735	63,852	7,666	7,278	2,939	—	—	—
1919	85,090	65,991	8,061	7,801	3,237	—	—	—
1920	88,100	65,787	8,826	8,931	4,556	—	—	—
1921	88,482	64,788	8,508	10,030	5,156	—	—	—
1922	82,636	59,778	7,861	10,209	4,788	—	—	—
1923	80,647	58,281	8,049	10,467	3,850	—	—	—
1924	73,259	51,686	8,051	10,258	3,264	—	—	—
1925	76,130	51,481	8,112	9,680	6,857	—	—	—
1926	75,644	49,394	8,335	9,088	8,827	—	—	—
1927	75,095	49,092	8,281	8,980	8,742	—	—	—
1928	75,298	47,880	8,683	8,995	9,740	—	—	—
1929	70,678	43,222	8,502	9,359	9,595	—	—	—
1930	70,267	43,181	8,313	9,367	9,406	—	—	—
1931	70,515	43,720	8,116	9,442	9,237	—	—	—
1932	68,714	42,923	7,872	9,297	8,622	—	—	—
1933	72,921	48,236	7,887	9,292	7,506	—	—	—
1934	85,536	61,064	7,912	9,448	7,112	—	—	—
1935	93,885	69,852	7,566	9,812	6,655	—	—	—
1936	99,422	74,727	7,435	10,521	6,739	—	—	—
1937	107,794	82,622	7,557	10,489	7,126	—	—	—
1938	112,017	86,125	7,901	10,360	7,631	—	—	—
1939	113,144	87,451	7,486	10,385	7,822	—	—	—
1940	112,191	86,363	7,451	10,439	7,938	—	—	—
1941	111,919	86,895	6,764	10,531	7,729	—	—	—
1942	112,085	86,889	6,784	10,490	7,922	—	—	—
1943	110,491	84,718	6,771	10,547	8,455	—	—	—
1944	111,789	83,732	7,738	11,125	9,194	—	—	—
1945	114,155	84,877	7,908	11,416	9,954	—	—	—
1946	120,142	89,968	8,238	12,560	9,376	—	—	—
1947	137,812	105,702	9,220	15,205	7,685	—	—	—
1948	144,294	109,635	9,345	17,169	8,145	—	—	—
1949	142,756	108,555	8,297	18,491	7,413	52,317	90,439	63·4
1950	157,901	121,065	7,951	19,772	9,113	57,115	100,786	63·8
1951	162,358	122,878	8,741	21,571	9,168	55,546	106,812	65·8
1952	173,188	127,196	9,024	26,686	10,282	56,625	116,563	67·3
1953	197,359	140,615	8,988	34,513	13,243	61,523	135,836	68·8
1954	218,465	149,695	8,871	45,563	14,336	57,371	161,094	73·7
1955	233,735	164,371	9,158	44,562	15,644	57,047	176,688	75·6
1956	237,616	166,507	7,912	46,617	16,580	60,776	176,840	74·4
1957	254,141	170,163	8,091	57,644	18,243	60,775	193,366	76·1
1958	245,336	161,330	8,075	57,380	18,551	59,961	185,375	75·6
1959 (R000)	461,732	347,770	15,694	53,432	44,836	105,215	451,847	81·0
1960	501,225	377,848	15,389	59,397	48,591	116,515	391,011	78·0
1961	529,080	402,673	15,282	60,834	50,291	126,803	412,564	78·0

SOURCES: Union of South Africa, Bureau of Census and Statistics, *Union statistics for fifty years,* for 1911–58; and Republic of South Africa, *Statistical yearbook, 1966,* for 1959–61.

Table 61. *Dividends declared by South African mining companies, 1911–61*
(£000 for 1911–58, R000 for 1959–61)

Year	Total	Type of mine				Outside Union	In Union	Percentage in Union
		Gold	Diamonds	Coal	Other			
1911 (£000)	264	64	196	3	1	—	—	—
1912	11,856	8,303	3,019	310	224	—	—	—
1913	12,623	8,597	3,443	354	229	—	—	—
1914	10,065	8,411	1,154	401	99	—	—	—
1915	8,198	7,734	—	398	66	—	—	—
1916	10,131	7,283	2,242	460	146	—	—	—
1917	10,289	6,726	3,022	360	181	—	—	—
1918	8,573	5,342	2,682	395	154	—	—	—
1919	11,170	6,103	4,659	389	19	—	—	—
1920	13,011	8,475	3,918	536	82	—	—	—
1921	8,469	7,260	500	700	9	—	—	—
1922	6,919	5,695	806	400	18	—	—	—
1923	11,063	8,538	2,065	435	25	—	—	—
1924	12,750	9,693	2,342	644	71	—	—	—
1925	11,658	8,302	2,621	642	93	—	—	—
1926	12,534	8,444	3,163	760	167	—	—	—
1927	11,697	8,476	2,197	777	247	—	—	—
1928	11,393	8,506	1,969	678	240	—	—	—
1929	11,496	8,485	1,974	751	286	—	—	—
1930	10,582	8,716	982	722	162	—	—	—
1931	9,198	8,590	23	543	42	—	—	—
1932	9,578	9,043	—	479	56	—	—	—
1933	14,414	13,684	56	583	91	—	—	—
1934	16,914	16,038	42	716	118	—	—	—
1935	18,045	16,778	449	789	29	10,737	7,308	40·5
1936	21,962	17,533	3,338	990	201	13,381	8,581	39·1
1937	21,250	16,999	2,973	1,047	231	13,075	8,175	38·5
1938	19,303	17,331	400	1,173	399	11,225	8,078	41·9
1939	22,575	19,999	800	1,349	427	12,617	9,958	44·1
1940	23,876	21,223	869	1,255	529	12,620	11,256	47·1
1941	23,722	19,575	2,079	1,529	539	11,588	12,134	51·2
1942	21,993	17,616	2,115	1,514	748	10,372	11,621	52·8
1943	21,600	15,592	3,080	1,618	1,310	9,880	11,720	54·3
1944	19,124	13,977	2,787	1,440	920	8,478	10,646	55·7
1945	18,799	13,359	2,838	1,531	1,071	8,941	9,858	52·4
1946	19,803	13,568	3,516	1,662	1,057	9,512	10,391	52·5
1947	20,414	12,798	4,510	1,924	1,192	9,278	11,136	54·6
1948	22,860	14,085	4,458	2,662	1,655	10,321	12,539	54·9
1949	26,587	18,055	4,393	2,251	1,888	12,160	14,427	54·3
1950	36,566	26,471	4,404	2,428	3,263	16,486	20,080	54·9
1951	40,720	24,344	6,518	2,763	7,095	18,456	22,264	54·7
1952	41,808	21,991	9,851	3,197	6,769	19,471	22,337	53·4
1953	40,173	20,136	9,021	3,317	7,699	18,756	21,417	53·3
1954	40,311	21,109	9,105	3,299	6,798	18,247	22,064	54·7
1955	46,366	24,633	9,161	3,610	8,962	21,023	25,343	54·7
1956	54,404	30,558	9,210	4,217	10,419	23,181	31,223	57·4
1957	61,578	39,266	9,260	4,770	8,282	22,790	38,788	63·0
1958	60,726	42,360	9,224	4,891	4,251	21,435	39,291	64·7
1959 (R000)	142,286	98,899	20,432	10,546	12,509	47,563	94,823	66·6
1960	157,256	102,029	23,407	12,067	19,753	49,355	107,901	68·6
1961	153,826	102,035	23,035	10,406	18,080	47,944	105,882	68·8

SOURCES: Union of South Africa, Bureau of Census and Statistics, *Union statistics for fifty years* for 1911–1958; and Republic of South Africa, *Statistical yearbook, 1966*, for 1959–61.

Table 62. *Relative size of mining finance-houses, South Africa, 1936 and 1969*

Name [a]	Date of establish-ment	No. of mines [b]		Employment (black labour) percentage		Gold production (fine oz.) percentage		Approximate percentage of group's funds invested in gold and uranium, 1960
		1936	1969	1936	1969	1936	1969	
Consolidated Gold Fields of South Africa, Ltd	1887	9	11	12	17	11	17	55
Johannesburg Consolidated Investment Company, Ltd	1889	7	4	23	4	24	3	13
Rand Mines, Ltd	1893	14	7	36	17	34	12	50
General Mining and Finance Corp., Ltd	1895	2	3	4	10	5	7	86
Union Corp., Ltd	1897	6	8	6	13	8	13	n.a.
Anglo American Corp. of South Africa, Ltd	1917	5	12	13	29	14	41	40
Anglo-Transvaal Consolidated Investment Co., Ltd	1933	1	5	2	10	1	6	50
Sundry companies		4	1	4	0	2	—	—
Total		48	51	100	100	100	100	

	Total number	Total production (millions)
	302,000 337,000	11·0 30·9

[a] This table is no more than a rough guide, as it does not show the involvement of each group with mines under the control of other groups.   [b] Including non-producing mines.

SOURCE: Francis Wilson, *Labour in the South African gold mines, 1911–1969* (Cambridge University Press,

Table 63. *Distribution of South African gold-mines, according to profitability between mining houses, 1936 and 1961*

Group	No. of producing mines		Rich		Average		Poor		No. of poor mines more than 30 years old	
	1936	1961	1936	1961	1936	1961	1936	1961	1936	1961
Anglo American	4	12	—	3	3	3	1	6	—	5
Anglo-Transvaal	1	4	—	—	—	1	1	3	—	1
Rand Mines/Central	11	8	—	1	4	1	7	6	7	6
General Mining	2	3	—	—	1	2	1	1	1	—
Consolidated Gold Fields	5	11	1	1	2	2	2	8	2	5
Union Corporation	2	7	—	—	2	5	—	2	—	2
Johannesburg Consolidated Investment	7	2	—	—	2	—	5	2	3	—

NOTE: Mines are graded according to their wealth, measured by the working profit per ton milled, as follows:

	Working profit/tons milled (current cents)	
	1936	1961
Poor	0–9·9	0–19·9
Average	10–29·9	20–59·9
Rich	⩾30	⩾60

SOURCE: Francis Wilson, *Labour in the South African gold mines, 1911–69* (Cambridge University Press, 1972), p. 108.

credits. Over the years, however, the greater part of the company's capital has been drawn from South African and British sources. Direct American participation has been negligible. By virtue of its success in developing gold-mines in the Orange Free State after the Second World War, Anglo American became banker to the entire industry. In addition to its own direct holdings, it is in a position to control the Johannesburg Consolidated Investment Company and Rand Mines, and has a substantial stake in the General Mining and Finance Corporation. It holds a 20 per cent share in Consolidated Gold Fields' most valuable South African assets also, and through the Charter Consolidated Company is the largest single shareholder in the Union Corporation. Its interests have spread beyond Africa and into fields other than gold and diamonds.

One of the biggest questions about South African gold-mining over the years has concerned return on capital invested. In the short term, very high profits from some mines were counterbalanced by low or negative yields from others. Despite the fact that the international market in gold shares was highly developed, the belief grew and persisted that more capital had been sunk in gold-mines than had been returned in the form of dividends or capital repayments. Professor R. A. Lehfeldt was the first to attack this view, when he showed that for the period 1907–26 the average yield on gold-mining investment, after allowing for all capital gains and losses, was 6·2 per cent. Professor Frankel later calculated that the average annual return for 1887–1936 was 4·2 per cent, and taking an even longer-term view, for the years 1887–1965, 5·2 per cent. Notwithstanding these scientific refutations of the idea that gold-mining investment was unprofitable, the mines have continued to appeal only to a very narrow segment of the investing public, except in boom times. Unlike the diamond industry, gold-mining always relied heavily on international money markets, although an increasing proportion of the capital employed in South African mining generally came from domestic sources. Tables 60, 61, 64 and 65 provide a partial picture of capital investment and returns.

There was further co-operation within the industry through the Chamber of Mines, which was formed in 1889 out of a Diggers' Committee set up three years earlier. The initial aim of the Chamber of Mines was to co-ordinate the recruitment of African labour for all the Transvaal mines. Although this is still a major part of its activity, it has in addition become the industry's representative in negotiations with white trade unions; it carries out much of the training of personnel, conducts research into new mining methods, and formulates policy regarding legislation and relations with the government. It is also through the Chamber that the mining companies keep one another informed about factor costs, techniques and so on. Because the demand for gold has been infinitely elastic and because the selling price is determined entirely by external forces, there is little if anything to be gained by competition among the companies either in the technical sphere or with regard to wages. Until the early 1960s, collusion among the companies to keep African wages at a low level was complete. The only area of competition has been in connexion with acquiring new leases.

North of the Limpopo river, investment in mining was in the early days even more highly speculative than investment in the Rand. Information from Africans, old legends and superficial prospecting were the only bases for initial decisions. It was therefore largely a matter of faith on the part of Rhodes and his colleagues to form the British South Africa Company (Chartered) to exploit mineral deposits, primarily gold, in what was to become Southern Rhodesia. Both De Beers and Gold Fields of South Africa took up large numbers of shares in the new company. From the 'Second Rand' Rhodes had counted on finding, he expected to be able not only to derive substantial profit but also to cover the cost of administering the vast territory held under the company's royal charter. The 'Second Rand' failed to materialize. Large amounts of gold were indeed to be found in Southern Rhodesia, but in small, scattered and heavily faulted deposits. In its original mining regulations, Chartered had required the formation of a company to work any mine found and could initially demand a 50 per-cent share of the authorized capital. (In practice, their share was usually closer to 30 per cent.) 'Blanket prospectors', so-called because they gave blankets to Africans in exchange for information about potential mineral sources, sold any promising claims which they found to land and mining companies, to whom concessions were granted, but who generally met with little success. Company promoters in London were more concerned with their own commissions than with providing working capital for the mines. Money available for development work was limited also by the fact that Chartered paid nothing for its share in the companies. Furthermore, the supervision of work on the spot and the business acumen of many of the people involved left much to be desired.

Table 64. Capital invested in the South African gold-mining industry, 1887–1965

Years	Capital of mines closed (1) £ m.	New capital (2) £ m.	Accumulated new capital (3) £ m.	Accumulated capital of mines existing at end of period (4) £ m.	Percentage of (2) on (4) (5) %	New capital * (6) £ m.	Accumulated new capital * (7) £ m.	Accumulated capital of mines existing at end of period * (8) £ m.	Percentage of (6) on (8) (9) %
1887–1903				95·1				93·1	
1904–13	5·1 (5·8%)	29·7 (4·7%)	29·7	119·8	24·8	31·1 (8·6%)	31·1	119·3	26·1
1914–24	26·6 (30·1%)	11·7 (1·8%)	41·4	104·8	11·2	8·8 (2·5%)	39·9	101·5	8·7
1925–32	9·7 (11·0%)	10·5 (1·7%)	51·9	105·5	10·0	8·3 (2·3%)	48·2	100·4	8·3
1933–42	3·1 (3·5%)	108·9 (17·2%)	160·8	211·5	51·5	93·4 (25·9%)	141·6	191·0	48·9
1943–52	10·4 (11·8%)	219·6 (34·8%)	380·4	420·7	52·2	123·1 (34·1%)	264·7	303·8	40·5
1953–65	33·3 (37·8%)	251·2 (39·8%)	631·6	638·5	39·3	96·0 (26·6%)	360·7	373·0	25·7
Total	88·2 (100·0%)	631·6 (100·0%)				360·7 (100·0%)			

* Real terms: 1913 = 100

SOURCE: S. Herbert Frankel, Investment and the return to equity capital in the South African gold mining industry, 1887–1965 (Oxford, 1967). p. 21.

Table 65. *Rates of return lump-sum in money terms, South African gold-mining industry, for periods of five years, 1919–24 to 1958–63*

Years	Consols after tax	Gold-mines after tax and lease	U.K. equities after tax	Finance companies after tax
1919–24	2·0	11·3	9·8	5·2
1920–5	5·6	9·2	5·6	6·6
1921–6	7·8	10·5	19·3	12·3
1922–7	5·2	17·7	21·9	23·8
1923–8	3·5	16·9	15·6	21·3
1924–9	3·8	12·7	17·6	22·7
1925–30	2·0	9·6	10·6	15·1
1926–31	4·4	7·4	2·0	3·2
1927–32	3·8	7·0	−1·7	−4·0
1928–33	9·1	1·9	0·0	−5·6
1929–34	8·7	19·4	0·8	7·5
1930–5	14·7	29·9	8·3	15·0
1931–6	11·5	33·2	14·5	23·7
1932–7	12·1	35·0	23·7	35·7
1933–8	2·6	34·7	13·6	30·8
1934–9	1·5	12·1	5·3	12·3
1935–40	−3·6	1·7	0·8	−1·2
1936–41	−0·3	2·0	−3·2	−3·0
1937–42	1·4	1·8	−3·6	−3·9
1938–43	4·0	4·7	2·2	−0·8
1939–44	4·4	5·7	6·9	7·5
1940–5	5·3	10·8	9·0	22·4
1941–6	5·0	11·5	11·8	28·1
1942–7	5·0	4·8	10·9	22·0
1943–8	1·5	7·6	7·0	21·9
1944–9	1·8	−0·3	4·0	6·9
1945–50	−1·1	4·4	0·4	8·5
1946–51	−3·3	0·6	1·1	1·6
1947–52	−7·3	4·8	−1·0	0·0
1948–53	−4·6	1·5	−0·7	−4·1
1949–54	−2·5	3·5	4·3	−2·4
1950–5	0·6	1·7	14·1	0·6
1951–6	−2·3	1·3	14·3	5·2
1952–7	−0·8	−2·2	10·8	1·5
1953–8	−1·8	1·2	11·2	8·1
1954–9	−1·7	6·9	14·6	14·9
1955–60	−2·8	7·2	14·9	12·7
1956–61	−2·0	8·9	13·2	10·1
1957–62	−2·9	13·1	16·5	13·4
1958–63	2·6	16·5	17·7	18·1

NOTE: Rates of return are after taxation and lease payments paid by gold-mines, but before deduction of any U.K. taxation.

SOURCE: S. Herbert Frankel, *Investment and the return to equity capital in the South African gold mining industry, 1887–1965* (Cambridge, Mass., Harvard University Press, 1967), p. 79.

In 1904, by ending the requirement that companies be formed to exploit any claims found, and by substituting a sliding scale of royalties for their fixed share, Chartered began to encourage individuals to retain and to work their claims. Individuals were often able to make a profit from deposits too small or low-grade to be of interest to the companies, but also opened up some mines that could be worked on a large scale. In either case, once again as diggings went deeper, capital was needed for machinery. Some individuals pooled their resources to meet these needs, but from 1909 onwards the major finance houses of the Rand took up interests in Southern Rhodesian gold. The flow of capital from Johannesburg was never sufficient to make the Southern Rhodesian gold-mining industry financially independent of Chartered and the London money market. Many small mines continued in production, but a few large producers became the source of the greater proportion of total output. By 1914–15, the larger producers were responsible for 45 per cent of total output (see Table 66). By the early 1960s, twelve out of the 235 mines being worked accounted for the greatest part of total production.

Table 66. *Gold-mining, Southern Rhodesia, 1915–37*

Year	Value of total gold output (£000)	Total number of contributors to output	Large producers	
			Number	Contribution to total output (per cent)
1915	3,823	508	8	45·2
1919	2,409	314	10	67·8
1928	2,438	—	—	77·3
1929	2,374	290	8	73·6
1930	2,317	332	9	74·8
1931	2,274	454	9	69·0
1932	3,366	782	10	61·4
1933	4,014	1,188	11	52·3
1934	4,696	1,636	11	43·7
1935	5,090	1,754	9	38·1
1936	5,636	1,707	10	37·2
1937	5,657	1,572	11	39·1

SOURCE: S. Herbert Frankel, *Capital investment in Africa* (London, Oxford University Press, 1938), p. 236.

Many other minerals have been found and exploited in southern Africa, but with the exception of coal and iron ore (see below, p. 401) they did not have an impact on the economy in any way comparable to that of diamonds and gold. Mines and other industries throughout Africa have depended heavily on the vast supplies of cheap, easily won coal found in Natal, the Orange Free State, the Transvaal and Southern Rhodesia. Coal was mined in Natal as early as 1840, but it was only when the gold-mines were opened and the railways built that large-scale exploitation began. In the Transvaal, the collieries were worked as an integral part of gold-mining operations (see Tables 67 and 68). The Wankie coal-fields in Southern Rhodesia contain vast reserves of high-quality coal that

Table 67. *South African output of gold, diamonds, iron ore and coal, 1910–61*

	Gold		Diamonds			Iron ore			Coal		
	Sales		Production	Sales		Production	Sales		Production	Sales	
Year	1,000 oz.	£1,000	Carats 1,000	Carats 1,000	£1,000	1,000 ton	1,000 ton	£1,000	1,000 ton	1,000 ton	£1,000
1910	7,531	31,991	5,601	—	8,189	—	—	—	—	7,112	1,867
1911	8,251	35,049	5,022	5,002	8,549	—	—	—	7,667	7,595	1,935
1912	9,109	38,692	5,206	4,898	9,565	—	—	—	8,138	8,117	1,999
1913	8,799	37,375	5,300	5,685	12,089	—	—	—	8,905	8,801	2,240
1914	8,396	35,664	2,875	3,453	6,759	—	—	—	8,632	8,478	2,259
1915	9,096	38,639	106	567	1,460	—	—	—	8,462	8,281	2,142
1916	9,297	39,491	2,409	2,353	5,228	—	—	—	10,239	10,008	2,740
1917	9,018	38,308	2,979	2,480	6,171	—	—	—	10,949	10,383	3,276
1918	8,418	35,759	2,605	2,712	7,233	4·6	4·9	2·7	10,425	9,877	3,225
1919	8,332	39,280	2,657	2,719	13,380	3·6	3·6	1·1	10,855	10,266	3,416
1920	8,158	45,606	2,613	1,813	10,328	3·9	2·6	0·8	12,040	11,473	4,520
1921	8,129	43,082	828	544	2,162	2·4	2·4	0·7	11,922	11,397	5,072
1922	7,010	32,343	670	1,231	3,766	2·1	2·1	0·9	10,221	9,734	3,395
1923	9,149	41,575	2,053	2,584	7,733	0·6	0·6	0·2	12,404	11,917	3,714
1924	9,575	44,739	2,440	2,041	6,752	—	—	—	13,029	12,492	3,825
1925	9,598	40,768	2,430	2,598	8,665	52·0	52·0	17·0	13,582	13,000	3,862
1926	9,955	42,285	3,218	3,178	10,962	85·5	85·5	29·7	14,275	13,734	4,047
1927	10,122	42,998	4,708	4,256	11,819	23·0	23·0	7·5	13,867	13,303	3,826
1928	10,354	43,982	4,373	3,687	11,079	42·2	42·2	13·4	13,896	13,403	3,673
1929	10,412	44,229	3,661	3,084	12,454	—	—	—	14,350	13,913	3,778
1930	10,716	45,520	3,164	1,877	5,883	56·9	56·9	19·9	13,473	13,106	3,494
1931	10,878	46,206	2,119	1,449	2,727	17·0	17·0	6·6	11,994	11,639	3,033
1932	11,559	49,766	798	868	1,523	34·9	34·9	11·8	10,936	10,650	2,733

1933	11,014	68,687	507	646	1,859	75·6	66·2	20·8	11,811	11,528	2,918
1934	10,480	72,311	440	1,262	2,494	257·0	252·3	97·7	13,442	13,117	3,154
1935	10,774	76,533	677	2,373	2,945	335·2	335·2	145·0	14,963	14,608	3,540
1936	11,336	79,495	624	1,098	3,227	402·3	401·6	94·1	16,360	15,996	3,950
1937	11,735	82,557	1,030	949	3,769	509·0	509·0	118·6	17,076	16,718	4,206
1938	12,161	86,670	1,239	519	1,323	557·0	557·0	134·6	17,950	17,536	4,729
1939	12,822	98,943	1,250	522	1,853	530·4	529·7	116·6	18,618	18,106	4,824
1940	14,047	117,991	543	1,128	2,482	694·0	683·0	272·4	19,283	18,934	5,326
1941	14,408	121,024	158	660	2,971	863·8	864·6	448·9	20,590	20,213	5,910
1942	14,127	118,666	119	652	2,725	774·7	779·2	312·5	22,496	22,102	6,562
1943	12,804	107,557	302	624	4,931	800·7	799·2	290·1	22,664	22,287	6,716
1944	12,280	103,149	934	719	5,052	831·6	827·2	333·9	25,339	24,907	8,036
1945	12,225	105,285	1,223	1,256	8,732	929·5	929·4	399·0	25,964	25,466	8,509
1946	11,927	102,872	1,349	1,332	10,741	1,010·9	1,007·7	465·3	26,017	25,634	8,733
1947	11,200	96,602	1,242	1,295	9,818	1,238·5	1,238·5	543·0	25,902	25,415	8,691
1948	11,585	99,919	1,382	1,368	10,210	1,234·1	1,232·5	579·5	26,482	25,968	9,143
1949	11,705	115,084	1,265	1,495	10,035	1,301·5	1,299·1	563·7	28,105	27,427	12,962
1950	11,664	146,899	1,732	1,926	14,389	1,233·7	1,241·2	615·5	29,182	28,665	14,797
1951	11,516	149,641	2,229	2,163	16,345	1,496·7	1,490·5	805·8	29,357	28,768	13,559
1952	11,819	150,829	2,383	2,350	14,776	1,893·0	1,887·4	1,015·7	30,936	30,038	14,640
1953	11,941	149,499	2,718	2,627	13,993	2,172·3	2,136·6	1,156·3	31,371	30,570	16,464
1954	13,237	164,688	2,859	2,891	13,235	2,086·8	2,060·5	1,175·7	32,313	30,844	16,122
1955	14,601	182,745	2,629	2,633	13,186	2,203·4	2,210·2	1,410·4	35,396	33,061	17,338
1956	15,897	198,500	2,586	2,577	13,419	2,275·5	2,288·7	1,517·4	37,040	35,570	20,774
1957	17,031	212,585	2,579	2,552	14,460	2,293·1	2,294·4	1,540·6	38,326	37,687	21,657
1958	17,656	220,025	2,702	2,747	15,554	2,438·7	2,429·8	1,919·5	40,879	39,940	23,623
		R 1,000			R 1,000			R 1,000			R 1,000
1959	20,066	500,272	2,838	2,843	31,316	3,187	3,093	5,367	40,182	39,193	49,420
1960	21,383	536,018	3,141	2,998	33,852	3,385	3,342	7,162	42,079	41,962	55,103
1961	22,942	574,900	3,788	3,719	38,370	4,366	4,111	9,580	43,613	44,627	59,624

SOURCES: Union of South Africa, Bureau of Census and Statistics, *Union statistics for fifty years*, for 1910–58; and Republic of South Africa, *Statistical Yearbook, 1966*, for 1959–61.

373

Table 68. *Coal output by province, South Africa, 1918–53*

	1918		1928		1938		1953	
	Output (short tons)	Per cent	Output (short tons)	Per cent	Output (short tons)	Per cent	Output (short tons)	Per cent
Cape	4,654	0·5	5,059		3,108			
Natal	2,607,133	26·3	4,641,145	34·6	4,447,977	25·4	5,754,344	18·3
Transvaal	6,438,961	64·7	7,669,102	57·2	11,518,304	65·6	21,666,396	69·1
O.F.S.	826,577	8·5	1,088,109	8·1	1,566,838	8·9	3,950,281	12·6
Union	9,877,325	100·0	13,403,415	100·0	17,536,227	100·0	31,371,021	100·0

SOURCE: Monica Cole, *South Africa* (London, 1961), p. 347.

produces excellent metallurgical coke. As none of the coal found north of the Zambezi could be used for smelting purposes, Wankie has been a prime source of supply for both Katanga and the Copper Belt.

Ironically, it was in Northern Rhodesia, where Rhodes had not initially expected to find much of commercial value that the 'Second Rand' was found, but this wealth was not exploitable on a large scale until after the First World War. The search for minerals north of the Zambezi had begun almost as soon as the company had been formed, but the deposits found at first were worked only sporadically, and did not produce favourable results. It was one of these early attempts to develop Northern Rhodesia's minerals that led to the opening up of the 'scandalously rich' copper-fields of Katanga. In 1895, wanting to help the Countess of Warwick resolve her financial difficulties, the Prince of Wales (later King Edward VII) asked Rhodes to grant a concession to a syndicate in which the Countess was the major participant. It was only in 1899 that Robert (later Sir Robert) Williams, an associate of Rhodes who had been involved in gold-mining in Southern Rhodesia, formed Tanganyika Concessions, Ltd (Tanks) to locate the concession and to work any mines found within it. (Tanks derived its name from the fact that its concession included a grant of land on the south shore of Lake Tanganyika. It had no connexion with Tanganyika Territory, which at the time was in any case known as German East Africa.) An expedition under George Grey (brother of Sir Edward Grey, British Foreign Secretary), with the help of information from local Africans located the Kansanshi mine, which appeared very promising but was in fact of very little value. The historical importance of Kansanshi lay in the fact that Grey used it as a base for clandestine investigations on the Katanga side of the Northern Rhodesia–Congo border.

King Leopold and his Belgian financial backers had known of the existence of copper in Katanga for many years; but preliminary, and unfortunately superficial, investigations by the geologist Jules Cornet indicated that the deposits were not sufficiently rich to justify the heavy capital outlay that would be necessary to bring the mines to production, to carry out preliminary refining, and to build railways to carry copper to the coast. At the end of 1900, Williams secured a concession to prospect in Katanga and sent Grey on a second expedition, the findings of which strongly contradicted Cornet's conclusions. Belgian pessimism was only slowly overcome, and political considerations delayed full-scale exploitation until 1906, when the Union Minière du Haut-Katanga was formed, with Tanks having a 40 per cent interest. After some technical problems with the smelting plant, commercial production began in 1912.

Among other minerals mined in the Congo, most important economically were diamonds. In 1906 the Société Internationale Forestière et Minière (Forminière) was founded with American and Belgian capital to exploit extensive deposits in the Kasai region. Although diamond mining promoted wider economic development, its impact on the Congo's economy was less than that of copper mining.

The First World War provided an important stimulus to the mining industry.

Table 69. *Production of coal, gold, asbestos and chrome in Southern Rhodesia, 1908–61*

Year	Coal (short tons)	Gold (fine oz.)	Asbestos (short tons)	Chrome ore (short tons)
1908	164,114	3,208,790 [a]	55	13,358
1909	170,893	623,388	272	25,620
1910	180,068	609,955	332	44,002
1911	212,529	628,521	460	52,363
1912	216,140	647,807	—	69,261
1913	243,328	689,954	290	63,383
1914	349,459	854,480	487	48,207
1915	409,763	915,029	2,010	60,581
1916	491,582	930,356	6,157	88,871
1917	548,954	834,230	9,562	72,962
1918	491,268	631,358	8,574	31,286
1919	510,040	593,222	9,800	35,283
1920	578,492	552,498	18,823	60,269
1921	574,753	585,525	19,529	50,188
1922	515,650	652,791	14,249	93,475
1923	617,297	647,491	20,364	96,675
1924	652,049	627,729	26,141	172,724
1925	759,718	581,504	34,349	135,827
1926	963,579	593,429	33,344	181,194
1927	1,001,724	581,438	33,176	218,018
1928	1,206,864	576,112	39,960	219,428
1929	1,142,900	560,813	42,634	293,116
1930	1,034,785	547,630	37,766	226,671
1931	587 [b]	532 [c]	24 [d]	90 [d]
1932	438	574	16	17
1933	484	642	30	39
1934	643	691	32	79
1935	695	726	43	117
1936	705	797	56	202
1937	1,029	804	57	304
1938	1,044	814	59	205
1939	1,208	796	58	153
1940	1,291	826	56	273
1941	1,412	790	44	357
1942	1,561	760	56	384
1943	1,779	657	58	317
1944	1,808	593	58	305

Table 69. *Production of coal, gold asbestos and crome in Southern Rhodesia, 1908–61 (Continued)*

Year	Coal (short tons)	Gold (fine oz.)	Asbestos (short tons)	Chrome ore (short tons)
1945	1,669 [b]	568 [c]	56 [d]	205 [d]
1946	1,613	545	56	167
1947	1,508	523	54	171
1948	1,696	514	69	254
1949	1,920	528	80	268
1950	2,124	511	72	321
1951	2,304	487	78	331
1952	2,556	497	85	862 [e]
1953	2,616	501	88	463
1954	2,748	536	80	443
1955	3,315	525	105	449
1956	3,553	535	119	449
1957	3,853	537	132	654
1958	3,535	555	127	619
1959	3,758	567	120	543
1960	3,559	17,502 kg	121·5 [f]	291·1 [f]
1961	3,073	17,732 kg	146·6 [f]	257·3 [f]

[a] Total output from beginning of production to the end of 1908.   [b] 000 metric tons 1931–59.
[c] 000 fine oz. 1931–59.   [d] From 1931, figures indicate 000 tons.
[e] Including 508,704 tons stockpiled.   [f] Metric tons.

SOURCES: Southern Rhodesia, *Official Yearbook*, vols. II and III; William J. Barber, *The Economy of British Central Africa* (London, Oxford University Press, 1961), p. 127; United Nations, *Statistical Yearbook*, various years.

Production of base minerals such as asbestos and chrome, which came to have particular importance for Southern Rhodesia, expanded rapidly to meet wartime demand (see Table 69). The market for copper also grew, and Union Minière was able to increase its output substantially during hostilities. In order to do this, however, Union Minière had to deplete seriously the available reserves of high-grade ores. The Katanga ores up to the end of the war had an average copper content of 15 per cent, compared with less than 2 per cent in American ores and the 3–4 per cent on the Zambian Copper Belt. A major expansion programme was necessary to make it possible to treat the relatively poor ores and to increase production to take advantage of the artificially high price maintained by American producers who agreed to limit production (Table 70).

The expansion of the copper industry in Northern Rhodesia was made possible by a combination of geological and technological discoveries. Systematic prospecting shed new light on the vast extent of Northern Rhodesia's copper reserves. Metallurgists, moreover, discovered new processes that enabled them to treat low-grade ores in a profitable manner. The so-called Perkins process, invented by an American engineer for treating oxidized ores, especially played a major part in the post-war expansion of Northern Rhodesia's mining industry. The Bwana Mkubwa mine had large reserves of such ores, but had been worked only intermittently since its discovery in 1902. In 1922 Edmund (later Sir Edmund) Davis and Mr (later Sir) A. Chester Beatty decided to attempt to

Table 70. *Copper output, Union Minière du Haut-Katanga, 1911–60*

Year	Output (metric tons)	Year	Output (metric tons)	Year	Output (metric tons)
1911	998	1928	112,456	1945	160,211
1912	2,492	1929	136,992	1946	143,855
1913	7,407	1930	138,949	1947	150,840
1914	10,722	1931	120,000	1948	155,520
1915	14,042	1932	54,000	1949	141,399
1916	22,167	1933	66,596	1950	175,920
1917	27,462	1934	110,085	1951	191,959
1918	20,238	1935	107,682	1952	205,749
1919	23,019	1936	95,667	1953	214,116
1920	18,962	1937	150,467	1954	223,791
1921	30,464	1938	123,943	1955	234,673
1922	43,362	1939	122,649	1956	247,452
1923	57,886	1940	148,829	1957	240,280
1924	85,570	1941	162,167	1958	235,586
1925	90,104	1942	165,940	1959	280,403
1926	80,639·3	1943	156,850	1960	300,675
1927	89,155	1944	163,610		

SOURCES: Tanganyika Concessions, Ltd and Union Minière du Haut-Katanga annual reports.

put production on a permanent, profitable footing. Davis was an Australian who, after coming to South Africa, had become involved in a wide range of mining and related enterprises in South Africa itself, South-West Africa, the Rhodesias and Angola. He acquired an excellent reputation in mining-finance circles and became a director of more than forty companies, including the Wankie Colliery Company, and all but one of the companies were connected with mining in Northern Rhodesia. Beatty was an American mining expert, almost unique in being able to draw on large financial resources and on technical expertise. In 1913 he established the Selection Trust, Ltd., a London finance house, which served as the base for his work with Davis in Northern Rhodesia. The two men reorganized the Bwana Mkubwa Copper Mining Company with an authorized capital of £1·5 million, then considered a fairly large sum for such an undertaking. They were joined on the board of directors by Ernest Oppenheimer and Dougal O. Malcolm of the British South Africa Company.

In 1923 Chartered, which retained the mineral rights in the territory, decided to grant mining concessions to groups commanding substantial financial resources rather than to allow the system of smallholdings that prevailed in Southern Rhodesia to develop. Beatty and Oppenheimer formed the Rhodesia Congo Border Concession Company (later the Rhokana Corporation, Ltd), the first of six companies to receive exclusively grants covering all of Northern Rhodesia outside Barotseland and the north-eastern region, a total area some 26,100 square miles larger than the British Isles (see Table 71).

Bwana Mkubwa was a high-cost producer, and was ultimately forced to close down. It was in the extensive sulphide deposits located at depth in the Copper Belt that the country's vast wealth was found. These were drawn primarily from four mines: Roan Antelope and Mufulira, which were controlled by Beatty's Selection Trust (reorganized in 1926 as Rhodesian Selection Trust), and the Nkana and Nchanga mines, controlled by Rhodesian Anglo American,

Table 71. *Distribution of mineral concessions in Northern Rhodesia, 1923–6*

Company	Date registered	Sponsor	Original capital	Area covered (sq. mi.)
Rhodesia Congo Border Concession	16·2·23	Copper Ventures, Ltd [a]	£500,000 in £1 shares	50,000
Nkana Concession	21·2·24	Copper Ventures, sold to Bwana Mkubwa Copper Mining Co.	[b]	1,800
Rhodesian Minerals Concession	4·6·24	Copper Ventures	£200,000 in £1 shares	12,500
Loangwa Concession	4·11·25	Gold Fields of South Africa and Broken Hill Co.	£200,000 in 5s shares	13,000
Serenje Concession	16·1·26	Chartered and General Exploration Co.	£225,000 in £1 shares	46,000
Kasempa Concession	24·2·26	Chartered and United Exploration Co.	£225,000 in £1 shares	25,000
				148,300

[a] Half the capital was provided by Minerals Separation, Ltd, a London metallurgical firm, half by Beatty and some of his associates.
[b] Bwana Mkubwa paid £60,000 cash and allotted 575,000 fully paid shares for the concession.

SOURCE: Sir Theodor Gregory, *Ernest Oppenheimer and the economic development of Southern Africa* (Cape Town, Oxford University Press, 1962), p. 394.

which was formed in 1928. Other mines, including Bancroft and Chibuluma, were opened later. In Northern Rhodesia, as on the Rand, individual companies were floated for the mines. The parent organizations provided managerial, administrative and technical services. It was through Beatty and the Selection Trust that American interests, particularly the Hochschild family and their American Metal Company (American Metal Climax, Incorporated), became involved in the Copper Belt. American Metal began buying shares in Roan Antelope in 1927, and two years later provided the largest part of a £1·5 million loan to the Selection Trust. In 1930 the American firm bought 800,000 shares in Roan Antelope and 1 million in the Selection Trust, coming to hold 51 per cent of the latter by 1933 and this percentage was later increased considerably). Although Oppenheimer was pleased to have access to American mining expertise, he did not want Americans to gain too much control over the Northern Rhodesian copper industry. In 1928–29 he prevented Bwana Mkubwa from falling almost entirely into American Metal's hands, and with the help of the Rothschilds and the Rio Tinto Zinc Corporation made Nchanga a definite part of his own empire. The two parent companies were not entirely separate, although Oppenheimer would have preferred them to move even closer together. The Rhodesian Selection Trust remained independent, although Rhodesian Anglo American was the dominant of the two in both the financial and technical spheres.

The only other significant mining operations in Northern Rhodesia outside the Copper Belt were carried out at Broken Hill, where zinc, lead and vanadium deposits were found in 1902 (see Table 72). Davis formed the Broken Hill Development Syndicate (later Rhodesia Broken Hill Development Company) to work the mines. Technical difficulties in separating the lead and zinc where they occurred together meant that the full value of the fields could be

Table 72. *Quantities and values of major minerals produced in Northern Rhodesia, 1925–58*

Year	Copper, blister (long tons 000)	Value (£000)	Copper, electrolytic (long tons 000)	Value (£000)	Zinc (long tons 000)	Value (£000)	Lead (long tons 000)	Value (£000)
1925	0·1	6	—	—	0·2	6	3·4	52
1926	0·7	27	—	—	0·7	2	3·8	231
1927	3	197	—	—	0·3	8	5·8	143
1928	6	383	—	—	13	331	4·7	99
1929	5	408	—	—	22	548	1·6	39
1930	6	344	—	—	20	340	a	a
1931	9	346	—	—	7	62	a	a
1932	68	2,095	—	—	a	a	a	a
1933	104	3,403	—	—	19	292	a	a
1934	137	4,147	0·6	19	19·5	266	0·2	2
1935	120	3,786	24	845	21	290	0·2	3
1936	114	4,464	28	1,205	21	209	0·3	5
1937	117	9,715	31	1,849	14	333	0·5	12
1938	182	7,445	31	1,441	10	142	0·3	4
1939	182	7,990	30	1,468	13	191	0·2	3
1940	236	11,249	27	1,430	13	353	0·3	6
1941	204	9,288	24	1,223	14	409	0·4	8
1942	202	9,089	45	2,287	13	472	1·1	47
1943	190	8,550	61	3,093	13	561	1·2	51
1944	159	7,172	62	3,124	14	611	1·0	39
1945	133	7,432	61	3,815	15	696	1·7	64
1946	129	8,470	54	3,956	17	870	8·2	486
1947	136	13,945	56	6,445	21	1,301	15·6	1,297
1948	152	18,161	61	7,695	22	1,700	13·0	1,243
1949	195	23,549	64	7,706	23	1,973	13·9	1,404
1950	199	30,678	78	12,732	23	3,127	13·7	1,538
1951	206	41,167	103	21,043	23	3,928	14·0	2,364
1952	201	45,969	112	26,415	23	2,859	12·6	1,582
1953	210	51,475	153	38,196	25	1,897	11·5	1,047
1954	204	48,008	174	43,136	27	2,075	15·0	1,446
1955	165	52,827	178	62,462	28	2,530	16·1	1,700
1956	157	47,271	226	73,730	29	2,828	15·4	1,768
1957	170	34,200	247	54,416	29	2,396	15·4	1,437
1958	133	23,192	242	46,659	30	1,995	13·4	949

a Negligible.

SOURCE: William J. Barber, *The economy of British Central Africa* (London, Oxford University Press, 1961), p. 127.

379

realized only after the war, when refining techniques had improved and when vanadium, which was also found at Broken Hill, was in greater demand. It was on Davis' assurance that a large amount of traffic would be available from these mines that the railway was extended from Kalomo to Broken Hill (see below, p. 391).

Copper became Northern Rhodesia's economic mainstay. After suffering some setbacks during the Depression, output increased until the Second World War. Indeed, it was only the outbreak of war that removed the potential problem of overproduction. Both Northern Rhodesian and Katanga mines expanded output during the war, selling most of it to Britain. After the war, demand generally remained high, leading to further plant expansion in the 1950s. It was in West Africa, however, that the most remarkable developments in the mining industry occurred after 1945.

Mining never had as much impact on the West African economies during the colonial period as it did in the south. European gold-mining operations began in 1880 at Tarkwa, but later the centre of production shifted. About 90 per cent of total output comes from an area within a sixty-mile radius of Dunkwa. Ghana has become the world's fifth largest producer of gold, and ranks third in world diamond production. (The Congo comes first, South Africa second.) Diamonds were first found near the Birim river in 1919. Companies were formed to exploit the deposits, but individual African diggers remained important, their share of output sometimes being much greater than that of the companies (see Table 73). The largest firm, Consolidated African Selection Trust (CAST), an offshoot of De Beers, never had a monopoly of diamond rights, a situation that raised difficulties for the control of world-wide production.

Individual diggers subsequently declined in importance and have recently become insignificant producers. Other minerals found in Ghana include manganese, shipments of which began in 1916, and bauxite, which is found over a wide area, but has never been worked on a large scale.

Sierra Leone also has large diamond deposits, but unlike Ghana, where all stones are of industrial quality, many are gem stones. In 1932, the Sierra Leone Selection Trust, a wholly owned subsidiary of CAST, was given a monopoly of diamond-working throughout the country. In 1952, Africans began working alluvial deposits and 'potholing', a particularly wasteful form of mining that picks the eye out of a mine and recovers only about a fourth of the stones, but

Table 73. *Gold Coast diamond exports, 1947–53*

Period April to March	Mining co.— carats	African diggers— carats	F.o.b. value per carat (£)
1947–8	746,000	111,000	1·2
1948–9	746,000	282,000	1·5
1949–50	527,000	452,000	1·6
1950–1	549,000	387,000	2·2
1951–2	870,000	914,000	3·7
1952–3	741,000	1,350,000	2·3

SOURCE: F. J. Pedler, *Economic geography of West Africa* (London, 1955), p. 101.

often makes it uneconomic for a company to go over the ground again. Illicit diamond-buying resulted, a practice that the government has never been able to bring under control. Many of Sierra Leone's diamonds find their way to Liberia and Guinea, artificially swelling those countries' diamond-export figures (see Table 74). Sierra Leone's other major mineral resource is iron, deposits of which were opened in 1933 by the Sierra Leone Development Company, Ltd (Delco). By 1938, minerals accounted for 57 per cent of the value of the country's domestic exports, whereas by 1961, diamonds alone provided about 65 per cent.

Table 74. *Tropical African diamond production, 1956–68*

	1956	1957	1966	1967	1968
Production (000 carats)					
Congo (Zaire)	14,010	15,647	12,429	13,153	11,353
Ghana	2,539	3,125	2,819	2,537	2,447
Angola	740	864	1,268	1,289	1,667
Sierra Leone	648	863	1,462	1,400	1,522
Tanzania	359	391	947	986	702
Central African Republic	143	108	541	521	609
Export value ($ m.)					
Congo (Zaire)	28	31	26	24	30
Ghana	22	25	15	15	17
Angola	12	15	39	42	47
Sierra Leone	10	18	44	36	55
Tanzania	8	9	25	31	19
Central African Republic	3	2	16	14	17

SOURCE: A. M. O'Connor *The geography of tropical African development* (Oxford, 1971), p. 82.

Until very recently, Nigeria's major mineral resource was tin, found in the form of alluvial cassiterite on the Jos plateau. Working began in 1902, when the Niger Company began to take out mining leases. Other groups followed the Niger Company's lead, and by 1951 thirty-nine tin-mining firms were operating, in addition to which there were seventy-six private operators. Among the labour force is a group called tributers, who do not receive a fixed wage but work a section of ground, paying the owner of the mining rights a percentage of the ore's value.

Nigeria is the only West African country where commercially valuable deposits of coal have been found. The fields at Enugu, which were discovered in 1909, could be developed only when the railway had been built (see below, p. 396). In 1950, the Nigerian Coal Corporation was established to take over the mines from the railway. Unlike the tin mines, which have adopted mechanical and hydraulic methods in addition to hand labour, the collieries have introduced very little mechanization because of the adequate supply of labour near the mine and the fear of resulting unemployment.

In 1957, after extensive reserves had been found under the Niger Delta and the surrounding coastal plain, Nigeria joined the ranks of the world's oil-producing countries. Several international companies were interested, the most successful of which has been Shell-BP, whose wells in the Eastern Region produce the greater part of the country's total output. More recently production has begun in the mid-west and the west, as well as in some off-shore locations. The only other areas of Africa where oil in commercial quantities has been proved are in Angola and Gabon. The successful search began in Angola in 1952, with strikes south of Luanda and later in the Cabinda enclave. In Gabon, production began in 1956. Angola uses all its oil output, whereas Nigeria exports a good share, retaining only sufficient supplies for such domestic use as the generation of electricity and the supply of diesel power for the railways (see Table 75).

Table 75. *Tropical African oil production, 1956–69*

	1956	1957	1958	1966	1967	1968	1969
Production (000 tons)							
Angola	9	10	51	630	535	752	511
Gabon	0	173	505	1,447	3,450	4,642	5,050
Nigeria	0	1	260	21,110	15,600	7,028	26,630
Export value ($ m.)							
Angola				All used locally			
Gabon	0	3	7	16	36	42	50
Nigeria	0	0	3	258	201	104	381

SOURCE: A. M. O'Connor, *The geography of tropical African development* (Oxford, 1971), p. 73.

Little attempt was made during the colonial period to develop minerals in the French West African colonies, in part because of the general French preference for *rentier*-type investment and the general French predilection for European rather than overseas investment. After the Second World War, French attitudes began to change. In 1948 the Bureau Minier de la France d'Outre-Mer was established by the government to promote prospecting and mineral development. By 1954, minerals accounted for 2·8 per cent of French West Africa's total exports. Guinea and Mauritania are the two former French territories best endowed with mineral resources. In 1952, a subsidiary of Aluminium, Ltd of Canada began mining bauxite on Kassa Island off Conakry. Reserves there are low, but production increased from 60,000 tons in 1952 to 540,000 tons in 1960. The undertaking was nationalized in 1962, as was the working of the larger deposits at Sangaridi, near Boke. A subsidiary of Alcan, Bauxites du Midi, had begun operations there in 1958. After nationalization, an American firm, Harvey Aluminum, negotiated a new contract to resume work. By far the most important deposits found are those at Fria, which are exploited by an international consortium owned 48½ per cent by Olin Mathieson, 26½ per cent by Pechiney-Ugine of France, 10 per cent by British Aluminium, Ltd, and 15 per cent by Swiss and German concerns. A $150 million alumina plant was built at Kimba, near Fria, in 1960, and the following year 390,000 tons were exported. Part of the alumina was shipped to Norway for refining, part to the Alucam plant at Edea in Cameroun. This plant, built in the early 1950s by a subsidiary of Pechiney-Ugine, treats alumina from Provence and Marseille factories as well as from Fria, and enables Cameroun to rank fifth among non-communist countries in aluminium production. French and British capital is involved also in exploiting iron ore in the Kaloum peninsula, while a consortium of Japanese and European banks is interested in the iron deposits of the Nimba mountains. Diamonds and gold also contribute to Guinea's mineral output, which in 1961 accounted for 66·7 per cent of the total value of exports.

Africa's iron became important after the Second World War because of the general depletion of European and American sources. It is in Mauritania that the most outstanding developments have taken place. An iron mountain was said to exist near Fort Gouraud in 1912, but this was confirmed only in 1935. Fourteen years later the Bethlehem Steel Corporation became interested in the deposits, but then shifted its attention to Venezuela. In 1952 the Société Anonyme des Mines de Fer de Mauritanie (Miferma) was formed, but preparations for exploitation began only in 1960, by which time the company was owned 62 per cent by French interests, including the government, 20 per cent by British, 15 per cent by Italian and 3 per cent by German shareholders.

Liberia, for long considered little more than the Firestone Rubber Company's plantation, has since 1950 undergone a dramatic change. German, Swedish and American capital has gone into the formation of four iron-mining firms operating in various parts of the country. The Liberian government has a share in the profits of these firms, ranging from 25 to 50 per cent. Alluvial diamonds along the Lofa river began to attract attention in 1953, and have been worked by smallholders. Although output is difficult to estimate because of smuggling from Guinea and Sierra Leone, in 1961 iron ore and diamonds accounted for roughly 52 per cent of the value of Liberia's domestic exports.

During the colonial period Africa became an increasingly important supplier of metals and other minerals to world markets, as shown in Table 76. This trend has continued in the decade since most of the continent became independent. In addition to wide-ranging socio-economic developments generated by mining, many changes took place within the industry itself. The most dramatic was the decrease in the mortality among both European and African mine-workers. In the early days of mining, the mortality rate was alarmingly high. Among Africans on the Southern Rhodesian mines, for example, the rate in 1906 was 75·94 per thousand. Concerted efforts by mining companies and administrative officials to bring this down to an 'acceptable' level brought the figure to 21·68 per thousand in 1917 (see Table 77). The battle against disease had to be fought on two fronts, one involving the mining industry almost exclusively, the other having much wider ramifications.

African mine-workers seemed to be highly susceptible to disease, particularly scurvy and pneumonia. This is hardly surprising, as the men had to live in compounds without the care normally provided by their wives or mothers, often in crowded conditions with inadequate sanitary arrangements. The quantity of food provided may have been sufficient, but the quality was not. No one gathered or provided the herbs which in the men's homes were served as relishes that provided essential vitamins. Added to this was the fact that they were doing more concentrated physical labour than they normally did, in a climate in many cases much harsher than that to which they were accustomed. This meant that in addition to being easy prey to scurvy because of dietary

Table 76. *African mineral production at the end
of the colonial era*

	Per cent of world production				Per cent of world production		
		Average				Average	
	1938	1955–7	1961		1938	1955–7	1961
Base metals				Other metallic			
Copper	18·0	23·9	22·2	minerals			
Tin	12·0	14·9	9·9	Lithium ores	nil	97·6	98·7 a,b
Lead	3·2	11·5	8·2	Beryl		39·8	40·3
Zinc	1·3	8·9	7·3	Uranium ores			15·2 a
Ferroalloys				Zirconium		3·9	8·3
Columbium-	nil	75·5	82·3	Bauxite	nil	3·1	6·7
tantalum				Titanium			
Cobalt	87·0	67·0	76·9 a	concentrates			
Chromite	35·0	35·0	34·5	Ilmenite		2·1	6·6
Vanadium	47·5	8·7	30·9 a	Rutile		0·4	4·5
Manganese	22·0	21·8	21·8	Barite	0·4	2·0	4·2
Antimony	4·0	30·8	21·7	Iron ore	3·5	3·7	3·2
Cadmium	0·3	3·6	5·6	Energy minerals			
Tungsten	1·9	5·6	2·5	Coal	1·0	3·4	2·3
Nickel	0·5	1·3	0·8	Petroleum	0·1	0·2	2·2
Precious metals				Other nonmetallics			
and stones				Kyanite			68·6 b
Diamonds				Phosphates	33·0	34·0	26·4
Industrial	98·5	99·9	97·4	Vermiculite		23·6	25·6
Gem		78·8	94·4	Asbestos	16·0	19·6	14·1
Gold	40·0	62·7	52·2	Graphite	7·4	6·2	4·0
Platinum	9·2	47·8	30·0	Mica	6·1	2·7	2·2
Silver	0·3	4·3	4·7 a				

a Excluding Sino-Soviet bloc.   b 1960.

SOURCE: William A. Hance, *The geography of modern Africa* (New York, Columbia University Press, 1964), p. 9.

Table 77. *Mortality of Northern Rhodesians employed
on Southern Rhodesian mines, 1912–20*

Year	Deaths per thousand
1912	65·43
1913	50·15
1914	43·81
1915	24·06
1916	27·76
1917	26·21
1918	127·96 a
1919	23·32
1920	20·94

a The abnormally high rate in 1918 was due to the widespread influenza epidemic that year.

SOURCE: Michael Gelfand, *Northern Rhodesia in the days of the Charter* (Oxford, 1961), p. 106.

deficiencies, they were also liable to contract pneumonia, as well as other less serious illnesses, because of lowered resistance.

In the Transvaal, the difficulties of nutrition and sanitation were less severe than elsewhere because the gold-mining companies had, and were prepared to spend, the money necessary to provide better rations and more adequate housing facilities. However, the mortality rate from pneumonia, especially among Africans coming from tropical areas was so high that in 1913 the Union government, in an attempt to resolve the problem, halted labour recruitment for the Transvaal in areas north of 22° latitude. In the same year the Witwatersrand Native Labour Association (see below, p. 412) established the South African Institute of Medical Research to investigate ways of controlling the disease. The Institute developed the Lister anti-pneumococcal vaccine, which proved a very effective preventative and was widely used in the Rhodesias and Katanga as well as in South Africa. The sulphonamide drugs introduced in Europe in the 1930s to treat pneumonia tended to replace the vaccine, but more recently the trend has been reversed. By the end of 1933 the Chamber of Mines was able to convince the government to lift, in part, the restrictions on tropical recruiting.

In Southern Rhodesia the first attempts by the administration to ensure the reasonable care of African workers was made in 1903, when regulations were issued requiring the appointment of a compound manager on larger mines, medical supervision, regular inspections by officials, improved sanitation and hygiene, adequate housing and hospitals and better food rations. Subsequent ordinances stiffened the requirements and gradually extended them to smaller undertakings, rather to the dismay of the small entrepreneur who felt he could not afford to comply with the law. Southern Rhodesia's medical director, Dr A. M. Fleming, was able to show that what appeared to be a significant difference in mortality between recruited and volunteer workers was in fact a difference between those who were already accustomed by previous experience to the work and climate of the mines and those who were not. Little could be done by law to enforce an acclimatization period for all new recruits. The companies tended to allow new employees some time to rest before putting them to work underground. The law could, and in 1913 did, empower the administration to limit the number of hours of continuous employment allowed, the number of men in a shift and the number of blasting shifts in a day. If they thought necessary, officials could withdraw men from work on all or any part of a mine. In Northern Rhodesia similar legislation was adopted; but in the years preceding the opening of the Copper Belt, the administrations' primary concern was to ensure the medical fitness of Northern Rhodesians going to work on the mines in Katanga and the south, the adequacy of their food rations while travelling to and from the mines as well as while they were at work and the provision of satisfactory housing.

As mining operations became more settled, the companies provided better medical and hospital facilities for their workers. Governments and administrative officials were also able to develop and expand their own medical and supervisory services. Government health services became responsible for looking after men employed by individuals and small concerns that were not in a position to do so themselves. Afflictions such as scurvy and pneumonia were, then, brought under control fairly quickly, but this resolved only part of the problem. Insect-borne diseases, especially malaria and human trypanosomiasis (sleeping-sickness) were responsible for the deaths of hundreds of people, both European and African. Although the advice given to northbound travellers at Cape Town not to bother taking a return ticket as no one ever came back may have been an exaggeration, the reality was harsh indeed.

Africans were widely believed to be immune to malaria, but in the Southern Rhodesian mines, for example, of the 282 Africans who died in 1934, malaria alone accounted for 24, and in combination with scurvy for another 16. (Pneumonia took 113 of these lives, scurvy alone 42.) The Rhodesian administrations and the larger companies provided quinine for those employees who would take it, screened living quarters and made some attempts to attack the problem at its source by eliminating mosquito breeding-grounds. The greatest single effort in this direction was the programme inaugurated in 1929 by the Rhodesian Selection Trust. Beatty asked the Ross Institute of Tropical Hygiene in London to advise on the control of malaria. A team headed by Sir Malcolm Watson went to the Copper Belt and began draining swamps, spraying houses and oiling rivers. Larvae were collected and adult insects caught; and hospital facilities and procedures for treating malaria cases were greatly improved. Some idea of the success of the measures taken may be gained from Tables 78 and 79. These measures were quickly adopted by all the mines on the Copper Belt and elsewhere.

Table 78. *Death-rate per 1,000 persons employed on the Copper Belt, 1929–48*

| | | Africans | | |
Year	Europeans (disease only)	Disease	Accidents and violence	Total
April 1929–March 1930	22·4	—	—	—
1930	13·2	32·3	2·3	34·6
1931	6·4	15·8	3·0	18·8
1932	12·5	8·2	1·7	9·9
1933	2·2	5·2	4·5	9·7
1934	10·4	12·9	2·7	15·6
1935	1·7	5·3	2·2	7·5
1936	5·7	4·6	1·3	5·9
1937	5·7	6·4	2·3	8·7
1938	6·1	4·9	1·7	6·6
1939	6·2	3·4	1·1	4·5
1940	nil	2·2	1·5	3·7
1941	3·2	3·6	2·8	6·4
1942	7·7	3·1	0·94	4·04
1943	3·5	4·2	1·93	6·1
1944	5·5	5·4	2·28	7·7
1945	4·1	4·2	0·55	4·75
1946	1·98	2·01	0·89	2·9
1947	4·45	3·9	1·52	5·42
1948	4·84	3·45	1·77	5·22

SOURCE: Sir Malcolm Watson, *African highway: the battle for health in Central Africa* (London, 1953), p. 77.

Table 79. *Total malaria cases among Mufulira mine employees and dependants, 1944–9*

	1944	1945	1946	1947	1948	1949
Totals	311	369	117	50	40	46
Average rate per 1,000 per annum	177·81	213·17	65·03	24·95	16·97	17·42
Average number of employees and dependants	1,749	1,731	1,799	2,004	2,357	2,640

SOURCE: Sir Malcolm Watson, *African highway: the battle for health in Central Africa* (London, 1953), p. 116.

The prevalence of trypanosomiasis in large areas of Northern Rhodesia and Katanga led to many difficulties too, not only as a result of the deaths and illness it caused but also because attempts made to contain it and to prevent its spread into places believed free of it hampered the unrestricted movement of labour. This caused hardship in north-eastern Rhodesia, where there was little local opportunity for employment. It was originally thought that only one tsetse-fly—*Glossina palpalis*—which frequented river banks, was responsible for the spread of the disease. The Rhodesian authorities co-operated with one another and with the Congolese government and Union Minière to control the movement of people to, from and through places known to harbour the flies. River crossings were regulated and medical check-points established. The British South Africa Company sponsored a Sleeping Sickness Commission to look into the transmission of trypanosomes. In 1912 the commission confirmed that another fly—*Glossina morsitans*—found throughout the Rhodesian bush, also carried them, thus greatly enlarging the scope of the problem. The First World War interrupted research, but in 1921, with the co-operation of Chartered and the British government, a team under Dr F. K. Kleine, director of the Koch Institute in Germany, was able to carry out experiments in Northern Rhodesia to prove the effectiveness of the drug Bayer 205 in curing sleeping-sickness. Another of Africa's ravaging diseases was thus controllable.

In the first years of full-scale operations, Union Minière was restricted by financial stringencies in the facilities it could provide. During the war, pressure from the Northern Rhodesian administration, alarmed by the continuing high mortality among Rhodesians employed on the Katanga mines, and from the Belgian government in response to rising humanitarian protests, led to an acceleration of the plans for improvement. Diet and housing were gradually improved, and closer supervision of compounds maintained. Quinine was given to all workers and better hospital facilities were built. It was in conjunction with the policy of stabilizing its labour force (see below, p. 416) that the company made the greatest strides in this sphere.

The lowering of the mortality rate in the mines removed one of the strongest reasons for African unwillingness to work on them, and therefore contributed significantly to the industry's growth and prosperity over the years. The health and housing facilities provided by the mining companies served as an example for other industries, notably the railways. By helping to bring malaria and sleeping-sickness under control, the mining companies were instrumental in removing one of the most serious obstacles to Africa's economic growth.[2]

Transportation

In 1854, the Cape was essentially an agrarian country, with 80 per cent of its white population employed on the land. The only existing railway line, which was operated by a private company, was designed to serve the farming region of the south-west and covered no more than sixty-five miles. It was only after the discovery in 1870 of the diamantiferous 'dry diggings' at Kimberley that railway construction began in earnest. The line from the Cape, as well as another short line serving Port Elizabeth, was taken over by the Cape government and extended to Kimberley. The only obstacles to the completion of the line, which was financed by the public treasury, were geographical; and the resulting difficulties were more easily overcome than some of the financial and political problems that arose farther north.

When gold began to be worked at the Witwatersrand from 1886 onwards, the Transvaal became a new target for railway-builders. The Transvaal, however, wanted to secure an outlet to the sea at Delagoa Bay, outside British control, before allowing any lines from the Cape or Natal to enter the Republic. The route to Delagoa Bay, which was the shortest and the most economical for Transvaal traffic, would, in addition to its political advantages for the Transvaal, open up for the port of Lourenço Marques a hinterland of much greater value than Moçambique itself could provide. In 1875, the Portuguese and Transvaal governments signed an agreement for the construction of a railway over this route, but when President Burgers of the Transvaal tried to raise the necessary money in Holland, he was able to send only a small consignment of rails to Lourenço Marques, where they were unloaded and left to rust. The Portuguese awarded a concession for the construction of the line through Moçambique to an American, Edward McMurdo, a Kentucky-style colonel of dubious reputation. It was only with considerable difficulty that McMurdo was able to form a British company to undertake construction. But financial difficulty continued to dog the project and to delay completion.[3] When the 55 miles of track were completed in 1887, extensive modifications were needed immediately to bring the light, badly laid line up to an acceptable standard. The Netherlands South African Railway Company continued the line through the Transvaal to the Rand, but financial and geographical obstacles made progress very slow.

Because much of the initial financing and impetus for the development of the gold-fields came from people already involved in the diamond mines farther south, people like Rhodes pressed for the extension of the Cape's railways

---

[2] One disease, pneumoconiosis (also known as silicosis or miner's phthisis), remained a serious problem, as it is for virtually all underground mine-workers. By introducing hoses to spray water on areas that have just been blasted and by using water-fed drills, the mining companies have done what they can to control dust in the mines. The greatest efforts, however, have been concentrated on treating the disease and the tuberculosis to which it makes men particularly susceptible. The South African Chamber of Mines, for example, bears about half the cost of the pneumoconiosis research unit set up in 1956, and in addition maintains the Springkell Sanitorium for white miners suffering from tuberculosis.

[3] In 1889 the Portuguese cancelled the concession, for which a Swiss arbitrator made them pay McMurdo's widow a million dollars.

through the Orange Free State to the Transvaal. The Free State, which stood to gain substantial benefits for its agriculture, offered little opposition. When the line from the Cape reached the Transvaal border, President Kruger refused to allow it to cross until the link with Delagoa Bay had been completed. Continuing financial stringencies, however, forced him to capitulate in exchange for a loan from the Cape government towards the finance needed. The Cape line reached the Rand in 1892, two years before the Lourenço Marques track, and a third line from Durban opened for traffic in 1895. The Cape ports and Durban as well as the Cape and Natal railways competed heavily with Lourenço Marques for Transvaal traffic, waging rate-wars to keep the Portuguese port and railway from taking any significant portion of it. The Portuguese, who undertook extensive improvement of port facilities, were able to attract a very large proportion of the traffic in both directions, partly because of the natural advantages of these routes for the Transvaal, partly because Kruger insisted as a matter of policy that the line be used as much as possible. Even after the Boer War, in the face of increasing demands that Transvaal traffic should go entirely through the Cape and Natal, Lourenço Marques continued to handle much of the traffic because the Portuguese insisted that a substantial portion go through Moçambique in exchange for granting the Transvaal Chamber of Mines permission to recruit labour in Portuguese territory. As the gold-mines suffered from a chronic labour shortage, and came to rely increasingly on men from Moçambique, pressure from the Cape and Natal was to no avail. A *modus vivendi* guaranteeing a minimum of 47½ per cent of Transvaal traffic to Lourenço Marques in return for recruiting rights was reached in 1902; a full convention followed in 1909 and was subsequently renewed. Even today Moçambique workers constitute a substantial part of the work force on the Rand mines (see Table 80).

While the three lines to the Transvaal were moving towards Pretoria, Cecil

Table 80. *Geographical sources of black labour employed[a] by the Chamber of Mines, South Africa, 1896–1969[b]*

	1896–8 (%)	1906 (%)	1916 (%)	1926 (%)	1936 (%)	1946 (%)	1956 (%)	1966 (%)	1969 (%)
Transvaal	23·4	4·0	10·3	8·4	7·0	7·6	5·5	4·8	3·8
Natal and Zululand	1·0	4·8	5·3	2·6	4·9	4·4	3·8	2·4	1·9
Swaziland		0·7	1·9	2·1	2·2	1·8	1·6	1·1	1·4
Cape Province	11·1	13·7	33·0	29·8	39·2	27·8	24·4	24·8	23·6
Lesotho		2·6	7·9	10·9	14·5	12·5	11·9	16·8	17·5
Orange Free State		0·3	0·6	0·5	1·1	1·5	1·0	2·1	2·1
Botswana	3·9	0·4	1·8	1·0	2·3	2·3	3·1	5·0	4·0
Moçambique	60·2	65·4	38·1	44·5	27·8	31·5	30·8	28·4	26·9
North of latitude 22°s	0·5	8·0	1·1	0·2	1·1	10·6	17·9	14·7	18·8
Total (000s)	54	81	219	203	318	305	334	383	371

[a] As at 31 December. The figures include employment on the Transvaal coal mines, which recruit labour through the Chamber of Mines.

[b] Apart from 1896–8, the Moçambique figures exclude men from north of latitude 22°s.

SOURCE: Francis Wilson, *Labour in the South African gold mines, 1911–69* (Cambridge University Press, 1972), p. 70.

Rhodes was embarking on his plans to acquire as much of Central Africa as he could for the British South Africa Company. One of the provisions of the charter granted to the company in 1889 was that they build a railway from the south to the northern limits (unspecified in the charter) of their territory. In 1889, Rhodes agreed to build a line from Kimberley to Vryburg for the Cape government, who took it over when it was completed. From Vryburg the line was built by private companies organized by Chartered. Before work began on this, however, a line from Fontesvilla on the Pungwe river in northern Moçambique began moving towards Salisbury to provide Chartered with a shorter route to the coast.

Rhodes had felt he should be allowed to include most of northern Moçambique in Chartered territory, but received no official support for his rather bizarre claims. In 1890, the British and Portuguese governments signed a convention establishing the boundaries of their territories in Central Africa. The Portuguese agreed to build, or to allow to be built, a railway from the mouth of the Pungwe to the frontier of British territory. With the hope of keeping Chartered from controlling this railway, the Portuguese gave a concession to H. T. van Laun, a company promoter of, apparently, Dutch nationality.

With the support of the British Foreign Office, Chartered was able to acquire van Laun's concession, forming the Beira Railway Company to build and operate the line. Actual construction was under the supervision of George Pauling, a contractor who built most of Rhodesia's railway system as well as lines in Russia and Latin America. He gained an excellent reputation, based largely on his uncanny ability to cut costs to an absolute minimum without sacrificing the quality of the work done. On the Beira Railway he had to face considerable obstacles: floods, lions, tsetse-flies and assorted fevers combined to make progress very slow. The first 75 miles took almost two years to complete, the next 38 miles another three. It was only in 1898 that the Beira Railway reached the Southern Rhodesian frontier at Umtali (being connected to Salisbury the following year), an average annual construction rate of just over 31 miles, compared with the one mile per day Pauling was often able to achieve in Southern Rhodesia.

Because the money available for construction had been very limited, it had been necessary to lay a narrow-gauge track, which it was evident even before completion would be inadequate. In 1900, work began on widening it to what had become the standard South Africa gauge, 3 ft. 6ins. By 1895 it had become obvious also that Fontesvilla was not suitable as a terminus. Shifting sand-banks and widely fluctuating river levels made it impossible to maintain a lighter service between Fontesvilla and the seaport at Beira. As the Beira Railway Company was in serious financial straits, it was necessary to form a new company, the Beira Junction Railway Company, to link Fontesvilla and Beira by rail. By the time the entire line was completed, it had to support an average debt of over £6,500 per mile, which did not include the cost of widening the line. Working receipts were insufficient to cover this debt, and over the years the financial structure of the two companies had to be reorganized. In 1930 they were amalgamated.

By comparison with this, construction northwards from Vryburg was straightforward and uncomplicated. In 1893 the Bechuanaland Railway Company was formed, and the construction contract awarded to Pauling, who completed the line to Mafeking, a distance of 106 miles, in seventeen months. After a delay during which various difficulties between Chartered and the British government were resolved, the line reached Bulawayo in 1897. Five years later it was linked to Salisbury. In 1894 extensive coal deposits were found at Wankie's near Victoria Falls, and the Mashonaland Railway Company was formed to provide rail access to them. That section of line was completed and carried across the Zambezi river as far as Kalomo in 1905. A number of branch lines were also built to connect various gold-mines to the main system.

It had always been Rhodes's claim that he wanted to build a railway from the Cape to Cairo, a scheme for which he aroused great public enthusiasm, but which economically and politically was completely impracticable. It is only because Rhodes is known to have seriously believed in a number of rather far-fetched ideas that it is possible to think that he ever intended the Cape-to-Cairo 'dream' to be anything more than a romantic notion designed to attract investors. His projected line would only have added a third north-south transport route to the two already provided for Africa by the Atlantic and Indian oceans and the Suez Canal. Even people who generally supported Rhodes maintained that such a railway would be useless and a financial disaster. What was needed, and what was in fact created, was a series of railways tapping the interior and feeding as closely as possible the nearest seaport. Nonetheless, Rhodes, and the Chartered Company after his death, continued to talk in terms of a railway to the southern shore of Lake Tanganyika as part of the Cape-to-Cairo route. It was originally intended to carry the line northwards from Salisbury, but the next section was in fact built from Kalomo to Broken Hill to serve the zinc- and lead-mines. The new construction was to involve Chartered in further financial problems, adding to the existing burden of the Beira line.

When Davis formed the Broken Hill Development Syndicate to work the zinc and lead deposits, he assured Chartered that there would be sufficient traffic for the railway to provide adequate revenue to cover the costs of operation and servicing the debentures issued to finance construction. On this basis Chartered agreed to guarantee the debentures issued by the Mashonaland Railway Company, which built the line, without requiring any prior guarantee from the syndicate. By the time the line reached Broken Hill in 1907, traffic was far below expectations (see above, pages 379–80), the railway could not meet its debt and Chartered had to fulfil its guarantee. The only possible source of sufficient traffic to make the Rhodesian railways profitable was the Katanga copper-mines.

When Williams had acquired his 40 per cent interest in Katanga's mineral wealth in 1900, he immediately began negotiating with Rhodes for the extension of the Rhodesian line to the Katanga frontier. Because Rhodes and Alfred Beit insisted on being given a half-interest in the Katanga enterprise in exchange, these talks failed. King Leopold II refused to agree to the arrangement because he not unnaturally wanted to keep as much as possible of the profits from Katanga in Belgian hands. He was particularly loath to allow Rhodes to have any share of the Congo State's wealth, as relations between the two men had been anything but cordial. Leopold preferred to place his hope for providing adequate transport for Katanga on a line running through Congolese territory from the mines to Leopoldville or the port of Matadi, and on a combined rail and river system that would use the navigable portions of the Congo river, with railway lines where necessary to by-pass rapids and waterfalls. The king also wanted to link this rail river system by rail to the navigable Nile, and used his opposition to the idea of Chartered's line coming to Katanga as a weapon in his fight to fulfil his dream of controlling at least a small part of that great river.

By 1908, Chartered's financial difficulties made them more amenable. Dropping their demands for a half-interest in the Katanga mines, they agreed with the Congo State and Williams to form the Rhodesia-Katanga Junction Railway and Mineral Company to build the line to the frontier from Broken Hill and to take over the Kansanshi mine and the other interests that had been given to Tanks in Northern Rhodesia. Pauling began work on this line in February 1909, and reached the frontier at Sakania before the end of the year. By arrangement with a Belgian construction firm, he was able to build the Chemin de fer du Katanga (CFK) to the Etoile du Congo mine, near Elisabethville, which he reached in September 1910. Until 1928, virtually all of Katanga's mineral traffic used this route, providing substantial revenues for the six railway companies involved. Ironically, the Katanga railway, being the shortest, profited least.

Williams and some of his Belgian colleagues had always been convinced that additional access routes would become necessary as production expanded. In 1902, having despaired of reaching an agreement with Chartered, Williams had secured a concession from the Portuguese to build a railway from Lobito Bay in Angola to the Katanga border, by way of Benguela, the old terminus of the Central African slave route. The Portuguese government had begun a railway from Benguela some years previously, but had made very little progress. Williams's success in securing this concession within two months of introducing his request was in part due to the support he received from the Countess of Warwick, who had helped him get his Katanga concession, and who received a half-interest in the railway enterprise for her efforts. King Edward VII, quite discreetly, lent his support as well.

The Benguela Railway concession met with strong opposition from many quarters. Chartered and South African interests generally did not want it built, since they preferred to control access to the interior of Central Africa on their own terms. As Chartered had an important share in the South-west Africa Company, they joined the German government in opposing the concession because the Germans had been trying unsuccessfully for many years to secure a concession for a railway from Tiger Bay in southern Angola to the Otavi mining region.

None of this opposition would have mattered at all if Williams had been able to secure firm assurances from Leopold that once the Benguela Railway reached the Congolese frontier it would be connected to the mines. Leopold was using Williams as another pawn in his attempt to gain access to the Nile, however, and refused to give the assurances, without which Williams was unable to secure the necessary finance. An agreement regarding the Nile was reached by the Congo State and Britain in 1906. Although Leopold was not very happy with the arrangement, he withdrew his show of opposition to Williams's line, and in 1908 approved an agreement whereby the Benguela Railway, the Katanga Railway and the Bas-Congo to Katanga Railway would pool their receipts, sharing them in proportion to their respective mileage. Leopold also agreed to build the Katanga section of the line.

The Benguela Railway Company was formed in 1903, but because of the obstacles to securing finance, construction began only in 1905, with the firm of John (later Sir John) Norton-Griffiths undertaking the work. The terrain was extremely difficult, rising steeply from 10 m above sea level at Benguela to 902 m at Fortela, a distance of only 60 km. The gradient was so steep at one point that a rack-and-pinion section of track had to be installed over 8 km. (This was not removed until after the Second World War, when extensive realignment was carried out.) By the time the First World War broke out, the most difficult terrain had been passed. Had finance and equipment been available, the line could have been completed without too many problems. As this was not the case, construction was delayed until after the war. By this time costs had nearly doubled, and the Portuguese government was unwilling or unable to provide financial support. Some Belgians and Germans were prepared to assist, but wanted control of the line. This Williams was not willing to give. Because of opposition from General Smuts and Southern Rhodesia, the British government refused to guarantee a Benguela Railway Company debenture issue under the terms of the Trade Facilities Act, which was first passed in 1921 in an attempt to generate employment, particularly in the British iron and steel industry. Smuts opposed the guarantee because the Benguela Railway would compete with the Rhodesian lines, which he hoped would become part of the South African system if Southern Rhodesia joined the Union. Southern Rhodesia was opposed quite naturally because Katanga traffic was the mainstay of its railways, without which it would be forced to charge considerably higher rates for other traffic.

Northern Rhodesia, on the other hand, tended to favour British support for anything that would increase the market in Katanga for its agricultural produce. Even after Southern Rhodesia voted for responsible government, Smuts continued to oppose the guarantee on the grounds that British support should not be given to a foreign railway, and that in any case the Belgians would not, he was convinced, honour their obligations under the 1908 agreement to build the Katanga section of the line. It was only after Smuts was voted out of office in 1924 that South African objections were withdrawn, and that Williams, with the aid of the British government's guarantee, was able to raise the rest of the money needed to complete the line. By the time the Benguela Railway reached the frontier in 1929, however, another access route for Katanga had already become available.

In 1906 the Compagnie du chemin de fer du Bas-Congo au Katanga (BCK) had been formed to build a line from Katanga to Matadi. Construction had not begun then because the line was not considered imperative and because available funds were needed more urgently elsewhere. After the war, rising Belgian economic nationalism led to the decision to create a *voie nationale,* a viable access route for Katanga that would run entirely through Congolese territory, a route that in turn would help promote the development of the Kasai province. Part of the line was built between Port Francqui (Ilebo) on the Kasai river and Katanga. It was begun in 1923 and completed in 1928, when the BCK withdrew from the pooling provisions of the 1908 pooling agreement. When the Benguela Railway was finally linked to the Katanga rail system at Tenke in 1931, the world depression had hit the copper market and production did not expand as rapidly as had been expected. Traffic that might have gone over the Benguela line was deflected to the *voie nationale* by artificial pricing policies.

The financial straits in which the Benguela Railway Company found itself were so serious that it could only keep from going into liquidation with the support of Tanganyika Concessions, which had given a prior guarantee on the entire debt incurred for construction, had taken up a large portion of the debentures and had reduced its holding in Union Minière from a high of 45 per cent to 14·5 per cent. The Benguela Railway Company paid its maiden dividend in 1956, more than half a century after its inception.

Katanga was thus served directly by three major railways, with additional access to the railway to Dar es Salaam via Lake Tanganyika and part of the line operated by the Compagnie du chemin de fer du Congo Supérieur des Grands Lacs Africains (CFL). The CFL also made it possible to ship copper by rail and river via Stanleyville. Because of the number of trans-shipments involved, this route was used very little. When the Northern Rhodesian Copper Belt was being developed, it was necessary to build only short branch lines from the already existing main line. Most Copper Belt traffic went via Rhodesia Railways and Beira, as did a considerable portion of Katanga's traffic. Union Minière had to guarantee a certain portion of its traffic to Rhodesian Railways in order to be certain of receiving essential coke and coal supplies from Wankie. The 20 per cent of Katanga's traffic secured to the Benguela Railway provided insufficient revenue for the railway to live up to Williams's early expectations of it (see Tables 81–84).

With the increase in Copper Belt production and the general economic growth in the Rhodesias after the Second World War, the Rhodesian rail system had mounting difficulty in meeting traffic demands. When the lines were nationalized in 1947, carrying capacity doubled; but even this was inadequate. In addition, the port of Beira, for which Nyasaland was also becoming an increasingly important hinterland, was very overcrowded, ships sometimes having to wait for nearly four months for a berth. To ease this congestion a railway was extended from Lourenço Marques, where surplus capacity was available, to the Rhodesian line at Bannockburn. Construction of the Limpopo Line, carried out in record time, was completed in 1955. This line also helped development in south-eastern Rhodesia, which was now becoming the major outlet for asbestos as well as for agricultural goods. Another measure to relieve pressure on Beira was the Tripartite Agreement signed in 1957 by Rhodesia Railways, the Benguela Railway Company and the BCK, setting a through rate for Copper Belt traffic to any of the three ports, Lobito, Beira or Lourenço Marques. For the first time, Northern Rhodesian traffic could use the Benguela Railway, but only for up to 20 per cent of its total exports. Very little Copper Belt traffic, in fact, used the Benguela line, because in 1960, Rhodesia Railways, contravening the Tripartite Agreement, offered a substantial discount on that portion of traffic that could use Lobito.[4]

West Africa's railways, which were constructed by the colonial governments and do not pass through foreign territory, did not have to face the financial and

---

[4] The possible use of the Benguela Railway, which has ample surplus capacity, for Zambian exports became a major question when Rhodesia declared its independence. Apart from the political considerations that make the use of a Portuguese line unacceptable to Zambia, the line through Katanga is, as is the general rule in Central Africa, single-track. The section of line between Lubumbashi (Elisabethville) and Tenke serves not only the Benguela Railway but also the BCK and CFL as well, severely limiting the amount of Copper Belt traffic that can be sent over this route.

Table 81. *Proportion of Katanga copper passing
through different ports, 1927–60*

Year	Matadi via Port Francqui 1,000 metric tons	Matadi via Port Francqui Per cent	Matadi via Stanleyville 1,000 metric tons	Matadi via Stanleyville Per cent	Beira 1,000 metric tons	Beira Per cent	Lobito 1,000 metric tons	Lobito Per cent	Dar es Salaam [a] 1,000 metric tons	Dar es Salaam [a] Per cent	Total 1,000 metric tons
1927	—	—	—	—	67	73·9	—	—	24	26·1	91
1928	11	9·6	—	—	75	64·9	—	—	29	25·5	115
1929	30	23·7	—	—	76	59·0	—	—	22	17·3	128
1930	42	27·8	—	—	81	53·4	—	—	29	18·8	152
1931	42	38·1	—	—	36	32·3	20	18·1	13	11·5	111
1932	19	36·4	1	2·7	17	34·1	14	26·8	—	—	51
1933	33	41·9	3	3·5	23	28·7	20	25·9	—	—	79
1934	54	49·1	5	4·5	33	30·0	18	16·4	—	—	110
1935	62	51·2	5	4·1	36	29·8	18	14·9	—	—	121
1936	46	46·3	5	4·9	30	30·3	19	18·5	—	—	100
1937	64	42·4	3	2·1	51	33·9	33	21·6	—	—	151
1938	59	44·9	4	2·8	39	29·8	30	22·5	—	—	132
1939	53	43·1	5	4·1	38	30·8	27	22·0	—	—	123
1940	68	43·2	4	2·2	51	32·6	35	22·0	—	—	158
1941	70	40·0	4	2·6	77	44·1	23	13·3	—	—	174
1942	78	45·5	5	2·7	61	35·5	28	16·3	—	—	172
1943	74	45·4	4	2·2	57	35·1	28	17·3	—	—	163
1944	72	43·2	2	1·4	56	33·6	36	21·8	—	—	166
1945	76	43·4	4	2·5	58	33·5	36	20·6	—	—	174
1946	72	49·3	2	1·4	43	29·4	29	19·9	—	—	146
1947	75	48·4	5	3·2	39	25·2	36	23·2	—	—	155
1948	74	46·5	5	3·0	40	25·0	41	25·5	—	—	160
1949	66	45·0	2	1·7	41	27·8	37	25·5	—	—	146
1950	82	47·4	3	1·7	48	27·4	41	23·5	—	—	174
1951	85	45·2	5	2·6	60	31·5	39	20·7	—	—	189
1952	100	48·9	4	2·0	52	25·4	48	23·7	—	—	204
1953	97	45·9	4	1·6	67	31·7	44	20·8	—	· —	212
1954	102	44·9	6	2·6	70	30·8	50	21·7	—	—	228
1955	108	45·6	5	2·4	71	29·9	52	22·1	—	—	236
1956	117	46·1	5	1·9	76	30·1	56	21·9	—	—	254
1957	110	46·0	5	2·0	72	30·0	53	22·0	—	—	240
1958	80	39·6	4	1·9	69	34·2	49	24·2	—	—	202
1959	100	40·7	4	1·6	82	33·3	60	24·4	—	—	246
1960	58	20·0	—	—	117	40·0	114	40·0	—	—	289

[a] In 1963, some copper again began going out through Dar es Salaam.

SOURCE: André Huybrechts, 'Les voies d'accès et d'évacuation du Congo', *Cahiers Economiques et Sociaux,* 1969, **7,** 63.

Table 82. *Passenger, goods and mineral traffic, Benguela Railway, 1908–34*

	Passengers		Goods		Minerals [c]		
Year	Number	Receipts 000 escudos)	Tonnage [a]	Receipts (000 escudos) [b]	Tonnage	Receipts (000 escudos)	Kilometres run
1908	25,957	17·9	7,151	£6,068	—	—	n.a.
1909	30,771	20·2	10,107	£8,780	—	—	n.a.
1910	38,449	33·6	18,456	£45,838	—	—	147,535
1911	48,606	49·5	32,863	£61,976	—	—	154,097
1912	50,818	52·7	38,474	£77,685	—	—	207,596
1913	63,333	53·2	47,533	283·6	—	—	226,087
1914	109,308	63·7	35,582	277·4	—	—	242,218
1915	116,224	100·3	42,071	390·7	—	—	267,977
1916	107,104	87·4	43,289	455·0	—	—	303,972
1917	126,612	93·2	71,543	511·7	—	—	350,492
1918	169,864	146·7	104,891	617·9	—	—	389,516
1919	200,254	160·1	117,394	772·2	—	—	390,920
1920	170,303	341·8	107,304	1,655·8	—	—	430,457
1921	159,045	574·7	124,275	2,872·4	—	—	400,322
1922	179,126	922·8	158,800	n.a.	—	—	481,418
1923	213,283	1,815·9	178,800	10,337·3	—	—	472,085
1924	225,458	3,106·7	188,539	18,236·4	—	—	530,058
1925	233,875	2,555·9	189,464	18,109·5	—	—	556,211
1926	227,699	2,293·6	178,641	21,062·3	—	—	596,920
1927	236,735	2,182·3	236,735	24,606·2	—	—	642,777
1928	224,167	2,191·7	224,167	26,447·2	—	—	706,494
1929	240,871	2,666·7	275,381	40,482·2	—	—	964,322
1930	257,984	2,567·6	267,864	24,436·3	—	—	970,060
1931	237,599	3,234·8	247,715	22,202·7	—	—	982,153
1932	183,558	3,746·6	221,044	21,369·8	19,285	7,262·2	925,899
1933	156,272	2,666·1	298,331	21,976·7	29,317	7,178·3	965,502
1934	157,802	2,227·5	271,434	20,827·9	24,460	6,200·2	958,907

[a] Including mineral traffic, all years.   [b] Except as indicated.
[c] Not regularly classified separately before 1932.

SOURCES: Benguela Railway Co. and Tanganyika Concessions, Ltd annual reports, various years.

political problems that arose in the south. Many lines were not built to serve mineral areas, but those that did were generally the most economically viable as they had reasonably assured high-rated traffic. Other lines tended to be cheaply built and inadequate for any heavier traffic that subsequently developed.

In the Gold Coast, for example, it was pressure from gold-mining interests that led the government to construct a railway from Sekondi to Tarkwa, a line that had the added strategic advantage of improving communications with the recently subdued Ashanti region. A similar combination of economic and strategic considerations led to the extension of the line to Kumasi in 1903. In Nigeria, the line from Port Harcourt to Enugu made it possible to exploit the coal deposits there. It was later extended to the tin mines of the Jos plateau. In some cases, minerals—chrome at Kenema, Sierra Leone, and manganese at

Table 83. *Earnings of Rhodesia Railways from mineral traffic and from stores imported by the Northern Rhodesian and Union Minière copper-mines, 1927–36*

	1927	1928	1929	1930	1931	1932	1933	1934	1935	1936
	£	£	£	£	£	£	£	£	£	£
Coal and coke for the public	717,295	918,702	934,865	714,907	402,702	282,946	247,446	380,980	454,629	387,363
Copper for export	417,229	557,446	558,371	509,623	316,651	358,628	497,728	718,370	829,385	732,587
Chrome ore	265,858	196,382	237,190	247,329	83,477	32,084	22,058	56,558	90,361	137,548
Asbestos	60,771	90,844	126,638	109,788	85,438	32,778	108,552	102,989	148,605	186,015
Other minerals	49,542	72,162	120,870	117,355	78,583	38,199	73,201	112,241	120,231	145,509
Stores for Northern Rhodesian and Congo copper-mines	....	208,823	300,477	399,322	425,845	45,607	57,777	250,427	284,643	110,801
£	1,510,695	2,044,359	2,278,411	2,098,324	1,392,696	790,242	1,006,762	1,621,565	1,927,854	1,699,823
Total revenue £	4,908,519	5,105,460	5,428,232	5,297,768	4,130,837	2,634,266	2,887,677	3,895,490	4,558,632	4,450,426
Percentage of mineral traffic and stores for copper-mines to total revenue	30·78%	40·04%	41·97%	39·61%	33·71%	30·00%	34·86%	41·63%	42·29%	38·19%

SOURCE: S. Herbert Frankel, *Capital investment in Africa* (London, Oxford University Press, 1938), p. 403.

Table 84. *Copper tonnage and revenue of Rhodesia Railways in relation to total rail tonnage and revenue, 1950–63* [a]
(tonnage in short tons)

	Copper tonnage (1,000)	Total freight tons (1,000)	Copper tonnage as percentage of total freight tonnage	Copper revenue (£1,000)	Total rail revenue (£1,000)	Copper revenue as percentage of total revenue	Copper price (£ per long ton)
1950	341·3	5,755·2	5·9	1,010·4	9,955·2	10·1	179·0
1951	377·1	6,689·3	5·6	1,358·1	11,960·2	11·4	220·7
1952	419·1	7,296·4	5·7	1,638·4	13,115·2	12·5	259·5
1953	420·9	7,894·8	5·3	1,714·9	15,628·0	11·0	256·3
1954	507·0	8,615·2	5·9	2,155·6	17,383·9	12·4	249·3
1955	463·9	9,106·5	5·1	2,833·1	21,161·2	13·4	351·7
1956	511·3	10,065·1	5·1	3,174·8	23,540·8	13·5	328·7
1957	580·2	11,250·7	5·2	4,945·9	27,191·7	18·2	219·4
1958	639·6	12,024·3	5·3	8,153·9	36,591·0	22·3	197·7
1959	697·5	11,159·5	6·3	5,866·6	26,603·3	22·1	237·7
1960	905·9	12,179·5	7·4	7,760·2	31,357·1	24·7	245·8
1961	1,024·8	12,242·1	8·4	8,783·8	32,127·5	27·3	229·7
1962	977·3	11,992·3	8·1	8,312·0	30,921·0	26·9	234·0
1963	947·6	11,630·3	8·1	8,868·6	32,175·4	27·6	234·4

[a] Prior to 1958, Rhodesia Railways operated on a fiscal year from 1 April through 31 March. Beginning in 1958, the fiscal year was changed to terminate on 30 June. Therefore, the 1958 figures include railway tonnage and revenues generated for a fifteen-month period from 1 April 1957 to 30 June 1958.

SOURCE: Edwin T. Haefele and Eleanor B. Steinberg, *Government controls on transport: an African case* (Washington, D.C., Brookings Institution, 1965), p. 38.

Nsuta, Ghana, were commercially exploitable immediately, inasmuch as they happened to be found near existing rail lines. A more recent example of the dependence of mining on railways is seen in the iron deposits in Mauritania. The company exploiting them has built a railway to the port at Nouadhibou, Port Etienne (see above, p. 383).

Closely associated with railway development has been the growth of ports, which, like the railways, depend heavily on mineral traffic. In South Africa, Durban became the most important port for the Transvaal. Traffic here rose from 4·8 million tons in 1938 to 10·1 million tons in 1961. Transvaal traffic uses Port Elizabeth and East London also, not because Durban lacks sufficient capacity but because growing congestion on South African railways since the Second World War has made it necessary to use all available lines. Cape Town, the country's second-ranking port, which is used more for agricultural, passenger and general commercial traffic, has the southern hemisphere's largest dry dock. None of these ports are located on really good natural harbours. All have required extensive dredging and land reclamation to be able to handle larger ships and increased tonnages.

By contrast, Lourenço Marques on Delagoa Bay has the east coast's finest natural shelter, outside the normal cyclone path and shielded from the south-eastern winds coming off the Indian Ocean. One of Africa's first deep-water berths was completed there in 1903, a year before such facilities were available at Durban. Further improvements were carried on steadily until 1914. Only minor extensions were needed in 1930 and 1951 to enable fifteen ocean-going vessels to berth alongside its 2,430 yards of marginal quay. (A further 1,000 feet of quay was added in 1966.) Lourenço Marques, because it is 119 miles closer to Johannesburg than is Durban, and because of the terms of the Moçambique Convention, became the third most important port for South Africa. Railway congestion often contributed to bringing the Lourenço Marques share of Transvaal traffic well above the 47½ per cent minimum. Development in Moçambique itself, as well as the completion of the Limpopo line to Southern Rhodesia, has increased the scope of the port's hinterland and lessened its dependence on South Africa.

Beira's importance for, and heavy reliance on, Rhodesian and Katanga traffic has already been indicated. Copper, chrome ore and other minerals have remained the most important commodities going out through the port. These products, in spite of growing agricultural production in Nyasaland and Moçambique, as well as in Southern Rhodesia, accounted for some 65 per cent of cargo embarked in 1954. Beira's natural deficiencies as a port, coupled with financial limitations on the private companies that operated it until 1948, made it impossible to expand facilities sufficiently to cope with increasing traffic pressure. Widely varying tides, heavy silting from the Pungwe and Buzi rivers and shifting sand-banks have always made navigation and loading operations very difficult, sometimes impossible. The very unstable ground forming the foreshore also inhibits expansion, making it necessary to continue using lighters. Beira's inability to handle more traffic has also been one of the factors leading to the development of other ports in Moçambique, such as Nacala.

On the west coast, Lobito Bay forms one of Africa's finest harbours. Here ships can enter without pilots. The development and use of the harbour, which was officially opened in 1928, have been almost entirely determined by the

Benguela Railway; and, like the railway, it has never been used to full capacity. Farther north, the port of Matadi is also an important outlet for Katanga's minerals, which arrive there via the BCK line, the Kasai and Congo rivers and the Kinshasa-Matadi railway. The economic disadvantages of this route, which requires two transhipments, were overcome by the artificial-rates policy designed to encourage the use of the *voie nationale*. This route is also the only one in which river transport has direct importance for the mining industry; rivers for the most part are unsuitable for mineral traffic, as they do not provide dependable year-round access directly from the mines to the coast. The cost of transhipment between rail and water usually nullifies the advantages to be gained from the generally lower cost of water transport.

In West Africa, the mining industry provides a considerable portion of the traffic passing through several ports. This has been increasingly true since 1945. Older ports, such as Sekondi and Port Harcourt, were important mineral outlets for a long time, although newer ones, such as the Nouadhibou, have their *raison d'être* almost entirely in the needs of a recently developed mining area.

Once built, railways and their terminal ports provided a basic part of the infrastructure on which further economic development depended. Although mining provided much of the initial stimulus for such development, in many respects railways are more important because they will be able to continue to serve and promote industry and agriculture after mining has lost its dominant position, as has already occurred in South Africa (see Table 85).

Other industries

The first ancillary industries to grow up around mining were those most directly connected with it, and for the most part run by the mining companies themselves as an integral part of their operations. The cost of transport to the coast made it necessary to carry out at least the first stages of refining in Africa rather than to ship untreated ores.[5] Mining companies established smelting plants, which, in the case of copper and zinc, had to be fairly extensive. In Katanga, at a site near Elisabethville on the Lubumbashi river, Union Minière set up its first smelting plant, beginning successful operations after some initial technical difficulties in 1912. As production expanded, it became necessary to install more sophisticated equipment, although the final stages of refining to meet the highest requirements for purity continued to be carried out in Germany and the United States. The original smelters were replaced by reverberatory furnaces in the 1920s and by an electrolytic refining plant that was put into operation near Jadotville. A broadly similar pattern emerged on the Copper Belt. On the Rand, the greatest changes concerned the winning of the ore rather than refining it, which involves a straightforward chemical process requiring little labour. The Transvaal gold deposits had to be mined at increasing depth. Over the years, more mechanization has been necessary to make this profitable. Mines and railways also had to set up their own workshops for the repair and maintenance of equipment.

Mining stimulated the growth of manufacturing industries in Africa, initially

[5] This was not the case after the Second World War, when ores, especially iron, were shipped without being smelted.

by providing a market for products directly involved in mining and smelting operations, notably coke and chemicals. Before the Boer War, the only manufacturing industry of any importance at all in the Transvaal was explosives. The South African Explosives Manufacturing Company, Ltd was formed in 1894 with capital from Alfred Nobel's French and German explosives trusts. President Kruger granted this company a monopoly of the manufacture and sale of explosives in the Transvaal, forcing the gold-mining companies to pay more for this essential item than they would have if they could have imported it from elsewhere. This monopoly, which was one of the grievances against the Transvaal that led to the Jameson Raid, was estimated to have cost the gold industry some £600,000. The company's first plant was built at Modderfontein, about 12 miles from Johannesburg, and became, it is now claimed, the largest explosives factory in the world. Another major plant was established near Durban by a Birmingham firm, and the De Beers Company built its own factory in the hope of being able to supply cheaper explosives for the diamond-mines. In 1924, all three factories were amalgamated as South African Explosives and Chemical Industries, which subsequently became a subsidiary of Imperial Chemical Industries, Ltd.

By 1953, South Africa used about two-thirds of its output of explosives, most of the remainder being exported to the mines in the Rhodesias and Katanga and some to Asia. Other chemicals are also produced for the mining industry, but most of the developments in the chemical industry have been in the area of fertilizers and petrochemicals using oil made from coal. In Southern Rhodesia, fertilizers are the most important chemical industry, although oil, soap, paints, explosives, pharmaceuticals and other such items are also produced. In Katanga, the Société Générale Industrielle et Chimique du Katanga (Sogéchim) began producing sulphuric acid for use in leaching, a process of concentrating ores before they are smelted.

Absolutely essential for the smelting of copper was a large supply of high-quality metallurgical coke. Union Minière relied initially on imports from Europe. With full-scale working, however, this became prohibitively expensive, because it made the cost of producing a ton of copper in Katanga twice its market price in Europe. The solution to the problem lay in the Wankie coalfields. Union Minière erected its own coke ovens to use Wankie coal and also took up shares in the Wankie Colliery Company to enable that company to erect more coke ovens of its own. The importance of coal and coke supplied from Wankie was largely responsible for making Union Minière continue to ship a substantial proportion of its output over Rhodesian Railways after 1928. This traffic was also an important source of revenue for the railways.

In South Africa, coke was less important, because only small quantities were needed for gold assay work. The diamond- and gold-mines relied on Transvaal coal, which was of poor coking quality, to produce whatever power they needed. When South Africa began developing its own iron and steel industry, it became necessary to mix Transvaal coal with better coal from Natal. Iron ore is abundant in South Africa; it is found in the Transvaal, as well as in Natal and the northern Cape. Limestone used as a flux in smelting iron is also found in the Transvaal in sufficient quantity to enable South Africa to maintain the industry without importing any basic materials. Between 1911 and 1916, attempts were made to manufacture steel from scrap iron in small electric fur-

Table 85. *South African foreign trade statistics,* [a] *1910–62*
(£000,000)

	Merchandise imports £	Domestic produce exported (incl. gold)	Gold exports		Diamond exports (cut and uncut)		All mineral exports		Agricultural exports		Imports as percentage of national income
			£	%	£	%	£	%	£	%	
1910	36·7	51·8	31·8	61·4	8·5	16·4	42·0	81·1	9·5	18·3	
1911	36·9	54·9	35·1	63·9	8·3	15·1	45·3	82·5	9·2	16·8	
1912	38·8	61·0	38·3	62·9	9·2	15·0	49·4	81·0	11·2	18·3	29·6
1913	41·8	64·5	37·6	58·2	12·0	18·6	51·9	80·3	12·0	19·0	
1914	35·8	52·8	35·3	67·0	5·5	10·5	43·3	82·0	9·1	17·2	
1915	31·8	52·8	38·3	72·6	1·7	3·2	42·2	80·0	8·9	18·8	
1916	40·4	62·1	39·1	63·0	5·3	8·5	48·0	77·4	12·9	20·8	
1917	36·5	66·1	38·0	57·4	6·1	9·2	48·5	73·4	16·3	24·7	
1918	49·5	65·7	35·4	53·9	7·1	10·7	46·2	70·2	18·2	27·7	29·2
1919	50·8	88·8	39·0	43·9	11·5	13·0	54·3	61·1	33·1	37·2	26·4
1920	101·8	91·7	46·8	51·0	11·6	12·6	64·3	70·1	25·6	27·9	41·1
1921	57·8	68·8	43·0	62·5	1·4	2·0	49·8	72·4	17·9	26·0	28·0
1922	51·4	60·9	31·8	52·7	4·4	7·3	39·6	65·6	19·4	32·1	28·8
1923	57·8	76·8	41·7	54·3	7·2	9·4	53·1	69·2	22·6	29·4	27·8
1924	65·8	80·7	44·2	54·8	7·1	8·8	55·8	69·1	23·9	29·6	29·2
1925	67·9	85·6	41·4	48·3	8·6	10·1	54·5	63·7	29·8	34·9	29·5
1926	73·2	80·5	42·6	52·9	10·7	13·3	58·3	72·4	21·3	26·5	30·8
1927	74·1	89·4	43·6	48·8	12·3	13·7	60·5	67·7	27·8	31·1	29·6
1928	79·1	89·0	42·8	48·1	8·9	10·0	55·9	62·9	31·8	35·8	29·2
1929	83·4	89·0	45·0	50·6	12·1	13·6	61·5	69·1	26·3	29·6	30·6

Year											
1930	64·6	76·7	46·3	60·4	5·5	7·1	55·6	72·5	19·9	25·9	25·6
1931	52·9	65·1	45·1	69·4	3·6	5·5	51·6	79·3	12·8	19·7	22·3
1932	32·7	66·2	48·5	73·3	2·0	3·0	52·2	79·0	13·4	20·9	15·2
1933	49·1	92·0	69·9	76·0	2·1	2·3	74·3	80·7	16·9	18·4	20·8
1934	66·3	78·1	56·2	72·0	2·8	3·6	61·4	78·7	16·1	20·6	23·7
1935	75·3	97·9	71·4	72·9	3·0	3·0	77·5	79·0	20·0	20·4	25·0
1936	86·3	109·3	82·7	75·7	3·3	3·0	89·2	81·6	19·1	17·5	26·1
1937	103·4	119·6	82·9	69·3	3·3	2·8	90·1	75·3	28·1	23·5	27·8
1938	95·6	102·9	73·3	71·3	2·4	2·3	79·8	77·6	20·5	20·0	26·7
1946	212	190	102 b	53·6	12·1	6·4	125·7	66·1	49·2	25·9	30·3
1947	303	197	97	49·2	10·9	5·6	a		46·3	25·0	41·3
1948	354	231	99	42·8	11·4	4·8	a		70·1	30·3	43·1
1949	314	254	115	44·9	10·8	4·3	a		71·0	28·0	35·8
1950	305	352	143	41·7	20·1	5·7	a		105	29·8	29·7
1951	467	403	143	35·5	25	6·2	a		136	33·7	37·2
1952	417	393	151	38·4	17	4·3	a		115	29·2	32·0
1953	425	410	149	36·3	29	7·1	a		130	31·7	29·3
1954	439	459	165	35·9	27	5·9	a		139	30·3	27·9
1955	481	515	183	35·5	32	6·2	a		156	30·3	28·5
1956	495	569	199	35·0	32	5·6	a		169	29·7	27·3
1957	550	615	213	34·6	35	5·7	a		183	29·8	27·7
1958	556	578	220	38·0	36	6·2	a		161	27·9	27·5
1959	489	645	250	38·8	38	5·9	a		167	25·9	23·4
1960	556	668	268	40·1	34	5·1	a		162	24·3	24·6
1961	503	712	287	40·3	42	5·9	a		193	27·1	21·0
1962	514	750	319	42·5	37	4·9	a		215	28·7	20·5

a Not classified.   b Gold exports are taken to be the equivalent of gold output from 1946.

SOURCE: Leo Katzen, *Gold and the South African economy* (Cape Town, 1964), pp. 60–1.

naces. It was only in 1917, when the war interrupted imported supplies, that experiments with South Africa's own ores began. Development was hampered by the post-war depression, but a system of bounties instituted by the government in 1922 led to the construction of a blast furnace at Newcastle in Natal and a steelworks at Vereeniging in the Transvaal. Both plants began production in 1926; and the Iron and Steel Corporation of South Africa (ISCOR) was formed in 1928 to take over the entire industry. During the 1930s, the expansion of gold-mining resulting from the increased demand for gold at higher prices when major countries abandoned the gold standard led to increased need for steel. This enabled the industry to expand still further. By the eve of the Second World War, about two-thirds of the demand for steel in South Africa was met by domestic producers. Following the war, the industry continued to grow and to produce higher-quality specialized steels, lessening still further the reliance on imports. Good iron-ore deposits were also found in Southern Rhodesia, in the area around Que Que. A smelting plant was erected there in 1943. In both countries the mines and railways have continued to provide the major markets for the industry's output, but the establishment of the steel industry on a firm footing has itself promoted the development of various engineering enterprises. Here again, the demand for equipment from the mines and railways has been the primary stimulus; but the need for agricultural machinery, electrical equipment, motor vehicles and so on, has led to a significant diversification of production.

An important difference between the steel industries of South Africa and Southern Rhodesia is that South Africa has had a large expanding domestic market, whereas Southern Rhodesia could not expand, let alone maintain, the industry without establishing an export market for pig iron. Negotiations along these lines with Japan were interrupted by the sanctions imposed following the unilateral declaration of independence.

Many lighter industries, such as textiles, clothing, leather goods and food processing, benefited from the markets created by the mines, but were also part of the wider growth of service and manufacturing industries to meet the demands of the Europeans and Africans in the cities and towns that grew up, primarily though not exclusively, around the mines. This wider industrial development is of great importance for the economic future of Africa because of the political pressures to substitute domestic manufactures for imports, and because minerals are essentially a wasting asset.

Apart from transportation, the most important service industry for the mines was the generation of electricity. Electric power was needed for lighting, for running machinery, for raising ores from greater depths than was possible with steam-power and for electrolytic copper-refining. The diamond-mines led the way; and in 1882, they not only supplied their own power, but also made Kimberley the first town in Africa with electrically lit streets. In this respect, in fact, they were far in advance of many towns in Europe. The first major electricity undertaking other than municipal generators was the Victoria Falls and Transvaal Power Company, formed in 1906 to generate power at the Falls and to transmit it overland to the Rand. The estimated cost of transmission was so high that the company decided to erect coal-fired stations to supply both the gold-mines and the Witbank collieries. In 1923, the Electricity Supply Commission was set up by the South African government to regulate the supply of power to the entire country, including the railways, which were then embarking on electrification of the lines over the escarpment. Because large supplies of cheap coal were available and because the country's rivers cannot provide adequate flows of water throughout the year without extensive dam-building, hydro-electric power provides only an insignificant portion of South Africa's total electricity output. Farther north the situation was again somewhat different.

Union Minière began planning a hydro-electric scheme as early as 1908, but lack of finance and the outbreak of war made it impossible to proceed until 1926, when the Société Générale des Forces Hydro-Electriques (Sogéfor) began work on a dam and generating installation at the Cornet (Mwadingusha) Falls on the Lufira river. This produced electricity for general use in Elisabethville, Jadotville and Kolwezi, as well as for the mines and the electrolytic refining plant. Other dams and generators were subsequently built, but were unable to meet the demand for power. Steam generators using coal from Katanga's Luena coal-fields had to be built as well. In 1953, Union Minière reached an agreement with the American government and the two Northern Rhodesian copper companies, for the construction of the Marinel hydro-electric installation on the Lualaba river with a loan of £8 million from the Import-Export Bank, repayable in shipments of copper and cobalt, and £7 million from the copper companies. The Rhodesian mines were by this time finding it impossible to meet their electricity needs from their own steam generators because Rhodesian Railways was unable to carry sufficient coal to them from Wankie. Importing current from the Congo was the quickest way of resolving the difficulty, but this was only a temporary solution.

Northern Rhodesia's first electricity-generating plant was a hydro-electric installation on the Mulungushi river, built in 1926 by the Rhodesia Broken Hill Development Corporation as part of its expansion programme. Another generator was installed on the Lusemfwa river in 1945. The copper companies had to rely on coal, each of the four major mines having its own generators. For more efficient operation, the electricity supplies of the mines were linked just before the Second World War. In 1952, the Rhodesia Congo Border Company took over responsibility for distributing power to the mines and the townships that had grown up around them, and for the transmission of at least 500 million kwh of power from the Marinel plant to the Copper Belt through a central switching point at Kitwe. (In 1958, for example, some 663 million kwh were in fact imported.)

The growth of industry in Southern Rhodesia and the anticipated expansion of copper production meant that additional capacity would soon be needed. Two hydro-electric schemes were proposed, one on the Kafue river at Keshima Gorge, the other on the Zambezi at Kariba. The copper companies favoured Kafue, which could have been completed sooner. But they were not too concerned when the government of the Federation of Rhodesia and Nyasaland decided on the Kariba scheme, with the generating equipment to be sited on the southern side of the river. This decision has been considered by many to have been a purely political one based on Southern Rhodesia's fear of allowing the north to have control over a vital economic resource. Such a view does not take account of several technical factors that made Kariba the better plan. A report by two French consultants maintained that power could begin flowing from

Kariba considerably earlier than had been expected, and that current from the completed Kariba plant would be considerably cheaper than from Kafue. This was a consideration that appeared to outweigh the additional cost, which was estimated at £85·75 million as compared with £55 million for Kafue. The most important technical question was whether the Kafue would provide sufficient water flow. Data on this point were thought insufficient to satisfy the International Bank for Reconstruction and Development, from whom it was hoped to secure a large part of the necessary funds. The Kafue scheme would have been ample to meet the needs of the copper-mines, but not necessarily those of other industries. The planners intended to build generators on the north bank of the river. When this phase was completed, Kariba was expected to supply all the demands made on it for the foreseeable future.

To finance Kariba, the Northern Rhodesian copper companies each loaned the federal government £20 million at 4½ per cent interest. (The British bank rate was then 5½ per cent). The British South Africa Company provided £4 million, while the Standard Bank of South Africa and Barclays Bank, DCO, put up £2 million each. The Colonial Development Corporation provided £15 million, the Commonwealth Development Finance Corporation £5 million and the International Bank £28½ million. The major contracts for the first phase were awarded to a consortium of Italian firms, although much of the equipment was manufactured in Britain. Work began in 1955, and power began to flow to the Copper Belt in January 1960. The Queen Mother officially opened the station the following May. The copper-mines were able to reduce the output of their thermal stations, because they had to draw only 30 per cent of their requirements from them.[6]

In West Africa, the generation of electricity has been primarily on a small scale, serving local needs with thermal generators. The first hydro-electric installation was built on the Senegal river, but the first major plant was in operation at the Jos tin-mines by the time the railway reached them. As early as 1915, there was discussion of harnessing the Volta river to provide power, and the idea was put forward again in 1924 in connexion with the possibility of working some of the Gold Coast's extensive bauxite deposits; but it was only in 1956 that full preparatory surveys were completed. The Volta River Project illustrates more clearly than Kariba the important role that electricity can play in promoting not only mineral production, but also more general industrial development (see Table 86). An integral part of the project, and in many respects a more important and more urgent one, was the development of Tema as a port and industrial centre.

A 17-mile rail link between Accra and Tema was completed in 1954; and full facilities were available at the port, which was half again as large as Takoradi, in 1960. By that time the United Africa Company was operating a motor assembly plant there, the Italian ENI an oil refinery. ICI had opened an insecticide factory, and a steel mill had been constructed. It was only in 1962, largely because of American fears that the Soviet Union would finance an alternative scheme, that work began on the dam itself. There was no shortage of aluminium at this time. Demand was not increasing rapidly, and for the fore-

---

[6] Kariba's second phase had not been begun when the Federation was dissolved and Northern Rhodesia became independent. The great increase in demand for copper had not in fact materialized. In 1971 an agreement was reached to go ahead.

Table 86. *Electricity production and energy consumption in sub-Saharan Africa, 1948 and 1961*

	Electricity production				Energy consumption	
	Total (in millions of kwh)		Hydro (in millions of kwh)		Total, 1961 (in millions of metric tons of coal equivalent)	Per capita, 1961 (in kg. of coal equivalent)
	1948	1961	1948	1961		
Sudan	17	103	—	—	·64	52
Former French West Africa [a]	34	c. 300	...	c. 84	·89	37
Togo	1	6	—	...	·04	28
Gambia	1	6	—	—	·01	41
Sierra Leone	5	50	—	—	·13	52
Ghana	171	390	19	176	·64	92
Nigeria	108	662	57	101	1·71	47
Liberia	10	120	6	20	·08	56
Cameroun	2	920	—	910	·28	66
Former French Equatorial Africa [b]	...	71	—	40	·27	49
Congo (Leopoldville)	497	2,600	...	2,500	1·25	64
Ethiopia	34	124	15	69	·19	9
French Somaliland	1	10	—	—	·02	278
Somalia	...	11	—	—	·05	24
Kenya	59	215	...	132 ⎫		
Uganda	8	435	—	435 ⎬ 1·64		69
Tanganyika	30	164	17	93 ⎭		
Zanzibar	2	12	—	—	·02	51
Northern Rhodesia	...	659	...	233 ⎫		
Southern Rhodesia	230	2,782	—	2,206 [c] ⎬ 3·92		460
Nyasaland	...	35	—	2 ⎭		
Angola	23	160	—	130	·35	71
Moçambique	39	220	18	110	·82	124
South Africa	9,259	24,556	—	—	43·52	2,414
Madagascar	27	113	—	82	·18	32
Réunion	1	20	—	—	·04	114
Mauritius	16	63	15	20	·08	115
Totals [d]	13,400	43,100	...	9,670	70·37	

[a] 1961 output of electricity in million kwh was as follows: Senegal, 152; Niger, 9·2; Dahomey, 9·6; Upper Volta, 10; Ivory Coast, 92·8 (of which, hydro 73·8). Output for Mali in 1960 was 15·3. No figures available for Mauritania or Guinea.

[b] 1961 output of electricity in million kwh was as follows: Chad, 9·0; Congo (Brazzaville), 30·9; C.A.R., 9·4 (of which, hydro 9·3); Gabon, 21·7.   [c] Federal Power Board (Kariba).

[d] Includes estimates where data are not given and for countries not listed.

... = Data not available.   — = Nil or negligible.

SOURCE: William A. Hance, *The geography of modern Africa* (New York, Columbia University Press, 1964), p. 40.

seeable future could be satisfied from existing sources. It was only because of Cold War considerations that the American government helped to finance the building of the dam and backed a consortium of American, British and Canadian interests in forming the Volta Aluminium Company (Valco), which built a smelting plant at Tema. Using only imported ores, not any mined in Ghana, the plant began operations in 1967, the year after current began to flow from the Volta dam.

Hydro-electric installations also made water available for irrigation and made it possible for a fishing industry to flourish. As the shores of the lakes behind the dams spread, so too, apparently, did some diseases.[7] Dam construction provided an important market for cement as well, an industry to be found in close proximity to virtually all mining and other industrial or urban centres. The Chilanga cement-works benefited enormously from the Kariba project, but was forced to close after the first phase had been completed. On the Rand, cement manufacture was of direct importance for mining. A cementation process, developed after the First World War, that impeded water seepage allowed mining at greater depths than would otherwise have been possible. Elsewhere, cement was needed for general construction as well as for building on the mines.

Agriculture

The two major obstacles to the development of agriculture in Africa were, first, the lack of a large domestic market and second, the difficulty of transporting export crops to the coast. The second problem was to a great extent eliminated by the building of the railways, although mining, by bringing together large numbers of Europeans and Africans outside the subsistence economy, helped to overcome the first. The diamond-mines had little difficulty in obtaining the food they needed from the reasonably well-developed agriculture of the Cape and Orange Free State. In the Transvaal, the long years of limited outlets, combined with unscientific methods, made it virtually impossible for farmers to respond at all to the increased demand. Many sold their holdings to land companies and went prospecting on their own or took up what was apparently the more congenial and, certainly, in the years before the arrival of the railways more profitable, occupation of transport riding. After the Boer War, the government took a more active part in promoting improved farming methods, but for many years the Transvaal remained heavily dependent on imported food supplies.

Farmers wanting to settle in Southern Rhodesia in the early days received very little encouragement from the British South Africa Company beyond grants of land to members of the Pioneer Column or the force that subdued the Matabele. It was only when the 'Second Rand', on which the company was counting for its success, began to prove illusory that it turned to agriculture as a potential source of commercial profit. More care was taken in the selection of settlers, preference being given to men from South Africa, who seemed to adjust better to soil conditions and climate than people coming directly from Europe. Because Southern Rhodesia's mineral resources are scattered, they did not provide the centralized markets to be found in Katanga and later on the Copper Belt. The railways did make the cultivation of maize and tobacco for export, initially to South Africa, quite profitable, and helped agriculture to become the dominant sector of Southern Rhodesia's economy. They were not,

---

[7] In connexion with the plans for the Aswan Dam, too, the fear of spreading disease was a point of controversy.

however, entirely without their disadvantages. Built to serve the mines, the lines followed higher ground, avoiding the more unhealthy, but generally more fertile, lowlands. European farmers moved into the areas along the line of rail, forcing the Africans out. Convenience of transport was gained at the expense of soil quality. The growth of a road network feeding the railway later overcame this problem.

Road construction was generally of more direct advantage to agriculture and commerce than to mining. New areas could be opened to farming, produce being transported cheaply over relatively short distances to the railway. The mines did need roads for the transport of people and equipment between their different installations. Union Minière, for example, built many miles of roads on its own account during the inter-war years, but could not use roads economically for transport to the coast.[8]

As land prices in Southern Rhodesia rose, men with little or no capital began to move north of the Zambezi, where poor soil, extensive tsetse-fly-infested areas and, once again, the lack of markets forced them to eke out a bare existence by trading African cattle and by transport riding. As the railway moved towards Katanga, Europeans settled along the line and began sending maize and cattle north. The Katanga trade was the mainstay of European agriculture in Northern Rhodesia, beginning to decline in importance only after 1928, when the BCK and the CFL made produce from Kasai and Kivu easily available. At the same time, the growth of markets and the development of transport facilities and of agricultural services also gave a stimulus to African farming, especially among the Tonga people.

The early interdependence of Northern Rhodesia and Katanga illustrates one of the problems created by the arbitrary drawing of Africa's boundaries by the European powers. Southern Katanga was geologically, historically and culturally more closely linked to the neighbouring areas of Northern Rhodesia than it was to the rest of the Congo, from which it was further divided by a wide tsetse-fly belt and, until 1928, by virtually non-existent means of communication. King Leopold II of the Belgians, by a sweep of his hand across a map in 1885 when none of the major powers had any interests in that part of the interior, had included Katanga in the territory of the Congo Free State. He was probably aware of the existence of copper there, but was more concerned with the exploitation of his domain's natural rubber and ivory resources, which required relatively little capital, than in developing minerals that could pay returns only after a long span of time and heavy expenditure. It was only when Cecil Rhodes began to cast covetous eyes in the direction of Katanga that Leopold took any positive action to secure his position. Even then, the impetus for developing the copper deposits came from British interests in the south, as did much of the skilled mining personnel. It became an important point of Belgian policy to resist the many forces tending to draw Katanga into the British orbit, and to keep in Belgian hands as much as possible of the profits to be derived from its exploitation. This was a major consideration in the decision to construct the *voie nationale,* but was not of prime importance in determining agricultural policy, although agriculture did benefit.

In the late 1930s Northern Rhodesia's growing population began to impose a

---

[8] Less bulky minerals could, of course, benefit from roads. The output of the Dunda diamondfields in Angola, for example, is taken by road to the Benguela Railway.

severe strain on the ability of African-held land to support the people living on it. With men increasingly drawn to the Copper Belt towns in search of work, the problem of urban African unemployment began. Among the many attempts made to improve the situation, one of the first was a land resettlement scheme begun in 1941 with the aim of increasing the amount of land available for African cultivation. This and later similar schemes helped to relieve some of the pressure but did not eliminate it entirely. At the end of the war, about 85 per cent of the families in the Tonga maize-growing region were still subsistence farmers, despite the fact that they were living in one of the country's most progressive districts. The problem involved more than a general shortage of good land; it was complicated by a lack of capital, which most people found difficult to accumulate. For some, this was because of the heavy burden of family obligations imposed by polygamous marriages. There was also a widespread suspicion of any government-sponsored schemes.

In 1948, the first of a number of Peasant Farming Schemes was started in the Eastern Province. With the help of supervision and training from the Agricultural Department, farmers involved in this began to use modern techniques of contour ploughing, manuring and crop rotation. Along with the subsidies for buying machinery and the department's extension services, these and other programmes enabled a number of Africans to do quite well for themselves, a very few exceptionally so. By 1949 it was estimated that about 85 per cent of the produce sold by African farmers had been grown specifically for market. For the most part, however, farming techniques over large areas remained fundamentally unchanged, with the result that Africans were unable to compete with European farmers in the export trade. The mines and towns continued to attract men whether jobs were available for them or not.

In the Congo the situation was rather different. European settlement was not encouraged. Land was alienated, not for farmers but for concessionary companies wanting to exploit natural resources—minerals, rubber and palm-oil. Most Europeans in Katanga were employees of the large companies—Union Minière and the railways—on fixed-term contracts, without their families. Others, generally not Belgians, came as merchants or to provide some of the professional and technical services demanded in a growing urban area. Although restrictions on settlement were lifted after 1933, no large group of European farmers emerged as a powerful political force, in contrast with what had happened in the Rhodesias and South Africa. African land rights were strongly, and quite successfully, defended by humanitarian pressures both inside and outside the Belgian government. Some of the early attempts to establish European farms in Katanga, and elsewhere, were not conspicuous for their success. Belgian farming methods were not at all suitable for local conditions.

The government decided that the best policy for developing agriculture was to encourage Africans to expand production within their traditional farming system and to enter the export trade as much as possible. The educational system placed strong emphasis on technical and agricultural skills. A research body, the Institut National pour l'Etude Agronomique de Congo Belge (INEAC), set up experimental stations, and in 1936 began the first *paysannat,* on which family units were helped to use new techniques of planting, fertilizing and crop rotation. Later, *fermettes* based on individual holdings that could be inherited but not sold were also organized. Much of the pressure for the expansion of the *paysannat* system came from cotton companies alarmed by falling production and the unsuccessful attempts to make independent African farmers grow cotton in preference to other crops. In rotation with cotton, which was the *paysannats'* major crop, were maize, ground-nuts, cassava and bananas. In some areas, coffee was grown as well. Because the expansion programme was disrupted by the events following the Congo's independence, it is difficult to draw any conclusions about the long-term success or failure of the schemes.

In general, the government support for African farming, though not entirely free from abuse, did make it possible for Africans to participate to a much greater degree than was the case farther south, in the production of cash-crops for both European and African domestic consumers as well as for exports. European farming did develop in Katanga, but relied on markets outside the mining industry, since Union Minière and the BCK got their food supplies primarily from Kivu and Kasai.

In West Africa, mines also provided markets for agricultural produce, but the heavy involvement of Africans in the cultivation of cash-crops made these markets much less important. As in Southern Rhodesia, the greatest impetus for agricultural development came from the export market and the railways. Market towns grew up along the lines, and easy access to northern rail terminals, in Ghana and Nigeria, for example, marked the limits of attempts to develop and expand agricultural output.

Labour and social change

One of the greatest needs of the mining industry was for cheap African labour, a need that was not apparent in the early days. When settlers from Natal with no skill or training in mining first began working the 'river diggings' at Pniel and Klipdrift, for example, whites and blacks shared the work, even the heaviest labour. When experienced miners were later brought in from Australia and Cornwall, whites gradually confined themselves to skilled and supervisory jobs. As mining expanded, the demand for African workers grew tremendously. A growing supply of cheap labour was considered essential if the mines were to overcome the disadvantage of distance from markets and to remain low-cost producers. Africa's relatively sparse population made it difficult to maintain adequate work forces, while the growth of agriculture and other industries exacerbated the situation by increasing the competition for the limited labour available. Africans became wage earners in order to pay taxes imposed primarily to make them do just that, and to be able to purchase manufactured goods. Initially, most were prepared to work for only short periods—long enough to satisfy immediate needs and to meet a set target—and at times when their help was not needed at home to clear land or assist in some other way. The mines demanded a constant influx of workers to replace those completing their short-term (usually three to nine months) contracts. For many Africans, work on the mines became a normal part of a year's activities, alternating with time at home. As the attraction for goods obtainable from wages grew, and as population pressure on land increased and the lure of urban life in the towns around the mines became stronger, more and more people were prepared to work for longer periods, and often to establish their homes near the mines on a more or less permanent basis. They thus tended to weaken or to sever completely their ties with their rural communities, but by the same token made it possible for many mines to stabilize their labour forces.

As may be seen from Table 87, the diamond-mines consistently offered higher wages than other employers (for many years making the wages payable in guns and ammunition, a practice that apparently caused many chiefs to send their followers to work), and were thus able to rely almost entirely on men who presented themselves for work of their own accord. Comparatively little use was made of independent labour recruiters (also known as touts, agents or contractors), who generally had somewhat unsavoury reputations, and no organized recruiting by the diamond industry was necessary. The only other major mining area that was able to meet its labour requirements from volunteers was the Copper Belt. By the time the mines in this area were brought to production, many Northern Rhodesians had already had considerable experience of mine work in the south or in Katanga, and were attracted to the mines by the social and economic advantages they felt they could gain and to which they had become accustomed. In the Transvaal, Southern Rhodesia and Katanga, extensive recruiting organizations had to be established.

Table 87. *Wages of Africans employed on gold, coal and diamond mines, South Africa, 1913–37* *

| | Gold | Coal | | Diamonds | |
| | | | | | |
	Witwatersrand	Transvaal	Rand	Cape of Good Hope	Transvaal
1913	52s 0d	41s 3d	43s 9d	89s 7d	78s 0d
1921	58s 7d	52s 3d	57s 6d	103s 7d	90s 5d
1932	57s 7d	53s 7d	49s 4d	72s 4d	79s 1d
1937	58s 4d	51s 11d	48s 1d	78s 0d	69s 0d

* Average wages per month of twenty-six working days.

SOURCE: Sheila T. van der Horst, *Native labour in South Africa* (London, Oxford University Press, 1942), p. 227.

In the early days, the Rand mining companies recruited labour individually. They competed heavily with one another to attract workers, to the detriment of all. Recruiting costs rose rapidly to twice the cost of wages or more, which led the companies to form the Transvaal Chamber of Mines (see above, p. 368) to reduce recruiting costs and to co-ordinate the labour supply. The Chamber created two organizations: the Witwatersrand Native Labour Association (WNLA), to recruit Africans from outside South Africa, and the Native Recruiting Corporation (NRC), to recruit within the country and in the High Commission Territories. Recruiting and distributing labour to all the mines in the Transvaal and the Orange Free State became the sole responsibility of these two organizations. As alternative employment opportunities grew, the gold-mines relied increasingly on labour from Moçambique (recruited under the terms of the Moçambique Convention), Nyasaland and Northern Rhodesia.

Part of the labour problem stemmed from the spasmodic nature of the supply. In an attempt to create a more stable labour force, the Chamber of Mines at the turn of the century began recruiting indentured Chinese. This policy had a number of drawbacks: the Chinese tended to react more strongly than Africans to pressures from supervisory staff, which caused friction, sometimes riots. Rather than spend their wages on manufactured goods, they gambled widely among themselves, and indebtedness became a serious problem. The British House of Commons was so shocked to learn of the prevalence of sodomy among the Chinese that both humanitarian and political pressure from Britain put an end to the recruiting experiment. This forced those in Southern Rhodesia who saw the employment of Chinese as the only way of solving the labour problem there to abandon the idea. It was pointed out to Robert Williams, who investigated the possibility of recruiting Chinese for work in Katanga, that in addition to the obvious reasons for not doing so, there was the added point that if any one of them died, his body had to be shipped back to China—at considerably greater cost than the passage for a living man.

The Transvaal gold-mines never completely solved their labour difficulties. The politically inspired principle of job reservation, although not as rigidly enforced as it might be, has limited the opportunities for Africans to advance to higher-paying, more responsible jobs. The general, although not absolute, refusal to allow a stabilized labour force to live more or less permanently in the vicinity of the mines, coupled with the unwillingness even to allow men to bring their wives with them while they are on short-term contracts, makes mining even less attractive than it inherently is. Africans with experience of working in the European sector of the economy usually prefer to seek other, better-paid, jobs (see Table 88), while the mines have had to rely on inexperienced

Table 88. *Cash earnings in different sectors, South Africa, 1936 and 1961*

	1936				1961			
	Black	Coloured	Indian	White	Black	Coloured	Indian	White
Manufacturing								
R/annum	84	158	120	452	370	566	602	2030
Index [a]	100	188	143	538	100	153	163	549
Construction								
R/annum	90	200	214	560	338	712	770	1926
Index	100	222	238	622	100	210	228	570
Gold mines								
R/annum	68	—	196	786	146	—	504	2478
Index	100	—	288	1156	100	—	345	1697
Agriculture								
R/annum	n.a.	n.a.	n.a.	n.a.	68	132	198	1416
Index					100	194	291	2082

NOTE: Figures for agriculture were obtained by dividing total wage bill by the total number of farm employees, including domestic servants but excluding casual employees. Whilst the figures for agriculture may be subject to a considerable degree of error, those for other sectors are probably more accurate. Figures for manufacturing include construction (i.e., 'building and contracting') and refer to private establishments (i.e., state enterprise is excluded).
[a] Black = 100

SOURCE: Francis Wilson, *Labour in the South African gold mines, 1911–1969* (Cambridge University Press, 1972), p. 169.

recruits. These men find it easier to enter the maze of industrial employment with the paternal assistance of the recruiting agencies, which furnish transportation to and from the mines as well as food *en route,* in addition to carrying out the necessary legal formalities. It was the task of providing these services rather than recruiting itself that became the major concern of the WNLA and the NRC.

In Southern Rhodesia, labour bureaux were organized as early as 1895 in an attempt to provide sufficient labour for the mines and to meet the strong objections raised against pressure to work being put on Africans by local administrative officers. The bureaux were not particularly successful, nor was the Southern Rhodesian Native Labour Board, formed originally in 1903 and subsequently reorganized several times. Part of the board's difficulty (it was unable to provide more than about 10 per cent of the men needed) stemmed from the conflict between mining interests and farmers. In 1914, a convention similar to the Moçambique Convention of 1909 opened northern Moçambique to recruiting for Southern Rhodesia, although men from Nyasaland and Northern Rhodesia, recruits or volunteers, made up the bulk of the work force (see Tables 89–91). It was only in the 1950s that reliance on foreigners began to lessen, but even then only 45 per cent of all workers came from Southern Rhodesia itself. By this time, the role of the Labour Board had become, as in the Transvaal, more one of providing services for volunteers than of actual recruiting.

Table 89. *Average number of Africans employed in Southern Rhodesia in mining, European agriculture and secondary industries, and percentage of aggregate employment for selected post-World War II years*

	Mining (000s)	Per cent	European agriculture (000s)	Per cent	Secondary industries (000s)	Per cent
1946	70·6	19	135·8	37	57·0	15
1948	63·4	16	147·3	36	72·3	18
1951	60·7	12	181·4	36	98·5	20
1954	56·5	10	194·3	35	—	—
1956	55·8	9	203·3	34	138·7	23

SOURCE: William J. Barber, *The economy of British Central Africa* (London, Oxford University Press, 1961), p. 210.

Table 90. *Africans employed in Southern Rhodesia coming from outside the territory, selected years*

	1931	1936	1941	1946	1951	1956
Nyasaland	49,487	70,362	71,505	80,480	86,287	123,025
Northern Rhodesia	35,542	46,884	48,163	45,413	48,514	39,580
Portuguese territory	14,896	25,215	45,970	72,120	101,618	105,406
Others	2,983	2,440	2,468	4,399	10,353	8,796

SOURCE: William J. Barber, *The economy of British Central Africa* (London, Oxford University Press, 1961), p. 210.

Table 91. *Average number of Nyasaland Africans employed on Southern Rhodesian mines, 1919–44*

Year	Number	Year	Number	Year	Number
1919	8,114	1928	13,494	1937	29,576
1920	12,539	1929	15,156	1938	29,349
1921	13,777	1930	15,632	1939	28,232
1922	13,208	1931	13,555	1940	28,168
1923	12,893	1932	13,404	1941	26,286
1924	14,020	1933	16,208	1942	25,618
1925	13,151	1934	20,007	1943	23,301
1926	13,422	1935	25,582	1944	22,404
1927	12,833	1936	28,030		

SOURCE: Robert R. Kuczynski, *Demographic survey of the British colonial empire,* vol. II (London, Oxford University Press, 1949), p. 558.

In Katanga, recruiting operations on a scale comparable to that of the Transvaal had to be mounted. In 1911, the Belgian government joined Union Minière, the railways and other prospective employers in Katanga to form the Bourse du Travail du Katanga, which was given the monopoly of supplying workers for the entire province. The Bourse had a formidable task, given the exceptionally sparse population in southern Katanga itself, the poor communications with the rest of the country and the nearness of the tsetse-fly belt. It could thus hardly have been adequately organized quickly enough to meet the heavy demand for labour on the copper mines and the smelting plant then being built. Union Minière was authorized to recruit on its own account outside the Congo, paying the Bourse an indemnity for each recruit until such time as the Bourse was itself in a position to meet the demand. Robert Williams, through his firm of mining engineers, Robert Williams & Company, reached an agreement with the administrator of north-eastern Rhodesia to recruit a specified number of men in certain areas. There was strong opposition to this from people who were afraid that Rhodesians would be treated in a way similar to that recently revealed by the investigations into the 'Congo atrocities'. Others felt that Rhodesians should not be recruited for work in a foreign colony when labour was so scarce in some British territories. The administrator justified the agreement by pointing out that many men went and would undoubtedly continue to go to Katanga on their own to earn the higher wages being offered there. Much better for all concerned than uncontrolled migration was a recruiting system that provided set conditions of rations, specified routes to be followed to and from Katanga and the right to have an inspector of natives resident at the mines. Northern Rhodesia became a major source of labour for Katanga (see Table 92), though Union Minière was forced to rely heavily on independent contractors, whose treatment of Africans left much to be desired.

During the First World War, when men were needed to carry military supplies to East Africa, the situation became worse. Attempts to bring in labour from other areas met with limited success. After the war, when more men were needed for work in Northern Rhodesia itself, recruiting was restricted. For a short time, Union Minière employed men from Ruanda-Urundi, but the government, wishing to avoid criticism from the League of Nations, did not allow this

Table 92. *Africans employed by Union Minière du Haut-Katanga, classified by country of origin, 1911–24* [a]

Country	1911	1912	1915	1916	1917	1918	1919	1920	1921	1922	1923	1924
Northern Rhodesia (north-eastern region)	306	1,421	1,426	776	553	904	5,447	5,481	5,310	3,036	4,204	6,846
Northern Rhodesia (north-western region) [b]	733	0	83	1,453	40	125	187	193	249	33	16	20
Congo	72	382	1,400	2,349	2,911	3,155	5,162	5,373	3,767	3,906	5,333	5,971
Nyasaland [c]	38	37		182	250	420	563	374	327	277	247	266
Angola	—	—	—	10	906	1,401	856	414	227	196	257	320
Others	2		906 [d]					1	2	3	1	2	[e]

[a] Numbers of recruits and volunteers on company's books as of 31 December 1911 and 1915–24 and 31 October 1912.
[b] Including Barotseland, where recruiting was carried out under separate arrangements. None of the Africans employed in 1911 was a recruit.　　[c] All volunteers.
[d] Including volunteers who, in this year only, were not classified by country of origin.
[e] Included with figure for Nyasaland.

SOURCES: Native Labour Department returns, Robert Williams & Co., 1911–18; Union Minière du Haut-Katanga, 1919–24.

to continue. In 1923, the problem was further exacerbated by the decision to go ahead with the construction of the BCK railway line to Ilebo (Port Francqui) and by the strong pressures put on Africans to work on construction.

An entirely new approach to the labour question was needed if Union Minière was to be able to make a success of the expansion plans that they were initiating. This involved a shift from the general policy of employing Africans on short-term contracts to one of stabilizing the work force. The first step was to introduce three-year contracts. British opponents of the change saw this as a form of forced labour, but opposition died down as soon as it became clear that Northern Rhodesians would not be involved. Some Belgians feared that Africans would be 'corrupted' by prolonged contact with Europeans. Besides, Union Minière wanted its African employees to maintain close links with their traditional societies, but not out of any sentimental considerations. The company wanted to be free to send back to their home villages any men they dismissed for economic or disciplinary reasons. Men who came to work on long-term contracts were not expected to become permanent residents in the mining camp, but rather, on completion of their contracts, to return home for a time before coming back to the mines if they so desired (see Table 93).

While men were at work, a variety of social services had to be provided for them, the most fundamental being accommodation for them and for their wives and children. Men were more willing to work for three years at a time if they were not separated from their families. In 1923, one of Union Minière's doctors pointed out that sanitation would be very much improved if men lived with their wives, who could be expected to reduce the number of prostitutes and the incidence of venereal disease. Having men bring their wives with them became such an important part of the company's labour policy that it set up marriage

Table 93. *Proportion of recruits in Union Minière's work force
for five-year periods, 1921–55* *

	1921–5	1926–30	1931–5	1936–40	1941–5	1946–50	1951–5
Total no. of workers	10,568	15,678	7,265	11,136	17,442	15,974	19,060
No. of recruits	10,112	9,805	529	1,247	1,662	454	1,362
Percentage	96%	63%	7%	11%	10%	3%	7%

* Average figures.

SOURCE: André Lux, *Le marché du travail en Afrique noire* (Louvain, Institut de Recherches Economiques, Sociales et Politiques, 1962), p. 61.

bureaux and paid bride wealth for single employees wanting to marry. Some areas experienced a considerable inflation of bride price as a result. Housing was so limited, however, that only a man's wife and children could live with him, other relations being restricted to short visits. In many cases, indeed, for lack of space children had to be sent to live with grandparents. Hospital and medical facilities were constantly improved, and considerable effort was made by the Organisation pour la Protection de l'Enfance Noire (OPEN), set up by Union Minière, to help women learn more about nutrition and child care, and in general to improve child health. Schooling at the primary level was available, with teaching being done by Benedictines. Technical education was provided as well, in addition to on-the-job training for the men. Union Minière did not generally want its African employees to have a broad education.

In Northern Rhodesia the copper companies, seeing the advantages to be gained from a stabilized labour force, introduced a similar system in 1931 (see Table 94). They too, considered it particularly important that the mine-workers should not constitute a permanent urban community. Wives and children were allowed to live on the mines, although single men did not have the help of company-sponsored marriage brokering. In both the Congo and Northern Rhodesia this policy was very successful. By 1951 the average term of employment in Katanga mines was eleven years, on the Copper Belt five years. In both the Congo and Northern Rhodesia an urban African community also grew up quite separately. People moved into the *cités indigènes* (*centres extra-coutumiers*) or municipal townships of their own accord, without being tied to a particular job. Some came directly from their rural villages, whereas others came from the

Table 94. *Changes in the proportion of married workers, length of stay and
turn-over of Africans employed on Roan Antelope mine, 1927–35*

	1927	1928	1929	1930	1931	1932	1933	1934	1935
Married workers (%)	20%	20%	21%	22%	27%	37%	43%	50%	52%
Average length of stay (months)	3	5	5	6	6	14	14	16	24
Turn-over (%)	24%	22%	17%	17%	11%	10%	7·5%	7%	3%

SOURCE: André Lux, *Le marché du travail en Afrique noire* (Louvain, Institut de Recherches Economiques, Sociales et Politiques, 1962), p. 39.

mines, often without completing their contracts. The Belgian government encouraged Africans to settle permanently near industrial and commercial centres and made it possible for them to buy plots of land. This they did primarily in order to establish a pool of labour for small companies, which, unlike the mines and railways, were not in a position to maintain their own workers' camps. So long as work was available, men in these urban communities were free to work when they wished at jobs of their own choice. They paid for this freedom by being subject to greater insecurity and a generally lower level of social services than were men on the mines. On the other hand, mine-workers were much more tied to their jobs. They were dependent on the companies not only for their jobs but for their homes as well, and in the case of many men in Katanga, for their wives. Still, men on the mines were more sheltered from the economic vicissitudes and realities of life than were their urban counterparts.

One of the greatest advantages that Africans gained from working on the mines or railways was that they acquired technical skills that opened up a variety of job opportunities, and mining companies often had difficulty in keeping trained men. Union Minière was more advanced than the Copper Belt companies in promoting technically qualified Africans into more skilled job categories. By 1934, 5 per cent of Union Minière's African work force were doing jobs previously done by Europeans, while the railway companies had gone even farther: over 60 per cent of their men were in such positions. With no effective European labour-union organization, the companies in Katanga did not have to face strong opposition to this policy. In the absence of the requirement of 'equal pay for equal work' demanded by the white miners' union in Northern Rhodesia, replacing Europeans with Africans at lower wages made sound economic sense.

Both as migrant workers and as part of a stabilized work force, Africans employed on the mines came into contact with a wide range of new ideas, both European and African. They gained an awareness of political and social problems outside their extended family units and tribal groupings. With increased skill and education, as in Europe in the eighteenth and nineteenth centuries, a middle class began to emerge. Common interests began to be identified, not only those concerning working conditions and wages but also with regard to the general relationship between Europeans and Africans and to the potential strength of African opposition to European domination. Even in Katanga, where no workers were allowed to strike or form unions, Africans learned the value of organized opposition to the government as well as to employers. In Northern Rhodesia, not only did the white unions limit African advancement into more skilled jobs; they also provided a good example for Africans to follow in organizing themselves. Many Africans were only indirectly affected by the changing attitudes emerging from the mines and urban areas, and some not at all. Though traditional mores and ties were still powerful, many roots of nationalist movements may be found in these more or less detribalized communities. The continuing process of change, of integrating new ideas into traditional patterns, had begun.

The mining industry, because it had been at the base of so much of Africa's economic growth during the colonial period, was largely responsible for the dual economies that developed. Within the economies of the African countries are two distinct economic systems: the modern, industrialized money economy on the one hand; the traditional agrarian subsistence economy on the other. (This phenomenon is, of course, not unique to Africa, nor even to countries that have been subject to colonial rule. It will be found wherever a subsistence or semi-subsistence economy continues while a complex, capital-intensive economy grows up alongside it.) One of the criticisms levelled against colonial rule is that the dual economy has operated to the detriment of many Africans, but there are positive as well as negative aspects of the impact it has had on African society.

On the negative side, there are the severe economic, social and political imbalances that arose. Political power was in the hands of Europeans. The division of the economy was reflected in racial separation and segregation. Most serious was the fact that the modern sector of the economy involved a relatively small number of Africans; the great majority remained within the traditional sector, gaining only marginal benefits from industrial growth. Those Africans who did become part of the modern sector and accepted its socio-economic values often found themselves in conflict with traditional customs and ideas, conflicts that could not easily be resolved and that led to considerable discontent. The social and political problems created by these imbalances have continued to face independent African countries.

On the positive side, there is the fact that industry in general and mining in particular have made significant contributions to the national wealth of many countries. Two indications of this record of accomplishment may be seen in Tables 95 and 96. As I have shown, the economic spin-off from mining was widespread. Mining has been far more than an extractive industry taking wealth from the ground and profits from the African continent. It has contributed to general welfare in a variety of ways, of which improved health conditions are only one aspect. Mining companies have subsidized development and research in other fields both by direct contributions and, indirectly, by the large amount of taxation in various forms that they and their employees have paid. In the long term, what will probably prove to have been mining's most important single contribution to Africa's economy is the development among Africans of the technical skills and expertise that had been seriously lacking at the beginning of the colonial period, skills that can serve as a foundation for continuing industrialization.

It is interesting to look more closely at Northern Rhodesia, where mining makes a more important contribution to national wealth than in any other sub-Saharan country. Although other industries, as they appeared, absorbed an increasing proportion of the African population into the money economy (see Table 97) mining continued to provide employment for a substantial number. As may be seen from Tables 98–100, the copper-mines provided a large part of the total revenue of the entire Federation. The mining companies, despite European opposition, increased the number of African artisans in skilled jobs. Furthermore, in order to meet the need for greater technical education—in skills not limited to the mining industry—they established the Copperbelt Technical Foundation, which set up technical institutions in the major towns. At a different level, Anglo American in 1955 gave Leeds University a grant of £100,000 to establish an Institute of African Geology to carry out fundamental research into the origin of ore deposits generally and into Africa's geological structure in particular.

Table 95. *Industrial source of the gross domestic product of independent African countries south of the Sahara* (in percentage, latest years available)

	Agriculture	Mining	Manufacturing	Construction	Electricity, gas and water	Transport and communication	Trade and finance	Public admin. and defence	Other branches
Botswana	46·9	0·1	7·5	5·4	0·8	7·8	13·0	4·1	14·4
Burundi	60·0	7·0	—	—	—	—	—	—	—
Cameroun	37·3	—	11·4	3·7	1·0	7·6	22·0	13·4	3·6
Central African Republic	49·0	—	12·0	—	—	—	—	—	—
Chad	54·1	—	4·0	4·1	—	1·1	19·9	13·6	3·2
Congo (Brazzaville)	23·4	—	17·0	—	—	34·2	—	25·4	—
Congo (Kinshasa)	21·5	6·4	15·9	2·6	0·9	6·4	16·1	18·1	12·0
Dahomey	45·9	—	2·8	5·5	0·6	6·9	18·8	15·0	4·5
Equatorial Guinea	—	—	—	—	—	—	—	—	—
Ethiopia	63·8	0·3	6·9	3·0	0·4	3·4	8·4	4·9	8·9
Gabon	22·9	18·1	5·9	8·8	—	9·7	10·0	—	24·6
Gambia	—	—	—	—	—	—	—	—	—
Ghana	51·4	2·5	19·2	4·4	—	—	—	7·4	15·1
Guinea	53·8	8·9	2·6	1·0	1·0	3·0	4·8	12·6	12·3
Ivory Coast	33·7	0·5	9·4	5·5	3·7	8·5	22·6	10·5	5·6
Kenya	35·7	0·4	11·1	4·4	2·0	8·4	14·7	12·3	11·0
Lesotho	65·3	1·6	0·8	1·9	0·6	1·0	4·7	9·9	14·2
Liberia	25·4	29·4	5·1	5·1	—	6·0	11·4	9·0	9·6
Malagasy Republic	31·7	—	10·9	—	—	10·3	18·4	20·1	8·6
Malawi	46·7	—	4·6	5·3	1·1	6·0	15·7	4·9	13·1
Mali	54·0	—	6·0	5·0	1·0	5·0	15·0	11·0	3·0
Mauritania	37·7	27·2	1·0	2·0	—	2·0	13·5	11·5	5·1
Mauritius	24·0	0·1	15·2	6·6	2·8	12·5	12·6	5·7	20·5
Niger	62·0	—	—	—	—	—	—	7·0	—
Nigeria	55·7	3·0	7·4	4·9	—	6·0	12·2	8·5	2·3
Rwanda	69·0	2·0	14·0	—	—	—	—	7·0	—
Senegal	33·1	2·5	14·0	2·7	—	4·5	34·4	17·5	7·6
Sierra Leone	31·4	19·2	6·3	3·6	0·8	7·7	15·0	5·2	10·8
Somalia	—	—	—	—	—	—	—	—	—
South Africa	10·2	12·2	22·4	3·3	2·5	9·5	17·6	9·4	12·9
Sudan	54·3	0·1	5·6	5·8	0·5	—	15·1	10·3	8·3
Swaziland	36·0	14·0	1·0	—	—	—	14·0	—	35·0
Tanzania (excluding Zanzibar)	53·5	2·6	5·0	3·1	0·9	4·5	14·1	7·0	9·3
Togo ·	44·9	9·2	4·5	3·3	2·2	6·0	18·3	7·1	4·5
Uganda	58·5	2·3	7·8	1·9	1·6	3·0	10·5	4·1	10·3
Upper Volta	58·0	—	2·0	—	—	—	—	—	40·0
Zambia	9·5	37·2	7·9	10·0	1·1	5·0	13·1	5·9	10·3

SOURCE: Andrew M. Kamarck, *The economics of African development*, rev. ed. (New York, 1971), p. 313.

Table 96. *Exports of Africa south of the Sahara*

	Total domestic exports (£ million)	Mineral exports as percentage of total for each territory	Mineral exports (£ million)	Mineral exports As percentage of total for all territories
Central African Federation (1959)	190·0	68·9	131·0	23·2
Belgian Congo and Ruanda-Urundi (1959)	177·0	56·5	100·0	17·7
Nigeria (1959)	160·0	3·8	6·0	1·1
French West Africa (1956) *	122·5	4·1	5·0	0·9
Ghana (1959)	113·0	23·0	26·0	4·6
Tanganyika (1959)	45·0	17·8	8·0	1·4
Uganda (1959)	42·0	7·1	3·0	0·5
Madagascar (1956) *	33·2	6·0	2·0	0·4
Kenya (1959)	33·0	6·1	2·0	0·4
French Equatorial Africa (1956) *	28·2	8·5	2·4	0·4
French Cameroun (1956) *	26·8	0·7	0·2	negligible
Total tropical Africa	970·7	29·4	285·6	50·6
Union of South Africa (1958)	579·0	48·2	279·0	49·4
GRAND TOTAL	1549·7	36·4	564·6	100·0

NOTE: 'Exports' in all cases includes gold bullion but excludes specie.
* Mineral exports are for 1957.

SOURCE: S. Herbert Frankel, 'Capital and capital supply in relation to the development of Africa', in *Economic development for Africa south of the Sahara*, E. A. G. Robinson, ed. (London, 1964), p. 427.

Table 97. *Estimated average numbers of Africans employed for wages in Northern Rhodesia and proportion in mining and European agriculture, 1929–56*

Year	Total 000s	Mining 000s	Mining Per cent	European agriculture 000s	European agriculture Per cent
1929	56·7	16·6	29	10·1	18
1930	70·5	21·8	31	10·9	15
1933	37·5	8·1	22	5·6	15
1936	53·5	15·1	28	9·2	17
1939	88·5	29·5	33	13·5	15
1945	100·3	33·0	33	15·0	15
1946	140·6	31·0	22	26·0	18
1948	158·4	36·5	23	25·0	16
1950	160·2	40·0	25	32·5	20
1953	269·0	46·0	17	44·2	16
1955	255·3	44·7	18	35·7	14
1956	265·9	46·0	17	31·6	12

SOURCE: William J. Barber, *The economy of British Central Africa* (London, Oxford University Press, 1961), pp. 202 and 228.

Table 98. *Estimated contribution of the Northern Rhodesia copper-mining industry to the net domestic product of the Federation of Rhodesia and Nyasaland and of Northern Rhodesia, 1954–62*

	Net domestic product		Contribution of Northern Rhodesia copper-mining industry		
Year	Federation (£ millions)	N. Rhodesia (£ millions)	Total (£ millions)	of Federation (per cent)	of N. Rhodesia (per cent)
1954	324	132	72	22	54
1955	375	162	93	25	58
1956	420	181	99	23	54
1957	409	144	56	14	38
1958	405	128	40	10	31
1959	464	178	83	18	46
1960	491	193	95	19	49
1961	495	184	84	17	45
1962	494	180	81	16	44

SOURCE: Northern Rhodesia, Chamber of Mines, *Yearbook,* 1963, p. 21.

Table 100. *Contribution of the Northern Rhodesia copper-mining industry to domestic exports, 1954–62*

	Value of domestic exports [a] from		Value of copper and cobalt exports from Northern Rhodesia [c] (£ millions)	Percentage contribution of copper and cobalt to exports of	
Year	Rhodesia and Nyasaland (£ millions)	Northern Rhodesia [b] (£ millions)		Rhodesia and Nyasaland [c]	Northern Rhodesia
1954	150·3	93·7	88·2	58·7	94·1
1955	176·2	117·5	112·0	63·6	95·3
1956	185·4	123·0	115·8	62·5	94·2
1957	159·3	91·3	84·7	53·2	92·8
1958	138·2	74·7	69·6	50·4	93·2
1959	189·7	117·5	109·6	57·8	93·3
1960	207·1	129·2	121·6	58·7	94·1
1961	207·3	119·7	111·5	53·8	93·1
1962	209·5	119·6	110·4	52·7	92·3

[a] Domestic exports of merchandise F.O.R. plus net gold sales.
[b] Exports to destinations outside the Federation of Rhodesia and Nyasaland.
[c] Revised figures.

SOURCE: Northern Rhodesia, Chamber of Mines, *Yearbook,* 1963, p. 22.

The companies have helped, in addition, to finance a number of research projects outside the mining field. One of the most important of these, for example, was an investigation into the production of nitrogenous fertilizers. The companies also supported an agricultural survey of the Kafue Flats, where the fishing industry and sugar cultivation have considerably developed over recent years. By expanding their activities, and also by assuming wider responsi-

Table 99. *Estimated taxation paid by the Northern Rhodesia copper-mining industry, 1954–62*
(calendar years)

	1954 £000s	1955 £000s	1956 £000s	1957 £000s	1958 £000s	1959 £000s	1960 £000s	1961 £000s	1962 £000s
Paid by copper mining companies									
Income tax on profits	17,442	16,491	21,421	24,169	12,556	6,643	14,272	17,872	16,315
Customs duties on imports	200	200	234	223	125	92	137	131	143
Mining, vehicle licences, etc.	20	20	41	19	13	22	28	28	30
Paid by British South Africa Company									
Northern Rhodesia minerals tax on copper mining industry royalties	1,762	2,714	2,762	1,795	1,365	2,568	2,786	2,607	2,548
Income tax attributable to copper-mining industry royalties	2,869	2,686	3,693	4,446	3,148	2,174	3,399	4,600	3,982
Paid by employees (including head-office staff)									
Income tax	634	712	1,115	1,476	760	602	1,158	1,305	1,370
Other	390	490	560	540	520	570	620	660	690
Total	23,317	23,313	29,826	32,668	18,487	12,671	22,400	27,203	25,078
of which accruing to									
Federal government	11,735	11,266	14,778	16,819	9,158	5,418	10,413	13,014	11,968
Northern Rhodesia government	8,246	8,874	10,854	11,027	6,604	5,651	8,797	10,161	9,428
Southern Rhodesia government	2,283	2,171	2,871	3,304	1,895	1,126	2,238	2,827	2,586
Nyasaland government	1,053	1,002	1,323	1,518	830	476	952	1,201	1,096
Total revenue of federal and territorial governments, excluding inter-government payments	54,400	69,600	80,900	90,100	84,200	82,700	92,100	107,300	113,600
Percentage paid by Northern Rhodesia copper-mining industry	42·9%	33·5%	36·9%	36·3%	22·0%	15·3%	24·3%	25·4%	22·1%

NOTE: Income tax includes basic tax and territorial surcharge except in the case of individuals resident in Northern Rhodesia who paid basic tax only.

SOURCE: Northern Rhodesia, Chamber of Mines, *Yearbook*, 1963, p. 23.

bilities, the mining concerns have taken a first step towards eliminating the disparities of the dual economy that the companies created in the first place. Much remains to be done before the economic and social problems created by the growth of mining and related industries can be resolved and the benefits accruing from the economic development promoted by mining shared by the mass of African people.

BIBLIOGRAPHY

Allan, William. *The African husbandman*. New York, 1965.

Baldwin, Robert E. *Economic development and export growth: a study of Northern Rhodesia, 1920–1960*. Los Angeles and Berkeley, University of California Press, 1966.

Barber, William J. *The economy of British Central Africa: a case study of economic development in a dualistic society*. London, Oxford University Press, 1961.

Bertieaux, Raymond. *Aspects de l'industrialisation en Afrique centrale*. Brussels, Institut des Relations Internationales, 1953.

Cole, Monica M. *South Africa*. London, 1961.

Collins, Robert O. *King Leopold, England and the Upper Nile, 1899–1909*. New Haven and London, Yale University Press, 1968.

Davis, J. Merle. *Modern industry and the African*. London, 1933.

Day, John R. *Railways of southern Africa*. London, 1963.

d'Erlanger, Emile B., baron. *The history of the construction and finance of the Rhodesian transport system*. London, 1938.

Duffy, James. *Portuguese Africa*. Cambridge, Mass., Harvard University Press, 1959.

Fetter, Bruce S. 'Elisabethville and Lubumbashi: the segmentary growth of a colonial city, 1910–1945'. Ph.D. thesis, University of Wisconsin, 1968.

Frankel, S. Herbert. 'Capital and capital supply in relation to the development of Africa', in *Economic development for Africa south of the Sahara*, E. A. G. Robinson, ed. London, 1964.

Capital investment in Africa: its course and effects. London, Oxford University Press, 1938.

Gold and international equity investment. London, Institute of Economic Affairs, 1969.

Investment and the return to equity capital in the South African gold mining industry, 1887–1965: an international comparison. Cambridge, Mass., Harvard University Press, 1967.

Gann, L. H. *The birth of a plural society: the development of Northern Rhodesia under the British South Africa Company, 1894–1914*. Manchester University Press, 1958.

'The Northern Rhodesian copper industry and the world of copper, 1923–1952', *Rhodes-Livingstone Journal*, 1955, no. 18.

A history of Northern Rhodesia: early days to 1953. London, 1964.

A history of Southern Rhodesia: early days to 1934. London, 1965.

Gann, L. H., and Michael Gelfand. *Huggins of Rhodesia*. London, 1964.

Gelfand, Michael. *Tropical victory: an account of the influence of medicine on the history of Southern Rhodesia*. Cape Town, 1953.

Northern Rhodesia in the days of the Charter: a medical and social study, 1878–1924. Oxford, 1961.

Gould, Peter R. *The development of the transportation pattern in Ghana*. Evanston, Northwestern University, 1960.

Gregory, Sir Theodor. *Ernest Oppenheimer and the economic development of Southern Africa*. Cape Town, Oxford University Press, 1962.

424

Haefele, Edwin T., and Eleanor B. Steinberg. *Government controls on transport: an African case*. Washington, Brookings Institution, 1965.

Hammond, Richard J. *Portugal and Africa, 1815–1910: a study in uneconomic imperialism*. Stanford University Press, 1966.

Hance, William A. *The geography of modern Africa*. New York, Columbia University Press, 1964.

Hance, William A., and Irene S. van Dongen, 'Beira, Mozambique, Gateway to Central Africa', *Annals of the Association of American Geographers*, 1957, **47**, no. 4.

'Lourenço Marques in Delagoa Bay', *Economic Geography*, 1957, **33**.

'The port of Lobito and the Benguela Railway', *Geographical Review*, 1956, **46**, no. 4.

Hellen, John A. *Rural economic development in Zambia, 1890–1964*. Munich, Institut für Wirtschaftsforschung, München Afrika-Studienstelle, 1968.

Horwitz, Ralph. *The political economy of South Africa*. London, 1967.

Hoyle, B. S., and D. Hilling, eds. *Seaports and development in tropical Africa*. London, 1970.

Hutchinson, Robert, and George Martelli. *Robert's people: the life of Sir Robert Williams, Bart., 1860–1938*. London, 1971.

Huybrechts, André, 'Les voies d'accès et d'évacuation du Congo', *Cahiers Economiques et Sociaux*, 1969, **7**, no. 1.

Transports et structures de développement au Congo: étude du progrès économique de 1900 à 1970. Université de Louvain, 1970.

International African Institute. *Social implications of industrialization and urbanization in Africa south of the Sahara*. Paris, UNESCO, 1956.

Kamarck, Andrew M. *The economics of African development*. Rev. ed. New York, 1971.

Katzen, Leo. *Gold and the South African economy*. Cape Town, 1964.

Katzenellenbogen, Simon E. *Railways and the Copper Mines of Katanga*. London, 1973.

Kuczynski, Robert R. *Demographic survey of the British colonial empire*. vol. II. London, Oxford University Press, 1949.

Lux, André. *Le marché du travail en Afrique noire*. Louvain, Institut de Recherches Economiques, Sociales et Politiques, 1962.

Morgan, W. B., and J. C. Pugh. *West Africa*. London, 1969.

O'Connor, A. M. *The geography of tropical African development*. Oxford, 1971.

Pedler, F. J. *Economic geography of West Africa*. London, 1955.

Pim, Sir Alan. *Colonial agricultural production: the contribution made by native peasants and by foreign enterprise*. London, Oxford University Press, 1946.

Prain, Sir R. L. 'The stabilization of labour on the Rhodesian Copperbelt', *African Affairs*, 1956, **55**.

Raphael, Lois A. C. *The Cape-to-Cairo dream: a study in British imperialism*. New York, Columbia University Press, 1936.

Shaffer, N. Manfred. *The competitive position of the port of Durban*. Evanston, Northwestern University, Department of Geography, 1965.

Stengers, Jean. 'Léopold II et la fixation des frontières du Congo', *Le Flambeau*, 1963, **46**.

Swindell, Kenneth. 'Iron ore mining in West Africa: some recent developments in Guinea, Sierra Leone, and Liberia', *Economic Geography*, 1967, **43**.

Taylor, John V., and Dorothea A. Lehmán. *Christians of the Copperbelt: the growth of the church in Northern Rhodesia*. London, 1961.

Thompson, C. H., and H. W. Woodruff. *Economic development in Rhodesia and Nyasaland*. London, 1955.

Union Minière du Haut-Katanga, 1906–1956. Brussels, 1956.

Van der Horst, Sheila T. *Native labour in South Africa*. London, Oxford University Press, 1942; reissue, London, 1971.

Watson, Sir Malcolm. *African highway: the battle for health in Central Africa*. London, 1953.

White, H. P., and M. B. Gleave. *An economic geography of West Africa*. London, 1971.

Wills, A. J. *An introduction to the history of Central Africa*. London, Oxford University Press, 1964.

Wilson, Francis. *Labour in the South African gold mines, 1911–1969*. Cambridge University Press, 1972.

EXTERNAL TRADE AND
INTERNAL DEVELOPMENT

by

GERALD M. MEIER

This chapter examines the impact of international trade on domestic development. To do this, it applies models from the theory of comparative advantage and from the theory of export-led growth. We must take care to note that these are both descriptive and normative models: descriptive in the sense that they use positive language to explain what is or what might have been; normative in the sense that they also use prescriptive language in stating what ought to be. Thus, when applied to the problems of foreign trade and internal development in Africa over the period 1870–1960, our models may not only illuminate what actually did occur but may also evaluate the deviation of the 'actual' from the 'ideal'.

The problem

After 1870, Africa began increasingly to be opened to world markets. Trade outside was in many respects easier than within the continent. Although Africa is a late-comer to world trade, the increases in mineral exports and exports of commercial crops have been rapid. Although it is well known that mineral exports rose markedly after the discovery of the Kimberley diamond-mines in 1867 and the Rand gold deposits in 1886, it is not so commonly realized that African exports of commercial crops have grown more rapidly than the exports of most of the tropical countries of Asia and Latin America.[1]

Our problem is to assess the significance of this rise in exports for the development of African economies. Did international trade contribute positively to domestic development? Or, on the contrary, did production for export actually restrain the pace and impair the quality of domestic development?

To be equipped to answer these questions, we first turn to the theoretical foundations of this problem. It will be seen that theory offers three different views of the relationship between trade and development—a positive, a negative and an eclectic view.

The positive view

The orthodox interpretation as expounded by classical and neo-classical economists is that foreign trade can be a propelling force in development. Adam Smith's model of foreign trade postulates the existence of idle land and labour before a country is opened to world markets. The excess resources are used to

[1] W. Arthur Lewis, *Aspects of tropical trade, 1883–1965* (Stockholm, 1969), p. 15. In 1913, sub-Saharan Africa's exports were only 6·2 per cent of tropical trade. By 1937 they were 13·3; by 1955, 18·2; and by 1965, 21·4 per cent of tropical trade.

427

produce a surplus of goods for export, and trade thereby 'vents' a surplus productive capacity that would otherwise be unused. In Smith's words,

Between whatever places foreign trade is carried on, they all of them derive two distinct benefits from it. It carries out that surplus part of the produce of their land and labour for which there is no demand among them, and brings back in return for it something else for which there is a demand. It gives a value to their superfluities, by exchanging them for something else, which may satisfy a part of their wants, and increase their enjoyments. By means of it, the narrowness of the home market does not hinder the division of labour in any particular branch of art or manufacture from being carried to the highest perfection. By opening a more extensive market for whatever part of the produce of their labour may exceed the home consumption, it encourages them to improve its production powers, and to augment its annual produce to the utmost, and thereby to increase the real revenue and wealth of the society.[2]

This idea of 'vent for surplus' assumes that resources are not fully employed prior to trade, and that exports are increased without a decrease in domestic production, with the result that trade raises the level of economic activity. As Smith expresses it:

When the produce of any particular branch of industry exceeds what the demand of the country requires, the surplus must be sent abroad, and exchanged for something for which there is a demand at home. Without such exportation, a part of the productive labour of the country must cease, and the value of its annual produce diminish.[3]

More generally, classical economists considered comparative advantage as determining the pattern of trade. Not the use of surplus resources but resource reallocation allowed trade to benefit a country by promoting a more efficient international allocation of resources. Without any increase in resources or technological change, every trading country is able to enjoy a higher real income by specializing in production according to its comparative advantage and trading. The exports have instrumental significance as the intermediate goods used for the 'indirect production' of imports: exports allow the country to 'buy' imports on more favourable terms than if produced directly at home. The gain from trade is on the import side; and it is significant that the gains are also mutual, realized by all the trading countries. By specializing in commodities for which its costs are comparatively lowest, a trading nation would, in Ricardo's words, increase 'the sum of commodities and mass of enjoyments'; in modern jargon, trade-optimized production.

Although specialization according to comparative advantage yields the direct benefits of international exchange, there are in addition dynamic aspects of trade that are relevant for the growth-transmitting effects of trade above and

[2] Adam Smith, *An inquiry into the nature and causes of the wealth of nations,* Edwin Cannan, ed. (New York, 1937), p. 415.

[3] For more detailed discussion of Smith's theory, See Hla Myint, 'The classical theory of international trade and the underdeveloped countries', *Economic Journal,* 1958, **68,** pp. 317–31. Myint indicates that Smith's concept of surplus productive capacity is not merely a matter of surplus land by itself but surplus land combined with surplus labour; and the surplus labour is then linked up with his concept of 'unproductive labour' (p. 323). This interpretation allows Smith's vent-for-surplus model of trade and growth to be consistent with W. Arthur Lewis's model of development with unlimited supplies of labour. See R. E. Caves, ' "Vent for surplus" models of trade and growth', in R. E. Baldwin *et al., Trade, growth, and the balance of payments: essays in honor of Gottfried Haberler* (Chicago, 1965), pp. 95–115.

beyond the static gains. Classical and neo-classical economists did not make the dynamic aspects of trade central to their thought; but to the extent that they did consider the effects of trade on development, they saw no conflict between a country's conformity with its comparative advantage and the acceleration of its development. Indeed, John Stuart Mill stated that trade, according to comparative advantage, results in a 'more efficient employment of the productive forces of the world', and that this might be considered the 'direct economical advantage of foreign trade. But there are, besides, indirect effects, which must be counted as benefits of a high order.' A most important 'indirect' dynamic benefit, according to Mill, is

the tendency of every extension of the market to improve the processes of production. A country which produces for a larger market than its own, can introduce a more extended division of labour, can make greater use of machinery, and is more likely to make inventions and improvements in the processes of production.

Widening the extent of the market, inducing innovations and increasing productivity through foreign trade allow a country to overcome the diseconomies of being a small country.

Another important consideration, according to Mill, 'principally applicable to an early age of industrial advancement', is that

a people may be in a quiescent, indolent, uncultivated state, with all their tastes either fully satisfied or entirely undeveloped, and they may fail to put forth the whole of their productive energies for want of any sufficient object of desire. The opening of a foreign trade, by making them acquainted with new objects, or tempting them by the easier acquisition of things which they had not previously thought attainable, sometimes works a sort of industrial revolution in a country whose resources were previously undeveloped for want of energy and ambition in the people: inducing those who were satisfied with scanty comforts and little work, to work harder for the gratification of their new tastes, and even to save, and accumulate capital, for still more complete satisfaction of those tastes at a future time.[4]

Further, Mill stated that trade benefits the less developed countries through

the introduction of foreign arts, which raises the returns derivable from additional capital to a rate corresponding to the low strength of accumulation; and the importation of foreign capital which renders the increase of production no longer exclusively dependent on the thrift or providence of the inhabitants themselves, while it places before them a stimulating example, and by instilling new ideas and breaking the chain of habit, if not by improving the actual condition of the population, tends to create in them new wants, increased ambition, and greater thought for the future.[5]

The indirect benefits of trade on development are therefore of three kinds: (1) those that widen the extent of the market, induce innovations and increase productivity; (2) those that increase savings and capital accumulation; and (3) those that have an educative effect in instilling new wants and tastes and in transferring technology, skills and entrepreneurship. This emphasis is on the supply side of the development process—the opportunity that trade gives a poor country to remove domestic shortages, to overcome the diseconomies of the small size of its domestic market and to accelerate the 'learning rate' of its economy.

[4] John Stuart Mill, *Principles of political economy*, 2 vols. (London, 1848), vol. II, bk. III, sec. 5, ch. 17.　　　　　　　[5] *Ibid.*, vol. I, bk. I, sec. 1, ch. 13.

For these several reasons, the traditional conclusion has been that the gains from trade do not result merely in a once-over change in resource allocation, but are also continually merging with the gains from development: international trade transforms existing production functions and increases the productivity of the economy over time. If trade increases the capacity for development, then the larger the volume of trade, the greater should be the potential for development.

More recently, various export-based models of growth have been formulated to present a macro-dynamic view of how an economy's growth can be determined by expansion in its exports. One version of the export-based model is that of the staple theory of growth.

The term 'staple' designates a raw material or resource-intensive commodity occupying a dominant position in the country's exports. It has a structural similarity to the vent-for-surplus view in so far as 'surplus' resources initially exist and are subsequently exported. It also has some affinity with Lewis's model of development with an unlimited supply of labour when the surplus to be vented through trade is one of labour and not natural resources.[6]

The staple theory postulates that with the discovery of a primary product in which the country has a comparative advantage, or with an increase in the demand for its comparative advantage commodity, there is an expansion of a resource-based export commodity; this in turn induces higher rates of growth of aggregate and *per capita* income. Previously idle or undiscovered resources are brought into use, creating a return to these resources and being consistent with venting a surplus through trade. The export of a primary product also has effects on the rest of the economy through diminishing underemployment or unemployment, inducing a higher rate of domestic saving and investment, attracting an inflow of factor inputs into the expanding export sector and establishing linkages with other sectors of the economy. Although the rise in exports is induced by greater demand, there are supply responses within the economy that increase the productivity of the exporting economy.

The staple theory has some relation also to Rostow's leading-sector analysis in so far as the staple-export sector may be the leading sector of the economy, growing more rapidly and propelling the rest of the economy along with its growth. In Rostow's analysis, however, a primary-producing sector can be a leading sector only if it also involves processing of the primary product.

A more general analysis of the effects of trade on the rate of growth has been considered by Corden.[7] Instead of the 'demand-motored' model of the staple theory, Corden analyses a 'supply-motored' model that emphasizes growth in factor supplies and productivity. After a country is opened to world trade, five different effects may be distinguished. First is the 'impact effect' corresponding to the static gain from trade: current real income is raised. Then there may be the 'capital-accumulation effect': an increase in capital accumulation results when parts of the static gain are invested. This amounts to a transfer of real income from the present to the future instead of an increase in present consump-

[6] W. Arthur Lewis, 'Economic development with unlimited supplies of labour', *Manchester School of Economic and Social Studies*, May 1954, **20**, pp. 139–91; 'Unlimited labour: further notes', *Manchester School of Economic and Social Studies*, Jan. 1958, **26**, pp. 1–32.

[7] W. Max Corden, 'The effects of trade on the rate of growth', in *Trade, balance of payments and growth*, Jagdish N. Bhagwati *et al.*, eds. (Amsterdam, 1971), pp. 117–43.

tion. Third may be the 'substitution effect'. This may result from a possible fall in the relative price of investment goods to consumption goods if investment goods are import-intensive. This would lead to an increase in the ratio of investment to consumption and an increase in the rate of growth. The fourth possibility is an 'income-distribution effect': there will be a shift in income towards the factors that are used intensively in the production of exports. If the savings propensities differ between sectors or factors, this will have an effect on the overall savings propensity and hence on capital accumulation. Finally, there is the 'factor-weight effect'. This considers the relative productivity of capital and labour and recognizes that if the rate of growth of output is a weighted average of capital and labour growth rates (with a consant returns-to-scale aggregate production function), then if exports rise, and exports use the faster-growing factor of production, the rate of growth of exports will rise more rapidly. These effects are all cumulative, and intensify the increase in real income over time as a result of opening a country to foreign trade.

The positive view of trade and development thus emphasizes the direct gain that comes from international specialization plus the additional support to a country's development through a number of spread effects within the domestic economy.

The negative view

Opposing the preceding analysis are critics who state that international trade has actually operated to the detriment of the poor country's development. An older group of critics concentrated on the unfavourable effects of imperialism or 'colonial exploitation'. The neo-Marxian or 'revisionist' formulation of empire-building is rooted in the development of capitalism and a deliberately exploitative mercantile-type of colonialism that, it is alleged, conquers, plunders and extorts tribute.[8]

More recent critics do not base their critique on any notion of deliberate exploitation by the advanced countries but instead emphasize the disequalizing effects of the free play of international market forces. As argued by Gunnar Myrdal, for instance, 'Market forces will tend cumulatively to accentuate international inequalities', and 'a quite normal result of unhampered trade between two countries, of which one is industrial and the other underdeveloped, is the initiation of a cumulative process towards the impoverishment and stagnation of the latter'.[9]

According to this view, international trade may set up not only spread effects but also backwash effects. For the less developed countries, the backwash effects may be stronger and more pervasive, thereby inhibiting their development. Myrdal states that

---

[8] For some clarification of the ambiguous and emotive notions that surround the use of the term 'imperialism', see Sir William Keith Hancock, 'Agenda for the study of British imperial history, 1850–1950', *Journal of Economic History*, 1953, **13**, pp. 257 ff.; D. K. Fieldhouse, 'Imperialism: an historiographical revision', *Economic History Review*, 2nd ser., Dec. 1961, **14**, no. 2, pp. 187–209; David S. Landes, 'Some thoughts on the nature of economic imperialism', *Journal of Economic History*, Dec. 1961, **21**, no. 4, pp. 496–512; and Jean Suret-Canale, *French colonialism in tropical Africa, 1900–1945* (New York, 1971). See also Robert Rhodes, 'Bibliography: on studying imperialism', *Review of Radical Political Economics*, Spring 1971, **3**, no. 1, pp. 80–5. [9] Gunnar Myrdal, *An international economy* (New York, 1956), pp. 55 and 95.

if left to take its own course, economic development is a process of circular and cumulative causation which tends to award its favors to those who are already endowed and even to thwart the efforts of those who happen to live in regions that are lagging behind. The back setting effects of economic expansion in other regions dominate the more powerful, the poorer a country is.[10]

There appear to be three main strands in the argument of those who uphold this negative view. It is alleged that development has been retarded by, first, the unfavourable effects of international factor movements; second, the international operation of the 'demonstration effect' on consumption; and third, a secular deterioration in the terms of trade for a primary-producing, less developed country.

The effects of international factor movements, it is claimed, have been adverse in creating a highly unbalanced structure of production. The inflow of foreign capital develops only the country's natural resources for export, to the neglect of production in the domestic sector. Foreign enterprises may transform the export sector into the most advanced sector of the economy, but this remains a foreign enclave which does not spill over into the indigenous economy. When the enclaves have been enlarged, as in mining or in the plantation system, they have seldom been integrated into the local economy, but have remained attached to the interests of a metropolitan state. The result, it is alleged, has simply been the creation of a dual economy in which production is export-biased, and the export sector remains an island of development surrounded by a backward, low-productivity sector.

One version of the dualistic character of poor countries emphasizes the 'factor proportions problem' or the 'technological dualism' associated with the differences in factor endowment and techniques of production in the advanced 'capitalist' sector and the backward 'pre-industrial' or traditional sector. The advanced sector is composed of plantation or other large-scale commercial agriculture, mines, oil-fields or refineries which produce for export, whereas the backward rural sector is dominated by peasant agriculture, handicrafts and small-scale industry producing for local demand. It is contended that the result of this dualism has been that capital, especially foreign capital, flowed into the advanced sector to produce mineral and agricultural products for export markets. But the rate of investment in this sector and the labour employment opportunities in the capital-intensive activities did not keep pace with population growth. Nor did the techniques of production in the advanced sector induce an increase in productivity or greater output elsewhere in the economy.

It is argued also that foreign-owned plantations, mining enterprises and foreign trading firms have frequently acquired monopsony and monopoly positions. As labourers, the indigenous population has confronted the monopsonistic power of foreign plantations and mining concerns. As peasant producers, they have faced a small group of exporting and processing firms with monopsonistic power in buying the native crop, and as consumers they have had to purchase imported commodities from monopolistic sellers or distributors of these commodities.

Further, it is said that the stimulating income effects of foreign investment have been lost through income leakages overseas. Not only has there been a

[10] Gunnar Myrdal, *Development and underdevelopment* (Cairo, 1956), pp. 9–10.

drain of profits and interest to the metropolitan countries, but the poor recipient countries have also had to import from the richer countries the capital equipment associated with any investment that has been induced by a growth in their exports. The implication is that a given amount of investment in the poor country has generated a much smaller amount of income than the same amount of investment would have generated in a more advanced and less dependent country.

It is believed also that the immigration of unskilled labour into poor countries has reinforced the dualistic structure of their economies. In some countries that were at one time sparsely inhabited, the mass immigration of labour into plantations and mines allowed the supply of labour to remain elastic at a conventional low wage rate. In other countries, labour immigration to richer countries has not been sufficient to exert an upward pressure on wages. Thus it is argued that the international migration of capital and labour have not been conducive to development but instead have had backwash effects.

Beyond the adverse consequences of international factor movements, it is claimed also that the international operation of the demonstration effect has been a handicap for the developing country. It is asserted that the demonstration of advanced consumption standards in richer countries has excessively raised the propensity to consume in the poorer countries and has thereby limited capital accumulation.

The third major criticism of international forces rests on the contention that there has been an international transfer of income from the poor to the rich countries through a secular deterioration in the commodity terms of trade of the poor countries. One thesis is that the commodity terms of trade between industrial and primary-producing countries shift in favour of industrial allegedly because monopolistic elements in their product and factor markets allow these countries to retain the benefit of their technical progress in the form of rising factor incomes, whereas in primary-producing countries the gains in productivity are distributed in price reductions.

Another group of dissenters now emphasizes not the market relations, as in the preceding allegations, but 'power relations'. Thus, Hymer and Resnick stress the importance of what they term the missing political equations in international trade theory and attempt to explain why the growth of the international economy over the course of the past few centuries has failed to equalize factor prices, but instead has created a dualism between the developed and underdeveloped areas of the world.[11] Considering shifts in the power structures that have resulted from trade, Hymer and Resnick construct a model of trade which might be summarized in the following simple balance equation of the gains and losses from trade:

$$\begin{matrix} \text{Gains to élite} \\ \text{in Europe} \end{matrix} + \begin{matrix} \text{Gains (or losses) to} \\ \text{majority in Europe} \end{matrix} = \begin{matrix} \text{Gains from} \\ \text{trade} \end{matrix}$$

$$- \begin{matrix} \text{Gains to élite} \\ \text{in underdeveloped} \\ \text{countries} \end{matrix} + \begin{matrix} \text{Losses of} \\ \text{exploited} \end{matrix} - \begin{matrix} \text{Deadweight} \\ \text{loss} \end{matrix}$$

[11] Stephen H. Hymer and Steven A. Resnick, 'International trade and uneven development', in *Trade, balance of payments and growth*, pp. 473–94.

The deadweight loss has some affinity to the creation of surplus value in neo-Marxist doctrine.

Referring specifically to the role of colonies in trade, Hymer and Resnick have contended that colonial policy 'squeezed the traditional economy to create an elastic supply of labour' and that it biased infrastructure towards exports 'in order to transfer the surplus to the center in the form of lower prices'. The authors argue that this was accomplished by a variety of devices: labour taxes or poll taxes 'to stimulate an exodus from the "traditional" economy into the "commercial" economy'; government seizure of land or creation of a landlord class, 'thus reducing the opportunity cost of wage labour'; land concentration, intensification of tenure arrangements and the growth of indebtedness.

The main contention of Hymer and Resnick is that 'the gains from trade generated . . . were shared unevenly' between the colony and the centre. 'The striking feature . . . is that the standard of living for the vast majority of the population of Africa . . . rose very slowly in sharp contrast to the progress at the center.'

Another significant part of Hymer and Resnick's argument is that

the gains from trade were partly captured by local élites (some of whom were foreigners from the mother country) who accumulated land, capital, education, or the rights to higher paying employment in the government bureaucracy or in the commercial economy. Often an alien complex of production was established where the peasant cultivated the soil or worked in the mines, a foreign mercantile class grew in strength . . . and the Europeans controlled the import-export trade as well as determined colonial expenditure and labour policies. The distribution of income reflected the political power of this economic structure.[12]

The gains from export growth, it is contended, went to the government (in the form of increased revenues), to the urban centres and to local and foreign élites.

According to this variant of the negative view of transmitting development through trade, Hymer and Resnick conclude that they 'would argue that political factors were an important if not dominant determinant. In our view, the observed uneven development represented uneven power, and the resulting distribution of income and demand was a social phenomenon rather than a technical one.'[13]

The eclectic view

Instead of over-generalizing in terms of either the positive or negative view of the transmission of development through trade, we adopt an approach that allows some elements of each view to be present or not in different cases. The essence of the development-through-trade model is that the export sector should not remain an enclave, separate from the rest of the economy, but that an integrated process should be established. Avoiding the polarity of the preceding views, a more eclectic view would consider the integrative process by focusing on the varying strength of the stimuli in different countries from their exports according to the nature of their export base, and on the different response mechanisms within the exporting countries. The strength of the potential for de-

[12] *Ibid.*, pp. 485–6.　　　　　　[13] *Ibid.*, p. 488.

velopment through trade will differ according to the strength of the forces in the integrative process.

Different export commodities will provide different stimuli, according to the technological characteristics of their production. The nature of the export-goods production function (namely, the technical relationship between physical inputs of the factors of production and the resultant physical output) has a close bearing on the extent of other secondary changes elsewhere in the economy beyond the primary increase in export output. With the use of different combinations of inputs to produce different types of export commodities, there will be different rates of learning and different linkage effects. The degree to which the various exports are processed is highly significant in the determination of external economies associated with the learning process: the processing of primary-product exports by modern methods is likely to benefit other activities through the spread of technical knowledge, training of labour, demonstration of new production techniques that might be adapted elsewhere in the economy and the acquisition of organizational and supervisory skills.

In contrast, growth of the export sector will have a negligible carry-over if its techniques of production are the same as those already in use in other sectors, or if its expansion occurs by a simple widening of production without any change in production functions. If the introduction or expansion of export crops involves simple methods of production that do not differ markedly from the traditional techniques already used in subsistence agriculture, the stimulus to development will clearly be less than if the growth in exports entailed the introduction of new skills and more productive recombinations of factors of production. More favourable linkages may stem from exports that require skilled labour than from those using unskilled labour. The influence of skill requirements may operate in various ways: greater incentives for capital formation may be provided through education; on-the-job training in the export sector may be disseminated at little real cost through the movement of workers into other sectors or occupations; skilled workers may be a source of entrepreneurship; skilled workers may save more of their wage incomes than unskilled workers.[14] The level of entrepreneurial skill induced by the development of an export is also highly significant. The level will be expanded if the development of the export commodity offers sufficient challenge and instils abilities usable in other sectors, but is not so high as to require the importing of a transient class of skilled managerial labour.

Although the processing of a primary product provides forward linkages in the sense that the output of one sector becomes an input for another sector, it is also important to have backward linkages. When some exports grow, they provide a strong stimulus for expansion in the input-supplying industries elsewhere in the economy. These backward linkages may be in agriculture or in other industries supplying inputs to the expanding export sector, or in social overhead capital. The importance of linkages has been stressed by Hirschman.[15]

The notion is emphasized also by Perroux, who refers to a developing enterprise as a 'motor unit' when it increases its demands on its suppliers for raw

[14] Richard E. Caves, 'Export-led growth and the new economic history', in *Trade, balance of payments and growth*, pp. 403–42.

[15] Albert O. Hirschman, *The strategy of economic development* (New Haven, Yale University Press, 1958), ch. 6.

materials or communicates new techniques to another enterprise. The 'induction effect' that the motor unit exerts upon another unit may be considered in two components that frequently occur in combination: (1) a dimension effect that is augmentation of demand by one enterprise to another by increasing its supply; and (2), an innovation effect that introduces an innovation which for a given quantity of factors of production yields the same quantity of production at a lower price and/or a better quality. When a motor unit is interlinked with its surrounding environment, Perroux refers to a growth pole or a development pole.[16] The emphasis on generating new skills, innovations in the export sector or other sectors linked to exports and technical change are important in determining the learning rate of the economy.

Beyond this, the nature of the production function of the exports commodity will also determine the distribution of income, and, in turn, the pattern of local demand and impact on local employment. The use of different factor combinations affects the distribution of income in the sense that the relative shares of profits, wages, interest and rent will vary according to the labour intensity or capital intensity of the export production and the nature of its organization—whether it is mining, plantation agriculture or peasant farming. If the internal distribution of the export income favours groups with a higher propensity to consume domestic goods than to import, the resultant distribution of income will be more effective in raising the demand for home-produced products; and to the extent that these home-produced products are labour-intensive, there will be more of an impact on employment. In contrast, if income is distributed to those who have a higher propensity to import, the leakage through consumption of imported goods will be greater. If income increments go to those who are likely to save large portions, the export sector may also make a greater contribution to the financing of growth in other sectors.

If the export commodity is subject to substantial economies of scale in its production, this will tend to imply large capital requirements for the establishment of enterprises, and hence extra-regional or foreign borrowing. This may then lead to an outward flow of profits instead of providing profit income for local reinvestment. But this is only part of the impact of the foreign investment. For a full appraisal, it would be necessary to consider all the benefits and costs of the foreign investment. And these too will vary according to the nature of the export sector in which the foreign investment occurs.

Finally, the repercussions from exports will also differ according to the degree of fluctuation in export proceeds. Disruptions in the flow of foreign-exchange receipts make the development process discontinuous; the greater the degree of instability, the more difficult it is to maintain steady employment, because there will be disturbing effects on real income, government revenue, capital formation, resource allocation and the capacity to import according to the degree of amplitude of fluctuation in foreign-exchange receipts. To the extent that different exports vary in their degree of fluctuation, and in revenue earned and retained at home, their repercussions on the domestic economy will also differ. Depending on the various characteristics of the country's export, we

---

[16] François Perroux, 'Multinational investment and the analysis of development and integration poles', in *Multinational investment in the economic development and integration of Latin America* (Bogotá, Inter-American Development Bank, April 1968), pp. 99–103.

may thus infer how the strength of the integrative process, in terms of the stimulus from exports, will differ among countries.

In summary, we would normally expect the stimulating forces of the integrative process to be stronger under the following conditions: the higher the growth rate of the export sector, the greater the direct impact of the export sector on employment and personal income; the more the expansion of exports has a 'learning effect' in terms of increasing productivity and instilling new skills, the more the export sector is supplied through domestic inputs instead of imports; the more the distribution of export income favours those with a marginal propensity to consume domestic goods instead of imports, the more productive is the investment resulting from any saving of export income; the more extensive are the externalities and linkages connected with the export sector, the more stable are the export receipts that are retained at home.

After analysing the character of a country's export base for an indication of the strength of the stimulus to development provided by its export commodities, we must go on to examine the strength of the response or diffusion mechanism within the domestic economy for evidence of how receptive the domestic economy is to the stimulus from exports. The strength of the integrative process, in terms of the response mechanism to the export stimulus, will depend on the extent of market imperfections in the domestic economy and also on non-economic barriers in the general environment. The integrative forces are stronger under the following conditions: the more developed the infrastructure of the economy, the more market institutions are developed, the more extensive the development of human resources, the less are the price distortions that affect resource allocations and the greater is the capacity to bear risks. Our view of the carry-over should stress not only the mechanical linkages but also a more evolutionary (and hence biological rather than mechanical) analogy that recognizes societal responses. What matters is not simply the creation of modern enterprise or modern sectors but modernization as a process. This involves not simply physical production or mechanical linkages but a change in socio-economic traits throughout the society, and an intangible atmosphere that relates to change in values, in character, in attitudes, in the learning of new behaviour patterns and in institutions.

In sum, the effects of a strong integrative process will be the following: (1) an acceleration in the learning rate of the economy; (2) an enrichment of the economic and social infrastructure (transportation, public services, health, education); (3) an expansion of the supply of entrepreneurship (and a managerial and administrative class); and (4) a mobilization of a larger surplus above consumption in the form of taxation and saving. These effects constitute the country's development foundations. Once these foundations are laid, the country's economy can be more readily transformed through diversification in primary production and the service industries, new commodity exports, and industrialization via import substitution and export substitution.

According to the eclectic view, we would therefore give more emphasis to the integrative process of which the export sector is a part. The essence is the avoidance of an enclave type of development that contributes little to the country's learning rate, infrastructure, entrepreneurship or general financial capacity for development. If there is this lack of carry-over, trade will not promote development (unlike the positive view); but the lack of carry-over may be the result of domestic impediments that cut short the stimulus, and not of the character of international trade (unlike the assertions of the negative view).

Empirical considerations

To be comprehensive, our response to the questions posed in the preceding sections would have to cover not only the nature and scope of the development that actually did occur, but also the alternatives of what might have been, as well as what ought to have been, for each African country during the precolonial and colonial eras. This is clearly an impossible undertaking within the confines of the present study. To be manageable, our empirical considerations must perforce be reduced to a few cases, selected to yield some insights of a comparative analysis. At best, we can hope to provide only some type of interpretative framework for the more extensive country and industry studies.

A typology might therefore be helpful. Various typologies are possible—ranging from considerations of geography and transportation facilities to political and administrative practices. For our purposes, the most instructive typology might focus on the economic organization of the country's export base—distinguishing whether the exports were foodstuffs, industrial raw materials or minerals, and whether the export production was characterized by peasant production, estates or plantations, or mines. From this typology we can select for special consideration cocoa exports from the Gold Coast (Ghana), palm products from Nigeria, and copper exports from Northern Rhodesia (Zambia).

The general context of world production and trade should first be noted. For the period 1870–1950 we have the statistical summary of Table 101. Another summary of changes in the value, prices and quantum of world exports is offered in Table 102. In Table 103, the growth in world trade is compared with the growth in world population and the increase in world manufacturing production.

In the general context of world trade, the trade of Africa has remained only a small share of the total. An early estimate of the trade of Africa in 1897 is given in Table 104. At that time, exports from South Africa amounted to more than 70 per cent of total African exports. Only five commodities—gold, diamonds, wool, rubber and palm products—accounted for more than 72 per cent of the total African exports. As a percentage of world exports, African exports did not amount to as much as 5 per cent until the 1930s: in 1913, African exports amounted to only 3·7 per cent; in 1928, only 4·0 per cent; and in 1937, 5·3 per cent.[17] But as distinct from its share of world trade, Africa's share of tropical trade has risen markedly. In 1913, sub-Saharan Africa's exports were only 6·2 per cent of tropical trade. By 1937, they were 13·3; by 1955, 18·2; and by 1965, 21·4 per cent.[18]

The growth of African exports before 1913 was pronounced not only in South Africa but also in West and Central Africa. With the decline in transportation costs and the increasing pace of industrialization in Europe and North America, the demand for tropical exports rose, with the result that the index number of value of exports from all tropical countries was 271 in 1913 com-

[17] P. Lamartine Yates, *Forty years of foreign trade* (New York, 1959), p. 32.
[18] Lewis, *Aspects of tropical trade,* p. 15. Tropical countries are defined as those lying approximately between 30°N and 30°S.

Table IOI. *World production and trade, 1870–1950*

	Production			Trade		
	Manufactures		Food	Manufactures ratio, %	Primary products	
	A	B			Value	Quantum
	I	2	3	4	5	6
1870	19·8	23·8	—	—	—	—
1871	21·5	25·9	—	—	—	—
1872	23·6	27·9	—	—	—	—
1873	23·5	28·0	—	—	—	—
1874	23·5	28·2	—	—	—	—
1875	22·8	27·4	—	—	—	—
1876	23·6	28·7	—	—	—	—
1877	24·2	29·I	—	—	—	—
1878	24·7	29·3	—	—	—	—
1879	25·I	28·8	—	—	—	—
1880	27·4	30·4	—	—	—	—
1881	28·8	31·5	—	35·6	36·4	36·2
1882	30·8	34·I	—	36·6	37·5	37·I
1883	31·9	35·4	—	36·5	37·8	38·7
1884	31·0	34·7	—	37·7	36·0	39·0
1885	30·7	35·0	—	37·9	33·9	39·2
1886	32·6	34·8	—	38·2	33·4	41·I
1887	34·9	37·7	—	38·I	34·3	42·5
1888	36·8	40·2	—	39·2	36·2	43·4
1889	39·8	43·8	—	37·4	40·0	46·8
1890	41·9	45·2	—	37·0	41·6	48·4
1891	42·3	45·4	—	34·7	43·I	50·0
1892	42·8	44·5	—	34·3	40·7	49·5
1893	41·2	44·8	—	35·3	39·9	49·I
1894	42·5	47·6	—	35·2	39·6	52·7
1895	46·7	50·3	—	35·6	40·4	56·4
1896	47·7	53·8	—	37·I	42·3	57·9
1897	50·0	55·9	—	36·0	44·8	61·0
1898	54·5	59·7	—	33·9	47·5	64·7
1899	58·5	63·3	—	35·2	50·4	65·6
1900	58·7	63·I	—	34·4	53·9	62·5
1901	60·9	62·5	—	34·8	53·9	65·6
1902	65·9	66·3	—	35·I	55·6	68·8
1903	67·3	67·6	—	34·9	59·5	72·0
1904	67·5	70·4	—	35·6	61·2	73·9
1905	74·7	74·7	—	36·6	65·2	78·4
1906	78·I	76·8	—	36·I	71·4	80·4
1907	80·6	80·I	—	36·I	75·I	80·4
1908	73·5	77·5	—	38·9	69·0	77·7
1909	81·0	81·7	—	36·3	76·4	85·7
1910	86·4	87·4	—	35·0	84·7	87·0
1911	87·8	91·6	—	35·7	88·2	92·6
1912	95·4	96·6	—	36·0	97·5	99·7
1913	100·0	100·0	100	37·0	100·0	100·0
1921	85·5	77·7	96	41·5	104·5	79·7
1922	104·8	92·2	104	41·I	112·5	92·I
1923	109·9	90·9	108	39·6	122·I	85·5
1924	116·3	106·2	107	38·0	40·0	99·0

439

Table 101. *World production and trade, 1870–1950* (continued)

	Production			Trade		
	Manufactures			Manufactures	Primary products	
	A	B	Food	ratio, %	Value	Quantum
	I	2	3	4	5	6
1925	125·4	111·9	113	35·9	165·0	110·8
1926	129·9	114·3	112	36·8	155·0	109·0
1927	138·9	128·4	117	36·8	163·0	120·1
1928	144·4	133·3	122	38·3	164·7	124·8
1929	154·8	139·3	121	38·7	167·0	132·3
1930	135·5	127·9	121	38·8	136·1	130·1
1931	116·7	113·8	123	39·2	`95·6	122·3
1932	100·0	103·9	125	36·5	67·3	114·8
1933	112·9	113·7	127	37·0	59·5	111·9
1934	125·3	127·4	126	37·6	56·4	110·2
1935	139·8	139·4	124	37·0	58·4	117·3
1936	157·4	149·5	128	36·5	63·7	121·6
1937	172·6	164·6	131	36·7	78·3	133·6
1938	154·5	161·4	133	40·1	63·8	118·6
1950	250·3	200·9	139	36·4	184·0	147·9

Series 1. World production of manufactures, including the U.S.A., but excluding the U.S.S.R.
Series 2. World production of manufactures, excluding both the U.S.A. and the U.S.S.R.
Series 3. World production of food, excluding the U.S.S.R.
Series 4. Ratio of the value of manufactures imported by all countries, to the value of all imports.
Series 5. The value of primary products entering into international trade.
Series 6. The quantity of primary products entering into international trade.
(All series are index numbers, with 1913 as base, except Series 4.)
SOURCE: W. Arthur Lewis, 'World Production, prices and trade, 1870–1960', *Manchester School of Economic and Social Studies,* Aug. 1952, **20,** 106–107.

Table 102. *World exports and imports: indices of actual values, unit values and quantum, 1876–1956*

Period	Actual values	Dollar unit values	Quantum
		World in 1913 = 100	
1876–80	30·9	102·4	30·1
1896–1900	44·7	82·5	54·1
1911–13	94·2	97·9	96·2
1926–9	162	139·6	116
1936–8	117 *	105 *	112
	World (excluding Iron Curtain countries) in 1913 = 100		
1936–8 (excluding Iron Curtain countries)	120	(105)	114
1954–6	469	255	184

* These and subsequent figures are based on data in new (devalued) dollars.

SOURCE: P. Lamartine Yates, *Forty years of foreign trade* (New York, 1959), p. 30.

Table 103. *World trade, population and manufactures, 1911–56*

Period	Export volume	Population 1876–80 = 100	Manufacturing production
1911–13	319	126	378
		1913 = 100	
1929	125	111	155
1938	110	120	158
1948	111	132	226
		1948 = 100	
1956	177	116	158

SOURCE: P. Lamartine Yates, *Forty years of foreign trade* (New York, 1959), p. 31.

Table 104. *Trade of Africa in 1897*

	Imports £(000)	Exports £(000)		Imports £(000)	Exports £(000)
Southern Africa [a]	23,915	20,467	Guinea	306	269
			Senegal	1,167	843
Lagos	771	811	Ivory Coast	188	189
Niger Protectorate	640	750	Dahomey	330	231
Gold Coast	911	858	French Congo	143	211
Sierra Leone	457	401			
Gambia	140	164	Total French	2,134	1,743
	2,919	2,984	German East Africa	479	262
			South-West Africa	244	62
British Somaliland	348	350	Togoland	99	39
Egyptian Sudan	91	66	Kamerun	295	185
British East Africa	298	73			
Zanzibar and Pemba	144	81	Total German	1,117	548
British Central Africa	86	27			
			Congo Free State	950	537
	967	597			
			Grand totals	37,391	28,347
Portuguese					
East Africa [a]	4,350	273			
Angola	1,031 [c]	1,195 [c]			
Guinea [b]	8	3			
Total Portuguese	5,389	1,471			

[a] Including goods in transit to and from the hinterland.   [b] Trade with and *via* Portugal only.
[c] 1898.

SOURCE: S. Herbert Frankel, *The tyranny of economic paternalism in Africa* (Johannesburg, 1960), p. 17.

pared with 100 in 1883. But for the peasant economies of West Africa the value index stood at 548, and for the newly opened mining economies of Central Africa the index was 498.[19] The volume of exports grew even more rapidly than these value indices indicate, because export prices were lower in 1913 than in 1883. The degree of variation in exports from different African countries is apparent in Table 105.

Table 105. *Exports from tropical Africa, 1883, 1899, 1913*
(U.S. $ million)

	1883	1899	1913
Angola	2·0	8·6	5·6
Belgian Congo	2·2	7·0	11·7
British Somalia	2·3	1·8	1·0
Cameroons	0·6	1·2	2·9
Cape Verde	0·2	0·4	0·4
Egypt	60·8	75·9	156·5
Eritrea	0·3	0·4	2·3
Ethiopia	1·0	0·2	4·2
French Equatorial Africa	—	1·6	7·1
French Somalia	—	0·1	9·2
French West Africa	4·0	12·4	24·4
Gambia	1·0	1·2	3·2
Gold Coast	1·8	5·4	26·4
Italian Somalia	0·1	0·1	0·4
Kenya-Uganda	0·3	0·6	7·2
Liberia	0·3	0·7	1·1
Madagascar	1·5	2·2	10·9
Mauritius	18·7	8·1	10·4
Moçambique	1·1	1·5	5·3
Nigeria	7·9	8·5	33·0
Northern Rhodesia	—	—	1·0
Nyasaland	—	0·2	1·1
Portuguese Guinea	0·3	0·5	0·5
Réunion	4·5	3·7	3·2
São Tomé	3·0	3·8	9·0
Seychelles	0·2	0·6	0·8
Sierra Leone	2·2	1·6	6·7
Southern Rhodesia	0·1	1·3	2·0
Sudan	0·6	1·5	5·8
Tanganyika	0·3	1·0	3·9
Togo	0·1	0·5	0·6
Zanzibar	6·8	7·4	3·0

SOURCE: Charles C. Stover, 'Tropical exports', in *Tropical development 1880–1913*, W. Arthur Lewis, ed. (Evanston, Northwestern University Press, 1970), pp. 46–7.

According to Charles Stover's calculations, the quantum of tropical trade grew by 3·6 per cent per annum between 1883 and 1913, a rate slightly higher than the rate of growth in industrial production in the four leading countries— the United States, Britain, Germany and France. However, the rate of growth of tropical trade fell to 2·2 per cent per annum between 1913 and 1955—a

[19] W. Arthur Lewis, ed., *Tropical development 1880–1913* (Evanston, Northwestern University Press, 1970), p. 15.

Table 106. *Exports and imports of selected African territories, 1907–59*

	Kenya[b] 1959	Tanganyika[b] 1959	Uganda[b] 1959	Nyasaland[m] 1953	Northern Rhodesia[m] 1953	Southern Rhodesia[m] 1953	Central African Federation[n] 1959	Nigeria 1959	Ghana 1959	Congo[h] 1959
1. Domestic exports[a]	£m33[c]	£m45[c]	£m42[c]	£m7[f]	£m84[k]	£m64[c,l]	£m190[c]	£m160	£m113[c]	£m177
2. Imports[d]	£m61	£m34	£m25	£m7	£m51	£m77	£m150	£m179	£m113	£m110
3. Gross domestic product in money economy	£m163	£m106	£m89	£m11	£m112	£m144	£m429	£m812[e,f]	£m341[g,f]	£m470
4. Agricultural exports	£m30	£m37	£m39	£m7	£m2	£m19	£m41	£m144	£m82	£m73
5. Mineral exports	£m2[c]	£m8[c]	£m3[c]	N	£m80	£m18[c]	£m131[c]	£m6	£m26	£m100
6. Domestic exports as percentage of gross domestic product	20	42	47	66	75	44	44	19[i]	33[i]	39
7. Agricultural exports as percentage of domestic exports	90	82	93	99	2	30	21	88	73	41
8. Mineral exports as percentage of domestic exports	6	13	7	N	96	29	70	4	24	56
9. Percentage of domestic exports sent to United Kingdom	24	36	20	N.A.	41	47	45	44	38	9
10. Percentage of domestic exports sent to EEC	33	25	19	under 10	under 5	under 6	18	31[g]	31	51
11. Domestic exports 1907	£m·157	£m·625	£m·140	£m·054	£m·096	£m2·3	N.A.	£m3·6	£m2·5	£m2·3
12. Domestic exports 1928	£m3·3	£m3·9	£m3·4	£m·676	£m·784	£m3·3	N.A.	£m16·9	£m13·6	£m7·1
13. Mineral exports as percentage of domestic exports 1935	6[o]	11	6[o]	N	96	80	N.A.	15	41	62

[a] The exports of goods produced within a particular territory. Re-exports not included. [b] Excluding domestic produce sent to other East African territories.
[c] Including non-monetary gold. [d] Net. Excluding goods subsequently re-exported. [e] 1956–57. [f] Including subsistence. [g] 1958.
[h] Including Ruanda-Urundi. [i] This proportion is not strictly comparable with other territories as the GNP includes subsistence production.
[j] Including exports to Northern Rhodesia and Southern Rhodesia. [k] Including exports to Southern Rhodesia. [l] Including exports to Northern Rhodesia.
[m] After 1953 the accounts of current transactions for each of the separate territories are not obtainable as they became combined in the Central African Federation.
[n] Transactions between Northern Rhodesia, Southern Rhodesia and Nyasaland not included. [o] Combined Kenya/Uganda percentage.
N = Nil or negligible. N.A. = Not available or not applicable.

SOURCE: Guy Hunter, *The new societies of tropical Africa* (London, Oxford University Press, 1962), p. 55.

period characterized by W. Arthur Lewis as a long depression, associated with world wars and adverse terms of trade. And yet three African territories are to be found in the list of ten countries or territories that developed their foreign commerce the most (in percentage terms) between 1913 and 1953: French West Africa, 1,113 per cent; Nigeria, 1,055 per cent; the Gold Coast, 938 per cent.[20]

Table 106 provides additional data on the growth of exports from selected African territories over the period 1907–59, share of exports in gross domestic product and composition of exports.

Let us now examine more closely two particular cases of agricultural export expansion—cocoa in the Gold Coast and palm products in Nigeria. Both crops were grown by indigenous African farmers who owned the means of production. Both crops, unlike settler-grown crops such as Virginia tobacco in Rhodesia or sisal in Tanganyika, required but a simple technology and minimal capital investment.

Cocoa and the Gold Coast

The introduction of cocoa into the Gold Coast in the 1880s, its subsequent extensive cultivation through areas of largely uncultivated forest and the rapid increase in its exportation provide an impressive illustration of Smith's vent-for-surplus theory of trade. Surplus labour-time was used to bring idle land into cultivation. And the expansion of the commercial crop of cocoa was not at the expense of food production; the opportunity cost of exporting cocoa was low.

As Lewis remarks,

Adam Smith had said that trade enriches a country by enabling a country to use resources that would otherwise be idle . . . Insofar as concerns the tropical farmers, Adam Smith turns out to have been right. Nowadays they will switch from foodstuffs to more profitable crops, but at the end of the nineteenth century, when they were only just learning to produce for distant world markets, this was a risk that few were prepared to take. The expansion of commercial crops was not at the expense of production, and could therefore occur.

The zest with which this was done was remarkable . . .[T]he farmers of the Gold Coast created the largest cocoa industry in the world between 1880 and 1913, without even waiting for a proper transportation network.[21]

Nor was this a case of establishing agriculture for the benefit of foreigners at the expense of Africans, as in other parts of Africa where indigenous land rights were disregarded and Africans were confined to reserves with a subsequent restriction of output. The colonial government did not declare the right of eminent domain over what it considered as vacant lands (as was done in some other colonies), and land was not made available to foreigners for development on a plantation basis. Instead, development in Ghana was based on small-scale farms, and the land-tenure arrangements of the export economy evolved out of traditional systems.

The transfer of land from unproductive use in the traditional village subsistence economy to productive uses was effected rapidly and efficiently. Polly Hill has analysed how groups of cocoa farmers were able to migrate from one area to another and to buy land from those who had an excess supply, or to rent it at low rates; thus enabling organized groups of migrant farmers (chiefly the

[20] Yates, *Forty years of foreign trade,* p. 160.   [21] Lewis, *Aspects of tropical trade,* pp. 10–11.

Akwapim and Krobo) to operate with tracts of scores and even hundreds of acres that were divided into strip-farms or into a mosaic pattern of individual occupancy. Miss Hill notes that the farmers evolved two types of migratory groups that were entirely new to them: the *company,* which was an Akwapim modification of a system of group land-purchase; and another type of land-purchasing group which bought family lands.[22]

A distinct feature of the migration was the practice, which extends over the generations, of investing a part of the proceeds of one cocoa-land in the purchase of another, so that most migrant farmers acquired several lands. The operation was capitalistic in that it promoted saving and investing in roundabout production. It is also significant that the organization of land owning and the form of land development did not inhibit individual economic achievement.[23]

The development of commercial cocoa production for export thus depended on several crucial factors introduced from outside the Gold Coast economy. There are various accounts of the introduction of cocoa into the Gold Coast, but all involve the bringing of cocoa pods into the country from overseas. The increased supplies of seeds and planting material for the cocoa crop also initially depended heavily on the efforts of missionaries (and later on supplies and advice from the government and especially the Aburi Gardens after 1903). The earlier export of palm produce and rubber also provided a source of finance for the purchase of land for cocoa-growing. Through their earlier trade in palm produce for export, the Akwapim were already familiar with the cash economy, and this earlier export crop provided the principal source of finance for buying land for cocoa-growing.[24] The group organization for purchasing land had also been anticipated when the Manya-Krobo people of the south-east organized themselves into groups in the 1860s to buy large blocks of forest land (called *huzas*) for the production of palm-oil for export. It was the accumulation of capital in this trade that helped them to turn to cocoa from the 1890s.[25] Another essential condition for the development of cocoa-growing was that European produce-buying firms (mainly German rather than British firms in the earliest period) had already been established on the coast and were willing to handle the new crops.

Although exogenous factors account for the introduction of cocoa production, the subsequent expansionary process was fuelled, however, by endogenous forces, not the least of which was the purely motivational. Polly Hill has observed that the

expansionary process soon became desirable for its own sake—it was creative, adventurous and all-absorbing . . . [M]any Akwapim men had highly expandible sets of wants when the process first began . . . The need to secure the future was involved with the idea, so reasonable in Africa, that there is no resting-place between stagnation and growth; a business cannot be healthy unless it is expanding.

[22] Polly Hill, *The migrant cocoa-farmers of southern Ghana: a study in rural capitalism* (Cambridge University Press, 1963), pp. 2–3. The migratory process in the Ashanti region differed radically from that of the southern farmers, mainly because Ashanti chiefs seldom sell land outright to strangers, but 'rent' it on some system of usufructuary tenure.

[23] *Ibid.,* pp. 16, 73, 183–5.   [24] *Ibid.,* pp. 15 and 167.

[25] M. J. Field, 'The agricultural system of the Manya-Krobo of the Gold Coast', *Africa,* 1943, **14,** 54–65; M. A. Havinden, 'The history of crop cultivation in West Africa: a bibliographical guide', *Economic History Review,* 2nd ser., Dec. 1970, **32,** no. 3, p. 546.

Miss Hill further notes that the expansionary process was much encouraged by the fact that it tended to involve all the inhabitants of the main Akwapim towns.

As it was everyone's aspiration to participate, so there was no question of men being motivated by a desire to free themselves from rapacious kin—in practical (not legal) terms the new lands were considered as an extension of the homeland, and there was no idea of leaving home for good.[26]

Upon this foundation of outside initiatory factors and the indigenous expansionary process, the Gold Coast was transformed in only two decades—1891 to 1911—from a traditional economy based on subsistence production into one dominated by a cash-crop that has become a major staple in international trade. An authoritative study of the structural changes in the economy during this period emphasizes how unique was the transformation in terms of its speed, magnitude and structural significance. From an economy dominated in 1891 by indigenous activities and by 'trade flows whose nature in terms of organisation, conveyance, spatial incidence and types of commodities had not changed significantly over centuries', the Gold Coast had become twenty years later the world's largest exporter of cocoa, with a railway network, new sectors of activity and a transformed economic structure. The study proceeds to emphasize, however, that 'what is even more interesting, the transformations of this period largely determined the structure of the economy for the next fifty years, and it can be maintained that the pattern established in 1911 still largely persisted in 1960'.[27]

Total exports of cocoa rose from nil in 1891 to 13 tons in 1895, 536 tons in 1900, 5,093 tons in 1905, 22,629 tons in 1910 and over 50,000 tons in 1913. The trend of exports after the First World War is indicated in Table 107. From a value of £500 in 1895, Gold Coast exports of cocoa rose to a value of £27,000 in 1900, £187,000 in 1905, £867,000 in 1910 and to almost £2,500,000 in 1913.[28] The average value rose from £4,145,000 between 1915

Table 107. *Gold Coast cocoa exports, 1916–60*

Annual average for the five years	000 tons
1916–20	106
1921–5	186
1926–30	219
1931–5	243
1936–40	263
1941–5	193
1946–50	232
1951–5	220
1956–60	249

SOURCE: Polly Hill, *The migrant cocoa-farmers of southern Ghana* (Cambridge University Press, 1963), p. 217.

[26] Hill, *Migrant cocoa-farmers*, pp. 180–1.
[27] Robert Szereszewski, *Structural changes in the economy of Ghana, 1891–1911* (London, 1965), pp. 1–2.　　　　[28] Hill, *Migrant cocoa-farmers*, pp. 176–7.

and 1919, to £10,012,000 between 1925 and 1929, fell as low as £3,654,000 during 1940–4, and rose again to almost £60,000,000 between 1955 and 1959.

It is noteworthy that food imports did not have to increase, as export production was not at the cost of food-crop production. As was generally true in Africa, food production was able to keep pace with the growth of population through the provision of colonial peace, improvements in transportation, spread of new food-crops, diffusion of better agricultural methods and agricultural extension activities of missionaries and departments of agriculture.[29]

Aggregative measures of the performance of the Gold Coast's economy are presented in Table 108. The gross domestic product, excluding traditional consumption (that is, production and consumption of foodstuffs and services in the traditional indigenous sector), increased from £1·95 million to £8·37 million at constant 1911 prices. This implied an average annual growth rate of 7·6 per cent compound. On a *per capita* basis, the average annual rate of increase was 6·5 per cent.[30]

Table 108. *Estimated expenditure on the Gold Coast's gross domestic product, 1891, 1901, 1911*
(1911 prices, in £000)

Items	1891	1901	1911
1. Export production	872	740	3,612
2. Private consumption of imported goods	1,595	2,741	4,310
3–4. Consumption of government and public services	150	490	635
5. Gross capital formation			
a. buildings and construction	98	837	800
b. equipment	56	287	490
c. cocoa	4	169	1,573
d. net accumulation of specie *	73	257	560
e. changes in stocks of imported goods	8	17	−3
6. Traditional consumption	9,200	10,000	11,100
7. Imports of goods and non-factor services			
a. imports of merchandise and non-factor services	−835	−1,870	−3,050
b. net imports of specie *	−73	−257	−550
Total: (A) including 6	11,148	13,411	19,467
(B) excluding 6	1,948	3,411	8,367
Per capita (£): (A)	6·8	7·5	9·7
(B)	1·2	1·9	4·2

* The figures are inflated here according to the index of the whole aggregate; the relevant magnitudes according to the index of prices of the economy excluding traditional consumption are 79 and 247 for 1891 and 1901 respectively.

SOURCE: Robert Szereszewski, *Structural changes in the economy of Ghana, 1891–1911* (London, 1965), p. 149.

[29] Bruce F. Johnston, 'Changes in agricultural productivity', in *Economic transition in Africa*, Melville J. Herskovits and Mitchell Harwitz, eds. (Evanston, Northwestern University Press, 1964), p. 152.   [30] Szereszewski, *Structural changes*, p. 73.

Although the gross domestic product was rising so rapidly, the share of traditional consumption in national expenditure was declining markedly. From constituting 84 per cent of domestic product in 1891, traditional consumption declined to 74 per cent by 1901 and to 57 per cent in 1911.[31] At the same time, however, the consumption of imported goods, government services and investment expenditures, as shown in Table 108, all rose markedly.

Underlying the increase in gross domestic product was the significant expansion in exports from £0·8 million in 1891 to more than £3·6 million in 1911. From being nil in 1891, cocoa exports had expanded to almost one-half the total value of the Gold Coast exports in 1911; and cocoa acreage had reached more than 425,000 acres, with an estimated investment value of more than £3·5 million at 1911 prices.[32] By 1938, there were some 300,000 cocoa farms with a total acreage of between 1,250,000 and 1,500,000 acres.

What was the carry-over from this rapid expansion of cocoa exports to the rest of the economy? To what extent did the trade in cocoa also act as an engine of domestic growth? Table 108 gives a general impression of domestic growth, but the specific contribution of cocoa exports should be summarized more precisely.

Cocoa production allowed surplus unskilled labour to be combined with idle land in a relatively uncomplicated method of cultivation and processing to meet an expanding overseas demand. This process of growth had many of the features of the classical model of migration of surplus labour from the traditional subsistence sector to a modern export sector. In this process, an increasing supply of labour services was absorbed and the return per unit of labour services increased as well. It is estimated that the increase in the labour intake of the cocoa industry, excluding transport, rose from about 100,000 labour-days in 1891 to 37 million in 1911.[33] In the earliest stages, the migrant farmers depended on family labour on their farms, but many 'outsiders' were employed as carriers. Some of these saved money for purchasing land and soon became cocoa farmers themselves. At a later stage, starting around 1900, when the cocoa trees had begun to bear, many of the larger farmers began to employ farm labourers who earned a share of the crop they harvested and who also assisted in establishing new farms. By 1910, there may have been as many farm labourers as farmers.[34]

In his study of the Gold Coast economy, Robert Szereszewski concluded that the most efficient growth pattern would be one based on rural labour and natural resources, utilizing the highest possible ratio of natural resources to labour in production.

Cocoa fulfilled these conditions admirably: improving the conversion rate of labour services to income, it activated labour resources; the expansion into the forest was an expression of the natural resource-intensity of cocoa farming; the capitalisation of current labour into cocoa farms was another labour-saving procedure, enhancing the productivity of labour over time.

The result was 'an increase in export-oriented economic activity' that 'was the main vehicle of the process of growth in the Gold Coast, and at the same time

[31] *Ibid.*, pp. 35, 45, 65.   [32] *Ibid.*, p. 60.   [33] *Ibid.*, p. 75.
[34] Hill, *Migrant cocoa-farmers*, p. 17. For details on the employment of labourers, see *ibid.*, pp. 187–90 and 213–14.

the substance of its originality'.[35] This was made possible by the technical conditions of cocoa farming, the labour-supply conditions, an expanding world market and the existence of introduced elements that could support an increase in export production.

Beyond the direct absorption of labour in cocoa-growing, the expansion in cocoa exports also gave rise to the employment of carriers of the cocoa to the ports, and to the emergence of a class of middlemen. From the European produce-buying firms and trading posts established on the coast, there developed a widespread network of African middlemen who carried trade into the interior. A trade and distribution system was stimulated by the consumption of imports.

Exports clearly expanded the capacity to import. And this constituted a gain in two senses: first, exports had instrumental significance as an intermediate good that allowed the country to 'buy' imports on more favourable terms than if the imports had had to be produced domestically; second, to the extent that investment goods were imported, the exchange of an export commodity, such as cocoa, represented the trade of a low-growth potential commodity for higher-growth potential import commodities. The second type of gain is especially important for a developing country.

The composition of imports to the Gold Coast reflects these gains. Over the period 1891–1911, textiles and 'provisions' remained about one-half of total consumption-goods imports, but the percentage of spirits and tobaccos declined, whereas miscellaneous merchandise increased. After the First World War, the range of non-durable and durable consumer goods in the miscellaneous category expanded. It might be argued, however, that this increase in consumption imports was at the expense of greater domestic saving or taxation. There may be truth to this; but on the other side, due weight must be given to the view that consumption imports may also act as incentive goods, increasing the supply of productive activity and the marketable surplus of cash-crops in order to fulfil the aspiration to consume. The spread of the exchange economy must have been stimulated by the desire to satisfy new wants created by new types of consumer imports.

Also significant is the increasing share of investment goods in total imports. Whereas private consumption goods accounted for 75 per cent of imports in 1891, this percentage had declined to 62 per cent by 1911, while investment goods had risen from 24 per cent of total imports in 1891 to 34 per cent in 1911.[36] Investment-goods imports were mainly equipment, transport machinery and tools.

It may be noted also that the composition of imports does not indicate that the rise in imports destroyed existing import-competing industries in the Gold Coast. But if local industry was not destroyed by foreign trade, neither was it stimulated to any significant extent. It was generally neglected, as the foreign traders were not interested; domestic industrial entrepreneurs were lacking; and the colonial government did not positively promote domestic industry. There were Lebanese trading firms, some of which later went into industry in the 1960s. But in the earlier period the domestic economy was not sufficiently integrated, and domestic markets remained too narrow and fragmented to induce

[35] Szereszewski, *Structural changes*, pp. 104–105.   [36] *Ibid.*, pp. 33, 50, 70.

such industrial investment. In the decade before the First World War some manufacturing industry was started—a sawmill, a brick and tile factory, an establishment producing mineral water and a workshop for repairing transport launches. But industrial expansion was slow, and it is of interest, as Szereszewski remarks, that the first four establishments are so characteristic of the present structure of Ghana's industry: timber processing, supply of construction inputs, light consumer-goods industries based on imported inputs and repair and maintenance establishments.[37] The narrow domestic market, limited financial capacity and deficiencies in skills have continued to constrain industrial development.[38]

Besides absorbing labour and raising the capacity to import, the expansion of cocoa exports had a backward linkage to construction and transportation facilities. The increase of capital formation in buildings and construction may be noted in Table 108. By 1911, almost one-third of the non-traditional capital stock consisted of constructions. While the export of gold induced railway expansion in the west, there was also by 1912 the Accra-Korforidua railway, the development of the railway-based port of Accra and a fairly extensive road network from the cocoa areas converging on Accra and Nsawam. By 1914, the rail carried more than three-quarters of the cocoa crop. In the 1920s the cocoa belt was linked to the coast by another rail line from Tarkwa to Sekondi. After this, cheap motor transport expanded and more roads assisted the export of cocoa.

The cocoa industry helped also to create employment for village artisans. During the 1930s, for instance, the settlement of Akokoaso in the Gold Coast comprised some 1,181 inhabitants, including 267 independent and 87 dependent cocoa farmers. But, as Sir Keith Hancock observed in his classic study of Akokoaso, the farmers often combined their farm work with some craft work (palm-wine tapping, shoemaking, smithing, potting), whereas other members of the community were wholly specialized in a craft and did no farming at all (for example, full-time palm-wine tappers, blacksmiths, petty traders, midwives, teachers, carpenters and cocoa buyers). Although those who worked only in a non-agricultural occupation were fewer than those who combined farming and a craft, 'nevertheless, this little village contains 66 persons whose entire income is derived from a trade or profession. It is plain that the division of labour has already advanced a considerable distance.' Further, Hancock emphasized that

participation in the world's business has brought to the people of Akokoaso a great increase of wealth . . . [T]he average income per family from all sources is £21· 18s· 6d·, of which £14· 18s· 6d· is from 'external sources' (chiefly the proceeds of the sale of cocoa) and in cash. By peasant standards this average is extremely high. There is nothing to compare with it in rural Africa.[39]

Significant as the foregoing contributions were, the export of cocoa did not have much of an impact on other elements that we would include in a country's 'development foundations'—namely, the learning rate of the economy, its social infrastructure, supply of entrepreneurship and expanded financial capacity.

[37] *Ibid.,* p. 63.
[38] For details on growth of manufacturing during the colonial period, see Kilby's essay in this volume.
[39] Sir William Keith Hancock, *Survey of British Commonwealth affairs,* vol. II: *Problems of economic policy, 1918–1939* (London, Oxford University Press, 1940–2), pt. 2, p. 277.

The extension of cocoa cultivation was essentially a widening process, with more labour being applied to more land, but without a significant increase in productivity through technical innovations. On the whole, the productivity of resources in the cocoa industry remained constant. Cocoa cultivation was for long a pure labour-axe-cutlass activity, and the processing was a simple activity with little forward linkage. The educative process of cocoa cultivation was thus slight, and the carry-over of skills to other activities minimal.

Right from the start, however, the British made some attempt at improving agricultural education. Already between 1890 and 1911, when the British administrative personnel in the colony numbered no more than a few dozen, the Gold Coast agricultural service expanded from two to twenty-seven officials. The Department of Agriculture distributed free cocoa seeds and plants, and it demonstrated the basic techniques of cocoa-growing to the people. Agriculture stations were opened—in 1901 (Christianborg Coconut Plantation), 1903 (Tarkwa Agricultural Station), 1906 (Kumasi Agricultural Station), 1907 (Assuantsi Station) and 1909 (Tamale Agricultural Station). These stations served many roles: they gave information to farmers, demonstrated newer techniques and crops and provided good seed and plants. In 1938, the Agricultural Department opened a research station at New Tafo to study the cause of and possible remedies for swollen shoot and other prevalent cocoa diseases. Six years later the station was taken over by the West African Cocoa Research Institute, an intercolonial agency supported by British funds, with an enlarged staff of experts devoted to the task of saving the industry. The institute also did work on the rehabilitation of soils and on seeking disease-resistant cocoa strains.

Despite its agricultural services, the colonial government failed to spend any substantial amounts on education and what would now be considered as an extensive policy of human-resource development. Education was left almost exclusively to the missionaries, whose resources were inadequate. In consequence, the country's need for trained manpower was met mainly by importation, not only of university graduates, but also of secondary and technical personnel. It has been argued that the neglect of education was perhaps the greatest failure of the colonial government, because the cost of importing intermediate personnel and the shortage of this kind of manpower continued to be a brake on economic progress throughout the pre-independence period.[40]

There is, however, some counter-evidence that indicates that the colonial government assisted the missionary effort by grants in aid, and achieved a good deal in the form of educational progress. Between 1935 and 1957 the number of children in primary schools increased from 63,000 to 456,000. Secondary school education for a long time lagged far behind elementary education. The first major change occurred in 1924, when the government founded Achimota College, which for a time provided education from kindergarten to college level, and which later developed into a full-fledged university. From 1938 to 1955, the number of secondary-school students expanded from 919 to 7,711.[41] This development had far-reaching consequences.

Cocoa farming may have promoted the managerial function,[42] but it made no sizeable contribution to increasing the general supply of entrepreneurship. The cocoa farmers' objective remained investment in additional cocoa-land, house-

[40] A. Baron Holmes, 'The Gold Coast and Nigeria', in *Tropical development*, p. 174.
[41] See W. E. F. Ward, *A history of Ghana* (London, 1963), pp. 409–10.
[42] Cf. Hill, *Migrant cocoa-farmers*, p. 186.

building and lorry ownership and operation—not diversification into commercial or industrial activities. Conditions for industrial development were unfavourable, and the dominant position of European import–export houses relegated Africans to the minor role of unorganized petty traders. There was not a capitalized commercial élite that could give rise to industrial entrepreneurs.[43] Aside from produce-buying, the purchase of lorries for commercial operation was the only common form of economic enterprise that sprang directly from cocoa farming.[44] Thus the profits from cocoa growing were not used in other investments to diversify the economy; nor did the government undertake any special effort to mobilize resources for a scale of expenditure that would now properly be considered a development programme.

In its most effective form, the revenue drawn from the cocoa industry contributed to the construction of a logistic infrastructure. In earlier days, head porters carried cocoa along winding jungle tracks. Palm-oil was rolled in eighty-four-gallon casks from the forests to the coast, where surf boats took all cargoes to ocean-going freighters. In 1898, the British built the first railway. The new means of transportation facilitated the spread of cocoa farms inland and freed carriers for other forms of employment. Inadequate transportation facilities, however, for long remained one of the country's main economic weaknesses. Hence the colony's first Ten-Year Development Plan, initiated under Governor Sir Gordon Guggisberg in 1919, laid special emphasis on the expansion of railways, on the creation of an artificial harbour at Takoradi and on the building of roads. By 1927, the colony had a road system extending over 4,688 motor miles, and Ford trucks began to revolutionize the transport in the backwoods. In addition, Guggisberg was responsible for other improvements: waterworks, forestry reserves, telephone and telegraph services, academic and technical education and new hospitals.

Finally, we must emphasize that the carry-over was limited by the pervasiveness of domestic market imperfections. The monetary export sector was in itself small relative to the traditional sector. Impressive as was the amount of labour absorption of cocoa farming, it is estimated that by 1911 this still amounted to the employment of only some 185,000 people out of the total population of the colony and Ashanti of 1.5 million. In terms of size, the cocoa-export sector was quite marginal compared with the amount of surplus labour-time that could be absorbed from the traditional sector.

What limited the rate of labour absorption into the exchange economy, however, was not the character of international trade as much as impediments in the domestic economy and non-economic barriers in the general socio-cultural environment. When intersectoral interrelationships are many, and the response to an expansion in exports is rapid and extensive in scope, then even a weak stimulus from exports can result in a significant carry-over. In contrast, there were formidable domestic impediments in the Gold Coast economy that cut short the stimulus from exports. The carry-over from exports was restrained by factor immobility into other activities outside of cocoa farming, narrow and isolated markets, ignorance of technological possibilities, limited infrastructure and slow rate of human-resource development. As long as the domestic economy

---

[43] Holmes, 'Gold Coast and Nigeria', p. 174. For a different interpretation of what held back economic progress in Africa, see the essay in this volume by the Dotsons.

[44] Hill, *Migrant cocoa-farmers*, p. 190.

remained fragmented and compartmentalized, the transfer of resources to more productive employment was restricted, and the linkage of markets and their subsequent extension were limited.[45]

The price system has a role to play not only in allocating resources at a given moment of time, but also in achieving intertemporal efficiency in the utilization of resources. But the functions of the price system were poorly articulated during the colonial period, when markets remained localized, subsistence production continued to account for a substantial proportion of national product and traditional rules and customary obligations prevailed. Under these conditions, the price system was too rudimentary to operate on an economy-wide basis as an instrument for development—either through decentralized choice or through deliberate governmental policy. Monetary and fiscal policies, for instance, cannot be effective without a fairly extensive market system. To allow the price system to have more penetrative powers, the colonial government would have had to underwrite on a much larger scale the development of human resources, and it would have had to engage in more institution-building, especially more market institutions. Without more extensive market institutions that widen the product markets, deepen the financial markets and counteract many monopolistic restrictions in both product and factor markets, there cannot be an effective mobilization and allocation of resources.

In the final analysis, trade may transmit growth, but only if there are also latent indigenous forces of development that can be released through trade. In the absence of receptivity elsewhere in the domestic economy, the stimulus from exports can initiate only a limited integrative process. So it was for the Gold Coast. There were favourable features of cocoa production that made the stimulus a strong one; but there was at the same time a neglect of some of the crucial development foundations and an insufficiently responsive domestic economic structure.[46]

As a result, the rate of economic expansion slowed down during the four to five decades after 1911, and the structure of the economy in 1960 bore a striking resemblance to that in 1911. After the remarkable episode of cocoa expansion, during the earlier decades of 1891–1911, the transformation of the economy was limited. The absolute level of non-traditional consumption had increased considerably. But in relative terms, in 1960, traditional consumption was still as high as 43 percent of gross domestic product (GDP);[47] the ratio for foreign trade to GDP was considerably higher, amounting to 58 per cent of GDP as against 38 per cent in 1911,[48] and cocoa amounted to 54 per cent of total exports in 1960 as against 45 per cent in 1911. Most significantly, by

---

[45] In a similar vein, P. T. Bauer observed: 'The lack of specialization which affects a large section of West African economic life derives from narrow markets which are an aspect of the low level of the local economy. In turn it impedes efficiency and retards economic progress. Thus it is both a symptom and a cause of the low standard of living.' P. T. Bauer, *West African trade: a study of competition, oligopoly and monopoly in a changing economy* (London, 1954), p. 12.

[46] For an alternative explanation, closer to some aspects of the 'negative view' discussed above, see G. B. Kay, ed., *The political economy of colonialism in Ghana* (Cambridge University Press, 1972), especially pp. 3–37. It is submitted, however, that the interpretation proposed here may have more explanatory power than the alternative, more emotive account of 'foreign political domination' and 'external economic dependence', and the caricature of the 'vision of the ideal colony in the minds of the colonial administrators that informed their practice'.

[47] Szereszewski, *Structural changes*, p. 93.　　　　[48] *Ibid.*, p. 94.

1960 the proportion of imports destined for final demand-uses, instead of being imported intermediate inputs, was 71 per cent, as compared with 91 per cent in 1911. This would indicate a more complex input-output network of the economy, but the change over half a century was still not marked; and in 1960 the major proportion of imports was still destined for final use as finished consumer goods or capital equipment. Thus Szereszewski concludes that the absence of domestic linkages is indicated 'by the fact that only about 8% of the output of the ten sectors of the economy [in a constructed input-output matrix for 1960 production] was absorbed as inputs in the production system'. The development of the manufacturing sector, construction, modern services and related activities from 1910 to 1960 'was not sufficiently rapid in relation to the growth of the total GDP in order to reshape the economy fundamentally'. The process of structural change was slow after 1911, and 'Ghana of 1960 could still belong to the same category of structures as the 1911 Gold Coast, albeit at a generally higher (double) level of GDP per capita'.[49]

Other agricultural exports [50]

A comparison between the different development-stimulating effects of other agricultural exports from African colonies would be most instructive. Unfortunately there is insufficient statistical information to do this in any comprehensive fashion. Some differences may be observed, however, in the social and economic organization of the export base of different colonies. The major contrast is between cash-crop production by smallholders and larger-scale modern farming on estates or plantations. The smallholder pattern of export growth was important not only for cocoa exports from the Gold Coast, but also for cocoa and palm-oil from Nigeria, coffee from the Ivory Coast and coffee and cotton from Uganda and Tanganyika. Based on indigenous enterprise and capital, this 'peasant-type' production of exports was highly significant in the enlargement of the monetary sector in African economies. In contrast with the larger-scale farming on plantations, it might be argued that peasant production ensured a wider diffusion of the benefits of growth. But there were variations among countries and commodities.

In their record of rapid expansion, palm-product exports from Nigeria, for example, bear some resemblance to cocoa exports from the Gold Coast. According to Helleiner, the value of Nigeria's exports increased more than sevenfold between 1900 and 1929; the volume of exports, fivefold. This implied compounded annual growth rates of 7 per cent in export value and 5½ per cent in export volume. But although palm-oil and palm-kernels accounted for 80 to

---

[49] *Ibid.*, p. 97. For a criticism of this conclusion, see Polly Hill's review of Szereszewski in *Economic Development and Cultural Change*, Oct. 1967, **16**, no. 1, pp. 131–7.

[50] EDITORS' NOTE: Although the colonial governments played only a small role in promoting cocoa cultivation, they took a much more important part in introducing and improving other crops, such as cotton, coffee and tobacco. (See Yudelman's essay in this volume for details.) Crops like cotton and tobacco necessitated a more extensive transfer of skills and produced greater technological changes. For instance, companies active in Nigeria promoted the cultivation of tobacco on the part of Africans; in addition, they sponsored research in the production of high-quality tobacco. Seedlings were provided to farmers, as well as loans, supplies, technical advice and other aid. Company officials also supervised the construction of small tobacco barns; and over the years, the Nigerian Tobacco Company taught Africans how to grow better brands and helped them form co-operatives and producers' groups.

90 per cent of total value of Nigerian exports in 1900, with the expansion of new exports of ground-nuts, cocoa and tin they had declined to only 47 per cent of exports in 1929.[51] Table 109 shows the annual quantity of palm-kernels and palm-oil exported between 1900 and 1960. The value of exports of palm products is indicated in Table 110.

Table 109. *Quantity of exports of palm products, Nigeria, 1900–1960*
(long tons)

Year	Palm-kernels	Palm-oil	Year	Palm-kernels	Palm-oil
1900	85,624	45,508	1931	254,454	118,179
1901	114,046	56,766	1932	309,061	116,060
1902	132,556	64,167	1933	259,945	128,696
1903	131,898	54,257	1934	289,447	112,773
1904	139,788	57,947	1935	312,746	142,628
1905	108,822	50,562	1936	386,145	162,778
1906	113,347	57,260	1937	337,749	145,718
1907	133,630	65,473	1938	312,048	110,243
1908	136,558	70,460	1939	299,943	121,042
1909	158,849	82,130	1940	235,521	132,723
1910	172,907	76,851	1941	378,124	127,778
1911	176,390	79,387	1942	344,569	151,287
1912	184,625	76,994	1943	331,292	135,268
1913	174,718	83,090	1944	313,530	124,829
1914	162,452	72,531	1945	292,588	114,199
1915	153,319	72,994	1946	277,242	100,885
1916	161,439	67,422	1947	316,376	125,954
1917	185,998	74,619	1948	327,174	139,204
1918	205,167	86,425	1949	375,835	170,145
1919	216,913	100,967	1950	415,906	173,010
1920	207,010	84,856	1951	347,013	149,752
1921	153,354	52,771	1952	374,163	167,288
1922	178,723	87,609	1953	402,872	201,345
1923	223,172	99,439	1954	464,111	208,482
1924	252,847	127,083	1955	433,234	182,143
1925	272,925	128,113	1956	451,069	185,235
1926	249,100	113,267	1957	406,200	166,200
1927	257,206	113,240	1958	441,228	170,508
1928	246,638	127,111	1959	430,608	163,692
1929	251,477	131,845	1960	418,176	183,360
1930	260,022	135,801			

SOURCE: G. K. Helleiner, *Peasant agriculture, government and economic growth in Nigeria* (Homewood, Ill., 1966), Table IV-A-8.

Beyond the indications of the growth of exports, some major indicators of internal growth have been assembled by Stolper for selected years. These are presented in Table 111. As observed by Stolper, these data indicate the harm which both the wars and the Great Depression have done to the development of Nigeria. 'In fact, in looking at the statistics, it appears as though the helpless-

[51] G. K. Helleiner, *Peasant agriculture, government and economic growth in Nigeria* (Homewood, Ill., 1966), pp. 5 and 8. For earlier export statistics, see Patrick Manning, 'Some export statistics for Nigeria, 1880–1904', *Nigerian Journal of Economic and Social Studies*, July 1967, **9**, no. 2, pp. 229–34.

Table 110. *Value of exports of palm products, Nigeria, 1900–1960*
(£000)

Year	Palm-kernels	Palm-oil	Year	Palm-kernels	Palm-oil
1900	834	681	1931	2,132	1,542
1901	948	813	1932	2,696	1,514
1902	1,274	958	1933	1,899	1,384
1903	1,094	848	1934	1,591	885
1904	1,278	929	1935	2,245	1,656
1905	1,090	858	1936	3,637	2,079
1906	1,194	1,002	1937	3,648	2,364
1907	1,658	1,314	1938	2,172	984
1908	1,425	1,155	1939	1,873	930
1909	1,816	1,447	1940	1,500	1,099
1910	2,451	1,742	1941	2,283	1,047
1911	2,574	1,697	1942	2,458	1,427
1912	2,797	1,655	1943	3,117	1,587
1913	3,110	1,854	1944	3,637	2,030
1914	2,541	1,572	1945	3,496	1,894
1915	1,693	1,462	1946	4,164	2,052
1916	1,740	1,403	1947	9,491	5,038
1917	2,582	1,883	1948	11,451	9,048
1918	3,226	2,704	1949	16,913	11,910
1919	4,948	4,246	1950	16,694	12,072
1920	5,718	4,677	1951	20,059	12,949
1921	2,832	1,656	1952	22,767	17,091
1922	2,810	2,676	1953	22,185	13,020
1923	3,741	2,982	1954	22,791	13,431
1924	4,461	3,911	1955	19,196	13,151
1925	4,937	4,166	1956	20,440	14,866
1926	4,440	3,616	1957	17,959	13,801
1927	4,439	3,375	1958	20,450	12,663
1928	4,423	3,751	1959	25,971	13,808
1929	4,265	3,767	1960	26,062	13,982
1930	3,679	3,250			

SOURCE: G. K. Helleiner, *Peasant agriculture, government and economic growth in Nigeria* (Homewood, Ill., 1966), Table IV-A-7.

ness in coping with the great depression and the aftermath of the First World War accounts for almost all the lack of development that underdeveloped countries feel they owe to colonialism.' [52]

The export-base of Nigerian development differed, however, in at least two fundamental respects from that of the Gold Coast. First, in terms of trading arrangements, oil-palm products from Nigeria were dominated by the Royal Niger Company, acting as a chartered company from 1886–1900, and then its successor, the Niger Company (later merged into the United Africa Company). In its royal charter, the company was prohibited from establishing a monopoly, and it was stated that trade was to be free for all British subjects and foreigners and liable only to customs duties for revenue purposes. But in practice the company acted as a monopsonist [53] vis-à-vis the African producers from whom it

[52] Wolfgang F. Stolper, 'Economic development in Nigeria', *Journal of Economic History,* Dec. 1963, **23**, no. 4, p. 398.

[53] EDITORS' NOTE: The Royal Niger Company never fully enforced a monopoly. Thus Hancock writes in *Survey of British Commonwealth affairs,* vol. II, pt. 2, pp. 167–8: 'Some of the Liver-

Table III. *Indicators of Nigerian long-range development*

	1899–1901	1919–21	1929–31	1935–7	1951	1960
1. Public revenues (£000)	639	6,814	6,045–4,887	7,342	70,088	151,219
2. Public expenditures (£000)	735	6,493	6,290–5,036	7,376	53,106	146,939
3. Shipping cleared (000 tons) in foreign trade	1,070	1,425		2,243		5,859
4. Length of railway (miles)	—	1,126	1,800	1,900	1,900	about 1,900
5. Length of tarred roads (miles)	—	—	—	—	1,114	5,267
6. Electricity generated (million units)	—	—	n.a.	14,549	116,703	430,559
7. Coal production (000 tons)	—	181	250	310	551	562
8. Value of exports (£ million)	2·0	14·7–9·7	17·6–8·6	19·2	116·6	161·0
9. Value of imports (£ million)	1·9	11·6–10·7	13·2–6·5	14·6	84·6	215·3
10. *Exports*						
Palm oil (000 tons)	14	80	129	150	150	183
Palm kernels (000 tons)	52	192	255	346	347	418
Ground-nuts (000 tons)	—	45	151	242	141	333
Cocoa (£000)	—	20	53	91	122	154
Mineral oil (000 tons)	—	—	—	—	—	847
Tin ore (000 tons)	—	—	—	15	12	10
Columbite (000 tons)	—	—	—	1	2	2
11. *Imports*						
Cotton piece goods (million yds.)	27	68	89	151	121	214
Wheat flour (000 cwt.)	—	27	78	57	272	607
Sugar (000 tons)	0·2	0·7	4·7	9·8	11	66·7
Cement (000 tons)	—	15	48	51	261	262·5
Motor fuels (000 tons)	—	—	16	25	167	280
Kerosene (000 tons)	—	8	11	11	43	118
Bicycles (000)	n.a.	n.a.	n.a.	45	153	160
Motor cars, trucks, buses	—	—	1,127–899	3,307	6,068	19,126

SOURCE: Wolfgang F. Stolper, 'Economic development in Nigeria', *Journal of Economic History*, Dec. 1963, **23**, no. 4, 397.

purchased exportables, and drove the producers' prices down to levels below those paid in contiguous areas where the monopsony was not in effect.[54]

Another difference between West African palm-oil production and cocoa production is that palm-oil exports faced competition from plantation enterprises elsewhere, especially during the inter-war period from Sumatra and

pool firms harried the Company by intriguing with the middleman-tribes and enticing the trade down branches of the Niger which the Company did not control. The Native traders of Brass took direct action; they equipped an expedition which sacked the Company's factory at Acassa.' It is inconceivable that the company, with its slender administrative and military resources, could, in fact, have enforced a full-fledged monopoly over such a huge area with its tremendous system of waterways.

[54] Scott R. Pearson, 'The economic imperialism of the Royal Niger Company', *Food Research Institute Studies*, 1971, **10**, no. 1, p. 73. More generally, Professor Bauer pointed out that 'newcomers in West African trade have to surmount a high threshold which acts as a partial barrier to entry. This naturally strengthens the position of those already established, and enables them to increase the difficulties of entry for new firms. As a result, natural (inevitable) scarcities and contrived (institutional) obstacles interact to raise the threshold and to restrict entry.' (Bauer, *West African trade*, p. 109.)

Malaya, where yields were high under large-scale plantation organization. Smallholder production from naturally growing trees was able to sustain its rapid growth without encountering serious competitive problems. Because the collection of wild palm fruit could be easily integrated with the peasant cultivation of forest food-crops, this state of affairs continued so long as world demand was expanding, until about 1929. But West African palm-oil was increasingly threatened by the superior-quality oil that could be grown on plantations. At the same time, colonial authorities refused permission to Lever Brothers and the United Africa Company to establish plantations in Nigeria, in place of the traditional system of land ownership and management.

In contrast to smallholder cultivation was the large-scale modern farming on estates or plantations in a number of African colonies. If a tropical export crop required large-scale cultivation to provide a marketable bulk or quantities sufficient for economic quality processing, it was better suited to large-scale plantation enterprise than to smallholder production. Plantation cultivation, based on immigration of settlers from metropolitan countries, was a feature of Kenya, Rhodesia, Moçambique and South Africa, and to a lesser extent in Tanganyika, Northern Rhodesia and the Belgian Congo.

Because of technical requirements or the necessarily large capital expenditures that were beyond the means of smallholders, plantation production characterized sisal in East Africa (chiefly Tanganyika); tea in Kenya, Nyasaland, and Uganda; sugar in East Africa, Mauritius and Natal; rubber in Liberia and the Congo (Leopoldville); bananas in Cameroun, Somalia and the Ivory Coast; coffee in Angola, the Belgian Congo, Tanganyika and Kenya.[55] A major feature of plantation development in East Africa was the land policy, designed to encourage white colonization. By 1914, 3·4 million acres had been alienated, much on 99- and 999-year leases.

Unlike the peasant export sector, expansion of plantation production was based on external resources—initially on foreign settlers bringing capital and technology from outside. The plantation sector was the 'modern' sector with advanced management, capital and technology. As with smallholders, the expansion in cultivation was for the most part horizontal, utilizing more land in a widening process.

Helleiner concluded for Nigeria that

Beyond offering peasant farmers a vent for their potential surplus production the foreigner did next to nothing to alter the technological backwardness of the economy. Since production functions were left largely untouched, he cannot be accused of introducing an export bias to the economy. All that he did was to dangle sufficiently attractive prizes before the producers' noses to persuade them to convert potential into actual surpluses by increasing their inputs. The (relative) switch from food to export cropping was not a switch from backward to modern agriculture. But the increased utilization of available factor inputs produced an increase in overall per capita income.[56]

Plantations did hire more labour than in peasant export production, and there were more improvements over time in methods of cultivation. Nonetheless, al-

---

[55] Originally, all coffee in East Africa was grown by Europeans in the highlands; but with the introduction of more easily grown types, peasant participation increased, and by the 1950s the smallholder was definitely of increasing importance in African coffee production.

[56] Helleiner, *Peasant agriculture,* p. 12.

though plantation labour was the route for entering the market economy, most Africans entered as unskilled labour, and the plantation economy did little to inculcate new labour skills. Nor was the low-productivity, casual labour force transformed into a high-productivity, permanent labour force. The migrant labour system that characterized so much of Africa meant that labour was in joint supply to the subsistence sector and the plantation sector.

As Myint reminds us, the migrant-labour system reinforced the pattern of low wages and low productivity in a number of ways. With the high rate of labour turn-over associated with the migrant-labour system, it was not possible nor worth while to select and train indigenous labour for skilled work. There was no obligation to pay adult single males who had left their families behind in the subsistence economy wages sufficient to maintain the worker and his family or to invest in housing and other welfare projects to enable him to settle permanently with his family on the location of his work. And during slumps in the export market, the redundant labour could be laid off and returned to the subsistence sector without continuing responsibility for them. The convention of maintaining low wages for a casual labour force was perpetuated as long as possible.

All the domestic market imperfections that we previously considered as inhibiting the carry-over from primary exports—when these were from the peasant export sector—applied as well to exports from plantations. But in addition, to the extent that their low-wage policy induced plantations 'to use labour extravagantly' as a low-productivity, 'cheap' labour force, the entry of unskilled labourers into the money economy through plantation labour was without much integrative force.[57] As Myint concludes,

The failure of plantations to become the 'leading sector' in the underdeveloped countries was due, not to their producing primary exports as such, but to their cheap labour policy which has perpetuated the pattern of low wages and low productivity. With the system of using indigenous labour mainly as an undifferentiated mass of brawnpower, it is not surprising that Adam Smith's vision of growth of the exchange economy and the division of labour, 'improving the skill and dexterity of the people', should remain unfulfilled.[58]

Mineral exports

A third type of export base was provided by mineral development that proved to be of especial importance in Africa.[59] By 1935, the 'special mining territories' of the Rhodesias and the Belgian Congo accounted for more than two-thirds of the total value of exports from Africa, and minerals accounted for 78

[57] EDITORS' NOTE: Scholars disagree on the role of plantation labour. Our studies show, for example, that in Nigeria plantation wages (including fringe benefits) have commonly been higher than the industrial wages of 'permanent labour'. Similarly, in the Belgian Congo and Liberia, Firestone Rubber Company paid wages above the local scale. Workers would sit outside the company hiring office and be willing to wait weeks for a job. As regards promotion of local skills, Firestone also encouraged peasant rubber production by providing seeds for independent rubber-growers and supplied trained instructors. See Raymond L. Buell, *Liberia: a century of survival, 1847–1947* (Philadelphia, 1947), pp. 49–50.

[58] Hla Myint, *The economics of the developing countries* (London, 1964), p. 64.

[59] For details on mining and railroad expansion during the colonial period, see the essay by Katzenellenbogen in this volume.

per cent of the exports from these territories.[60] The rise in value of mineral exports from South Africa and the two Rhodesias was particularly strong. Mineral exports from South Africa rose from £51.8 million in 1913 to £61.5 million in 1929 and to £77.5 million by 1935. From Southern Rhodesia, mineral exports were £3.0 million in 1913, £4.4 million in 1929 and £6.5 million in 1935. From Northern Rhodesia, mineral exports increased from only £52,000 in 1913 to £557,000 in 1929 and to £4.5 million by 1935.[61]

The extension of the miners' frontier and the frontier of investment in South Africa has been described by Hancock and by Frankel.[62] Their accounts conform with our emphasis on domestic market conditions as being strongly determinant of the extent of the carry-over from exports of diamonds and gold. Thus, Frankel is concerned with the 'tyranny of economic paternalism' as contrasted to development through the aid of market forces. He states that

if there had been no colour bar, no economic frontier between Black and White, no paternalistic interference with market forces, there would . . . have been a normal growth of urban areas comprising a settled non-European working population, the supply of which would have adapted itself to a growing demand in mining, as well as to the steady expansion of the manufacturing industries and tertiary services. If the whole paternalistic network of restrictions on Natives . . . had been lifted, there might well have been an organic economic development which would have raised wages, living standards, and the national income at a rate sufficient to enable European standards generally to be safeguarded without retarding the development of the skill and potentialities of progressive non-Europeans.[63, 64]

More recently, Baldwin's study of Northern Rhodesia's development has been conducted within a framework of analysis that is in several respects close to that suggested here. Baldwin's study is especially instructive in emphasizing the technological nature of the production function of the export commodity as the key relationship among the basic productive characteristics of the developing economy. The rise in copper production was rapid. Mines began to be developed in the late 1920s by the Rhodesian Selection Trust and the Anglo American Corporation of South Africa. From a negligible quantity in 1930, output rose to 138,000 long tons in 1934, to a pre-war peak of 251,000 long tons in 1943 and then to 579,000 long tons by 1960. Between 1945 and 1953, copper exports accounted for an average of 86.5 per cent of the value of all exports, and the exports of mineral commodities equalled 69.3 per cent of Northern Rhodesia's gross domestic product during these years.[65] Nonetheless,

[60] S. Herbert Frankel, *Capital investment in Africa: its course and effects* (London, Oxford University Press, 1938; reprint, New York, 1969), p. 213.   [61] *Ibid.*, p. 212.

[62] Hancock, *Survey of British Commonwealth affairs*, vol. II, pt. 1, pp. 10–15; II, pt. 2, pp. 1–153; Frankel, *Capital investment in Africa*, chs. 3 and 4.

[63] S. Herbert Frankel, *The tyranny of economic paternalism in Africa: a study of frontier mentality, 1860–1960* (Johannesburg, 1960).

[64] EDITORS' NOTE: Frankel's explanation has been criticized, however. Uganda, for instance, had no white settlers and no industrial colour bar. But Gutkind and Southall's researches in Kampala, a city without segregation laws or apartheid-minded settlers, showed a semi-migrant black population essentially similar in character to migrant labour in Rhodesian and South African towns. After two generations of town life, black workmen in Uganda were still leaving their wives in the rural areas. Concubinage was rife, and family life hardly existed. (See A. W. Southall and P. C. W. Gutkind, 'Townsmen in the making: Kampala and its suburbs', in *East African Studies*, 1956, no. 9.)

[65] R. E. Baldwin, *Economic development and export growth: a study of Northern Rhodesia, 1920–1960* (Berkeley, University of California Press, 1966), pp. 32–3 and 36.

Northern Rhodesians continued to confront the fundamental problem that an increase in their copper exports did not induce additional domestic spending and production on a sufficiently substantial scale: 'An expansion of their export industry was incapable of triggering the development of a diversified domestic industrial structure.' [66] Whereas the growth rate of real gross domestic product (in the monetary sector) averaged 5·8 per cent for the period 1938–61,[67] the development process has been confined to only a small part of the total economy. As a modern, highly mechanized industry, copper has been superimposed upon a rural, backward economy—and as late as 1960, more than 70 per cent of the population remained engaged in subsistence production.

Why did the high rate of growth in copper exports not support a broader pattern of development? Much of the answer in Baldwin's analysis rests on the technological characteristics of copper production. These are a low aggregate labour coefficient in which the skilled-labour component is comparatively large, significant economies of scale, and moderately high capital coefficient. The low labour coefficient (number of employees per $1,000 of annual gross output) means that the copper sector was a small-scale employer of labour. Moreover, during the earlier period of the industry, European workers proved to be less expensive than the African worker for jobs requiring almost any significant degree of skill: even though the African's real wage may have been only one-twentieth of the European worker's, the cost of training him, in relation to the length of time he was likely to remain in employment, was sufficiently high that the European worker's 'efficiency wages' were actually lower for almost any level of skilled job. Initially, therefore, the mines employed Africans in only the most rudimentary tasks. The direct employment and immediate skill-imparting effects on African labour were consequently comparatively slight.

During the 1930s and 1940s, however, there was considerable improvement in the efficiency of African labour, and consequently a relatively greater utilization of Africans in mining activity. In addition, more opportunities and training were provided for the advancement of unskilled workers to higher skilled activities in the copper industry; and in some cases the skills were transferable to other industries. But the process of African advancement remained slow and the total impact on direct employment small. Two non-competing groups of labour emerged—the higher-skilled, high-wage Europeans; and the lower-skilled African workers, whose wage rate was initially related to the much lower alternative income that could be earned in the subsistence sector. But this large wage differential of the 1920s and 1930s could not have been perpetuated in the 1940s and 1950s if the labour market had been more competitive without the monopolistic pressures from the European Mineworkers Union and governmental policies. By setting the wage pattern for other sectors of the economy, the high-wage policy in mining aggravated the problem of providing sufficient employment opportunities to absorb labour from the subsistence sector into other secondary and tertiary activities.

The other technological characteristics—economies of scale and high capital coefficient—made it necessary to import both foreign capital and management. Small-scale domestic mining units were simply uncompetitive, and only the large-scale, foreign-operated mining enterprise could survive in competition on

---

[66] *Ibid.*, p. 218. [67] *Ibid.*, p. 29.

world markets. The large amount of capital and the high degree of technological knowledge required in copper production also militated against domestic ownership or management. Baldwin concludes that because of the technological constraints in copper mining, the Northern Rhodesian copper industry was 'well adapted to the plentiful supply of copper resources but not to the other relative factor conditions of the economy—an abundant supply of unskilled labor and a relatively small stock of capital'. It was therefore necessary to import capital and skilled labour in order to establish a profitable copper industry. 'The direct impact on existing factor conditions other than natural resources was comparatively small.' [68]

If conditions on the supply side were not favourable for a widespread carry-over from export production, they were limited as well on the demand side. The strongest influence on the demand side was on the growth of market-oriented agriculture because the mining industry provided the major market outlet for cattle and maize. Until the mid-1950s, European employers directly supplied African workers with foodstuffs. After money payments substituted for rations, the African employees still provided the greatest demand for domestic foodstuffs. And although much of the demand was met by European farmers, an increasing share—especially of maize—was produced by African farmers. This was important in inducing the movement of African farmers out of the subsistence economy into cash-crops. The movement into the market economy to meet an increased demand in turn stimulated the adoption of better agricultural techniques by subsistence cultivators, and the larger market made the introduction of improved productive techniques more feasible. The stimulus to greater production of cash-crops by African farmers was cut short, however, by governmental policies that were designed to benefit European settlers.

Baldwin has analysed in some detail how, when the interests of the African farmers were believed to conflict with those of the European population, the Africans were largely ignored or discriminated against through the land policy adopted by the government, the measures enacted to control grain prices and the steps taken to influence cattle prices. [69] An appraisal of these policies leads to the following conclusion:

The agricultural policy of Northern Rhodesia was based upon the premise that European farmers were entitled to preferential treatment . . . The European government . . . apparently believed that the African people had no right to share as agricultural producers in the demands generated by the copper industry and, moreover, were incapable of responding to the market demand. When the fallaciousness of this latter view was demonstrated by a rapid growth in the African share of the commercial agricultural market during the early thirties, the government introduced controls that clearly were designed to give preference to European farmers. [70]

Whereas the demand from African workers in the mines was confined to foodstuffs, the consumption spending of the skilled European workers had only a marginal effect on the demand for local products. Because of their high income levels and their foreign-oriented taste patterns, the demand of the European workers for imported goods was much higher. The distribution of income remained highly unequal (as late as 1959, only 4 per cent of the wealthiest families received 35 per cent of all personal income), [71] and this also biased con-

[68] *Ibid.*, pp. 80–1.   [69] *Ibid.*, pp. 144 ff.   [70] *Ibid.*, p. 159.   [71] *Ibid.*, pp. 42 and 184.

sumption demand towards imports. Beyond foodstuffs, the demand for locally produced goods was therefore extremely limited, and the inducement to local industry negligible. Secondary industry was confined to construction activity, cement, clothing, drink and tobacco, furniture and some small-scale metal-works.[72]

Expansion of the copper industry did in itself, of course, induce a demand for inputs from secondary industry. But, apart from local building and construction materials, the demand for complex machinery and specialized equipment was filled by imports. Mining machinery, structural steel, electrical apparatus, vehicles, explosives, bearings, rails, fittings and piping were all imported. Some small industrial firms were, however, eventually established in the Copper Belt to manufacture less specialized repair and distributive materials. It is of interest that many of these firms were organized by former European employees of the mines who had acquired specialized knowledge at the mines, and that many of the African employees who were later able to enter manufacturing employment had gained simple skills and industrial work habits in the mines. Some small-scale local secondary industries also arose during the 1950s.[73]

Apart from agriculture, the major impact of mining on the industrial structure was confined to rail transportation, electric power and some public services. The extension of copper production gave the impetus to railway construction, and in the mid-1950s more than 60 per cent of railway revenue was derived from the copper industry. The railways, in turn, demanded some local inputs, and in 1960 employed almost 6,000 Africans. Although built in response to the mining activity, the extension of the railway was also instrumental in promoting the marketing of cash-crops.

The next most important secondary repercussion from the copper industry was on the electric-power industry, the establishment of which was linked to copper expansion. As of 1957, the copper companies were still purchasing directly as much as 63 per cent of the gross output of the electric-power industry, although not many African employees were affected.

As in the other African colonies, a whole host of domestic obstacles limited the repercussions from the export sector. A more vigorous carry-over from export was not possible without a more strongly defined price system, a wider network of market relationships and a diminution of the forces of traditionalism. Not only was the facilitative support of a wider-spread market economy missing, but there were actually inhibitions through the use of monopolistic power by special groups—namely, organized European unions and European settlers who, with the aid of governmental policies, managed to retain for themselves a major share of the economic gains from Rhodesia's growth. As Baldwin concludes, European monopolistic efforts affected not only the distribution of income, but even more, the overall rate of development itself. If there had not been monopolistic government and union policies, there would have been a larger skilled labour-force that could have been employed in

[72] EDITORS' NOTE: Economists have yet to explain fully why this is so. Nigeria and Uganda had no settlers, but until recently the same pattern of secondary industrial growth was found in those countries as in Northern Rhodesia.

[73] For the value of industrial output, see Federation of Rhodesia and Nyasaland, *Survey of economic developments since 1953* (Salisbury, 1960), p. 497.

the production of more copper and in more numerous secondary industries than at present exist. Even though the economy would still be dualistic and dominated by the copper industry, nonetheless, 'compared with its present extreme narrowness, the faster, more-balanced growth that would have resulted could have made an important contribution to the country's present development goals'.[74, 75]

A distinctive feature of the Rhodesian case, however, was the dependence of the export sector on foreign investment. The problem of export-led development acquires an additional dimension when the export growth is linked to direct private foreign investment. An assessment of the contribution of exports to the country's development must then involve consideration of the benefits and costs of the foreign investment over time. Some of the benefits to be considered are these: (1) foreign savings are made available to the host country; (2) foreign exchange is made available; (3) to the extent that the investment contributes more to output than is appropriated by foreign investors, there must be a distribution of the gain in product in the form of either higher wages, greater income to domestic suppliers and/or revenues to government; (4) managerial knowledge, including overseas contacts is provided; (5) labour is trained; (6) technology of more advanced countries is introduced; and (7) the country enjoys the 'spill-over' or educative effects of the advanced management, trained labour force and technology.

Against these benefits are to be set the possible costs of private foreign investment: (1) special concessions made by the host government in order to attract the foreign investment; (2) a possibly negative effect on domestic saving if the foreign investment competes with domestic investment or limits the supply of domestic entrepreneurship; (3) the cost of balance-of-payments adjustment when the inflow of new capital is insufficient to cover the return outflow of interest, dividends and profits; and (4) political and social costs through the possible loss of national autonomy in domestic policy-making if the foreign enterprise or the foreign investor's government exerts undue influence on the host government's policies.[76]

In the case of foreign investment in Northern Rhodesia's copper industry, there were definite contributions in helping to fill the savings, foreign exchange, management and technological gaps of the initially backward subsistence economy. Over time as the investment operated, the major domestic beneficiaries of part of the increase in real national income were African labourers and the Northern Rhodesian government. Government revenue increased al-

[74] Baldwin, *Economic development and export growth,* p. 217.

[75] EDITORS' NOTE: European farmers, especially tobacco- and maize-growers, however, continued to play a major part in Zambian agriculture at a time when the country was approaching independence, and when the government was no longer as favourable to their interests as it had been in the 1930s. Europeans had the advantage of technological and agronomical skills, and of having greater capital reserves than the great majority of African cultivators. Between the 1930s and the 1960s there were fundamental changes within the structure of European farming. According to Republic of Zambia, *First National Development Plan, 1966–1970* (Lusaka, 1966), p. 2, in 1964 some 700 white farmers thus still accounted for the bulk of the cash-crops. The Europeans, working 180,000 acres, accounted for £7·7 million of the country's total agricultural sales. The African cultivators, working an area of about 5 million acres, produced agricultural sales to the value of £3·2 million.

[76] EDITORS' NOTE: For a different interpretation of what impeded African economic progress during the colonial period, see the essays in this volume by the Dotsons and by Katzenellenbogen.

most a hundredfold between the mid-1920s and 1959–60; and by 1938 the mining industry was furnishing some 43 per cent of all government revenue. During the mid-fifties, when copper profits were extremely high, over 60 per cent of all government revenue came from the mining industry.[77] At the same time, however, remittances abroad in the form of net interest, net dividends and net profits were substantial: between 1951 and 1953 over 17 per cent of the income earned within the country was remitted abroad in this form.[78] Moreover, with the very high import content to both exports and investment, the leakages abroad from domestic expenditures were large, and the domestic multipliers were correspondingly low. Estimates for the early 1950s are of an export multiplier between 1.25 and 1.8 and an investment multiplier of approximately 0.6.[79]

We cannot engage here in any attempt at a full-scale statistical exercise of calculating the benefits and costs of foreign investment in Rhodesia's exports. But we might conclude from the readily available evidence that the benefit/cost ratio was greater than unity. The ratio would have been greater, however, if governmental policies had sought to retain more of the benefits within Rhodesia and to secure more of an impact on the longer-term productive capabilities of the Rhodesian economy.[80]

Conclusion

This essay has reviewed three different interpretations of how international trade may affect a country's development, and has considered their applicability to a number of African economies. We have had to consider many different countries and complex forces, and our data have often been sparse. Hence our analysis has of necessity been more superficial than exhaustive, and more impressionistic than precisely quantitative. Future studies of individual countries possibly using more advanced econometric techniques of the 'new economic history', may remove these deficiencies. At present, however, we must be content with suggesting a few central propositions:

(A) The opportunity to trade overseas provided the initial stimulus to development in many of the African colonies, and the export sector was the leading sector. But the development of most colonies remained highly uneven, and Africans entered the money economy either through production of cash-crops or through wage employment without substantial change in the traditional sector. Large rural subsistence sectors remained at the end of the colonial period.

(B) The effectiveness of the export sector in initiating an integrative process of development depended on the strength of the initial stimulus, as determined mainly by the technological aspects of the export's production function, and on the receptivity of the domestic economy, as determined by the widespread existence of market institutions and market relationships. There were differential

---

[77] *Ibid.*, pp. 187 and 189.   [78] *Ibid.*, p. 47.

[79] Based on calculations for both Rhodesia and Nyasaland by A. G. Irvine, *The balance of payments of Rhodesia and Nyasaland, 1945–1954* (London, 1959), pp. 598–608. This means that a £1 million increase in exports and in investment, respectively, would increase gross national product only by £1·25–1·8 million and £0·6 million, respectively. Comparable figures for Northern Rhodesia alone would undoubtedly be even lower because of a higher import content than for the Federation as a whole.

[80] For details on growth of industries during the colonial period, see Kilby's essay in this volume.

stimuli from exports, but the domestic impediments—broadly interpreted as market imperfections—were common in all the colonies.

(C) An illuminating typology for analysing the nature of the initial stimuli for exports is that of smallholder cultivation, plantation cultivation and mineral production.

(D) The extent to which the export enterprise is indigenous or foreign-owned also raises issues of benefits and costs that extend beyond simply the productivity of the investment in the export sector.

(E) In all cases, the stimulus from foreign trade produced some positive carry-over. There is no evidence of 'immiserization through trade.' But the diffusion mechanism was weak, not because of limited wants or lack of response to price and income incentives, but because of the absence of market information, high risks, insufficient market opportunities, lack of marketing facilities, as well as of integrative market forces.

(F) It is not difficult to envisage an alternative course of historical development that would have been more conducive to a widespread and more even process of development. Such a course would, however, have had to depend on more positive and deliberate governmental policies, especially in promoting market institutions fostering human-resource development, reducing the market imperfections and securing for the host country a larger share of the rents accruing to foreign investment. The villain in the piece was not that exports of the colonial economies were primary products, but rather the absence of more active policy-making by colonial governments.

If colonial governments did not solve these problems, the development programmes of post-independence governments must. Sir Keith Hancock anticipated this when he concluded:

The traditional outlook and policy of the West African administrations need to be modified and modernized, not obliterated. Something new is most emphatically needed. Economic policy must be given the place which is its due . . . Different generations choose different aspirations and concepts to guide them in their political endeavour: 'indirect rule' was the watchword of the decade which followed the last war; 'development and welfare' will probably be the cry which follows the present one.[81]

Just as colonial rule was not responsible for the underdevelopment of Africa, so will decolonization not in itself produce development. The importance of decolonization from the standpoint of facilitating export-led growth is that it may allow the post-colonial governments to use a greater variety of discretionary policy instruments. The potentialities for 'development through trade' are present in abundance, and it is now incumbent upon the new African governments to formulate policies that will lay the sound foundations necessary to support a more extensive restructuring of their societies.

BIBLIOGRAPHY

Baldwin, R. E. *Economic development and export growth: a study of Northern Rhodesia, 1920–1960.* Berkeley, University of California Press, 1966.
  'Export technology and development from a subsistence level', *Economic Journal,* March 1963, **63.**

[81] Hancock, *Survey of British Commonwealth affairs,* vol. II, pt. 2, pp. 266–7.

'Patterns of development in newly settled regions'. *Manchester School of Economic and Social Studies,* May 1954, **24**.

ed. *Trade, growth, and the balance of payments: essays in honor of Gottfried Haberler.* Chicago, 1965.

Barber, William J. *The economy of British Central Africa.* Stanford University Press, 1961.

Bauer, P. T. *West African trade: a study of competition, oligopoly and monopoly in a changing economy.* Cambridge University Press, 1954.

Berril, K. 'International trade and the rate of economic growth'. *Economic History Review,* April 1960, **12**.

Bhagwati, Jagdish N., Ronald W. Jones, Robert A. Mundell and Jaroslav Vanek, eds. *Trade, balance of payments and growth: papers in international economics in honor of Charles P. Kindleberger.* Amsterdam, 1971.

Cambridge history of the British Empire, vol. III: *The Empire-Commonwealth, 1870–1919.* Cambridge University Press, 1959.

Caves, Richard E. 'Export-led growth and the new economic history', in *Trade, balance of payments and growth: papers in international economics in honor of Charles P. Kindleberger,* Jagdish N. Bhagwati *et al.,* eds. Amsterdam, 1971.

'' 'Vent for surplus'' models of trade and growth,' in R. E. Baldwin *et al., Trade, growth and the balance of payments: essays in honor of Gottfried Haberler.* Chicago, 1965.

Corden, W. Max. 'The effects of trade on the rate of growth', in *Trade, balance of payments and growth: papers in international economics in honor of Charles P. Kindleberger,* Jagdish N. Bhagwati *et al.,* eds. Amsterdam, 1971.

Dike, K. O. *Trade and politics in the Niger Delta.* Oxford, Clarendon Press, 1956.

Federation of Rhodesia and Nyasaland. *Survey of economic developments since 1953.* Salisbury, 1960.

Field, M. J. 'The agricultural system of the Manya-Krobo of the Gold Coast', *Africa,* 1943, **14**.

Fieldhouse, D. K. *The colonial empire.* London, 1966.

'Imperialism: an historiographical revision', *Economic History Review,* 2nd ser., Dec. 1961, **14**, no. 4.

Frankel, S. Herbert. *Capital investment in Africa: its course and effects.* London, Oxford University Press, 1938; reprint, New York, 1969.

The tyranny of economic paternalism in Africa: a study of frontier mentality 1860–1960. Johannesburg, 1960.

Gann, L. H. *A history of Northern Rhodesia: early days to 1953.* London, 1964.

'The Northern Rhodesian copper industry and the world of copper: 1923–1952', *Rhodes-Livingstone Journal,* 1955, **18**.

Gann, L. H., and Peter Duignan. *Burden of empire: an appraisal of Western colonialism in Africa south of the Sahara.* New York, 1967.

Hailey, William Malcolm Hailey, 1st baron. *An African survey: a study of problems arising in Africa south of the Sahara.* London, Oxford University Press, 1957.

Hancock, Sir William Keith. 'Agenda for the study of British imperial history, 1850–1950', *Journal of Economic History,* 1953, **13**.

Survey of British Commonwealth affairs, vol. II: *Problems of economic policy, 1918–1939,* pts. 1 and 2. London, Oxford University Press, 1940–2.

Wealth of colonies. Cambridge University Press, 1950.

Havinden, M. A. 'The history of crop cultivation in West Africa: a bibliographical guide', *Economic History Review,* 2nd ser., Dec. 1970, **23**, no. 3.

Helleiner, G. K. *Peasant agriculture, government and economic growth in Nigeria.* Homewood, Ill., 1966.

Herskovits, Melville, and Mitchell Harwitz, eds. *Economic transition in Africa.* Evanston, Northwestern University Press, 1964.

Hill, Polly. *The Gold Coast cocoa farmer*. London, Oxford University Press, 1956.

The migrant cocoa-farmers of southern Ghana: a study in rural capitalism. Cambridge University Press, 1963.

Review of Robert Szereszewski's *Structural changes in the economy of Ghana*, in *Economic Development and Cultural Change*, Oct. 1957, **16**, no. 1.

Hirschman, Albert O. *The strategy of economic development*. New Haven, Yale University Press, 1958.

Hodgkin, Thomas. 'Islam and politics in Africa' (nine articles), *West Africa*, 15 Sept.–10 Nov. 1956.

Hunter, Guy. *The new societies of tropical Africa: a selective study*. London, Oxford University Press, 1962.

Hymer, Stephen H., and Steven A. Resnick. 'International trade and uneven development', in *Trade, balance of payments and growth: papers in international economics in honor of Charles P. Kindleberger*, Jagdish N. Bhagwati *et al.*, eds. Amsterdam, 1971.

Irvine, A. G. *The balance of payments of Rhodesia and Nyasaland, 1945–1954*. London, 1956.

Johnston, Bruce F. 'Changes in agricultural productivity', in *Economic transition in Africa*, Melville J. Herskovits and Mitchell Harwitz, eds. Evanston, Northwestern University Press, 1964.

Kamarck, Andrew M. *The economics of African development*. New York, 1967.

Kay, G. B., ed. *The political economy of colonialism in Ghana*. Cambridge University Press, 1972.

Landes, David S. 'Some thoughts on the nature of economic imperialism', *Journal of Economic History*, Dec. 1961, **21**, no. 4.

Lewis, W. Arthur. *Aspects of tropical trade, 1883–1965*. Stockholm, 1960.

'Economic development with unlimited supplies of labour', *Manchester School of Economic and Social Studies*, May 1954, **20.**

'Unlimited labour: further notes', *Manchester School of Economic and Social Studies*, Jan. 1958, **26.**

'World production, prices and trade, 1870–1960', *Manchester School of Economic and Social Studies*, May 1952, **20**, no. 2.

ed. *Tropical development 1880–1913*. Evanston, Northwestern University Press, 1970.

Manning, Patrick. 'Some export statistics for Nigeria, 1880–1904', *Nigerian Journal of Economic and Social Studies*, July 1967, **9**, no. 2.

Metcalf, G. E., ed. *Great Britain and Ghana: documents of Ghana history, 1807–1957*. London, 1964.

Mill, John Stuart. *Principles of political economy*, vols. I and II. London, 1848.

Mungeam, G. H. *British rule in Kenya, 1895–1921*. London, Oxford University Press, 1966.

Myint, Hla. 'The classical theory of international trade and the underdeveloped countries', *Economic Journal*, 1958, **68.**

The economics of the developing countries. London, 1964.

Myrdal, Gunnar. *Development and underdevelopment*. Cairo, 1956.

An international economy. New York, 1956.

Neumark, S. Daniel. *Foreign trade and economic development in Africa: a historical perspective*. Stanford, Food Research Institute, 1964.

New Cambridge modern history, vol. XI: *Material progress and world-wide problems, 1870–1898*. Cambridge University Press, 1962.

Pearson, Scott R. 'The economic imperialism of the Royal Niger Company', *Food Research Institute Studies*, 1971, **10**, no. 1.

Perroux, François. 'Multinational investment and the analysis of development and integration poles', in *Multinational investment in the economic development and integration of Latin America*. Bogotá, Inter-American Development Bank, April 1968.

Rhodes, Robert. 'Bibliography: on studying imperialism', *Review of Radical Political Economics*, Spring 1971, **3,** no. 1.

Smith, Adam. *An inquiry into the nature and causes of the wealth of nations,* Edwin Cannan, ed. New York, 1937.

Stolper, Wolfgang. 'Economic development in Nigeria', *Journal of Economic History,* Dec. 1963, **23,** no 4.

Stover, Charles. 'Tropical exports', in *Tropical development 1880–1913,* W. Arthur Lewis, ed. Evanston, Northwestern University Press, 1970.

Suret-Canale, Jean. *French colonialism in tropical Africa, 1900–1945.* New York, 1971.

Szereszewski, Robert. *Structural changes in the economy of Ghana, 1891–1911.* London, 1965.

Thompson, C. H., and H. W. Woodruff. *Economic development in Rhodesia and Nyasaland.* London, 1954.

Ward, W. E. F. *A history of Ghana.* London, 1963.

Woods, I. R. 'Some aspects of South Africa's foreign trade in relation to her aggregate income, 1910–1954', *South African Journal of Economics,* June 1958, **26.**

Yates, P. Lamartine. *Forty years of foreign trade.* New York, 1959.

CHAPTER 12

MANUFACTURING IN COLONIAL AFRICA

by

PETER KILBY

Chronicling the development of manufacturing in African countries that have been at one time or another colonial dependencies is an unmanageably large task, comprehending as it does virtually the entire continent. To reduce the enterprise to more modest proportions, we shall at the outset place to one side the old commercial economies of the Arab states and the Republic of South Africa. This still leaves an extremely heterogeneous collection of countries, yet nevertheless a collection that is differentiated from the continent's northern and southern extremities by some important unifying characteristics.

Four such common characteristics will be identified, although a considerably longer list could no doubt be assembled. These are all tropical or semi-tropical countries in which black Africans constitute over 95 per cent of the population. Politically, all these territories were subject to colonial rule only during the twentieth century, and virtually all gained their independence within five years of 1960. In terms of the economic structure, they all entered colonial subjugation as subsistence agrarian economies without the most rudimentary infrastructure—(without, for example, facilities for wheeled transport or primary schools)—or the legal and institutional supports upon which significant economic growth depends. And, owing to the late start of economic modernization in tropical Africa and to various obstacles thwarting African participation in large-scale commercial ventures, in all these countries manufacturing has been pioneered by non-African entrepreneurs, who remained dominant throughout the colonial period. These elements, then, define the geographic scope of our narrative, as well as provide the context in which to judge the record of industrial achievement.

The essay that follows is divided into five parts. The first part presents a statistical overview of the extent of manufacturing in a large number of countries and discusses some of the broad determinants of differential achievement. The second part seeks to examine the historical patterns in white settler colonies; a brief inspection of Kenya and Uganda is followed by an extended coverage of the Southern Rhodesian experience. The third part focuses on the peasant economies of West Africa; after a review of developments in Senegal, the Ivory Coast and the Gold Coast, Nigeria is singled out for more intensive study. Emergent African entrepreneurship is the subject of the fourth part. The fifth draws together such generalizations as our narrative permits about the colonial industrial experience and appraises the value of this heritage to the postcolonial African states.

Throughout the essay, our concern will be narrowly confined to the establishment of manufacturing enterprise, with some attention to entrepreneurial factors and immediate economic conditions that bore on the investment decision and subsequent performance. Business firms engaged in construction, mining, electricity generation and transportation are excluded.[1] Nor is more than passing consideration given to such matters as labour commitments, technical education and infrastructure and government incentive policies. These ingredients, although seldom a binding constraint, are significant and have been neglected only because the prior task of assembling the basic historical facts about colonial manufacturing fully absorbed the writer's energies.[2]

The extent of manufacturing in colonial Africa

In order to obtain a notion of the quantitative significance of the phenomenon under investigation, we begin with a review of the level of manufacturing output that had been reached by the end of the colonial period. Whereas these measures are subject to a very wide margin of error—although perhaps no greater than for any other statistic on Black Africa—they do give a fair indication of orders of magnitude.[3] Table 112 presents figures on the absolute size of industrial output and its relative share in national output for some eighteen

[1] EDITORS' NOTE: Professor Kilby's essay does not treat either mining enterprise or the development of transport. Both these areas are discussed in the Meier and the Katzenellenbogen studies in this volume. Clearly, such economic boundary lines have necessarily been somewhat arbitrarily drawn. Mining in Zambia, for instance, was not confined merely to digging ore from the ground. Modern copper-mining involved a complex set of industrial processes. It created, besides, a host of subsidiary enterprises that Professor Kilby has not considered in detail. The same consideration applies to the provision of transport.

Though railway-building is designed primarily to speed up and to multiply the movement of men and merchandise, railways act also as multiple accelerators of economic progress. As Marx pointed out more than a century ago with regard to British railway construction in India: 'You cannot maintain a network of railways over an immense country without introducing all those industrial processes necessary to meet the immediate and current wants of railway locomotion, and out of which there must grow the application of machinery to those branches of industry not immediately connected with railways. The railway system will therefore become, in India, truly the forerunner of modern industry.' (Karl Marx, 'The future results of British rule in India', *Karl Marx on colonialism: his despatches and other writings* . . . in Shlomo Avineri, ed., [New York, 1968], pp. 128–9.) The provision of railways thus created a need for railway workshops and repair shops. The Kilby analysis, moreover, does not deal with service industries connected with road-building and the running of railways, ports and airways.

[2] The writer is indebted to Marianne Baer Kilby and Robert Siegel for extensive research assistance with respect to French West Africa and Kenya-Uganda-Rhodesia, respectively. Their work of screening widely scattered narrative and statistical sources was made possible by funds from Wesleyan University.

[3] The principal sources of error occur with respect to incomplete coverage of agricultural processing, cottage craft production, artisan industries, and smaller establishments in the modern sector. Although the statisticians make allowance for these exclusions in the construction of their output estimates, their method of doing so varies greatly, with the result that figures for manufacturing are not strictly comparable between countries.

There is also a tendency to exaggerate the rate of growth of industry as a consequence of widening statistical collection. The Ugandan case is typical: 'The estimate in the GDP series for 1963 was £12·1 million of value added in the manufacturing sector, while the 1963 Survey reported a figure of £16·8 million. For 1964, the figures were £12·8 million and £17·1 million respectively. These revisions threw rather serious doubts on the accuracy of earlier estimates of manufacturing product in the GDP estimates and, indeed, on the estimate of Gross Domestic Product as a whole. The Second Five Year Plan concludes on the basis of this recent evidence that the official GDP figures are probably underestimated by at least 10 percent.' (E. J. Stoutjesdijk, *Uganda's manufacturing sector* [Nairobi, 1967], p. 20.)

Table 112. *Population, income and manufacturing output
in selected African countries, 1960*

	Population (million)	Gross domestic product ($ million)	Per capita income ($)	Manufacturing production ($ million)	Share of mfg. in GDP (per cent)
Nigeria	40·0	3,500	88	157·5	4·5
Ethiopia	20·7	1,021	49	61·3	6·0
Belgian Congo	14·1	910	58	127·4	14·0
Sudan	11·8	909	77	43·6	4·8
Tanganyika	9·6	671	67	20·1	3·0
Kenya	8·1	641	79	60·9	9·5
Gold Coast	6·8	1,503	222	94·7	6·3
Uganda	6·7	583	87	37·9	6·5
Angola	4·8	726	151	31·2	4·3
Cameroun	4·7	511	109	30·6	6·0
Southern Rhodesia	3·6	751	206	120·2	16·0
Northern Rhodesia	3·2	511	155	28·1	5·5
Ivory Coast	3·2	584	181	31·0	5·3
Senegal	3·1	678	218	64·4	9·5
Dahomey (1965)	2·4	175	74	4·6	2·6
Sierra Leone (1965)	2·3	316	133	19·9	6·3
Togo (1965)	1·6	150	92	6·2	4·1
Gabon	0·4	131	294	8·0	6·1

NOTE: Manufacturing excludes utilities and construction. All values expressed in U.S. 1964 dollars.

SOURCES: Population data from Organization for Co-operation and Economic Development, Development Centre, *Population of less developed countries* (Paris, 1967). For Nigeria, income data from Nigeria, Federal Office of Statistics, *Gross domestic product of Nigeria 1958–1966* (Lagos, 1968). For the Gold Coast, columns 4 and 5 from Peter Robson and D. A, Lury, *The economies of Africa* (Evanston, Northwestern University Press, 1969), p. 112. All other data from International Bank for Reconstruction and Development, Economics Department, *World tables* (Washington, D.C., 1968).

countries, along with demographic and income data. The countries are listed by order of population.

At the end of the colonial period, Nigeria, the Belgian Congo and Southern Rhodesia had, by a substantial margin, the largest industrial sectors. Annual net output for these countries ranged from $120 to $160 million. The most common production levels were a third or less that of the 'big three', eight of the eighteen countries falling between $44 and $20 million. If we look at size of manufacturing relative to national product, Nigeria drops out, leaving the Belgian Congo and Southern Rhodesia as the clear leaders at 14 and 16 per cent respectively. The great bulk of our sample (fourteen countries) appears in the bottom range of 2·5 to 6·5 per cent, with only two countries—Kenya and Senegal—falling in an intermediate position of 9·5 per cent.

What general characteristics of these economies, if any, appear to be related to the size of the manufacturing sector? Clearly, population is one such factor, associated with the high levels of industrial production (in an absolute sense) in Nigeria and Ethiopia, and the extremely low levels in Dahomey, Togo and Gabon. A second significant variable, seeming to explain the relatively good performance of the Gold Coast and the poor one for Tanganyika, is *per capita* income. Lastly, a high share of manufacturing in gross domestic output (above 6 per cent) is in every case associated with the presence of a large resident European community.

In exactly what way do the above factors contribute to the establishment of manufacturing? In the case of a sizeable population, even though *per capita* income may be very low, there is always enough discretionary expenditure for the purchase of simple consumer goods (for example, textiles, beer or cigarettes) and construction materials (e.g., cement), with the result that large numbers soon create national or, as in the case of Nigeria, regional markets equal to the volume of production of an efficient-sized manufacturing plant. When this occurs, assuming the government is willing to extend modest tariff protection, replacing the imported commodity with local production is likely to become a profitable undertaking. On the other hand, for very small countries with comparable levels of average income, the diseconomies of small-scale production have meant that under normal circumstances investment in import-substituting manufacturing is neither privately profitable not socially beneficial.

In contrast to population size, the principal impact of a resident European community is on the 'supply side'.[4] Although a significant number of relatively wealthy Europeans may by their demand sustain certain industries, for any given level of *per capita* income the African population has that much less to spend; and it is the simpler commodities purchased by the latter that offer the best prospects for competitive local production. Thus, on balance, from the point of view of market demand, the distribution of income implied by the presence of a substantial European community is less favourable for import substitution than when such groups are absent.

From the supply side, however, resident Europeans have provided investible savings, technical and managerial skills and entrepreneurship, which, given the extreme scarcity of these ingredients among the African population, has historically far outweighed the less favourable contribution on the demand side. Because the bulk of industrial output in countries without settler communities has been accounted for by foreign investment, it is also appropriate to ask how the resident Europeans have added to what the large foreign firms would have achieved acting alone. The answer is twofold. Because of their greater number, their lower cost of obtaining local information and their proximity to a wider range of emerging opportunities, especially for small-scale ventures related to their farming and merchandising activities, resident Europeans were likely to act earlier and in more fields than large investors located abroad. Second, the strong political leverage of settler interest-groups on cautious colonial administrations meant that they could more easily extract the necessary government support for their proposed industrial ventures.

We now come to the third general factor influencing the level of industrial development. In the long run, over the course of decades, forces associated with a rising *per capita* income are the most potent determinants of industrialization. These forces act upon both demand and supply. With rising in-

---

[4] We define a sizeable European community as one that is in excess of fifty thousand. The countries that possessed such communities in 1960 were the Congo, Southern Rhodesia, Kenya, Senegal, Moçambique and Angola. Only in the Portuguese territories is the predicted effect on manufacturing absent.

come, the share of household expenditures on food diminishes, whereas that devoted to manufactured goods and services expands. As demand shifts in favour of manufacturing, changes in the productive structure of the economy alter comparative advantage in a similar direction. Growing specialization in product and factor markets, rising savings with subsequent growth in public and private capital stock, a movement to larger and more specialized productive units, the assimilation of superior technologies, higher levels of education—all these changes, which are linked to rising national productivity, successively create capabilities for efficient manufacturing production where none existed before.

The statistical association between *per capita* income and the changing shares of agriculture and industry in national output has been examined in a number of works by Simon Kuznets and by Hollis Chenery and Lance Taylor.[5] On the basis of 1950–63 inter-country comparisons for forty-eight countries relating sectoral output share to *per capita* income, Chenery and Taylor estimated a normal functional relationship for three types of countries: large (population over 15 million); small, primary export-oriented; and small, industry-oriented. The majority of African economies fall into the small, primary export-oriented category, although only four African countries were included in the Chenery-Taylor sample. For the forty-eight countries the level of *per capita* income explained about 80 per cent of observed variation in sectoral shares. If we apply the appropriate regression equations to the countries in Table 112 and make allowance for our exclusion of construction and utilities, Kenya and the Congo exhibit an average-sized industrial sector relative to their income, Southern Rhodesia is well above average and all the other countries are very much below the norm. Although there are both statistical and theoretical difficulties with any such estimated normal pattern,[6] in light of the relatively short period of widespread monetization, of adequate infrastructure, of education and the like, the discovery that most African territories at the close of the colonial era were below average in the size of their manufacturing sector conforms to our expectations.

The composition of industrial output in African economies in 1960 exhibited considerable uniformity. Food and beverages (grain milling, baking, margarine, beer, soft drinks), cigarettes, cotton textiles and cement constitute more than half of manufactures in all but a handful of countries. Other light consumer industries typically present include furniture, clothing, footwear, soap and perfume. Export processing—smelting, oil-seed crushing, sawmilling, cotton-ginning and so on—is proportionately diminished from earlier years but still looms large. Noticeably absent in all but two or three of these economies are iron and steel, engineering industries and industrial chemicals. In sum, the overall pattern is one of manufacturing based on the processing of local food and raw materials, some construction materials and miscellaneous light consumer goods. Absent is any significant production of intermediate products or capital equipment.

So far, we have been focusing on industrial production at the close of the co-

---

[5] For their most recent works, see Simon Kuznets, *Economic growth of nations* (Cambridge, Mass., Harvard University Press, 1971); and H. B. Chenery and Lance Taylor, 'Development patterns: among nations and over time', *Review of economics and statistics*, November 1968, **50**, no. 4.   [6] See Kuznets, *Economic growth of nations*, chs. 3 and 4.

lonial period. How recent a phenomenon is manufacturing in colonial Africa? In West Africa it is largely a post-Korean War occurrence. If we exclude crafts, in Nigeria the share of manufacturing in national output was calculated to be 0·6 per cent in 1950; in the Gold Coast the figure was 0·8 per cent as late as 1954.[7] Given the very much lower levels of gross domestic product in the early 1950s, the absolute size of industrial output was modest indeed. No aggregate statistics are available for the French colonies, but, in view of the limited number of industrial establishments and recorded employment, it is likely that the proportionate magnitudes were, with the exception of Senegal, little different from those in Nigeria and the Gold Coast. The bulk of value added in these countries derived from export processing: sawmilling, ground-nut and palm-fruit oil extraction, cotton ginning and treatment of minerals.

In other parts of colonial Africa, manufacturing reaches back farther. Southern Rhodesia takes pride of place, boasting its first factory serving the home market before the turn of the century; at the outbreak of the Second World War, manufacturing contributed about 9 per cent of national output. Kenya and the Belgian Congo were probably around the 5-per-cent mark at that time. The first official national accounts in 1954 show Kenya with 8·9 per cent of its output from manufacturing and Uganda with 7·2 per cent; considerably lower, but still well ahead of West Africa, were Northern Rhodesia at 4·0 per cent and Tanganyika at 2·6 per cent.[8] We will see from the country studies that follow that the later development of discretionary industrial processing [9] and import-substitute manufacturing in West Africa is related in significant measure to the particular type of European enterprise that was dominant in these territories.

Historical patterns in white settler colonies

The first group of African colonies whose industrial history we shall explore are those territories located in the eastern and southern portions of the continent with significant resident non-African populations. Southern and Northern Rhodesia, the Belgian Congo, Moçambique, Angola and the three British East African colonies constitute this group. We will briefly chronicle events in Uganda and Kenya, and then turn to Southern Rhodesia for a systematic analysis of industrialization in one white-settler economy.

Uganda and Kenya

The beginning of the modern period in Kenya and Uganda can be fixed at 1902, when the railway from Mombasa on the coast reached Kisumu on Lake Victoria. Although the construction of this railway was politically motivated, intending to secure Uganda, it opened up the hinterlands of Kenya no less than

---

[7] Calculated from P. N. C. Okigbo, *Nigerian national accounts, 1950–57* (Enugu, 1962), p. 21; and Peter Robson and D. A. Lury, *The Economies of Africa* (Evanston, Northwestern University Press, 1969), p. 83. [8] Robson and Lury, *Economies of Africa*, chs. 7 and 8.

[9] We may define mandatory processing as those instances where extreme weight-loss or perishability makes primary production and processing a compulsory joint-product, e.g., cotton ginning, sawmilling, palm-fruit oil extraction. Where these two characteristics are not present, the processing activity may be located in either the producing or the consuming country, depending upon the balance of a wide variety of factors. Examples of discretionary industrial processing relevant to Africa are ground-nut crushing, tin smelting, cocoa-butter extraction, tanning and palm-kernel oil extraction.

the land-locked protectorate to the west. In both colonies cotton was introduced early. The crop took hold in Uganda but not in Kenya. Because cotton became Uganda's leading crop, the industrial processing associated with it—the mandatory ginning and the discretionary extraction of edible oil from the seed—early became the country's principal manufacturing activity.

The first ginnery was opened in Kampala in 1904 by the missionary-inspired Uganda Company. Two more ginneries were established in 1907, one by the French trading firm L. Besson et Cie and the other by James Buckley, a former mechanic with the Uganda Company. In 1914, Allidina Visram (1863–1916) opened the first ginnery operated by an Asian. Unlike West Africa, where the trader's frontier was manned by Europeans, in East Africa it was the Indian merchant with his *duka,* imported goods and rupee currency who brought African producers into the money economy. And so in 1903 when cotton production began, Indian traders were well placed to purchase the crop. Arguing that African farmers needed protection from the 'sharp practices' of Indian middlemen, the European ginners were finally able to persuade the government in 1913 to require that cotton be sold directly to the processors to forestall any abuse. This, of course, knocked the Indians out of the trade and conferred monopsony powers on the ginners to fix lower prices for the farmers' cotton. So threatened, Visram, the largest of the Indian merchants (commanding a network of some 240 *dukas* in four countries), pressed on by a large number of his colleagues, decided to make the sizeable industrial investment necessary to protect his stake in the market. This is but the first instance of many that we will encounter of a defensive, market-protection motive for an industrial investment, where the object of the act is primarily to protect an existing source of income rather than to acquire a new one.

Other Indian merchants followed Visram: in 1919, of fifty-eight ginneries, seventeen were Indian-owned; six years later, 100 out of 155 were Indian-owned. Indian ginners outbid English ginners, and Bombay outbid Lancashire: in 1916, the United Kingdom took 74 per cent of Uganda's cotton exports and India 12 per cent; by 1922, England's share had dropped to 29 per cent and during the 1930s Bombay, both as an ultimate market and as an entrepôt for the Japanese trade, was taking as much as 90 per cent. (So much for colonies as a source of raw materials for the metropolitan power!) The crushing of cotton-seed for edible oil, which had started during the Second World War when the curtailment of ocean shipping prevented export of the seed and simultaneously created a scarcity of margarine and cooking oil, has also been in Asian hands. By 1948, there were twenty-eight mills.

Visram's trading interests led him into other processing activities besides cotton ginning. Between 1907 and 1915 he established a leather tannery, furniture workshops in Kampala and Entebbe, several sawmills, and a soap factory at Mombasa. Two other Indian merchants who played a leading role in East African manufacturing were N. K. Mehta and Muljibhai Madhvani. During a period when English planters in Uganda were failing with coffee and rubber, in 1924 Mehta acquired 5,000 acres of derelict plantation land for the purpose of growing sugar and built a processing plant at Lugazi, near Jinja. In addition to some 5,000 tons of refined sugar, Mehta was also producing 150,000 gallons of industrial alcohol by 1928. Madhvani came into production with a similar plantation-cum-factory in 1929. From Ugandan sugar these two entrepreneurs branched out into a wide range of industries. By the 1960s, Madhvani investments in East Africa amounted to some £20 million and included three large sugar factories, a rayon textile mill, a cotton textile mill, a match factory, paper-sack production, three glass factories, a soap works, steel re-rolling, coffee processing, margarine and cotton-seed crushing. A number of these ventures were in partnership with the Uganda Development Corporation or with Mehta. The latter's principal manufacturing investments beyond those in sugar and in partnership with Madhvani included a large iron foundry, the manufacture of agricultural implements, vehicle assembly and a distillery.

Save for four or five large entrepreneurs, Asian industrial activities outside of processing before the Second World War were on a small scale and in such lines as light engineering, printing and wearing apparel. The only sizeable foreign industrial venture was a cigarette factory established in 1937 at Jinja by the British-American Tobacco Company.

In Kenya, where the Asians were less dominant and subject to greater discrimination, ethnic shares in manufacturing were quite different. The processing of grain, pyrethrum, sisal and coffee was in the hands of the European settlers, as were also printing, beer brewing, baking and food processing. British overseas investments were to be found in soda ash (Imperial Chemical Industries, 1924), in tea (Brooke Bond and Finlay, 1925), in wattle extract (Forestal, 1932) and in cement grinding of imported clinker (Associated Portland Cement Manufacturers, 1933). Indians were prominent in sugar, cotton ginning, seed crushing, furniture and wearing apparel.

Following the post-war boom in export earnings, the pace of industrialization began to accelerate, particularly in Kenya, where foreign investment was substantial. There are many reasons why foreign investors tended to concentrate on Kenya rather than on Uganda or Tanganyika: a more developed network of supply firms, a better location for serving the three territories, previous commercial connexions with white Kenyans, proximity to a seaport and living preferences of management staff. Most of these firms were British and had long supplied the East African market from England. Indian, American, European and Japanese investors took a very distant second through fifth place.[10] The tendency for industry investments to cluster (for example, three paint factories in two years) suggests that protection of now sizeable markets was one of the motives at work.

In Uganda, the two propelling forces in the post-1950 phase of import substitution have been the large Asian entrepreneurs and the Uganda Development Corporation. The latter, probably Africa's most successful development corporation, was formed by the colonial government in 1952 with an equity of £5 million.[11] Despite some unsuccessful ventures, the Uganda Development Corporation has earned after-tax profit every year and by 1965 had accumulated assets at cost of £9·7 million. (Its market value was no doubt considerably higher.) Fixed assets of its subsidiaries and associated companies were £19·8 million with 18,279 employees. Approximately half the corporation's resources have been invested in the manufacturing sector, in five subsidiaries and six

[10] For a wealth of information on this subject, see National Christian Council of Kenya, *Who controls industry in Kenya?* (Nairobi, 1968).

[11] This discussion of the Uganda Development Corporation is largely based upon Stoutjesdijk, *Uganda's manufacturing sector,* ch. 2.

associated companies. In 1963, the five subsidiaries engaged 3,905 persons and contributed £2·4 million to net national product, representing something over a fifth of value added and employment in import-substitute industries (that is, manufacturing exclusive of agricultural processing), as shown in Table 113.

The Uganda Development Corporation's maiden manufacturing venture was an integrated cement factory (East Africa's first), a project that was begun by the colonial government in the late 1940s and that looked to the demand for cement generated by the construction of the Owen Falls Dam. With natural protection from transport costs adding more than 100 per cent to the ex-factory price of overseas supplies, this undertaking has been successful since 1953 without any tariff protection. (However, quotas have been placed on the sales of nearby, lower-cost Kenyan cement producers.) Subsequent smaller, linked projects were asbestos-cement tiles and paper sacks. In the case of its largest venture, a cotton-textile plant, profitability was not achieved until tariffs ranging from 30 per cent upward were imposed in 1958. Established by Calico Printers of Manchester as East Africa's first integrated spinning and weaving operation in 1954, this ailing company was purchased by the Development Corporation in 1957. Since 1959, the rate of return on equity (£2 million in 1963) ranged between 18 and 36 per cent. Just as Calico Printers was retained as the managing agent, Duncan, Gilbey and Matheson, Ltd was recruited as the technical partner in East African distilleries, established in 1963. An enamel and metal products factory (1957) and a super-phosphate fertilizer plant (1960) were unable to achieve profitable operation by 1965, despite considerable tariff protection in the case of the former and transport protection in the case of the latter.

Table 113 provides a picture of the manufacturing sector in Kenya and

Table 113. *Manufacturing employment and output in Kenya and Uganda, 1963*

	Uganda		Kenya	
Industry	Number employed	Value added (£000)	Number employed	Value added (£000)
Total	38,175	16,321	49,829	28,580
Agriculture processing	20,562	6,656	5,425	4,759
Sugar, tobacco, beverages	3,407	3,851	5,199	5,085
Bakery and misc. food	808	218	1,621	689
Textile, apparel, footwear	3,250	1,779	3,701	1,584
Cordage, rope, twine	—	—	2,233	655
Wood products	3,106	610	6,837	1,484
Printing and paper	1,005	353	3,683	2,864
Paint, soap, etc.	366	122	1,898	2,508
Industrial chemicals	389	14	1,561	1,475
Rubber products	159	213	276	189
Glass, cement, clay products	1,872	761	1,761	1,883
Metal products and machinery	1,868	1,158	3,832	2,295
Rolling stock	—	—	6,392	1,012
Shipbuilding and repair	—	—	2,107	663
Motor vehicles and repair	1,383	549	1,819	815

SOURCES: Uganda, *Survey of Industrial Production, 1963;* Kenya, *Statistical Abstract, 1965.*

Uganda in 1963. Agricultural processing remains the largest subsector in Uganda, with cotton ginning and coffee processing accounting for the bulk of both output and employment; cotton-seed crushing, tea processing, grain milling and the processing of meat and fish contribute less than a fifth to this category. Principal items in Kenya's agricultural processing are grain milling and meat and dairy products. Because of its ports and major railway line, Kenya gains considerable employment and modest output from shipbuilding and rolling stock. If we take the remaining categories as common import substitute industries, we find that Kenya's output in this field is some 2·3 times that of its westerly neighbour. This reflects not only larger production of cigarettes, beer, furniture and so on, but also the presence of several technically more advanced product lines in paper, industrial chemicals and light machinery.

Southern Rhodesia

The early history

Of all the countries under review, Southern Rhodesia has the longest history of manufacturing. In 1898, eight years after the 'pioneer column' from South Africa had implanted European settlement, the manufacture of lager beer commenced at the Salisbury Brewery.[12] About the same time, the first small engineering concerns of Johnson and Fletcher and E. W. Tarry Ltd started operations as suppliers of parts and equipment to the gold-mining companies. Johnson and Fletcher, like the three partners who established the Salisbury Brewery, were Rhodesian settlers; E. W. Tarry Ltd had been established two decades earlier at the Kimberley diamond-fields and now boasted a number of branches as well as having Cecil Rhodes on its board of directors. In the same year that these two firms were setting up (1897), railway workshops opened at Salisbury and Bulawayo; from these workshops four years later came armoured trains for the Boer War. The last of the early engineering facilities was founded in 1904 by W. S. Craster, a former ricksha-fleet operator, who in 1912 opened the country's first commercial foundry.

Other early industrial activities including baking, animal slaughtering, saw-milling and furniture manufacture. Tobacco was an important crop by 1900, and cigars, cigarettes and pipe tobacco were being produced for the local market by two small factories as early as 1903.[13] However, then as now, the curing, grading, cleaning and packing of tobacco leaf for export represented the single largest agricultural processing activity carried on in the country.

The British South Africa Company, in contrast to the performance of French and British chartered companies in other parts of Africa, was active in fostering considerable industrial development.[14] Its first ventures were in food processing: pork and bacon, cheese and butter. In 1915, the company erected a cement mill with a capacity of 7,000 tons per annum. In 1920, the BSA launched the Rhodesia Milling Company, the country's second flour mill (the first mill had

[12] The principal sources for this paragraph and the two that follow are various 'Commercial Rhodesiana' features published in *Illustrated Life Rhodesia* (Salisbury) over the period 1968–70.
[13] The British South Africa Company, *Annual report*, 1903, p. 28; and *Annual report*, 1904, p. 25.
[14] BSA circumstances were, of course, very different from those of the other chartered companies. The BSA was long-lived and generously capitalized; its manufacturing ventures served proven European markets and were staffed by a predominantly European labour force.

been established in 1916 by a young British produce merchant, Mark Harris). A large BSA-affiliated chemical fertilizer factory was completed in 1930, to which was shortly added the manufacture of explosives. During this period, however, the bulk of the BSA's commercial investments were directed not to industry but to mining, timber and farming (tobacco, cattle, citrus, maize).

The first census of manufacturing was carried out in 1938. In that year, some three hundred manufacturing establishments were recorded, producing a net output of £2·3 million.[15] Most of the concerns were very small. Five-sixths of the 299 firms, in fact, had sales of less than £20,000; only two firms had sales over £250,000. European employment was 2,798, and that of Africans and others 14,756. As Table 114 shows, in terms of employment, agriculture and mining were still far ahead of manufacturing in 1938.

Table 114. *Employment of Europeans and Africans in various sectors of the Southern Rhodesian economy, 1938*

| | Number employed | |
Activity	Europeans	Africans
Agriculture	4,633	92,051
Mining	3,120	87,847
Construction and utilities	2,123	22,399
Manufacturing	2,798	14,756
Commerce and transport	6,811	
Public service	4,962	37,244
Other	1,335	

Under the spur of wartime scarcities and a marked shift of government policies in favour of industrialization, manufacturing output, measured in constant prices, doubled between 1939 and 1945. As imported supplies of consumer goods were cut off, domestic production of processed foods, sugar, spirits, footwear, clothing, soap and cigarettes doubled and tripled, supplying not only the home market but Northern Rhodesia and Nyasaland as well. Military demand stimulated the manufacturing of smoke bombs, aeroplane parts and a wide range of light engineering products.

Southern Rhodesian industry continued to expand rapidly after the war. Export earnings—led by tobacco, asbestos fibre, gold, chrome ore and clothing—tripled between 1945 and 1953. This stimulated manufacturing both directly, in terms of export processing and the production of wearing apparel for South African markets, and indirectly, by means of rising domestic purchasing power. The other major stimulant was large-scale European immigration, which brought in its wake a construction boom. Domestic output of cement, clay products, asbestos-cement tile and pipe, sawmilling, furniture, metal doors and windows, steel construction rods, and nails leaped ahead. In aggregate, net manufacturing output (measured in 1938 prices) rose from £4·7 million in 1945 to £10·7 million in 1953. At the same time, the industrial sector had

[15] The statistics in the paragraph are drawn from Table 114 and from *Official yearbook of Southern Rhodesia*, no. 4 (Salisbury, 1952), ch. 19.

become more diversified and technologically more sophisticated with the beginnings of three new industrial groups: iron and steel, cotton spinning and textiles, and industrial chemicals.

The statistics in Table 115 describe several aspects of the alterations that occurred in Southern Rhodesia's manufacturing economy over the period 1938–53. Even allowing for an average price rise of 160 per cent, absolute output advanced in every group. The faster-growing industries were textiles and wearing apparel and metal products, which enlarged their share in aggregate manufacturing output from 2·3 to 11·8 per cent and 8·4 to 14·9 per cent, respectively. As would be expected, the relative importance of food and tobacco processing fell. The lower panel in Table 115 records the rapid growth in the number of firms and the even more rapid shift to larger-scale units of production. The very much greater investment and technical and managerial requirements associated with larger-scale units have more often than not exceeded local capabilities, with the result that the role of foreign corporations has grown

Table 115. *Southern Rhodesia's changing industrial structure*

	Net output			
	Value in £000		Per cent	
Industry group	1938	1953	1938	1953
Food processing	394	3,118	16·9	11·8
Beverage	201	2,272	8·6	8·7
Tobacco	304	2,625	13·0	9·9
Textiles and wearing apparel	55	3,110	2·3	11·8
Wood products	121	1,638	5·2	6·2
Nonmetallic mineral products	163	2,338	7·0	8·9
Rubber products	12	117	0·5	0·4
Chemicals	124	1,359	5·3	5·2
Metal products	196	3,872	8·4	14·9
Transport equipment	442	3,427	18·9	13·0
Paper and printing	252	1,571	10·8	6·0
Miscellaneous	68	636	2·9	2·4
Total	2,332	26,084	100·0	100·0

	Number of firms			Per cent of gross output		
Size of firm by sales	1938	1953	1957	1938	1953	1957
Under £5,000	159	85	73	6	1	—
£5,000–19,999	96	244	292	18	5	3
£20,000–49,999	28	168	244	16	8	7
£50,000–250,000	20	164	224	44	27	22
Over £250,000	2	54	85	16	59	68
Total	299	714	918	100	100	100

SOURCE: Data from Central African Statistical Office as compiled in Leonard Tow, *The manufacturing economy of Southern Rhodesia* (Washington, D.C., National Academy of Sciences, 1960), pp. 13 and 16.

in importance. By 1953, total industrial employment, not shown in the table, had risen to 70,000. In terms of the contribution of manufacturing to national output, its share in GDP rose from 9 per cent in 1938 to 14 per cent in 1953.[16]

The year 1953 marked the entrance of Southern Rhodesia into a common market with Northern Rhodesia and Nyasaland. The federation, which lasted eleven years, sprang from historical seed, nurtured by economic and political considerations. From the early 1950s, federation promised somewhat enlarged markets for Rhodesian manufactures (mainly in Nyasaland) and a share in the copper revenues of Northern Rhodesia. The Imperial government had remained wary of Salisbury's racial policies. Nevertheless, the British had to conciliate Southern Rhodesia, which had supplied much-needed rail facilities and coal for Northern Rhodesia. Advocates of federation looked to a more balanced and a more credit-worthy economy. The larger political unit would become a British bastion capable of standing on its own, independent of both an Afrikaner-dominated South Africa and a 'black' north.

The state as entrepreneur

Before1940, the government had pursued a neutral policy via-à-vis industry: although the industrial field was reserved for private enterprise and new undertakings were welcomed, they could not expect any public assistance in the way of loan capital, income tax relief or tariff protection. Wartime scarcities created political pressures that abruptly altered this posture.[17] In 1940, an Industrial Development Advisory Committee was appointed. In early 1942, after eighteen months of inaction, the Tory Prime Minister, Sir Godfrey Huggins, much to the disbelief and consternation of the mercantile community, opted for state enterprise as the vehicle to pioneer industrialization. The government's directive read as follows:

The Government's policy is to nationalize under Commissions or Government Utility Companies basic industries such as iron and steel and cotton spinning, the object being to make semi-finished products so that private enterprise can obtain semi-manufactured material at the lowest prices, and so enable them to compete with imported manufactures. This will also prevent monopolies from being established by the cornering of semi-manufactured products. The Government believes that all creameries, bacon factories, and the processing of certain perishables, such as meat, should be co-operative or be done by a Commission or utility company.[18]

The government proceeded to nationalize the Iron and Steel Corporation in Bulawayo, the South African Cold Storage Company and, in 1944, the Triangle Sugar Estates. Also, in 1942 the Cotton Research and Industries Board was constituted to develop a cotton-spinning industry.

The Iron and Steel Corporation was founded in 1938 by a group of Bulawayo businessmen; somewhat ironically, the protesting leader of this group of expropriated capitalists was Donald Macintyre, head of the Rhodesia Labour Party. The works consisted of an electric furnace for reducing scrap, a small rolling mill and a forge, with an annual capacity of 11,000 tons of steel. When the

[16] The 1938 figure is reported in Giovanni Arrighi, *The political economy of Rhodesia* (The Hague, 1967), p. 44.
[17] For a perceptive analysis of pressure-group politics and policy formation, see D. J. Murray, *The governmental system in Southern Rhodesia* (Oxford, Clarendon Press, 1970).
[18] *Ibid.*, p. 177.

company was taken over by the government's Rhodesian Iron and Steel Commission (RISCOM), construction of a second, integrated works was started near Que Que at the site of iron-ore and limestone deposits, deposits soon found to be extremely large and of high grade. Although planned to meet wartime needs, the Que Que facility did not begin operation until 1948. In favour of local production were low-cost raw-material assemblage and labour. Moreover, transport charges equal to one-quarter of the foreign suppliers' ex-factory price provided a measure of natural protection from external competition. Conscious of the dangers of raising the cost of iron and steel and thereby undermining the competitiveness of customer industries, RISCOM set its prices somewhat below the landed cost of imports. Working against the home industry were marked diseconomies of small scale both for the hot metal and for the various items of finished steel. Teething problems, scale factors and inept management among them resulted in deficits in most years. Production consisted of pig-iron and steel ingots for sale to private foundries, billets for tube making, bar, rod, small shapes and small flats.

In 1952, with the prospect of the enlarged market from federation, plans were laid to expand capacity from 25,000 to 65,000 tons of finished steel. This level of output was achieved in 1956; but operations were still not profitable despite an embargo placed upon all competing imports. In 1957, the industry was turned over to a consortium of British and South African firms.[19] The assets of the state enterprise were valued at £4·3 million, for which the government took up shares in the new company. The private firms invested £8 million for reconstruction and expansion to increase capacity to 150,000 tons.

The government's initiative in textiles was the first to bear fruit. An experimental spinning unit with a thousand spindles began production in 1943 at Gatooma, the site of the cotton-research station. Once it had been established that Rhodesian cotton and African labour were up to the mark, a full-scale spinning mill of 17,500 spindles was erected in 1948; a second mill of the same size began operations in 1952. The Cotton Research and Industry Board also operated the country's sole ginnery. Small private weaving and knitting factories converted Gatooma yarn into cotton drills, interlock fabric, tobacco netting, towels and blankets; in addition, a large fraction of yarn output was exported to the South African weaving industry. In 1953, the first large weaving mill was established by David Whitehead & Sons of Lancashire, the same firm that would be involved in Nigeria's first textile venture three years later. Several other large mills were subsequently established by South African firms. In contrast to RISCOM, the Gatooma spinning venture showed modest profits in most years, although it too was sold to private interests in 1960.

What was the impact on the country's industrial development of the government's initiative in steel and textiles? The large export of clothing to the south—a windfall for Rhodesia of India's embargo on exports to South Africa—was not based on local cloth, but rather on imported Indian piece goods. Similarly, at least until the early 1960s, most of the grey cloth used in textile printing for the local market was produced in Asia. (This has also been true in West Africa.) As for the stimulation of cotton-growing, local production has actually fallen, and the bulk of cotton lint has had to be purchased abroad.

[19] The group consisted of Lancashire Steel Corporation, Stewarts & Lloyds, Anglo American, Rhodesian Selection Trust, BSA, Messina (Transvaal), and Tanganyika Concessions.

Likewise, many of the steel-fabricating industries—metal containers, wire, nails, construction members, fencing—have sprung up in most other African countries, none of which produces iron and steel. On the other hand, Lancashire Steel Corporation's tube factory was set up on the basis of a local steel-billet supply. In the long run, as the production of intermediate goods grows and foreign exchange shortages make importing difficult, more internal linkages will be realized. Although the textile industry would probably have developed with a slight lag in much the same way without public enterprise, in the absence of RISCOM the discovery of the large ore-fields might have waited several decades. The £2 million loss borne by the Rhodesian tax-payer in RISCOM deficits and capital write-off was probably a good investment.

The sale of the Gatooma mills ended the government's adventure in industrial entrepreneurship. The sugar project, a consistent financial loser, had been sold to a South African syndicate in 1954. As early as 1950, official statements of policy had shifted to the traditional narrow view of the role of government in a free enterprise system.[20]

It is instructive to compare Southern Rhodesian experience with publicly managed industrial enterprise to that of other African countries such as Nigeria and Ghana. They have more in common than one might suppose. In most cases the projects are influenced by economic nationalism. Huggins not only responded to wartime British patriotism; he also feared economic dominance and potential monopolistic exploitation by South African firms, and lack of initiative from domestic investors. Political pressures have influenced key management appointments and staffing levels. Projects have generally suffered from insufficient technical expertise and from an inability to move quickly. Most of the ventures have been unsuccessful from a commercial point of view. Finally, in the absence of local capitalists with sufficient resources (financial, technical, managerial), the government's only option for handing over to the private sector has been to sell out to foreign investors.

The differences between Southern Rhodesia and other African countries are fewer in number but more critical in their consequence. In the case of Southern Rhodesia, product prices, as described for steel, were held to the level of the duty-free import alternative, with all operational losses being underwritten by the government. Following the more common practice, other African countries have employed protective devices that enable the infant firms to cover the costs of inefficiency by charging substantially higher prices to the buyer. The former practice insulates user industries from cost distortions and clearly signals the need for corrective action; the latter practice does neither. The second difference between Southern Rhodesia and the other countries is that the government did sell its enterprises to more efficient private foreign operators, whereas no black government has in practice been willing to take this step.[21] Of course, the psychological and political difficulties of selling off state enterprises to

---

[20] Murray, *Governmental system in Southern Rhodesia*, p. 187.

[21] Despite an official policy since 1966 of selling off its money-losing manufacturing enterprises (i.e., nineteen out of twenty companies), five years later the Ghana Industrial Holding Corporation had still to relinquish controlling interest in a single case. Minority participation for a foreign investor—including a management contract—had occurred in four instances. See Leslie E. Grayson, 'A conglomerate in Africa: public sector manufacturing enterprises in Ghana, 1962–1971', mimeographed (African Studies Association, Nov. 1971). The Nigerian case, reviewed below, is similar.

overseas firms are far greater for the latter. One may reasonably doubt that the Rhodesian government would have sold its projects if the only customers were Chinese investors.

Trade and investment

As we have indicated, protective tariffs did not play an important role in Southern Rhodesia's industrialization prior to federation with Northern Rhodesia and Nyasaland in 1953—and even then probably not until 1962.[22] Tariffs were for revenue and were generally low. In 1946, for example, just under half of all imports bore no tariff, while only 3·6 per cent of incoming goods incurred a duty in excess of 25 per cent.[23] The only fiscal assistance to local industry was import-duty relief on raw materials and equipment, dating from 1925. Tariff policy has, however, been important in its effects upon the direction of trade. In Southern Rhodesia, as in other African countries, foreign investors have been drawn overwhelmingly from the ranks of foreign suppliers of imports. From this point of view, a four-tiered preference system (South Africa, the United Kingdom, British dominions and the rest of the world, favoured in the order given) has added to historic connexions that explain the dominance of firms controlled from South Africa and Britain in Rhodesia's manufacturing sector. These two countries have accounted for two-thirds to three-quarters of all imports. And South Africa has been the principal market for Southern Rhodesian manufactured exports (principally clothing, cotton yarn, rubber footwear, toys, suitcases and radios).

Given the relative maturity of Rhodesian industry and the presence of a large European population, it is somewhat surprising that the proportionate share of foreign investment is not significantly different from that in Black African countries. A survey for 1962 revealed that 63 per cent of manufacturing profits were earned by firms controlled from abroad, principally England and South Africa.[24] British investment is somewhat greater and concentrated in larger-scale industries. A glance at the Johannesburg Financial Directory turns up companies operating in Rhodesia manufacturing such items as baby food, flour, beer, matches, paint, furniture, paper, electrical insulators and cement.

These investments have come about in many ways, but most of them have been associated with the prior development of a Rhodesian market. Lancashire Steel Corporation had first exported tubing to Rhodesia before investing in a local plant; later, concern over its source of billet led to involvement in the RISCOM purchase. Bata built up a sizeable interest in the shoe trade that antedated the erection of its domestic factory in 1943. Turner and Newall, although involved in mining Rhodesian asbestos for its European plants, supplied the local demand for tile and pipe from England until the expansion of Porter Cement Industries threatened its position in the growing market. Porter Ce-

[22] See R. L. Cole, 'The tariff policy in Rhodesia, 1899–1963', *Rhodesian Journal of Economics,* June 1968, **5.**

[23] The data refer to January–March and are given in 'Report of the Committee of Enquiry into the Protection of Secondary Industries in Southern Rhodesia, 1946', typescript (Salisbury), p. 270.

[24] D. S. Pearson, 'Industrial development in Rhodesia', *Rhodesian Journal of Economics,* March 1968, **5.** Data showing comparable ratios of foreign to total investment in manufacturing for nineteen African countries are given in John de Wilde, 'The development of African private enterprise', vol. II, mimeographed (Washington, D.C., International Bank for Reconstruction and Development, 1971), p. 107.

ment, founded by an Australian immigrant in 1945, was bought out by Turner and Newall in 1953. Of the country's earliest ventures, the Salisbury Brewery was taken over by South African Breweries, Ltd in 1910, although Mark Harris's son did not sell Gloria Flour mills to its principal competitor, the Rhodesian Milling Company (owned by Anglo American), until 1956.

The failure of white Rhodesians to attain a commanding position in their own industrial sector by the early 1960s is no doubt the product of many circumstances. The pace of economic development in the decade and a half following the Second World War meant that economy-wide investment requirements outran domestic savings. The increase in factory scale and technological sophistication is another element. Because foreign investors were English cousins (once removed in the case of South Africa), the force of reactive nationalism and government policies to indigenize the manufacturing sector were weaker than they otherwise would have been. More interesting, and probably more fundamental, have been entrepreneurial factors. Not unlike the pattern in Black African countries, Rhodesians have directed their own investments not to industry, but rather into commerce and real estate. Compared to Japan or Taiwan, there has been little inclination to pursue technical training or otherwise develop modern specialist skills in the industrial arts. The performance of Rhodesians as managers and supervisors has frequently been sub-standard, and this is one of the reasons why a large share of senior positions in industry is filled by non-Rhodesians or recent immigrants. Attributing the failure to attitudes as well as to lack of acquired skills, Leonard Tow concluded in 1960 that 'inept and inadequate management has clearly been one of the more significant handicaps to industrial development'.[25]

African participation

Our narrative so far has dealt only with the white community. What has been the impact of manufacturing upon the Africans who constitute some 95 per cent of the population? The principal effect has been in the area of employment. The number of Africans engaged in manufacturing grew from 15,000 in 1938 to 73,400 in 1962, accounting for 12 per cent of the black labour force in the latter year. Average incomes rose, especially in industry. (Between 1954 and 1962, the Africans' average wage in manufacturing went up from £65 to £164.) But disparities of incomes between the different racial groups remained vast. Whereas Africans accounted for 81 per cent of manufacturing employment, they received only 35 per cent of wage and salary payments.[26] This wide disparity was, at least in part, occasioned by a colour bar by which European workers entrenched their standard of living in the cities through the 'rate-for-the-job' principle, which prevented the great majority of Africans from holding jobs above the semi-skilled level.

Industrialization provided a need for a literate African labour force. Southern Rhodesia therefore made some advances in African education. (Indeed, the

---

[25] Leonard Tow, *The manufacturing economy of Southern Rhodesia* (Washington, D.C., National Academy of Sciences, 1960), p. 107.

[26] The statistics here and in the paragraph that follows are drawn from R. B. Sutcliffe, 'Stagnation and inequality in Rhodesia, 1946–1968', *Bulletin of the Oxford University Institute of Economics and Statistics,* Feb. 1971, **33**; and Southern Rhodesia, *Economic survey of Rhodesia for 1965* (Salisbury, 1966).

schooling given to Africans in Southern Rhodesia generally compared favourably with the facilities provided to black people under the auspices of the British Colonial Office in Northern Rhodesia and Nyasaland.) But the Southern Rhodesian educational system, like the system in Northern Rhodesia, remained separate and unequal. Educational deficiencies and the unwillingness of most white workers to accept Africans as superiors, or even as equals at the work-bench, combined with a lack of capital, of technical expertise and of business experience to prevent Africans from participating in the establishment and ownership of small and medium-scale industrial enterprises of the kind set up in West Africa.

Industrialization helped to change the economic perspectives of the mercantile and manufacturing segment within the European bourgeoisie. Africans, for the first time, came to be considered as customers as well as wage workers. A few Africans indeed began to make money as entrepreneurs, by supplying goods and services to fellow Africans as craftsmen, store owners or transport contractors. Industrial development also increased the market for African agricultural products. By 1962, for instance, African farming accounted for 9·2 per cent of the country's gross domestic product (as against 14 per cent of non-African farming). But the effects of discriminatory racial policies continued to operate in every sector of the economy. The allocation of much, though not all, of Southern Rhodesia's best farmland to Europeans, a lop-sided distribution of agricultural assistance and price-support programmes in favour of non-Africans, restrictions on where Africans might live and acquire property and a host of other administrative measures all helped to relegate the bulk of the black population to impoverished subsistence farming in the native reserves or to the lowest rungs of the monetized economy. Thus in 1946, Southern Rhodesian whites (including a few thousand Asians and Coloureds), who constituted 3·8 per cent of the population, received 49 per cent of the national income (subsistence production included). In 1960, the whites accounted for 6·2 per cent of the total population and received 61 per cent of the national income.

This same pattern of exclusion of Africans from positions of industrial proprietorship and a racially lop-sided distribution of the national income is found also in pre-independence Northern Rhodesia and Kenya, colonies which pursued approximately the same set of discriminatory policies that have been enumerated for Southern Rhodesia. The economic cost of Southern Rhodesia's social injustice has been a more limited market for the kinds of products for which a comparative advantage exists and an inability to draw upon the full potential of its human resources—factors that more likely than not have some bearing on the economy's relative stagnation since 1960.[27]

Peasant economies of West Africa

Turning to West Africa, we find a pattern of economic development quite different from that of the white-settler countries of eastern and southern Africa. European and Levantine enterprise was significant, but for the most part limited to commerce and the extraction of natural resources. Outside the Cameroons

[27] National income reached a peak of £67 per head in 1960, began to decline in 1962 and was £60 in 1968 (all at 1954 prices). Data from Sutcliffe, 'Stagnation and inequality', p. 36.

and a few plantations in the Ivory Coast and Nigeria, agricultural production for the market—both domestic foodstuffs and primary exports—has been in the hands of peasant farmers. The economic and social consequences of African primacy in commercial agriculture have proved far-reaching.

The economic consequences have been twofold. With some exceptions (the opulence of subsistence in parts of Uganda, the confiscatory régime in French Equatorial Africa), the average West African has enjoyed during most of the present century a higher material standard of living than his East African counterpart, and this as a result of the sale of cash-crops. Although European farming in eastern and southern Africa entrained considerable wage employment, the persons so engaged were never more than a small fraction of the economically active population, the bulk of which remained in the traditional economy. More important from the perspective of African development, the lack of preemption by better-equipped aliens, on the one hand, and the provision of financial means and self-confidence from the experience with export crops, on the other, enabled large numbers of Africans to move out of farming into produce-buying, retail and wholesale distribution, transport and a wide range of artisan trades. These activities in turn generated the technical skills, social traditions and market networks that would lead, *inter alia,* to the development of a substantial amount of small-scale industry. We shall return later to this subject of African industrial entrepreneurship.

French and British Africa

Although Africans were responsible for primary-export production and the lower reaches of the import distribution network, they did not possess sufficient financial resources, organizational skills or market power to take over the commanding heights of the ocean-borne import-export trade. This position was initially held by a large number of relatively small European trading concerns operating from Liverpool, Manchester, Marseille, Bordeaux and Hamburg. From 1879 onwards, trade wars and amalgamations continually reduced their number; by 1930, four companies accounted for some 60 per cent of the export-import trade in the British and French West African colonies. These companies were Unilever, Compagnie Française de L'Afrique Occidentale (CFAO), John Holt and Société Commerciale de L'Ouest Africain (SCOA).[28] The economic power of these concerns was even greater than their dominant market share would suggest, because by means of fully owned subsidiaries and interlocking directorates they exercised partial or complete control over the principal shipping lines and banks operating in their territories. It is not surprising that the interests and policies of these large firms played a central role in the timing of industrialization in their territories.

What was the extent of industrial activity in West Africa before the Second World War? The country that was most industrialized was Senegal, the home of the administrative capital for all of French West Africa (AOF) and hence of a sizeable European population. Table 116 describes Senegal's industrial prog-

---

[28] Unilever was represented by the Nouvelle Société Commerciale Africaine in Senegal, the Compagnie du Niger Français in the Sudan, the Compagnie Française de la Côte d'Ivoire in the Ivory Coast and the United Africa Company in the four British colonies. A full discussion of the origin and scope of all the larger trading firms can be found in Jean Suret-Canale, *French colonialism in tropical Africa, 1900–1945* (London, 1971), pp. 159 ff.

Table 116. *Senegalese industrial firms with fifty or more
employees, pre-1925 to 1965*

Year of start-up	Ground-nut oil	Food	Textiles and shoes	Metal eng.	Chemicals	Construction material	Misc.	Cumulative total
pre-1925	1	—	—	—	—	—	—	1
1926–30	2	1	—	—	1	2	—	7
1931–5	—	1	—	—	—	—	—	8
1936–40	1	—	2	1	—	—	1	13
1941–5	2	2	—	1	1	—	—	19
1946–50	—	—	1	2	2	5	5	34
1951–5	1	2	2	2	—	1	2	44
1956–60	—	5	3	2	—	—	1	55
1961–5	—	2	1	2	1	—	—	61
Total	7	13	9	10	5	8	9	

SOURCE: Guy Pfeffermann, *Industrial labour in the Republic of Senegal* (New York, 1968), p. 6.

ress, starting with its first ground-nut oil-mills established by the Compagnie Générale des Colonies in 1920 and 1922.[29] At first these small mills served only the local market, but gradually as they expanded capacity exports developed, surpassing 5,000 tons of oil in 1937 (equivalent to about 3 per cent of ground-nut exports). At the instigation of metropolitan oil-millers, a quota of 5,800 tons was imposed on AOF producers in April 1938. Beyond the oil-millers, there were nine other manufacturing establishments in 1940 employing fifty or more workers. These included a soap works, a sisal cordage and bag factory, an arsenal, a brick works and railway and construction workshops. Smaller units not shown in the table would include a network of bakeries operated by Maurel et Prom and several printing presses. Lebanese entrepreneurs were engaged in producing furniture and wrought iron.

The principal industries in AOF outside of Senegal consisted of two palm-oil mills in Dahomey and the Ivory Coast, several sawmills, a few cotton ginneries and the Gonfreville textile works. The Gonfreville works, Black Africa's first cotton-spinning and weaving factory, was established in Bouaké, Ivory Coast, in 1921, by a former Native Affairs official. Robert Gonfreville saw in the Bouaké region three ingredients upon which to build his enterprise: a native spinning-weaving-dyeing industry that would supply a labour force adaptable to modern textile processes, the availability of raw cotton well under world prices as a result of a compulsory cultivation scheme and a market that in terms of cloth width and texture was poorly served by imports. The plant was enlarged in 1928, 1933 and 1951. Although Gonfreville supplied but a small fraction of the AOF market, it was not until 1952 that the first of four additional firms commenced production in Senegal.

The situation in Nigeria and the Gold Coast was very much the same. In

[29] Apparently only one of these mills employed more than fifty workers and thus appears in Table 116. The Compagnie Générale des Colonies was established in 1920 by a consortium of French banks and construction companies. Its principal investments were made in Indo-China and North Africa. All the later ground-nut crushing mills were connected with merchant firms engaged in the ground-nut trade (e.g., Lesieur Petersen).

Nigeria in 1940 the British Cotton Growing Association operated four ginneries in the Northern Region. There were half-a-dozen sawmills, mostly in the Sapele-Benin area. A soap works in Lagos (1924), two palm-oil bulking plants (1924), a cigarette factory at Ibadan (1937) and a metal-drum plant (1939) complete the list of sizeable private industrial ventures. The government operated a sawmill, two small Public Works Department furniture factories and a boat yard. Pioneered by the West Indian A. W. Schackleford, bread baking was in the hands of Africans in both Lagos and Accra. The Gold Coast boasted a Swiss brewery (1932) but lacked production of either soap or cigarettes.

In West Africa, wartime scarcities brought extreme hardship. Unlike the Southern Rhodesian case, the cloud of privation had no silver lining: without a minimum industrial base to germinate from, high prices and potentially enormous profits induced no flowering of home industries. Because it had the largest base and received subsidies from the Vichy government for the purpose, Senegal was a partial exception. As shown in Table 116, two new oil-mills and four other factories employing fifty or more were founded between 1941 and 1945. The pace of industrial development in the Dakar area, the manufacturing centre for the AOF common market of 17 million people, continued after the war with the help of extensive colonial subsidies. The export quota on the Dakar oil-mills was lifted during the war, reimposed in 1946 but successively adjusted upwards thereafter. Investment activity subsided after 1958 with the break-up of the federation (AOF).

The overall picture for colonial West Africa, then, is one of very limited industrial development until the late 1950s, with Senegal being somewhat of an exception. In 1957, industrial output, exclusive of craft production, was less than 2 per cent of national income in Nigeria, the Gold Coast and the Ivory Coast. Then, starting about 1958, we see a rapid spurt of industrialization that carried on into the mid-1960s, raising the share of manufacturing in NNP from about 2 per cent to 6–8 per cent. Two questions arise. Why, in contrast to Uganda, Kenya and Southern Rhodesia, were virtually no industries serving the home market established in the four decades following the First World War? What caused the sudden transformation of somnolence into frantic investment activity starting in about 1958?

The influence of market structure

A major part of the answer to both questions is to be found in the structure of the product market. An intriguing problem for the economic historian is to trace through the differential mixture of technical factors (minimum capital requirement, economies of scale) and historic events (the prior arrival of Indian traders and white settlers in East Africa) that produced a monopolistic market structure in the import-export trade in one region and an open, competitive structure in another. Whatever the causes, the tendency towards a high degree of concentration in West African markets down to the wholesale level was well under way by the turn of the century and culminated in 1929 with the formation of Unilever. For the quarter century that followed, some 60 per cent of imports and exports—the principal items of market exchange in these economies—were controlled by four firms. The six next largest concerns—Paterson-Zochonis,

Union Trading Company, Peyrissac, G. B. Ollivant,[30] Maurel et Prom, Vezia— probably accounted for another 20 per cent.

A comparison between East and West Africa of the largest market share held by a single seller provides striking evidence of the monopoly power that had been built up in West Africa. In the three East African territories, in the early 1950s Gailey & Roberts handled less than 4 per cent of merchandise imports. In Nigeria and the Gold Coast, the United Africa Company controlled between 35 and 40 per cent of the import market during the same period. Nor can this difference in achieved market dominance be attributed simply to the greater financial resources of the United Africa Company, because Gailey & Roberts was itself part of that organization.[31]

Given their carefully buttressed monopoly position, the merchant houses enjoyed a stable and highly favourable market situation.[32] Not only did they have positive incentives to remain fully committed to the import-export trade; there were also disincentives to enter manufacturing or to let others do so. In many cases the trading firms had a contractual relationship with metropolitan producers. In other cases, such as Unilever's British Oil and Cake Mills Ltd or Maurel's ground-nut-crushing operations in Bordeaux, the merchants had a direct stake in maintaining the existing division of labour. Similarly with the affiliates of Palm Line, Guinea Gulf Line and Fabre et Frassinet, displacement of imported goods by local manufacturing would reduce the earnings of their own shipping companies, and raise freight cost to all trading firms. To the extent that the banks were free to pursue their independent interests, financing the self-liquidating cycles of produce and provisions was comfortably remunerative and a low-risk activity that required little exertion. A final strand in this web of commercial interests was the internal make-up of the merchant houses: they had no experience in running industrial enterprise, they lacked personnel with the requisite skills and they were averse to long-term fixed investments which entailed sacrificing manœverability, that essential element of the merchant's art.

Some scholars allege that colonial administrations intentionally discouraged local manufacturing in order to maintain outlets for metropolitan industry and to ensure that the dependencies bent their full efforts to providing the imperial power with needed raw materials. Although such a proposition is consistent with the observed pattern of trade, the policies of colonial governments were motivated by quite different concerns. Professor Nicolson has shown (for British West Africa at least) that the majority of colonial governors and their ad-

---

[30] G. B. Ollivant was purchased by Unilever in 1938.

[31] Gailey and Roberts, former surveyors for the construction of the Uganda railway, established their trading concern in Nairobi in 1904. By 1937, when they sold to the United Africa Company, they had establishments throughout the three countries. See United Africa Company, *Statistical and Economic Review*, March 1956, no. 17, pp. 29 ff. For the company's West African market share, see P. T. Bauer, *West African trade*, new ed. (London, 1963), ch. 5.

[32] In addition to the natural barriers against new competitors—high capital requirements of maintaining overseas buying offices, of storage and handling facilities for a geographically extensive but shallow market, of credit for distributors, plus knowledge of the market and contacts accumulated for years—the firms also pursued a conscious policy of pre-empting the market by handling all ranges of merchandise, by establishing formal cartel arrangements and by undertaking specific actions (below-cost pricing, credit squeeze) to drive smaller competitors out of business. Moreover, government import rationing on a quota system guaranteed their market position during the period 1940–9. See Bauer, *West African trade*, chs. 6–14.

ministrations were very much concerned with advancing African welfare, that is, with raising money incomes and providing more medical facilities, school and roads.[33] It was their judgement that in the context of predominantly subsistence economies, where labour and land were not fully utilized, this could best be brought about by encouraging African producers to grow crops for sale to the export market. After 1900, despite the efforts of Empire enthusiasts, the electorate in England and France were decidedly uninterested in their colonial estates, and their parliamentary representatives could not be persuaded to allocate sums for the exploitation of these holdings. Thus the colonies had to be self-financing. And because the only source of revenue was taxes on exports and imports, the desire to provide amenities for the African population pointed in the same direction as that of raising African money incomes—namely, the encouragement of agricultural exports.

From this perspective, import-substitute manufacturing held little promise. Quite apart from increased demand for government-provided facilities, manufacturing entails a net loss in public revenue, because whatever wage and profit taxes can be collected are virtually always far more than offset by the lost tariff revenue from the displaced import. As yet we have no information about the number of requests for tariff protection that were made prior to the mid-1940s. At that time colonial governments, no longer starved for income thanks to FIDES (Fonds d'Investissement pour le Développement Economique et Social) and CDW (Colonial Development and Welfare) schemes, shifted to a positive policy of encouraging import substitution. However, we do know that during the 1930s the Swiss brewery in the Gold Coast and the British-American Tobacco Company's cigarette factory in Nigeria both received substantial fiscal subsidy by virtue of an excise tax well below the import duty. From 1946 onwards an increasing number of tax incentives were available but apparently had little effect.

What about difficulties on the production side? Clearly, the lack of a pool of experienced industrial labourers, problems of factory construction and availability of utilities and the absence of a network of supplying firms made the establishment of factories very difficult. Yet the situation was initially not very different in East Africa or Southern Rhodesia. Moreover, enough scattered enterprises were set up in West Africa during the 1920s and 1930s—Gonfreville, the Dakar oil-mills, the Accra brewery, the Ibadan tobacco factory, sawmilling, soap works and so on—to indicate that such barriers were not insurmountable. Rather, the principal explanation for limited industrialization in West Africa during the period 1929–57 is to be found in the highly concentrated market for manufactured goods. Because the distributive channels were so concentrated, there were few individuals or firms with the requisite qualifications (close contact with consumer demand, access to capital, organizing skills) who were in a position to develop an industrial incentive to undertake an industrial investment. Once the barriers that maintained the oligopoly were eroded, competition in these same markets became a major propellant for the post-1957 spurt of industrialization. We will examine how this second aspect of market structure operated, drawing material from the Nigerian experience. Because of the size

[33] I. F. Nicolson, *Administration in Nigeria, 1900–1960* (Oxford, Clarendon Press, 1969), *passim*.

of its economy, the market-protection investment motive was particularly powerful in Nigeria.

Nigeria

What caused the monopolistic structure of the Nigerian merchandise market to be altered in the mid-1950s? What relationship did that change have with the spurt of industrialization that followed—industrialization led by private foreign investors in a period characterized by a deteriorating balance of payments, growing uncertainty about political stability and weakening governmental administration? [34]

The answer to the first question is that the barriers to entry to new sellers were greatly reduced by the explosive growth in demand that took place during the 1950s. From £20 million pounds in 1946, the value of imports rose to £62 million in 1950, to £114 million in 1954 and to £166 million in 1958. This enrichment of the market, itself a result of the surge in earnings from peasant agricultural exports, meant that an importer/distributor could now specialize in one or two commodities and limit his operations to a few locations. As a consequence, the capital needed to engage in import trade was cut to a small fraction of what it had been a decade earlier, when a break-even volume of sales necessitated handling a wide range of goods distributed from a large number of trading posts. The new sellers who entered the market may be divided into three groups: merchant firms, manufacturers' sales agencies and Nigerian traders.

The first group of importers/distributors who grew to importance in the Nigerian market, contributing to the rising tide of competition, were in existence before the Second World War but on a very small scale. These were the Indian merchants K. Chelleram & Sons, J. T. Chanrai & Company, Bhojson, Indian Emporium and Inlaks. By the late 1950s, K. Chelleram, for instance, had become Nigeria's fifth largest importer. A second group of new merchants, probably quantitatively more significant, were former Greek and Levantine produce buyers and numerous Lebanese retailers who found the import trade more profitable than their previous activities.[35] Outstanding in this group were Mandilas & Karibaris, Nassars, Arab Brothers, S. Raccah and A. G. Leventis. Leventis, a Cypriot Greek who started out as a produce buyer in 1938, developed the importing side of his business to an annual volume of £15 million, ranking third after the United Africa Company and John Holt.[36]

---

[34] The discussion of Nigeria that follows is based on the writer's *Industrialization in an open economy: Nigeria 1945–1966* (Cambridge University Press, 1969). The tables and a number of passages are drawn directly from the book.

[35] The term 'Levantine' is used loosely to apply to some 15,000 Lebanese, Palestinians, Cypriots, Syrians and Greeks whose families came to Nigeria between 1910 and 1940. Initially engaged in transport and small-scale trade (the majority of Lebanese are still in retail and wholesale trade, primarily in Northern Nigeria), the enterprising Levantines have from small beginnings developed many important industrial concerns (e.g., soap, ground-nut crushing, plastics, rubber crêping). Levantine enterprise is distinguished from European commercial activity by (1) family rather than corporate organization, (2) more labour-intensive and smaller-scale operation, (3) lower levels of education, and (4) quasi-permanent residence in Nigeria.

[36] Leventis, who had begun trading in Africa at the age of eighteen, had worked his way up to general manager of G. B. Ollivant's operations in the Gold Coast when Ollivant's was bought out by the UAC in 1937. The dramatic rise of Leventis as a major importer-exporter in the Gold Coast and attempts by the Association of West African Merchants and certain individuals in the

The second important group to enter the import-wholesale trade were overseas manufacturers. As the economy expanded, the potential demand for specific products grew to the point where Nigeria became a very important concern, both to those manufacturers already supplying the market and to those looking for new markets. The traditional stocking and distribution arrangement of the general merchants was no longer adequate; advertising, intensive promotion, specialized distribution and after-service were required to maximize the sales of their particular brand. Many manufacturers—Nestlés, Tate & Lyle, Imperial Chemical Industries, Philips, National Cash Register, British Paints, to name but a few—accordingly set up their own machinery of importation, market promotion and wholesale distribution. Other manufacturers arrangeed exclusive agencies among established importers, including the general merchants.

The third group who encroached on the traditional preserve of the expatriate trading companies were Nigerian traders. From a figure of about 5 per cent in 1949, the Office of Statistics estimates that in 1963 Nigerians were responsible for approximately a fifth of the country's imports.[37] To some extent this has been a result of the gradually increasing skill and capital resources of Nigerian traders. Two other factors, however, were quantitatively more important in explaining the recorded increase. The first was the growing practice by market-seeking overseas manufacturers of financing the Nigerian importer on the basis of ninety-day credit and providing him with the services of a local expatriate confirming and warehousing agent. Second, since 1958–9, when the UAC and John Holt began their withdrawal from general importing as a result of the already intense competition, they both, presumably to avoid any major dislocations, provided their former Nigerian customers with clearance, warehousing and credit facilities for a flat 10-per-cent commission. Assisted in this manner, Nigerian wholesalers were able to become importers on their own account.

Thus the enrichment of the market attracted a host of new distributors into the import trade. Moreover, the established trading concerns found themselves not only threatened but also at a competitive disadvantage. Carrying with them a country-wide distribution network, foreign buying offices and ponderous administrative machinery from an earlier era when their market position rested upon horizontal integration and self-sufficiency, the general merchants were now burdened with higher overhead costs and less flexibility as they faced intense competition from numerous purveyors specializing in specific products and limiting themselves to the richest geographic areas. A measure of the magnitude of the resultant changes in market structure may be obtained by an examination of changes in the share of the leading merchant firms in the distribu-

colonial administration to drive him out of business—events which led, through the Martindale and Sachs investigations, to the Accra riots of 1948—are chronicled by Bauer, *West African trade,* ch. 6. An interview with members of the Leventis family in 1964 provides information on one lacuna in Bauer's excellent narrative: how Leventis managed in two years to become the third largest importer in the Gold Coast. When the farmers ended the cocoa hold-up in April 1938, the established firms were carrying full inventories. Leventis, on the other hand, was just starting up and thus appeared as the largest importer for the year 1938. When supplies became short in late 1939, manufacturers in Britain rationed sales to merchants in West Africa on the basis of average share in the trade over the previous three years. What would otherwise have been a temporary advantage for Leventis was made permanent by the imposition in 1941 of governmental quotas on the same basis.

[37] Bauer, *West African trade,* ch. 5, for 1949; for 1963, data supplied by the Nigerian Federal Office of Statistics.

tion of imported goods. In 1949, the three largest importers accounted for 49 per cent of all traded commodities; in 1963, the three leading importers accounted for about 16 per cent, or one-third of the earlier figures.[38]

Market protection and industrial investment

The response of the merchant firms to the rising tide of competition, which was reducing both their unit profit margins and their share of the market, was to transform themselves from general trading companies into many smaller semi-autonomous specialized marketing and manufacturing units. In so doing they rid themselves of the redundant overhead facilities and at the same time capitalized on their accumulated experience, operating methods, local contacts and knowledge of the market. In terms of market strategy, specialized merchandising represented an attempt to concentrate in the least competitive markets (namely, those lines requiring considerable capital and technical servicing skills). The establishment of manufacturing, involving greater risk, had the effect of denying the market to competitors altogether.

By going into manufacturing, the merchant firm could protect its stake in the market and at the same time re-create its earlier monopolistic position. This aspect of infant industry protection, although neglected by economists, is fully appreciated by businessmen. Because the intended effect of a protective tariff is to provide local industry with an assured market (that is, to provide local industry not with equal costs but with a decisive cost advantage vis-à-vis overseas suppliers), the imposition of a protective duty establishes the condition for a sharp contraction in competition. In consequence of the elimination of competition, the firm or firms willing to risk an industrial investment are able, first, to expand total sales, and second, to increase net earnings by an ever greater proportion as a result of a tariff-enhanced unit profit margin. Not only does the tariff secure the seller who makes an industrial commitment against the competition of similar products, but it also shields him to a substantial degree from technically more advanced varieties or otherwise superior articles that in the absence of fiscal discrimination might pre-empt the market. Hence, for both the overseas manufacturer and the distributing merchant firm, the optimum solution to mounting competition and threatened markets was often to establish a local factory.

That this mechanism of market protection was the catalyst in the first phase of Nigeria's industrialization—as opposed to the more conventional view that when the market approaches a size that will support a plant of near-optimum efficiency (the 'technological threshold'), fiscal incentives induce a profit-seeking investor to establish the industry—is demonstrated by Table 117. From the second and third columns it may be seen that in most cases industrial investments occurred long after the technological threshold had been reached. Then, once the first firm had taken the plunge, several competitors immediately followed suit. The sole exception is flour milling, where the first investor installed capacity to cover more than adequately the entire market. Fortunately, additional in-

---

[38] Should the reader doubt that the entry of new sellers far more than offset the growth in demand, with consequent pressure on profit margins, he is referred to company reports (published for the United Africa Company, John Holt, Paterson-Zochonis) for evidence on the losses that were sustained in the general import lines prior to the merchants' withdrawal from these areas. See also the article 'Redeployment', in United Africa Company, *Statistical and Economic Review*, April 1963, no. 28.

Table 117. *Technological threshold and import substitution, Nigeria*

Product and minimum-size plant	Minimum-size plant attained	Start-up	Imports at start-up	Additional plants 3 years [a]	Total plants 1965
Asbestos-cement products (17,000 t) [b]	1955	1961	28,359 t	1	3
Galvanized iron sheet (20,000 t) [b]	1951	1964	36,567 t	2	3
Cement (30,000 t)	1923	1957	510,237 t	—	7
Cotton textiles (8 m. yds.)	1890s	1957	156 m. yds.	—	10
Tyres and tubes (2,500 t) [b]	...	1962	... [c]	1	2
Flour (25,000 t)	1953	1962	61,152 t	—	1
Biscuits (2,000 t) [b]	1953	1961	4,000 t	2	3
Leather shoes and sandals (75,000 p)	1947	1963	3·2 m.p.	2	3
Rubber and canvas shoes (250,000 p)	1947	1959	3·6 m.p.	3	6
Paint (120,000 g)	...	1962	... [c]	7	8
Bicycle assembly (30,000) [b]	1946	1958	114,753	2	3
Aluminium holloware (n.a.)	...	1960	470 t	2	3
Enamelware (n.a.)	...	1959	17,300 t	3	5
Gramophone records (50,000 r) [b]	1944	1962	1·3 m.r.	1	2
Steel door/window frames (400 t) [b]	pre-1954	1958	2,700 t	2	5
Candy (500 t)	1947	1959	2,400 t	2	6

NOTE: t = tons; g = gallons; p = pairs; r = single records; m = millions.
[a] Additional plants established within three years of the first plant.
[b] Announced capacity of first plant to go into production.
[c] Not available in comparable units.

SOURCES: Nigeria, Federal Ministry of Commerce and Industry, *Industrial directory 1965* (Lagos, 1966); Nigeria, Federal Office of Statistics, *Nigeria trade summary*, various years.

formation gained by interviews with the firms involved is available to supplement the inferential evidence of Table 117. We shall begin with the merchants and then proceed to the overseas manufacturers.

Of all the firms engaged in distribution, the United Africa Company has redirected the highest proportion of its resources into manufacturing. From its constituent companies the UAC inherited two processing industries which had grown out of the produce trade—a large sawmill at Sapele established by Miller Brothers in 1917 and two (later expanded to six) palm-oil bulking plants dating from 1924. In 1948, a plywood factory was added to the sawmill. The resulting company, African Timber and Plywood Ltd, employs fixed capital of £3 million and a labour force of 3,200—one of the country's largest industrial establishments. The bulk oil plants, on the other hand, have gradually been nationalized by the marketing boards, whose subsidiary, the Nigerian Produce Marketing Company, took up a third of the capital in 1946 and the other two-thirds in 1961. In 1953, following the lead of John Holt, the UAC induced the British construction firm of Taylor Woodrow to come to Nigeria and provided half of the capital. Through this holding, the UAC has interests in three furniture factories (1953, 1955, 1958) and a company producing pre-stressed concrete products (1954).

The UAC's first industrial investment other than processing was the Nigerian Breweries, Ltd in 1949, one of the earliest instances of import-substitution.[39] The primary motive for the UAC's initiative was market protection: the company's beer trade had already been displaced in Ghana (1932) and the Congo (1935) as a result of the establishment of local breweries by Swiss entrepreneurs. It was apparent that the Nigerian market would soon be richer than either of these and that unless the UAC took the initiative, a valuable merchant interest might be jeopardized.

The relatively early date of the investment in beer (the project had been mooted as early as 1937) suggests that the shift from trade to manufacture, which did not become a conscious policy as such until the late 1950s, grew out of earlier precedents. Taking another example, the UAC's entry into modern consumer retailing, a field which the company pioneered, developed out of a sudden hunch in 1947 of a visiting London director that a new building with a long frontage on a main street in Lagos, intended as the company's administrative headquarters in Nigeria, should instead be converted into West Africa's first department store, making extensive use of window displays. More than a decade later, this form of merchandising provided a fully explored and proven avenue for redeployment (annual turnover of the Lagos Kingsway having reached £3 million). Second and third stores opened in Ibadan in 1962 and in Port Harcourt in 1963.

It was not until about 1957 that conscious redeployment actually commenced. In 1958, the company began its withdrawal from the produce trade and the closing down (or transfer to Nigerians) of small outlying trading stations, and set up its first assembly plants (Bedford lorries and Raleigh bicycles). Table 118 sets forth details of the individual investments in which the UAC has an interest. All save one of the twenty-eight projects are directly connected to marketing activities.[40] The production of reconstituted milk, ice cream, meat products and pigs developed from retailing activities of the Kingsway stores. As a general rule of thumb the UAC will consider an industrial investment only if it represents the protection of an established merchant interest that is both sizeable and profitable. Regarding production, the industry must be within the competence of the company, the Unilever organization or a principal supplier who can be persuaded to join the venture as a technical partner.

Such products as cosmetics and meat products are relatively simple to produce and thus could be handled completely by the UAC. Ice cream, packaging materials and (since 1961) plastics are manufacturing activities in which Unilever is engaged and is consequently able to provide the technical know-how. In the case of lager beer, mattresses and beds, yarn, printed textiles and matchets, the UAC was able to persuade one of its suppliers to embark upon a joint venture. For cigarettes and vehicle assembly, the UAC went out and employed qualified technical managers. This can be a risky practice, as the fate of many government projects attests, because in the event of serious problems

---

[39] Although this was a joint venture with the technical partner, Heinekens, and other merchant firms, the project was initiated and organized by the UAC, which is also the managing agent. United Africa Company, *Statistical and Economic Review,* Sept. 1953, no. 12, p. 8.

[40] The exception was the plastics factory, Nipol, a goodwill venture undertaken in partnership with the Western Nigeria Development Corporation, which was built in advance of the market; losses were made for six of the first seven years of operation. When demand began to develop, a Greco-Lebanese firm established and captured the bulk of the market.

Table 118. *Industrial investments of the United Africa Company in Nigeria, 1948–65*

Company	Product	Year of start-up	Fixed capital [a] (£000)	UAC equity (per cent)
African Timber and Plywood	timber and plywood	1948	3,000	100
Nigerian Breweries (3 plants)	beer and minerals	1949	3,500	33
Taylor Woodrow	building contractors	1953	500 [b]	50
Nigerian Joinery (3 plants)	woodwork and furniture	1953	100 [b]	50
Prestress	pre-stressed concrete	1954	40	20
Nipol	plastic products	1957	105	35
Raleigh Industries (3 plants)	cycle assembly	1958	75	50
Vehicle Assembly Plant	Bedford lorries	1958	500	100
Minna Farm	pigs	1959	35	80
Northern Construction Co.	building contractors	1960	100	30
W. A. Thread	sewing thread	1961	450	20
W. A. Portland Cement	cement	1961	4,500	10
W. A. Cold Storage	meat products	1961	250	100
Walls	ice cream	1961	90	100
Vono Products	beds, mattresses	1961	80	38
Cement Paints	cement paint	1962	35	16
Guinness	stout	1963	2,000	33
Fan Milk	re-constituted milk	1963	100	45
Nigerian Sugar Co.	sugar and by-products	1963	3,800	7
Norspin	cotton yarn	1963	1,100	53
Pye	radio assembly	1963	40	50
Vitafoam	foam-rubber products	1963	100	50
A. J. Seward	perfumery and cosmetics	1964	200	100
Bordpak	fibre-board cartons	1964	800	100
Kwara Tobacco Co.	cigarettes	1964	500	80
Associated Battery Mfgs.	vehicle batteries	1965	65 [b]	22
Crocodile Matchets	matchets	1965	120	51
Textile Printers	printed textiles	1965	3,250	68

[a] Equity, capital reserves and long-term debt as of 1965.   [b] Author's estimate.

SOURCES: Information supplied by the United Africa Company, except for 'fixed capital', which was compiled from the UAC house magazine *Link,* press releases, and the Registrar of Companies, Nigerian Ministry of Commerce and Industry.

there is no reserve of technical knowledge to fall back on, as contrasted to the case of a technical partner where the resources of an entire manufacturing firm can be drawn upon. And finally, in the case of sewing thread, cement, stout, cement paint and radio assembly, it was the manufacturer who took the primary initiative and invited the UAC to join for its contribution by way of local knowledge, commercial management and distribution facilities.

Nigeria's second largest merchant firm is John Holt & Company. This family venture was founded in 1867 and is the oldest surviving trading concern in West Africa.[41] Both river- and ocean-transport interests developed as adjuncts of the merchandise-produce trade soon after the turn of the century.[42] Until just before the Second World War, John Holt differed little from the United Africa

[41] Much of the narrative that follows is taken from *Merchant adventure,* a book published privately by John Holt & Co. about 1950.

Company in its organization and the nature of its activities—except in size, its turn-over in Nigeria being approximately a quarter of the UAC's. However, in the late 1930s French colonial trade preferences induced the company, which was also trading in the French territories, to establish a French subsidiary. Subsidiaries were also set up in the United States and South Africa for reasons of procurement. These subsidiaries gradually developed interests of their own independent of West African trade. Thus, when the pressure of competition became intense in Nigeria, John Holt, unlike the UAC, had the option of shifting away from Africa and concentrating on other areas.

Pre-dating the UAC's connection with Taylor Woodrow, John Holt formed a partnership in 1947 with the British construction firm Richard Costain Ltd for a Nigerian venture, to take part in the execution of large-scale construction projects contained in the 1947 ten-year plan. Most of Holt's 45-per-cent share was later sold to provide capital for industrial investments more closely linked with its distributive activities. In recent years the company has followed the standard pattern of withdrawal from produce buying, urban concentration and import specialization. The major imports handled are drugs and cosmetics (retailed through its West African Drug Company), automobiles, engineering and electrical equipment and hardware. John Holt is one of the few merchants not to have gone into department-store merchandising. On the other hand, the company has redeployed into such activities as shipping and travel services, harbour dredging, real estate, insurance discount banking and stock brokerage.

In the field of industrial processing, from its interest in produce which the company has 'backed' into tanning of hides and skins, ground-nut crushing (partial acquisition of an established producer) and rubber crêping. Table 119 lists these investments as well as import-replacing industries. A minority share in a biscuit factory (1961), not shown, was sold to the Nigerian Tobacco Company, because of a conflict of interest in the marketing field. The holding in the Nigerian Canning Company, a project developed by government agencies, parallels the UAC's participation in the plastics venture. The factory was built well ahead of demand and, although highly protected, did not get into the black until 1964, still only on one shift a day (a third of capacity).

The next largest distributor in Nigeria, A. G. Leventis, has, like the others, redeployed from the produce/general import trade to specialized merchandising (six department stores, office equipment, electrical goods, lorries and cars) and industry. The industrial interests include three Coca-Cola bottling plants, a vehicle assembly plant, production of industrial gases and a 10-per-cent interest in West African Breweries. Leventis also owns two hotels.

We turn now to Levantine former produce-buyers (later importers). The firm of S. Raccah has established a factory producing brass hollow-ware and has participated in another making cotton blankets, both articles he had earlier handled as imports. The Gazal brothers shifted from general importing to the production of terrazzo tiles, candles and singlets. The Nassar family, prominent in large-scale food retailing, has established two large biscuit factories. Other redeploying Levantine importer/wholesalers have gone into the manufacture of perfume (four establishments), hard candy (four), soft drinks, interlock fabric, plastic sandals (two), umbrella assembly, wrought iron and metal furniture

---

[42] The ocean shipping company, Guinea Gulf Line, was sold to Elder Dempster's in 1964 for £1·5 million.

Table 119. *Industrial investments of John Holt & Company in Nigeria*

Company	Description	Year	Equity capital (£000)	Holt's equity (per cent)
Costains	construction	1948	400	6
Holt Tanneries	...	1949	150	53
P. S. Mandrides	ground-nut crushing	1960	625	10
Holt Rubber Co.	rubber crêping	1962	120	100
Thomas Wyatt	stationery	1948	220	30
Nigerian Breweries	...	1949	1,500	7
Nigerian Canning Co.	corned beef	1956	100	30
Critall-Hope	metal doors, etc.	1958	160	14
Asbestos Cement Products	...	1960	1,000	3
Nigerian Enamelware Co.	...	1961	130	50
Haco	perfume and plastics	1963	175	51

NOTE: Equity capital is not comparable to fixed investment in Table 118, which includes capital reserves and long-term debt as well. The 51 per cent of Haco's equity was purchased for £310,000.

SOURCE: Data supplied by John Holt & Company of Liverpool.

(five), and terrazzo tiles (two). In a number of the cases cited the small-scale entrepreneur, suffering from the same pressure on distributive margins as the large trading houses, did not possess the technical competence and was unable to recruit a technical partner to manufacture the article he formerly traded. In these cases the choice of industry was dictated by capital and skill requirements.

Although the greatest part of Levantine investment is a reaction to falling margins in the distributive trade, other motives are not absent. In the case of the three out of four Kano ground-nut crushers who expanded into import-replacing industry (aluminium holloware, rubber and canvas shoes, soft-drink bottling) and of Mandilas and Karibaris, who participated in a steel rolling-mill, the motive was the classical attraction to a profitable market opportunity rather than the compulsion of competition. It would seem significant that none of these ventures, where the entrepreneur lacked an intimate prior knowledge of the product or its market, has been particularly successful.

Returning to the original European merchant firms, we find that Paterson and Zochonis's first industrial investment was in partnership with a Greek soap-maker, P. B. Nicholas, in 1949. The motive was the profitability of soap manufacture combined with the assurance of a local source of supply for Paterson-Zochonis's marketing requirements. In 1952, the company bought out Nicholas's interest and recruited its own technical personnel. In 1963, operations were extended to include perfume and cosmetics. In 1962, Paterson-Zochonis joined their principal paint supplier in establishing a factory in order to hold their position in that market (four other competing plants were opened in the same year). In 1964, a similarly motivated joint venture began production of galvanized iron sheet (a competing Japanese concern also started up that year).

Of all the merchants, the French firms of CFAO and SCOA and the Swiss Union Trading Company have gone into industry least—with the consequence that their position in the market relative to the other merchant houses has

500

declined appreciably. Each of the French companies has gone into partial assembly of the lorries they distribute; all three of the firms have made small trade investments (usually less than 10 per cent) in industries manufacturing products which they sell—for example, metal doors and windows, paint, galvanized iron sheet.

Of the Indian merchants only the largest, K. Chelleram, has so far gone into industry. Since 1962, he has bought two factories producing luggage, and cosmetics and candles, respectively. Chelleram also took minority participation in a varnish factory in 1964. Finally, the smaller merchants and agent/importers have gone into a variety of industries (such as proprietary drugs, cosmetics, louvre windows, packing materials), usually as commercial partners with their former suppliers.

A number of market-protecting investments by overseas suppliers have already been referred to. At this point we will review a few of the larger investments of foreign suppliers not already mentioned; the important cases of cement and textile will be considered subsequently. Over 95 per cent of the asbestos-cement import market was held by two firms, Turner and Newall of England and Eternit of Belgium. Given their large stakes in the Nigerian market and the active rivalry between the two firms, both began investigating the possibilities for establishing a plant in the Lagos area in 1959, four years after the technological threshold had been achieved. When Eternit formed a partnership with the Western Nigeria Development Corporation in 1960 to build a £600,000 plant in Ikeja to produce flat and corrugated sheet, Turner and Newall, despite the fact that the market could not at the time support two plants, went to the east and launched a venture of comparable size at Emene near Enugu.[43]

In early 1964, both firms began to construct £350,000 pipe-forming plants and adjoining their existing operations. Later in that year, when the Northern Nigeria Development Corporation indirectly let the Ikeja and Emene firms know that it was negotiating with an Indian producer, both the Belgian and English companies came forward with counter-proposals. In March 1965, the government of Northern Nigeria announced that an agreement had been signed with Turner and Newall for the establishment of a £400,000 factory at Kaduna.

The establishment of two tyre factories in 1962 and 1963, representing an investment of about £5 million, was a dramatic and unamibiguous example of manufacturers' market protection. As in the case of asbestos-cement products, market shares were highly concentrated, with Michelin and Dunlop supplying about four-fifths of all imports. Both firms had had their own marketing organizations in Nigeria for some years. In 1960, Michelin began discussions with the federal government about the possibility of constructing a factory in the Lagos area; a negotiating team from Dunlop arrived soon afterwards. Shortly after Nigeria's severance of diplomatic relations with France over the atomic explosion in the Sahara, federal approval was given to Dunlop's proposal. The British firm, however, made no move to go ahead with its project, now that the Michelin threat had been turned aside. Meanwhile, the latter had quietly approached the regional government in Enugu, and in March 1961 Michelin an-

---

[43] Tariff protection was 10 per cent until 1964, when it was raised to 20 per cent. More important are the following elements of natural protection: transportation costs, 25 per cent; breakage, 10 per cent; and ship handling, 3 per cent.

nounced that it was beginning construction of a plant in Port Harcourt. Dunlop, despite a statement by one of its directors in the Federation of British Industries investment survey that Nigeria could only support one tyre factory,[44] formally launched its own venture in October of that year.[45]

A majority of the industries listed in Table 117 also represent manufacturers' market protection. Perhaps the most spectacular instance was the establishment of five paint factories in a single year, each sponsored by a leading British firm: Imperial Chemical Industries, British Paints, Permacem, International Paints and Pinchin Johnson (Courtaulds). In 1963 and 1964, the three major suppliers (one British, two Japanese) of galvanized iron sheet began local production. In like manner, multi-investments occurred in the cases of Hong Kong enamelware and British metal door and window frames. In other cases, not easily presented in tabular form, single investments were undertaken to hold a market. Such an instance is English Sewing Cotton's West African Thread venture, whose purpose was to secure its Nigerian sales from the severe competitive pressure being applied by its chief rival, J. and P. Coates.

Although English Sewing Cotton's 'Crown' and 'Parrot' thread held 60 per cent of the market, the competition from Coates's 'Comb' thread had reduced margins to the point where ESC had been making net losses on its Nigerian trade for two years prior to its decision to undertake local manufacture. Coates was supplying the market from a low-cost Indian subsidiary factory, whereas ESC's 'Crown' and 'Parrot' were manufactured only in England.

So far we have dealt only with investors who had a prior stake in the market and whose decision to go into manufacturing was in some measure a defensive act. Although these firms have been responsible for the major part of industrial output and employment, other private investors, strangers to Nigeria seeking new sources of income, have also played a role. The decision of the Southern Star Shipping Company to establish a port-side flour mill was related to the economies that would accrue to its principal activity: the ability to fill its charter ships with American hard wheat on the inward voyage allowed it to bid successfully for carriage of Nigerian produce exports. The Anglo-Canadian Cement Company, a port-side plant that was started up in 1963 to grind imported clinker, was sponsored by a shipping firm for the same reason. Indian Head Mills promoted a £2·7 million textile venture at Aba to which it contributed £72,000 and forty-year-old equipment from its American plants in return for 70 per cent of the equity.

Although there are undoubtedly more, the writer knows of only two instances—Alcan and Charles Pfizer—where straightforward, entrepreneur-financed manufacturing investments were made by firms that had no prior stake in the market. These cases might be considered similar to the 1920 investment of the Compagnie Générale des Colonies in ground-nut crushing in Dakar. Regarding investments by individuals not already distributors, E. A. Seroussi's

---

[44] Federation of British Industries, *Nigeria: an industrial reconnaissance* (London, Feb. 1961), p. 12.

[45] A revenue tariff of 20 per cent was raised to 33 per cent at the request of Michelin, and then 60–70 per cent at the request of Dunlop, whose prior share in the car- and lorry tyre market was considerably smaller. For bicycle tyres, a field already dominated by Dunlop, no tariff increase was requested. Closing off the importation of used tyres substantially aided the second producer (Dunlop) in getting out of the red by its third year of operation (1965).

Kaduna textile plant can be compared in its uniqueness with that of Robert Gonfreville four decades earlier at Bouaké.

Some government initiatives

What about the role of government? Starting in 1946, the colonial government sponsored sustained programmes in technical education, applied industrial research, mechanized palm-oil extraction and indigenous entrepreneurial development (loans, technical assistance, nursery estates).[46] In aggregate, the contribution of these efforts to the growth of manufacturing output has been small. Legislated fiscal incentives for industrial investment—accelerated depreciation (1943), pioneer income-tax holiday (1952), import-duty relief (1956)—formalized benefits that earlier had been negotiated individually.[47] Interviews with the firms involved revealed that accelerated depreciation and unlimited loss carry-forward, plus less than exacting standards for the granting of tariff protection, were important permissive factors in the investment decision.[48]

The government also provided investment capital in various forms. In addition to making direct equity investments, various branches of the federal and regional government were involved in development banking operations in collaboration with foreign aid agencies.[49] By taking some of the foreign investor's risk without demanding a commensurate share in profits, such lending was important in attracting investors of the non-market protecting type.[50] We have already mentioned government involvement with the UAC in plastics and John Holt in meat canning. Far more successful was the initiative of the federal government and regional development corporations in launching the pioneering firms in cement production and textiles. We shall briefly review these develop-

---

[46] A full treatment of these programmes may be found in Kilby, *Industrialization in an open economy,* chs. 5, 6, 8, 10.

[47] Before 1939, there was no income tax whatever. Because there are no tax-sparing treaties, the principal beneficiary of tax holidays is the investor's home-country treasury. Before 1956, import-duty relief was provided by the creation of new tariff categories, e.g., 'tobacco to be used in the manufacture of cigarettes'.

[48] For a detailed discussion of Nigeria's tariff-making process and the role of fiscal incentives in the investment decision, see Kilby, *Industrialization in an open economy,* pp. 48–9, 58–9, 132–3.

A study by Yair Aharoni of a large number of American firms that invested in Latin America tends to substantiate the primacy of the market-protection motive and the secondary nature of fiscal incentives as a general phenomenon. From his interviews with management, Aharoni identifies four initiating forces leading to the *consideration* of an overseas investment, each of which can be interpreted as a specific kind of market threat. Using organizational theory, he formulates the *decision* itself as being a function of the level of personal and organizational 'commitment' to making the investment. In all but a few of the cases he cites, the commitment varied with the volume of sales involved, i.e., the size of the stake in the market. See Yair Aharoni, *The foreign investment decision process* (Boston, Harvard Business School, 1966), chs. 5–7. For evidence from Asia, see Helen Hughs and Y. P. Seng, eds., *Foreign investment and industrialization in Singapore* (Madison, University of Wisconsin Press, 1969).

[49] The institutions were the Investment Company of Nigeria, established in Lagos in 1959 and expanded into the Nigerian Industrial Development Bank in 1964; Indag, located in Enugu; and Northern Nigeria Investments Ltd., located in Kaduna. Launched by the Colonial Development Corporation, later contributors to the investment companies were the International Finance Corporation, Commonwealth Development Finance Company and several international banks.

[50] For details as to which firms received risk-shifting loans, see Kilby, *Industrialization in an open economy,* pp. 101–2 and 118–23.

ments and then turn to the area where public investment has been greatest, in state-owned turnkey projects.

Of all import-replacing industries, none possesses so great a comparative advantage as the production of cement. The cost of carriage to a Nigerian seaport adds some 70 per cent to the ex-factory price of the overseas manufacturer. Beyond this natural protection, cement has carried the usual revenue tariff, which ranged between 9 and 16 per cent of the c.i.f. value prior to the establishment of local production. For inland producers serving inland markets, the cost of land transport provides further protection, the equivalent of 20 per cent of the cost of manufacture for every hundred miles. Given the size of this transport-savings incentive, it might be expected that the manufacture of cement would be one of the first instances of import-substitution, occurring as soon as the market reached the technological threshold—the capacity of a single vertical kiln, 30,000 tons. In fact, because the industry is characterized by large firms, a market of a mere 30,000 tons is far below the *minimum sensible*. It was not until 1954, when imports were 368,000 tons, thirty-one years after the technological threshold had been reached (1923), that a company to produce cement in Nigeria was formed—and this at the initiative of the government.

As with most other goods, imports of cement were more or less static during the two decades before 1945. Thereafter, consumption grew rapidly, rising from 100,000 tons in 1947 to 1,137,000 in 1966. In 1950, the federal government invited the British combine Associated Portland Cement Manufacturers (the world's largest producer), which supplied over half of Nigeria's imports, to establish a local plant. After nearly two years of surveying the country's limestone deposits, negotiating and deliberating, APCM declined to go ahead with the project. Unable to interest private investors, the government determined to undertake the major burden of the investment itself, setting aside £1.2 million in 1952. After two and a half years of searching in Belgium and America for a technical partner, the Nigeria government finally reached agreement with the Danish firm of F. L. Smidth, the world's largest manufacturer of cement-making machinery, and its British associate, Tunnel Portland Cement Company, to join in a venture as consulting engineers and managing agent, respectively. Both private firms agreed to take up a small incentive-creating share of the equity capital.

Once the government shouldered the entrepreneurial risk itself and succeeded in attracting a competent technical partner, APCM was faced with the prospect of losing a large and growing market. As in most of the cases we have reviewed, there was a certain natural disposition to supply Nigeria from APCM's efficient well-written-down home plants. More important, the major part of Nigeria's cement consumption was in the Lagos-Ibadan area—markets that could not easily be supplied from the one proven site at Nkalagu in the northern corner of the Eastern Region. This unfavourable location, conjoined with the moderate size of the overall market in 1951, was not attractive enough to APCM to establish a local plant, nor was it likely in the company's judgement to be sufficiently attractive to other investors. Proved wrong by the rapid growth in consumption and by the determined efforts of the government to recruit a technical partner, APCM acted immediately to protect its market lest a second mill be established in the west. Within a month of the formation of the Nigerian Cement Company, APCM set up a syndicate with the Western Nigeria

Development Corporation to search for viable limestone deposits. When these were uncovered at Ewekoro in 1957, the West African Portland Cement Company was formed.

The establishment of a smelting industry in 1961–2 parallels in some respects the start-up of Nigeria's cement industry. Tin ore (cassiterite) has been mined in Northern Nigeria on the Jos plateau since 1909. For many years the Ministry of Mines and Power had urged the traditional processor of Nigerian ore, William Harvey and Company of Liverpool, to establish a local smelting plant. Apparently interested in the project, the Liverpool firm continually delayed taking any action. When a Portuguese entrepreneur connected with smelters in Brazil and Portugal proposed in 1960 to establish a smelter at Jos based on a new capital-saving electrometallurgical process, the government immediately accepted his offer. The Nigerian Embel Tin Smelting Company was to have eight electric furnaces with an aggregate processing capacity of 17,000 tons per annum at a planned investment of £250,000. Despite the fact that the Embel plant had more than enough capacity to smelt Nigeria's entire ore output, Consolidated Tin Smelters, Ltd of London, the parent company of William Harvey, announced its intention a few months later to establish a second smelter, Makeri Smelting Company, with a two-furnace capacity of 30,000 tons and costing £500,000.

Embel began smelting in 1961. Theoretically, the Portuguese venture possessed a number of advantages over its pursuing rival. Unlike the conventional reverberatory oil-burning furnaces employed by Makeri, Embel's electrometallurgical process utilized only domestic imputs—wood, coal from Enugu and local limestone. Because of their capacity to reach very high temperatures, the electric furnaces were capable of re-smelting the slag, thereby achieving a higher extraction rate. However, owing to the lack of availability of a sufficient supply of electricity, only one (later two) furnaces could be used, and operation of these was hampered because of high silica content in the local limestone. In 1961, only 600 tons of tin metal were produced, the balance of the cassiterite being shipped to Embel's plant in Portugal.[51]

In January 1962, Makeri commenced operations. Its output of tin metal for the year was 7,300 tons as compared to ailing Embel's 200 tons. In January 1963, the Nigerian Embel Tin Smelting Company declared itself bankrupt.

The position of Consolidated Tin Smelters was analogous to that of Associated Portland Cement Manufacturers. Given the significant diseconomies of small smelters (for example, those employed by Makeri) and the more than sufficient capacity already existing in Britain, Consolidated Tin Smelters was reluctant to make an 'unnecessary' investment and to shoulder the risks and inconvenience that a Nigerian smelter involved. Once threatened, to go ahead

---

[51] There is some indirect evidence to suggest that the promoters of Embel did not intend to process all of Nigeria's ore in their Jos plant. The generation of electricity in the Jos area has for many years lagged behind demand; most firms are compelled to install their own auxiliary generating equipment. Embel's smelting process required 250 kw for each of its eight furnaces (compared with 100 kw total requirement for Makeri); yet no auxiliary generators were installed. The plant was inefficient and of old design. Even with the plant operating at full capacity, unit costs would have been far higher than the conventional process, which relies on imported inputs. However, if Embel had been the only smelter, which its promoters had no doubt anticipated, it would have automatic purchasing rights over all Nigerian cassiterite, as was the case in 1961. The unsmelted cassiterite could then be shunted to the home plant in Portugal, which, although it enjoys a protected market, has difficulty in securing an adequate supply of ore.

with such an investment, as it had already done in the case of Malaya, became a requisite of survival. Unlike the British oil-seed crushing industry, which has been able to maintain operations near full capacity by substituting U.S. soybeans for the shrinking supply of raw produce from the former colonial territories, metropolitan tin smelters must take themselves to the producing countries or perish.

The cotton-textile industry has been one of the major areas of industrialization for nearly every developing country in the twentieth century. There are a number of reasons for this. In low-income societies not only does the purchase of cloth account for a significant portion of all consumer expenditures (about 7 per cent for Nigeria), but as an import, cotton textiles are the largest single user of foreign exchange—in the case of Nigeria over £21 million as late as 1965. From the supply side, as a modern industry textile production is moderately labour-intensive and yet does not require a highly skilled work force—features that make the industry particularly attractive to countries with an abundance of untrained labour. Excess capacity in both the textile and textile-machinery industries in advanced economies means that new and used equipment is available at favourable prices and that competent partners can be recruited. Moreover, Nigeria possesses the further advantage of producing some 50,000 tons of high-grade, medium-staple cotton each year.

There are, however, two factors that have worked against the early establishment of cotton-textile manufacturing. The first is the very slight degree of natural protection afforded by transportation, conjoined with the existence of highly efficient, low-cost exporting producers in the Far East. Second, and more important, the market-protection incentive for the overseas manufacturer to establish locally is not as strong as in other industries. This stems from the fact that the major importing firms maintain buying offices in Madras, Hong Kong, Tokyo and elsewhere, and purchase from a large number of suppliers in each country, thus spreading the stake in the Nigerian market over a wide number of producers. Consequently, government initiative and special concessions have played a particularly important role in the creation of the textile industry.

Nigeria's first textile plant came into operation in 1950. With technical and financial assistance from the government, Kano Citizens Trading Company, an enterprise formed by leading members of the Hausa trading community in Kano, began weaving operations using fifty second-hand power looms imported from Lancashire. In 1952 a similar mill, J. F. Kamson & Company, comprising sixty looms and a spinning section, went into production on the outskirts of Lagos. This too was a private Nigerian venture extensively assisted by the government. Primarily as a result of bad management, neither of these projects has expanded nor enjoyed any marked degree of success.

Although a number of schemes were proposed in 1952 and 1953, it was not until 1955 that a major project was launched at the initiative of the regional government in Kaduna. The capital about £1 million, was provided by the regional marketing board and the Northern Nigeria Development Corporation. David Whitehead & Sons of Lancashire, which had recently established a mill in Southern Rhodesia, was approached and subsequently recruited as the technical partner. Production of unbleached grey baft commenced in January 1958; spinning operations, using Nigerian cotton, had begun two months earlier.

Kaduna Textiles Limited (KTL) was an unqualified success. Earning a profit from the first month of operation, an exceptional feat, the factory reached full capacity in the second year. In proving that Nigerian labour was readily adaptable to textile operations and that Nigerian cotton was of the requisite quality without the supplementary use of imported lint, the Kaduna venture had removed major elements of risk for future investors in the textile industry.

The country's second large textile project, Nigerian Textile Mills at Ikeja near Lagos, was also a result of the initiative of a public body; but in this case more than half of the capital was provided by private interests. The Western Nigeria Development Corporation (WNDC) had been trying to interest British and continental manufacturers in undertaking a project in the Western Region since 1955. It was not until February 1959, more than a year after KTL had begun profitable operation, that an acceptable proposal was received from a consortium of Trans-Continental Mercantile Company of Milan, Maurer Textile Consultants of Geneva and the Chase-Manhattan Investment Company of New York. Unlike KTL, which only spun and wove grey cloth, NTM undertook the full range of spinning, weaving, bleaching and printing. None of the private investors had a prior interest in the Nigerian market. However, one of the lines of activity of the Milan firm, a co-promoter of the project with WNDC, was selling textile machinery.

Nigerian Textile Mills opened in 1962. In the following year, two more plants began production in Kaduna. The first was Nortex, producing 8 million yards of grey and bleached cloth. Its promoter and principal private investor was E. A. Seroussi, a Sudanese entrepreneur. The second plant, Norspin, was a cotton-spinning factory designed to supply handloom yarn for the United Africa Company's merchandise trade, yarn for conversion into sewing thread in English Sewing Cotton's Lagos factory and cotton cord for Dunlop's tyre factory. The bulk of Norspin's risk capital was provided by the UAC and English Sewing Cotton, who also shared the management of the enterprise, with ESC being responsible for the technical side.

Three more textile plants came into production in 1964. The first was Aba Textile Mills, designed to produce 7 million yards of grey and bleached cloth, plus printing 24 million yards of imported Japanese grey cloth. The private investor behind this project was the American firm Indian Head Mills, whose major capital contribution was redundant equipment from its U.S. plants. The second and third projects, both in Kaduna, were undertaken as part of a move to protect overseas markets of oriental producers. Arewa, with a capacity of 10 million yards of grey and bleached cloth, was sponsored by a consortium of ten Japanese cotton-spinning firms. United Nigerian Textiles was established by Chinese Dyeworks (Hong Kong) to print 15 million yards of imported grey cloth. Table 120 gives the 1965 figures for Nigerian textile production.

Two factories began operation in 1965. The United Africa Company and its technical associates, protecting a merchant interest, established Textile Printers of Nigeria at Onitsha to print 24 million yards of Japanese grey cloth.[52] Zamfra, E. A. Seroussi's second joint project with the Northern Nigeria Development Corporation, started production at Gasau, with a planned output of 8 million yards of grey, bleached and dyed cloth. Also in 1965, construction

---

[52] The technical partners, Calico Printers and two Dutch firms, had long printed for the West African market under contract to the UAC, using rollers and Japanese grey cloth supplied by the UAC.

Table 120. *Nigerian textile industry, 1965*

Product	No. of plants	Employment	Sales (£000)	Value added (£000)
Total	17	12,117	20,855	9,893
Yarn	1	8·9%	4·3%	2·7%
Woven piece-goods, exclusive of prints	7	59·6%	47·1%	60·4%
Prints	2	14·2%	34·4%	26·2%
Towels and blankets	3	11·4%	6·9%	4·1%
Knit piece-goods	4	6·0%	7·3%	6·5%
		100·0%	100·0%	100·0%

NOTE: Percentages may not add to 100 because of rounding.

SOURCE: Arthur D. Little, Inc., *The Nigerian textile industry outlook in 1967* (Cambridge, Mass. [1967?]).

began on Nigeria's first turnkey textile project, at Asaba, sold to the Mid-Western Nigeria Development Corporation. The capacity of this £4·2 million factory (500 looms) was 20 million yards of grey, bleached and printed cloth.

Buying factories

The Asaba textile mill is an example of the type of large-scale state enterprise that became increasingly important after 1961. The regional development corporations in the early 1950s launched a number of small- and medium-scale processing and manufacturing projects that they owned and operated. The biggest venture, begun by the Nigeria Local Development Board in 1946, was the pioneer oil-mill scheme; by 1960, 145 of these mills had been erected at a cost in excess of £2 million. By 1965, the bulk of these mills had ceased operation; about twenty of those remaining were earning a profit. The other development corporation projects were soft-drink bottling (two), fruit canning, rubber processing and boat building (three). The rubber-processing firm earned net profits on the average of every third year, whereas the others never got into the black. These projects were researched, planned, financed and staffed by the development corporations.

The distinctive features of public-sector manufacturing investment during the 1960s were large scale, financing by external credits and project initiation and execution by machinery merchants. Some of the larger turnkey factories purchased by the federal and regional governments between 1961 and 1965 are listed below, with location and cost in parentheses:

Brewery (Umuahia, £1·0 million)
Brewery (Abeokuta, £1·0m)
Glass factory (Port Harcourt, £1·2m)
Glass factory (Ughelli, £1·3m)
Cement factory (Ukpilla, £4·6m)
Textile mill (Asaba, £4·2m)

Paper mill (Jebba, £2·3m)
Kenaf factory (Badagri, £1·5m)
Palm-kernel crushing (Ikeja, £1·4m)
Cocoa processing (Ikeja, £1·9m)
Palm-kernel crushing (Port Harcourt, £1·6m)
Palm-kernel/cocoa (Sapele, £2·1m)

The shift to turnkey projects was partially attributable to the psychological desire for quicker and more visible progress towards industrialization. Short-term supplier credits appeared to overcome the shortage of public investment funds, because only 10-per-cent down payment was required. No less important, these prestigious capital-intensive projects provided well-paid directorships for politicians as well as jobs for the unemployed, and they opened up a rich source of party finance by means of the kick-back. Subsequent commissions of inquiry, in both Ghana and Nigeria, have laid bare the shortcomings of this type of investment: the extensive promotion of political and personal corruption, inflated capital costs (usually on the order of 100 per cent), selection of industry and location without regard to comparative advantage and inadequate provision of management. The burden of supplier credits precipitated Ghana's balance-of-payments crisis, devaluation and debt rescheduling—a fate that Nigeria escaped only because of its burgeoning oil revenues.[53]

The foregoing list does not exhaust the difficulties encountered in turnkey projects. Although the equipment supplied by the machinery merchant is always new in the sense of not having been used before, it is usually not of the latest design. Moreover, because the machinery-merchant shops around for the best bargains, the various pieces of process equipment may not be made by the same manufacturer and thus may not be well matched in terms of capacity or rate of through-put. The effect is to make factory operations difficult, to create a serious spare-parts problem and in general to increase the burden on management.

Perhaps the most critical weakness of the turnkey project is the method by which management staff is provided. Recruited individually by means of advertisements in professional journals in developed countries, such personnel are not an adequate substitute for a corporate technical partner, such as a David Whitehead & Sons (Kaduna Textiles) or a Tunnel Portland Cement Company (Nigerian Cement Company). (For the reasons enumerated in the paragraphs above, reputable manufacturers were generally unwilling to become involved in turnkey projects.) First, there is great variation in the technical competence of the individuals so hired. Second, for a host of reasons the duration of their tenure tends to be short. Third, with no externally protected job security, these individuals do not have the power to resist the unremitting pressures to overstaff. Lastly, they lack the resources of technical knowledge and organizational strength available to a management team that is being backstopped by an entire firm in Europe or America. The management factor is as important as any other in explaining why not a single turnkey project was earning a profit when the civil war erupted in 1967.

If we set aside the special handicaps that arise from the human weakness of politicians, what general observations can be made about the problems of publicly managed industrial enterprises in Nigeria and Ghana? [54] A first set of

---

[53] The Federal Ministry of Industries in 1968 estimated that repayment costs for 'mislocated' turnkey plants were in excess of £40 million. See Katherine Langley, 'Financing development in Nigeria: an appraisal', in *South of the Sahara: development in African economies*, Sayre P. Schatz, ed. (Philadelphia, Temple University Press, 1972), p. 228.

[54] One might want to argue, as W. Arthur Lewis did in 1968, that this is an important structural factor that ought *not* be set aside: 'as for public ownership, its reputation stinks in West Africa because the politicians have used it as a field of patronage and corruption. A country is not ready for public management of property until it has solved the problem of maintaining honest and efficient government. Most of Africa is, regrettably, still far from this.' (Aggrey Memorial Lectures, Legon, 1968, cited in Grayson, 'A conglomerate in Africa.'

For details on Ghana's equally unhappy experience with state enterprise, see Grayson; and,

factors that had an effect on their performance operated either not at all or to a much lesser extent for private firms. Irrespective of their market position, public enterprises were expected to be model employers, paying high wages and generous fringe benefits in terms of housing, medical care, paid holidays and leave allowance. Pressures to add new jobs and resistance to any rationalization in the labour force were great. Customer opposition to price increases by state corporations often meant that increased costs were offset by a price increase only after long delay. Authority to take certain managerial actions—purchase of additional capital equipment, a shift in marketing policy, a new supply source for raw materials—had to be obtained from the Ministry of Commerce and Industry or the Ministry of Finance. As in the preceding case, long delays resulted in sizeable losses in net income.

Publicly managed industrial firms also face most of the problems confronting the private entrepreneur in technology, in management organization and in marketing. Technical difficulties in the production process (stemming from the deviation of local raw-material characteristics, temperature and humidity from those for which the imported technology had been designed) created product-quality problems in varying proportions for about two-thirds of the undertakings. Also related to control over product quality was a very imprecise knowledge of consumer tastes, their regional variation, competing substitute goods and the peculiarities of the various distribution channels. Although less acute for experienced manufacturers, these same problems of an unfamiliar product line were encountered by the UAC in its Kwara cigarette investment, by Mandilas & Karibaris in steel re-rolling and by the new ventures of the Kano oil-millers. In the realm of managerial organization, inadequate spare-parts inventory, irregular equipment maintenance and a lack of co-ordination between raw material stocks and customer orders were the most common causes of frequent shutdown. Defective systems of financial and cost control and poor standards of supervision permitted high levels of raw material wastage, product damage, pilferage and embezzlement. These managerial problems also constitute the principal bottleneck to the more rapid emergence of African industrial entrepreneurs, to whom we shall turn shortly.

The composition of manufacturing output and employment in Nigeria in 1965 is shown in Table 121. Urban small-scale industry employing fewer than ten would add perhaps another 80,000 to the employment figure and £12 million in value added. Looking at the top three items in the table, we see that the once-dominant export-processing activities now comprise about 10 per cent of manufacturing output. Although some three times larger, the industrial composition of Nigerian output is very similar to that of Kenya. As in the East African territories, import-substituting textiles, beer and cigarettes are the largest industries. If we regard 'metal products and machinery' and 'industrial chemicals' as indicators of technological maturity, Nigeria would rank above Uganda, just below Kenya and well below Southern Rhodesia.

To what extent were Nigerians participating in the manufacturing sector in 1965? Aliens accounted for only 2 per cent of the labour force. These were, however, the critical managerial and technical positions, as may be inferred

for the 1950s, Tony Killick, 'Manufacturing and construction', in *A study of contemporary Ghana*, vol. 1: *The economy of Ghana*, Walter Birmingham et al., eds. (London, 1966), pp. 289–93.

Table 121. *Employment and output in establishments*
of ten or more, Nigeria, 1965

Industry	Number of establishments	Number employed	Value added (£000)
Vegetable-oil milling	62	7,014	4,912
Tanning	8	724	662
Sawmilling	46	8,077	3,376
Meat and dairy products	14	1,321	759
Grain-mill products	6	536	2,142
Bakery products	70	2,407	1,182
Sugar and confectionery	9	3,803	1,120
Tobacco and miscellaneous food	9	2,563	11,783
Beer	6	2,984	11,257
Soft drinks	13	851	948
Textiles, apparel and footwear	76	15,123	9,166
Furniture and fixtures	59	4,043	1,921
Printing and paper	85	6,207	2,632
Rubber products	35	6,823	4,944
Paint, soap, etc.	35	4,269	6,572
Industrial chemicals	6	295	524
Glass, cement and clay products	31	5,089	6,163
Metal products and machinery	53	8,038	6,651
Motor-vehicle and bicycle assembly	11	1,863	1,556
Motor-vehicle repairs	121	11,514	6,772
Other	31	2,070	1,253
Total	776	95,614	86,296

SOURCE: Nigeria, Federal Office of Statistics, *Industrial Survey of Nigeria, 1964 and 1965* (Lagos, 1968).

from their share in the total wage bill—25 per cent. The foreigners' share in ownership and profits was much higher: private foreign firms accounted for 62 per cent of paid-up equity, and foreign development banks for another 4 per cent. However, when debt capital, which contributed in about equal measure to fixed assets, is brought into the equation, the Nigerian share in ownership (but not profits) rises well above one-third. The publicly owned turnkey factories are the principal element here, although development (bank) loans to foreign investment projects are also a factor. Private Nigerian ownership in paid-up capital was 11 per cent. Because of a much smaller proportion of debt financing, control over fixed assets would probably be in the neighbourhood of 8 or 9 per cent. As for industry, Nigerian firms were dominant in baking, wearing apparel, sawmilling, furniture and printing. To this should be added some twenty or thirty thousand small urban artisan firms that employ fewer than ten.

Emergent African Entrepreneurship

Complex organisms—whether they be plant, animal or social—do not spring into existence robust and fully operational. They develop from fragile beginnings, gaining strength over time. If the environment furnishes little nourishment and competing organisms are numerous, the process of development is arrested at the start. In less hostile surroundings, development goes ahead at a faster or a slower pace in accordance with the relative advantages provided by external circumstances and the generative powers internal to the organism. Such a process appears to have governed the emergence and development of African industrial enterprise.

In eastern and southern Africa, where colonial policies limited the opportunities for meaningful commercial farming (Uganda excepted) and where European and Asian competition in distribution and the artisan trade precluded African entry, the learning or growth process was not even begun. When sixty years of colonial rule came to an end, not a single African-owned and -operated manufacturing firm employing ten or more was recorded in Kenya, Uganda or Northern Rhodesia. There were about five such firms in Nyasaland and Tanganyika.[55]

By contrast, in West Africa in the early 1960s small manufacturing units employed in a given country anywhere from 5,000 to 100,000 workers. Although the bulk of these enterprises consisted of craft and service industries (tailoring, woodworking, goldsmithing, motor repair, tinsmithing), there was a significant number of firms engaged in baking, printing, rubber processing, tire retreading, soft-drink bottling, sawmilling and the manufacture of nails, singlets, mattresses, electric motors, plastic bags, soap and cosmetics. Of course, the extent of indigenous manufacturing development has varied considerably between countries, depending upon differences in opportunity and differences in sociological factors (authority structure, achievement orientation and the like). On the basis of John de Wilde's multi-country survey, Nigeria, Ghana and Senegal appear to be at the top of the scale, whereas Sierra Leone, Niger and Togo occupy the lowest rungs.

The Nigerian case

We shall confine our attention to Nigeria. We estimated in the preceding section that on the basis of the most inclusive definition of indigenous manufacturing, there were some twenty to thirty thousand urban units employing fewer than ten. On the basis of field surveys by four independent investigators whose collective work encompassed the entire federation, a considerably more reliable estimate may be made for indigenous firms engaging ten and above.[56] In 1965, such firms numbered in the neighbourhood of 900. Of these, approximately 220 employed more than twenty workers, with the largest firm—the sawmilling and rubber-processing activities of Joseph Asaboro—boasting over 1,000 employees and a net worth of £1·2 million.

Table 122 presents data gathered by Mary Rowe and John Harris on the occupational background of some 260 of Nigeria's largest manufacturing entrepreneurs, as well as that of their fathers and grandfathers. With the exception of 4 per cent, all the entrepreneurs came from the non-farm modern economy.

[55] Existing statistical data and official guesses on the extent of African manufacturing activity in the early and mid-1960s for nineteen countries are carefully reviewed, along with government assistance programmes, in de Wilde, 'Development of African private enterprise', vol. II.

[56] The dissertation research on entrepreneurship was done by Mary Rowe, John Harris and Wayne Nafziger (see bibliography), and enumerations were supervised by the writer in Eastern Nigeria. The incompatibility of the estimate of 900 firms with the census figures in Table 121 is an index to the short-fall in coverage of smaller establishments in the official statistics.

Table 122. *Occupational background of Nigerian entrepreneurs and of their fathers and grandfathers*

			Entrepreneur	
	Grandfather (N-209)	Father (N-263)	Initial (N-263)	Previous (N-261)
Subsistence farmer	44%	25%	3%	—%
Cash-crop farmer	19	19	1	—
Small trader	4	4	6	4
Larger trader	12	18	1	14
Employed artisan	—	4	28	12
Self-employed artisan, contractor, transporter	6	17	19	46
Clerical work	—	2	22	7
Teacher	—	1	12	2
Government service	1	5	7	11
Professional	2	2	2	4
Traditional chief	12	3	—	—
Total	100	100	100	100

NOTE: Percentages may not add to 100 because of rounding.

SOURCE: J. R. Harris, 'Industrial entrepreneurship in Nigeria' (Ph.D. dissertation, Northwestern University, 1967), chap. 3.

This same pattern was found for an earlier sample of 300 somewhat smaller entrepreneurs surveyed by the writer.[57] Moreover, the departure from the traditional subsistence economy is not just a matter of one generation. In the Harris-Rowe sample, for instance, nearly three-quarters of the fathers and more than two-fifths of the grandfathers gained their livelihood in the market economy. It is precisely the presence of this broad base of traders, contractors, craftsmen and the like that differentiates West African countries such as Nigeria, Ghana and Senegal from other regions of the continent where significant numbers of manufacturing entrepreneurs have yet to emerge.

Three brief case histories of entrepreneurs prominent in the early 1960s provide insight not only into occupational background but into other characteristics of Nigerian entrepreneurial endeavour as well.[58] C. T. Onyekwelu, born a farmer's son in 1898 in Nawafia, Onitsha Province, did not complete his primary education until age twenty. During the period 1918–24 he was successively a catechist for the Christian Mission Society, a railway labourer, a police cadet and a farmer. He took up trading in Onitsha in 1924, first on a small scale selling palm-kernels to the United Africa Company, next importing rice from Burma and then importing spare parts for bicycles and sewing machines from the United Kingdom. In the rice and spare-parts ventures, he enjoyed a highly profitable year before being imitated and bested by the trading houses. In 1929, he turned to gramophones and records. In this instance the expatriate firms could not compete, because, unlike Onyekwelu, they were unable to predict

[57] Kilby, *Industrialization in an open economy*, p. 339.
[58] The first two cases are based on 1964 interviews with the principals and prior observation of their activities; the information on Chief Ekotie Eboh is drawn from press releases and newspaper reporting.

which records would be popular with the public. Onyekwelu's advantage over his Nigerian competitors lay in his ability to spot new trading opportunities and to seek out overseas suppliers willing to extend credit to an African.

With the exception of a brief flirtation with a sock-knitting factory in 1934, Onyekwelu remained with records, gramophones and radios to become one of Eastern Nigeria's largest importer/distributors. In 1939, he began to organize singers and musicians to perform at local functions. Tapes of these popular Nigerian songs were then sent by CFAO to a European record-pressing company. The entrepreneur was thus able to import and distribute records of Nigerian music bearing his personal label. In 1952, he purchased his own recording machine, but neither he nor the British technician he hired could operate it. After two trips to Europe and a refusal from Decca to be his technical partner, he determined to build his own studio and record-pressing factory in Onitsha. Despite collateral of urban real estate 'worth £100,000', the Eastern Nigeria Development Corporation turned down his request in 1955 for a £50,000 loan. Four years later he did secure £35,000 from the Federal Loans Board. Construction on the factory was delayed for a year by an ownership dispute over the factory site. After factory construction moved ahead, there was further delay in the installation of equipment, and it became clear that the hired German technician did not have all the knowledge necessary to run the operation. At this point, with all funds exhausted, the Dutch firm of Philips entered the picture (no doubt at the urging of the project's creditors), providing additional capital and taking over the production management of the 125-employee factory. The entrepreneur, who retained approximately half the equity, was responsible for both the recording side and marketing.

The reference groups from which C. T. Onyekwelu, like almost all Nigerian entrepreneurs, sought recognition were the village community of his origin and the opinion leaders in the modern urban sector. Standing in the village is related to the amount of employment, scholarships and community gifts which the entrepreneur provides, as well as to the visible display of personal wealth—the Mercedes, the multi-storeyed house and the retinue. In the town, it is this last factor, as well as the number of people for whom he is providing jobs, that determines social prestige. Our next entrepreneur, Nigeria's most prominent baker, was exceptional (although not unique) in seeking recognition from an additional group, the European governmental and mercantile community. In his successful pursuit of the substance and image of an idealized European standard of personal probity and an emphasis on quality, cleanliness and order that bore little relation to the market environment, Joshua Ade Tuyo achieved status in European eyes at the cost of more modest success in the other two areas.

Born in Ijebu-Ode in 1902, Joshua Tuyo's father mixed farming with tailoring. His mother was an indigo trader. After completing primary school, Joshua Tuyo entered a mission teacher-training programme in conformity with his parents' wishes. Health problems forced Tuyo after three years to switch from teaching to a clerical career in the Railway Department. During this period (1921–4) he also took correspondence courses in shorthand and business management. In 1924, Tuyo obtained employment with the Bank of West Africa, where he stayed for a dozen years before returning to the Railway Department. With the exception of a three-year stint in the Ministry of Commerce and Industry (1948–51), Tuyo remained with the Railway Department as chief clerk until his retirement in 1953.

In 1926, while stationed in Onitsha with the bank, Joshua Tuyo had met a young Ijebu girl, Alice Idowu, in the course of trading with her mother in the Onitsha market. They married the following year, and Alice, with the aid of her husband, gradually developed into a large wholesale-trader specializing in textiles, sporting goods and cement. In 1950, after a major theft took her entire stock-in-trade, Mrs Tuyo determined to take up baking as a more profitable and less risky occupation.[59] Her husband insisted on proper training and helped finance her to a two-year course at the Borough Polytechnic Institute in the United Kingdom. When Tuyo's first post-retirement project, trading in produce and textiles, proved disappointing, he began to take note of the high returns in bread baking. With some financial assistance from a British friend, a four-man bakery was launched in 1955. Capitalizing on his wife's training and the interest of the Ministry of Commerce and Industry in promoting baking as an indigenous industry, he applied to the Federal Loans Board for a £15,000 loan. This was issued to De Facto Works, Ltd in 1956, and a second loan of £6,000 was made in 1959.

By the mid-1960s the De Facto bakery was one of the country's largest, with more than 200 employees engaged in the production and distribution of bread. The manufacturing process was by far the most modern and capital-intensive of Nigeria's several hundred mechanized bakeries. In addition to operating with water-tempering and measuring devices, flour sifters, oil-fired reel and draw-plate ovens (in contrast to wood-fired peel ovens) and embossed english bread pans, the bakery made bread that included such atypical ingredients as full-cream dried milk and malt extract. The principal market for De Facto's high-quality, high-cost bread was the hotels and the food stores servicing the large Lagos European community. Even allowing for a higher sales price, heavy overhead costs in the form of a large administrative staff (nearly a quarter of all employees), and the services of an English accounting firm gave De Facto a considerably lower profit margin on sales than that of its competitors who catered to the mass market. Nevertheless, its earnings and its ability to borrow were sufficient to finance a De Facto restaurant and five retail bake-shops, as well as to take a small interest in a Swedish-sponsored reconstituted-milk factory.

From an Ibo trader and a Yoruba civil servant to a mid-west politician, Chief Festus Sam Ekotie Eboh was not only Nigeria's most colorful minister; he was also one of its wealthiest businessmen. He was born in 1912, son of a minor Itsekiri chief. After completing Standard Six, his first position was that of assessment clerk for the Sapele township, followed by four years as a teacher in a Baptist primary school. In 1935, he joined the Warri branch of the Bata Shoe Company. He advanced in this company to become deputy manager of the regional office in Sapele by 1943. In this same year he launched the first of a

---

[59] Mrs Tuyo's brother, E. A. Idowu, also a retired civil servant, had established a very successful bakery in Ibadan two years earlier. Profits in the rapidly expanding bread industry were extremely high prior to 1954, when a major invention by Idowu lowered capital entry requirements and greatly increased competition. See chs. 2, 7 and 8 in Peter Kilby, *African enterprise: the Nigerian bread industry* (Stanford, Hoover Institution, 1965).

string of five schools. In 1947, Bata sent their able young manager to Czechoslovakia for further training. The following year he returned with diplomas in business administration and chiropody. Soon afterwards, Ekotie Eboh struck out on his own in the timber and rubber trade. In 1951, he was elected to the Western Region House of Representatives and in 1954 to the Federal Parliament in Lagos. He was made Minister of Labour in 1955 and then Minister of Finance in 1957, a position he still held at the time of his assassination in January 1966.

Chief Ekotie Eboh's first wholly owned industrial venture was a rubber-crêping factory opened in 1958. This, like the Omimi rubber and canvas shoe factory (opened in 1963), was run by a succession of hired expatriate managers. Despite the Ministry of Finance's much publicized excise tax of 1964, which discriminated against competing leather and plastic footwear, Omimi never achieved profitability. In other ventures, the Mid-West Cement Company and Unameji Cabinet Works, management was provided by the co-investors, Cutinho Caro and Dissengoff, respectively. These co-investors were two of the machinery-merchant firms whose activities, which were subject to the veto of the Minister of Finance, were described in the preceding section. Mrs Ekotie Eboh, the former manageress of her husband's schools, was also active in the business world, holding directorships in a number of overseas companies doing business in Nigeria.

As the three vignettes well illustrate, Nigeria's entrepreneurs have been aggressive in seeking out market opportunities; nor have they hesitated to risk their savings in manufacturing investments. They have shown energy and resourcefulness in launching pioneering ventures. They have performed less well, however, in applying themselves to solving the technological problems of their enterprises once established and in exerting efficient management control. Although all students of the subject agree on this assessment, they offer divergent opinions as to the cause of technological-managerial problems. In his exhaustive essay 'Development in an adverse economic environment,' Sayre Schatz has stressed the severely limited access of small-scale entrepreneurs in West Africa to technological knowledge in all its forms: information on the scores of alternative machines and production processes available from sources in Japan, America and Europe; the technical competence of the entrepreneur's most skilled workers; the external problem-solving capabilities that can be brought to bear from supplier firms, industrial consulting services, research institutes and so on.[60] Others have placed their emphasis on the more general education factor, as it relates both to the organizational and problem-solving capabilities of the entrepreneur and to the technical knowledge possessed by his labour force.

Although these factors clearly condition the environment in fundamental ways, there is considerable evidence that they are not the binding constraints. The investigations of Harris, Rowe, Nafziger and the writer all revealed the absence of a significant statistical association between the entrepreneur's educational background and the success (profitability and rate of growth) of his firm. On the other hand, schooling and travel are correlated; and it is travel that has led to most of the entrepreneur 'innovations'—namely, the introduction of new

---

[60] Ch. 3 in Schatz, ed., *South of the Sahara.*

products and equipment first observed abroad. Yet the 'innovators' have shown no more inclination than their less educated counterparts to supervise productive operations closely, to make systematic use of written records, to delegate authority and to study technical problems relating to their plant layout, product quality and the like.

That such management factors are responsible for the modest levels of efficiency and technological progressiveness among Nigerian industrial firms, rather than environmental impediments beyond the entrepreneur's control, is suggested not only by simple observation but also by the performance of comparable non-Nigerian firms. In her study of Lagos, Mary Rowe compared the capital/labour and capital/output ratios and returns to capital of Nigerian firms to equally novice Lebanese and Greek undertakings of the same size, in the same industry and utilizing the same equipment.[61] As a result of far higher levels of machine utilization (for example, 60 per cent versus 20 per cent) the Lebanese and Greek entrepreneurs had lower capital/labour and capital/output ratios, and returns to capital were two to three times those of the Nigerian firms. Even more marked contrasts in efficiency between Greek and Nigerian firms were recorded in a 1960 inter-firm productivity comparison in the rubber-crêping industry.[62]

The present writer is among those who are persuaded that socio-psychological factors, deriving from certain cultural and historical antecedents, play an important part in explaining current management performance in Africa. Several interrelated circumstances, it is postulated, have had a significant formative effect. In traditional agriculture and traditional crafts the production process is a series of sequential steps carried out by the same individual. Production of a commodity involving a large number of people simultaneously engaged in different tasks is very rare. The absence of intra-commodity specialization, with its concomitant requirements of co-ordination, supervision and control, means that there is no management tradition upon which to build. In terms of contemporary social recognition, establishing a factory and providing employment bring a high degree of status respect; but there is no parallel respect for efficient role-performance as a manager. Mary Rowe, who questioned her sample extensively on self-image, reports a marked lack of confidence in their abilities to cope with technological problems. She is inclined to attribute this to colonialism, both in its acts of disparagement and in the set of occupational models it provided. Power, status and high income among the British élite appeared to be the monopoly of political leaders, civil servants, doctors and lawyers, whereas the wealth and prestige of British industrial capitalists were hidden from view. Thus both long-standing traditions and recent history conspire to make the managerial learning process an arduous one.

Whatever the merits of such speculations, there can be little doubt that the future of any meaningful industrialization in Africa is very much bound up with the development of appropriate managerial and technological orientations.

[61] M. P. Rowe, 'The supply of Nigerian industrial enterpreneurs in the post-independence period', Ph.D. dissertation, Columbia University, 1970, ch. 4.
[62] Kilby, *Industrialization in an open economy,* pp. 228 ff.

Conclusions

What generalizations can we draw from the historical material that has been presented? Statements about causal factors or the balance of cost and benefit are laden with danger. Hence we will begin with the far easier descriptive generalizations. At the turn of the century there was virtually no industry in any of the colonial territories. In all countries the pattern of growth in manufacturing output has been similar, with processing of primary exports holding initial dominance but later being outpaced by production for the home market. The latter consisted for the most part of food processing, light consumer goods and construction materials. Only in the case of Southern Rhodesia was there a movement into the technologically more demanding intermediate goods such as industrial chemicals and iron and steel. The drastic curtailment of imports during the Second World War acted as a stimulant for local industry only where a sizable industrial base already existed, most notably Southern Rhodesia and Senegal. The last decade of the colonial period saw first a tremendous surge in export earnings and later large inflows of foreign aid. Both led to an accelerated growth in manufacturing output.

Manufacturing developed far earlier and to a much greater extent in territories with substantial non-African populations. At the same time, the presence of European and Asian groups drastically curtailed the opportunities for Africans in multiracial territories to learn critical entrepreneurial and technical skills. There was therefore much greater private African participation (in absolute as well as in relative terms) in the industrial sector of many Black African countries by the end of the colonial period. In white-settler and Black Africa alike, ownership and control of manufacturing enterprise, its initiation and operation, were left predominantly in private hands. Finally, foreign corporate entrepreneurship and foreign capital played a very large role in colonial industrial development, irrespective of the presence or absence of substantial numbers of Europeans or Asians.

The most important actions of the colonial rulers for all aspects of economic advance were those that set the terms on which Africans were allowed to participate in commercial agriculture. Where a pattern of inequality of access was established in agriculture, it was naturally applied in subsequent spheres—the distributive trades, promotion to skilled jobs, access to technical and managerial education and so on. Here the trustees in multiracial territories must stand condemned of grievous wrong. As Professor Bauer discusses elsewhere in this volume, marketing boards, particularly in West Africa, also had the effect of retarding the expansion of a commercial economy. But these ills were largely the unintended effects of expediency and incompetence. If there is reason to suppose (and there is) that post-independence African policy-makers would have embraced marketing boards, state enterprise and other crude forms of interventionism even in the absence of colonial tutoring in such practices, then on both practical and moral grounds we may judge these deviations from a régime based on free individual initiative to have been venial rather than mortal sin.

Turning to the narrower issue of active efforts to promote industrial development, it is difficult to construct a standard against which to assess the record. Judging by the performance of former Japanese dependencies, Korea and Taiwan, the African colonies were poorly served. On the other hand, a comparison with Ethiopia and Liberia, where initial conditions were more nearly identical, suggests that the colonial contribution was a positive one. Certainly during the 1920s more could have been done to promote industry, but at that time it would have had to have been based on European labour for all but the least skilled jobs, thereby exacerbating the problem of entrenched racial monopoly. Between 1930 and 1947, economic conditions precluded any significant development initiatives. When resources were available during the last decade and a half of the colonial period, wide-ranging efforts were made both to attract foreign investment (fiscal incentives, debenture capital, industrial estates) and, particularly in West Africa, to develop African entrepreneurial and industrial skills (lending schemes, government procurement, technical-training institutes).

Other policies, not specifically related to the promotion of manufacturing, had in fact a greater bearing on the pattern of industrial development. Colonial monetary systems, combined with traditions of a balanced budget, prevented the kind of inflation that in post-colonial Africa has lifted domestic prices far above world prices. Inflated domestic prices, coupled with privileged access to undervalued foreign exchange, enhance the profitability of investment in import-substitute industries. They do so, however, at the cost of undermining the discipline of comparative advantage. Although the rate of industrial growth was slower during the colonial period, its proportionate contribution to real national income was greater. Whereas colonial monetary policies and sparing use of the protective tariff fostered a comparatively high degree of competitiveness with the world economy, restrictive immigration policies (especially in Black Africa) limited the number of competitors within the domestic market. The resultant monopolistic structure of the merchandise trade, reinforced by officially supported cartels such as the Association of West African Merchants, undercut a major agent of industrialization. Without the threatened loss of market share to competitors, the 'push' to undertake the risk and expense of a manufacturing investment was absent.

What is the heritage of the colonial manufacturing experience for policy-makers in the new states? The attitudes and actions of African politicians and economic planners are remarkably similar to those of their counterparts in other late-developing Asian and Latin American countries. Rapid industrialization is fervently desired. There is impatience with the gradual, accretionary pace of learning and capital accumulation being achieved by indigenous businessmen. Foreign investment is sought but distrusted. Nationalization is a frequent recourse. Legislated prices, direct controls and state enterprise are viewed not only as morally preferable but in many, if not most, cases, as being more efficacious than the invisible hand of the market and the profit motive. Perhaps colonialism has had something to do with all of this, but then again there may be no colonial heritage at all.

BIBLIOGRAPHY

Arrighi, Giovanni. *The political economy of Rhodesia.* The Hague, 1967.

Bauer, P. T. *West African trade.* New ed. London, 1963.

Birmingham, Walter, I. Neustadt, and E. N. Omaboe, eds. *A study of contemporary Ghana,* vol. I: *The economy of Ghana.* London, 1966.

British South Africa Company. *Annual reports,* 1903–22.

Chenery, H. B., and Lance Taylor. 'Development patterns: among nations and over time', *Review of Economics and Statistics,* Nov. 1968, **50**, no. 4.

Cole, R. L.. 'The tariff policy of Rhodesia, 1899–1963', *Rhodesian Journal of Economics*, June 1958,**5.**

De Wilde, John. 'The development of African private enterprise', vol. II. Mimeographed. Washington, D.C., International Bank for Reconstruction and Development, 1971.

Grayson, Leslie E. 'A conglomerate in Africa: public sector manufacturing enterprises in Ghana, 1962–1971'. Mimeographed. African Studies Association, 1971.

'The role of suppliers' credits in the industrialization of Ghana, Nigeria, and Sierra Leone'. Mimeographed. African Studies Association, 1970.

Harris, J. R. 'Industrial entrepreneurship in Nigeria'. Ph. D. dissertation, Northwestern University, 1967.

Illustrated Life Rhodesia, 1968–70. Salisbury.

Ismaïl, Toufik. *L'industrie dans l'économie de l'Afrique centrale: Sénégal, Côte d'Ivoire, Cameroun, Congo (Kinshasa)*. Louvain, Faculté des Sciences Economiques, Sociales et Politiques de l'Université Catholique de Louvain, 1970.

Kilby, Peter. *African enterprise: the Nigerian bread industry*. Stanford, Hoover Institution, 1965.

Industrialization in an open economy: Nigeria 1945–1966. Cambridge University Press, 1969.

Kuznets, Simon. *Economic growth of nations*. Cambridge, Mass., Harvard University Press, 1971.

Marris, Peter, and Anthony Somerset. *The African entrepreneur*. New York, 1972.

Murray, D. J. *The governmental system in Southern Rhodesia*. Oxford, Clarendon Press, 1970.

Nafziger, E. W. 'Nigerian entrepreneurship: a study of indigenous businessmen in the footwear industry'. Ph. D. dissertation, University of Illinois, 1967.

National Christian Council. *Who controls industry in Kenya*. Nairobi, 1968.

Nicolson, I. F. *Administration in Nigeria, 1900–1960*. Oxford, Clarendon Press, 1969.

Okigbo, P. N. C. *Nigerian national accounts, 1950–57*. Enugu, Government Printer, 1962.

Pearson, D. S. 'Industrial development in Rhodesia', *Rhodesian Journal of Economics,* March 1968, **5.**

Pfeffermann, Guy. *Industrial labour in the Republic of Senegal*. New York, 1968.

'Report of the Committee of Enquiry into the Protection of Secondary Industries in Southern Rhodesia, 1946'. Typescript. Salisbury.

Robson, Peter, and D. A. Lury. *The economies of Africa*. Evanston, Northwestern University Press, 1969.

Rowe, M. P. 'The supply of Nigerian industrial entrepreneurs in the post-independence period'. Ph.D. dissertation, Columbia University, 1970.

Saylor, R. G. *The economic system of Sierra Leone*. Durham, N. C., Duke University Press, 1967.

Schatz, S. P., ed. *South of the Sahara: development in African economies*. Philadelphia, Temple University Press, 1972.

Statistical and Economic Review. London, United Africa Company, 1948–63.

Stoutjesdijk, E. J. *Uganda's manufacturing sector*. Nairobi, 1967.

Suret-Canale, Jean. *French colonialism in tropical Africa, 1900–1945*. London, 1971.

Sutcliffe, R. B. 'Stagnation and inequality in Rhodesia, 1946–1968', *Bulletin of the Oxford University Institute of Economics and Statistics,* Feb. 1971,**33.**

Thompson, Virginia, and Richard Adloff. *French West Africa*. Stanford University Press,1958.

Tow, Leonard. *The manufacturing economy of Southern Rhodesia*. Washington, D.C., National Academy of Sciences, 1960.

Zajadacz, Paul, ed. *Studies in production and trade in East Africa*. Munich, 1970.

PART FOUR

SOCIAL IMPLICATIONS

CHAPTER 13

HISTORICAL ASPECTS OF MANPOWER
AND MIGRATION IN AFRICA
SOUTH OF THE SAHARA

by

COLIN W. NEWBURY

One of the common assumptions used to justify European occupation of much of Africa in the nineteenth century was that economic development would follow the substitution of the slave-trade by trade in tropical produce. 'Our primary object is to establish free-labour cultivation', explained two of the early apostles of African regeneration, 'thus providing wholesome and profitable occupation.' [1] An echo of this optimism of the 1841 Niger expedition may be found in such widely differing enterprises as plans for French expansion up the Senegal in the 1850s, in Sir George Goldie's 'abolition' of slavery after his campaign against Nupe and Ilorin, in Sir Harry Johnston's wars in Nyasaland and Northern Rhodesia or, finally, in Catholic and Protestant missionary experiments with 'industrial education' in Uganda and East Africa at the end of the century. [2] If Africa was to be delivered 'by calling forth her own resources', in Buxton's memorable phrase, the liberated African was at hand to perform the task.

Thus, having taken over enormous areas and populations, alien planters, administrators, miners and businessmen faced the problem of utilizing Africa's major resource. Nowhere was the transition from rural employment to rural or urban wage contracts made easily, or without considerable displacement of African peoples. Administrators' reports—German, French or British—at the turn of the century stress the shortage, not the abundance, of workers willing to assist European investment in building, farming and public works. Even in the older and more developed areas of European agriculture and mining in South Africa the 'labour situation in 1902 was critical as the demand for labour for public works, railways, the reconstruction of the farms and mining far exceeded the supply'. [3]

---

[1] Dr S. Lushington and Sir T. F. Buxton to Lord John Russell, 7 Aug. 1840, in Great Britain, *Parliamentary papers*, 1843, vol. XLVIII (472), cited in C. W. Newbury, *British policy towards West Africa: select documents 1786–1874* (Oxford, Clarendon Press, 1965), p. 108.

[2] Instruction to Faidherbe, 13 Nov. 1855, cited in Christian Schéfer, *Instructions générales données de 1763 à 1870 aux gouverneurs et ordonnateurs des établissements français en Afrique occidentale* (Paris, 1927), vol. II, p. 293; and for expansion into Cayor to protect indigenous agriculture, *ibid.*, vol. II, pp. 316–26; S. Vandeleur, *Campaigning on the Upper Nile and Niger* (London, 1898); Roland Oliver, *The missionary factor in East Africa* (London, 1952), pp. 213–14; C. P. Groves, 'Missionary and humanitarian aspects of imperialism from 1870 to 1914', in *Colonialism in Africa 1870–1960, vol. I: The history and politics of colonialism 1870–1914*, L. H. Gann and Peter Duignan, eds. (Cambridge University Press, 1969), pp. 485–6.

[3] D. Hobart Houghton, 'Economic development, 1865–1965', in *The Oxford history of South Africa*, vol. II: *South Africa 1870–1966*, Monica Wilson and Leonard Thompson, eds. (Oxford, Clarendon Press, 1971), p. 15.

To meet this demand, South African experience during the first century of that country's economic history implied that some rural areas would be destined to serve as labour reservoirs. For already by the 1890s, the gold-fields employed just over 100,000 African labourers, most of whom came from Moçambique and the High Commission Territories. But was it sufficient to leave labour supplies to professional recruiters? Few other colonies could match the mining companies' ability to consolidate their interests by handing over their labour problems to a single agency—the Witwatersrand Native Labour Association, or the Native Recruiting Corporation established later in 1912. Clearly, in the less endowed regions of imperial expansion and settlement in West, Central and East Africa, other methods would have to be used.

The paradox of much of the earlier growth of exportable staples—palm produce, rubber, ground-nuts, timber and cotton—in the mercantile economies of these regions was that Buxtonian 'free-labour cultivation' was not enough. Nor were local labour markets sufficient to assure an infrastructure of railways, roads and administrative centres, without recourse to non-Buxtonian measures, direct and indirect, to bring forth a supply of men. In some parts of Africa— notably the British 'protected' areas, and German and French West Africa— domestic slavery existed to assist the transformation of agriculture from subsistence to cash-crops.[4] Elsewhere, military and civil administrations in the 1890s used the labour of 'liberated slave' colonies, or recruited through indigenous rulers or shifted contract labour from one colony to another.[5] Indeed, it has been argued that 'the rise of legitimate commerce, far from bringing about the abolition of internal slavery, increased the demand for cheap labour in Africa itself, and slave raiding continued in order to meet growing domestic needs'.[6]

This viewpoint has not passed without criticism (historically, it would apply best to Western Africa prior to the 1890s). But it is probably a more realistic starting-point for a general study of the formation of an African wage-labour force than the rural-urban migration emphasis in works that concentrate on late colonial economic and sociological aspects of African manpower.[7]

[4] There is no study of the aftermath of the abolition of the external slave-trade in West Africa, as there is for the West Indies. But see W. E. F. Ward, *A history of the Gold Coast* (London, 1952), pp. 347–8; Sierra Leone, *Despatches relating to domestic slavery in Sierra Leone,* Sierra Leone Legislative Council, Sessional paper no. 5 (Freetown, 1926); Karin Hausen, *Deutsche Kolonialherrschaft in Afrika: Wirtschaftsinteressen und Kolonialverwaltung in Kamerun vor 1914* (Zurich, 1970), pp. 148–54 and 274–90.
   It is interesting that Lugard, who played an important part in the drafting of the slave-trade abolition convention of 1926, had been careful, when in Nigeria, not to tamper with domestic slavery: 'The Abolition of Slavery has never been decreed by the Govt. The status of domestic slavery exists and there is no obstacle to traders transporting goods by their domestic slaves— provided the slaves themselves are not sold.' Lugard to Scarbrough, 14 March 1903, Royal Niger Company papers, vol. x, f. 481, Oxford, Rhodes House Library.
[5] See especially Denise Bouche, *Les villages de liberté en Afrique noire française* (Paris, 1968), chs. 5 and 9; C. W. Newbury, *The western Slave Coast and its rulers* (Oxford, Clarendon Press, 1961), pp. 144, 155, 169, 174, 181, 189; Thea Büttner, 'On the social-economic structure of Adamawa in the 19th century: slavery or serfdom?'in *African Studies,* Walter Markov, ed. (Leipzig, Karl-Marx-Universität, 1967), pp. 43–61.
[6] A. G. Hopkins, 'Economic imperialism in West Africa: Lagos 1880–1892', *Economic History Review,* 1968, **21**, no. 3, 587.
[7] For sources, see Hans E. Panofsky, 'A bibliography of labour migration in Africa south of the Sahara', in Inter-African Labour Institute, *Migrant labour in Africa south of the Sahara* (Abidjan, Commission for Technical Co-operation in Africa South of the Sahara, 1962), sec. 4; G. E.

Similarly, in East African history there is a tendency to assume a quick transition from systems of forced to free employment, because such systems are held to have been mutually incompatible:

A system of slave labour could not exist side by side with a system of wage labour. The European mining managers and railway engineers needed African labour. However, they did not want to 'own' Africans and keep them till their dying days. They did not want women. They wanted African adult labourers for limited periods, working for wages and bound to them by contract. They did not want to mobilize their labour through forcible abduction. They were willing and able to recruit labour and return it to the villages. They were prepared to pay wages. Wages combined with the indirect inducement of taxation, the lure of new trade goods and the facilities of efficient recruiting organizations, would produce the required hands.[8]

This may well have been an accurate summary of expectations in the Rhodesias, Kenya or Uganda; but how far were they historically justified? Were wage levels (even with taxes as an additional spur) everywhere sufficient to account for the rise of migratory wage-labour forces in these territories and the later mandated areas of Tanganyika and Nyasaland?

Other evidence suggests that the transition was made with difficulty. On the Kenya-Uganda railway in 1899 Africans made up less than 20 per cent of the mainly Indian labour force: the idea of organized labour was reported to be 'utterly foreign to most of the tribesmen'.[9] The origins of labour recruitment in Northern Rhodesia were marked by hut-burnings to secure administration carriers and to enforce payment of the head tax introduced after 1900.[10] In Southern Rhodesia, chiefs could be compelled by the 1897 Native Regulations to furnish labourers; and although these were cancelled almost immediately, district commissioners still doubled as recruiters. In 1903 the Southern Rhodesian Native Labour Bureau assisted them in this task. In Kenya (East African Protectorate), administrative 'pressure' was used freely by the same date to furnish posts with cultivated crops; but low wages (5s 4d per month), reported the assistant secretary, attracted little labour where it was urgently required for 'porters . . . office and domestic servants, labour for the Zanzibar and Pemba clove plantations, soldiers, policemen and other kinds of permanent labour'.[11] Caught between Colonial Office instructions to avoid compulsion and the imperatives of increasing settler demands, Kenya officials and chiefs resorted to exhortation and intimidation. Once again, taxation was seen as 'the only possible method of compelling the native to leave his reserve for the purpose of seeking work'.[12]

and C. W. Newbury, 'Annotated bibliography of Commonwealth migrations: the tropical territories: 1 Africa' (Oxford, Institute of Commonwealth Studies, 1969).

[8] Lewis H. Gann, 'The end of the slave trade in British Central Africa: 1889–1912', *Rhodes-Livingstone Institute Journal*, 1954, no. 16, p. 41.

[9] Sir Guildford Molesworth, cited in M. F. Hill, *Permanent way: the story of the Kenya and Uganda Railway* (Nairobi, East African Railways and Harbours, n.d.), p. 182. By 1900, 23,379 labourers had been imported from India.

[10] Lewis H. Gann, *A history of Northern Rhodesia: early days to 1953* (London, 1964), pp. 102–11; A. J. Wills, *An introduction to the history of Central Africa* (London, 1967), p. 213.

[11] W. J. Monson, 'Report on slavery and free labour in the British East African Protectorate', in Great Britain, *Parliamentary papers*, Cd 1631 (London, 1903), p. 5.

[12] Sir Percy Girouard, in *East African Standard*, 8 Feb. 1913, cited in Raymond L. Buell, *The native problem in Africa*, 2nd reprint (London, 1965), vol. I, p. 331.

But taxation was not always a sufficient stimulus either. In Uganda, where a hut tax helped to produce a voluntary labour supply after 1900, competition from cotton-growing among the Baganda by 1908 had reduced labour available for porterage and road-building. A remedy was sought in compulsory paid labour (*kasanvu*) by every able-bodied male for one month a year; and so till 1922, when this system was abolished, 'the labour market in Uganda was no longer open to the free play of demand and supply'.[13] Between the sale of men and the sale of staples there was a structural change in the use of African manpower in many areas of monetized economic growth; but the element of compulsion implicit in both bondage and forced recruitment did not immediately disappear.

Compulsory labour was not unique to these territories at the early stages of their occupation and development.[14] It is evident to anyone looking at the history of the Congo, the Portuguese territories or twentieth-century Liberia that 'economic incentives' do not by themselves explain a 'swift and massive incorporation of Africans in industrial employment in urban areas' over the last half-century or more.[15] The pace, except in recent decades, has been uneven and slow. The African did not always come forward willingly as a wage-labourer; and where he did, his links with his rural base remained intact till relatively late in the history of African urbanization. Part of the historical explanation for his incorporation in a monetized and wage-labour economy must include an account of the ways in which administrations, by one means or another, have sought to 'prime the pump' and induce labour to leave the land.

Such a history is not yet written.[16] Much of the evidence on which to base a study of forced labour was made public only during instances of notorious colonial 'scandals' at the turn of the century. Other materials were collected and examined by the Committee of Experts on Native Labour for the International

[13] P. G. Powesland, *Economic policy and labour,* East African studies, no. 10 (Kampala, East African Institute of Social Research, 1957), p. 18. This policy was confirmed by the Uganda Development Commission in 1920.

[14] In general, see Buell, *Native problem in Africa,* vol. I; W. Kloosterboer, *Involuntary labour since the abolition of slavery: a survey of compulsory labour throughout the world* (Leiden, 1960); International Labour Organization (ILO), International Labour Conference, 12th Session, *Forced labour report and draft questionnaire* (Geneva, 1929); Lord Hailey, *An African survey: a study of problems arising in Africa south of the Sahara* (London, Oxford University Press, 1938), chs. 11 and 25; Sheila T. van der Horst, *Native labour in South Africa* (London, Oxford University Press, 1942).

[15] *Social implications of industrialization and urbanization in Africa south of the Sahara* (London, International African Institute and UNESCO, 1956), p. 34.

[16] Much of the following is based on International Labour Organization records, especially Committee of Experts on Native Labour (CENL), *Minutes* (Geneva, 1927), and CENL, *Report* (Geneva, 1927); CENL, 'Minutes', 1928–30, mimeographed; League of Nations, Temporary Slavery Commission, 'Memorandum by Mr. H. A. Grimshaw (representative of the International Labour Organisation) on the question of slavery', CTE 31, mimeographed (Geneva, 15 April 1925); League of Nations, Temporary Slavery Commission, *Report,* A. 19 (Geneva, 25 July 1925), p. vi; Edward Alsworth Ross, *Report on employment of native labor in Portuguese Africa* (New York, 1925); 'Rapport de la Commission pour l'étude du problème de la main-d'oeuvre au Congo belge', *Congo: Revue Générale de la Colonie Belge,* May 1925, **1,** no. 5, pp. 693–714, and June 1925, **2,** no. 1, pp. 1–12; ILO, International Labour Conference, 19th Session, *The recruiting of labour in colonies and in other territories with analogous labour conditions* (Geneva, 1935); ILO, *Report of the Ad Hoc Committee on Forced Labour* (Geneva, 1953); League of Nations, International Commission of Enquiry in Liberia, *Communication by the government of Liberia . . . December 15, 1930,* C. 658, M. 272 (Geneva, 1930).

Labour Organization (ILO) in the 1920s. Much remains in the records of colonial administrations. It would be generally agreed, however, that the period of direct constraints on African labour lasted well into the 1930s in Belgian, French and Portuguese territories, though there would be less agreement about the economic contribution of compulsory work. It would also become clear that in South Africa there was less need to employ direct methods of compulsion as the economy reached a more advanced level. The problem of finding labour was replaced by the problem of stabilization in the face of European unwillingness to tolerate undifferentiated wage levels or permanent urban settlement by Africans.

Direct and indirect methods of recruitment

In all the territories covered by the ILO investigation of the 1920s and by other investigators such as Hailey and Buell, one or more of the following techniques has been used by colonial administrations to build up a migratory or semi-permanent labour force:

(*A*) Unregulated recruitment for planters and concessionary companies
(*B*) Regulated recruitment for porterage and other public services (including road and railway construction), on demand, or as a labour tax
(*C*) Forced cultivation of exportable crops and food requisitioning
(*D*) Recruitment to military forces and labour brigades
(*E*) Regulated recruitment by private agents with official assistance
(*F*) Taxation
(*G*) Land transfers and resettlement on reserves
(*H*) Official labour bureaux, *bourses du travail* and provision of transport, transit camps, medical inspection
(*I*) Labour contracts with penal sanctions
(*J*) Mobility controls, passes, residence permits

Of these techniques, the first five may be considered as direct methods and were the special target of humanitarian and international reformers in the 1920s. Examples from the first category were well identified in the earlier economic history of French Equatorial Africa, Angola, Moçambique, Liberia, the Belgian Congo and Kenya.[17] The practice of using officials to recruit for private interests sometimes survived metropolitan condemnation; it was specifically rejected in the Forced Labour Convention of 1930 and disappeared in British territories. Only in Portuguese possessions did a 'moral and legal obligation' to work remain with the force of law and serve as a basis for official encouragement of recruitment.[18]

Official action under the second category of recruitment provided the original labour forces for most of the railway network of French West Africa, the Leopoldville-Matadi line and the Baro-Kano and Uasin-Gishu lines in Nigeria

---

[17] ILO, CENL, 'Minutes', 1928–30; Catherine Coquery-Vidrovitch, 'French colonization in Africa to 1920: administration and economic development', in *Colonialism in Africa,* vol. 1, pp. 179 and 184–91; William A. Cadbury, *Labour in Portuguese West Africa* (London, 1910); W. McGregor Ross, *Kenya from within: a short political history* (London, 1927).
[18] Details of the application of Convention 29 are to be found in ILO, International Labour Conference, 25th Session, *Summary of annual reports under article 22 of the constitution of the I.L.O.* (Geneva, 1939); ILO, *Summary of reports on ratified conventions* (Geneva, 1950).

and Kenya. Often, such early labour formed the nucleus of a regular wage-labour force, as noted by a British official who inspected the Senegal-Niger railway in 1904:

As the natives of the country were not prepared to work of their own accord, recourse had to be had to what really amounts to forced labour. The number of workmen required are recruited by the civil administration, each district having to supply a given number of men. They are enlisted for one year, during which time they are fed and paid. The rate of pay is from 60 centimes to 1 franc a day, and the ration ½ kilo of rice, or 1 kilo millet, 30 grammes mutton, 15 grammes salt. After the expiration of their year the men are at liberty to return to their districts, and many do so, but on the other hand many having got used to the work remain voluntarily. For instance in October 1903, of 5,000 workmen employed 3,000 are old hands who have remained voluntarily after finishing their year. After the capture of Samory, 500 of his Sofas (or soldiers) who had been taken prisoners were sent to work on the railway. The Administration found them as a rule more intelligent than the Bambaras, and most of them have become useful artisans, masons etc. These men, although long since released as prisoners, have all remained on the railway of their own accord.[19]

Possibly this was a recurring pattern in the early transition from obligatory to voluntary paid labour—a colonial apprenticeship that is one of the starting-points for the development of migratory flows. Nor is there a shortage of evidence for the use of forced labour in the construction of colonial road systems; and regulations to secure labour for periodic repairs are among the longest survivals of official labour recruitment.

Another important example of forced recruitment which has been little examined was the military contingents raised for the First World War, particularly in French and Equatorial Africa, where forces numbering some 162,000 men were formed in 1916 and 1918.[20] The impact of their demobilization, along with several thousands of voluntary and conscripted British and German labour brigades, on local labour markets has never been studied.

Category (E) above covers the major recruiting companies located in South Africa and dates from the formation of a Native Labour Department in 1893 by the Chamber of Mines. After difficult beginnings, when very low wage rates and a high mortality rate among recruited workers resulted in a critical shortage, the Chamber turned to Chinese coolies and (less controversially) to Africans in the three British protectorates. Since 1910, the proportion of 'foreign' African labourers in the gold-mining industry has never been less than 60 per cent to 70 per cent; and absolute numbers of these workers have risen from just under 100,000 in 1910 to nearly 320,000 annually by 1972.[21] Wage attraction

---

[19] C. F. Cromie, 'Report on the Senegal-Niger Railway', in Great Britain, Colonial Office, *Construction of railways in West Africa,* Confidential Print no. 765 (London, 1905). See, too, Great Britain, *Report by the Hon. W. G. H. Ormsby-Gore on his visit to West Africa during the year 1926,* Cmd 2744 (London, 1926). One may compare road works to the Jos plateau mines in 1910, where half the labour had been previously employed by the Niger Company as a carrier force during railway construction in Northern Nigeria. The other half was 'political' labour, paid 6d per day (voluntary labour was paid 9d), recruited by force within Zaria Province. All labour lived off villages along the route. (Royal Niger Company papers, vol. XIV, f. 97 and f. 239.)

[20] See Marc Michel, 'La genèse du recrutement de 1918 en Afrique noire française', *Revue Française d'Histoire d'Outre-Mer,* 1971, **58,** no. 213, pp. 433–50.

[21] Francis Wilson, *Labour in the South African gold mines 1911–1969* (Cambridge University Press, 1972), appendix 3; and the same author's *Migrant labour* (Johannesburg, 1972), ch. 6; *Gold,* supplement to *Financial Mail,* 17 Nov. 1972, p. 73.

undoubtedly accounts for the continuation of this regulated migration (and for the larger regulated and clandestine foreign migration into railway, construction and agricultural employment). But it should be kept in mind that labour movements from Lesotho, Moçambique, Malawi, Botswana and Swaziland are also a function of local taxation, experience of a harsher wage-labour system under the chartered concessionary companies which controlled two-thirds of Moçambique by 1900, compulsory cultivation schemes also in Moçambique and a general deterioration of land under pressure of population settlement, especially in Lesotho.[22]

The five indirect factors in recruitment have usually operated in various degrees in combination. Taxes and pressure on land have probably been the most consequential in encouraging wage-labour displacement in areas of European settlement. Native reserves were set aside as early as 1894 in Southern Rhodesia and 1904 in Kenya, leading to a spatial restriction of some tribes on inferior soils. Nearly half of available land was alienated to non-Africans in Southern Rhodesia and some 89 per cent in South Africa. Increased population and the arbitrary creation of native trust lands, native purchase areas, game and forest reserves and various other categories in Kenya, South Africa and the Rhodesias have had far-reaching and dislocatory consequences for many of the tribes concerned. Official policies by the 1930s were aimed at lessening the impact of such changes by inspection and control of mobility. But, once set in motion by factors dating from the nineteenth century, the migratory labour patterns that emerged and that were only briefly checked by the Great Depression were sufficiently well established to be accepted as an integral part of development in the areas of white settlement, as they were in areas of African cash-crop farming in West Africa.

International standards

As a result of the work of the Temporary Slavery Commission of the League of Nations, attention by 1926 began to focus on labour conditions in the colonies. Pressure came from two main quarters: British humanitarian societies, supported to some extent by the Colonial Office; and special committees set up by the League itself. Forced labour was already prohibited in B and C Class Mandates, except for essential public works and services; and the obligation to abolish direct forms of forced labour was written into the International Slavery Convention of 1926. The drafting of the first of a series of international conventions on labour in 1928 and 1929 was the occasion of further debate, not merely on the use of colonial labour, but also about the aims of development and the quality of administration required to achieve these aims. The Forced Labour Convention, which was approved by the International Labour Convention in 1930 in order to attract ratification, was, however, a compromise with a number of loop-holes.[23]

Excluded from the general definition of 'forced labour' (meaning work ex-

---

[22] J. A. Hellen, 'Colonial administrative policies and agricultural patterns in tropical Africa', in *Environment and land use in Africa,* M. F. Thomas and G. W. Whittington, eds. (London, 1969), pp. 321–52.

[23] There is a summary of the text in G. St J. Orde Browne, *The African labourer* (London, International African Institute, 1933), pp. 217ff.

acted 'under the menace of any penalty') were compulsory military service, penal labour, if not hired to private employers, emergency services and minor communal services performed for chiefs. The main prohibition was against recruitment by officials on behalf of private employers and agencies.

Even so, a number of governments viewed the Forced Labour Convention as an unwarranted extension by the ILO of international supervision of the Mandates to colonies in general; and they viewed with suspicion British support for the prohibition of conscripted labour as a 'desire of the British to hinder the development (the *mise en valeur*) of the colonies of other nations'.[24] In practice, it was possible for France and Belgium to circumvent the requirement that military labour should be restricted to works of a 'military' nature, even after they ratified the Convention in 1937 and 1944.[25] Portugal had ratified by 1956, but did not enforce it.[26] South Africa has not ratified at all.

Nevertheless, despite its weaknesses, the Convention of 1930 did contain some advances, particularly in the limitation of all conscripted labour to a period of sixty days. And it was followed by the less well-known (and less ratified) conventions of 1936 and 1939 on recruitment and contracts, which also provided new norms for labour management.[27] But it could not end forced labour completely—not even in British territories where it was still allowed by law in the 1930s in the Gold Coast, Togoland, Kenya, Nigeria, the Cameroons, Nyasaland, Sierra Leone, Tanganyika and Uganda. The Second World War, too, renewed and temporarily extended labour conscription in Kenya, Nigeria and Tanganyika—though only a very small proportion of the total labour force had to be raised in this way.[28] By 1950, very few of the colonial powers, except Great Britain, tried to observe all the pre-war standards set by the ILO on recruitment and contracts; and only Britain and Southern Rhodesia by ratification of Convention 65, on penal sanctions, had moved towards ending one of the important 'indirect' methods of keeping labour under control by making desertion a criminal offence. And even in Southern Rhodesia, which accepted the Convention in principle, it was thought that 'the immediate or even early abolition of criminal penalties would be likely, not only to upset the stability of labour, but to increase lawlessness'.[29]

[24] Weaver (ILO) to Lugard, 27 July 1930, Lugard papers, Series S/9, Oxford, Rhodes House Library. See, too, J. Bouret Aubertôt in *Législation et finances coloniales* (Paris, 1930), p. 383, for an attack on ILO policy.

[25] ILO *Summary of reports on ratified conventions*. Such provisions as France accepted were replaced by the French Labour Code after 1952.

[26] ILO, *Report of the Ad Hoc Committee on Forced Labour*, pp. 318–34. But forced labour for private employers was prohibited by the Portuguese Labour Code of 1928. Portugal defended its policy on the grounds that metropolitan legislation went beyond the 1930 Convention, but retained compulsory labour for public works.

[27] ILO, *Summary reports on ratified conventions*, pp. 224–67.

[28] G. St J. Orde Browne, *Labour conditions in East Africa*, Colonial report no. 193 (London, 1946), pp. 13–26; Kenya, *Report of the committee appointed to inquire into the question of the introduction of conscription of African labour for essential services* (Nairobi, 1942).

[29] 'Convention concerning penal sanctions for breaches of contracts of employment by indigenous workers' (1948), in ILO, *Summary of reports on ratified conventions*, p. 267. Southern Rhodesia did not formally ratify (as a non-self-governing dominion), but adopted the convention voluntarily.

The growth of wage-labour forces

It was not till relatively late in the period of European administration that sufficient demographic and economic data were collected to form a picture of the expansion of African wage-labour.[30] Allowing for the doubtful quality of some of the statistics and difficulties in the definition of 'economically active populations', it would seem that the number of wage-earners in African countries expanded most rapidly between about 1930 and 1955; and, thereafter, there has been a tendency for wage-labour forces, as a percentage of the economically active population, to level off. Secondly, population and land resources altered considerably during the same period, though in what proportion it is difficult to say without detailed case studies. But, as an ILO survey of 1958 pointed out: 'The populations of Africa, although small, are still too large in relation to the means of subsistence obtained from the soil.' [31]

This imbalance between subsistence production and the availability of temporary employment—rural or urban—is quite basic to an understanding of the pattern and persistence of migratory flows. But it should be remembered that the broad orders of magnitude indicate that farming for cash or food is still the predominant occupation of Africans, with rural or urban wage-labour as a supplement in most areas outside of South Africa and Southern Rhodesia: 'On the average 27 per cent of men over 15 years of age were engaged in cash-crop agriculture [in the 1950s] while 60 per cent were still at work in subsistence agriculture and 13 per cent were wage earners.' [32]

In other words, although the number of wage-earners has increased much faster in Africa than the population in the last few decades, the proportion of able-bodied men thus employed is small and extremely varied between territories—from 4 per cent of the active population in Nigeria to nearly 50 per cent in Central Africa. A later analysis by the ILO rounded off earlier data, as shown in Table 123.

Comparisons with earlier data collected by the ILO for the 1930s are difficult to make. But it would seem that the higher percentages of wage-earners attributed to Malawi, Tanzania, Zambia and Angola in 1938 can be explained only by including migrants from those countries in their total work force. Migrant labour was included in the statistics of the country of census. Southern Rhodesian figures for African employment in 1956 also show that 300,000 labourers were 'non-indigenous'—or about half the country's African wage-earners. For South Africa, the Tomlinson Report noted that by 1951 there were about 650,000 'extra-Union Natives' in the country, of whom perhaps one-third were permanent settlers.[33]

Conversely, for some of the neighbouring 'reservoirs' of labour, these movements have meant that unusually large proportions of the indigenous labour force are working in another state. To take two extreme cases, in 1956 there were almost as many Nyasaland Africans employed in Northern and Southern

---

[30] I[nternational] L[abour] O[ffice], *African labour survey* (Geneva, 1958), esp. ch. 4; ILO, African Advisory Committee, 'Employment policy in Africa', 3rd sess., AF/A.C./111/3 (Dakar, 1967). [31] ILO, *African labour survey*, p. 107. [32] *Ibid.*, p. 111.
[33] South Africa, *Summary of the report of the Commission for the Socio-economic Development of the Bantu Areas within the Union of South Africa* (Pretoria, 1955), pp. 40–1.

Table 123. *Wage employment in African countries*

Country	Year	Total wage employment as percentage of economically active population	1938	Non-agricultural wage employment as percentage of economically active population
Ethiopia	1960	6·7		4·0
Kenya	1960	20·5	26·2%	11·6
Malawi	1961	16·3	44·1	10·6
Moçambique	1960	30·5		24·1
Tanzania	1962	10·1	16·2	4·9
Uganda	1960	8·9	7·9	6·6
Zambia	1961	25·4	44·1	22·7
Southern Rhodesia	1956	52·0	33·5	33·0
South Africa	1960	66·8		52·7
Angola	1954–5	27·0	40·1	(not available)
Cameroun	1962	5·1		(not available)
Chad	1961	3·0 *AEF*	13·2(1955)	2·7
Congo (Brazzaville)	1960	10·2		8·2
Congo (Kinshasa)	1955	19·1	21·8	14·5
Gabon	1963	20·0		14·1
Dahomey	1961	3·9		3·8
Ghana	1960	19·9	8·3	14·3
Guinea	1954–5	2·8		2·4
Ivory Coast	1961	12·7 *AOF*	4·8	7·1
Liberia	1961	19·1		10·3
Mali	1961	(not available)		0·9
Niger	1963	0·9		0·9
Nigeria	1962	5·1	4·7	5·0
Sierra Leone	1963	6·0	4·6	5·7
Togo	1961	4·1		2·9
Upper Volta	1961	1·2		1·2

SOURCE: International Labour Office, *African labour survey* (Geneva, 1958), p. 666. For some territories (French West and Equatorial Africa, Belgian Congo, Sierra Leone, Angola), male and female labour statistics were combined; the remaining territories furnished male labour statistics only. See, too, International Labour Organization, African Advisory Committee, 'Employment policy in Africa', AF/A.C./111 (Dakar, 1957), p. 6.

Rhodesia as in their country of origin.[34] Or in the case of Basutoland in 1960, there were perhaps 131,000 persons temporarily absent in South Africa, including a high proportion of able-bodied males, out of a total population of about 800,000.[35]

A further point suggested by Table 123 is the considerable disproportion between wage-labour forces in western Africa and former French territories in Equatorial Africa, compared with East and Central Africa. Some of this difference is explained by the relative absence of an agricultural wage-earning sector in Dahomey, Niger, Upper Volta, Chad, Nigeria and Sierra Leone. This factor probably accounts for the fairly high wage employment percentage in

[34] Great Britain, Advisory Commission on the Review of the Constitution of the Federation of Rhodesia and Nyasaland, *Report: Appendix VI, Survey of developments since 1953,* Cmnd 1149 (London, 1960), p. 336.

[35] ILO, *Report to the government of Basutoland on the manpower situation,* TAP/Basutoland/R. 1 (1964), table 3, p. 8 (projected from 1946 census).

Moçambique and Kenya in the 1930s. But more striking is the impact in wage labour terms of mining, manufacturing, construction and commerce in areas of European settlement and investment. The largest additions to the wage-labour force between 1933 and 1955 were made in South Africa (300-per-cent increase), Kenya and Southern Rhodesia (200-per-cent increase). The labour force of the Belgian Congo increased by about a third over the same period. Even in countries with small wage-labour forces, substantial progress from low base-lines was made in Nigeria, Tanganyika and, more especially, in Ghana, where both mining and an expanding cocoa industry increased the wage-labour force by about 30 per cent in the two decades 1930–50. Finally, it is noticeable in more recent statistics, as shown in Table 124 that following this period of expansion, a number of wage-labour forces have shown a tendency to remain static, or even to decline, as percentages of the economically active population.

Table 124. *General level of employment in selected countries* (indices: 1958 = 100 per cent)

	1959	1960	1961	1962	1963	1964	1965
Cameroun	95·3%	76·6%	80·1%	69·9%	77·6%	75·4%	78·3%
Kenya	100·6	104·9	99·4	97·7	89·9	99·4	100·1
Malawi	98·8	96·4	93·3	86·6	83·1	(not available)	
Nigeria	98·8	104·5	88·4	108·5	92·3	(not available)	
S. Rhodesia	100·3	102·2	100·4	98·7	97·6	99·2	101·1
Tanzania	99·4	99·9	98·9	95·5	82·1	83·7	79·1
Zambia	95·7	94·5	92·3	90·1	87·8	92·0	95·5

SOURCE: International Labour Organization, African Advisory Committee, 'Employment policy in Africa', AF/A.C./111 (Dakar, 1967), p. 11.

Some territories, then, have experienced a considerable labour boom since the 1930s; others, even in the populous area of West Africa, have been slow to develop a wage-labour force; and yet others, after considerable development, have fallen behind in their struggle against underemployment. By about 1960, total wage employment amounted to some 19 million wage-earners on the African continent (excluding North Africa); and of these, nearly four million were employed in South Africa. The total represented about 19 per cent of the economically active population—a norm most West African and Equatorial African countries failed to reach. Within this wage-labour force inter-territorial migratory labour amounted to perhaps one and a quarter million, or over one quarter: some 560,000 for southern Africa, 400,000 for West Africa, 137,000 for East Africa and 40,000–50,000 for the Congo.

Migratory and stabilized labour

From the foregoing it will be recognized that it is easier to stress the contrasts than to find similarities in the emergence of regional labour forces during the colonial period in Africa. There is a considerable literature devoted to the social and economic problems of migratory (or oscillating) labour that must serve as a point of departure for any historian investigating the dynamics of African labour supplies. The emphasis in particular and general studies of labour migration has, on the whole, been placed on motivation and effect within tribal societies and on the accommodation of tribesmen to an urban environment. It is only recently that the broader aspects of population displacement, in relation to land, capital and government intervention in the labour market, have received attention. And these attempts to synthesize and compare labour migrations have resulted in at least two models relevant to any explanation of the development and perpetuation of migratory patterns and their transformation into stabilized work forces.

A quite simple model of the exchange of labour between indigenous and money economies includes as its main variables the pull of wages and the counter-attraction of cash-crop agriculture within a social system that 'tends to act centripetally'.[36] The theory which this model serves to demonstrate has been criticized for emphasizing the 'supply side' of the equation at the expense of the 'demand' or employers' side. The explanation for the continuation of 'oscillating' labour in the work of Francis Wilson stresses that such migrations may be preferred by employers, because low wages are supplemented by the migrant's economic and social support in his rural base.[37] Thus, migrants are not merely attracted 'centripetally', but are also pushed out of the urban workplace for reasons of wages policy. The earlier model by Clyde Mitchell has therefore been modified by Wilson to include the following variables:

Rural pressures: supply	*Urban pressures: demand*
Need for money to pay for food, lobola, school fees, taxes, etc.	Need for labour.
Push → Supplemented by social forces, e.g., 'bright lights', desire to prove manhood, etc.	→ Pull
Pull ← Need to maintain agricultural production, land rights, and social connexion for purpose of security in old age. Supplemented by desire to live in familiar social and geographical surroundings. ←	Necessity for employees to be based in rural areas in order that their wages may be kept low, and so that employers need not be responsible for housing families of workers. ← Push

It has been argued, therefore, mainly from the example of South African mining labour, that the 'oscillating' system, characteristic of long periods of South African wage-labour, depends on a balance of push-and-pull factors; and furthermore that where any or all of the four factors weaken, the system can be continued only by 'legislative action' preventing a stabilization of the wage-labour force in the area of employment.[38]

There is much to be said for this schematic summary of causal factors in African migrations. In any study of the origins of wage-labour, each of the variables has a place, though there are some regions such as the Western Sudan and the Congo where, historically, the influence of trade routes, indigenous mar-

[36] Clyde Mitchell, 'The causes of labour migration', in Inter-African Labour Institute, *Migrant labour in Africa,* pp. 275–6.
[37] Wilson, *Labour in the South African gold mines,* pp. 120–3; see, too, Joseph Gugler, 'The theory of labour migration', mimeographed, University of East Africa Social Science Conference, Dar es Salaam, 1968. [38] Wilson, *Labour in the South African gold mines,* p. 123.

kets, and some occupational specialization by different tribal groups would have to be taken into account in any discussion of later population movements between the interior and the coast.[39] Secondly, from what has been said above, it would appear necessary to account for 'rural pressures' also in terms of early administrative intervention leading to spatial restriction and shortage of productive resources. In the history of Bantu migration in South Africa, the far-reaching effects of the 1913 Land Act, which aimed at eliminating an African tenant peasantry and curtailing African land purchase, are also to be seen as a remedy for labour demands. The results of spatial restriction and land degradation within Northern Rhodesian reserves can be correlated with the high incidence of migrant labour provided by the Kunda, Ngoni and Nsenga people of Eastern Province and the Bemba of Northern Province in the 1930s. And for other tribes, such as those in Kasempa district, Western Province, historic reasons connected with early forced recruitment for the Katanga mines cannot be discounted among the varieties of official intervention.[40] It follows from what has been argued earlier on forced labour that this factor would also have to be added under the rubric of 'rural pressures'. Ideally, too, the discussion of a migration model should also include sources of wage-labour external to Africa—Chinese and Indian coolies, and European immigration and settlement as a factor differentiating regions.

The latter point raises the question whether levels of public and private investment accompanying European controls and settlement should not be worked into the variable 'urban pressures' as fundamental to demand. One would expect migratory flows to bear some relationship to this investment, given that the bulk of it was in extractive industries, construction and manufacturing, and to a lesser extent in plantations or African lands (see Table 125).

Unfortunately, the table is incomplete (there are no figures for labour in French Equatorial Africa for 1938, for example). But a fair degree of correspondence exists between investment levels in relation to population and the formation of wage-labour forces in the late 1930s. It should be remembered, however, that the Portuguese African wage-earner totals are distorted by counting in absent migrants who belong in the South African or Rhodesian figures. There are probably similar distortions in the percentages for Tanganyika and Nyasaland. If the figures for Uganda and Kenya are subtracted from the East African totals, Tanganyika and Nyasaland are left with a very small share of capital investment in proportion to their relatively high individual wage-labour percentages (16·6 per cent and 44·1 per cent, respectively, in 1938). This wage-labour followed investment in the Rhodesias and in South Africa.

Given that demand for labour was a consequence of this investment, it remains to be seen whether wage levels were manipulated in the manner suggested by Wilson for South Africa, so as to use the migrant's rural base in order to avoid the expense of stabilization.

Data on which to base a complete comparative survey of wage levels from the end of the nineteenth century are not available. But it is not difficult to doc-

---

[39] M. Piault, 'The migration of workers in West Africa', in Inter-African Labour Institute, *Migrant labour in Africa,* pp. 323–38.

[40] Great Britain, *Report of the Commission Appointed to Enquire into the Financial and Economic Position of Northern Rhodesia* (Colonial, no. 145; London, 1938), pp. 30–6, and appendix 6, p. 362.

Table 125. *Relation between investment levels and economically
active population, 1936–8*

	Capital per head of population 1936	Wage-earners as percentage of economically active population 1938
South Africa	55·8	(not available)
Northern Rhodesia	38·4	44·1
Southern Rhodesia		33·5
Belgian Congo	13·0	21·8
Angola, Moçambique	9·8	35·1
Kenya, Uganda, Tanganyika, Nyasaland	8·1	23·6
Kenya, Uganda	6·8	17·0
British West Africa	4·8	5·8
Nigeria	3·9	4·7
French West Africa	2·1	4·8

SOURCES: S. Herbert Frankel, *Capital investment in Africa: its course and effects* (London, Oxford University Press, 1938), p. 170; and International Labour Office, *African labour survey* (Geneva, 1958), p. 6.

ument some of the assumptions which fairly consistently depressed African wages and contributed to a perpetuation of oscillating flows. It has been shown that administrative low-wage policy in Nigeria was intimately connected with the belief that 'urban wages had to be kept more or less at parity with agricultural wages' and made no allowance for a differential to defray the rural labourer's costs in displacing himself from the land to the town.[41] This tends to confirm the ILO survey's observation that

throughout most of Africa the principal occupation to be taken into consideration when estimating the general wage level is agriculture, including both subsistence and cash-crop farming. It is largely in terms of the needs and desires of men many of whom are engaged in a communal form of agriculture that the levels of remuneration in wage-earning activities have been determined. These needs and desires have been, and are still in the main, of such a nature as to exercise a generally depressing effect on wage levels. The need for the rural African to seek wage-paid work is often not urgent; frequently the object is to acquire a certain sum of money for a limited purpose, and the money wage accepted, particularly if the employer also provides food and accommodation, may have little relation to anything except the reasonableness or otherwise, in the worker's eyes, of staying away from home long enough to earn enough to buy the objects coveted, whose range in any case is limited because of his own limited experience.[42]

Furthermore, it has been pointed out that there existed a fairly common belief among European employers in West, Central and southern Africa that to raise wages for such target workers would satisfy their wants more quickly and thus lead to a decrease in labour supplies. The fallacies in this view of inelastic supply and the backward-sloping supply curve have been sufficiently exposed, and the point need not be laboured here.[43] What is not sufficiently explained is

[41] A. G. Hopkins, 'The Lagos strike of 1897: an exploration in Nigerian labour history', *Past and Present: a Journal of Historical Studies*, 1966, no. 35, p. 146.
[42] ILO, *African labour survey*, p. 259.
[43] See, especially, Elliot Berg, 'Backward sloping supply functions in dual economies: the Africa case', *Quarterly Journal of Economics*, 1961, **75**, 473–89.

the long period of relative stability in depressed wage-levels in West, South and Central Africa until the period of the Second World War. How were labour forces in some territories built up during the 1930s, without increasing wages, at a period of increasing costs for imported items of clothing, fuel and food-stuffs?

Part of the answer lies in price competition between wage-earning sectors and between neighboring territories. In the case of Nigeria, large numbers of unskilled workers left Lagos between 1900 and 1902 to seek marginally higher rates of pay on the Sekondi railway and the gold-mines. There is no evidence as yet that Nigerian labour continued this pattern into the 1930s, but migrant labour from Niger and Upper Volta certainly did. In the case of South African mine labour, the long depression of wages at a period of rising retail prices, according to Katzen, led to a diversion of workers to other fields in secondary industry where price competition was stronger.[44] The shortages were made up presumably only by increasing supplies of imported labour from the High Commission Territories, Moçambique and other territories north of latitude 22° S. But the statistics for the geographical sources of mine labour collected by Wilson do not support this proposition till relatively late, during the period of industrial expansion after the Second World War.[45] The percentages of immigrant labour have always been high—higher indeed in 1906 than at any period since. There is, however, some decline in the aggregate of black South Africans employed by the Chamber of Mines, between 1936 and 1969, compared with a rise in the numbers recruited from the north and from the High Commission territories. And this is explained not only by increased competition for labour in the Union, but also by the monopoly of imported labour achieved by the Chamber of Mines after 1937.

Price competition is more evident if one considers the labour situation in the Rhodesias, Nyasaland and Tanganyika in the 1930s. In Northern Rhodesia and in the two mandates, wages showed a downward trend during the slump years and only a partial recovery after 1932:

> It was not uncommon for labourers to work at 3s. or 4s. a month on the poorer class of farms. The general rates of wages both agricultural and industrial are decidedly lower than in Southern Rhodesia and the difference is even greater when comparison is made with the corresponding rates in the Union of South Africa. It is therefore hardly surprising that local labour should tend to drift southwards.[46]

This drift was assisted by the 1936 agreement between Rhodesian, Nyasaland and Transvaal Chamber of Mines representatives concerning recruitment centres, transport and repatriation, as well as by a 'demonstration effect' in the return of Barotse from the Rand, bringing with them sums averaging £11 at the end of twelve months' contract. A similar agreement to provide rest camps and cheap transport, a remittance system and repatriation was concluded among the three administrations of the British territories. Some indication of the pattern of immigrant employment in Southern Rhodesia is shown in Table 126.

[44] Leo Katzen, *Gold and the South African economy* (Cape Town, 1964), pp. 22–7.

[45] Wilson, *Labour in the South African gold mines,* pp. 70–1.

[46] Great Britain, *Report of the Commission Appointed to Enquire into the Financial and Economic Position of Northern Rhodesia,* p. 52. Compare the wages policy of the Nigerian Chamber of Mines, whose members pledged themselves to keep the daily rate at a maximum of 9d in 1912 and eliminate wage competition (Royal Niger Company papers, vol. VI, f. 315). Wages rose

Table 126. *Africans in employment in Southern Rhodesia*

	Country of origin						
	Southern Rhodesia	Nyasa- land	Northern Rhodesia	Portuguese East Africa	Other	Total non- indigenous	Total
1936	107,581	70,362	46,884	25,215	2,440	144,901	252,482
1946	160,932	80,480	45,413	72,120	4,399	202,412	363,344
1956	300,178	132,643	42,253	122,607	12,272	309,775	609,953

SOURCE: Great Britain, Advisory Commission on the Review of the Constitution of the Federation of Rhodesia and Nyasaland. *Report:* Appendix VI, *Survey of Developments since 1953,* Cmd 1149 (London, 1960), p. 336.

With one exception, in every census year since 1936 non-indigenous Africans formed over half the total number of Africans in employment in Southern Rhodesia. But by 1956 the migrant-labour agreements that had helped regulate this flow were terminated in favour of a policy of stabilizing the local labour force. Similar policies had been in operation in Northern Rhodesia on the Copper Belt and in the Belgian Congo on the mines of the Union Minière.

Probably this belated attention to stabilization came too late to remedy the problem of urban unemployment which had begun to be noticed in the more developed centres of wage employment by the 1950s. The long wage depression in British Central Africa which lasted from 1930 to about 1949 was radically ended. The minimum African wage increased by 73 per cent, 1954–58, in Southern Rhodesia; skilled employment rates expanded even faster; the gap between rural and urban wages grew, and relatively poorer areas such as Nyasaland had smaller *per capita* wage increases than Southern Rhodesia with its expanding municipalities and peri-urban townships. The working of the Native Land Husbandry Act of 1951 probably assisted this rural-urban migration, at the same time as pass laws in urban local authority areas aimed at controlling it.

The official viewpoint of unemployment, however, was that it did not exist in the Federation, except in Nyasaland, where, 'as pressure on the land increases . . . and as the outside market for Nyasaland labour approaches saturation, unemployment is beginning to appear. It has not yet attained serious proportions; but there is already a problem so far as Standard VI African school leavers are concerned.' [47] The idea that rural areas offered an alternative to wage employment died hard.

Conclusion

From the many studies of migrant labour that have accumulated it would be fairly easy to conclude that African manpower has been divided between two different economies and has been forced and/or stimulated to flow from an unintegrated, traditional, 'subsistence' area into a monetary or exchange area in which mining and manufacturing are outstanding growth points. The 'oscilla-

slightly after the war, but fell during 1927–38. See Margery Perham, ed., *Mining, commerce and finance in Nigeria* (London, 1948), p. 11, and table 10, p. 97.

[47] Great Britain, Advisory Commission . . . *Report:* Appendix VI, p. 357.

tion' of labour is explained by low wages, social ties and communal rights in land. Such a view, I believe, distorts, and even denies some of the more interesting features of African economic history, though its prevalence in much of the literature must be laid at the door of historians and not sociologists or economists. The roots of this dualistic theory, moreover, are to be found in older European assumptions that Africa was to be developed as a source of tropical staples, on the whole, apart from a few areas favoured with mineral deposits. The desire to preserve Africans from the pernicious effects of 'detribalization' encouraged this belief, after the early effects of forced labour were perceived, and took the form of an administrative paternalism characteristic of the inter-war period. As late as Hailey's *African survey* it was still considered advisable and possible to stimulate 'the cultivation of subsistence crops where natives have become unduly dependent on wage earning'.[48] An echo of this sentiment is to be found in the Tomlinson Report, which supported government policy for development of Bantu areas 'to enable them to make their proper contribution to the production of food' and to provide economic islands of employment and even vertical mobility apart from the economy of the "non-Bantu areas". [49]

Not the least weakness of the theory of 'dual' African economies is the difficulty encountered when seeking an explanation for mushrooming unemployment since the 1950s. Suddenly, it would seem, after long periods of labour shortages within the monetized economy and a relative surplus in the 'subsistence' zone, there has been an influx that is greater than employers' demand. For long, the problem of development was that manpower had to be coerced and carefully regulated to meet this demand, at a period of low wage levels and patchy investment. The paradox of rising wage levels since the Second World War is that economic expansion in Africa, modest though it is, has not been able to absorb all the manpower available. Where did the 'dual' economy break down?

Explanations for the change, in these terms, run into a semantic, as well as a conceptual, difficulty, over notions of 'employment', 'underemployment' and 'semi-employment'. Or else an appeal is made to an educational surplus—the 'school-leavers' who have upset the labour market operating between the two economies.

Historically, in many parts of Africa this 'dualism' looks much less significant as our information about the early growth and fluctuation of trade, markets and entrepreneurial activities accumulates.[50] It is possible to view the incorporation of much of the so-called subsistence sector within a single economy developed and taken over by a colonial state and inherited by independent governments. The feature of such economies is their high degree of dependence on outside markets and the slow linkages established over scattered areas of pro-

---

[48] Hailey, *African survey,* p. 1648. See, too, J. H. Boeke, *Economics and economic policy in dual societies* (New York, 1953), pp. 318–19.

[49] South Africa, *Summary of the report of the Commission for the Socio-economic Development of the Bantu Areas,* p. 109.

[50] See the essays in Claude Meillassoux, ed., *Development of indigenous trade and markets in West Africa* (London, Oxford University Press, 1971); Richard Gray and David Birmingham, eds., *Pre-colonial African trade: essays on trade in Central and Eastern Africa before 1900* (London, Oxford University Press, 1970).

duction through the interpenetration of the import-export trading sector and the rural markets. In western Africa this interpenetration was already well established by the date of European expansion and consolidation; and in South Africa, as early as the 1860s, with the development of daily and seasonal migrant labour—both black and white—working for cash and kind, there was already laid an uneven and fragile foundation for a series of economies within the states that eventually made up the Union. Our growing understanding of Central and East African pre-colonial markets, small as they were, means that they will have to be reconsidered as part of the colonial economies which took over enterprises begun by the Kambu, Nyamwezi, Yao, Bisa, Cokwe and Tonga. In most areas of European settlement, it is true, the economic gap between black and white widened, and occasionally between successful cash-crop farmers who were African and their less fortunate neighbours. But this gap does not stem from a 'dual' economy, but from an import-export mercantile economy in which resources were unevenly spread and in which labour was one of these resources.

The important and unexplored topic in such African economic history is the level of regional incomes in relation to land pressures, population, taxation and communications—fundamentals of migratory movements. In West Africa, migrations arising from these factors brought interior traders and labourers (in earlier times, slaves) to the coastal markets and port towns. There already existed by the 1860s, thinly spread, elements of an exchange economy in the interior and urban and village entrepreneurial groups. As coastal trade grew, the scale of the 'internal market' that was starved of capital decreased relatively, compared with the new urban centres. By 1900, there were many pockets of limited growth, partially monetized. There were target workers, seeking rural and urban employment, and there were also target employers, seeking labour at low rates for specific works programmes or seasonal agriculture. Migration served the immediate ends of both groups. It is possible, too, to find in Lagos or Accra in the 1890s examples of urban unemployment, when demand decreased, or when wages were too low.

But none of this slow rural and urban formation of a temporary wage-labour force can be said to have resulted from the coexistence of 'two' economies, or from an economic 'frontier' between money and subsistence; rather, it was the result of interpenetration of rural markets by the import sector concentrated on the coast. Urban and rural labour responded fitfully to this stimulus. But during the half-century 1890–1940, when wages remained low and prices rose, labour continued to come forward, as the internal market demand for consumer goods increased.[51]

The status of wage-labourer, however, must not be thought of as a constant

---

[51] An early example from Nigerian labour history in 1919 makes this point clear: 'The natives are acquiring wants and the goods they need are possibly 300% dearer than in pre-war times. A labourer on the mines obtained 6d. per day ten years ago practically at the commencement of the active stage of the Mining Industry. Today he is only obtaining 9d. to 1/-per day and with the high prices ruling for Groundnuts, Hides, Skins etc., he can readily obtain elsewhere a much higher price for his services.' (Annual report on the Niger Company's Mining Department, 23 Jan. 1919, Royal Niger Company papers, vol. XVI, f. 160.) The alternative of payment for 'services' in the staple cash-crops was reduced by the sharp recession of 1920 and by other fluctuations after 1928.

factor in the monetized economy. It is a temporary, rather than a permanent, economic category; for, as in South Africa,

at some time during his life a married man will have cultivated, herded, worked as a migrant labourer and, in come cases, carried out small-scale mining; and it is part of a young man's general education to acquire all these skills and to learn to adapt himself to life of occupational alternatives.[52]

It could be argued that it is the existence of these alternatives, rather than stabilized wage-labour, which has been the historical characteristic of a low-wage-earning sector within the monetized economy of states in Africa. Much subsistence will also exist, but this is not an alternative for the migrant worker whose wants have already been stimulated to undertake a variety of occupations. In a sense, it is his needs, not his occupation, that have been stabilized.

As an example, one may look at the Belgian Congo, where there was a fairly steady growth rate, 1920–56, of 8 per cent per annum for exports and 11·2 per cent for industrial production. Demand for labour was constant; and the labour force grew from 53,000 workers in 1918 to 416,000 by 1926, rising to 1,200,000 by 1955. In some provinces such as Leopoldville, Katanga and Kivu, as much as 45 per cent of the male population was employed for wages.[53] But after 1955, demand dropped. Urban unemployment was already a problem, because the rural villages had long entered the cash and market economy, assisted by half a century of forced labour, cash-crop production and wage recruitment. The step from peasant producer to wage-labourer by the 1930s was a short one, and it was made many times, before urban settlement brought into the *centre extra-coutumier* a labourer whose expectations were no longer met by oscillation between farm and factory or plantation. Decrease in demand left him as an urban proletarian, and not as a migrant labourer dependent on a remote 'subsistence' economy.

In other parts of Central and South Africa such proletarians are still required to oscillate by legal and social restrictions on urban settlement. And in this sense the economy subscribes to the older view that the 'reserves' are a sufficient alternative for workers who have been accustomed to a number of alternative employments to satisfy their aspirations. The 'targets' of these workers, moreover, may well include urban housing, schooling and other social services lacking in their rural environment.

African wage-labour, then, should perhaps be viewed as a linear progression, rather than as a dual development within two 'economies', stimulated by forced labour, cash-crops and occasional paid employment towards the satisfaction of internal market demands. Contemporary urban unemployment is a painful and politically dangerous discontinuity in the labour market, as the rising expectations of the migrants are frustrated by the uneven and regressive state of the economy.

This means that the usual static model offered to account for push-pull factors requires some modification, if the historical growth and continuation of urban wage-labour are to be understood. To the usual factors of land shortage,

---

[52] W. Peter Carstens, *The social structure of a Cape Coloured reserve: a study of racial integration and segregation in South Africa* (Cape Town, 1966), p. 74.
[53] A. Lux, *Le marché du travail en Afrique noire* (Louvain, 1962), pp. 48–50.

wage attraction and employers' demands, there must be added the consumer needs of the migrant from within the rural market—a factor that has been underestimated and that explains the rise of urban unemployment since the 1950s. Such migrants do not go back to the land unless they are compelled to do so. Even as late as 1957 it was still assumed that migratory movements would continue to be typical of African wage-labour: 'Traditionally there has been an over-supply of Native labour since the appeal of the money economy has taken hold of African society.' [54]

But historically this begs the important question, how and when did African societies become enmeshed in the 'money economy'? A more accurate sequence would be extreme shortage of labour at the outset of the establishment of European mercantile and industrial enterprise in Africa, followed by forced labour and indirect methods of stimulating migration, leading to established African consumer patterns. Only then, and not 'traditionally', does the proposition of over-supply hold true; and it is expressed increasingly in urban, not merely rural, unemployment.

BIBLIOGRAPHY

Aubertôt, J. Bouret. *Législation et finances coloniales*. Paris, 1930.
Berg, Elliot. 'Backward sloping supply functions in dual economies: the Africa case', *Quarterly Journal of Economics, 1961*,**75.**
Boeke, J. H. *Economics and economic policy in dual societies*. New York, 1953.
Bouche, Denise. *Les villages de liberté en Afrique noire française*. Paris, 1968.
Buell, Raymond L. *The native problem in Africa*. 2 vols. 2nd reprint. London, 1965.
Büttner, Thea. 'On the social-economic structure of Adamawa in the 19th century: slavery or serfdom?' in *African studies*, Walter Markov, ed. Leipzig, Karl-Marx-Universität, 1967.
Cadbury, William A. *Labour in Portuguese West Africa*. London, 1910.
Carstens, W. Peter. *The social structure of a Cape Coloured reserve: a study of racial integration and segregation in South Africa*. Cape Town, 1966.
Coquery-Vidrovitch, Catherine. 'French colonization in Africa to 1920: administration and economic development', in *Colonialism in Africa 1870–1960,* vol. 1: *The history and politics of colonialism 1870–1914,* L. H. Gann and Peter Dugnan, eds. Cambridge University Press, 1969.
Frankel, S. Herbert. *Capital investment in Africa: its course and effects*. London, Oxford University Press, 1938.
Gann, Lewis H. 'The end of the slave trade in British Central Africa: 1889–1912', *Rhodes-Livingstone Institute Journal,* 1954, no. 16.
A history of Northern Rhodesia: early days to 1953. London, 1964.
Gray, Richard, and David Birmingham, eds. *Pre-colonial African trade: essays on trade in Central and Eastern Africa before 1900*. London, Oxford University Press, 1970.
Great Britain. *Parliamentary papers*. Cd. 1631. 'Report on slavery and free labour in the British East African Protectorate'. London, 1903.
Great Britain. *Report by the Hon. W. G. H. Ormsby-Gore on his visit to West Africa during the year 1926*. Cmd 2744. London, 1926.

[54] 'Inter-territorial migrations of Africans south of the Sahara', *International Labour Review,* 1957, **76,** no. 3, 307.

Great Britain. *Report of the Commission Appointed to Enquire into the Financial and Economic Position of Northern Rhodesia.* (Colonial No. 145.) London, 1938.

Great Britain. Advisory Commission on the Review of the Constitution of the Federation of Rhodesia and Nyasaland. *Report:* Appendix VI, *Survey of developments since 1953.* Cmnd 1149. London, 1960.

Great Britain. Colonial Office. *Construction of railways in West Africa.* Confidential print No. 765. London, 1905.

Groves, Charles Pelham. 'Missionary and humanitarian aspects of imperialism from 1870 to 1914', in *Colonialism in Africa 1870–1960,* vol. I: *The history and politics of colonialism 1870–1914,* L. H. Gann and Peter Duignan, eds. Cambridge University Press, 1969.

Gugler, Joseph. 'The theory of labour migration'. Mimeographed. University of East Africa Social Science Conference, Dar es Salaam, 1968.

Hailey, William Malcolm Hailey, 1st baron. *An African survey: a study of problems arising in Africa south of the Sahara.* London, Oxford University Press, 1938.

Hausen, Karin. *Deutsche Kolonialherrschaft in Afrika: Wirtschaftsinteressen und Kolonialverwaltung in Kamerun vor 1914.* Zurich, 1970.

Hellen, J. A. 'Colonial administrative policies and agricultural patterns in tropical Africa', in *Environment and land use in Africa,* M. F. Thomas and G. W. Whittington, eds. London, 1969.

Hill, M. F. *Permanent way: the story of the Kenya and Uganda Railway.* Nairobi, n.d.

Hopkins, A. G. 'Economic imperialism in West Africa: Lagos 1880–1892', *Economic History Review,* 1968, **21,** no. 3.

'The Lagos strike of 1897: an exploration in Nigerian labour history', *Past and Present: a Journal of Historical Studies,* 1966, no. 35.

Houghton, D. Hobart. 'Economic development, 1865–1965', in *The Oxford history of South Africa,* vol. II: *South Africa 1870–1966,* Monica Wilson and Leonard Thompson, eds. Oxford, Clarendon Press, 1971.

I[nternational] L[abour] O[ffice]. African labour survey. Geneva, 1958.

International Labour Organization. *Report of the Ad Hoc Committee on Forced Labour.* Geneva, 1953.

Report to the government of Basutoland on the manpower situation. TAP/Basutoland/R. 1. 1964.

Summary of reports on ratified conventions. Geneva, 1950.

International Labour Organization. African Advisory Committee. 'Employment policy in Africa'. AF/A.C./111; 3rd sess., AF/A.C./111/3. Dakar, 1967.

International Labour Organization. Committee of Experts on Native Labour. *Minutes.* Geneva, 1927.

'Minutes', 1928–30. Mimeographed.

Report. Geneva, 1927.

International Labour Organization. International Labour Conference, 12th Session. *Forced labour report and draft questionnaire.* Geneva, 1929.

19th Session. *The recruiting of labour in colonies and in other territories with analogous labour conditions.* Geneva, 1935.

25th Session. *Summary of annual reports under article 22 of the constitution of the I. L. O.* Geneva, 1939.

'Inter-territorial migrations of Africans south of the Sahara', *International Labour Review,* 1957, **76,** no. 3.

Katzen, Leo. *Gold and the South African economy.* Cape Town, 1964.

Kenya. *Report of the committee appointed to inquire into the question of the introduction of conscription of African labour for essential services.* Nairobi, 1942.

Kloosterboer, W. *Involuntary labour since the abolition of slavery: a survey of compulsory labour throughout the world.* Leiden, 1960.

League of Nations. International Commission of Enquiry in Liberia. *Communication by the government of Liberia . . . December 15, 1930.* C. 658, M. 272. Geneva, 1930.

League of Nations. Temporary Slavery Commission. 'Memorandum by Mr. H. A. Grimshaw (representative of the International Labour Organisation) on the question of slavery'. C.T.E. 31. Mimeographed. Geneva, 15 April 1925.

Report. A. 19. Geneva, 25 July 1925.

Lugard papers. Series S/9. Oxford, Rhodes House Library.

Lux, A. *Le marché du travail en Afrique noire.* Louvain, 1962.

Meillassoux, Claude, ed. *Development of indigenous trade and markets in West Africa.* London, Oxford University Press, 1971.

Michel, Marc. 'La genèse du recrutement de 1918 en Afrique noire française', *Revue Française d'Histoire d'Outre-Mer,* 1971,**58,** no. 213.

Mitchell, Clyde. 'The causes of labour migration', in Inter-African Labour Institute, *Migrant labour in Africa south of the Sahara.* Abidjan, Commission for Technical Co-operation in Africa South of the Sahara, 1962.

Newbury, Colin W. *British policy towards West Africa: select documents 1786–1874.* Oxford, Clarendon Press, 1965.

The western Slave Coast and its rulers. Oxford, Clarendon Press, 1961.

Newbury, G. E., and C. W. Newbury. 'Annotated bibliography of Commonwealth migrations: the tropical territories; 1 Africa'. Oxford, Institute of Commonwealth Studies, 1969.

Oliver, Roland. *The missionary factor in East Africa.* London, 1952.

Orde Browne, G. St J. *The African labourer.* London, International African Institute, 1933.

Labour conditions in East Africa. Colonial report no. 193. London, 1946.

Panofsky, Hans E. 'A bibliography of labour migration in Africa south of the Sahara', in Inter-African Labour Institute, *Migrant labour in Africa south of the Sahara.* Abidjan, Commission for Technical Co-operation in Africa South of the Sahara, 1962.

Perham, Margery, ed. *Mining, commerce and finance in Nigeria.* London, 1948.

Piault, M. 'The migration of workers in West Africa', in Inter-African Labour Institute, *Migrant labour in Africa south of the Sahara.* Abidjan, Commission for Technical Co-operation in Africa South of the Sahara, 1962.

Powesland, P. G. *Economic policy and labour.* East African studies, no. 10. Kampala, East African Institute of Social Research, 1957.

'Rapport de la Commission pour l'étude du problème de la main-d'oeuvre au Congo belge', *Congo: Revue Générale de la Colonie Belge,* May 1925, **1,** no. 5; June 1925, **2,** no. 1.

Ross, Edward Alsworth. *Report on employment of native labor in Portuguese Africa.* New York, 1925.

Ross, W. McGregor. *Kenya from within: a short political history.* London, 1927.

Royal Niger Company papers. Oxford, Rhodes House Library.

Schéfer, Christian. *Instructions générales données de 1763 à 1870 aux gouverneurs et ordonnateurs des établissements français en Afrique occidentale.* 2 vols. Paris, 1927.

Sierra Leone. *Despatches relating to domestic slavery in Sierra Leone.* Sierra Leone Legislative Council, Sessional paper no. 5. Freetown, 1926.

Social implications of industrialization and urbanization in Africa south of the Sahara. London, International African Institute and UNESCO, 1958.

South Africa. *Summary of the report of the Commission for the Socio-economic Development of the Bantu Areas within the Union of South Africa.* Pretoria, 1955.

Vandeleur, S. *Campaigning on the Upper Nile and Niger.* London, 1898.

Van der Horst, Sheila T. *Native labour in South Africa*. London, Oxford University Press, 1942.

Ward, W. E. F. *A history of the Gold Coast*. London, 1952.

Wills, A. J. *An introduction to the history of Central Africa*. London, 1967.

Wilson, Francis. *Labour in the South African gold mines 1911–1969*. Cambridge University Press, 1972.

  Migrant labour. Johannesburg, 1972.

CHAPTER 14

THE RISE OF NEW INDIGENOUS ÉLITES

by

PETER C. LLOYD

The economic and political developments of the colonial period have wrought great changes in the social structure of the African peoples and, not least, in the patterns of social stratification. In a few instances the dominant social groups in the pre-colonial era were able to exploit to their own advantage the new opportunities offered and so to perpetuate their dominance. In most cases new social groups have emerged, recruited from the hitherto underprivileged mass of the population. This upward and downward displacement of persons has occurred in part because the rules of social mobility have altered; in particular, Western education is now one of the prime determinants of social ranking. But new élites have emerged because the major political units have increased in scale. The modern state is supreme, although the traditional kingdoms and tribes form units of local government. In fact we see in the African state the emergence of two new élites, a national élite and a plethora of local élites.

The national élite comprises the professionals, the category which, in most cases, wrested power from the metropolitan government; the bureaucrats, who man the increasingly complex machinery of state; and the businessmen, who are variously employed as managers in the expatriate companies, as co-partners with expatriates in smaller enterprises, and as owners of their own, usually quite small, firms. These men are almost invariably Western-educated, often to a very high degree.[1] Their overt style of life has far more in common with an international 'middle-class' standard than with that of their traditional homes. The local élites, on the other hand, comprise the traditional rulers and chiefs; the various local government functionaries; and the rich farmers, traders, transport owners and the like. These men usually have minimal education and are more oriented towards traditional society, still respecting its values and norms.

This dichotomy between national and local élites would seem to parallel many other conventional distinctions—the 'dual economy', the modern and traditional sectors of society, the progressive and conservative elements. In a limited sense the distinction is convenient in that the origin and the growth of the two élites may often be considered separately. But certain dangers are inherent in such a rigid distinction. All too often specific characteristics are falsely attributed to each of the pair. Thus it is just not true to say that ascribed status predominates in traditional African societies, achieved status in modern. (The example given below of Yoruba society shows how difficult it is to apply such terms.) Again, many individuals cannot be neatly described as either national or local élite: some members of a local élite are highly educated; some, too, may have a national reputation. Perhaps the greatest handicap in distinguishing sharply between national and local élites lies in the danger of over-

[1] See P. C. Lloyd, ed., *The new élites of tropical Africa* (London, Oxford University Press, 1966).

looking the dependence between them. It is this interdependence that I wish to examine in the present discussion. I shall stress two situations; first, one in which the emergent national élite, largely professionals, seeks the support of the local élites in its efforts to win political power; second, one in which the distinction between the rapidly growing national élite and the local élite becomes increasingly occluded. These are not mere academic issues but matters of considerable political importance. For in most African states the political party in power is dependent upon the elector support of the masses—and this is often controlled by the local élites. But the national ideology, conceived by professionals and intellectuals, often runs counter to the interests expressed by the local élites. This is especially so where the national ideology is couched in terms of socialism and equality whilst the local élite are clearly enriching themselves in a manner described as the capitalist exploitation of their fellow men.

I believe the process that I shall describe is common, in very general terms, to most of colonial Africa, for there are, in fact, universal themes in the political and economic history of the colonial era. I wish, however, to illustrate this process with reference to one small area of Africa that I know particularly well, that area of south-west Nigeria peopled by the Yoruba and embraced by the successive administrative units—Western Provinces, Western Region, Western State.[2]

In stressing the uniformity of the process, one must indicate also the major variables that determine the individual differences between one area and another. I would cite three such variables. First, we must consider the traditional social structure. Some African societies were relatively open—all men could aspire to great wealth or high political office—whereas others were closed, office being restricted to a few families or individuals. Second, the metropolitan country must be taken into account, for there are significant differences between the administrative methods of the colonial powers. A third variable lies in the nature of economic development. Some areas are suitable for exported cash-crops, whereas others, though they may be agriculturally barren, have exploitable mineral wealth. These three variables limit the opportunities that are open to aspiring élites at any one time and constrain the succession of choices they make, so determining the course of their history.

Traditional Yoruba society

The Yoruba, today numbering over nine million persons, share a common culture in terms of language, dress and other such traits. Yet their social and political structure shows some marked internal differences. Thus agnatic or patrilineal descent prevails among the northern Yoruba, cognatic or bilineal descent among the southern Yoruba of Ijebu and Ondo.[3] Although the kingdom of Oyo grew, in the eighteenth century, into a mighty empire covering 30,000 square miles, the village communities of the Kabba Yoruba lacked even kingship.[4] The following description of Yoruba society is thus both highly generalized and simplified, though in its essentials it is sufficiently accurate for our purposes.

[2] See P. C. Lloyd, 'The Yoruba', in *Peoples of Africa*, James L. Gibbs, ed. (New York, 1965).
[3] See P. C. Lloyd, 'Agnatic and cognatic descent among the Yoruba', *Man*, 1966, n.s. **1**, no. 4.
[4] See P. C. Lloyd, 'The traditional political system of the Yoruba', *Southwestern Journal of Anthropology*, 1954, **10**, no. 4.

The Yoruba are a town-dwelling people. In the nineteenth and earlier centuries, the capitals of the larger kingdoms had populations approaching 50,000. Ibadan today, if its citizens living temporarily in farm hamlets are included, numbers over a million inhabitants; and the population of several other towns exceeds 100,000. The towns were formerly dense agglomerations of mud-built compounds encircled by a substantial wall or earth rampart and ditch. Yet these settlements could not be called urban, for in the past, as now, the greater part of their people, often over three-quarters, were engaged directly in agriculture. Men and women either walk daily to and from their farms, a combined distance of up to eight miles, or live temporarily in hamlets. Sociologically, too, one hesitates to use the term 'urban,' for the town comprised a number of descent groups, numbering perhaps a thousand or more persons. The members of such groups trace their descent in a usually foreshortened genealogy from a founder who migrated to the town. They corporately hold rights to land both in the town, on which the compound is built, and in the surrounding farming area. They usually hold rights to a political office and constitute administrative units. They have deities and ancestors, facial marks and food taboos peculiar to themselves. By African standards these descent groups were, in the past, very strongly corporate bodies. Today certain factors, such as emigration, weaken them; but other factors work in the reverse direction. The scarcity and the increasing cash value of land for instance encourage men to guard jealously their right in descent-group land—to claim their share of building or farm land or a share in the income from its alienation.

Before the colonial era the Yoruba were a wealthy people. Their agriculture was quite diversified, with yams, cassava, maize and sorghum as staple crops and a wide variety of other produce. Handicrafts were strongly developed, producing both articles for general consumption, such as baskets and pottery, elaborate clothes, metalwork, and for royal and ritual purposes. Many of these crafts were hereditary within descent groups. Trading was well organized, for not only did large caravans traverse Yoruba country trading in highly valued commodities and, until the early nineteenth century, slaves, but there was also an intricate exchange of goods between the towns and the farm areas. Yoruba women rarely helped their husbands in the basic agricultural tasks; they marketed the produce, prepared food for sale or engaged in crafts. Because they were allowed to retain the profits of their activity for their own use, they were economically independent of their husbands. During the nineteenth century, most of the Yoruba kingdoms were engaged in intermittent warfare, and professional warriors, with their private armies, often overshadowed the traditional rulers of their polities.

Great differences in power and wealth have for long existed in Yoruba society. Some men ruled kingdoms with populations of tens or hundreds of thousands. Their wealth was most overtly demonstrated by polygyny. A chief or wealthy trader might have as many as twenty wives, whilst kings often possessed a hundred. The affluent household would also contain many domestic slaves. But Yoruba society was egalitarian, in that positions of wealth and power were open to most freeborn men.

Let us look first at the political system.[5] The town and kingdom were ruled

---

[5] See P. C. Lloyd, 'Sacred kingship and government among the Yoruba', *Africa*, 1960, **30**, no. 3.

by an oba, usually termed the 'king'. This title was indeed hereditary, being restricted to those men who were born to a reigning monarch—that is, born on the throne. But because the title rotated between two or more segments of the royal lineage, a son might never directly succeed his father. The oba was a consecrated ruler, the rituals of installation endowing him with vast supernatural power. Secular power lay not with his close kin but with a council of commoner chiefs. In fact the members of the royal lineage were not only usually debarred from political office and even from personal contact with the ruler, but they held little land and had in consequence little prestige in the town. Among the northern Yoruba, the chiefs were elected by and from among the members of their own descent groups. Here too the title rotated between the segments of the group, though it was not restricted to those men whose fathers had once held the title. Every man, in fact, was eligible; the qualities deemed necessary for success were usually wealth and personality. Many men who attained these titles were in practice sons or grandsons of past chiefs; but given the high rate of polygyny, a very large proportion of the descent group could claim this qualification.

Wealth, a prerequisite for titled office inasmuch as the competition was severe and candidates had to buy support, was gained from farming and trade, rarely from crafts. Because land was corporately held by the descent group, the individual could acquire a right to use as much as he needed; he could not own or alienate land surplus to these needs. The rich farmer was one with a number of sons or slaves, one who was probably a hard worker himself. The big fortunes generally came from trade (and, in certain periods, from war). Here success was dependent on capital accumulation through skill and hard work, though helpers may have provided the original capital. The astute trader appreciated market conditions and the credit-worthiness of his customers. He perhaps employed others as his agents but was the sole manager of his business and since written records were nonexistent until the late nineteenth century, retained in his head a record of all transactions.

By Yoruba rules of inheritance a man's wealth was divided at his death into as many equal parts as he had wives with children.[6] In such a polygynous society the individual child thus received very little, certainly not enough to endow him immediately with the same prestigious status occupied by his father. During their lifetimes, too, fathers tended not to favour one son at the expense of others for fear of generating even more hostility between co-wives. In practice, an old man often had little wealth at his death. Traders reached the peak of their ability in their forties and fifties; they then sought titled office if eligible (and thus ceased to trade) and tended to live off their capital. When one asks, in the Yoruba town, about the wealthy traders of past decades, one is told of men who rose to prominence from very humble origins. The descendants of these men may be observed working in a variety of occupations. In fact, they are fairly representative of the total population; they are distinguished in maintaining the honour of their esteemed ancestor by their own good behaviour.

The wealthy and powerful Yoruba men could not, as I have described, transmit their privileged status to their own children, thus creating a self-perpetuating privileged category. Furthermore, during their own lifetimes they hardly

---

[6] See P. C. Lloyd, *Yoruba land law* (London, Oxford University Press, 1962), ch. 9.

constituted a social group. They lived in their own compounds alongside poorer relatives. Their status was symbolized in their number of wives, in their richer diet and in their freedom from manual work; but their speech patterns, their leisure interests and, in general, their culture were those of the people living around them. In these circumstances it is not surprising that although vernacular Yoruba has terms denoting the possession of power and of wealth of varying types, there are no terms to denote a social class.[7]

The Yoruba man saw his society as open, one in which mobility from humble origins to the most privileged positions was not only possible, but could, on occasion, be achieved very rapidly. At first sight this attitude may seem incompatible with a belief in destiny. For the Yoruba held that, on entering the world, a man is given by the high god his personal 'fate'. This was often a fate of the individual's own choosing, though from his birth he was ignorant both of its details and of his own part in selecting it. However, this belief in destiny did not produce apathy. Firstly, one had a chance of modifying one's fate; and secondly, one felt a need, like some early puritans, to strive to fulfil one's destiny. A poor fate might be rectified if, by divination, it was elucidated early in one's life and one could take action to avoid the threatened crises. Again, the continual service of one's tutelary deity could modify an adverse fate. Character, too, was important; a good fate might be spoiled by rashness in trying to overachieve. 'A person is not to expect an automatic fulfillment of a good destiny. He must co-operate to make his destiny successful by acquiring and practising good character.'[8]

Good character was reflected, too, in observance of the values of the society. The chief was elected by his descent group; the trader was dependent upon his customers. Both had to be popular men. The Yoruba ideal was the *gbajumo,* the extrovert, always willing to help others with advice, recommendations or money. The generous man was admired, the miser despised. For the average Yoruba man social advancement came not so much from individual achievement as from membership of a descent group which was, corporately, growing in wealth or power, or from identification with a patron whose star was in the ascendant. Those Yoruba who were successful, even to a moderate degree, tended to emphasize not their own genius but the help received from others. Every man must have a backer, a patron. In this recognition of one's social debts (and in many cases in the exaggeration of the magnitude of the debt), one may see the desire to maintain past relationships and to be seen to have an influential patron on whose aid one can still rely in the highly competitive society.

Finally, the search for extra-personal factors to account for one's success or failure is illustrated by the belief in witchcraft and the supernatural as means of social mobility. If a man suddenly became rich, it was suggested, Faustus-like, that he had used medicine to this end. The costs of this were alleged to be in the death of his wives or children. The poor man similarly explained his poverty by the evil machinations of others. (Conversely, the rich man did not attribute his own fortune to the supernatural; and the poverty of others was attributed by their peers to laziness.)

[7] See P. C. Lloyd, 'Class consciousness among the Yoruba', in *New élites of tropical Africa.*
[8] E. B. Idowu, *Olódùmarè: God in Yoruba belief* (London, 1962), p. 181.

The new local élite

I have described traditional Yoruba society mainly in the past tense, though in the rural areas and in the smaller provincial towns it remains relatively unchanged at the present time. Furthermore, as they relate to the rise of the new local élites, traditional patterns of social mobility remain largely appropriate. This applies more to the economic sector, as a consequence of cocoa growing, than to the political sector, with the institution of methods of native administration.

Cocoa was introduced into Nigeria at the end of the nineteenth century, some of the first plantations being established on the outskirts of Lagos by the educated professional élite of that city. After a slow start, production expanded rapidly, first northwards towards Ibadan and then eastwards through the forest zone to Ondo Province. In 1915, 9,000 tons were marketed; in 1939, 114,000 tons; and in the decade 1955–64, production fluctuated between 80,000 tons in a very bad year and over 200,000 tons in a good year. The annual value of cocoa exports in the early 1960s was over £30 million.

Cocoa in Nigeria is a peasant crop. In most areas of Western Nigeria one-half or more of the cocoa-farmers have less than two and a half acres of cocoa, and in few areas do more than 10 per cent of the farmers have holdings of more than ten acres.[9] In 1951, the average cocoa-farming family received from this crop an income of less than £100; but only a third of the farmers in the cocoa belt actually grew cocoa.[10] Men planted cocoa on suitably forested fallow land held by their descent group and have been able to maintain the small plots with family labour. A few rich cocoa farmers there certainly are. These are men who had the capital necessary to establish more than a small holding and the influence, perhaps, to acquire the necessary land. However, the labour requirements of large cocoa farms are relatively modest. An Etiki farmer who in 1950 sold cocoa to the value of £4,000 had ten permanent labourers living on his land.

The purchase of the cocoa crop is ultimately the responsibility of the Cocoa Marketing Board.[11] Until Independence, expatriate firms dominated the market, five of them accounting in 1950 for more than three-quarters of the crop. These firms were served by produce buyers and their agents, estimated to number between 25,000 and 35,000 in 1950, to whom the farmers brought their crop.[12] The farmers received a good price for their harvest; yet the small profit margin allowed to the produce buyers made the largest of them among the wealthiest men in their towns.

The same expatriate firms that dominated the export trade of Nigeria similarly controlled the import trade. In fact one firm, the United Africa Company, was responsible for a third of Nigeria's trade.[13] These companies, again through their factors and commission agents, retailed imported goods to the consumer and to petty traders who carried them to the most remote local markets. A further source of wealth derived from transport, for most of the cocoa and imported goods were carried by road. The lorry, built locally onto

---

[9] R. Galletti, K. D. S. Baldwin and I. O. Dina, *Nigerian cocoa farmers* (London, Oxford University Press, 1956), p. 643.
[10] Gerald K. Helleiner, *Peasant agriculture, government, and economic growth in Nigeria* (Homewood, Ill., 1966), p. 78.   [11] See P. T. Bauer, *West African trade* (London, 1954).
[12] Galletti *et al.*, *Nigerian cocoa farmers*, p. 40.   [13] Bauer, *West African trade*, pp. 71 and 220.

imported chassis, carried both goods and passengers with equal felicity. Though often poorly maintained, the lorry earned its owner a handsome return.

The wealthy local businessman tended to combine all three of the above activities—produce buying, wholesaling and retailing of imported goods and transporting—for all were interlinked. Typically, his rise to success followed the same path as that of traders in the pre-colonial era. He came from a humble home and in his youth was employed in quite menial tasks. The richest man in Ado-Ekiti in the early 1950s, for example, had started by hawking chickens from his town to Ilorin, a hundred miles away. He had subsequently joined the United Africa Company (as a labourer), where he had risen rapidly to prosperity. The typical businessman usually had little or no formal education, though he may have picked up a smattering of English in his dealings with government officials and the agents of the firms. It is my impression that many of these businessmen came from descent groups that did not hold large areas of farmland or rights to high titled office.

A further category within the local élite were the building contractors. Much of the money received, directly or indirectly, from cocoa was used for house improvement, such as the addition of a corrugated iron roof in place of thatch, the cement plastering of walls and the installing of windows, or the construction of two-storey houses. The contractor was usually a man of limited technical knowledge, but he did have the capital and the reputation to enable him to bring together the various teams of craftsmen. His entrepreneurial abilities brought him a rich reward compared with a craftsman's wages.

These businessmen built flamboyant mansions in a modified 'Brazilian' style diffused from Lagos, on the land of their own compounds. Often these had an upstairs parlour lavishly outfitted with imported furniture for the entertainment of expatriates and other members of the local élite, and a spare downstairs parlour for conducting business with customers and clients. Their several wives and children lived in a courtyard behind the house. Besides receiving the support of members of their descent group, these men established large networks of clients and customers. For both groups they served as benefactors, giving advice, settling disputes, granting small loans, paying school fees. To a considerable extent they supplanted the traditional chiefs who, in their poverty, lost prestige in the sight of their people. The wealthy local élite with their lavish styles of living and most conspicuous consumption patterns were a source of pride to the inhabitants of the Yoruba town, hopefully setting their own town ahead of neighbouring rivals.

The British Colonial Service employed very few expatriates at the local level. A typical province of a million people was administered by a Resident, three or four District Officers and perhaps ten Assistant District Officers. From the outset these men governed through the traditional obas and their chiefs; and from 1917 the chiefs were gazetted as Native Authorities (N.A.'s), responsible both for the traditional functions of town government and for those consequent upon British administration—primarily, of course, the collection of taxes. In these circumstances it was the policy of the administration to maintain the prestige of obas and chiefs, and it was recognized that it was essential that they should continue to be selected and installed by their people (subject to the overriding approval of the British officials) in the customary manner. In their capacity as N.A.'s (and as Native Court judges, too), obas and chiefs received salaries that were intended to replace all customary forms of income and per-quisites. The salaries of obas tended to be generous. In 1950, for example, the five major obas received approximately £2,500 per annum; the Ewi of Ado-Ekiti, a kingdom of 50,000 at that time, received £600, and other rulers were similarly paid according to the size of their kingdoms. The chiefs, however, tended to share a sum equal to the salary of their oba, and thus earned between £18 per annum for the lowest-ranking to £120 for the more senior.

From the late 1920s the traditional kingship began to attract literate candi-dates, for apart from the prestige of the office and the opportunities it gave to improve the town, the salary was often much higher than the candidate could expect to earn, given his educational qualifications, in the civil service.[14] In the 1930s, when the British administration sought to use the N.A.'s as agents of change, they too sought educated men as obas and chiefs. During this period and the decade that followed, several such men were appointed. The wealthy educated oba tended to live in a style similar to that of the big traders, building a modern house near the traditional palace. He set aside a room as his office and would spend much of each day dealing with files sent by the District Of-ficers. The low salaries of the chiefs were, on the other hand, a deterrent to liter-ate men; and those who did assume such an office were often in difficulty, as their legitimate income was clearly insufficient for them to maintain the style of life commensurate with their education. Thus elderly and illiterate men tended to dominate the council of chiefs.

From an early period the British administration sought to involve members of the local trading and clerical élite in the work of the Native Authorities. In the twenties and thirties they set up 'advisory boards' selected by themselves and the oba and chiefs. These bodies tended to include the top élite of the commu-nity. In the immediate post-war period, the late 1940s councillors were elected in their wards by acclamation. The men so chosen tended to be locally popular but not necessarily wealthy, since the active businessman was apt to feel that the functions of the N.A. were too petty to occupy his time. In the fifties, local government councils were instituted by the new, Action Group-controlled, Regional Government. Councillors, who outnumbered traditional members by three to one, were directly elected. Not only were the tasks of the local govern-ment council clearly specified in the law, but the increased income from taxes and grants made this body the prime determinant of local development. Coun-cillors thus tended to be literate men; and many small towns and villages that felt that they had hitherto been exploited by their larger neighbours elected very well-educated men.

In the first half of the present century the scale of local administration slowly increased. Schools and churches grew in number. But the clerks, teachers and priests usually worked away from their home towns and were, in addition, sub-ject to frequent transfer. They tended to show little interest in the communities of their temporary sojourn and sought their social life among those similarly ex-patriate. Though retired clerks and teachers were to be found in many Yoruba towns, their social position was ambiguous. As travelled men they were held in respect, but their continual criticism of the corruption and inefficiency of the

[14] See P. C. Lloyd, 'Traditional rulers', in *Political parties and national integration in tropical Africa,* James S. Coleman and Carl G. Rosberg, Jr., eds. (Berkeley and Los Angeles, University of California Press, 1964).

obas, chiefs and local élite tended to lose them the support of the masses and thus deprived them of a traditional or modern political office through which their views might be legitimately expressed.

In any study of élites, attention is likely to be focused upon the conflicts that develop between the new élite and that which it is supplanting. Three types of such conflict recur in Yoruba towns. Let us discuss first the conflict between literate oba and chiefs. The role of the traditional oba, as conceived by his chiefs, was to ordain the decisions reached by them. The Native Authority system made the oba far more dependent upon his District Officer than upon his chiefs; and the literate ruler of the thirties and forties was apt to become very autocratic, revelling in the powers devolved upon him and scornful of the ignorance of his chiefs. Many clashes occurred in which the oba suffered temporary exile, but the chiefs, poor and lacking in prestige, could never win this battle unaided; and the literate oba was supported not only by the administration but also, in most cases, by the local educated and wealthy élite.

The autocratic literate oba tended to be popular in his town both with the mass of the people—he symbolized the prosperity of the town and was instrumental in obtaining new social services—and with the local élite who were generally content with their roles as businessmen or clerks. In many cases the oba was the most highly educated resident native of the town, his scholastic peers being strangers and the traders only barely literate. In some towns, however, a bitter contest for power developed between the oba and his most prominent commoner citizen. Such a power-struggle occurred in Ijebu-Ode (and in very similar circumstances in Benin, a neighbouring but non-Yoruba town),[15] In each case the oba was literate and his adversary comparatively well educated. In both cases, furthermore, the adversaries were not only very wealthy businessmen, but had reached the fringes of the national élite as members of the Legislative Council. Both had attained very high-ranking chieftaincy titles in their respective towns, and in each case the traditional role of these titles had been to protect the interests of commoners against the palace. Thus a traditional cleavage in the society was reawakened in the new situation. The institution of local government councils in the fifties saw the autocracy of the literate obas challenged by the newly elected councillors, who sought not only to wield the powers granted to them, but also to receive the usual perquisites, such as bribes for granting licences and promoting appointments. The obas strove to maintain their former roles and their illicit incomes. It followed that those who were politically inept in such situations quickly lost the respect of their people.

In each of the conflicts cited here party politics intruded after 1951 and further complicated the issue. This theme I develop below.

The rise of the national élite

At the beginning of the nineteenth century, Lagos was an important port for the export of slaves from the Yoruba hinterland. In the 1840s, Christian missionaries landed at nearby Badagry and travelled to Lagos, Abeokuta and other interior towns. In 1851, British warships shelled Lagos and ten years later the British annexed the town. During this period several thousand Yoruba who had

---

[15] See R. E. Bradbury, 'Continuities in pre-colonial and colonial Benin politics (1897–1951)', in *History and social anthropology*, I. M. Lewis, ed. (London, 1968).

a few decades earlier been sold into slavery returned to their homeland and settled, mostly in Lagos. Those from Brazil included many trained craftsmen who brought Lagos its distinctive house styles. Those from Sierra Leone had been converted to Christianity and had been given a more formal education. It was members of this group who reached high positions in state and church before the end of the century. The colonial government and missionaries placed their emphasis on primary and technical education; but the creole group, who demanded secondary schools, were instrumental in founding many such institutions in Lagos during the second half of the century.[16]

On the one hand, this creole aristocracy in Lagos sought, and were in large measure granted, social parity with the European community. One still sees their family photographs with wives in crinolines, husbands in formal morning suits and children in sailor suits. On the other hand, some made greater efforts to establish links with their communities of origin, intervening in local politics and writing tracts on local history and customs. Their impact on traditional society, however, was very slight. The establishment of the Protectorate in 1901, with its improved health conditions and the increasing missionary interest consequent upon evangelical revivals in England, set back severely the efforts of these men. During the five decades that followed, it was to become rare for an African to rise to a state or church office superior in rank to that held by a European. (By 1939, there were but three Africans in the 'Senior Service'.) Nationalist attitudes were now intensified. In the first decade of the present century the African churches of Lagos seceded from their Protestant parent mission churches. The very few Nigerians who received a university education turned to the independent professions. In the early twenties, there were fifteen African barristers and twelve doctors, mostly Yoruba and almost all working in Lagos. Even by 1945, there were only 193 Nigerian students in Britain. Of these more than a hundred were studying law and medicine, with all but two privately financed. Of the remainder, forty-two were receiving government scholarships. At the turn of the century, Lagos had a number of African businessmen some of whom rivalled the expatriate firms. But the African-run businesses tended to decline as their founders died and their children, rather than go into trade, turned to professional and clerical occupations, their education financed by investments in landed property. The expatriate firms amalgamated and grew to the position of dominance already cited, rendering competition from independent Nigerian businessmen well-nigh impossible. Many Nigerians did prosper, however, often acting as agents of the expatriate firms at least until they had accumulated enough capital to start on their own.

The early nationalist political movements, which were dominated by this Lagos élite, were liberal in outlook.[17] They demanded an extension of elective government, more educational facilities, free trade and Africanization of the public services. Under the leadership of Herbert Macauley the movement played an active role in the internal politics of Lagos town, but took little interest in the affairs of Yoruba towns farther afield. With Macauley's death, leader-

---

[16] See J. F. Ade Ajayi, *Christian missions in Nigeria, 1841–1891: the making of a new élite* (London, 1965); also Jean Herskovits Kopytoff, *A preface to modern Nigeria: the 'Sierra Leoneans' in Yoruba, 1830–1890* (Madison, University of Wisconsin Press, 1965).

[17] See James S. Coleman, *Nigeria: background to nationalism* (Berkeley and Los Angeles, University of California Press, 1958).

ship passed to Nnamdi Azikiwe, an Ibo. The rising tide of Ibo ethnic consciousness led to a split in the movement and to the founding in 1947, by Obafemi Awolowo, of the Action Group, a predominantly Yoruba party composed, at that time, of a small number of professionals, teachers and wealthy traders. A large proportion of them worked in Lagos.[18] With this division, the Action Group appeared in Lagos as the party of the 'bourgeoisie', whereas the National Council of Nigeria and the Cameroons—Azikiwe's party—represented the 'proletariat'. In the elections of 1951 the Action Group won the majority of seats in the Western Region and formed the government during the ensuing decade.

It was only with the growing awareness that Nigeria would, in the not too distant future, become an independent state that any marked effort was made to expand the country's educational facilities. After the war the number of government scholarships was increased; in 1948 a University College, associated with the University of London, was opened at Ibadan. In the fifties, great strides were made simultaneously at all educational levels. Free and, it was hoped, universal primary schooling was instituted in the Western Region in 1956. With tremendous enthusiasm from local communities the number of secondary grammar schools, trebled in less than a decade—from fifty-nine in 1954 to 177 in 1961. New universities were opened in Lagos and Ile Ife. With this rapidly increasing output of scholars, the Nigerianization of the public services (although themselves rapidly expanding) was quickly achieved. The regular intake of expatriates into the administrative service ceased in 1953, and the first wave of Nigerians entered in the following year. In 1960, the Western Region government Nigerianized all but one of the posts of permanent secretary. In the mid-sixties, more than 800 civil servants were in the administrative grades (usually denoting the possession of a university degree), and more than 1,300 were graduate teachers. Of Nigeria's two thousand lawyers, the greater part were in Lagos and the Western Region.

From what social groups did these new bureaucrats come? Though the educated creole aristocracy of Lagos tended to give their children a good education, they were numerically a small group. The very rapidity of educational expansion necessitated the recruitment of scholars from a wide social base. Thus illiterate chiefs or traders would send one or two sons to school so that they might help them with their correspondence and accounts, although they feared public disgrace when these sons flouted local taboos. Conversely, humble men with less to lose, and little hope of a rise in social rank in their community, educated as many sons as they could. The story of Awolowo, as told in his own autobiography, is not an atypical picture of the poor boy who seeks an education, moving from one school or one patron to another.[19]

The wealthy illiterate man was willing to pay the fees of any of his own children, or those of friends or relatives, who won a place in grammar school or university; but he tended to regard this scholarship as an aspect of the boy's destiny and was not unduly troubled that other children might be less bright and would become farmers or poor craftsmen. The educated man, however, not only believes that all his children can be educated but also that he can ensure

---

[18] Richard L. Sklar, *Nigerian political parties* (Princeton University Press, 1963), pp. 101–12.

[19] See Obafemi Awolowo, *Awo: the autobiography of Chief Obafemi Awolowo* (Cambridge University Press, 1960).

their success through the influence of the home environment, by his ability to pay the fees and through his influence in gaining admission to the prestigious schools. Thus the educated élite becomes a self-perpetuating category.

As is well known, the university-educated Nigerian, in assuming a post previously held by an expatriate (or a new post of similar status), acceded to the salary scales and perquisites—generous leave and travel allowances, subsidized housing—received by the expatriate. Although some of the perquisites have in recent years been reduced, the great disparity in annual income between the primary-school leaver (£100–£250), the grammar-school leaver (£250–£500) and the university graduate (£700–£3,000) remains. These incomes are, of course, matched by styles of living. The graduate, for instance, has a modern house and car and consumes more imported food.

This bureaucratic élite is concentrated in the affluent suburbs of the national and regional capitals. They mingle as social equals almost exclusively with persons of similar education and income. They meet together in a number of clubs, some obviously restricted, such as Old Boys' Associations, others open in theory to all comers but in practice highly exclusive. One image of the educated national élite stresses this corporate activity and emphasizes the manner in which they attempt to maintain their own privileged status in the independent state and ensure a like status for their children.

Individually, however, these men remain closely tied to their families and communities of origin. They are predominantly young, and their parents and many of their siblings remain at home. The affective ties of kinship are strong. Men whose education has been financed by relatives feel obliged to repay this generosity by educating not only their own children but their nephews, nieces and cousins. Some argue that they ought to train all close relatives so that none may, in poverty, bring disgrace to the family name. Parents, to increase their own prestige locally, are anxious to demonstrate that their sons have won fame. Communities wishing to build a new road, or a school, seek the advice of their sons in the capital and expect them to use their influence to steer applications for grants-in-aid or official approval through the appropriate ministries. The man who aspires ultimately to a political or business career feels the need of a local base of support and so accedes to the requests made. Furthermore, a man who generously gives of his time and money to help his community is respected by all.

In discussing the national élite I have up to this point made no mention of the modern business element—mainly because it remains so small. To establish a competitive manufacturing industry, both high levels of technical skill and considerable capital are needed, and educated Nigerians have neither of these.[20] Many men have prospered in businesses of an intermediate scale, such as bakery, printing or furniture making. Studies of such entrepreneurs suggest that education is not an important factor in their success. Many of them are self-made men who started with very little capital. In 1971, the Nigerian federal government reserved a number of small-scale manufacturing industries for Nigerians. The expatriate firms, for their part, in order to retain their popular image, have extensively Nigerianized their staff. At the higher levels Nigerians have been appointed to nominal directorships and to posts involving public

[20] See Peter Kilby, *Industrialization in an open economy: Nigeria 1945–1966* (Cambridge University Press, 1969).

relations and labour management. Less often are they allowed to determine the economic policies of the company. For those so employed, the pattern of work and the style of living differ very little from those in the public services.

The politicizing of the local élite

So far in this study I have dealt separately with the local and the national élites. I come now to consider their mutual interaction.

The very anglicized Lagos creole élite had few links with Yoruba society in the provincial towns or in the rural areas. Even those men who in the thirties and forties became comparatively well educated and found jobs in Lagos tended to visit their homes infrequently, for there was little in their political activity to excite their interest. There were, of course, some exceptions. Awolowo, for instance, intervened actively in title disputes in his home town of Ikenne; Ikenne, however, is only thirty-five miles from Lagos. For the most part, the rural masses looked upon the national élite as alien, and would argue that rule by British administrators was preferable to government by this African élite. The British officials took the position, with some justification, that they understood the interests of the mass of the people better than those of their countrymen who so rarely moved outside Lagos.

With the first elections to national and regional parliaments in 1951, many of the politically active members of the national élite found themselves without a constituency, for a candidate had to be a native of the area in which he stood for election.[21] One or two did try to exploit rather tenuous links with a rural area, but were rejected either by the electorate or by the judiciary. The local communities put forward instead a large number of members of the local élite, both the wealthy traders and, more often, young schoolmasters. Few of these had ever engaged in any form of nationalist political activity, and in their manifestos rarely mentioned any political allegiance. They stressed rather the efforts which they had already made, or would make in the future, on behalf of their local communities.

The Action Group at this time was little more than a clique of educated professionals and businessmen with a very rudimentary party organization. In touring the provinces the leaders tended to visit the obas, as courtesy indeed demanded, and to rely on them to ensure the success of their nominees. The National Council of Nigeria and the Cameroons (NCNC) leaders, in contrast, did hold a few public meetings. The Action Group lobbied a few candidates and claimed them as its nominees, while the NCNC tended to claim many of the remainder. At this period the party leaders regarded their task as identifying the likely winners and attracting them to their fold. When the Action Group won the 1951 election in the Western Region, some winning candidates who had stood on the NCNC platform promptly changed sides.

When the Action Group party first assembled in Ibadan, it contained a nucleus of active politicians, to whom went most of the ministerial posts, together with a large group of almost apolitical members interested only in the welfare of their own towns. To the leaders fell the task of welding these into a group

[21] See P. C. Lloyd, 'The development of political parties in Western Nigeria', *American Political Science Review*, Sept. 1955, **49**.

and instructing them in party discipline. For the support of their party, they contributed one-tenth of their salaries to party funds.[22]

Party politics gradually seeped into the local communities of Yoruba country. It became generally accepted procedure for a town that wished to have its due share of those social services distributed by the apparently affluent government to support, at least overtly, the dominant party, and not to allow its elected representative to ally with the opposition, the NCNC. Furthermore, all manner of local conflicts and rivalries were exploited in the name of the parties. Thus the Ibadan had little love for the Ijebu, whom they regarded as traders and landlords draining the wealth of their town; and since the Ijebu were identified with the Action Group (Awolowo and many of the Lagos businessmen in the party were from that area), the Ibadan tended to support the NCNC. Again the rival factions in a chieftancy dispute would assume the party labels associated with their participants, backers or lawyers.

The educated élite represented by the Action Group did not wish to share power with the traditional rulers and chiefs.[23] Yet they both recognized the popular support enjoyed by the obas in their own communities and shared with all Yoruba the respect for that kingship which symbolized the culture and differentiated the Yoruba from neighbouring ethnic groups. The party's policy towards the obas seemed to rest on an ambivalence and on expediency. The obas and some of the senior chiefs constituted a House of Chiefs, many of whose members were educated. One oba, the Odemo of Ishara, had formerly been active in nationalist politics in Lagos, whilst others had belonged to the same social categories as maintained the Action Group. To curb the powers of the obas the Action Group tried successively during the fifties, first, to restrict obas to the ceremonial presidency of local government councils in lieu of the more active office of chairman; then to rule that in a contest for a traditional throne a literate candidate should have priority over an illiterate one; and finally, to give control over 'communal land' customarily vested in obas and chiefs to the elected councillors. Each of these manœuvres was defeated by the obas, though their victories were more apparent than real.

The obas, whilst retaining their rights and privileges, became increasingly dependent upon the Action Group. The powers to appoint and depose obas wielded by the colonial administration and scathingly criticized by Awolowo before 1949 were nevertheless retained by his government. As obas ran into trouble with their elected councils, the government could use its discretion in supporting them. A council's ultimate effective sanction lay in reducing or stopping the oba's salary, but the ministry could order it restored. Obas who overtly supported the NCNC, perhaps because it was the locally popular party, could be punished. The Alafin of Oyo was deposed in 1956 as an example to others. It is perhaps significant that the obas who accepted office as ministers without portfolio tended to be those in deepest conflict with their subjects.

After 1951, both the Action Group and the NCNC attempted to create a network of local party branches with a strong card-carrying membership. Their efforts were short-lived, however, and by 1953 little local organization existed. In 1954, the Action Group was heavily defeated in the Yoruba constituencies in the federal parliamentary elections; new taxes had been imposed in 1953 and

[22] *Ibid.*, p. 701.   [23] See Lloyd, 'Traditional rulers'.

the benefits were not yet apparent. To re-establish its reputation it participated much more actively in the ensuing local government elections, with the result that henceforth these were contested on a party basis. The elected councillors became, in effect, the core of the local party organization, anxious to sustain the government and thus their own privileged and often lucrative offices. In the late fifties and early sixties, as regional government politicians became more alienated from their electorate, as the Action Group split into factions led by Awolowo and his deputy Samuel Akintola, as political life became much more vicious and corrupt, so did these local politicians pay, often dearly, for their identification with one or other party.

Modern trends

Driving through the Yoruba countryside today, through the provincial towns and villages, one is struck by the absence of flamboyant new 'Brazilian' houses. In fact, many of those started in the fifties still remain uncompleted. Instead, on the margins of the towns, a ribbon development along the main roads, appear new houses of very modern design. But these, owned by members of the national élite—civil servants, professionals, businessmen living in Ibadan and Lagos—are week-end country residences. The absence of conspicuous housing does not necessarily mean that a local élite, of the type described in an earlier section, has ceased to exist. It does suggest, however, that the character of this group has radically altered. Some of the factors that account for the changes in local and national élites I shall consider in these concluding pages.

One reason for the apparent stagnation of the rural areas is the fall in real incomes from cocoa. In the early fifties, world prices for cocoa rose dramatically, though the farmers received but a small share of this increase (the remainder being appropriated by the Cocoa Marketing Board). In the succeeding years the producer price fixed by marketing boards has fluctuated without even reaching the earlier levels, whilst the cost of living has risen. Thus Helleiner estimates that the producer price in the early sixties was less than half that of a decade earlier.[24] The real *income* of the farmers did not fall quite as much, for the output of cocoa, largely as a result of disease control, increased somewhat. The costs of spraying, however, reduced the farmers' profits. This depression in turn must certainly have affected the incomes of the produce buyers and transporters.

In the second place, the wealthy local élite are probably spending their incomes in a different manner. The large house and car were but modern symbols for traditional values. The illiterate rich man, moreover, saw nothing untoward in sending one of his many sons to university and apprenticing another to a local craftsman; their differences in academic attainment were seen as a matter of destiny. Today, because an increasing number of men realize that education is a prerequisite for almost all occupations likely to confer élite status, they are sending more of their children to secondary-grammar schools. The growing number of these schools makes this possible. Furthermore, in devoting more of their income to the education of their own children, they not only have less to spend on more conspicuous consumption but also less to devote to sons of poor parents who gain admission to grammar schools but cannot afford the high fees

[24] Helleiner, *Peasant agriculture,* p. 90.

for tuition and board, now approximately £80 per annum, or equivalent to the total annual wage of a labourer. Again, one of the most lucrative forms of investment in the fifties and sixties was house-building in the cities. The rents paid by the immigrants often yielded the owner an annual return of 15 per cent or more. Such an income could be used to finance the education of children when one, in later years, had ceased active trading.

In the next place, the scale of operations in produce-buying and transporting has altered. In the early fifties almost all the produce buyers were agents of expatriate firms and were dependent on the favours of the local European agent. They were working for the most part, within their own towns and districts. Now that the expatriate firms have been withdrawn, Yoruba buyers have become licensed agents, selling directly to the Marketing Board. Similarly, with the expansion in internal trade some men have become very wealthy transporters operating large fleets of lorries. Their operations cover much wider areas than hitherto, sometimes making it necessary for them to move from their home towns to places more central to their activities. They thus become less dependent upon the goodwill and custom of the people of their home areas.

Still another explanation for the change in status, a corollary to the previous point, is that these businessmen are far more dependent upon their regional or federal government. Produce buyers must be licensed; contractors are graded, their category determining the value of official contracts they are allowed to undertake. The prosperity and the success of these men have thus become increasingly dependent on their relationships with strategically placed civil servants, with politicians and ministers, with military rulers.

For this reason, the patronage role of the local élite is changing substantially. To a decreasing degree are they local benefactors. They spend rather to ensure their children's future status than to attain popularity in their home towns. Political events, too, have modified this role. In the early fifties the local élite seem to have been universally admired. The autocratic, literate oba was popular with his people if not with his chiefs. Traders were rated according to their generosity. But in the course of the decade the population of the Yoruba towns became more deeply divided as local factions were enhanced by party rivalry. The oba, leaning heavily on the Action Group for support against hostile chiefs or elected councillors, ceased to enjoy the respect of those of his people who supported the NCNC. The later rift between the two Action Group factions led by Awolowo and Akintola, resulting in the imprisonment of Awolowo and the supporting of Akintola as regional premier by the Northern-dominated federal government, brought even more bitterness to local politics and considerable violence at election times. Men who had grasped the opportunity of allying themselves with the new rulers in Ibadan in order to gain favours, such as more contracts or the presidency of a customary court, later suffered as the tide of local opinion turned and their homes were looted, their cars burned. Few men emerged in the mid-sixties with their reputations untarnished.

Military rule has further diminished the patronage of the local élite. Since 1966, party political activity has been banned and all local government councils dissolved. The local government advisors, civil servants in the Ministry of Local Government, administer the provinces and districts directly through the pre-existing council offices. In some cases they are now assisted by advisory boards; in orders they consult local opinion as they please, selecting obas, chiefs, rich men, local teachers according not only to their presumed intelligence or influence but also to the whims of the administrator.

In the earlier period the members of the local élite, as staunch supporters of the party in power, acted as brokers between the senior politicians and the masses. In fact, the local businessman with the ear of a powerful minister could often get an administrative decision unfavourable to his client reversed. Such channels are now virtually closed, for the military élite has had few links with the rural area (though there are indications that the politically powerful among the high-ranking officers are beginning to behave in the manner associated with politicians). The military rulers are advised by the civil servants, whose influence has been strengthened by recent events.

As has been mentioned earlier, well-educated men with posts in Ibadan or Lagos tended, before 1950, to make infrequent visits to their home towns; they felt too alien there. Those with political aspirations did become locally active in the ensuing years. At the same time, the growing cadre of bureaucrats also began to play an active role in the affairs of their natal community. They were encouraged to pay frequent visits to and use their influence in the capital on behalf of the local projects. The more affluent among them have built the substantial houses of which we have spoken and return to them for periods of relaxation. It might be expected that the social life of the cities would restrict the opportunities for such visits. Improved mortuary facilities, however, now make it possible to hold the funerals of locally important people on the Saturday following death instead of within twenty-four hours, and even a week later if the social calendar becomes too crowded. No longer can the national élite plead that their work makes it impossible to attend such ceremonies. In consequence, it is at such gatherings, as well as at the week-day cocktail parties, that matters of importance are discussed; furthermore, these events draw the national élite far more closely into local affairs. It is now the civil servants and wealthy businessmen from Ibadan and Lagos, influential in the ministerial corridors, who are assuming the mantles of local patronage.

In describing the role of the literate oba I have said that he was often the most educated man in his town, and that his salary often approximated the incomes of affluent local businessmen. Few Nigerian senior civil servants were posted in the provinces at this period; the local executive class were lowly paid and usually subject to frequent transfer. This position has now changed. With the growth of the government machine and the Nigerianization of senior posts, divisional and district headquarters now have a substantial number of resident officials, though few of these are local men. More significant is the growth in numbers of secondary-grammar schools. In order to establish these institutions, local communities often 'conscripted' a university graduate from their own area, impressing upon him his duty towards his community. Other teachers, too, work in or near the place of their birth and, as highly educated and relatively affluent men, now exert considerable influence on the local scene.

Conclusion

In this discussion I have restricted myself to a somewhat narrow theme. I have described the origin and growth of two separate indigenous African élites: the one, a national élite, created through the establishment of secondary and university education and of bureaucratic structures in administration and business; the other, the local élites made up of traditional rulers and chiefs, farmers and businessmen, who exploited new economic and political opportunities consequent upon colonial rule. These two groups developed separately and for several decades remained socially distinct. But since Independence the members of the local élites have been drawn increasingly into political and economic activity at the national level. In the process they have, variously, withdrawn from the local scene or have lost their local prestige and influence. At the same time, members of the national élite have become increasingly involved in local affairs, and in many spheres of activity have to a large extent supplanted the local élite. I have illustrated this process from but one small part of Africa, one with which I am intimately familiar. I believe that the same process, subject to the variables outlined at the beginning of this study, is taking place elsewhere in Africa, although this sociological phenomenon may not have been documented by scholars. Political scientists have rarely studied the local community, and social anthropologists have preferred the village to the small provincial town. For Ghana, Owusu has chronicled political developments in Swedru and has shown how members of the local élite used the Convention People's Party to further their interests in the community.[25]

Another way of looking at this development of élites would be to focus upon emergent patterns of social stratification. How far have differences in income, life-style or power led, in the rural areas, to the growth of social classes and class consciousness? The growth of a category of wealthy farmers has been impeded, in most African states, by the absence of major technological improvements in agriculture (Africa has as yet had no green revolution) and by the communal holding of land; save in a few areas, landless agricultural labourers do not exist in any number. The emergence of wealthy traders and businessmen has already been described. These men have the money and influence to ensure that their children are well enough educated to become, in turn, members not so much of the local but of the national élite. But divisions in rural society based upon wealth have been overlaid by others, based upon kinship and ethnic ties, upon factions and relationships of clientage. The achievements of the trader with humble origins are admired and to be emulated. He is not seen as exploiting his neighbours; it is rather the functional interdependence of members of the community that is stressed.

The penetration of the national élite into the rural area in the manner described, and the growing dependence of the local élite upon the national élite has, however, made more apparent the development of a national social stratification. The oft-cited distinction between urban and rural areas, modern and traditional modes of life, is perpetuated with the identification of the modern towns with affluence, the traditional rural areas with poverty. But these are not to be seen as two discrete spheres. They are parts of a single economic system in which wealth is transferred from the rural areas to maintain the lavish styles of living of the national élite living in the capital and major provincial towns. A growing polarization between the élite—often loosely termed the 'government' by the poor—and the masses is to be seen in most African states, though the protests of the masses still remain to be effectively articulated.

[25] See M. Owusu, *Uses and abuses of political power* (University of Chicago Press, 1970).

BIBLIOGRAPHY

Ajayi, J. F. Ade. *Christian missions in Nigeria, 1841–1891: the making of a new élite.* London, 1965.

Awolowo, Obafemi. *Awo: the autobiography of Chief Obafemi Awolowo.* Cambridge University Press, 1960.

Bauer, P. T. *West African trade* . . . London, 1954.

Bradbury, R. E. 'Continuities in pre-colonial and colonial Benin politics (1897–1951)', in *History and social anthropology*, I. M. Lewis, ed. London, 1968.

Coleman, James S. *Nigeria: background to nationalism.* Berkeley and Los Angeles, University of California Press, 1958.

Galletti, R., K. D. S. Baldwin and I. O. Dina. *Nigerian cocoa farmers: an economic survey of Yoruba cocoa farming families* . . . London, Oxford University Press, 1956.

Helleiner, Gerald K. *Peasant agriculture, government, and economic growth in Nigeria.* Homewood, Ill., 1966.

Hopkins, A. G. 'Economic aspects of political movements in Nigeria and the Gold Coast 1918–1939', *Journal of African History*, 1966, **7**, no. 1.

Idowu, E. B. *Olódùmarè: God in Yoruba belief.* London, 1962.

Kilby, Peter. *Industrialization in an open economy: Nigeria 1945–1966.* Cambridge University Press, 1969.

Kopytoff, Jean Herskovits. *A preface to modern Nigeria: the 'Sierra Leoneans' in Yoruba, 1830–1890.* Madison, University of Wisconsin, 1965.

Lloyd, P. C. 'Agnatic and cognatic descent among the Yoruba', *Man*, 1966, n.s. **1**, no. 4.

'The development of political parties in Western Nigeria', *American Political Science Review*, Sept. 1955, **49.**

'Sacred kingship and government among the Yoruba', *Africa*, 1960, **30**, no. 3.

'The traditional political system of the Yoruba', *Southwestern Journal of Anthropology*, 1954, **10**, no. 4.

'Traditional rulers', in *Political parties and national integration in tropical Africa*, James S. Coleman and Carl G. Rosberg, Jr., eds.

'The Yoruba', in *Peoples of Africa*, James L. Gibbs, ed. New York, 1965.

Yoruba land law. London, Oxford University Press, 1962.

ed. *The new élites of tropical Africa.* London, Oxford University Press, 1966.

Owusu, M. *Uses and abuses of political power: a case study of continuity and change in the politics of Ghana.* University of Chicago Press, 1970.

Sklar, Richard L. *Nigerian political parties.* Princeton University Press, 1963.

CHAPTER 15

THE ECONOMIC ROLE OF NON-INDIGENOUS ETHNIC MINORITIES IN COLONIAL AFRICA

by

FLOYD DOTSON *and* LILLIAN O. DOTSON

The summer of 1860 found nine Europeans, six of whom were artisan missionaries trained at the Swiss Chrischona Institute near Basel, busy setting up a substantial workshop at Gafat, in the dominions of the reigning Ethiopian emperor, Theodore II.[1] They were assisted by a large work-force of Ethiopians reported to number a thousand. The shop that emerged is described as well-equipped with 'various machines' and a 'large and powerful' water-wheel. The primary intention, of course, was not production *per se* but rather to impart Christian faith and virtue, reinforced by a knowledge of the industrial arts sufficient to enable the beneficiaries to live a civilized life.

Missionaries were received by the Ethiopian emperors of this period with a large measure of ambivalence—an ambivalence shared to some degree with virtually every other indigenous ruler in Africa. But in Ethiopia this ambivalence was compounded: in their own eyes, if not in the view of outsiders, the Amharic overlords of the country *were* Christians, and they deeply resented the implication that their people needed any instruction in this sphere. On the other hand, missionaries with industrial or scientific skills appeared to be worth tolerating, and this particular group had been warmly welcomed.

Relations turned tense, however, when an order came down from the emperor to produce a cannon. The missionaries demurred at Theodore's request, not on pacifist grounds but on the perfectly reasonable ones of lack of competence. None of them, they pointed out, was experienced in founding.[2] But Theodore was a vitriolically tempered autocrat, not used to taking no for an answer. He demanded that the missionary artisans carry out his order forthwith. To reinforce his point, he put their Ethiopian servants in chains and announced that they would not be released until the cannon was produced.

Any of these intelligent and ingenious men would presumably have ranked high on David C. McClelland's *n*-achievement scale.[3] Fortunately, they were also literate. By consulting technical manuals they were able to form some

---

[1] Richard Pankhurst, *Economic history of Ethiopia: 1800–1935* (Addis Ababa, Haile Sellassie I University Press, 1968), pp. 53–5.

[2] One of the three non-missionaries was a French gunsmith; another, of vaguely Polish origins, seems to have been an ex-soldier. These cosmopolitan adventurers had found their way independently to Ethiopia (*ibid.*, p. 54).

[3] David C. McClelland, *The achieving society* (Princeton, 1961). Most of the contemporary research in the substantive area of this essay—in what we will call group-specific capabilities—is psychologically oriented, *à la* McClelland. As the reference to the critical importance of literacy in the next sentence suggests, our emphasis here is historical, cultural and sociological rather than psychological. But there is no inherent contradiction between the two approaches, which are in fact complementary.

conception of how to proceed. Although their initial efforts were failures, on the third try they produced a workable mortar complete with an explosive shell. When the time came for an official demonstration, the first ball from the first cannon to be produced entirely in Ethiopia of local materials roared through the air and exploded with a resounding crash among the nearby hills. Theodore was intensely delighted at this technical *tour de force* of 'his' Europeans—and so, we may safely guess, were his hostages.[4]

From the perspective to be developed in this essay, the case of Ethiopia becomes an especially interesting one, since it provides a kind of 'natural experiment', as it were, in which the strictly economic attractions offered by non-African immigrants may be studied in a 'free market' context, apart from the coercive framework of imperial political control. If we may discount the brief Italian occupation after 1936, Ethiopia was the only country in Africa except Liberia that retained its independence throughout the colonial period. It did so, of course, because it was able to organize sufficient military power to protect itself, not through any extraordinary benevolence of the Europeans.

That the Ethiopians were able to organize an effective response to armed imperialistic assault furnishes in itself conclusive evidence that they already had in fact what elsewhere in modern Africa had to be created out of myth and half-forgotten legend: a 'great empire' and a 'great civilization'.[5] Without going into details—amply provided by Richard Pankhurst—we may make the general observation that the indigenous economy and technology of Ethiopia were in many respects as advanced (compared to the rest of Africa *circa* 1870) as its literate religious tradition and its relatively complex political institutions. Yet in terms of strictly modern cultural and socio-economic characteristics taken for granted today in the poorest countries of the world, the list of Ethiopia's deficiencies down to the twentieth century is formidable indeed. Roads were nothing but worn paths. Bridges across the numerous rivers and streams of this mountainous country were nonexistent. The native building tradition was rudimentary: bricks were imported into Addis Ababa until a local supply became available in 1907 through European initiative. Until the early part of the century, there was no local currency, the common medium of exchange being salt. There were no inns or hotels, and of course no doctors or dentists. A little local trade had always existed; and from time immemorial some foreign trade in slaves, gold, ivory and civet musk had been conducted by Arabs and native Muslims across the Red Sea. But modern trade involving credit facilities and written communication with distant suppliers of manufactured goods awaited introduction by foreigners.

Ethiopian interest in foreigners, as we have seen in the story of the missionary artisans, was dominated in the first instance by a desire for arms and munitions. Nonetheless, Theodore and his successors, particularly Menilek II,

---

[4] The missionaries were well rewarded: they were given 'shirts of honour, horses and mules with gold and silver trappings, and 1,000 [Maria Theresa] dollars apiece'—all this *and* Ethiopian wives, as an inducement to stay in the country (Pankhurst, *Economic history of Ethiopia*, p. 55).

[5] In terms of later political and economic developments, there is no question that the Ethiopians ultimately paid a very heavy price for their independence. But that is a different theme from the one pursued here. See Francis A. J. Ianni, 'Ethiopia: a special case', in *The transformation of East Africa: studies in political anthropology*, Stanley Diamond and Fred G. Burke, eds. (New York, 1966), pp. 407–27; also L. H. Gann and Peter Duignan, *Burden of empire: an appraisal of Western colonialism in Africa south of the Sahara* (New York, 1967), pp. 365–7.

were able to see that Ethiopia needed more of Western culture than arms alone.[6] Under Menilek's aggressive policy of general modernization, the flow of non-African immigrants into Ethiopia increased greatly towards the end of the nineteenth century. These tended to concentrate in the capital, the very construction of which depended upon their artisan skills. By 1910, the non-African population resident in the country stood at something like a thousand. By 1935, it had increased to about 14,500.[7]

This 'foreign community', as Pankhurst points out, was much more cosmopolitan than in the colonial dependencies, where most non-Africans were by the nature of the case citizens of the imperial power.[8] In terms of ethnic origin, Arabs, Greeks, Indians and Armenians were the most numerous. After them, in numbers, came the French and the Italians. Of the dozen or so other nationalities represented the most numerous were British and Americans. A few Swedes and Russians are mentioned, too.

Functionally, two broad groupings appear clearly in Pankhurst's description—advanced Western Europeans and Orientals—with the suggestion of a third made up of marginal Europeans.

The French, who were the most important of the smaller communities, were both wealthy and influential, and included several large traders [in arms, particularly] . . . The Germans included . . . a small number of professional people, among them one or two doctors and a pharmacist . . . The British community comprised the governor of the Bank of Abyssinia and several members of his staff, as well as a handful of merchants and missionaries . . . The Swiss included several wealthy traders . . . The Russians . . . consisted of several military officers as well as some hospital doctors and an artist.[9]

The Orientals, too, were a diversified population, with Arabs, Armenians and Indians predominating. Foreign Jews (estimated at only 125 persons in 1935) were never numerous; nor, strange as it may seem, were Lebanese. On the functional level, Orientals participated in the local economy in two main areas: as artisans and in small- and medium-scale trade. Pankhurst describes Arabs, for example, as 'largely merchants, camel drivers and sellers and readers of the Koran'; Arab merchants were 'in many cases in close commercial contact with trading houses in Aden'.[10] Armenians were for the most part humble people 'engaged in small-scale trade and handicrafts . . . as ironmongers, goldsmiths, saddlers, tailors, embroiderers, upholsterers and photographers'.[11] Indians first entered the country as artisans and builders 'who . . . could knock-up buildings for half the price demanded by Greeks or a quarter of that required by Italians'.[12] After the turn of the century, however, Indians became increasingly prominent in trade and 'flooded the market with cotton cloths, spices, perfumes and other imports mainly from the East'. Pankhurst adds, in the already stereotyped terminology of his source, 'The longer established French firms found great difficulty in competing'.[13]

---

[6] Theodore, in the unfortunate correspondence with Queen Victoria that eventually led to his ruin, had specifically asked for engineers and doctors from England (Pankhurst, *Economic history of Ethiopia*, p. 11).   [7] *Ibid.*, pp. 62 and 65. For more recent statistics, see Table 131.
[8] Pankhurst, *Economic history of Ethiopia*, p. 61. Although formally correct, Pankhurst's generalization may leave an impression of greater homogeneity in the colonies than in fact existed. See Tables 129 and 130.   [9] Pankhurst, *Economic history of Ethiopia*, p. 63.
[10] *Ibid.*   [11] *Ibid.*   [12] *Ibid.*   [13] *Ibid.*, p. 398.

This broad and fundamental distinction between, on the one hand, an advanced Western European group performing functions related to high finance, international trade, science and technology, and, on the other, a larger diversified group of Orientals engaged in highly skilled but traditional-type handicraft industry and small-scale trade, might suggest an invidiously 'racial' division of labour if it were not contradicted by the prominent presence of some marginal Europeans. Italians, for example, had high status not only as 'architects and entrepreneurs' but also as 'employees of the Ministry of Posts and Telegraphs'.[14] But many Italians were merely manual labourers in a country that traditionally denigrated any form of manual work. The point is even sharper with respect to the Greeks, some of whom again were successful as traders and as restaurant and bar proprietors. But even more Greeks than Italians were humble manual labourers, an identification that seems to have given all Greeks a peculiarly low status. In the words of a contemporary observer, as quoted by Pankhurst, 'they were often referred to as *yafaranje barya,* or "slave of the foreigners", it being popularly believed that they were slaves in Europe'.[15]

Ethnic specific capabilities

What foreigners in their varying capacities imported into Ethiopia was in the main 'non-material capital' in the sense in which S. Herbert Frankel used the term in his pioneer work on African economic development nearly forty years ago.[16] As Frankel points out in an intellectually penetrating (if somewhat clumsily phrased) passage, non-material capital consists of more than merely skills and technical knowledge; and, for a given time and place, it tends to be highly *group* specific. It is not, in short, the freely available, free-floating entity that it is too often and too lightly assumed to be.

Much confusion . . . arises from the fact that trade and international investment are considered abstractly. In practice, the provision of capital, the development of new products and the expansion of commerce are not processes that occur *in vacuo.* Their success inevitably depends on innumerable personal and political connections of, and on the vast store of accumulated knowledge and experience possessed by countless special groups in the metropolitan countries and their commercial and financial representatives in Africa.[17]

Among Frankel's great virtues as a social and economic analyst is his unrelenting sense of realism in a field where, unfortunately, unrealism abounds. Economic change in modern Africa, we are reminded in the passage just

[14] *Ibid.,* p. 63. [15] *Ibid.,* p. 64.
[16] S. Herbert Frankel, *Capital investment in Africa: its course and effects* (London, Oxford University Press, 1938), p. 4: 'The term "capital" will be used both in its narrow sense, and in a wider sense to include things which are not easily valued in money or easily saleable or purchasable. This is very necessary if the importance to Africa of the resources on which it has been able to draw from Europe, and the use of those resources are to be properly assessed. There is, in fact, no hard and fast line between that which is, and that which is not capital, or between "material" and "non-material" capital.' On occasion, Frankel uses Cannan's more colourful but less precise phrase, 'the heritage of improvement', as a synonym for non-material capital (*ibid.*). See also Frankel, 'Some aspects of investment and economic development in the continent of Africa', *Africa,* 1952, **22**, no. 1, pp. 50–8. [17] Frankel, *Capital investment,* p. 28.

quoted, has not happened magically *in vacuo,* nor simply as a result of a vague and mysterious intellectual contagion from Europe and elsewhere. Instead, it has taken place (and could only have taken place in the form in which it has) *through a linked chain of social groups and individuals with very specific historically determined characteristics.* By no means are all such economically relevant characteristics *ethnically* specific. But many of them are, and it is this fact that provides us with our particular focus of attention in the present essay.

'Non-material capital' will be retained here for occasional reference, particularly when the connotation is 'investment' as Frankel originally conceived it. Yet implicitly, if not quite explicitly, Frankel himself recognized that nonmaterial capital is composed of two fundamentally different components, which for our purposes it is important to separate analytically. One of these is *cultural:* 'accumulated knowledge and experience'. The other is *social* or organizational: Frankel's 'personal and political connections'. Together, these constitute the foundation for effective action and are in practice always tightly interrelated functionally. But phenomenologically they are not the same thing, and they may and do vary independently.

Realistically viewed, people can do only what they cognitively know how to do. The thousand Ethiopians at Gafat, for instance, could not have produced a cannon unaided if they had sweated at the task to the end of their days. Narrowly defined, this is the strictly cultural component in ethnic specific capabilities of economic significance. But it is also true that all significant human behaviour, economic and otherwise, is socially organized. What people learn, culturally, is always in the first place a direct function of their group membership. Moreover, in a given concrete case, what people can or cannot do is often as much or more a matter of their 'personal and political connections' as it is of 'knowledge and experience' as such. The fact must be frankly faced, especially in Africa but certainly not peculiar to it, that group-specific capabilities may include the social and political power to restrict and control the acquisition and exercise of 'knowledge and experience' by others.[18] It is this social

[18] For a concrete case conveniently exemplifying these generalizations, we may consider a little drama that used to take place daily on the Northern Rhodesia–Congo frontier. From the driver's seat of trains coming south from Elisabethville, a black African stepped down to be replaced by a white Rhodesian. Explaining why a black African, anywhere in Africa, drives a locomotive ultimately involves an exercise in cultural history. Locomotives, like nearly everything else 'manmade . . . that stands more than six feet above the ground', were brought to the Congo by Europeans; and the requisite skills and cognitive knowledge necessary to drive them were without question ethnically specific to Europeans up to the time they were imparted to Africans. But culture alone, quite obviously, does not explain why Africans drove locomotives in the Congo *circa* 1960 and not in Northern Rhodesia. For this we must move beyond the sphere of culture *per se* to that of social organization, which universally includes principles—of sex, age, class, race or 'ability'—for determining who in the given social order has access to particular known cultural content and, conversely, who is to be denied such access.

Group capacity—defined simply, straightforwardly and empirically, as to what people can (or, negatively, cannot) do—involves both determinants, and both therefore must be taken into account in realistic and comprehensive analysis.

The reference to the Congo is from George Martelli, *Leopold to Lumumba: a history of the Belgian Congo 1877–1960* (London, 1962), p. 215. For a brief discussion of the differentiating circumstances under which Africans were trained as skilled railway workers in the Congo, see Lewis H. Gann, *The birth of a plural society: the development of Northern Rhodesia under the British South Africa Company 1894–1914* (Manchester University Press, 1958), p. 131, n. 5.

and political projection of ethnic phenomena, culturally and economically defined, that turns the ethnic group into the 'ethnic minority', as the term 'ethnic minority' is currently understood in the modern social sciences.

Advanced and less advanced minorities

A minority, by existing sociological usage, is defined as a disadvantaged, underprivileged, politically weak group that is exploited and discriminated against by a dominant power-holding group. In a working democracy, the social minority tends to be a statistical minority as well; but sophisticated sociologists have long refused to recognize sheer numbers as the determining criterion of minority status. It is pointed out, for example, that whites throughout the 'black-belt' counties of the American Old South are by definition less numerous than blacks. Yet no American sociologist would dream of calling these whites a minority. By extension, the same sociologists are apt to point to the social structure of South Africa as a virtually identical situation, in which a small dominant group holds coercive sway over a 'minority' composed of 80 per cent of the population.[19]

This is, to say the least, terminologically straining the legitimate point that what creates minority status is social and political power and not sheer numbers alone. The Europeans of Rhodesia today are clearly the dominant group. To call them a minority, which statistically speaking they certainly are, directly flies in the face of established usage. On the other hand, to call the 95 per cent of the population that is African a minority violates—if nothing else—one's sense of arithmetical proportion. To complicate matters, established terminological order again happily reigns across the Zambezi. There, Europeans, many of whom are blood-related to the white Rhodesians, are now clearly a minority, politically speaking.

It is apparent from these examples that something much more fundamental than mere terminological confusion is at issue. As so often happens in social science, technical terms and their associated concepts that are appropriate in one context are bound to that context and do not have universal applicability. The fact is that 'minorities' in modern Africa and minorities in the liberal democracy of the industrialized West are empirically different phenomena that cannot easily be equated. Algerians and West Africans in France, West Indians and Pakistanis in Britain, Puerto Ricans and southern blacks in the northern cities of the United States have in common, despite their great variation in ethnographic detail, an origin in economically backward or depressed areas. Not only are they subjectively perceived by the members of the receiving host society as inferior (and thus suitable for discrimination); objectively speaking they lack the culturally engendered capabilities that would fit them for socioeconomic participation at an equal level. By contrast, the immigrant minorities of the old colonial dependencies of Africa and South-East Asia derived, virtually without exception, from societies more technologically and economically

---

[19] This standard conception of the minority, complete with the two empirical illustrations cited, can be found in Arnold M. Rose, 'Minorities', *International encyclopedia of the social sciences* (New York, 1968), vol. x, pp. 365–71. For an application to Africa, which implicitly (but not explicitly) recognizes some of the conceptual complications dealt with here, see Elizabeth Hopkins, 'Racial minorities in British East Africa', in *Transformation of East Africa,* pp. 83–153.

advanced than the one to which they came. Judged by capacity to perform in a 'modern' as opposed to a 'traditional' setting, they were objectively superior to the local people; and this superiority was perceived subjectively not only by themselves but also (however grudgingly) by the host population as well. In such situations, where relations of superiority and inferiority are diametrically reversed from what they are in the liberal democracy, it follows inevitably that the dynamics of inter-group interaction are not and cannot be the same, nor do the usual sociological assumptions based upon Western experience apply.[20] The truer parallel to the African situation, as Lewis H. Gann has suggested in a highly original and illuminating observation, is that of Eastern Europe during the early modern period, where culturally advanced white 'minorities' confronted culturally backward and economically underdeveloped white 'majorities'—or, as we would prefer to call them, base populations.[21]

Perhaps, given these ambiguities, it would be best to avoid the term 'minority' altogether, or to confine it to such situations as that of relations between Bantu and Bushman, where the traditional usage applies without modification.[22] Actually, 'minority' conveys little meaning not adequately covered by the more neutrally toned 'ethnic group', except a vague connotation of political and social grievance. The term, nonetheless, like many others equally unsatisfactory in the social sciences, is very firmly established; and we take the position that it is not profitable to quarrel over words. What is essential is to recognize empirically significant differences between ethnic groups where they exist: specifically, in the present instance, those differences in cultural evolution that translate into important differences in economic capabilities.[23]

[20] We are quite aware that 'superiority' and 'inferiority' are terms so heavily loaded with negative connotations that most social scientists now assiduously avoid them in discussions of inter-ethnic relations. In the process, however, some very real problems of socio-cultural evolution and contemporary organization, understandable only in terms of profoundly important group differences, tend to be either swept out of sight or hopelessly muffled in euphemisms. We have argued elsewhere at some length that the now all but universally accepted doctrine of cultural relativism is a primary stumbling-block to the development of adequate 'minority group' theory. (Floyd Dotson and Lillian O. Dotson, *The Indian minority of Zambia, Rhodesia, and Malawi* [New Haven, Yale University Press, 1968], *passim*, but esp. pp. 395–409.)

It must be understood, nonetheless, that 'superiority' and 'inferiority' are meaningless terms unless we are specific as to what, precisely, is being compared. Close examination within context will usually show that what the relativist maintains so earnestly is the inherent moral worth and dignity of all cultures when evaluated in their own terms. But this premise is not at issue in the present essay. We are concerned here with empirical capabilities of economic relevance in what we believe to be an entirely objective sense. Surely, it can be agreed, the artisan missionaries at Gafat were superior to the indigenous Ethiopians in their capabilities *for cannon production*—and it is in this strictly empirical sense that our use of the terms 'superior' and 'inferior', 'advanced' and 'less advanced' is to be construed.

[21] Lewis H. Gann, 'Liberal interpretations of South African history', *Rhodes–Livingstone Institute Journal*, 1959, no. 25, pp. 40–58. See also Lewis H. Gann and Peter Guignan, *White settlers in tropical Africa* (Baltimore, 1962), pp. 67–8 and 124–6; and Dotson and Dotson, *Indian minority*, pp. 1–3.

[22] For some concrete examples, see Adam Kuper, *Kalahari village politics: an African democracy* (Cambridge University Press, 1970). The point is very incidental to Kuper's major emphasis; nonetheless, a reading of this short monograph alone should correct the easy notion that abuse and exploitation of weak groups by stronger ones are peculiarly European phenomena, even in contemporary Africa.

[23] In a comment upon an earlier version of this section, our editors pointed out that not all minorities in 'the liberal democracies of the industrialized West' fit without qualification the picture drawn in the text, and that in the liberal democracies, too, 'the word "minority" is used in an

Afrikaners: a negative case

Except for the administrative personnel of the colonial services and the settler-farmers of some highly localized areas, the advanced Western Europeans, the Orientals and the European marginals who came to Ethiopia are broadly representative of non-indigenous immigration into Africa after 1870; and it is significant of the structure of world-wide socio-economic developments at the time that these immigrants came in roles and even in proportions not so very different from those of the rest of the continent. The British banker, the German doctor and the Indian trader resident in Ethiopia *circa* 1910 had exact functional counterparts elsewhere, although they may have been Belgian, French or Lebanese by nationality.

The largest single non-indigenous ethnic group in contemporary Africa, however, was not represented in Ethiopia, nor is it composed of recent immigrants. In recognition of their near-indigenous status, Afrikaners quite self-consciously call themselves Africans, which is all that 'Afrikaner' means in Afrikaans. From our point of view, they become exceedingly interesting as still another 'natural experiment', this time with the factor of 'race' being held constant. Although Western European in origin, it was the Afrikaners' paradoxical fate, through long isolation and special socio-economic adaptation, to become a backward 'minority' vis-à-vis later culturally advanced immigrants of essentially similar genetic composition. From this perspective, therefore, much of the Afrikaners' frontier history reads as if they were simply another indigenous African people, forced by the exigencies of invasion and conquest to come to terms with a more economically and technologically advanced ethnic group.

Of course this is only partially and imperfectly true. 'Advanced' and 'less advanced', as we have been careful to point out, are relative terms that acquire concrete meaning only through comparison and contrast. Vis-à-vis Africans, the trekboers had three possessions associated with the cultural tradition of their European past that proved decisive in military conflict: the horse, the ox wagon and the rifle. Of great significance, too, is the fact that Afrikaners never lost, either in their own eyes or in those of others, their psycho-social identity as Europeans; and morally and politically this European identity was critical to them for re-entry (if that is quite the word) into the modern world. Furthermore, it

ambiguous and sometimes an arbitrary fashion'. They went on to say: 'For some, a minority is a separate group with its own ethnic, religious, or cultural identity. For others, the word "minority" has humanitarian connotations; "minorities" are thus defined only if they are, or if they are believed to be, subject to specific disabilities. For instance, some would regard the Jews in Great Britain as a minority with distinctive characteristics, subject to prejudice on the part of many of their compatriots. Others argue that Jews are fully integrated into British society, that prejudice has not prevented Jews from gaining wealth, position, or social esteem. Hence Jews are no longer a "true" minority in Great Britain. Minority status is thus accorded only to more recent immigrants, to West Indians, Nigerians, or Pakistanis, who not only have their own cultural characteristics, but may also be subject to economic discrimination. Many British people moreover believe dark-skinned newcomers to be socially and culturally inferior to the majority in a manner not attributed to British subjects of, say, Polish or Jewish origins.

'By comparison, the immigrant minorities of the colonial dependencies are easily and unambiguously identified. They are, on the average, much wealthier, even though they do not necessarily owe their income to their ability to manipulate the state machinery. (Neither the Chinese in Indonesia, the Indians in Kenya, nor the Lebanese in West Africa were ever accorded special rights, even though politicians often accused them of being "privileged".) But in economic terms, they came from relatively advanced groups deriving from alien societies.'

must be remembered that Afrikaners taken as a whole were far from being entirely homogeneous. By comparison with contemporary European immigrants, the old-style *platteland* Boer *circa* 1870 was distinctly backward in certain critical respects. But the wealthy wine-grower of the Western Cape or the respectable burgher of the Old World port city of Cape Town was very different from the rough and semi-literate frontiersman. And even with respect to this frontiersman, the archetype of the Afrikaner to come, selective emphasis from what in fact was a considerable array of wealth and status groupings can all too easily make the trekboer out as either more primitive or more civilized than he actually was.

Fortunately for us, narrowing the focus down to group-specific economic capabilities makes the problem much simpler. However varied in his other characteristics, the trekboer, as Gann and Duignan describe him, was a 'frontier-farmer specialist'. In this capacity he was adept and resourceful, but he had no other skills.[24] For goods and services that he did not produce, he depended entirely upon foreigners. The *smous* who brought him sugar and coffee, clothing and cloth, simple hardware and the all-important shot and gunpowder was British or, increasingly as the nineteenth century advanced, a Jew. Even the *predikant* of the Dutch Reformed Church during most of the nineteenth century was a foreigner, as were the majority of the few clerks and secretaries of the Boer governments. The constitutions of both the Orange Free State and the South African Republic (Transvaal) were drafted in good part, not accidentally it would seem, by immigrant Hollanders.[25] In a direct parallel with his contemporary, the Emperor Menilek, President Kruger imported British artisans from Natal for the construction of government buildings at his capital, Pretoria.

The established order which Afrikaners traditionally knew upon the basis of two hundred years of adaptation was as rudely shattered by thrusts from the outside as it was for any other African people. After the diamond discoveries at Kimberley, the economic foundations of South African society shifted rapidly from backward pastoral agriculture to highly sophisticated industry, one of the most technologically advanced and demanding in the world in fact. For this transition the Afrikaner was completely unprepared. As Laurence Salomon notes, 'No laboring class, skilled or unskilled, existed among the white population [of South Africa], and the Coloured artisans of the small Cape enterprises were neither numerous nor available.' Initially, therefore, skilled labour for the mines had to be imported, as it did (with many Afrikaners now included) into the Northern Rhodesian Copper Belt half a century later. Only gradually did Afrikaners enter the mines. 'In 1910, forty years after the Kimberley fields were opened and 18 years after the beginning of deep level mining on the Witwatersrand, 72·8 per cent of the 7,255 white, skilled mine employees were immigrants.'[26]

With a few minor exceptions, such as transport and haulage, Afrikaners were at first unable to take advantage of the opportunities in secondary industry and

[24] Gann and Duignan, *White settlers*, pp. 28–9; Gann and Duignan, *Burden of Empire*, pp. 177–8.

[25] Leonard Thompson, 'Co-operation and conflict: the high veld', in *The Oxford history of South Africa*, vol. I: *South Africa to 1870*, Monica Wilson and Leonard Thompson, eds. (New York, Oxford University Press, 1969), pp. 428–9.

[26] Laurence Salomon, 'The economic background to the revival of Afrikaner nationalism', in *Boston University Papers in African History*, vol. I, Jeffrey Butler, ed. (Boston University Press, 1966), pp. 223 and 225.

commerce suddenly created by the emergence of mining. The shops in the little *dorps* that sprang up over the high veld after the coming of the money economy were commonly operated by Jews, most of whom were recent immigrants among the 400,000 Europeans who flooded into South Africa between 1875 and 1904.[27] Even in agriculture the Afrikaner found himself largely frustrated. After the railways were built, it was sometimes cheaper to import food from agriculturally efficient areas overseas than to produce it in South Africa; and after 1870, for most of the rapidly growing rural population the old-style pastoral agriculture became an increasingly obsolete option as a way of life.

The result of these converging forces was the 'Poor White' problem, long the staple component in South African sociology, but now half-forgotten in the light of recent prosperity and politics. The statistics gathering dust on library shelves are startling to one exposed to them for the first time. Nearly half of South Africa's white population, the half consisting almost entirely of Afrikaners, was classified as 'poor' by the Carnegie Commission of 1931; and no less than 17·5 per cent of these met the 'Poor White' criteria, meaning 'in dire poverty' or unable to live except by 'charity'.[28]

The fundamental reason for the Afrikaner's poverty was inability to participate fully in the most productive part of the economy, a not unusual situation in advanced industrial societies. An occupational breakdown of the 1921 census by birth (South African and foreign-born) shows that from two-thirds to three-fourths of all independent professionals, merchants and corporate executives were immigrants; even half the plumbers and carpenters were. By contrast, only 10 per cent and 5·8 per cent of the white unskilled labourers and farmers, respectively, were born outside South Africa.

Marked social and economic progress among Afrikaners was hardly apparent before 1920, and real prosperity was delayed until the Second World War. Generally speaking, however, the economic disparity between Afrikaners and other whites in South Africa remained great throughout the period covered in the present volume; and, although continually narrowing, it still exists today. Calculations from 1951 census figures show *per capita* income of Afrikaners of the Witwatersrand region to be only £182, or not much more than half the £349 enjoyed by English-speaking whites.[29] Interestingly and perhaps very significantly, because in both cases we are considering depressed groups of a formerly rural and agricultural people caught up in the demands of a highly developed urban and industrial way of life, this differential is remarkably similar to that between whites and blacks in the United States for the same period.[30]

Economic standing tends universally to correspond fairly closely with social class—or, better in this instance, with what Max Weber called 'social honour'.

[27] A brief reference to these Jewish shopkeepers is made by Edwin S. Munger, *African field reports: 1952–1961* (Cape Town, 1961), p. 494.

[28] Salomon, 'Economic background to . . . Afrikaner nationalism', pp. 231–2.

[29] *Ibid.*, p. 235. See also Sheila Patterson, *The last trek: a study of the Boer people and the Afrikaner nation* (London, 1957), pp. 163 and 171. For more recent data of a similar nature, see David Welsh, 'Urbanisation and the solidarity of Afrikaner nationalism', *Journal of Modern African Studies*, 1969, **7**, no. 2, p. 270.

[30] In 1950, the ratio of non-white to white median family income was 0.54 (U.S., Bureau of the Census, *Statistical abstract of the United States: 1971* [Washington, D.C., 1971], p. 316). Estimated *per capita* income and family income are not, we recognize, directly comparable statistics.

In the complicated society of South Africa—at once so sophisticated and so miserably backward—Afrikaners have consistently found themselves at the bottom of the European population in respect to overall status. And significantly it is not only the British, as it might be assumed, who have taken this down-the-nose attitude. The degree to which the Afrikaners' social honour has been determined economically and culturally is better illustrated by their relations to two groups with whom they might be expected to identify more closely.

The relatively well-to-do and better-educated German settlers of South-West Africa, it is reported by Edwin S. Munger, have generally adopted a patronizing manner towards Afrikaners, both for their uncouthness (as perceived by Germans) and for their poverty, which to the German mind indicates incompetence and slothfulness.[31] An even more instructive case is provided by Afrikaner relations with immigrant Hollanders, who have come to southern and eastern Africa in considerable numbers since the Second World War. Urbane and well-educated for the most part, the new arrivals have quickly established themselves in the economy and society of South Africa at a level commensurate with their superior skills. Some Afrikaners are reported by Munger to envy and resent the intrusion of these *kaaskoppe* (cheese-heads), while a good many Hollanders profess to be embarrassed by the 'crudity' of their ethnic cousins and by the linguistic peculiarities of Afrikaans.[32]

However, group-specific capabilities, we must remember, include by our definition more than mere technical skills and special knowledge. Political capabilities are just as real, and often they are more effective. Using parliamentary institutions bequeathed them by the British, Afrikaners of the Union long sought (and with considerable success) political solutions to their economic problems. *In this they have reacted, as in so many other respects, in ways highly typical of modern Africa, black or white as the case may be.* Their support of the farmers' bloc succeeded at first in diverting vast sums earned from the mines into subsidies for their often under-capitalized and inadequately managed agriculture. Later, Nationalist leaders tried to serve their Afrikaner con-

---

[31] Munger, *African field reports,* pp. 456–7. Theodor Leutwein, the administrator of German South-West Africa between 1894 and 1905, discouraged the settlement of Boers whose cattle-raising methods he regarded as too backward for the modern rational ranching he envisaged for the area (Helmut Bley, 'Social discord in South West Africa, 1894–1904', in *Britain and Germany in Africa: imperial rivalry and colonial rule,* Prosser Gifford and William R. Louis, eds., assisted by Alison Smith [New Haven, Yale University Press, 1967], p. 613).

[32] Munger, *African field reports,* pp. 471–8.

EDITORS' NOTE: Despite current stereotypes expressed in ethnic jokes such as the 'Van der Merwe' stories, Afrikaners did advance in the economic field. The process began when the country's economy became more diversified and South Africa's economic frontier began to shift northward. During the second part of the nineteenth century, enterprising Afrikaners, reared on farms, began to enter into a variety of middle-level jobs, become artisans, prospectors, labour managers, military officers, mine supervisors and also entering service occupations. A picturesque case history is provided by the career of Johannes Wilhelm Colenbrander (1855–1918). The son of a Dutch settler in Natal, Colenbrander became successively a trumpeter in the Natal Mounted Rifles, a frontier trader in Zululand and in Swaziland, an agent of the British South Africa Company at the court of Lobengula in Matabeleland, the leader of a Coloured mercenary unit during the Matabele rising in 1896, a cattle-dealer, a labour recruiter, a mining claims-inspector and manager of the Redrup's Kop Mine in Rhodesia. After an adventurous life, Colenbrander was accidentally drowned when acting the part of the British commander-in-chief in a movie depicting the Zulu War of 1879. For his papers, see Historical Manuscripts Collection of the National Archives of Rhodesia (MS NA), CO 4.

stituents through a government-enforced colour-bar in industry. (Significantly, they were initially coached in these matters by the more politically experienced British trade unionists.) Finally, in 1948, Afrikaners achieved their ultimate political goal: undisputed control of the Union government, with its entrenched system of politically imposed economic restrictions, privileges, and prerogatives.

Non-Afrikaner farmers

Afrikaners were the pioneer European farmers in Africa, and they still constitute by a wide margin the largest single non-African ethnic group in agriculture. But the modern Afrikaner farmer, now as thoroughly westernized in his conception of agriculture as in other spheres of life, is a far cry indeed from the eighteenth- and nineteenth-century frontiersman, who was a product of a long period of informal and largely unconscious adaptation. (For an example, see Case I, pp. 602–3.) In some respects, particularly in his herding methods and use of auxiliary labour, the trekboer of old was closer to the aboriginal pastoralist of the Cape than he was to the progressive European farmer in Western Europe and North America, *circa* 1870.

By 1870, in Western Europe and North America, the scientific and technological revolution in agriculture was far advanced. Ethnically, however, this revolution was then strictly confined to Western Europeans. Its transfer to Africa, therefore, depended as much upon the immigration of representatives of this group as from the fields of medicine and engineering. Scientific agriculture, quite patently, could not have come from either the Africans or the trekboers.

The British settlement of Natal offers an instructive example of some of the socio-cultural processes involved in this transfer. Natal, as Alan F. Hattersley points out, attracted a rather special type of settler. In this period poor Britons without either money or skills were much more likely to go to America or Australia. Many of the original Natal immigrants were farmers from the most progressive agricultural regions of England. Some, particularly those responsible for the establishment of the sugar industry, were experienced planters from Mauritius and the West Indies.[33]

It is noteworthy, however, that some of the most innovative people in agricultural development had had no previous agricultural background; and the same pattern was later to be repeated many times in the Rhodesias and Kenya. Daniel de Pass is a prime early example. Son of a well-to-do Jewish mercantile family of Cape Town, de Pass purchased an estate in Natal in the late 1860s. In the early 1880s, after much experimentation, he introduced the first fully satisfactory strain of sugar-cane to be adapted to African conditions, the cuttings of which he obtained from Calcutta. His case is instructive. What de Pass did have, which proved more important than an agricultural background *per se,* were the three indispensable ingredients for a successful farming career in tropical Africa: capital, education and motivation.

Capital. The establishment of commercial agriculture anywhere in tropical Africa has been, by and large, an uphill business, with far more failures than

---

[33] Alan F. Hattersley, *The British settlement of Natal: a study in imperial migration* (Cambridge University Press, 1950), pp. 118–19, 149–52, 235–6 and *passim.*

successes. Climate and ecology seem almost deliberately to conspire against it. Livestock of a sufficiently refined strain to produce meat or fibre of commercial quality are subject to a lengthy list of parasites and diseases. Without dips and other costly prophylactic veterinarian measures, profitable animal husbandry is usually impossible. Soils, where usable at all, commonly require elaborate treatment and very heavy fertilization. Plant crops are as subject to diseases as are animals; and such plants, if exotic, as most necessarily are, may react in unpredictable ways when transferred to the African habitat. For these reasons, constant experimentation has been necessary in order to discover adaptable crops and the best methods for their production.

The best-documented case illustrating concretely some of these problems and some solutions is the career of Hugh Cholmondeley, Lord Delamere (1870–1931).[34] In a pattern common to his time and social status, Delamere was first attracted to Africa for sport, to which he was single-mindedly devoted. On his sixth trip to Africa (dignified as scientific museum collection, like that of Theodore Roosevelt a few years later), he entered from Mombasa by the still incomplete Uganda Railway. Upon reaching Nairobi he naturally called upon Sir Charles Eliot, first commissioner of the infant protectorate. In the course of their conversations, Delamere found the polestar that guided the rest of his life. Granted a large leasehold of 100,000 acres, he began his long series of experiments to prove what he and Eliot believed but what many well-informed men doubted: the feasibility of European settlement in the East African Highlands.

Delamere imported sheep, but they died of foot-rot, liver fluke and a mysterious grub that bored its way into their brains through the sinuses. He also imported cattle and, very intelligently and correctly, domesticated grasses to sustain them. The pastures flourished, but the cattle sickened from what eventually was shown to be a mineral deficiency, easily cured by adding cobalt to the animals' salt ration. He tried wheat, not once but several times. It grew luxuriantly to the point of maturity, only to crumble into useless dust from rust. Severely shaken but undaunted, Delamere brought to Africa at his own expense (since governmentally supported experiment stations were yet to come) a wheat scientist, who shortly provided a rust-resistant strain. This came about, however, only after the expenditure of six years and £40,000.

It would be all too easy to paint a grossly distorted picture of the record of British settler-farmers in tropical Africa by paying too much attention to Lord Delamere, who was certainly most unrepresentative of the run-of-the-mill Kenyan settler of his day, and still less of those of other areas.[35] Very few indeed could match either his resources or his passionate devotion to his experimental goals, which he pursued as relentlessly as he had the unfortunate lions of his youth. Nonetheless, essentially the same prerequisites, scaled down as they necessarily were to fit more modest gifts and circumstances, held for the more typical settlers. These people came from the most varied backgrounds, counting among their ranks former engineers, policemen, retired civil servants on pension and a host of others. Amounts and original sources of the money brought

[34] Cf. Elspeth Huxley, *White man's country: Lord Delamere and the making of Kenya* (New York, 1968).

[35] Cf. M. P. K. Sorrenson, *Origins of European settlement in Kenya* (Nairobi, Oxford University Press, 1968), pp. 65–7 and 229–31.

with them naturally varied as greatly. What was required in any case was sufficient capital to establish themselves initially for lengthy periods when income was often exceeded by expenses. In many cases, this initial capital was provided by an inheritance.[36] In others, it was derived from other occupations, such as trading or prospecting.[37]

With few exceptions, therefore, tropical Africa proved quite unsuitable for the kind of small homesteader with scanty capital who was predominantly responsible for bringing most of the arable land in the United States and Canada under the plough. As a result, by the time European farming in East Africa

[36] In addition to being a prolific journalist and novelist, Lord Delamere's biographer, Elspeth Huxley, happens to be a university-trained agronomist, with an enduring interest in agriculture and farming. Her two volumes of memoirs of a Kenyan childhood, skilfully written for the trade market, contain, adroitly worked in here and there, many tidbits providing excellent case material on pioneer British settler-farmers of a kind not easily obtainable elsewhere. See *The flame trees of Thika: memories of an African childhood* (New York, 1959); and *On the edge of the Rift* (New York, 1962).

The Grants, Mrs Huxley's family, arrived in Kenya in 1913. Socially, they were well-connected upper-middle-class people; but, financially, they were far from being wealthy, nor did they become so in the fifteen years or so covered in Mrs Huxley's two volumes. For most of this time they lived in their initial grass house, constructed for something like £10. (*Flame trees of Thika*, p. 36.) Such residences, free adaptations on a more spacious scale of African architecture, were first houses for everyone. But moneyed settlers like the neighbouring Palmers built stone houses soon after arrival.

Mrs Huxley's father paid £4 an acre for his 500 acres of completely raw bush in the rolling upland hills some forty-five miles north of Nairobi, the red laterite soil of which was thought especially suitable for coffee. Even at this early date land prices in accessible regions had been driven up to this high figure by intense speculation. (On land speculation in early Kenya, see Norman Leys, *Kenya* [London, 1924], pp. 149–50.) We are not told how much this initial payment of £2,000 left the Grants; but since coffee trees take three or four years to bear at all and something like eight to reach full maturity, prospective growers of this crop necessarily had to have enough capital left after paying for their land to live on for an extended period, as well as enough to pay African labour, the chief item of development cost. In this particular instance, however, World War I intervened and upset calculations. Most young plantations were ruined through neglect while their owners were away on military service, and returning farmers had pretty much to start from scratch again. Fortunately for them, where the land was paid for and planting was proceeding on schedule, banks were willing to extend credit in the form of overdrafts. Mrs Huxley estimates that her parents were £3,000 in debt in the years just after the war, which must have been the larger part of the current market value of their farm. (*Edge of the Rift*, p. 21.)

Clearing and planting, all done by hand and animal labour, proceeded slowly in this pre-bulldozer age. Something around ten to fifteen acres of new *shamba* were created a year. At this rate, Mrs Huxley remarks, it would have taken her parents twenty years to bring their farm into full production. Assuming that 300 of the total 500 acres were planted in coffee selling at the officially supported prices prevailing in the late 1950s, this farm would then have brought in a net annual income of perhaps £9,000. (For price and production figures to derive these estimates, see *The economic development of Kenya* [Baltimore, Johns Hopkins Press for the International Bank for Reconstruction and Development, 1963], p. 117.) But ever restless as true pioneers tend to be, the Grants sold out long before full production was reached in order to buy a new and completely virgin farm in the highlands to the west overlooking the Rift valley.

[37] EDITORS' NOTE: A Rhodesian example was Herbert George Robins (1867–1939), a frontier farmer and prospector. In 1902 Robins entered the service of Tanganyika Concessions, Ltd to prospect in what was then the Congo Free State. By 1913, when his contract had expired, Robins had accumulated a capital of £10,000, then a considerable sum, which enabled him to become a substantial cattle rancher in the Wankie area, as well as a recluse and an experimenter with scientific instruments.

had reached peak efficiency (*circa* 1960) immigrant agricultural enterprise was mostly on a large scale.[38]

Education. Although initial capital is absolutely essential, it has to be intelligently used if it is not to be wasted. Deliberate and controlled experimentation, as distinguished from informal, gradual adaptation of the trekboer variety, demands trained abstract thinking of a fairly high order, the essential elements of which are a clear-cut intellectual conception of goals and a firm cognitive grasp of possible alternative procedures, as gained from the collective experience of others. If the planter is really new in a given geographical area, neither goals nor alternatives can be directly acquired by experience; hence they can be obtained only from technical literature.[39] To read and comprehend such literature requires, in turn, not necessarily a university degree, but an education well beyond mere sign-your-name literacy and with some focus upon the elements of scientific method.[40] The successful European farmer in Africa *circa* 1960, whether Rhodesian, Kenyan, Algerian *colon* or German rancher of the South-West territory, was necessarily a fairly well-educated and scientifically minded individual, however reactionary his politics might appear to outsiders.

[38] EDITORS' NOTE: The acreages of European and Asian landholdings in Kenya in 1961 were as follows:

Acreage	Percentage of holdings	Percentage of area
20–499	34·0	2·9
500–999	20·9	7·1
1,000–4,999	37·4	34·3
5,000–49,999	7·5	44·2
50,000 and over	0·3	11·5

SOURCE: William A. Hance, *The geography of modern Africa* (New York, Columbia University Press, 1964), p. 398.

[39] Like most of the would-be coffee planters who poured into Kenya just before World War I, the Grants had had no prior experience in agriculture. 'Robin' is shown taking first lessons in ox-breaking and ploughing from a 'Mr Roos', a crusty Boer. (Huxley, *Flame trees of Thika*, p. 48.) The essentials of soil preparation, planting, tree care and harvesting seem to have been absorbed from the pooled knowledge of the emerging settler community. In other matters, however, the highly literate and bookish Grants tried to extend their knowledge through a 'lively correspondence with seedsmen, poultry breeders, herbalists, handicraft experts and others who possessed some skill, or purveyed some new or unusual product' (Huxley, *Edge of the Rift*, pp. 98–9). At one point the ebullient young Mrs Grant, really the more enthusiastic farmer of Mrs Huxley's parents, is shown citrus-grafting, 'illustrated book' in hand (*Flame trees of Thika*, p. 172).

[40] Mrs Huxley again provides us with a concrete example. The bringing of large-boned native Boran cattle from the north to the highlands seems to have been first done by the ubiquitous Lord Delamere. (*White man's country*, vol. 1, p. 142.) But the decisive step in the creation of the improved, pure-bred strain of Borans that eventually became 'famous and sought-after' among Kenyan farmers appears to have been done primarily the work of an obscurely ordinary British South African by the name of Oram. Disdaining the usual policy of upgrading native stock by cross-breeding, Oram put his faith and his efforts into a carefully conducted programme of selective breeding, a home-grown experiment that in this particular instance paid off. (*Edge of the Rift*, p. 47.)

This educational prerequisite helps to explain, although obviously it is by itself insufficient to do so entirely, why a direct transfer from Europe of an illiterate peasantry proved infeasible, although it was tried in a number of instances. In the first decade of the twentieth century, for example the Germans attempted to settle a group of ethnic Germans from southern Russia in German East Africa. These settlers, though ill-educated in a formal sense, had coped successfully with the multiple hardships of life on the plains of Eastern Europe. But they proved unable to make a satisfactory adjustment to the African bush, where natural conditions were strange to them and where transport and marketing facilities were inadequate.[41]

Motivation. Beyond education as such, the German case just cited suggests the presence and operation of sufficiently strong motivation. After testing the Marxian thesis of economic determinism against his vast knowledge of history, Max Weber concluded that man is driven motivationally by *both* material and ideal interests. The lesson seems to apply forcefully to the history of European agriculture in tropical Africa, which has on the whole been difficult and unprofitable enough to preclude a strictly 'economic' interpretation.

Separating material and ideal interests is, to be sure, easier done analytically and abstractly than concretely in the given case. A pioneer as flamboyantly idealistic (in the peculiarly Weberian sense) as Lord Delamere was at the same time an 'economic man'. His many experiments with different strains of plants and beasts were conducted not solely for the fun of it, but with an eye towards the very mundane goal of making farming pay—for others, certainly, but also for himself. Having spent all he had and all he could borrow on his East African ventures, he was of course interested in recovering his large losses and rebuilding the family fortune.[42] Still less could the ordinary European farmer of

[41] The most extensive of the several attempts to settle European peasants in Africa is that of the Portuguese, which to date would appear to show only limited success. See James Duffy, *Portuguese Africa* (Cambridge, Mass., Harvard University Press, 1959), pp. 337–8, 378 n. 16; James Duffy, 'Portuguese Africa, 1930 to 1960', in *Colonialism in Africa: 1870–1960*, vol. II: *The history and politics of colonialism: 1914–1960*, L. H. Gann and Peter Duignan, eds. (Cambridge University Press, 1970), p. 178; Ronald H. Chilcote, *Portuguese Africa* (Englewood Cliffs, N.J., 1967), pp. 9 and 61. For a discussion of various abortive proposals to establish colonies of Indian peasants in British East Africa, see J. S. Mangat, *A history of the Asians in East Africa: c. 1886 to 1945* (Oxford, Clarendon Press, 1969), pp. 66–71.

Significantly, the one group of Europeans without much education or capital who could live in British 'settler' areas were Afrikaners. 'However poor a British farmer thought himself', Mrs Huxley remarks, 'the Dutch looked upon him as a sort of a Croesus' (*Flame trees of Thika*, p. 248). Theoretically, each family in the van Rensberg contingent of Afrikaners whom the government settled in the then remote (and therefore virtually valueless) Uasin Gishu plateau, of which the town of Eldoret eventually became the rail head, was supposed to have had £500 in observable assets. In fact, few if any possessed anything like that amount. Nonetheless, they had what they needed, since Boers could live almost entirely off the country. All they bought was 'salt, paraffin, coffee and tobacco'. And 'even the paraffin could be done without, at a pinch' (*Flame trees of Thika*, p. 248). In time, the Afrikaners of Kenya did establish themselves as prosperous farmers and in other skilled and professional capacities. Furthermore, their role in helping to open up the country can hardly be disputed. Yet quite clearly the initiative for scientifically based agriculture did not and could not have come from them.

[42] By standards prevailing among the English nobility of his day, Delamere was a 'poor' man, whose capital resources were less property than credit. At the age of twenty-four, having already disposed of £27,000 on his shooting and exploring expeditions, he was left, his biographer tells us, 'with a net income of less than £1500 a year'. (Huxley, *White man's country*, vol. I, p. 16.)

later Kenya and Rhodesia ignore the economic imperative, since, with few and well-advertised exceptions, he lacked sufficient inherited resources upon which to live indefinitely.

Yet, after this is granted, a conspicuous 'ideal' factor in his motivation remains. The typical settler-farmer of tropical Africa farmed, not because he had no other alternatives, but because farming represented to him the good life, what he wanted most to do. Idealism of the Weberian kind inspired those settlers from Wilhelmian Germany who invested some of their profits from sheep- or cattle-farming in strange replicas of Teutonic castles incongruously placed on the South-West African veld. In the British case, the ethnic linkage to some powerful Victorian upper-middle-class values is equally obvious from even the most superficial appraisal. In that culture the status of gentleman-farmer has long represented a social ideal, held superior traditionally to a career in commerce or industry. Associatively, the land, the outdoors, horses and dogs, wildlife and sport have been idealized in contrast to—and partly in op-position to—the intellectualistic, artistic, epicurean and gregarious urban values prevailing, let us say, along the Mediterranean or in Central Europe. It is dif-ficult to imagine a group of middle-class Spaniards or Austrians, for example, settling down contentedly at an Abercorn, *circa* 1910. In the same light, it is perhaps not merely or entirely poverty and isolation that kept the Nyasaland highlands from being pre-empted by Portuguese planters.

At times, this extra-economic motivation produced behaviour negative in its impact upon development. Because, as C. C. Wrigley notes, the earliest 'gen-tlemen-settlers' of Kenya 'preferred the types of agriculture to which they were accustomed—the breeding of sheep and cattle and the growing of wheat', they were slow to turn to the growing of coffee, for which East Africa was more ecologically suited.[43] Still, the ideal factor in their behaviour seems clearly a positive rather than a negative one in relation to economic development. Pre-cisely because he did not think solely or even primarily in terms of an 'eco-nomic' balance sheet, the British pioneer persevered in the face of obstacles and disappointments that would have utterly discouraged others.[44]

Indians provide a partial and admittedly imperfect test of these assumptions. The Indians now in Africa, as we shall see later, were commonly from land-holding families in India; and among Indian pioneers there were a large number of market gardeners (an early Indian occupational speciality that persists in

The money spent so lavishly on his early agricultural experiments was thus almost entirely bor-rowed. The family estate in England was so heavily and repeatedly mortgaged that at one time it passed into receivership. (*Ibid.*, p. 170.)

[43] C. C. Wrigley, 'Kenya: the patterns of economic life, 1902–1945', in *History of East Africa,* vol. II, Vincent Harlow and E. M. Chilver, eds., assisted by Alison Smith (Oxford, Clarendon Press, 1965), pp. 217–18.

[44] On the question of basic motivation, as applied to her family, Mrs Huxley makes a brief, explicit statement. Her parents, she concludes, were 'questers' rather than 'squatters'. The quest they themselves perceived as 'a fortune', but it was not: what they really wanted was to plant seeds, sometimes literally, sometimes in a general sense: seeds of change, of enterprise, of improvement' (*Edge of the Rift,* pp. 227–8).

To make ideal conform to practice, and therefore to be idealists in the Weberian sense, demands that people have the luxury of choice. The Grants were not, of course, compelled to live in Kenya, nor did they have to be farmers. They had alternatives (although on the face of it less attractive ones); and that, realistically speaking, is the essence of choice in any question of human motivation.

South Africa but that has disappeared elsewhere). Given this background in agriculture, one wonders why Indians were not attracted to the land in Africa in greater numbers. In some areas, of course, good and sufficient reasons are immediately apparent. In Kenya, for example, where Indians were most numerous outside South Africa, they were never allowed to acquire land in quantity; and no immigrants of any race were allowed land in Uganda. In Tanganyika, Nyasaland and Northern Rhodesia, however, these statutory limitations either did not exist or were less stringently applied; yet significantly, in these territories Indians never engaged in agriculture in numbers. Among the principal isolated exceptions were a few market gardeners and tea- and cotton-planters. Specifically, in Nyasaland and Northern Rhodesia, where Indians could have bought land freely (or as freely as anyone else), very few did. Most, of course, were too poor. Nonetheless, it seems indicative of real ethnic differences in this respect that the few who did acquire capital in sufficient quantity to buy land preferred to invest their money in commercial business, where opportunities for a rapid and dependable return were much greater.

In keeping with its partly extra-economic motivation, European agricultural enterprise in Africa remained on the whole remarkably individualistic in its social organization.[45] Although predominant in certain limited areas, plantation agriculture has never played a significant role in the total economy. Perhaps if the German presence had been greater and had remained unbroken, more agricultural development would have assumed this form. After the turn of the century the Germans, in the limited areas under their control, established briefly a lead in scientific development. Institutions such as the Biologisch-Landwirtschaftliches Institut, Amani, in East Africa, set up in 1902, and the Versuchsanstalt für Landeskultur, organized in Kamerun in 1905, vigorously pursued the double goal of promoting a scientifically based plantation agriculture and of improving African peasant cultivation for the market.[46] A few German *Kleinsiedler* tried their hands at intensive farming in South-West Africa, but the country proved far more suitable for cattle ranching and the raising of karakul sheep.

Except for terminology, the large family farm and the small plantation may, in fact, be indistinguishable. In its social organization, the really large commercial plantation, such as those of the Firestone or Lever Brothers enterprises of West Africa, clearly belongs to the bureaucratic sector of the economy. It is to this sector that we now turn our attention.

[45] Plantation agriculture, Wrigley points out, did not accord with many gentleman-settlers' ideal of what a British colony should be ('Kenya: the patterns of economic life', p. 218). Individualism in this context, however, should not be construed to mean a *laissez-faire* rejection of governmental support. The British settler-farmers of Kenya, in particular, came to be the recipients of a good deal of sympathetic assistance from their local government, not only in the area of basic research, but also through the provision of very expensive infrastructure in the form of roads and schools. Surveying the scene in the early 1930s from the perspective of classical academic economic liberalism, young Frankel clearly doubted whether they were worth it. (Frankel, *Capital investment,* pp. 266–7.)

[46] On the importance attached by the Germans to both scientific research and the development of plantation economies, see Prosser Gifford, 'Indirect rule: touchstone or tombstone for colonial policy?' in *Britain and Germany in Africa*, p. 369; also W. O. Henderson, 'German East Africa, 1884–1918', in *History of East Africa,* vol. II, p. 144.

The bureaucratic sector

Historically, two types of bureaucratic organization have predominated in the development of Africa. The first of these—somewhat paradoxically, because it was originally not intended to play such a role—was that erected by the imperial governments themselves. Some of the contributors to the first volume of the present series have furnished details of how, in keeping with the prevailing faith in private initiative and *laissez-faire,* the imperial powers tried at first to govern through concessionary companies. The failure of these experiments soon forced the metropolitan governments into a reluctant economic intervention. To maintain even the skeleton, constabulary type of administration that prevailed throughout the inter-war period required heavy investments, particularly in railways. The second great area of bureaucratic organization has been that of the mining industry, especially in gold and copper. In sheerly quantitative terms, these two great engines have been responsible for most of whatever economic development has so far taken place on the continent. Writing in 1952, Frankel summed up the overwhelming role of government and mining as follows:

It is significant that of the total capital invested in Africa from 1870 to 1936 nearly half was supplied by governments or public authorities. Of the remainder a large part has been connected with mining and exploration activities.[47]

To these historic bureaucracies, we must add the great private trading companies, which have long dominated commerce on the west coast, and the large agricultural plantations briefly mentioned above. These hierarchies might become interlocked, as some senior civil servants acquired directorships in companies on their retirement, or as successful businessmen would be called to serve on the boards of public corporations.[48] In recent years, particularly since the Second World War, these older bureaucracies have been joined by other significant, if less imposing, organizations: for example, insurance companies, construction concerns, chain stores and automobile dealerships.

Given the present context, our interest in the bureaucracy is confined to the manner in which it attracts, directs, controls and limits non-indigenous immigration. Even in this connexion, however, certain of its well-defined sociological characteristics are relevant. Among these is its more or less firmly fixed 'table of organization'. Recruitment for vacant positions is based upon formally

---

[47] Frankel, 'Some aspects of investment, p. 52.

[48] EDITORS' NOTE: An interesting career is that of Sir Francis Percy Drummond Chaplin (1866–1933). In 1910 Chaplin, a former British newspaper correspondent with extensive foreign experience, was appointed by Cecil Rhodes to become joint manager at Johannesburg for the Consolidated Gold Fields of South Africa, Ltd. In addition, Chaplin became director of many of Rhodes's subsidiary companies. He likewise acquired interests in the Wernher-Beit group of ·mines. In 1905 he rose to be president of the Transvaal Chamber of Mines. Chaplin, a spokesman for the mining interests, a convinced supporter of Lord Milner, and a strong opponent of the Liberal policy of restoring self-government to the conquered Transvaal, entered the Union House of Assembly in 1910. In 1914 the British South Africa Company appointed him administrator (that is to say, chief executive) of Southern Rhodesia, a post he held until Southern Rhodesia attained self-government in 1923. He subsequently became a director of the British South Africa Company, director of Rhodesian Anglo American, Ltd, and chairman of the Wireless Telegraph Company of South Africa and of various other concerns.

defined skill requirements. Given the close association of many bureaucracies with science and advanced technology, these may be of a very high order. *It is fundamental to an understanding of the social structure of modern Africa to appreciate that its colonization, particularly in the interior, was delayed until ethnically specific Western science, medicine and technology were far advanced.* Remuneration of employees is in terms of a fixed salary; and, of special significance in the African context, such remuneration may be quite independent of the short-run profitability of the enterprise in question.[49] Employment is understood as constituting a phased career, with retirement and pension following a fixed term of service. Certain kinds of perquisites, which augment very substantially the value of monetary compensation, are nearly always provided in corporate systems. Familiar examples in the colonial context are company housing, medical services and long periods of home leave.

Defined in the strictest, original Weberian sense, the term 'bureaucracy' applies only to the 'line' or managerial personnel of an enterprise. In practice, however, professional 'staff' (engineers, accountants or doctors, for example) tend to be included; and this inclusion is especially necessary in the colonial situation, where professionals (such as doctors in a government hospital) commonly have important executive functions. In terms of skill level, entry into the bureaucracy narrowly defined would therefore be that of junior management; but again in colonial Africa, many skilled workers, down to, let us say, the factory-trained mechanic of the automobile dealership, may have to be recruited from abroad on bureaucratic terms, because adequate local supplies of such labour, especially in the earlier phases of development, are typically not available.[50]

Unskilled labour, on the other hand, is indigenous. It is, in general, poorly disciplined (again, particularly so in the earliest phases of development) and inefficient (in good part because of very serious health deficiencies); and such labour tends to be short-term or cyclical. It is therefore unstable and undependable, although in the abstract it may appear to be abundant. Unskilled labour is paid at an extremely low level, although probably in most cases at a rate fairly commensurate with its marginal productivity. However, wage rates are not set through strictly rational considerations. The necessity for high pay for skilled labour, taken together with the extremely high materials and overhead costs typical of the underdeveloped area, provides a powerful incentive to 'economize' on the pay of the unskilled. The whole remuneration system thus tends rapidly to become customary and rigid to an extraordinary degree. These rigidities, as Frankel has brilliantly shown, seem to be the inevitable consequence of imposing technically advanced economic enterprise upon economies otherwise at the level of agricultural subsistence.[51]

---

[49] Railways provide an extreme example. It is doubtful whether any railway in Africa has ever been, in strictly economic terms, a paying proposition. Virtually none had, in any case, up to the 1930s. (Frankel, *Capital investment,* pp. 374–420.) On the other hand, even governments cannot be completely oblivious to long-term account balancing. Administrative attempts to keep costs in some relation to income go a long way towards explaining the sketchy constabulary character of colonial government in the inter-war period.

[50] Until indigenous personnel could be trained, the lower levels of bureaucratic enterprise throughout Africa, with one notable exception, were European. Owing to the peculiar history of the region, Indians participated in the lower ranks of the East African civil service from the beginning.   [51] Frankel, 'Some aspects of investment', pp. 50–8.

The presence of a technically, culturally and organizationally advanced bureaucratic sector artificially implanted within the framework of a subsistence economy goes a long way towards explaining the pronouncedly dual character of colonial economies and the very peculiar social structure associated with them. The high level of skill requirements in the bureaucracy, together with the relative indifference to short-term profitability, translates socially into a compact group of well-paid élite at the top, who typically become tightly organized into a cohesive community. Their 'high' pay, which is invariably held against them by hostile critics, is in fact basically set by impersonal, external market forces outside the local system. At a minimum these people cannot be paid less than they would get at home or elsewhere in an equally advanced economy. In practice, they must be paid somewhat more as an inducement to their serving in the colonial situation, where living conditions, once the initial romantic attractions have dimmed, may be somewhat trying.[52]

Much of what we have just said has often been commented upon and is widely familiar. It is less generally appreciated that the high 'civilized standard' of living created and maintained by the structural requirements of the advanced bureaucratic sector imposed an equally high standard of economic 'success' (and therefore negatively 'failure') upon the few Europeans outside its organizational boundaries. In this category are the independent artisan, the professional and the small businessman.[53] The results, however, were not entirely negative. For those capable of exploiting it, the small but rich market provided by the presence of a privileged bureaucratic élite was at once highly attractive and very strictly limited. Furthermore, the pay-out to that part of the indigenous population employed by the bureaucratic sector, small as it was in the individual case, might in the aggregate be considerable. Feeding such workers provided a market for nearby farmers, indigenous or non-indigenous as the case might be.[54] Finally, supplying the indigenous working population with the very

[52] This generalization applies better to private than to governmental bureaucracies. Specialists in the British colonial service or in the employment of the now defunct Federation of Rhodesia ard Nyasaland often received less money than they might have obtained in corresponding positions in Canada or in the United States. The difference was made up by 'psychic income' in the form of an intricate system of Honours, used to reward successful administrative, scientific and technical officers by giving them status in terms of an older complex of rural-gentry values that we have just seen operating in the case of British settler-farmers.

[53] The bureaucratic sector tended to loom large everywhere in late colonial Africa. There were, of course, important variations in the degree of its dominance. The Belgian Congo was the 'company colony' *par excellence*. Northern Rhodesia may be compared to it in this respect, although Northern Rhodesia's giant copper companies never succeeded in completely dominating the territory. By contrast, Southern Rhodesia, with its large population of European farmers, was notably individualistic in economic organization; even the mining industry there was remarkably atomistic before World War II. Senegal, site of the federal capital of French West Africa, Dakar, had, along with its many large corporate businesses, a relatively large population of *petits blancs* engaged in individualistic enterprise. (See Paul Mercier, 'Le groupement européen de Dakar: orientation d'une enquête', *Cahiers Internationaux de Sociologie*, 1955, **19**, 130–46.)

[54] Emphasis upon the bureaucratic sector as the major engine of African development should not obscure the fact that its impact was in good part indirect or secondary rather than in the form of direct wage payments. For Africans, specifically, there were two major sources of such secondarily derived money income: the sale of agricultural and other primary products (fish and 'wild' palm-oil, for example); and wages for work on European farms. Other sources, which gradually became more significant as general development proceeded, were domestic employment in the cities and employment in small, unincorporated enterprises.

On the west coast, the sale of African-grown crops and products was and remains the single

limited range of goods for which it could pay provided the economic niche filled by the middleman-trader.

Middlemen-traders

Considered as a market, the African trade had (and still retains for the most part) some distinctive features that formed both its economic and its social parameters. Economically, the amount of money in the hands of any one potential customer was small, given the prevailingly low income of the African population. Individual purchases were therefore correspondingly small, and these were restricted to a narrow range of goods, of which textiles led in volume by a wide margin. Socially, until cities and towns provided some concentration, the consuming population, too, was dispersed widely over a given area. The result was small shops, geographically scattered, all offering essentially the same narrow line of goods. The small turn-over of such shops thus translated into a relatively small income for the shopkeeper, an income much too small to attract an educated Western European capable of participating at any level in the bureaucratic sector.[55] Shopkeeping therefore fell by default to either marginal Europeans (mainly, but not quite exclusively, Greeks, Cypriots or Jews recently immigrated from Russia), to Orientals, or, in those limited areas where the indigenous population was sufficiently prepared for it, to Africans themselves.

most important source of money income for Africans: 'Agricultural products provided nearly two-thirds of West Africa's exports in 1961, with almost all these crops grown by African peasant producers' (Peter S. Lloyd, *Africa in social change* [Harmondsworth, 1967], p. 69). In Kenya and Southern Rhodesia, the single largest source of paid employment for Africans is European-owned agriculture—some 45 per cent of all paid employees in Kenya (1959) and 44 per cent in Southern Rhodesia (1964) (M. W. Forrester, *Kenya today: social prerequisites for economic development* [The Hague, 1962], pp. 101–2; Rhodesia, *Monthly Digest of Statistics,* Feb. 1966).

In relation to the still undeveloped potential of African agriculture in Central and East Africa, the rapidity and extent to which Africans were brought into the market economy provided by European settlement are remarkable. Less than a decade after the occupation of Southern Rhodesia, the Chief Native Commissioner reported: 'Most of the mines have this year been supplied locally with grain . . . I anticipate that the amount grown during this year will be far in excess of previous seasons. It is estimated that about 100,000 bags of grain, varying in prices from 10s. to 15s., were traded by the natives last year.' ('Report of the Chief Native Commissioner [Mr. H. J. Taylor], Matabeleland, for the period ended 31st March, 1900', British South Africa Company, *Reports on the administration of Rhodesia 1898–1900,* printed for the information of shareholders [London, n.d.].)

'The first business in what is now Lusaka', writes a son of one of the Jewish pioneers, 'was that of Mr. Rapport, who set up to trade cattle and grain, which he was under contract to supply Robert Williams and Company, who were then constructing the railway between Kafue and Broken Hill.' 'Cattle and grain were plentiful', this informant goes on to explain, 'because this was a district free from the tsetse fly.' (*Central African Post,* 14 May 1954.) Yet fifty years later the total annual value of the African-grown agricultural product was only about £0.7 million (*A brief guide to Northern Rhodesia* [Lusaka, Northern Rhodesia Information Department, 1960], p. 100). This is a good example of the principle that few socio-economic processes are unilinear. It appears obvious that European settlement both stimulated and inhibited the development of African commercial agriculture in this region.

[55] Describing the situation existing in the late 1950s in Northern Rhodesia, we wrote as follows: 'The average net return from a small Indian shop is probably something like fifty pounds a month—a little less than a European woman would earn as a secretary and not much more than half the wage that an experienced European automobile mechanic would command.' (Dotson and Dotson, *Indian minority,* p. 67.) Earlier, during the 1930s, net return probably averaged out to something like £10.

In much of Africa, however, the indigenous population was unable to exercise this economic function initially upon the basis of the existing traditional culture.

The successful operation of even a small shop demands a complex of skills of a fairly high order, skills that tend to be grossly underestimated by the uninitiated, because they are not tangible as are those of a bricklayer or a doctor. A measure of literacy, although not indispensable for the very small business firmly integrated into a larger organization, is a great asset. What is really essential is enough arithmetic to keep track of transactions and stock. This need not be acquired in school if it can be learned as part of an established apprenticeship training. (See the case study of an Indian businessman provided in Case IV, pp. 608–11 below.) Less obvious, but absolutely essential, is a clear-cut perception of the difference between working capital and net income for consumption. Beyond this perception itself—and people lacking it find it difficult to grasp its importance—is the discipline necessary to maintain it. Otherwise the would-be shopkeeper soon finds that he, or in many cases his relatives, have eaten up his capital. Such self-discipline is part of a character structure (as the psychologist might call it) that includes, among other essential components, a willingness to take risks and a trained ability to defer gratification. In other words, the shopkeeper requires a long-term rather than a present-time orientation. Necessary, too, are patience and the capacity to apply effort steadily over a long period of time, without much immediate reinforcement. These qualities of personality or character, however, are still not enough. Some fairly high-order cognitive knowledge is essential also. The shopkeeper must know his market—what will and what will not sell—and his customers. In addition, he must, of course, have a dependable source of supply of both goods and credit. This ultimately means contact—if not in his own person, then through an organized series of intermediaries—with wholesalers, bankers, manufacturers' representatives and customs agents.

A final prerequisite, perhaps the most critically important of all, is that of motivation. Motivation, which is often thought of too narrowly in terms of individual psychology, is in the last analysis socio-cultural, because it is grounded in fundamental life conditions. Shopkeeping must be perceived as a welcome opportunity within a range of less attractive occupational choices. People who could in the abstract operate a shop if they had to may not want to for the very uncomplicated reason that other and more attractive choices are available. On the other hand, it clearly does not obversely follow that those who might be attracted by the modest income from shopkeeping can necessarily perform the role. To do so they must have the requisite capability. In a population of subsistence farmers, this never exists until it is developed there; it must initially be brought in from the outside in the persons of immigrants, just as surely as is the case with the skills necessary for the operation of schools and hospitals.

Taking Africa as a whole during the period covered in the present volume, the largest single ethnic group of middlemen-traders was the Indians. Indians came to Africa through early connexions with Arabs and Portuguese and even more importantly through channels created for them by their prior connexion with the British. They were thus naturally more prominent in the British territories of South, East and Central Africa than elsewhere. However, Indians were by no means the only group to occupy the middlemen-trader's role; and in some areas where they eventually did so they were not the first. Eastern European Jews were pioneer bush-traders in various parts of South and south-east Central Africa. These people, who came in considerable numbers from the turn of the century onward, were typically European marginals in the sense previously suggested. As a group, they were culturally different from the more advanced Western European Jews of an earlier vintage, of whom Daniel de Pass and Maximilian Thalwitzer (German-born and a pioneer of the South African merino-wool industry) would be good examples.[56] In contrast to the sophisticated Jews of the advanced Western type, the generally lower living standards and modest expectations from life characteristic of the Eastern European Jews pre-adapted them to the middleman-trader's role. Greeks, who were, as we have seen, among the very first foreigners to come to Ethiopia, were the chief middleman-trading group in the Sudan and the Congo. Some Greeks settled in Southern Rhodesia, where early (1923) restrictions upon Indian immigration helped to relieve them of those formidable competitors.[57] Greeks in small numbers were to be found in a great many other areas, too, particularly on the west coast.[58] But here the more typical middleman group was composed of 'Syrians', to use the older term for what in fact were almost entirely Lebanese by contemporary terminology.

The Lebanese began coming to West Africa around 1900—significantly, in the same period when Indians were coming to Ethiopia, to the Portuguese territories and to British East and Central Africa. Whether their eventual destination was a French or a British territory, virtually all of the Lebanese boarded ship at Marseille. They came to Africa, which in the early period was almost entirely free of restrictions, as a second or third choice, when either for economic or for

[56] EDITORS' NOTE: A marginal Western European who made good in Rhodesia was Jacob Hendrik Smit (1881–1959). Smit was destined for a teaching career, but instead took a position as a bank clerk. He left his post in 1899 and went to the Transvaal. Failing to establish himself in South Africa, he went next to Beira, where he tried to make a living as a tobacconist. He then migrated to Rhodesia, where for a time he was reduced to selling victuals from a barrow, and later from a mule cart. In 1914 he opened a grocery and hardware store that afforded him an acceptable living. He later went into politics and became one of Sir Godfrey Huggins's ministers, known for his unimpeachable financial orthodoxy and for his firm belief in 'parallel development' for Africans. [57] Dotson and Dotson, *Indian minority*, pp. 41–2.

[58] Of all the literatures on the major non-indigenous ethnic groups, that on the Greeks in Africa is perhaps the scantiest. Furthermore, the Greeks, partly because of their unusual geographic dispersion, but even more because of their immense social and economic diversity, defy a neat, summary classification. Although in the earliest periods they were primarily middlemen-traders in most areas, a certain number of them have always been found in farming and other businesses in some regions. As of 1964–65, Georgulas reports that of the thirty-seven adult Greek males in the small community of Moshi, Tanzania, only two were in commerce. Most of them—as have been the Greeks in this area since their arrival in the 1890s—were coffee farmers. (Nikos Georgulas, 'Minority assimilation in Africa: the Greeks in Moshi—an example', Syracuse University, Maxwell Graduate School of Citizenship and Public Affairs, Program of Eastern African Studies, *Occasional Paper*, no. 22, 1966, pp. 25–6.)

A significant feature of this interesting short study is Georgulas's attempt to calculate in precise terms the economic 'input' of Greeks into the local economy. 'In terms of *per capita* expenditure Greek enterprise contributed at the rate of £2,960 per individual annually, in addition to tax contributions' (*ibid.*, p. 29). In terms of investment in the narrower sense, Georgulas estimates this at £640 per person on improvements and extensions alone. This, he notes, 'is four times as great as that envisaged in the National Plan for the average "private enterprise community" as a whole' (*ibid.*, p. 30).

health reasons they were unable to follow the much greater stream of their compatriots migrating to North or South America.[59]

The total number of Lebanese in Africa nonetheless remained small.[60] In the earliest period, when entry was easy, West Africa was too underdeveloped economically to attract many. By the time it had become more attractive, highly restrictive regulations had been imposed by the colonial authorities. These were aimed at protecting indigenous traders who, as a class, were also expanding rapidly. In sharp contrast to most of the rest of the continent, West Africa has always had a large volume of purely indigenous trade. Under Western stimulus, this has increased greatly, with some indigenous groups (the Ibo of Nigeria are an outstanding example) assuming a middleman-trader's role. The swift rise of Lebanese from back-pedlars to rich department-store owners and industrialists, however, shows that Lebanese possessed group-specific capabilities in business not widely shared by even the most economically sophisticated West Africans.[61]

Unlike such historic trading peoples as the Greeks and the Jews, neither the Indians nor the Lebanese who came to Africa were typically traders in their lands of origin. In both instances they came overwhelmingly from peasant families, but from peasants who possessed those indispensable 'personal and political connections' commented upon by Frankel with traders already established in Africa.

Although quite different in major ethnological characteristics, these two Oriental peoples were remarkably similar in those aspects of traditional culture and social structure that predisposed them to success in business. Both, for example, possessed a family system extended beyond the immediate 'nuclear' unit of parents and dependent offspring. The extended family is conducive to successful business entrepreneurship in two ways. At the value level, the strong sense of obligation and family continuity inculcated by it helps to create and constantly reinforce the future orientation that we have described as a shopkeeping prerequisite. Organizationally, on the other hand, the small, tightly knit unit so created provides the foundation for co-operative action, capable of transcending the limitations of either the capital resources or the functional capabilities of single individuals. Particularly when initial resources are small, this capacity gives such a group tremendous competitive advantages over isolated individuals.

Neither the Lebanese nor the Indian family, however, was *too* tightly knit, nor was it integrated into a larger societal structure based entirely upon subsistence agriculture. These facts explain why so many African family systems, which were also extended in form, did not function in the same way. African kinsmen, demanding assistance from their better-off relations, made their claims in the normative tradition of a society not only agricultural, but agricul-

[59] On Lebanese immigration patterns, see R. Bayley Winder, 'The Lebanese in West Africa', *Comparative Studies in Society and History*, April 1962, **4**, no. 3, pp. 296–333.

[60] Official statistics on the Lebanese population appear to be singularly unreliable. Piecing together data of admittedly uneven adequacy, Winder concluded in 1962 that Lebanese and Syrians in West Africa totalled somewhere between 30,000 and 40,000 (*ibid.*, p. 303).

[61] P. T. Bauer, *West African trade: a study of competition, oligopoly and monopoly in a changing economy* (Cambridge University Press, 1954), p. 161. See also Peter C. Garlick, *African traders and economic development in Ghana* (Oxford, Clarendon Press, 1971).

tural at a strictly subsistence level.[62] Indians and Lebanese came from peasant villages, it is true; but as Orientals they also came from *societies* in which commerce and trade were anciently established and well understood in principle, even by their peasant populations.

In both the Lebanese and the Indian instances, the highly organized but still *gemeinschaftliche* homeland village played a consequential supportive role, apart from and in addition to the kinship unit. Sustaining the neophyte immigrant of these groups—typically a youth of sixteen to twenty suffering severely from overwork and loneliness in Africa—was a vision of himself as an important and respected personage making a triumphal return to the village of his birth. Unlike many dreams, this one had a fair chance of being realized. This was being constantly demonstrated, in fact, as successful businessmen from overseas returned for more or less extended visits.

For the Lebanese and the Indian, family and village together provided the social foundation for an African trading career. From the perspective of the raw peasant recruit, a previously established organization existed that served this end. It gave him an initial sponsor and the financial means to make the journey to Africa. Once there, he was provided by the same system not only with an indispensable period of apprenticeship within which trading skills (including the difficult one of learning a new language) could be acquired, but also with the supportive framework for psychological adjustment to a new and thoroughly alien environment.

Admittedly, this was never easy. Most immigrants earned only a moderate competence, and there were many failures. (According to the Kenya Development Plan 1964–70, for instance, in 1962 10·3 per cent of the Asian tax-payers had an annual income of less than £200; 13 per cent earned between £200 and £300 only. The corresponding figures for European tax-payers were 5·3 per cent and 2·5 per cent.) The necessary discipline was rigorous in the extreme. In both the Lebanese and the Indian cases the system was, in fact, highly exploitative of its younger members and was typically so perceived by them. Nonetheless, in the course of a few years the neophyte emerged as a knowledgeable, resourceful, full-fledged businessman in his own right. complete with a small initial capital normally furnished by his sponsor. From there, he was expected to sink or swim on his own initiative within the ruthlessly competitive rules that defined his relationships not only with outsiders, but with other traders within his own ethnic community as well.[63]

Ethnic succession

Ethnic group position, we have argued, is fundamentally grounded in an economic and cultural context. This situational context has a relatively fixed and determined character. It is not, in other words, simply fortuitous. Although the reasons may be morally repugnant from particular points of view, there are good and sufficient explanations for the manner of distribution of the various

---

[62] For a more elaborated comparison between Indians and Africans as businessmen, see Dotson and Dotson, *Indian minority,* pp. 78–84.

[63] Cf. Fuad I. Khuri, 'Kinship, emigration, and trade partnership among the Lebanese of West Africa', *Africa,* Oct. 1965, **35,** no. 4, pp. 385–95; and Dotson and Dotson, *Indian minority,* pp. 73–8 and 198–210.

component groups. To say this, however, is not to deny either the possibility or the concrete fact of change. It is only to suggest that change, when in occurs (as it constantly does), is ordered or, in a meaningful sense, lawful.

Although it may quite legitimately be argued that change has been slower in Africa than might have been ideally desirable, it is patent that great changes have taken place. The readers of these volumes need scarcely be reminded, for instance, that for better or for worse Africa in 1960 was emphatically not the Africa of 1870. The years in between saw the establishment, the expansion and the consolidation of modern public administration, with its correlated services of communications and transport. It saw the coming and the spread of formal education and medical care, the development of mines, the expansion of both indigenous and non-African agriculture, the growth of towns and cities, the emergence of some manufacturing. These developments everywhere created jobs that had not existed before and increased the flow of money into both African and non-African hands. Urbanization aggregated population into ever larger units, and the total population itself increased tremendously in the final decades of the colonial era.

All these familiar changes, seen from the perspective of the individuals and the groups so able to perceive them, constituted new economic and social opportunities. For the sociologist, the same phenomena translate into well-marked patterns of ethnic succession, in which members of one group tend to follow and replace others in the same (or a similar) functional role.

The socio-economic history of the Afrikaner people since 1870 might, for example, be written almost exclusively in these terms. The Boer of 1870 was precisely that and nothing else—a farmer. Even the village schoolmaster and the Dutch Reformed *predikant* were, as we have seen, originally foreigners, Scotsmen in a few cases or, more likely, Hollanders. With the emergence of the Afrikaner universities, the professorate was originally foreign, mainly English-speaking or Hollander.[64] Now, of course, education and the church have long since been Afrikanerized. The replacement of foreigners—mainly but not quite entirely British—has been a slow process in the mines; but it is now largely accomplished. What was true in the mines was true also of artisans and foremen in private business, particularly construction. The coming of Nationalist government in South Africa greatly speeded up the replacement of non-Afrikaners by Afrikaners throughout the civil service and the armed forces. In addition, Afrikaners began to make their mark in large-scale private industry and in banking and commerce, as well as in public corporations. By the 1960s wealthy Afrikaners, though proportionately not yet as numerous as entrepreneurs of British and Jewish ancestry, had begun to play a conspicuous part in the country's economy, as well as in its administration.[65]

---

[64] Munger, *African field notes*, pp. 504–5. Of the six professors under whom young Jan Christiaan Smuts studied in the late 1880s while at tiny Victoria College, Stellenbosch, three were Scotsmen and one a Hollander. The Theological Faculty did already contain at least one Afrikaner, a certain J. I. Marais, who befriended Smuts and who exerted a considerable influence in establishing his socio-political identity. At this time, however, instruction was in English. (W. K. Hancock, *Smuts: the sanguine years 1870–1919* [Cambridge University Press, 1962], pp. 19–20.)

[65] EDITORS' NOTE: Sociological data for the economic diversification of the Afrikaner people may be gathered from numerous printed sources, including the *Who's who of Southern Africa* (Cape Town), which emphasizes business and provides details concerning company directorships. A

In Central Africa, where we can speak from our own field data, a well-marked tendency toward ethnic succession may be seen in the areas of private non-corporate business and the professions. Ethnically, the very earliest traders were mainly British, but these were soon joined by Jews. The employees of the old-style trading company that persisted for a long time in Northern Rhodesia and Nyasaland were typically Scots. Throughout Southern Rhodesia and up the line-of-rail to the Northern Rhodesian Copper Belt, however, the earliest independent shopkeepers were Jews. But Jews in the African trade soon gave way to Greeks and Indians. From the African trade, Jews turned to wholesale, European-oriented department stores and specialized businesses such as office equipment. Increasingly, too, the offspring of Jewish businessmen entered the professions.

Indians in their turn, in so far as they have been permitted, have followed much the same pattern. By the early 1960s less than half the Asian working population in Tanganyika and Uganda, for example, derived its income from commerce.[66] Successful Indians almost invariably moved from the African retail trade to the more profitable wholesale business, where they again competed with Jews. Those equipped with good English and a thorough knowledge of European habits and tastes established department stores, patronized at first solely by Europeans in the days of strict segregation. A few Indians in recent years have trained for the professions, and some have turned to manufacturing (especially agricultural processing industries), where none had existed before. Much the same kind of evolution is reported on the west coast among the Lebanese, except that this group seems to have been able to expand and diversify its enterprises even more rapidly than the Indians.[67]

characteristic case history is the career of Dr Albert Hertzog, son of General James Barry Munnik Hertzog, a former prime minister. Albert Hertzog, an advocate educated at Stellenbosch, Oxford and Leiden, became chairman of the National Board of Trustees, in which capacity he helped to extend Afrikaner influence in the trade-union field. He was also a co-founder of the Volkskas, a major Afrikaner bank; the Koopkrag Spaarbank, a savings institution; and the Afrikaanse Pers Beperk, an important publisher. In addition, he served as a cabinet minister in the Nationalist government (1958–68).

[66] EDITORS' NOTE: Broadly speaking, between 45 and 50 per cent of the economically active population in both countries derived its living from commerce (defined in the broadest sense so that it includes wholesale and retail trade, banking and insurance). Manufacturing and public services each accounted for another 10 per cent of the working population. In Tanganyika, transport and communications employed an additional 9 per cent of the working population. In Uganda, some 9 per cent were employed in agriculture, including cotton ginning and coffee curing, rudimentary industries founded upon an agricultural base. The remainder of the population derived its income from the provision of various services and construction. In Kenya, an even higher percentage depended on wages and salaries obtained in the public services, transport, communications and miscellaneous areas. (See Dharam P. Ghai, *Portrait of a minority: Asians in East Africa* [Nairobi, Oxford University Press, 1965], pp. 94–5.)

[67] EDITORS' NOTE: Lebanese as well as Cypriots in Nigeria played a major part in setting up small, modestly financed, individually or family-owned concerns employing rudimentary production processes. By the 1960s, these embraced several hundred indigenous firms engaged in soap-making, metal-working, saw-milling, rubber crêping, baking, umbrella assembly, singlet manufacture, construction, etc. Lebanese and Cypriots dominated ground-nut crushing, an important processing industry. On the other hand, European firms, larger in scale and more capital-intensive in technique, accounted for the output of tin smelting, cotton ginning and plywood, as well as soap factories and other enterprises employing more complex techniques. (See Peter Kilby, *Industrialization in an open economy: Nigeria 1945–1966* [Cambridge University Press, 1969], pp. 138–9 and 358.)

The history of ethnic succession suggests that in a freely developing economy most members of the old middlemen-trading groups would within two or three decades move spontaneously out of the African trade entirely, leaving it in African hands. Pushed by seemingly irresistible pressures for greater indigenous participation in the economy, independent governments have attempted to speed up the process by direct intervention, thus providing still another concrete instance in which the ethnic group, culturally and economically defined, is transformed into a social and political minority.

Monopolistic closure

Abstractly, the formula for the economic development of Africa is straightforwardly simple in its major components, and within that formula a continuing role for culturally advanced immigrant groups would seem beyond argument. Rapid development demands massive importation of capital, non-material as well as material. Of the two forms, it is perhaps the non-material that is the more important.[68] Until a high level of literacy has been attained by the base population, there is no alternative way of bringing non-material capital into a country except in the persons of those who possess it.

This is not to deny the importance of indigenous unskilled labour. There is a sense in which the now common insistence that modern Africa is a product of *African* hands is profoundly true. Yet it is inescapably true also that without the skills of the trained artisan, the organizational effectiveness of the entrepreneur and the cognitive knowledge of the scientist and technician, such labour can accomplish nothing more than traditional tasks. The cannon at Gafat, to revert for the last time to our initial example, was produced by the labour of a thousand Ethiopians *plus* that of nine Europeans; and the nine Europeans were clearly the critical factor.[69] Similarly, the gold of the Witwatersrand would have remained locked there forever if the extraction of it had depended on the semi-literate Boers who wandered over the area periodically in search of grass.

Following this logic, P. T. Bauer has shown in a detailed and closely reasoned argument how restrictions upon immigration have impeded commercial development even in West Africa, where indigenous trade was quite advanced.[70] Speaking more generally, in an earlier publication our editors have flatly stated their conviction that Africa needs 'neither restrictions nor birth control but immigrants . . . Africa, like America in the past, needs to import labour as fast as it can'.[71]

Impeccable as abstract economic logic, this is poor sociology if we look upon sociology as a realistic appraisal of actual relationships in historically concrete situations. Africa is not and never has been an America. In respect to its observed capacity to absorb foreign immigration, the entire continent has not

---

[68] As Frankel remarks in *Capital investment*, p. 148: 'In the last resort, economic progress [in Africa] depends on the aptitude effectively to organize the efforts of the population and to educate and train its backward members, and . . . there is no real substitute for this slow and difficult task.'

[69] On the respective roles of entrepreneurial and unskilled labour, cf. Gann and Duignan, *White settlers*, p. 120. Our editors comment here upon the bias in favour of the unskilled factor exerted by the Marxist labour theory of value.

[70] Bauer, *West African trade*, pp. 156–71.   [71] Gann and Duignan, *White settlers*, pp. 94 and 96.

even been an Argentina.[72] This historical fact is now most unlikely to be reversed: since 1960, the inflow of non-Africans has been greatly exceeded by the outflow, although the details of the balance between the two movements are complex.

Just as complex are the reasons why the many millions of Europeans and Orientals that enthusiastic pioneers as diverse as Livingstone and Johnston envisaged flooding into the 'empty' spaces of Africa never materialized. Immigration restrictions *per se,* however, are certainly not the primary answer. Legal restrictions on the free movement of people are a result, not a cause. They mirror something more basic. In the case of Africa, this fundamental factor, we think, is that underlined by the interpretive school of De Kiewiet and Frankel: that is, the poverty of the continent in arable land and other easily exploitable natural resources sufficiently great to provide the all-important *initial* impetus to development. The Kimberley diamond deposits constituted one of the few real bonanzas in the economic history of modern Africa. The fortunes made by a handful of diggers enabled the diamond industry to finance its own growth, as well as to supply funds for the development of the South African gold industry. A great deal of money was rapidly made, too, in the development of the Tanganyikan diamond industry.[73] By and large, however, wealth from mines,

---

[72] In 1870, the non-indigenous population of the African continent, taken as a whole, was exceedingly small; and these few numbers were highly concentrated at its extreme poles, north and south. By 1960, roughly 7 million non-Africans lived in Africa, excluding those in Egypt, North African Jews (450,000), South African Coloureds (1.5 million) and East African Arabs (100,000), all of whom present special problems of definition. The polar concentrations of 1870, however, remained in 1960: something like 80 per cent of the 7 million cited above were either below the Limpopo river or north of the Atlas-Aurès mountains. This fact suggests what upon a closer look indeed proves to be the case: that a very large proportion of this population had been created by natural increase, not by immigration. This is almost entirely true of the largest single non-indigenous ethnic group: the seventeenth- and eighteenth-century immigrant progenitors of the contemporary 1.8 million Afrikaners of South Africa scarcely added up to more than a few hundred people.

Separation of immigrants from African-born elsewhere is more complicated. By 1960, however, many of the *pieds noirs* among the *colons* of French North Africa were fourth or fifth generation. A fair number of British South Africans could trace their ancestry in South Africa back to 1820, and a good many more to, let us say, 1900. Nor should it be forgotten that a great many of the 'immigrants' to British territories north of the Limpopo were South African in origin, largely British but also Boer. (It is commonly estimated, for example, that on the eve of independence Northern Rhodesia's European population was about 40-per-cent Afrikaner.)

After these necessary caveats are entered, it of course remains true that most of the non-African population in the vast area between the Limpopo and the Mediterranean littoral, totalling about 1,400,000 in 1960, were fairly recent immigrants. In sheer volume, most of this immigration took place in the last fifteen years of our period, i.e., after 1945. (More detailed demographic data and sources are presented in Tables 127–9.)

To the African nationalist seriously intent upon turning Africa back to Africans, 7 million non-Africans may appear to be 7 million too many. Yet in world-wide comparative terms, this number is a small one indeed. Between 1856 and 1932, 6.4 million people immigrated to Argentina. Most informed demographers, if asked point blank, would probably classify twentieth-century immigration to Cuba as insignificant. The fact is, however, that more people immigrated to Cuba between 1901 and 1932 (857,000) than to South Africa (852,000) for roughly the same period (1881–1932). (A. M. Carr-Saunders, *World population: past growth and present trends* [Oxford, Clarendon Press, 1936], p. 49.)

[73] EDITORS' NOTE: The career of Cecil John Rhodes (1853–1902), an English parson's son, whose fortunes were built first on Kimberley diamonds and later on gold, is well known. A more recent diamond magnate, also an immigrant, was John Thoburn Williamson (1907–58), a Canadian.

plantations and farms capable of providing the primary foundation for secondary industry and tertiary services has been exceedingly hard won. The African El Dorados, described in such glowing terms by so many Victorian explorers and company promoters, turned out to be chimeras. The exploitation of Africa's wealth generally required far more skill and capital than the pioneers had thought possible.

It is in this light that the restrictive psychology respecting immigration that has been (and remains) characteristic of much of Africa has to be understood. Ordinary people and their political leaders cannot realistically be expected to act consistently in terms of comprehensively rational plans for long-range socio-economic welfare. What they can be expected to do is to act in terms of what they *perceive* as their immediate interests, such perceptions always being made in a socio-cultural context of historically concrete situations rather than according to the dictates of abstract logic. More often than not, the result is what Max Weber terms monopolistic closure. With the wonderful simplicity of genius, he provides us with the universally applicable rule governing open versus closed relationships:

If [group] participants expect that the admission of others will lead to an improvement of their situation . . . their interest will be in keeping the relationship open. If, on the other hand, their expectations are of improving their position by monopolistic tactics, their interest is in a closed relationship.[74]

Demonstrably, what most people of all races in modern Africa perceive from the vantage-point of their experience is not a generous vision of potential abundance for everyone, but rather an ungenerous and niggardly conviction of scarcity for all but the lucky and organized few. There is something symbolic, perhaps, in the fact that the history of European settlement in Africa should have begun within the narrowly monopolistic psychology of the Dutch East India Company. Once established on the continent, Afrikaners fought Africans bitterly and bloodily for the land, only to discover after they had acquired some 90 per cent of it that even this was still not enough for their rapidly growing population. The coming of industry brought the colour bar—as crude an example of monopolistic closure as one could hope to find.[75] It is not on record that the British white settlers of Southern Rhodesia welcomed with open arms

Having begun his career as a university demonstrator of mineralogy and geology, Williamson later acquired extensive experience in Canada, Rhodesia and South Africa. He then spent six years exploring what he believed to be diamondiferous country in Tanganyika. In 1940, he located the Mwadui diamond 'pipe', the largest ever found, three times the size of the Premier pipe in South Africa. In 1942 Williamson became governing and sole director of Williamson Diamonds, Ltd, and in 1946 director of Buhemba Mines, Ltd.

[74] Max Weber, *Economy and society: an outline of interpretive sociology,* Guenther Roth and Claus Wittich, eds. (New York, 1968), p. 43.
[75] The coming of industry produced also some instructive examples of how much human behaviour in the concrete instance is determined by perceived group interests, and how little by abstract ideology. Flush with the recent Bolshevik victory, the socialist South African Industrial Federation met in 1919 and passed two resolutions: one condemning allied intervention in Russia as a capitalist plot against the working class, and another barring the admission of Coloured delegates to the convention. (H. J. and R. E. Simons, *Class and colour in South Africa: 1850–1950* [Harmondsworth, England, 1969], p. 220.) Three years later, in the heat of the turmoil created by the 1922 general strike, the Communist Party of South Africa issued the battle-cry, 'Workers of the world, unite for a white South Africa!' (Eric A. Walker, *A history of Southern Africa* [London, 1959], p. 591.)

the half-starved Poor White Afrikaners who appeared on their borders during the lean decades of the 1920s and 1930s. Southern Rhodesia consistently maintained a policy of 'selective' white immigration, designed to exclude unskilled whites as well as any unduly large number of European continentals. Over three-quarters of a century, a succession of schemes were concocted in South Africa, though not adopted, to move the Indian minority bodily back to India. Virtually the first official act of the settler-dominated Federation of Rhodesia and Nyasaland, when that ill-fated state came into existence, was to cut off further Indian immigration.[76] The only reason there are Indians in East and Central Africa today was British Colonial Office policy, based upon empire-wide considerations, which resisted discriminatory regulations against holders of British passports, irrespective of their origin. Nonetheless, the same Colonial Office favoured highly restrictive measures aimed at the non-empire Lebanese of West Africa, and it was these measures that effectively kept out other potentially productive immigrants as well.[77]

Seen against this background of restriction and organized efforts for group protection, contemporary policies of independent African states towards both immigration and resident non-African minorities have more continuity with the colonial past than might otherwise appear on the surface. The power-wielding group has differently coloured faces. But the broad thrust of policy and administrative effort is familiar: monopolistic closure, of which Africanization is a special but by no means unique case.

Neither space nor data permit a full-scale review of the post-independence fate of non-indigenous ethnic groups in Africa, but a few summary observations seem to be in order.

(A) Generally speaking, the overall tendency is clearly towards restriction and exodus. These trends are in part contradictory, and the situation taken as a whole is still fluid. The largest single exodus has been that of some 800,000 *colons* fleeing Algeria. Nonetheless, it has been reported in a recent survey that there are still a quarter of a million French-speaking foreigners in the former French territories of West Africa.[78] In some areas there are as many French as there ever were, and in Abidjan, capital of the Ivory Coast, their numbers are said to have trebled since independence. Nor should it be forgotten that not all of those who left Africa in the wake of decolonization have stayed away. Many have in fact returned. This is particularly true of Zaire (the former Belgian Congo); but it is true also of Kenya, and to a lesser extent of other areas. With a facilitating shift of either government or policy, it is not beyond the realm of possibility that at least some of Uganda's recently expelled Indians will eventually return to that country.

(B) A second very general observation seems to be called for if we are to maintain a sense of proportion while reviewing the fate of non-indigenous

<hr />

[76] Dotson and Dotson, *Indian minority*, p. 303.

[77] John Holt, founder of a vast trading concern who began his career in West Africa as a poor clerk, could not later, as Bauer points out, have met capital requirements for immigration (*West African trade*, p. 162). Young Rhodes, supposedly dying of tuberculosis, would have been refused entry into present-day Rhodesia (L. H. Gann and Peter Duignan, 'Changing patterns of a white élite: Rhodesian and other settlers', in *Colonialism in Africa*, vol. II, p. 145).

[78] *New York Times*, 8 Feb. 1971.

minorities in volatile post-independence Africa. Putting Algeria aside as a somewhat special case, it is quite clear that to date non-Africans have on the whole suffered much less from the strains of decolonization than have certain indigenous groups. No foreign ethnic minority has yet been treated anywhere else in Africa as ferociously as the Hutu of Burundi, an estimated 100,000 of whom have reportedly been slaughtered in the latest (at this writing) round of their ongoing conflict with the Tutsi. Massacre on a lesser scale was the fate also, it might be remembered, of Ibo caught on the eve of the civil war in the north of Nigeria, and, before them, of a large portion of the Arabs of Zanzibar. It is possible, if the facts were accurately known, that the black Christian peoples of southern Sudan have suffered even more proportionately from their long-drawn-out war with the Arabic north. Short of murder, many thousands of Africans have, in numerous areas, been declared *personae non gratae* and driven from their jobs and homes. For example, the Busia government, upon assuming control of Ghana, expelled 150,000 aliens, virtually all of whom were Africans, but with some Indians and Greeks among them. What such expulsion means in terms of comparative hardship is difficult to assess. But in sheer numbers this single act affected three times as many people as did President Amin's orders to the alien Indians of Uganda. Important as they are intrinsically, however, these inter-African ethnic conflicts are not our proper business in this essay.

(C) A sociologically instructive feature of post-independence 'race' relations has been the feeble correspondence between leadership rhetoric before independence and that since. Tanzania is a prime example. The contrast between Zambia and Malawi provides another, with still a different twist in Kenya. European settlers, who feared Kenyatta as an apostle of the Mau Mau terror, have lived to see him as an admired and hopeful symbol of post-independence stability.[79] Similarly, Dr Banda badly frightened the Indians of Malawi by a series of harshly anti-Indian statements while rising to power. But Indians have felt far safer and more secure in Malawi under his government than have Indians in neighbouring Zambia and Tanzania, where presidents Kaunda and Nyerere assiduously preached non-racialism and brotherly tolerance.

The chief reason for this interesting discrepancy is not obscure, nor does it necessarily indicate more hypocrisy than can reasonably be expected of working politicians. All leaders of the new African states without exception have had to give lip service to the ideals of 'African socialism', the precise meaning of which is usually vague and contradictory—*except* as it bears upon the future role of non-Africans, where its implications are manifest and unambiguous. Africa belongs, in the basic tenet of this creed, to Africans. Both government and the economy therefore should be Africanized, meaning in concrete terms that Africans should acquire through political means the jobs, land and businesses of non-Africans. Seen from the perspective of African eyes, this is simple equity, a necessary rebalancing of the accounts left by the heritage of imperialism.

This much, it appears, is universally agreed upon in principle. But there are

[79] Peter Knauss, 'From devil to father figure: the transformation of Jomo Kenyatta by Kenya whites', *Journal of Modern African Studies*, 1971, **9**, no. 1, pp. 131–7.

wide differences in what is seen as immediately practicable, because it is recognized that the goal of equity conflicts with that of economic development.[80] To the occasionally unsophisticated minds of some of the newer African leaders, the demand for instantaneous equity can outweigh all other considerations, practical or moral. Other leaders, both more sophisticated and more experienced, are more cautious, however sympathetic they may personally be to the ultimate goal of complete Africanization. In their states, which constitute the current majority, the extent to which non-indigenous minorities are threatened varies directly with the degree to which the doctrines of African socialism are taken literally as guides to legislation and administration. Algeria, Tanzania, Zambia and Kenya might be cited, at present writing, as concretely illustrating midway positions upon such a spectrum of policy and action. Finally, at the opposite extreme from a Uganda, minorities are in practice left pretty much alone in such pragmatically and non-ideologically ruled states as the Ivory Coast and Malawi. However, given the inherent instability throughout the entire region, in no African state is the future of any non-indigenous minority indefinitely and unambiguously assured.[81]

(D) Still another broad pattern emerges with considerable clarity. Gann and Duignan have observed of Kenya that 'the local burden of decolonization' was 'borne by the immigrant communities rather than by the imperial power', and their generalization applies elsewhere.[82] Where both Europeans and Orientals have been present, however, this 'burden of decolonization' has fallen far more heavily upon the Orientals than upon the Europeans. To many Europeans in the salaried bureaucratic sector, the loss of their jobs through Africanization has meant little more than a transfer, a new job in Great Britain, Australia or North America, or early retirement on a more or less generous pension. Likewise, the relatively few settler-farmers of Kenya who have been displaced to date have been compensated. More broadly speaking, the European artisans, professionals or white-collar workers anywhere who have been forced to leave independent Africa have had the option of returning to a Europe prosperous and labour-hungry as never before in history, or of going to a booming South Africa or to Australia or Canada.

Indians and, to a lesser extent, Lebanese face a far grimmer set of alternatives. Most of these people have limited formal education, small capital and no skills other than those of trading. For them, to move at all is difficult, and to move advantageously impossible. Furthermore, Orientals have clearly been treated much less gently by Africans than have Europeans. Traditionally, Orientals have been disliked more; but more importantly, they have much less external political protection. Weak African states, still dependent upon the good-

---

[80] Donald Rothchild, 'Kenya's Africanization program: priorities of development and equity', *American Political Science Review*, Sept. 1970, **64**, no. 3, pp. 737–53.

[81] Morocco may be cited more or less at random as a pertinent example. The 90,000 resident French and other foreign nationals have been repeatedly reassured by King Hassan II that there would be no hurried Moroccanization or arbitrary confiscations (*France Soir*, 25 August 1972). Attempted coups against Hassan have so far proved unsuccessful–but a successful one would no doubt bring into question continuation of the king's 'liberal' policy with respect to foreign nationals.

[82] Gann and Duignan, *Burden of empire*, p. 350.

will and assistance of their former colonizers, have been generally restrained in their treatment of Europeans; but the same constraints do not necessarily apply equally to Orientals. The Tanzanians, for example, are reported to be confiscating Indian property under their nationalization laws disproportionately and discriminatorily compared to that of Europeans.

The expulsion of some 50,000 Indians from Uganda by the Amin government (1972) constitutes the sharpest single blow that this group has yet suffered in Africa.[83] This sudden and dramatic event, however, should not obscure what in the aggregate are perhaps equally important trends elsewhere. Shorn of trading licences and civil-service jobs, as well as positions in schools and universities as pupils and students, something like 36,000 Indians left Kenya between 1962 and 1969.[84] Figures for other areas are unfortunately less readily available. What we can say for a certainty is that Indians have come under heavy and perhaps accelerating political and economic pressures throughout the East and Central African regions where they are found in appreciable numbers, and that in response many have emigrated.[85] We can add that by now many more undoubtedly would have left if the British passports provided them in lieu of citizenship in the African state where they resided at the time of independence had been honoured in Britain. Until Amin's action forced the British government to reconsider existing policy, they were not honoured.

The citizenship issue emerges quickly as the dominant theme in virtually all post-independence discussion, whether journalistic or scholarly, of the Indians' future in Africa. The very explicit judgement is usually made that if Indians had opted for citizenship when it was offered and had made a sincere effort to integrate with Africans and identify with their emerging states, they would not be finding themselves in their present predicament. To our mind, these judgements are both excessively legalistic and sociologically obtuse.[86] Indians with very few exceptions wanted and hoped to stay in Africa. The decision not to take citizenship when it was formally offered after independence was therefore negatively, not positively, motivated. Nothing in their experience had convinced them that citizenship *per se* offered much protection to either their property or their persons.[87] European settlers, significantly enough, arrived at the

---

[83] On the eve of the 8 November 1972 deadline, it was reported that out of a total population of 82,000 'Asians', 55,000 would be affected by the expulsion order (*New York Times,* 8 Nov. 1972). All such statistics must obviously be regarded as tentative and approximate.

[84] See *Africa contemporary record: annual survey and documents, 1970–71,* Colin Legum, ed. (London, 1971), pp. B119–20; and Donald Rothchild, *Racial bargaining in independent Kenya: a study of minorities and decolonization* (London, Oxford University Press, 1973).

[85] Since President Kaunda's 1968 Mulungushi declaration of the Zambian 'economic revolution', trading licences of aliens have been restricted to the ten major towns—where Indians had already recently concentrated for purely social and economic reasons (see Kenneth Kaunda, 'Zambia's economic reforms', *African Affairs,* Oct. 1968, **67,** no. 269, p. 297; also Dotson and Dotson, *Indian minority,* p. 362).

[86] On the problem of citizenship, see Donald Rothchild, 'Citizenship and national integration: the non-African crisis in Kenya', in University of Denver, Graduate School of International Studies, Center on International Race Relations, *Studies in race and nations,* **1,** no. 3 (Denver, 1969–70); also Dotson and Dotson, *Indian minority,* pp. 363–79.

[87] The fate of the Shia Ismailis—a large and in some areas (e.g., Uganda) predominant Muslim sub-group in East Africa—will in time provide a convenient test of these assumptions. With the approach of independence, Ismailis were encouraged by their authoritative religious head, the Aga Khan, to take citizenship and identify with the Africans. How much difference this policy

same conclusion: even fewer of them chose citizenship than did Indians. Of course, the fact that most Indians are now aliens provides African governments with a conveniently legal excuse for denying responsibility for them. Yet, even if the Indians had not been so obliging, other and less subtle measures doubtless would have been found to accomplish the same ends.[88]

Nonetheless, despite these mounting uncertainties and anxieties, a measure of scholarly caution is in order before we succumb to an utterly apocalyptic vision of the fate of Africa's non-indigenous minorities. This applies to Indians as well as to Europeans. As recent Ugandan history so convincingly shows, demagogic demands for Africanization and the expulsion of foreigners are politically popular. Furthermore, the same events suggest that in contemporary Africa, as has been all too abundantly illustrated elsewhere in history, making scapegoats of helpless minorities has all but irresistible appeal to political leadership of questionable legitimacy, fighting to maintain power in situations fraught with serious internal conflict. Yet, although granting this, we must at the same time recognize that socio-political processes are not typically unilinear. They are to an important degree self-correcting when it becomes apparent that certain changes desired in principle may carry price-tags too high to be comfortably borne. Thus the first lesson taught by Amin's Uganda, how easy it is to get rid of unwanted minorities if one sets one's mind resolutely to the task, is certain to be countered in time by a second lesson, how costly such a policy is, both economically and in terms of international goodwill.[89]

These equilibrating forces can already be observed in operation. At the mass level, there is probably little difference between Uganda and Kenya in basic sentiment with respect to their minorities, and Kenyan politicians are certainly not lacking who would gladly imitate General Amin if they had the opportunity. Up to the present writing, however, the Kenyan government has successfully resisted popular pressures for more drastic action against its alien Indians beyond the rather onerous ones it has already applied. As the *Africa contemporary record* notes, there is a conscious and recognized 'element of self-interest' in this policy, 'for Kenya wants their skills, experience and capital'.[90] The

will ultimately make remains to be seen. Ismailis in Tanzania with real property have already suffered expropriation—carried out in democratic fashion along with that of Indian aliens and with the properties, largely nonexistent, of Africans.

[88] In a moment of irritation at criticism of his order expelling alien Indians from Uganda, President Amin startled the world by announcing that citizens would have to go also. The sharp international reaction, including for the first time that of African leaders, brought a quick 'clarification' negating this abrupt extension of the original order. But understandably, it left many Indians wondering what citizenship was worth in Uganda. (*International Herald Tribune*, 22 and 23 Aug. 1972.) In reply to his African critics, among whom the most outspoken was President Julius Nyerere, Amin is reported to have reminded Nyerere that he (Nyerere) was moving toward the same goals through his nationalization policies but 'at a snail's pace' (*ibid.*, 23 Aug. 1972).

[89] Modern nations, particularly small ones, do not exist in either economic or political isolation. Negative reverberations from President Amin's Asian policy were being felt in surrounding countries even before appreciable numbers of Indians had left Uganda. 'In 1971 Kenya, which by African standards is a booming economic success, sent 20 per cent of her exports to Uganda, and this market is gravely endangered by Uganda's growing inability to pay' (*New York Times*, 10 Oct. 1972).

[90] *Africa contemporary record, 1970–71*, p. B119.

same considerations have clearly offered some protection to the former 'white highlands' farmers, most of whom remain.[91] Zambia, by contrast, has paid a very heavy price for the voluntary emigration of several hundred of its small contingent of European farmers. Between 1964 and 1969 'the [total] cost of imported foodstuffs more than doubled', and 'it was estimated [in 1969] that 1970's bill would be even higher'. Nor has Zambia found it possible to dispense with the services of Europeans even in government, where the pressures for Africanization are most acute. 'At the year-end [1970] a massive recruitment drive started overseas for 450 skilled expatriates to fill local authority jobs such as electrical engineers and town clerks.' [92] These jobs had been previously held by Europeans, who left under the rigours of 'decolonization'. But given the current level of Zambia's social evolution, the jobs simply could not be filled—except by other Europeans.

Modern social science has recognized from the beginning that human societies are constituted of a precarious and awesome balance between rational and non-rational forces. No historical society has ever been entirely rational; but, on the other hand, in no society is rationality ever entirely absent. It is a simple empirical observation that to date most governing African leaders, in the face of exceedingly strong temptations, have demonstrated a measure of moderation in their treatment of non-indigenous minorities. Economic rationality counsels continuation in this path, since it is an ineluctable fact that Africa, now as in the past, remains dependent to a considerable degree upon the capital and the capabilities of foreigners, and that this dependency will continue for an indefinite time.

* * *

Four careers

An essay covering ninety years of colonial history and all the non-indigenous ethnic groups of Africa must depend primarily upon secondary sources and must be cast more or less continuously at an exceedingly high level of generalization. Here, as a small counterweight to this unrelieved abstraction, material of an entirely different kind is offered without apology for its somewhat informal character.

The brief case studies that follow, stressing occupational capabilities, motivation, income and associated living standards, are drawn from our own field-work in Central Africa between September 1959 and August 1961, and extended by a two-month return visit in 1966. No claim is made, of course, for representativeness in any meaningful statistical sense. Yet, since man is a social animal moulded by subcultures and relational structures far larger than his individual self, we are confident that our Messrs. A, B, C and D reflect experiences, values and destinies widely shared by roughly similar people. If they do not, social science has no validity.

[91] 'In 1967 . . . agricultural commodities accounted for 60 per cent of the nation's export earnings; large-scale farming, overwhelmingly owned and controlled by whites, accounted for 75 per cent of the total volume of Kenya's marketed agricultural products.' (Knauss, 'From devil to father figure', p. 136.)

[92] *Africa contemporary record, 1970–71*, pp. B225 and 229.

Case I: a modern Afrikaner farmer

Mr A's family of orientation, to adopt the useful designation of W. Lloyd Warner, were among the pioneer Afrikaner farmers and transport riders described by Frederick Selous as already established in Southern Rhodesia by the mid-1890s.[93] From that territory they trekked north, crossed the Zambezi ahead of the railway (which reached Victoria Falls in 1902) and settled for a time near the site of the modern city of Lusaka.

This was well before Mr A was born in Northern Rhodesia around 1910. His father, mother and most of his numerous siblings returned to South Africa in the late 1920s. He stayed on, worked for neighbouring farmers and then for a stretch of several years on the maintenance crew of the railway. Just before the beginning of the Second World War he entered the copper-mines, where he laboured until 1954. Intelligent, staid and responsible, Mr A there rose as far as he could go with his limited formal education. He was on the Copper Belt when for a brief period the annual pay of exceptionally skilled and experienced European workers pushed upward beyond £3,000. Yet despite the good pay, Mr A never liked the mines. Early in 1954 he quit his job, cashed in his substantial savings and bought a new black Mercedes sedan (then the universally recognized success-symbol in Central Africa). This still left him with enough money to acquire the 300-acre farm where he was living with his ex-school-teacher wife when we came to know them in the fall of 1959.

Mr A's farm was small by local standards, the more typical European holdings in Northern Rhodesia at this time being between 1,200 and 5,000 acres.[94] The soil, however, was good, and this particular farm was unusual in the high limestone plateau area where it was located in that it was blessed with a perennial spring of considerable volume. Before Mr A's occupancy, this spring had been used only to water livestock and an orchard of citrus trees, since its outlet lay in a deep crevice-like ravine well below the general level of the land. By investing in a diesel-driven pump and an extensive system of pipes, Mr A brought the water to the surface and used it to irrigate a hundred acres upon which he was growing wheat during the otherwise dormant dry season, which in this region extends from May to November. In addition, he grew the usual maize during the rainy season and a good deal of fruit, and kept a few head of cattle. Given adequate public facilities for cold storage and processing, his fruit might very well have been his most profitable product. But unfortunately for him such facilities were still nonexistent. Mr A's fruit matured at a time when every backyard in Northern Rhodesia was loaded with home-grown mangoes and oranges, thereby temporarily depressing prices to a point where it barely paid Mr A to harvest all of his crop.

Being preoccupied at the time with our Indian study, we did not collect detailed notes on the operation of this farm as an economic enterprise. Some crude estimates sufficiently precise for the present purposes are nonetheless fairly easily calculated. On the assumption that Mr A's land produced seven bags of wheat to the acre, selling at the officially supported price of 50s per bag, this crop alone would have brought in a gross income of £1,750.[95] If we

---

[93] Frederick C. Selous, *Sunshine and storm in Rhodesia* (London, 1896), pp. 241–2.

[94] *Brief guide to Northern Rhodesia*, p. 76.

[95] Production estimates and prices are taken from *ibid.*, p. 85, intended mainly as information for prospective immigrants.

may assume again that his maize, fruit and cattle produced a slightly greater amount, the total gross income from the farm would have been something like £4,000. From this, a considerable bill for fertilizers, diesel fuel, taxes and African labour would have to be extracted, to say nothing of fencing and machine parts. Payments upon outstanding debt, in all likelihood, consumed most of whatever was left. On the other hand, since the As grew most of their food and paid nothing for rent, their living costs were minimal.

However costs and income might have balanced out, it seemed clear to us that Mr A had not gained economically by exchanging his mining career for that of a farmer. He and his wife lived in classic rural Boer simplicity. Their small four-room house had been inherited from their predecessor. Already two or three decades old, it was still unimproved. Typical of its region and period, it was constructed of crude local masonry, set on a raised concrete floor, roofed with corrugated iron nailed to pole rafters and left unceiled. No attempt had been made to maintain a lawn or shrubbery. But the ageing and always carefully washed and polished Mercedes stood grandly before the door, in a yard made untidy by a squawking flock of geese and ducks happily supplied with water from an open irrigation ditch that ran beside the house.

Although the strictly monetary return from the property could not have been more than modest, its psychic income to the As was obviously very substantial. Mr A was proud of his farm and enormously proud of his achievement in developing his irrigation system and of the resulting wheat, which composed a not inconsiderable part of Northern Rhodesia's tiny production, then only about 5,000 bags a year.[96] Nor had the As ever expected to make a fortune. This was not their motive when they bought the farm. Rather, it was to provide a retirement home and a secure income for their old age. But already in late 1959 they were wondering how long they could continue to stay in a country where the 'bloody Munts' were threatening to acquire control. Dispirited also by the loss of their only child (a youth who had been killed in an accident a couple of years before), they talked much of giving up and 'going south', where Mr A was confident he could still get a job in the mines despite his advancing years.

Severe petrol restrictions made it unfeasible to visit the farm when we were last in Zambia in 1966, and no one was left among our common acquaintances who could tell us what had happened to the As. It seems likely, however, that they were among the several hundred of Zambia's small contingent of European farmers who simply abandoned their land and left the country after the coming of independence.

Case II: an English technician

When we first met Mr B in 1959, he was several years past forty. He had grown up in the slums of East London, and in speech and manner retained many of the distinctive characteristics of the Cockney subculture. Under circumstances that never became clear to us, he acquired in his youth the technical skills of a locksmith. During the Second World War he served Great Britain, usefully applying his talents to the delicate and dangerous task of defusing unexploded Nazi bombs. Soon after the war he emigrated, alone, to Northern

---

[96] Great Britain, Advisory Commission on the Review of the Constitution of Rhodesia and Nyasaland, *Report: Appendix VI, Survey of developments since 1953*, Cmnd. 1149 (London, 1960), p. 372.

Rhodesia, leaving behind in England the wife whom he seems to have had for only a very short time.

Circa 1960, Mr B was one of two people in Lusaka capable of opening a balky safe; and at least to hear Mr B tell it, he was the expert and the other man the amateur, despite the fact that the latter got most of the business. Like all accomplished artisans, Mr B was proud of his skill. Given any encouragement, he would tell stories by the hour of how he had solved difficult problems after everyone else had failed. Faced with a sufficient array of stuck or broken safes, Mr B would have been both happy and prosperous, since he put a high monetary value on his professional time. Yet in fact he was neither.

As is usual in cases of career success and failure, both structural and personal factors were involved in Mr B's predicament. Structurally, the simple and elementary fact confronting him was that safes, balky or otherwise, were not as yet very numerous in Lusaka and its surrounding metropolitan region, and, as we have already pointed out, there were two qualified experts to share what little business there was.

We have already discussed above the remarkable degree to which European business and its associated technical skills, in the Northern Rhodesia of this time, were corporate and bureaucratic in organization. Mr B's competitor provides a concrete example. He was regularly employed as a salesman-technician by a large British-South African hardware and implement concern. Safe-work for him was simply an incidental part of his duties in their totality; it did not matter, in terms of income, how much or how little of it he did. But Mr B was too individualistic to seek a like solution. Through what was doubtless a very complicated mixture of choice and necessity, he tried to live as an independent businessman. Between all-too-infrequent calls for safe- and lock-work, he maintained a tiny shop for key-making and minor gun-repair. These tasks were in fact performed under Mr B's supervision by an African assistant, since he himself loftily disdained them as beneath his professional and European dignity. But as is not uncommonly the case, the dignity so acquired came at a high price. Combined, the work of both himself and the assistant might have occupied Mr B a quarter of his time, and he could certainly have used to good purpose the £9 a month that was theoretically paid the assistant, since this was often enough more than his own net income.

It might be correctly observed, therefore, that Mr B lived in good part through a rather crude exploitation of African labour. The level of living so gained, however, would come as something of a shock, as indeed it did to us, to those British and American liberals who simply assume that all Europeans in Africa live in the style of maharajas. When we first came to know him, Mr B slept on a dirty cot in a half-open shed behind his shop, where he himself prepared most of his meals over makeshift cooking facilities. (These arrangements were feasible, since the premises, originally built for Indians, contained basic plumbing.) Later, after an unwary automobile dealer had sold him a used Volkswagen microbus on hire-purchase, Mr B took up residence in what had been an abandoned farmhouse some fifteen miles out of town. This move to a grander, suburban style of living of course necessitated an African 'houseboy', who was accordingly added to his staff.

Seen in purely rational terms, Mr B's poverty was a gross and unintelligible contradiction. Although eccentric and erratic, Mr B was certainly no fool, not in the literal sense. If he could not make a living in Lusaka from the very useful skills he possessed, why then did he not move to a place where a better market for them existed—for example, back home to England? The answer is not that Mr B was indifferent to material rewards in principle. On the contrary, he continually and bitterly complained of his severely straitened circumstances, for which he seemed to hold his creditors primarily responsible. The real answer is that Mr B was at heart less a locksmith and a businessman than a poet.

In what is surely one of the most perceptive books on colonial Africa ever written, H. Alan C. Cairns remarks that the ill-assorted pioneers whom he surveyed from the pre-imperial period can be neatly divided into two categories: those who wanted to bring civilization to the Dark Continent and those who wished to escape from it.[97] Belatedly, Mr B fell within the second of Cairns's categories, and from this fact largely flowed the remainder of his difficulties. Mr B did not come to Africa to be a locksmith, although these skills were the mundane reason why immigration officials let him in. He came to be a White Hunter.

Incredible as it might seem to anyone who knew Mr B as we knew him, he had actually taken initial steps in the achievement of his highly elusive ambition. Shortly after his arrival in Africa he had teamed up with a partner, presumably better prepared financially and personally than he. Together they managed to organize and carry out several cut-rate safaris, the clients being for the most part local people interested in meat. It is even possible that this venture may have received some official encouragement. For a brief period, just before and just after Federation, there had been some highly inflated official hopes of establishing a profitable safari business modelled on that of East Africa. But under the rapid European influx and the resulting inroads of economic development, Northern Rhodesia's game population declined precipitously, necessitating stringent regulations to save the remnant. The scope for the safari business, never very great to begin with, was thereby drastically reduced; and Mr B had neither the capital, the social skills nor the political connexions to exploit its remaining small potential. As a second best, he then tried ivory poaching in a remote (and at this time poorly patrolled) corner of eastern Angola. But this, too, proved unprofitable—less, it appears, from the considerable risks involved than from a lack of sufficient elephants in the area.

Thus in the period when we knew him Mr B lived the life of a frustrated poet-of-action. Bored, virtually unemployed, moneyless and entangled ever deeper in debt, he acquired the reputation of an undependable and vaguely unsavoury character. Consequently, he must have found it a great relief when salvation unexpectedly presented itself. During the period when most Europeans were fleeing the Congo after the July 1960 *débâcle*, Mr B suddenly disappeared one day over that frontier, presumably in hopes of offering his services to one of the mercenary military units in the process of forming there.

Case III: an English civil servant

It so happens—the fact is really of only incidental interest—that Mr B and Mr C were acquainted although not on particularly friendly terms. A not inconsid-

[97] H. A. C. Cairns, *The clash of cultures: early race relations in Central Africa* (New York, 1965), p. 34.

erable part of Mr C's duties as a middle-range executive officer in the Northern Rhodesian administration bore directly upon the activities of the police and the courts. Mr B was well known in these circles, although to the best of our knowledge he was never actively prosecuted. Mr C once gave us a fatherly admonition to the effect that the less we had to do with Mr B the better.

Mr C came from a lower-middle-class southern England family, too poor to send him to a university. As an alternative he joined the Indian police in the mid-1930s. He did well, attracted the favourable attention of his superiors and, following independence in India, went as a District Officer to Nigeria. From there he applied for and obtained the similar but somewhat better post he occupied when we came to know him in Northern Rhodesia.

A supremely self-assured and intelligently opinionated man, Mr C believed that he stood out sharply from his fellow civil servants as one more humanly sensitive, more liberally inclined and more energetically and positively moral. Certainly he was possessed of all these qualities in abundant measure. It is simply inconceivable to us, for example, that he would ever, under any provocation, have spoken rudely to an African menial. He thoroughly disapproved nonetheless of the physical and moral slackness, what he termed fecklessness, that he thought he saw in the indigenous population. But he was inclined to be indulgent of these failings, for he interpreted them as behaviour to be expected, given the usual treatment meted out to Africans by non-Africans. As for Indians, whom he believed he understood thoroughly upon the basis of his long residence in India, he applied to them a much sterner standard of judgement. Because they had had the benefit of superior tutelage for a longer period, naturally more could be expected of them than of Africans. Yet the truth was that the local community sorely disappointed Mr C.

It was his fellow Europeans, however, whom Mr C judged most harshly of all. Here we refer not to the tiny minority of Mr Bs (for whom he would have had no mercy, once they were caught firmly beyond the line of the law), but to the ordinary run-of-the-mill of the settler population. In particular and of most interest to us in the present context, he held their extravagant level of living against them. That a less-than-competent European automobile mechanic should be paid £80 a month to stand by and watch Africans paid £7 or £8 change tyres was in his eyes monstrously immoral. That the mechanic's wife should be lazily collecting an additional £45 for selling lingerie in an Indian-owned department store only added fuel to his indignation. The wife's job, he would correctly observe, was made possible by the fact that her pre-school children were tended in a *crèche* run (but not owned) by Coloured women earning £10 to £15, while her domestic chores were assumed by an African 'houseboy' earning £6 or £7. Anything if not consistent, Mr C was always quick to add that his own (base) salary of £1,700 a year was more than adequate, and we are confident that he would have cheerfully accepted less if that had been really necessary.

We have pointed out that Mr C viewed himself as unusual among his civil-servant peers in these attitudes and evaluations, and certainly few of them were either so harshly critical of their fellow Europeans or so masochistically ascetic. Yet, we believe that Mr C, like most people, erred in thinking of himself as in a fundamental sense extraordinary. From the vantage-point of foreigners and sociologists, it appeared to us that he merely participated more enthusiastically than most of his colleagues in the distinctive subculture of their group, into which he had received an early and particularly intensive socialization. Be this as it may, the overridingly significant fact is that the Mr Cs of the British colonial service provided the territories under their jurisdiction with an efficient, humane and devotedly well-intentioned public administration.

In keeping with these high standards of administrative efficiency, the government of Northern Rhodesia sought and used the advice of competent economic experts in a variety of technical capacities. Nonetheless, we concluded from our own field-work experience that its Mr Cs were not, generally speaking, economically minded. To cite the main supporting evidence that forced itself upon our attention, they had little understanding of, and still less sympathy for, the middleman-traders and their economic function. It might be objected that this was simply anti-Indian, anti-Semitic or anti-Greek prejudice, which of course it effectively came to in manifest practice. But such an interpretation would miss our essential point that they thought more easily in moralistic terms than in economic ones, and that they seemed not readily to appreciate economic motivation either in themselves or in others.

Here again it might correctly be pointed out that thinking economically, if you were a Mr C, was simply not your job as defined in the bureaucratic hierarchy, and that, as far as you yourself were concerned, your economic needs were served by adequate compensation, much of which was in the form of hidden but valuable perquisites. It is also true that 'adequate', in this case, was defined normatively as that appropriate to a European standard of living, and that top administrators saw the maintenance of such a standard as absolutely necessary to the prestige (and therefore authority) of their government, irrespective of sheer economic rationality. Furthermore, it is true that this standard was in fact very high indeed *if measured against the prevailing poverty of the indigenous population.* But if the terms of the argument are shifted, as is seldom done in the usual discussion, and if we compare the level of living enjoyed by the Mr Cs of the African colonial services with that of Western Europeans *elsewhere than in Africa,* a rather different perspective emerges.

The Cs, to follow through on their example, maintained a small car. Along with virtually every other European and Indian family in Lusaka at that time, they had an African servant. They were substantially housed in a government-owned bungalow, for which they paid a sub-economic rent. This bungalow, it is also true, was located in the next-to-the-best residential district in town, a district made up very largely of almost identical bungalows. The typical house here was equipped with a small refrigerator, but it had no washing-machine or dryer. Laundry was commonly done in the bathtub, and along with the ironing constituted one of the principal duties of the servant. In other respects, too, the house was rather simply furnished. Furthermore, the Cs dispensed with one of the major luxuries commonly indulged in by people at their status level, a fairly elaborate garden, which would have required an additional 'boy' to maintain. This luxury, for reasons of both economy and moral principle, they were unwilling to take on.

In short, the Cs lived comfortably but hardly luxuriously by standards now taken for granted by middle-class people in every developed country in the world. Indeed, they could hardly have lived otherwise, not on £1,700 a year.

The Cs' case would have little significance if they were truly exceptional, which they were not. There were, of course, a good many Europeans in Lusaka with larger incomes. They themselves would have had somewhat more if Mrs C had worked, as most wives in European families did. Nonetheless, not so very many people had much higher income than the Cs, nor did this category include more than a very few with incomes of, let us say, twice as much. Lusaka, with a non-African population of about 15,000, was essentially a government town. Of the Europeans not in government, most were employees of local branches of corporate enterprises. Their salaries, except for the top positions, paralleled rather closely those of the government hierarchy. The quite striking result of these facts was that there were virtually no really wealthy Europeans, nor many substantial property owners. The two richest men in town, significantly, were a second-generation Jew, the proprietor of the largest department store; and an ageing Indian pioneer, who, among his other numerous holdings, was owner of the largest and most imposing office-building.

The Cs, who never had the slightest intention of remaining permanently in Northern Rhodesia, were the only psychological expatriates among our four cases. Well ahead of the eventual Africanization of Mr C's job, the family returned to England. There they bought a small cottage and took relatively humble jobs to bolster his modest civil-service pension—he at first as a secondary-school teacher, and then, more appropriate in terms of his previous experience, as a social-work counsellor at a prison. Lower-level employment after retirement is, of course, quite in keeping with the English civil-service tradition. Very much in the same tradition, Mr C amuses himself by writing of his adventures and retailing to a not-very-interested world his somewhat old-fashioned moral judgements and opinions.

Case IV: an Indian businessman

Mr D is still a comparatively young man, only now approaching middle age. The fact that he is an immigrant is thus somewhat unusual, since most of his demographic cohorts in East and Central Africa are African-born. With some hundreds of his compatriots, he helped to swell the immigration chart to its highest point just before the inaugural of the Federation of Rhodesia and Nyasaland (3 September 1953), after which entry into the new state was closed to economically productive Indian males.

In still another respect, Mr D is somewhat unusual. Most Indian immigrants were 'called' to East and Central Africa through a patron-client system in which the established patron (usually but not necessarily a close kinsman) acted as a sponsor and initial employer. But in the last-chance press to get into the Federation, this system had broken down. Mr D was therefore actually 'called' by his slightly older brother, who himself had been in Africa only a year or so and who was still working as a shop assistant. Partly for this reason, but only partly, since the patron-client system in its older form was already disintegrating, Mr D has always been considerably more independent than was typical of his immediate predecessors.

By 'community' (the commonly used euphemism for a caste), Mr D is a Patidar and therefore a representative of the most numerous Hindu group in East and Central Africa. The Patidars were traditionally small landholding farmers. Many of those living in the rich old Charotar district of Gujarat from which Mr D originated were growers of cotton and tobacco, crops sold for cash rather than used for subsistence. On such income some Patidars were able to provide an education for their sons, thus preparing them for the civil service and the professions or, alternatively, with capital for business ventures. Few of these people, who were well established, emigrated because they had no compelling motive to do so. But they did manifest in their careers an active tradition outside agriculture that could be emulated by peasant boys like Mr D who boarded ship for Africa.

Like all Indian immigrants to Northern Rhodesia in recent times, Mr D had to pass an English test. For this he had been prepared by a primary-school education that included a foundation in that language as well as literacy in Gujarati and elementary mathematics. To this day the mathematics is indeed a primary tool for Mr D, who, like most successful businessmen, is a calculating man and therefore a rational one in the Weberian sense of that term.

When we first came to know him—and he was one of our very first contacts in the Indian community—Mr D worked as a shop assistant in a prosperous grocery with a European-oriented clientele. He was then making £45 a month, the top wage being paid to superior assistants. This was sharply above the £10 to £15 he had earned just a few years previously, and it represented an impressive victory of collective action on the part of shop assistants as a class, helped along and encouraged in their struggle by the local labour office. (Incidentally, £40–45 a month was the going wage for European *female* shop assistants.) Only a very few European males were so situated, unless the term is broadly defined to include the salesmen of such businesses as hardware and implement concerns. If their jobs demanded technical knowledge, they were paid more. Mr B's competitor would be a good example.

Most of Mr D's salary at that time (the autumn of 1959) was absorbed by traditional family obligations, although for a brief period he and his brother did splurge to the extent of buying and maintaining an old car. He was still unmarried. Because no single Indian ever lived alone, he lodged with his married brother, his brother's rapidly expanding family and the similarly young and numerous families of two cousins, all in a small new modern house in the segregated Indian residential district of Lusaka.

These arrangements, however, did not last long—as nothing else seemingly has for the ambitious and upwardly mobile Mr D. He liked to practise his English, which was why he tolerated us initially; and he had for this reason become friendly with a European executive of a large corporate firm of manufacturers' representatives, with headquarters on the Copper Belt. This man occasionally shopped at the grocery and was impressed with the speed and accuracy of Mr D's mental arithmetic. After considerable persuasion on Mr D's part, he finally agreed to arrange a job for him in his firm. This was breaking new ground for both of them, because Indians did not commonly hold 'European' jobs in European firms.

Mr D moved to the Copper Belt and worked in his new position as warehouse clerk for just over a year, rising to a top pay of £60 a month. He got along well with his employers, as he invariably has with Europeans. Nonetheless, he felt himself discriminated against in terms of pay, which was probably objectively the case. More importantly, he had no intention of spending his life on a salary. When he quit his job to go to India to get married, therefore, he did not return to it. Instead, he and his newly acquired wife moved to Salisbury, where he set up shop in the traditional fashion in the old secondary trading district.

The times, as Mr D very well knew, were hardly auspicious for such a venture. Darkened political horizons had depressed the economy generally; and the sudden emergence of a large cohort of young Mr Ds, all anxious to establish themselves in business, had dampened prospects in the African trade in particular. But Mr D was confident that skill, persistence and intelligence would put him ahead of his competitors. Time proved that this self-confidence was not misplaced.

The reason Mr D chose the African trade for entry into independent entrepreneurship is also much more rational than might appear at a glance. His trip to India and its associated family-kinship obligations had drained him of most of his accumulated savings. But in the African trade lack of capital was not an insurmountable handicap. For experienced hands like Mr D, the £1,500 of stock necessary to set up a minimal shop could easily be obtained on credit. What was indispensable was a small back-log of capital large enough to meet rent payments and living expenses until he was established.

Nonetheless, for a year or more the Ds had a very rough time of it. There were months when their total gross income did not exceed £35, out of which they had to pay £25 in rent to their Indian landlord. Fortunately, this included their old-fashioned (and theoretically illegal) living quarters behind the shop. But they had no money for furnishings. When we visited them during this period, we ate on upturned packing cases, and the Ds were sleeping on a mattress thrown upon the floor. As a sign of the changing times, however, there was *one* item of furniture: a television set bought on hire-purchase. This, together with card games with friends on Sundays, constituted the sum total of the Ds' recreation. Yet even on Sundays the Ds discreetly kept the shop door slightly ajar for a possible knowing customer, although shops were supposedly closed by order of the municipal council.

When the shop next door went vacant, Mr D was provided with the opportunity for which he had been waiting. He rented the vacated store and installed a fruit-and-vegetable counter, which by law had to be separate from his other premises. While he was away at the central wholesale market every morning acquiring fresh produce, his wife took care of both shops, a simple enough task given the scarcity of customers for either.

As Mr D expected, the fruit-and-vegetable counter was soon doing a much larger volume of business than his other shop; and it was also shortly the most popular of several similar such counters in the neighbourhood. The reason was simple: the produce was always the freshest and the best obtainable, and the price was dependably a penny or two below the competition. These secrets of success had been acquired by Mr D in his old employment back in Lusaka. There his employers had done a better business in fruit and vegetables than almost anyone else in town, precisely because they made a speciality of it and paid strict attention to the rigorous and somewhat peculiar demands of the trade.

Mr D's shop was just off the central business district of Salisbury and just inside, as we have said, of the old secondary African trading area. Many of Mr D's new customers, however, were working-class Europeans, and among these he established a regular and dependable clientele. (Africans less typically develop the 'regular customer' relationship.) As soon as he felt secure enough in this regular clientele, Mr D closed both his shops and moved into more commodious premises around the corner, where he sold nothing but fruit and vegetables. Then, when he was doing well enough for his books to show a steady and rising turn-over, Mr D went to a bank and borrowed £3,000 for a used walk-in refrigerator. With this equipment installed, he was able to store produce and keep it fresh almost indefinitely, thus offsetting to a very considerable extent the effects of the otherwise volatile seasonal cycle. Because his was the only refrigerator of its kind in the immediate neighbourhood, Mr D was able also to corner his local off-season market, with the result that his neighbourhood competitors were compelled either to buy from him, which some of them did at near retail prices, or to suspend sales temporarily.

The refrigerator was the essential key to Mr D's rapid ascent from a tiny bazaar-type trader of the traditional kind in the African trade to the status of a substantial small businessman. The refrigerator was soon followed by a new van to bring produce from the market. (Hitherto, Mr D had depended upon the taxi service provided hawkers, most of them Africans.) The van was shortly followed by a second, and the old refrigerator by a new and larger one. When we last heard from the Ds in 1968 with the news of these developments, they were busily planning a new house in the Indian suburb.

Table 127. *European populations in Africa, pre-World War II and pre-independence*

	Pre-World War II		Pre-independence	
	Year	Number	Year	Number
Extreme north				
Algeria	1931	920,788	1954	910,000
Morocco	1931	195,000	1954	615,000
Tunisia	1931	195,293	1954	245,000
Total		1,311,081		1,770,000
Extreme south				
Basutoland	1935–6	1,434	1956	1,926
Bechuanaland	1935–6	1,899	1956	3,173
South-West Africa	1935–6	31,049	1960	73,464
Swaziland	1935–6	2,735	1956	5,919
Union of South Africa	1935–6	2,003,512	1960	3,088,492
Total		2,040,629		3,172,974
Rest of Africa				
Angola	1935–6	30,000	1960	172,529
Cameroons (Br.)	1935–6	354	1952–3	758
Cameroun	1935–6	2,257	1952	13,173
Congo (Belg.)	1935–6	18,680	1958	109,457
Ethiopia	1935	5,000	1957	15,000
Fr. Equatorial Africa	1935–6	4,463	1953	21,885
Fr. West Africa	1935–6	19,061	1953	62,236
Gambia	1935–6	217	1963	300
Gold Coast	1935–6	2,800	1953	7,100
Kenya	1935–6	17,997	1962	55,759
Moçambique	1935–6	10,000	1955	65,798
Nigeria	1935–6	5,246	1952–3	15,339
Northern Rhodesia	1935–6	9,913	1961	74,540
Nyasaland	1935–6	1,781	1961	8,750
Ruanda-Urundi	1935–6	893	1958	7,109
São Tomé and Príncipe	N.A.		1960	2,520
Sierra Leone	1935–6	718	1947–8	964
Southern Rhodesia	1935–6	55,419	1961	221,490
Sp. Equatorial Africa	N.A.		1960	7,086
Sudan	N.A.		1956	6,882
Tanganyika	1935–6	8,455	1957	20,598
Togoland (Br.)	1935–6	43	1953	100
Togoland (Fr.)	1935–6	418	1952	1,427
Uganda	1935–6	1,994	1959	10,866
Zanzibar	N.A.		1958	507
Total		195,709		902,173
Grand Total		3,547,419		5,845,147

SOURCES: United Nations, *Demographic yearbook 1963, Demographic yearbook 1964;* Lord Hailey, *An African survey: a study of problems arising in Africa south of the Sahara* (London, Oxford University Press, 1938), and *An African survey: revised 1956* (London, Oxford University Press, 1957); *Statesman's yearbook;* Richard M. Brace, *Morocco, Algeria, Tunisia* (Englewood Cliffs, N.J., 1964).

Table 128. *Oriental populations in Africa, pre-World War II and pre-independence*

	Pre-World War II		Pre-independence	
	Year	Number	Year	Number
Extreme south				
Basutoland	1921	172	1956	247
Bechuanaland	1936	62	1956	248
Union of South Africa	1936	219,691	1960	477,125
Total		219,925		477,620
Rest of Africa				
Congo (Belg.)		N.A.	1958	1,233
Ethiopia	1935	10,000	1959	44,500 *
Kenya	1931	43,623	1962	176,613
Moçambique	1931	5,000	1955	17,180
Northern Rhodesia	1931	176	1961	7,790
Nyasaland	1931	1,591	1961	10,630
Ruanda-Urundi		N.A.	1958	2,320
Southern Rhodesia	1931	1,700	1961	7,260
Sudan		N.A.	1956	12,837
Tanganyika	1931	23,422	1957	76,536
Uganda	1931	13,026	1959	71,933
West Africa	1931	8,410	c. 1960	35,000
Zanzibar	1931	14,242	1958	18,334
Total		121,190		482,166
Grand Total		341,115		959,786

* Of this number, 42,000 are Saudi Arabians and Yemeni.

SOURCES: United Nations, *Demographic yearbook 1963; India yearbook;* Floyd Dotson and Lillian O. Dotson, *The Indian minority of Zambia, Rhodesia, and Malawi* (New Haven, Yale University Press, 1968); R. B. Winder, 'The Lebanese in West Africa', *Comparative Studies in Society and History,* April 1962, **4,** no. 3.

Table 129. *Birthplace of non-indigenous populations in selected countries*

	Number	Per cent		Number	Per cent
Europeans, Algeria, 1948 [a]			Europeans, Northern and Southern Rhodesia, 1961 [b]		
Foreign-born					
Africa			Foreign-born		
Tunisia	6,090		Africa		
Morocco	4,092		South Africa	83,102	
Europe			Elsewhere in		
France	106,988		southern Africa	926	
Spain	47,704		Br. eastern Africa		
Italy	12,568		(incl. Malawi)	1,549	
Other	10,392		Congo	480	
Total	187,834	20·2	Port. Africa	644	
Native-born	743,907	79·8	Other	1,434	
Grand Total	931,741	100·0	Europe		
			United Kingdom and Ireland	80,190	
			Western Europe		
			Netherlands	2,399	
			Germany	1,991	
			Other	1,579	
			Southern Europe		
			Italy	2,827	
			Portugal	1,812	
			Greece	1,646	
			Spain	103	
			Eastern Europe		
Non-Moroccans, Morocco, 1951 [a]			Poland	984	
Foreign-born			Lithuania	424	
Africa			Other	857	
Algeria	63,026		Scandinavia	601	
Tunisia	6,213		Other	717	
Other	2,487		Asia		
Europe			India and Pakistan	1,894	
France	114,535		Other	1,406	
Spain	15,907		Oceania	1,352	
Italy	5,547		North America		
Portugal	3,321		U.S.A.	1,550	
Other	9,624		Canada	766	
Asia			Other	31	
Turkey	593		South America	289	
Other	948		Not stated or born		
North America	1,213		at sea	702	
South America	232		Total	192,255	65·0
Total	223,646	62·6	Native-born		
Unknown	1,498	0·4	(Northern or Southern		
Native-born	131,894	37·0	Rhodesia)	103,798	35·0
Grand Total	357,038	100·0	Grand Total	296,053	100·0

[a] United Nations, *Demographic yearbook 1956.*
[b] Zambia, *Final report of the September 1961 censuses of non-Africans and employees* (Lusaka, 1965); Rhodesia, *1961 census of the European, Asian and Coloured population* (Salisbury, n.d.).

Table 129 (*continued*)

	Number	Per cent		Number	Per cent
Asians, Northern and Southern Rhodesia, 1961 [b]			*Asiatics, South Africa, 1960* [c]		
Foreign-born			Foreign-born		
Africa			Rest of Africa	283	
South Africa	189		Asia	25,565	
Elsewhere in southern Africa	4		Other	61	
Br. eastern Africa			Unknown	247	
Malawi	129		Total	26,156	5·5
Other	67		Native-born	450,969	94·5
Congo	4				
Port. Africa	103		Grand Total	477,125	100·0
Other	26				
Asia			*Asiatics, South Africa, 1951* [c]		
India	6,024		Foreign-born		
Pakistan	31		Rest of Africa	113	
Other	192		Asia		
Other	14		India and Pakistan	31,295	
Not stated or born at sea	15		China	2,108	
Total	6,798	45·2	Other	202	
Native-born			Other	540	
(Northern or Southern Rhodesia)	8,245	54·8	Unknown	423	
			Total	34,681	9·5
Grand Total	15,043	100·0	Native-born	331,983	90·5
			Grand Total	366,664	100·0
Whites, South Africa, 1960 [c]			*Whites, South-West Africa, 1946* [a]		
Foreign-born			Foreign-born		
Africa			Africa		
South-West Africa	10,328		South Africa	14,133	
Fed. of Rhodesia and Nyasaland	12,544		Angola	1,148	
Other	13,888		Other	136	
Europe			Europe		
United Kingdom and Ireland	136,721		Germany	4,426	
Netherlands	30,279		United Kingdom	250	
Germany	26,267		Other	552	
Other	63,755		Asia	23	
Asia	8,571		Oceania	11	
Oceania	5,080		North America	26	
America	5,317		Total	20,705	54·7
Unknown	2,737		Native-born	17,028	45·0
Total	315,487	10·2	Unknown	125	0·3
Native-born	2,773,005	89·8			
Grand Total	3,088,492	100·0	Grand Total	37,858	100·0

[a] United Nations, *Demographic yearbook 1956*.
[b] Zambia, *Final report of the September 1961 censuses of non-Africans and employees* (Lusaka, 1965); Rhodesia, *1961 census of the European, Asian and Coloured population* (Salisbury, n.d.).
[c] Republic of South Africa, *Statistical yearbook 1964* (Pretoria, 1964).

Table 130. *National origin of Europeans, Nyasaland, 1896*

	Number		Number
British		Non-British	
English and Welsh	123	German	13
Scottish	119	Dutch	8
South African	23	Austro-Hungarian	5
Irish	7	Italian	2
Eurasian	3	French	1
Australian	2	Portuguese	1
Anglo-Indian	1	Total	30
Total	278		
		Grand Total	308

SOURCE: H. H. Johnston, *British Central Africa* (London, 1897), pp. 146–7.

Table 132. *Industrial distribution of economically active non-indigenous populations in selected countries*

	Year	Economically active population — Number	Agriculture, forestry, hunting and fishing — Per cent	Mining and quarrying — Per cent	Manufacturing — Per cent	Construction — Per cent
Algeria	1948	331,595	14·5	0·8	19·2	8·2
Fr. Equatorial Africa	1951	12,123	4·7	4·5	5·7	9·5
Morocco	1951	137,705	7·0	3·5	14·0	8·2
Moçambique	1950	37,141	11·1	0·6	12·0	6·5
Northern Rhodesia	1961	35,911	4·3	20·9	7·1	7·3
Nyasaland	1961	7,570	6·2 +	( )	7·4 +	5·6 +
South Africa	1960	1,266,289	10·0	5·0	20·7	5·9
South-West Africa	1960	27,340	23·8	6·2	10·2	10·1
Southern Rhodesia	1961	101,070	9·0	2·9	15·5	7·3
Tanganyika	1957	39,179	7·5	2·1	6·7	2·9
Uganda	1959	28,507	6·8	1·1	8·0	3·3

Table 131. *Nationality of resident foreigners, Ethiopia, 1957*

	Number		Number
British	3,819	Yemeni	25,164
French	2,530	Saudi-Arabian	16,921
American	1,773	Indian	2,383
Swedish	1,229	Total	44,468
German	476		
Canadian	417	Sudanese	970
Russian	351	Other	2,447
Dutch	310	Total	3,417
Yugoslav	260		
Total	11,165	Grand Total	62,650
Greek	2,256		
Italian	1,344		
Total	3,600		

SOURCE: Ethiopia, *Statistical abstract 1965* (Addis Ababa, n.d.).

Table 132 (*continued*)

	Electricity, gas, water and sanitary services	Commerce	Transport, storage and communications	Services	Activities not adequately described	
	Per cent	Per cent	Per cent	Per cent	Per cent	
Algeria	1·1	22·0	10·0	22·2	2·0	100·0%
Fr. Equatorial Africa	1·0	19·3	10·0	45·3	—	100·0
Morocco	1·3	16·7	8·6	26·2	14·5	100·0
Moçambique	0·3	28·1	17·5	23·4	0·5	100·0
Northern Rhodesia	0·8	22·1	8·6	27·7	1·2	100·0
Nyasaland	( )	39·5	5·4 +	30·1	( )	94·2 +
South Africa	0·8	20·6	9·9	21·7	5·4	100·0
South-West Africa	0·6	18·0	10·7	18·5	1·9	100·0
Southern Rhodesia	1·5	26·3	9·4	26·5	1·6	100·0
Tanganyika	0·5	39·3	6·9	24·8	9·3	100·0
Uganda	1·0	39·6	1·4	14·3	24·5	100·0

SOURCES: United Nations, *Demographic yearbook 1956* and *Demographic yearbook 1964;* Zambia, *Final report of the September 1961 censuses of non-Africans and employees* (Lusaka, 1965); Rhodesia, *1961 census of the European, Asian and Coloured population* (Salisbury, n.d.); Republic of South Africa, *Statistical yearbook 1964* (Pretoria, 1964).

Table 133. *Occupational distribution of economically active non-indigenous populations in selected countries*

	Year	Economically active population — Number	Professional, technical and related — Per cent	Managerial, administrative, clerical and related — Per cent	Sales workers — Per cent	Farmers, fishermen, hunters, lumbermen and related — Per cent	Workers in mines, quarries and related — Per cent
Fr. Equatorial Africa	1951	11,962	12·4	29·3	13·0	2·6	1·3
Northern Rhodesia	1961	35,911	17·3	29·7	9·9	3·7	7·2
Nyasaland	1961	7,570	20·1	25·0 +	26·9 +	N.A.	N.A.
South Africa	1960	1,268,711	10·9	27·5	9·5	9·9	2·5
Southern Rhodesia	1961	101,070	14·6	36·8	9·4	8·1	1·0
Tanganyika	1952	39,868	16·9	37·5	6·5	5·5	0·5

Table 133 (*continued*)

	Workers in operating transport	Craftsmen, production process workers and labourers not elsewhere classified	Service workers	Armed forces	Not classifiable elsewhere	
	Per cent	Per cent	Per cent	Per cent	Per cent	
Fr. Equatorial Africa	0·8	21·0	0·6	19·0	—	100·0%
Northern Rhodesia	4·0	20·0	5·0	2·1	1·1	100·0
Nyasaland	N.A.	11·0 +	N.A.	N.A.	N.A.	83·0 +
South Africa	6·3	24·4	5·7	—	3·3	100·0
Southern Rhodesia	3·9	18·4	4·8	1·7	1·3	100·0
Tanganyika	0·7	12·4	1·9	...	18·1	100·0

SOURCES: United Nations, *Demographic yearbook 1956* and *Demographic yearbook 1964;* Zambia, *Final report of the September 1961 censuses of non-Africans and employees* (Lusaka, 1965); Rhodesia, *1961 census of the European, Asian and Coloured population* (Salisbury, n.d.); Republic of South Africa, *Statistical yearbook 1964* (Pretoria, 1964).

Table 134. *Occupational distribution of economically active Europeans and Asians in southern Africa*

	Year	Economically active population Number	Professional, technical and related Per cent	Administrative, executive and managerial Per cent	Clerical workers Per cent	Sales workers Per cent	Farmers, fishermen and lumbermen Per cent
Europeans							
Northern Rhodesia	1961	33,267	18·4	9·7	21·4	5·7	3·8
Southern Rhodesia	1961	96,117	15·1	10·9	26·9	8·6	8·4
South Africa	1960	1,142,821	11·6	5·0	24·6	8·6	10·1
South-West Africa	1946	14,973	—————26·8—————				44·5
Asians							
Northern and Southern Rhodesia	1961	4,228	3·0	14·1	5·4	62·2	0·7
South Africa	1960	125,890	4·1	2·0	6·5	17·8	8·0

Table 134 (*continued*)

	Miners, quarrymen and related	Workers in transport and communications	Craftsmen, production workers and labourers	Service workers	Armed forces	Not classifiable or stated	
	Per cent	Per cent	Per cent	Per cent	Per cent	Per cent	
Europeans							
Northern Rhodesia	7·8	4·2	20·5	5·2	2·3	1·0	100·0%
Southern Rhodesia	1·0	3·8	17·8	4·7	1·7	1·1	100·0
South Africa	2·8	6·4	23·8	5·1	...	2·0	100·0
South-West Africa	0·5	7·0	14·3	4·1	...	2·8	100·0
Asians							
Northern and Southern Rhodesia	—	1·6	8·1	2·5	—	2·4	100·0
South Africa	0·1	6·0	29·5	11·0	—	15·0	100·0

SOURCES: Zambia, *Final report of the September 1961 censuses of non-Africans and employees* (Lusaka, 1965); Rhodesia, *1961 census of the European, Asian and Coloured population* (Salisbury, n.d.); Republic of South Africa, *Statistical yearbook 1964* (Pretoria, 1964); United Nations, *Demographic yearbook 1956*.

Table 135. *Employment status distribution of economically active non-indigenous populations in selected countries*

	Year	Economically active population Number	Employers Per cent	Workers on own account Per cent	Employees Per cent	Unpaid family workers Per cent	Not classifiable Per cent	
Algeria	1948	331,595	25·9	...	74·1	...	—	100·0%
Fr. Equatorial Africa	1951	12,113	11·0	3·9	85·1	—	—	100·0
Fr. West Africa	1951	34,026	10·3	10·0	79·7	—	—	100·0
Morocco	1951	137,705	14·3	8·9	75·4	—	1·4	100·0
Moçambique	1950	37,141	12·2	6·3	81·3	0·2	—	100·0
Northern Rhodesia	1961	35,911	8·0	0·3	91·3	0·4	...	100·0
Nyasaland	1961	7,570	20·7	N.A.	73·5	N.A.	N.A.	94·2 +
South-West Africa	1960	27,340	27·5		69·8	0·8	1·9	100·0
Southern Rhodesia	1961	101,070	9·2	0·5	89·7	0·6	...	100·0
Tanganyika	1957	39,179	10·5	21·6	61·2	...	6·7	100·0
Uganda	1959	28,507	9·2	18·3	57·6	3·0	11·9	100·0

SOURCES: United Nations, *Demographic yearbook 1956* and *Demographic yearbook 1964*; Zambia, *Final report of the September 1961 censuses of non-Africans and employees* (Lusaka, 1965); Rhodesia, *1961 census of the European, Asian and Coloured population* (Salisbury, n.d.).

Table 136. *Income distribution of non-Africans by sex,*
Federation of Rhodesia and Nyasaland, 1961

Year's income (pounds)	Males Per cent	Females Per cent
Under £300	5·7	24·6
300–599	9·5	35·6
600–999	17·9	28·4
1,000–1,499	34·8	
1,500–3,999	27·8	8·4 (£1,000–4,000 +)
4,000 and over	2·6	
Not stated	1·7	3·0
	100·0	100·0
Persons with income	101,610	49,710
Persons with no income	74,630	118,720
Total persons	176,240	168,430

SOURCE: Federation of Rhodesia and Nyasaland, *Preliminary results of September 1961 federal censuses of population and of employees: (3) Results of a ten per cent sample of the non-African census forms* (Salisbury, 1962).

Table 137. *Income distribution of Europeans and Asians by sex,*
Northern and Southern Rhodesia, 1961

Year's income (pounds)	European Males Per cent	European Females Per cent	Asian Males * Per cent
Under £300	4·7	22·2	8·8
300–599	8·2	33·7	27·5
600–999	16·6	31·5	32·1
1,000–1,499	37·0	6·6	15·3
1,500–3,999	28·8	1·8	11·6
4,000–7,499	2·2		1·2
7,500–14,999	0·6	0·2 (£4,000–15,000 +)	—
15,000 and over	0·2		—
Not stated	1·7	4·0	3·5
	100·0	100·0	100·0
Persons with income	90,571	47,314	3,770
Persons with no income	60,363	97,806	4,209
Total persons	150,934	145,120	7,979

* Of the total Asian females (7,064), only 517 are reported having any income.

SOURCES: Zambia, *Final report of the September 1961 censuses of non-Africans and employees* (Lusaka, 1965); Rhodesia, *1961 census of the European, Asian and Coloured population* (Salisbury, n.d.).

Table 138. *Income distribution of whites and Asiatics by sex, South Africa, 1960*

Year's income (rands)	White			Asiatic	
	Males Per cent	Females Per cent		Males Per cent	Females Per cent
Under R600	11·5	35·4		63·2	79·3
600–1,199	17·4	39·7		23·6	9·6
1,200–1,999	30·0	14·9		6·5	1·3
2,000–2,999	23·7	3·4		1·7	0·6
3,000–7,999	13·9	1·8			
8,000–14,999	1·4	0·2 (R8,000 –	1·6 (R3,000 –	0·4 (R3,000 –
15,000 and over	0·4	15,000 +)	15,000 +)	15,000 +)
Not stated	1·7	4·6		3·4	8·8
	100·0	100·0		100·0	100·0
Persons with income	902,069	417,101		98,971	14,145
Persons with no income	637,034	1,132,288		142,666	221,343
Total persons	1,539,103	1,549,389		241,637	235,488

SOURCE: Republic of South Africa, *Statistical yearbook 1964* (Pretoria, 1964).

Table 139. *Earnings distribution of regular European male employees, Kenya, 1960*

Year's earnings (pounds)	Private industry and commerce (excluding agriculture) Per cent	Public service Per cent
Under £600	6·5	2·0
600–1,199	24·2	24·7
1,200–1,799	40·5	51·5
1,800–2,399	16·8	15·6
2,400 and over	12·0	6·2
	100·0	100·0

SOURCE: Kenya, *Statistical abstract 1966* (Nairobi, 1966).

Table 140. *Earnings distribution of regular Asian
male employees, Kenya, 1960*

Year's earnings (pounds)	Private industry and commerce (excluding agriculture) Per cent	Public service Per cent
Under £180	9·2	4·5
180–359	23·8	20·8
360–719	51·2	48·6
720 and over	15·8	26·1
	100·0	100·0

SOURCE: Kenya, *Statistical abstract 1966* (Nairobi, 1966).

Table 141. *Average annual cash wages of non-African
male employees by industry, Uganda, 1965*
(in pounds)

	Private industry		Public services	
	Europeans	Asians and other non-Africans	Europeans	Asians and other non-Africans
Agriculture	2,049	520	1,339	854
Cotton ginning	...	567	—	—
Coffee curing	4,125	812	—	—
Forestry, fishing and hunting	...	602	1,781	580
Mining and quarrying	1,898	882	—	...
Manufacture of food products	2,030	664	—	—
Misc. manufacturing	2,167	612	2,898	882
Construction	1,774	599	2,175	708
Commerce	2,410	675	...	—
Transport and communications	1,669	568	1,964	659
Government (administration and misc.)	—	—	2,392	913
Local government	—	—	2,576	741
Educational and medical services	1,723	650	1,792	1,018
Misc. services	1,899	524	2,016	1,009
Overall average	1,979	634	1,987	886
Number of employees	1,456	7,827	894	1,189

SOURCE: Uganda, *1966 statistical abstract* (Entebbe, n.d.).

Table 142. *Average monthly earnings of European and other non-African
employees by industry, Federation of Rhodesia and Nyasaland, 1961* *
(in pounds)

	Europeans	Other non-Africans
Agriculture	68·8	36·8
Mining and quarrying	133·2	40·7
Manufacturing	101·7	52·4
Construction	105·1	61·1
Electricity, water and sanitary services	110·9	58·7
Commerce and finance	80·6	40·8
Transport and communications	90·6	55·1
Services	83·0	34·2
Activities not adequately described	71·7	—
Overall average	91·9	45·9

* Cash earnings during the 30 days ended 26 September 1961, excluding annual or less frequent bonuses, allowances, etc.

SOURCE: Federation of Rhodesia and Nyasaland, *Preliminary results of federal censuses of population and employees: (1) Industrial and racial distribution of employees* (Salisbury, 1962).

Table 143. *Average monthly earnings of non-Africans
by industry, Ghana, 1961* [a]
(in Ghana pounds) [b]

Agriculture, forestry, fishing	146
Mining and quarrying	154
Manufacturing	177
Construction	151
Electricity, water, sanitary services	139
Commerce	156
Transport, storage, communications	179
Services	127
Overall average	151

[a] Earnings at December in reporting establishments. [b] Ghana pound = pound sterling.

SOURCE: Ghana, *1963 statistical yearbook* (Accra, 1966).

Table 144. *Average basic monthly pay of Europeans in
selected occupations, Northern Rhodesia, 1960*
(in pounds)

Males	
Accountants	143
Bakers	84
Barbers	91
Carpenters	111
Civil engineers	125
Clerks (insurance)	61
Editors	136
Electricians	102
Fitters/turners (construction)	109
Managers (retail trade)	129
Mechanics (automobile)	96
Storemen (automobile parts)	78
Tobacco graders	87
Females	
Cashiers (retail trade)	50
Hairdressers	63
Housekeepers (hotel)	39
Pharmacists	81
Shop assistants	41
Stenographers	61

SOURCE: Northern Rhodesia, *Annual report of the Department of Labour 1960* (Lusaka, 1961).

Table 145. *Average weekly earnings of whites in selected occupations,
Witwatersrand, South Africa, 1959 **
(in rands)

Carpenters	39
Fitter/turners	44
Mechanics (automobile)	39
Shop assistants (male)	34
Shop assistants (female)	18
Storemen (commerce)	32
Typesetters	54

* Includes overtime earnings, cost-of-living and all other allowances, but excludes payments in kind.

SOURCE: Republic of South Africa, *Statistical yearbook 1964* (Pretoria, 1964).

Table 146. *Typical wages for daily paid European copper-mine workers, Northern Rhodesia, 1959* *
(in pounds, shillings, pence)

	Total wage per shift	Total monthly wage (26 shifts)
Underground		
Artisan charge hands	88s 5d	£114 18s 10d
Certificated winding-engine drivers	89s 6d	116 7s 0d
Lowest rate	66s 5d	86 6s 10d
General surface		
Highest rate	72s 6d	94 5s 0d
Lowest rate	64s 3d	83 10s 6d
Refinery and leach plant		
Highest rate	70s 10d	92 1s 8d
Lowest rate	65s 4d	84 18s 8d

* Includes cost-of-living allowance.

SOURCE: Northern Rhodesia, *Annual report of the Department of Labour for the year 1959* (Lusaka, 1960).

Table 147. *Average wages for white mine-workers, South Africa, 1959* *
(in rands)

	Per shift	Per month
Shiftboss		
Gold		216·80
Coal		199·40
Diamonds		187·85
Miner-machine stoping		
Gold (contract)	8·16	
Gold (day)	6·56	
Coal	6·02	
Diamonds	4·36	
Onsetter and skipman		
Gold	3·80	
Coal	4·13	
Diamonds	3·43	
Fitter		
Gold	4·89	
Coal	4·64	
Diamonds	4·62	

* Excludes overtime payments and cost-of-living and other allowances.

SOURCE: Republic of South Africa, *Statistical yearbook 1964* (Pretoria, 1964).

BIBLIOGRAPHY

Bauer, P. T. *West African trade: a study of competition, oligopoly and monopoly in a changing economy*. Cambridge University Press, 1954.

Bennett, George. 'British settlers north of the Zambezi, 1920 to 1960', in *Colonialism in Africa 1870–1960*, vol. II: *The history and politics of colonialism 1914–1960*, L. H. Gann and Peter Duignan, eds. Cambridge University Press, 1970.

Bley, Helmut. 'Social discord in South West Africa, 1894–1904', in *Britain and Germany in Africa: imperial rivalry and colonial rule*, Prosser Gifford and William R. Louis, eds., assisted by Alison Smith. New Haven, Yale University Press, 1967.

Bourdieu, Pierre. *The Algerians*. Alan C. M. Ross, trans. Boston, 1962.

Brace, Richard M. *Morocco, Algeria, Tunisia*. Englewood Cliffs, N.J., 1964.

A brief guide to Northern Rhodesia. Lusaka, Northern Rhodesia Information Department, 1960.

Cairns, H. Alan C. *The clash of cultures: early race relations in Central Africa*. New York, 1965.

Carr-Saunders, A. M. *World population: past growth and present trends*. Oxford, Clarendon Press, 1936.

Chilcote, Ronald H. *Portuguese Africa*. Englewood Cliffs, N.J., 1967.

De Kiewiet, C. W. *A history of South Africa: social and economic*. London, Oxford University Press, 1941.

Diamond, Stanley, and Fred G. Burke, eds. *The transformation of East Africa: studies in political anthropology*. New York, 1966.

Dotson, Floyd, and Lillian O. Dotson. *The Indian minority of Zambia, Rhodesia, and Malawi*. New Haven, Yale University Press, 1968.

Doxey, G. V. *The industrial colour bar in South Africa*. Cape Town, Oxford University Press, 1961.

Duffy, James. 'Portuguese Africa, 1930 to 1960', in *Colonialism in Africa 1870–1960*, vol. II: *The history and politics of colonialism in Africa 1914–1960*, L. H. Gann and Peter Duignan, eds. Cambridge University Press, 1970.

Portuguese Africa. Cambridge, Mass., Harvard University Press, 1959.

The economic development of Kenya. Baltimore, Johns Hopkins Press for the International Bank for Reconstruction and Development, 1963.

Esseks, John D. 'Government and indigenous private enterprise in Ghana', *Journal of Modern African Studies*, 1971, **9**, no. 1.

Forrester, M. W. *Kenya today: social prerequisites for economic development*. The Hague, 1962.

Frankel, S. Herbert. *Capital investment in Africa: its course and its effects*. London, Oxford University Press, 1938.

'Some aspects of investment and economic development in the continent of Africa', *Africa*, Jan. 1952, **22**, no. 1.

Gann, Lewis H. *The birth of a plural society: the development of Northern Rhodesia under the British South Africa Company 1894–1914*. Manchester University Press, 1958.

'Liberal interpretations of South African history', *Rhodes–Livingstone Institute Journal*, 1959, no. 25.

Gann, Lewis H., and Peter Duignan. *Burden of empire: an appraisal of Western colonialism in Africa south of the Sahara*. New York, 1967.

'Changing patterns of a white élite: Rhodesian and other settlers', in *Colonialism in Africa 1870–1960*, vol. II: *The history and politics of colonialism 1914–1960*, L. H. Gann and Peter Duignan, eds. Cambridge University Press, 1970.

White settlers in tropical Africa. Baltimore, 1962.

Garlick, Peter C. *African traders and economic development in Ghana*. Oxford, Clarendon Press, 1971.

Georgulas, Nikos. 'Minority assimilation in Africa: the Greeks in Moshi—an example'. *Occasional paper*, no. 22. Syracuse University, Maxwell Graduate School of Citizenship and Public Affairs, Program of Eastern African Studies, 1966.

Ghai, Dharam P., ed. *Portrait of a minority: Asians in East Africa*. Nairobi, Oxford University Press, 1965.

Gifford, Prosser. 'Indirect rule: touchstone or tombstone for colonial policy?' in *Britain and Germany in Africa: imperial rivalry and colonial rule,* Prosser Gifford and William R. Louis, eds., assisted by Alison Smith. New Haven, Yale University Press, 1967.

Gifford, Prosser, and William R. Louis, eds., assisted by Alison Smith. *Britain and Germany in Africa: imperial rivalry and colonial rule*. New Haven, Yale University Press, 1967.

Great Britain. Advisory Commission on the Review of the Constitution of Rhodesia and Nyasaland. *Report: Appendix VI, Survey of developments since 1953*. Cmd 1149. London, 1960.

Hailey, William Malcolm Hailey, 1st baron. *An African survey: a study of problems arising in Africa south of the Sahara*. London, Oxford University Press, 1938.
An African survey: revised 1956. London, Oxford University Press, 1957.

Hance, William A. *The geography of modern Africa*. New York, Columbia University Press, 1964.

Hancock, W. K. *Smuts: the sanguine years 1870–1919*. Cambridge University Press, 1962.

Harlow, Vincent, and E. M. Chilver, eds., assisted by Alison Smith. *History of East Africa,* vol II. Oxford, Clarendon Press, 1965.

Hattersley, Alan F. *The British settlement of Natal: a study in imperial migration*. Cambridge University Press, 1950.

Henderson, W. O. 'German East Africa, 1884–1918', in *History of East Africa,* vol. II, Vincent Harlow and E. M. Chilver, eds., assisted by Alison Smith. Oxford, Clarendon Press, 1965.

Hopkins, Elizabeth. 'Racial minorities in British East Africa', in *The transformation of East Africa: studies in political anthropology,* Stanley Diamond and Fred G. Burke, eds. New York, 1966.

Huxley, Elspeth. *The flame trees of Thika: memories of an African childhood*. New York, 1959.
On the edge of the Rift. New York, 1962.
White man's country: Lord Delamere and the making of Kenya. New York, 1968.

Ianni, Francis A. J. 'Ethiopia: a special case', in *The transformation of East Africa: studies in political anthropology,* Stanley Diamond and Fred G. Burke, eds. New York, 1966.

Johnston, H. H. *British Central Africa*. London, 1897.

Kapferer, Bruce. *Strategy and transaction in an African factory: African workers and Indian management in a Zambian town*. Manchester University Press, 1972.

Kaunda, Kenneth. 'Zambia's economic reforms', *African Affairs*, Oct. 1968, **67,** no. 269.

Khuri, Fuad I. 'Kinship, emigration, and trade partnership among the Lebanese of West Africa', *Africa*, Oct. 1965, **35,** no. 4.

Kilby, Peter. *Industrialization in an open economy: Nigeria 1945–1966*. Cambridge University Press, 1969.

Knauss, Peter. 'From devil to father figure: the transformation of Jomo Kenyatta by Kenya whites', *Journal of Modern African Studies*, 1971, **9,** no. 1.

Kuper, Adam. *Kalahari village politics: an African democracy*. Cambridge University Press, 1970.

Legum, Colin, ed. *Africa contemporary record: annual survey and documents, 1970–71*. London, 1971.

Leys, Norman. *Kenya*. London, 1924.
Lloyd, Peter S. *Africa in social change*. Harmondsworth, Middlesex, 1967.
McClelland, David C. *The achieving society*. Princeton, 1961.
Mangat, J. S. *A history of the Asians in East Africa: c. 1886 to 1945*. Oxford, Clarendon Press, 1969.
Martelli, George. *Leopold to Lumumba: a history of the Belgian Congo 1877–1960*. London, 1962.
Mercier, Paul. 'Le groupement européen de Dakar: orientation d'une enquête', *Cahiers Internationaux de Sociologie*, 1955, **19.**
Munger, Edwin S. *African field reports: 1952–1961*. Cape Town, 1961.
Neumark, S. Daniel. *Economic influences on the South African frontier: 1652–1836*. Stanford University Press, 1957.
Pankhurst, Richard. *Economic history of Ethiopia: 1800–1935*. Addis Ababa, Haile Sellassie I University Press, 1968.
Patterson, Sheila. *The last trek: a study of the Boer people and the Afrikaner nation*. London, 1957.
Rose, Arnold M. 'Minorities', *International encyclopedia of the social sciences*, vol. x. New York, 1968.
Rothchild, Donald. 'Citizenship and national integration: the non-African crisis in Kenya', in University of Denver, Graduate School of International Studies, Center on International Race Relations, *Studies in race and nations*, **1**, no. 3, Denver, 1969–70.
'Kenya's Africanization program: priorities of development and equity', *American Political Science Review*, Sept. 1970, **64,** no. 3.
Racial bargaining in independent Kenya: a study of minorities and decolonization London, Oxford University Press, 1973.
Salomon, Laurence. 'The economic background to the revival of Afrikaner nationalism', in *Boston University Papers in African History*, vol. I, Jeffrey Butler, ed. Boston University Press, 1966.
Selous, Frederick C. *Sunshine and storm in Rhodesia*. London, 1896.
Simons, H. J. and R. E. *Class and colour in South Africa: 1850–1950*. Harmondsworth, Middlesex, 1969.
Sorrenson, M. P. K. *Origins of European settlement in Kenya*. Nairobi, Oxford University Press, 1968.
Thompson, Leonard. 'Co-operation and conflict: the high veld', in *The Oxford history of South Africa*, vol. I: *South Africa to 1870*, Monica Wilson and Leonard Thompson, eds. New York, Oxford University Press, 1969.
Walker, Eric A. *A history of Southern Africa*. London, 1959.
Weber, Max. *Economy and society: an outline of interpretive sociology*, Guenther Roth and Claus Wittich, eds. New York, 1968.
Welsh, David. 'Urbanisation and the solidarity of Afrikaner nationalism', *Journal of Modern African Studies*, 1969, **7,** no. 2.
Wilson, Monica, and Leonard Thompson, eds. *The Oxford history of South Africa*, vol. I: *South Africa to 1870*. New York, Oxford University Press, 1969.
Winder, R. Bayley. 'The Lebanese in West Africa', *Comparative Studies in Society and History*, April 1962, **4,** no. 3.
Wrigley, C. C. 'Kenya: the patterns of economic life, 1902–1945', in *History of East Africa*, vol. II, Vincent Harlow and E. M. Chilver, eds., assisted by Alison Smith. Oxford, Clarendon Press, 1965.

CHAPTER 16

BRITISH COLONIAL AFRICA: ECONOMIC RETROSPECT AND AFTERMATH

by

P. T. BAUER

Many scholars and politicians nowadays assume as self-evident that in Africa as elsewhere in the less developed world, the colonial period was one of stagnation. According to General Principle XIV of the first United Nations Conference on Trade and Development (UNCTAD), for instance: 'Complete decolonisation . . . is a necessary condition for economic development and the exercise of sovereign rights over natural resources.'

Another example is from the annex to the report of the Commission for International Development, the celebrated Pearson Commission:

Compared to the rest of the developing world, Africa has been a late starter in economic development. Only three countries, UAR, Ethiopia and Liberia, were independent before 1950, and most attained independence between 1955 and 1963. Despite the late start there have been impressive growth performances in such countries as the Ivory Coast, Kenya and the main oil exporting countries. The relatively recent start on development programmes and in many cases the past failing of colonial administration explain to a large measure Africa's great scarcity of skilled personnel.[1]

Finally, some remarks by Kwame Nkrumah, who in his time was perhaps the most influential African politician:

Without exception, they [the colonial powers] left us nothing but our resentment . . . It was when they had gone and we were faced with the stark realities, as in Ghana on the morrow of our independence, that the destitution of the land after long years of colonial rule was brought sharply home to us.[2]

Nkrumah was a politician, but his views were widely respected and quoted in the West, particularly in the United States.

If these opinions were true, the contents of this volume could be reduced to a single sentence noting the absence of change. However, the passages quoted bear no relation to reality.

Economic change in the colonial period

It is manifestly untrue that colonial status as such precludes economic progress. Some of the richest countries were colonies in their earlier history, notably the United States, Canada, Australia and New Zealand, and they were already very

---

[1] *Partners in development: report of the Commission on International Development* (London and New York, 1969), p. 262. The annex, published within the same covers as the report, was prepared by the expert staff of the commission, and according to the commissioners formed the basis of a considerable part of their conclusions.

[2] Kwame Nkrumah, *Africa must unite* (London, 1963), p. xiii.

prosperous while still colonies. Nor did colonial status preclude progress in Africa. Many African colonies in East, West and Central Africa developed rapidly over the colonial period. Familiar examples include Nigeria, the Gold Coast, the Ivory Coast, Kenya, Uganda, Southern Rhodesia and parts of the Congo.

Material progress was especially pronounced and extensive in the Gold Coast and Nigeria. Major aspects of this advance are noted elsewhere in this volume, especially in the essays by Professors Kilby and Meier. The references in Professor Meier's essay note the phenomenal rise in the major exports of these countries over the colonial period from nil or negligible amounts to leading staples of world commerce; and they refer also, albeit more briefly, to the corresponding rise in imports. And in West Africa these exports were produced by Africans, and almost all imports were for the use of Africans.

Statistics of population growth, government revenues, school attendance, public health, literacy rates, all reflect rapid and large-scale material advance. For instance, in the early 1890s there were about three thousand children at school in the Gold Coast; by the mid-1950s there were over half a million. In the early 1890s there were neither railways nor roads but only a few jungle paths, and transport of goods was entirely by human porterage or by canoe. By the 1930s there was a considerable railway mileage and a good road system; and journeys by road required fewer hours than they had required days in 1890.

This kind of information cannot by itself convey the far-reaching and pervasive change that took place over the colonial period in these areas. In many parts of Africa the period saw a total or virtual elimination of slavery, slave-raiding and famine and a great reduction of endemic and epidemic disease. For instance, in much of Nigeria, slave-raiding was still widespread at the end of the nineteenth century, when some of the larger towns of Northern Nigeria were still regular slave markets; by the 1930s they had become centres of the ground-nut trade.

The profound changes in the conditions of life, and the material progress that made them possible, brought about a large fall in mortality, with consequent longer life expectation and a substantial increase in population, which in turn represented a betterment of conditions. There has been a significant improvement in living standards. The reality of this improvement is often overlooked because conventional statistics do not include health and life expectation in estimates of *per capita* incomes or even of living standards.

Economic change was not uniform even within individual colonies, especially the larger ones, and even less so over the vast and diverse regions of British colonial Africa. For instance, in Nigeria the economic progress during the colonial period was very different in, say, parts of Southern Nigeria from what they were among the Tiv in the north. The economic experience of the many and diverse societies of British colonial Africa range from comparatively little change to large-scale and pervasive transformation of conditions. Nor is this diversity of experience unexpected.

Differences between regions and groups in economic attainment and progress are familiar throughout the world both within countries and across frontiers. Such differences are inescapable in the early stages of economic development because economic advance necessarily starts in certain areas and sectors. Its outward spread depends on people's capacities, attitudes, institutions and political arrangements, as well as on physical communications. The differences are likely to be pronounced when the area under review is large and is inhabited by ethnically different peoples with different institutions, and separated by large distances and poor physical communications. The differences are accentuated when change is initiated largely by foreigners and by contacts established with the area by materially more advanced societies. All these conditions were present in British colonial Africa, and of course even more so in colonial Africa as a whole.

The characteristic experience of the many and diverse societies of colonial Africa was not stagnation but uneven material progress. It was uneven both in that it affected some groups sooner and more pervasively than others and in that it affected some activities, attitudes and institutions much more than others. As we shall note at greater length subsequently, these differences and instances of material advance were themselves among the problems set up by sudden emergence from material backwardness as a result of contacts established by the West.

Far-reaching diversity of social, economic and physical conditions substantially limits the usefulness of averaging and of aggregation. Simple averages are useless for summarizing the conditions of deeply heterogeneous societies. Moreover, as Professor Dan Usher has cogently argued, the estimates and international comparisons of the national incomes of less developed countries (ldcs) are subject to biases and errors often amounting to 500 per cent, which compounds the shortcomings of averaging and aggregation of widely different conditions. These considerations should help to put into perspective statistical exercises that claim to estimate changes in *per capita* incomes of African countries to within 1 or 2 per cent.

Change and diversity

Recognition that the period was one of rapid and uneven development and not of stagnation is important on several grounds. It is important first for the sake of historical accuracy and thus of scholarship. It should help also to engender a more critical attitude towards emphatic and apparently authoritative statements such as those quoted earlier in this essay. And appreciation of the historical process should promote a time perspective appropriate to the context of African development. Much of the discussion on this subject ignores both the many centuries of development in the West before the Industrial Revolution and the material backwardness of pre-colonial Africa. Such a lack of time perspective, or at any rate its drastic foreshortening, is reflected in the insistence on instant development and in the expressions of disappointment (genuine or pretended) over the alleged absence of progress or its supposedly inadequate rate. What may be a limiting case in this context is a suggestion, in an ostensibly serious publication, that the cocoa industry has not served as an effective instrument for the development of Gold Coast–Ghana because the level of economic attainment there is still below that of North America and Great Britain. The suggestion that colonial rule precludes material progress compounds the lack of time perspective in that it presents a misleading picture of the colonial period, as well as of the conditions prevailing at the conclusion of colonial rule.

Contemplation of the African scene throughout the colonial period, and especially in its earlier stages, should also throw into relief the importance of economic capacities, attitudes and social institutions as determinants of material progress. These factors are all too often overlooked in discussions that treat humanity as a standardized, undifferentiated mass, whose components differ only in conventionally measured incomes, discussions that also consider monetary investment as the principal determinant of development, or even as its only determinant. These ideas, together with the disturbing lack of time perspective just mentioned, are apparent in some of the essays in this volume, which register surprise or disappointment that the progress even of West Africa has not been faster, or that Africans are still poorer than Asians or Europeans in their midst. The practice of referring to the colonial period as one of stagnation in part also reflects and confirms the habit of envisaging the peoples of Africa as a uniform undifferentiated mass, instead of as the rich variety of humanity which they encompass. In Africa, as in other parts of the world, individuals, groups and societies differ greatly in their economic aptitudes, attitudes and mores both within countries and across frontiers.

Many perplexing and intractable problems facing colonial governments (and their successors) arose not from stagnation, but from the impact of change: personal and social difficulties deriving from the transformation of a subsistence economy into a money economy; changes in land use, property rights and inheritance laws; detribalization and urbanization; congestion in the ports or on the railways. Allegations that the African colonies were stagnant societies deny the presence of these problems and divert attention from the most effective ways of dealing with them.

The extent and speed of social and economic change served also to deprive the governments and their advisers of time for sufficient examination of the background and implications of such change. This consideration explains at least partly the land policies of the British colonial governments, notably the decision to reserve large areas of land for particular sectors of the population, including the establishment of native reserves and the promotion of what is usually termed communal tenure of land. Although various influences lay behind these arrangements, a major factor was the belief that they were necessary to protect the indigenous population: humanitarians and missionaries were among the most influential advocates of the creation of native reserves.

In recent years these arrangements have been much criticized. For instance, Professor Frankel has emphatically argued that they have obstructed the material progress of both the indigenous and the non-indigenous population, besides increasing political tension.[3] Even more radical is the argument of Professor Colson's essay on land use in Volume 3 of this *Colonialism in Africa* series. She argues there that the promotion of communal tenure fundamentally misunderstood both the needs of the population and the nature of the pre-colonial systems of land usage in Africa.

It is at least possible, and perhaps even probable, that had the colonial governments been less pressed by rapid change, their land policies would have been based on a more thorough understanding of social realities. The radical and recent nature of the change of opinion in this area of discourse is evident

[3] S. Herbert Frankel, *The tyranny of economic paternalism in Africa: a study of frontier mentality 1860–1960* (Johannesburg, 1960).

from a comparison of the arguments of Professor Frankel and Professor Colson with the publications of C. K. Meek and of other authorities in the 1940s and 1950s.

Rapid change: impact and implications

The difficulties and complexities of change were aggravated by the extremely low level of material attainment of pre-colonial Africa and by the role of external contacts in initiating and promoting change. In most parts of sub-Saharan Africa, there were practically no Western-type schools; literacy was rare; there were virtually no man-made communications, except for simple bush tracks. Most of this huge area depended entirely on muscle power for transport and communications.

The foundations and ingredients of modern social and economic life were brought to Africa during the colonial period: public security and law and order; wheeled traffic (there were few wheels and no wheeled traffic in pre-colonial times); mechanized transport (that is, transport powered by steam or petrol instead of muscle, overwhelmingly human muscle), railways, roads and large, man-made ports; modern forms of money, instead of barter or commodity money, such as bars of iron, bottles of gin or cowrie shells; the application of science and technology to agriculture, animal husbandry, water control, forestry and mining; modern commerce; towns with substantial buildings, water and sewerage; hospitals, public-health measures and the control of endemic and epidemic disease; formal education and the idea of scholarship; and even the idea of material progress.

These elements and components of modern social and economic life, as well as many others, were introduced by the colonial administrations or by foreign private organizations or persons under the comparative security of colonial rule and in the face of formidable and varied obstacles. These results, or at least accompaniments, of colonial rule are widely ignored in contemporary discussion.

Although much recent literature ignores the radical changes that occurred throughout the colonial era, many knowledgeable and authoritative writers over the past eighty years recognized that rapid changes were taking place, that these changes were initiated by external contacts and that the repercussions of such changes presented major social, political and administrative problems.

Mary Kingsley admonished politicians and administrators at the turn of the century in the following terms:

If you will try science [i.e., anthropology] all the evils of the clash between two culture periods could be avoided, and you could assist these West Africans in their thirteenth-century state to rise into their nineteenth-century state without having the hard fight for it which you have had.[4]

Mary Kingsley's hopes of the potentialities of anthropology (or of any other form of knowledge) in solving social and political problems may have been too sanguine, but the recognition of rapid change is plain.

A generation or so later, but well before economic development became an international political issue, McPhee, in *The economic revolution in British West Africa,* wrote along the following lines:

[4] *West African studies* (London, 1901), pp. 326–7.

The process since the 'Nineties of last century has been the superimposition of the twentieth century after Christ on the twentieth century before Christ, and a large part of the problem of native policy is concerned with the clash of such widely different cultures and with the protection of the natives during the difficulties of transition . . . The transition has been from the growth of subsistence crops and the collection of sylvan produce to the cultivation of exchange crops, with the necessary implication of a transition from a 'Natural' economy to a 'Monetary' economy, and the innumerable important reactions from the latter phase.[5]

The title of the book is revealing. McPhee noted that broadly similar changes were occurring in East Africa.

Finally, Sir William Keith Hancock wrote:

In some periods of European history—in our own day, for example, or in the day of the first steam-engines and power mills—the European world has seemed to be transformed; Europe nevertheless has remained the same world, spinning very much faster. But in Africa change means more than acceleration. Europe's commerce and its money-measurements really have brought the African into a new world . . . He retains something of his old social and religious and mental life and habit—these things are very slow in dying—but they are distinct from his new economic life and habit.[6]

Hancock's emphatic observations are of special interest because they were written towards the close of the colonial period, and by an economic historian critical of much of colonial policy.

These writers and many others recognized that the manifest and readily observable changes in colonial Africa resulted from contacts established by much more advanced countries, where attitudes and institutions had been adapted for centuries to a monetary economy; and that exposure of Africans to a vastly different and materially successful system was bound to pose baffling problems of adjustment.

Colonial rule and material progress

It is easy to dispose of the allegations that colonial Africa stagnated. Whether colonial rule promoted or retarded progress cannot be shown so conclusively because one cannot say for certain what would have happened without it. But I think it may be said confidently that colonial rule promoted rather than obstructed progress, and was even necessary for it.

Economic change in Africa was initiated by external contacts. These were the channels for the large-scale inflow of skills and of financial and physical capital that initiated or promoted material progress. These contacts also brought new commodities to the local population and simultaneously opened up large markets for local products. By improving communications and increasing public security they were instrumental not only in linking Africa to the outside world, but also in establishing links within Africa. The external contacts induced an inflow of new ideas, methods, crops and wants. They often brought about radical changes in attitudes and institutions, or even first acquainted the population with the idea and possibility of material advance.

---

[5] Allan McPhee, *The economic revolution in British West Africa* (London, 1926; 2nd ed., London, 1971), pp. 8–9.

[6] Sir William Keith Hancock, *Survey of British Commonwealth affairs,* vol. II: *Problems of economic policy, 1918–1939,* pt. 2 (London, Oxford University Press, 1942), p. 283.

A vast number of external contacts existed in pre-colonial Africa. And, as is clear from the essay in this volume by Professor Duignan and Professor Gann, such contacts were increasing in frequency and in range during the nineteenth century. But it is certain that the comparative security provided by the colonial governments vastly enlarged their volume, variety and effectiveness. A few examples of some generality will illustrate these major or even decisive considerations.

Colonial rule and metropolitan support were necessary to secure the inflow of administrative and technical skills and of the capital required for the construction of railways, ports and practically all the roads in Africa, which in turn were necessary both to link Africa to the outside world and to expand links between different parts of the interior. In the absence of railways and roads, and with very little public security, communication in Africa was difficult even over relatively short distances, and the typical communities were generally small and isolated. Without basic transport facilities and some public security there could have been no substantial development of the production of cash-crops away from the coast, let alone substantial production of minerals. The railways, which altered the conditions of existence over large parts of East, West and Central Africa, could not have been built in the nineteenth and early twentieth centuries in the absence of colonial rule, with the result that these areas would have had to continue to depend on exceedingly expensive and wasteful human porterage, supplemented by canoe traffic.

The railways and roads of the colonial period have come to be so much taken for granted that their role as agents of change has been ignored. McPhee, who wrote in the 1920s, was well aware of their significance. In his book he quotes at length contemporary accounts of the lack of communications in West Africa, of the absence of roads and bridges, of the obstacles to the movement of people and goods even over short distances and of the high cost of human porterage. And he discusses in detail the cost and difficulties of the construction of roads and even more of railways, and their profound effects in establishing public security, preventing the recrudescence of slavery, promoting peaceful contacts, breaking down social and tribal barriers and developing cash-crops. In both East and West Africa, the construction of railways was made possible by colonial rule. And it is noteworthy that even in 1973 Africa depends largely on transport facilities constructed by foreigners.

In an earlier section of this essay we mentioned briefly the expansion of the export of cash-crops from Nigeria and the Gold Coast during the colonial period. The outlines of this notable episode of economic history are familiar, but some of its aspects warrant further discussion. In British West Africa all major export crops were produced on farms established, owned and operated by Africans, with the exception of palm-oil and palm-kernels, which are derived from naturally occurring trees. The same applies largely to Ugandan cotton and coffee. The development of these crops required much direct investment in agricultural properties. These sequences in turn show that there are hundreds of thousands of enterprising Africans who respond to familiar economic incentives, though the form of their enterprise, namely the establishment and production of cash-crops or small-scale transport and trading activity (often associated with the production of cash-crops), differs substantially from that found in more advanced economies. These developments throw into relief the inappropriateness of disregarding direct investment in agriculture in discussions on capital formation. The large-scale expansion of these exports shows also that Africans can produce competitively for world markets, although the external marketing may be carried out by expatriates.

In parts of West Africa, especially Yoruba country, there was a long tradition of settled agriculture, and the concept of bounded land emerged well before the end of the nineteenth century. There was also a long history of intermittent commercial contact with the West and the Mediterranean area. Though the historical background may have contributed to the readiness of the response of the local population to the new economic opportunities, this possibility still does not make the response any less impressive.

Some of these cash-crops, primarily cocoa and kola-nuts in West Africa and coffee in East Africa, are derived from bushes and trees that do not produce until about four to six years after planting. Their extensive adoption by Africans disposes of the opinion, which anthropologists have long known to be unfounded, that individual Africans cannot or will not take a long view in economic matters. This unfounded opinion is widely held at two ends of the political spectrum. It is espoused by people who use it as an argument for suggesting that all major economic decisions should be taken by governments, on the ground that private individuals in less developed countries suffer from economic myopia. And it is espoused also by people who think that Africans are incapable of taking a long view in economic matters.

The economic history of these areas is a particularly convincing refutation of the fanciful notion that external contacts are somehow damaging to material progress, a notion frequently encountered in the recent development literature. This idea is inconsistent with ample empirical evidence, notably so in Africa. There, as practically throughout the less developed world, the most advanced regions are those with which the West has established contact, and the most backward are those with the fewest external contacts.

Finally, the West African development experience shows up clearly the inappropriateness of describing the advanced sectors and activities of African economies as mere enclaves, owned and operated by foreigners, that do not benefit the local people, or even as enclaves that have somehow been extracted from them. Even where advanced sectors are in fact owned and largely manned by expatriates, they still serve the indigenous population by providing employment opportunities and government revenues, and usually in other ways as well. But the large-scale production of cash-crops by Africans on their own properties shows up especially clearly the hollowness of the notion that the advanced sectors of African economies are mere enclaves, as would appear from some observations in Professor Meier's essay in this volume.

Economic colonialism: some costs and benefits

As we have seen, the ingredients of modern social and economic life in colonial Africa were introduced during the colonial rule and the use of them was largely promoted by the colonial presence. Assessment of the cost of material progress involves much more subjective judgement. Moreover, the costs were usually of a kind not readily commensurable with material advances, a fact that precludes meaningful comparisons. All we can do is to set down some pertinent observations and considerations, recognizing that there is scope for wide and legitimate difference of opinion in this area of discourse.

Colonial conquest was usually attended by bloodshed. As is clear from the most cursory knowledge of Africa, as well as from the essays in Volume I of *Colonialism in Africa,* the extent of bloodshed and of other forms of coercion that attended colonial conquest differed greatly in the different areas. In the British colonies it was generally modest, especially in East Africa; in West Africa, especially in Ashanti and in Nigeria, it was on a larger scale. But on the eve of colonial conquest, civil wars, local wars, slavery and slave-raiding were endemic in most areas, notably in West Africa, especially Northern Nigeria. Indeed, these conditions usually provided the occasion or the excuse for external intervention. It is highly probable that over most of British Africa colonial conquest saved lives rather than destroyed them: this is a virtual certainty in Northern Nigeria. (The loss of life in the course of conquest and the suppression of local revolt was much larger in some other territories, especially German South-West Africa, with which this essay is not concerned.)

After the establishment of colonial rule, coercion was also often used in the recruitment of labour for public employment and at times for private employment. This was thought necessary because of the absence of a cash economy, the sparse population, large distances and poor natural lines of communication, a combination of circumstances that greatly increased the cost of establishing the infrastructure and the difficulties of financing it from taxation, when its construction was necessary for public security and material progress.

The extent and nature of coercion differed greatly in form, in intensity and in duration. In most of British colonial Africa, forced labour for private purposes disappeared by the end of the First World War. Government-instigated coercion to press porters into service for district commissioners or to impose other services for public purposes continued longer; for instance, in some relatively backward areas, such as the Northern Territories of the Gold Coast, coercion continued sporadically until the mid-1920s. (Elsewhere in colonial Africa the use of forced labour, or compulsion to produce prescribed amounts of specified crops, endured longer, until sometime around the Second World War and even beyond.) The rate at which this type of direct compulsion diminished in British colonial Africa depended partly on political and moral pressures, but chiefly on the spread of economic progress, especially the extension of the cash economy.

In the British colonies, the exercise of compulsion was limited in extent and duration. But of course it can be argued that even where it promoted the progress of the indigenous population, coercion was objectionable, especially when applied by alien governments or agencies whose ways were often incomprehensible to their subjects and who were often ignorant of the sentiments and mores of the population; hence coercion involved greater hardship than if it had been exercised by rulers closer to their subjects. In incompletely monetized economies forced labour is a familiar form of taxation by both indigenous and alien governments. It represents a form of taxation in kind. In East Africa, in the early days of British rule some backward groups were first allowed to pay taxes in cattle. But this system had to be abandoned because people paid in old and diseased beasts that died on the collectors' hands. Similarly, chiefs required to supply men for forced labour were apt to enlist the weakest and least efficient men for the work.

All taxation implies compulsory levies. The burden of forced labour is difficult to measure meaningfully because of the importance of non-quantifiable attendant conditions. In the British colonies, the periods to be served were usually relatively short and conditions comparatively humane. And use of forced labour diminished as the money economy made headway. We cannot assume that without colonial rule the population would have experienced less coercion. As we have already noted, local wars, slavery and slave-raiding were widespread and endemic before colonial rule. The British occupation did away with pre-colonial forms of coercion. Hence the great majority of people came to live longer, more securely and with a greater degree of freedom than before. The situation in present-day Liberia and Ethiopia and over much of post-colonial Africa—for example, in Burundi, the Sudan, Tanzania and Uganda—suggests that colonial rule probably diminished rather than increased the extent and intensity of coercion.

It is sometimes urged that there would have been progress sooner or later even without colonial rule; and, further, that even apart from coercion, colonial rule brought about social disruption as a result of large-scale migration. The suggestion of eventual progress without colonial rule envisages a time-span that not only far exceeds the colonial era, but is also open-ended. Without colonial rule there would have been far fewer external contacts and much less progress. The public security, the more advanced transport system and the public-health measures of colonial rule not only made possible the survival of many millions of Africans, but lengthened their life-span and gave them greater security. Furthermore, improved communications and the widening of peaceful contacts without and within Africa also meant that progress extended beyond the material aspects of life.

The extent of disruption in social and family life caused by large-scale migration of labour is a much disputed matter. Where migration was an aspect of forced labour, it no doubt involved considerable hardship and disruption. But forced labour was a small proportion of total migration. The greater part, probably the great bulk, was voluntary response to wider opportunities, especially for earning a cash income for underemployed rural people, who as a result of greater public security were able safely to travel over long distances. This judgment is supported by various forms of evidence from many regions in Africa and elsewhere: the large-scale, long-distance voluntary migration to the cocoa-producing areas of the Gold Coast; the continuing inflow into the towns throughout Africa; the sustained attempts and efforts of many Africans from distant countries to find employment on the Copper Belt, in Southern Rhodesia and in South Africa; the large-scale voluntary labour migration from China and India to different parts of South-East Asia, the Caribbean and elsewhere; and the importance of the backward parts of Europe and Asia as sources of mercenary soldiers from the sixteenth to the twentieth century.

Single men predominated in most of these migrations; and many migrants at first regarded migration as merely a temporary absence from home. These characteristics were perhaps especially pronounced in colonial Africa. But the influence behind these features came from the supply side rather than the demand side: tribal chiefs preferred temporary movement of single men to more permanent migration of families, as the movement of families would have disrupted and diminished the tribe much more. Therefore the chiefs exercised pressure accordingly. Moreover, the migrants often wished to retain the right in the tribal lands, and this would have been endangered by permanent or family migration. These factors were quite as important in shaping the character of the migration as any preference of the colonial authorities or of the employers for single men. Thus neither extensive migration of labour nor the preponderance of single men was confined to colonial Africa. And in the great expansion of labour migration, the widening of opportunities and the greater security of movement were overall almost certainly much more significant than the temporary exercise of compulsion. It is of course arguable that the social disruption caused by economic change brought unhappiness and was thus objectionable. But this charge raises issues about economic progress that are not peculiar to colonialism as such and that cannot be pursued here.

The balancing of the costs and benefits of economic changes so vast as those brought about by colonial rule in Africa is an exercise that involves large elements of arbitrary judgement and that is almost always unconvincing. But it may be said with confidence that the far-reaching changes provided the colonial territories with such elements of a modern society and economy as there are in Africa. These changes were achieved in the face of great difficulties. The force and coercion employed and the hardships inflicted, though by no means negligible, were nevertheless modest in view of the conditions of pre-colonial Africa and of the extent of the changes. The number of Africans who lived longer, more securely, in materially better conditions and in peaceful contacts with their fellow men, was much greater, probably by orders of magnitude, than the numbers who were harmed. And it may be said also that the experience of colonial Africa was unusual in that the rulers addressed themselves to a considerable extent to the improvement in the conditions of their subjects, and did so with some success.

These observations are not intended to support either the establishment of colonial rule or the methods employed. They may serve as a reminder that in political action and judgement the change is usually between courses that many people would regard as evils. In a subsequent section of this essay we shall, however, note a very important damaging legacy of colonial rule that is unrelated to the usual criticisms of the system, but that can be considered only after we have noted some of the policies of the terminal years of colonial rule.

Resumption of state control

From the inception of colonial rule to the early 1930s, direct compulsion and direct state intervention in economic life gradually retreated. This trend reflected various factors, such as the increase in population, which made it easier to dispense with forced labour, especially in conditions of economic advance indicated by the spread of the money economy and the increase in the volume and diversity of economic activity.

Foreign commerce under the Union Jack was at first relatively unrestricted. During the 1920s and the early 1930s, Great Britain itself moved from a system of free trade to one of full protection and the grant of imperial preferences. But in Africa this policy swing had but limited effects. British colonial governments were apt to look with a more friendly eye upon tenders advanced by British, rather than by foreign, businessmen in the construction of public-works projects. But there was no deliberate exclusion of foreigners. Southern Rhodesia, Sierra Leone and the Gambia gave small preferences to British producers. The imperial authorities made some attempts also at giving most favoured treatment for Britain's own exports by means of tariff devices such as the imposition, after 1934, of a textile quota directed against Japanese competition. By and large, however, the British colonial empire in Africa maintained an 'open door' policy, and British industrialists had to compete against foreign firms on a level of equality.

Right from the start, there was state intervention in the construction of a transportation network. As Professor Katzenellenbogen shows in his essay, the great majority of railways, and also the port facilities and airfields, were built by the various colonial governments. Sir Frederick Pedler points out in his contribution how men such as Chamberlain and Sir Gordon Guggisberg were determined to develop what they considered to be the undeveloped African estates by the creation of a logistic infrastructure, by promoting education and research, by encouraging what the Germans called scientific colonization. To give just one example, Guggisberg, as governor of the Gold Coast between 1919 and 1927, initiated construction of the port of Takoradi; he was only one of many officials concerned with expanding the role of the state in the economy. According to the calculations made by S. H. Frankel in his standard work *Capital investment in Africa: its course and effects* (1938), public-listed capital placed in British Africa between 1870 and 1936 thus amounted to £546,345,000, nearly as much as the total of all private investments (estimated at £580,827,000). These investments were concentrated above all in the field of transport, but they included also monies put into schemes such as the Gezira irrigation project in the Sudan, where the Sennar dam was opened in 1926.

From the 1930s, the pace of state intervention increased. So did its scope. The operation of state power had many different aspects. After 1938, for example, the pound sterling ceased to be freely convertible. Colonial trade was controlled in the interests of maintaining British reserves of gold and hard currency. According to British policy-makers, the necessities of the Second World War required a system in which colonial earnings of hard currency, especially of dollars, were pooled in London. The colonies might no longer import goods from outside the sterling area, except with specific permission from the British authorities. These currency restrictions facilitated control over colonial trade, and reinforced controls brought about by quotas, tariffs and other means.

At the same time, other controls over the exchange sector were expanded, too. At first the rate of acceleration was limited. As Sir Frederick Pedler points out, colonial governments before 1945 possessed no powers to restrict the free choice of private consumers; they lacked central banks to direct the local monetary system. They were deficient in statistical data required for planning. Private competitive trade remained the mainspring of economic activity. The gradual expansion of controls over the exchange sector gathered momentum during the latter part of the colonial era and during its aftermath. Controls ranged from such comparatively limited though not insignificant measures as the prescription of markets in which producers could sell their produce, or the insistence that they had to sell without using the intermediaries, to comprehensive state export monopolies over all cash-crops. The range of these controls and the intensity of their application varied in the different British colonies and elsewhere. Nor was their operation always easily ascertainable. Many of the controls were embodied in readily available enactments or ordinances. But many others were announced in local regulations and notices, or emerged in administrative practice, or were conveyed verbally to organizations primarily affected. In Nigeria in the 1930s, for instance, the important decision to bar expatriates from trading in local foodstuffs was conveyed to the United Africa Company without public announcement. In Northern Nigeria various restrictions on southerners were applied informally. Various restrictions on the employment of expatriates or of strangers, or the establishment of minimum charges, often emerged from administrative practice. But the general pattern was unambiguous. By the time of decolonization, the exchange or monetized sector of the colonial economies (that is, economic activity outside the subsistence sector) was subject to extensive and close state control.

The principal components of state control of the economy included state monopoly of the export of the major cash-crops, as well as of other branches of trade and industry; the establishment of many state-owned and -operated enterprises, some of which were rather inaccurately termed 'co-operative societies'; official prescription and definition of the numbers and categories of traders permitted to operate in certain areas and of the commodities that could be traded; extensive licensing of commerce and industrial activities, including imports, exports and foreign exchange; large-scale subsidies to certain activities and enterprises; formal or informal restrictions on the employment both of expatriates and of African strangers (internal migrants); and prescription of minimum wages.[7] In examining the re-emergence and extension of state control, we shall have to confine ourselves to some major components and implications of the process and of its outcome. But any element of judgement or even of arbitrariness is relatively unimportant in this context because of the unequivocal nature both of the overall process and of its outcome.

Since the earliest days of colonial rule in British Africa, especially in East and Central Africa, restrictions were imposed on the number or nationality of traders who were allowed to operate in certain areas. Many of these measures were thought necessary to protect Africans from contact with more resourceful expatriates. In the 1930s, these restrictions increased in number, coverage and intensity. By the 1940s in East and Central Africa a close network of controls prescribed the numbers, the ethnic origins of traders and processors and the categories of enterprise (for instance, co-operatives or state trading and processing organizations) permitted to operate in specified places, areas or even entire colonies, and also the commodities, especially agricultural produce, in which trading was permitted.

The influences behind these controls differed geographically and varied through time. They included the tidiness complex of administrators, which was often coupled with the belief that the activity of private traders was wasteful or even anti-social; the desire of civil servants for greater power and influence; pressure by private sectional interests, first mainly expatriate and subsequently also African interests, for the restriction of competition; and, especially towards

---

[7] The inclusion of minimum wages in this list may need explanation. With exceptions irrelevant in this context, minimum wages imply the restriction of employment opportunities, both because total employment is diminished and because those willing to work at lower wages cannot secure employment. Minimum wages also assist employers to ward off competition from other employers willing to use cheap labour.

the end of colonial rule, a desire by administrators to placate articulate and influential African traders and politicians by reserving for them a substantial share of certain activities.

Although hostility to traders and expatriates was no doubt a factor, straightforward economic restrictionism was generally a strong influence. This was evident in such measures as the restrictions on the disposal of maize in Northern Rhodesia and even more unequivocally so in the restrictive licensing of cotton ginneries in Uganda. Until the 1950s, this restrictive licensing benefited expatriate owners of ginneries. From the 1950s, the system was increasingly used to assure profits to ginneries owned by state-sponsored co-operative societies.

From the 1930s to well into the 1950s, the major beneficiaries of the restrictions on trading and processing in East and Central Africa were expatriates. The system was gradually developed to protect influential African traders. The cost was invariably borne by the would-be entrants excluded from these activities, and by the unorganized farmers and consumers whose terms of trade were worsened—those of the farmers often sufficiently to inhibit them from production for sale.

Under African conditions, the familiar effects of such a maze of restrictions were pronounced: fragmentation of the economy; restriction on the movement of people and commodities; retardation of the spread of the exchange economy; obstruction of the establishment and extension of low-cost producers; provocation of political tension; retardation of capital formation and of the emergence and extension of corruption. All these results are especially significant in the early stages of development when subsistence production is relatively important and emergence and spread of the exchange economy necessary for material progress.

In Africa, the adverse effects were further exacerbated by the multi-racial character and the ethnic diversity of the population of many colonies. Restrictionism is most easily aroused and administered against groups readily distinguishable from the rulers or from the advocates of restrictions on ethnic and linguistic grounds. And the restriction on the activities of minorities is of special significance because of the decisive role of Asians, Europeans and Levantines in the progress of much of Africa and of their further potential usefulness especially in the extension of the exchange economy. Restrictions were freely directed also against African strangers; ethnic or tribal diversity often extends to differences overlooked by outsiders.

In the 1930s, the restrictions on trade and processing activities were appreciably more significant in British East Africa and Central Africa than in West Africa. But they spread to West Africa during and after the Second World War. Indeed, two major categories of restrictive control that were of altogether special significance—extensive licensing of imports and state monopoly of exports—were introduced first in West Africa and spread subsequently to East Africa. The increased centralization of policy-making in secretariats and in the Colonial Office in the 1930s and 1940s promoted the spread of state economic control between districts, areas and colonies.

Control of imports

The licensing of imports, including foreign exchange for their purchase, played a major role in the political and economic life of the British African colonies between the early 1940s and decolonization. Both in its origin and in its result, import licensing is a form of restrictionism that shields recipients of licences from competition and secures them a specified share of the trade. With few exceptions, mainly the result of treaty obligations that preclude the imposition of tariffs but not of import quotas, a given measure of import restriction can normally be achieved by means of tariffs without the restrictive implications of specific licensing.

There was no significant licensing of imports in British African colonies before the Second World War. Licensing was introduced shortly after the outbreak of the war and gradually extended to cover practically the entire range of imports in West Africa and in varying measure in the other British African colonies. And although it was intermittently relaxed, a large measure of import licensing remained in force in British colonial Africa over most of the two terminal decades of colonial rule.

In African conditions, the operation of import licensing has certain consequences that transcend the familiar results of this type of economic control. In particular, it is frequently attended by substantial windfall profits. Recipients of licences secure imports at a cost substantially below the prices prevailing at the retail level after allowing for marketing costs. As effective rationing is rarely possible at the ultimate retail stage, the consumer normally pays the price at which demand balances the available supply, and this price usually much exceeds the landed price and the cost of distribution. There is therefore a windfall profit inherent in the situation. As long as effective rationing and price control at the retail level are impracticable (which is normally the case, at any rate, in the rural areas of less developed countries), the presence and the size of the windfalls are not affected by attempts to control prices at the earlier stages of marketing, though these attempts may affect the share-out of the windfall. The level of the windfall profits in the situation is usually ascertainable by a comparison of the effective retail prices with the landed costs, or with the controlled prices that importers are supposed to charge.

The windfalls are shared in different and varying proportions among the import merchants, their employees and the various intermediaries who stand between importers and ultimate consumers, and also the politicians and administrators who allocate the licences. Effectiveness of price control is generally in a descending order from the first stage of importing; but even at the first stage, any price control is usually only partially effective. The incomplete observance of price control at the import stage is generally unavoidable, because the windfall profits in the situation set up an insatiable demand for licences and supplies.

These windfalls were largest during the Second World War and in the years immediately following it. Whenever such windfalls are appreciable, the allocation of supplies or licences is tantamount to a cash gift. This situation in turn makes corruption practically unavoidable. The closer the adherence by the importers to the officially prescribed or agreed prices, the more insistent becomes the demand for supplies and licences, because the riskless windfall profits become correspondingly greater. Similar considerations apply to the level of bribes. The lower the customary or expected level of bribes relative to the windfalls, the more insistent becomes the demand for supplies and licences. The operation of controls during the Second World War and its aftermath provided many local politicians and administrators with their first insight into the benefits to be derived from the operation of economic controls.

In principle, the windfalls that derive from the excess of demand for supplies and licences at controlled prices can always be eliminated by the imposition of duties or the raising of existing duties, measures that would not affect the retail price paid by the majority of consumers, who in any case pay the price at which available supplies balance demand. But in practice this course is often difficult to apply, partly because supply and demand conditions are apt to change rapidly, and also because the situation benefits and always has benefited influential interests both African and expatriate. However, it also seems that quite often the administrators, especially the colonial administrators, failed to appreciate the fundamentally simple economics of the situation, and also underestimated the political tensions of a situation in which the allocation of supplies was attended by large, assured and readily ascertainable windfall profits. Thus they did not investigate to any great extent the possibilities of eliminating or reducing the windfalls by such devices as the auctioning of licences or of supplies, the raising of duties or the floating of the exchange rate.

State export monopolies

By the end of colonial rule, the bulk of non-mineral exports from the British African colonies, including practically all exports produced by Africans, was handled by state export monopolies usually known as marketing boards. These organizations, which were introduced in West Africa in the early years of the war and which subsequently spread to East and Central Africa, became the most important single instrument of state economic control in the British colonies. Their operation is the subject of extensive and readily available literature. For this reason only their outline is reviewed here, largely in terms of the West African experience; the operation of similar bodies in East Africa, of which the cotton and coffee export monopolies of Uganda were the most important, closely resembled those of their West African counterparts, which were, however, much larger.

The establishment of the West African export monopolies was a fortuitous by-product of an instance of restrictionism. The export monopoly over cocoa was introduced in the 1939–40 cocoa season when the British government announced that it would buy all West African cocoa at seasonally fixed prices to avert a threatened collapse of the local price in the face of a shortage of shipping and the closure of important overseas markets. The export monopoly was subsequently extended to every major West African cash-crop, especially oils and oil seeds, ostensibly to stimulate their output following the Japanese conquest of South-East Asia. Monopoly of export was in fact not required for either of these purposes. A government guarantee to act as residual buyer at stated prices would have sufficed to maintain the price of cocoa. And monopoly of export was clearly unnecessary for the expansion of supplies of oils and oil seeds, which in fact it obstructed, because throughout the war the relevant marketing board paid farmers much less than the market price, or the price paid by the Ministry of Food for bulk supplies from other sources.

The export monopolies were established at the suggestion of the West African merchants, who had not only proposed it to the Colonial Office within a week of the outbreak of war but had also put forward a detailed scheme for its operation. This scheme, which was adopted by the Colonial Office, provided for a monopoly of export and for the purchase of the crops by the merchants as agents of the monopoly in accordance with officially determined quotas based on pre-war performances. The scheme provided also for penalty payments by those who exceeded their quotas for the benefit of those who were under-bought. These quotas were paradoxical because the market was unlimited, since the British authorities undertook to purchase the entire exportable output both of cocoa and of oil and oil seeds. The paradox was reflected in the quotas themselves, which did not refer to fixed amounts but were shares in unspecified and indeed unlimited totals.

The quotas were the clue to the establishment of state monopoly of export. They represented statutory extension and enforcement of the pre-war market-sharing arrangements (pools) of the West African merchants that were designed to protect profit margins by restraining buying competition. Such measures are easier to administer and to enforce when there is only one buyer, especially if that buyer arranges settlements between those overbought and those under-bought. This is why the merchants promoted the establishment of state export monopolies. And the arrangements for the calculation of the quotas and for the penalties and compensations for excess and shortfall of purchases were identical with those of the 1937 Gold Coast cocoa-buying agreement of the merchants, the terms of which had been made public and which sparked off the producers' strike of that year.

Within a few years of the establishment of the export monopolies, the British government and the colonial authorities decided to make them permanent. The decision was announced in a series of official publications. The main theme of these documents was the need to continue these monopolies for the purpose of price stabilization. By virtue of their sole right to purchase for export and to export the controlled crops, these powerful organizations were able to dissociate the producer price from the market price, and thus to determine effectively or rather to limit the incomes and the livelihood of the producers. They were empowered also to license processors and traders dealing in the controlled crops even for local sale. In these documents the British government and the colonial administrations gave the most emphatic and unequivocal assurances that the marketing boards would on no account be used as instruments of taxation and would indeed act as agents and trustees of the producers.

Even official statements were rarely discredited so speedily and completely as were these assurances. The boards, which immediately became instruments of severe taxation, continued this role to the end of colonial rule. In addition, they exercised close control over processors and traders. Neither during colonial rule nor thereafter did the operation of these organizations bear any resemblance to their ostensible objectives.

It is not possible here to present detailed statistics of the operations of the boards; but on the basis of available figures, it is estimated that between the establishment of these organizations and 1962, the state export monopolies withheld from the producers of the controlled crops in Nigeria and the Gold Coast between one-third and one-half the commercial value of the yield. In absolute terms, the sums for these two territories over this period exceeded £700 million. These retentions generally represented rates of taxation applicable in Britain to surtax payers. After various adjustments, especially for the costs of production and transport to convert gross proceeds into incomes, the proportion of proceeds withheld from producers represented rates of taxation borne in Britain only by persons with incomes of many thousands of pounds a year. The producers of some of the controlled crops, especially of Nigerian ground-nuts and cotton, were small farmers. Their cash proceeds from the sale of these crops in the 1950s were only about £4–5 annually after the payment of these levies. Of course, the producers still had to pay local taxes and consumption taxes.[8]

The heavy special taxation reduced correspondingly the tax burden on the rest of the population. No other group with similar incomes was taxed at rates comparable to those imposed on these producers. It is notable that in Gold Coast–Ghana the surpluses of the Cocoa Board and the export duties in most years far exceeded total government gross capital expenditure. By the mid-1950s even the pretence of stabilization (a term of little meaning without specific definition not attempted in the official documents) was abandoned, and monopoly of export was used frankly for taxation. In fact, monopoly of export was not only unnecessary for stabilization in any meaningful sense, but was not necessary even for taxation. If it had been thought desirable to tax producers of certain cash-crops specially severely, this could have been achieved largely by export duties without state export monopolies—that is, without organizations that denied alternative outlets for farmers, and that subjected producers, traders and processors to the mercy of those in charge of the monopolies.

Some effects of state monopoly of export

The severe taxation imposed by the state export monopolies had certain familiar results, such as the obstruction of the spread of cash-crops, the accumulation of private capital and the development of a prosperous peasantry and of an independent middle class. But there were other, possibly even more far-reaching, results. The huge sums collected by the state export monopolies passed through the hands of administrators and politicians, at first primarily expatriate, subsequently largely African. Many of these men were unaccustomed to controlling such huge sums, which they often regarded as instruments for the promotion of their personal interests or political power. Moreover, their livelihoods often depended, not on their obligations to abstract entities or to nebulous concepts such as the public good of a large area, but on their obligations to their relatives, friends or political allies. Thus the cocoa funds (both the accumulated reserves and the current revenues) served for years both before and after complete independence as a major financial base for Dr Nkrumah's political operations, as well as for large-scale personal spending by himself and his allies and for indiscriminate public spending. The economic usefulness of the huge expenditure of the Nkrumah government may be gauged from the fact that after the rapid expenditure of the large reserves of the Gold Coast–Ghana export monopolies and of current cocoa revenues, the government incurred debts on which it had to default, in spite of many years of acute dearth of consumer goods in the country.

The very large sums that accrued to governments and their agencies through the state export monopolies reinforced the effects of other state controls, espe-

[8] I discussed this taxation at length in two papers reproduced, respectively, as essay 9 in P. T. Bauer and B. S. Yamey, *Markets, market control and marketing reform* (London, 1968); and as essay 12 in my book *Dissent on development: studies and debates in development economics* (London, 1972). The first of these papers draws in part on two papers by Professor Gerald K. Helleiner and Mr. A. T. Killick, respectively, to which reference will be found in that essay.

cially of import licensing, in promoting large-scale corruption. This was especially pronounced in West Africa, where both the export monopolies and import licensing were established longest, where their coverage was most comprehensive, and the sums at stake the largest. These various influences helped to turn the West African polities into kleptocracies, to borrow Professor Andreski's felicitous term.

Even where the large-scale expenditure was not blatantly political or corrupt, it was undertaken with little regard to economic usefulness or welfare. It was often allocated for prestige projects or in directions dictated by intellectual fashion, such as heavily subsidized industrial or commercial ventures, expensive government buildings, unsuccessful co-operatives. This was not surprising, since the politicians and administrators were quite unprepared for these large sums of money. The tendency for wasteful spending was reinforced by the familiar practice in contemporary economic and political discussion of treating an activity or its output as a net addition to income, thus ignoring its cost in terms of the alternative use of resources. Moreover, in British Africa as elsewhere, the effectiveness of public spending is often measured by its volume, which assumes that expenditure is productive or worth-while in itself, a practice often genuinely unavoidable in the assessment of public expenditure. In these conditions, ineffective or outright wasteful spending of marketing board funds, reserves and revenues was practically inevitable. The last course desired by the politicians and administrators in Britain or Africa was to return the funds to the African producers of cash-crops, who in most of British Africa were inarticulate, unorganized and politically far less effective than the urban population.

We have already noted some of the major adverse effects of restrictive controls on economic development in emerging economies. And for reasons that we have also noted earlier, the adverse effects are likely to be especially pronounced when the controls restrict external economic contacts. In Africa, these contacts are potent instruments of change, of mores and customs uncongenial to material progress. They are thus instruments for that modernization of the kind that is a prime condition of material advance. They are most effective for these purposes when they are diverse, and when they are widely dispersed among the population. State export monopolies and import licensing restrict the volume and variety of these contacts, and their dispersal among the population.

Moreover, extensive state economic controls politicize social and economic life. The prizes of political power increase greatly. In these conditions it becomes all-important who has the government. The stakes in the fight for political power increase greatly and so does the intensity of the struggle for it, especially, but not only, in multi-racial societies. These sequences exacerbate political tension and struggle at least until all opposition is suppressed. And when political action becomes all-important, the energies and activities of the ambitious and resourceful men are diverted from economic activity to political life (sometimes from choice, often from necessity) because people's economic prospects, or even their economic or physical survival, come to depend on political developments; and this diversion of energy from economic activity to political life inhibits economic progress.

All these adverse effects of state control were manifest throughout British Africa in the terminal years of colonial rule, and have remained manifest since independence. The state export monopolies have been of special significance because of their comprehensive control over the incomes of farmers, their right to deny alternative marketing outlets for producers and processors, their exclusive right to export the crops and the unavoidable restriction on external contacts that attends their operation. And their huge revenues have been a major factor in increasing the prizes of political power.

Increased concern for the well-being of Africans?

The extension of state control, the expansion of government expenditure and the increase in Colonial Development and Welfare funds in the closing decades of colonial rule are widely regarded as evidence of increased concern on the part of the colonial powers, especially the British government, for the well-being of the local population on the eve of independence. And the terminal period of colonialism is accordingly often contrasted favourably with the period before the Second World War, which was allegedly one of neglect or even of exploitation. This interpretation is misleading.

Some pre-war administrations might well have spent with advantage more on education, health and agricultural extension work or concerned themselves more with the adaptation of traditional institutions to the needs of an exchange economy—though the merits of such policies would of course have depended on their specific contents and circumstances, including the method of collection of the required funds. The financial problems appear much simpler in retrospect than in the pre-war years, when the market prospects of export crops were very different from what they become later. However, greater attention to some of the problems just noted would have called for little additional expenditure.

But not much of the greatly increased government expenditure in the final years of colonial rule was derived from the metropolitan tax-payer. It was largely financed from local funds, chiefly from the taxation of export crops, and to a lesser extent from mining royalties and corporation taxes, together with some external loans under foreign-aid schemes, and with some contributions from Colonial Development and Welfare funds. Some of the greatly expanded expenditure was presumably productive, as, for instance, on the roads in Northern Nigeria and Kenya. But as already noted, a very large proportion was spent on projects and activities that were uneconomic at best, mere prestige projects, or total failures, or instruments for personal enrichment and political patronage. It is facile to take it for granted that increased government spending promotes the welfare of the population or reflects greater concern for it.

Some of the results and implications of the increased expenditure that we have noted are familiar concomitants of rapid and discontinuous expansion of public spending. In the terminal years of British colonial rule in Africa, the results were especially pronounced because of the differences in political effectiveness between the politicians and administrators and the tax-payers, who were principally inarticulate farmers or expatriate companies and firms who feared for their future. The difference in effectiveness in turn reflected partly the play of political forces and partly the administrative arrangements of the late colonial period.

The most distinctive feature of economic policy of the closing years of colonial rule was a great extension of state control of the exchange sector, of which the increased government spending was one component. The controls benefited mostly articulate and influential sectional interests at the expense of the population at large. They were not intended or operated to raise general living standards. Indeed, for the most part they inhibited substantially any improvement in conditions, most obviously in the case of the state export monopolies. These systematically depressed the incomes of the producers, which is hardly the way to raise living standards. But this was only a limiting case of the operation of these controls. The unequivocal result was the creation of closely controlled economies in which people's livelihoods came to depend largely on political and administrative decisions. This was in contrast to the policy of colonial governments of the inter-war period. These governments were also authoritarian in the sense of being non-elective, but they did not attempt close comprehensive control over their economies.

Nor did the state controls reflect economic planning in any meaningful sense, such as systematic examination of their likely social, political and economic results, or even attempted cost-benefit analysis in the narrower sense. They mirrored very largely the play of political forces, the operation of sectional interests emanating from the public or the private sector, the vagaries of intellectual fashion or short-term administrative convenience. The operation of these controls imposed no financial sacrifice on the British tax-payer, and often benefited influential British interests such as certain categories of exporters or expatriate administrators or advisers.

Genuine concern for the welfare of the African population would have involved reflection on the difficult and delicate problems of promoting types of institutional change likely to smoothe the transition to modern forms of economic activity. It would also have involved attempts to explain to some sections of the population that the required institutional change means more than the expropriation or expulsion of unpopular or ineffective groups. It might also have involved attempts to make clear to local opinion the costs of various types of government activity, including state-sponsored or -supported activities (both the more specific and direct economic costs, and also some wider repercussions, such as those on the progress of the exchange economy), as well as attempts to consider how far certain objectives of policy could be achieved by methods involving less political tension than the methods usually employed (as, for instance, control of imports by tariffs rather than by specific licensing, or attempted income stabilization without export monopolies).

There is no evidence that the departing governments gave any thought to these matters. They promoted institutional and political arrangements that inhibited material progress and exacerbated political tension. The operation of import licensing was the inception of large-scale corruption, to be reinforced shortly by the sudden expansion of government expenditure. The establishment and operation of the state export monopolies entailed immediate large-scale breaches of formal undertakings by the British authorities, thereby providing examples of political conduct that was instructive and possibly helpful to the incoming African governments. The results of this conduct were compounded by the irresponsibility of handing over control over the livelihood of producers and over vast sums of money to politicians and administrators with little interest in the welfare of their subjects. In many ways, the ready-made framework of a totalitarian government was handed over to the incoming African governments.

It is conjectural how far such policies might have emerged without colonial rule. In the contemporary intellectual climate, independent African governments would in any case have attempted extensive state economic controls; and in such attempts they would have enjoyed the support of the international organizations. But it is doubtful whether such far-reaching and extensive controls could have been effectively established and operated without the administrative and financial resources of the colonial governments, including their personnel, some of whom they have left behind and for the maintenance of whom they provided financial support. It is also doubtful how far some of these controls would have been introduced without the examples set by the colonial governments in the 1940s and 1950s. The experience of Liberia and Ethiopia suggests that without colonial rule state controls would not have been so comprehensive and effective.

Nor is it possible to foretell how lasting and effective the results of state control will be in these territories. This is likely to be much affected by external factors, especially the presence of expatriate personnel supplied under various aid schemes. The experience of the first decade or so of independence suggests that some effects and repercussions will extend over a considerable period or may even be lasting. For instance, if economic life had not been politicized so thoroughly, the treatment of expatriates in the private sector might not have been so harsh. It is doubtful also whether there would have been civil war on such a large scale as that which occurred in Nigeria.

We have seen that there was considerable state coercion in the early days of British rule that gradually receded under various influences, especially the spread of the exchange economy. In the closing years of colonial rule the sustained extension of state control represented the recurrence of coercion, less direct but more pervasive than that of the earlier period. The new controls were increasingly exercised by Africans, though usually by Africans rather unrepresentative of the population at large. A given degree of coercion or control may be more acceptable to Africans when exercised by other Africans rather than by expatriates, though this is not necessarily so and has in fact been disputed. What is clear is that the controls introduced during the terminal years of colonial rule have exacerbated political tension in these ethnically heterogeneous countries.

We have emphasized that virtually all components of modern social and economic life in Africa date from the colonial period, and that colonial rule has greatly accelerated material progress and has even made it possible. Over the last two decades of colonial rule the conclusion is more equivocal. Without colonial rule the progress might have been slower even over this period. But the past decade or two might not have been fraught with such large-scale corruption, intense political struggle and mass expulsion of highly productive minorities.

Nkrumah enjoined African politicians first to seek the political kingdom, because if they attained that, all else would be added unto them. It is because the closing years of colonial rule lent support to this policy that at this point I find the balance sheet of colonialism more difficult to read than I would have a generation earlier.

BIBLIOGRAPHY

Andreski, Stanislav. *The African predicament*. London, 1971.

Bauer, P. T. *Dissent on development: studies and debates in development economics*. London, 1972.

    West African trade: a study of competition, oligopoly and monopoly in a changing economy. Cambridge University Press, 1954.

Bauer, P. T., and B. S. Yamey. *Markets, market control and marketing reform*. London, 1968.

Commission on International Development. *Partners in Development: report of the Commission on International Development*. London and New York, 1969.

Deane, Phyllis. *Colonial social accounting*. Cambridge University Press, 1953.

East Africa Royal Commission. *Report*. London, 1955.

Frankel, S. Herbert. *Capital investment in Africa: its course and effects*. London, Oxford University Press, 1938.

    The economic impact on under-developed societies: essays on international investments and social change. Oxford, 1953.

Gann, L. H., and Peter Duignan. *Burden of empire: an appraisal of Western colonialism in Africa south of the Sahara*. New York, 1967.

Hailey, William Malcolm Hailey, 1st baron. *An African survey: revised 1956*. London, 1957.

Hancock, Sir William Keith. *A survey of British Commonwealth affairs,* vol. II: *Problems of economic policy, 1918–1939,* pt. 2. London, Oxford University Press, 1942.

    Wealth of colonies. Cambridge University Press, 1950.

Herskovits, Melville J., and Mitchell Harwitz, eds. *Economic transition in Africa*. London, 1964.

Jackson, E. F., ed. *Economic development in Africa*. Oxford, 1965.

Kamarck, Andrew M. *The economics of African development*. New York, 1967.

Kilby, Peter. *Industrialization in an open economy: Nigeria, 1945–1966*. Cambridge University Press, 1969.

Kingsley, Mary. *West African studies*. London, 1901.

Lewis, W. Arthur. *Development planning: the essentials of economic policy*. London, 1966.

McPhee, Allan. *The economic revolution in British West Africa*. London, 1926; 2nd ed., London, 1971.

Myint, Hla. *Economic theory and the underdeveloped countries*. London, 1971.

Nkrumah, Kwame. *Africa must unite*. London, 1963.

Perham, Margery, ed. *Mining, commerce and finance in Nigeria*. London, 1948.

    The native economies of Nigeria. London, 1946.

Prest, A. R. *Public finance in underdeveloped countries*. 2nd ed. London, 1972.

Prest, A. R., and I. G. Stewart. *The national income of Nigeria, 1950–51*. London, 1953.

Robinson, E. A. G., ed. *Economic development in Africa south of the Sahara*. London, 1964.

Stolper, Wolfgang F. *Planning without facts*. Cambridge, Mass., Harvard University Press, 1966.

Usher, Dan. *The price mechanism and the meaning of national income statistics*. Oxford, 1968.

CHAPTER 17

HOW PEOPLE CAME TO LIVE IN TOWNS

by

WALTER ELKAN *and* ROGER VAN ZWANENBERG

A salient feature of twentieth-century Africa has been the growth of towns. In West Africa, large towns were already in existence by the turn of the century; but several of the towns of East Africa came only with colonial development. They therefore not only reflect the different ways in which each territory developed, but are of course also very much a product of the twentieth century. This essay is concerned principally with these East African towns, especially with Kampala and Nairobi; but some comparisons are made with West Africa in order to focus attention on the distinguishing characteristics of the East African towns. We begin by outlining some of the main features in the growth of towns in Africa generally.

Principal features of the growth of towns in Africa

As has often been pointed out, towns existed in West Africa long before there were colonial governments, although their size and nature have not always been very clearly understood. Thus, the capitals of the Hausa and Yoruba states, about which so much has been written, never exceeded fifty thousand inhabitants, of whom between one-half and four-fifths were farmers. The Hausa towns had something of the character of mediaeval European cities in that they served as administrative and commercial capitals of the surrounding rural areas, whilst the Yoruba towns also were centres of craft industries, especially cloth-making.

But most of today's large towns of West Africa were very small before the First World War. Lagos had 18,000 inhabitants in 1901 and Accra 21,000 in the same year. Abidjan had still only 10,000 people as late as 1931; and only Ibadan was really big, with an estimated population of 200,000 in 1900. East Africa, too, had two towns, Mombasa with roughly 30,000 people in 1906 and Dar es Salaam with 20,000. In both West and East Africa, most of the growth of large towns took place *after* the beginning of colonial government. Some, like Nairobi, did not exist at all, so that the rapid development of towns has been a direct outcome of the political and economic changes that we associate with the period of colonial government.

Although towns grew rapidly, their growth was usually much slower than in the years since independence. The earlier growth seemed rapid only because percentage increases from small beginnings always appear more dramatic than the growth itself. Most of the discussions have concentrated on explaining the rapid growth of towns, whereas it would really be more instructive to ask why they did not grow faster. This is especially the case in East Africa, where at the time of independence the proportion of the African population living in towns

655

of 2,000 inhabitants or more was no more than 5·3 per cent in Kenya—the most urbanized of the three territories.

The main reason is, of course, that in contrast with much of European experience in the nineteenth century, the economic development that did take place took the form of the growth not of manufacturing but of agriculture. Some manufacturing industries were indeed established, especially in Southern Rhodesia and South Africa, but also, for example, in Nigeria and Kenya, usually as subsidiaries of overseas firms anxious to dominate the local market. Yet as an engine of growth, the development of manufacturing was nowhere to be compared with the development of cash-crops for export, except, mainly in South Africa, Northern Rhodesia (now Zambia) and the Belgian Congo (now Zaire), where mineral production formed this role.

The rising demand in the industrial countries for tropical food, raw materials and minerals was one of the main economic reasons for colonization in the late nineteenth and early twentieth centuries, and this of course implied rural, not urban, development. In most of the territories that came to export agricultural produce, any industrial development that occurred before 1939 tended mainly to be the processing of agricultural products, many of which had by their nature to be rural-based. Thus the decortication of sisal, the drying and hulling of coffee, the extraction of sugar and even cotton ginning had to take place in close proximity to where the crops were grown. The creation of rural money-incomes generated a demand for manufactured consumer goods that might have been manufactured locally in towns; but they were, in fact, mostly imported from the industrial countries. In most of the colonial territories the development of manufacturing industries would have required deliberate government intervention— protective tariffs, industrial training, harnessing of capital—and this was ruled out, at any rate until the Second World War, by the prevailing policy of colonial administration and by pre-Keynesian ideas of economic management that looked to retrenchment, not to foreign aid, as the way to combat unemployment at home. There is also evidence that opposition from overseas suppliers, who were not anxious to see their markets in Africa eroded, played a part. Some urban industries did develop; and others, like the West African hand-made cloth industries, expanded. They were in general those that were protected from overseas competition by high costs of transport or perishability, and that at the same time were technologically simple, like the manufacture of furniture, brewing, baking and newspaper printing.

At any rate, until the last decade or two of colonial government, the growth of towns other than in South Africa and Southern Rhodesia was only to a slight degree a response to industrial employment opportunities. As a result, urban growth did not become an important feature of most African economies until the last twenty years, when the growth of import substitution industries began to change the character of the towns. Until the 1950s, most tropical African towns, like the towns of mediaeval Europe, grew because they became the centres of administration, of transport and of trade; and like them also, they remained small, nowhere except in Southern Rhodesia accommodating as much as 10 per cent of the population and generally much less.

Only in Northern Rhodesia and the Belgian Congo, where development was based on mining rather than on agriculture, did a different kind of town develop; and it is even questionable whether 'town' is a proper description for the mining communities that grew up in Katanga and on the Rhodesian Copper Belt. These are to be compared more with company towns such as Bourneville in England, whose sole reason for existence is the presence of one major employer. Their character was therefore also very different. They were closely controlled by the mining companies in much the same way as armies control the accommodation of their troops. Houses were built in an orderly manner and were equipped with running water, sewerage and cooking facilities; and there was a place for everything and everything was in its place. From 1926, when the labour policy in the Congo had altered, an attempt was made to stabilize the labour force, at least for the semi-skilled grades upwards. Because short-term migrant labour had been found to be inefficient, measures were taken to create a healthy and adequately nourished work force. The result was the provision of sanitary, albeit rather dreary, company towns.

The thesis that—mining towns apart—most African towns grew in response to the growth of administration, of transport and of trade is well illustrated by the composition of Nairobi's working population. An occupational census of 1939 estimated that a total of some 28,000 employees were distributed as shown in Table 148.

Table 148. *Occupational census, Nairobi, 1939*

Domestic servants	8,457
Employees of central administration, municipality, and railway	9,049
Skilled workers—tailors, bakers, messengers	4,756
Headmen, garage hands, etc.	5,507
	27,769

SOURCE: E. R. St Davies, 'Some problems arising from the conditions of housing and employment of natives in Nairobi', Kenya National Archives, no. 9·1707·70: 257 (Nairobi, 1939).

It is a rather bizarre classification, and of course relates only to employees—not to those earning a livelihood as hawkers, water carriers, ricksha-men, or vegetable sellers. Even so, it is not clear whether the employees of the soda-water factory, of the brewery or the *East African Standard Press* were included. There existed also a variety of small workshops mostly Indian-owned and operated, and it is not clear whether the small number of Africans they employed as 'boys' are included in the tabulation. But by the side of the 8,000 domestic servants and 9,000 employed by the government, the muncipality and the railways, they pale in any case into insignificance.

Relationship between growth of towns and general development of colony

The characteristics of a particular town reflect the way the territory in which it is located has developed. One would expect towns in countries that have developed on the basis of cash-crop production by small indigenous cultivators to be different from towns in countries that were developed by European settlers. This emerges clearly from an examination of Kampala and Nairobi.

From negligible beginnings at the turn of the century, by the time of independence in the early 1960s, Nairobi has grown to about a quarter of a million inhabitants and Kampala to over a hundred thousand. Within these totals were minorities of Europeans and Asians. In Nairobi, there were about 20,000 Europeans and 70,000 Asians; whereas in Kampala, Europeans accounted for only some 3,000 and Asians for 20,000 of the total. The minorities were substantial by West African standards, but much smaller in Kampala than in Nairobi. The difference in the size of these minorities is not accidental, but rather reflects the difference in the character of Kenya's and Uganda's economic development. Kenya had developed on the basis of settlers, mostly from Great Britain, who had established large farms and estates, whereas Uganda's expansion in output, especially since the twenties, had been accomplished by small African cultivators who had added cash-crops—cotton, and later coffee—to those they had always grown for their own consumption.

Although both Kampala and Nairobi were centres of government, Kenya's settler population constituted a much larger and more complex market for urban services, and this explains both Nairobi's larger European *and* Asian populations. Nairobi had also established itself as the entrepôt for Kenya and Uganda, if not for East Africa as a whole. On the export side, each town handled the crops of its own hinterland, but imported goods were often re-exported to Uganda from Nairobi; and the big importing houses and commission agents that operated throughout East Africa had their headquarters in Nairobi, as had the railways, the post office, the income tax department and some of the other services that were operated on an inter-territorial basis.[1]

None of this in itself explains the presence of substantial non-African minorities, because presumably all these activities could have been carried on by Africans, as indeed they were to a much greater extent in West Africa and have been in East Africa since independence. But West Africa, as has often been pointed out, had had a much longer connexion with Europe, which had fostered aptitudes and skills that were conspicuously absent in East Africa. However, West Africa, too, relied heavily in its foreign trade on Levantine traders; and the big import-export businesses were managed by people from Europe. East Africa also had a readily accessible and cheap supply of people from abroad with relevant skills; and although the choice lay between training Africans or allowing free immigration from Britain and especially India, there was never much doubt as to how it should be exercised. The expense of training African carpenters or plumbers, for example, would have been infinitely greater than importing highly skilled Sikhs. Why create an expensive educational system to produce clerks and accountants when Goans were only too eager to accept such work, and at much lower pay than any Englishman would accept? Furthermore, if cash-crops were to be grown by small-scale cultivators, as in Uganda, there had to be traders to buy them and to offer the opportunity to acquire imported consumer goods with the proceeds. Indians had these skills and were prepared to come and to go to very remote districts and work for returns that no European would accept. It seemed the obvious answer in the short run, and the long run seemed altogether too remote.

Non-Africans thus came to play a much more important role in Uganda and

---

[1] Walter Elkan and Leslie Nulty, 'Economic links between Kenya, Uganda and Tanganyika', in *History of East Africa*, vol. III, A. R. Low, ed. (Oxford, Clarendon Press, forthcoming).

Kenya than in West Africa, but there are important differences in the parts they played in the development of their principal towns, Kampala and Nairobi. We therefore turn now to a more detailed account of the growth of these two towns.

Growth of Kampala

Kampala as such came into existence only seventy years ago, but it had been preceded by the capital of the kingdom of Buganda, which had been in Mengo—later to be simply one of the hills of Kampala—since the last quarter of the nineteenth century. Then in 1890 Sir Frederick Lugard established his camp and with it British authority on the neighbouring hill called Old Kampala, where it remained until some fifteen years later. At that time the British administration headquarters for Buganda, having outgrown the very limited space available at Old Kampala, was moved to Nakasero hill.

The subsequent development of Kampala cannot be understood except by reference to the 1900 Uganda Agreement that divided authority over the town between the British and the Buganda administrations. Under this famous agreement, 8,000 square miles of Buganda land was given in freehold to the senior Baganda chiefs and 1,000 square miles to the Kabaka in person. Included in these areas were the parts of Kampala—the Kibuga—adjacent to the Buganda capital. The remainder was administered by the colonial administration under a township—and later municipal form of government. The significance of this division of authority is that it gave rise to a dual standard of urban administration. The colonial administration evolved an elaborate system of rules and regulations designed to safeguard public health and welfare. It introduced a rating system and with the proceeds built and paved roads, laid drains and sewers, collected garbage and provided a piped supply of clean water. The Baganda, by contrast, did nothing except draw rents and defend their rights against all attempts by the municipality to encroach upon their terrain in order to improve conditions of life. They refused to rate or tax owners or occupiers, and indeed there was no separate Buganda urban authority; the Kibuga was ruled as part of the unitary Buganda government.

A natural consequence of this division of authority was, of course, that life in the municipality was healthy but expensive, whereas in the Kibuga, which made no attempt to provide any sort of services, it was insanitary and cheap. Given the racial distribution of income, this led naturally to a racial distribution of residence. Africans came to live in slums in the Kibuga whilst Asians and Europeans settled in the more salubrious municipality. This racial segregation was not, of course, complete. Domestic servants lived in quarters provided by their European and Asian employers, and some squatter settlements also developed at Wandageya and elsewhere within the municipal boundary. But in general, Africans could not afford to live in the municipality, and in consequence there developed along its borders a series of peri-urban slums, as close as possible to the places of employment.

Almost no East African had any previous experience of the problems of permanent town life. Consequently, the majority who stayed in the towns replicated their rural way of living. As population increased, houses grew ever closer to one another, and standards of building, sanitation and so on, that would be acceptable on isolated farmsteads, became oppressive and a danger to health as population densities rose in one area after another, as they did in the

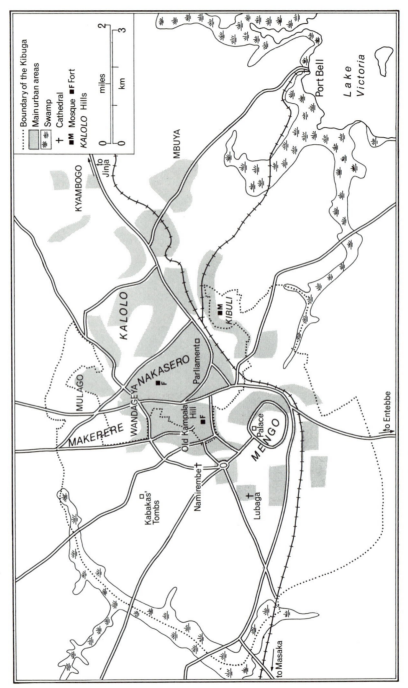

8. Kampala and environs, showing the Kibuga boundary as at 1955

Kibuga. It did not occur to people who had never seen a town or even a village to build houses along roads, and this in turn made it the more difficult subsequently to provide sanitary services such as sewers, even if the will to do so had existed.

One solution that was strongly advocated in the years before the First World War was racial segregation, but in Kampala it was neither statutorily enacted nor implemented as a deliberate act of policy because there was in fact no need to do so. All that was necessary was that the government should lay down high enough building standards in the municipality; the price mechanism could be relied upon to do the rest. Some will of course argue that the government deliberately laid down these standards in order to discourage Africans from living in the municipality; and it is certainly true that few Europeans relished the prospect of having much poorer Africans live cheek by jowl with them. But one has to remember that many of the colonial administrators saw themselves as imbued with a paternalistic concern for African welfare in the tradition of Lord Shaftsbury and the English public health movement, though few pursued it with the same vigour and single-mindedness. A dominant theme in the thinking of many of them had always been how to bring about development without what they thought of as the evil consequences of the English Industrial Revolution. Unfortunately, an elementary understanding of the economic consequences of administrative action was never regarded as a necessary qualification for colonial administrators, and the development of segregation and slum dwelling in Kampala was just one of many examples of inadvertent, undesirable consequences resulting from acts of administration that were intended for other purposes.

Growth of Nairobi

Nairobi presents a different picture. Even more than Kampala, it is a town that came into existence only as the result of colonial development. As has often been remarked, there appears not even to have been a settlement of any kind until the builders of the Uganda Railway decided to make it their halfway staging post and headquarters. Nairobi may have been a trading post between Masai and Kikuyu women, but what is better substantiated is that the coastal caravans used to shop for supplies at neighbouring Ngong. But to all intents and purposes Nairobi was started from *tabula rasa* in the area between the present River Road and Tom Mboya Street where the Railway Administration established its headquarters in 1899. Given the crucial importance of the railway in the economic development of East Africa, it is not difficult to see why Nairobi should soon also be chosen as the capital city. The provincial headquarters of Ukamba had moved there from Machakos in the same year. Until 1905, the capital of the East Africa Protectorate (as Kenya was then called) had been Mombasa; but with the growth of the railway and the development of comparatively easy communication inland, it proved administratively convenient to move the capital from the coast to the centre of the country. It could, of course equally well have been removed to Naivasha or Nakuru, but the choice of Nairobi by the railway made that the natural place to move.[2]

[2] William T. W. Morgan, 'The location of Nairobi', in *Ostafrikanische Studien—Ernst Weigt zum 60. Geburtstag,* ed. Herfried Berger (Nürnberg, 1968).

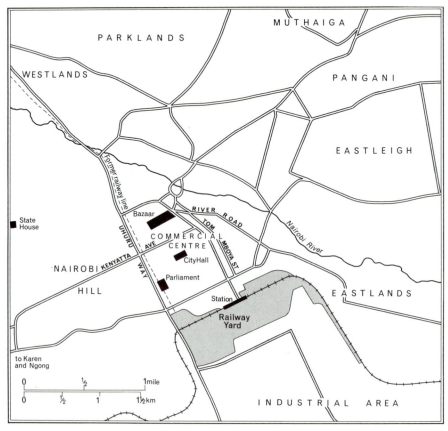

9. Central Nairobi

By 1906, the town had mushroomed to eleven thousand people living in five distinct areas within a one-and-a-half-mile radius of the government offices. The Europeans settled on the wooded ridges to the north and west of the railway centre. To the south and east were to be found the Indian railway workers' huts, or coolies' *landhies* as they were called. Adjacent to them were the washermen's (*dhobi*) quarters and the houses that constituted the Indian Bazaar. This, together with the European business district that developed a little later, set the pattern for the future city centre. Because the railway was constructed by Indian rather than African workers, the population of Nairobi was initially predominantly Indian, but by 1921 the balance had shifted. Indian indentured railway workers had left the country and some twelve thousand Africans were estimated to be living in eight separate 'villages' in Nairobi.[3]

The growth of Nairobi was rapid—though not by the standards of the decade since independence. From some fourteen thousand in 1906 it had grown to over a quarter of a million by the time of the 1962 census. By 1969 it was half a

[3] David Etherton, ed., *Mathare Valley: a case study of uncontrolled settlement in Nairobi* (University of Nairobi, Housing Research and Development Unit, 1970).

million. Its growth was accelerated by the arrival of British and South African settlers for whom it was the base camp from which they set forth to start their new farms, all within a radius of a hundred and fifty miles and mostly much closer. From Nairobi they obtained their supplies; it was there that they went when they fell ill; it was their centre of recreation when the loneliness of their isolated farmsteads got them down. And Nairobi, as we saw earlier, became not only the political capital of Kenya but also the commercial capital of East Africa.

Like Kampala, Nairobi soon came to exhibit a dual aspect in its growth. There were the European residential areas, including Westlands, Karen and Ngong, which surpassed in space and prettiness anything that had been dreamed of by the new school of garden-suburb planners in England. No house was set in less than an acre of land and the owners vied with one another in laying out their beautiful gardens. The Indians in Parklands were already more confined, and their more modest ambition was to replicate the houses in the suburbs of Bombay.

But the majority of Indians lived in the Bazaar and, like the Africans, they lived in slums. It is important to notice that the earliest outbreaks of plague occurred in the Bazaar, not in the African settlements. The point needs to be stressed, because it is nowadays so often forgotten that the Indian communities that were later to prosper were by no means born with silver spoons in their mouths. The reaction of the government to the outbreak of plague in the Bazaar was to burn it down. To quote J. H. Patterson, divisional engineer during the early years of Nairobi's history, 'A case or two of plague broke out [in the Bazaar], so I gave the natives and Indians who inhabited it an hour's notice to clear out, and on my own responsibility promptly burned the whole place to the ground.' [4] There were in fact several outbreaks of plague before 1914; and because contagious disease is no respecter of class or race, there was much concern among the European community about standards of hygiene and sanitation, especially in the African areas. In this situation there were two possible alternatives. It was possible to lay down minimal standards for the whole town: ensure that the water was clean, the rubbish was collected, the sewage evacuated and so forth. Or the new authorities could draw a *cordon sanitaire* around the area to be protected from contagion and thus create enclaves where, in the words of the poet, 'tout est ordre et beauté'. They chose the second alternative—or at any rate tried to do so.

Successive commissions of inquiry, following the outbreaks of plague, urged strict residential segregation and the development of African locations on the South African pattern. This policy seemed to the municipal administration to have three things to commend it. First, as we have seen, it was a way of combating the contagion of disease. Secondly, it would facilitate control of the African population and thus strengthen the physical security of Europeans and Asians. Thirdly, segregation would facilitate the control of movement into Nairobi. Africans were wanted only as employees in the town, and a policy of segregation, coupled with a restriction of entry by special passes issued only to those who had 'legitimate' employment, would ensure that 'undesirables' were effectively excluded.

[4] M. F. Hill, *Permanent way* (Nairobi, 1949), p. 191.

The African locations were of course not to be entirely neglected. Employers were legally required to erect housing (never 'houses'), and the new locations were to be provided with services by the municipal authority. Professor Sir William Simpson, who had been requested in 1913 by the Secretary of State for the Colonies to investigate sanitation in Nairobi, recommended that 'well defined and separate quarters be established for Europeans, Indians and Africans'.[5] Racial segregation expressed as frankly as this was, however, unacceptable to the Colonial Office, and the famous Command Paper no. 1922 of 1923, *Indians in Kenya,* would have none of it, although it pointed out that 'it may well prove that in practice the different races will by affinity keep together in separate quarters'. But to effect such segregation by legislative enactment, except on the strongest medical grounds, would not be justifiable in the British government's opinion. The Command Paper went on, however, to explain that 'the rigid enforcement of sanitary, police and building regulations without any racial discrimination by the Colonial and municipal authority will (in any case) suffice'.[6]

The Command Paper was largely irrelevant, because segregation does not really need the force of law but only, as the paper itself implicitly recognized, a sufficiently unequal distribution of income along racial lines. What would have been more helpful would have been some recognition of the political and economic factors underlying the existence of the African slums. A muncipality dominated by Europeans and Asians found itself unable to resist the temptation to arrogate to itself the greater part of municipal revenue and to devote the major share of finance to the provision of services in the European and Asian areas. Moreover, it was pointed out in justification that, because the Europeans were spread out over such a wide area, the provision of municipal services proved immensely costly and really left little to spare for the African areas! Mary Parker has shown that between 1932 and 1947 services provided to African areas absorbed only a very small portion of the municipality's total expenditure.

A related question was why, almost from the outset, there appeared to be a chronic shortage of houses for people to live in. To document this housing shortage runs up against the age-old problem of determining what constitutes an adequate supply of houses. Standards of adequacy are a function of time and place and cannot be absolute. Yet some conditions are clearly intolerable by any standards, and the municipal authorities became very concerned every now and then when, after a midnight or dawn raid, they discovered conditions that were totally unacceptable. For instance, in 1937 a raid disclosed that 325 persons were living in fifteen houses, and other raids disclosed similar situations. We are, however, still left to answer two questions: first, why more houses were not built, and secondly, why so much of the accommodation, especially that provided by employers, was clearly designed to cater for single men rather than for families.

The answer to the first question is twofold. First, much of the onus of building houses was placed on employers, because it was assumed that any African in Nairobi was an employee and it was therefore deemed the duty of employers

---

[5] Quoted in Great Britain, *Master plan for a colonial capital,* L. W. Thornton White, L. Silberman and P. R. Anderson, eds. (London, 1948), p. 15. [6] Quoted in *ibid.*

to see to it that they had somewhere to live. Employers, however, and this included the government and the municipality, had no enthusiasm for doing so and failed lamentably to carry out what the government regarded as their duty—principally because they had no difficulty in obtaining workers even without the offer of accommodation. Houses were built on the Copper Belt and on the Tanganyikan sisal estates because there was clearly no alternative. In Nairobi there was. Some private housing was available, and many Nairobi employers took the view that their workers should look for their own housing and pay for it out of their wages.

But there were not enough houses because potential African private builders were discouraged by the fact that they had little capital and that the rents to be obtained were restricted by the low wages of their prospective tenants. Above all, they were discouraged by the fact that they had absolutely no security of tenure of any land on which they might build. They could be evicted at any time and their houses torn down, and this was indeed a frequent occurrence. It was and remains a vicious circle. Landlords put up the flimsiest of structures and charged what were comparatively high rents in relation to wage levels in order to recoup the cost quickly before the municipal authorities could knock them down again. Multiple occupancy of small rooms was the obvious consequence, which then quickly attracted the attention of the authorities and led them the sooner to destroy their houses in the sacred name of slum clearance.

We have argued that in Kampala the existence of slums was in part the result of a failure to understand the economic consequences of administrative action. And so it proved to be in Nairobi. Low wages, lack of capital, failure to enforce the law, the greed of landlords, reluctance of the rich to pay for the services of the poor—all these played their part. But the housing problem would have been less acute if the public authorities had been more adroit in harnessing private enterprise in the pursuit of public goals instead of discouraging self-help. As it was, many people were forced to sleep on verandas and in latrines because the municipality was unable and unwilling to provide sufficient houses that would meet its self-imposed standards of adequacy while it prevented others from building any at all.

There was, however, another reason for the inadequate supply of houses. Despite official policy, Nairobi was not in fact the exclusive preserve of employees or even of those seeking employment. Any growing town provides great opportunities for earning a living in other ways, and what has recently been baptized 'the informal sector' by a visiting International Labour Office team was born a long time ago. People were quick to seize the opportunity to sell food, to brew and distil liquor, to carry water from the nearest standpipe, to cook meals, to supply charcoal, to collect and sell old clothes and bottles, to draw handcarts or rickshas and to sell sex. They, too, needed somewhere to live, and they had not even employers nominally responsible for providing them with somewhere to live; hence they added further pressure on the already hard-pressed supply of houses. The administration had always tried to keep their number to a minimum, having never understood the vital economic role that these self-employed entrepreneurs performed. They were invariably confused with the criminals who, of course, also found rich pickings in Nairobi. Criminals and the self-employed were lumped together and referred to indiscriminately as vagrants, and both the Vagrancy Laws and the Pass Laws were used to try to keep them out or to remove them.[7]

Lack of family housing in the towns

We have still to answer the question why so many of the houses that were officially provided were specifically designed to serve the needs of single men rather than of families—bachelor housing, as it was called. The view commonly held by Europeans was that Africans had their real homes in the countryside and were not interested in bringing their families with them for the relatively short periods for which they came to Kampala or Nairobi. Bachelor housing was then seen as the natural response to the situation confronting the authorities. But there was also another view, namely, that wages in Nairobi and Kampala were so low and the cost of living so high that Africans could not afford to bring their families, and that this was the real reason why they left them behind in the reserves. This view received powerful support from the Carpenter Report on Urban Wages of 1954, which argued the case for a substantial rise in urban wages and for the provision of family housing and of social security arrangements, in the hope that this would cause increasing numbers to sever their ties with the rural areas and to become permanent town-dwellers. We shall show that both views contain elements of the truth and that only when taken together do they provide a satisfactory explanation of the prevailing system of short-term circular male-labour migration.

As has frequently been documented, urban real wages were indeed low, and there is evidence that the Kenya government may have deliberately kept them so. The government was under pressure from private employers to do so, and being itself a large employer it regarded low wages as in its own best interest. But, even though urban wages were low—around twelve to eighteen shillings per month for much of the inter-war period, plus various fringe benefits that were not, however, always paid—it is clear that they were at least 50 per cent above the wages paid by European farmers and the government in rural areas, and were therefore well above the supply price of labour. Hence there was hardly ever a shortage of labour in either Nairobi or Kampala. Compared with earnings in agriculture—either small-scale or on big farms and estates—urban wages proved attractive in the sense that they drew a more than sufficient supply of labour.

Some will of course retort, with justification, that this is not support for the adequacy of urban wages (it is not intended to be!) but only an eloquent indication of the lack of alternative opportunities for workers to earn comparable sums in rural areas, either through wage employment or through the sale of crops. In Kenya, small-scale farmers were for much of the time legally precluded from growing coffee, the most lucrative of the export crops, and were not encouraged to grow other export crops. After 1934, Africans could for the first time be licensed to grow arabica coffee; but as late as 1953 only some fifteen thousand had been so licensed, and the acreage of coffee grown by them was under four thousand.[8] Although, throughout the period, there were limited

[7] R. M. A. van Zwanenberg, 'History and theory of urban poverty in Nairobi: the problem of slum development', *Journal of Eastern African Research and Development*, 1972, **2**, no. 2, 195.
[8] Lord Hailey, *An African survey: revised 1956* (London, Oxford University Press, 1957), p. 834.

opportunities for selling other crops, for the majority it would be true to say that in the main, if they were to earn cash, it had to be through wage employment. This was especially so for unmarried young men who did not yet have a farm of their own. Because urban wages were higher than either rural wages or the income to be earned from growing crops for sale, it might well be assumed that no further explanation is needed for the well-attested coexistence of labour shortage in the White Highlands and labour surplus in towns. The same phenomenon was found in Uganda. But what we have explained so far is simply why, despite what must be regarded as low urban wages in an absolute sense, people nevertheless moved to the towns in search of work. We have not yet addressed ourselves to the question of why they stayed there only for short periods and then returned to their villages of origin. In other words, we have still to explain why labour migration was not only short-term but also circular.

The most common explanation, as we have seen, is that given by the Carpenter Committee, which concentrates exclusively on conditions in the towns. We shall, however, now argue that this is only one part of the explanation and that factors operating in the rural areas need also to be brought into the picture.

It has always been assumed to be part of the order of nature that all urban growth shall follow the same pattern, and that the classical case of this pattern was the growth of towns in England in the early nineteenth century. This growth was thought to be the result of the once-and-for-all movement of unemployed or dispossessed families from the countryside who came to man the new factories that were propelling the growth of employment opportunities in the towns. That this picture of what actually happened in Britain is itself highly stylized and largely erroneous need not concern us here. What matters is that this was what those concerned with interpretation of the growth of African towns, and who were charged with policy, actually believed. They recognized that there was one difference between twentieth-century Africa and nineteenth-century Britain, namely, that 'every African had his shamba (small farm) to go back to'; and so the great majority did and still do. Some of the shambas were very small indeed, and there were the Sudanese ex-soldiers and others in Nairobi who had no such shambas. But as a broad generalization the belief was well founded.[9] What was not realized was that this was in marked contrast with early nineteenth-century Britain, where those who came to the towns had nothing to go back to because the great majority who migrated had not been farmers but second- or third-generation agricultural labourers owning at most certain rights in the 'commons', such as the right to graze a cow or two or to collect firewood. Because these rights had been progressively eroded during the latter part of the eighteenth century, what had emerged was a rural proletariat in the sense of a distinct category of people who had nothing to sell except their labour. They sold it where they could and where wages were highest. Given much rural unemployment and very low rural wages, they tried their luck in towns.

In East Africa, as elsewhere in the continent, those who came to the towns still retained smallholdings in the places they came from. But in most parts, the terms on which land was held were such that the rights to their land were dependent upon its being farmed; and consequently the only way to safeguard

[9] Walter Elkan, 'Circular migration and the growth of towns in eastern Africa', *International Labour Review*, 1967, **96**, no. 6, 581–9.

this right was to leave one's wife or other kin behind. Because it was in any case customary for women to do much of the daily work in the fields, especially in the case of subsistence crops, the departure of men in search of wage employment did not greatly diminish farm productivity so long as it was only temporary, and on the contrary added a cash income to the income in kind generated by the farm. This division of labour was therefore a rational way to maximize family income. If this analysis is accepted, then it must follow that bachelor housing in the towns was not perhaps primarily the cause of, but rather a response to, this pattern of migration.

One might of course object and say that if only family accommodation had been available and higher wages paid, people would have 'sold up' in the countryside and moved to the towns, lock, stock and barrel. But there were at least two reasons why they were unlikely to do so. First, land everywhere in Africa remains the special security against sickness, unemployment, old age and political upheaval; and there may even be an emotional attachment to land that goes beyond such practical considerations.

Secondly, it was not actually open to them to *sell* their land, as it was only theirs to use, but not to sell. Land generally was regulated by membership of a clan and was allocated in intricate though well-established ways, but there was no way in which it could be legally bought or sold. Because land produces an income, not to mention security in times of sickness, unemployment and old age, it would not have made good sense to abandon it without some form of compensation, because total family income would have been correspondingly smaller, irrespective of the level of urban wages and of other urban amenities. Even if land *could* have been sold—if, in other words, there had been some sort of freehold tenure—it is doubtful if that would have greatly altered the situation, because the price paid for land would have been very low in relation to the income to be earned from it in future years. For this there are two reasons. First, in the absence of lending institutions prepared to advance part of the purchase price on a mortgage against the security of the land, land prices would have been depressed by the low level of accumulated savings. Secondly, in large parts of East Africa there is still no shortage of good land; and this too would have depressed prices well below the value of land in terms of its anticipated future stream of income.

Interestingly, a land market had in fact developed, despite the absence of legal provisions for purchase and sale, in those areas where there was a shortage of land, especially in the Kikuyu reserves and in the densely populated parts of South and North Nyanza. Here land prices were of course still further depressed by the fact that the purchaser could not until the late 1950s obtain any legal title.

Once again we are driven to the conclusion that much of the misery of urban life was the result not so much of positive policy, but in part of a failure by the government to intervene actively and effectively to raise wages until almost the end of the colonial period and in part a by-product of the legal and institutional framework. This framework, which was largely inherited, not created by colonial administrations, was intended to ensure an equitable distribution of land and to serve as an instrument by which society could apply sanctions and thus secure adherence to its norms. Colonial officials and employers, of course, soon recognized that if people continued to have land, this might have the effect of keeping wages low and of minimizing the cost of providing urban amenities. But what was seldom understood was the actual connexion between the system of land tenure and the nature of labour migration. The Carpenter Committee of 1954 had quite failed to take this into account.

The moment this is recognized, the phenomenon of short-term circular male-migration can no longer be viewed exclusively in the light of (for example) the Carpenter Committee, which regarded the continued maintenance of a rural home as simply the result of low urban wages and of lack of urban amenities suitable for family settlement. People migrate to *supplement,* not to supersede, their rural incomes, and if that is accepted it explains both why they left their families behind and why they did not remain permanently in the towns. In Uganda, especially, urban employment was often undertaken by young men who did not yet have their own farms or had only land but neither the wife nor the capital to make it yield a cash income. A few years in Kampala, working for wages, was then seen as the quickest way to accumulate savings to spend on bride-wealth, on a bicycle on which to carry crops to the market and on coffee trees that would ultimately produce a much higher income than employment ever could. Yet wages were no higher than in Nairobi.

This points to a further facet of the observed poverty, namely, that it was not only the result of low wages but of even lower levels of consumption. Because often the prime motive for seeking urban employment was to accumulate savings, people were willing for limited periods to put up with an inadequate diet and overcrowding in order the more rapidly to accumulate these savings. Nor is that unprecedented in human history: the Irish who entered Manchester and Liverpool in the early nineteenth century did exactly the same, with the same consequences. They saved because their real aim in coming to England was to accumulate the fare that would take them on to America. For the sake of that they were prepared to starve themselves and to live in hovels.

Results of labour migration

One consequence of this pattern of labour migration was a substantial imbalance between the sexes in the towns. Men greatly outnumbered women, as indeed they continue to do. In this respect there is a marked contrast between East and West Africa. In West African towns the sexes have always been much more evenly balanced. A further explanation of the comparatively small percentage of women in the towns of East Africa may lie in the frequently observed phenomenon that in poor countries all members of the family must contribute to production if there is to be enough for all to live on. Thus in Europe both female and child labour were the accepted practice until well into the nineteenth century, and the same is of course true of the rural parts of Africa today. But in East Africa, once a family moves into town it becomes largely dependent on the income of the male head of household. A few women manage to get jobs as domestic servants, shop assistants or—if they are sufficiently educated—clerks and typists. Their number has actually increased somewhat since independence. Perhaps slightly larger numbers engage in illegal brewing and in prostitution, whilst others are to be found 'sitting in market stalls and selling sisal rope or basketwork'. The contrast with West Africa is most striking. There women play a most important role in commerce, transport and even manufacture. They trade substantially in produce and own many of the lorries and buses, and the traditional textile industry is largely in their hands. Why there should be this marked difference between East and West Africa has never been satisfactorily explained. But one consequence must clearly be that it is easier in West than in East African towns for both men and women to contribute to family income, and this helps to explain the greater prevalence of short-term male migration in East Africa during the period of colonial government.

One possible refutation of the explanation for short-term migration advanced in this essay is that people appear to be staying in towns much longer now than they did a decade ago and that there has been some improvement in the sex ratio. Both phenomena are attributed to the marked increase in wages that has occurred since shortly before independence, and it is said that at these higher wages men can now afford to have their families living with them in town. The facts are not in dispute, but they are susceptible to more than one interpretation and there are other facts to consider before these arguments may be considered a refutation.

First, the reason why people stay longer has as much to do with the increasing difficulty of obtaining one of the highly paid jobs as with the high pay itself. Having secured a job yielding a much higher income than can now be obtained by farming, people naturally cling to it for much longer than was formerly the case. Secondly, the evidence that improvement in the sex balance is the result of a greater proclivity to bring one's family to town is rather slight. It is certainly the case with people in middle-class or professional jobs; and part of the improvement in the sex radio is simply that there are probably not only a greater number but even a greater proportion of Africans who now have such jobs. This has been a result of rapid Africanization in the government and of jobs formerly held by Europeans or Asians, as well as of an absolute increase in such jobs. In these categories of occupations it is certainly now much more common for people to lead settled family lives in Nairobi. It is *their* pressure for somewhere to live that explains why overwhelmingly the greater part of official house-building in Nairobi since independence has been for middle-income earners and above. Those earning less than, say, K£300 a year have had largely to fend for themselves as before, with the result that housing conditions for the poor have probably deteriorated, or, at any rate, not improved.

Interestingly, however, Kikuyu entrepreneurs have moved in to take advantage of the opportunities offered by the housing shortage for the poor. The structures they have built, however, are not family dwellings, but wooden-frame houses with six or eight rooms, each with its own entrance, so that each room constitutes a separate dwelling. Some of these rooms have come to be occupied by families, but the majority are shared, as they have always been, not by a man and his wife, but by several men who share the rent. Perhaps people share rooms because they cannot afford to pay the rent alone, but at the same time a recent study revealed that over one-fifth of the income of low- and middle-income earners is remitted each month to relatives outside Nairobi. In these circumstances, it seems unwise to maintain that higher wages have really altered the basic structure of migration to the towns. The evidence seems to indicate that the arguments listed earlier as to why people leave their families at home continue to apply with almost equal force.

BIBLIOGRAPHY

Berg, Elliot J. 'Economics of the migrant labor system', in *Urbanization and migration in West Africa*, Hilda Kuper, ed. San Francisco and Los Angeles, University of California Press, 1965.

Brett, E. A. *Colonialism and underdevelopment in East Africa*. London, 1973.

Colson, Elizabeth. 'The impact of the colonial period on the definition of land rights', in *Colonialism in Africa 1870–1960*, vol. III: *Profiles of change: African society and colonial rule*, Victor Turner, ed. Cambridge University Press, 1971.

Davies, E. R. St 'Some problems arising from the conditions of housing and employment of natives in Nairobi', Kenya National Archives, no. 9.1707.70. Nairobi, 1939.

Ehrlich, Cyril. 'Some social and economic policy implications of paternalism in Uganda', *Journal of African History*, 1963, **4.**

Elkan, Walter. 'Circular migration and the growth of towns in eastern Africa', *International Labour Review*, 1967, **96,** no. 6.

Migrants and proletarians: urban labour in the economic development of Uganda. London, Oxford University Press, 1960.

Elkan, Walter, and Leslie Nulty. 'Economic links between Kenya, Uganda and Tanganyika', in *History of East Africa*, vol. III, A. R. Low, ed. Oxford, Clarendon Press, forthcoming.

Etherton, David, ed. *Mathare Valley: a case study of uncontrolled settlement in Nairobi.* University of Nairobi, Housing Research and Development Unit, 1970.

Ferraro, G. P. 'Kikuyu kinship interaction: a rural urban comparison'. Ph.D. thesis, Syracuse University, 1971.

Great Britain. *Master plan for a colonial capital*. L. W. Thornton White, L. Silberman, and P. R. Anderson, eds. London, HMSO, 1948.

Great Britain. East Africa Royal Commission. Cmd 9475. *Report, 1953–1955.* London, 1955.

Gutkind, P. C. W. *Royal capital of Buganda: a study of internal conflict and external ambiguity.* The Hague, Institute of Social Studies, 1963.

Hailey, William Malcolm Hailey, 1st baron. *An African survey revised*. London, Oxford University Press, 1957.

Hance, William A. *Population migration and urbanization in Africa*. New York, Columbia University Press, 1970.

Hill, M. F. *Permanent way*. Nairobi, 1949.

Huxley, Elspeth. *The Flame trees of Thika: memories of an African childhood*. London, 1959.

International Labour Office. *Employment incomes and equality: a strategy for increasing productive employment in Kenya*. Geneva, 1972.

Johnson, G. E., and W. E. Whitelaw. 'An estimated remittances function', *Economic Development and Cultural Change*, April 1974, **22,** no. 3.

Kenya. *Report of the committee on African wages* (Carpenter Report). Nairobi, 1954.

Ministry of Finance and Economic Planning. *Population census 1962: tables*, vol. I. Nairobi, 1964.

Lloyd, P. C. *Africa in social change*. Harmondsworth, Middlesex, 1967.

Morgan, William T. W. 'The location of Nairobi', in *Ostafrikanische Studien—Ernst Weigt zum 60. Geburtstag*, ed. Herfried Berger. Nürnberg, 1968.

Oram, Nigel. *Towns in Africa*. London, Oxford University Press, 1965.

Parker, Mary. 'Political and social aspects of the development of municipal government in Kenya with special reference to Nairobi'. Ph.D. thesis, London University, 1949.

Powesland, Philip. *Labour and economic policy in Uganda*. London, 1958.

Southall, A. W., and P. C. W. Gutkind. *Townsmen in the making*. London, 1957.

Van Zwanenberg, R. M. A. 'History and theory of urban poverty in Nairobi: the problem of slum development', *Journal of Eastern African Research and Development*, 1972, **2,** no. 2.

'Primitive colonial accumulation: a study in the processes and determinants of the supply of labour in Kenya 1919–39'. D.Phil. thesis, University of Sussex, 1971.

CHAPTER 18

ECONOMIC ACHIEVEMENTS OF THE COLONIZERS: AN ASSESSMENT

by

PETER DUIGNAN *and* L. H. GANN

Our contributors have presented an array of new data and new ideas on economic development in sub-Saharan Africa during the colonial period. But many questions remain unanswered; many others remain subject to dispute. What, for instance, was the total impact of imperial rule on African economies by the end of the imperial era? Historians supply contradictory answers. Conditions, after all, differed immensely, not only from one territory to another but even within the same territory. According to many critics of colonialism, trade and investment profited only Europe: mining took wealth from African soils without contributing to the colonies' economic development, and, save in a few enclaves, agriculture remained basically unaltered. In the colonial period, it is charged, there was growth without development; because of increased population pressure on the land, African living standards remained stationary or rose only slightly. The story of colonialism was, then, the tale of *How Europe underdeveloped Africa*.[1] Our own conclusions are at variance with this interpretation.

Trade and Investment

In the days of empire, when men like Rhodes, Ferry and King Leopold II advocated expansion in Africa, the case for investing money in the colonies was put forward by imperialists with much enthusiasm. Overseas dependencies were supposed to provide the motherland with convenient markets and with inexpensive raw materials, thereby enabling the metropolitan countries to shift the terms of trade in their favour. Investments in exotic countries, where raw materials and labour were cheaper than at home, it was believed, would yield splendid profits for entrepreneurs as well as provide work for the unemployed at home. If Great Britain wanted to avoid civil war, Rhodes argued, Great Britain must become imperialist.

Critics of empire subsequently used the polemics of empire—except that they stood them on their head. Imperialism, they said, entailed the manipulation of world commerce in favour of the colonialists or the ruthless exploitation of colonial labour, raw materials and markets. For a time, they argued, social peace at home was bought by the colonizing countries by territorial aggrandizement abroad. The only sufferers were the colonies, whose economic progress under imperial tutelage was either retarded or distorted. The reasons for this state of affairs were many. But much hinged on the question of trade and investment.

[1] See, for instance, Walter Rodney, *How Europe underdeveloped Africa* (London, 1972); and E. A. Brett, *Colonialism and underdevelopment in East Africa 1919–1939* (London, 1973).

The critics of empire argued that either investments had been inadequate, thereby leaving the colonies stagnant backwaters, or it had been the very extent of European investments that had fuelled the disastrous drive for colonies in the first place.

Each of the various colonial powers had its separate national 'style', which was influenced by its domestic traditions. Though there were exceptions, the British African empire was essentially founded upon the principle of the 'open door'. Even after the British had swung to a protection system and imperial preference during 1931 and 1932, this swing had but slight effects on their African dependencies. German trade polices were relatively liberal in the Kaiser's possessions, where British enterprise always had a considerable stake. The Congo Basin and West, East and Central Africa had been declared free-trade areas in 1885 and 1890. Hence these areas were open to the traffic of all nations. On the other hand, France and Portugal (at least under the republic), were highly protectionist powers, though tariffs differed considerably within the various parts of their respective colonies.[2]

The existence of free-trade régimes did not, of course, prevent the rulers from manipulating the commerce of their colonies in indirect ways. The iniquities of Leopold's régime in the Congo and the malpractices of the Royal Niger Company are well known. Even the British colonial authorities proper managed to give different advantages to their compatriots—for instance, by granting railway contracts to their own nationals rather than to foreign firms. Nevertheless, British terms of trade seem to have been surprisingly little affected by the expansion and control of colonies. In fact, the British terms of trade, as shown in Table 149, were worse in 1890, at the heyday of the Victorian empire, than they were sixty years later. The changes seem to have had little to do with the policies followed or not followed by colonial administrators.

Table 149. *British terms of trade*
(1913 = 100)

Year	Import prices	Export prices	Terms of trade (import prices as a percentage of export prices)
1880	107	89	120
1890	88	81	109
1900	85	85	100
1910	99	93	106
1920	286	360	79
1930	118	153	77
1940	159	199	80
1950	352	427	82
1958	408	552	74

SOURCE: John Strachey, *The end of empire,* paperback ed. (New York, 1964), pp. 149–51.

[2] For an excellent discussion of this and of associated subjects, see David K. Fieldhouse, 'The economic exploitation of Africa: some British and French comparisons', in *France and Britain in Africa: imperial rivalry and colonial rule,* Prosser Gifford and William Roger Louis, eds. (New Haven, Yale University Press, 1971), pp. 593–662, which includes also excellent statistical material.

The extent and profitability of foreign investment are also difficult to assess. The brilliant pioneering study of S. H. Frankel, *Capital investment in Africa: its course and effects* (1938), has been extended and brought up to date (1967). Even the most accomplished statistician, however, cannot provide more than roughly approximate figures. The problem of collecting all relevant information defies solution. The national/aggregate statistics accumulated by experts such as Frankel can therefore serve but an illustrative function. They do show that by the late 1930s the bulk of all foreign capital was invested in South Africa and South-West Africa. From the investor's point of view, the second most important group was British colonial Africa, with the French and the Portuguese colonies coming last.

The funds placed in Africa played but a small part in British and French overseas investments as a whole. Tropical Africa was neither a major nor a necessary field for German, French or British investors. (In 1928, French total investments abroad supposedly amounted to something like £719 million, with just over £70 million of this sum going to French tropical Africa. British total investments overseas stood at about £4,500 million in 1938, of which just under £373 million went to British colonial Africa.) In local African terms, however, given the backward nature of most African economies, the relatively small size of the local markets, the difficulties in the way of communication and the nature of the risks involved, these sums amounted to a great deal. Europeans could not earn profits in Africa without building an entirely new infrastructure: transportation problems had to be solved; labour had to be trained and its productivity increased. The colonial rulers, like their successors, were forced to cope with enormous natural difficulties posed by soils, climates and diseases of men, plants and animals. In addition, it was necessary for the Europeans to make the right decisions with regard to economic priorities. In many cases, for example, foreign lenders disbursed excessive amounts of money that went into enterprises, such as railways, that lacked sufficient traffic to yield profits.

Africa was not the tropical treasure-house envisaged either by the Marxist-Leninist theoreticians or by the more imaginative or the more dishonest kind of company promoter. One of the most profitable industries in Africa was the South African gold-mining industry, endowed with the world's most extensive auriferous resources and worked by what appeared to be cheap African migrant labour. Some firms did make enormous profits. But at the same time these gains, which are shown in Table 150, were often counterbalanced by substantial losses in unprofitable mines or in other barren ventures. Hence the overall profit rate throughout the heyday of British financial influence fluctuated sharply. The average rate of return for all South African gold-mines during the period 1887 to 1965 has been calculated in several different ways. Frankel has assessed the average rate for the period at 5·2 per cent, on the assumption that all the capital invested (including capital that was lost) was carried forward from the date when it was first issued. Using a revised method, Frankel arrives at 9 per cent. Investors who put their money in South African gold-mines usually obtained better returns than those of their colleagues who had placed their savings in British equities or British financial companies. Even so, the South African gold-mines yielded nothing like the astronomical profits attributed to them alike by Marxist theoreticians, Afrikaner nationalists and the more irresponsible kind of share-pusher. (For a comparison of earnings, see Table 150. Overall, something like 40 per cent of the mines yielded nothing after taxes and lease expenses; 25 per cent had a yield below 5 per cent; the remainder earned much higher dividends.)

The Belgian Congo was likewise famed for its wealth. Some investors reaped a great harvest, but others did not. Once again, exact figures are hard to obtain. According to the calculations made by Georges Hostelet, a Belgian scholar (anxious to prove how valuable the colony was), something like 23,000 million gold francs was invested in the territory between the start of colonization in 1885 and the year 1935. (About 20 per cent of this was foreign capital.) Yields varied widely, depending on the period and the enterprise involved. A good deal of capital, moreover, was lost. Mining did better than any other sector. Between 1920 and 1939, for instance, the mining companies earned an average of 7·9 per cent per annum; the banks 7·4 per cent; cotton-producers 7·1 per cent; construction firms 5 per cent; palm-oil and soap producers 1·3 per cent; trading firms 1·0 per cent. On the other hand, farming and pastoral concerns sustained an average annual loss of 1·9 per cent per annum, while food-processors and brewers lost about 3·2 per cent. After examining various estimates, Hostelet concludes that between 1927 and 1939 the average net yield on capital invested in colonial companies amounted to 8·3 per cent per annum, while annual dividends distributed to shareholders stood at about 5·7

Table 150. *Average yield of capital, after tax deductions and leases, from South African gold-mines, U.K. equities and U.K. finance companies* (in per cent)

	Real terms, constant money amounts		
No. of 10-year periods (years at 1 January)	South African gold-mines	U.K. equities	U.K. finance companies
Average of five periods from 1919–29, etc., to 1923–33	11·7	11·8	10·7
Average of ten periods from 1919–29, etc., to 1928–38	17·2	11·3	13·9
Average of six periods from 1923–33, etc., to 1928–38	20·5	10·3	15·3
Average of nineteen periods from 1935–45, etc., to 1953–63	1·0	3·2	4·4
Average of nine periods from 1945–55, etc., to 1953–63	1·8	7·7	3·8
Average of thirty-five periods from 1919–29 to 1953–63	7·4	5·2	7·7

SOURCE: S. Herbert Frankel, *Investment and the return of equity capital in the South African gold mining industry 1887–1965: an international comparison* (Cambridge, Mass., Harvard University Press, 1967), pp. 7–8, 32, 44, 46.

per cent.[3] The gains accruing to the more fortunate investors were therefore substantial. But again, they do not bear out the assumption that colonial investments as a whole yielded superprofits.

Africa did not return to its investors and traders what earlier imperialists and promoters had hoped for. As Fieldhouse has noted, 'Economic return was in direct proportion to effort made.' Insufficient capital was invested to develop Africa's potential. Government policies were not designed by economists anxious to achieve maximum economic growth. Before 1945, colonial officials saw themselves as law-makers and teachers rather than as economic planners. There were enormous difficulties to overcome. Knowledge was limited, statistics and administrative methods inadequate. Two world wars, depressions, falling demands for tropical materials, the backwardness of the population, the lack of roads, ports and rail facilities—all these were brakes on development. Still, trade and investment did accomplish a good deal: there was significant though uneven economic growth dependent above all on export crops and mineral production.

Before 1945 no colonial power had the desire, the resources or the economic techniques to make the extraordinary efforts required for rapid economic expansion. Once they had recovered from the ravages of the Second World War, Britain, Belgium and France improved upon their earlier record (see Table 151). The Portuguese did not do so much until 1961 when, in order to hold on to their colonies, they launched large-scale development schemes and encouraged foreign investment. (According to the Portuguese, the total value of internal production, measured in million U.S. dollars, increased between 1962 and 1970 from 803·7 to 1,888·5 in Angola; from 835·5 to 1,872·0 in Moçambique; and from 85·1 to 125·8 in Portuguese Guinea.)

As part of the post-war colonial expansion programme, educational and social services were increased. There were large-scale projects to improve indigenous farming—for example, the Swynnerton project in Kenya, the Gezira project in the Sudan, the Senegal river project in French West Africa. New ports, roads and airfields were constructed. The total investment figures, private and public, are hard to calculate. However, as noted below, it seems clear that, except for the Belgian Congo, the greater part consisted of public investment. According to Fieldhouse, between 1946 and 1964 the French government placed something like $8,293 million in grants and aid in its Black African colonies. British government grants and loans may have amounted to approximately $1,417 million for this period, though this estimate may well be too low. Belgian government expenditure in the Congo has been assessed at 6,930 million francs between 1950 and 1958, during the years that elapsed between Belgium's recovery from the German occupation and the onset of Congolese independence. Between 1950 and 1958, Belgian net investments in the Belgian Congo amounted to something like 7,340 million francs. Out of a total of 130 milliard francs invested in the Belgian Congo from its inception to the early 1960s, something like 100 milliard francs represented private investments.

In other colonies, however, private investments were considerably less important than public investments. For Angola and Moçambique, for example,

---

[3] Georges Hostelet, *L'œuvre civilisatrice de la Belgique au Congo, de 1885 à 1953* (Brussels, Académie Royale des Sciences Coloniales, 1954), vol. II, pp. 27–32.

Table 151. *Sub-Saharan Africa: net international flow of long-term capital and official donations, by country, 1951–5 and 1956–9* (millions of dollars, annual average)

Country or territory	Total		Net official donations		Net long-term capital					
					Total		Official and banking		Private	
	1951-5	1956-9	1951-5	1956-9	1951-5	1956-9	1951-5	1956-9	1951-5	1956-9
British East Africa	...	94	...	24	...	70	...	26	...	44
British West Africa	...	81	...	13	...	54	...	5	...	63
Congo (Leopoldville)	38	41	...	3	38	39	34	63	4	-24
Ghana	-37	-5	-1	1	-36	-5	-40	3	5	-3
Liberia	10	11	...	...	10	11	2	3	8	7
Rhodesia and Nyasaland	69	98	4	...	65	98	36	38	29	60
Sudan	-3	2	...	2	-4	-1	-3	...	-1	-1
Union of South Africa	129	2	...	...	129	2	36	6	93	-4
Franc area	(510)	(639)	(299)	(519)	(211)	(120)	(211)	(120)	...	(350)
Total of amounts shown (excluding British East and West Africa and private capital to franc area)	716	788	302	525	413	264	276	234	138	35
All underdeveloped countries	2,400	3,776	878	1,328	1,524	2,447	628	906	894	1,542

SOURCE: United Nations, Economic Commission for Africa, *International economic assistance to Africa*, 1960, E/CN.14/152 (New York, 1960), cited by Walter A. Chudson, 'Trends in African exports and capital inflows', in *Economic transition in Africa*, Melville Herskovits and Mitchell Harwitz, eds. (London, 1964), p. 355.

the planned investment under the Six-Year Plan, 1968–73, amounted to 42,608·2 million escudos. Public investment was expected to account for 26,721·2 million escudos—that is to say, more than half the projected total. Foreign investments were set at 15,887·2 million escudos, just over one-third of all the planned investments. Between 1945 and 1963 the French put some £348 million ($976 million) into French Black Africa, whereas the British invested £280 million in British Africa from 1936 to 1962. Only 5·5 per cent of British private investments went to Africa after 1945, whereas before 1945 they amounted to about 6 per cent, most of them going to South Africa. The bulk of French investments were destined for Algeria, where there was also a large settler group that created opportunities for capital use.

There was accordingly no great rush to make private investments in Africa. African investments accounted for a negligible proportion of metropolitan investments as a whole. This was true even in the case of a minor power such as Belgium, the value of whose total domestic savings in 1956 (39 milliard francs) was equal to nearly one-third of the total invested in the Belgian Congo since the beginning of the colonial period. The average rate of profits is hard to calculate, both for statistical reasons and because of the investors' proclivity to understate their profits for purposes of tax avoidance. But according to the best available sources, including the British Board of Trade figures (1962), average earnings in Africa were by no means excessive (South Africa 9·8 per cent, Central Africa 8·1 per cent, Ghana 7·9 per cent, Kenya 7·1 per cent).

Certainly, the metropolitan powers benefited in many ways from colonialism. Merchants and investors received direct or indirect favours. At a minimum, they could not be excluded from colonial markets: their investments were safe from confiscation; their nationals enjoyed physical security; they benefited from controlling the banking and currency systems. Some metropolitan merchant fleets profited from trade controls and other devices. The metropolitan powers had secure supplies of raw materials and a large share of the available African market. From 1950 to 1957, for instance, 37 per cent of the Belgian Congo imports derived from Belgium, 47 per cent of the imports of British Africa came from Great Britain, and 67 per cent of the imports of the French franc countries in Africa originated in France. But neither in imports nor in exports did the African market represent a major share of the total trade of any industralized colonial power. In 1956, for example, 12·8 per cent of British exports went to British Africa and 9·8 per cent of British imports derived from British Africa. In 1959, 28·2 per cent of French exports were sent to the French African territories, whilst 20·3 per cent of French imports came from French Africa. In 1958, the Belgo-Luxembourg Economic Union accounted for 18·9 per cent of the exports of the Belgian Congo and Ruanda-Urundi, and 36 per cent of their imports.

Generally speaking, European merchants in Africa encountered great difficulties. They were commonly accused of exploiting Africans by paying too little for the peasants' crops or for charging too much for the goods they sold. But the prices received and paid by Africans were more often than not determined by the high expense of transport, by the extent of customs duties and handling charges and by risk factors, rather than by inflated profit margins supposedly enjoyed by European trading concerns. In British Africa, the system of government purchases through marketing boards did lead to exploitation of African producers and reduced the peasants' profits considerably. For most years, African producers were paid lower than world market prices for their goods. Even at its most productive, African trade was usually marginal and inefficient. Although Africans suffered for this, their loss did not bring about vast imperialist gain.

It may be argued that Africans paid more for their goods because they were tied to the metropole. The French, Portuguese and Belgians controlled a large share of the import-export trade of their colonies; hence imperial buyers and sellers benefited. But the French also paid more than the world prices for some goods from their colonies. In effect, metropolitan consumers thereby furnished a subsidy to local producers. In the British colonies there was more economic freedom; producers usually sold where they could get the best price, unless they were limited by marketing boards. The British, for example, had introduced cotton into East Africa in part to gain a secure, cheap supply for British mills. Yet British mills in India wound up by buying the bulk of Uganda's cotton.

Agriculture

An enormous increase in agricultural productivity and trade during the colonial era was brought about by a transfer of new techniques, by the introduction of new crops and by the development of markets and transport facilities. The clearest indicators of this heightened productivity were the sustained rise in agricultural exports and the growth in population, as shown in Table 152. Population increased significantly, and at the same time life expectancy was lengthened, both signs of improved material well-being.

Cheap transportation facilitated the rapid development of the export markets of the tropics. Steamships were not only faster but also could carry three or four times as much cargo as sailing-ships. Macgregor Laird's development of the small, shallow-draught steamboat revolutionized river transport by enabling the boats to penetrate the Gambia, Niger and Senegal rivers. The needs of the industrialized West stimulated tropical African exports—cocoa, coffee, tobacco, palm-kernels and oil, ground-nuts, cotton, sisal and rubber. African societies, spurred on by missionaries, by commercial concerns and by the colonial governments, responded to this demand and increased their exports. The period from 1880 to 1913 was especially productive. Gold Coast exports grew from £390,000 in 1882–4 to £5,427,000 in 1913, or an average growth-rate per annum of 9·2 per cent. Southern Nigeria expanded its exports from £1,608,000 in 1899 to £7,099,000 in 1913, or a 12 per cent growth-rate per annum. A period of depression from 1913 to 1950 resulted from the decline in world trade growth caused by two world wars and the depression of the 1930s. Post-war growth, however, was dramatic and sustained, and led to the partial industrialization of certain areas in Africa. (For the 1938–58 period, see Table 153.)

By and large, the development of export crops accompanied an expansion of food crops. At first, when export crops were produced in addition to food crops, they represented a net addition to farm output. Although export production of commodities such as cotton, sisal, cocoa and palm-oil was enormously increased from 1880 to 1960, food production kept pace with population

Table 152. *Population growth in colonial Africa*

1. Population of British African territories, 1901 and 1961

	1901	1961
South Africa	4,992,188	16,122,000
Swaziland	85,491	266,000
Basutoland	348,848	697,000
Bechuanaland	120,776	288,000
The Rhodesias	1,250,000 ⎱ 1,956,000	8,510,000
Nyasaland	706,000 ⎰	
Uganda	4,500,000	6,845,000
Kenya and Zanzibar	2,960,000	7,602,000
Nigeria	13,606,093	35,752,000
Gold Coast	1,486,433	6,943,000
Sierra Leone	1,027,000	2,450,000
Gambia	90,354	267,000

2. Population of French African territories

	1911 (unless otherwise indicated)	1959
Algeria	5,563,800	10,930,000
Tunisia	1,939,087	3,935,000
Morocco	3,533,786 (1921)	10,550,000
Madagascar	2,966,000 (1909)	5,287,000
French West Africa	11,343,000	20,884,000
French Equatorial Africa	2,851,000 (1921)	5,000,000
The Cameroons	2,110,000 (1924)	3,225,000
Togo	731,000 (1922)	1,442,000

SOURCE: David K. Fieldhouse, 'The economic exploitation of Africa: some British and French comparisons', in *France and Britain in Africa: imperial rivalry and colonial rule,* Prosser Gifford and William Roger Louis, eds. (New Haven, Yale University Press, 1971), p. 661.

growth. (Ground-nut production in Senegal was an exception, for it led to a decline in food production and the importing of rice.) The colonial *pax,* better transportation systems, the introduction of new food crops and the spread of better agricultural methods and tools, as well as agricultural extension work by missionaries and departments of agriculture, improved the food supply in tropical Africa. Bruce Johnston suggests that food imports in 1960 accounted for less than 3 per cent of total supplies to tropical Africa.[4] Thus domestic production of food crops enabled the expanding population to be fed during the colonial period. Meanwhile, crops for export also increased dramatically. Most of the rise in agricultural productivity during the colonial period resulted from 'spontaneous changes in traditional agriculture and from the super-imposition of an export crop and its associated technology on the pre-existing food economy'.

However, many obstacles to increasing the productivity of traditional agricultural systems based on shifting cultivation presented themselves. Production on small plots for a year or two made it difficult to bulk, process and transport produce. Agricultural improvement was not easily achieved on communally held land. Johnston has concluded:

[4] See Bruce F. Johnston, 'Changes in agricultural productivity', in *Economic transition in Africa,* Melville J. Herskovits and Mitchell Harwitz, eds. (London, 1964), pp. 151–78.

Table 153. *Principal agricultural exports of selected African territories for selected years, 1938–58*

	Quantity (1,000 metric tons)			Value (1,000 U.S. dollars)		
Item	1938	1950	1955–8	1938	1950	1955–8
Cocoa						
French West Africa	52·7	61·8	66·0	4,968	26,933	43,072
Ghana	267·5	271·2	228·3	22,166	152,891	160,869
Nigeria	98·7	101·6	109·1	7,648	53,155	72,102
Total	418·9	435·1	403·3	34,782	232,979	276,943
Index	100	104	96	100	670	796
Coffee						
Angola	16·6	33·9	72·8	1,576	23,920	49,644
Belgian Congo	22·5	33·4	58·9	3,638	25,578	50,443
British East Africa	43·3	57·2	120·0	6,933	42,731	107,020
French West Africa	14·5	57·7	115·4	510	40,815	88,819
Malagasy Republic	41·2	44·8	49·0	7,529	37,132	37,678
Total	138·1	227·0	416·1	20,186	170,176	333,604
Index	100	164	301	100	843	1,653
Cotton						
Belgian Congo	43·0	51·0	42·0	7,604	35,620	28,815
British East Africa	84·2	71·1	93·4	19,214	51,433	70,395
Nigeria	5·8	12·8	30·5	1,206	8,330	21,473
Sudan	62·7	66·5	86·7	17,276	65,673	85,307
Total	195·8	201·4	254·8	45,300	161,056	205,989
Index	100	103	130	100	356	455
Maize						
Angola	128·7	189·4	95·8	3,015	8,961	4,694
Union of South Africa	200·0	19·6	910·7	4,648	1,064	47,110
Total	328·7	209·0	1,006·4	7,663	10,025	51,804
Index	100	64	306	100	131	676
Palm-kernels						
French West Africa	70·8	84·5	87·3	3,041	12,758	10,962
Ghana	5·3	4·2	9·2	195	367	1,033
Nigeria	317·1	416·8	440·3	10,582	46,743	54,632
Total	393·2	505·5	536·7	13,818	59,868	66,627
Index	100	129	137	100	433	482
Palm-oil						
Angola	3·6	13·8	8·8	202	2,939	1,634
Belgian Congo	70·3	132·0	140·2	4,126	26,656	29,107
French West Africa	13·7	11·8	15·2	657	2,681	3,575
Nigeria	112·0	175·8	179·2	4,788	33,802	38,143
Total	199·6	333·4	343·4	9,773	66,078	72,369
Index	100	167	172	100	676	741
Ground-nuts						
French West Africa	169·4	200·3	306·5	6,644	33,034	67,204
Nigeria	183·0	321·9	422·1	6,374	42,664	68,589
Sudan	5·8	4·7	63·7	201	603	10,445
Total	358·2	526·9	792·3	13,219	76,301	146,238
Index	100	147	221	100	577	1,107
Ground-nut oil						
French West Africa	5·7	71·4	98·5	665	29,947	45,799
Index	100	1,253	1,728	100	4,503	6,887

Table 153. (continued)

Item	Quantity (1,000 metric tons)			Value (1,000 U.S. dollars)		
	1938	1950	1955–8	1938	1950	1955–8
Sisal						
Angola	6·5	20·6	44·1	459	6,436	6,798
British East Africa	123·3	163·3	226·5	9,225	51,562	34,347
Total	129·8	183·9	270·6	9,684	57,998	41,144
Index	100	142	208	100	599	425
Sugar						
Angola	32·1	43·0	34·3	1,639	3,158	3,121
South Africa	215·3	63·8	204·2	9,198	5,936	16,968
Total	247·4	106·8	238·4	10,837	9,094	20,089
Index	100	43	96	100	84	185
Tobacco						
Rhodesia and Nyasaland	11·1	43·4	64·8	6,501	51,156	76,051
Index	100	393	586	100	787	1,170
Wool						
South Africa (greasy)	107·6	78·6	99·1	41,103	147,728	133,224
South Africa (others)	3·2	11·1	13·5	2,421	26,516	28,182
Total	110·8	89·7	112·6	43,524	174,244	161,406
Index	100	81	102	100	400	371

SOURCE: S. Daniel Neumark, *Foreign trade and economic development in Africa: a historical perspective* (Stanford, Food Research Institute, 1964), pp. 157–8.

There is little incentive for investing labour or other resources in improving land that is held only in temporary usufruct, and long-term planning and rational management of a well-defined farm unit is impossible. These factors have impaired the effectiveness of agricultural extension programs, and have limited the responsiveness of African farmers to technical innovations that would increase output and productivity.[5]

Economists such as Johnston and W. Arthur Lewis have concluded that the colonial governments' approach to enhancing agricultural productivity, by working through the traditional agricultural framework and by introducing technological innovations (such as ploughs, manure fertilizer, crop rotation, irrigation) and new crops, was sound; indeed, that it was the best way that agriculture could have been improved. The first impetus for rapid economic change derived mainly from the colonial period. The logistic, administrative and scientific infrastructure essential for promoting change likewise had its beginnings in this era.

The expansion of trade that resulted from production for export served also to increase the bulk and variety of consumer goods available to Africans. In the Belgian Congo, for instance, as shown in Table 154, overall African consumption nearly doubled between 1950 and 1958. Certain quantitative analyses, of course, purport to prove that the export trade still did not increase enough, or did not substantively change the economic system. But as we see it, these critics miss the essential point—the function of trade as a means of reshuffling goods to provide more economic choices.

[5] *Ibid.*, p. 176.

Table 154. *Rise in African consumption in the Belgian Congo, 1950–8*

	Nominal value of African consumption	Official cost of living index	Actual value of African consumption weighed by cost of living index
1950	100	100	100
1954	178	118·8	149·8
1958	214·2	121	177

SOURCE: Belgium, Office de l'Information et des Relations Publiques pour le Congo belge et le Ruanda-Urundi, *Belgian Congo* (Brussels, 1960), II, 76.

Wage labour and cash-cropping transformed the peoples and the economies of Africa. As Africans entered the market economy, the receptivity of diverse peoples to economic change varied considerably. The Arusha of Tanganyika, for instance, had been self-sufficient agriculturalists. To pay their taxes and to buy extra food and new goods they entered into market exchanges. Af first they sold just enough of their traditional crops to get money for food and taxes; they did not produce simply for the market or to make profits. Gradually, pressure on their land forced them reluctantly to change production to meet market demands for certain goods. While the Arusha hesitated to commit themselves to produce for the market, the Kipsigi in Kenya were eager to do so. They switched from a pastoral economy to farming for the market. Similarly, whereas the Lele in the Belgian Congo preferred to sacrifice economic development to protect traditional ways of life, their neighbours, the Bushong, saw hard work and individual effort as an opportunity to acquire wealth and gain status.[6]

Because of the wide regional variations, the indirect effects of agricultural expansion are hard to assess. A brilliant micro-study of Akokoasa on the Gold Coast, made by W. H. Beckett, an agricultural officer, during the 1930s, shows how the growth of cocoa cultivation stimulated not only trade but also local crafts such as carpentry and shoemaking. The Gold Coast, with so valuable an export crop as cocoa, represented one end of the spectrum. A contemporary observer in the 1930s would have found an infinitely more depressing picture, say, in an isolated Lenje or Ila community in Northern Rhodesia. But progress occurred even in some of the remoter regions, as, for instance, among the Lovale in what is now north-western Zambia.[7]

Long before the arrival of the British, the Lovale had become habituated to trading in wild rubber, slaves and guns. Trading caravans had to be provisioned; hence foreign commerce stimulated food production, crops acquired exchange value and the Lovale were introduced to the vagaries of market fluctuations in wild rubber. The tribe subsequently made good use of expanding

[6] The classic example of receptivity to economic change was the Akwapim and Krobo people of Ghana, who took to growing cocoa in the 1880s and by the 1900s were among the world's leading producers. They had to migrate to new lands, and wait several years for the trees to bear and then compete in a world market.

[7] See Sir William Keith Hancock, *Survey of British Commonwealth affairs,* vol. II: *Problems of economic policy 1918–1939,* pt. 2 (London, Oxford University Press, 1942), pp. 273 ff. For a study of the Lovale, see C. M. N. White, *A preliminary survey of the Luvale rural economy,* Rhodes-Livingstone paper, no. 29 (Manchester University Press, 1959).

markets in the Northern Rhodesian towns. Hawkers sold fish, dried caterpillars and grain to the cities along the Northern Rhodesian railway belt. Portuguese traders purchased ground-nuts, dried fish and bees-wax. In addition, Lovale cassava went to the Barotse valley in return for slaughter-cattle. Agriculture thus stimulated trade. The more substantial Lovale dealers employed agents to produce the wanted commodities and to supervise their transport and to market them in the towns. Smaller traders operated on their own, or in concert with relatives. The steady increase in the Lovale cash-economy was remarkable in many respects: for example, it took place in a relatively isolated area; it owed little to British agricultural advice; and agricultural expansion procèeded without any corresponding increase in population. For reasons that remain unclear, and that would puzzle Malthusian economists, the opportunities available to the Lovale grew without their having to be shared out among a growing number of people.

The development of mining

Mining was still another engine of development in Africa. In 1867, the first diamonds were discovered at the Cape. At that time the mineral production of Africa, in total quantities, was negligible. Sub-Saharan Africa's mineral exports were minuscule. Less than a century later, a number of sub-Saharan countries had reached the position attained by South Africa alone in the first decade of the present century, before South Africa had embarked on the path of economic diversification (see Table 155).

Large-scale mining—unlike, say, alluvial mining, which is carried out by simple technological means—requires an elaborate technology and a variety of new skills. Mining on such a scale, therefore, stimulates wide learning experiences. Mining also tends to promote ancillary industries concerned with such operations as the treatment and processing of ores, the production of hydroelectric power, construction, cement plants and repair shops. A great deal, of course, depends on local circumstances. But there is no doubt that the modern industrial economies of Zaire, Zambia and Rhodesia were built on the basis of extractive enterprises. The same was true of South Africa, where mining, urbanization, and the rail-transport system prepared the necessary conditions for large-scale manufacturing.

Evidence tends to show that the extractive industries had an effect on raising levels of consumption.[8] They had an impact also on African entrepreneurship.

---

[8] In colonies that had mining industries or export crops, consumption certainly increased. In the Belgian Congo, for instance, the consumption of manufactured products increased something like four times between 1938 and 1951, despite the impact of the war and its aftermath. This rise is illustrated by Hostelet, *L'œuvre civilisatrice*, vol. II, p. 191, as follows:

	1938	1948	1951
Food	82	96	122
Beer	17	84	174
Clothes	61	92	95
Cotton cloth	40	98	149
Blankets	23	95	127

(continued on p. 686)

Table 155. *Value of domestic exports of sub-Saharan Africa for selected years, 1939–58*

	1938	1950	1955	1956	1957	1958
	Million U.S. dollars					
Total	1,006·8	2,771·5	4,370·6	4,735·0	4,727·1	4,619·8
Mineral	580·1	873·2	1,642·9	1,840·2	1,814·3	1,690·7
Nonmineral	426·7	1,898·3	2,727·7	2,894·8	2,912·8	2,929·1
Union of South Africa	509·5	894·9	1,427·2	1,577·2	1,733·2	1,622·6
Mineral	384·6	467·3	797·2	893·5	984·5	979·4
Nonmineral	124·9	427·6	630·0	683·7	748·7	643·2
Belgian Congo and Ruanda-Urundi	66·3	266·9	464·4	543·5	480·1	413·4
Mineral	40·9	132·9	296·4	358·4	285·2	224·5
Nonmineral	25·4	134·0	168·0	185·1	194·9	188·9
Rhodesia and Nyasaland	105·4	284·2	493·3	519·1	446·0	386·9
Mineral	85·7	172·4	375·7	398·6	317·1	264·5
Nonmineral	19·7	111·8	117·6	120·5	128·9	122·4
All others	325·6	1,325·5	1,985·7	2,095·2	2,067·8	2,196·9
Mineral	68·9	100·6	173·6	189·7	227·5	222·3
Nonmineral	256·7	1,224·9	1,812·1	1,905·5	1,840·3	1,974·6
	Per cent					
Total	100·0	100·0	100·0	100·0	100·0	100·0
Mineral	57·6	31·5	37·6	38·9	38·4	38·6
Nonmineral	42·4	68·5	62·4	61·1	61·6	63·4
Union of South Africa	50·6	32·3	32·7	33·3	36·7	35·1
Mineral	38·2	16·9	18·2	18·9	20·8	21·2
Nonmineral	12·4	15·4	14·5	14·4	15·9	13·9
Belgian Congo and Ruanda-Urundi	6·6	9·6	10·6	11·5	10·2	8·9
Mineral	4·1	4·8	6·8	7·6	6·0	4·9
Nonmineral	2·5	4·8	3·8	3·9	4·2	4·0
Rhodesia and Nyasaland	10·5	10·3	11·3	11·0	9·4	8·4
Mineral	8·5	6·2	8·6	8·4	6·7	5·7
Nonmineral	2·0	4·1	2·7	2·6	2·7	2·7
All others	32·3	47·8	45·4	44·2	43·7	47·6
Mineral	6·8	3·6	4·0	4·0	4·8	4·8
Nonmineral	25·5	44·2	41·4	40·2	38·9	42·8

SOURCE: S. Daniel Neumark, *Foreign trade and economic development in Africa: a historical perspective* (Stanford, Food Research Institute, 1964), p. 155.

footnote 8 (continued)

	1938	1948	1951
Shoes	53	83	238
Durable household goods	41	96	197
Non-durable household goods	11	96	122
Tobacco, etc.	28	81	164
Pharmaceutical products	41	93	170
General average	39·7	99·4	155·8

Already in the 1930s, when the mining industry was just getting under way in Northern Rhodesia, some enterprising workers there used the money made on the Copper Belt to good purpose. An ex-miner might buy a camera and set himself up as a member of a new service occupation. Another might become a professional bicycle-repairer. A third might buy a bicycle for trading second-hand clothes in backwoods villages. Some of these hawkers, in turn, would open stores and join the ranks of the petty bourgeoisie. Still others might purchase a sewing machine and begin to repair clothes or make up new garments for sale. Clearly, the assumed contrast between extractive industries and productive industries has been exaggerated by many historians. The correlation between the two was much closer than the pessimistic school suggests. The diversification of the urban economy also created new job opportunities in the rural areas. By 1951, for instance, the African labour force of Marandellas, a village some forty-five miles from Salisbury in Southern Rhodesia, included not only general labourers, but also a whole range of new occupations unknown in the township a generation earlier—African truck-drivers, garage hands, tobacco graders, builders, telephone operators and carpenters.[9] Some men accumulated enough cash to go into a business of their own. By 1953, in the Belgian Congo, for example, there were 1,937 enterprises run by Africans. The history of African enterprise remains to be written, though such scholars as Kilby have done important pioneering work.

Contributions of the immigrants

Given the general backwardness of African labour, a substantial proportion of the new skills required in industry and commerce was supplied by foreigners. Except in Southern Africa, these immigrants, whether Europeans, Indians or Lebanese, remained few in number, as shown in Table 156. In economic terms, however, the role of non-Africans was enormous. Economic change in Africa, as the Dotsons point out in their essay, has taken place 'through a linked chain of social groups and individuals with very specific historically determined characteristics'. These newcomers brought not only physical capital but also non-material capital, consisting of accumulated knowledge and experience as well as organizational capacity. In addition they possessed special elements of social cohesion that facilitated the creation of new economic networks cemented by the bonds of ethnicity. Immigrant merchants instinctively preferred men of their own stock to strangers.[10]

[9] For details, including data on their wages, see J. Wilson Vera, 'Report on a survey of African conditions in Marandellas, Southern Rhodesia . . .' mimeographed (Bulawayo, Federation of African Welfare Societies, 1951).

[10] As Kipling put it:

The Stranger within my gate	The men of my own stock
He may be true or kind	They may do ill or well
But he does not talk my talk—	But they tell the lies I am wonted to,
I cannot feel his mind	They are used to the lies I tell;
I see the face and the eyes and the mouth,	And we do not need interpreters
But not the soul behind.	When we go to buy and sell.

(*Rudyard Kipling's verse: definitive edition* (Garden City, N.Y., 1939), p. 549.

Table 156. *Distribution of total population by ethnic composition* (in percentage)

County	Year	Indigenous (African)	European (White)	Mixed	Asian	Others
West						
Togoland	1948	100·0	0·0	—	—	—
Ghana	1948	99·9	0·1	—	0·0	—
	1960	99·8		0·2		
Upper Volta	1960–1	99·8		0·2		
Portuguese Guinea	1950	98·7	0·4	0·9	0·0	—
Senegal	1960–1	98·1	1·2	0·2	0·5	0·0
Gambia (former colony only)	1951	98·0		2·0		
Cape Verde Islands	1950	28·4	2·0	69·6	0·0	0·0
Central						
Rwanda	1958	99·9	0·1	0·0	0·0	—
Burundi	1958	99·7	0·2	0·0	0·1	—
Congo (Leopoldville)	1958	99·2	0·8	0·0	0·0	0·0
Gabon	1960–1	98·7		1·3		
Spanish Equatorial Region	1950	98·0	2·0	—	—	—
	1960	97·1	2·9	—	—	—
São Tomé and Príncipe	1950	91·0	1·9	7·1	—	0·0
	1960	85·6	4·0	10·4	—	0·0
East						
Comoro Islands	1958	99·4		0·6		
Uganda	1948	99·2	0·1	0·0	0·7	0·0
	1959	98·7	0·2	0·0	1·1	0·0
Tanganyika	1957	98·6	0·2	0·0	1·1	0·1
Moçambique	1955	98·1	1·1	0·5	0·3	—
Madagascar	1962	98·1	0·8	—	0·4	0·7
Kenya	1962	96·9	0·7	—	2·4	0·0
Zanzibar and Pemba	1948	93·8	0·1	—	6·0	0·1
	1958	93·7	0·2	—	6·1	0·0
French Somaliland	1956	93·1		6·9		
Mauritius ex.dep.	1952	66·9	— 29·5 —		3·6	—
	1962	66·7	— 29·9 —		3·4	—
Seychelles	1947	— 98·8 —			1·2	
South						
Basutoland	1946	99·6	0·3	0·1	0·0	—
	1956	99·6	0·3	0·1	0·0	—
Malawi	1962	99·2	0·3	0·0	0·5	—
Bechuanaland	1946	98·8	0·8	0·4	0·0	—
	1956	98·7	0·1	0·2	1·0	—
Zambia	1950–1	97·8	2·0	0·1	0·1	—
	1962	97·5	2·1	—	0·3	0·1
Angola	1950	97·4	1·9	0·7	—	0·0
Swaziland	1946	97·9	1·7	0·4	—	—
	1956	96·9	2·5	0·6	0·0	—
Rhodesia	1956	93·9	5·6	0·3	0·2	—
	1962	94·1	5·4	0·3	0·2	—
South-West Africa	1951	84·2	11·7	4·1	0·0	—
	1960	81·5	14·0	4·5	0·0	—
South Africa	1946	68·6	20·8	8·1	2·5	—
	1951	67·5	20·9	8·7	2·9	—
	1960	68·3	19·3	9·4	3·0	—

SOURCE: United Nations, *Economic Bulletin for Africa*, Jan. 1965, **5,** 48–9.

Where immigrants wielded political power, they were able to manipulate the colonial administration to their purpose. But neither Lebanese nor Indians owed their success only to governmental intervention on their behalf. In fact, excessive government controls restricted their opportunities and limited their freedom of action. In the same way, the success of European settlers did not necessarily derive from legislation on their behalf. For instance, white farmers, especially tobacco- and maize-growers, continued to play an important part in Zambian agriculture after independence, even though the government was no longer pushing the cause of white settlement. The Europeans had the advantage of technological and agronomical skills, and also of having greater financial reserves than the great majority of African cultivators. Hence, to give a particular instance, some seven hundred white farmers in 1964 produced the bulk of Zambia's cash-crops on less than 4 per cent of the country's cultivated acreage. According to statistics cited by the Republic of Zambia, *First National Plan, 1966–70* (Lusaka, 1966), the value of total agricultural sales for European farmers (with 180,000 acres) was £77 million, whereas for African farmers (with approximately 5 million acres) it was £3·2 million.

The colonial impact

By the end of the colonial era, the African continent as a whole remained economically backward, still dependent to a considerable extent on fairly simple forms of farming. With about one-fourth of the world's total land surface, Africa by the early 1960s supposedly contained about 273 million people, or barely 9 per cent of the world's population. The population of Africa was said to be increasing at the rate of roughly 2·4 or 2·5 per cent per annum. The area of land under cultivation *per capita* was about three times as high as in Western Europe. The number of livestock *per capita* was twice as high, and the grazing area per unit of livestock nearly seven times as high. The bulk of the population were still farmers or herders. (Probably no more than 9 per cent of the total African population lived in cities, compared with 35 per cent in Europe and 42 per cent in North America.) According to contemporary United Nations estimates, the overall *per capita* income in Africa, excluding South Africa, amounted to no more than $90 a year, compared with something like $1,200 in the industrially advanced countries. However it may be assessed, the economic gap between Africa and Western Europe remained extremely wide.

These figures, nevertheless, must be seen against the material poverty and the technological backwardness that characterized the various economies of sub-Saharan Africa during the pre-colonial era. Economic progress in Africa, we are well aware, did not begin with the colonizers. Long before the Union Jack, the Tricolour and the German imperial colours were raised on the west coast, African farmers had begun to respond to the pull of the world market. West Africa's agricultural revolution, which substituted the export of groundnuts and oil-palm products for the sale of slaves, had begun long before the coming of empire. European colonization, however, greatly accelerated the rate of economic change. Viewed in this historical context, the brief span that elapsed between the onset of late-Victorian imperialism and decolonization in Africa was in fact marked by astonishing progress in many fields, as has been documented by our contributors. Within the lifetime of a single worker, Africa was pulled out of the Early Iron Age into the era of steam-power and the internal-combustion engine.

Progress was bought at a heavy price. Colonial development was accompanied by a vast number of abuses, by physical exploitation of the kind objected to not only by Marx but also by such colonial reformers as Bernhard Dernburg. Economic coercion was applied at various times in many different ways, ranging from indirect pressure to the compulsory cultivation of crops and the use of forced labour. By and large, the colonial rulers, up to the end of the imperial era, failed to see the importance of the emerging African middle class and gave inadequate consideration, or none at all, to their economic interests. Development was widely held back by a mixture of paternalism and statism whose economic consequences were often misunderstood by its protagonists.

The transfer of resources—ideological, technical and material—from Western Europe to Africa was, however, considerable. Government grants and aid, public and private investments, not to mention the skills and techniques which individuals and companies brought to Africa, all represented a significant transfer of resources and technology. Almost never assessed in accounts of colonial economic benefits is the input of missionaries in terms of men and money. Thousands of missionaries went to Africa and tens of millions of dollars flowed annually from church groups in Western Europe and the United States to build and to run schools, dispensaries and hospitals. Certainly, African labour and resources were important in laying the bases for modern economies in Africa; but without the capital and skills and markets provided by Europe, development would have been greatly retarded.

We disagree with those who maintain that Europe prevented colonial development. With benefit of hindsight, economists may argue that the colonizers did not do enough, or that they neglected investment for social needs and rather sought profits. We cannot, however, fault earlier generations for not having used deficit-spending techniques or central-planning procedures before these were invented and widely used by governments in the West.

Africa was developed, above all, to supply export crops and raw materials to meet the needs of Europe. Colonies did provide a small market for European manufactured goods and capital. Yet colonies were not acquired just for trade and investment outlets, or just for raw materials. European colonial nations traded more with one another than they did with their colonies; they invested far greater sums outside than within their colonies. Where natural resources existed that could be economically developed, there was development. Where resources were absent or hard to exploit, there was little development. Mining and mineral industries did transform the economic landscape of certain colonies. Crops for export produced rapid economic development in some areas. The continent became a world leader in the production of minerals, wood and tropical crops. This led to the expansion of harbours, roads and railways (see Maps 10 and 11), to the growth of towns and processing industries, to new opportunities for jobs and to increased government services and agricultural supplies.

The impact of development and change was extremely uneven. But a survey of the economic history of the African colonies shows certain general trends. The initial stimulus to economic development came mostly from trade and mineral exploitation. The export sector developed in an extremely uneven fashion.

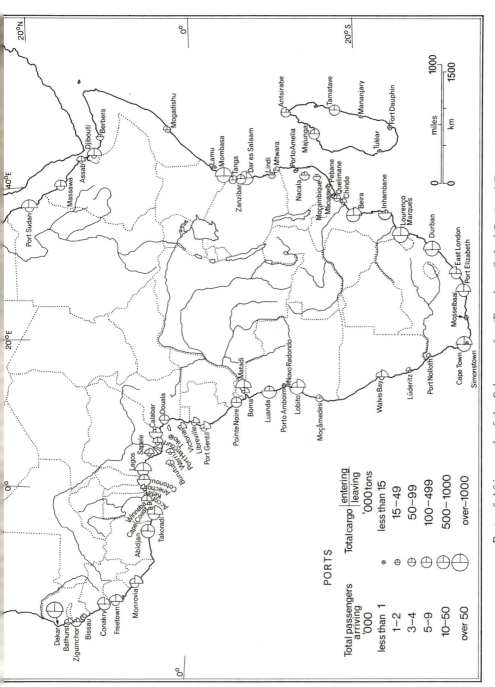

10. Ports of Africa south of the Sahara, 1962. (Based on *Oxford Regional Economic Atlas of Africa*, published by Oxford University Press.)

PORTS

Total passengers arriving '000		Total cargo	entering / leaving '000 tons
less than 1			less than 15
1–2			15–49
3–4			50–99
5–9			100–499
10–50			500–1000
over 50			over–1000

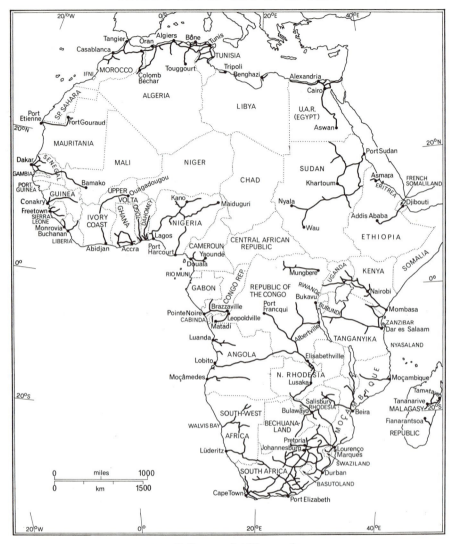

11. Railways of Africa, 1960

Even by the end of the colonial period the subsistence sectors of many regions accounted for 80 or 90 per cent of the local economies. But foreign trade did produce development rather than increased misery for the masses. Commerce indeed had a positive carry-over effect in modernizing the economy. The failure to accomplish more resulted, above all, from imperfections in the domestic African market. These included such factors as the absence of adequate market information, high risks owing to insufficient market opportunities and facilities, unwise governmental interference (including the use of economic coercion), a widespread reduction of demand for many African raw materials (1914 to

1939) and the relative absence of integrative market forces. All these short-comings tended to brake the diffusion mechanism of foreign trade.

As noted earlier, colonial governments and private concerns were handi-capped by their inexperience with Africa's enormous problems, by their lim-ited resources and by the restrictions caused by wars, depressions and the decline in world demand for tropical goods. Before the outbreak of the Second World War, moreover, the colonial official considered himself primarily as a judge and a teacher. His basic aims were to impose law and order, to promote hygiene and to improve agriculture. He did not usually feel called upon to change traditional subsistence systems in a rapid fashion or to impose Western economic practices throughout his district. He did try to make the existing economies more productive, but he did not wish to replace them. He en-couraged trade, but he did not much approve of traders and middlemen, whom he often considered to be parasites and materialists. In their efforts to control commerce and to protect Africans, colonial officials often resorted to measures that impeded the growth of African trading and the development of the middle classes. Their desideratum often seemed to be productive villages rather than productive towns. City Africans were widely distrusted and disliked. 'Town air makes free,' says a German proverb; town life also stimulated trade and the acquisition of new skills. The European officials' paternalism and their anti-urban bias at times slowed down Africa commerical development and impeded the modernization processes.

After 1945, the new philosophy of development became more widely ac-cepted. New economic attitudes and techniques led to major development pro-grammes. But too little time remained before independence. Ghana, for ex-ample, became a sovereign state in 1957; and most of the remaining territories in sub-Saharan Africa followed suit between 1958 and 1964 (see Map 12). Only a limited amount of time was available therefore to promote new market institutions, to provide new infrastructures, to develop more human resources, and to transfer additional skills and capital. The colonizers did create what have been called by some 'islands of development', linked economically both to the more backward hinterland and to the world at large. But even at the present stage, 85 per cent of the wealth in Black Africa is produced by 5 per cent of its geographical area.

The European rulers, however, did provide the basic infrastructure for Black Africa; they encouraged mining and mineral industries, plantation and peasant farming for export. They began secondary industrial growth. The colonialists also built the support services of education, social services and government research necessary for future growth. The European administrators and their an-cillary agents—European missionaries, businessmen and technicians—introduced new skills and new occupations and created many new needs. The colonial period thus forced Africa into the world economy; colonialism sup-plied the engines for progress and modernization. The successor states could only follow in the paths laid down by the colonialists.

'The bourgeoisie, during its rule of scarce one hundred years', wrote Karl Marx in 1848,

has created more massive and more colossal productive forces than have all preceding generations together. Subjection of Nature's forces to man, machinery, application of

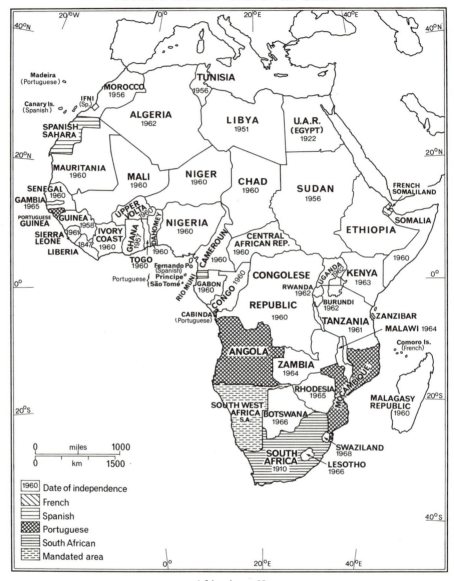

12. Africa in 1968

chemistry to industry and agriculture, steam-navigation, railways, electric telegraphs, clearing of whole continents for cultivation, canalization of rivers, whole populations conjured out of the ground—what earlier century had even a presentiment that such productive forces slumbered in the lap of social labor? . . .

. . . The bourgeoisie, by the rapid improvement of all instruments of production, by the immensely facilitated means of communications, draws all, even the most barbarian nations, into civilization.[11]

[11] Karl Marx, *The Communist manifesto,* paperback ed. (Chicago, 1965), p. 23 and pp. 21–2.

Marx was Victorian to the core. Had he been able to foresee the economic history of Africa during the eighty years following his death in 1883, he would have found no reason for altering his judgement. No era in the history of Africa saw economic change on a scale similar to the imperial epoch. What is more, these achievements took place during an astonishingly short period of time, within the life-span of a single person. Over much of Africa, the economic basis of life was transformed. A wholly new system of states came into being. The population increased several times over. Progress obviously was bought at a price, psychological as well as material. As Marx put it,

Constant revolutionizing of production, uninterrupted disturbance of all social conditions, everlasting uncertainty and agitation distinguish the bourgeois epoch from all earlier ones. All fixed, fast-frozen relations with their train of ancient and venerable prejudices and opinions are swept away, all newly-formed ones become antiquated before they can ossify. All that is solid melts into air, all that is holy is profaned.[12]

The very speed of the colonial impact created profound contradictions and caused a deep-seated sense of malaise among the peoples of Africa. To the heirs of empire remains the task of mastering the processes of modernization unleashed by the colonial experience. Yesterday's rulers have seldom understood what forces for change, good and evil, they left in their wake.

BIBLIOGRAPHY

Belgium. Office de l'Information et des Relations Publiques pour le Congo Belge et le Ruanda-Urundi. *Belgian Congo,* vol. II. Brussels. 1960.

Brett, E. A. *Colonialism and underdevelopment in East Africa 1919–1939.* London, 1973.

Chudson, Walter A. 'Trends in African exports and capital inflows', in *Economic transition in Africa,* Melville J. Herskovits and Mitchell Harwitz, eds. London, 1964.

Fieldhouse, David K. 'The economic exploitation of Africa: some British and French comparisons', in *France and Britain in Africa: imperial rivalry and colonial rule,* Prosser Gifford and William Roger Louis, eds. New Haven, Yale University Press, 1971.

Frankel, S. Herbert. *Capital investment in Africa: its course and effects.* London, Oxford University Press, 1938.

Investment and the return to equity capital in the South African gold mining industry 1887–1965: an international comparison. Cambridge, Mass., Harvard University Press, 1967.

Hancock, Sir William Keith. *Survey of British Commonwealth affairs,* vol. II: *Problems of economic policy 1918–1939,* pt. 2. London, Oxford University Press, 1942.

Hostelet, Georges. *L'oeuvre civilisatrice de la Belgique au Congo, de 1885 à 1953,* vol. II. Brussels, Académie Royale des Sciences Coloniales, 1954.

Johnston, Bruce F. 'Changes in agricultural productivity', in *Economic transition in Africa,* Melville J. Herskovits and Mitchell Harwitz, eds. London, 1964.

Marx, Karl. *The Communist manifesto.* Paperback ed. Chicago, 1965.

Neumark, S. Daniel. *Foreign trade and economic development in Africa: a historical perspective.* Stanford, Food Research Institute, 1964.

Rodney, Walter. *How Europe underdeveloped Africa.* London, 1972.

[12] *Ibid.,* p. 20.

Strachey, John. *The end of empire*. Paperback ed. New York, 1964.

United Nations. *Economic Bulletin for Africa,* Jan. 1965, **5.**

Vera, J. Wilson. 'Report on a survey of African conditions in Marandellas, Southern Rhodesia . . .' Mimeographed. Bulawayo, Federation of African Welfare Societies, 1951.

White, C. M. N. *A preliminary survey of the Luvale rural economy*. Rhodes-Livingstone paper, no. 29. Manchester University Press, 1959.

Zambia. *First National Plan, 1966–70*. Lusaka, 1966.

INDEX

83–4, 89, 310–11, 638; in Belgian Congo, 84, 192, 344, 676; and capital formation, 300, 321, 445; and development of palm-kernel oil, 291, 342; exports of, 85, 142, 144, 250 n., 287, 291, 306, 310, 342, 438, 455, 680, 682, 689; in French colonies, 345–6, 489; in German West Africa, 221, 237; in Gold Coast, 445, 452; and Lever, 81–2, 105–6, 180, 189, 344, 458; and Loder process, 342; and marketing boards, 647–8; in Nigeria, 83–4, 105–6, 303, 310–11, 323, 344, 347, 454–9, 490, 496, 503; on plantations, 457–8; pre-colonial, 310, 689; price of, 83, 291, 321, 342; processing, 490, 496, 503, profitability of, 676; trade, 3, 5, 6, 7, 12, 39, 43, 58–9, 61, 82, 85, 96, 104, 228, 287, 310–11, 342

Pankhurst, Richard, 566, 567, 568

Pass, Daniel de, 576, 588

Pass laws, 538, 666

Pastoralism, 35, 224, 251, 576

Paternalism: colonial, 11, 97, 106, 190, 238–9, 539, 661, 693; economic, 460, 690

Pauling, George, 390–2

Peasant farming, 12, 487–8, 551

Pedler, Sir Frederick, 12, 643

Pemba Bay, 260, 525

Peters, Karl, 76, 213

Petroleum industry, 384; in Angola, 274, 382; in Gabon, 151; in Nigeria, 381–2; and palm-oil trade, 342; in USA, 291

Planning: see government intervention

Plantation farming; in British colonies, 105–7, 344, 454, 458; of coffee, 12, 106, 229, 458; development of, 458, 582; in French colonies, 142, 345; in German colonies, 220, 229, 232, 236–42 passim 247, 249 n., 582; investment in, 535; and labour, 275, 303, 458–9, 525, 527; management of, 218; and monopoly, 432; outside Africa, 44, 88; of palm products, 12, 344, 457–8; in Portuguese colonies, 44, 262, 275; profitability of, 247, 249 n.; vs. small holder cultivation, 457–8. See also prazos

Plastics industry, 154, 497 n., 499, 504, 512

Police, 10, 179, 235, 277, 525

Politicization of economic life, 649–53

Politics, party, 554–6, 558–60, 561–2

Polygamy, 410, 548–50

Population: density, 263, 289, 290–1, 336; distribution, 37, 148, 156, 234, 275, 655–6, 658, 689; ethnic distribution, 688; increase, 54, 57 n., 79, 113, 158, 271, 447, 633, 680–1, 689, 695; and industry, 472; and means of subsistence, 531; pressure, 11, 36, 168, 263, 529, 540, 673; sex distribution, 669, 670. See also miscegenation

Port Harcourt, 296; industry in, 502; and mineral exports, 400; and railway, 295, 396; and retail trade, 497

Porterage: in cocoa trade, 452; cost of, 55, 293–4, 296, 313, 638; inefficiency of, 638;

supply of labour for, 525–6, 527; use of forced and slave labour for, 15, 16, 19, 294, 338, 640

Porto Novo, 296, 312

Ports in Africa, 28, 60, 219; congestion in, 296, 635; construction of, 10, 240, 638, 677; growth of, 399, 690–1; improvement of, 131, 150, 296–7; and Transvaal traffic, 389, 399. *See also* entries for individual ports

Portugal: colonial policy of, 73, 77, 256–79, 352 n.; economy of, 256–7, 269, 276; emigration from, 256, 272; growth of empire, 256–8; labour policies of, 527, 530; land policies of, 12; military forces of, 265–6, 267, 278; and slave trade, 44, 258–9, 261, 316; social structure of, 272, 276–7; and trade with Africa, 9, 10, 61, 263, 287–8, 299. *See also* colonial economic policies; illiteracy; investment, foreign

Portuguese Guinea (Guiné): conquest of, 262; economic development of, 259, 262, 677; ground-nut production in, 263; liberation movement in, 277–9; and threatened French and British takeover, 263; and trade, 258, 263

Power supply: *see* electricity

Prazos (estates): and exports, 259; owners of, 46, 61, 258

Preference system, 9, 485, 499; imperial, 121, 144, 642, 674

Price controls, 189, 190, 519, 646; in transport, 203–7

Price fluctuations, 85, 108, 172, 283, 648

Price support, 137, 145, 350, 487

Price system, 463; and efficiency, 452; and protection of home industry, 484; and resource allocation, 452

Primary products: demand for, 193, 692–3; and development, 89, 430; exports of, 89, 165, 673, 679, 690; and import duty relief, 485; processing of, 435, 474–9, 518, 592 n., 645; processing of agricultural, 27, 88, 314, 451, 476–7, 479, 482–3, 489, 496, 502, 508, 645, 656; processing of mineral, 28, 382–3, 400–1, 404, 483–4, 502, 505–6, 685; and world prices, 23, 25, 58, 89, 108, 119, 144, 145, 148, 186, 190, 208, 228, 269, 270, 292, 680

Príncipe, 262, 273, 275

Processing, industrial, 499–502, 645. *See also under* primary products

Productivity: of agriculture, 36–7, 139, 141, 171, 194, 196; and development, 429, 432, 474; of industry, 193, 194, 196; of labour, 448 (*see also* labour, yield of); of mining, 184, 193, 194; of transport, 184, 194

Profit: and industry, 517; and mining, 86, 370, 675–6; rates of, 72, 167, 249 n., 676, 679; repatriation of, 166, 196, 198, 433, 436, 465; and transport, 205–6; understatement of, 679; windfall, 646–7

Protectionism: *see* preference system

Public debt, 197–8, 206

188, 302, 329, 348, 411, 525–7, 529, 534; of export crops, 651; forced labour as, 14–15, 18, 25; in German colonies, 232, 235, 237, 248 n.; head tax (hut tax, poll tax), 8, 18, 135, 155, 175, 188, 275, 277, 302–3, 313, 434, 525–6; indirect, 135; and investment, 8; in kind, 170–1, 175, 177, 187, 320, 640–1; reform of, 16; through marketing boards, 648–9; transfer of revenues to metropolis, 23
Tea cultivation, 293, 332, 339, 458, 477, 479
Technological development: in agriculture, 3, 36, 51–3, 185, 224, 314, 315, 329–57, 410, 435, 462, 563, 576–7, 636, 683 (*see also* agricultural machinery); and development, 64–6, 89, 335, 429, 432, 636; and labour savings, 190, 334; metallurgical, 47, 51, 52, 360–1, 400; in mining, 360–2, 363, 368, 376, 380, 400, 636, 685; resulting from trade, 40
Tema; aluminium smelting at, 408; port, 406
Terms of trade, 196, 433, 444, 673, 674
Territorial annexation, 14, 18; economic motives for, 7, 72–6, 167; forcible, 523, 595, 640; political motives for, 673; in Portuguese empire, 262; role of railways in, 241; through chartered companies, 62–4, 77
Textile industry, African, 6, 37, 39, 287, 315, 316, 473, 474, 477, 506, 655, 656; manufacturing, 151, 478, 483–4, 489, 502–3, 506–8; trade, 85, 449, 586
Theodore II, 565–6
Timber industry: *see* forestry
Timbuktu: and food imports, 38–9, 287, 336; and trade, 3, 37–8, 42, 48, 54, 298
Tin industry: canning, 151, 291, 499, 504, 508; mining, 295, 381, 384, 396, 406, 505; smelting, 505–6
Tobacco: cigarette manufacture, 118, 154, 474, 477, 479, 480, 490, 492, 510; cultivation, 51, 337, 341, 342, 344, 408, 444, 454 n.; exports of, 680, 683; trade, 287, 293, 298, 479
Togo: administration of, 128, 242; agricultural research and development in, 8, 304, 343; cotton cultivation in, 232, 237, 242, 343; development of, 236; education in, 243, 244 n., 245, 246, 304, 338 n.; industry in, 472, 512; investment in, 135, 218; and labour, 156, 530; land ownership in, 12; palm-oil trade in, 237, 250 n.; taxation in, 303; trade in, 248 n., 250 n., transport and communications in, 237, 239–40, 250, 296
Tonga: and agriculture, 339, 409, 410; and trade, 40, 540
Tourism, 275, 605
Towns: building of new, 18; growth of, 591, 655–66, 690; sanitation services in, 10, 18, 657, 659, 661, 663–4
Tractor, introduction of, 333–4
Trade, external
in agricultural produce, 5, 41, 59–62, 79, 84, 103–4, 108, 143, 196, 309–24, 683

with Belgium, 10, 171, 173, 679, 680
with Britain, 9, 85, 643, 679–80; Central African, 20, 485; East African, 314, 680; South African, 5, 20, 485; West African, 5, 20, 96–100, 110, 310, 322
and economic development, 21, 40, 219, 338, 427–66
with France, 9–10, 85, 143–8, 151, 679–80; Algerian, 10; Equatorial African, 20; Madagascar, 20; West African, 20, 60, 96, 310, 317
with Germany, 6–7, 10, 61, 217–19, 319, 488
with Holland, 85
and imperialism, 75–6, 78, 80
import-export, 4–6, 122, 297–300, 441–3, 540; and chartered companies, 59–64, 80, 97–100, 102, 110, 131; diversification of, 84–5; as proportion of metropolitan trade, 4, 9–10, 95–6, 217–18; and trading companies, 488, 491, 493–5
with Italy, 10
maritime, 3, 69, 220–1, 258, 297
models of, 427–31
nineteenth century, 4–6, 58–62, 80, 95–100, 131, 177
with Portugal, 10, 61–2, 680
pre-colonial, 3, 40–3, 64, 284–5, 567, 685
quotas, 9, 643
regulation, 104, 144, 188, 643, 679
supposed immiseration through, 466, 692
unfavourable effects of, 431–4, 673. *See also* chartered companies; entrepôt trade; free trade in Africa; slave trade; terms of trade
Trade, internal: in agricultural produce, 39, 41, 84, 107, 284–7, 306–10, 336, 488, 513, 561, 586 n., 644; artisan, 512; and development, 540; European intervention in, 62; by immigrants, 586–93, 609–11, 644; petty, 16, 188–9, 272, 450, 452, 488, 551, 567, 574, 586, 665; pre-colonial, 1–3, 34, 38–43, 47, 98–9, 284–7, 306–10, 548–9, 684; subsistence-market-oriented, 38–40, 142. *See also* distribution; gold trade; long distance trade; middlemen
Trade routes: influence on population movements, 534–5; control of, 40, 41
Trade unions: *see* labour organizations
Trading companies, 592; and agricultural development, 188–9, 299–300, 341; and cocoa trade, 60; and development, 99–100, 488, 490–1, 583; and ground-nut trade, 100; and import-export trade, 61, 96, 99, 121, 490–5; and palm-oil production, 311; profitability of, 676; and shift to manufacturing, 495–7, 501, 507. *See also* chartered companies; *compagnies à charte,* concession companies
Transport: and agricultural development, 329, 408, 444, 638, 680; in British colonies, 294–6, 313, 315, 551–2, 561; in Congo, 174, 178, 199–209; cost of, 56, 203–8, 287–97 *passim,*